KISSINGER:
The Price of Power

KISSINGER:
The Price of Power

HENRY KISSINGER IN
THE NIXON WHITE HOUSE

SEYMOUR M. HERSH

faber and faber
LONDON·BOSTON

First published in the United States of America in 1983
First published in Great Britain in 1983
by Faber and Faber Limited
3 Queen Square London WC1N 3AU
Printed in the United States of America
All rights reserved

British Library Cataloguing in Publication Data

Hersh, Seymour M.
Kissinger: the price of power.
1. United States — Foreign relations — 1945–1976
2. United States — Foreign relations — 1977–
I. Title
327.73   E87Z
ISBN 0-571-13175-1

FOR ELIZABETH, MATTHEW, MELISSA, AND JOSHUA

CONTENTS

Introduction

THIS BOOK is an account of the foreign policy of the United States, presided over by Henry Kissinger, during Richard Nixon's first term in the White House. It is also an account of the relationship between two men who collaborated on what seemed to be a remarkable series of diplomatic triumphs. These were the years when China was reclaimed by American diplomacy; when a much-praised agreement on strategic arms limitation (SALT) was negotiated with the Soviet Union; when a complex dispute in West Berlin was settled; and when American participation in the war in Vietnam, the most crucial issue facing the American presidency, was brought to a dramatic end with the signing of the Paris peace accords in January 1973, three days after Nixon was inaugurated for a second term.

The book had its beginnings in my experiences as a Washington reporter for the *New York Times* during those Watergate years when the press—and the nation—became aware of the distance between the truth and what we were told had happened. But even at the height of the outcry over the methods and morality of the men at the top, foreign policy remained sacrosanct.

I began my research certain that, despite all that has been written, there was more to be known about the conduct of foreign affairs. It was no surprise to discover that personal ambition was sometimes entwined with diplomatic and strategic goals, that successful bargaining whether in White House meetings or at a summit was never an open process. No experienced reporter or government official expects otherwise. But as my interviewing proceeded I came to realize that even sophisticated public servants perceived something crucially different about the conduct of foreign policy in the Nixon White House. That difference and its cost both to the participants and to the country is what I have tried to describe.

My basic sources are more than 1,000 interviews with American and international officials—some retired, some still in government—who were directly involved in making and executing policy. Most of the people I talked with agreed to be quoted by name. I also relied on internal documents and on the published memoirs of those who themselves participated in the history of that time. Despite my many requests, neither Kissinger nor Nixon agreed to be interviewed for this book.

1

THE
JOB SEEKER

AFTER THE ELECTION, there would be much fancier offices, with antique desks, hand-woven rugs, possibly a view of the Rose Garden, and fireplaces that were kept burning year-round.

But now it was mid-September 1968, with the presidential election less than two months away, and the men who were responsible for drafting the foreign and domestic policy statements of the Nixon campaign were hard at work in their sparsely furnished New York City offices in what had once been the American Bible Society's headquarters. The old six-story building at Fifty-seventh Street and Park Avenue, scheduled for demolition, had been leased by the Nixon campaign that fall.

Richard M. Nixon was running far ahead of Vice President Hubert H. Humphrey in both the Harris and Gallup polls, but he and his staff knew that the race was far from over. For one thing, former Vice President Nixon had lost his last two elections—the presidency to Senator John F. Kennedy in 1960 and the governorship of California to Governor Edmund G. (Pat) Brown in 1962.

And then there was Vietnam.

Humphrey had yet to break with President Lyndon B. Johnson on the war, but what if he did? And what if Johnson decided to sue for peace in Vietnam in an effort to pull out the election for his Vice President and his party? Nixon's vague campaign promise—that he would find an "honorable solution" to the war—would pale beside the real thing.

Most of the senior Nixon advisers were convinced that Nixon's chance to become President hinged on Vietnam and the issues associated with it. One adviser, Bryce N. Harlow, a former speech writer and aide in the Eisenhower Administration, had already established liaison with a high official inside the Johnson White House, who was ready and willing to supply information about any last-ditch administration plans to settle the war. And clandestine contact had been made with President Nguyen Van Thieu of South Vietnam, in a carefully concealed effort to discourage him from participating in any peace talks prior to the election.

Given the immense stakes involved, Richard V. Allen, Nixon's thirty-two-year-old coordinator for foreign policy research, was an important member of the Nixon campaign team. He was assigned a private office on the top floor of the old Bible Society Building, where, amid battered metal desks and squeaky typists' chairs, he provided the traveling presidential candidate with drafts of speeches and statements.

Allen had been among the few to offer his support to Nixon in the months after his disastrous defeat in California. He believed even then that Nixon would be resurrected as President, or Secretary of State, or, at the least, as an *éminence grise* in the Republican Party. Allen is a man of medium height, with the horn-rim eyeglasses, cherubic round face, and short hair that seemed the required style for the bright young Nixon men. By the mid-1960s he had become a minor figure among the conservative anti-Communist right in America, warning repeatedly in his articles and books that the Soviet call for peaceful coexistence was no more than a shield for its plan of world domination. By June 1968, when Nixon personally recruited him for his campaign staff, Allen had studied for a doctorate in political science at the University of Munich and was now a fellow at the Hoover Institution on War, Revolution, and Peace at Stanford University. He had not earned the doctorate but others thought he had. Throughout the 1968 campaign, his associates and the press often called him Dr. Allen.

For all his pretensions and rigid ideology, Allen could also be good company, and he enjoyed laughing at himself. Moreover, he realized that he did not yet have enough experience and expertise to serve as national security adviser in a Nixon administration. Allen did, however, have his personal choice for the job—Henry A. Kissinger, a Harvard professor of government who had served as New York Governor Nelson A. Rockefeller's foreign policy adviser during Rockefeller's campaign for the Republican presidential nomination earlier that year. He and Kissinger had first met in 1962, and Allen had renewed their acquaintance, shortly after he joined Nixon's campaign, by telephoning Kissinger—his counterpart with Nelson Rockefeller.

Allen had long admired Kissinger's hard line toward the Soviets and his published works on nuclear threats and deterrents, especially his *Nuclear Weapons and Foreign Policy,* which had been a best seller in 1957. Allen, then twenty-six, was among the founders of the Center for Strategic and International Studies at Georgetown University, in Washington, D.C.—one of the nation's first conservative think tanks—and Kissinger contributed to a collection of papers that Allen helped edit for the Center.

It made eminent sense for the two advisers to arrange breakfast together before the Republican National Convention in Miami Beach and agree to work together to avoid a bitter floor fight over Vietnam: Their collaboration resulted in a compromise plank, endorsed in advance by the Nixon and Rockefeller forces, that emphasized negotiations, not confrontation. The language was accepted without challenge at the convention. Allen had enjoyed staging clandestine meetings with Kissinger in Miami Beach, and somehow to escape the notice of the hordes of newspapermen who were everywhere that week.

A few weeks after the convention, Allen again sought out Kissinger—still thought by his friends at Harvard and elsewhere to be in mourning over Rockefeller's defeat—and asked him to serve as a member of candidate Nixon's foreign affairs advisory group. Kissinger hesitated a few days and then told Allen that it would be better for the Nixon campaign if he did not formally join it. "I can do you more good by not coming out for you publicly," he said.

Not long afterward, on about September 10, Allen, in his office at campaign headquarters, was told that Henry Kissinger was on the telephone. Speaking very seriously, Kissinger reminded Allen—who hardly needed to be told—that he still had many good friends and associates involved in the Johnson Administration's Paris peace negotiations. Kissinger explained that he "had a way to contact them," Allen recalls. Would the Nixon campaign be interested?

Allen was excited. "When he called, it was a continuation of our team. This was Mr. 'Nuclear Weapons and Foreign Policy.' This was a guy who'd written a seminal book on nuclear strategy."

Kissinger was also a member of the Council on Foreign Relations and was part of the Eastern Establishment that had always—so Nixon and his aides thought—rejected Nixon as a serious student of foreign affairs. Former colleagues at Harvard recall that Kissinger was a Democrat at least through the early 1960s, when his academic and Democratic Party contacts were good enough to propel him into an unhappy part-time White House consultancy during the Kennedy Administration. His shift to the Republican Party was apparently made sometime before 1964, when he was a foreign policy consultant to the Republican Platform Committee. Richard Allen knew that Kissinger had been active as a consultant on Vietnam for the Johnson Administration, and that, even though he was on Rockefeller's staff, he had worked out of offices in the State Department.

"He had access and I figured that the Nixon campaign would get something out of him," Allen explains. He had no illusions about what Kissinger wanted in return. "We didn't have enough qualified Republicans and Henry was a hard-nosed son-of-a-bitch. Already I knew that Nixon would never pick a conservative like me for the job [as national security adviser] and Henry was obviously the most qualified card-carrying Republican around. I knew he was the best guy for the job. And so," Allen says with a laugh, "I became a handmaiden of Henry Kissinger's drive for power."

"I *was* naïve," Allen concedes. "I had my zipper wide open. But I thought, Damn it, we changed the course of history at Miami Beach. We didn't have any floor fight at the convention."

Within hours, Kissinger's offer was relayed to the pleased candidate. As a secret operative Kissinger was a prize catch, because Nixon knew the Johnson Administration was involved in a desperate attempt to get some kind of substantive peace talks under way in Paris, and thus improve Humphrey's chances in the election. Kissinger's access inside the Democratic administration was first-class. His career at Harvard and his work in the Kennedy White House had put him in close touch with State Department advisers on NATO and Western European affairs. Under Johnson, he had expanded his contacts to include the top officials of the White House, the Pentagon, and the State Department who were seeking a way to settle the Vietnam War.

What Allen and the Nixon entourage could not know was the extent of Kissinger's maneuvering. In funneling information from Paris to the Nixon campaign, he would not only be taking advantage of professional friendships but also betraying people with whom he had worked on the still-secret Vietnam negotiating efforts. At the same time he would continue telling colleagues at Harvard and friends in Cambridge, Martha's Vineyard, and New York about his contempt for Nixon and his anger at Rockefeller's defeat in Miami Beach.

A few weeks after the Republican convention, in a letter to a fellow political scientist at the University of Denver, Kissinger described Nixon's behavior after his nomination in Miami Beach as "astounding—ungenerous, petty and, I should have thought, against his long-term interests." He made similar comments about Nixon throughout the fall, repeatedly expressing concern for the fate of the nation if Nixon were to be elected.

And he went further. While dealing covertly with Richard Allen, Kissinger also talked with an old acquaintance in the Humphrey camp and offered to help accumulate information to discredit Nixon. The first known contact came within a week or so after the Miami Beach convention, in a telephone conversation with Zbigniew Brzezinski, Humphrey's foreign policy coordinator. Brzezinski had called to see whether Kissinger would be willing to comment on some of the Humphrey foreign policy papers. Kissinger seemed eager to help. "Look," he said, "I've hated Nixon for years." He surprised Brzezinski by announcing that he had already been in direct contact with Humphrey, and then offered to do more than review policy papers—he would make available Rockefeller's private files on Nixon. The papers were known as the Nixon "shit files," Kissinger explained, and were among his personal documents at Harvard. He would let Brzezinski see them if the arrangement was kept quiet, and if Humphrey himself was told of Kissinger's help.

The Democratic convention, held in Chicago in August, was marked by violent confrontations over the war. Humphrey won the nomination, defeating Senator Eugene J. McCarthy, the antiwar candidate. Afterward, Brzezinski and John E. Rielly, another of Humphrey's foreign policy advisers, agreed that someone would make the trip to Cambridge to inspect the files. In mid-September, with Humphrey far behind Nixon in the public opinion polls, Brzezinski telephoned Kissinger's office and told his secretary what he wanted. She said, "You know, Dr. Brzezinski, that Dr. Kissinger is working for Nixon now?" There was a long pause. The Humphrey campaign heard no more about the Nixon files.

Max Kampelman, Humphrey's long-time adviser and friend, remembers being told by Humphrey shortly before the election that Kissinger was working with him. Kampelman also recalls that Humphrey told him, "if he got elected, he thought he'd put Henry in the national security spot." The same word was later passed to Brzezinski.

Kissinger's offer to report secretly on the peace talks for Nixon would have astonished his friends in the Paris delegation, who continued to trust him in the weeks before the election as if he were still a part of the team seeking a settlement of the Vietnam War.

By 1968, Kissinger had established a considerable reputation as an expert on the war. He had made his first trip to South Vietnam as a State Department consultant in 1965, discussing the war with, among others, Daniel Ellsberg, who was then a pacification official in the U.S. Embassy in Saigon. Kissinger made two more trips in 1966, again meeting Ellsberg and also renewing a friendship with Daniel I. Davidson, a junior State Department official who would later become an aide to Ambassador W. Averell Harriman, the chief American negotiator at the Paris peace talks in 1968.*

In 1967, Kissinger earned the respect of the top echelon of the Johnson Administration, including the President and Secretary of Defense Robert S. McNamara, by his discreet involvement in a four-month exchange of messages between Hanoi and Washington in which the United States sought to trade a halt to the bombing of North Vietnam for Hanoi's agreement to begin serious peace negotiations. Johnson Administration officials now acknowledge that Kissinger played a far more important role than was known at the time in creating a much-needed reevaluation of American policy in the summer of 1967; his work indirectly led to the public peace talks between North Vietnam and the United States that began in Paris in May 1968.

Paul C. Warnke, then a senior Pentagon official, recalls that Kissinger visited McNamara early that summer and offered to relay messages to Hanoi through two French intellectuals, one of them a close friend of Ho Chi Minh, North Vietnam's chief of state. McNamara was intrigued by the new channel of communication and asked Warnke to frame a fresh offer for Kissinger to carry to his friends in Paris.

Warnke turned to one of his brightest aides, Morton H. Halperin, who had been a Kissinger associate at Harvard. "Warnke pulled me in and said that Kissinger had just come back [from Paris] and told McNamara of a new chance for a settlement and nobody in the White House was taking it seriously," Halperin says. Until that point, the American negotiating position had been rigid and unproductive, with President Johnson insisting that he would not stop the bombing of North Vietnam until Hanoi promised to stop the infiltration of men and matériel into South Vietnam. Hanoi, in turn, insisted that it would not begin talks until the American bombing of the North was unconditionally ended.

Encouraged by Kissinger's offer, McNamara wanted a new approach. "Paul and I sat down and in a half-hour we wrote it out," Halperin remembers. "We thought it was crazy to believe the North Vietnamese were going to totally stop the infiltration in return for stopping the bombing, when the fact was that the bombing could not stop the infiltration anyway. We couldn't ask North Vietnam to stop doing what we couldn't force them not to do." The Warnke-Halperin proposal was to tell Hanoi that the United States would "assume" that it would reduce infiltration in response to a bombing halt, Halperin says. President Johnson later made the proposal public policy in a speech at San Antonio, Texas, in September 1967.

---

* Ellsberg first met Richard Nixon in 1964. The former Vice President was passing through Vietnam on a visit and arranged a lunch at the Saigon home of retired Major General Edward G. Lansdale, a free-wheeling expert on counterinsurgency who had known Nixon during the Eisenhower years. Lansdale, who was then the embassy's senior liaison officer with the South Vietnamese, wanted the support of Nixon—who was still a major voice in Republican affairs—in urging the Saigon government not to interfere with its pending national elections. Lansdale's team, including Ellsberg, assembled for the meal, and Nixon asked Lansdale what he and his men were up to. "We want to . . . make this the most honest election that's ever been held in Vietnam," Lansdale replied. "Oh sure, honest, yes, honest, that's right," Nixon said. *"So long as you win."* With that, Ellsberg later wrote, Nixon "winked, drove his elbow hard into Lansdale's arm, and, in a return motion, slapped his own knee. My teammates turned to stone."

According to Halperin, "Kissinger was a catalyst in McNamara's thinking." Thus Kissinger became a trusted addition to the small group of Johnson Administration officials who were dedicated to turning the Vietnam War around. He began to spend more and more time in a State Department office, where he consulted regularly with Harriman, then a special assistant for the Vietnam negotiations.

Paul Warnke also recalls that Kissinger was "regarded as being a trusted consultant," particularly after he was able to stimulate the new approach to negotiations. "If he had come to see me and begun talking about a secret negotiation," Warnke says, "I would have assumed he was talking about it legitimately and I'd have had no problem talking to him about it."

Kissinger's 1967 negotiating efforts took him to Paris at least four times between June and October. Not a word leaked to the press. By then, Kissinger's reputation was also high in the White House; friends from Harvard recall a Vermont weekend in early October when he ran up a huge telephone bill at a colleague's vacation retreat talking to President Johnson and others. But they never found out from him what was up.

Kissinger protected his secrets, but he made sure that everyone knew how trusted he was. In July of 1968, he ran into John D. Negroponte, a young Foreign Service officer with whom he'd traveled during his first visit to South Vietnam in 1965. Negroponte had just been reassigned to the Paris peace talks, and, making small talk, told Kissinger that he could not tell him much—meaning that he did not know very much about the secret talks at that stage. Kissinger misunderstood. "Oh yes," he said, "you can tell me anything because I have been cleared for everything now."

In September 1968, Richard Allen did not know all the specifics about Kissinger's work with the Johnson Administration, but he quickly learned that Kissinger was exceedingly cautious about their contacts. During the last two months of the campaign, the two men had four or five transatlantic conversations, with Kissinger initiating each call from pay telephones—to avoid interception, so Allen assumed. During one call, Kissinger startled Allen by asking, "You speak German, don't you, Dick?" and the two men self-consciously exchanged a few sentences in German. Allen says that, to his surprise, his own German was more fluent than Kissinger's. In subsequent telephone talks, Allen recalls, "all the important stuff was in English."

One of Allen's main contacts in his dealings with Kissinger was John N. Mitchell, Nixon's law partner and campaign manager, who was to become Nixon's Attorney General and closest confidant. Allen recalls telling Mitchell about the Kissinger connection and insisting that it be very closely held. "I laid heavy stress on protecting the source," Allen says, "because it was a matter of high stakes. It was important that it [Kissinger's role] be protected in the national interest."

Allen also discreetly kept Kissinger's name off the list of foreign affairs advisers that the Nixon campaign made public. Kissinger, as Allen informed Nixon in a private memorandum of September 22, 1968, preferred to "advise on an informal basis for the time being." By then, Kissinger had been in Paris for five days, having told Daniel Davidson, now Harriman's aide in Paris, that he was arriving on personal business September 17. Davidson had looked forward to the visit. Not only was Kissinger a trusted adviser known for his discretion, he was also caustic, bright, and witty—"fun to be with." Harriman, now spending more time in Paris, enjoyed his visits, too.

Kissinger sailed on the *Île de France,* along with Davidson's mother. Davidson offered to pick them both up at Le Havre and drive them to Paris. A day or two before the vessel was to arrive, Kissinger telephoned ship-to-shore to tell Davidson that, having had longer experience with Jewish mothers, he recommended that Davidson drive his mother alone. He would take the train, Kissinger said. It was a thoughtful suggestion, made with the special panache that only Kissinger seemed to have.

Davidson's mother was coming to celebrate his thirty-second birthday, which was September 19, and the *Île de France* arrived two days earlier. While in Paris, Kissinger visited with Davidson and had dinner at least once with Cyrus R. Vance, the former Deputy Secretary of Defense who was Harriman's chief deputy at the peace talks. Harriman had just flown back to Paris with important news from Washington: A breakthrough had finally been made in the long-stalled American negotiating position. Kissinger's timing was perfect.

On September 17, President Johnson agreed to another last-ditch effort to get the Paris peace talks working before the presidential election on November 5. There was near-panic in the Democratic ranks: Humphrey was fourteen points behind Nixon in the Harris poll and still going nowhere. The peace formula conceded one of Hanoi's basic bargaining points, a bombing halt without any formal preconditions, if it would agree to immediate peace talks. North Vietnam need not reciprocate before the bombs actually stopped falling, although the Johnson formula made it clear that Hanoi was expected to restrain its military activities afterward. Similar proposals had been privately advanced to Hanoi for more than a year, with no progress, because Johnson had insisted that North Vietnam, once at the peace talks, commit itself to serious negotiations and a quick resolution of the war. With less than two months left in the campaign, Johnson had finally agreed to drop that requirement. The new formula would lead to a breakthrough in the talks in early October and to President Johnson's order to halt the bombing of North Vietnam on November 1.

Secrecy was essential in these talks, for the Johnson Administration needed to be able to control the flow of information to the press, to the Nixon campaign, and to Nguyen Van Thieu, the President of South Vietnam. If word of a possible agreement leaked out, the Thieu government might be tempted by the Republicans to stall the negotiations or find other ways to make it impossible to reach agreement before the election. Lyndon Johnson and his aides were already suspicious of the role of Richard Nixon. Johnson told an adviser a week after the Democratic defeat that in early October he and President Thieu had agreed on a joint statement supporting negotiations, but Thieu had suddenly backed away. Jack Valenti, one of Johnson's closest confidants, quotes Johnson in his memoirs as saying that "hard information had come to him that representatives of Nixon reached President Thieu and urged him not to accept" any last-ditch negotiations, suggesting he would get a better deal if Nixon won the election.

Exactly how much Henry Kissinger was able to learn during the few days he spent in Paris in late September is not clear. Davidson was not fully briefed on the new initiatives at the time of the Kissinger visit, although he knew "something was going on." He says that he would certainly have discussed whatever he knew with Kissinger. During his stay Kissinger often spoke of the presidential election: "Henry told me, 'Six days a week I'm for Hubert, but on the seventh day, I think they're both awful.' " Another matter was also discussed. Kissinger was reasonably certain he would be offered a post in either a Humphrey or a Nixon administration, probably as an Assistant Secretary of State or of Defense. When that happened, he promised, Davidson would become his principal deputy.

The best source for what happened next is Richard Nixon himself, in his memoirs, *RN,* published in 1978. Johnson's bombing halt, Nixon wrote, "came as no real surprise to me. I had known for several weeks that plans were being made for such an action . . . I had learned of the plan through a highly unusual channel. It began on September 12, when Haldeman brought me a report from John Mitchell that Rockefeller's foreign policy adviser, Henry Kissinger, was available to assist us with advice." *

Nixon goes on: "I knew that Rockefeller had been offering Kissinger's assistance and urging that I make use of it ever since the convention. I told Haldeman that Mitchell should continue as liaison with Kissinger and that we should honor his desire to keep his role completely confidential."

On September 26, two weeks after Mitchell's first contact with Kissinger, Nixon wrote, "Kissinger called again. He said that he had just returned from Paris, where he had picked up word that something big was afoot regarding Vietnam. He advised that if I had to say anything about Vietnam during the following week, I should avoid any new ideas or proposals."

Nixon took the advice. He immediately issued a memorandum to his staff advisers and speech writers ordering them, as he wrote, "to put the Vietnam monkey on Humphrey's back, *not* Johnson's. I wanted to make it clear that I thought it was Humphrey rather than the President who was playing politics with the war." Over the next few weeks, Nixon spoke cautiously, as Kissinger advised, about the war, going so far as to tell a rally in Johnstown, Pennsylvania, that he would support a bombing pause if it would increase the chance for peace and not endanger American lives. "And the one man who can make that determination," Nixon added, "is the President of the United States."

Nixon writes that Kissinger had advised him he considered it "proper and reasonable" to warn the candidate against "making any statements that might be undercut by negotiations I was not aware of." Yet John Mitchell remembers that his direct link to Kissinger was considered one of the campaign's most important secrets—so vital that the trusted Bryce Harlow and even Richard Allen, who was busily reporting about his own communications with Kissinger, were kept in the dark. "I thought Henry was doing it because Nelson wanted him to," Mitchell says. "Nelson asked Henry to help and he did."

There could be little doubt about the magnitude of Kissinger's personal risk in providing help for the Nixon camp. Harriman, former Governor of New York and Ambassador to the Soviet Union, was one of the Democratic Party's most prominent members; his elegant home in Georgetown had been the scene

---

* Former Nixon associates told me in late 1979 that Nixon based this part of his autobiography on handwritten notes provided by H. R. (Bob) Haldeman, his White House Chief of Staff.

of many of the party's successful fund raisers and its most glittering social occasions. One close Harriman aide, asked later what his boss would have thought of Kissinger's go-between role, cited Harriman's deep loyalty to the Democrats and added: "He would have regarded the use of anything he told Kissinger to assist Richard Nixon as a personal betrayal."

Nixon and his close advisers—Haldeman and Mitchell among them—were impressed by Kissinger's work. On September 27, shortly after Kissinger passed the warning of a possible breakthrough in Paris, Nixon had an off-the-record chat with Joseph Kraft, the syndicated columnist, whom the Nixon forces considered one of the few balanced reporters on the campaign.* On a flight from Chattanooga to Tampa, as the two men discussed foreign policy jobs in a Republican White House, Kraft was surprised when Nixon told him Kissinger was the leading contender for the job of Special Assistant for National Security Affairs. Nixon described Kissinger as being tough-minded and obviously "had a very, very high opinion of him. . . . It was clear to me that [Kissinger] was the guy who was going to get the job."

In an interview in 1977, filmed but not broadcast for public television, Kraft further recalled that he bumped into Kissinger a few days later. "I had been seeing quite a little bit of him because he was weaving in and out as one of the Vietnam negotiators. He was extremely secretive and would never say anything about what he was doing—at least to me." Nonetheless, Kraft said, "I mentioned it to Henry, who immediately acted the way he did in those days, and to a certain extent still does when some good fortune comes his way—he became a totally scared rabbit, and he said, 'Please don't mention this to anybody else.' And then he called me several times during the day—once from the Washington airport, another time from the airport in New York, another time from the airport [in Boston], then from his house in Cambridge—each time telling me, 'Please don't mention it; keep it a secret.' "† Kraft, of course, had no way of knowing about Kissinger's most recent, self-generated involvement in the peace process.

The columnist was not the only person telling Kissinger that he was in line for the national security adviser's job under Nixon. Sometime in late September, Richard Allen advised Kissinger to make it clear to the men at the top that he was available. "You're the guy for the job," Allen said. Kissinger played coy, telling Allen, "I would not seek the job, but if asked, I'd consider it." The conversation was relayed to the top echelon of the Nixon staff.

It was also in late September that the Nixon campaign got its second report from Kissinger, relayed by Haldeman and Mitchell. Nixon recalls in his memoirs that Kissinger warned that "there is a better than even chance that Johnson will order a bombing halt at approximately mid-October." A Haldeman memo, referring to Kissinger as "our source," included the following advice: "Our source does not believe that it is practical to oppose a bombing halt but does feel thought should be given to the fact that it may happen—that we may

* Kraft and Walter Lippmann, generally considered Democratic columnists, were both writing that Nixon would be freer and able to do more to end the war than Hubert Humphrey.
† Nixon floated Kissinger's name with another reporter, Theodore H. White. In his book on the 1972 campaign, White recalled a conversation in September of 1968. He wanted a young team, Nixon told the journalist, men between thirty and forty who could move hard and fast. The candidate suddenly asked, "What did I think of Henry Kissinger for foreign affairs?" White did not record his answer.

want to anticipate it—and that we certainly will want to be ready at the time it does happen." And again, "Our source is *extremely* concerned about the moves Johnson may take and expects that he will take some action before the election."

Kissinger was right. On October 9, at the regular weekly meeting in Paris between the North Vietnamese and United States delegations, there was another breakthrough. The North Vietnamese specifically asked Ambassador Harriman whether the new United States position meant that the bombing of North Vietnam would be stopped if the Hanoi government agreed to change its policy and sit at the Paris conference table with representatives of the South Vietnamese government, led by Nguyen Van Thieu. Harriman said yes, adding that North Vietnam must agree to respect the demilitarized zone between North and South Vietnam and must also agree to refrain from violence against the cities of South Vietnam.

Hanoi's representatives then asked a direct question: "Will you stop the bombing if we give you an affirmative clear answer to the question of Saigon government participation?" The Johnson Administration began a series of intensive consultations in Saigon and Washington in an effort to arrive at an answer. One implicit aspect of the bargain was that South Vietnam would finally be in negotiations with the National Liberation Front, the opposition guerrilla force in the South known as the Vietcong, which was part of the North Vietnamese delegation.

On October 12, Kissinger telephoned Allen again and reported, according to the Nixon memoirs, that "there was a strong possibility that the administration would move before October 23." Kissinger "rather cryptically . . . reported that there was 'more to this than meets the eye.' " Two days later, the Johnson Administration decided that the answer to Hanoi's question would be yes, leading to the final negotiations that produced the bombing halt on November 1.

Kissinger's last telephone call before the election was his most dramatic. Some twelve hours before the bombing halt, Kissinger telephoned Allen and excitedly announced, "I've got important information." He went on to say that in Paris Harriman and Vance had "broken open the champagne" because a bombing halt had been negotiated and would soon be announced. Kissinger's latest information was "absolutely hot stuff," Allen says. "My heart went into my mouth."

By this time, Humphrey's campaign had taken hold, sparked by the constant rumors of a breakthrough in Paris and by his new willingness to separate himself from the President on the war. The latest polls showed him two points behind Nixon. The election was going to be very close.

There was a direct telephone line from the New York campaign headquarters to Nixon, and Allen quickly relayed Kissinger's last-minute information about the champagne party. Allen later said, "My attitude was that it was inevitable that Kissinger would have to be part of our administration. . . . Kissinger had proven his mettle by tipping us. It took some balls to give us those tips." Allen was well aware that it was "a pretty dangerous thing for him to be screwing around with the national security."

John Mitchell was impressed, too: "Henry's information was basic. We were getting all of our information from him."

The last weeks of the campaign must have been agonizing ones for Kissinger, as he watched Humphrey climb steadily in the polls. In late October, while he was still in telephone contact with the Nixon advisers, Kissinger wrote a letter to Humphrey, criticizing Nixon and offering his services to a Humphrey administration. The letter came to the attention of Ted Van Dyke, one of Humphrey's closest aides, a man who, as it happened, knew of Kissinger's aborted promise to give the Humphrey campaign his secret files on Nixon.

"Later we get this letter—when the gap begins to close in the last month—from Kissinger indicating his distaste for Nixon and his willingness to serve," Van Dyke recalls. "It was so grotesque." Humphrey had corresponded with hundreds of academics in his years of campaigning, the aide adds, but to his knowledge Kissinger had never written to Humphrey before. "I wasn't angry at him," Van Dyke says. "I remember Henry being a both-sides-of-the-street kind of guy."

It is still impossible to assess the full significance of Kissinger's role in Nixon's election victory; how much he did and how important his information was is not in the record. But it is certain that the Nixon campaign, alerted by Kissinger to the impending success of the peace talks, was able to get a series of messages to the Thieu government making it clear that a Nixon presidency would have different views on the peace negotiations.

Two days after the White House announced that South Vietnam would participate in the Paris peace talks, and three days before the American election, Thieu sabotaged the agreement. In a speech in Saigon on November 2, he said his government would not participate as long as the North Vietnamese were representing the Vietcong. President Johnson, enraged by intelligence reports alleging that the Nixon campaign was deliberately trying to disrupt the peace talks, ordered the Federal Bureau of Investigation and the Central Intelligence Agency to find out who was leaking details of the Paris negotiations to the Republicans.

Johnson never got his man—or woman. Not until 1980, when she published her autobiography, *The Education of Anna,* did Mrs. Anna Chennault, a leading Republican fund raiser and ardent supporter of Taiwan and South Vietnam, acknowledge what was reported by intelligence agencies in 1968: that before the election she was in regular contact with Nixon and Mitchell about Saigon's future. A few days before the election, she wrote, Mitchell telephoned with an urgent message. "Anna," she quotes him as saying, "I'm speaking on behalf of Mr. Nixon. It's very important that our Vietnamese friends understand our Republican position and I hope you have made that clear to them."

In an interview with the author in early 1982, Mrs. Chennault insisted that Nguyen Van Thieu did not need Richard Nixon or John Mitchell to tell him that his government would do better by not participating in the Paris talks. (Thieu was quite capable, as he would demonstrate to Nixon and Kissinger in late 1972, of making up his own mind.) "Thieu was saying to me, I don't care who's going to be the next President. There are no peace talks in Paris. It's just a smokescreen. I'm not going to Paris until after the elections." Officials with first-hand knowledge of events in the fall of 1968 recall, however, that both Nixon and Johnson were convinced that Thieu's attitude toward the peace talks could be influenced by American pressure. In the last weeks of the election campaign, they say, there was intense intelligence agency traffic on Madame Chennault, who was code-named "The Little Flower." "The agencies had caught on that Chennault was the go-between between Nixon and his people and President Thieu in Saigon," a former Johnson Cabinet official recalls. "The idea was to bring things to a stop in Paris and prevent any show of progress." According to this official, Lyndon Johnson decided not to make the information public for two reasons: the sensitivity of the methods used to collect the intelligence and the fact that Johnson, angry at Humphrey's defection on the war, "had no interest in defeating Nixon. He wasn't going to do anything for the purpose of seeing Nixon discredited." Mrs. Chennault, in her 1982 interview, said that Nixon and Mitchell went to great lengths after the election to seek reassurances that she would not talk. She told of many conversations with Mitchell, who became her neighbor and frequent dinner guest in Washington's Watergate apartment complex. The high point of Mitchell's anxiety, she said, came after his nomination as Attorney General; "he was concerned even after he was confirmed." At a White House reception in early 1969, President Nixon took her aside and said, "Anna, you're a good soldier and we are grateful." She understood what the President meant. Nixon remained anxious about both the failure of the preelection peace talks and what the Democrats might have learned about his role in insuring that failure. It was not until much later, Mrs. Chennault added, that Mitchell confided to her the name of the man responsible for supplying the inside information about Lyndon Johnson's attempt to make a last-minute settlement of the war—Henry Kissinger.

In the first volume of his memoirs, *White House Years,* published in 1979, Kissinger discussed only a few of his preelection contacts with the Nixon campaign. "During the national campaign in 1968," he wrote, "several Nixon emissaries—some self-appointed—telephoned me for counsel. I took the position that I would answer specific questions on foreign policy, but that I would not offer general advice or volunteer suggestions." * He specifically denied any direct contact during the campaign.

Kissinger wrote that his direct contact with the Nixon camp began a few weeks after the election, when Dwight Chapin, who was to become Nixon's appointments secretary, invited Kissinger to meet with the President-elect on November 25. The call came while Kissinger was attending a luncheon strategy session in Manhattan with Nelson Rockefeller and a few associates to deal with the question whether Rockefeller should take a Cabinet position in the Nixon Administration if one were offered. After the call, Kissinger wrote, the men resumed their conversation "as if nothing had happened. No one at the

* William F. Buckley, Jr., editor of the conservative *National Review,* has a different recollection. In his 1974 memoir, *United Nations Journal: A Delegate's Odyssey,* he wrote that Kissinger invited him to lunch shortly after the Republican convention. Kissinger "had a few ideas he thought would be interesting to Nixon, in framing his foreign policy campaign speeches. But these ideas he must advance discreetly, as he would not wish it to appear, having just now left the dismantled Rockefeller staff, to be job-seeking." Buckley dutifully telephoned Nixon's headquarters and praised Kissinger and his suggestions, but nothing, apparently, came of that contact.

lunch could conceive that the purpose of the call would be to offer me a major position in the new Administration.''

Other sources, with direct access to Kissinger, make clear that Kissinger expected his high-risk reporting for the Nixon campaign to project him into the post of national security adviser. According to a biography of Kissinger by Marvin and Bernard Kalb—which, as the authors acknowledge, was prepared with Kissinger's cooperation—Kissinger had earlier discussed that job with Helmut Sonnenfeldt, a State Department intelligence official who, like Kissinger, had come to the United States as a refugee from Nazi Germany and who had been in the Army in Germany with Kissinger at the end of World War II. The Kalbs' book quoted Sonnenfeldt as telling Kissinger shortly after the Republican convention that he, Kissinger, had the best credentials for the job. Kissinger "demurred," but did manage to offer Sonnenfeldt a chance to join him at the NSC if the job should materialize.

What the Kalbs did not report is that shortly after the election Kissinger sought again to bring himself to Nixon's attention via an alarming report to William Buckley. On that day, November 12, Secretary of Defense Clark M. Clifford had publicly warned Thieu that unless he agreed to participate in the Paris peace talks, the United States would be compelled to proceed without him. At a news conference, Clifford made no effort to conceal his anger, according to a report in the *New York Times,* at Thieu's last-minute objections to the Johnson bombing halt negotiations.

"Nixon should be told," Kissinger told Buckley, "that it is probably an objective of Clifford to depose Thieu before Nixon is inaugurated. Word should be gotten to Nixon that if Thieu meets the same fate as Diem, the word will go out to the nations of the world that it may be dangerous to be America's enemy, but to be America's friend is fatal." Kissinger urged Buckley to relay the information to the President-elect to prevent any such action. Buckley telephoned Frank Shakespeare, a senior vice president of CBS whom Nixon was about to nominate as director of the United States Information Agency, and told him, as Shakespeare recalls, "This is an important matter." Shakespeare, as Buckley knew, had access to the Nixon inner circle, and he quickly set up the first Nixon-Kissinger meeting with a telephone call to John Mitchell.*

The fact that there was no known basis for Kissinger's concern about high-level Democratic assassination plots proved to be irrelevant over the next few days. Kissinger, with his warnings of such plots, was once again proving him-

* Buckley, citing his "notes" of the conversation, described the Kissinger call in his 1974 *United Nations* memoir. Earlier, however, he gave a far more dramatic version. Edward J. Rozek, a conservative Republican with close ties to the Nixon White House, recalls that in mid-1971 Buckley told friends in the Pentagon that Kissinger claimed, in the telephone call, to have heard that the Johnson Administration was planning to assassinate Thieu. Rozek, who later became director of the Institute of Comparative Politics and Ideologies at the University of Colorado, wrote about the Buckley conversation in a 1980 review of Kissinger's memoirs. He remembered discussing the matter with Frank Shakespeare a year or so later, when Shakespeare made a speech at the University of Colorado. At that time, Rozek wrote, Shakespeare also linked Kissinger's call to an alleged assassination. In a conversation with me in early 1982, however, Shakespeare said he could not remember any mention of assassination. Buckley, through his office, also said Kissinger had not mentioned assassination. Rozek wrote to me that he would stand by his account, which was published in *Survey* magazine in London. He was convinced that "there was no truth" to Kissinger's claim that Thieu's life was in danger.

self a loyalist—and his fealty was undoubtedly linked to Nixon's decision to grant the interview on November 25. By then, there was ample reason for Nixon to believe that Kissinger had established sufficient credentials to be considered for the national security adviser's position.

Richard Allen recalls that a few days after the election, James Keogh, a senior campaign aide, asked him—as Nixon's foreign affairs coordinator in the campaign—whom he would recommend for national security adviser. Allen answered without hesitation. He "thought Henry was the best and the brightest."

A few days later, Peter M. Flanigan, Nixon's deputy campaign manager, who was responsible for political appointments, asked Allen what he thought of Kissinger for the NSC job. Allen quickly filled Flanigan in on Kissinger's behind-the-scenes activity during the campaign. "I told Flanigan that Henry helped us a lot," Allen says.

Nixon, discussing how he came to pick Kissinger, made it plain in his memoirs that he viewed the secret reporting as vital: "During the last days of the campaign, when Kissinger was providing us with information about the bombing halt, I became more aware of both his knowledge and his influence." Nixon was impressed not only by Kissinger's extensive knowledge and contacts, but also by his willingness to make use of those assets. "I had a strong intuition about Henry Kissinger," he wrote.

Nixon had found his man, and, after the two had another talk on November 27, he offered Kissinger the job—which, Nixon said, was immediately accepted.

Kissinger, not surprisingly, had a different recollection. In *his* memoirs, he described himself as unsure about what job was really being offered when he first talked with Nixon. And then, Kissinger wrote, upon being specifically told before the second meeting that he was being offered the NSC position he coveted, he asked the President-elect to give him a week to decide. Two days later he said yes.

During those days, while Nixon believed Kissinger had agreed to take the job, Kissinger went to friends at Harvard and elsewhere, sharing his secret and asking advice. At an academic conference that week at Princeton University, for example, Kissinger ran into Carl Kaysen, former deputy assistant for national security affairs in the Kennedy Administration, and talked with him privately. "Henry told me that he'd gotten a call from Nixon and, to his utter astonishment, Nixon had asked him to be his national security adviser," Kaysen says. " 'Am I equal to the task, Carl?' he asked me. 'I'm so scared.' "

Of the many colleagues and friends who were sought out for advice, most recall their amused conviction that the only advice Kissinger wanted was that he take the job.

2

A NEW
NSC SYSTEM

HENRY KISSINGER'S PERFORMANCE in the two months between his selection
as Special Assistant for National Security Affairs and the inauguration of Richard Nixon seemed flawless. His academic credentials were widely praised in
the press. He assembled a first-rate staff, and he successfully met his first
presidential demand: new guidelines for the control of foreign policy. Nixon
and Kissinger wanted authority shifted to the White House and thus to themselves. In a pattern that was to become typical, Nixon stayed largely in the
background during the struggle over the new NSC system in late December
and January. It was Kissinger who dealt with the resentment of the State
Department and of its newly appointed Secretary, William P. Rogers. And it
was Kissinger, representing the insistent demands of his patron, who seemed
to win the major victory over Rogers.

Kissinger's goal was institutional power. The NSC had been set up, at the
same time as the Central Intelligence Agency, by the National Security Act of
1947, which assigned it the task of advising the President "with respect to the
integration of domestic, foreign and military policies relating to national security." But the NSC was to be more than a clearing house for competing interests in the bureaucracy. Congress also ordered it to independently "assess and
appraise the objectives, commitments, and risks of the United States in relation to our actual and potential military power." Statutory NSC members
included the President, the Vice President, the Secretaries of State and Defense, and the director of the Office of Emergency Planning, with the chairman
of the Joint Chiefs of Staff and the director of Central Intelligence serving as
advisers.

The 1947 legislation also called for an executive director of the National
Security Council, who, in theory, was to have immense influence on the control and monitoring of the overseas operations of the armed forces and the
intelligence agencies. But each President, beginning with Harry S Truman,
tended to delegate responsibility for national security affairs to a special assistant on his White House staff who operated independently of the NSC and its
executive director. During the Eisenhower Administration, the NSC system
became heavily bureaucratized, with the establishment of a formal Planning
Board that monitored all foreign policy papers going to the President for review. The result was cautious consensus and generalized policy guidance that
diluted the influence of the NSC and did little to challenge the authority of

Secretary of State John Foster Dulles, who had close personal and philosophical ties to the President. President Kennedy further eschewed the NSC's formal apparatus and moved the job of assistant to the President for national security affairs into the limelight with the appointment of McGeorge Bundy, a Harvard professor and dean of faculty. In crises Kennedy consistently bypassed the NSC, with its interagency discussions and disputes, and brought decision making into the White House on an ad hoc basis. During the Cuban missile crisis in the fall of 1962, for example, decisions were made and ratified through what was called the Excomm, a hastily assembled committee of Kennedy insiders, on which Bundy played a significant role. The NSC and its executive director continued to operate in these years, but had increasingly little of import to do. President Johnson also chose to maneuver informally on key issues, especially in dealing with the war in Vietnam, and eventually set up a regular Tuesday lunch at which the administration's principals, including Walt W. Rostow, who became special assistant after Bundy resigned in 1966, would meet to discuss and formulate policy without any advance memoranda or planning. During those years, the staff aides on the NSC routinely found themselves serving in support of the President's assistant for national security affairs, and the size of the NSC staff steadily increased. By the early 1960s, NSC staff aides were filling dozens of offices in the White House and the Executive Office Building. The NSC executive director, with his small staff, also maintained offices in the Executive Office Building. The two staffs were not formally consolidated until Richard Nixon took office.

Of the men closest to the President-elect in December 1968, Kissinger was the most experienced in national security affairs. He had been a consultant to the NSC under Kennedy, and was far from a newcomer to covert intelligence operations. He had served in the Army Counterintelligence Corps at the close of World War II and stayed on active duty in occupied West Germany after the war. He was eventually assigned to the 970th CIC Detachment, whose functions included support for the recruitment of ex-Nazi intelligence officers for anti-Soviet operations inside the Soviet bloc.* After entering Harvard as an undergraduate in 1947, at age twenty-four, he retained his ties, as a reserve officer, to military intelligence. By 1950, he was a graduate student and was working part time for the Defense Department—one of the first at Harvard to begin regular shuttles to Washington—as a consultant to its Operations Re-

* The 970th Detachment, later known as the 66th CIC Detachment, was under orders after the war to collect information on ex-Nazis who could be utilized for anti-Soviet intelligence operations. Documents from the 66th Detachment later made available to Justice Department officials showed that among the unit's functions was the compiling of research for use in a series of anti-Soviet operations in the Ukraine and elsewhere inside Russia. Such work was carried out at secret bases in Germany. Kissinger later transferred to the Army's Military Intelligence Service and became an instructor at the Army's European Command Intelligence School at Oberammergau, in western Germany, at the same time the facility was training American intelligence officers to exploit the use of Nazi collaborators who had fled from Eastern Europe to the displaced persons camps of western Germany. Kissinger stayed on at Oberammergau as a civilian instructor for a year after being mustered out of Army military intelligence in May of 1946. There is no evidence that Kissinger knew what was going on in the 970th CIC Detachment or at Oberammergau, in terms of the recruitment and use of former Nazi partisans for operations against the Soviet Union, but such activities, although highly classified, were an open secret among many military intelligence and CIC personnel in western Germany at the time.

search Office. That unit, under the direct control of the Joint Chiefs of Staff, conducted highly classified studies on such topics as the utilization of former German operatives and Nazi partisan supporters in CIA clandestine activities. In 1952, Kissinger was named a consultant to the director of the Psychological Strategy Board, an operating arm of the National Security Council for covert psychological and paramilitary operations. In 1954, President Eisenhower appointed Nelson Rockefeller his Special Assistant for Cold War Planning, a position that involved the monitoring and approval of covert CIA operations. These were the days of CIA successes in Iran, where the Shah was installed on the throne, and in Guatemala, where the government of Jacobo Arbenz, considered anti-American and antibusiness, was overthrown. In 1955, Kissinger, already known to insiders for his closeness to Rockefeller and Rockefeller's reliance on him, was named a consultant to the NSC's Operations Coordinating Board, which was then the highest policy-making board for implementing clandestine operations against foreign governments.

Kissinger has written and said little about his high-level exposure to clandestine operations in the early 1950s. Former intelligence officials recall that the young Harvard scholar had come to the attention of Allen Dulles, Eisenhower's influential CIA director, even before the Rockefeller appointment. "He was highly regarded," according to Elmer B. Staats, who was executive director of the Operations Coordinating Board from 1953 to 1958. "Allen spoke of his meetings with him. He and Walt Rostow [who then was a professor at MIT] were considered kind of a team."

One little-known fact is that in late 1955 Rockefeller was replaced as the presidential adviser on Cold War strategy by Vice President Nixon. There is no record of Nixon's having met Kissinger in those days, although many former intelligence aides consider it highly likely that Nixon was aware of Kissinger's intelligence work.

There is evidence, however, that Nixon and Kissinger, within days of Kissinger's appointment, were working in far more harmony than outsiders—and many Nixon insiders—could perceive. The grab for control had been signaled at President-elect Nixon's news conference on December 2, 1968, at which he made the formal announcement of Kissinger's appointment and introduced his national security adviser to the press. Nixon told the press that Kissinger would move immediately to revitalize the National Security Council system. He would set up "a very exciting new procedure for seeing to it that the next President of the United States does not hear just what he wants to hear, which is always a temptation for White House staffers, but that he hears points of view covering the spectrum. . . ." In addition, "Dr. Kissinger is keenly aware of the necessity not to set himself up as a wall between the President and the Secretary of State or the Secretary of Defense. I intend to have a very strong Secretary of State."

Nixon's public statements had little to do with what he wanted done. At their first meeting, on November 25, according to Kissinger's memoirs, Nixon talked about "a massive organizational problem . . . He had very little confidence in the State Department. Its personnel had no loyalty to him; the Foreign Service had disdained him as Vice President and ignored him the moment he was out of office. He was determined to run foreign policy from the White House. He thought the Johnson Administration had ignored the military and

27

that its decision-making procedures gave the President no real options. He felt it imperative to exclude the CIA from the formulation of policy; it was staffed by Ivy League liberals who behind the façade of analytical objectivity were usually pushing their own preferences. They had always opposed him politically.''

Kissinger records himself as merely agreeing that ''there was a need for a more formal decision-making process.'' Nixon recalls much enthusiasm. In his memoirs, he even credits Kissinger with actually articulating the notion of centralizing power in the NSC inside the White House: ''Kissinger said he was delighted that I was thinking in such terms. He said that if I intended to operate on such a wide-ranging basis, I was going to need the best possible system for getting advice. . . . Kissinger recommended that I structure a national security apparatus within the White House that, in addition to coordinating foreign and defense policy, could also develop policy options for me to consider before making decisions.''

The dispute between Kissinger and Nixon over who proposed what remains, but the fact is that what they discussed in private that November—the centralization of power in the White House—was not hinted at in their news conference. Kissinger attributed Nixon's misleading remarks to the press to the President-elect's fear of criticism over the proposed NSC restructuring. ''In his eagerness to deflect any possible criticism,'' Kissinger wrote in his memoirs, Nixon ''announced a program substantially at variance with what he had told me.'' Kissinger was untroubled by such discrepancies. ''The pledges of each new Administration,'' he explained, ''are like leaves on a turbulent sea.''

The press was handled readily enough, as it would be throughout their first term, but the President-elect and his new adviser had a much more formidable task convincing some of Nixon's senior campaign staff that all authority should reside in the President's office. During this intense and secret preinaugural struggle to gain control of the NSC, Nixon came out of the shadows at least once, to help Kissinger manipulate and deceive a senior member of the staff. Their first opponent was Bryce Harlow, the former Eisenhower aide, who had served Nixon faithfully during the 1968 campaign and who seemed to have authority in those early days. His first recommendation about the NSC was accepted, and Nixon brought in General Andrew J. Goodpaster, deputy commander of the American forces in South Vietnam, to serve as his temporary military adviser.

General Goodpaster had been on the White House staff during the Eisenhower Administration, handling national security matters. Those were the years, in Harlow's eyes, when the NSC functioned as an advisory and analytic group rather than a policy maker, as it did under such strong-willed men as McGeorge Bundy and Walt Rostow in the Kennedy and Johnson administrations. In mid-December, Harlow presented these views to Kissinger and Nixon. ''My idea,'' he says, ''was that Kissinger should be a faceless, anonymous professional whose role is to produce papers for the great to work their will on. I told them they had to return the NSC to its rightful role.'' He left pleased with the meeting and with Kissinger's apparent assent, but he was already a marked man. Named as one of four presidential assistants after the inauguration, he quickly found his title meaningless and his duties constricted in a White House run by Nixon, H. R. Haldeman as Chief of Staff, John D. Ehrlichman, then White House Counsel, and Henry Kissinger.

Harlow would come to understand later that Kissinger and Nixon did not want the NSC to be an anonymous funnel, but to seize control, to tell the bureaucracies what to research and when to report. Setting up the new machinery was Kissinger's first, and most vital, assignment. But heretofore he had served only as a part-time White House consultant and knew little of the day-to-day workings of the special assistant's office and the National Security Council. How to begin? At this point, he turned to Morton Halperin, the thirty-year-old Deputy Assistant Secretary of Defense. Halperin, aggressive, secretive, and ambitious, was considered among the brightest administrators in the Pentagon. He had played an important role in helping the Johnson Administration begin to reverse its policies in Vietnam, and had become a major force in that administration's planning on strategic arms control. Working for the Nixon Administration posed no problem for him; he was a Republican who had been one of the founders of the liberal Republican Ripon Society in the mid-1960s. Early in 1967, when he was in the Pentagon, he had even been approached about becoming Nixon's international policy adviser during the 1968 presidential primaries. He had also spent six years teaching a series of defense policy courses at Harvard with Kissinger, beginning in 1961, the year he earned his doctorate in political science at Yale. He had been lobbying for a NSC job since Kissinger's appointment was announced.

Halperin was in the right spot at the right time. He was scheduled to give a lecture on December 16 to Kissinger's national security policy seminar at Harvard—a Government Department course attended by many military and civilian officials in mid-career—and it turned out to be Kissinger's last Cambridge appearance. The two men talked and Kissinger asked Halperin to join his staff. His first assignment would be to prepare a paper on systems-analysis techniques that could be used in foreign-policy decision making. Halperin, seizing the opportunity, took it upon himself to draft a broad memorandum that placed nearly all the power in the hands of the national security adviser.

Halperin understood the needs of his master as well as Kissinger understood the needs of his. The projected system gave Kissinger the power to decide the agenda for National Security Council meetings and also made him chairman of the review group that considered the various option papers prepared by the bureaucracy. Under the existing machinery, that function had been controlled by the State Department. In addition, Halperin's memorandum gave Kissinger direct authority to order State and other agencies to prepare option papers on specific subjects; such orders were to be known as National Security Study Memoranda. The President's policy decision, to be made after a National Security Council meeting, would take the form of a highly classified National Security Decision Memorandum written by Kissinger and his staff. Subsequent implementation of the President's policy would be in the hands of an under secretary's committee to be chaired by a State Department representative— the only important policy group that would still be led by State. That group would also handle issues not important enough for the full NSC. Under the proposed system, even the lower-level working groups for each geographical region would report directly to White House officials. Halperin's paper was endorsed in full by Kissinger and became the basis for the subsequent NSC reorganization that Nixon approved.

It was now late December and Kissinger had begun assembling a temporary staff at Nixon's postelection headquarters in the Hotel Pierre. One of the first aides was Lawrence S. Eagleburger, a Foreign Service officer with impeccable Republican credentials who was to emerge over the next few weeks as Kissinger's personal aide and one of his closest deputies. Eagleburger, then thirty-eight years old, was a witty extrovert from Stevens Point, Wisconsin, with a very tough side—he was harshly anti-Soviet and a strong supporter of the use of force in diplomacy. His mother had worked in the local campaigns of Melvin R. Laird, the Wisconsin congressman whom Nixon had just nominated as Secretary of Defense. Kissinger turned the Halperin memorandum over to Eagleburger, directing him to recast it as a memorandum from Kissinger to the President—and to do so without telling Halperin. Another Kissinger aide, Roger Morris, also a Foreign Service officer, recalls Eagleburger's immediate reaction to the Halperin paper: "Whatever happened to the Secretary of State?"

Eagleburger was nonplused by the Halperin document. Since he did not know enough about the procedural background to judge it, he quietly sought Halperin's help and advice, as is normal in bureaucracy.* Despite their different backgrounds, Kissinger, Halperin, and Eagleburger were all superbly skilled at the bureaucratic game—with one exception: Kissinger did not at first seem to realize that he, as a senior government official, would certainly be the target of such maneuvers.

Halperin took the intrigue in stride: "I gave the paper to Henry and never saw it again. The next thing I knew Eagleburger saw me and said Henry wanted his help in redoing the memo for the President. Henry had told Eagleburger not to tell me, and so Eagleburger asked me not to say anything. Henry didn't know that I knew what he'd done with my memo." Halperin, eager for a major role on Kissinger's staff, was not about to spoil his chances with unnecessary talk.

But Halperin had to suffer one minor indignity even then. Kissinger was afraid Goodpaster would want to leave his combat assignment permanently and remain the White House senior military adviser, as General Maxwell D. Taylor had been for Kennedy in 1961. Goodpaster would then be a direct competitor. Kissinger's solution, Halperin says, was to demonstrate repeatedly to Goodpaster that the national security was in the hands of a tough-minded pragmatist. Since Halperin was viewed with suspicion by many Pentagon military men, he was to be kept out of sight. And so, as Halperin puts it, "One of Eagleburger's jobs in the Hotel Pierre was to kick me out of Henry's office if Goodpaster was coming."

Goodpaster had been among the first to urge the President-elect to

---

* Some would go further and argue that in the national-security area, trading information is a necessary part of the bureaucratic makeup. Openness, in this view, is a detriment. In 1965, Daniel Ellsberg was working for the late John T. McNaughton, a Pentagon official who played a key role on Vietnam issues in the Johnson Administration. "One day," Ellsberg recalls, "just to flatter McNaughton in a friendly way, I told him that I'd had lunch at the State Department with someone who said to me, 'The nice thing about your boss is he's absolutely open and straightforward.' I want you to know I defended your honor," Ellsberg quotes himself as telling McNaughton. "I told him you were the most devious man I knew. He laughed and said, 'Thank you.' "

strengthen his control over the NSC. His goal, he told colleagues, was to provide a mechanism for presidential intervention on major policy decisions, thus preventing the Secretaries of State and Defense from getting locked into disputes from which they could not gracefully retreat. Goodpaster, of course, had no idea that his modest suggestions would be seized on to justify the drastic Nixon-Kissinger reorganization, which eliminated the potential for dispute between the Pentagon and State by eliminating the role of the latter. Under the new NSC procedure, senior military men would be able to present their important proposals directly to Kissinger without the prior clearance of the Secretary of Defense or his deputy.

On December 27, having successfully fooled Bryce Harlow and neutralized General Goodpaster, Kissinger submitted Halperin's ten-page reorganization proposal to the President-elect. In a covering note, he apologized for the document's length—even in 1967, ten pages was obviously too long for Nixon— and noted that General Goodpaster "agrees with my recommendations." Nixon initialed his approval that day. The next day, the new administration's principal foreign policy advisers were summoned to Nixon's vacation home in Key Biscayne, Florida, for a five-hour meeting on foreign affairs. In attendance, along with Kissinger, were Laird, Rogers, Harlow, Goodpaster, and Spiro T. Agnew, the Vice President-elect. Kissinger had prepared a talking paper for the discussion, and Nixon, making it clear that he had already agreed to the reorganization, presented it for his advisers' pro forma approval. He got it.

The press, briefed about the meeting on a background basis, was deliberately misled. Journalists were told, as the *New York Times* reported next morning, that Nixon intended to "enlarge the role of the National Security Council" and had ordered Kissinger to submit a reorganization plan for doing so "in the next few weeks . . . The President-elect is expected to give a sympathetic reception," the *Times* said. The first stories on the proposed reorganization took what Kissinger and Nixon said at face value. James Reston, the eminent columnist for the *Times,* began what was to be a close relationship with Kissinger by noting two days after his appointment as national security adviser that it was "reassuring" that one of the new administration's goals would be to rebuild the NSC and restore "the authority it had under President Eisenhower." In an analytical article a few days later, Max Frankel, then the Washington bureau chief of the *Times,* elevated Kissinger's academic standing to near-greatness. "At 45," Frankel wrote, "he has become . . . a leader in the first generation of atomic-age scholars attempting to cope with the consequences of the balance of terror." The warm notices for Kissinger undoubtedly reflected the Washington press corps' immense relief that Nixon had not chosen someone with more right-wing views or of lesser intelligence. Another factor may have been the aura of Harvard. In any case, it seems clear that Kissinger did not have to cultivate a favorable press: It came with the job.

Within a few days, as word about the Kissinger-Nixon coup spread through the top ranks of the State Department, opposition mounted. But the would-be protesters first had to convince the newly nominated Secretary of State.

One of the mysteries of the Nixon era is why the President-elect decided to name William P. Rogers Secretary of State. Rogers, fifty-five years old at the time of his nomination, was a ranking Republican who had served as Attorney General in the Eisenhower Administration and who, with his wife, had befriended the Nixons in their years of crises while Nixon was Eisenhower's Vice President. As Rogers grew more prosperous in his corporate law practice in New York City and Washington in the 1960s, he and Nixon, who had also begun practicing law in New York after his defeat in the California gubernatorial election, drifted apart. Rogers was not Nixon's first choice for Secretary of State.* Nonetheless, Bryce Harlow recalls that when Nixon first discussed naming Rogers, it was agreed that he would be able to handle negotiations with the Russians. "He's cold, mean and tough," in Harlow's assessment. Asked why, in that case, Rogers let himself and his department be overrun by Kissinger, Harlow could only say, "Rogers didn't try. He could have whipped Kissinger easily."

In reality, Kissinger won his bureaucratic wars not because Rogers did not try, but because Nixon wanted it that way. Rogers agreed to serve as Secretary of State with the knowledge that foreign affairs would be run from the White House and that he would have little to do with them. When Nixon first mentioned the job to him, Rogers says, he expressed reluctance to leave his law firm and recommended that the job be offered to Nelson Rockefeller. Rogers also told the President-elect that he knew little about foreign affairs. It was that ignorance, Nixon replied, that made the job his. "I was prepared to play a subordinate role," Rogers recalls. "I recognized that he wanted to be his own foreign policy leader and did not want others to share that role. After all, the man who ran for office and won deserves [to make his own decisions]. I knew that Nixon would be the principal actor and, when Kissinger came along, I recognized that he would be a very valuable asset to the presidency."

Rogers' willingness to take a back seat insured the success of the bureaucratic restructuring. For all its failings, the new system might have operated in harmony—Nixon was, after all, the President—if Kissinger had not decided, sometime in his first years in office, that he should be Secretary of State in title as well as in practice. Rogers did seem to accept the limits of his role. One of Rogers' aides remembers that in late December 1967 he urged his boss to discuss the revised guidelines directly with the President, but "Rogers told me that if we did go to the President, we wouldn't win. He said it was better to 'wedge out' what we could."

Rogers' insight was correct—he was never to play a major role in the Nixon-Kissinger foreign policy. Although most published accounts of the Nixon-Rogers relationship have stressed their personal friendship, there is evidence that at best it was bittersweet; according to Rogers, the two men saw each other only rarely during the years they both lived in New York. Many of Rogers' friends believe that Nixon was jealous of Rogers' success as a corporate lawyer, and also of his attractiveness to and ease with women. Rogers'

* Nixon's first choice was reported to be Thomas E. Dewey, the former New York governor who narrowly lost the 1948 presidential election to Harry S. Truman. It's not known whether the offer, if made, was a serious one. Nixon wrote in his memoirs that he had sounded out Dewey, through John Mitchell, to serve as Chief Justice of the Supreme Court in 1969 after the resignation of Abe Fortas. "But, as I expected," Nixon wrote, "he ruled himself out because of his age." According to the Kissinger memoirs, Dewey was also one of three men, including Kissinger, whom Nixon later considered for the job of emissary to China during the secret Washington-Peking talks.

social graces, unfortunately, did little to make up for his lack of experience in foreign affairs. Kissinger and many of his aides wrote him off as uninformed, even stupid, and a coward. From the moment of his first talk with the President-elect at the Hotel Pierre, he was marked as an ineffectual Secretary of State—with substantial consequences for the foreign policy of the Nixon Administration, since he was one of the few inclined to be conciliatory in moments of international crisis. Advice from a man who was viewed as having participated in his own beheading simply provoked further Nixon-Kissinger estrangement from the State Department and its "soft" diplomats.

Some senior State Department officials concluded years later that much of Rogers' problem with Nixon was his own doing. Elliot L. Richardson, who was Under Secretary of State, offers one explanation: "Rogers could not psychologically bring himself to subordinate himself to Nixon, and that played right into Henry's hands. Rogers felt that in terms of character and judgment he was a better man and he could not subordinate himself, which an effective Secretary of State must do. It's true that Rogers didn't have any inclination to engage in the strategic planning process—but he didn't try."

Rogers' reluctance to fight created an immediate loss of morale in the State Department. Even before the Halperin memorandum on the NSC was presented to Nixon in Key Biscayne, Eagleburger had told Roger Morris about it in confidence.* Out of loyalty to the Foreign Service, the two aides had then told Arthur A. Hartman, a career diplomat who was in charge of the State Department's Senior Interdepartment Group, which until the Kissinger era held the major responsibility for monitoring the flow of papers inside the State Department. "We said," Morris recalls, " 'You're going to get screwed; you're going to lose all kinds of power. We don't think this building should be cut out.' " Hartman, who later became an Assistant Secretary of State under

* Morris' complex relationship with Eagleburger is a good illustration of one path to success in the Foreign Service. Eagleburger rose quickly in the State Department by getting the right assignments at the right time. During the early 1960s, he was a junior officer in Belgrade, Yugoslavia; then he returned to Washington to serve as a line officer in the State Department's executive secretariat, the clearing house for all communications between Washington and American embassies throughout the world. During the 1966 crisis, when France withdrew from NATO, President Johnson summoned former Secretary of State Dean Acheson as his special assistant and consultant on NATO matters. Acheson selected Eagleburger, known as a hardliner, as his aide, and Eagleburger, with the advantage of having an office in State and working for the White House, immediately began a sophisticated intelligence operation. He would sit in meetings at State and relay anything significant to Francis M. Bator, the National Security Council's aide for NATO. By providing Bator with such inside information, he was aiding Bator in his job and building up a credit. When Acheson retired later in the year, Eagleburger naturally found himself with a job working with Bator in the NSC. While Eagleburger was making those moves, Morris was assigned, as a very junior Foreign Service officer, to work in the State Department's European Bureau as a special assistant to John Leddy, Assistant Secretary of State for European Affairs. Morris quickly began passing information covertly from the European Bureau to Bator's office in the White House, helping both Bator and Eagleburger. In June 1967, McGeorge Bundy, who had been national security adviser to President John F. Kennedy, was recruited by the Johnson Administration for a special assignment and asked Bator, an old colleague from Harvard, for a bright young assistant. Bator assigned Morris to Bundy's staff; eventually Walt Rostow asked Morris to stay on the White House staff. Eagleburger, meanwhile, had been reassigned as a deputy to Nicholas de B. Katzenbach, the Johnson Administration's Under Secretary of State, after Bator left the White House. It was Katzenbach, among others, who recommended Eagleburger to Kissinger in December 1968, when Kissinger was looking for a compatible Foreign Service officer to be an aide. "These games, and this espionage, were gentlemanly in the Johnson Administration," Morris insists. "It was not malicious compared to what happened later."

33

Kissinger, apologetically explained that no one wanted to fight Kissinger. "We can't get anyone to step forward," Hartman told Morris.

Morris and Eagleburger were upset and angry. "It was basically a lost cause," Morris saw. "State's idea was to wait it out and see if once the first wave of White House enthusiasm had passed, the bureaucratic flow would go back to State."

U. Alexis Johnson was the most experienced by far of Rogers' senior appointees and the most aggrieved by what was happening. As Deputy Under Secretary for Political Affairs in the Johnson Administration, he fit the mold of the tough-minded, relentlessly anti-Communist State Department official who was the essence of discretion. He was a hawk on Vietnam, and this, plus his long tours in Washington, finally earned him a post he had long desired: In 1966 he was appointed Ambassador to Japan. Rogers brought him back before the inauguration, promising to upgrade his title to Under Secretary of State and assuring him he would have full authority as the senior operating Foreign Service officer. All these promises, Johnson learned in a few moments at the Hotel Pierre, were in jeopardy. He had helped restructure the NSC in the Eisenhower years, and had been instrumental in establishing State's Senior Interdepartment Group, which Henry Kissinger had now dismantled. There was a brief and unpleasant meeting with Kissinger. "I told Henry I'd heard what was up and told him what was wrong with it," Johnson says. "We had a vigorous five-minute exchange. I was seeking to get the same kind of relationship we had with McGeorge Bundy. I wanted it clear when it was the President who wanted something or when it was he." Kissinger was equally direct: "It's already been decided and this is the way it's going to be." Johnson realized, after brief chats with Rogers and Richardson, that neither "had any notion what it was all about." He returned to Japan to make his farewells, knowing that "we weren't going to have the same kind of relationship with Kissinger as with Mac." He sent Richardson a private message from Tokyo outlining his reservations, but it was too late. Returning to Washington he learned that "it was a *fait accompli*." When Johnson, ever the bureaucrat, began working closely with Kissinger, he was reviled by many in the State Department, but in his view he was only doing what was necessary. "He honestly believed," one of his aides explains, "that it was in the best interest of the country; that he had to be subservient to Henry to protect the Foreign Service."

As word of the White House takeover seeped through State, even junior officers perceived what Kissinger understood very early—that despite all of the public talk about "policy options" and free-flowing dissent, Nixon wanted to chart the future course of the United States in secret and without opposition. And only with Kissinger. The irony that the President and his chief advisers were refusing to listen to dissent over a policy allegedly designed to open up channels for dissent obviously escaped Kissinger, who minimized his role and the Johnson encounter in his memoirs. Johnson, Kissinger wrote, had only made a foolish effort "to encourage Bill Rogers to fight a rearguard action to defend the preëminence of the State Department—which even five minutes' conversation with Nixon could leave no doubt that the President-elect would ever tolerate."

One staff member who looked on at the process was Richard M. Moose, another former Foreign Service officer who had worked for Rostow's NSC and

was an early Kissinger recruit. A liberal Democrat by background and inclination, he watched bemused as the State Department cut its own throat. "I
had come down, may God forgive me," Moose recalls with a grin, "for a very
strong NSC. The more the State Department fought, the worse they dug themselves in." Protests from Alexis Johnson and others in State "allowed Henry
to appear to be protecting the President and the State Department to be defending the status quo."

The next step—imposing the system on the bureaucracy—was the most
crucial. Three National Security Decision Memoranda formally promulgating
the new procedures were drafted by Halperin and Eagleburger, approved and
signed by Nixon, and circulated on Inauguration Day. In addition, Kissinger
ordered his staff to begin writing National Security Study Memoranda on topics ranging from Vietnam to foreign aid. The formal requests for the NSSMs
were distributed to government offices on January 21.

This first batch of "requests" seemed to have three goals: First, they were
a sincere effort to get the bureaucracy to begin thinking in terms of different
options to foreign policy questions; second, they asserted the ascendancy of
the Kissinger apparatus; and finally, with their requirements of lengthy studies
and impossibly short deadlines, they were intended to overwhelm the "faceless civil servants" so despised by Nixon. In its first month in office, Kissinger's staff issued twenty-two NSSMs requesting broad studies on every
important issue before the new administration. Yet, as Kissinger concedes in
his memoirs, the most important decisions were made without informing the
bureaucracy, and without the use of NSSMs or NSDMs.

Morton Halperin, analyzing the NSC in a scholarly article years later, argued
that the initiation of the system was not a "cynical act. The President certainly
wanted it and some on Kissinger's staff struggled to make it work." Nonetheless, Halperin conceded, the system, as it evolved, seemed best equipped to
deal with the secondary problems of the Nixon Administration.*

Richard Allen recalls that he and Kissinger discussed the system before the
Nixon inauguration and Kissinger "knew at the time that the best of these
studies wouldn't see the light for a year. He kept them busy. He wanted to
demoralize the bureaucracy by keeping them overwhelmed."

In his memoirs, Kissinger dismissed the disputes over the revised National
Security Council procedures as "important less in terms of real power than in
appearance . . . Nor was it a crucial grant of power to me to the degree that
was often alleged." He repeatedly purveyed that view in his first years in the
White House, telling one group of reporters that "I cannot believe that with
seven people I am going to be able to take over both the State Department and

---

* One notable success, cited by many former National Security Council aides, was the Nixon-
Kissinger decision to ban chemical and biological weapons unilaterally. In National Security Decision Memorandum No. 35 on November 25, 1969, the White House proclaimed, after a series of
internal NSC reviews, that it was renouncing the first use of lethal and incapacitating chemical
weapons and submitting to the 1925 Geneva Protocol barring all use of asphyxiating, poisonous, or
other gases. A similar renunciation of biological agents was announced, along with a major cutback
in the Army's budget for the weaponry. Roger Morris has argued that the National Security Council
review process was essential in achieving the renunciations. Kissinger saw, Morris wrote in Uncertain Greatness, his 1977 study of Kissinger, "the prospect of a relatively painless unilateral arms
control initiative valuable in setting the stage for later diplomacy with the Soviet Union." Another
factor, perhaps, was the chance for the White House to make a public announcement that would
undercut the antiwar movement, then protesting, among other things, the My Lai massacre.

the Defense Department," and insisting that it was the President, and not he, who made the final decisions. In the Kalbs' biography, he is quoted as saying, "There is no 'Kissinger policy' on the questions of substance. My task is to convey the full range of policy options to the President. If there were a 'Kissinger policy,' the whole new mechanism we have set up in the National Security Council—not to speak of relations between the governmental agencies—would be in shambles."

But, of course, revised national security procedures insured that, far from providing options to a President Nixon who brooked no dissent, Kissinger would be in sole control of the flow of documents for the President to study. And since one of the most carefully kept secrets of the administration was how little independent consulting and study the President actually did, only a very few understood that Kissinger's private advice was inevitably the one most relied upon by Nixon.

Even Halperin, who prided himself on his pragmatism and who had as much to do with the new NSC system as anyone besides Kissinger, did not at the outset fully comprehend Kissinger's real objectives. On January 25, 1969, five days into the administration, the NSC was convened for its first meeting. The issue was Vietnam, and Halperin, now clearly Kissinger's top aide, was assigned to summarize all the papers and prepare a covering memorandum for the President. He carefully listed the various options in the two- or three-page summary, leaving boxes for the President to initial his choices. The idea was to reduce the President's work load: If Nixon chose not to read the attached documents, he could merely review Halperin's summary (which, of course, came with Kissinger's imprimatur) and make his decision. "Henry loved the summary and thought it was terrific. But, 'Mort,' he said, 'you haven't told the President what options we should choose.' "

"I thought to myself," Halperin recalls, "we're not supposed to be giving positions; we're just supposed to send summaries of the options." Years later, Halperin would realize how naïve he had been: "Henry had been publicly saying that we were just going to sort out the issues for the President. I didn't know that Henry wanted to give him the decisions he should take. I was surprised—because I still believed what Henry had said." The Kissinger summary papers, with their recommendations, would become the most secret documents in the Nixon White House.

3

CONSOLIDATING AUTHORITY

HENRY KISSINGER ENTERED the White House on Inauguration Day with immense power and no illusions about its source. He understood that his authority would never be disputed as long as he kept his sole client—Richard Nixon —pleased. Kissinger knew that as an outsider he would never be totally trusted by Haldeman, Ehrlichman and other Nixon loyalists on the White House staff. But he also realized that he was an oasis of intellect and of knowledge about foreign policy in the Nixon White House.

Morale was high among the members of Henry Kissinger's reorganized National Security Council staff. They considered themselves a hand-picked elite, assembled not as a result of postelection patronage but solely on the basis of their expertise in foreign affairs and policy making. Eight members of the roughly thirty-man staff held doctorates; eight had served in the State Department; six were former members of the Johnson Administration's NSC who had been asked to stay on; some came from the Pentagon, the Central Intelligence Agency, and academia. Many were Democrats who viscerally disliked Richard Nixon, but Kissinger had been persuasive from the start in promising that his National Security Council would be above politics.

Roger Morris had handled African affairs for Walt Rostow and had been flattered to be asked to meet with Kissinger late in December 1968, at a time when the new Nixon appointees were still feeling their way around Washington. Kissinger was late for the interview—as he would be for nearly every meeting in the next eight years—and asked Morris to ride with him to his next appointment. Once in the car, Kissinger was direct. "You're a Democrat, aren't you?" Before Morris could answer, Kissinger said, "Well, you've got to remember that I didn't support this man either. I worked for Nelson Rockefeller. I was asked to take this job and I was astonished to be asked to take it, but I consider that I am working for the presidency, for the institution, and I expect everyone on my staff to consider that we are not a part of the political side of the White House. I want the best people I can get regardless of their personal affiliation. I expect to have Democrats and Republicans and I expect decisions to be made and advice given to me entirely independent of partisan considerations. You are working for the presidency; do not consider you are working for the man."

Morris readily agreed to stay on the NSC staff. Bureaucratic life in the last year of the Johnson Administration had been stifling: The White House's foreign policy had been intertwined with the Vietnam War to the exclusion of nearly all other issues. This would change, Morris was told. There would be an open system in which all options would be analyzed and then presented to the President for his decision.

Clearly, what Haldeman and others saw as an essential virtue in White House staff members—personal loyalty to Nixon—was being given a much lower priority by Kissinger. The President's men, whose criteria placed such loyalty above all else, were inevitably suspicious of Kissinger's generally young and moderate professional staff. Yet Haldeman, obviously acting on Nixon's instructions, had not insisted on placing any of his people on Kissinger's staff. There was tension, but even so, Kissinger immediately felt secure enough to take on and subdue Richard Allen, one of the few certified conservatives and Nixon loyalists on his newly formed staff, the man who had served so discreetly and loyally as the go-between while Kissinger was betraying both the peace talks and the Democrats that fall.

Allen had accepted a job as one of Kissinger's chief aides in the National Security Council, and had even been introduced to the press along with Kissinger at the December 2 press conference. Kissinger had telephoned him a few days before to praise him effusively and invite him to breakfast. At breakfast, as part of the job offer, he promised to relay every one of Allen's memoranda to Nixon "without any markings": Allen's access would be total. Kissinger then asked if Allen would escort his parents, who lived in New York, to the press conference. Allen was flattered. "I was sure of my role with Kissinger," he recalls ruefully.

Allen learned much later that in those early weeks of December Kissinger privately complained to Nixon and Haldeman about an interview Allen gave shortly after the election to U.S. News & World Report, in which he suggested that the banning of antiballistic missile systems was an area "where agreement would be good for both sides." Allen was told that Kissinger warned Nixon that the interview would "provoke" the Soviets. In mid-month, the New York Times published a friendly piece about Allen, describing him as "a hard worker, bright, articulate, open in manner, and plain-spoken." The Times went on to note, without explaining further, that Allen had "maintained discreet contact with Dr. Kissinger" during the Nixon campaign.

The next blow fell two weeks after that. Allen, in Los Angeles for a meeting, was in a taxicab the day after Christmas when he happened upon a syndicated column by Rowland Evans and Robert Novak in the Los Angeles Times. The column title was: "Nixon's Bizarre Choice."

"I remember looking down and saying to myself, 'Who is this poor man?' I started reading and it is I." The columnists, calling Allen a member of the "sandbox right," wrote that "the gap between Kissinger's sophisticated, adult anti-communism and Allen's simplistic version is a chasm." They further quoted Nixon aides as "apologetically" pointing out that Allen was no longer an assistant to Nixon, as he had been during the campaign, but "was specifically named as an assistant to the mature Dr. Kissinger."

The day before the inauguration, after Allen had been assigned an office in the Executive Office Building, Evans and Novak reported, "A decision has been made at high levels of the new Administration . . . to isolate him from substantive duties." It was the first Allen had heard of such a decision, but the column was prophetic. Indeed, as Allen well remembers, he was soon isolated and shunted aside by Kissinger, and widely believed to be a "spy" for Nixon by his more liberal colleagues on the National Security staff.* Cut off from all significant assignments, Allen resigned late in 1969. "I was still loyal to Nixon," he says of his quiet departure. "I really was."

Within days a major reason for Kissinger's confidence became apparent in the White House, Patrick Buchanan, the most conservative of Nixon's speech writers, recalls. "All you had to do was talk to Bill Rogers, and you knew who was going to come out on top."†

On January 20, as Rogers was participating in the Nixon inaugural, Kissinger's staff was already dispatching the first of more than a dozen personal letters from Nixon to the heads of foreign governments, including France, Yugoslavia, Romania, and the Soviet Union. The letters were sent over Nixon's signature and hand delivered by NSC aides to the various Washington embassies. Rogers spent the day celebrating and was told nothing of these high-level contacts. The letters were merely perfunctory expressions of good will; yet they were also, in a sense, the first official Nixon-Kissinger secret. One NSC aide described them as even more significant: They were "the beginning of the effort to establish channels directly from the White House."

In February 1969, barely a month into his presidency, Nixon flew to Europe for a series of meetings with heads of state that were designed to "show the world," as Nixon reported in his memoirs, "that the new American President was not completely obsessed with Vietnam." On the flight across the Atlantic, the President read an essay on French President Charles de Gaulle that had been adapted from Kissinger's highly publicized book on NATO, *The Troubled Partnership*. Nixon was proud of the Harvard professor who saw eye to eye with him.

The relationship quickly became hostage: Nixon had a consuming need for

---

* Allen "was regarded as a very conservative element who had a line to Nixon that predated the NSC," according to Donald R. Lesh, a junior Foreign Service officer who worked for Kissinger in 1969. Richard Moose, the first NSC staff secretary, recalls Kissinger's telling him "right off the bat" that "Allen was to be put in a pigeonhole on the corner of a desk someplace and that Allen was not really going to figure in Henry's operation." Martin Anderson, a young White House economist and Nixon campaign worker who had become friendly with Allen, watched with fascination as Kissinger worked his will in the White House. Anderson says he was told of a high-level foreign policy meeting in the Oval Office sometime early in 1969 at which Nixon—seemingly concerned about the future of his former campaign aide—turned to Kissinger and said, "Have Dick Allen do this." Kissinger agreed but, as Anderson subsequently learned, never discussed it with Allen. Weeks later, Anderson was told of a second meeting in the President's office at which Nixon asked again about the project for Allen and Kissinger responded, in effect: I'm sorry. That man does not produce. I cannot get him to produce.

† Buchanan first met Kissinger at the Florida White House in Key Biscayne, shortly after the inauguration. Swimming laps in a pool used by the senior White House staff, he noticed Kissinger beside the pool, his briefcase open and top-secret documents spilling out. Buchanan got out of the water, walked over, and said hello. Kissinger immediately responded, "You know, Burnham is right." He was referring to James Burnham, the senior editor of the conservative *National Review*, whose columns repeatedly criticized American policy makers for their failure to support dissent inside the Communist bloc, beginning with the short-lived revolt in East Germany in July of 1953. Burnham was, as Kissinger obviously knew, an intellectual hero to Buchanan.

flattery and Kissinger a consuming need to provide it. Thus, after Nixon's first meeting with Soviet Ambassador Anatoliy Dobrynin, on February 17, 1969, the President repeatedly summoned Kissinger. "It was characteristic of Nixon's insecurity with personal encounters," wrote Kissinger, "that he called me into his office four times that day for reassurance that he had done well. He thought there had been a tough confrontation. My impression was rather the opposite—that the meeting had been on the conciliatory side." Nixon did not discuss the February 17 meeting in his memoirs, but he reported Kissinger's glowing assessment of his performance after a meeting with Dobrynin later that year: "Kissinger came back in after he had seen Dobrynin to the door. 'I'll wager that no one has ever talked to him that way in his entire career!' he said. 'It was extraordinary! No president has ever laid it on the line to them like that.' "

Kissinger's fawning was obviously a significant part of the job, but it was not the only reason for his accumulation of power. He and Nixon had seized the government from the beginning, and less than a month after the inauguration they were in the process of applying a joint stranglehold. Both acknowledged in their memoirs that Rogers had been deliberately excluded from that first meeting with Dobrynin. "From the beginning," Kissinger wrote, "Nixon was determined to dominate the most important negotiations. He excluded his Secretary of State, for example, from his first meeting with Soviet Ambassador Anatoliy Dobrynin . . . ." Kissinger begged off any responsibility for the treatment of Rogers, however, insisting that Nixon had been solely responsible— "it would have been inconceivable for me to suggest such a procedure." The former President naturally had a different account: "Kissinger had suggested that we develop a private channel between Dobrynin and him," Nixon wrote. "I agreed that Dobrynin might be more forthcoming in strictly private and unpublicized meetings and we arranged for him to arrive unseen through a seldom-used East Wing door so that no one need know they had met. Within a short time, they were meeting weekly, often over lunch."

The significant point is that the practice of excluding Rogers was to continue throughout Nixon's first term. Nixon and Kissinger were going to run the foreign policy of the United States from the White House, and Rogers was to be no more than an easily maneuvered and sometimes flattered pawn. Little was left to chance. By late March, Nixon and Kissinger had begun the practice of summoning senior American ambassadors to an Oval Office meeting and offering them a chance to please the new President by reporting sensitive information directly to Kissinger. The first ambassador known to have been approached was Jacob D. Beam, whom Nixon nominated in early 1969 as Ambassador to the Soviet Union. Beam was a career Foreign Service officer who had loyally worked with Nixon in 1959, when he made a highly successful vice presidential visit to Poland; eight years later, as Ambassador to Czechoslovakia, Beam was again a gracious host when Nixon the private citizen visited Prague.

Before leaving for his new assignment in Moscow, Beam was invited to lunch with Kissinger and Dobrynin at the Soviet Embassy, where, to Beam's astonishment, Kissinger told both ambassadors that Nixon specifically wanted him to attend "all discussions with foreign officials." A few days later Beam met with Nixon and Kissinger at the White House and was asked to help draft a presidential letter to Alexei Kosygin, the Soviet Premier, outlining a new proposal for U.S.-Soviet relations. Beam was told he must treat the letter with the utmost secrecy. The discreet professional diplomat did so, of course, but also found it natural to write a private summary of the meeting to the Secretary of State. "All hell broke loose," Beam remembers. Rogers was upset, and complained to the President. Nixon, in turn, sent word of his distress at Beam's indiscretion through one of Kissinger's aides; he had considered their conversation "purely a private talk." Telling the Secretary of State about a presidential letter to the Premier of the Soviet Union wouldn't do. Beam would pay a high price for his innocence. He was cut out of U.S.-Soviet policy making just as Rogers was, and his function was reduced to the ceremonial and routine, even during the 1972 Moscow summit.

To the dismay of his staff, Rogers chose to ignore the evidence and not make a stand against such White House operations. "I was aware and spoke to Nixon about it," Rogers recalls impassively, "and he'd say, 'I'll see that it won't happen again.' And it would happen again." Rogers was clearly not sure who would win in a confrontation, and he obviously knew who the real mastermind of the gamesmanship was: "I heard that Nixon was telling [foreign] ambassadors: 'If you really want to get something done, call Henry.' "

Alexis Johnson has offered this personal explanation for Rogers' inability to get angry: "I think Bill had an awfully hard time accepting the fact that this fellow he'd worked so hard for would treat him as dirty as he did."

Throughout this early period, there were only faint hints in public about what was really going on. In early April, *U.S. News & World Report* took notice of the Kissinger dominance that had been suggested during Nixon's February trip to Europe. It was Kissinger "who seemed to be holding most of the background briefings for reporters" and Kissinger who was speaking for the President. Trying to be even-handed, however, *U.S. News* also reminded its readers that it was Rogers who was "a close friend and confidant" of the President, with "access that few in the Administration can match."

Some administration officials knew the truth, but they weren't talking. Attorney General Mitchell was among the insiders who made no secret to his immediate staff of his contempt for Rogers. One aide recalls dashing into Mitchell's office on a Justice Department matter early in 1969 only to find Kissinger there, intent in conversation. Mitchell waved his aide off and later cautioned him: "You must not tell anybody that you saw Kissinger here. He and I were pretty unhappy about Rogers." Some months later, the aide was answering telephones for Mitchell during an out-of-town trip when Rogers telephoned. "He asked for Mitchell, but Mitchell said, 'Tell him I'm not in.' " Faced with the prospect of lying to the Secretary of State, the staff man said only that Mitchell couldn't come to the telephone. "Please tell him I don't understand what's happening in Paris," Rogers pleaded, distraught. "Something's going on and I don't know about it." When the aide reported Rogers' request, Mitchell said without explanation, "He's not supposed to know." Later, the aide realized that at the time Kissinger was meeting secretly with Le Duc Tho, the chief peace negotiator for the North Vietnamese.

Other relative outsiders were also appalled by such goings-on. So were some officials who considered themselves insiders. Paul H. Nitze, a distinguished public servant who had served Republican and Democratic administrations for twenty-five years, was asked that June by Rogers to serve as a senior member of the United States delegation to the strategic arms limitation talks with the Soviets, working under Gerard C. Smith, Nixon's new head of the Arms Control and Disarmament Agency and chief delegate to the SALT talks in Geneva.

Nitze said yes. "I had always gotten along well with Nixon," he recalls, "and Rogers said I had to go see Nixon and Kissinger. And so I went over." Rogers was not invited. Nitze quickly found out why. "Nixon says, 'Paul, I don't have any confidence in Bill Rogers with respect to SALT. I don't think he understands anything about it. And frankly, I don't have real confidence in Gerard Smith." The astonished Nitze said nothing. "I want you to go there and report directly to me about what's going on," Nixon said.

"Mr. President, that's not the way it works," Nitze replied. "I can't go there and report secretly to you. I must have confidence in Smith and he must have confidence in me. The delegation can't keep any secrets from the Secretary and Smith." It was inconceivable to Nitze that anyone would ask him to spy on Smith; the two men were old friends with high regard for each other.

Nixon quickly retreated. "The situation might arise where you have to get in touch," he said, and he then explained that Kissinger and the Joint Chiefs of Staff had set up a separate, private line of communication—known in the government as a backchannel—to enable Nitze and other specially selected SALT delegates to communicate directly with the White House without Smith's knowledge. These communication systems, as Nitze knew, with their encoded messages and guarded printout terminals, were an essential part of Washington bureaucracy, and the men at the top depended on such quick, private access to subordinates.* If Nitze saw the need, the President continued, he could use a backchannel to communicate directly with Kissinger, who in turn would relay Nitze's report to his office. Kissinger said little, and the meeting concluded rather lamely. "They knew that I was not going to do anything like that," Nitze says.

Not everyone had Nitze's experience or his scruples. Throughout his career as national security adviser, and later as Secretary of State, Kissinger would repeatedly urge senior officials to report directly to him by backchannel, in an effort not only to keep control of an ongoing negotiation but also to prevent his peers and subordinates from finding out what was going on. Kissinger usually initiated such conversations—amid much flattery—but in the case of Nitze, who had advised such eminent men as Dean Acheson, when he was Secretary of State in the Truman Administration, Kissinger obviously felt the need to have Nixon make the backchannel pitch himself.

Sometimes Nixon refused to go along. In August 1969, William J. Porter, a

---

* Most backchannel messages are routed through the facilities of the Central Intelligence Agency and of the National Security Agency—which is under the aegis of the Defense Department—where such messages are seen by only a few clerks and no copies are kept. One NSA official recalls that there were scores of informal government teletype links around the world in the late 1960s that were used for "OTR" (off-the-record) messages as well as highly classified reports. The Pentagon has a separate backchannel facility for its senior officers, who can use the system to complain about presidential policy or to make golf dates and hunting plans with the knowledge that the message will remain secure.

veteran career diplomat who was then Ambassador to South Korea, came home for consultations and was summoned to meet with Kissinger and then with Nixon. The Ambassador recorded his impressions in his diary:

[Kissinger] greeted me effusively . . . provided me with compliments about the President's high regard, and his own, for my performance. . . . The President had asked him to take up an important matter with me. He said that though the President had a low opinion of the State Department, he was aware that there were some "good officers" ("like you, Bill") in it, but as a whole the Department was proving to be a disappointment. To counteract the inefficiency of the Department, and to avail himself of the services of able officers, the President had authorized him, Kissinger said, to open direct and private communications with half a dozen "key Ambassadors" around the world ("like you, Bill"). What did I think? he inquired.

I said it sounded like an impressive honor. Did "direct and private" mean through the Secretary of State?

Kissinger: Absolutely not. No one would know about this arrangement.

Porter: About what would I be reporting?

Kissinger: Anything you believe of interest to us. No subject limitation.

Porter: You say this has the President's approval?

Kissinger: That's correct. He'll mention the subject when he sees you in a few minutes from now. Do you accept the proposal?

Porter reluctantly agreed. "The President is the boss. If he wants it that way, I'll cooperate." He asked Kissinger what would happen if Bill Rogers heard about the arrangement. Kissinger responded, Porter recalls, "That's our problem." The national security adviser "seemed rather elated" about their conversation, and Porter, with his thirty-two years in the Foreign Service, thought to himself, "Here's the Nixon-Kissinger secret diplomatic service shaping up, secret codes and all."

A few minutes later he had a pleasant private meeting with Nixon, who said nothing about the secret reporting arrangement. Porter's account continues:

I returned to Kissinger's quarters. He inquired whether the subject had come up. I said it had not. He then commented that lack of mention didn't mean anything because it was all approved. He said we'd be in touch, at which point I took my leave of him.

During the long return flight to Seoul, I mulled over the meaning of Kissinger's proposal. . . . Pretty rough on Rogers . . . They've only been in office a few months . . . if the President agreed to create a super-net of ambassadors under his security adviser without the knowledge of the Secretary of State something new was happening in American history. . . . I concluded that I was just a country boy and I'd keep my head down.

When he returned to Seoul, Porter tested the secret communications system, which had been arranged by the CIA. His test signal was promptly acknowledged. He remembers that he used the backchannel only once, to transmit a minor item about China, before leaving South Korea in 1971.

Nixon's decision not to follow the prearranged agenda for his talk with Porter must have given Kissinger pause: Nixon, when he was angry with his national security adviser, invariably relayed that anger indirectly. He would, for example, refuse to take Kissinger's telephone calls, or not summon him to Oval Office meetings, or, as with Porter, decide at the last minute not to go along with a stratagem. There is no evidence that Nixon ever confronted Kissinger with a complaint. Confrontations, always difficult for Nixon, were perhaps made even more complicated in Kissinger's case by Kissinger's overwhelming obsequiousness.

Inevitably, then, one of Kissinger's early methods of determining the President's attitude toward him in moments of stress was to measure the attitude of Haldeman and Ehrlichman. If they angrily complained to him about press leaks or another of the incessant admiring magazine articles about his NSC operation, Kissinger knew they were relaying Nixon's views. What seemed to be Kissinger's occasional attacks of paranoia about the White House "palace guard" were, in some cases, merely a rational fear of the only man who mattered for him in that administration. When Haldeman was representing Nixon, he was to be feared. But when he was trying to protect his own White House turf, he was not a threat—as Haldeman quickly learned.

Bryce Harlow recalls how Kissinger wriggled his way out of Haldeman's control early in the Nixon Administration. During the first few months after the inauguration, Harlow says, while he was still an insider, he would join Kissinger, Haldeman, and Ehrlichman in the President's office every morning and afternoon for meetings. Haldeman, who from the very beginning "wanted to control everything," soon demanded that the meetings with Nixon be preceded by short planning sessions in his office. "Henry started to skip those meetings right away, [and] I told Bob, 'Don't you let him do that to you.' We had to relate foreign policy to domestic policy. Well, Bob'd force him in there —but then Henry just began slipping and slipping"—arriving later and later. "Finally, it ended up with Kissinger meeting alone with Nixon."

Robert Finch, the California Republican who was Nixon's first Secretary of Health, Education and Welfare, remembers Haldeman's early worries about Kissinger's role. "He thought Henry was consuming too much of Nixon's time," Finch says. "It was clear that Nixon's preoccupation with foreign policy was a restraint on Haldeman's ability to control Nixon's schedule." Haldeman's dream, as Finch puts it, was to elevate the role of John Ehrlichman, who had been placed in charge of domestic affairs in November 1969, to a status equaling that of Kissinger in foreign affairs. "Then Haldeman could balance it," said Finch. "They both would have to come through him" to Nixon. It was another unfulfilled White House dream.

Haldeman could not intimidate Kissinger, but he did serve as an effective role model. The way Haldeman ran his office was obviously the way Nixon wanted things done. Over the first few months of 1969, Kissinger emulated the tactics of his patron's chief assistant. If Haldeman ruthlessly cut staff access to Nixon, so did Kissinger. If Haldeman moved swiftly against Harlow and Arthur Burns, senior aides with independent views, so Kissinger moved against those on his staff who might be dangerous to him. The first casualty was Richard Allen, who had direct access to Nixon and knew the secret of Kissinger's campaign activities. Then Kissinger turned on those, such as Morton Halperin, whom Nixon and his chief aides considered too liberal.

Coping with Nixon, pleasing him, and trying to find out what he really wanted were the most important priorities for Kissinger. They would become even more important than his own convictions about American foreign policy. Even more important than finding a way out of the war in Vietnam.

4

VIETNAM:
THE POLICY

HENRY KISSINGER CAME into the Nixon White House profoundly skeptical about the Vietnam War. He was not a dove; he believed, as Richard Nixon did, that the United States had to find a way to end the war "honorably" or else face a crippling loss of prestige throughout the world. But Kissinger's criticisms of the war were nonetheless profound and based on firsthand experience. Kissinger's trip to South Vietnam in late 1965, at the request of Ambassador Henry Cabot Lodge, had been a free-wheeling two weeks spent talking extensively to Vietnamese and American officials. Among those he impressed was Daniel Ellsberg, who was in the process of becoming a State Department expert on the provinces and districts outside Saigon. Ellsberg gave Kissinger a list of knowledgeable Americans and Vietnamese throughout the country and urged Kissinger to talk with them informally, so they would speak frankly. Robert S. McNamara, Johnson's Secretary of Defense, had been misled year after year during his visits to South Vietnam, Ellsberg told him, by permitting senior officers to monitor all his briefings. Ellsberg gave the same advice to many visitors, but Kissinger was one of the few who took it.

"He was a talented and incisive questioner," Ellsberg recalls. "He took notes and listened carefully and did learn an unusual amount." Just before he left Saigon, in early November, Kissinger had lunch with a small group of American correspondents and expressed his dismay at what he termed the almost total lack of political maturity and unselfish political motivation among current and future leaders of South Vietnam. Specifically included in that denunciation were the current Premier, Nguyen Cao Ky, and the chief of state, Nguyen Van Thieu, who was soon to become President. Kissinger further complained, during the off-the-record luncheon, that the Ky-Thieu government was in no sense democratic or representative, because the peasants, 80 percent of the South Vietnamese population, had little or no voice in the government.*

---

* The lunch turned out to be a fiasco for Kissinger. It enmeshed him in an immediate—if private—dispute with the White House, the press corps in Saigon, and Clark Clifford, a distinguished Washington lawyer and former Truman Administration official who would later become Johnson's Secretary of Defense. Clifford, who was touring Vietnam as a member of the President's Foreign Intelligence Advisory Board, had not attended the lunch, but Jack Foisie of the *Los Angeles Times,* who was there, published a dispatch in which he attributed Kissinger's expressions of dismay and disappointment to both Kissinger and Clifford. The story caused resentment among the political leadership in Saigon, and Clifford wrote to President Johnson dissociating himself from the incident and stating that he had not met with any journalists during his trip. Bill D. Moyers, the White House

In 1966, Kissinger visited South Vietnam twice more, as a consultant to a State Department program aimed at finding new ways to induce members of the National Liberation Front, the antigovernment coalition of Communists and nationalists that Hanoi had organized in South Vietnam in 1960, to defect to the South Vietnamese government. The concept, as Kissinger explained it at the time, was to give individual members of the NLF, known to Americans as Vietcong, a chance to participate in government at the provincial or village level. Since the South Vietnamese constitution banned the Communist Party, a way had to be found for Communists to work at equivalent positions as individuals, not as Party members, inside the political structure. As Ellsberg recalls it, Kissinger and a few other farsighted analysts believed the South Vietnamese government might have to give the Vietcong *de facto* control of some of the rural provinces to induce them to end the war. "This was the right direction," Ellsberg says, "but the Vietcong were not going to buy it. They weren't looking for a way to lose the war gracefully, which is what we were offering them." Kissinger made it clear that he had "no interest" per se in this pacification program, "which he properly read as a loser." *

Over the next two years, Kissinger's views sharpened. By 1968 Ellsberg was back in the United States, working in Santa Monica, California, for the Rand Corporation, a leading think tank, and doing some consulting for the Pentagon. In the middle of that year, he attended two conferences on Vietnam at which Kissinger expressed the almost radical view that the only United States objective in Vietnam should be the assurance of a "decent interval" between the final exodus of American troops and a Communist-led takeover of the South Vietnamese government. His analysis came after the seeming success of a major NLF offensive during Tet, the Vietnamese New Year, in February, in which guerrilla forces staged uprisings throughout the country.

In the summer of 1968, just after the Republican convention, Kissinger began work on a lengthy analysis of the Vietnam negotiating dilemma for publication in the January 1969 issue of *Foreign Affairs,* the distinguished journal of the Council on Foreign Affairs. The article, which he circulated privately before it appeared, served not only to express his views but also to advertise his wares to the next President, whether Nixon or Humphrey.

In the article, Kissinger described the 1968 Tet offensive as the "watershed of the American effort. Henceforth, no matter how effective our actions the

press secretary, immediately made the Clifford denial public and pointedly told the press that Kissinger's views were "his and not the government's." Kissinger then wrote to Moyers disavowing Foisie's article and apparently also suggesting that Moyers had attacked him personally. Moyers' response to Kissinger, now in the archives at the Lyndon B. Johnson Library in Austin, Texas, provided little solace: "Under the circumstances, Dr. Kissinger, knowing how much pain [Foisie's] false account had created in Saigon, and not having the opportunity to talk with you before I was questioned on the subject, I did what I felt had to be done . . . not because I wished to attack you but because a dilatory or vague response to the question at my briefing would only have compounded what you have already admitted was the 'damage done to American policy' by the views attributed to you."

    * Kissinger went even further in his criticism after returning to Harvard that fall. Over a sherry one afternoon with Dr. Matthew Meselson, a Harvard microbiologist who was a State Department consultant on arms control, Kissinger expressed profound distress over the war: "Matt, now I know what the good Germans felt." Meselson came away from the conversation convinced that Kissinger believed the Vietnam War was a moral wrong. Another possibility, of course, is that Kissinger was telling Meselson what he thought the avowedly antiwar scientist wanted to hear.

prevalent [American] strategy could no longer achieve its objectives within a period or with force levels politically acceptable to the American people." Tet made the American commitment to a political solution in South Vietnam inevitable. Kissinger also warned that the United States could not and should not rely on the Soviet Union to bring an end to the war. He noted that the United States had done little in reaction to the Soviet invasion of Czechoslovakia in August 1968; therefore, America "would compound the heavy costs of our pallid reaction . . . if our allies could blame it on a quid pro quo for Soviet assistance in extricating us from Southeast Asia. Washington therefore requires great delicacy in dealing with Moscow on the Vietnam issue. It cannot be in the American interest to add fuel to the already widespread charge that the superpowers are sacrificing their allies to maintain spheres of influence."*

Thus Kissinger entered the Nixon Administration on record as deeply pessimistic about the Vietnam War, as convinced that the Soviet Union should not be a conduit for negotiations, and as believing that any negotiated settlement had to end the war in an honorable fashion, if only for the sake of American prestige and continued international order. That belief, many of Kissinger's associates thought, did not necessarily rule out a pro-Communist government in the South, provided a "decent interval" could be guaranteed.

Within a few weeks of the announcement of his appointment as national security adviser, Kissinger telephoned Henry Rowen, president of Rand, and asked him to put together a list of possible options for the Vietnam War. The request was natural: Kissinger had become a consultant there and a friend of Fred C. Iklé, head of the Social Science Division.† Rowen, a former member of the Kennedy Administration, put Ellsberg in charge. By this time, Ellsberg and the Rand Corporation as a whole were widely regarded inside the bureau-

---

* The *Foreign Affairs* article, widely praised at the time of its publication, is replete with contradictions. For example, Kissinger wrote—correctly, as it turned out in 1975—that "it is beyond imagination that parties that have been murdering and betraying each other for 25 years could work together as a team giving joint instructions to the entire country." A few pages further on, however, he suggested that "while a coalition government is undesirable, a mixed commission to develop and supervise a political process to reintegrate the country—including free elections—could be useful." Similarly, in a much-quoted phrase, he cited with approval what he said was a cardinal maxim of guerrilla war: "the guerrilla wins if he does not lose; the conventional army loses if it does not win." By that definition the North Vietnamese and Vietcong forces were winning the war by 1969 and the United States was losing. But then Kissinger went on to declare that the American military position had begun to improve, and "As a result, we have achieved our minimum objective: Hanoi is unable to gain a military victory." He did not explain how denying Hanoi a military victory was a measure of success in light of the concept that Hanoi did not need a victory in order to win.

† Kissinger's relationship with the analysts at Rand had been soured in the late 1950s by a scathing review of his *Nuclear Weapons and Foreign Policy* by William W. Kaufmann of Rand. Several Rand people were known to have contributed ideas to the review, which was published in *World Politics* magazine in July 1958 and debunked, at great length, Kissinger's reasoning and strategy concepts. The review, innocuously entitled "The Crisis in Military Affairs," accused Kissinger of muddling his facts, arguing inconsistently, and changing his assumptions depending "on what point he is trying to prove." As for Kissinger's main thesis, the possibility of waging a limited nuclear war, Kaufmann raised a serious objection: Kissinger "has omitted to consider the precedent-setting effects of initiating the use of atomic weapons and has also overlooked the impact upon allied and neutral nations of our having taken this step. Presumably," Kaufmann added caustically, "any war that is limited in scope is bound to have a great many interested onlookers." Kissinger was pained by the review, Kaufmann recalls: "I got one of his six-page letters." Kissinger eventually revised his views on the viability of limited nuclear warfare, and Kaufmann, who became director of the Social Science Division at Rand in 1961, ended their impasse by offering him a consultancy.

cracy as having gone "dovish" on Vietnam. Kissinger had insisted that Rand's involvement with the policy be kept secret, a condition to which Ellsberg and Rowen agreed.

Ellsberg was fresh from researching a detailed secret history of American involvement in the Vietnam War that had been assembled in the Pentagon, at McNamara's direction, by a team headed by Morton Halperin and Leslie H. Gelb, then deputy director of the Planning Staff. Ellsberg consulted with Halperin and Gelb on the Kissinger option study, in which he analyzed contingencies ranging from an invasion of North Vietnam to a unilateral withdrawal. The selection of Ellsberg to head the study raised no eyebrows. Kissinger himself had praised his knowledge of Vietnam issues at a Rand seminar shortly after the 1968 election, telling the group, "I have learned more from Dan Ellsberg than from anyone else in Vietnam." On Christmas Day, 1968, Ellsberg, Rowen, and another Rand official flew to New York to present the options paper to Kissinger, Halperin, and Thomas C. Schelling, a Kissinger colleague from Harvard. Kissinger and Schelling had one immediate criticism of the paper: It did not include a threat option. Schelling also told Ellsberg that the paper did not include a "win" option. "Here we have a set of papers going to a new President," Schelling said, "and you're not telling any way that he could possibly win." Ellsberg recalls telling Schelling and Kissinger, "I don't believe there is a win option in Vietnam."

Ellsberg readily agreed to include an analysis of a threat option, but he told Kissinger, "I don't see how threatening bombing is going to influence the enemy because they have experienced four years of bombing." Ellsberg remembers arguing that the only effective threat "would be simply a threat to stay there for a long time; not to win, but if you could stay there in terms of domestic politics"—by reducing casualties and financial costs—"that would impress them. You might get some small concessions out of them." According to Ellsberg, "Henry then said, 'But how can you conduct negotiations without a credible threat of escalation?' I said, 'People negotiate all the time without threatening bombing.' "

A few of the early recruits to Kissinger's NSC staff were surprised to meet Ellsberg during his brief visit to the Pierre headquarters. John C. Court, a former Pentagon analyst who was coming to work under Kissinger, was introduced to Ellsberg and told he was "an old friend of Kissinger's. I'd heard of Ellsberg," Court says. "He was a wild man."

Ellsberg's options paper was accepted and submitted to the President-elect sometime around the first of the year. In those weeks, Kissinger was obviously learning more about the man he was serving, and what he learned was reflected in a change he ordered in the study. He asked Iklé whether Rand would mind if the withdrawal option was deleted. That option called for the United States to withdraw unilaterally within a fixed period, regardless of events inside South Vietnam. Ellsberg was later told that General Goodpaster had dropped his copy of the study on Kissinger's desk and said coldly, "I have not commented on the final option [withdrawal], which is not an option." The option was deleted from the final draft of the study, edited by Iklé, that was turned over to the NSC.

Out of that first study came a second Kissinger assignment for Ellsberg. In the options paper, Ellsberg had summarized some of the intelligence questions about the Vietnam War and its progress that were dividing the bureaucracy. At breakfast with Kissinger at the Hotel Pierre, Ellsberg told him how McNamara had overwhelmed the bureaucracy immediately after taking charge of the Pentagon by ordering the Joint Chiefs of Staff to respond to ninety-six questions. The questions, soon referred to as the "ninety-six trombones," after the popular show tune "Seventy-six Trombones," had the immediate effect of letting the military know that he, McNamara, had direct knowledge of many lower-level rivalries and disputes. If the military leaders sought to manipulate him or lie to him in their answers, McNamara was saying, they faced exposure and embarrassment. Kissinger was intrigued, says Ellsberg, and readily agreed that a similar effort to seize and challenge the bureaucracy should begin at once, using the same technique: a list of tough questions. Ellsberg was impressed at Kissinger's courage in agreeing to expand the questions and to "send them out in the President's name to all these agencies." Ellsberg also knew the significance of the current "lull" in Vietnam, with the military insisting that it was a sign the war was being won and other agencies claiming that the lull merely reflected a Vietcong and North Vietnamese desire not to act. With Kissinger's approval, he expanded his questionnaire for the bureaucracy, and then returned to Rand.

In February, Kissinger summoned Ellsberg back for special White House duty. The answers to the questionnaire, which had been distributed to the bureaucracy as National Security Study Memorandum 1, were flooding in and help was needed to coordinate the answers. Ellsberg spent nearly all of March in Washington, working in secret.

At his suggestion, the questionnaire had posed its questions separately to the Pentagon, the State Department, and the Central Intelligence Agency, and the responses were to be returned separately. Ellsberg's idea was to allow the President to see firsthand the extent of disagreement in the government about the course of the war. The responses were generally negative and pessimistic. Doubts were expressed about the efficacy of bombing and of pacification, and about the South Vietnamese Army's ability to stand up to the North Vietnamese and the Vietcong without heavy American air support. The Pentagon also conceded for the first time that the Vietnam War was not even near the point where attrition of enemy soldiers would exceed their replacement, though the so-called crossover point theory had been the underlying basis of the Johnson Administration's military strategy.

The implications of these replies to NSSM 1 were far-reaching. Even the most optimistic assessment from staunchly prowar military officers was that it would take a minimum of 8.3 years more to completely pacify and control the Vietcong areas of the South. Pessimists, including civilian advisers in the State Department and Pentagon, thought it would take at least 13.4 years. Such responses made it clear that the war in the South could not be won at all without a continuing American presence, at least in the air, no matter how extensively the South Vietnamese Army was augmented and improved. But in fact Nixon and Kissinger never relied on NSSM 1 and its replies except as a method of forcing the bureaucracy to do busywork and removing it from decision making. The documents were kept top secret: The public would have been deeply disillusioned to learn in 1969 that while Nixon and Kissinger had embarked on a policy of building up the South Vietnamese Army—"Vietnamization"—they already knew that the end result, short of a most unlikely capitulation by Hanoi, would be a continuing American Air Force role in the South for years to come. But the conclusions of the NSSM 1 papers—and the man who was responsible for them—would haunt the White House over the next four years.

Kissinger did not permit himself to link NSSM 1's dreary long-range implications to his innate pessimism about the war. Whatever Nixon believed Kissinger soon found himself advocating. Nixon had won the presidency by telling the American people that he had a plan to end the war with honor. He had not made his plan public; had he done so, he might not have been elected. Nixon's plan was not merely to end the war but to win it. He and Kissinger agreed immediately on the one overriding principle that would guide Vietnam policy for the next four years: South Vietnam must remain non-Communist forever.

The Nixon-Kissinger plan, as it evolved over the first year, had three basic elements. Most important, the Hanoi government must be shown that the Nixon Administration would stop at nothing—not even the physical destruction of North Vietnam's cities and waterworks—to end the war on terms it declared to be honorable. Second, the Soviet Union would be warned that its relationships with the United States in all areas, especially foreign trade, would be linked to its continuing support for Hanoi. When these threats failed to force Hanoi to make concessions at the peace table, a third major policy goal emerged: The antiwar movement in the United States would be challenged and neutralized, to gain enough time to pursue complete military victory.

An essential facet of the policy was secrecy. Only without public knowledge and public protests could Richard Nixon carry out his plan to threaten North Vietnam so strongly that it would be forced to sue for peace. In his memoirs, Nixon wrote that shortly after taking office, "I confidently told the Cabinet that I expected the war to be over in a year." But his Cabinet, like the rest of the government, was kept in the dark about the real reason for his confidence.

Nixon's secret policy had its roots in the Eisenhower era.

As the newly elected Vice President in 1953, Nixon watched Dwight Eisenhower fulfill a campaign promise and end the Korean War six months after taking office. In *Mandate for Change, 1953–56*, Eisenhower revealed what was not said publicly at the time: that he had explicitly threatened to use atomic weapons to end the war. When he took office, Eisenhower wrote, a military offensive in North Korea was being considered by the U.S.-led United Nations forces helping South Korea defend itself: "To keep the attack from becoming costly, it was clear that we would have to use atomic weapons." Eisenhower decided, as he wrote, "to let the Communist authorities understand that, in the absence of satisfactory progress, we intended to move decisively without inhibition in our use of weapons, and would no longer be responsible for confining hostilities to the Korean Peninsula. We would not be limited by any world-wide gentlemen's agreement." According to Eisenhower, word was quietly passed to the Chinese Communists and the Soviet Union, and the end of the war was quickly negotiated. Eisenhower's long-time assistant and confidant, Sherman Adams, wrote that the President told him later that he had made the threat "sure that there was not the remotest chance we would actually have to carry out our threat; the Communists would simply throw up their hands and the war would be over."

Along with the nuclear threat, Eisenhower ordered a sharp escalation of the air war over North Korea. In early May 1953, American bombers destroyed hydroelectric power plants on the Yalu River, destroying dams and creating floods that swamped twenty-seven miles of farmland. It was the first deliberate military attack on irrigation targets since Hitler's Luftwaffe destroyed dikes and dams in Holland late in World War II.*

Nixon's attempt in 1969 to emulate Dwight Eisenhower's methods of extricating America from an unpopular war was not an unconscious act of hero worship but a carefully thought-out strategy. Nixon had spelled out his policy the previous August in what he thought was an off-the-record talk to a group of southern delegates at the Republican convention.† "How do you bring a war to a conclusion?" Nixon said in response to a question. "I'll tell you how Korea was ended. We got in there and had this messy war on our hands. Eisenhower let the word go out—let the word go out diplomatically—to the Chinese and the North Koreans that we would not tolerate this continual ground war of attrition. And within a matter of months, they negotiated. Well, as far as negotiation [in Vietnam] is concerned that should be our position. . . . I'll tell you one thing. I played a little poker when I was in the Navy . . . I learned this—when a guy didn't have the cards, he talked awfully big. But when he had the cards, he just sat there—had that cold look in his eyes. Now we've got the cards. . . . What we've got to do is walk softly and carry a big stick. And that is what we are going to do."

Nixon did not mention nuclear weapons in his talk to the delegates, but before the convention he had told Richard J. Whalen, one of his speech writers and advisers, that if elected President, "I *would* use nuclear weapons." Nixon quickly added, as Whalen later recorded, that he did not mean he would use them in Vietnam, only that he would be willing "to threaten their use in appropriate circumstances."

As President, however, Nixon was aware that his threat could work only if North Vietnam believed he was capable of anything. Sometime early in 1969, he explained his secret strategy for ending the war to Haldeman as they strolled along the beach at Key Biscayne. He told Haldeman about the Eisenhower nuclear threats in 1953 and how those threats had quickly ended the Korean War. Eisenhower's military career—he had been commander of the Allied

---

* An official analysis of the bombings in North Korea, published in the *Air University Quarterly Review,* described the dams targeted for destruction as responsible for 75 percent of the water supply for North Korea's rice production. ". . . [T]o the Communists the smashing of the dams meant primarily the destruction of their chief sustenance—rice. The Westerner can little conceive the awesome meaning which the loss of this staple food commodity has for the Asian—starvation and slow death." The Air Force study concluded that "These strikes, largely passed over by the press, the military observers and news commentators in favor of attention-arresting but less meaningful operations events, constituted one of the significant air operations of the Korean War."

† An enterprising reporter for the *Miami Herald* apparently persuaded one of the delegates to tape record the session and the *Herald* published the text on August 7, placing its exclusive story across eight columns on page 1: "What Dick Nixon Told Southern Delegates."

Forces in World War II—had convinced the Communists that the threats were real. Nixon said he planned to use the same principle: the threat of maximum force. "I call it the madman theory, Bob," he said.* "I want the North Vietnamese to believe I've reached the point where I might do *anything* to stop the war. We'll just slip the word to them that, 'for God's sake, you know Nixon is obsessed about Communists. We can't restrain him when he's angry—and he has his hand on the nuclear button'—and Ho Chi Minh himself will be in Paris in two days begging for peace."

There was a basic flaw in Nixon's "madman theory." Eisenhower's threat had been made at a time when the United States had a virtual monopoly on nuclear weapons. That situation did not exist in the late 1960s, and the credibility of Nixon's threat was reduced by the possibility that the Soviet Union, or even Communist China, would retaliate after an American first use of nuclear weapons. Another drawback was the fact that Richard Nixon did not have Dwight Eisenhower's military background. Nonetheless, Haldeman wrote, Nixon believed that the Communists regarded him as an uncompromising enemy whose hatred for their philosophy had been repeatedly made clear in his two decades of public life. "They'll believe any threat of force that Nixon makes because it's Nixon," Haldeman quoted the President as saying. Nixon not only *wanted* to end the war, Haldeman added, he was absolutely convinced he *would* end it in his first year. "I'm the one man in this country who can do it, Bob," he told Haldeman.

The administration's immediate problem was one of technique: how to convey its ominous message to the Hanoi government. It was not that easy. For one thing, such a threat had to be kept totally secret. To do otherwise would trigger renewed antiwar demonstrations and perhaps destroy the traditional honeymoon Nixon was enjoying in the first months of his presidency. The question was how to "signal" the other side that Richard Nixon was prepared to be far more ruthless than Lyndon B. Johnson. The men in the White House found a quick answer.

---

* It is highly likely that Kissinger was responsible for Nixon's adoption of the phrase "the madman theory." In 1959, Ellsberg had presented two lectures to Kissinger's Harvard seminar on the conscious political use of irrational military threats. Ellsberg called the theory "The Political Uses of Madness." In essence, he described a problem in bargaining theory: what to do when the available threat is so extreme or costly as to make it seem unlikely that a sane and reasonable person would carry it out. On the other hand, since the threat is so extreme, Ellsberg noted, it does not have to be very likely to be used in order to be effective, particularly if the nation posing the threat is making only moderate negotiating demands. Ellsberg postulated that one way of making the threat somewhat credible—which, in this case, was all that would be necessary—would be for the person making the threat to appear not to be fully rational. In effect, an application of this was implicit in Kissinger's *Nuclear Weapons and Foreign Policy*, which advocated, among other things, a "strategy of ambiguity" in connection with United States use of tactical nuclear weapons. In his Harvard lectures, Ellsberg cited as his main example Hitler's conscious use of his reputation as a madman to win victories without firing a shot in the Rhineland, Austria, and Munich before World War II. As his model of Hitler indicated, Ellsberg regarded such a strategy as reckless and utterly dangerous for the world, but a possibility to be anticipated from opponents because, in connection with a nuclear threat, it might work. "I didn't even imagine that an American president could consider such a strategy," Ellsberg says.

5

CAMBODIA:
THE SECRET BOMBING

IN THE FIRST FEW WEEKS of the new administration, Kissinger ordered the Pentagon to present a highly classified briefing on bombing options available in the Vietnam War. The task fell to Air Force Colonel Ray B. Sitton, an experienced Strategic Air Command officer serving the Joint Chiefs of Staff. Sitton was known in the Pentagon as "Mr. B-52."

It was an unusual exercise, Sitton says. "I drew up a big list—on a board about three feet high and eight or nine feet wide—of military steps you might make that would signal North Vietnam that we meant business. Kissinger wanted them to know that we were serious about possible escalation."

Nixon and Kissinger had found the right signal to send: By mid-March 1969 they would secretly begin bombing Cambodia with B-52 aircraft, the eight-engine jets that were the core of the strategic bombing fleet. The bombing became a turning point not only in the war but also in the mentality of the White House. The secret of that bombing—and hundreds of later missions—would be kept for five years. Eventually, the secret became more important to the White House than the bombing.

There was, in the Pentagon's view, a legitimate military reason to assault Cambodia directly. Tens of thousands of North Vietnamese soldiers had established bases and supply depots there and were using the sanctuaries as jumping-off points for ground battles in South Vietnam, just across the border. Somewhere in that area, too, was the Communist headquarters for the guerrilla war in South Vietnam, known as the Central Office for South Vietnam, or COSVN. The Cambodian sanctuaries had been made necessary in part by the heavy bombings inside South Vietnam.

The Joint Chiefs of Staff had long urged the Johnson White House to divert some of the B-52 missions from South Vietnam to the Cambodian sanctuaries, but without success. The political arguments against such bombing were obvious. The United States was not at war with Cambodia, whose government was headed by Prince Norodom Sihanouk. The official American position was one of respect for Sihanouk's neutrality, as North Vietnam's was also. Sihanouk was engaged in a diplomatic balancing act whose goal was to insulate his nation of seven million from the Vietnam War. And, of course, there was the antiwar movement at home to be considered.

The issue came up again a few days after the outgoing Johnson Administration had finally resolved a series of procedural disputes with the North Vietnamese in Paris, permitting the long-delayed peace talks to begin. On January 21, the day after Nixon's inauguration, both sides announced that the first Paris plenary session would be held in four days.* Nixon, shortly before taking office, had let it be known that he favored the compromises in Paris.

The Pentagon chose that week, Nixon's first in office, to propose formally that the bombing of North Vietnam be renewed. That was politically impossible—which should have been obvious—and was rejected out of hand.† In early February 1969, the Pentagon tried anew: It told the White House that it had received evidence from a North Vietnamese defector pinpointing the location of COSVN. Kissinger was further assured, according to top-secret military documents later declassified and released under the Freedom of Information Act, that "all of our information, generally confirmed by imagery interpretation, provides us with a firm basis for targeting COSVN hqs [headquarters]." The documents also show that General Earle G. Wheeler, chairman of the Joint Chiefs of Staff, endorsed a recommendation for a "short-duration, concentrated B-52 attack" on COSVN, in an effort to disrupt a North Vietnamese offensive that was correctly believed to be imminent. Ellsworth Bunker, the American Ambassador in Saigon, also endorsed the proposed mission.

Kissinger turned for advice to Richard L. Sneider, his National Security Council aide for East Asia. Sneider was dubious. "It didn't make military sense," he recalls. He had studied an earlier proposal to use B-52 aircraft against the North Vietnamese sanctuaries in Cambodia, and concluded then that the bombing would disperse the North Vietnamese soldiers from border areas farther west into Cambodia, thus putting more of Cambodia under Communist control. Sneider had another reason, too, for his skepticism: "I knew we wouldn't hit COSVN."

Alexander M. Haig, Jr., the Army colonel who was Kissinger's newly named military aide, wanted the strikes and argued forcefully for them with Kissinger. "Haig was the guy who pushed the goddamn thing," Sneider says. "Henry didn't know what was going on in terms of military operations." One aspect of Haig's qualifications was particularly impressive to his civilian colleagues: He confided to a few that while serving in Vietnam he had participated in one of a regular series of highly classified ground reconnaissance missions inside Cambodia. The Americans who went on such missions, whose existence did not become publicly known until 1973, wore specially manufactured replicas of North Vietnamese uniforms and carried captured gear and weapons. They

* The talks initially were held up by, among other problems, a demand by the United States and the South Vietnamese governments that only North Vietnam, and not the National Liberation Front, be formally included in the talks. The solution, calling for the use of a round table, provided a compromise of sorts: Washington and Saigon would continue publicly depicting the conference as "two-sided," while also agreeing to sit at the round table with representatives of Hanoi and the NLF. A dispute over the size and shape of the table to be used during the proceedings further held up the expanded talks for ten weeks.

† The new administration felt free in early 1969, however, to order a sharp increase in the number of B-52 missions over the Ho Chi Minh Trail in southern Laos. The bombing had begun in December of 1965, when the United States became directly involved in the ground war in South Vietnam. The Laotian missions totaled 3,377 in 1968 and rose to 5,567 in 1969, according to official Pentagon statistics, as the B-52s, no longer permitted to bomb North Vietnam under the November 1968 bombing halt agreement, were increasingly diverted to Laos. Nearly 160,000 tons of bombs were dropped over the Ho Chi Minh Trail in 1969, a 60 percent increase from 1968. Such increases were apparently not considered enough of a "signal" of the Nixon Administration's intent to prosecute the war harshly.

went in "sterile," that is, without any identification or markings to indicate that they were Americans—except, of course, their white or black skin, large body size, and fluent knowledge of English.

No record has been found that Haig did in fact participate in such a mission. Former junior officers who served in Haig's unit in South Vietnam and who regularly went on cross-border operations had no knowledge that he or any other field-grade officer took part. Haig's military record was exemplary without such derring-do. Haig, forty-four years old, had served as deputy commandant at West Point, a traditional stepping stone to high Army rank, before being assigned as Kissinger's military assistant shortly before the inauguration. With every staff stumble and change, Haig grew in importance to Kissinger. His most obvious attributes were the most important ones for Kissinger: He was a no-argument, "can-do" military man all the way, a hardliner on Vietnam, the kind of man who would appeal to Nixon and the White House staff.

In 1969, Haig seemed to be the consummate staff officer. An average student at West Point—214th in a class of 310—he had graduated in 1947 and been assigned to the American Army of Occupation in Japan, where he became a social aide on the staff of General Douglas MacArthur's headquarters. In 1950, he married the daughter of MacArthur's deputy chief of staff, to whom Haig was now aide-de-camp. He won a Silver Star while serving, again as an aide-de-camp, in a corps headquarters during the Korean War, where he participated in MacArthur's landing at Inchon. After Korea, Haig continued on the upwardly mobile track, attending the right Army schools and serving in the right staff jobs. In 1962, after a tour as a staff officer of a tank battalion in Europe, he received a master's degree in international relations from Georgetown University. His next assignment was at the Pentagon, where he was selected over many other applicants to become a staff aide to a Kennedy Administration task force on Cuba directed by Cyrus Vance, then Secretary of the Army, and Joseph A. Califano, Jr., then the Army's general counsel. He was, by all accounts, a superb assistant to Vance and Califano: tireless and loyal, personable, and with a flair for organization.

It was at this stage in his career that Lieutenant Colonel Haig was exposed to covert CIA operations. Pentagon documents show that he was assigned in June 1963 to serve as Califano's assistant on "all matters pertaining to Cuba." At the time, the CIA and the military were in the midst of an intense secret war, authorized by President Kennedy, to overthrow the government of Fidel Castro. Haig was also officially designated to serve as the Pentagon's representative on a highly classified unit known as the "Subcommittee on Subversion" —whose basic target was obviously Cuba. In 1966 and 1967, as a combat officer with the First Division in Vietnam, he won the Distinguished Service Cross and became the youngest lieutenant colonel to serve as a brigade commander. Now riding on the Army's fastest track, he left Vietnam for West Point. After Nixon's election, Haig, by then a full colonel, was formally recommended to Kissinger by the Army, and informally endorsed by many military and civilian officials, including Califano and General Goodpaster.

From the beginning Haig was immensely popular with the young, bright, and ambitious Kissinger crew. He was not viewed as an intellectual threat—his first assignment was the routine task of preparing the President's daily intelligence summary—and he struck most of his colleagues as open and self-effacing. He laughed easily, held his gin well, and had a lively scatological wit.

None of the NSC members, in scores of interviews many years later, was quite sure how Haig did it, but within months he had managed to become indispensable to Henry Kissinger. His loyalty was astonishing; he worked seemingly all the time—every day, every night, every weekend—insuring that the flow of documents in and out of Kissinger's chaotic office was uninterrupted. He had access to the vast flow of backchannel messages from Kissinger's office to American officials throughout the world. He saw, as few other NSC staff people could, the dimensions of the takeover that Kissinger and Nixon were trying to accomplish. As an adroit bureaucrat, he knew that more power for Kissinger meant more power for him. Along with his institutional loyalty, there was a personal one: He understood that his relationship to Kissinger was as important to his career as Kissinger's relationship to the President was to his. Haig was no minor-league courtier himself; he had learned from his days as an aide-de-camp and in the Pentagon the art of flattering a superior.

Like most senior military men, and like Henry Kissinger, Haig was a believer in military force—especially in Vietnam—and saw the war as vital to American credibility and world stability. He quickly expressed his views to his fellow National Security Council staff members. Sometimes things got unpleasant.

Richard Moose, staff secretary for the National Security Council during most of 1969, shared space with Haig and Eagleburger just outside Kissinger's main office, in the White House basement; the rest of the Council staff was across the street in the Executive Office Building. Before he went to work for the Pentagon's Institute of Defense Analysis, and from there to Walt Rostow's NSC, Moose, a native of Arkansas, had spent five months on the staff of Senator J. William Fulbright, the Arkansas Democrat and Vietnam war critic who was chairman of the Senate Foreign Relations Committee—and thus one of Richard Nixon's instant enemies. Early in the administration, Moose earnestly—and naïvely—wrote Kissinger a memorandum saying he had worked with Fulbright and offering to use his relationship if needed. Kissinger, already under siege because of the "moderates" on his staff, did not respond. A few weeks later, Moose accidentally encountered Fulbright in the White House after a presidential meeting. They chatted amiably. Haig walked by, saw them, and, as Moose recalled later, "looked as if he'd seen the devil."

Things quickly became difficult for Moose in the small office. Eagleburger shared the views of Haig, the hard-liner, who was aggressive and full of certitude about Vietnam; Moose, critical of the war, was not. And so Haig moved in on the unresisting Moose and was soon handling much of the daily document flow. Moose was being cut out. "I soon came not to care," Moose says, "except I did really." Within a few months Moose resigned, his NSC position swallowed up by Haig. As Allen was for Kissinger, Moose was Haig's first victim.

Al Haig, always working, always loyal, soon began undermining others on the NSC staff whose integrity and independence made them potential threats, among them Morton Halperin and Richard Sneider. The rest of the staff—ever sensitive to bureaucratic pecking order—soon came to realize that Haig's aggressiveness was being encouraged by his patron. For Kissinger, Haig's very presence in his outer office served as a way of demonstrating to the senior military men in the Pentagon and to the hawks in Congress and on the President's staff—even to Richard Nixon—that Kissinger was reliable. "Haig was the guy Henry could point to," as one former NSC staff man puts it, "and say, 'If I were a Harvard liberal, a left-wing kook, would I have Al Haig working for me?' He was Henry's insurance policy."

Haig was that, but there was much more. As Sneider recalls, "Haig moved in on Henry and he moved in from the very beginning. First of all, he was Henry's butler and his chauffeur. Henry never knew the kinds of perks that could be arranged—private planes for trips to New York for dinner, limousines —and he loved it.* Haig was also very shrewd politically where Henry was naïve. He was advising Henry at first on how to handle Haldeman and Ehrlichman. When Henry had to wear a white tie and tails for his first White House dinner, it was Haig who went to Henry's house and helped him dress . . ."

Even more important, Sneider said, was Haig's understanding from the beginning "that the fight for the soul of Henry Kissinger would be between the civilians and military on the National Security Council staff—and that's why he put the knife in the Foreign Service officers and that's why he was so competitive with Mort Halperin."

Haig's authority and power on the NSC were to increase with each staff defection and each crisis. Eventually he would accomplish the one thing Kissinger found intolerable—a separate relationship with Richard Nixon—and the two men would become bitter enemies. And eventually Kissinger would come to realize that Alexander Haig was not Kissinger's Kissinger, as the newspapers would later characterize him, but Haig's Haig.

In the early months, however, Haig's ambition was not yet a threat. Kissinger was relying on his enthusiasm and his firmly expressed professional opinion that the B-52 bombing in Cambodia would succeed in destroying the Vietnamese sanctuaries. The Joint Chiefs of Staff also urged the bombing, and, as Nixon and Kissinger both explained in their memoirs, those urgings were given more weight after Hanoi initiated a spring offensive throughout South Vietnam on February 22. Although the attacks were on a far less ambitious scale than the Tet offensive the year before, Nixon's immediate instinct was to retaliate. He and Kissinger believed the offensive, coming before the new administration had had any substantive meetings with the North Vietnam delegation in Paris —and on the day before the President was to depart for his ceremonial ten-day visit to Europe—was deliberately timed to humiliate him.†

* Kissinger learned quickly. William Buckley, in his *United Nations* memoir, recalled his first visit with Kissinger in the White House, on a Friday in the spring of 1969. Buckley was pressed for time; he was soon to go off on a lecture tour. "I will send a jet for you," Kissinger said. Buckley offered to take the Eastern Airlines shuttle, which flew hourly between New York and Washington. "No," Kissinger said, "the jet will take you back." Kissinger couldn't resist adding, Buckley wrote, "This is going to ruin academic life." Buckley's escort officer for the private flight, he wrote, "was an amiable young-looking colonel—Alexander Haig."

† The evidence is clear, in fact, that the North Vietnamese and Vietcong attacks were in response to a previously authorized increase in American operations. Pentagon statistics show that the number of battalion-sized operations initiated by American units rose from 727 in November 1968, the month the Johnson Administration's bombing halt began, to 1,077 in January 1969—an increase

Nixon wrote that his first response was to order Kissinger to warn Soviet Ambassador Dobrynin that the United States would retaliate if the North Vietnamese kept up the offensive. Kissinger wrote that the next day, en route from Washington to Brussels, the first stop on the European tour, Nixon decided to authorize the bombing, but was persuaded by Kissinger to delay its implementation. "I wanted to go over the military operations once again and to work out a diplomatic plan," Kissinger explained. Kissinger then ordered Colonels Haig and Sitton to fly to Brussels.

It was a Sunday evening in suburban Washington, and Sitton, enjoying a day off, was looking forward to a dinner party he and his wife were giving in a few hours. The telephone call from Haig came while he was in the shower. He was crisply ordered to pack his bags and rendezvous with Haig at the Pentagon as soon as possible. The two men would then go to nearby Andrews Air Force Base, Haig told him, and take an Air Force jet to New York, where they were to take a commercial overseas flight to Brussels. There they were to brief the President and his national security adviser on the proposed B-52 strikes.

Sitton moved fast, but by the time he reached the Pentagon, there had been a change in plans. The hurried jet ride to New York and the commercial flight to Europe were out; instead, Haig told the properly awed Sitton, they were going to be the sole occupants of a backup presidential plane that would whisk them directly to Brussels. Haig was never reluctant to make use of the enormous authority available to him.

There was time for a quick visit to the quarters of General Wheeler at Fort Myer, Virginia, a few miles from the Pentagon. Sitton worried about his new assignment as Haig and the chairman of the Joint Chiefs of Staff discussed the presidential briefing. "There's one more problem, General," Sitton found himself telling Wheeler. "Am I giving an informational briefing or am I selling this program?" Wheeler's answer was deft: "Go over there and follow your nose. If it's your opinion that they want to do this, you're a salesman." As Sitton remembers it, he and Haig, two colonels suddenly propelled up to the highest level of decision making, laughed nervously at Wheeler's remark.

Once in Brussels, ushered to the President's personal airplane, Haig and Sitton learned that Nixon would not, after all, be meeting with them. Kissinger explained that he had tried to get the President to participate but there was other pressing business. And so the three men, sitting in a small but elaborate

---

of nearly 48 percent. Some of these operations were among the most brutal of the war in terms of civilian casualties in the South. For example, Operation Speedy Express, initiated on December 1, 1968, was an unrestricted shelling and bombing of Kien Hoa Province in the Mekong Delta that caused the death or forced relocation of thousands of peasants. Kevin Buckley, a reporter for *Newsweek* magazine, later quoted American officials as estimating that as many as 5,000 noncombatant civilians were killed "by U.S. firepower to 'pacify' Kien Hoa. The death toll there made the My Lai massacre look trifling in comparison. . . ." In a "pacification" operation farther north, as many as 12,000 peasants were driven from their homes. It was in response to such attacks that the Vietcong and North Vietnamese increased their military activities. Nonetheless, at a briefing in May 1969, Kissinger—identified only as a White House official—told the White House press corps that the number of American battalion-sized operations had "not significantly increased since last November." Describing that stage of the war in his memoirs, Kissinger was again misleading. He wrote that General Creighton W. Abrams, the new commander of American forces in South Vietnam, had only "concentrated on protecting the population" in the last half of 1968, as part of a more aggressive American pacification effort.

conference room in the back of Air Force One as the Nixon entourage flew to London, began talking about the bombing of Cambodia.

Kissinger's overwhelming concern was secrecy. "That was the concern—even above wanting to do it," Sitton says. "We've got to do it with total secrecy." The Air Force colonel recalls Kissinger's attitude vividly: "He was still wringing his hands and seeking moral support to be sure that we could do it and do it without having it in the newspapers."

There was no talk of international law or diplomatic niceties, says Sitton. Nor was any concern expressed about Prince Sihanouk's response. Kissinger insisted that the missions had to be conducted without the knowledge of the Strategic Air Command's normal command and control system—highly classified in itself—which monitors for budgetary requirements such items as fuel usage and bomb tonnage deployed. At one point, Kissinger wanted the Cambodian bombing arranged so that crew members aboard the B-52s would not know they were bombing Cambodia. Sitton balked. He warned Kissinger that if the pilots and bombardiers were not officially told, they would nonetheless quickly figure out where they were bombing and begin gossiping about it.

Sitton won his point, but only after guaranteeing that he could devise a method to set up cover missions and false reporting requirements that would keep the normal chain of command from finding out that Cambodia was under attack. He was under no illusions about Haig's and Kissinger's purpose in bringing him aboard Air Force One: "I was the operations guy who knew how to make it happen." If it did not happen correctly—that is, secretly—and word of the bombing leaked to the press and led to antiwar and anti-Nixon protests, he knew he would be the one saddled with the blame.

Near the end of the flight, Nixon walked back to the briefing room. "He thanked us for coming, apologized for not being there and said he'd discuss it with Kissinger," Sitton says. "It was obvious that Henry's recommendation would carry a lot of weight."

There was another brief interruption. Bob Haldeman also joined the conference for a few minutes, long enough for Kissinger to explain carefully and fully what he, Haig, and Sitton were talking about. "Henry was very comfortable with him," Sitton recalls. And yet it was clear to him that Haldeman really wasn't that interested. "He acknowledged it [Kissinger's briefing] with a nod. He didn't really care. Why Kissinger felt he had to tell him I don't know."*

Kissinger says in his memoirs that he wanted the bombings because a failure to react to Hanoi's "cynical" offensive "could doom our hopes for negotiations; it could only be read by Hanoi as a sign of Nixon's helplessness in the face of domestic pressure. . . ." Back in Washington, he tried to persuade Sneider that, while the missions would not be militarily useful, they would fit into his theory of "always keep the enemy guessing," the Nixon "madman theory." Characteristically, Kissinger seems to have told everyone what he thought was wanted, since Nixon, in his memoirs, depicted a tough-minded

* A few days after the airborne planning session, the President flew on to Paris for his much publicized ceremonial meeting with Charles de Gaulle. In Paris, Nixon and Kissinger also summoned Henry Cabot Lodge, the newly named chief delegate to the Paris peace talks, to a three-hour Vietnam strategy review session in a secure room in the American Embassy in Paris. Also at the talks were Secretary of State Rogers and Marshall Green, Assistant Secretary of State for East Asia and Pacific Affairs, who was temporarily attached to the Paris negotiating team. Green recalls no mention of plans for the B-52 missions.

national security adviser whose steadfast support of the bombing helped him override Laird's and Rogers' opposition. At a critical moment, Nixon wrote, Kissinger carried the day by telling the President: "What do we care if the *New York Times* clobbers us now if it helps us end the war sooner?" The President added: "I agreed with him."

Laird and Rogers warned the President that he would run into intense criticism from Congress and the press if word of the missions became known, as both Cabinet members thought highly likely. Laird was fully in support of the bombing but argued vigorously against keeping it a state secret. "I was for going public right away," he says. "I wasn't worried about Sihanouk. I considered it a sanctuary not in the control of Cambodia . . . North Vietnamese territory. There was nothing much he [Sihanouk] could do about it." Kissinger and Rogers "went the other way," Laird recalls, expressing fear that if the bombings became known "we'd have all kinds of trouble in the United Nations and with Sihanouk."

Laird and Rogers made the error of telling the President what they really thought. Kissinger knew better.

Despite the brave talk about standing up to the *New York Times,* Nixon and Kissinger were obsessed, of course, about Congress and the media. The B-52 bombings, whose early justification had been the need to respond immediately to the North Vietnamese challenge, were delayed long enough for Colonel Sitton to perfect a reporting procedure that would insure secrecy. And in the meantime Nixon ordered a top-secret cable sent to Ambassador Bunker in Saigon, explaining that all discussions of B-52 bombings of Cambodia had been suspended. Such a cable, despite its classification, would routinely be read and filed by dozens of senior officers and military clerks. At the same time he had a backchannel message sent directly to General Creighton W. Abrams, commander of the American forces in Vietnam, telling him to ignore the message to Bunker and continue planning for the B-52 missions.

Sitton went back to the drawing board and soon devised a plan that seemed foolproof. Sixty B-52 aircraft would be sent on the mission. Twelve of them would drop their bombs on legitimate targets inside South Vietnam; the others would be bombing Cambodia.

Sitton's process was to become known as the dual reporting system. The B-52 pilots would be briefed en masse before their mission on targets that were in South Vietnam—that is, the cover targets. After the normal briefing, some crews would be taken aside and told that shortly before their bombing run they would receive special instructions from a ground radar station inside South Vietnam. The radar sites, using sophisticated computers, would in effect take over the flying of the B-52s for the final moments, guiding them to their real targets over Cambodia and computing the precise moment to drop the bombs. After the mission, all the pilots and crews would return to their home base and debrief the missions as if they had been over South Vietnam. Their successes and failures would then be routinely reported in the Pentagon's secret command and control system as having been in South Vietnam.

The small contingent of officers and men who worked inside the four ground radar sites in South Vietnam were to be provided with top-secret target instructions for the Cambodian bombings by special courier flights from Saigon that arrived a few hours before each mission. The men on the ground knew Cambodia was being bombed, but none of them reported that fact until the Watergate investigations of 1973. The men had no illusions about why the secrecy was necessary. Hal Knight, Jr., of Memphis, Tennessee, was the first to talk. Knight, who resigned from the Air Force as a captain in 1972, after being passed over for promotion twice, told the Senate Armed Services Committee in July 1973 that he had believed the bombings were being kept secret to hide them from the American public and the Senate Foreign Relations Committee. There was another concern, too, Knight said: "The thing that disturbs me a little bit is the fact that at least once, if I had had a nervous breakdown . . . I could have gone to a typewriter, picked me out a town, say, within a reasonable distance of the actual aiming point, changed the coordinates of the aiming point to those of that town . . . and no one would have known the difference."

The final reporting process, as approved by the National Security Council, flew in the face of a basic military principle. "We were all trained to the idea that those reports were just pretty near sacred," Knight testified, "and that falsifying a report could result in the gravest disciplinary action against the person who did it."* Knight did not add in his testimony that he and his colleagues had been trained to deal with B-52 missions involving the basic mission of the Strategic Air Command—the carrying of nuclear weapons. Nixon and Kissinger were casually tampering with the command and control system of America's nuclear deterrent, a system necessarily under constant high-level analysis to prevent accidents or unauthorized nuclear bombings.

Sitton's plan, as approved by Kissinger and Haig, included elaborate precautions in case reporters in Saigon or Washington began asking questions about the missions over Cambodia. If that should happen, they were to be told by a press spokesman that, yes, B-52s did strike on routine missions in South Vietnam adjacent to the Cambodian border. The spokesman, wrote Sitton, is to "state that he has no details and will look into this question. Should the press persist in its inquiries or in the event of a Cambodian protest concerning U.S. strikes in Cambodia, U.S. spokesmen will neither confirm nor deny reports of attacks on Cambodia but state it will be investigated. After delivering a reply to any Cambodian protest, Washington will inform the press that we have apologized and offered compensation."

Sitton was ordered to draft the initial set of press guidelines—and all subsequent guidelines for dealing with the press during the clandestine bombing—in the most secure manner possible. Only a few men inside the Pentagon—including the Secretary of Defense, the Joint Chiefs of Staff, and Sitton's two imme-

* The bombing of Cambodia, concealed from Congress as from the public, was considered as an article in the impeachment of Nixon in the House Judiciary Committee's impeachment inquiry in 1974. The article was voted down 26 to 12, and ten members who had voted in favor of the article filed a dissent in which they said, "By failing to recommend the impeachment of President Nixon for the deception of Congress and the American public as to an issue as grave as the systematic bombing of a neutral country, we implicitly accept the argument that any ends—even those a President believes are legitimate—justify unconstitutional means." The committee was unable to learn how the dual bookkeeping system originated. The Senate Armed Services Committee, in hearings a year earlier, had also been unable to fix responsibility for authorization of the dual system. The first hint of Sitton's involvement, and his direct contact with Kissinger and Haig, was given to me by a senior Pentagon official in mid-1979. Sitton, retired and living in Georgia, readily described his activities on behalf of the White House.

diate superiors—were to know what the White House was doing. Any paperwork in connection with the bombing was to be hand carried by Sitton to his superiors; nothing was to be put into the normal lines of communication.

Nixon and Kissinger wanted the bombing, but they preferred to bomb with the concurrence of Laird and Rogers. By mid-March, Laird had been brought around, although he still had reservations about the secrecy aspect, but Rogers was still opposed.

On March 15, Nixon formally authorized the Joint Chiefs to schedule the attack for March 18. Neither Rogers nor Laird was told that the command order had been given. The next step was to concoct an Oval Office meeting for Rogers and Laird. As Kissinger recalled it, the March 16 meeting "followed predictable lines." Laird and General Wheeler, chairman of the Joint Chiefs of Staff, advocated the bombing; Rogers objected on the ground that it would create domestic turmoil. Kissinger's revealing account continues: "There were several hours of discussion during which Nixon permitted himself to be persuaded by Laird and Wheeler to do what he had already ordered. Having previously submitted my thoughts in a memorandum, I did not speak."

Two days later Kissinger was talking with Halperin when Haig broke in and handed Kissinger a cable. Kissinger smiled. The first raids on Cambodia had gone without a hitch and the crew members, in their initial debriefings, reported seventy-three secondary explosions, some as much as five times the normal intensity. Vietcong headquarters, with its presumably vast stores of munitions, must have been hit. Kissinger expansively shared the report with Halperin and then sternly warned him that the bombing of Cambodia was a vital secret that they had to protect; only a very few people knew of it.

Kissinger did not report in his memoirs that the initial report of numerous secondary explosions, like so many of the reports official Washington received from the battlefield during the Vietnam War, was exaggerated. Those first raids did not, in fact, accomplish their basic mission—the destruction of COSVN. And within hours that failure cost American and South Vietnamese lives.

On the same day Kissinger was sharing his secret with Halperin, a Special Forces group, twelve thousand miles from the White House basement, also learned for the first time of the B-52 attacks. The men, operating out of a makeshift base near the Cambodian-South Vietnamese border, were told that they were going to be inserted by helicopter into the COSVN area right after the bombing raids, literally before the dust and smoke had a chance to settle. Two members of the reconnaissance unit were Americans; the rest were specially trained South Vietnamese soldiers. Listening excitedly was Randolph Harrison, a Green Beret lieutenant who was not scheduled for the mission. He and his fellow officers had long urged using B-52 strikes to destroy the North Vietnamese sanctuaries, and he recalls the briefing vividly: "We were told that we would go in and pick some of these guys [COSVN personnel] up. If there was anybody still alive out there they would be so stunned that all you will have to do is walk over and lead him by the arm to the helicopter. This is what they told us. We had no reason to doubt this. . . . We had been told that B-52 strikes will annihilate anyone down there."

Moments after the bombing, the helicopter rolled over the still-smoking bomb site and unloaded the thirteen-man reconnaissance team. There was instant carnage. "The visible effect [of the B-52 bombing] on the North Vietnamese who were there was the same as taking a beehive the size of a basketball and poking it with a stick," Harrison says. "They were mad." Only four members of the team lived long enough to find cover in the woods. "I'm sure there are instances wherein tremendous damage has been done by B-52s," Harrison says. "But my original enthusiasm has been tempered somewhat."

There was an order from military headquarters in Saigon to insert a second Green Beret team that morning, he recalls. No one wanted to go. "They said, 'Fuck you.' " The second mission did not take place.

There is no evidence that the Pentagon informed the White House of the slaughter of the intelligence team in the jungles of Cambodia. Neither Kissinger nor Nixon mentions the deaths in his memoirs. There was White House concern, however, about the failure to knock out COSVN. Richard Sneider thinks Haig may have been embarrassed by the lack of results, but he was among those urgently recommending a second attempt on COSVN. "The military kept on saying, 'We'll get it next time,' " Sneider says. Colonel Sitton recalls hearing right away that the reconnaissance team had been "shot up." It caused him no undue worry. "We weren't surprised. It was a complete and total headquarters," he said of COSVN. "The more bombs we laid on it, the more we learned how big it was. We could find air vents sticking up above ground but couldn't tell which way they were going underground."

Such accounts of the size and permanence of COSVN emplacements would have amazed North Vietnam's leaders in Hanoi. They had issued orders early in the war that COSVN was never to stay in one place for more than ten days. The enemy headquarters moved constantly throughout the war, constantly managing to leave a false trail for American intelligence. COSVN was never destroyed.

Nevertheless, the White House did not seem to consider the March 18 attack on COSVN a military failure. In his memoirs, Kissinger insisted that the bombing was kept secret solely for diplomatic and military reasons: "[A] public announcement [would have been] a gratuitous blow to the Cambodian government, which might have forced its demand that we stop; it might have encouraged a North Vietnamese retaliation (since how could they fail to react if we had announced we were doing it?)." If the bombing had been made public, Kissinger added, "It would surely have been supported by the American public." Richard Nixon was more honest. There was concern about Prince Sihanouk's position, he wrote in *RN,* but "Another reason for secrecy was the problem of domestic antiwar protest. My administration was only two months old, and I wanted to provoke as little public outcry as possible at the outset."

Within the next few months, the secret bombing of Cambodia would become far more intense, and Colonel Sitton would be rewarded for his work with a promotion to brigadier general; later he would become a lieutenant general, the second-highest rank in the Air Force.

Sitton had been promoted for helping to institute a policy that would enable a few men, operating without written instructions, to change the flight path and bombing patterns of a Strategic Air Command bomber. In his view, he had been a good officer, carrying out orders that he knew had come from the very top of the government: "My job was picking the right target and putting the bombs there. If the government chooses to bomb in secret, that's a political decision."

Over a fourteen-month period, ending in April 1970, Nixon and Kissinger authorized a total of 3,630 flights over Cambodia; by the Pentagon's count, the planes dropped 110,000 tons of bombs.

In 1973, when the full story of the secret B-52 bombings became known, Kissinger was among the first to condemn the fact that the bombs were officially reported to have fallen not on Cambodia but on South Vietnam. Speaking at the height of the outcry over Watergate, Kissinger told the author, then a reporter in Washington for the *New York Times,* that the White House "neither ordered nor was it aware of any falsification of records" of the bombing. He added that the White House had begun its own investigation into the official mishandling of the records. "I think it's deplorable," he said.

6

KOREA:
THE FIRST CRISIS

THROUGHOUT THE 1968 presidential campaign, Nixon had privately told his foreign policy aides that he believed the quickest way to end the war was through Moscow. In late March 1968, his staff had persuaded him to publicize his solution to the war. In a speech prepared for delivery on March 31, Nixon declared, "The Soviets hold a position of extraordinary advantage in Vietnam. . . . If the Soviets were disposed to see the war ended and a compromise settlement negotiated, they have the means to move Ho Chi Minh to the conference table. . . . The real centers of decision are Washington and Moscow." The speech was never given. President Johnson chose that night for his dramatic announcement that he was not a candidate for reelection, and Nixon, ever cautious, decided then to keep his plan to himself—and did so throughout the long campaign.

Kissinger, however, who had made it clear in his *Foreign Affairs* article that he did not think the road to peace in Vietnam led through the Soviet Union, was faced with a potentially profound disagreement with Nixon on the new administration's most crucial area of foreign policy. Within weeks, he managed to suppress his doubts about the value of such intervention and to become a passionate advocate of Nixon's plan to end the war by threatening the Soviet Union. On March 20, for example, he sent Nixon a top-secret memorandum, "Vietnam Situation and Options," that had been drafted by Morton Halperin. "There is no question," Kissinger wrote, "that the Soviets could play a major role in bringing the war to an end if they decide to put pressure on Hanoi." He concluded that the Soviets would become involved, and pay the consequent price in the world Communist movement, "only if after a careful calculation of costs and gains they decide that it is in their interest to do so." He was telling the President what he wanted to hear.

It was at this time, Kissinger wrote in his memoirs, that he decided to ask Cyrus Vance, who in February had resigned the post of deputy chief of the Paris peace talks delegation, to take on a mission that "was tailor-made for his qualities. It was nothing less than to enlist the Soviet Union in a rapid settlement of the Vietnam War." The plan was to send Vance to Moscow in an attempt to link what Moscow wanted—the opening of strategic arms limitation talks—to a Vietnam solution. The linkage was pure Nixon. On April 3, Kissinger formally proposed the Vance mission to Nixon.

Kissinger's proposal was carefully thought out and put him in a no-lose position. Its basic thesis was flattering to the President, who had been describing Moscow as the key to a Hanoi solution for more than a year. Kissinger recommended that Nixon accompany the proposal by warning Ambassador Dobrynin that United States-Soviet relations were "at a crossroads." There would be very tough talk to the Soviets—something that always delighted Nixon—and Dobrynin would be told that none of his country's major needs could be met as long as the Vietnam War continued to be an obstacle. If the Vance mission failed, Kissinger recommended a military showdown with Hanoi. If the mission was a success, the Soviets would be told that Nixon would then consider a possible summit meeting—another of Nixon's eagerly sought goals.

Kissinger's price for all this advice was carefully shielded but explicit nonetheless, as his memoirs made clear. His April 3 proposal for the Vance mission included this important proviso: "Our government has to be sufficiently disciplined to speak with the same voice." Kissinger, of course, was to be that voice.

Kissinger kept his proposal very quiet, not even telling Halperin, at the time his closest aide on Vietnam matters in the NSC. Kissinger had good reasons for not telling. Halperin was aware that Kissinger had discussed substantially the same mission with Averell Harriman, the former chief negotiator at the peace talks. "I knew Henry was meeting with Harriman and telling him he would send him to Moscow to settle the war," Halperin recalls. "I always thought the purpose was to keep Harriman quiet." Halperin, furthermore, was extremely skeptical, as he knew Kissinger was, of the prospect of settling the Vietnam War in Moscow.

The Vance mission suited Kissinger's internal needs perfectly. In his memoirs, Kissinger repeatedly portrayed himself as frustrated by the free-wheeling atmosphere at the top of the Nixon Administration that spring; he conceived of the Vance mission, he wrote, as a "means of bringing matters to a head." His doubts about the value of such intervention with the Soviet Union, as expressed to Halperin and recorded in *Foreign Affairs,* were beside the point. The Vance proposal gave him a bureaucratic vehicle for enthusiastically endorsing the Nixon threat policy as well as a further chance to consolidate bureaucratic power.

The Vance mission never took place—the Soviet Union dealt with the impossible proposal by simply never responding to it. Moscow could not solve the Vietnam War. But Kissinger was beginning to achieve his goal of becoming the administration's voice on foreign policy. It was possible, he was learning, to use the great issues, as he had done in his dealings with Vance and Harriman, to bolster his personal standing with the President and diminish that of his peers.

By mid-April, Kissinger was well on his way toward the neutralization of Laird and Rogers, but his bureaucratic battles were not fully won. His overriding concern in March and early April, as he and the NSC staff struggled to find an effective Vietnam policy, was the continuing signs of independence from the Secretaries of State and Defense. On March 8, in a private conversation with Ambassador Dobrynin of the Soviet Union, Rogers had gone too far, in Kissinger's view, by suggesting that the Nixon Administration was prepared to begin secret peace talks with North Vietnam on military issues and also to begin discussing political matters in four-party talks that would involve the South Vietnamese and the National Liberation Front. Rogers' comments to Dobrynin came a few days after a Vietcong shelling of Saigon, thus providing Kissinger with a chance to undercut the Secretary of State with the President by characterizing him as soft. In an eleven-page memorandum of March 10 (marked "Top Secret/Sensitive"), Kissinger told Nixon that Rogers was undermining the administration's negotiating policy by offering secret talks without "getting anything in return" from the other side.

"We have combined heavy military pressure with a deliberate pace in Paris," Kissinger declared. "We have specifically refrained from taking the initiative on opening private talks and have made clear that when such talks were possible we would talk only to the NVM [North Vietnamese] and only about mutual withdrawal." Rogers' conversation with Dobrynin had made it "difficult to resist early private talks . . . By lobbing a few shells into Saigon, Hanoi has induced us to change our position . . ."

On April 1, Laird, who had previously urged Nixon to begin withdrawing American troops from South Vietnam unilaterally, publicly announced a 10 percent cutback—for budgetary reasons—in the number of B-52 missions in Vietnam; the statement was issued without prior presidential clearance. But Kissinger was already strongly on record against any deescalation of the war, a view he knew agreed with Nixon's. In a memorandum to the President three weeks earlier, he had argued that "Our military effort leaves a great deal to be desired, but it remains one of our few bargaining weapons." He added that North Vietnam had begun withdrawing its main force units from the South, enabling American and South Vietnamese troops to devote "substantial forces to anti-guerrilla action. If we now de-escalate, Hanoi will get for nothing what it has had to pay heavy, perhaps excessive casualties to obtain: the effective neutralization of U.S. forces . . ."

The Laird and Rogers actions proved to be inconsequential in terms of serious peace negotiations, which had yet to begin in Paris, but they tormented Kissinger, who was driving to instill his will and influence throughout the bureaucracy. In his memoirs, Kissinger tried to show that his outrage was solely in terms of the damage to the American negotiating position. Rogers, he wrote, "was dissipating assets for one day's headlines" by making commitments to Dobrynin. Furthermore, "The Paris delegation [which was under State Department control] lacked discipline; our internal divisions made it unlikely that we could present a coherent policy or prevent oscillation between extremes." Thus Rogers was a poor bargainer, a publicity seeker, and an incompetent administrator.

As for Laird, wrote Kissinger, his announcement of a unilateral cutback in B-52 operations could be perceived by the North Vietnamese as a withdrawal of American forces. Kissinger did not explain in his memoirs how Hanoi could come to that conclusion less than two weeks after he and Nixon had initiated the first of the secret B-52 bombings of Cambodia.

Kissinger, aided by what he and Nixon saw as the diplomatic gaffes of Rogers and Laird, had greatly strengthened his position in regard to foreign policy inside the White House. He would take another great leap toward ultimate control in the administration's first foreign policy crisis.

The crisis began late in the afternoon of Monday, April 14, 1969, when a North Korean jet fighter shot down, without warning and without provocation, a U. S. Navy electronic espionage aircraft known as EC-121. The four-engine propeller-driven plane, unarmed and weighted down with eavesdropping equipment, was attacked about ninety nautical miles off the coast of North Korea in international waters. All thirty-one men aboard were killed.

Nixon's immediate response was to meet force with force, as the White House had done in Cambodia after the North Vietnamese offensive two months earlier. There was immediate talk of another B-52 strike. Nixon was angry, and adding to his anger was the obvious parallel between the EC-121 shooting and the North Koreans' seizure in January 1968 of the U. S. Navy spy ship *Pueblo,* whose crew was held captive for eleven months. During his campaign for the presidential nomination, Nixon had repeatedly criticized the Johnson Administration for failing to retaliate, and he had returned to that theme in his acceptance address at the convention: "I say to you tonight that when respect for the United States falls so low that a fourth-rate military power like Korea will seize an American naval vessel on the high seas, it's time for new leadership to restore respect for the United States of America."

Kissinger lost no time in picking up the call for retaliation. He turned again to Colonel Sitton, to ask: Was it also possible to put a secret B-52 bombing mission into North Korea? Colonel Sitton, who had helped to draw up the Pentagon's contingency plans after the *Pueblo* seizure, had a number of military options—"ranging from hitting one airfield to taking out everything"—ready to go when the White House called. He spent the next four days shuttling back and forth between the Pentagon and the White House with new attack plans for North Korea.

Over those four days, however, Nixon and Kissinger were unable to control the bureaucracy. That is, during the many meetings of the National Security Council, they were unable to prevent Laird, Rogers, and Richard Helms, director of the Central Intelligence Agency, from expressing their doubts about the necessity for and the risks of military retaliation. Kissinger's and Nixon's newly revised National Security Council system worked during the EC-121 crisis in a way that the two men made sure it never would again: to produce frank debate at the highest levels. When the Secretaries of Defense and State and the director of the CIA urged diplomatic action only, Kissinger and Nixon were confronted with Cabinet-level officials who were on record against retaliation before the two men had a firm plan on how to retaliate.

There was a basic—and until now unreported—reason for caution: a series of highly classified intelligence intercepts which demonstrated that—contrary to Nixon's belief—the North Koreans had not shot down the EC-121 in a deliberate act of defiance. The plane had indeed been shot down in cold blood, but the National Security Agency, which intercepts and monitors communications all over the world, concluded soon afterward that the incident was apparently a command-and-control error involving a single North Korean airplane. There was no evidence that the North Korean government knew of the attack in advance, as it had, for example, before the *Pueblo* was seized. The NSA

69

also concluded that the Soviet Union was "appalled" over the incident; it had quickly sent patrol craft out to help in the U.S. Navy's search for survivors. One former NSA analyst recalls: "There was evidence it was a screw-up. The North Koreans are ruthless but careful. It would be very much out of their pattern" to gratuitously provoke the United States by deliberately shooting down one of its aircraft ninety miles offshore.

Amazingly, there is no evidence that senior policy makers in the White House were ever officially told of the NSA's findings. Halperin, who worked closely with Kissinger during the crisis, does not recall receiving any indication that the EC-121 had not been provocatively shot down by the North Koreans. According to Halperin, if Kissinger knew otherwise, he kept it to himself. The NSA analyst, who was directly involved in the crisis, acknowledges that the staff of his agency would have been reluctant to report its conclusion to the White House, which had concluded from the start that North Korea was a deliberate aggressor. "It wouldn't have been accepted," he explains. "They wouldn't have believed it." If any cautionary report was sent, he thinks it would have gone backchannel as an off-the-record message.

Not everyone in the White House was eager to accept the incident at face value. Richard Sneider, the experienced East Asia aide, expressed doubts that were ignored. "I was the only one on the NSC staff who had second thoughts," he says. "And I wrote Henry a memo saying in effect, We've got enough trouble now in Vietnam. The initial response domestically will be positive, but there will be a kickback." Sneider "knew Henry was very serious about retaliation, but nobody else was. I remember telling Alex Johnson, 'This is serious.' He just laughed, and I said, 'No, Alex, we're serious about this.' " One of Kissinger's ideas, Sneider says, called for what he termed a "sterile" strike over a North Korean airfield. "It was one of those things Henry said that nobody really understood. He wanted to send a couple of bombers over to clobber the airfield. The Pentagon said we can't send planes over without air cover."

Alexis Johnson "raised questions not because I thought we shouldn't do it," he recalls, "but because of no feasible plan. How would the North Koreans know when they saw those [U.S.] planes that this was just a retaliatory raid? What if they retaliated and hit our airfields in South Korea?" Kissinger proposed ordering all the American planes in South Korea into the air. Then, Johnson persisted, what if North Korea considered that move another stage of the attack? Kissinger's response made the folly of any retaliation apparent to all, in Johnson's view: "We'd have to communicate with Kim Il-sung [the North Korean premier] and tell him it's only a retaliation." Johnson insists that much of Kissinger's behavior during the crisis was theatrical. In reality he "recognized that if you're going to do something like that you have to do it immediately—not two or three days later."

Kissinger's audience in all this was, of course, not the senior aides in the government, but the President. Richard Nixon wanted retaliation, and thus so did he. Their underlying instinct was that a sharp military response was a necessary part of their secret threat strategy in the Vietnam War. If there were those in the administration who had reservations, they were the enemy.

Melvin Laird was among those most strongly opposed to the concept of a retaliatory strike, and he had even put his opposition in writing. The EC-121 issue was to lead to a direct and bitter confrontation between Kissinger and Laird. It was an inevitable collision, for Laird was correctly perceived by Kissinger as his one substantial threat to total domination of the bureaucracy. Laird's public image as a hawk and a hardliner masked his intense desire to get the United States out of Vietnam. He had already surprised the President and his national security adviser, who knew less about the Secretary of Defense than they thought, by constantly urging—in private, of course—a disengagement from the war.* There was no talk from Laird of massive escalation, or the threat of escalation, as there was from Nixon and Kissinger. Laird wanted to begin the immediate withdrawal of Americans from South Vietnam. In their place, he proposed additional military training and economic aid for the South. His proposals on disengagement would eventually be adopted by a reluctant White House, for his influence in Washington was immense, and he was independent of the presidency. He had spent sixteen years in Congress, eventually becoming a respected leading member of the House Appropriations Committee, with control over defense spending. He had also spent years intensely involved with the appropriations subcommittee that handled finances for the CIA and other intelligence agencies. He understood the world of foreign policy and intelligence as well as, if not better than, anyone in the White House. He also seemed to understand what Kissinger and Nixon were up to. In his memoirs, Kissinger described Laird as others would have depicted Kissinger: "Laird acted on the assumption that he had a Constitutional right to seek to outsmart and outmaneuver anyone with whom his office brought him into contact."

Nixon and Kissinger chose to deal with Laird by trying to work around him. His office was to be avoided.

"We always heard about it last," says Robert E. Pursley, an Air Force colonel who was Laird's military assistant. Pursley, who had been military adviser to Secretaries of Defense Robert McNamara and Clark Clifford at the time the Johnson Administration began its slow turnabout on the Vietnam War, was an extremely controversial figure, resented by many senior officers, including Haig and Wheeler, as being a dove on Vietnam. Many people thought that Pursley, whose intelligence and common sense were highly respected by Clifford and Laird, had more real power than a military assistant was entitled to have. His cautious views were to be very influential in the EC-121 crisis.

"The White House reached into the JCS [Joint Chiefs of Staff] general staff," Pursley remembers, "and there was an endless stream of options. Our position"—that is, the position enunciated by Laird in memoranda written by Pursley—"was let's not worry about the options. The issue is whether to

---

* Nixon had originally settled on Senator Henry M. ("Scoop") Jackson, the senior Democrat from Washington, to serve as Defense Secretary, and Jackson had accepted. In early December 1968, a day or two before Nixon was to unveil his new Cabinet, Jackson—who still dreamed of one day becoming a Democratic presidential candidate—telephoned to say he had changed his mind. He would stay in the Senate and take his chances. Laird had been instrumental in persuading Nixon to appoint Jackson, a process that, at Jackson's insistence, included negotiating a commitment from Daniel J. Evans, the Republican governor of Washington, to appoint a Democrat to replace Jackson in the Senate. Nixon, not unnaturally, was enraged at Laird. Laird recalls his saying, "You son-of-a-bitch. You talked me into this. Now you've got to do it"—take the Defense Secretary's job. Laird wanted to stay in the House, and had already turned down the Cabinet post of Secretary of Health, Education and Welfare. But now, feeling guilty, he agreed to serve one term in the Pentagon: "I got sandbagged into it."

retaliate at all or not—forget the options. The first question you have to study is whether you would run the risk of getting involved in a second-front war." The Laird position, as spelled out to Kissinger and Nixon over the next few days, was that if the administration decided to retaliate, it would have to face the possibility of a general mobilization of men and women for the armed forces. "The North Koreans most certainly would respond" to an American attack, Pursley and Laird argued in their memoranda. The basic question that wasn't being considered, Pursley says, was "just what in hell do you do after they respond? There was just no thought on that."

"Kissinger was so limited in his thinking," Pursley recalls. "His attitude was: 'Don't bother me. We'll get the supplies from somewhere.' We said let's think it all the way through. But then it takes time to think it through and that's what burned them up."

Nevertheless, in those first days after the EC-121 incident, Kissinger ordered updated studies made of all options, including the possible use of tactical nuclear weapons. Six or seven were produced by the Joint Chiefs of Staff, ranging from retaliatory strikes on North Korean airfields to the mass destruction of hydroelectric plants.*

Nixon wanted to hit hard, too. "Kissinger and I continued to feel that retaliation was important," Nixon wrote. "As he put it, a strong reaction from the United States would be a signal that for the first time in years the United States was sure of itself. It would shore up the morale of our allies and give pause to our enemies. We discussed the possibility that the North Koreans would respond with an attack on South Korea. Kissinger said that he did not believe that would happen, but, if it did, we had to be prepared to take whatever steps were necessary to bring the North Koreans to their knees."

Rogers recalls a lot of tough talk from Nixon at an Oval Office meeting the morning after the shootdown. "The President said, 'We're going to show them.' I told him that's what Lyndon Johnson said about Vietnam and we're still there," Rogers recalled. Rogers argued against a second confrontation in Asia and listened as Kissinger argued "the other way." A few days later, Kissinger began privately telling the press that Rogers was "soft." The day after the meeting, Rogers, who had yet to learn that he was not expected to act like a Secretary of State, took it upon himself to indicate publicly that no significant retaliation against North Korea would be taken. In a speech before a meeting of the American Society of Newspaper Editors in Washington, he declared that "The weak can be rash. The powerful must be more restrained. Complexity in world affairs should teach us the need to act responsibly, to substitute cooperation for coercion and to move from confrontation to negotiation on the issues that divide nations."

The day after the speech, more and more frustrated by his inability to gain government-wide support for immediate retaliation, Kissinger exploded. He stormed over to Laird's office and, as Pursley recalls, "ricocheted all over the walls" in rage. "He was livid, and said that we had 'usurped the President's

---

* In *The Ends of Power,* Haldeman wrote that Kissinger conceded that the American use of nuclear weapons might become necessary if the United States retaliated for the loss of the EC-121 and the North Koreans counterattacked. It is conceivable, however, that Kissinger was deliberately talking tough to bolster his position and his image at this early stage of his career. In the Nixon White House, no one's reputation ever seemed to suffer because of such talk.

authority.' Henry saw everything as a plot. That's why it was so hard to deal with him. Mel Laird would tell them over and over—'you guys are your own worst enemies.' "

In addition to cautions from Laird, Helms, Rogers, and Sneider, Kissinger also received prudent advice from William Porter, the Ambassador to South Korea. Porter, upon learning that the White House was considering bombing North Korea's ports, sent a go-slow cable. "I stressed that a strong American reaction, which could not be revealed in advance to President Park [of South Korea], would be taken as a signal by the South Koreans to go North," Porter says. "I said that they would believe that we had acted that way—in not consulting with them—in order to say that we did not urge them to go in." The cable ended with the suggestion that the White House "be careful."

Despite all this advice, Kissinger obviously expected retaliation to be authorized. He ordered a draft speech prepared in which the President would explain why it was necessary. And, in a futile attempt to make sure the National Security Council would decide the way he wanted it to decide, he ordered two interagency papers prepared. "Henry played a typical game," says Sneider, who, as the ranking NSC official for East Asia, was to prepare the briefing papers for the NSC. "At the same time I was doing the interagency paper, Henry had Mort [Halperin] and Larry [Eagleburger] writing another paper. He was sure my report would be too soft." Both Halperin and Eagleburger, as Kissinger knew, supported an immediate bombing raid.

Kissinger finally recommended one strike on a North Korean airfield from an American aircraft carrier, with enough planes involved to destroy all the planes on the airstrip. Nixon agreed to the one strike, but postponed ordering it—in part, he said in his memoirs, because of Porter's warning. The final decision was put off until after Nixon's news conference on April 18, which had been scheduled before the crisis arose. Nixon was preoccupied with elaborate briefings to insure that he would not stumble. The news conference may have been "a further source of inhibition," Kissinger suggested in his memoirs. "It was an experience that usually filled him with such a combination of dread and exhilaration as to leave no energy for other reflection."

Despite Nixon's careful preparation, the news conference was a botch. Nixon announced that the reconnaissance flights, which had been discontinued since the EC-121 shootdown, would immediately be resumed and would be protected. He and Kissinger had agreed on that statement before the news conference, thinking it would be perceived as a "signal" that retaliation was still a live possibility. They were wrong. Their intended message was ignored or missed, and people in Congress and the media praised Nixon's restrained handling of the crisis.*

In addition, Nixon made an extremely damaging breach of intelligence by revealing to the press that the NSA was able to monitor and recreate both

---

* It was also ignored by Laird, who, as the White House learned later, had canceled all reconnaissance flights not only near North Korea but also near the Soviet Union, China, and Cuba, and in the Mediterranean. Laird continued the embargo on such operations, despite violent protests from Kissinger, until early May. Halperin recalls Kissinger's explosion upon hearing that Laird had not reinstated the flights: "How can he do this? How can he do this? He has a direct order from the President." Halperin saw the irony of Kissinger's despair. "The notion that the bureaucracy doesn't obey the President is repeated throughout his books, but still he was outraged. It was happening to him."

North Korean and Soviet radar signals. Emphasizing that the EC-121 was in international waters, Nixon told reporters, "There was no uncertainty whatever as to where this plane was, because we know what their radar showed. We, incidentally, know what the Russian radar showed. And all three radars [Russian, United States, and North Korean] showed exactly the same thing."

The Nixon statement created near-pandemonium at the NSA. "I died when I heard it," one official said. "This was my business. I just fell out of my chair —I literally did." He considered the Nixon statement equivalent to "Black Tuesday," the day in 1960 when two NSA cryptologists who had defected to the Soviet Union were unveiled at a Moscow news conference. The NSA men, William H. Martin and Vernon F. Mitchell, gave away more secrets than ever before in the NSA's eight-year history, and the revision of interception and signal communications that their betrayal caused took years to accomplish.*

After Nixon's statement about the EC-121, the NSA official says, "The Soviet Union and other countries changed every frequency, every crypt system, every net structure—all at once. It took months to work it out." At the time of Nixon's blunder, the Soviets, North Koreans, and Chinese were using relatively simple codes in their radar analyses and the NSA had been able to break those codes and recreate their radar patterns in its systems, giving the United States the incalculable advantage of knowing what the other side was seeing.

There was also dismay in the White House Situation Room, the lead-shielded basement office where the most highly classified materials could be discussed without fear of interception. Kissinger and his aides had gathered there before the news conference to continue their planning for air strikes in North Korea; there was also a quick intelligence briefing on how little the President could say publicly about the radar intercepts. The meeting was adjourned to enable Kissinger to attend the press conference. When he returned, Halperin recalls, Alexis Johnson, who had been horrified by Nixon's comments, attempted a weak joke: "We're going to take the President's clearances away." Kissinger said nothing.

Later that day, Nixon and Kissinger convened a meeting of the National Security Council and listened to the formal objections to retaliation from Laird, Rogers, and Helms. Nixon and Kissinger wavered in the face of such united opposition. "Kissinger agreed that we could ill afford a Cabinet insurrection at such an early date in the Administration," Nixon wrote. In the future, important decisions would be made before the National Security Council met.

Kissinger confirmed that he recommended against a retaliatory attack after the April 18 Security Council meeting. But it was Nixon, he insisted, who really backed down. "I never had the impression Nixon had his heart in a retaliatory attack," Kissinger wrote. "He had procrastinated too much; he had

---

* For example, shortly after the defection, the North Vietnamese changed their code to high-level ciphers and the NSA lost its ability to read Hanoi's communications and instructions to its cadre scattered throughout South Vietnam. The North Vietnamese code was not broken again by NSA cryptographers for at least six years. Since "Black Tuesday" refers, not to the day that Martin and Mitchell defected from the United States, but to the day they told the world what they had been telling the Soviets, it can be argued that the stringent security measures regarding communications intelligence are not designed merely to keep such information from the Soviets, whose own skills in the area are great, but also from American allies and Third World nations whose communication facilities are far less advanced.

not engaged in the relentless maneuvering by which he bypassed opposition when his mind was made up. Now that he had in effect an alibi, he raged against his advisers. He would get rid of Rogers and Laird at the earliest opportunity; he would never consult them again in a crisis. . . . But the bottom line was that he would make no military response against North Korea."

Kissinger made clear his contempt for the advice of Rogers, Laird, and Helms. "There was no discussion of the fundamental issue: whether our failure to respond to the shootdown of an unarmed reconnaissance plane over international waters might not create an impression that it would encourage our enemies in Hanoi and embolden opponents elsewhere." Kissinger did not record the underlying reason for his concern: that the failure to respond militarily would be a setback for the "madman theory." The other senior officials, not knowing the real strategy, could not understand why Nixon and Kissinger had insisted on a brutal response.

There was a lingering attempt to salvage a sense of American unpredictability. The "madman theory," as Nixon had told Haldeman, involved the use, or threatened use, of excessive force. To that end, late on April 17 the Navy was ordered to assemble a flotilla of aircraft carriers and warships and steam to the waters off North Korea for the air attacks—if they were authorized. Twenty-four ships, including four aircraft carriers, subsequently formed a task force and, receiving no orders to launch strikes, merely steamed about the Sea of Japan for a few days before returning to their duty stations.

Their slow pace in reaching the area further frustrated Kissinger, who accused Laird and Pursley of deliberately delaying the flotilla to prevent any possible utilization of a military response. One intelligence official who monitored the EC-121 operation recalls that Kissinger "had an expectation that he could push a button and things would get done. He didn't understand organizational routines. It took us three days to assemble the fleet and to go from the Tonkin Gulf to North Korea." What complicated matters was that Nixon and Kissinger had ordered "the most enormous armada since the invasion of Normandy in World War II."

Nixon and Kissinger agreed on a second military measure, also aimed at giving a "signal" to the North Koreans and the North Vietnamese. Sitton was called back to the White House and asked whether he could plan another secret B-52 mission over Cambodia. Sitton was eager to please. "How big a mission do you want?" he asked. "Do you want a bigger one?" Of course the answer was yes, and within days, ninety-six B-52s made another secret bombing run over Cambodia—more than twice as many as on the first raid in March. Once again a reconnaissance team was sent in to survey the damage and attempt to retrieve prisoners. And once again the team was badly shot up, with only a few men surviving to be rescued by helicopters.

Nixon was convinced, he said in his memoirs, that the B-52 attacks on Cambodia were "an effective way to impress the Communist leaders of both North Korea and North Vietnam with our resolve to support our allies and resist aggression." Sitton wasn't so sure. "Henry is the world's greatest signal sender," he said, "but I don't know if the message he sent was the one he wanted."

In his memoirs, Kissinger gave no hint of Nixon's intelligence gaffe, nor did he indicate that the White House had been told of the vital information about North Korea's intentions that the NSA had gathered shortly after the EC-121 was shot down. Nonetheless, he wrote that "The EC-121 incident was a blessing in disguise. It made us dramatically tighten our procedures." What he meant was that he and Nixon had decided to collaborate in isolation, away from the advice of those in the Cabinet who might disagree. In early May, Nixon sent a memorandum to the bureaucracy announcing the formation of a special team to deal with crises, the Washington Special Action Group. Its members would not be Cabinet officials but their deputies. In the case of State, neither Rogers nor Under Secretary Richardson would serve; the State Department representative would be Alexis Johnson, who, Kissinger knew, could be trusted to perform his national security functions with no back talk and no leaking. The Pentagon representative would be the deputy Secretary of Defense, David Packard. The Secretary of State and the Secretary of Defense would no longer be involved in day-to-day crisis management. If they had a complaint, they could take it to the Oval Office.

Kissinger was careful to protect himself, and the President, throughout the crisis. On the second day, at a time when Kissinger was insisting that the Joint Chiefs of Staff provide military options, the *New York Times* and the *Washington Post* were told, as a page-one *Times* account by Max Frankel put it, "Diplomatic action rather than military response will be the Nixon Administration's essential response . . ."

A few weeks later, Kissinger was interviewed by Patrick Anderson, who was writing a profile of him for the *New York Times Magazine*. The article, like all articles on Kissinger at that time, was friendly. It noted that President Nixon had been on the edge of ordering a retaliatory strike against North Korea. "Kissinger does not discuss his advice to the President," the article continued. "It is reported that when some officials argued for a quick retaliatory strike, Kissinger replied that if the U.S. did bomb North Korea there was no need to hurry, that it would be better to act in cold calculation than in the heat of passion, and that while it is always easy to get into wars, it is much harder to get out of them. People who know Kissinger's thinking find it very hard to believe that he would want the U.S. to risk confrontation with China and/or Russia over the loss of one intelligence plane."

Kissinger was also misleading in his comments to the Kalb brothers for their biography. After Nixon decided on April 18 not to retaliate, the Kalbs wrote, "Kissinger was pleased that he had reached his decision only after a full range of options had been examined." In his memoirs, however, Kissinger was sharply critical of the procedures he had set up in January: "The NSC system became a device to accumulate options without supplying perspective or a sense of direction."

It was an early instance of what would increasingly emerge as another essential White House role for Kissinger: liaison to the liberal press. His function in the various interviews and briefings was not merely to garner favorable publicity for Nixon and his policies, but to shield the real goals and strategy of the administration from view. By doing so, Kissinger was also weakening the antiwar movement, and one White House goal—perhaps never completely articulated even in private by either Nixon or Kissinger—was to isolate the antiwar activists from the many millions of citizens who were also against the war but had yet to take to the streets in protest.

Kissinger's adroit handling of the press did little to pacify those on his staff who, understanding Nixon's strategy of threat, were distressed over his failure to demonstrate American nerve. After the crisis, Haig complained bitterly to one staff member, "I'm going to resign if we don't get a President with balls." Months later, Lawrence Eagleburger harshly criticized the White House's handling of the incident, telling an American diplomat that he and Kissinger were "disgusted with pusillanimous politicians such as Nixon who talk tough but back down under pressure."

Kissinger's desire to demonstrate America's toughness, although futile in the EC-121 case, had a built-in personal bonus: It stood him in good stead with Nixon, Haldeman, and their all-important loyalists in the White House. In his memoirs, Haldeman wrote that Nixon "believes that Kissinger overreacted on the hawkish side . . . [by] conceding the possible necessity of nuclear bombs as a bottom line if the North Koreans counterattacked." One could never go wrong in that White House by being too far right. Nixon, Haldeman, and the other confidants now had their secret: Kissinger, the favorite of the liberal press and the antiwar columnists, could be tougher than even "the old man" in a pressure situation.

Kissinger was always careful not to show his hard line in public. He would continue with impunity for the next four years to argue heatedly in private for bombing—whether in North Korea or North Vietnam—and present himself in public and to the press as a force for restraint.

By late April, having survived the EC-121 incident with no loss of public esteem, the Nixon Administration began to put into effect its basic plan to end the war. North Vietnam would first be offered what Nixon and Kissinger believed was a generous peace—far more than anything suggested during the Johnson Administration. The offer would be accompanied by a direct threat to Hanoi and Moscow. If North Vietnam did not respond to the new peace proposal, it would be privately warned to expect a major, and perhaps irrational, escalation by the United States. In underworld language, Hanoi was being given an offer it couldn't refuse. Public opinion would be assuaged, in case there was an escalation, by the initiation of Laird's "Vietnamization" program —the publicly announced reduction of American forces and the increased training of South Vietnamese Army units.

The overall Vietnam policy was Nixon's. It followed, to a remarkable degree, his view as he had spelled it out in his August 1968 talk to the group of southern convention delegates: "Critical to the settlement of Vietnam is relations with the Soviet Union. That is why I have said over and over again that it is going to be necessary for the next President to sit down and talk with the Soviet leaders—and talk directly, not only about Vietnam, you've got to broaden the canvas—because in Vietnam, they have no reason to end that war. It's hurting us more than it's hurting them." Along with direct threats to the Soviets and Hanoi, "We need a massive training program so that the South

Vietnamese can be trained to take over the fighting—that they can be phased in as we phase out.''

Kissinger's role throughout this early period was that of the tactician dutifully executing orders from the strategist. Under his leadership, in February and March the National Security Council devised a new Vietnam negotiating strategy. Its major change was to alter drastically the basic American negotiating position as laid down by the Johnson Administration in October 1966, the so-called Manila formula. Under that formula, the war would be settled only when Hanoi withdrew its troops from the South, to be followed by the withdrawal of all American forces within six months. In short, the Johnson Administration had offered North Vietnam only a phased withdrawal, with Hanoi's troops to leave first.

On April 1, the Nixon Administration issued a top-secret National Security Decision Memorandum, NSDM 9, which specifically revoked the Manila formula and proposed a mutually timed withdrawal of North Vietnamese and American forces from Southeast Asia, with political settlements to be negotiated by the South Vietnamese and the Vietcong. That was the offer Cyrus Vance would have made in Moscow, if the Soviet Union had permitted him to go.

On May 14, in his first presidential address on Vietnam, President Nixon disclosed the new proposal. He specifically abandoned the Manila formula— without saying as much—and proposed mutual withdrawal from South Vietnam, Laos, and Cambodia, as well as an internationally supervised ceasefire and supervised elections in the South. The nationally televised speech also provided the first clue to the soon-to-be-announced Vietnamization program. "... [A]part from any development that may occur in the negotiation in Paris," Nixon said, "the time is approaching when the South Vietnamese forces will be able to take over some of the fighting fronts now being manned by Americans." Nixon also restated his belief in the overwhelming importance of the war: "If we simply abandoned our effort in Vietnam, the cause of peace might not survive the damage that would be done to other nations' confidence in our reliability. . . . It would threaten our long-term hopes for peace in the world. A great nation cannot renege on its pledges. A great nation must be worthy of trust." Hanoi, the President declared, was reported to have "given up hope for a military victory" in the South, but was "counting on a collapse of American will in the United States." These were the themes that would dominate Vietnam debate over the next four years.

The new public offer was accompanied by private threats, as planned. Ambassador Dobrynin was summoned to Kissinger's office shortly before Nixon's speech and warned that, as Kissinger later told the Kalb brothers, if the Russians "didn't produce a settlement," the United States would "escalate the war." Kissinger's threat, which had been carefully worked out with Nixon, was meant to be a secret even from NSC staff members who worked directly on Vietnam problems and who had helped write the President's speech—men such as Halperin. Eagleburger, however, had surreptitiously shown Halperin a copy of the "talking paper" for the meeting with Dobrynin. Eagleburger's action was not disloyalty to Kissinger, but once again a normal part of inner-office bureaucratic procedure.

Later, Halperin would link the Dobrynin warning to his knowledge of the secret bombings in Cambodia, and would draw some correct conclusions about the real Nixon-Kissinger policy in Vietnam. At the time, however, he managed to persuade himself that real progress toward peace had been made through the change in American policy announced on May 14. He believed Nixon and Kissinger were certain that a quick settlement was possible that spring. Halperin was correct in his guess that the President and his national security adviser expected a quick settlement, but he and the other Vietnam War critics in the White House were convinced—as Kissinger and Nixon wanted them to be—that the high-level optimism was based solely on the change in the Vietnam negotiating policy. "It looks silly now," Halperin says, "but at the time it *was* a big change of policy. The State Department was still holding out for the Manila formula."

Nixon and Kissinger, as well as the National Security Council staff, were disappointed by the results of the May 14 speech, which the press and many congressional leaders regarded as conciliatory. North Vietnam and the National Liberation Front waited less than a day to denounce Nixon's new proposal publicly and to claim that its essential element—mutual withdrawal— was unacceptable because it put withdrawal of the American GIs on the same basis as withdrawal of the North Vietnamese Army. Nixon, the NLF said in Paris, now "places the aggressor and the resisting victims of aggression on the same footing, a proposal that we have repeatedly rejected." In a broadcast from Hanoi, North Vietnam stated, "The plan of the Nixon Administration is not to end the war but to replace the war of aggression fought by U.S. troops with a war of aggression fought by the puppet army of the United States." And the expected give did not materialize at the weekly peace talks in Paris, which had quickly become propaganda rituals and were to remain so for the next four years.

Nor did the May 14 speech quiet the growing domestic dissent over the administration's war policies. On May 15, eight Democratic members of the House, six of them from New York, introduced legislation calling for a ceasefire and the unilateral withdrawal of 100,000 American troops. Senator Frank Church, the Idaho Democrat who was a leading critic of the war, described the speech as a "bitter disappointment" because, he said, it showed that the Nixon Administration's plan for ending the war was "the same as the Johnson plan."

The war was still raging, at home and abroad, and casualties on all sides were mounting.

To those who asked, Kissinger and Nixon had but one message in the spring of 1969: Give us time. "The way we're going now," Kissinger told Patrick Anderson for the *Times Magazine* profile, "we can settle the war on acceptable terms. What we've lost in these past few years is time—time and public patience and public confidence in the Government." Time, of course, was necessary for the secret-threat strategy to have its effect. When two liberal Republican congressmen, Paul N. (Pete) McCloskey, Jr., of California and Donald W. Riegle, Jr., of Michigan, visited Kissinger in his basement office, Kissinger said, as Riegle later wrote, "Be patient. Give us another sixty or ninety days. Please, stay silent for the time being." The two congressmen, who had sharply criticized the Johnson Administration's handling of the war, agreed to hold off.

In his memoirs, Kissinger wrote rather plaintively of the May 14 offer: "We knew too little of Hanoi at that point to understand that its leaders were interested in victory, not a ceasefire, and in political control, not a role in free elections." He did not mention the threat to Dobrynin nor the fact that the notion of "free elections" existed neither in Washington nor in Saigon.

From May 14 on, the Nixon Administration was committed to a negotiating policy that could not succeed; and the obstacles were not solely in Washington and Hanoi. While the administration was making secret threats and publicly talking about mutual withdrawal and free elections, President Nguyen Van Thieu of South Vietnam was proclaiming repeatedly, as he did in early March of 1969, that he was simply not prepared to accept members of the National Liberation Front in his Saigon government. There could be no coalition government and "no Communist party as such" in Vietnam, he said. The NLF would be treated merely as another political party running for office. His aides later told journalists that Thieu was talking of NLF participation only in village and senatorial elections.

The North Vietnamese leaders were unimpressed by the May 14 offer for a number of reasons, as they later explained.* First, they believed President Thieu's public remarks about the political future of the NLF were far truer than any abstract promises by Nixon of what would happen after a mutual withdrawal.

In an interview in Hanoi, Nguyen Co Thach, who was a senior member of the secret negotiating team in Paris and later became North Vietnam's foreign minister, said that throughout the talks a major stumbling block was the refusal of the Nixon Administration to offer the NLF a true share of political power in the South. "In all of the negotiations," he said, "the Saigon government was to be the lawful government of South Vietnam and the NLF was only to be a political party inside the framework of the Saigon constitution. We told Kissinger that we could not accept the constitution of the Saigon government."

Thach put it succinctly: "The biggest mistake of Kissinger and Nixon was to want to have the whole cake, and not to share with others even a small slice."

A second point of contention was Hanoi's belief that there could be no reciprocity for the withdrawal of American troops, just as Hanoi had refused in late 1968 to make any concessions in return for the end of the American bombing. To match American withdrawals with similar removal of its troops from the South would be to obliterate the distinction, as a North Vietnamese official said, between the "aggressor" and the "victim of aggression." A third reason for not taking the new offer seriously, Thach said, was the weakness of the Vietcong troops in the South. The Central Intelligence Agency's assassination program in South Vietnam, known as Operation Phoenix, had slaugh-

* In July and August of 1979, I visited Hanoi to discuss the secret peace talks and the Vietnam War with senior members of the Vietnamese government, including staff members and aides who had participated in the talks. The Vietnamese repeatedly checked their written records of the peace talks and permitted all our interviews to be tape recorded for my use.

tered far more than the 21,000 officially listed by the United States.* "We had many weaknesses in the South," Thach said, "because of Phoenix." In some provinces, 95 percent of the Communist cadre had been assassinated or compromised by the Phoenix operation.† And finally, Thach said, although the top leaders of North Vietnam were aware that the Nixon Administration would consider escalation, they did not fear it. "All the threats were useless," Thach said, "because during the whole war we never retreated from our position. If we were afraid, we could not go to war, and if we were afraid, we could not be very tough."

Hanoi's failure to respond favorably to the May 14 speech—no such response, Thach said, was ever considered—hardened the Nixon-Kissinger attitude. "I had never thought that peace in Vietnam would come easily," Nixon wrote; "for the first time I had to consider the possibility that it might not come at all. Nonetheless, I decided to continue on the course we had planned." The May 14 speech had been the carrot; now Hanoi would feel the stick.

Kissinger was by now firmly in control of the bureaucracy—the May 14 speech was drafted and cleared by his NSC staff, and, far more important, Nixon waited until the last minute to allow Secretary Rogers, who was leaving for Southeast Asia on May 12, to review it. Kissinger and Nixon were more than a little careful with the Secretary of State; Halperin recalls that the plane bearing Rogers and his entourage was in final boarding preparations when the draft speech was delivered to the airport. There was a dual reason for cutting it so fine—to make sure Rogers could not cancel or delay his trip, and also to prevent his having the draft reviewed by one of the department's Vietnam experts. Kissinger had made it: Rogers was now an outsider, a person to be conned and duped by the men running the White House. Kissinger was now an enthusiastic supporter and endorser of Nixon's secret-threat strategy. His doubts about the possibility of victory in South Vietnam, as expressed to Daniel Ellsberg and many others in 1965 and 1966, were banished. The United States, he declared in his memoirs, now had a "duty" to defeat the Vietnamese, in part because they had had the audacity to defy a presidential threat:

"The North Vietnamese were cocksure; it was our duty to prove them wrong. I myself pursued the ambiguities of our complex policy with a heavy heart and not a little foreboding. But there was no acceptable alternative. We had the duty to see it through in a manner that best served its chances for success—because a defeat would not affect our destiny alone: the future of other people depended on their confidence in America."

Nixon and Kissinger had no way of perceiving the scope of the American intelligence failure in those first months of 1969. The Vietcong had been stag-

* South Vietnamese government statistics listed the number of Phoenix casualties at 40,994 in the period beginning August 1968 and ending in mid-1971. The casualties were described as suspected enemy civilians.

† Another factor, undoubtedly, but one not discussed with me, was that Tet, the Vietcong's political and public relations victory, had also produced thousands of casualties. During the offensive, the Communist troops had emerged publicly in provincial and district capitals throughout South Vietnam, obviously thinking that the United States and South Vietnamese forces would not bomb the populated areas. The Vietcong were wrong, and casualties—of soldiers and civilians alike—were high.

gered by the Tet offensive, just as Johnson's men, their credibility in shreds, had insisted. Hanoi, weakened by the Phoenix program, by pacification, and by the Tet offensive, could not consider a ceasefire in 1969, because North Vietnamese theoreticians knew that the Vietcong forces in the South would have no chance to topple Thieu, even with American troop withdrawal, as long as he maintained his American air support. Hanoi's goal was a political solution: the ouster of Nguyen Van Thieu. Negotiations would give North Vietnam the time needed to rebuild its forces in the South to the point where an offensive could be chanced if the negotiations failed. The war would have to continue.

By summer, Nixon and Kissinger were convinced that Hanoi and the Soviet Union were calling their bluff. Hanoi would be threatened with a major escalation in the air and ground war unless it accepted the American peace terms. Kissinger, in his meetings with NSC staff members, began talking about "breaking points" and the inability of a "fourth-rate power" like Hanoi to withstand the punishment he and Nixon were preparing. The threat option was going into effect.

The policy was bankrupt, and as it failed to work, the White House's perception of its enemies began to expand. By early fall it included not only the antiwar marchers in the streets but those in Congress who were no longer willing to keep their peace.

In September, Representatives Riegle and McCloskey visited Kissinger a second time. It was a courtesy call: The conscientious Republicans wanted to warn him, and through him the President, that they could no longer maintain their silence about the administration's Vietnam policy. Kissinger conceded that the initial plan to end the war, involving the good offices of the Soviet Union, had failed. Another plan was being prepared, he said—not indicating, of course, that it called for escalation.

A few days later Representative Riegle was chastised for his antiwar views by House Republican leader Gerald R. Ford. Riegle was shocked when Ford said he had read a transcript of the conversation with McCloskey and Kissinger. "I had assumed that this was a personal conversation," Riegle wrote Kissinger on October 1, "and would not be discussed outside the Executive offices. Under the circumstances, I feel the need to have a personal copy of that discussion to refresh myself on all aspects so that I can discuss it further with Gerry Ford."

Kissinger quickly wrote back denying that there had been a transcript— there was only a "brief summary record" prepared by one of his staff members. But the cat was out of the bag—if only for a moment. Kissinger may not have been monitoring conversations in his own office, but he was eavesdropping, through the FBI, on those of friend and foe alike throughout the NSC staff, the bureaucracy, and the press.

7

THE WIRETAPS

ROGER MORRIS QUICKLY WON Henry Kissinger's trust in the early months of the Nixon presidency. Morris was not only a good friend of Eagleburger, who became, next to Haig, Kissinger's closest confidant on the NSC staff; he was also a bright, articulate, appropriately caustic thirty-one-year-old Harvard Ph.D. Morris' memo on the situation in Nigeria, where the government was waging a bloody civil war with Biafran separatists, impressed both Kissinger and Nixon.

It was not surprising, then, that Eagleburger asked Morris to sit in Kissinger's office and "cover" it one weekend day in the spring of 1969. Kissinger was spending the weekend in New York, quietly visiting Nancy Maginnes, the woman he would later marry; it was a trip he often made in those early years. Haig, who usually worked seven days a week, had taken some rare time off, and Eagleburger needed a relief man so he could keep an appointment.

Morris moved into Kissinger's office. At one point during the quiet morning, an FBI courier came in and left a sealed envelope for Kissinger. Morris brooded about the document. Should he call Henry? As Morris tells it, he could imagine Kissinger's angry impatience at his caution: "Idiot! Of course open it." And so he opened it.

The envelope was from J. Edgar Hoover, for Kissinger's "eyes only." "It was this long, detailed account of Martin Luther King's sex life. There were transcripts, and indications that photographs were available." Some of the women with Dr. King had obviously been FBI informants. Morris was appalled.

When Eagleburger returned that afternoon, Morris quickly showed the documents to him. "I was speaking as an old friend and as a Foreign Service colleague and I said, 'This is absolutely scurrilous stuff.' Larry just glanced at the first page or two, with the ho-hum attitude of an aide reading a telephone directory, and said, 'Oh, yeah, we get these all the time.' " Eagleburger then opened a nearby file cabinet and pulled out Hoover files on members of the NSC staff—including Morton Halperin. Files were being kept on Martin Luther King, Eagleburger reassured his colleague, "to blunt the black antiwar movement." Morris was not reassured, but kept his peace.

Kissinger was far from an innocent about the FBI by the time he reached the White House. In 1953, while an instructor in the Department of Goverment at Harvard, he reported to the Boston office of the FBI that someone had tried to circulate what he considered subversive literature to members of an international seminar of which he was executive director. Kissinger described himself as being strongly sympathetic to the FBI's work and said he was a consultant to the United States Army, having served in counterintelligence during World War II. In its report to Hoover, the FBI's Boston office said it would seek to make the patriotic Harvard instructor a future confidential source.*

Proving his loyalty remained an obsession for Kissinger in the Nixon White House. His support for the bombings of Cambodia and his hardline stance on the EC-121 incident had strengthened his position, but Nixon still seemed unwilling to isolate Laird and Rogers from White House decision making. There was another reason for Kissinger's nervousness: the fact that he was a Jew.

There were days when Nixon would directly castigate liberal Jews in front of Kissinger.

"Nixon would talk about Jewish traitors, and the Eastern Jewish Establishment—Jews at Harvard," John Ehrlichman recalls. "And he'd play off Kissinger. 'Isn't that right, Henry? Don't you agree?' And Henry would respond: 'Well, Mr. President, there are Jews and Jews.' " Ehrlichman remembers that when Jerome B. Wiesner, who had been a science adviser to the Kennedy Administration, criticized Nixon's March 1969 decision to deploy a limited antiballistic missile system, Nixon angrily denounced Wiesner in front of Kissinger as "another one of those Jews."

By midsummer of 1969, three Jews, Morton Halperin, Daniel Davidson, and Richard Sneider, had left or were in the process of leaving the National Security Council. Davidson, whom Kissinger had cultivated in Paris during the Johnson Administration's last round of peace talks, had been recruited a month after the election and put to work on Vietnam and Middle East issues. Sneider, a widely respected Foreign Service officer who was an expert on Japan, had joined the staff after the inauguration to work on Asian affairs.† All three came to share the belief that Nixon was anti-Semitic.

There is no evidence that Kissinger was in any way ashamed of his Jewishness or was an anti-Semitic Jew. But being Jewish was a chink in his armor, a vulnerability that could threaten his position in the White House. And Nixon

* The FBI document, released under the Freedom of Information Act, was published on November 10, 1979, in the *Nation* magazine. No related FBI documents were made public at that time, and it is not known whether Kissinger maintained that early contact.

† Kissinger had hired Sneider reluctantly, at the urging of Halperin, who had worked with Sneider on the Johnson Administration's negotiations over reverting the island of Okinawa to Japan. Halperin recalls that he and Eagleburger insisted that Kissinger interview Sneider, and that Kissinger, having done so, was "too embarrassed not to hire him." Kissinger's own choice was a former West Point officer, John H. Holdridge, also in the Foreign Service, whom Halperin and Eagleburger considered far less knowledgeable. "Henry wanted somebody [such as Holdridge] who would do what he told him without worrying about being cut out," Halperin says. "He thought they would be more willing to work on just what they were told to work on—and not assert their right to see everything." Sneider, for example, was upset early in 1969 when he learned from the Indonesian Ambassador that President Nixon was planning to visit. The Ambassador had been told about the impending trip by Kissinger, who enjoyed relaying good news. Sneider, of course, felt that he, as the NSC specialist for Indonesia, among other Asian countries, should have been told of Nixon's plan as soon as the decision was made; he also felt he should have been the one to pass along the information to the Indonesians.

himself clearly viewed it as a drawback, at least during the early years. Immediately after taking office, the President decided to permit Secretary of State Rogers to operate publicly on Middle East issues, his only such area of seeming responsibility. In truth, of course, Nixon and Kissinger were determined to control initiatives in the Middle East as thoroughly as they watched over the Soviet Union and Vietnam, but Rogers had the appearance of authority, and Kissinger could do little to undercut him publicly. Thus for Kissinger, eager to control Rogers as well as the whole bureaucracy, being a Jew was an immediate disadvantage. As he said in his memoirs, "He [Nixon] . . . suspected that my Jewish origin might cause me to lean too much toward Israel."

Kissinger seemed constantly to be sensitizing the Jews on his staff to his patron's attitude. When Davidson was first hired, Kissinger—in an obvious reference to Halperin—told him with a laugh that there were "not too many goyim [non-Jews]" on the staff. Davidson reported to work before the inauguration and Kissinger ordered him squirreled away in an office in the Executive Office Building next to the White House, where he was assigned to read and summarize briefing books on the Middle East from previous administrations. Kissinger told Davidson that he did not want the Nixon transition team to know he was involved in Middle East affairs.

Shortly after the inauguration, when Nixon's February trip to Europe was being planned, Kissinger removed Helmut Sonnenfeldt, who had been his longtime friend and associate in the State Department before coming to the NSC staff, from the list of those to make the trip in the presidential plane. Sonnenfeldt told Davidson later that Kissinger had explained his reassignment to the White House backup plane by saying, "I don't think too many Jews should be around."

Halperin recalls a National Security Council meeting in May 1969 to discuss new intelligence on Israel's capacity to manufacture nuclear weapons.* It was the first meeting of what would become known as the Senior Review Group, involving administration officials of under secretary rank and above. Richard Helms, the newly reappointed director of the Central Intelligence Agency, had not only urged the high-level meeting but also sought to limit its attendance.

Halperin expected to go to the meeting just as he normally went to all such meetings. Harold H. Saunders, a former CIA official who was the NSC's staff man for the Middle East, also assumed he would attend. Shortly before the meeting, as Halperin was helping to draft the briefing papers for the session,

---

* The meeting dealt with CIA and FBI evidence that the Israeli intelligence service, Mossad, had been responsible sometime in the mid-1960s for diverting highly enriched uranium from a private company, the Nuclear Materials and Equipments Corporation, in Apollo, Pennsylvania. Its owner, Dr. Zalman Shapiro, was known to have close ties to the Israeli Consulate in New York. Some officials believed that the processing plant, which did classified contract work for the U. S. Navy and authorized foreign countries, primarily NATO allies, had been set up with Israeli-supplied funds —and might have been created solely to divert enriched uranium for Israeli nuclear weapon production. The implications of the investigation were enormous for America's staunchest ally in the Middle East, and for the Nixon Administration's foreign policy. Dr. Shapiro, formally interviewed by investigators for the Atomic Energy Commission in August 1969, denied the allegations and the matter was allowed to rest there. One Kissinger aide who reviewed the file in the early 1970s considers the CIA and FBI evidence "very circumstantial. We didn't know whether it would stand up in court." There was another reason for not continuing the inquiry: "You don't mess with the Israelis."

Kissinger telephoned. "I can't have you there," Kissinger said. "I've told the other people not to bring staff and I can't show up with three people from the NSC—two of them Jewish."

Halperin said nothing to Kissinger, but he was strongly tempted to ask, "Henry, who's the second Jew?" A moment later, even madder, he daydreamed a better remark: "Henry, I didn't know Hal [Saunders] was Jewish." The phone call came at a time when Halperin had already begun keeping a list of reasons to resign.

That spring, Morton Halperin became a dominant concern. During the last years of the Johnson Administration, he had become a marked man in the Pentagon—notably with General Wheeler, chairman of the Joint Chiefs of Staff —for his role in persuading the Johnson Administration to offer the bombing halt. Wheeler was among the first to complain to Kissinger when he asked Halperin to join his staff. Senator Barry Goldwater also complained, in a letter of April 22, 1969, to Attorney General Mitchell. Goldwater described Halperin as among those who "made it so hard for the military to operate in the Pentagon by their strategic papers which were forced down the throats of the Joint Chiefs and Commanders."

Hoover, too, repeatedly complained about Halperin's loyalty; among other things, he told the White House, Halperin had once sponsored an antiwar teach-in at Harvard.

Kissinger knew better, of course. Halperin had sponsored the demonstration as a *supporter* of the war. He had been among those advocating a strong military response to the EC-121 incident; he had helped set up Kissinger's tight National Security Council system; his advice on issues ranging from strategic disarmament talks to the Vietnam War was highly regarded; he was a tireless worker who believed that the Nixon Administration was committed to getting out of Vietnam. Throughout the spring of 1969, Halperin praised the Nixon-Kissinger team to friends in Washington and Boston. He was not disloyal.*

But Hoover and Mitchell and Goldwater and Nixon thought he was, and so Kissinger began to savage Halperin behind his back. John Ehrlichman took notes, as was his custom, on conversations in the Oval Office that spring between Kissinger and Nixon. The men were discussing possible leakers and Kissinger mentioned Halperin, Ehrlichman said, "as being singularly untrustworthy. I gathered from the context of the conversation that Dr. Kissinger knew him, knew him quite well." During these conversations, Kissinger depicted Halperin as "philosophically in disagreement" with the President on matters of policy. Ehrlichman says it was his impression that Halperin did more than merely disapprove of the Nixon-Kissinger decisions: "I gather that he sabotaged them." Another Kissinger aide "was also the subject of considerable anguish" during those Nixon-Kissinger conversations, Ehrlichman said —Richard Sneider, who had been deeply involved in the EC-121 deliberations.

The White House wiretaps were initiated on May 9, a few hours after William Beecher, the military correspondent for the *New York Times*, published a page-one dispatch from Washington accurately describing the first of the B-52 bombing raids on Cambodia. The dispatch did not describe the fraudulent

* Halperin told Ellsberg sometime late that spring, "For the first time I can remember, I am not in disagreement with an administration policy on Vietnam."

record keeping involved in the bombing, but did say that the missions were designed to "signal" Hanoi that the Nixon Administration would be tougher and far more willing to take military risks for peace. That day Kissinger talked four times with Hoover, asking him to find the leakers and declaring, according to a Hoover memorandum, that the White House "will destroy whoever did this if we can find him, no matter where he is." The investigation was to be a "major effort"—though with one caveat, Hoover reported. Kissinger characteristically urged that the FBI conduct its investigations discreetly, "so no stories will get out." Hoover was not troubled by Kissinger's attempt to tell him and the FBI how to conduct its business. Far from it. "I told him that is what we are doing at the present time," Hoover noted in his memorandum to four senior assistants.

Kissinger's telephone conversations with Hoover were primarily exercises in self-protection. He had his own suspect for the leak, and chose to deal with him directly. Melvin Laird told friends later that Kissinger had him paged off a golf course in Washington to bitterly accuse him—"you son-of-a-bitch"—of leaking the story to Beecher. At that point, at least, Kissinger did not suspect Halperin.* Later, attempting to deny responsibility for starting the wiretaps, Kissinger told reporters that on the day the article was published, he had met with Mitchell, Hoover, and Nixon to discuss newspaper leaks. He subsequently changed that account and said that the meeting had taken place, according to his "sporadic and undeveloped" office logs and memoranda, on April 25 in the Oval Office.

In all his comments and testimony about the wiretapping, Kissinger depicted himself as a passive participant in the decision, made by his superiors, to begin the surveillance. "I can say that the idea that this was not common practice or that this was in any sense illegal simply never crossed my mind," he told the Senate Foreign Relations Committee in September 1973. "I do not from my own knowledge know that this program was carried out in previous administrations."† In his memoirs, Kissinger provided a further explanation: His motive in going along with the wiretapping "was to prevent the jeopardizing of American and South Vietnamese lives by individuals . . . who disclosed military information entrusted to them in order to undermine policies decided upon after prayerful consideration. . . ."

In truth, Beecher's article merely provided the rationale for the wiretaps; it was the catalyst but not the sole factor. Kissinger and Nixon were also concerned about a series of leaks in late April and early May in regard to some of the hardline options discussed after the EC-121 incident.

Nixon himself later provided the most specific testimony linking the wiretapping to events besides the B-52 leak. This statement appears in a deposition,

* Kissinger told a former Harvard colleague early in 1969 that he couldn't "afford to keep Mort" on his White House staff because the Joint Chiefs of Staff "will tag me as a softy." The colleague, who had also taught courses with Halperin, added: "I didn't tell Mort what Henry said, but I did urge him to quit when he talked of quitting."

† The usually careful Kissinger stumbled in testimony before the Senate committee in July 1974. He testified that he knew Sonnenfeldt had been wiretapped "because when I put him on my staff the FBI brought me the records of the wiretaps going back to 1960 in order to dissuade me from hiring him, and I overruled the FBI recommendation and put him on my staff anyway."

dated January 15, 1976, given in a lawsuit that Halperin filed in 1973.* "A great deal of attention has been put on the Cambodian so-called 'secret' bombing," Nixon said, "but I think Dr. Halperin will probably recall the EC-121 conversations." Nixon went on to say that the basic decisions in that crisis had been made in a closely held Oval Office meeting, not in the National Security Council. Revelation of those discussions, he testified, had added to his concern at the time because "I had to consider some other highly confidential material which had not yet leaked."

On May 6, three days before the B-52 story, William Beecher had published a detailed and accurate account of some of the secret deliberations about the EC-121 incident, revealing that Nixon and Kissinger had considered bombing airfields in North Korea as well as the use of nuclear weapons. The Beecher account was not taken up as an important story by other newspapers and radio and television, although it flatly contradicted the White House's version that Nixon and Kissinger calmly and coolly decided not to take action.

For Nixon and Kissinger, Beecher's May 6 account may have brought additional chills. They could not be sure how much the *Times* reporter knew about the nuclear planning or about one of the truly important secrets of the EC-121 incident. Did Beecher know that Nixon had become violently drunk early in the crisis?

Nixon's drinking had yet to be perceived as a significant problem by Kissinger and his immediate staff and the incident was quickly hushed up. Neither Halperin nor Sneider was told. But when Eagleburger kept a standing lunch date with an old friend that first week after the EC-121 shootdown, he was obviously upset. "Here's the President of the United States, ranting and raving —drunk in the middle of the crisis," the shaken Eagleburger told his friend. Nixon's drinking would soon become a source of distress among other NSC aides.

There was more to protect, too. Both Nixon and Kissinger knew by early May that if the North Vietnamese did not respond to the administration's offer of mutual withdrawal, to be formally presented in the Paris peace talks and to the American public within days, the response would be escalation. And Kissinger knew, too, that Halperin's support of the administration's policy in Vietnam was based on what Halperin thought that policy was, not on what Nixon and Kissinger knew it to be. The same held for Halperin's dovish colleagues on the staff of the NSC.

Another factor in the increasingly discordant White House was Alexander Haig. He had come as a certified hardliner on Vietnam, and he had little use for the doubts and concerns of the NSC moderates. Halperin was a special target, not only because of his key role in the Johnson Administration but because he was close to Kissinger. There was open staff rivalry for Kissinger's attention, as well as for the unfilled post of deputy to the national security

* Halperin instituted a damage suit in federal court in Washington on June 14, 1973, naming Mitchell and Kissinger, among others, as defendants. (Nixon was not made a defendant in the case until September 30, 1974, seven weeks after he left office.) Halperin argued that the White House wiretaps violated federal law in that they were issued without a warrant, and he further claimed that his "political ideas and associations" were the real targets of the wiretap, and the sole reason the White House continued the surveillance for nearly eighteen months after he formally left the National Security Council. The suit was still pending as of mid-1983.

adviser. Kissinger had chosen to have no deputy in those early months rather than appoint Richard Allen, who had been promised the job. There was no lack of candidates, nonetheless, including Haig, Eagleburger, Sonnenfeldt, and, of course, Halperin. "Halperin was the once and future menace for everybody," Morris observes. "In essence, everyone believed that Mort was doing what in fact Haig did—moving in on Henry. Nobody gave Haig any credit for moving in."

Haig moved in because Kissinger allowed him to. There was no question that spring of his loyalty to Kissinger and to Nixon-Kissinger policies. Haig also knew far more about wiretapping and the government procedures involved than anyone else in the White House; he had been exposed to FBI wiretap materials while working as a special assistant in the Pentagon during the mid-1960s, and had struck up a friendship with William C. Sullivan, an FBI assistant director who was in charge of domestic intelligence activities.*

Wiretapping NSC aides was a dirty business, and everybody in the White House and the FBI knew it. Kissinger's method of handling it was simple: He put Haig in charge. It was Haig who, over the next two years, would formally transmit the names of NSC staff members and reporters to be wiretapped. It was Haig who repeatedly went to Sullivan's FBI office to read wiretap transcripts and summaries. And it was Haig who transmitted the orders to curtail the surveillances.

Haig truly seemed to enjoy the snooping. He constantly checked up on younger staff members to see that they did not meet with journalists. One junior NSC official recalls being braced by Haig for not getting advance clearance for one such lunch. The conversation left a distinct impression that Big Brother was constantly watching. "Haig relished it," the NSC man remembers. "He loved it."

It was Haig, too, who gave Kissinger his basic alibi for his role in the wiretapping. "I would not say that I ever said to the FBI, please tap this individual," Kissinger told the Senate Foreign Relations Committee in July 1974. "My perception is that I would not have said anything to the FBI. That was done by Haig. I would have said to Haig, we have had this leak, give the names of the people who had access to the information."

If Haig had any doubts about what he was doing, he concealed them well. Years later, he told a reporter who asked about his role in the wiretapping, "I have absolutely no apologies to make. The wiretaps for the purposes were justified and anyone who claims otherwise is not filled in."†

* Haig had learned enough in the Johnson Administration to insist during his talks with Sullivan in 1969 that the White House wiretapping be zealously protected. In testimony during the Halperin lawsuit, Haig explained that he had wanted FBI paperwork on the wiretaps kept to a minimum because "I recall back when I worked for Bob McNamara, when J. Edgar Hoover sent over a report on King, Martin Luther King, which just about blew the Pentagon apart. It was so—you know, anti-King in character, and hand-tailored by Mr. Hoover to be damaging. And it was flushed all through the bureaucracy. I remember Mr. McNamara thought that was a deliberate thing by the Director to jeopardize Mr. King, and I think that is the kind of concerns that we had." Haig's point seemed to be that he and Kissinger were not going to make Hoover's mistake and let their surveillance activities be "flushed all through the bureaucracy."

† The comment was made in an interview with me on May 16, 1973, in the White House. Haig, whom Nixon had just named White House chief of staff, repeatedly urged me not to write an article for the *New York Times* directly linking Kissinger to the wiretaps. At first Haig portrayed the

In the various investigations and legal proceedings after the wiretaps first became known in May 1973, Kissinger sought to blur the issue of his responsibility, repeatedly claiming that he did not "initiate" the wiretaps. But who "initiated" what is less important than the fact that Kissinger seized upon the wiretaps not only as a way of proving anew his loyalty to Nixon, but also as a means of verifying the personal loyalty of his staff. And, equally important, the wiretapping would enable Kissinger and Nixon to monitor the loyalty of Melvin Laird.

Inside the White House, hatred for Laird and Pursley, his aide, had become palpable. Kissinger's outrage over their refusal to go along with the White House plans to retaliate for the EC-121 shootdown had not diminished, and there had been even more serious disagreements on key policy issues, such as the pending nuclear disarmament talks and withdrawal from South Vietnam. To Kissinger's dismay, Laird still insisted on making the decisions about when and where American troops would be withdrawn. "Cutting out Mel Laird is what we did for a living," says Laurence E. Lynn, Jr., one of Kissinger's senior NSC aides. "Henry used to joke about Laird's horrible syntax. He'd let us listen in on their conversations and Henry would predict accurately what Laird was going to say and then make gestures and smirk at us as they talked." Another senior National Security Council aide recalls with a laugh that "For a long time I thought Laird's last name was crook. 'Mel Laird's a crook,' Henry would always say."

Haig's attitude was similar. Charles M. Cooke, Jr., a former Pentagon official who resigned his Air Force commission to join Elliot Richardson's State Department staff early in 1969, speaks of a lunch with Haig in the White House mess. It was his first meeting with Haig, who began the conversation by reminiscing about his relationship with Cooke's father, a four-star Navy admiral who had once briefed Douglas MacArthur's staff in Japan. It began as a pleasant conversation. "I didn't know much about Haig. Then he starts telling me what a traitor Mel Laird is. Haig said, 'He's a traitor to the country and will destroy the armed forces.' " Cooke, appalled, said nothing as Haig continued to rail. "Haig said Laird was trying to destroy our capability to destroy our enemies and our capability to hit North Vietnam," and one specific complaint stood out: Haig cited Laird's effort to recall the Air Force's F-105 fighter-bombers from duty over North Vietnam because of the planes' high loss rate in combat. A similar proposal had been hotly debated in the Johnson Administration.

That complaint was especially memorable to Cooke, a former Air Force major who had taught at the Air Force Academy in Colorado Springs for years,

<hr/>

wiretaps as legal and justified, and therefore not a legitimate newspaper story; later he warned that my story would lead to Kissinger's resignation; then, as the deadline for filing the story approached, there was this final appeal: "You're Jewish, aren't you, Seymour?" I told him yes. "Let me ask you one question, then," Haig said. "Do you honestly believe that Henry Kissinger, a Jewish refugee from Germany who lost thirteen members of his family to the Nazis, could engage in such police-state tactics as wiretapping his own aides? If there's any doubt," Haig persisted, "you owe it to yourself, your beliefs, and your nation to give us one day to prove that your story is wrong." The *Times* published the story nonetheless.

because he agreed with Laird. After that lunch, Cooke says, "My decision was that I could not deal with Al Haig—and I never did deal with him again."

The first group of White House wiretaps can be assessed against this background of distrust. The first man to be wiretapped was Halperin, whose home telephone was under surveillance shortly after 6:00 P.M. on the evening of May 9, the day the second Beecher story was published and three days before Attorney General Mitchell formally signed the FBI authorization for the tap.* Three other wiretaps—on Davidson, Sonnenfeldt, and Pursley—were installed on May 12. On May 20, Richard Sneider and Richard Moose, the one-time aide to Senator Fulbright who had run afoul of Haig, were wiretapped. Oddly enough, William Beecher, whose articles had so alarmed the White House, would not be wiretapped for another year.

Haig, believing that anybody who was against the war was an enemy of the state, may indeed have believed in the necessity for the taps. But Kissinger knew better. For him, the wiretaps provided more security, more proof to Nixon, Hoover, and Mitchell that he could be trusted. An ardent leaker himself, Kissinger knew, as any important official in Washington quickly learns, what to say and what not to say on the telephone. Years later, Halperin summed up the situation: "The notion that you can find out who's leaking and the notion—which Henry keeps putting forward—that you can prove that somebody was not leaking or exonerate somebody by tapping their phone is absolutely preposterous. I'm not going to come home at night and dial Bill Beecher and say, 'Hey, Bill, we're bombing Cambodia.' I'm sure the FBI knows that Beecher lives about ten minutes from me and in that particular year we happened to have theater tickets together with our wives. We used to drive down to the Arena Stage together and obviously if I was going to tell him anything, which I wasn't, I would have done so [near] the Arena Stage and not on the telephone. You just don't find out whether people are leaking by wiretapping and I think they knew it, too."

In Kissinger's view, the most nearly legitimate wiretap must have been the one on Colonel Pursley, because Kissinger and Nixon believed throughout Nixon's first term that Laird was constantly leaking stories, both to ingratiate himself with the press as a secret dove and to fight Kissinger's growing power.

The other wiretaps served a multitude of purposes for Kissinger. To begin with, four of those tapped—Davidson, Halperin, Sneider, and Sonnenfeldt—were Jewish; tapping them not only played to the anti-Semitism in the Oval

---

* Halperin spent that day at Key Biscayne with Kissinger, at work on NSC matters. He discussed the Beecher story at length with Kissinger and convinced him, so Halperin thought, that he could not have been Beecher's source, largely because he knew very little about the B-52 bombing. Halperin agreed without hesitation to Kissinger's seemingly reasonable solution: "He proposed that he cut off my access to very sensitive material so that if something like this happened again, he could say, 'Look, it wasn't Halperin. He didn't even know about it.'" Although Halperin was unaware of it at the time, he would no longer have access to any highly classified material, a virtual death knell in the White House, where secrets, and access to them, were so important. Describing the scene in *The American Police State*, David Wise wrote: "Under the palm trees, Morton Halperin had just had his head chopped off. But Kissinger had done it so skillfully that Halperin never felt the blade pass through his neck."

Office but also demonstrated that Kissinger was able to rise above his religious background and not protect those aides who were Jewish. The FBI already had in its files what was claimed to be adverse information on Davidson, Halperin, and Sonnenfeldt—none of which had much to do with the EC-121 and B-52 leaks, however—and by permitting them to be tapped, Kissinger was increasing his stature with Hoover and Mitchell.* In addition, Davidson was considered one of Averell Harriman's protégés, and that wiretap might give Kissinger information about the liberal Democratic Establishment, the group he was privately beseeching not to criticize the Nixon policies. Finally, and perhaps most important, the wiretaps on Moose, Sneider, Davidson, and Halperin would tell much about what those men—all known to favor a quickly negotiated settlement in Vietnam—thought of him.

On May 20, according to one of Sullivan's memoranda to Hoover, Kissinger and Haig came to the FBI offices in downtown Washington to read wiretap logs. The Sullivan memorandum continues: "On doing this, he [Kissinger] said 'it is clear that I don't have anybody in my office that I can trust except Colonel Haig here.' He mentioned that he was under great pressures to adopt a soft line on foreign policy. But he said he is not going to do so." Kissinger later denied making the visit, and Sullivan would testify that he had no recollection of it. But the memorandum, found in the FBI files during an inquiry into the wiretaps four years later, remains.

The next step was to wiretap reporters. By September, the names of three —Hedrick Smith of the *New York Times,* Henry Brandon of the London *Sunday Times,* and Marvin Kalb of CBS News—were forwarded to the FBI. Brandon and Kalb were close to Kissinger and were direct recipients of many briefings and leaks. National security surely was not a factor in those wiretaps, since Kissinger knew that he was the source of much of their classified information. J. Edgar Hoover had long considered Brandon, who was born in Prague, Czechoslovakia, to be an agent for the Czech and British intelligence services, and Richard Nixon and others in the White House were told by Kissinger late in 1969 that Kalb was an agent of the Romanian government.†

* The only two items in Halperin's security files that relate to possible security lapses are trivial at best. In August 1966, while filling out an extensive government security form, Halperin did not list his visits to Greece, Yugoslavia, and the Soviet Union in describing a round-the-world trip two and a half years before. He explained to security officials that his Pentagon typist had inadvertently deleted those countries in copying the papers. Halperin had reported these stops on prior security forms on file with the government. In July 1968, Halperin told security officials that he had identified the wrong Russian when he reported on a conversation with the man. He failed to file a written memorandum correcting the error, but a month later he was granted one of the nation's highest security clearances, Talent-Keyhole, which gave him access to satellite and U-2 photography. Halperin also had a separate SI (Special Intelligence) clearance that enabled him to receive, among other things, communications intelligence. His SI clearance remained in effect until he resigned from the NSC in September 1969.

† Kissinger reported Hoover's suspicions about Brandon to the Senate Foreign Relations Committee during his secret testimony on July 23, 1974. His comment to Nixon about Kalb was made, astonishingly, in front of at least three other White House aides, Pat Buchanan, Jeb Stuart Magruder, and Herb Klein, with whom Nixon was discussing the press and television response to his major Vietnam speech in November 1969. Buchanan reported, as Magruder later wrote, that the response had been favorable, except for one analysis by a network correspondent. Magruder did not cite Kalb by name in his memoirs, although it was known to some in the White House that the journalist was the subject of classified FBI reports alleging that he had met socially with representatives of the Romanian Embassy in Washington. It was at this point, Magruder wrote, that Kissin-

Kissinger knew the allegations against Kalb and Brandon were preposterous. His interest in the wiretaps had nothing to do with such beliefs, but was personal: He wanted to learn the identities of Brandon's and Kalb's other sources in the government and perhaps find out as well what the two reporters were saying behind his back. Brandon, one of the few reporters in Washington who had some access to Nixon, was also known to be talking to Halperin. (The FBI had supplied the White House with photographs of the two men meeting for lunch.) But ultimately, Brandon was beholden to Kissinger, a fact Kissinger understood.

This relationship ran two ways. Brandon enjoyed high-level access and Kissinger was able to insure that his views were reported in the influential London *Sunday Times*. Brandon submitted typed chapters of his 1973 book on the Nixon-Kissinger foreign policy to the National Security Council for advance screening, a price he presumably thought was fair since Kissinger had generously given him access to classified information.

In his testimony to the Senate committee, Kissinger suggested that the Brandon wiretap might also have been aimed at him.* "I must have been tapped frequently on that tap because Brandon was the only journalist I knew socially when I came to Washington, and I spoke to him very frequently and I had no conceivable interest in tapping Brandon." There is no evidence, however, that Kissinger was a target of the FBI or the Oval Office in that first year of the Nixon Administration. Such close aides as Eagleburger and Haig were not wiretapped, although theoretically they also had access to the most sensitive information about the EC-121 incident and the B-52 bombings. And, as Kissinger knew, Eagleburger was among those who had been leaking to favored columnists and reporters. By the spring of 1969, for example, Eagleburger had established rapport with Robert Novak, the widely syndicated columnist, and at Kissinger's direction had begun passing along a consistent series of leaks. "We called it 'feeding the animals,' " Roger Morris says.

The wiretap on Hedrick Smith provides the clearest evidence of Kissinger's direct role. The tap was authorized on June 4, 1969, the day Smith reported in the *Times* that a summit meeting between President Nixon and General Nguyen Van Thieu of South Vietnam—scheduled for June 8 at Midway Island— might result in the announcement of a reduction in American troops in Vietnam. By that late date, however, the Nixon Administration's tentative decision to begin withdrawing American troops had been widely reported, and a similar story had appeared in the Washington *Evening Star* the day before. Perhaps more significant to Nixon, and thus to Kissinger, was Smith's exclusive story in the *Times* of June 3, which reported that Nixon was willing to return Oki-

ger broke in and said, "Well, Mr. President, that man is an agent of the Romanian government." He explained that Kalb was being paid by the Romanian government to provide reports from Washington. And Romania, of course, is a Communist government, Kissinger added. "That's right," the President responded angrily. "That guy is a Communist." Kissinger's comment was taken as the gospel at the time. Klein, who was director of White House communications, subsequently informed at least one other staff aide that Kalb was "a Romanian spy."

* An uncensored version of Kissinger's testimony before the Foreign Relations Committee was made available to me. The transcript released by the Senate included no names of those wiretapped or under investigation.

nawa to Japanese control and withdraw American nuclear weapons from the American bases there. Smith did not, however, report the essence of the bargain, which assured continued American use of the Okinawa bases.

The Smith story was published six days after issuance of a top-secret National Security Decision Memorandum (NSDM 13), which, as a directive to the negotiating team on the elements to be discussed, spelled out the compromise in its last sentence: "Our desire [is] to retain nuclear weapons, but indicating that the President is prepared to consider, at the final stages of negotiations, the withdrawal of the weapons while retaining emergency storage and transit rights, if other elements of the Okinawan agreement are satisfactory."

"Our fallback position was thus in print before our negotiations had even begun," Kissinger complained in his memoirs. In the mid-1960s, Nixon had often visited Japan on behalf of two clients, Pepsi-Cola and Precision Valve, and was in close touch with conservative members of the government. He too complained about the Smith story in his memoirs.

One reason for this amount of anger seems obvious. The American position was conciliatory; it was "soft"; it was the wrong "signal" for Asia. Complicating the question of who leaked was the fact that Halperin and Sneider, who were monitoring the negotiations, had already been wiretapped.*

On June 4, Kissinger was scheduled to meet with Hoover at the FBI, and in preparation for it, Haig, ever the alert deputy, presented his boss with a memorandum (marked Top Secret—Sensitive) summarizing some of the issues to be discussed. Kissinger was first to express his appreciation to Hoover and William Sullivan "for their outstanding support in recent weeks in uncovering security problems within the NSC." He was also to ask Hoover "for his views on how we should proceed with Halperin, who has been involved in indiscretions and who obviously has a reputation for liberal views but who has yet to be firmly linked with a security breach." Third, Kissinger was to ask Hoover "if he has any additional information or guidance which he feels would be helpful in this very difficult situation."

There was one other problem, Haig's memorandum suggested. Nixon was apparently having second thoughts about the wiretapping, because Haig urged Kissinger to "inquire about the requirement for prolonging the taps, making it clear that the President wishes to terminate them as soon as possible." Haig added his opinion that the wiretaps on Halperin and another NSC staff member "should be kept on for at least another two weeks so that a pattern of innocence can be firmly established." In Halperin's case, the wiretaps remained on until February 1971, a total of twenty-one months, surely more than enough time to prove his innocence.

The Smith wiretap was authorized within hours after Kissinger's meeting

* Kissinger and Nixon were clearly overstating the significance of Smith's story, in the view of some officials who were involved in the Okinawa negotiations. The *Times* dispatch, far from being damaging, was meant to signal the always cautious Japanese government to continue bargaining and not back down in the face of what seemed to be strong Pentagon opposition to withdrawing the nuclear weapons. There was concern that an impasse would be reached and the security treaty, which was subject to renunciation with one year's notice beginning in 1970, would become the subject of political confrontation inside Japan, a situation that could lead to deteriorating relations. Smith's story "added to the mood music" of encouragement, one official recalls. Kissinger, in his own private talks with the Japanese, may also have passed the same message.

with Hoover, and, in a memorandum, William Sullivan specifically cited Kissinger as the official who made the request—the only time Kissinger was so named in the FBI's wiretap files. Sullivan wrote, "Today Dr. Kissinger requested that a telephone surveillance be placed on Hedrick Smith, who has been in contact with individuals on whom we have telephone coverage in this case." In his Senate testimony in 1974, Kissinger discussed an FBI report that Smith had been overheard talking to Daniel Davidson on the wiretaps. But neither he nor any other government official was able to supply evidence linking those conversations to any of Smith's stories.

Smith's dispatches came at a trying time for Kissinger. There was renewed pressure from Nixon about leaks, and Laird was still trying to control the administration's Vietnamization plan and direct the timing of American force reductions. The reduction plan was extremely damaging to Kissinger's Vietnam negotiating strategy. How could he negotiate a mutual withdrawal of United States and North Vietnamese forces when Laird and Nixon were beginning to withdraw troops unilaterally? Another problem, undoubtedly, was the necessity to choose Midway Island for the Nixon-Thieu summit. Kissinger wrote in his memoirs that Midway was chosen for fear "that a visit by Thieu to the United States would provoke riots." (Hawaii was also rejected because Johnson had met with Thieu there.) "It was a symptom of the morass into which the Vietnam War had plunged our society," Kissinger thought, "that a meeting between the President and the leader for whose country over thirty thousand Americans had died, had to take place on an uninhabited island in the middle of the Pacific."

It seems clear that Smith's two stories were much on Kissinger's mind when he visited Hoover the morning of June 4. Yet in his later testimony to the Senate, Kissinger said he could not remember whether they came up. "I am confident I did not . . . request a tap from Mr. Hoover," Kissinger testified, "but what else was said in this conversation would be very hard for me to reconstruct. These conversations one has to see in the context. It is the wrong idea to assume that one went to Mr. Hoover who passively listened to descriptions of security violations and then reluctantly went along with orders. Usually what happened was that the Director would give one an enormous amount of alleged security violations to which one tried to make a more or less reasonable response." Hoover had died in 1972. Kissinger could suggest in 1973, without fear of contradiction, that he too was one of Hoover's victims.

There is evidence, however, that Hoover, far from badgering Kissinger, was protecting him. During the twenty-one months that Halperin's home telephone was wiretapped, the FBI sent thirty-four letters to Kissinger, Nixon, and Haldeman summarizing the information overheard. Nothing was reported, however, about a long telephone conversation between Halperin and Kissinger on a Saturday afternoon, August 9, 1969. By then, Halperin had been wiretapped for three months and no derogatory information had been obtained. Yet Kissinger had been increasingly isolating him from classified materials inside the NSC and Halperin was on the verge of resignation. Urging Halperin to stay, Kissinger spoke very frankly that Saturday, though he had to know the talk was being transcribed since he had called Halperin at home. Many of Kissinger's statements would have outraged President Nixon. In an FBI transcript of the conversation, Kissinger is quoted as praising Halperin's work as extraordinary and urging him not to leave the White House. Kissinger even promised to talk about Halperin's role with Nixon and Mitchell—a promise he knew he would not keep—to see "if they feel we can't tailor something [for Halperin] right now."

The conversation was self-serving on Kissinger's part; his only concern was to insure that Halperin would keep his peace. Nonetheless, Kissinger would not have spoken as he did if he had thought there was any chance that the FBI would routinely forward a transcript to the White House. To have to explain to Nixon how manipulative and misleading he was in his talk with Halperin could have raised questions about all his conversations, whether with his staff or with the President.*

In a conversation with the author in 1973, conducted at the time on a not-for-attribution basis, William Sullivan said that none of the NSC wiretaps produced any evidence of wrongdoing.† "There wasn't one member of the staff who was disloyal to the country. But they were disloyal to Kissinger and they were giving him real problems. Some of them began to disagree with him and they weren't with him," Sullivan added. "Actually they *were* disloyal—not to the country but to him."

Richard Nixon, in a White House tape recording that was made public during the 1974 impeachment hearings, strongly implied that it was Kissinger who urged the wiretapping. Discussing the wiretaps on Halperin and W. Anthony Lake, a young Foreign Service officer who had joined the NSC staff in June 1969, Nixon said, "I know that he [Kissinger] asked that it be done. And I assumed that it was. Lake and Halperin. They're both bad. But the taps were, too. They never helped us. Just gobs and gobs of material: gossip and bullshitting—the tapping was a very, very unproductive thing."

In his various public statements, Nixon consistently based his approval of the wiretaps on grounds of national security. Kissinger did the same. During testimony before the Senate Foreign Relations Committee in 1974, Kissinger was asked whether any of his aides were fired because of indiscretions. His answer, classified and thus deleted from the published transcript, was: "As a result of this program, there were two violations that I remember. In the case of one person, he was separated from the staff over a period of months in such a way that it did not appear that he'd been fired for a security violation. I thought it was an indiscretion. I did not want to blight his whole career, so first I had him transferred out of the National Security Council to another government position and suggested to him as a friend that he resign after a decent interval. . . . It was clearly an indiscretion, but I did not want to have him blighted."

* A transcript of all Halperin's telephone calls on August 9 was made available by the Justice Department to Halperin's counsel in his lawsuit. It provides a glimpse of the sort of staff gossip that Kissinger and Haig could find irresistible. After his talk with Kissinger, Halperin called Leslie Gelb, his former Pentagon colleague, and the two agreed, according to the transcript, that Haig was "that God-damn gossip." The transcript further quotes them as saying that Haig "knows everything about everybody," and continues, "Neither could understand when he had time for this as he was in the office from 7 a.m. to 10 or 11 p.m. and he tells everybody." At one point Halperin laughed and said that "there isn't anybody on the [Kissinger] staff who isn't unhappy and seriously thinking about leaving."

† William Sullivan was killed in a hunting accident near his home in New Hampshire in October 1977, four years after he retired from government service.

Kissinger was referring to Davidson, as Haig told the author years later. But Davidson was never accused of any leaks, nor was he transferred to another job, nor did he have a conversation with Kissinger in which he was advised to "resign after a decent interval." Davidson was intensely loyal to Kissinger at the time. "At that early stage, most of us liked him very much," he says. "He was a hypnotic guy." According to Davidson, Haig told him in mid-1969 that his resignation was desired and he was offered his choice of a new post. Instead, he left government to practice law in Washington.

In his testimony to the Senate, Kissinger also talked about what he described as the second security violation, which was Halperin's. "In the case of another person, we suddenly separated him from classified documents to a point where he felt he wanted to resign, but that was an attempt on my part to minimize the damage to the individuals themselves. If there had been overwhelming security violations," Kissinger said, "we would have thrown them out. They were borderline cases, where you erred on the side of protecting the security but did not feel justified in blighting the whole career of the man."

Kissinger, testifying in 1976 in Halperin's lawsuit, significantly altered his account. He said that as of August 1969, when he had the long and friendly conversation with Halperin in which he urged him to stay on at the NSC, "I had no information that would—on security grounds—make me change my mind about keeping him." It was "my judgment" that Halperin was not a security risk, Kissinger said.

By the fall of 1969, the wiretapping, the lying, and the failure of the Nixon-Kissinger Vietnam policies were taking their toll. Kissinger's NSC staff was beginning to crumble. In secret.

8

DECAY

SOME RECALLED that the first portent came early—at a meeting in the Executive Office Building of the new NSC staff a day or so after Nixon's inauguration. Kissinger came in with Eagleburger, Haig, and Moose, the three aides who shared his office space in the White House basement. There was the obligatory joke: "I've been in office now for hours and I haven't had a thought yet." Everyone laughed. "I took this job to think," Kissinger went on, "and all I've been doing is reading cables, putting out fires, and trying to keep the Department of State from selling us down the river." More laughter.

Someone then asked whether the National Security Council staff would have mess privileges in the White House. Kissinger said no; he had discussed the matter with Haldeman and it had been decided that only the domestic staff personnel would have such privileges. The mood changed abruptly. Without mess privileges, NSC people who worked through the evening and late into the night—as most knew they would—would be forced to rely on vending machine food, since the employee cafeteria in the Executive Office Building closed after normal working hours. The NSC staff was being told that it would not have top-level status inside the White House. The message was that the NSC people were to be judged, and carefully, by the men around Richard Nixon—and also by Kissinger.

Some staff members, notably Sonnenfeldt, the former State Department intelligence official, felt that their prerogatives were being slighted. What was the point of being in the White House if one couldn't enjoy the perquisites? Kissinger was sympathetic and promised to "see what I can do." His audience did not know, of course, that it had been Kissinger's idea to isolate his staff from the White House. He meant to control his staff, and its access to the President and his men, as thoroughly as he meant to control the rest of the bureaucracy.

Kissinger's next topic was equally important to this control: NSC staff members were to sever all relations with the press. "If anybody leaks in this administration I will be the one to leak," Kissinger said. "To your friends in the press you are simply not in from here on in."

There was one exception, Kissinger added. He might, on occasion, direct various staff members to see newspapermen. Within weeks, such an occasion arose. Kissinger was to be on the cover of *Time* magazine, the beginning of a close relationship that continued—amid constantly fawning reportage—even after he left public office. The staff was told that they could talk to *Time* reporters.

Such goings-on were normal in any bureaucracy, and in those first months the NSC was by all accounts a reasonably happy place to work. Kissinger could be a demanding boss, but many bosses were demanding. He could rant and rave, but those who stood up to him found that he could shorten his tantrums. Indeed, Kissinger developed what some staff members called the "lollipop treatment." After an unpleasant show of temper, or an excessive number of late-night meetings, flowers would be delivered to an angry wife, or ballet tickets to an overworked secretary, or a staff member would be asked to pay a social call, on behalf of the White House, on a prominent ambassador. Haig's easy humor often soothed the bruised feelings of staff members who had been called back to the White House at 10:00 P.M. because "Henry needs you" and found themselves waiting outside his office for hours.

Kissinger himself worked long hours, as newspapers and magazines constantly reported, but they were his hours, set by himself for himself. White House social life was important to him, for obvious reasons; so were the parties at the Alsops' or the Harrimans' in elegant Georgetown, just across the Potomac. He would disappear for dinner and return late that night. Staff members learned to work through the evening preparing papers for Kissinger to pore over after his outings. Much of his time during the day was lost to his staff because it was taken up with interminable briefings for newspaper and television reporters. The regulars included Max Frankel, James Reston, Joseph Alsop, Henry Brandon, Joe Kraft, Marvin Kalb, Rowland Evans, Murray Marder of the *Washington Post,* and Hugh Sidey of *Time.*

The first to leave was Spurgeon M. Keeny, Jr., a defense and arms control expert who had worked both for the National Security Council and as assistant to the President's science adviser since the Eisenhower Administration. In 1968, Keeny was a sophisticated forty-four-year-old bureaucrat who got no public recognition but was known in the government as one of the key men in high-technology analysis and management. The Kennedy and Johnson administrations had relied on his judgment and had given him the authority to clear policy cables to points overseas from the State Department and the Pentagon. This was no small responsibility, for every department must have approval— the White House "chop"—before authorizing any activity anywhere else in the world. Thus a State Department decision, endorsed by the Secretary, to supply humanitarian aid to a famine-stricken nation in Africa, or a Pentagon decision, endorsed by the Joint Chiefs of Staff, to supply arms to a new Third World regime, would need prior approval from Kissinger's office in the White House.

Keeny was pleased to be asked to stay on in the Nixon White House, but there was one immediate change: He would no longer have the authority to clear cables. That was to be solely Kissinger's responsibility. Before long, Keeny recalls, "The whole process of government was coming to a stop. Henry didn't want to delegate authority and so every night there'd be people at 9:00 P.M. lining up outside his office, waiting to explain things." Keeny was troubled at the discrepancy between Kissinger's constant talk about the desire for openness and the reality of his demand that only he control policy.

There was another problem. Under Kennedy and Johnson, the President's science adviser had played a key role in defense and arms control issues. Under Kissinger, Lee A. DuBridge, the newly appointed Nixon adviser, was being isolated. Keeny told Kissinger and Haig that DuBridge's office, with its many outside consultants, could be a valuable resource in the debates to come over U.S.-Soviet strategic arms control. "Weeks went by," Keeny says, "and DuBridge was too proud and too much of a gentleman to force himself." Kissinger finally agreed to meet with DuBridge and Keeny in the basement office, but as the meeting began, Kissinger took a call from a friend and stayed on the phone for many minutes. The two men listened silently, and Kissinger's point was made. "Henry had no intention of sharing power."

DuBridge was doomed from the start, and Keeny took the first opportunity to get out. When Gerard C. Smith, a wealthy Republican who had contributed substantially to the Nixon election effort, was appointed head of the Arms Control and Disarmament Agency, he offered Keeny a chance to become assistant director for science and technology. "Henry was very pleasant about it," Keeny said, "and I went almost immediately."

There were more important struggles in the first few months of Kissinger's regime. One was over who would be Kissinger's principal staff assistant during the negotiations on a strategic arms limitation agreement with the Soviet Union. Competition was fierce between Halperin, who had had major responsibility for such talks in the Johnson Administration; Lynn, the economist and systems analyst from the Pentagon; and Sonnenfeldt, the Soviet expert from the State Department.

The second struggle was less substantive but just as bitterly contested: Who on the NSC staff would become Henry Kissinger's deputy? Eagleburger, one of the main candidates, was an intense worker who arrived at the office before Kissinger and stayed on the job till late at night. Eagleburger quickly burned out. Sometime in June he suffered what some NSC aides describe as a nervous breakdown and others thought was a stroke. To his close friends, Eagleburger's illness was no surprise—he was simply working too hard. He often brought a change of clothes to the office because he perspired so profusely under the work load during the day.*

* Kissinger's reaction to Eagleburger's collapse upset many NSC staff members. He fell ill one afternoon while Kissinger was meeting with Arthur Burns, Nixon's chief economic adviser, and Burns's aide, Martin Anderson. Anderson recalls what happened: "As we walked out of his office, Henry turned to one of his secretaries and said, 'Where is Eagleburger?' She said, 'I'm sorry, but while you were in the meeting Larry collapsed and he's unconscious.' The extraordinary thing is that he didn't hesitate but said, 'But I need him.' Then he said to her, 'Get me [Patrick] Buchanan,' and went into his office and closed the door." Eagleburger was taken by ambulance to the Washington Hospital Center and, after a rest, was reassigned as a Foreign Service officer at NATO headquarters in Brussels. Later that year Kissinger astonished his aides by criticizing Eagleburger in his annual State Department efficiency report. He said that Eagleburger was an outstanding and brilliant officer, Roger Morris recalls, but that he had little organizational ability. Knowing such a verdict would be fatal for a Foreign Service officer, Morris and a colleague sneaked it off Haig's desk and rewrote it. "We sent it back to be signed, and Henry—who doesn't notice such things

Much of the tension inside the NSC seems to have been intentionally created by Kissinger. In June, just before Eagleburger's collapse and after the Nixon-Thieu meeting on Midway, at which the South Vietnamese President approved the plan to begin withdrawing American combat troops, Richard Sneider decided that he'd had enough. He arranged to have a breakfast meeting with Kissinger at which he asked to be released from the NSC. Before joining Kissinger's staff, Sneider had been considered a rising star in the Foreign Service. He was of course concerned about his future: Would Kissinger punish him for leaving? Sneider, who was privy to the administration's most important secrets of the moment, the EC-121 deliberations and the B-52 bombing of Cambodia, paid a visit to Eagleburger after the Kissinger breakfast and made it clear that if his next assignment was not appropriate, he was going to start talking about some of the seamy operations inside the NSC. Four days later he was assigned as minister in charge of the Okinawa reversion negotiations, and by the end of the year he was Deputy Chief of Mission at the United States Embassy in Tokyo.

By midsummer of that first year, jockeying inside the NSC had gone far beyond the normal limits of bureaucratic intrigue. The White House wiretaps added a whole new dimension.

Not long after Eagleburger became ill, Morris went to visit him in the hospital. "He was lying there as we talked," Morris recalls. "Tears welled up and he said, 'Don't say anything on your phone. You're being tapped.' " Eagleburger also confided that Halperin was finished in the White House.

Morris may have been the first to know, but soon the word was out: Halperin was in trouble. The messenger was Haig. Laurence Lynn was in a running battle with Halperin over control of NSC studies on the SALT talks; both men passed memoranda to Kissinger without informing the other. At one point, Lynn was offered another spot in the Nixon Administration and—no amateur in the ways of bureaucracy—sought to pass the word to Kissinger through Haig. Haig immediately made it clear that Lynn's rival was in trouble with the President and with Senator Barry Goldwater, and was being "monitored." Lynn stayed on the job.

Early that summer Davidson left the staff, and word quickly filtered through that he had been caught leaking on a wiretap. Eagleburger added to the rumors by telling Morris that Halperin's name had shown up on a National Security Agency intercept of a Japanese Embassy transmission: Halperin had been discussing the Okinawa reversion negotiations with Japanese officials in Washington, and they had cabled the conversation to the Tokyo Foreign Office. Morris got the impression that Al Haig and others in the White House believed a criminal case could be made against Halperin for giving away secrets to a

---

—signed it," Morris said. In September 1973, Kissinger, newly appointed Secretary of State, summoned Eagleburger back to the department as his own executive secretary. Later, Kissinger appointed Eagleburger Under Secretary for Management, which placed him in direct administrative control of the State Department. After serving as Ambassador to Yugoslavia in the Carter Administration, Eagleburger became Assistant Secretary for European Affairs in the Reagan Administration and was later named Under Secretary for Political Affairs.

foreign government.* By summer, Richard Moose was also reported to be on the way out—likewise rumored to be a victim of wiretapping.

Sometime in June, W. Anthony Lake arrived from a sabbatical leave at Princeton University, formally replacing Eagleburger as Kissinger's special assistant. There was an immediate change in the outside office of Kissinger's cramped basement quarters.† Haig moved to Eagleburger's desk, a few feet from Kissinger's private office, and Lake slipped into the desk Haig vacated. The significance of the shift was not lost on the NSC staff, who knew that Haig was getting close to the job many wanted—that of deputy. Within months, Lake later told Watergate prosecutors, he became aware of the wiretapping and also suspected that wiretap summaries forwarded by the FBI were kept in a top-secret safe in the Situation Room in the basement. The safe, designed for the storage of the nation's nuclear targeting materials, as well as the codes to activate and arm America's nuclear weapons, was under twenty-four-hour guard. Lake and Morris, fellow Foreign Service officers, became close friends, and Lake soon shared his information about the Situation Room safe.

Robert Houdek, a junior Foreign Service officer who was assigned the relatively meaningless task of NSC liaison with the White House press office, learned early in the spring that Morton Halperin "was *malodor*." As a Foreign Service colleague, he tried to warn Lake about the wiretapping. "I remember so well," Houdek says. "I was approaching Tony as a friend and he one-upped me. 'You don't have to tell me anything; I've already been briefed.' " Over the next two years, a number of personal aides would rotate in and out of Kissinger's personal office; all quickly learned that the White House was wiretapping some of the NSC staff. Except for such occasional attempts to warn each other, the young men kept their secret well.

By fall, Kissinger had stripped his staff of many of those considered offensive to the man in the Oval Office. Halperin formally resigned in September; Sneider and Davidson were long gone; Moose was on the way out. All went quietly, telling the few reporters who asked that their resignation had nothing to do with foreign policy. In a sense that was true—they were not opposed to the policy as they understood it to be. Kissinger had made sure that neither Halperin nor Moose, who remained on the NSC staff throughout the summer, was fully informed.

Cutting certain people out of the flow of information was a way of life in the

* Halperin had held private talks with Japanese officials in which he made clear that if they made enough concessions, the United States would capitulate on the nuclear storage issue. He had held similar conversations during the Johnson Administration and considered it good bargaining. "The Japanese kept saying to us, 'Do you have to keep nuclear weapons?' And I'd say, 'As long as you ask us that question, we're going to say yes.' " Halperin says, "Nobody authorized me to say anything, but the question of what you say to foreign diplomats is a matter of discretion; and the question of what I had authority to say is a matter of judgment."

† Some of Kissinger's friends didn't think his offices were appropriate to the job. Guido Goldman, a Harvard professor who had been a Kissinger teaching assistant, seemed to be reflecting Kissinger's private complaints when he told a television interviewer in September 1976 that Kissinger's office had been "a very small room, with a very low ceiling. No private entry, and every time you wanted to go use the bathroom, you had to go out to meet whoever was waiting to see you, so you couldn't even play the game that you weren't in or something like that. . . . It was not a prestigious office in the sense of its internal dimensions."

Nixon-Kissinger White House, far more so than in previous administrations. Most of Kissinger's staff simply did not know what he was doing. Halperin recalls that Nixon and Kissinger would plan presidential trips overseas and initiate correspondence with foreign leaders not only without informing the State Department but without telling the NSC staff specialists for the areas involved. "The Kissinger operation right from the beginning was a one-man operation."

Kissinger's personal aides, who at various times in 1969 included Eagleburger, Haig, and Lake, were somewhat more trusted. In August, William Watts, a colleague of Kissinger in Rockefeller's campaign for the presidential nomination, arrived to replace Moose as staff secretary. He was immediately given more responsibility—assigned, for example, to the NSC in the West Wing basement offices when Kissinger was traveling. These men saw the highly classified documents that streamed into Kissinger's office, and were aware of his effort to isolate other staff members from the decision-making process. They also saw many of the FBI documents Hoover sent to Kissinger, including the wiretap summaries. Lake and Morris were responsible for editing Kissinger's diary entries and insuring that no copies of those notes strayed from his personal files. The personal staff was also responsible for monitoring the flow of memoranda from Kissinger to Nixon.

Yet the always careful Kissinger managed to sharply limit their role, too. He never told these aides what he and the President discussed in their daily morning talks, which often lasted two hours or more. "Kissinger would never, never say what he had recommended to the President," Lake recalls, "not even to Haig during those days and not to me. . . . And the very hot ones would get handled in those meetings."

Lake and others were aware that Kissinger had one great advantage in his dealings with Nixon. One of the NSC's most important functions—at least in the President's and Haldeman's eyes—was to prepare briefing books before presidential press conferences. For all his disdain of the press, Nixon would "sit twenty-four, forty-eight hours," according to Lake, "just going over and over these books which would list a question and then the possible answers." Lake and occasionally Morris were assigned to summarize the possible questions and answers that were routinely forwarded from the State Department. Then Kissinger would come in, Lake remembers, "and there would be this flurry of papers being thrown around and screams of outrage and we would redo them again the way Kissinger wanted, usually adding things because Kissinger's theory was that this was the best way we could both educate the President and get Kissinger's points across."

Invariably Haldeman's office would complain that the answers were too long and involved, too much reading for Nixon. Lake and Morris finally decided to provide long and short answers for each question, to meet Haldeman's objections and at the same time advance Kissinger's educational project.*

* Haldeman remained a critic of the Kissinger briefing process. Watts recalls that the chief of staff would telephone Kissinger after a presidential news conference and declare, "Henry, I give him a C-minus on foreign affairs. You didn't prepare him well enough." Nixon never heard such talk, however. The President would telephone Kissinger after the news conference and be effusively praised. According to Watts, Kissinger would say, "Mr. President, you did such a beautiful job," or "Mr. President, you were so impressive." After hanging up, Kissinger would then make some denigrating comment to his staff.

After Nixon's period of isolation with the briefing books, they would be returned to Kissinger and, Lake recalls, "in the margins you could see the President's notes to himself. Those comments were bureaucratic gold because they showed what the President was thinking." Lake, who spent ten months in 1969 and 1970 as Kissinger's personal aide, does not remember many times when the President disagreed with Kissinger on major policy issues. Kissinger's staff came to realize that his success in the White House stemmed from his insight into what the President wanted as well as his refusal to question it.

Kissinger knew instinctively what Lake ultimately came to understand: "This President is not about to be persuaded by opposing points of view. He feels threatened by them, obviously doesn't want to hear them. When ambassadors would go in [to pay courtesy calls] it became almost a joke. You know, American ambassadors going abroad would see the President and always raise two or three things, parochial concerns in those countries. I never sat in but would hear about them later. Nixon would start getting very cool and friendly and smile and appear to be agreeing and obviously had no intention of doing it but wasn't about to argue it through or confront it. Let the ambassadors say it and go away and then write them off as fools for having misused their time with the President to try to get something out of him."

Halperin too perceived the secret of Kissinger's success. Kissinger was "very good at figuring out how to handle Richard Nixon, which many people were not. Nixon basically is a man who doesn't like to be pushed into a corner. If you got in to see him while he was President, and you asked for something and you pushed it—eventually he would say, 'Okay, you can have it.' And then when you walked out the door, he would pick up the phone and call Haldeman and say, 'I've just promised the Secretary of Transportation—or whoever—something. One, he is not to get it, and two, I never want to see that man again.' And then the Cabinet officer would go around town trying to get what Nixon had promised him. He would never get it; he could never get in again. And that's really where Haldeman's bad reputation came in, because they would assume it was Haldeman because they knew the President agreed with them."

Halperin realized that "the trick with Nixon was never to push him into that kind of corner; it was always to talk around the problem until he came around and bought your viewpoint. And Kissinger understood that very quickly, and therefore Nixon became very comfortable with seeing him—because he knew he was not going to be pressed into a corner, which is what he didn't want."

Most of the NSC staff got a chance to see Nixon in action in the first few months of 1969, usually at NSC meetings. The President was impressive. Staff members recall that he seemed to have done his homework and to understand the intricacies of the foreign policy matters under discussion.

In February, less than a month after he took office, the NSC discussed the burgeoning crisis in the Nigerian civil war with secessionist Biafra. Should America recognize Biafra, as a few other nations had done? Or should it side with the federal government in Nigeria, and continue to be perceived throughout emerging Africa as antirevolutionary? Roger Morris recalls being "absolutely astonished at the level of knowledge of Nixon and Kissinger. I had become accustomed in the Johnson Administration to a sort of scatter-shot approach. Whatever you sent up you never assumed that Johnson necessarily assimilated it. In this case Nixon had clearly been doing his homework."

NSC meetings traditionally opened with a briefing from Helms of the CIA. At this meeting Helms began by listing the countries that had recognized Biafra. At one point, as Morris tells it, "Nixon stopped him and said, 'Look, Dick, you've left out a couple of countries—Zambia and the Ivory Coast.' Helms sort of stopped a moment and looked slightly shaken. Helms then said something else, about tribal rivalries within Nigeria being part of the origin of the civil war and a complicating factor in the politics of the war, and Nixon stopped him and said, 'Yes. And this is a problem which really goes back in the history of that country. The British colonial policy favored the Moslem Hausas in the north and that aggravated the tensions and there's cultural as well as economic and political factors here. It's a very, very tragic problem.' I was sitting there in utter amazement: 'My God, this man has actually read his briefing papers—and he's not only read it but he's understood it.' "

Other Kissinger staff aides have similar recollections. Richard Sneider remembers that Nixon was often the "star performer" at meetings about Asian issues. Over the next few months, however, these formal meetings were recast as caricatures, rituals through which the President could be exposed to his Cabinet and his senior advisers under tightly controlled conditions. By mid-year, Kissinger was ordering his staff to include the admonishment that "no decisions will be made here" in presidential briefing papers submitted before the NSC meetings.

By then, too, Nixon seemed to be giving far less attention to the formal meetings, and far less thought to the studies prepared by the NSC staff. The talking papers prepared for Nixon before the meetings soon began to include word-for-word dialogue. One staff aide vividly recalls the first of many such papers he wrote for Nixon: "It was like a first-grade primer—a 'Run, Spot, run' kind of thing." In his script, Nixon began the meeting by stating, "Gentlemen: Today we are dealing with etc., etc. There are four issues: first, we have, etc., etc." After listing the issues, Nixon was then to call on Kissinger and ask him to summarize the available options. When Kissinger had done so, the script called for Nixon to say, "Thank you, Dr. Kissinger." Then Nixon was supposed to say, "Now it's Mr. so-and-so's turn," and bring in a Cabinet member for discussion. The astonishing thing, the aide recalls, was that Nixon followed the script exactly.

The Pentagon analyst John Court, who became a deputy in Lynn's program analysis office, recalls writing his first talking paper and listening as Nixon followed it precisely. As Nixon was reading, "I was thinking to myself, 'Hell, I'm not a foreign policy analyst; I'm a script writer for a White House performance.' "

One of Court's NSC scripts called for Nixon, after he and Kissinger had outlined the issues and options, to turn to Melvin Laird. When Laird concluded his comments, Nixon was to express disagreement with Laird's remarks, whose gist Kissinger seemed, somehow, to know in advance. Again Nixon followed the scenario precisely.

Laird was an anomaly to the NSC staff members. He was bright and articulate when he was interested in the topic under discussion, but when it did not directly concern the Pentagon, or relate to a domestic political situation, he seemed to fade. He and his closest aides had another characteristic that separated them from the rest of the NSC—they did not always share the awe for Nixon that seemed obligatory in the upper echelons of the administration. For example, David Packard, Laird's deputy, invited Ivan Selin, the Pentagon's Acting Assistant Secretary for Systems Analysis, who had worked in the Johnson Administration, to come along to a White House meeting on the military budget. During the meeting, Nixon incorrectly recited a statistic, and Selin, who had written Nixon's briefing paper, abruptly corrected him. "No, Mr. President," he said, and went on to explain the error. After that meeting Kissinger specified that only principals—that is, Laird and Packard—would be welcome at future meetings on the Pentagon budget. Haig was more graphic. He telephoned Robert Pursley and said, Pursley recalls, "I can't believe these bastards from systems analysis." Nonetheless, Packard brought Selin to a follow-up meeting a week or so later.

If Laird occasionally impressed Kissinger's staff aides, Secretary of State Rogers did not. Watts recalls a meeting in late 1969 at which Latin American policy was being discussed in the aftermath of Nelson Rockefeller's well-publicized trip to South America earlier that year, a trip orchestrated by Kissinger and Nixon as a show of Republican unity. During the meeting, Nixon suddenly exclaimed that a new theme was needed for the relationship between Latin America and the United States. The Alliance for Progress, Nixon said, was a holdover from the Kennedy Administration and not acceptable. He turned to Rogers and asked him to have one of his "wordsmiths" at the State Department devise a new phrase. After a moment, Watts recalls, Rogers suggested that the name be broadened to demonstrate the North American commitment to Latin America. Why not "The Hemispheric Alliance for Progress"? There was embarrassed silence throughout the room, Watts says, broken only when Nixon remarked, "Oh yeah, then we could let that fucking Trudeau grow a beard and go play with Castro." Pierre Trudeau, Canada's Prime Minister, had infuriated the Nixon White House by continuing normal trade and diplomatic relations with Castro's Cuba and by criticizing American involvement in the Vietnam War.*

NSC staff members were also contemptuous of other important NSC participants. Admiral Thomas H. Moorer, who became chairman of the Joint Chiefs of Staff in the summer of 1970, was known to the staff as Admiral Mormon. (Nixon had introduced him by that name at one of the first NSC meetings he attended.) Vice President Agnew was considered a know-nothing on foreign policy matters; he "just read his notes."

Elliot Richardson also came in for his share of criticism. One staff member recalls that Kissinger on occasion was forced to defend Richardson from violent attacks by Nixon, who didn't like Richardson's manner. Not only did Richardson occasionally object to policy decisions, but his carefully measured and didactic style of speaking could cause considerable impatience in a

---

* Canada's support for Cuba had a business basis, for Canadian companies had been quick to pick up much of the trade in food and heavy equipment that had gone to American firms before 1961, when the Kennedy Administration imposed an embargo. Even Air Canada profited from the relationship by working out a leasing arrangement for its aircraft with Cubana de Aviación, Cuba's national airline.

President who knew that the decision under discussion had already been made.*

By the end of the year, the constant sniping and behind-the-back criticism of their government superiors had become part of the process for the men who worked for Henry Kissinger. And an even darker tone—brought on in part by the wiretaps, the intense intrigues, and the constant bureaucratic bitching—was developing: malevolence. This was ultimately Kissinger's responsibility. The NSC staff was simply following the example of its leader.

* For all his integrity and intelligence, Richardson could be surprisingly compliant on occasion. In early 1970, during a White House meeting on drug control chaired by John Ehrlichman, it was agreed that the quickest solution to solving the nation's heroin problem was to ban all opium products. Dr. Roger Egeberg, a senior health official from the Department of Health, Education and Welfare, recalls being asked whether he would open talks with the American Medical Association to see whether its support could be obtained if the White House were to ban opium. The theory seemed to be, Egeberg says, that if all opium products were declared illegal, police and courts could conclude that anyone with the drug in his possession was automatically guilty. Egeberg knew the proposal was ridiculous, since the medical need for such opium derivatives as morphine, codeine, and paregoric was immense. "I was shocked at the attitude that we could stamp out the use of these drugs in this country," Egeberg says. He was also shocked that everybody at the meeting, including Ehrlichman, Kissinger, and Richardson, obviously thought the proposal was valid. He was further troubled by the unsupported assumption that opium imported for medical use was a major source of street sales of heroin. "They thought they really could stamp out heroin usage" by winning over the AMA. Another shock came later, when Richardson made it a point to remind Egeberg several times over the next weeks that he was expected to talk to AMA officials and urge their support. It was clear to Egeberg that Nixon, who had not attended the meeting, was behind the proposal and that Richardson was doing what the White House wanted, even when it was preposterous.

9

INTRIGUES

KISSINGER'S BACKBITING BEGAN almost immediately. Rogers was a corrupt "fag" who had some strange hold over Richard Nixon; Laird was a megalomaniac who constantly leaked anti-Kissinger stories to the press; Richard Nixon was a secret drunk of dubious intelligence.

There was a steady stream of invective from Kissinger, and his personal aides heard it all. At one time Kissinger told some of his staff that a prominent Georgetown columnist had confided to him that Rogers was keeping a house in Georgetown with a young male paramour in it. Kissinger went further one evening, Roger Morris recalls, telling some of his close aides that Haldeman had once hinted that Rogers and Nixon had "indulged" in the past. No one believed there was evidence for such remarks.

Morris and others whom Kissinger trusted, including Anthony Lake, found themselves enthralled as they worked on Kissinger's private diary, which was transcribed and edited nearly every night. On some days, Morris remembers, Kissinger's entries filled fifteen pages, not with high-level diplomatic strategy but with low-level gossip. "We caught glimpses of Nixon, Laird, Rogers, and Kissinger in action," Morris says. "Nixon drank exceptionally at night and there were many nights when you couldn't reach him at Camp David," the presidential retreat in Maryland.

The diary was treated as if it were the most sensitive document in the government—which it may have been. Stored in an electronically wired safe in Kissinger's office, along with materials from the secret negotiations with North Vietnam in Paris, it was a "gold mine of bureaucratic duplicity and maneuver," Morris says. "When Henry went home at night, he didn't discuss policy; he discussed the nature of people. He is really interested in personalities and their weaknesses; he analyzed issues and people the way a good boxer analyzes his opponent's boxing style."

Morris often listened in on Kissinger's conversations with an obviously drunken Nixon. "There were many times when a cable would come in late and Henry would say, 'There's no sense waking him up—he'd be incoherent,' " he remembers. The young aide, frightened at the thought of a President who was not fully competent after sundown, often wondered what would happen if the Soviet Union attacked at night.

Morris did not mention such things to friends outside the White House. "It's hard to explain," he said later. "It's a constant barrage. You go around taking it for granted that Nixon's nuts. Henry and others go around wringing their hands for the President and saying Rogers is a fag. After a while, you lose your perspective. You don't feel a sense of outrage. All of the things that you think about later—the drunkenness, the wiretapping—you've become inured to while in the White House. It isn't a matter of constant moral torment when you're there.''

Kissinger told his personal staff more than once about his first formal White House reception and his first meeting with Mrs. Nixon. Naturally, he said, he began to praise the President lavishly, but Mrs. Nixon leaned over and interrupted him, saying, "Haven't you seen through him yet?" Morris recalls that Kissinger would tell the anecdote to the staff and joke about it, "as if to say, 'This man is not stable.' ''

"It's a curious paradox about Henry," Morris says. "Nobody schemed or planned about his enemies more than Kissinger—and yet nobody was as careless. He didn't really conceal his contempt for all these people, except in face-to-face dealings.''

Colonel Pursley says that Kissinger and Haig would seek his support—and Laird's—for a White House stratagem "by telling me, 'We've got a madman on our hands.' They'd always say that to me; it was a continual thing.''

Just how serious was Nixon's drinking problem? Many of his former associates and aides, such as Charles W. Colson, dismiss its significance by saying that the President had a notoriously low capacity for alcohol, that he would slur his words and appear to be somewhat drunk after one or two highballs. Yet John Ehrlichman recalls that he refused to work on Nixon's presidential campaign in 1968 unless Nixon promised to stop drinking. "Nixon promised to lay off during the campaign and he did," Ehrlichman says. "There were times when he got drunk—no question about it. But it wasn't that frequent and he had a sense of when he was on and when he was off duty.''

Another Kissinger aide remembers, however, that Nixon always seemed to be "off" during the many weekends he spent at the Florida White House in Key Biscayne. On those weekends, Nixon spent an inordinate amount of time drinking martinis with two old cronies, Charles G. (Bébé) Rebozo and Robert H. Abplanalp. "To the extent there was a problem," the aide recalls, "it was very real in Key Biscayne." Kissinger's main concern during those Florida trips, which were working weekends for the national security adviser and his staff, was avoiding social encounters with the Nixon entourage. "We always played hard to get for Nixon," says the aide, repeatedly turning down invitations. On occasion Nixon himself would telephone with a request and Kissinger would go. One night when he did go, Nixon stopped an attractive woman as he left a Miami restaurant—after having a few drinks too many—and offered her a job in the White House. "She looks like she's built for you, Henry," the President said. The Kissinger aide heard about the encounter, not from Kissinger but from a Secret Service man. "This kind of thing made my veins hurt," the aide remembers. "The President of the United States, drunk in a restaurant, making crude remarks and engaging in familiarity with a strange woman in a public place—all clearly attributable to martinis." Nonetheless, "I didn't think of his drinking as a real problem—although you sort of wondered what would happen if there was ever a nuclear threat." Most of the time, "it was one of the things you knew about in terms of handling papers—'Oh, no, this is not the time to get him to sign these.' "

Whatever the truth, Kissinger's staff—who rarely saw Nixon—were convinced that they were dealing with a defective President, and Kissinger did little to reassure them. Halperin recalls that even in the early days of the administration Kissinger would return from a private session with the President and say, "Maybe the President has two hours every morning to spend kibitzing about foreign policy, but I'm much too busy for that." Halperin got the distinct impression that Nixon "liked nothing better than to sit around every morning for several hours with Kissinger. For Nixon, this was a great thing. He was sitting with this distinguished Harvard professor, talking about the future of the world. And Kissinger would go up there every morning and disappear. And the appointments would back up, the work would back up—and he would come out two hours later, having had this seminar on foreign policy."

The NSC staff sympathized with Kissinger's plight, as he depicted it, in dealing with Nixon. They soon came to believe that the most closely held secrets in the White House did not deal with CIA operatives, communications intercepts, or satellite photography, but with the character of the man running the nation's government. Nixon's drinking was to be kept quiet at all costs; and so was his racism.

There seems to have been an unrelenting stream of anti-black remarks from the President during his first year in office. In his telephone conversations with Kissinger, he repeatedly referred to blacks as "niggers," "jigs," and "jigaboos." Some of the slurs were obviously results of Nixon drinking bouts, but NSC aides who monitored Kissinger-Nixon telephone calls came to believe that Richard Nixon, drunk or sober, was a racist. Far more disillusioning was their boss's attitude; Kissinger also repeatedly made clear his contempt for black people. Yet there was a constant stream of Kissinger asides to his staff about Nixon's racism.

One theme was that Nixon had always been a racist but did not know the correct derogatory words until he moved from California to New York in the 1960s. After Nixon had referred to blacks as "jungle bunnies" during one of his telephone talks with Kissinger in 1969, Morris recalls, Kissinger whimsically explained that Nixon had seen *Hair* while in New York "and gotten educated." (One scene in the play consists of a recitation, put to music, of various derogatory and slang phrases for blacks, including "jungle bunny.")*

The NSC staff aides understood what was acceptable behavior and what was not. They would join the laughter at Alexander Haig's antics during the rare staff meetings that dealt with African issues. Morris recalls that when he would enter the Situation Room laden with briefing books, "Haig would begin to beat his hands on the table, as if he was pounding a tom-tom. It was all very manly —a locker-room mentality. Haig would make Tarzan jokes—'Where's your pet ape?' or, talking about blacks, say, 'Henry can't stand the smell.' "

There were other comments. Sonnenfeldt would joke about the blacks in Washington moving into upper-middle-class white neighborhoods, Morris re-

* John Ehrlichman has a simpler explanation. He says "jungle bunny" happens to be one of Rebozo's favorite derogatory phrases for blacks.

members: "He called them niggers, jigs, spades, or your dusky friends." Another recurrent Sonnenfeldt complaint was that the African embassies in Washington were "taking all the good embassy spots; you couldn't live on Sixteenth Street any more unless you wanted to have 'dusky friends.' "

The racist joking invariably began whenever Morris sought White House action in the areas where he had major responsibility—Africa, AID, and the United Nations. "You couldn't find three subjects less important [to Kissinger] and more the object of ridicule."

Kissinger repeatedly made clear his lack of respect for the intelligence of blacks. When the State Department appointed C. Clyde Ferguson, a black law professor from Rutgers University, special relief coordinator during the Nigerian civil war, Kissinger asked fatuously, "Do you think he'll understand the cables?" Morris also recalls a disturbing conversation between Kissinger and Senator Fulbright. It was the spring of 1970 and the White House gave a reception and dinner for ambassadors, most of them black, who were in Washington for a meeting of the Organization of African Unity. Kissinger asked Morris to join him at the dinner, and as Morris and Kissinger were strolling from their basement offices they bumped into Senator Fulbright, also on his way to the party. "Henry walked up to him and initiated this racist conversation," Morris says. "He asked: 'I wonder what the dining room is going to smell like?' And Fulbright said, 'You never know who's going to be at your table.' It was amazing to me that Henry would say such outrageous things in public; this was in a crowded hallway with lots of people coming and going."

Sometimes the racist comments seemed almost surrealistic in the context of the White House and its foreign policy. After the Biafran rebellion collapsed in January 1970, Morris briefed Kissinger on the prospect for continued bloodshed between the victorious Nigerian troops and the defeated Ibos of Biafra. Morris explained, in response to Kissinger's question, that the Ibos of Biafra were more Negroid in appearance and the Nigerians tended to be more Semitic. Kissinger, Morris later wrote, was visibly surprised and confused. "But you have always told me the Ibos were more gifted and accomplished than the others. What do you mean 'more Negroid'?" Earlier, there had been a brief moment of panic when Ronald L. Ziegler, the White House press secretary, who knew and cared little about Africa and its civil wars, began a briefing by announcing he had a statement to read on the "Niggerian" war. Whether out of embarrassment or ignorance, none of the press commented on the slip, Morris says.

In February of 1970, when Kissinger and his staff were working in Key Biscayne, the President, at play with his friends Rebozo and Abplanalp, telephoned ship-to-shore with a request about the foreign policy paper they were drafting. "Make sure there's something in it for the jigs, Henry," Nixon said. A moment later, Morris recalls, Nixon asked again, "Is there something in it for the jigs?" Kissinger said yes. A few months earlier, when Secretary of State Rogers received good press coverage during a trip to Africa, Kissinger had been distraught with jealousy and anxiety. There had been a soothing telephone call from Nixon, also overheard by one of the NSC aides: "Henry, let's leave the niggers to Bill and we'll take care of the rest of the world." The remark became common knowledge to Morris and his colleagues.

Another strong feeling that Nixon and Kissinger shared was animus toward Laird. Early in the administration, Nixon would occasionally flip through the morning newspapers, criticize many of the stories, and wonder who was responsible for leaking them—the perennial White House obsession. Alexander P. Butterfield, a retired Air Force colonel whom Haldeman had hired as one of Nixon's personal aides, was in charge of writing staff memoranda about Nixon's wishes. The NSC people called these documents "Butterfieldgrams." One morning Haig summoned some of the younger staff to read a series of Butterfieldgrams based on Nixon's perusal of the morning papers. "It sent us all into hysteria," Morris says. "He would read the *Times* or the *Post* and he would go through story by story and identify the leaks and every leak was Laird's. This is Nixon looking through the paper and thinking out loud and Butterfield was taking these things down. They were on separate pieces of paper that came through Henry: 'I see this goddamn, cock-sucking story about troop levels. This is Laird again. The son-of-a-bitch up to his old games. What's he trying to do?' Next page. 'Henry, what is this goddamn, cock-sucking story by Beecher? Is this Laird? It must be Laird. It's Laird, isn't it?' Next page. 'What is this editorial in the *Post?* I've seen this before—it's the same kind of reasoning. You know who this is—this is Laird.'

"This particular batch was about five or six sheets like this and all of them were about Laird and Nixon treating his Secretary of Defense as a sort of foreign government out to get him. The level of suspicion between those two men was a source of constant amazement to us." But not to Kissinger.

The national security adviser did not try to restrain the President's suspicions about bureaucratic enemies and leaks. He shared them. He had a private fear, too—that an outsider would somehow get access to the confidential files of the Nixon presidency and produce a documented memoir before he was ready to write his own.

By September 1969, his NSC staff had grown to 114 members and secretaries. One addition was particularly important to Kissinger: that of Peter W. Rodman, a former student of his. From the moment Rodman arrived, some of Kissinger's aides realized that his mission was to assemble and prepare documents for Kissinger's memoirs. "He indexed everything that came in," according to Morris. Later, Morris became convinced that another Rodman mission was to be ready to "evacuate the personal files" within hours if Kissinger ever felt that he was on the verge of being forced out by Haldeman and Ehrlichman. Even as early as 1970, Morris says, Rodman was routinely shipping the files Kissinger considered most valuable to Nelson Rockefeller's estate at Pocantico Hills, New York.

The Rodman-collected papers were the only complete set of both official and unofficial documents in existence. By mid-1969, Kissinger had begun to shield many of the backchannel materials from the NSC file system pending his personal review. Jeanne W. Davis, the NSC official who was in charge of the files, said later that she was unable to estimate the volume of Kissinger documents that were not on file inside the system. Those not filed included the typed notes and transcripts of Kissinger's telephone conversations, his diaries, and the backchannel communications that Kissinger wanted to keep private even from Nixon. Many of the backchannel documents, it should be noted, dealing with such subjects as the SALT negotiations and the secret Vietnam peace talks, were left on file, at least in part, with Davis inside the White House.

Kissinger realized quickly that his effectiveness in controlling the bureaucracy would depend on how well he stifled the flow of information. Early in 1969, Halperin recalls, Laird informed the White House that he could accept a pending treaty barring the installation of nuclear weapons on the seabed—one of the administration's first arms control issues—if five relatively minor modifications were made. "Henry decided to see Gerard Smith and sell him on the changes as if they were his changes." It was an obvious attempt to demonstrate his bureaucratic clout to the new director of the Arms Control and Disarmament Agency. "As they began going through the proposed changes item by item," Halperin says, "Smith said at one point, 'I see you have the Laird paper.' " Kissinger was mortified, but managed to joke in telling his staff about it later.

"The key point in this," Halperin says, "is that Henry didn't understand the way the system worked: that everything was passed around; that people didn't like to conduct foreign policy as if it was a conspiracy." Laird had naturally given Smith a list of his proposed changes at the same time he sent them to the White House. "This is the way government works. No one likes surprises. But Henry didn't understand this in the beginning and later it led him to cut everybody out of everything. The lesson learned was to do it all in the White House, because everybody in the bureaucracy passes things along."

For all his sniping at Laird, the most consistent target for Kissinger was William Rogers. Morris recalls that Kissinger and Haig would repeatedly speculate about Rogers' relationship with Nixon. "Most of this was done to deprecate the general lack of 'manliness' of Rogers' communications" to Nixon about the EC-121 incident and the plans to escalate the Vietnam War. "Henry felt that there was something between Rogers and Nixon that he could never equal—some critical tie that would enable Rogers to get to see Nixon at a key time and say, 'Fire Henry,' and Nixon would. Henry would always say, 'He's got something on him.' "

Kissinger's anxiety about Rogers' friendship with the President was heightened by the fact that the Secretary of State and his wife were among the very few administration officials invited to dinner in the private quarters of the White House. There were not really many such evenings, but they were evenings of agony for Kissinger, as one close aide describes them. Kissinger, who was never invited to the family quarters in his first years in the White House, would pace back and forth in his office on the nights that Rogers was upstairs, not leaving until the Secret Service reported that the guests had gone. On those few occasions when Kissinger did not immediately agree with the President on a foreign policy issue, the aide recalls, Nixon would use Kissinger's anxiety to force acquiescence. "I guess I'll bring Bill Rogers in on this," was all the President had to say.

Another personal aide says that Kissinger repeatedly submitted memoranda to the President compiling the alleged sins of Rogers in the State Department. He would telephone the President later, saying that he "couldn't take it any longer," and threaten to resign if things weren't changed. Nixon would join in the game and placate his national security adviser by promising to talk to Rogers and straighten it out.

Occasionally the two officials became locked into petty battles. Late in 1969, for example, Kissinger and Rogers had a dispute over who was first with the idea of publishing an end-of-the-year report to the public on foreign policy. Lake, Morris, and Winston Lord were writing a comprehensive report for Kissinger when, as Lake remembers it, "suddenly this huge document—some 400 pages—comes over from State. There was stunned disbelief that they had done it." Rogers, in turn, was not notified of the Kissinger effort until he was out of the country on an official visit to Africa.

Indeed, Rogers seemed always to get the bad news while he was away from Washington. Richard Pederson, the State Department Counsel and one of Rogers' most trusted aides, recalls that he and the Secretary of State spent hours one night in the secure code room of the United States Embassy in Addis Ababa, Ethiopia, reading the text of the Kissinger report as it was filed, in code, page by page from the State Department. "The White House blanketed everything we were doing," Pederson recalled. "Rogers was very unhappy with it."

The next step was a meeting of proxies in Key Biscayne. Lake and Morris represented the NSC, and two of Rogers' aides represented the State Department. William Safire, the White House speech writer, also participated. Lake recalls "one of the main arguments was not over substance, but over how many times Henry's and Rogers' name would appear as heads of committees in the second chapter of the report." Safire helped to negotiate the dispute and was also involved in the editing of the combined reports.*

Kissinger intrigued not only against Cabinet members but also against his own staff, among them Helmut Sonnenfeldt. One aide thought Kissinger was convinced that his old friend Sonnenfeldt was a double agent—although, the aide says, it was never clear for whom Kissinger thought he was spying. Kissinger repeatedly routed parts of classified documents to Sonnenfeldt, and let it be known to others on the staff that some materials were being kept away from him.

Nixon might rant and rave about real or imagined enemies, but Kissinger went a step further. Once, during a high-level meeting on the SALT negotiations, Kissinger humiliated Sonnenfeldt before half a dozen of his peers among the government's experts on the Soviet Union. As one participant recalls the incident, Sonnenfeldt had come to the meeting wearing a back brace—the result, Sonnenfeldt explained, of tension and overwork. At one point, a paper clip on Kissinger's desk fell to the floor, perhaps accidentally, and Sonnenfeldt bent over and picked it up. A few moments later, the clip fell again, and again Sonnenfeldt laboriously reached over to retrieve it. Some of the participants noticed the interplay—with trepidation. When the clip fell for a third time, it was clear to everyone that Kissinger had deliberately pushed it off his desk.

* In his 1975 book about the Nixon Administration, *Before the Fall,* Safire described the rivalry over the two papers this way: ". . . [W]hen State officials saw the Kissinger-NSC 40,000-word white paper, they decided to join their own effort to this quality product. . . ."

Sonnenfeldt picked it up. "Everybody looked at Kissinger and he said, 'Some of you may wonder what Sonnenfeldt does here and now you know.' Everyone laughed sort of nervously, but it was not done in good fellowship. If anybody else had done it, it might have been funny, but given Sonnenfeldt's reputation as Henry's hatchet man, it was humiliating," the participant felt. "The important point is that Henry did understand what people thought of Sonnenfeldt. It was terribly embarrassing."

Another factor that undoubtedly militated against Sonnenfeldt was his repeated insistence on having direct access to Nixon. Donald R. Lesh, a Foreign Service Soviet specialist who came to the NSC as Sonnenfeldt's assistant, recalls that as a senior adviser to Kissinger Sonnenfeldt considered himself a senior adviser to the President. Late one afternoon in the spring of 1969, Eagleburger privately summoned Lesh over to the White House Situation Room. Following Eagleburger's instructions, Lesh did not tell Sonnenfeldt where he was going but simply pretended to be leaving for home. Once in the White House, he was literally locked into the Situation Room with a recently arrived note from the Soviet Union and a typewriter. Kissinger wanted him to assess the note and prepare a secret analysis. Sonnenfeldt was not to be told. And he was not.*

There was also discernible malice in Kissinger's day-to-day badinage with Haldeman and Ehrlichman. His aides never saw Kissinger lose his temper in the face of rudeness from the two men, but he made others pay—and Haig was one of his prime targets. Lynn recalls that Kissinger would often work Haig over, saying, for instance, "Al, how many times do I have to tell you things? Why didn't this get done?" Haig "would stand there with his jaw muscles twitching, saying nothing, in the classic military manner."

Haig learned the lessons of the Nixon White House fast. He was deferential to Kissinger in his presence, Morris recalls. "He stood to Henry as Henry stood to Nixon. But behind Henry's back, Haig called him pussy-whipped and cock-crazy. He would always say that Henry's got his mind in his pants—talk about him beating off" in the privacy of his office.† Like many others on the

---

* Despite the constant competition, Sonnenfeldt and Kissinger shared many values: Both were refugees from Nazi Germany and both were virulently anti-Communist. Both were also inveterate social climbers. Sonnenfeldt was never able to get close to Nixon, and a number of National Security Council aides recall with pleasure Sonnenfeldt's distress when Nixon, while on his February 1969 trip to Europe, went up to Sonnenfeldt and, clearly assuming he was a member of an official airport welcoming party, made small talk about the weather "you're having here."

† Morris soon learned that Haig had a double standard on sexual innuendoes in the White House: What was permissible in discussing Henry Kissinger would not do at all when it came to the President. Sometime late in 1969, a group of academics, including a team from Duke University, came to a NSC staff meeting to discuss a new technique in parapsychology, constructing abstract models of the personalities of world leaders. Theoretically, the verbal models—or machines, as the academics called them—could be used to simulate and predict the behavior of, for example, President Gamal Abdel Nasser of Egypt. Some of Nasser's weaknesses, notably for women, could be factored into the model. Lack of relevant data, the scientists explained, prevented them from building certain machines—there was nothing, for instance, on Leonid Brezhnev of the Soviet Union. But they could construct machines for such men as Ian Smith of Rhodesia and Kenneth Kaunda of Zambia. At this point, Morris exclaimed, "Look, it isn't the unpredictability of foreign governments that concerns us as much as it is the unpredictability of American government. If you could build us a Nixon machine, it'd be better." To Morris' surprise, nobody laughed. In fact, no

National Security Council staff, Morris came to dislike and fear Haig. "Al was the ultimate special assistant," he says. "There's a whole culture in the Defense Department and in the White House. The special assistant sits in front of the door and, like the priest telling the villagers what the gods did that day, he'd tell us the gods are venal and woman-crazed. The essence of all this was betrayal."

Haig also complained repeatedly about the President. After Nixon had him promoted from colonel to brigadier general in 1970, Haig described himself to John Court more than once as nothing more than a "gold-star" general, rewarded with verbal praise instead of Army promotions. By late 1972, Haig was nominated for promotion to full four-star general, the highest military rank possible in peacetime.

Lynn recalls that during the days when he was thinking of resigning from Kissinger's staff, Haig would be sent over to buck him up. "Al would work me by telling me seamy stories about Henry and the President," Lynn says. "He had enormous cunning and subtlety. He presented a kind of primitiveness on some of these issues and he mastered Henry. He came to feed a lot of Henry's conservatism." As months went by, Lynn says, he and his colleagues "came to realize that he was dangerous—and he got more dangerous."

Kissinger's reliance on Haig was a constant topic of conversation among the ambitious men in the National Security Council. Sonnenfeldt often theorized to other staff people that Kissinger wanted Haig around to testify in his defense at a war-crimes trial. Sonnenfeldt's thesis was that Kissinger's real fear was of a reaction from the right, and thus Haig was needed to testify to Kissinger's patriotism. When Haig began putting his own covering memoranda on NSC documents going from the staff to Kissinger's office, there was pandemonium, Lynn says. "All of us bitched about that, but Henry wanted Al's views."

By mid-1969, Kissinger and Haig were heavily involved in the wiretapping —and bound forever by what they knew about each other. Both men thought they were being wiretapped too, and Kissinger began having his personal office telephones swept for taps.

It was inevitable that the NSC staff would emulate their superior and begin to leak. It was almost innocent at first, the goal being not to thwart the Nixon-Kissinger policies but to further them. Morris acknowledges that he and Lake "began to leak in a major way late in '69 or '70," to Joe Kraft, the columnist, and to a number of reporters on the *New York Times,* including Hedrick Smith, Anthony Lewis, Peter Grose, Benjamin Welles, and Neil Sheehan, a neighbor of both Lake and William Watts. Morris recalls being in Lake's living room when Lake told a reporter about the Nixon Administration's hard line on Vietnam. "It was done pretty casually," Morris remembers, "although Tony was against the position. Leaking was almost a matter of habit."

---

one said anything at all. A few days later, Haig summoned Morris to his office and asked him to explain why he'd chosen to accuse Nixon in front of a group of nongovernment academics of having a voracious sexual appetite. Morris quickly denied making any such remark, and explained that the only sexual comments had been made about Nasser. As for Nixon's sex life, Morris said, "Al, I think the guy is like a carrot." Haig remained serious, and warned Morris that the remark—whether it had been made or not—could get back to Haldeman and Ehrlichman.

Morris also talked to some *Washington Post* reporters and to Elizabeth Drew, then of the *Atlantic* magazine. Others leaked to columnists, including Evans and Novak. "Were these national security violations?" Morris asks. "I don't think so. Mostly we were planting stuff on stories we were interested in." Other NSC members told reporters about specific decisions taken by specific aides, Morris adds. "Who's doing what to whom." When Haig put a covering memo on one of Sonnenfeldt's studies, shifting its position more closely to that recommended by the Pentagon, Sonnenfeldt promptly leaked the Haig memo to the *New York Times*. "This is the last time that son-of-a-bitch will put a cover memo on my stuff," Sonnenfeldt told Morris.

Eagleburger, who was not only involved with press leaks for Kissinger but had past experience with them as a special assistant to Nicholas de B. Katzenbach when he was Under Secretary of State in the Johnson Administration, knew what was going on. He once warned Morris: "I know you leak like a sieve and be careful." Kissinger also realized that his staff was leaking. "Henry would kid me on things that he didn't worry about," Morris says, "especially if it was favorable to the President. 'I see you've been talking to the press again,' Kissinger would say. He would often kid about James Doyle of the *Washington Star*. 'Well, your friend Doyle didn't get the story right. Next time make sure he's sober.' "*

Morris thinks that despite the leaks, the National Security Council staff "was not as disloyal at our worst as they thought. Most of the staff supported the war." By late 1969, only a handful of the staff had begun to dissent: Morris, Watts, Lake, and, to some extent, Lynn. And even they kept the important secrets secret.

But by then too, the constant bureaucratic intrigue and personal betrayal in the National Security Council were taking their toll. "There was a dawning recognition that this was a frightening place," Lynn recalls. "It was like walking into a room with a bad odor. After a while you get inured. You realized that this is not the way the government should work. I had to do a lot of things out of loyalty to Henry that I preferred not to do—the secrecy, the confinement of activities to certain people, the centralization of power. Henry used to kid me a lot. He used to say, 'You've got too much integrity.' "

Lynn, the Pentagon "Whiz Kid" who came into the Nixon-Kissinger White House with as much ambition as anyone, resigned from the National Security Council staff in 1970. So did William Watts, the young aide from the Rockefeller campaign. "I came down really full of idealism," he says. "It was a very exciting thing; an extraordinary chance. Starting on day two, it was a process of steady disillusionment and enormous unhappiness."

---

* Doyle, who later served as a press aide to the Watergate Special Prosecution Force and as chief political correspondent for *Newsweek* magazine, is in fact a very light drinker.

10

VIETNAM: PLANNING FOR GÖTTERDÄMMERUNG

BY THE EARLY SUMMER of 1969, Nixon and Kissinger had reached agreement in secret on a Götterdämmerung solution to the Vietnam War: North Vietnam would be threatened with a "savage, decisive blow"—a phrase Kissinger now used openly and repeatedly in meetings with the NSC staff that summer and fall—if it did not begin serious negotiations in Paris. There was tough war talk in the White House; Haldeman, Colson, and Robert F. Ellsworth, Nixon's Ambassador to the North Atlantic Treaty Alliance, were convinced that the President would stop at nothing to force Hanoi to sue for peace. Its refusal to accept the Nixon-Kissinger offer of mutual withdrawal as a starting point for serious negotiations had both baffled and enraged the President. Despite the continuing secret B-52 raids on Cambodia, the military was floundering in Vietnam. Frustrated by the lack of any sign that the war was slowing down, the antiwar movement was again becoming active, and Nixon's concern was that he could become a victim of Vietnam, as Lyndon Johnson had. Unless *something* was done, there would be no second term.

The administration's desperation was kept from the press, in large measure because of Kissinger's continued mastery of the media. But there were many public clues. Three times in his May 14 speech, his first on the war, the President had specifically barred total unilateral withdrawal. "We have also ruled out either a one-sided withdrawal from Vietnam," he said, "or the acceptance in Paris of terms that would amount to a disguised American retreat." On June 8, the President and Kissinger flew to Midway Island to meet with President Nguyen Van Thieu. There, Thieu reluctantly assented to the Vietnamization program, an immediate political boost for Nixon. One Nixon-Thieu meeting was interrupted after less than two hours, Kissinger wrote in his memoirs, to enable the President to announce the unilateral withdrawal of 25,000 American GIs in time for the morning papers' deadlines. The withdrawal, to be the first of many, Nixon said, would take place by the end of August. To offset that loss, there would be additional training and aid for the South Vietnamese Army to enable them to become more effective—the basic goal of Laird's Vietnamization policy.

"Nixon was jubilant," Kissinger wrote. "He considered the announcement a political triumph . . . [and] a public relations coup. . . . He thought it would buy him the time necessary for developing his strategy." Kissinger thought he knew better: Not only did the unilateral withdrawals vitiate the administration's negotiating goal of mutual withdrawal, but the new policy, Kissinger believed, "was likely to become irreversible. Henceforth, we would be in a race between the decline in our combat capabilities and the improvement of the South Vietnamese forces—a race whose outcome was at best uncertain."

Nixon's jubilation was, at least for the short term, more realistic than Kissinger's pessimism, which was undoubtedly based in part on the fact that Vietnamization was Laird's policy and not his. Nixon understood all too well what the public seemed slow to perceive in those early months—that there was a world of difference between reducing an army and removing it. The gradual reduction of American forces gave the administration a smokescreen for its real policy of coercion. Nixon, with Kissinger's help, seemed that summer and fall to be talking tough in public but also moving, with the Vietnamization program, to end the American commitment.

"Watch what we do and not what we say," John Mitchell had urged, in a widely quoted comment on administration policy. It was disingenuous advice. The President had also outlined his real beliefs in his May 14 speech: "If we simply abandoned our effort in Vietnam, the cause of peace might not survive the damage that would be done to other nations' confidence in our reliability."

But the contradiction, pointed out in Kissinger's memoirs, between the Vietnamization policy of unilateral withdrawal and the declared negotiating goal of mutual withdrawal was not the most pressing problem that summer. The immediate issue was how to respond to Hanoi's decision to ignore the May peace proposal. Hanoi had rejected the carrot of mutual withdrawal, and the administration, to Nixon's and Kissinger's consternation, was beginning to be criticized for not doing more. The next step was to turn the ratchet, to convince Hanoi's leaders that the "madman" in the White House was capable of anything. As always for Nixon, the chance to exhibit "toughness" was welcome; he would show his critics in Congress and on college campuses. Kissinger was with his President all the way: The only solution he saw for what he would call in his memoirs "The Agony of Vietnam" was to force Hanoi to its knees.

Americans as well as Vietnamese were continuing to die by the thousands in Vietnam, and the White House, hoping to avoid a widespread resurgence of the antiwar movement, set a new goal: to buy enough time for the threats to reach Hanoi and the "madman theory" to succeed. In May, Kissinger had met with a small group of Quakers—a few of the hundreds of demonstrators who staged a well-publicized day's vigil outside the White House—and appealed for patience. He promised substantial progress in Vietnam within "three months," one of the Quakers told a reporter.

Antiwar students, not surprisingly, had from the first expressed doubts about the real intent of Nixon's policy—whatever it was. In June, several hundred students at Brown University silently stood up and turned their backs as Kissinger was awarded an honorary degree during graduation ceremonies. It was the last time while he was in the White House that he accepted an honorary degree at commencement exercises. That summer, Kissinger bitterly criticized both student dissenters and conscientious objectors in a *Look* magazine interview: "Conscientious objection must be reserved for only the great moral issues, and Vietnam is not of this magnitude."

Ignored by the North Vietnamese, angered by the students, and painfully aware of the basic flaws in the administration's negotiating policies, Kissinger became increasingly enthusiastic about Nixon's demands for increased violence in North Vietnam. On July 15, Nixon wrote to Ho Chi Minh renewing his offer to negotiate an end to the war but proposing no new peace terms. The letter was hand carried to Hanoi by a Kissinger acquaintance, Jean Sainteny, a French diplomat who had served in Hanoi. Nixon reported in his memoirs that Sainteny was given an additional message, not in writing; he was to tell Ho Chi Minh that "unless some serious breakthrough had been achieved" by November 1, "I would regretfully find myself obliged to have recourse 'to measures of great consequences and force.' "* By the time he wrote the letter, Nixon said, he and Kissinger had decided to "go for broke" and "attempt to end the war one way or the other—either by negotiated agreement or by an increased use of force." He and Kissinger spent many hours discussing the new policy, and agreed on the deadline of November 1—by coincidence the first anniversary of the Johnson Administration's bombing halt—for the ultimatum to North Vietnam. The threat became known to its planners in the NSC as the November ultimatum.

Kissinger, working through Haig and a Navy captain assigned to the military liaison office in the National Security Council, commissioned top-secret studies for the proposed escalation in the North. Code named "Duck Hook," they were completed on July 20 by the Office of the Chief of Naval Operations without Melvin Laird's knowledge.†

Kissinger and Haig now had an extensive war plan. It called for the massive bombing of Hanoi, Haiphong, and other key areas in North Vietnam; the mining of harbors and rivers; the bombing of the dike system; a ground invasion of North Vietnam; the destruction—possibly with nuclear devices—of the main north-south passes along the Ho Chi Minh Trail; and the bombing of North Vietnam's main railroad links with China. There was a separate, even more secret study dealing with the implications of using tactical nuclear weapons on the rail lines, the main funnel for supplies from the Soviet Union as well as China. In all, twenty-nine major targets in North Vietnam were targeted for destruction in a series of air attacks planned to last four days and be renewed, if necessary, until Hanoi capitulated.

* Ho Chi Minh responded bluntly in a letter dated August 25. Peace in Vietnam would not come, he told Nixon, until the United States stopped "the war of aggression" and withdrew its troops, leaving the Vietnamese to settle the remaining political issue among themselves, "without foreign influence." Nixon considered the letter "a cold rebuff." On September 3, Ho Chi Minh died.

† The military liaison office had been set up during the Johnson Administration to insure a smooth flow of documents between the White House and the Pentagon. Kissinger insisted, over Laird's objections, that the office continue to function in the Nixon era. Laird correctly assumed that Kissinger would use the liaison unit to bypass Laird's office. At the time of the November ultimatum, the unit was directed by Captain Rembrandt C. Robinson, an ambitious Navy officer who worked with Haig to keep Kissinger's backchannel machinations secret from Laird. Admiral Moorer, who was then still Chief of Naval Operations, permitted his staff to work on the Duck Hook papers without informing Laird. Captain Robinson, who shared Haig's hardline views on the Vietnam War, ended up doing exactly what Laird had assumed would be done—deflecting the flow of Kissinger material instead of facilitating it. The Duck Hook documents were made available to me, in part, under the Freedom of Information Act, and they set forth some astonishing reasoning to justify the proposed assault on North Vietnam. Discussing the legality of mining Haiphong Harbor, the CNO papers noted: "The former simple dichotomy between state of peace and state of war no longer has legal or political validity. . . . Acts in self-defense are lawful under international law. Therefore, mining of Haiphong Harbor and its approaches, as described in this plan, is considered to be a lawful exercise of South Vietnam's right of self-defense against the aggression of North Vietnam."

As this secret planning continued, the administration publicly talked of moderation and cautious pushes toward peace. On June 19, shortly after Nixon's Midway announcement of American troop withdrawals from Vietnam, the President told a news conference that he expected to "beat" former Secretary of Defense Clark Clifford's proposal—published that month in *Foreign Affairs* —that 100,000 troops be pulled out of South Vietnam by the end of the year. On July 25, five days after he received the full plan to savage North Vietnam, he enunciated a new, peace-seeking U.S. doctrine for Asia. Fittingly enough, he spoke of this during a talk with American reporters in Guam, where he had gone to watch the splashdown of the American astronauts who were the first men on the moon. This statement, which made worldwide headlines as a new "Nixon Doctrine," declared that the United States would no longer assume the primary responsibility of defense for its allies around the world. America would honor its commitments, Nixon said, but it "must avoid the kind of policy that will make countries in Asia so dependent on us that we are dragged into conflicts such as the one that we have in Vietnam."*

In mid-August, Laird announced a change in the military mission of the United States troops in South Vietnam. Their objective was no longer to "defeat" the North Vietnamese and force them to return to North Vietnam; now the American troops were to focus on providing maximum assistance to the South Vietnamese Army in an effort to strengthen its ability to repel a North Vietnamese attack.†

On September 16, Nixon announced that 35,000 more American troops would be withdrawn from Vietnam by the end of the year, reducing the overall number there to fewer than 500,000. "The time has come to end this war," Nixon said in a statement recorded for radio and television broadcast. "The time for meaningful negotiations has . . . arrived."

The contradiction was growing between Nixon's increasing reliance in public on troop withdrawals and his private plans for escalation of the war—a goal unknown to the public, the press, the Congress, and most people working for his presidency. By late summer, Kissinger, far from being immersed in intensive planning for peace, had become heavily involved in the mechanics of war. He was picking targets for the B-52 strikes on Cambodia.

Colonel Sitton, the Joint Chiefs of Staff expert on B-52 missions, recalls that as Kissinger's involvement deepened, he began routinely overruling Sitton's office in its targeting recommendations for the bombings. When the military men presented a proposed bombing list, Kissinger would redesign the missions, shifting a dozen planes, perhaps, from one area to another, and altering the timing of the bombing runs. "Not only was Henry carefully screening the raids," Sitton says, "he was reading the raw intelligence"—the detailed post-

* The Nixon Doctrine followed to a remarkable, if coincidental, degree a set of principles outlined by Morton Halperin in a 1968 article published in the *Journal of International Affairs*, a Columbia University publication. Halperin had given a copy to a Nixon aide during the presidential campaign, at the time the Nixon camp was seeking to hire him as a foreign policy adviser.

† The always unpredictable Laird announced the change in orders unilaterally. Pursley recalls that around August 4 or 5, Laird sent Nixon and Kissinger a memorandum at the California White House in San Clemente, saying that the mission had been changed and if there was no objection by August 15, the new orders would go into effect. Somehow, Pursley said, the Laird note was overlooked and Kissinger did not learn of the change, which had been discussed and approved in earlier meetings in Washington, until it was made public. Of course, "Kissinger exploded." But it was too late.

strike reports and bomb damage assessment photographs. By August, the secret bombings, known as "Menu," were averaging more than ten missions a day, and Kissinger seemed to enjoy playing bombardier.* Sitton recalls one constant Kissinger directive: that the secret missions avoid civilian casualties and thus, it was hoped, a public protest from the Sihanouk government. Such public exposure might bring international protest that would require cancellation of the flights, which totaled 376 in August. It would certainly strengthen the antiwar movement at home.

In public, Kissinger continued to shine as the main spokesman for what he and Nixon chose to portray as the administration's policy for ending the war. There were constant press briefings as, to Nixon's immense satisfaction, Kissinger managed almost single-handedly to prevent senior members of the Washington press corps from signing on with the antiwar movement. There were some close calls, but the White House always seemed able to rally support. In early October, for example, six Vietnam experts from the Rand Corporation, among them Daniel Ellsberg, publicly broke with the administration in a joint letter published in the *Washington Post*. Their letter protested Washington's continued ties to the Nguyen Van Thieu regime, whose interest, they said, "is to perpetuate its status and power." They urged the administration to set a date for total withdrawal and an end to participation in the war within a year, and to stick to it—or face a never-ending war. The letter received scant attention in the press, and provoked a rebuke from Joseph Kraft. ". . . [M]ore than ever," he wrote, "there is an obligation on those of us with doubts about the government policy not to suspend our disbelief but to be careful, selective and discriminating in criticism." Henry Kissinger couldn't have put it better.

Kissinger also played an important role as a mediator with Congress, holding private meetings with senators and representatives in an effort to gain time. The legislators seemed almost guileless in their willingness to believe him. Years later, Kissinger told Donald Riegle that the Nixon Administration had "made a mistake in not trying to make a deal with the 'sincere' doves in 1969, asking them for a three-year moratorium on public comment about the war. That was his one major regret," Riegle wrote. Although as a White House adviser Kissinger repeatedly invoked executive privilege in refusing to testify formally before congressional committees, he kept in touch with Senator Fulbright of the Foreign Relations Committee. "Kissinger interested him," Seth Tillman, a former Fulbright aide, recalls. "He entertained the hell out of Fulbright, who found him articulate and plausible. Almost from the first time they had dealings, Fulbright was impressed with Henry's mind. He would just marvel at the eloquence of Henry—particularly when he agreed with what Henry said." Bryce Harlow, who remained in charge of White House liaison with Congress, recalls bringing Kissinger in to meet with Fulbright and other mem-

---

* The first B-52 mission, in March 1969, was code named Operation Breakfast—a reference to the South Vietnamese-Cambodian border area that was bombed. As the bombing became institutionalized, other target areas inside Cambodia were given equally macabre code names—dinner, dessert, snack, supper, and lunch. For obvious reasons, the overall program became known as the Menu bombing. None of the other code names for covert military activities in Southeast Asia was linked to meals or food. The clandestine B-52 bombing in Laos was code named Good Look, and the secret tactical air operations inside Cambodia were known as Patio and Freedom Deal.

bers of the Foreign Relations Committee in times of stress. "We did it time and time again. It was always funny. All these Senate doves would come over and Henry would sit down and they'd be ready to take him to camp. Within fifteen minutes at every one of these meetings, Henry was conducting a seminar. They'd be sitting there with their mouths open. Six weeks later, we'd have the same thing all over again."

But Kissinger's influence was not unlimited. Eleven antiwar resolutions were introduced in the House and Senate during one three-week period in the early fall, including a bill offered by Senator Charles Goodell, the liberal Republican from New York, that would bar the appropriation of funds for American troops in South Vietnam after December 1, 1970. These bills had no chance of passage, but they reflected growing disillusionment with the Nixon strategies. By fall, the nation was in turmoil, as it had been in the last years of the Johnson Administration. Campus antiwar dissent reached a high pitch, with demonstrations and riots. Sam Brown and David Mixner, who had worked in the antiwar presidential campaign of Senator Eugene J. McCarthy of Minnesota, announced plans for a series of Vietnam Moratoriums, mass demonstrations in cities around the country on the fifteenth of each month, beginning in October, until the war was over.

The battle lines were drawn and Kissinger knew where he stood: with the President. "Very few, if any, of the protesters ever appealed to Hanoi for even a little flexibility or were ready to grant that just conceivably their own government might be sincere," he wrote petulantly in his memoirs. "There was no civility or grace from the antiwar leaders; they mercilessly persecuted those they regarded as culpable." Kissinger did not speculate about how much more uncivil the students and congressional antiwar leaders would have been that fall if they had known what was being planned in the White House.

The direct warnings began in August.

From Guam, Nixon made several brief state visits in Asia, including a day's stopover in South Vietnam. On August 2, he arrived in Bucharest, Romania, en route home. In his talk with President Nicolae Ceauşescu, Nixon wrote in his memoirs, he conveyed a threat to Hanoi: "I said, 'We cannot indefinitely continue to have two hundred deaths a week in Vietnam and no progress in Paris. On November 1 this year—one year after the halt of the bombing, and after the withdrawal of some of the troops and several reasonable offers for peaceful negotiations—if there is no progress, we must re-evaluate our policy.' "

Nixon's use of Ceauşescu as a conduit was shrewd. He was an independent strongman who had carefully cultivated relations with China while avoiding any serious disputes with the Soviet Union. Romania also had excellent relations with North Vietnam. Any presidential ultimatum delivered in Bucharest was assured of being heard around the world.

Two days later, Kissinger held the first of what would be a four-year series of intermittent secret meetings with the North Vietnamese in Paris. There were no major new approaches on either side, but Kissinger warned, as Nixon wrote, that "if by November 1 no major progress has been made toward a solution, we will be compelled—with great reluctance—to take measures of the greatest consequence."*

In late September, with Hanoi not responding, Kissinger and Nixon collaborated on some theatrics in an effort to demonstrate to Ambassador Dobrynin that the threats were serious. By prearrangement, Nixon telephoned Kissinger while he was in a meeting with Dobrynin. The two men talked for a few minutes, and when Kissinger hung up, he said to Dobrynin, "The President has told me in that call that as far as Vietnam is concerned, the train has just left the station and is now headed down the track." What Dobrynin thought of the playlet is not known, but in the White House, the use of extreme force was growing more plausible.

Sometime in October, Nixon and Kissinger decided to send a direct military signal to the Soviet Union and its allies. For the first time since the Cuban missile crisis of 1962, the Strategic Air Command was ordered to place its nuclear-armed B-52 aircraft on "combat ready status"—a full alert. The aircraft were pulled off their routine training and surveillance duties and placed in take-off position on runways across the United States, fully armed, fueled, ready to fly attack missions anywhere in the world. No public announcement was made of the special alert, which originated in orders issued by Haig, representing Kissinger and the President, to Colonel Sitton. The alert amounted to a secret between the White House and the Soviet Union, whose military and political leaders were bound to realize that the United States had gone, without announcement and for no obvious reason, to the most advanced alert status possible, Def Con 1. "The guy on the other side saw what looked like a Def Con 1, but it wasn't announced," Sitton said. "They saw something that would make them say, 'What in the hell is he doing?' " Knowing that such an alert by the United States, even if unannounced, could lead to increases in Soviet activity, Sitton privately warned Pentagon officials to increase surveillance of Russian air, sea, and troop activities. "As far as I know," Sitton recalls, "the other guy didn't come up to alert status. All we know is that he did notice, and he wondered what we were doing."

So did Sitton. "I had no idea what we were trying to do, and so I asked Al what else he wanted." Haig's answer was cryptic, Sitton says: "You're doing all you need to do."

The alert lasted an almost unbelievable twenty-nine days without public knowledge.† It finally ended because SAC commanders complained that the

* In his memoirs, Kissinger conceded that such a threat was conveyed to the North Vietnamese in Paris, but added: "No plans yet existed to implement the threat if no progress resulted." By August 4, however, the date of the Paris meeting, the White House had been in possession of the Navy's Duck Hook plans for more than two weeks.

† There was at least one attempt to bring the alert to the attention of the press. The lengthy Def Con terrified Joseph P. Urgo, an Air Force Security Police sergeant on duty at a small Air Force detachment at the Atlantic City airport, who found himself helping to guard four F-106 fighter interceptor aircraft loaded with armed tactical nuclear weapons. Two of the fighters, assigned to Detachment 1 of the 52nd Fighter Group, were kept—with nuclear weapons attached—at the end of the runway. Urgo, who had enlisted in the Air Force in 1966 from his home in northern New Jersey, had recently completed a year-long tour of duty in South Vietnam and was skeptical of the war and of the men in Washington who were keeping it going. The alert triggered a sense of panic. "Nobody was telling us anything. All days off were canceled and it went on and on," Urgo recalls. "Putting those planes out on the runway freaked me out. All my experience told me that they would never take a chance by putting two nuclear-loaded airplanes out in the open"—where they would

aging B-52 fleet would begin to deteriorate if it was not given air time. The aircraft were allowed to phase gradually into their normal flight and training missions and the undeclared alert stuttered to an end, to join the lengthening list of White House secrets.

William Watts came to Washington in August of 1969 eager to start solving the world's problems. The day he came to work as NSC staff secretary, Watts discovered that Kissinger and his senior aides were at the California White House with the President. Two days later, "really full of idealism," Watts flew west to join them. That night, there was a dinner at a fancy restaurant with Kissinger, Haig, and Anthony Lake. The conversation was casual until someone used the phrase "Duck Hook," and Watts asked what it meant. "Everybody then began shushing me," Watts recalls. In the car later, Kissinger briefed him, and "I was stunned. The idea in broad terms was that 'We're going to show them that we're tough.' I felt that it was being discussed in glowing terms."

A few weeks later, on a working trip to the Florida White House, Watts was given a series of blue-covered documents, the Duck Hook papers as prepared by the Navy. On the cover was a drawing of an aircraft soaring away from a carrier, and inside were the plans for the escalation, replete with reconnaissance photographs of potential targets in North Vietnam. There were estimates of expected civilian casualties for each target, and Watts particularly remembers one busy central railroad station in Hanoi that was targeted with an expected loss of only four civilians. Later he expressed some doubts to Kissinger: "These are awfully high stakes; we've got to think about it." A day or so later, he again raised questions, asking Kissinger rhetorically, "How can you possibly say you're going to bomb a railroad station and just have four civilian casualties?"

Kissinger dismissed Watts's queries. "He trusted me," Watts explains, "but looked upon me as intellectually soft."

Watts was included when, sometime in late August or early September, Kissinger assembled a small working staff to analyze the Duck Hook attacks. Captain Robinson of the military liaison office was brought in, as were Haig and Lieutenant Colonel William J. Lemnitzer, assigned from the Army to the National Security Council. Only a few civilians were involved—Watts, Lake, Winston Lord, Peter Rodman, Sonnenfeldt, Morris, and, later, Laurence Lynn.*

---

be more vulnerable to sabotage. The other nuclear-armed planes remained secreted in hangars. "Obviously we were in some sort of a real situation," Urgo adds. "I kept scanning the newspapers but I couldn't find anything—no world situation to go along with this. One night I telephoned a wire service desk in New York, got some guy on the phone, and told him, 'There is something going on. We're on nuclear alert!' The guy was sleepy. I asked if there was anything—ships moving, etc.— to justify it. He said no. We went on and on and on and he didn't pursue it. He didn't even ask my name." Urgo could not recall whether he telephoned the Associated Press or United Press International. After being honorably discharged from the Air Force in 1970, Urgo, now a New York restaurant worker, became active in Vietnam Veterans Against the War.

* In early September, Morton Halperin attended his last staff meeting and formally left the National Security Council, knowing nothing specifically of the Duck Hook planning but suspecting the worst. He knew that Dobrynin had been warned of Vietnam escalations before the May 14 speech and he also knew that the sanctuaries in Cambodia had been bombed. That fall, he had

Morris recalls being summoned to Kissinger's office and told, "Look, for the moment I want you to put aside your African concerns. I'm forming a little group from certain people on the staff whom I trust to deal with a very, very sensitive matter." Morris assured Kissinger that he had no problems working on Vietnam and keeping it confidential. At the time he still believed that Nixon and Kissinger were actively seeking a negotiated settlement to end the war. Kissinger gave him a low-keyed explanation of Duck Hook, as Morris remembers it: "This is to be a special group on Vietnam; the war is not going well. You're here for a variety of reasons. Sonnenfeldt is here to look at the Soviet reaction, but I want most of you here because I want you to give fresh advice and I want you to devote a fresh perspective toward it. My view is that the bureaucracy is constitutionally unable to come up with a fresh initiative on the war. If there is to be a negotiated settlement, if the war is to end, I am convinced that I have to do it. I must take the President along with me and we must in turn carry the Congress and the American people."

Kissinger, said Morris, then gave the staff a pep talk: "I want this group to examine objectively a number of options with regard to the war and the first task will be the most difficult of all. We've had a series of secret talks with the North Vietnamese in Paris. We've been very forthcoming; we've attempted to make concessions which have been unrequited and I refuse to believe that a little fourth-rate power like North Vietnam does not have a breaking point. The Johnson Administration could never come to grips with this problem. We intend to come to grips. It shall be the assignment of this group to examine the option of a savage, decisive blow against North Vietnam. You start without any preconceptions at all. You are to sit down and map out what would be a savage blow."

Kissinger ordered his special staff to compile its findings in a large notebook and authorized Morris to coordinate everyone's research. Morris was also to draft a presidential speech announcing the escalation and explaining why it was necessary.

At one point, someone asked about the possible use of nuclear weapons. As Morris recalls it, Kissinger's response was: "It is the policy of this administration not to use nuclear weapons and we shall not, so these options exclude that one thing. But you are not to exclude the possibility of a nuclear device being used for purposes of a blockade in the pass to China if that seems to be the only way to close the pass." Morris thought Kissinger was referring to the railroad between North Vietnam and China.* Later he was shown nuclear target folders describing the predicted results of low-yield nuclear air bursts over at least two sites in North Vietnam.

---

soberly predicted to Daniel Ellsberg that, as Ellsberg recalls, "This administration will not go into the elections of 1972 without having mined Haiphong." Halperin had been able to perceive what the public was not to know—that Nixon and Kissinger did not want to end the war but to win it.

* Relevant portions of the Navy's Duck Hook papers are still classified by the Pentagon, but one type of nuclear device that may have been under consideration would not have caused an explosion but simply contaminated a specific area with radioactivity. Such devices were discussed at various times during the Vietnam War as an effective method of creating an enclave, or to seal off an area such as the demilitarized zone between North and South Vietnam to prevent North Vietnamese infiltration. In later interviews Kissinger's aides recalled no evidence that the use of a nuclear device was ever seriously considered by Nixon and Kissinger during the planning for Duck Hook. The aides also acknowledged that they were not aware of Nixon's "madman theory," as expounded by the President to Haldeman.

"Savage was a word that was used again and again . . . a savage unremitting blow on North Vietnam to bring them around," Morris says. "That was the whole point."

Morris did not know about the Cambodian bombings or Kissinger's threats to Dobrynin. It did not occur to him then that the "savage blow" was not only the whole point but the whole strategy.

Over the next few weeks Morris, Watts, and Lake began to forge a bond of dissent. For the first time, the young trio was directly involved in the war planning, and, Morris recalls, there was much that they did not like. "I argued to Tony and Bill that you could not politically sustain a repeated number of blows in domestic terms; the whole strategy was predicated on a savage, decisive blow and bringing North Vietnam to its knees. That just wasn't reasonable to expect unless one had prefaced it by a much more elaborate and probing negotiation. In fact, there had been no serious negotiations, only a series of ambiguous meetings on general principles."

On October 13, Watts wrote Kissinger a top-secret memorandum warning that the plan for November could provoke widespread domestic violence. He declared that America's "black and ghetto population" would perceive it as a sign that the government was unwilling to take strong leadership at home to solve domestic problems, but was prepared to move forcefully outside. "The resultant feeling of disappointment and rage could be hard to contain," Watts wrote. The rioters would be joined by students and other youths. Even antiwar intellectuals and concerned citizens would support such protests, he predicted, as would many of the major newspapers. "The nation could be thrown into internal physical turmoil. Should this happen, the Administration would have to be prepared to accept the consequences," Watts said. "Widespread mobilization of the National Guard could become inevitable, and use of U.S. Army units . . . could also ensue. The Administration would probably be faced with handling domestic dissension as brutally as it administered the November plan." Perhaps afraid that he sounded overwrought, Watts went on to remind his boss that he had spent four years working on domestic issues at the Ford Foundation and with Nelson Rockefeller. He was doing all he could to give Henry Kissinger pause.*

As his staff labored at contingency planning for escalation in November, Kissinger redoubled his efforts to convince the media and Congress that a new peace initiative was in the offing. His immediate goal was to defuse the first of the Vietnam Moratorium rallies on October 15. The Washington rally alone seemed sure to attract hundreds of thousands. By early October, as if on cue, there were repeated rumors in the press of a pending breakthrough in Vietnam. *Newsweek,* in a cover story entitled "Five Ways Out of Vietnam," quoted a "high official" in Washington as declaring that Nixon had flatly ruled out any attempt to seek victory in the Vietnam War. "Escalation of any kind is out,"

---

* Watts's memorandum proved prophetic the following spring when, after the Cambodian invasion, Ohio National Guardsmen fired upon and killed four demonstrators at Kent State University. The national outcry over Cambodia came after only one phase of the many-faceted November ultimatum was put into action.

the official was quoted as saying. "Forget it. . . . If that were the alternative to defeat, I am convinced that the President would choose defeat."

If journalists and other citizens were fooled, Kissinger's immediate staff was not. On October 21, six days after 250,000 Americans marched in Washington to protest the war, Lake and Morris sent Kissinger a long memorandum arguing that Vietnamization was doomed and ultimately would become unilateral withdrawal. Instead, they said, the Nixon Administration should give in on the basic sticking point in the talks and offer a "new caretaker government in Saigon, acceptable to both sides," to oversee a new election in the South. The Communists must be assured a major role in the transitional government.*

Knowing that their proposal would be vigorously opposed in Saigon, they included a tough option: "We would have to study carefully how to present the *fait accompli,* and fuzz the question of who initiated the bargain. . . . We must be prepared to exert means of imposing the settlement over Saigon's opposition. The stakes would warrant steps we have not contemplated since 1963." The allusion was to the assassination of South Vietnam President Ngo Dinh Diem in 1963, which Morris says he and Lake believed had American support: "I told Tony that we have to make it plain to Henry that we have to be willing to knock off Thieu." If Kissinger had any objection to such talk, he did not mention it.

Another NSC staff paper may have had more effect on postponement of the full Duck Hook plan. Laurence Lynn, the staff's senior systems analyst, did a study in these weeks which showed that air raids over the North would lead to heavy B-52 bomber casualties without seriously diminishing Hanoi's capacity to continue the war in the South. He also predicted that carpet bombing of the capital would lead to many civilian deaths and a reinforcement of the political will of the people. He was convinced that Kissinger was against the November option. "I vividly remember having a great time," he recalls. "Henry was encouraging me to write the meanest memo I could. As much as I could tell, at that particular point he didn't want that operation." †

If Kissinger's aides disagreed about where he stood on Duck Hook, the men around the President were convinced that he was very much for it; in fact, they believed that nuclear weapons might be used. Charles Colson remembers a late summer conversation with NATO Ambassador Robert Ellsworth, whose chief aide was now Lawrence Eagleburger. Eagleburger still maintained close ties with Kissinger. "One night," Colson recalls, "while sipping Scotch, Bob said, 'We'll be out of Vietnam before the year is out. But the Old Man is going to have to drop the bomb. He'll drop the bomb before the year is out and that will be the end of the war.' " When Colson joined the White House staff in

---

* The two aides showed their awareness of Nixon's and Kissinger's need for tough talk by coupling their proposal for a concession in Saigon with a recommendation that the Soviet Union be warned that "We are concerned. We are therefore dangerous. The Russians should see this as an authentic last grasp at a political solution, with the product of rejection [being] a U.S. humiliation carrying incalculable risks." In any event, their proposal was doomed because it hinged on mutual withdrawal from South Vietnam under international supervision, a concession that Hanoi would not make.

† Lynn also acknowledges that it was very difficult to know just what Kissinger really wanted at any point. "Henry could be egging Nixon on on one hand and trying to stop him in other channels." Often, Kissinger "did not want to be the one" to directly urge the President not to take action.

1970, he asked Haldeman about it, and "Haldeman told me that Kissinger had lobbied for nuclear options in the spring and fall of 1969."

Was Kissinger really prepared to go that far? Or was all the talk, as many of Kissinger's aides and colleagues later insisted, another method of ingratiating himself with the President? There is evidence that Kissinger took the nuclear option one step further that fall, without informing even those trusted aides who were involved in the Duck Hook planning. Two scientists who were known for their discretion and had participated in many studies for the Johnson Administration, including studies of the effectiveness of the bombing of North Vietnam, were asked to comment on the Duck Hook nuclear target folders. Both scientists were distressed at the nuclear option. "I knew that Henry was involved in the planning and that he wanted it," one of them says. "The implications went way beyond local tactical considerations. I was worried about bringing in the Chinese." Though communicating about such matters was not easy, they decided they must reach Kissinger somehow. After due thought, they approached Paul M. Doty, Jr., a leading Harvard biochemist who was a friend of Kissinger, and urged him to discourage the planning. A second approach was made to Haldeman, an old acquaintance of one of the scientists. Haldeman said he was against the option, the scientist recalls, "on the simple grounds of election politics." Using nuclear weapons in the Vietnam War would not help elect Richard Nixon in 1972.

In late September, as he recalled in his memoirs, Nixon decided to do some further signaling to the North Vietnamese himself, a chore he usually left to Kissinger. He summoned a group of Republican senators and deliberately let slip a part of the November plan—he was considering a blockade of Haiphong Harbor and an invasion of North Vietnam. A few days afterward, a report on his planning appeared in the Evans and Novak column. "I wanted this rumor to attract some attention in Hanoi," Nixon wrote. "Although I never knew for sure that it did, I do know that it attracted the attention of Mel Laird . . . and Bill Rogers." Laird and Rogers immediately made known their objections to such escalation, and their view was no surprise to Nixon and Kissinger.

The opposition that mattered was elsewhere. Sometime in mid-October the President realized that he had badly misjudged the strength of the antiwar movement. In his memoirs, he cited October 14 as the day "I knew for sure that my ultimatum [to Hanoi] had failed . . ." On that day, he wrote, Kissinger informed him that Radio Hanoi had broadcast a letter of encouragement to the American peace movement from Pham Van Dong, the Premier of North Vietnam. Vice President Agnew was immediately sent to the White House press room to denounce North Vietnamese interference in domestic affairs, but the media, wrote Nixon, did not share his outrage. Agnew's appearance was seen as a last-minute attempt by the White House to discredit the Vietnam Moratorium, whose army of protesters were flooding into Washington.

"I had to decide what to do about the ultimatum," Nixon wrote. "I knew that unless I had some indisputably good reason for not carrying out my threat of using increased force when the ultimatum expired on November 1, the Communists would become contemptuous of us and even more difficult to deal with. I knew, however, that after all the protests and the Moratorium, American public opinion would be seriously divided by any military escalation of the war."

With two weeks to go, Nixon backed down. There would be no escalation of the war on November 1.

He did not, however, tell his aides at the time, and the White House staff still considered escalation a strong possibility. Nixon had scheduled a major speech about Vietnam for November 3, and on October 16, the day after the Moratorium, Dwight Chapin, the President's appointments secretary, sent Haldeman a memorandum earnestly detailing how the speech might blunt the impact of the Moratorium's next rally, on November 15: "Key dates are now November 3 and November 15. If the President should determine that the war has to be escalated and it is announced November 3, unless the stage is properly set, the action will only fuel the November 15 movement. (If the President de-escalates the war on November 3, then the action can be built upon in order to head off November 15.)"*

Those Americans who marched in Washington on October 15 to protest the war had no idea of their impact; they were protesting the policies already adopted by the Nixon Administration and not those under consideration. Nixon came out of the crisis convinced that the protesters had forced him to back down. The protesters thought the Moratorium had been largely in vain.

Nixon was candid about the Moratorium's effect on him. A group of antiwar students had successfully foiled his "madman" strategy. In his memoirs, he portrayed himself as fatalistic; he would have to temporize in his speech on November 3; it could not be a war speech. On the night of the Moratorium, he began making preliminary notes and scrawled the following advice: "don't get rattled—don't waver—don't react." In his view, there was much "irony" in the result "of this protest for peace. It had, I believed, destroyed whatever small possibility may still have existed of ending the war in 1969."

Kissinger, in his book, gave the antiwar demonstrators no such significance. "I knew that Nixon was planning to take no action on November 1. . . . On his world trip he dropped less than subtle hints that his patience was running out and that if no progress had been made in Paris on November 1, he would take strong action. So far as I could tell, Nixon had only the vaguest idea of

* The Chapin memorandum, reprinted in *An American Life,* Jeb Stuart Magruder's 1974 autobiography, provided more evidence of Nixon's obsession with "p.r." Chapin urged that on November 15, the day of the second Vietnam Moratorium, Nixon should attend a college football game, to show that he was a "strong, confident" President who would not be "detoured" in his Vietnam policy by antiwar demonstrators. Nixon *was* officially reported to have watched an Ohio State football game on television that afternoon, as thousands demonstrated outside the White House. The extent of the panic inside the White House during the October and November Moratoriums did not become fully known until William Gulley, a former Marine who worked as director of the White House Military Office, published his memoirs in 1980. At Nixon's request, three hundred Army troops from the airborne training facility at Fort Bragg, N. C., were flown to Washington and hidden in the corridors of the White House and the Executive Office Building. The soldiers were armed with rifles and light machine guns. A detachment of Marines at Camp Lejeune, S. C., was also put on alert, and military aircraft were ordered to stand by to rush those troops to Washington if needed. "The Administration tried to play the demonstrations down," Gulley wrote, "but they were taken very seriously. . . . Unbeknownst to the people, the military was ready to move." In addition to the federal troops, Nixon also ordered that a special twenty-four-hour crisis control center be set up in an underground bomb shelter under the East Wing of the White House. There, amid telephone banks and television monitors, John Ehrlichman and his staff maintained overall control of the operation and continuously reported to the President. "Whenever we got word of a demonstration where violence might be expected," Gulley wrote, "the center was manned around the clock." Federal troops were also put on alert in May 1970, at the time of the large Washington demonstrations protesting the Cambodian invasion and the slayings at Kent State.

what he had in mind." There certainly was no prior staff planning, Kissinger wrote.

Morris and his Duck Hook planning colleagues would have disagreed. By September 27, Morris had completed a second draft of a presidential speech that would announce the escalation. "Our course is clear," Morris wrote. "Continued bloodshed on the battlefield and Hanoi's rigidity at the peace table have taught us there is but one other choice . . . to take action to prove to Hanoi that we mean to have an honorable peace in Vietnam. Today, pursuant to my order . . ." The phrase "pursuant to my order" had by now become an insider's joke among the increasingly bitter dissidents on Kissinger's staff.

Watts, Lake, and Morris were all assigned in the last days of October to prepare further drafts for Nixon's November speech on Vietnam. Watts took a break late one evening and walked outside the White House. There was yet another demonstration against the Vietnam War going on—hundreds of protesters marching in front of the White House carrying candles. Watts strolled to the gate to get a closer look and saw his wife and children go by, each holding a flickering candle. "I felt like throwing up," Watts says. "There they are demonstrating against me, and here I am inside writing a speech."

Nixon ignored the earlier tough-sounding NSC drafts and wrote much of the November speech himself. He seemingly took the hard line, warning Hanoi, "I shall not hesitate to take strong and effective action . . ." Nixon did not, however, specify what kind of escalation he had in mind. Instead, the President, in the nationally televised speech from his Oval Office, once again equated loyalty and morality with support for his war policies. He warned that "this first defeat in our Nation's history would result in a collapse of confidence in American leadership." His solution, he said, which was to try to "win America's peace," was not the "easy way. It is the right way . . . [A]ny hope the world has for the survival of peace and freedom will be determined by whether the American people have the moral stamina and the courage to meet the challenge of free world leadership." Nixon vowed to continue the war until Hanoi accepted his version of a "just peace." He appealed, in what would emerge as the most widely quoted line of the speech, for the support of "you, the great silent majority of my fellow Americans. . . ." American withdrawal, he said, would lead to "massacres" by the Communists in South Vietnam, and a reign based on slave-labor camps like those he claimed had been set up in North Vietnam after Ho Chi Minh took over in 1954.

A Gallup poll showed that 77 percent of those Americans who heard the "silent majority" speech supported Nixon's stance, with only 6 percent expressing direct opposition. The public reaction, manipulated in part by Haldeman, Colson, and the White House "p.r." contingent, was electric. It was announced that eighty thousand telegrams and letters, overwhelmingly in favor of the tough line, reached the White House within days. America, it seemed, strongly supported a President who sounded aggressive and sure.

Only a few noticed a curious ambivalence in the speech. Anthony Lewis, the *New York Times* columnist, sensed frustration in it. "Four times he [Nixon] warned against 'defeat,' twice he spoke of 'disaster,' and twice of 'humiliation,' " Lewis wrote in a commentary published November 8. Lewis, of course, had no way of knowing that Nixon was not, by his own standards, giving a tough speech. That speech had been drafted by Morris and discarded.

Nixon, in his memoirs, referred to the silent majority speech as one that changed "the course of history. . . . Now, for a time at least, the enemy could no longer count on dissent in America to give them the victory they could not win on the battlefield." Kissinger, Nixon wrote, also "felt that if we backed off, the Communists would become totally convinced that they could control our foreign policy through public opinion." In his memoirs, Kissinger praised Nixon's speech: "Against the recommendations of all of his cabinet he drew the line and made no concessions to the protesters. I agreed with his course." In an earlier interview, for the Kalbs' biography, Kissinger claimed that the speech had "turned public opinion around completely and the North Vietnamese softened their line." Like Lewis, the Kalbs had no knowledge of the November option and thus could not understand that it was Nixon and Kissinger, not the North Vietnamese, who had been forced to soften their line.

Over the next few weeks, Nixon and Kissinger moved brilliantly against their immediate enemy—the antiwar movement. Dwight Chapin's memorandum of October 16 had outlined a "game plan" that the White House put into effect with great success. Chapin urged that the congressmen who supported the October 15 Moratorium be warned to stay away from the November rally. "A full-fledged drive should be put against the media. . . . Letters, visits to editorial boards, ads, TV announcements, phone calls," Chapin recommended. "Cold turkey" should be talked to network officials in New York. The message was that the Moratorium leaders were not Democratic liberals who believed in the political system, but hard-core radicals espousing violence and repeating the propaganda of America's Communist enemies. On November 13, Vice President Agnew made a scurrilous—but also very successful—attack on the networks, accusing them of biased and selective reporting. He especially singled out the few television analysts who had commented critically on Nixon's speech. "Is it not fair and relevant," he asked rhetorically, to question the concentration of power "in the hands of a tiny, enclosed fraternity of privileged men, elected by no one and enjoying a monopoly sanctioned and licensed by Government? Perhaps the place to start looking for a credibility gap is not in the offices of the Government in Washington but in the studios of the networks in New York."

As effective as Agnew, though far less visible, was Henry Kissinger. The national security adviser spent dozens of hours before and after the Nixon address explaining to reporters and columnists that the tough speech—which, as he knew, could have been so much tougher—was really a peace speech. Given the language of the Nixon speech, Kissinger's message was audacious: The President was just trying to talk his way out of the saloon. Once again Kissinger was able to shape the thoughts of the country's most influential opinion makers. James Reston dutifully took the Kissinger line in a column of November 9 entitled "What Is the President Up To?": "The guess here is that he is determined to get out of the war, and like de Gaulle in Algeria, is covering his retreat in clouds of brave rhetoric. . . . He has taken the political offensive at home but is withdrawing his troops from Vietnam; and in a war of this kind, what he does is more significant than what he says. . . . Our guess is that the President . . . is acting for peace." A week later, Reston wrote, "The war is winding down in Vietnam, not winding up. . . . What we are arguing about now, in the main, is not so much the direction of policy as the pace of policy."

The White House's public pressure and Kissinger's private lobbying took the steam out of the November Moratorium. The number of demonstrators was large, but the leading congressional liberals did stay away. There was no live network television coverage, although the demonstration was, by any objective standard, a major story. The Moratorium planners had envisioned another massive three-day demonstration in December, but it would fizzle badly. The public seemed to believe that Vietnamization would end the war.

Nixon's speech marked a turning point for Kissinger. He had come around to full acceptance of the President's view that the quickest approach to a settlement in Vietnam—that is, victory—would be to make a seemingly generous offer to the North Vietnamese, "and then," as Nixon put it, "if rejected, to seek to impose it militarily." That approach, which was indeed started with the mutual withdrawal proposal on May 14, had to be suspended, at least temporarily, in November, because of the antiwar movement and the continuing dissent from Rogers and Laird. Further extension of the "madman theory" would have to wait until the White House got public opinion and the Cabinet under tighter control. And the key to that step, Kissinger had come to realize, was Vietnamization. "In the face of the domestic turmoil and the divisions within the Administration I did not fight for my theoretical analysis," he wrote. "I joined the general view that, all things considered, Vietnamization was the best amalgam of our international, military, and domestic imperatives." He might have grave doubts about Vietnamization, doubts that stemmed from his Vietnam experiences in 1965 and 1966, but he was even more fearful about losing his place in the administration. It made him more than willing to, as he wrote, accede to a policy that "I knew . . . would be painful and long."

The men directing the war in Hanoi knew nothing of the detailed planning for the November option; they knew nothing of Kissinger's skepticism about Vietnamization. And yet a captured Vietcong document dated July 1969 revealed their analysis of the Nixon-Kissinger policy to be amazingly accurate.

"Their present plan," said this document, known as COSVN resolution No. 9, "is to *de-Americanize and de-escalate the war step by step, to preserve their manpower and material as they de-escalate, especially to preserve U.S. troops, and to compete with us [in territory and population control] so as they can end the war on a definite strong position.*" The resolution, which in late 1969 was disseminated by the CIA to other intelligence agencies and the press in a 98-page translation, added that the United States would accelerate the pacification program "in order to gain control of the people and territory" and would ultimately seek to "find a political solution [which would allow them] to *end the war while still maintaining neocolonialism in South Viet-Nam to a certain extent and under a certain form; to create a 'neutral' South Viet-Nam whose real nature is pro-American and in which the U.S. lackeys still keep a strong force and hold advantageous positions* [which enable them] *to compete with us economically and politically after the war. . . .*" (The emphasis is in the original.)

COSVN 9 noted that the United States would either seek an early end to the war by agreeing to a North Vietnamese-imposed political settlement, or, if the Communist attacks were "not sufficiently strong," would strive to prolong the war in hopes of gaining a more favorable political solution. "In both these eventualities, especially in the case of a prolonged de-escalation, the Americans may, in certain circumstances, put pressure on us by threatening to broaden the war through the resumption of bombing in North Viet-Nam . . . or the expansion of the war into Laos or Cambodia."

In interviews in Hanoi in 1979, North Vietnamese officials insisted that they had not received any of the "signals" Kissinger and Nixon were sending about the November option. One senior member of the Foreign Ministry said that his government was aware after the death of Ho Chi Minh in August 1969 that "our position will be tough"—hence the language in COSVN 9 warning of future escalations. But no direct threats were ever relayed, he said.

Nguyen Co Thach, Foreign Minister of North Vietnam, who participated in most of the secret peace talks in Paris, also took issue with Kissinger's account of the warning that allegedly was given during the first session on August 4, 1969. "Never has Kissinger threatened us in the secret talks," Thach said. "Because if he threatens us, we would turn our backs. We would stop the talks. They could not threaten us for we knew that they could not stay in Vietnam forever, but Vietnam must stay in Vietnam forever."*

From November on, Nixon and Kissinger fought an increasingly bitter action against the antiwar movement. The FBI and the CIA were ordered to increase their spying on radicals and suspected radicals; the Justice Department initiated sweeping grand jury inquiries to compel dissidents to testify about their colleagues; the draft was replaced by a more equitable lottery system and its director, Lieutenant General Lewis B. Hershey, was promoted and retired; and, by early spring, Nixon had committed himself to the withdrawal of 200,000 more troops from Vietnam.

By then, the policy was beginning to work. Student demonstrations—deprived of one major focus, the inequities of the draft boards and the Selective Service System—began to dwindle. The antiwar movement became more polarized; there were increasing disputes between those willing to disrupt the system and go to jail and the majority, who viewed their participation in protests as symbolic. The administration had managed to convince many of America's liberals that they should not take direct action against the war. The Vietnam Moratorium Committee, which had twice proved its ability to turn out a quarter-million or more people to march against the war, was forced to shut its Washington office in April 1970, a victim of dwindling contributions and apathy. America seemed anxious to believe that withdrawing its troops

* Thach told me that Hanoi was fully aware of the public threats Nixon made in his various speeches and press conferences; the residents of Hanoi practiced bomb-evasion techniques and built shelters throughout the city. Obviously there was fear of the Nixon policies, with his B-52 bombing in Cambodia and elsewhere, but the North Vietnamese consistently refused to admit to such fear. Thach, for example, who had read some of Kissinger's earlier writings, recalled that at one point in the Paris talks he went up to Kissinger and teased him about his views on the strategies of threat bargaining. "It is Kissinger's idea," Thach said, "that it is a good thing to make a false threat that the enemy believes is a true threat. It is a bad thing if we are threatening an enemy with a true threat and the enemy believes it is a false threat. I told Kissinger that 'False or true, we Vietnamese don't mind. There must be a third category—for those who don't care whether the threat is true or false.'"

meant an end to the war, and Nixon and Kissinger did nothing to discourage that belief.

However, though overt protest wound down, quiet dismay over the war was increasing. In mid-November 1969, the American Army massacre of more than 350 South Vietnamese in the hamlet of My Lai became publicly known, and middle America got a glimpse of what its young men were learning in the villages and hamlets of Vietnam. "I gave them a good boy and they sent me back a murderer," the mother of one My Lai participant, a farm worker from rural Indiana, told a journalist.

Nixon was enraged. He ordered the military to spy on Ronald Ridenhour, the former GI who reported the incident first to the Army and then to Congress. One night, Alexander Butterfield recalls, Nixon spent more than two hours complaining about the publicity on My Lai. "It's those dirty rotten Jews from New York who are behind it," he kept saying. Kissinger was among those who soothed the President during this period. Morris recalls seeing a transcript of a conversation in which Kissinger told the President, "All they want to do is make a scapegoat." *

Near the end of the year, Nixon finally found a way to show that he was tough. Lynn remembers a meeting on the federal budget: Ehrlichman was there, along with Robert P. Mayo, director of the Bureau of the Budget, and a not very interested Nixon. Lynn was sitting in for Kissinger. A tedious budget meeting was one of the few occasions when Kissinger would permit an aide to sit in with the President.

The meeting moved along perfunctorily until discussion began on a proposed budget cut for the Provincial Reconnaissance Units in South Vietnam, small American-led assassination teams that theoretically were to target and "neutralize" members of the Vietcong shadow government—the "infrastructure" —living inside the society of the South. The PRUs, under the control of the Central Intelligence Agency, had by 1969 been responsible for thousands of assassinations in South Vietnam. Mayo argued that funds for the program should be cut back. At that point, Lynn recalls, "Nixon went into his reverie . . . that strange reverie. It may have lasted for thirty seconds. 'No,' Nixon said. 'We've got to have more of this. Assassinations. Killings. That's what they're doing [the other side].' " The funds were restored, Lynn says. "Who's going to argue with him?"

---

* On November 13, 1969, I published the first newspaper accounts of the My Lai massacre. During interviews for this book, Robert Houdek, a junior NSC staff member, told me that at the height of the outcry over My Lai he occasionally rode behind me on the morning commuter bus to downtown Washington. He eavesdropped on my conversations, Houdek said, and reported to Haig what he had learned.

11

A GREEK TRAGEDY
AND A CIVIL WAR IN AFRICA

FROM THE BEGINNING of their first year in office, Nixon and Kissinger were consumed with the great issues abroad—in Vietnam, the Soviet Union, and Europe—and the need to consolidate their control of foreign policy at home. The two American leaders had edged close to a dramatic escalation in Vietnam, only to pull back at the last moment in fear of public dissent at home. By the end of that year, Vietnam was entrenched as the main obsession of the men in the White House, whose policy of secret threats and public calls for patriotism was being offset by the turbulence and growing despair at home.

There was little room at the top for concern over what were seen as the lesser issues, such as human rights, and the problems of lesser countries, in Africa and Latin America; these were shunted into bureaucratic limbo. The vaunted Nixon-Kissinger NSC system continued to demand reams of studies and analyses, but by January 1970 the system had decayed into a crisis management unit incapable of dealing effectively and consistently with issues that did not personally interest the President or his national security adviser.

The human rights issue confronted the Nixon Administration most directly in Greece, where a military junta headed by Colonel George Papadopoulos had seized power in April 1967. The Johnson Administration had immediately authorized a partial suspension of the shipment of heavy arms, including aircraft, artillery, and tanks, despite protests from McNamara's Defense Department, which argued that the embargo on American military aid would damage Greece's ability to be a full participant in NATO. Over the next year and a half, the junta moved with increasing brutality to stifle dissent, and detailed reports of torture—many from victims and eyewitnesses—flooded the world. An inquiry by the European Commission on Human Rights produced evidence that torture was being routinely applied to political prisoners at, among other sites, a Greek military police facility less than a block from the American Embassy in Athens—and near a statue of President Harry S Truman, whose "Truman Doctrine" had in 1947 publicly heralded the beginning of the Cold War, America's worldwide effort to contain communism.*

---

* Truman, in an address on March 12, 1947, to a joint session of Congress, sought approval of a grant of $400 million in economic and military aid to help Greece and Turkey fight off what he called the threat of a Communist takeover. The speech marked the formal entry of the United States into the Cold War and set out an immense task for American policy planners: "We cannot allow changes in the status quo by such methods as coercion, or by such subterfuges as political infiltration."

Neither Kissinger nor Nixon mentioned Greece in his memoirs, nor did either seriously discuss the general issue of human rights.* NSC staff members recall that Kissinger viewed Greece geopolitically, in terms of its logistical importance in the worldwide struggle against communism. Greece served as an important strategic base for the Navy's Sixth Fleet, operating in the Mediterranean, and it permitted United States Air Force planes full overflight and landing rights. According to his aides, Kissinger's support for the junta was based on its strong stance against communism. "Henry regarded Greece as being one of those places that was going to embarrass us eventually," one of them recalls. "It was one of those countries where he had a feeling of prejudice —as if, given half a chance, the Greeks would stab us in the back."

Another factor in Kissinger's support was his knowledge that the CIA was among the junta's strongest backers in official Washington, a reflection of the Agency's long-standing dominant role there. The CIA, newly set up in 1947, spent hundreds of millions of dollars in the next three decades directly financing, training, and supplying the Greek intelligence service, KYP. During a trip to Greece in 1956, Kissinger, then a private citizen teaching at Harvard, was greeted by the CIA station chief, John H. Richardson, who arranged details during his stay. A prominent Athens journalist, Elias P. Demetracopoulos, was asked to be the host at a lunch for Kissinger that week; he recalls that Richardson reassured him of Kissinger's "importance." †

Nixon's support for the Greek junta was based on more than geopolitics, as investigators would learn much later. One of the junta's leading supporters was Thomas A. Pappas, a prominent Greek-American businessman with CIA connections who had raised millions of dollars for Republican candidates.

In the early 1960s, Pappas, who maintained homes in Athens and Boston and routinely commuted between them, had become a dominant financial force in Greece by persuading the government to grant him the right to construct a $125-million oil, steel, and chemical complex in partnership with Standard Oil of New Jersey. Pappas also promised to invest heavily in other businesses in Greece, and won favorable government terms for doing so. When the more liberal Center Union Party, headed by George Papandreou, was in power in 1963 and 1964, Pappas was forced to renegotiate downward many of those highly profitable contracts. Three years later the junta began rescinding Pappas' concessions and his business interests rapidly flourished.

Late in the presidential campaign of 1968, there were repeated press allegations that Pappas played a role in delivering campaign contributions from the Greek government to the Nixon forces. On October 31, just five days before the election, the *Boston Globe* reported that "the rumor mills of Boston and

Truman made it clear that American support would be forthcoming even in cases, as in Greece, where political disputes were within a nation and not a clash involving outside forces.

* In a conversation in Washington on May 8, 1975, with Patricio Carvajal, Foreign Minister of the Pinochet government in Chile, Kissinger declared: "I hold the strong view that human rights are not appropriate for discussion in a foreign policy context. I am alone in this. It is not shared by my colleagues in the Department of State or on the Hill." Pinochet's military junta had seized control of Chile in 1973 and still controlled dissent with extreme violence. Kissinger was Secretary of State when the conversation took place, and an official transcript of his remarks was prepared for internal use. The transcript was provided to me.

† Demetracopoulos fled Greece after the military takeover in 1967, went to live in Washington, and became one of the leading opponents of the junta.

Washington" were hinting that Pappas was "the conduit of campaign funds from the Greek junta to the Nixon-Agnew treasury."* No evidence could be found to support the allegation, the *Globe* said. That same day, Lawrence F. O'Brien, chairman of the Democratic National Committee, publicly called on Nixon to explain his relationship with Pappas. O'Brien acted after a series of private meetings that had begun weeks earlier at his Watergate offices with Demetracopoulos, who had turned to the Democrats after hearing from friends in Greece that, as he puts it, "hundreds of thousands of dollars from the Greek KYP, directly subsidized by the CIA, was being laundered through Pappas for the Nixon campaign." O'Brien's carefully hedged statement received little press attention, but left Demetracopoulos a marked man for the Nixon Administration. In July 1971, after testifying publicly against the regime and Pappas before a congressional committee, Demetracopoulos was warned by senior White House aides that he would be deported if he did not stop his activities. Nixon's old friend and political operative, Murray Chotiner, went so far as to tell the Greek exile at a luncheon meeting, Demetracopoulos recalls, to "lay off Pappas. It's not smart politics. You know Tom Pappas is a friend of the President." Nixon was "angry," said Chotiner.†

In 1972, Pappas served as a principal Nixon fund raiser and as a vice president of the finance committee of the Committee to Re-elect the President. It was not until 1976, however, that the House Intelligence Committee was able to confirm Demetracopoulos' allegations against Pappas. It received sworn evidence from Henry J. Tasca, a career Foreign Service officer who had been Nixon's Ambassador to Greece, that in 1968 Pappas had served as a conduit for campaign funds from the Greek government to the Nixon campaign. Tasca's statement was made off the record—at his insistence, according to a committee investigator—and was not published. Tasca died in an automobile accident in 1979, but the author was told by a senior State Department official, then serving abroad as an American ambassador, that he too had learned of Pappas' role as a conduit for campaign funds while dealing with Southern

---

* Agnew, meanwhile, had abruptly changed his view toward the junta. While governor of Maryland—and the highest-placed Greek-American in the United States—he had been steadfast in maintaining a neutral position after the 1967 military takeover, and had promised Elias Demetracopoulos, among others, that he would remain neutral. In late September 1968, when Agnew was Nixon's vice presidential candidate, Demetracopoulos learned that Agnew was being pressured to endorse the junta. A private meeting was quickly arranged, Demetracopoulos recalls, and Agnew insisted that no change was contemplated. A few days later, at a luncheon speech at the National Press Club in Washington, Agnew was asked about the junta and, as Demetracopoulos watched, pulled a two-page prepared statement out of his pocket in which he praised the military leadership for its role in combatting what he referred to as the Communist threat in Greece. The junta, he said, "has not proven itself to be as horrendous a spectre. . . as most people thought it would." The military leadership, he added, "does not wish to control the country absolutely, but only to provide a salutary climate in which a free elective system can take place." Agnew's comments, which at the time amounted to the strongest endorsement of the junta from any American officeholder, came two days before a national plebiscite in Greece on the military government. The junta, which widely disseminated Agnew's comments, won more than 90 percent of the votes cast, in an election that opposition forces debunked as rigged.

† Demetracopoulos subsequently learned from government files acquired under the Freedom of Information Act that Kissinger, while working for Presidents Nixon and Ford, had been—at the least—aware of the White House's persistent attempts to intimidate' him. One such document, dated October 18, 1974, cryptically noted that President Ford's briefing officer had "left the derogatory blind memo as well as the long Kissinger memo on Elias" with Air Force General Brent C. Scowcroft, who was then Kissinger's deputy at the National Security Council.

European affairs. "We were carrying out policy to support 'a Greek bearing gifts,' " the official said.*

The Nixon Administration formally retained the partial embargo on heavy arms shipments to Greece, but by mid-1969 the embargo had evolved into little more than a token of official disapproval. And it had never blocked the shipment of small arms and riot control equipment, which the junta was using to maintain control. Furthermore, the Pentagon, eager for any method of evasion, had begun selling defense matériel to the Greek government and officially describing it as "surplus" goods. Congressional investigators computed later that total delivery of military goods climbed by some $10 million annually after the junta seized power.

Throughout this period, as opposition to the junta mounted in Congress and among the public, Greece was not considered a significant issue inside the National Security Council. "It wasn't high on anybody's agenda," recalls Donald Lesh, who worked on European problems for the NSC. "I can't recall anybody worrying about it," says another NSC aide. Harold H. Saunders, the NSC staff member who was assigned to monitor Greece, among other nations, remembers that "Things had pretty well settled to a pattern [in Greece] by the time the Nixon-Kissinger team came. It doesn't stand out prominently in my mind." Still another aide specifically recalls that Pappas' influence was felt inside the NSC. "He was very close to the junta; one of those counseling us to 'go easy.' " Nobody asked too many questions. "We knew Pappas had a special relationship—access right at the top. One didn't ask on what it was based." This staff member had visited Greece and met with some of the junta while working for Kissinger. Upon his return, he made a point of assuring everyone who was interested how successful the government was: "If you wanted to score points with Henry, the hard line scored well."

Publicly the Nixon Administration continued to insist that the political embargo on military shipments was still in force, and would remain so until democratic reforms were made. Such claims, however, were left to Rogers and Laird. In July 1969, the Secretary of State told the Senate Foreign Relations Committee that the suspension of arms shipments would not be removed "unless the Greek junta made some progress toward more parliamentary government." Laird told the committee the next day, "I want it understood . . . we have a freeze on the aid as far as Greece is concerned, and that freeze is being continued and will be continued until progress is made toward more democratic procedures in the country."

* Nixon's unflinching support for the Greek junta was extensively investigated during the various Watergate inquiries. Although such contributions were not illegal at the time, suspicion centered on the role of Pappas in funneling unreported contributions from the junta to the White House. In a White House tape recording that was transcribed prior to the Watergate coverup trial, Nixon, Haldeman, and Ehrlichman were heard discussing Pappas on April 26, 1973, at a time when they were reconstructing prior conversations in an effort to determine who was guilty of what. Haldeman quoted John Dean, the White House Counsel, as recounting a conversation with John Mitchell about payoff money for the Watergate burglary defendants: "Dean says, 'Did you talk to the Greek?' Mitchell said, 'Yes, I have.' Dean says, 'Is the Greek bearing gifts?' Mitchell said, 'Well, I'm gonna call you tomorrow on that.' " Elsewhere in the conversation, which was first published in the *Washington Post* on May 1, 1977, it was clear that the "Greek bearing gifts" was a reference to Pappas, who eventually testified before the Watergate grand jury and denied contributing any Watergate payoff funds. Haldeman, Mitchell, and Ehrlichman were found guilty of charges that included conspiracy and obstruction of justice and each sentenced to prison terms of twenty months to five years.

In private, Nixon and Kissinger had decided to "tilt" toward the junta, as White House documents make clear. On November 14, 1969, National Security Decision Memorandum No. 34 informed the bureaucracy, in secret, that the White House had decided to suspend the embargo and was looking for a way to do so without creating controversy. Tasca, just appointed Ambassador to Greece, was to play a major role in a five-stage process that would lead to a renewed flow of heavy weapons. First, Tasca was to meet privately with Papadopoulos and inform him that the United States was prepared to resume normal military aid. The Ambassador was to "make clear" that some movement toward democracy "would ease U.S. problems in speeding the release of the suspended equipment." NSDM 34, which was signed by Kissinger, noted at this point: "This linkage is conceived as a means of improving the atmosphere for removing the suspension. . . ." The next paragraphs spelled out the extent of the White House's *fait accompli*. Point three: "The U.S. government, after the President has reviewed Ambassador Tasca's report of the Greek government's response, [is to begin] shipping the suspended items gradually, beginning with the less dramatic items." Point four: "After the President's final *review and approval* [emphasis added], the following public line will be taken with members of the Congress and the press as necessary: Overriding U.S. security interests were the principal factor in the decision to lift the suspension. The U.S. government will continue urging the government to move toward a constitutional situation." Finally, Tasca was ordered to "develop a relationship" with the junta in a way that would permit him to "exercise influence for democratic reform."

Before departing for Athens, Tasca was invited to meet with the President. Like many of Nixon's ambassadorial appointees, he, while serving as Ambassador to Morocco, had befriended the former Vice President during one of his overseas trips in the 1960s. Nixon made his policy explicit during the meeting, telling Tasca, as later reported in *The Wrong Horse,* by Laurence Stern of the *Washington Post:* "We've got to restore military aid; as far as the *rest* is concerned, make it look as good as you can."

The continuing uproar over the junta's human rights violations apparently forced Nixon and Kissinger to delay putting NSDM 34 into effect in late 1969. In June 1970, however, a new NSDM was issued, No. 67, marked "Exclusively Eyes Only," setting a target date of September 1 for the resumption of shipments. Nixon and Kissinger still wanted their "linkage": Tasca was instructed to inform Papadopoulos that "it is anticipated that there will be further specific steps which we can cite as further evidence of progress toward full constitutional government." The Greek Prime Minister was to be assured, NSDM 67 added, that the Nixon Administration would take "at face value and accept without reservation" any such assurances. The arms embargo was formally lifted on September 22, 1970, with little protest within the bureaucracy. The White House found an easy way to handle the story: Word was leaked a few days earlier to the *New York Times,* which reported that the renewed flow of arms was linked to an ongoing national security crisis in the Middle East. The decision to lift the embargo, the *Times* wrote, had apparently been taken just a week before, at the White House level.

Nixon's and Kissinger's ability to conceal their attitude toward Greece, despite the attention focused on the White House, was not atypical. Policy toward Africa quickly became one of contempt and neglect, even on the one African issue that truly intrigued Nixon, the civil war between the Federal Republic of Nigeria and its secessionist state, Biafra.

The Nigerian war had begun in May 1967, when Biafra declared its independence. The rebellion attracted strong support from both the left and the right in the United States. The Biafran Ibos were Christian, mainly Roman Catholic, in a war against Moslems. They were also seen as blacks battling for self-determination against far superior forces. Senators Edward M. Kennedy, the Massachusetts liberal, and Strom Thurmond, the South Carolina conservative, became strong supporters of the Biafran regime, and both urged relief organizations and the State Department to supply desperately needed funds. The war for independence went badly for Biafra from its inception; photographs of its starving children, staring with unblinking eyes at the cameras, seemed to fill the magazines and newspapers of the world.

During the 1968 presidential campaign, Richard Nixon spoke out at least twice in support of more relief aid for Biafra, and his wife publicly appeared on the steps of St. Patrick's Cathedral in New York to encourage donations. "This is not the time to stand on ceremony or go through channels or to observe the diplomatic niceties," Nixon said in a public statement. "While America is not the world's policeman, let us at least act as the world's conscience in this matter of life and death for millions. . . ."

The State Department's attitude remained fixed in support of the Nigerian government, at least partly because it was clear from the outset that the Biafrans had no chance of winning. Roger Morris had been frustrated in the Johnson White House at his inability to persuade the administration to increase its aid to Biafra, but there was reason to believe Nixon would change policy. Indeed, during the transition period after the election, Nixon asked Kissinger for a study paper on expanded relief to Biafra; and on January 24, 1969, four days after the inauguration, Biafra was the subject of one of the first National Security Study Memoranda Kissinger ordered. In the early months of his presidency, Morris recalls, Nixon repeatedly told Kissinger that he wanted formal recognition of Biafra, which would have provoked open opposition in the State Department. Yet the policy agreed upon at a February 1969 NSC meeting, at which Nixon presided, called for the United States to maintain official neutrality on the civil war, although continuing to supply relief for the Biafrans.

By May, however, Nixon had changed his mind and decided to recognize Biafra—largely, Morris concluded, to teach the State Department a lesson in authority. "He wants to recognize them," an astonished Kissinger aide told Morris and others after a meeting with Nixon. Morris' account, in *Uncertain Greatness*, his 1977 study of Kissinger's foreign policy, goes on: "Presidential musings on recognition continued through June, apparently sparked by intelligence reports or press summaries. . . . To each statement, Kissinger by his own account gave an unquestioning and sympathetic hearing. He then returned to his office and proceeded as if the conversation had never taken place, ordering his staff to do the same with a knowing smile and a reference to the increasingly common West Basement explanation of periodic behavior upstairs in the Oval Office: 'He's a little crazy, you know.' "

Kissinger, in his own memoirs, speculated that Nixon's support for the Biafrans was not a deeply felt view but a ploy: "I am inclined to believe that Nixon took the contrary view in part because he took no little pleasure in showing some of those who were wont to attack him for his alleged moral defects that they too were capable of expediency on the issue of human rights."

In early July, on a state visit to Washington, Emperor Haile Selassie of Ethiopia discussed the Biafran war with Nixon. Kissinger soon received a presidential directive from Alexander Butterfield, telling Kissinger, as Morris recalls, "I have decided, Henry, that I'm going to mediate the Biafra civil war (Haile Selassie agrees). Get on with it." Why Kissinger chose to obey that directive when he had ignored earlier presidential orders was not made clear to Morris, whom Kissinger told to negotiate secretly with the Foreign Minister of Biafra at the New York apartment of Norman Cousins, editor of the *Saturday Review*. "I'm looking at Henry like he's mad," Morris recalls. "I have no negotiating position; no instructions. Henry is saying, 'Just negotiate something that's sensible.' " Haig, who was in the meeting, slipped Morris a much-appreciated note: "Don't you understand? If you're successful, Kissinger gets the diamond. If not, you get the rocks." Haig winked at Morris as he read the note, and Morris was relieved: "I had an ally. Kissinger's given me an impossible job to do, which clearly Kissinger doesn't understand, because he's dead serious. He sees himself on the podium in Stockholm getting the Nobel Peace Prize. And I'm going up there without instructions and staff." At that point, Morris had only one person helping him handle African affairs, a young White House intern from Ohio State University.

The subsequent negotiations, kept secret from the State Department, were a fiasco. The meeting with the Biafrans at Cousins' apartment was inconclusive, and Morris later needed to clarify a point left unsettled. The Biafran officials, meanwhile, had gone on to Brussels, apparently to meet with NATO officials before returning home. Morris sent a backchannel message to Eagleburger, his former NSC benefactor who was now fully recuperated and reassigned out of the White House as a Foreign Service aide to Ambassador Ellsworth at NATO headquarters in Brussels, asking him to meet secretly with the Biafrans and resolve the issue. The message to Eagleburger, sent through CIA channels, was somehow deflected to the National Security Agency and from there to the State Department. The men at State were furious, not only because the White House seemed to be working against the official United States policy, but also because the department's official position, as cited repeatedly to the Biafrans at the United Nations, was that America would have nothing to do with any mediation efforts. "It's a little difficult to do these things when you're working against your government," as Morris puts it.

Elliot Richardson then paid Kissinger a visit and formally protested the White House intervention, carefully accusing only Morris of exceeding his authority. Kissinger expressed his regrets over Morris' "insubordination" and promised to reprimand him. Morris remembers the issue as "a sideshow par excellence. Henry called me in and told me to write a nice little note to Richardson. And then he asked me how it was going and reminded me that Nixon wanted it settled."

Later that summer, Dr. Jean Mayer, a leading expert on food supply and nutrition who taught at Harvard, visited his former colleague in the White House. Dr. Mayer had gone to Biafra early in 1969 to assess conditions there for a United Nations relief agency, and had been deeply shocked. "My estimate was that one and one-half million were dying from starvation," Dr. Mayer says. "I saw villages where no one over seven years of age was left." The scientist spent months without success trying to instill some urgency into the various U.S.-sponsored relief programs. In June, he was appointed a special consultant to President Nixon and assigned responsibility for planning a White House Conference on Food, Nutrition and Health to be held in December. Still haunted by the carnage he had witnessed in Biafra, Mayer took his crusade into the White House with him. He finally obtained an appointment with Kissinger, and it was one of Kissinger's more convincing performances.

"His attitude was very understandable," Dr. Mayer says. "His point was that he was concerned but he was the national security adviser to the President and it was difficult in his job not to overlap too much with the State Department. He was constantly resented by the State Department, he said, and so he found that the only behavior to avoid this was to limit himself strictly to those matters affecting the national security of the United States and only to deal where the actual security of the United States was threatened." Dr. Mayer left Kissinger's office convinced that the national security adviser shared his concern but was powerless to take on the State Department.

In fact, Kissinger was at an impasse with State over Biafra, but only because of his effort to negotiate behind the department's back. Kissinger risked a breach with Richardson, his most competent State Department ally, if he continued to meddle in Biafra; clearly, the possible starvation of hundreds of thousands of Biafrans mattered less than maintaining good relations, if only on the surface, with the few people in the bureaucracy whom he could rely on. Dr. Mayer, with his tales of horror and death in Africa, was mollified and sent away, and the Nigerian civil war disappeared as a significant issue in Washington.

By late fall, Biafran leaders were bitter over the Nixon Administration's refusal to do more than express sympathy and support for their position. "We are especially resentful of the ambivalent pretenses the United States makes, that it is trying to help us," Sir Louis Mbanefo, Biafra's Chief Justice, told a *Washington Post* reporter. "If we are condemned to die, all right, we will die. But at least let the world, and the United States, be honest about it." White House interest in the Nigerian civil war was not renewed until January 10, 1970, when word came that the collapse of the Biafran forces and the secessionist movement was imminent. The Biafrans surrendered twenty-four hours later.

Roger Morris quickly reminded his superiors of what Dr. Mayer had learned nearly a year before—that the lives of a huge number of Biafrans were in the balance. By January 20, Morris had forwarded to Kissinger an authoritative study, prepared by physicians from the U.S. Public Health Service, which predicted that more than one million Biafrans would, as Morris summarized the document, "be dying over the next 2-3 weeks unless there is a massive injection of high-protein food." In this secret memorandum, Morris was also careful to note that the American doctors "contend that in the Nigerian case, as in *every* recorded famine in modern history, initial observer reports have vastly underestimated the magnitude of the problem."

The major opponent of any large-scale relief effort was still the State Department, which, in its continuing attempts to avoid a rupture of relations with Nigeria, had been minimizing the peril. On January 14, for example, the *New York Times* quoted a State Department official as explaining that the Nixon Administration "was anxious to counter an impression there is a serious danger of starvation" in Biafra.

In Morris' view, Kissinger fully understood and sympathized with the gravity of the situation in those days of crisis; many of Morris' memoranda and documents were forwarded to the President. On January 23, in one of the secret memoranda Morris drafted for presentation to Nixon, Kissinger told the President about the American doctors' report indicating that more than a million Biafran lives were in imminent jeopardy, and strongly recommended that Nixon take action. He noted that he had discussed the issue with Senator Kennedy, Nixon's bête noire, who had urged that the United States pressure the Nigerian government to change its policy and permit an airlift directly into Biafra. "Firm Presidential action now to press the Nigerians does risk offending them. They could turn closer to the Soviets," Kissinger wrote, but on the other hand, "Mass deaths . . . will hardly make for good relations between the U.S. and Nigeria." And there was "also an important point to be made in terms of protecting you on this issue domestically. Acting strongly now to follow up our offers of assistance would probably gain support from many elements not usually in your camp. In this respect, Biafran relief would be similar to your decision on chemical and biological warfare. . . . But if mass starvation does take place, and we cannot point to a record of strong action, you will be vulnerable to criticism. . . . Elements who say this Administration is efficient but unfeeling might then charge we were neither in the case of Biafra."

Five days later, as the world's newspapers and television began reporting that conditions inside Biafra were worse than previously believed, Kissinger wrote Nixon again: Fatalities inside Biafra could reach 85 percent in some localities, and there had been a sharp increase in the roadside death rate (significant because only the strongest were able to walk). It was a picture, Kissinger wrote, "of deep need, Nigerian incompetence and potential mass deaths. . . . Our evidence is now overwhelming that the food and logistical situation in the enclave is desperate."

By then, it had been seventeen days since the fall of Biafra and only 200 tons of food had been airlifted into the area. In other memoranda, Morris was citing expert estimates indicating that at least 20,000 tons of food were needed immediately to prevent mass deaths.

January 28 was also the day the Nigerians did permit two American cargo planes to land in the capital, Lagos, and begin unloading supplies for the 300-mile drive to Biafran areas where the need was most acute. But the impact of the Nigerian-supervised relief program did not become noticeable to journalists on the scene until the middle of February. The number of Biafran children and noncombatants who starved to death in the five weeks between the end of the secessionist war and the beginning of an effective relief program is now known to far exceed the official estimate of 20,000.

What had gone wrong?

In his memoirs, Kissinger discussed the Nigerian civil war only briefly, dryly noting that "For some reason Biafra had become an issue in the American Presidential campaign of 1968." He and Nixon were aware of studies showing that more than a million Biafran lives were threatened with starvation, Kissinger said, and both supported Roger Morris in his efforts to get supplies directly to Biafra. But, he added, opposition from the British, who supported Nigeria, and "State Department procrastination soon made the issue moot. We never succeeded in establishing an independent relief program. . . . A curtain of silence descended."

Kissinger's and Nixon's unwillingness to take on the State Department—even with hundreds of thousands of lives possibly in the balance—frustrated and further disillusioned Morris. He later wrote that "Throughout this sequence of events, Kissinger and Nixon were suddenly transformed: the responsible, powerful men who had so forcefully seized control of other policies for the good or ill now remained distracted, cynically detached onlookers."

Nixon, preoccupied as usual with political issues, went into hibernation in the last half of January, working for long stretches in his hideaway office in the Executive Office Building on his first State of the Union address. After one meeting with Elliot Richardson and other State Department officials, all of whom downplayed the estimates of Biafran starvation, Nixon telephoned Kissinger and, Morris recalls, said simply of his State Department, "They're going to let them starve, aren't they, Henry?" Kissinger's answer, according to Morris, was "Yes." He and Nixon then began discussing some of the foreign policy passages in the State of the Union speech.

And of course there was theater at the NSC, as Kissinger was deciding not to do battle with Elliot Richardson over Biafra. Kissinger telephoned Senator Kennedy to say he was doing all that could be done, and Roger Morris recalls overhearing his boss say, "You remember, Ted, that I worked for your brother."

Dr. Mayer was also further soothed. His work on the White House Conference successfully concluded, he had been rewarded with a meeting with the President after the rebellion collapsed. Again he urged direct relief efforts, and Nixon authorized him to meet with Kissinger and Richardson. "The minute Henry was officially charged by the President to do something," Dr. Mayer recalls, "he was no longer resented by the State Department. He was extraordinarily effective. Once Kissinger got involved, things started moving."

Morris later wrote that Kissinger, after one meeting with Richardson and Dr. Mayer, took his former Harvard colleague aside and whispered, "You see what I'm up against. The State Department is incompetent." Dr. Mayer was left with the desired impression, Morris wrote, "that Kissinger was a lonely force for compassion against the lethargy and client-myopia of the rest of the government."

Years later, Morris concluded that Kissinger had, in fact, behaved "the worst" of all the senior officials in the Nixon Administration in not doing everything possible to obtain immediate relief in the first days after Biafra fell. "Henry understood the issues perfectly and"—unlike the State Department—

"had no bureaucratic rationale of protecting an interest. There really is a streak of compassion in him, yet everything is expendable. He had no rational reason for letting those kids starve; he was just afraid to alienate Richardson because he and Richardson had other fish to fry. And with the President, Henry just didn't want to bother him. He'd look soft."

Nothing and nobody in Africa was worth that.

12

SALT:
A MIRV MISTAKE

HENRY KISSINGER'S most formidable success in self-education as national security adviser was with SALT, the strategic arms limitations talks with the Soviet Union. It was a vital issue—an attempt to put a ceiling on the nuclear arms race between the two superpowers—and Kissinger, for all his writings on nuclear strategy, came into the White House knowing little about the complex technical issues of negotiating and verifying a nuclear arms ban.

Because of his ignorance, perhaps, and his awareness that SALT would be a dominant issue in the Nixon Administration, Kissinger began carefully. To those arms control experts in and out of the administration who favored sweeping limitations on nuclear arms, Kissinger portrayed himself as a faithful compatriot battling the hawks in the Pentagon and the Oval Office. To those in the Pentagon and the armed forces who worried about Soviet advances in nuclear arms, Kissinger professed himself to be even more concerned than they over the possibility of Soviet "cheating" on any arms control agreement.

His staff watched with awe as Kissinger, in a dramatic show of brilliance and determination, spent hundreds of hours in the first months of the administration mastering the technicalities of arms control negotiations. By mid-1969, he seemed to be the best-informed and most forceful administration voice on SALT and related issues. Laird, Rogers, and even Gerard Smith, Nixon's chief SALT negotiator, were left in his wake. Some NSC staff members came to understand that Kissinger's struggle to dominate the SALT process was as much a part of his drive to control the bureaucracy as a matter of intrinsic belief in the necessity of arms control. Morton Halperin, who in the early months was a leading adviser and educator on SALT, remembers Kissinger's basic apprehension about those who advocated arms control: "Arms controllers were interested in an agreement for its own sake. They'd get an agreement on SALT to get an agreement." Halperin says that Kissinger viewed the negotiations as a means to an end, a vehicle for extracting far-reaching concessions from the Soviets in other areas, such as Vietnam. "That's why he had to control the process—to make sure that things didn't get proposed that he didn't want."

Halperin became convinced that the White House permitted the formal SALT talks in Helsinki to begin as early as they did—in November of 1969—only because of Soviet pressure. "We were confronted with it, and it would

147

have been politically disastrous to Nixon and personally harmful to Henry not to go ahead with it." Over the next three years, Kissinger maintained more than rigid control over the delegation; he and Nixon negotiated behind its back and systematically kept from their SALT negotiators any insight into what the White House really wanted to accomplish. As with the other White House secrets, all outsiders—even those entrusted with negotiations on the fate of the world's arms race—were excluded.

At the outset, Nixon and Kissinger faced a pending arms control matter left over from the Johnson Administration. In the last months of his presidency, Johnson had been the driving force behind the signing by the United States and other countries of a treaty to halt the spread of nuclear weapons, formally known as the Treaty of the Non-Proliferation of Nuclear Weapons. Senate ratification of the treaty was stalled by the Soviet invasion of Czechoslovakia on August 21, 1968, and, at President-elect Nixon's request, was further delayed after the election.

On February 5, 1969, Nixon eased the fears of disarmament proponents by formally requesting the Senate to ratify the nonproliferation treaty. At a news conference the next day, he was asked whether he would urge France and West Germany—known to have reservations about it—to support the treaty. The President left the impression that he would indeed do what he could: "I will make it clear that I believe that ratification of the treaty by all governments, nuclear and nonnuclear, is in the interest of peace and in the interest of reducing the possibility of nuclear proliferation. . . . I think in the end, most of our friends in Western Europe will follow our lead."

In fact, as some NSC staff people knew, Nixon and Kissinger were privately hostile to the treaty and, the day before the news conference, had issued National Security Decision Memorandum No. 6, in effect disavowing all that the President would tell the world the next day. The NSDM stated: "The President directed that, associated with the decision to proceed with the United States' ratification of the Non-Proliferation Treaty, there should be no efforts by the United States government to pressure other nations, particularly the Federal Government of Germany, to follow suit. The government, in its public posture, should reflect a tone of optimism that other countries will sign or ratify, while clearly disassociating itself from any plan to bring pressure on these countries to sign or ratify."

"It was a major change in American policy from the Johnson Administration," says Halperin, who had played a major role in disarmament matters while in the Pentagon under the Democrats. "Nixon and Kissinger didn't believe in the treaty. Henry believed that it was good to spread nuclear weapons around the world." Kissinger's thesis was very pragmatic, as Halperin explains it. He was convinced that most of the major powers would eventually obtain nuclear weapons and the United States could benefit more by helping them in such efforts than by participating in an exercise in morality. Halperin recalls that in private, Kissinger repeatedly remarked to his staff that nations such as Israel and Japan would be better off with nuclear weapons.

The far more important arms control legacy from the Johnson Administration was, of course, SALT. In 1967, President Johnson had sought unsuccessfully to initiate disarmament talks with the Soviet Union about both nations' development of antiballistic missile defense systems (ABMs). In 1968, the Soviets, having invested billions in upgrading and expanding their strategic missile programs, had agreed to discuss offensive and defensive weapons. The August invasion of Czechoslovakia, which came on the eve of the planned announcement of a U.S.-Soviet summit meeting on SALT, made such negotiations politically impossible. After the November elections, Nixon and Kissinger specifically vetoed Lyndon Johnson's desire to hold a postelection summit by making it clear that their administration would not be bound by the results of any such meeting.

The Soviet Union continued to press for SALT, and on Inauguration Day the Soviet Foreign Ministry announced that the country was eager to start disarmament discussions of strategic offensive and defensive weapons systems. "When the Nixon Administration is ready to sit down at the negotiating table," the spokesman said, "we are ready to do so, too."

Nixon and Kissinger responded to the Soviet pressure by trying to extract diplomatic concessions on Vietnam and the Middle East. Asked about the possibility of disarmament talks at his first news conference on January 27, Nixon noted that "There is the proposition which is advanced by some that we should go forward with talks . . . clearly apart from any progress on political settlement." Rejecting that suggestion, he said, "What I want to do is to see to it that we have strategic arms talks in a way and at a time that will promote, if possible, progress on outstanding political problems at the same time." In his memoirs, Kissinger makes clear the real intention of this "linkage": "We would not ignore, as our predecessors had done, the role of the Soviet Union in making the war in Vietnam possible."

Thus within a few days after the inauguration, Nixon and Kissinger had concluded that disarmament talks were less important that their belief that the Soviet Union could control the pace of the war. In itself, such a belief was not corrupt or pernicious—it was simply wrong.

In early April, when Kissinger suggested that Cyrus Vance be sent to Moscow secretly, empowered to link the opening of SALT talks with an overall settlement in Vietnam, Nixon approved the idea and the Soviets ignored it. In his memoirs, Kissinger wrote that he even called in Soviet Ambassador Dobrynin and announced to him that "Nixon was prepared to send a high-level delegation to Moscow . . . to agree *immediately* on principles of strategic arms limitations [emphasis added]." The price, however, was a concurrent meeting in Moscow with a North Vietnamese official empowered to settle the war in Vietnam. Kissinger's account indicates that he and Nixon had no real opposition to immediate SALT talks, if the price was right.

White House refusal to seize the opportunity for arms control talks in early 1969, without any political payoff, would prove to be a tragic blunder that committed the United States and the Soviet Union to what occurred throughout the 1970s: a continuing and accelerating arms race. The ABM system, even then a highly publicized focal point for dissent among the antiwar members of Congress and the public, did not, however, pose a basic threat to nuclear stability among the superpowers, but there was a weapon that did: a complicated offensive missile system known as MIRV—a multiple, independently targeted reentry vehicle.* In essence, a MIRV is a Hydra-headed missile, one that can thrust as many as fourteen nuclear warheads into outer space, where, with the aid of complex electronics, each is capable of reentering the atmosphere and striking a target with almost unbelievable accuracy. To sophisticated arms control planners, MIRV was not just an improved weapons system but a great qualitative leap forward in the ability to wage nuclear war. The United States had begun developing the new missile system in the early 1960s, after Pentagon officials discovered that the number of nuclear targets inside the Soviet Union exceeded the number of warheads that could be deployed without MIRVs.† By August of 1968, the MIRV had undergone its first successful tests. But it had not been deployed as of 1969, and, in the view of many arms control experts, until that step was taken MIRV proliferation could, in theory, be controlled.

Kissinger was informed of all this very quickly by a small group of arms control experts, many of them colleagues from Cambridge, whom he had begun to assemble within weeks after being named national security adviser. The experts gave their advice in secret and kept their peace afterward, as Kissinger surely realized they would.

Kissinger's ad hoc group came to include many of the government's leading consultants on arms control and technical issues, among them Jack P. Ruina and George W. Rathjens, professors at the Massachusetts Institute of Technology; Carl Kaysen, the former NSC official who was director of the Institute of Advanced Studies at Princeton, N.J.; Sidney D. Drell and Wolfgang K. H. Panofsky, professors at the Stanford Linear Accelerator Center at Stanford University; and Richard L. Garwin, a senior research official for the IBM Corporation. All had served as high-level consultants or officials in the Kennedy and Johnson administrations; all held high security clearances.‡ Kissin-

* The ABM system was doomed even in 1969, the victim of repeated expert testimony before Congress by scientists who said that the system, designed to shoot down enemy missiles, simply would not work. In March of 1969, Nixon approved a thinned-down version of ABM, known as the Safeguard system, which theoretically would protect twelve strategically vital areas in the United States from Soviet missiles. The Senate approved the system by one vote on August 6, after a national debate of several months. By 1972, the number of Safeguard sites had been reduced to three, including one to protect the Washington, D.C., area. The SALT I treaty, signed in Moscow in May 1972, reduced the sites to two, and the treaty was amended in 1974 to permit only one site. In 1975, the United States unilaterally gave up the one site that was permitted. In his memoirs, Nixon wrote that he had sought approval for the ABM in 1969 "as a bargaining chip" for SALT negotiations with the Soviet Union. Kissinger, as his memoirs make clear, was in full agreement.

† Throughout the ABM debate in the late 1960s and early 1970s, the public was repeatedly told that the MIRV had been developed in response to the Soviet deployment of the Galosh ABM system around Moscow, a system whose effectiveness later turned out to be severely limited. The fact was, as Laird told the Senate Foreign Relations Committee in 1969, ". . . [W]e started appropriating funds for the deployment of this program [MIRV] prior to the time we knew the Galosh was in being."

‡ Ruina had directed the Pentagon's Advanced Research Projects Agency from 1961 to 1963 and had been a member of the President's Science Advisory Committee since 1963. Rathjens had served, under Ruina, as the chief scientist for ARPA and also worked for the Arms Control and Disarmament Agency. Kaysen had been a deputy special assistant for national security affairs in the Kennedy Administration. Drell had been a consultant to the White House Office of Science and Technology since 1960. Panofsky, director of the High Energy Physics Laboratory at Stanford, had been in the American delegation to disarmament talks in Geneva in 1959, and later a White House consultant in the Office of Science and Technology. Garwin first began consulting for the White House in 1958 and served on the President's Science Advisory Committee through succeeding

ger had attended American Academy of Arts and Sciences meetings and international seminars with some of the scientists before joining the Nixon Administration; he considered several of them good friends.

"It all started with the idea of giving him another perspective," Jack Ruina recalls. "Right after he came into the White House, a group of us from Cambridge went to see him on various issues, mostly on Vietnam. I was there to talk about strategic issues. My message was that there was no independent voice on arms control issues in the White House." Ruina had served with Garwin, Panofsky, and Drell on a highly classified subpanel on strategic issues for the President's Science Advisory Committee during the Johnson Administration; that group was still well informed, he assured Kissinger. Within a few months, Rathjens and Kaysen, who did not belong to PSAC, decided that their Saturday mornings could be better spent, leaving Ruina and his PSAC colleagues in the awkward position of being high-level consultants who were continuing to consult with Kissinger—but not as members of their PSAC subpanel. Kissinger was anxious to avoid even the appearance of relying on the Advisory Committee, which he disdained, and finessed the problem, Ruina recalls, by suggesting that "an outsider"—Paul Doty, the Harvard biochemist who was not then an expert on strategic issues—"come and be chairman of the little group. Henry said, 'Let's just make it like academic friends—just colleagues coming in to talk informally.' That's how the group started," Ruina says. "Doty was the outsider but he quickly came up to speed." Doty was also the only one in the group who was not a Jew.

The group met at least once a month early in 1969, usually over a Saturday morning breakfast in Kissinger's office. Kissinger was invariably late, but he did come, and often brought an aide or two. The Doty group soon realized— as the NSC staff was also realizing—that Kissinger was, as Ruina puts it, an "amazingly" quick learner. Dozens of papers were presented and Kissinger digested them; they included not only MIRV analyses but sometimes brutal attacks on the ABM and its poor chance of success against a Soviet missile attack. Highly classified papers on such topics as America's nuclear targeting capability were also prepared for Kissinger and his staff.

One theme, repeated incessantly in the meetings, was the danger of proceeding with the continued testing and scheduled deployment of MIRV, which the Doty group initially believed would take place sometime in 1971. In early June 1969, Rathjens and Ruina, the MIT colleagues, wrote a paper for Kissinger that cited three major points of jeopardy for the strategic balance: the ABM deployment, the continued growth of the Soviet missile force, and the development of MIRV by the United States and possibly the Soviet Union. Neither the ABM nor the Soviet decision to build up its SS-9 heavy missile fleet was as urgent a matter as MIRV development, the paper argued: "We see no way of precluding deployment of MIRVs by agreement, and of having sufficient confidence to verify compliance [of a MIRV ban], once test programs have proceeded to the point where such systems are ready for deployment. . . ." The two scientists warned that if the MIRV testing, already under way for ten

administrations. Panofsky and Garwin, both physicists, were among the most prominent and outspoken critics of the antiballistic missile defense system in early 1969, basing most of their objections on the premise that it would not fulfill its mission.

months, continued "even for only a few more weeks," the United States might develop the weapon's accuracy to such a point that the Soviet Union could see it as a first-strike threat. And if the United States could accomplish that, so could the Soviet Union; and the United States would then be in the position of having its Minuteman land-missile force—spread out across the Western plains —under threat of an accurate Soviet MIRV attack.*

"For the United States, and probably for the Soviet Union as well, what is really at issue," the paper said, "is the question of whether we will be able to rely on fixed-base ICBMs [intercontinental ballistic missiles] as a significant part of our deterrent in the mid-1970s. . . . This means, at least as far as we can now see, that a decision to go ahead with MIRV tests probably also implies eventual abandonment of Minuteman missiles by the United States." This prediction was made repeatedly by the Doty group in 1969—and rarely has a strategic prediction been so accurate. By the late 1970s, the Carter Administration, faced with a Minuteman force threatened by increasingly accurate Soviet MIRVed missiles, was urging the adoption of the mobile MX missile system, with the 200 missiles constantly shifted on a shuttle system containing more than 4,000 launching points, to avoid exposure to Soviet MIRVs, at a minimum cost of at least $33 billion.†

Ruina and Rathjens recommended that the United States take the unilateral step of stopping MIRV testing, and announce that the moratorium on testing would continue as long as the Soviet Union also stopped its testing of multiple warheads. Kissinger responded to the Ruina-Rathjens proposal three weeks later with a perfunctory note expressing his gratitude. Privately, however, NSC aides recall, he was outraged at the repeated urgings of the Doty group that the Nixon Administration must take unilateral steps to limit the deployment not only of the MIRV but also the ABM.

Adding to his anger, perhaps, was the fact that he knew, as Doty and his

* The Soviet Union, from the early days of the missile race, had emphasized the development of very large intercontinental ballistic missiles with launchers that utilize multiple clusters of engines. Intelligence experts believed the Soviet ICBM force had a larger "throw-weight" than the United States Minuteman missile force because the size of its launchers enabled the weapons to carry larger nuclear warheads with more explosive force. The United States, with its more sophisticated electronics skills, was less concerned with the size of warheads; instead, emphasis was placed on accuracy in delivering the payload. Planners were constantly pitting future American forces against future Soviet forces in war games; as early as the mid-1960s there were consistent findings that the deployment of MIRV missiles would initially give the United States a great advantage in the arms race, but that when both sides reached parity in the number of missiles, the Soviet Union would gain superiority because its missiles were larger and thus could carry more warheads; that is, they would have a greater throw-weight. This finding occurred consistently in internal studies and war games throughout the 1960s and early 1970s.

† The MX continued to bedevil the Reagan Administration, which backed away from the Carter plan after environmentalists and local officials made it clear that the mobile-based system would be a political liability. In October 1981, Reagan announced that he had approved a plan calling for a hundred MX missiles to be deployed by 1988, but there was still a dispute about where to put them. The initial Reagan plan called for thirty-six to be installed in silos previously constructed for the outmoded Titan intercontinental ballistic missiles. That plan was changed in late December 1981, after it was determined that modernization of the Titan silos would be more difficult than anticipated. By early 1982, Defense officials were suggesting that at least the first forty or fifty, and perhaps all of the hundred MX missiles, might end up deployed in existing Minuteman ICBM silos, which would probably be reinforced, or "hardened," to withstand Soviet attack. Reagan endorsed that "dense-pack" proposal in late November 1982, but Congress, during fiscal maneuvering a month later, stripped $998 million from the fiscal 1983 budget in production money for the troubled MX. Reagan then set up an eleven-member outside panel to consider new deployment options.

colleagues did not, that the Nixon Administration had decided by early summer to proceed with the deployment of MIRVs. Kissinger also knew that there were some on his staff who had doubts about that decision. On May 27, Halperin, who had yet to fully discover the extent of his eclipse as a Kissinger aide, caustically discussed MIRVs in a phone conversation with Leslie Gelb, his former Pentagon colleague. According to the FBI transcript, Gelb asked, "What's cooking with the arms talks?"

Mocking Kissinger, Halperin replied, "We're waiting for the propitious international climate."

Gelb: "Is it ever propitious?"

Halperin: "No. The Committee is supposed to meet tomorrow to approve a report which NSC will discuss soon after the President gets back, but the hostility on the NSC staff to it is enormous. I had a meeting with Hal [Sonnenfeldt] and Larry [Lynn] and those guys are convinced and have convinced Henry there is absolutely no strategic rationale for an arms control view."

Gelb: "That's fantastic."

Halperin: "And that we prefer a world in which both sides have MIRVs from . . . a level [in] which neither does."

Gelb: "You've got to be kidding."

Halperin: "No. Henry is telling this to reporters and to Senators—that they will be embarrassed opposing MIRVs because he is going to show that it's silly."

Gelb: "This is really nutty."

After Halperin's fall from grace—which could only have been expedited by such observations—Laurence Lynn became Kissinger's leading expert on the technical aspects of SALT. He shared Kissinger's skepticism about the Doty group members, who "used to come in and pour out their souls." Lynn's recollection is that "they got absolutely zero respect" from Kissinger. "Henry didn't like academics. He came away bitter from Harvard." Lynn recalls that Kissinger considered the Doty group "opportunistic"—that is, secretly hoping to play a major public role in getting a SALT treaty. "The more those scientists would come down and wait for hours for him," Lynn says, "the more contempt he had for them—contempt because they came back." But despite his doubts about the value of their advice, "Henry kept them coming—he kept his lines out. There were some advantages: He'd tell the President he was explaining the administration's policy to them, he was 'softening them up.' " Doty kept up his ties throughout Nixon's first term.*

Lynn said he shared Kissinger's distrust of the scientists' advice about MIRV, primarily because he thought they were underestimating the problems of making sure the Soviet Union would not cheat on a ban by secretly producing and testing the weapons. Kissinger and Nixon considered a MIRV ban virtually impossible to verify.

---

* And he, at least, remained loyal. As late as January 1981, in a paper presented to an international colloquium on disarmament in Paris, Doty was publicly apologizing for Kissinger. "Looking back over the last decade or more," he said, "it now appears that the most important arms control issue was left unattended. . . . This is the failure to control the MIRVing of strategic missiles. It is true that in the three years prior to its first deployment in 1970 there was considerable debate, but its strategic consequences were never clearly perceived by high Administration officials—by President Nixon and National Security Adviser Kissinger."

Lynn remembers that "Henry spent an enormous amount of time on MIRV. He knew that if he appeared to be smarter and better informed than the technical experts inside the government, it would be an enormous advantage. What would [Deputy Secretary of Defense] Dave Packard of the Pentagon think if Henry is dueling with the senior experts in the Pentagon on MIRV and winning? Henry felt he had to beat the analysts at their own game, and he did a hell of a lot of homework."

Undoubtedly some of Kissinger's expertise was a result of the hours he continued to spend with the Doty group. "Henry met with them regularly," recalls Walter B. Slocombe, who came to the NSC in early 1969 and spent nearly two years working on SALT, "but he had no confidence in their discretion and very little respect for their ability to confront the fact that they had to make hard decisions." Slocombe, a Harvard Law School graduate who had clerked for Supreme Court Justice Abe Fortas, recalls being warned by Kissinger after a session with the scientists, "Don't talk to those people about anything. They can't be trusted."

Most members of the group sooner or later became aware of Kissinger's distrust. But "my view," Sidney Drell explains, "was that Kissinger was in a central position in the government and we had an opportunity to talk with him. It was a no-lose game. I have only one country and it was an opportunity we had to take advantage of."

Richard Garwin recalls that he and his colleagues sensed "from the beginning" that Kissinger had contempt for the group. "But we persisted because this is what we wanted to do for our country. Henry would not believe this—he does not share these values." He and his colleagues were shocked, Garwin says, at Nixon's announcement in March 1969 that the Safeguard ABM system would be deployed. Neither the Doty group nor other arms control experts had been offered any opportunity to argue against it. "They announced it without having done the responsible thing: asking experts in the government about it."

Garwin recalls warning Kissinger that his refusal to share information with other arms control experts in the government was dangerous for the country. "I told him he was doing a terrible thing by working outside the State Department and Pentagon bureaucracy on SALT because they would go along working on their own plans and he would have no support for his proposals when he needed it. It was a terribly dangerous thing for the nation—nobody would know what he and Nixon were trying to accomplish. It was a high-risk policy to leave the bureaucracy in the dark. Kissinger misunderstood the democratic process: He thought he could do things better than anybody else."

The two scientists who abandoned the "seminars" almost immediately had no regrets. Carl Kaysen had given his views to Nixon and Kissinger even before joining the Doty group, as chairman of a Council of Foreign Relations study—presented to the Nixon Administration early in January 1969—that called for a unilateral moratorium on MIRVs. Kaysen went to two or three of the Saturday meetings, but then, "I was going down one night from Princeton to have breakfast with Henry and the train was delayed. I thought to myself, 'I'm going to have a meaningless breakfast with Henry.' So I got off the train at Philadelphia, rented a car, and went back home."

George Rathjens says, "To tell the truth, I didn't want to feel coopted. We weren't doing anything useful; it was like talking into a void. I figured I could be more influential writing and speaking on the outside." He also recalls being highly suspicious of the depth of Kissinger's widely assumed expertise on some of the more sophisticated aspects of SALT. One vital intelligence area was telemetry, the communication signals sent by intercontinental missiles to various ground stations to report, for example, how much fuel has been burned up. Monitoring and interpreting such signals are crucial in verifying compliance with a disarmament treaty, and would be a factor in determining whether the Soviets were secretly testing a MIRV missile. "I can remember Henry talking about the telemetry as if he really understood it," Rathjens says. "I was appalled. He seemed to really think he understood it. He was conveying the impression that he was into this very deeply—and he didn't really understand what he was talking about."

What Kissinger understood was that Nixon did not want to stop the development of MIRVs—unless the political payoff, in Vietnam or elsewhere, was high, and maybe not even then. Just how much Nixon really understood about the technical aspects of SALT is open to question: The discussion in his memoirs was extremely scanty, with no mention at all, for example, of the debate with Congress over a unilateral MIRV moratorium. Kissinger, in his memoirs, repeatedly described those in the antiwar movement and in Congress who were urging such a moratorium as "emotional" and illogical. His argument against such a moratorium was that it would have favored the Soviets and delayed a SALT agreement: "To abandon ABM and MIRV together"—as the Doty group and others were advocating—"would thus not only have undercut the prospects for any SALT agreement but probably guaranteed Soviet strategic superiority for a decade." But, as the Doty group was telling him in 1969, the failure to ban MIRVs had the same effect, and the American Minuteman force would be far more threatened by Soviet MIRVs in 1979 than it had been before MIRV deployment.

Throughout the first half of 1969, Nixon and Kissinger were under great pressure from the Joint Chiefs of Staff and Melvin Laird, who, although eager to end the American involvement in Vietnam (and perhaps because of that), joined the Chiefs in arguing strongly and heatedly against a MIRV agreement, insisting that there were no means of verifying Soviet compliance with such a ban. In addition, the Pentagon argued that it would jeopardize national security to permit the Soviet Union to balance, or at least neutralize through the SALT talks, the American lead in developing and deploying MIRVs. Kissinger understood that without a ban it was the United States that would some day be threatened in a MIRVed world. But he also understood the perils of telling Richard Nixon something he did not want to hear.*

* Years later, Kissinger sought to leave the impression that he had made a misjudgment about the significance of MIRV missiles. The seemingly heartfelt admission came in December 1974, shortly after another round of SALT negotiations with the Soviet Union—negotiations dealing largely with attempts to limit the number of MIRV missiles on both sides. During a background discussion with journalists, one reporter asked, "As you look back at it, now are you sorry you went ahead with the MIRV?" Kissinger responded, "I would say in retrospect that I wish I had thought through the implications of a MIRVed world more thoughtfully in 1969 and 1970 than I did." Of course, as the NSC aides who worked on SALT issues knew, he had thought about MIRV carefully in 1969 and 1970 and fully understood the consequences of his decisions.

Herbert (Pete) Scoville, Jr., a deputy director of the CIA for scientific intelligence and later an assistant director of the Arms Control and Disarmament Agency, was a leading public critic of MIRV and the ABM during the late 1960s and early 1970s. He watched as the Doty group slowly dissolved in the first years of the Nixon Administration. "Henry used Doty—he kept leading him on. Eventually Doty ended up being essentially the only contact." Scoville believes that there was a "chance" in 1969 and 1970 to persuade the Soviet Union to agree to a ban on MIRVs. Kissinger's decision not to seek such a ban, Scoville says, was "one of not fighting the bureaucracy. I'm not blaming Kissinger specifically—it would have taken real leadership—but the fact is that the United States muffed it. And here is Henry claiming to run the show. If he claims that he's the big boss, he's got to face up to the mistakes that it cost us later."

Jack Ruina put the thought another way: "It was on Henry's watch that we lost the opportunity to control MIRVs."

13

SALT: A MISTAKE
BECOMES A POLICY

ONE OF THE MYTHS of the early Nixon-Kissinger era revolved around indus-triousness: The White House and the National Security Council were por-trayed in countless books, newspaper and television reports, and magazine articles as the focal point of exhaustive studies, countless memoranda, relent-less efforts to seek out the available options on all major issues demanding a presidential decision. The myth reached new heights in contemporary accounts of the SALT process.*

The truth was far from mundane. Some officials involved in the SALT pro-cess—men such as Laird and Helms—were far too busy with day-to-day work to read and digest the lengthy SALT studies prepared by their staffs and Kis-singer's. Others, such as Rogers, were too lazy or indifferent. Most of the analyses were read in full only by those who wrote them; slimmed-down ver-sions, "Executive Summaries," were provided for those who made the deci-sions. Major reports were often summarized in twelve or fourteen paragraphs; others were boiled down to four paragraphs, or even two. On occasion senior officials would simply receive oral briefings before a meeting.

In mid-1969, the key technical issue in the SALT process, as the White House saw it, was still one of verifying whether the Soviets could cheat on an agreement. Kissinger took personal control of a special "verification panel" that became, in effect, the main White House tool in controlling the MIRV and ABM debate in the bureaucracy. The panel was a political device. No amount of expertise or analysis was going to convince Laird and the Joint Chiefs that the Soviets wouldn't find some way to cheat. With all its deliberations and studies, Kissinger used the verification panel in typical fashion: While the top SALT officials in the administration were considering, so they thought, Amer-ican SALT options, Kissinger was meeting secretly on SALT with Am-bassador Dobrynin. The results of the Kissinger-Dobrynin backchannel conversations, in the form of American proposals, would suddenly be flung, a

* See, for example, Henry Brandon's *The Retreat of American Power*, published in 1973. The London *Sunday Times* correspondent wrote that Nixon, facing a fateful decision on SALT, "wanted to learn to understand the essentials of the problem involved and to think them through. The behind-the-scenes preparations Kissinger organized in his meticulous and intellectual sagacity were unprecedented; he marshalled and co-ordinated every possible source of information with a bearing on the subject." Kissinger, the source for much of Brandon's information, painted a rather different picture of Nixon's thirst for knowledge in his memoirs.

fait accompli, to the SALT delegation in Europe without the approval or even the knowledge of the verification panel.

The major officials involved in SALT began with biases that remained intact. Laird was stridently against any effort to ban the MIRV regardless of its long-range peril to American security; he was joined by the Joint Chiefs of Staff. Nixon shared that view, and also the belief that the Soviet Union would cheat on any arms ban. On the other side were the CIA, whose experts believed that a MIRV ban could be verified, and the three ranking State Department officials involved in SALT—Rogers, Richardson, and Smith. Kissinger was responsible for coordinating the agenda of these discussions, but he and Nixon apparently agreed early that a MIRV ban would not do; even if the Soviets did not cheat, the political costs in opposition from Laird and the Joint Chiefs would be too high.

Kissinger's aides agreed. Even Halperin, considered the most passionate arms control advocate on the NSC staff, believed in early 1969 that it was politically impossible at that time to get Pentagon backing for a ban on both the ABM and the MIRV. He agreed with Kissinger that it was too late to halt MIRV testing and deployment: "Henry's position was that if [the Johnson Administration] hadn't started testing it in 1968, we never would have gone ahead. Now the momentum was too much."

Lynn, too, took a hard line. "A MIRV ban was regarded as virtually impossible to verify," he recalls. "None of us believed that the Soviets were prepared to negotiate" on MIRVs, and "Henry felt the CIA was giving inadequate information" about the Soviets' MIRV-testing programs.

A struggle among Halperin, Lynn, and Sonnenfeldt for the job of Kissinger's main deputy for SALT did not improve chances for objective inquiry and thoughtful proposals. Arguments on SALT were covertly funneled into Kissinger's office at night as the three men who shared skepticism about the verification of MIRV testing worked to outdo each other. The safest line in such circumstances, as Kissinger demonstrated by example, was the hard line.

Throughout the spring and summer of 1969, the United States continued its heavy MIRV test programs on both the land-based Minuteman missile forces and the sea-based Poseidon missiles. In April and May, the Soviet Union conducted a series of tests over the Pacific Ocean, firing a missile with three warheads. The Pentagon concluded—wrongly, as it turned out—that the Soviets had been testing a MIRV missile. Further analysis soon demonstrated that what the Americans had observed was the first of a series of Soviet tests of a multiple reentry vehicle that was able to fling three warheads, like pellets in a box, into the same general area. Its warheads were not independently targeted after separation from the launch missile; it was a MRV, not a MIRV, and the United States had been deploying MRVs on its Polaris submarine fleet since 1963. By MIRV standards, the new Soviet missile system was primitive.

Nevertheless, in a news conference on June 19, Nixon defended his proposed Safeguard ABM system, which had strong opposition in the Senate, by cryptically stating that the Soviets had tested "a multiple weapon." A Soviet MIRV, whether it existed or not, served White House purposes by providing a much-needed rationale for the ABM. At the time, there was a sharp disagreement over the Soviet tests inside the bureaucracy, with the Pentagon insisting that the missile was MIRVed, with three independently targeted warheads, and the CIA and State arguing that the weapon was far less sophisticated and did not involve separate guidance systems. Laird was among those publicly insisting that the Soviets now posed a threat that could be met only by the Safeguard ABM system.

Throughout the debate, Kissinger sided with Laird and thus with Nixon. In June 1969, he summoned Richard Helms to a meeting in the White House, where, according to a later Senate Intelligence Committee report, "Kissinger and the NSC staff made clear their view that the new Soviet missile was a MIRV and asked that Helms' draft be rewritten to provide more evidence" in support of the Laird position.* The CIA's intelligence estimate had been prepared by the Agency's Office of National Estimates, whose integrity had never been so directly challenged in its twenty-year history. John W. Huizenga, deputy director of the ONE, had no illusions about the purpose of the White House. "From the point of view of the CIA," he recalls, "the game was being played because the Soviet MIRV was necessary as a threat to justify the Safeguard [ABM] system. There's no doubt that the White House was determined that there should be an intelligence finding that the Soviets were engaged in MIRV testing." At the meeting, as Huizenga remembers it, Helms and his aides were asked to "clarify" their analysis. "Henry's line was that the paper lacked clarity—that it had editorial and presentational defects. He was saying this in order not to place himself in the position of demanding a change." After the meeting, Huizenga and his colleagues went through the motions of expanding their report, but still reached the same conclusion: The Russians had not tested a MIRV.

The CIA's refusal to change its estimate was "disloyalty," for which the Nixon-Kissinger solution was to begin systematically reducing the importance of the CIA's intelligence reporting.† It was not hard to convince the President of the CIA's infidelity. "Nixon considered the CIA a refuge of Ivy League intellectuals opposed to him," Kissinger wrote in his memoirs. "And he felt ill at ease with Helms personally, since he suspected that Helms was well liked by the liberal Georgetown social set to which Nixon ascribed many of his difficulties."

From that point on, the White House began to demand that Helms and the CIA turn over the raw data upon which CIA analyses were based. Kissinger and his staff were then free to make their own intelligence findings. But even with Helms out of the way, there was still the pitched battle over MIRV, as Kissinger opposed those who sought to bar the weapons. Sometimes things got dirty.

On April 16, Senator Edward W. Brooke, Republican of Massachusetts, was granted a rare private meeting with Nixon, in which he urged the President to slow down the MIRV test program; in effect, Brooke argued, such a move would amount to a unilateral move to defuse the arms race without an explicit

* The meeting is described by Helms and other CIA officials in the Final Report of the Senate Select Committee on Intelligence Activities, headed by Senator Frank Church, Democrat of Idaho, which investigated the CIA in 1975 and 1976.

† Huizenga, who later became director of ONE, told the Senate Intelligence Committee in 1976 that the Nixon-Kissinger hostility toward the CIA undoubtedly had a chilling effect on its intelligence-analysis function. "When intelligence producers have a general feeling that they are working in a hostile climate, what really happens is not so much that they tailor the product to please, although that's not been unknown, but more likely, they avoid the treatment of difficult issues."

decision to that effect, which might cause political problems with the Pentagon and Nixon's conservative constituency. In a private letter to Nixon, delivered at their meeting, Brooke pointed out that an early disruption of flight tests would be a major barrier to MIRV development. He took the issue to the public on April 24, in a speech in New York before a meeting of the American Newspaper Publishers' Association, explaining that MIRV was of far more strategic importance than the ABM. When the White House made no effort to cancel a MIRV test scheduled for May 24, Brooke again urged Nixon, in private communications, to delay. There was no response, and on June 17, Brooke, who had been active in educating his Senate colleagues on MIRV, introduced a resolution calling for, among other things, a unilateral moratorium on MIRV testing. Forty other senators joined Brooke in sponsoring the legislation. At his news conference two days later, Nixon was restrained about Brooke's initiative: "I know that it is certainly a very constructive proposal insofar as they, themselves, are thinking about . . . However, as far as any unilateral stopping of tests on our part, I do not think that would be in our interest." Privately, Nixon's rage was intense.

Brooke had left his meeting with Nixon—arranged because of his strong support of the Nixon-Agnew ticket during the 1968 campaign—convinced that Nixon did not fully understand the MIRV issue and was dependent on Kissinger, who, even then, was the only senior foreign policy aide with regular access to the President. Brooke, too, was a newcomer to arms control policy. Shortly after his election in 1966, he had begun to consult with Alton Frye, a disarmament expert from the Rand Corporation, who joined his Senate staff in early 1968. While at Rand, Frye had worked on a study of the stability of deterrence for the Air Force and had independently reached the same conclusion as the Doty group: that the Air Force's land-based missiles would eventually be threatened by a Soviet MIRV force.*

Frye, once at work in the Senate, quickly developed a reputation for MIRV expertise among Capitol Hill insiders. At a diplomatic reception early that summer, he ran into Yuli M. Vorontsov, a Soviet diplomat, and told him that the United States and his country should be talking about MIRVs. Frye recalls that Vorontsov replied heatedly, "We have nothing to do with this. It's your technology that's doing it. You're creating the problem. You ought to be doing something." Frye duly wrote a report of the conversation for Elliot Richardson, with whom he and Brooke maintained close rapport, and the State Department shared the information with the NSC.

A few days later, Frye recalls, the *New York Times* reported that some Washington officials were concerned that the Soviets were deliberately manipulating Senate staff aides on the MIRV issue. Frye and Brooke were outraged; they were convinced that Kissinger or one of his aides had deliberately leaked the story to embarrass them and damage Brooke's position in the Senate debate. The Senator and his staff had learned what Kissinger's staff already

---

* The analysts all agreed that the Soviets, with their traditional emphasis on constructing larger missile launchers capable of delivering bigger payloads, would be able to make more efficient use of the MIRV mechanism. Once the Soviets improved the accuracy of their MIRV delivery vehicles, a step deemed inevitable after more testing, they would be able to override any ABM defense surrounding the Air Force's Minuteman fleet. They would thus be more capable of successfully launching a first strike against the United States, since their fear of retaliation would be lessened.

knew: Kissinger always dealt severely with those who opposed him and who were less powerful, whether they were in the White House, the State Department, the Pentagon, and thus responsible to the President, or in the Congress, and thus responsible to the people.

In his memoirs, Kissinger made no attempt to understand the point of view of those in the Senate who sought a MIRV ban. Senator Brooke was described, in Kissinger's account of another arms control protest in 1970, as "engaged in his annual campaign against ABM and MIRV."*

Another challenge to the Nixon-Kissinger MIRV policy came from a most unlikely source: Gerard Smith, who was beginning to emerge as one of Nixon's most distinguished appointments. Smith had been a special assistant for atomic affairs to Secretary of State Dulles during the Eisenhower Administration; his long-term financial contributions to the Republican Party had assured him of a major appointment. Nixon seems to have made Smith director of the Arms Control and Disarmament Agency out of ignorance; he was considered safe and malleable. Nixon and Kissinger "probably figured ACDA was a throwaway job," one of Smith's aides recalls. "Gerry comes on rather pompous and they thought he'd be easily managed."

Smith was far from compliant even at the beginning. He soon joined ranks with those in the government who were urging the White House to drop its demand for "linkage" and immediately open wide-ranging SALT talks with the Soviet Union. Nixon and Kissinger responded to Smith's independence by trying to undercut him with his own delegation, as they did with Paul Nitze when they urged him to report directly to the White House by backchannel. Not all the complaints were made behind Smith's back. Late in 1969, Smith wrote in his book, *Doubletalk*, Nixon sent him and other disarmament negotiators a note warning that if they gave any encouragement to a moratorium on testing or deployment prior to a SALT agreement, they would be "first reprimanded and then discharged." Smith's troubles were not only with the President. Throughout the SALT talks, Kissinger wrote, Smith "was engaged with me in internal negotiations that were complex because we understood each other very well indeed. He wanted a freer hand and I was determined to prevent it."

Smith was quick to understand the implications of MIRV and soon became a strong advocate of a ban or moratorium. Worse still, he insisted upon discussing it, in his gentlemanly way, at meetings of the verification panel and the National Security Council. Philip J. Farley, one of his senior aides, recalls that Smith "was used to the business that, as head of a major agency, you should have a chance to argue your point of view with the President." A clash was inevitable. It came at an NSC meeting in which Smith once again fought for a MIRV ban, "Gerry was making a lawyerly and analytical argument on

---

* Brooke's sense-of-the-Senate resolution passed by a vote of seventy-two to six on April 9, 1970. It not only urged the White House to ban MIRV testing unilaterally, but called on both the United States and the Soviet Union to seek immediate suspension of further deployment of all offensive and defensive weapons systems pending the SALT talks—a freeze. The White House obviously had the votes in the Senate, at least in 1970, to go much further in the disarmament talks than it did.

MIRV," Farley says, "just talking common sense. He had at least two-thirds of the people in the room with him and it must have been obvious. Nixon looked at Smith with one of his evil looks and said, 'That's bullshit, Gerry, and you know it.' " Smith dropped the argument, and in the car going back to their office, he turned to Farley and said quietly, "Nobody's ever talked to me that way."

Kissinger moved against Smith quite early, and his first step was to prevent Smith from obtaining the staff he wanted to help him manage the SALT talks. One person Smith wanted from the beginning was Raymond L. Garthoff, a Foreign Service expert on the Soviet Union. Garthoff was a Yale Ph.D. who had written extensively on Soviet strategy and foreign policy intentions as a senior analyst in the CIA's Office of National Estimates. Later he had worked on the SALT initiatives proposed during the Johnson Administration, and by 1969 he was counselor to the American diplomatic mission at NATO headquarters in Brussels. During Nixon's European trip in February 1969, Kissinger renewed his acquaintance with Garthoff; the two had known each other in Washington during the late 1950s and the 1960s. Was Garthoff interested in a position with the National Security Council? Garthoff was, and Kissinger later had Eagleburger continue the conversation. "What became clear was that Henry had had some falling out with Hal Sonnenfeldt," Garthoff recalls, and he was being considered as a replacement. "I thought about it and told Larry I thought I'd be interested," Garthoff said. There was one hitch, however: "I told him I'd also been asked by Gerry Smith to go to ACDA as an assistant director."

Garthoff heard nothing for weeks, and then received a perfunctory note from Kissinger "thanking me for my 'interest' but explaining that things had changed and 'it couldn't be worked out'—as if I'd been the supplicant." Things quickly got worse. Smith telephoned to say, Garthoff recalls, that Rogers had told him the State Department had another "important job in line for me and that he couldn't release me" to the ACDA. Garthoff heard no more about the other "important job."* None of his acquaintances in the State Department could help, and Garthoff assumed that the order to keep him out of the ACDA "must have come from Henry."

By the end of 1969, Kissinger was involved in an elaborate balancing act to maintain control of SALT and prevent widespread discussion of a MIRV ban. He was placating the Doty group by seeming to take its advice seriously; he was struggling to keep his dominance over Gerard Smith and the arms control contingent at ACDA; and finally, he was denigrating the efforts of those in the Senate who wanted serious public discussion of these matters.†

---

* Garthoff, who was later assigned to a lesser position on the SALT negotiating team, remembers that Smith once told him "he was upset that his first choices for two top jobs had now been rejected —after he'd been promised a free hand by the President." Smith's other early rebuff had come when he wanted Henry D. Owen, a moderate Republican who had been on the State Department's policy planning staff from 1955 to 1962, as his top deputy.

† In November, shortly before the first SALT talks with the Soviet Union in Helsinki, Kissinger refused to let Smith and other ACDA aides brief a Senate Foreign Relations subcommittee. Senator Albert Gore, Democrat of Tennessee, who was chairman of the subcommittee, told reporters, "This is the first time to my knowledge that an agency charged with a responsibility in the field of foreign affairs has not been willing—or, in this case, free—to meet with the disarmament subcommittee on a subject on which the subcommittee has had jurisdiction." The Foreign Relations Committee,

Meanwhile, the administration quietly authorized a speeded-up series of MIRV tests and also expedited by six months the actual deployment of the warheads. In June 1969, without informing the MIRV critics in Congress, the Pentagon signed an $88-million contract with General Electric for the production of sixty-eight MIRV missiles. In March 1970, Robert C. Seamans, Jr., Secretary of the Air Force, told a congressional hearing that the United States would begin deployment of its MIRV missile fleet by early summer, well ahead of schedule. Two days later, the *Washington Post* quoted "high administration officials" as saying that Seamans' announcement had "somehow slipped through"; that is, the speeded-up deployment was to have been a secret.

Nixon—and thus Kissinger—was determined to have MIRV and did not waver in that determination even after the President's own General Advisory Committee on Arms Control and Disarmament urged that the testing be stopped. The GAC had been set up under the 1961 Arms Control and Disarmament Act, which also authorized the Arms Control and Disarmament Agency. The advisory committee was a separate entity, however, with its own staff and a chairman who, by law, was adviser directly to the President; he did not have to clear any GAC recommendations with the State Department or the Pentagon but could present them directly to Nixon. Nixon's chairman was John J. McCloy, former High Commissioner of Germany and former board chairman of the Chase Manhattan Bank, a major figure in the Republican Party and a staunch conservative who was considered one of the architects of the Cold War. McCloy's concern about continued MIRV testing was a serious political danger to Nixon, and the formidable makeup of the committee's advisory board increased that danger. Among the advisers were Dean Rusk, former Secretary of State; Cyrus Vance, the former senior Pentagon official; Harold Brown, former Secretary of the Air Force; William W. Scranton, a former governor of Pennsylvania who had been a foreign affairs adviser to Nixon during the 1968 campaign; and William J. Casey, another 1968 campaign aide, who was later appointed head of the Securities and Exchange Commission. Jack Ruina, the MIT expert who was still affiliated with the informal Doty group, was also appointed, and it was Ruina, other board members recall, who was instrumental in educating them on the dangers of MIRV. At one point, Ruina became so concerned over the Pentagon's enthusiasm for MIRV —an enthusiasm he was sure it would later rue—that he privately warned Air Force Secretary Seamans of the dangers to the Minuteman fleet that a future Soviet MIRV buildup would bring.*

Kissinger attended at least one full meeting of the GAC and promptly demonstrated that he understood the issues. As usual, he convinced each person

---

involved in a deep dispute with the Nixon Administration over the Vietnam War, did not protest further.

* Ruina also discussed the issue with John L. McLucas, the Air Force Under Secretary who wore the "black hat" in the Pentagon; that is, he was in charge of the National Reconnaissance Office, a secret unit responsible for the development, procurement, and targeting of intelligence satellites. The NRO, which is jointly staffed by CIA and military personnel, is perhaps the most highly classified unit in the government. Its existence is technically a secret. As the official with direct responsibility for the Air Force's satellite spy programs, McLucas, with his detailed knowledge of the threat that Soviet MIRVs would pose, should have been among those most eager for a MIRV ban. But neither he nor Seamans made an effort, as far as those who favored such a ban could tell, to argue against Laird and the Joint Chiefs of Staff.

that he was on his side. "He did not commit himself," one participant says, "except to leave a general feeling of support for a MIRV agreement."

The GAC, aware nonetheless of Kissinger's and Nixon's hostility to its views, formally recommended to the President, in March 1970, that MIRV testing be discontinued. Some GAC members believed that their recommendations, if the White House used them properly, could alleviate much of the pressure from the Pentagon. The fact that such prominent anti-Communists as John McCloy, Dean Rusk, and William Casey believed that a MIRV ban was in the best interests of the United States, even though the Pentagon was years ahead in the development of the weapon, could mitigate much of the military's opposition and perhaps even Laird's.

McCloy and his distinguished committee could no more change the President's mind than Doty's Saturday group and Smith's ACDA. In his memoirs, Kissinger caustically suggested that even McCloy was merely following public opinion in his opposition to MIRVs: ". . . [T]he President's General Advisory Committee on Arms Control and Disarmament, chaired by the stalwart John McCloy, reflected the prevailing mood and recommended . . . suspension of MIRV testing." Earlier in his memoirs, however, Kissinger had described McCloy, with whom he consulted frequently during the preinauguration weeks at the Hotel Pierre, as anything but a follower of prevailing moods. He was "a reliable pilot through treacherous shoals. He rarely supplied solutions to difficult problems, but he never failed to provide the psychological and moral reassurance that made solutions possible. . . . He was ever wise." But by early 1970, Kissinger, like Nixon, had come to believe that the only wise advice was the advice he wanted to hear.

The national security adviser and the President had already received—and rejected—formal MIRV ban proposals in writing from Smith, Richardson, and Rogers (Smith's first formal proposal had been delivered a year before, on April 16, 1969). Nixon and Kissinger had found it easy to ignore the proddings of these people in the government, but they needed to be more cautious with outsiders, especially the high-powered outsiders on the GAC. For this reason the GAC recommendations finally produced a show of movement.

In April 1970, only two months before the United States deployed its first MIRVed missiles, and six months after the SALT talks had begun, Nixon and Kissinger finally agreed to permit the SALT delegation to discuss a MIRV test ban with the Soviet delegates.* By then, there had been repeated hints from Moscow that such an American proposal would be seriously considered, although the Soviet delegation had said nothing about MIRVs in the formal talks. But Nixon and Kissinger, to the dismay of the American delegation, tied a tin can to the new offer: A MIRV test ban would not be discussed until the Soviets agreed to permit on-site inspection of their existing strategic offensive missiles as well as their ABM sites. The Nixon-Kissinger proposal also specified that

* The preliminary round of SALT talks had opened on November 17, 1969, at Smolna Palace in Helsinki. An immediate conflict emerged over the question of linkage, with the Soviet delegation announcing at the outset that it rejected the notion that progress on arms limitations must be dependent on any other issue. The delegations were able to reach some agreement, before the first round ended on December 22, 1969, about the areas to be studied, including the need to focus on ABM systems and the interrelationship between offensive and defensive arms systems—but no substantial progress was made. The second round of talks was to begin April 16, 1970, in Vienna; the negotiations would continue to rotate between Helsinki and Vienna.

the United States would continue to produce and stockpile MIRV missiles but not deploy them, an obvious advantage since the Soviets were not yet producing MIRVs; would not even begin testing until mid-1975; and could not deploy the new weapons without such tests. Finally, the ban was to be an inseparable part of a wide-ranging agreement that also called on the Soviets to unilaterally dismantle a newly deployed advanced air-defense radar system.

Neither the public nor most members of Congress knew the full details of the Nixon-Kissinger offer at the time, and there is no evidence that the few legislators who received oral briefings understood all the loopholes. In essence, the Nixon Administration, having completed the essential MIRV testing programs, would continue producing MIRVs but not deploy them, whereas the Soviet Union was not even to test the new weapon. Lawrence D. Weiler, who was on the SALT negotiating team, later wrote that the administration had much to gain domestically by its one-sided offer: "Making a MIRV proposal and letting it be known that such a proposal had been advanced helped pacify those outside the executive branch who wished to halt MIRVs. . . . With secrecy concealing the issues and developments in the [SALT] negotiations, a critical opportunity in efforts to control strategic arms was to be debated within a closed group, and let fall." *

As to the on-site-inspection aspect of the MIRV proposal, it was equally cynical. By the time the package was presented to the Soviets, Raymond Garthoff had managed, finally, to be assigned as executive officer of the SALT delegation, and was Gerard Smith's chief adviser on the negotiations in Helsinki and Vienna. Garthoff recalls that the on-site provisions were advocated at the last minute during an NSC meeting by, among others, John Mitchell and Spiro Agnew, two men whose NSC recommendations were much influenced by the White House and who knew very little about any aspect of arms control.

The disarmament experts knew, however, that even if the Soviet Union broke with its firm policy of not permitting outsiders to have access to its most sensitive military sites and accepted on-site inspection, the concession would do little to prevent Soviet cheating on a MIRV deployment ban. On-site inspection meant that American teams of experts would be permitted to look inside opened Soviet missile silos to see whether MIRV warheads were on the missiles; in theory, such inspection would insure that the Soviets would not deploy MIRVs after agreeing not to do so. But "even if they did let us do it," as one senior arms control official says, "what's to prevent the Soviets from switching from a warhead with one missile [after inspection] to a MIRV with ten warheads that's being stored in a shack nearby? It would take only a day to make the change, and they could still cheat."

One of Kissinger's NSC aides acknowledges that the on-site provision was put into the administration's MIRV offer "to make it unacceptable. It was put in with no illusions that it would be accepted or much help with verification if it were." At this stage of the negotiations, Kissinger's aides manufactured a lame in-house joke that, as recounted by Walter Slocombe, went something like this: An American on-site inspector would look into a single-warhead

* See "The Arms Race, Secret Negotiations and the Congress," by Lawrence D. Weiler, Occasional Paper No. 12, published in 1976 by the Stanley Foundation, Muscatine, Iowa.

missile and say to his Soviet counterpart, "Well, Ivan, you're clean." Ivan would say, "Of course." Then the American would ask, "Ivan, I know you don't have to answer this, but what's in that building over there?"—pointing to a nearby warehouse. Ivan's answer: "Oh, that's where we keep our MIRVs."*

In his memoirs, Kissinger wrote that he justified the on-site proposal to Nixon on two bases: It would "respond" to the congressional and bureaucratic supporters of a MIRV ban, and it "would give us the positive public posture of having favored comprehensive limitations."

The Soviets promptly responded with an offer to discuss a ban on MIRV production and deployment, and not on testing, a step that would favor them, since they would surely need to test their MIRVs before manufacturing and deploying them. The U.S. delegation sought permission to make the obvious counteroffer: "a ban," as Garthoff says, "on everything—production, testing, and deployment. And we were told not to do it. I don't know what the Soviets would have said but we never asked them."

By late summer, when it was clear that MIRVs would not be dealt with in the SALT negotiations, some Soviet delegates sought out Garthoff to say they regretted that "more hadn't been done on MIRV." The suggestion was left that the Soviet delegation was not in a position to push a MIRV ban, but might have been able to be responsive. "My counterparts were telling me that they were sorry that we weren't taking a lead on this."

None of the American officials involved in the 1969 and 1970 attempts to urge a MIRV ban is sure that such negotiations would have been successful; but there was widespread belief among the American SALT delegation that the Russians were ready to negotiate seriously. The delegation was never given permission to test its belief.† One SALT official was convinced that the Soviets "kept it open to see if there was any serious [American] interest in a MIRV ban. Once they concluded that the United States wasn't interested in MIRV, they decided to go just with the ABM limitation," which was finally agreed upon and signed in Moscow in May 1972.

The problems of verifying Soviet compliance with a MIRV ban were undoubtedly real and perhaps, as the Pentagon thought, insoluble; but that was not why the United States failed to negotiate seriously on the issue during the SALT negotiations of 1969 and 1970. Nixon and Kissinger had made a political judgment that only an ABM agreement was acceptable; for them, the price of forcing the Pentagon to accept a MIRV agreement that would ultimately benefit the national security was too high. The White House collaborators made a Mephistophelian bargain with Melvin Laird and the Joint Chiefs of Staff on

* The cynicism of the on-site proposal seems to have escaped former Vice President Agnew. In his 1980 memoirs, *Go Quietly . . . Or Else*, Agnew, who was forced to resign before Nixon did, recalled one NSC meeting at which he criticized the Soviet Union's rejection of on-site inspection. "Gentlemen," Agnew quoted himself as saying, "if two nations make an agreement to limit strategic nuclear weapons, and they intend to carry out that agreement, then neither should object to inspection to insure that the agreement is being performed. The only conclusion you can come to is that they're not going to play fair." Agnew wrote that the military men attending the NSC meeting agreed with him but "the doves looked at me as if I were Attila the Hun." The Vice President obviously did not understand the long-standing policy behind the Soviet rejection of on-site inspection, a condition that Nixon and Kissinger did little to alter.

† As Raymond Garthoff put it, in an evaluation of SALT published in 1978, "Never having asked, we shall never know."

SALT, trading the possibility of a MIRV ban for their agreement to a limitation on ABM sites in both the United States and the Soviet Union.

The folly of that bargain would be increasingly understood over the next few years, as Congress refused to authorize funds for constructing the ABM defense system and as American defense planners sought increasingly vast sums of money to finance a more sophisticated defense system, the MX, and to reinforce the existing silos for the Minuteman missile fleet in an attempt to limit its vulnerability to a Soviet MIRV attack.

Kissinger knew all he needed to know about MIRV and its implications in mid-1969, but he chose not to act on his knowledge. The nation's security was not aided by any of this—but Kissinger maintained his control over the SALT negotiations.

14

SOUTHEAST ASIA:
POLICY CHANGE AND ESCALATION

By EARLY 1970, with all hope for a quick Vietnam victory gone, Henry Kissinger had become a fervent, if belated, convert to a fallback position—Vietnamization. His deep doubts about the long-term efficacy of the program were swept aside as he decided that, yes, it was possible for the South Vietnamese government to stand up to the North Vietnamese and the Vietcong, with military and economic aid from the United States and the continued willingness of its President to escalate the war, irrationally if necessary.

Like most late converts, Kissinger became an even more ardent supporter than the true believers of long standing—in this case Melvin Laird and the Joint Chiefs of Staff. Full support of Vietnamization had many advantages, the most significant being to place Kissinger firmly on the same wave length as Richard Nixon, who, if he had any doubts about the policy, did not express them. Not surprisingly, Kissinger's conversion prompted a new series of studies in 1970, led by his National Security Council staff, which concluded that Vietnamization did after all have a chance of succeeding. It also led to escalations of the war in northern Laos and Cambodia, with the dual purpose of protecting Vietnamization and demonstrating anew to the North Vietnamese that Richard Nixon, though he had hesitated the previous November, was still not afraid to take chances.

The first move in the new offensive came in late January 1970, as the North Vietnamese and their allies in Laos, the Pathet Lao, began what had become their annual dry-season offensive in the hotly contested Plain of Jars area in the north. Laos had been a secret battleground for the United States since the early 1960s, with the CIA financing and leading indigenous tribesmen against the Communist forces. One of the Nixon Administration's first steps after taking office had been to divert American aircraft—which under the November 1968 bombing halt agreement could no longer bomb North Vietnam—to targets along the Ho Chi Minh Trail, Hanoi's main north-south supply line, in southern Laos. By the end of 1969, the number of American bombing missions over Laos had reached a total of 242,000, an average of more than 650 missions a day over a country not much larger than Cambodia. Some of that bombing was under the direct control of the American Ambassador to Laos, who worked covertly through military men and also through CIA officials under cover in the officially neutral country as employees of the Agency for International Development. The war in Laos, which had been conducted in secrecy throughout the 1960s, became a political issue by early 1970, with the White House getting harsh criticism from antiwar Democrats and Republicans in the Senate. Protest increased after the Nixon Administration authorized the use of B-52 aircraft on February 17 and 18 against the Pathet Lao and North Vietnamese forces in northern Laos. The expansion of B-52 bombing to the north of Laos was carried on the military's internal records as routine missions over South Vietnam or southern Laos, where bombing along the Ho Chi Minh Trail was conducted on a near-daily basis and fully reported. The secret reporting procedures ordered for the B-52 missions over northern Laos were the same as those then in effect for the secret B-52 "Menu" bombing in Cambodia, but, unlike the Cambodia bombing, the Laos escalation was reported in the *New York Times* the next day. Congressional criticism reached a high point on February 25, when six senators, three of them Republicans, made floor speeches deploring the administration's secrecy about the deepening American involvement in Laos. Senator Charles McC. Mathias, Jr., a freshman Republican from Maryland, Vice President Agnew's home state, went so far as to accuse the administration of subverting the will of Congress. The dispute threatened to bring to an end a period of congressional and public acquiescence that had followed Nixon's "silent majority" Vietnam speech of November 3. The administration's immediate defense—that it was helping the Laotian anti-Communist forces, headed by Premier Souvanna Phouma, fight off North Vietnamese aggression—did not satisfy the Senate. And thus, on March 6, President Nixon turned to Vietnamization. In a public statement prepared by Kissinger's office, Nixon acknowledged that he had increased American aid to Laos and defended it as a necessary part of Vietnamization: "We are trying above all to save American and allied lives in South Vietnam which are threatened by the continual infiltration of North Vietnamese troops and supplies along the Ho Chi Minh trail." The American role, Nixon said, "has been necessary to protect American lives in Vietnam."

Laos was being kept safe for Vietnamization.

In his memoirs, Kissinger acknowledged that as long as North Vietnam's main goal—to make sure its supply lines along the Ho Chi Minh Trail were not jeopardized—was met, the North was content to fight only hard enough to keep the war in "uneasy equilibrium." This policy changed in January 1970, Kissinger wrote, when North Vietnam suddenly sent 13,000 more troops into Laos, threatening the Souvanna Phouma regime—and, more important, threatening the Prince's acquiescence in the continuous bombing of the Ho Chi Minh Trail. Kissinger argued that the North Vietnamese offensive, if successful, could have led to a serious threat to Thailand, America's SEATO ally, which shares a long border with Laos along the Mekong River. And if that threat materialized, "We would almost certainly be denied use of the Thai airbases, essential for our B-52 and tactical air operations in Vietnam."

Kissinger did not discuss the bitter division over Laos inside the United States government. Opposition to the widening of the war was strong among the young aides of such State Department officials as Elliot Richardson, the Under Secretary, and Marshall Green, an Assistant Secretary. These aides, many of them experts on the Vietnam War, believed that North Vietnam sought nothing more in Laos than similar offensives had accomplished in the past: keeping the CIA-led mercenary army on the defensive and protecting the

Ho Chi Minh Trail. For Hanoi, these experts believed, the only real war was still in South Vietnam.

Kissinger's rationale notwithstanding, the fact is that he and Nixon decided to escalate the air war over Laos to show Hanoi the high price of prolonging the war. When Hanoi and the Pathet Lao began their annual offensive in 1970, they provided a peg on which the White House could hang its threat. Nixon was explicit in his memoirs: After the postponement of Duck Hook, he wrote, "We had to think about initiatives that we could undertake to show the enemy that we were still serious about our commitments in Vietnam."

Posing a credible threat was a major factor but not the sole one. Kissinger and Nixon were convinced, and apparently remained so as they wrote their memoirs, that the success of Vietnamization depended on the elimination of North Vietnamese sanctuaries in Laos and Cambodia. Many people in the government resisted the White House pressure, and there were heated meetings during the first months of 1970 as the State Department, the CIA, and even the Defense Department opposed Kissinger's and Nixon's recommendation for yet another escalation: sending Thai artillery battalions into the Laotian guerrilla war.

Charles Cooke, the Air Force officer who became an aide to Richardson, has described the struggle over the Thai battalions as one of the crucial battles inside the Nixon Administration: "We were all against it and we all held the line." Even the Defense Department argued that the risk was too high, Cooke recalls; in case of a debacle in the rugged terrain of Laos, it would take more troops than were available in either the South Vietnamese or the United States Army to relieve the Thai battalions. Cooke and others also had grave doubts about the need for the Thai units.*

None of these arguments mattered much, because nobody making them fully understood what the administration was trying to do. "What happened next was critical, at least to me," Cooke recalls. "Henry said the President wanted it done and that was that. We will not discuss it any more. He managed to crack the opposition. Once he'd done that, everybody started getting off their positions and began to rationalize why it should be done. Helms was the first to go."

"Once Henry broke the united front on Laos," Cooke says, "things began to move quickly and by May he's into Cambodia."

Kissinger's desire to dominate the bureaucracy almost undid him in the skirmishing over Laos. He had taken charge himself of drafting Nixon's March 6 statement, which justified the Laos escalations in terms of Vietnamization and which clung tenaciously to a legal rationale for increased involvement in Laos: "Our assistance has always been at the request of the legitimate government of Premier Souvanna Phouma which the North Vietnamese helped establish; it is directly related to North Vietnamese violations of the agreements." Nixon also described North Vietnam as intent on threatening all of Laos and

---

* In his memoirs, Kissinger credited the Thai units with being "decisive" in blunting the North Vietnamese offensive. Not everyone shared his enthusiasm, however. At one acrimonious meeting during this period, according to Cooke, Kissinger asked Dennis A. Doolin, a senior Pentagon official, whether the Thais had had a favorable kill ratio, or KIA, in comparison with American units. Doolin replied, "Well, you can't use KIA for the Thais. You've got to use DOF." "DOF? DOF? What is DOF?" Kissinger asked, exasperated. "Died of fright," Doolin responded.

insisted that North Vietnam's goal in its current offensive was to expand its area of operations "beyond the furthest line of past Communist advances." At the time, as Cooke recalls, only the Joint Chiefs of Staff held such views; the other agencies regarded that theory as a "myth."

The fact that Kissinger's statement for the President was replete with mistakes, lies, and half-truths could never by itself have jeopardized his relationship with Nixon.* But Nixon got caught on one lie, and he was furious. That lie was a categorical denial that any Americans stationed in Laos had been killed in ground operations, a denial that Nixon very much wanted to believe. On March 8, the *Los Angeles Times* published a graphic account of an American captain's death in a firefight on the western edge of the Plain of Jars. Accounts of similar combat casualties then began to leak in Washington, and the Pentagon was forced to announce that twenty-seven Americans had been killed there. Kissinger inadvertently showed in his memoirs how his eagerness to please led to the mistake: When the Pentagon supplied his staff with statistics on Americans killed in cross-border ground operations in Laos, he decided to ignore them on the ground that the deaths "were clearly related to the war in Vietnam . . ." When the story broke, "Nixon was furious at what he considered a failure of my vaunted staff; for a week I could not get an appointment to see him." There could be no harsher punishment.

Left unsaid in Kissinger's memoirs was the fact that the Nixon Administration had begun escalating the secret ground war in Laos from the moment it took office. Statistics made public by the Pentagon in 1973 showed that Army and Marine units had been conducting cross-border operations into Laos since 1965, but the number of those missions climbed to nearly nine hundred in 1969 and 1970, 50 percent higher than the number in 1967 and 1968. The Pentagon statistics also showed that in 1969 and 1970, the number of helicopter and fighter-bomber missions over Laos rose by about 50 percent over the figures for 1967 and 1968—to more than 4,000, nearly six a day. The extent of those operations was not made public by Nixon on March 6.

The 1970 Laotian crisis did not become one. As predicted, the North Vietnamese made no effort to sweep to the Thai border, and Senate indignation at the White House's escalation and deception was shunted aside by the other crisis of that spring—in Cambodia. Kissinger maintained his usual mastery over the press corps; none of the attacks on the March 6 statement traced responsibility to him.

Nonetheless, early 1970 was a parlous time for Kissinger. Some of his closest aides openly despaired of the lying and escalation, and it was clear that

---

* One egregious error concerned a basic statistic: the number of enemy troops in Laos. Jerome H. Doolittle, a United States Information Agency official who was a press attaché in Laos in 1970, recalls the shock at the White House decision to put out the March 6 statement without clearing it with any of the experts in the field or in the Pentagon and the State Department. The night before the statement was issued, Doolittle had told a press briefing in Vientiane that there were 40,000 North Vietnamese troops in the country. The next day, Nixon put the number at 70,000, "Suddenly we had this gigantic increase that'd occurred overnight," Doolittle recalls. "We had to ask for guidance from Washington and they came back saying they had good, solid intelligence. What they'd done was add up every conceivable estimate." Doolittle was so angry he was tempted to ask Washington why, if the information it had was so accurate, it wasn't being made available to the men whose job it was to fight the war.

more resignations were in the offing. The possibility increased that someone from the inside would tell the world what the Vietnam policy of the White House really was.

Two of Kissinger's men had become serious about leaving before the Laotian crisis erupted. In February 1970, Roger Morris and Anthony Lake talked about quitting—and how to do it—as they walked along the quiet beach at Key Biscayne late one evening. They had been writing and rewriting drafts of the White House's first Annual Report on United States Foreign Policy.

"Tony and I hadn't been that terribly close before," Morris recalls. "We were talking about our misgivings about this administration and both of us came to the conclusion that we probably would leave quietly and in a gentlemanly way at the end of the year—not because we wanted to leave Henry, but because we were so at odds with the administration. Both of us were genuinely worried about the direction that Henry was going; we worried that our departures would leave him, in effect, without any liberal input. We were both impressed by then with how much Henry was head and shoulders above anybody else in the administration. We had seen NSC meetings; we had seen what an incompetent Rogers was, what a cunning knave Laird was, and we both had a great deal of respect for Henry as a man and as a public servant. We were both anti-Nixon; he was about what we'd imagined him to be. He was brighter than I imagined, but every bit as venal and every bit as political. But Henry was different. I'd worked for Rostow and Bundy; Tony had worked for Katzenbach and Lodge, and neither one of us had seen a man with the grasp Henry had. Intellectually he was a delight to work for."

At that time, "there was no single motivation" for their decision. "We both had a feeling of being terribly uncomfortable. We felt that things were going badly and that things were going to end badly."

When he went back to Washington, Morris expressed some of his disillusionment to Kissinger and asked to be relieved of NSC staff responsibility for African affairs; he was still angry over the government's refusal to rush food and medical supplies to Biafra after the collapse of the revolution there. In response, Kissinger set up a new NSC Special Projects Office for Morris and Lake, and one of their first assignments was to write an amusing speech for him to give at the Gridiron Club, an association of Washington journalists whose annual off-the-record dinner party is a major event in the capital. Soon afterward, Kissinger took the two young men aside and shared a secret he knew they would find exciting: He had met privately in Paris the summer before with Xuan Thuy, the senior North Vietnamese negotiator in the peace talks; now the President had given permission for another private meeting, to be held in late February. This session might well be even more important, because Le Duc Tho, the fifth-ranking member of North Vietnam's ruling Politburo, would be there with Xuan Thuy. "It was sort of mind-boggling," Morris recalls. "He was negotiating the end of the war." Kissinger authorized Morris and Lake to tell W. Richard Smyser, a Foreign Service officer with Vietnam experience who had recently been assigned to the NSC, and to include him in the policy planning for the meeting. No one else was to know.

The three men wrote drafts of papers on American troop levels and the continuing question of how power in South Vietnam would be redistributed after a peace agreement. Kissinger seemed nervous about the meeting with Tho, who had the authority to make an agreement that Xuan Thuy clearly lacked. Morris remembers how he, Lake, and Smyser watched as Kissinger practiced his opening remarks to Tho. "He would pace back and forth and talk through his negotiating stance," Morris says: "We're both scholars, men with a sense of history. I want you to know that we begin these negotiations with an acute sense of the great sacrifice the people of North Vietnam have made in their struggle. I don't intend to negotiate any settlement which dishonors that sacrifice in any way. I look forward to the time when we can meet under different circumstances, when you can come to the United States and I can come to Hanoi."

In his memoirs, Kissinger wrote that he had urged the renewal of secret talks in early 1970 because he believed that the United States was in a strong position. In his November speech on Vietnam "the President had taken his case to the people and received substantial support." Another factor, perhaps, was Kissinger's belief that Hanoi had perceived the signal being given by the renewed American bombing in Laos. Nixon agreed to more talks with considerable reluctance, and his skepticism proved correct. Le Duc Tho made it clear in three sessions—in February, March, and April—that North Vietnam still insisted on a new government in the South as a condition to serious bargaining, a condition Nixon and Kissinger would refuse to meet throughout the peace talks. At the first session, Kissinger wrote, Le Duc Tho asked how the United States, which could not win the Vietnam War with 500,000 troops in South Vietnam, expected to win after it pulled out its troops. It was a question, Kissinger wrote, "that was also tormenting me." The answer, of course, one that Kissinger could not write, was that he and Nixon hoped the North Vietnamese would capitulate when directly threatened with massive bombing, or worse.*

Another serious issue in the three secret meetings was Kissinger's insistence that any "deadline" for the withdrawal of all American troops and support facilities was dependent on reaching a peace agreement first. The United States was still in the awkward negotiating position of seeking the mutual withdrawal of North Vietnamese and American troops from the South, while it continued to withdraw unilaterally. The North Vietnamese, however, demanded that the deadline for American withdrawal be unilateral, and not linked to the success or failure of peace talks. It was not serious bargaining. In interviews with the author in Hanoi in 1979, Nguyen Co Thach, a key aide to Le Duc Tho, casually dismissed the early 1970 meetings as containing "nothing new."

Kissinger misread the North Vietnamese mood that spring. In his memoirs,

* There is no evidence in their memoirs that Nixon or Kissinger ever fully analyzed their reliance on bombing as an effective threat measure, or as a key facet of the "madman theory." North Vietnam was not the first society to stand up to systematic bombing. Studies of World War II show that the English, Germans, Japanese, and Chinese all stood up to it very well, as the North Koreans did in the Korean War. In the late 1960s Konrad Kellen of the Rand Corporation produced a series of studies, based on interviews with captured North Vietnamese prisoners, showing that morale in the North had remained amazingly high during the Johnson Administration's heavy bombings. All these studies suggested that intensive bombing might well increase morale. Many intelligence officials predicted in the late 1960s that morale in the North would be much higher during the war than afterward—and their predictions seem to have been borne out.

he noted that his reporting to Nixon after each session was "extraordinarily sanguine . . . partly due to my desire to keep the channel alive." Nixon's memoirs quote Kissinger as claiming after his first meeting with Le Duc Tho that "this has been an important meeting, certainly the most important since the beginning of your administration and even since the beginning of the talks in 1968." Kissinger was even more carried away after the second secret session, on March 16, two days before the overthrow of Prince Sihanouk in Cambodia; he told Nixon that "Hanoi had hinted at a willingness to discuss mutual withdrawal." In his memoirs, Kissinger acknowledged that he learned at the third secret meeting, in April, that he had misunderstood totally: Hanoi would discuss removing its troops from the South only after the negotiation of a coalition government in Saigon that did not include Thieu.

At that early stage, Kissinger wrote in his memoirs, "We were still relative innocents about the theological subtleties of Hanoi's unrelenting warfare." But there was nothing subtle or even secretive about North Vietnam's position. Late in 1969, Richard J. Barnet, a former Kennedy Administration disarmament official who had become a leading antiwar theorist, visited Hanoi and met with Premier Pham Van Dong. Barnet described these talks in a meeting with Kissinger, explaining that Hanoi had no incentive to negotiate with Thieu because Thieu had repeatedly declared that he would not accept a coalition government with the Communists. "Such negotiations would be a ratification of a defeat on the battlefield, an event which had not happened and seems most unlikely to happen," Barnet wrote a few weeks later. "Nor are they enticed by the prospect that 'something interesting might develop' in the course of such negotiations. As they see it, Thieu's only interest is to block negotiations, and so long as he is in control, this is precisely what he will do." As Kissinger was to learn in 1972, Hanoi's analysis of Thieu's intentions was correct.

The early 1970 talks were a failure that generated no new bargaining concepts, but Nixon and Kissinger did succeed, so they thought, in keeping them secret. Not even Rogers was told until 1971, and Laird, according to Kissinger's memoirs, was never officially informed.

15

CAMBODIA: THE COUP

IN MARCH 1970, Prince Sihanouk's government was overthrown by a group of anti-Communist Cambodian officials led by Premier Lon Nol. The coup, staged when Sihanouk was out of the country, marked the beginning of the end of Cambodia. Ahead were new ties to the United States, civil war with Cambodian Communists, intensified American bombing, disintegration of the social order, and, in 1975, defeat for the Lon Nol government, which would lead to the Pol Pot Communist reign of genocide and war with the Democratic Republic of Vietnam.

The North Vietnamese, in both public statements and the secret talks with Kissinger, denounced Sihanouk's overthrow as American-inspired.

On April 30, American and South Vietnamese Army forces invaded Cambodia—the infamous "incursion," as the Nixon-Kissinger White House called it—and Cambodia became engulfed in war between Lon Nol's Cambodian army, aided by the United States and South Vietnam, and the Cambodian Communists, or Khmer Rouge, aided by North Vietnam and the Vietcong.

The invasion was a shock to the American public as well as the Cambodian populace. It inspired antiwar demonstrations all over the United States, and led, indirectly, to the killing of four students at Kent State University in Ohio. The domestic political consequences of the war in Cambodia drastically affected American foreign policy throughout the summer and fall.

Sihanouk, crowned king in 1941 and chief of state since 1960, had long been under pressure from the United States and South Vietnam for his tolerance of the North Vietnamese and Vietcong "sanctuaries" that, from March 1969 on, were being secretly bombed by American B-52s under the personal direction of Kissinger. The Joint Chiefs of Staff had repeatedly lobbied both the Johnson and the Nixon administrations for permission to invade the sanctuaries; their invariable solution for the failure to win the war in South Vietnam was to expand it. Nevertheless, Sihanouk carefully maintained his neutrality. In January 1970, Sihanouk left his capital, Phnom Penh, for a two-month vacation in France and a series of high-level meetings in the Soviet Union; Lon Nol, a former Minister of Defense with close ties to the American military, was in charge of the affairs of state.

In early March, Lon Nol encouraged violent attacks—really sackings—on North Vietnam's embassy in Phnom Penh, and on that of the Provisional Revolutionary Government, the Vietcong's government in exile that had been set up in June 1969 by the NLF and an alliance of anti-Thieu forces. On March 16, there were more riots at the Communist missions and Lon Nol met with

North Vietnamese and NLF officials in Phnom Penh to demand that they withdraw their troops from the sanctuaries. They refused. On March 17, a day before the Cambodian parliament formally deposed Sihanouk in a staged, unanimous vote, Lon Nol authorized a South Vietnamese Army task force to cross the Cambodian border on a military sweep against Communist strongholds.

. In his memoirs, Kissinger alloted eight pages to a denial of any American complicity in or advance knowledge of the coup. The White House, he wrote, would have "preferred" that the Prince remain in office. As with Chile, and the overthrow in September 1973 of its president, Salvador Allende Gossens, there is no conclusive evidence that the United States was directly responsible for Sihanouk's overthrow in 1970. But, as with Allende, such responsibility cannot be measured entirely in terms of actions taken or not taken in one day or week or month; Lon Nol seized power in Cambodia knowing that his regime would immediately be recognized and supported by the United States.

Sihanouk's harshest critics were in the American military, and they did more than complain. His immediate overthrow had been for years a high priority of the Green Berets reconnaissance units operating inside Cambodia since the late 1960s. There is also incontrovertible evidence that Lon Nol was approached by agents of American military intelligence in 1969 and asked to overthrow the Sihanouk government. Sihanouk made similar charges in his 1973 memoir, *My War with the CIA,* but they were not taken seriously then.

One factor may have been his many personal flaws: He was vain, indiscreet, and had a high tolerance for official corruption.* In a sense, some of these faults may also have been responsible for his success in maintaining neutrality amidst war—he was constantly talking, and those listening, if they chose to do so, could hear only what they wanted to hear. Thus when the secret bombing of Cambodia became known at the height of the outcry over Watergate in July 1973, Kissinger was able to cite many broadcast transcripts and official memoranda of conversations with Sihanouk in which he seemed to express acquiescence to the bombing. Critics of the bombing were able to cite other broadcast transcripts and newspaper interviews to show that Sihanouk did not endorse the bombing.

Sihanouk was consistent in one view, however, and he expressed it to most official visitors: The United States could not win the Vietnam War. On August 22, 1969, for example, he met with Senator Mike Mansfield, the Montana Democrat who was a ranking member of the Foreign Relations Committee. According to the almost verbatim notes of a member of Mansfield's party, the Prince urged the United States "to adopt a realistic approach regarding inevitability. Since a unified socialist Vietnam cannot be avoided, it is better to begin now by establishing normal diplomatic relations with that Vietnam [North Vietnam]. There is no other choice. . . . The question of establishing relations with Saigon doesn't exist. There is one Vietnam with which to deal

* I asked to interview Sihanouk, who was in Hanoi when I first visited there. It was a difficult time for both the North Vietnamese and Sihanouk, since Nixon had visited China the month before. Vietnamese guards outside Sihanouk's villa relayed my request and I was subsequently told by a Foreign Ministry official that Sihanouk was playing badminton and could not be disturbed. "He is a very strange fellow," the Vietnamese official said, "always playing badminton." When I tried again later, the guards at the villa told me the Prince had converted his dining room into a badminton court and played through the night.

—socialist Vietnam." Sihanouk explained that he had been unable to get the North Vietnamese and the Vietcong to leave their sanctuaries inside Cambodia. "The [American] press," he told Mansfield, "criticized Cambodia for providing sanctuaries. Cambodia could criticize the U. S. and her allies in Vietnam for pursuing the Viet Cong . . . into Cambodia. The United States should look at its own responsibility when criticizing Cambodia." Sihanouk went on to say that he knew of American bombing of the sanctuaries and would not protest such bombing as long as the areas under attack were not inhabited by Cambodians. "It is in one's own interest, sometimes, to be bombed," he said; "in this case, the United States kills foreigners who occupy Cambodian territory and does not kill Cambodians." Finally, the Prince suggested that there was a way to avoid any bombing incidents—an American withdrawal from Vietnam. "It would seem that it would be impossible to avoid withdrawal," Sihanouk correctly added. "If the United States were now to say that the time had come for the Vietnamese to deal with each other and were to let them solve their problems alone, that would be a good thing."

Sihanouk, in typical fashion, provided something for everybody in his talk with Mansfield. Kissinger, if he was permitted to review the notes of that meeting, could conclude that Sihanouk was prepared to tolerate even more bombing, as long as Cambodians were not being killed, and also that the Prince did not realize—or was not prepared to acknowledge publicly—that systematic B-52 bombing was occurring in his country. Shortly after Mansfield's trip, Kissinger became even more obsessed with personally picking targets for the secret bombings, to avoid civilian casualties at all costs, as Colonel Sitton recalls.*

But Sihanouk's message was stark: The United States should consider a strategic, face-saving retreat. It was too late to save South Vietnam. In the Nixon-Kissinger White House, the messenger carrying bad news was always beheaded. What Kissinger would not say in his memoirs has been said repeatedly by former intelligence operatives who served in South Vietnam: Sihanouk was considered an enemy of the United States.

As in Laos, Green Beret teams led by Americans constantly moved into Cambodia on secret intelligence-gathering trips. The number of such missions, at one time code named "Salem House," rose from fewer than 400 in 1967 and 1968 to more than 1,000 in 1969 and 1970. Some extremely sensitive operations inside Cambodia were conducted with the aid of the Khmer Serei, an anti-Communist Cambodian movement of mercenaries based in Thailand that was dedicated to the overthrow of the Sihanouk government. But the official policy then in effect for the Green Beret units ruled out the use of ethnic Cambodians while on operations inside the country, and the vast majority of such cross-border operations were conducted with Vietnamese, Chinese, or Thai mercenaries. The Khmer Serei and another ethnic Cambodian sect, the Khmer Kam-

---

* In his memoirs, which were written with the aid of Wilfred Burchett, the Australian radical journalist, Sihanouk had a different description of the bombing's effect on civilians: "It was from American bombs and shells that our peasants suffered in the frontier [border] areas—not from the occasional presence of the Vietcong. And in the areas most frequently and most heavily bombed, there had never been any trace of the Vietcong. The corpses found . . . were those of Cambodian peasants, including a high proportion of women and children." His different remarks to different people made it difficult for me to investigate seriously for the Times the many leads to CIA implication in his overthrow, as published in his book in 1973.

puchean Krom, were also involved in the Phoenix assassination program, aimed at killing suspected Vietcong officials inside South Vietnam.* Such operations were carried out by Green Beret special operations teams throughout Vietnam.

Randolph Harrison, the Green Beret lieutenant whose colleagues were killed in the aftermath of the first secret B-52 strike inside Cambodia in March 1969, recalls that Special Forces units operating in the border area at that time were constantly urged by their senior officers to avoid encounters with Cambodian civilians. After an operation in which a Green Beret unit inadvertently blew up a Cambodian civilian bus, causing heavy casualties, Harrison and other Green Berets were ordered to stop carrying American-made weapons while on missions. "There was no secret about what we were doing," Harrison says, "but we just didn't want to give Sihanouk material that he could use against us. Philosophically, we considered Sihanouk to be in bed with the North Vietnamese. We just knew that the North Vietnamese were all over the place."

Forrest B. Lindley was a Green Beret captain commanding a Special Forces team, which included 450 ethnic Vietnamese, near the Cambodian border. His main mission early in 1970 was to coordinate and inject intelligence teams inside Cambodia, and he was constantly pressured to keep the Cambodian sanctuary areas under surveillance. There were repeated complaints from the Sihanouk government about the operations of Lindley's unit, which routinely lobbed artillery shells into Cambodia. "In February of 1970," Lindley recalls, "I was told that there would be a change of government in Cambodia. My radio operator, an enlisted man, actually told me. He got it from the Special Forces B team [a higher command]; they told him that Sihanouk was taking off for France. The radio operator also told me that the Khmer Serei would be going into Cambodia." Lindley was later ordered to transfer two of the four companies under his command to another Green Beret unit as replacements for Khmer Serei units that were going into Cambodia. "Using Cambodians in Cambodia like this had never been done before," Lindley says. "The policy was not to use Cambodians there because of the political ramifications of the United States supporting mercenary troops against their own government. This was a policy change." Lindley was forced to cancel many operations which, until then, had been considered a very high priority. He knew at that point that something big was in the air.

Other Green Berets repeatedly told colleagues after the 1970 coup that a highly secret Special Forces unit, known as Project Gamma, was responsible for conducting anti-Sihanouk intelligence operations inside Cambodia before Sihanouk's ouster. Project Gamma, formally listed as Detachment B57, Fifth Special Forces Group in South Vietnam, used members of the Khmer Serei and the Khmer Kampuchean Krom in its activities inside Cambodia, former Green Beret officers said. One member of B57, Captain John J. McCarthy, Jr., was court-martialed in 1968 and sentenced to hard labor for life for killing a Khmer Serei operative believed to be a double agent. McCarthy's conviction

* The KKK were basically bandits from Cambodia who worked for the CIA in Vietnam and were violently anti-Sihanouk. Their political goal, theoretically, was to liberate former Cambodian provinces in the Delta region of South Vietnam and return them to Cambodian control. In practice, however, as a senior Green Beret officer recalled: "They would fight anybody provided there was something in it for them."

was reversed in 1971, after an appeals hearing in Washington in which the Army warned that public disclosure of evidence in the case would damage national security. An official Army history of the Green Berets, published after the Vietnam War, does not mention Project Gamma or Detachment B57. Although the Pentagon has declassified much material about Green Beret cross-border operations inside Laos and Cambodia, nothing on Project Gamma has been made available. One former senior officer of the unit, who left South Vietnam prior to 1970, says that Gamma utilized only ethnic Cambodians in its operations, which were designed to gather tactical intelligence from deep inside Cambodia—areas that the normal Green Beret cross-border operations were forbidden to penetrate. The Cambodians involved in such missions, which included many Khmer Serei and some Khmer Kampuchean Krom, were extremely anti-Sihanouk, the former officer recalls, but he knew of no plans to overthrow Sihanouk while he was involved in Gamma.

Other Americans besides the Green Berets were involved in plots and operations inside Cambodia in the late 1960s. Samuel R. Thornton, a Navy yeoman assigned in May 1968 as an intelligence specialist to the United States Navy command in Saigon, vividly recalls that major planning to overthrow and assassinate Sihanouk was initiated late in 1968 by a Lon Nol representative who was then a high official in the Sihanouk government. Lon Nol was seeking a commitment of American military, political, and economic support after he engineered the overthrow of Sihanouk. The message was relayed by Lon Nol's representative to a Cambodian merchant of Chinese ancestry who regularly traveled between Saigon and Phnom Penh, and who—as Lon Nol and his aides understood—served as an intelligence operative for the United States. The Cambodian merchant was debriefed immediately upon his return by his contact, or "case officer," an American working under cover as an AID adviser to the Vietnamese Customs Service in Saigon. "I was the first person the case officer spoke to after his debriefing of the agent," Thornton recalls.

According to Thornton, the United States did more than pledge its continued support to Lon Nol. It sought to participate in the coup directly. A highly classified operations proposal, initially code named "Dirty Tricks," called for the use of Khmer Kampuchean Krom mercenaries to infiltrate the Cambodian Army before the coup and provide military support if needed. In addition, "the plan included a request for authorization to insert a U.S.-trained assassination team disguised as Vietcong insurgents into Phnom Penh to kill Prince Sihanouk as a pretext for revolution."* After the assassination, "Dirty Tricks" called for Lon Nol to declare a state of national emergency and issue a public request for American military intervention in Cambodia. Such intervention would include assaults against the North Vietnamese and Vietcong sanctuaries along the Cambodian border.

"I was present at some of the discussions which resulted in this plan," Thornton says, "helped prepare the proposal to use Khmer Kampuchean Krom elements, and personally delivered this portion of the proposal to the action office of the MACV [Military Assistance Command headquarters for Vietnam in Saigon] intelligence staff." At least two briefings on "Dirty Tricks" were given to the senior intelligence staff at American military headquarters in

---

* Many of the CIA and Green Beret assassination teams that operated inside South Vietnam routinely dressed as Vietcong cadre while on missions.

Saigon. Thornton remembers that it was late February or early March of 1969 —shortly after Nixon's inauguration—when approval for the operation came from Washington; the message said that there was exceptional interest in the project at "the highest level of government." Thornton says that he and others in his unit interpreted that comment as indicating that President Nixon or one of his top advisers had given personal approval. At that point, the project was given a more discreet code name, "Sunshine Park," and was presented to Lon Nol for his approval.

Lon Nol surprised the Americans by vehemently objecting to the talk of assassinating Sihanouk, calling that part of the plan "criminal insanity." Lon Nol "doubted that either he or the United States Army would be able to control the popular uprising he felt would develop from an attempt to assassinate the Prince, successful or otherwise," Thornton says. Instead, Lon Nol proposed that he lead a coup when Sihanouk left the country for one of his periodic trips to France. Lon Nol stressed "that he had requested originally only overt United States military support for a possible coup, emphasized his impatience with the proposal, and renewed his original request."

Lon Nol's counterproposal was relayed to Washington, where the response was surprisingly cool. Officially, Washington ordered that Lon Nol be told that the United States would have to base a decision to commit American forces in support of a coup on the exigencies of the moment. "Unofficially," Lon Nol "was to be told that, although he could in fact have the requested support, he must understand that the United States was sensitive to international criticism on this point, so that he must be prepared for a show of vacillation and great reluctance." Lon Nol agreed to the American position, Thornton says, and requested that Khmer Kampuchean Krom troops be infiltrated into Cambodian Army units. He also requested a meeting with the KKK commander, who was an exiled Cambodian, and such a meeting did take place, Thornton remembers, in which the two men reached agreement on the infiltration.

Thornton's tour of duty ended in May 1969, by which time the KKK troops had completed their infiltration of Cambodian Army units that were allegedly loyal to Sihanouk.* Thornton was not in Asia when Lon Nol took power in 1970, and he has no firsthand information about any American role at that time. But he maintains that he was present earlier at many secret discussions which "resulted in the plan to overthrow the Sihanouk government and either helped

* Thornton, who was living in Phoenix, Arizona, at the time of my interviews with him, told me he presented his information to the Senate Intelligence Committee shortly after it began its investigations in 1976. To his knowledge, nothing came of that approach. In late 1979, Thornton tried again to make his information public. He wrote a detailed account of "Sunshine Park" to the editor of the London *Economist* after the magazine had published a letter from Henry Kissinger insisting that Sihanouk's "overthrow took us completely by surprise." Kissinger in turn was responding to an *Economist* review of *Sideshow,* an exposé of the Nixon Administration's involvement in Cambodia written by William Shawcross and published in 1979. Andrew Knight, editor of the *Economist,* did not publish Thornton's letter; he wrote Thornton that he had investigated the allegations and could not substantiate them. Among those who told Knight they had no knowledge of "Sunshine Park" was Richard Helms, who pleaded *nolo contendere* in 1977 to two charges of making false statements to a Senate subcommittee about the CIA's role in Chile. Knight had also queried Henry Kissinger and two Navy admirals, none of whom confirmed the story, and he concluded that, as he wrote Thornton, "it would be irresponsible" to publish his letter after receiving such denials. If all journalists used Knight's method of asking those at the very top about their possible misdeeds, none of the major investigative stories of the past two decades would have become public.

prepare or had occasion to handle most of the pertinent documents." Unable to obtain the "Sunshine Park" documents under the Freedom of Information Act, despite repeated requests, Thornton wants the story known and says he would be willing to undergo a lie detector test if necessary. No governmental or congressional unit seems eager to take him up on the offer.*

One military man who would not need a lie detector test to be persuaded of Thornton's allegations is Randolph Harrison, the Green Beret officer. A few weeks after Lon Nol took over, Harrison—on his second tour in Vietnam, this time as an Army information officer—happened to be in the Associated Press news office in Saigon when a German freelance photographer brought in some film from Cambodia. The photographs were of war atrocities—beheaded and disemboweled Cambodian Communist cadre killed, so the photographer reported, by the Cambodian troops who were also in the pictures, posing with their victims. Harrison watched as the photographs were processed and was astonished to see that the smiling soldiers were Khmer Serei who had served with him the year before in South Vietnam. "I knew those guys," Harrison says. "They'd been in my Special Forces unit."

Thornton's allegations, when added to the questions raised at the trial of Captain John McCarthy and the recollections of Green Beret officers Randolph Harrison and Forrest Lindley, provide hard-to-ignore evidence that at least some officials in the American government were actively encouraging the overthrow of Sihanouk before 1970. It is scarcely possible that all this activity was going on outside the purview of the White House and the National Security Council. But, if it did, that would in turn raise profound questions about the Nixon Administration's ability to monitor and control the way the Vietnam War was conducted, and especially about Kissinger's responsibility as national security adviser.

* At least two academic researchers have reported that the Khmer Kampuchean Krom were operating inside Cambodia before the March coup against Sihanouk. Gerald C. Hickey, an anthropologist financed by the government whose specialty is the ethnic and tribal groups of Southeast Asia, told the Pentagon that KKK soldiers had been involved in the sacking of the North Vietnamese and PRG embassies in Phnom Penh on March 16. Hickey's written report was made in October 1970, when he completed his research, to the Defense Department's Advanced Research Projects Agency. Two days after the coup, Hickey wrote, the KKK began full-scale military activities against North Vietnamese and Vietcong troops inside Cambodia. "With their dark green berets and U.S.-made jungle fatigues, gear, and weapons," Hickey wrote, the KKK forces "stand out among the Khmer troops. Also, they have a markedly different manner and style, which has earned them the designation of 'American Khmer.'"

The second report on KKK operations came from George McT. Kahin, director of the Southeast Asia program at Cornell University, who testified before the Senate Foreign Relations Committee on March 6, 1975. Kahin told the senators he had learned that as many as 4,800 KKK soldiers serving with the Green Berets and the South Vietnamese Army had been pulled from their units and flown by American aircraft into Cambodia within a few weeks of the coup, and he added that there was "some reason to believe" that KKK troops were involved in anti-Communist riots inside Cambodia on March 8. Such movements would have been impossible without the knowledge of the American military command in Saigon, which closely monitored all cross-border intelligence operations into Cambodia. Additional support for these accounts of KKK troop movements can be found in Sihanouk's memoirs. Sihanouk's account tracks closely to that outlined by Thornton and the academicians, although he repeatedly writes that it was the CIA, not Navy intelligence, that was "masterminding the affair." The KKK, Sihanouk writes, without citing any specific source for the statement, "were in fact moved into Phnom Penh before the coup and were among those who attacked the embassies and later massacred the Vietnamese."

Not all the evidence indicating American complicity has emanated from those on the scene in Southeast Asia, however. Stephen W. Linger was an enlisted man who believed utterly in the rectitude of the Vietnam War and the fight against communism when he joined the Army as a volunteer. His high IQ and his patriotism projected him in early 1970 into one of the most secret jobs in the Pentagon—handling top secret and "Eyes Only" messages for the back-channel communications link of the Joint Chiefs of Staff. The link, formally known as the Digital Information Relay Center, provided the military with a secure way of exchanging informal single-copy messages not meant to be filed or retained in any form. In a world of secret badges and secret rooms, the Relay Center stood at the pinnacle. It processed some of the most highly classified communications intelligence in the United States government—including intercepted material from the Soviet Union—and it handled messages between the highest military commanders. It was a vital means of communication for Henry Kissinger, who could relay messages to field commanders in Saigon and elsewhere without the State Department's knowledge and even without the knowledge of Laird or any of his aides in the Department of Defense.*

Linger was thrilled at his assignment and the inside look it gave him into the government's activities. Over the months, however, as he began to perceive the difference between what was happening in Southeast Asia and what the newspapers were reporting, he became distressed. By early 1971, Linger was in touch with Jack Anderson, the newspaper columnist, and had begun to relay some of the Relay Center's information to him. Anderson's columns that spring and summer were to stagger Washington—and Henry Kissinger and Richard Nixon.†

---

* The Relay Center was under twenty-four-hour watch by civilian guards from the General Services Administration, and access to its basement quarters was limited to the few senior officers with appropriate clearances. Thus, Linger recalls, it was even more appalling when, in December 1970, military guards were suddenly put on watch at the Relay Center and ordered to use physical means if necessary to prevent Defense Secretary Laird or any of his aides from entering the area. "We were told," Linger recalls, "not to allow anyone from the Secretary of Defense's office—whether in uniform or not—into the Center to read backchannel messages. This was told to us orally—not in writing." Linger was never told the reason for the change of guards and the barring of the Secretary of Defense, who, under the 1958 Defense Reorganization Act, was legally entitled to any information available to the Joint Chiefs of Staff and its chairman.

† Linger's backchannel material, which began appearing in Anderson's column in mid-March, caused immediate turmoil. On March 18, Anderson reported that the United States was secretly seeding the clouds in Indochina in an effort to increase the rainfall over the Ho Chi Minh Trail. Anderson revealed the operation's code name, Intermediatry-Compatriot, and also correctly noted that it had begun in 1967. A few days later, again relying on Linger, Anderson reported that Ambassador David K. E. Bruce, the newly appointed head of the U. S. delegation to the Paris peace talks, had been restricted by Kissinger to the most routine intelligence about the war whose end he was supposed to be negotiating. For example, Bruce did not know in advance of the extensive bombing raids over North Vietnam in late November 1970. When he asked for more information—in a "flash" message to the Pentagon—Admiral Moorer's office "sent back a detailed account of the raids from the *Washington Post*." Anderson's potentially most explosive story came on March 24: "Contingency plans for a devastating air attack upon North Vietnam, including the bombing and mining of Haiphong harbor, are being kept up to date for possible use. . . . The top-secret plans, drawn up last October by General Creighton Abrams, the American commander in Vietnam, were transmitted to the Pentagon on October 17. They offer options for a three-day, seven-day or ten-day aerial assault upon North Vietnam." That story, which attracted little attention from other journalists, threw the White House and Admiral Moorer's office into a panic. Anderson later reported that John Mitchell ordered an extensive investigation, and all enlisted men in the Relay Center were subjected to interrogations.

But on the evening of March 18, 1970, Stephen Linger was still new to his job, and the thought of providing information to a newspaper columnist was far off. Nonetheless, he was curious about what was really happening in Cambodia. There was a high-priority message from an overseas American embassy late that night: Sihanouk, in Moscow, had pleaded with a senior American official to "help me out." Linger followed his usual custom with such messages: He forwarded a copy for immediate dispatch to Kissinger's office and telephoned aides of General Wheeler, chairman of the Joint Chiefs of Staff, who would have to wake him up and read him the message. Linger's duty hours were over before an answer came back, but the next day he dug out the file to see what the United States government had decided to tell Sihanouk. The message, when he did locate it, was one he would never forget: America had decided to adopt a "laissez faire" attitude. "The basic thrust of the message was 'lay off and let Sihanouk get overthrown,' " Linger remembers. And there was other immediate backchannel traffic from Washington to Saigon in which the White House and the Pentagon "kept talking about the military requirements for the new regime."

In his memoirs, Kissinger wrote, "We neither encouraged Sihanouk's overthrow nor knew about it in advance. We did not even grasp its significance for many weeks. My own ignorance of what was going on is reflected in two memoranda to Nixon." * It was the only point in his 1,500-page memoir when Kissinger took any credit for ignorance.

There were other Linger-supplied reports on secret cross-border operations into Laos and Cambodia, with the disclosure of correct code names; accurate analyses of the faulty intelligence that led to the 1969 My Lai massacre; a factual account of the FBI's ability to wiretap the Soviet Embassy; and, finally, a report on American electronic eavesdropping on President Nguyen Van Thieu's palace in Saigon. That story, published April 30, also revealed that all the South Vietnamese government's secure communications facilities had been supplied by the National Security Agency, which, unbeknownst to the South Vietnamese, was able to routinely decode any of the system's messages. Anderson reported that such intercepts, known as "gamma controlled items," were identified by the code name "Gout," and were forwarded to Washington marked "Exclusive for Dr. Henry A. Kissinger/White House."

In all, Anderson wrote thirteen columns between March 18 and May 6, 1971, using Linger's information, and all were ignored by the rest of the press. In some cases, Anderson's information was recycled by other reporters in stories years later, and invariably each was treated as major news. For example, in early July 1972, I reported more extensively on the military's rain-making programs on the front pages of the New York Times; the White House had no official comment but secretly ordered the program shut down two days later. The failure of the press to follow up on his reports tells a little about Anderson's ambivalent status among his peers and a great deal about the Nixon Administration's ability to control events. Anderson did not become a quotable columnist until December 1971, when he got access to and published the famous "tilt" papers dealing with the India-Pakistan war. In 1972 he again published voluminous documents, dealing with ITT's involvement inside Chile, and again made front-page news. In retrospect, it looks as if Linger's leaking failed to change American policy because Linger did not take the step of actually giving Anderson top-secret documents from the Relay Center for publication. What was needed to cut through the administration's effective public relations front, at least through 1971, was the real thing.

* In Sideshow, William Shawcross reported that Kissinger, at a farewell lunch in January 1977 with a group of European journalists, defended his role in Cambodia and added that the United States had not been involved in Sihanouk's overthrow, "at least not at the top level."

16

VIETNAM:
A SPRING INVASION

APRIL 1970 was a difficult month for the men running the White House. Nixon was, by his own description, "tense" because of the coup in Cambodia and the unchanging military situation in South Vietnam. The tension seeped to Kissinger, who spent much of his working day worrying about—and trying to shape—the mood of his boss.

There was plenty to worry about. Kissinger's secret talks with the North Vietnamese had gone badly, and, by mid-April, Nixon and Kissinger were convinced that the North Vietnamese, far from negotiating an end to the war, planned to try to overthrow the Lon Nol government and take over Cambodia. The White House's options seemed limited, largely because of the recent escalation of bombing and ground war in Laos, which had led to a brief renewal of antiwar dissent in Congress and the media—dissent that had been forcefully neutralized, so Nixon and Kissinger thought, by the strong November speech and the administration's continuing reliance on Vietnamization.

There were other pressures, too. The doves in Congress were continuing their efforts to force the administration to seek a ban on the MIRV missile. And the Senate, having defeated Nixon's nomination of Clement F. Haynsworth, Sr., for a Supreme Court vacancy the previous November, turned back his second nominee, G. Harrold Carswell, on April 8. Nixon took the rejections of these southern judges personally. "If the Northern liberals had tasted victory in defeating my second nominee," he wrote in his memoirs, "I was determined that they would at least pay a political price for it in the South."

It was amid these political rebuffs that Nixon's aides and staff were invited to share the President's admiration for the movie *Patton,* a biography of the World War II Army hero. The movie glorified—as Hollywood invariably does —the violence of the war. General Patton was dramatized as unpredictable and independent almost to the point of insubordination—qualities that obviously appealed to Nixon. He had been forced to cancel plans to see his daughter Julie graduate from Smith College after the Secret Service warned that several student demonstrations were being planned. "Julie was also terribly disappointed," Nixon wrote in his memoirs. "She tried to hold back her tears." Vice President Agnew had some unwelcome advice for the President: " 'Don't let them intimidate you, Mr. President. You may be President, but you're her father, and a father should be able to attend his daughter's graduation.' "

But Nixon was not only a President who could not attend his daughter's graduation. He was also a President who, the year before, had canceled the Duck Hook escalation in North Vietnam and had done nothing in response when the North Koreans shot down an American plane. Hanoi still stubbornly refused to show any signs of lessened resolve, despite repeated warnings and savage "signals." The President was worried, Kissinger noted in his memoirs, that 1970 would not produce any major foreign policy achievements, and he did not want to let his policies in Southeast Asia be the major criteria for the voters in the November congressional elections.

Early in April, eager to retaliate against his real and imagined enemies but afraid of the political consequences, Nixon had instructed Kissinger to explore secretly the possibility of a summit meeting with the Soviet Union. Late that month, the Russians responded, as the White House viewed it, by increasing their combat personnel in Egypt and authorizing their pilots to begin flying defense missions there. Nixon did not publicly criticize the Russians. Instead, he was forced—again for political reasons—to make another concession to antiwar critics. On April 20, he announced that by the spring of 1971 an additional 150,000 American troops would be withdrawn from South Vietnam—the largest cutback so far.

A reaction was inevitable. It came during the last days of April, and it culminated in Nixon's formal order, issued in secret on April 28, that American troops invade Cambodia. Once again, the method in the madness was to show the North Vietnamese and the Soviets that they must not take risks with Richard Nixon's character. The order, when it was made public two days later by the President, would be justified as a response to increased "military aggression" by the North Vietnamese. Kissinger, in emotional discussions with NSC staff members before the invasion, repeatedly made it clear, though not in so many words, that Nixon's apparent instability was a usable and expandable bargaining resource.

Still, an intention to invoke the "madman theory" does not fully explain the Cambodian invasion. The decision was made by an angry, frightened, and unsure President whose main adviser—in a kind of reverse synergism—exploited those fears to establish, once and for all, his dominant position in the White House. Kissinger's participation in the Cambodian planning led to the resignation of at least four members of his staff, all of whom argued that the invasion of Cambodia by American troops would accomplish none of its objectives. It led to campus riots, the jailing and slaying of students, and Senate passage of the Cooper-Church Amendment demanding the removal of all American troops from Cambodia by July 1—the first such military restriction ever voted by Congress against a President in a time of war, declared or undeclared.

A ground assault into the Cambodian sanctuaries had always been high on the military's wish list. In February, Laird, accompanied by Robert Pursley, his military assistant, made an inspection trip to South Vietnam and discussed such an assault with General Creighton Abrams, head of American forces. Abrams was convinced, Pursley recalls, that the South Vietnamese Army could now handle such a ground assault by itself, with very little United States support.

Sihanouk's overthrow on March 18 removed a major obstacle, and, with

Lon Nol's acquiescence, the South Vietnamese Army began penetrating deeply and often into Cambodia. On March 20, two days after the coup, there were South Vietnamese Air Force attacks and ground probes inside Cambodia; a week later, a South Vietnamese armored unit crossed the border. On April 5, two South Vietnamese battalions moved ten miles into Cambodia. The official policy of the United States government at the time was that the South Vietnamese were operating on their own without American support, but few —either in the United States or in North Vietnam—were fooled.*

In postwar interviews, Nguyen Co Thach told the author that his government hoped at first that the Lon Nol regime would remain neutral and permit the North Vietnamese troops to continue operating out of their base areas along the border. The South Vietnamese invasion in April dashed that hope, and also put Hanoi's troops in jeopardy. Its forces found themselves caught in a pincer between the invading South Vietnamese Army and units of Lon Nol's Cambodian Army, which was made up, in many cases, of American-trained Khmer Serei and Khmer Kampuchean Krom, who had been infiltrated into regular Cambodian units after the ouster of Sihanouk, and, according to some Green Beret officers, even before his overthrow. The North Vietnamese troops, confronted with a classic military trap, had to break out of their base areas to protect their foothold inside Cambodia. "We went westward" in the skirmishing after Sihanouk's ouster, Thach explained, "but not to capture Phnom Penh." It would have been "militarily impossible" at that point to go into the main city, because the Khmer Rouge, the guerrilla Communist insurgents in Cambodia, were not strong enough. North Vietnam's goal in 1970, Thach said, was "to train the Khmer Rouge people so they could set up an army to liberate themselves."

Hanoi's decision to expand its activities in Cambodia was a military step that many advisers on Kissinger's National Security Council staff had anticipated. Watts and Lynn both remember warning Kissinger that an invasion of Cambodia would force the Communist troops out of their sanctuaries and drive them farther west—toward Phnom Penh; in essence, the aides were arguing that the invasion would in fact provoke the threat that Kissinger and Nixon were using to justify it—that Hanoi had plans to invade Phnom Penh.

John Court recalls seeing some evidence later on that the goal of the North Vietnamese, caught between the South Vietnamese and Cambodian Army operations, was to threaten Phnom Penh. "But it was not compelling. The North Vietnamese objective was to win in South Vietnam—not in Cambodia." It was only after the invasion that the possible threat to Phnom Penh appeared. "The evidence came to light as a result of the incursion," Court recalls. "The documents [captured then] showed that as the North Vietnamese moved west, they could threaten Phnom Penh. Henry talked like he wanted to believe it. It provided a neat reason after the fact."

There was similar skepticism at the Pentagon. Colonel Pursley concluded, after reviewing the available intelligence, that "there was no substantive basis" for the Nixon-Kissinger theory that Phnom Penh was directly threatened. "It's a theory that has to stand on its own." A senior civilian Pentagon

* Laird revealed to the Senate Foreign Relations Committee six weeks later that he had "approved and recommended" the April 5 mission and others.

official says he and his staff concluded that the North Vietnamese would not risk an overthrow of Lon Nol because it would be much criticized in the Third World. At the State Department, intelligence officials recall that the North Vietnamese began preparing for an attack from Lon Nol shortly after Sihanouk's ouster. North Vietnamese artillery was normally targeted to the east, at sites inside South Vietnam, rather than against Cambodia, to the west. But "They turned their guns around 180 degrees," one official said. "They were worried about their supply lines and their troops were terribly exposed." It was only then that the North Vietnamese began to expand their base areas inside Cambodia, seeking to protect their supply lines and, in the process, alarming Nixon, Kissinger, and some of the military. The State Department and senior civilian officials in the Pentagon urged that the United States limit its aid to the Lon Nol government; they argued that an immediate heavy shipment of arms and matériel could provoke the North Vietnamese into retaliating against the new regime.

Evidence and arguments were less important in the White House than Nixon's belief that Hanoi was defying him. By the third week in April he had developed a solution: to demonstrate his toughness by using American troops in the next cross-border invasion of Cambodia.

The policy was irrational and the intelligence used to justify it unpersuasive, and thus Nixon planned the Cambodian operation in secrecy, away from those in the Cabinet who might object. Laird and Rogers, while aware of the proposed escalation, were excluded from any serious involvement in its planning; in their place Nixon relied on Richard Helms, his newly compliant CIA director.* He also set up an extraordinary backchannel arrangement with General Abrams in Saigon, and with other military men who were experts at telling presidents what they wanted to hear. The same could be said for Kissinger. Between April 22, when Nixon first considered using Americans in Cambodia, and April 26, when he made the final decision to, as he put it in his memoirs, "go for broke" and commit 32,000 American troops to the invasion, there is no evidence that Kissinger raised any objections, although Laird, Rogers, and some of Kissinger's closest aides voiced heated dissent.

Watts, Lake, and Morris, who knew of the secret Paris peace talks with Le Duc Tho, were especially upset. Watts knew firsthand just how irrational Nixon's approach to the operation was. In one telephone call during the Cambodian planning, Watts was assigned to take notes as the President talked to Kissinger and said, speaking of the Senate rejection of Haynsworth and Carswell, "Those senators think they can push Nixon around on Haynsworth and

* Helms had been badly burned by Kissinger and the NSC staff in the debate over MIRVs and Soviet missile testing the previous fall. Being proved right in that argument hadn't helped his position with the White House; he knew Nixon and Kissinger were still constantly criticizing CIA reporting. His subsequent insecurity played into Kissinger's hands: Helms not only supported the use of American troops in Cambodia, but also suppressed a CIA analysis, completed in April 1970, which concluded that a major American and South Vietnamese Army attack on the sanctuaries in Cambodia, no matter how successful, "probably would not prevent [the North Vietnamese] from continuing the struggle in some form." The report was provided to Helms thirteen days before the Cambodian operation, but Helms returned it to his analysts, asking that it be considered again on June 1, six weeks later. John Huizenga, testifying before the Senate Intelligence Committee in 1976, described Helms's action as an example of "gross interference" with the intelligence product.

Carswell. Well, I'll show them who's tough.'' In another telephone conversation, Watts heard Nixon tell Kissinger, "The liberals are waiting to see Nixon let Cambodia go down the drain the way Eisenhower let Cuba go down the drain.'' The "madman theory" was now being directed at Congress.

Watts knew too that Nixon and Kissinger were excluding from their planning everyone who might raise objections. Shortly before a key meeting Kissinger ordered him to locate Admiral Moorer, acting chairman of the Joint Chiefs of Staff, and invite him to an Oval Office meeting as "the President's principal military adviser"—thus not as a representative of the Secretary of Defense. Obviously, "Laird was not to be invited."

Watts learned by Friday, April 24, six days before the invasion, that American troops would be involved in force. That evening, Lake, Morris, Lynn, and Winston Lord filed into Kissinger's office to discuss the invasion. As they did, Kissinger looked across the hall to Watts, working that day in his outer office, and said, "Do you want to sit in? This is my bleeding hearts club. Do you consider yourself a bleeding heart?" Lake remembers that moment well. "I could see Bill's future passing before his eyes because I think he knew what was going to happen. He said, 'Yes, I consider myself as such,' and we went in.''

The meeting itself dealt only with the possibility of an invasion of Cambodia by South Vietnamese troops with American advisers. Morris, Lynn, Lake, and Watts had each been privately told—and Lord may also have known—that American troops would also be used, but none of the aides knew whether the others had been told, so none of them brought up that aspect. At one point during the discussion, which remained low-keyed, Kissinger heard out Lake's arguments and said, "Well, Tony, I knew what you were going to say." Lake recalls thinking, " 'Well, I am out of the effectiveness trap. If I am predictable, if I can be dismissed that way, then there is no point in my staying around.' I decided to resign if they did it."

Lynn told Kissinger that a Cambodian invasion would not only drive the North Vietnamese deeper into Cambodia (where Nixon already had come to believe they were), but, more important, would leave the defense of South Vietnam that much more vulnerable and open to a Vietcong and North Vietnamese offensive. Kissinger made a special effort with Lynn, who was older and, with his background as a Pentagon analyst, seemed more mature and less agonized than the other dissidents. Lynn remembers hearing more than once during those frantic days Kissinger's explanation of the bargaining power of Nixon's seeming irrationality: "Henry talked about it so much, particularly at the time of Cambodia—that the Russians and North Vietnamese wouldn't run risks because of Nixon's character." By then, however, Lynn had become concerned about Nixon's real state of mind. "All of us were worried about this man's stability. We'd have glimpses of him and didn't know what to do with it."

A few days before the operation, when the Joint Chiefs' hastily drawn plans for the attack were submitted to the White House, Kissinger—as he had done with the Duck Hook planning papers—asked some of his staff to evaluate them. "The plan was just awful," Lynn recalls. "It was imprecise and vague. I was to write up all the questions I could think of—about refugees, the South Vietnamese Army, security, and I even queried the proposed result of the operation itself." Kissinger told Lynn his list was "terrific" and gave it to a military aide to present to the Joint Chiefs for a reply. Lynn heard nothing over the next few days and eventually asked Haig whether anything would come from his queries. Nothing did. Lynn had managed to convince himself after writing his tough critique of Duck Hook in the fall that Kissinger had not wanted those escalations, and he still thought so years later. He could have no such illusions about Cambodia. Lynn was to leave the NSC staff not long afterward.

Morris was among those who warned Kissinger about the domestic dangers of the Cambodian operation. He and Lake "said we thought there would be tremendous domestic consequences. We said something about 'blood in the streets,' but we had no idea what was going to happen at Kent State. I argued that Cambodia was a contradiction in terms for Henry, in that he was always talking about a savage blow and it was technically impossible to administer a savage blow in that terrain; this was another indecisive action and the war would simply go on. You might have political effects in Southeast Asia but you certainly would have political effects here at home."

None of the arguments mattered. Nixon had begun to personalize the war and no one, certainly not his national security adviser, dared to interfere. Until he made his dissent known, Morris had been involved in the flow of paper from Nixon's office to Kissinger, memoranda he later described as "stream-of-consciousness excursions into courage and aggression" that would "make extraordinary reading for historians if they survive." Nixon published only one such paper in his memoirs, a memo he wrote during the Cambodian planning. Kissinger published the same document in full.* Morris says the memoranda depicted "a man angry and obsessed with the idea that the other side was trying to push him around" in Cambodia. "Now what the hell are they trying to do, Henry? These intelligence reports are very disturbing. It looks as if there is an effort here to take advantage of the weakness of the new regime, an effort to take over large sections of the country, to upset the truce, to have some kind of decisive, indirect effect on politics in South Vietnam." Nixon's memoranda gave the sense "of being taken advantage of—a sense that the other side was trying to steal a march on the whole process and the tacit understanding by which Kissinger had begun the secret negotiations: which is that we were now at the stage of getting out and they were going to help us get out in a mutually advantageous way. Suddenly they had broken the rules of the game and we could not afford to let them do that. The constant refrain of these conversations was: How are we going to look? Where will we be after this if they do something dramatic in Cambodia? We can't let them do this."

Morris remembers Kissinger as very noncommittal in his telephone talks with Nixon during that time: "You're right, Mr. President, but on the other hand they could simply be testing us; they may not be going all the way. There was a lot of 'Yes, Mr. President' in it." Kissinger was talking "not as if he

* In the memorandum, written April 22 at five o'clock in the morning, Nixon castigated the "State Department jerks" who had successfully urged him the month before not to offer Lon Nol large-scale military aid and thus provoke the North Vietnamese. "They are romping in there," Nixon said of the North Vietnamese, "and the only government in Cambodia in the last twenty-five years that had the guts to take a pro-Western and pro-American stand is ready to fall." Nixon began the memorandum by noting, "I think we need a bold move into Cambodia. . . . In the event that I decide to go on this course . . . We are going to find out who our friends are. . . ."

were serving the President," Morris thought, "but as if he were treating him," as a doctor would his patient.

Morris and Lake resigned on April 29, in a joint letter to Kissinger expressing regret "because of our regard and respect for you."* They handed their letter to Haig and asked him not to give it to Kissinger until after the invasion. "Tony and I seriously discussed calling a news conference when we quit," Morris recalls, to tell the public about the wiretapping and Nixon's drinking. "I consider the failure to do so to be the biggest failure of my life. We didn't do so on the single calculation that it would destroy Henry. I knew the administration was squalid, but there still was this enormous illusion about Henry. I clung to the delusion that the man was still rational and that even his own strong sense of self-survival would keep him out of real trouble. In effect, it was my theory of the limits of the ruthlessness of Henry Kissinger; in truth, there were no limits."

Watts said nothing to Kissinger after the late meeting on Friday, but was more nervous and tense afterward than usual. Watts had become heavily involved in the Cambodian planning, a project he loathed. It was a hard weekend for Nixon, too, Watts recalls. Late Friday afternoon, the President flew to the presidential retreat at nearby Camp David, Maryland, with Bébé Rebozo. There was the usual heavy drinking. At some point that night, the President, his voice slurred, telephoned Kissinger at the White House and turned over the phone to Rebozo, who had a message that the President would never deliver himself. Watts, horrified, listened on the line as Rebozo said to Kissinger, "The President wants you to know that if this doesn't work, it's your ass."

On Saturday, Watts finally expressed some of his concerns about American troop involvement to Kissinger, who told him, "Don't worry. I've seen the Old Man and it'll never happen." Kissinger suddenly began to praise Watts, telling him the Cambodian planning had "separated the men from the boys" and asking him to be White House coordinator of the operation. "I was now considered okay," Watts says. "I got home utterly distraught. What the hell do you do?"

Sunday afternoon there was to be a typical Nixon-Kissinger ritual: Rogers and Laird were invited to a National Security Council meeting, supposedly to discuss the Cambodian invasion plans. They still did not know that the basic decisions had already been made. Watts was torn. That afternoon, half an hour before the meeting, he told Kissinger he could not attend. " 'When I came to work for you,' I said, 'my sense of loyalty was, first, to the American people, secondly, to you, and finally, to Richard Nixon. I'm against this action on every count and I'm resigning.' Henry didn't know I was going to do it. We had a very tense exchange—hostile and tense. He said, 'Your views represent

---

* Neither Morris nor Lake left the staff immediately, but both were cut off from all sensitive materials. Shortly before Morris left the NSC that fall to work for Senator Walter F. Mondale, Democrat of Minnesota, as a foreign policy aide, Haig offered him a chance to stay in the government at a high level. "We'll get you a job in the Peace Corps," Haig said. "You want to stay in government somewhere where you won't have to worry about these big matters. We'll handle that."

the cowardice of the Eastern Establishment.' " Watts was angry too; he stalked into the Situation Room and told Winston Lord what had happened. Haig suddenly charged in, also very angry, and said, as Watts recalls it, "What the hell did you say to Henry? He's furious." Kissinger was throwing papers around his office in a rage, Haig said. Then he told Watts: "You've just had an order from your Commander-in-Chief and you can't refuse." "Fuck you, Al," Watts replied. "I just have and I've resigned." Watts left the White House and went home, feeling better than he had in months.*

There was much solace for Kissinger, however. If his staff was defecting, the President was not. On the day before Watts resigned, Kissinger—the man who had waited out Rogers' visits to the White House in agony—had been invited to join Bébé Rebozo, John Mitchell, and the President on a hard-drinking cruise along the Potomac. "The tensions of the grim military planning were transformed into exaltation by the liquid refreshments," Kissinger noted in his memoirs, without explaining how that group of four nonmilitary men could conduct military planning. The high point of the afternoon's activities was another screening of *Patton,* Kissinger's second viewing at the President's behest.

Nixon wrote much of his April 30 speech himself, but he read his final draft to Kissinger and Haldeman for their approval. Kissinger, as he subsequently told the Kalb brothers, offered "only small comments." The speech included a number of major lies—notably Nixon's statement that the United States had previously done nothing to violate Cambodia's neutrality. His cataclysmic view of the ground activities in Cambodia was equally significant: "It is not our power but our will and character that is being tested tonight. The question all Americans must ask and answer tonight is this: Does the richest and strong-est nation in the history of the world have the character to meet a direct challenge by a group which rejects every effort to win a just peace, ignores our warning, tramples on solemn agreements, violates the neutrality of an unarmed people, and uses our prisoners as hostages?" In his memoirs, Kissinger de-fended the speech, saying that "behind the words, at once self-pitying and vainglorious, the merits of the case were overwhelming."

William Rogers had a different reaction to the speech. He was presented with a copy only hours before it was to be telecast, and only a few moments before he, as the administration's highest-ranking official in foreign affairs, was to brief the Cabinet on it. One aide recalls the scene: Rogers had his shirt and tie open that afternoon; he had found time to play golf at his country club in the morning and had exposed his neck too long to the sun. Rogers read the speech without emotion until he came, near the end, to Nixon's plea that the country unite behind his policy. Then his face flooded with outrage. He flung the speech down and said, in a rare outburst, "Unite the country! This will make the students puke."

At the Pentagon, Laird and Pursley were angry about Kissinger's and Nix-on's manipulation of General Abrams, who had assured Laird in February that

* Watts formally left the National Security Council staff in early July, after catching up with his task of typing the minutes of NSC meetings. The day before he left, Kissinger called him in and, in a friendly and solicitous manner, asked him what he was going to do. As he left, Watts said, "Goodbye and good luck. It's been fun." "Don't say that, Bill," Kissinger responded. "It's been interesting."

the South Vietnamese Army could handle a Cambodian invasion by itself. "What they were doing," Pursley says, "was feeding Abrams stuff in the backchannel." In the critical days in late April, when Nixon and Kissinger were trying to avoid an internal confrontation on Cambodia, Nixon suddenly announced in a meeting that he would ask Abrams for his private view on the use of American troops; Abrams recommended exactly what the President wanted. Pursley learned from Haig what Abrams was telling the White House, and he refused to believe it. There was a shouting match between the two officers. "Haig was really putting the pressure on me, calling me and saying 'The Pentagon better come around.' "

Kissinger had now routed his two biggest foes inside the bureaucracy, and moved even closer to the Oval Office. It was Kissinger who stood firm in the hours immediately before the Cambodian invasion, reassuring the White House staff that it was a necessary action. Kissinger also told the staff, according to William Safire's memoirs, "We're trying to shock the Soviets into calling a [summit] conference, and we can't promote this by appearing to be weak. . . . Anyone who wants to negotiate a peace must hang tough. If we get through this, we should have a negotiation by July or August." It was the essence of the "madman theory," as well as dramatic evidence of Kissinger's loyalty.*

All the internal debate over North Vietnam's intentions inside Cambodia was swept aside by the night of April 30, when Nixon announced the invasion of Cambodia in his televised address. Using a map, the nervous and perspiring President falsely declared that "thousands" of North Vietnamese soldiers "are invading the country from the sanctuaries; they are encircling the capital of Phnom Penh." It was a test of American resolve, Nixon added: "If, when the chips are down, the world's most powerful nation, the United States of America, acts like a pitiful, helpless giant, the forces of totalitarianism and anarchy will threaten free nations and free institutions throughout the world."

In his memoirs, Kissinger did not go quite that far, but he did describe the Cambodian invasion as necessary to save Cambodia and Vietnamization. "By April 21 we had a stark choice. We could permit North Vietnam to overrun the whole of Cambodia so that it was an indisputable part of the battlefield and then attack it by air and sea . . . Or we could resist Cambodia's absorption" into North Vietnam. "The basic issue had been laid bare by Hanoi's aggressiveness; it was whether Vietnamization was to be merely an alibi for an American collapse or a serious strategy designed to achieve an honorable peace."

Nixon continued to behave erratically. The morning after his speech, after only a few hours of sleep, he traveled to one of the few places where he could be assured of a warm reception—a briefing room in the Pentagon where he was to get a report on the offensive from the Joint Chiefs of Staff. To some of those at the briefing he seemed incoherent. "He was like a college coach giving a pep talk," a senior Pentagon official recalls. "He was, in effect, giving the Chiefs carte blanche" in the war. The official added, "He was a little bit out

---

* Safire did not note in his memoirs that Kissinger was wrong in his optimistic assessment of the impact of the Cambodian invasion on the Paris peace talks, as he had been and would be about nearly all aspects of the Vietnam War negotiations. But he included Haig's comment after Kissinger's presentation at the meeting: "The basic substance of this is, we have to be tough!"

of control. It scared the shit out of me." In his memoirs, Nixon wrote that there had been a strained moment during the briefing: "Everyone seemed to be waiting for someone else to speak. Usually I like to mull things over, but I made a very uncharacteristic on-the-spot decision. I said: 'I want to take out all of those sanctuaries. Make whatever plans are necessary, and then just do it. Knock them all out so that they can't be used against us, ever.' " There was a small group of employees and press people waiting to greet him afterward, and Nixon once again seemed incoherent. Asked by a reporter about the American troops in Vietnam, he suddenly denounced the antiwar movement, which had taken to the streets in instant protest against the invasion: "You see these bums, you know, blowing up the campuses. Listen, the boys that are on the college campuses today are the luckiest people in the world . . . and here they are burning up the books, I mean storming around on this issue—I mean you name it—get rid of the war; there will be another one. . . ." Nixon's remarks were tape recorded by the journalists, and the word "Bums" was in every headline the next morning. Many readers, of course, agreed with the President.

The political pressure grew on May 3, when William Beecher of the *New York Times* reported the renewed bombing of North Vietnam, which had not been announced by the White House. The President had authorized raids over two days on supply depots and populated areas that had been off-limits since the bombing halt of November 1968. One raid, Beecher wrote, involved attacks by as many as 128 American fighter-bombers in Quangbinh and Nghean provinces, and North Vietnam broadcast charges of extensive civilian casualties. The renewed bombing of the North was another jolt to the bureaucracy, because, as press and public did not know at the time, Nixon and Kissinger had ordered the attacks without Laird's approval. Instead, the order went directly to Admiral Moorer.

Kissinger had tried to stop publication of Beecher's story, and when that failed, he and Nixon turned again to wiretaps.* On the evening of May 2, shortly after Kissinger heard that Beecher's piece was going to be run, and the day after the Hanoi broadcasts, Haig cited Beecher's article as a "serious security violation" in a formal request to the FBI for four more wiretaps. Pursley was to be wiretapped again at home and in his office, the real target clearly being Laird. Richard Pederson, the State Department counselor who was known to be close to Rogers, was also to be wiretapped at home and office; he shared two private lines on his desk with the Secretary of State.

* The first report of the bombing was made by Hanoi Radio, and Beecher, the *Times*'s Pentagon correspondent, confirmed the account from sources in Washington and prepared to write his story. Kissinger telephoned Max Frankel, the Washington bureau chief of the *Times*, and, with Beecher listening on an extension, began arguing against publication. Frankel and Kissinger talked almost daily, and perhaps, Beecher thinks, there was something in Frankel's resistance or his tone of voice as he defended the planned publication that alerted Kissinger. He suddenly asked whether anyone was listening on an extension. Frankel quickly shooed Beecher off the telephone and continued the conversation, unaware that everything he was saying was being recorded and transcribed in Kissinger's office. Kissinger's motive for trying to prevent publication of the story—already known internationally—was obviously to avoid provoking Laird, who had been bypassed in the bombing decision and might retaliate. It seems obvious, of course, that Laird had learned almost immediately of the bombing, through his own sources, but chose to keep his counsel.

William H. Sullivan, the former Ambassador to Laos who was then a Deputy Assistant Secretary of State, was on the list. He was a close aide to Marshall Green, who had become, after his dissent on the Cambodian operation, a major bête noire in the White House.* Sullivan was also a protégé of Averell Harriman, yet another reason for suspicion. And finally, Beecher, whose articles had been a source of grief to the White House since early 1969, was to be wiretapped. That assignment was of special sensitivity. Haig, citing presidential authority, told the FBI the White House wanted Beecher's home and office telephones to be wiretapped. "Haig stated . . . that he fully realizes the difficulty in covering office phones in . . . *The New York Times*," an FBI memorandum said, "and knows that this might not be feasible." According to the memorandum, "General Haig was advised that we would check with the Attorney General for clearance."

There is no known evidence that Beecher's office telephone—and unavoidably those of other *Times* reporters—was wiretapped. It was not "feasible," apparently, to do so. The newspaper had a large switchboard. So do government agencies, and, as the Watergate Special Prosecution Force later concluded, none of the people wiretapped by Nixon and Kissinger in 1969 and 1970 was monitored at work.

The FBI wiretaps on Pursley, Pederson, Sullivan, and Beecher would stay on until February 10, 1971, when, apparently at Hoover's insistence, all of them were removed. Kissinger, in his 1974 testimony to the Senate Foreign Relations Committee, explained that the four were wiretapped because they had access "to the information, to sensitive information that had leaked," and thus could logically be considered suspects. In fact, as Kissinger had to know, none of them—not even Beecher at the time—was aware of the real secret involved in the May 3 story: Laird had not authorized the bombing but had been bypassed. Laird, for all his infighting with Kissinger over Vietnamization, was a good soldier and had suffered many indignities in silence, but the Nixon and Kissinger decision to ignore the chain of command was high-risk.

On May 4, the Kent State shootings took place. The campuses exploded; one-third of America's colleges were shut down by administrators and demonstrators within a week. Ever the political animal, Nixon now sought to quell the national uproar. On May 8, the day before a hundred thousand citizens were to demonstrate in Washington, Nixon held a news conference and announced that "the great majority" of the American units in Cambodia would leave by the second week in June. He also unilaterally announced that all

---

* When Beecher reported, in another exclusive dispatch on April 22, that Nixon had secretly authorized a supply of captured Communist weapons for the Lon Nol regime, Nixon telephoned Kissinger in a rage and demanded that Green be fired. Kissinger took no action and Nixon did not return to the subject. But Kissinger too was angry about the story. Shortly after the Cambodian invasion, he ran into Jonathan Moore, another aide to Green who had joined in dissent on the Cambodian operation, in a White House corridor. Obviously smarting about the April 22 leak, Kissinger asked Moore, "Jon, why do you give me so much trouble? Why are you so resistant?" Moore, who had attended some of Kissinger's defense strategies lectures at Harvard, replied, "It's simply a matter of analyzing the pros and cons of your options and projecting the consequences, just like you taught me, professor." Kissinger said nothing and slipped into a nearby bathroom. A moment later he walked out and found Moore still in the corridor, waiting to see Daniel P. Moynihan, a former Harvard professor who was Nixon's senior adviser on urban affairs. "Jonathan," he bellowed, "if I asked you to send *rifles* to our boys over there, you'd find a way not to do it."

American soldiers would be withdrawn by July 1, and that no Americans would be permitted to go farther than twenty-one miles inside Cambodia. Kissinger was upset with the orders, describing them in his memoirs as "panicky decision[s]" that were the "one concrete result of public pressures." Kissinger was concerned about Nixon's hesitancy because, as he put it in his memoirs, "The ambivalence of the government in Washington was bound to be transmitted to those in the field who soon sensed that Washington was not handing out prizes for imaginative and bold efforts to pursue the enemy in Cambodia." There was another, equally fundamental concern that was not spelled out in the memoirs: Nixon's decision to limit the Cambodia offensive demonstrated anew the ultimate power of the antiwar movement. The "signal" was one of weakness, and not the promise of continued irrationality worthy of a true "madman."

The night after his news conference was another sleepless one for the President. His telephone logs, as reproduced in William Safire's book, recorded fifty-one conversations between 9:22 P.M. and 4:22 the next morning. After the final call, Nixon, accompanied only by his personal valet, Manolo Sanchez, drove to the grounds of the Lincoln Memorial, where antiwar demonstrators had already begun to gather, and engaged some of the students in chitchat. There was talk of travel and environmental problems, as few of the young people dared to engage the President directly on the Cambodian issue. "I hope it was because he was tired," one student subsequently told reporters, "but most of what he was saying was absurd. Here we had come from a university that's completely uptight—on strike—and when we told him where we were from, he talked about the football team." Nixon, now joined by Secret Service men and White House aides, drove to the Capitol, where he and Sanchez found the doors to the House chamber locked. Finally a key was found, and Nixon then showed Sanchez where he had sat as a member of the House in the 1940s. Nixon, according to Safire, sat in the first row of the chamber and told Sanchez to make a speech. There were some comments from the valet on his pride at being an American, and applause from the President. Nixon ended the morning with breakfast in a downtown hotel shortly before 7:00 A.M., his first meal in a Washington restaurant since his inauguration. Nixon devoted nearly seven pages of his memoirs—far more space than he allotted to some major international events—to an attempt to explain this sequence of activities. He had deliberately chosen not to take any staff or press along, Nixon wrote, in an effort to engage the dissidents in serious talks. "Thus it was especially frustrating when the newspapers reported that I had been unable to communicate with the young people I met . . ." Not even his closest aides saw it his way, Nixon added. When John Ehrlichman referred a few days later to the "problems I had created by talking about sports to students who had traveled hundreds of miles to protest my war policies . . . I snapped at him about the problems a President has when even his own staff believes the false stories that are spread about him."

Nixon wrote that "Those few days after Kent State were among the darkest of my presidency." There were also stories in the press revealing that Rogers and Laird had opposed sending Americans into Cambodia, and Walter Hickel, the outspoken Secretary of the Interior, publicly criticized the President's failure to communicate with the dissenting students. Two hundred and fifty State Department officials went so far as to sign a public statement objecting to the administration's Cambodian policy.

Kissinger remained steadfast through it all, although the demonstrations after Kent State threatened to make him, as well as the President, a virtual prisoner. One night Kissinger slept in Nixon's bedroom in the bomb shelter to avoid the demonstrators who ringed the White House. While many officials in the administration—including Nixon—advocated further concessions to the demonstrators, Kissinger was adamant in his opposition to them. "He was appalled at the violence they provoked and at the ignorance of the real issues they displayed," Nixon wrote. "He felt strongly that I should not appear more flexible until after the Cambodian operation was successfully completed. As he put it, we had to make it clear that our foreign policy was not made by street protests." * It was vintage Kissinger. To the President, he was unrelenting and tough—even tougher than Nixon. To student groups, however, with whom he repeatedly held private meetings in the days after the Kent State shooting, the message was "Give me six months."

One of Kissinger's former colleagues from Cambridge, an academic dean, recalls being asked to sit in during one of these meetings. "I felt—naïvely— that he really cared about the students," the dean recalls. "We sat down and talked about a plan to increase his contact with campuses—it was exactly what a dean would expect from a Harvard professor. By the time Henry had finished with the students—he briefed them in the Situation Room—they were eating out of his hand. I was equally taken; I really saw it as the beginning of a dialogue that Henry was going to have with American students. He told them, 'Give me six months. If you only knew what I'm staving off from the right'— a suggestion that he did not fully agree with the plans of Nixon. He sent away a very docile group of young people." Once the crisis had passed, however, there were to be no more such meetings involving the dean, and "I became increasingly unimportant to Henry."

Kissinger also had a stormy meeting that week with a group of thirteen senior faculty members from Harvard, including Thomas Schelling and Paul Doty. The session ended with angry denunciations and many newspaper stories. Kissinger's break with Harvard as reported by the nation's press had a built-in benefit for him: It played well in the Oval Office.

---

* In his memoirs, Kissinger claimed that he had a "special feeling" for the students, who, he said, "had been brought up by skeptics, relativists and psychiatrists; now they were rudderless in a world from which they demanded certainty without sacrifice. My generation had failed them by encouraging self-indulgence and neglecting to provide roots." It could be argued that the students' concerns were far less complicated, and in fact were centered in moral outrage over a war that was destroying a society. In any case, there is evidence that Kissinger's feelings toward antiwar students were far less avuncular and more personal—he was more and more becoming a target of the antiwar movement. In mid-April 1970, for example, as the Cambodian invasion was being planned, Kissinger was invited to give a keynote address to a conference of graduate students at the Johns Hopkins School of International Studies in Washington. After he was introduced, a majority of the roughly one hundred students in attendance stood up and a student leader read a statement they had signed which denounced the administration's Indochina policies. Kissinger listened in silence and, forgoing his speech, threw the floor open for questions. The first was direct: "Dr. Kissinger, do you consider yourself a war criminal?" With no show of emotion, Kissinger turned to the chairman of the proceedings, said, "Mr. Chairman, get your audience in order," and walked out.

Perhaps the embattled President and his loyal adviser were able to get some pleasure from their "Top Secret—Eyes Only" world of intelligence and national security as, on May 9, upward of a hundred thousand students and other demonstrators, none of whom had access to White House secrets, marched around the White House to protest Cambodia and Kent State. On that day, the National Security Council bureaucracy ground out NSDM 59, dealing with one of the most highly classified areas in government—nuclear weapons. Nixon and Kissinger signed authorizations bringing the total number of warheads for nuclear weapons in American arsenals to 27,173, an increase of 1,139 over the previous fiscal year. Another NSDM, No. 60, was also promulgated as the demonstrators marched: It authorized the deployment of 8,951 of those nuclear warheads outside the United States, spreading the weapons to American military installations across the world. On that day, too, the White House wiretaps produced a conversation between Halperin and Ellsberg in which Halperin told his friend that he had decided, after the Cambodian invasion, to resign as a consultant to the National Security Council. Halperin also said, according to an FBI transcript, that "the major and most certain consequence" of the Cambodian invasion "is that a large number of Cambodian civilians will be killed and labeled Viet Cong." Two days later, J. Edgar Hoover rushed Nixon and Kissinger "Eyes Only" letters reporting Halperin's views. Earlier, Halperin had been overheard informing a caller that Laird and Rogers had disagreed with Nixon's decision on Cambodia. Halperin also said, as Hoover reported to the White House, that "in his opinion the President had never had the intention of getting out of Vietnam," and added that "the only effective way to oppose the present policy is to elect a Congress which will stop the war by cutting off funds." Halperin was also quoted as agreeing to work with Walter Pincus, a staff aide to the Senate Foreign Relations Committee, who had played a key role in the committee's inquiry into Laos.*

Nixon, Kissinger, and Haig have given conflicting accounts of what happened next, but it is known that the Halperin intercepts led to a frenzy of high-level action. On May 12, the FBI was requested by Haig, in Kissinger's name, to wiretap two more members of the NSC staff: Lake, who had just resigned, and Lord, a Halperin protégé who had proved his mettle, in Kissinger's and Haig's eyes, by not joining the others in resigning over Cambodia. Lake and Lord were wiretapped for the next nine months. The next day, Hoover participated in a White House meeting with Nixon and Haldeman, and perhaps others, at which he was told to deal from then on only with Haldeman on the

_____

* Pincus, a *Washington Post* reporter, served as staff consultant to the Foreign Relations Subcommittee on U.S. Security Agreements and Commitments Abroad, which was chaired by Senator Stuart Symington, Democrat of Missouri. Beginning early in 1969, Pincus and Roland Paul, the subcommittee's counsel, toured American installations overseas to plumb and record in detail exactly what the United States military was doing in each country. Their work was closely monitored by Kissinger and the National Security Council, and by their second trip that year, every interview Pincus and Paul conducted with American officials was tape recorded. It was during this investigation that Pincus and Paul uncovered the extent of the secret American involvement in Laos and convinced Symington and Fulbright they should make it public. The two investigators also looked into the status of the National Security Agency's highly classified relay and interception stations overseas—another area that put them into constant conflict with the White House.

White House wiretaps. Kissinger and his office were no longer to be on the mailing list for wiretap summaries. On that day, too, Hoover provided the White House with some of the FBI's verbatim logs of the Halperin wiretaps upon which the summaries had been made.

At this point, Kissinger had reached a new height of power and authority inside the Nixon White House, and it is inconceivable that Nixon intended to strip away his direct access to the wiretap information as a punishment. One obvious factor in the switch was Lake, who was going to remain for the next few months as Kissinger's personal aide and thus might learn of FBI reports on his own wiretap, just as he had learned of the wiretaps on others. Similarly, Winston Lord was going to play a far greater role in Kissinger's office, something that Kissinger surely knew, and would also be exposed to the FBI records. Lake was wiretapped not for any indiscretion, but because of what he knew and the White House's fear that he would begin talking—which he did not. Lord had been brought into the National Security Council by Halperin, for whom he had worked in the Pentagon, and was thus a prima facie suspect in the hysteria over Halperin that persisted in the Oval Office.

What is extraordinary about the mid-May maneuvering inside the White House is how everyone involved lied about it in subsequent investigations, and managed to get away with the lies. President Nixon told J. Edgar Hoover, as Hoover reported in a memorandum, that Haldeman was to be the sole recipient of the wiretap summaries, "inasmuch as the President is anxious to cut down leaks that are occurring at the present time." In his deposition in the Halperin wiretap lawsuit, however, Nixon volunteered a different reason for making the change: "General Haig came in to see me. He expressed great concern about Dr. Kissinger's very emotional and very concerned reactions to the Cambodian action, not that he was opposing it. . . . He said we have simply got to get some of the load off . . . and he wanted it transferred to someone else and suggested that it might be Mr. Haldeman." But Haig, in his deposition in the Halperin suit, said that he had learned of the switch in policy only when Kissinger told him about it. Kissinger "said the decision had been made that we are out of it and there was a decision that I welcomed," Haig testified. In testimony a few months earlier, before the Senate Foreign Relations Committee, however, Haig acknowledged that "I had urged Henry to disassociate the National Security Council staff, meaning me or anybody else, from what was essentially an internal security matter. . . . I know he took that matter up either with the President or Mr. Haldeman or somebody outside of our office, and he informed me that we would in fact be out of it." Kissinger, in his Senate testimony, explained that the transfer to Haldeman's office "was no climactic event. During the course of the spring it had become clear to me that while I was getting occasional reports, I was in no position to do anything with these reports and I would just look at them and throw them into my out basket. I, therefore, pointed out on a number of occasions to the President that my office would serve best if it concentrated on foreign policy matters and if internal security matters were shifted somewhere else." After Cambodia, Kissinger said, "when I had mass resignations from my staff . . . I believed then that it was probably decided that the combination of my preference and some of the difficulties that had existed on my staff made it desirable to accede to my recommendation and shift it to another office. I was informed of this as a routine matter several days later. . . . The President never spoke to me about it."

Kissinger, of course, did not testify about one conversation with John Mitchell that may explain why he now wanted to get out of the wiretap business. In an interview with the FBI after the Watergate scandal broke, Mitchell recalled discussing the White House wiretaps either with Haig and Kissinger or just Haig alone. The FBI quoted Mitchell as agreeing with Haig and/or Kissinger that "the wiretaps could become 'explosive' " and that the whole wiretap operation was "a dangerous game we were playing." Mitchell later recalled that, in his opinion, Kissinger simply "wanted to get out" of the wiretap operations that spring. "He was just ducking—running for cover."

Exactly what did provoke the procedural change remains a mystery. Although Kissinger and others have repeatedly emphasized the almost trivial nature of the wiretap information, it was considered far from routine in the Nixon White House. The day after Haldeman was authorized to be the sole recipient of the summaries, he called in a senior FBI official and reported that Nixon had specifically requested that the summaries were to be handed to him personally or to be given in a sealed envelope to his aide, Lawrence Higby. Haldeman then instructed Higby—in the presence of the FBI official—not to open them. Haldeman further told the FBI that it was no longer to initiate wiretaps on demand from Kissinger or Haig unless he had cleared them in advance.

The change in procedure removed Kissinger from direct control of the wiretap operation. By then, his NSC staff had been purged; the malcontents and the disaffected had already left his office or were in the process of resigning. Morris, Lake, Watts, and Lynn would be replaced over the next few months by others far less mercurial, independent, and brilliant—but far more trustworthy and dependable from Kissinger's point of view. The new NSC aides would learn to follow orders without question.

Cambodia was a watershed for Kissinger; he would no longer permit himself to become fond of those on his staff, as he had with Lake and Morris. Kissinger also began to delegate to Haig much of the work of dealing with the staff and their papers. He would now begin to involve himself even more closely with Nixon and the continuous centralization of power in the White House.

By the end of June, the Cambodian offensive had played itself out. In their meetings with staff aides and the press, Nixon and Kissinger repeatedly described it as a victory, but the military in the field knew better. In June 1970, General Abrams raised a profound problem in a cable to Washington. He noted that the South Vietnamese Army was scheduled that summer to assume more military responsibility inside South Vietnam under the Vietnamization program, but was still heavily engaged on the ground in Cambodia. Abrams strongly recommended that the South Vietnamese be permitted to slow down the timetable for Vietnamization and continue to operate in Cambodia "during the next few weeks . . . to prevent loss of major objectives"—that is, the loss of Cambodia. Far from aiding Vietnamization, the Cambodian operation was apparently hindering it. Laird summed up the dilemma in a staff meeting at the Pentagon: "The South Vietnamese are wandering all over Cambodia protecting the government while we, in turn, are in South Vietnam protecting the South Vietnamese."

It was even more complicated than that, for the United States Air Force was fully involved by then in bombing Communist targets in Cambodia; and would continue to bomb there until stopped by Congress in mid-1973. Ironically, the air war in Southeast Asia had been expanded at a time when Kissinger's and Nixon's cherished secret B-52 bombing of Cambodia had come to an end. The last improperly reported "Menu" bombing raid was on May 26; in its fourteen months of operation, the more than 108,000 tons of bombs that had fallen on Cambodia had all been officially recorded as falling on South Vietnam. That secret would remain safe for three more years.

The end of Menu did not mean the end of secret bombing, however. On April 24, a week before the Cambodian invasion, the United States Air Force was authorized to begin bombing targets with tactical fighter-bomber aircraft as far as eighteen miles inside Cambodia; these raids were officially recorded as having taken place in Laos. That secret bombing lasted for thirty days, under the code name "Patio." After the American troop pullout on June 30, more secret fighter-bomber missions were authorized and there was much less concern about where the bombs fell. Bombing could now be carried out over much of eastern Cambodia and officially reported as being somewhere else. Under the code name "Freedom Deal," more than 8,000 missions against North Vietnamese, Vietcong, and Khmer Rouge troops inside Cambodia were flown between July 1970 and February 1971, when the duplicitous reporting procedures were discarded. Many of those bombing missions also eventually came to involve B-52s.

The continued bombing, albeit secret, by American aircraft and the continued need for South Vietnamese troops in Cambodia were evidence of the failure of the invasion. The North Vietnamese sanctuaries had not been cleaned out—only relocated to the west. The air war had been vastly expanded and the White House was again resorting to secrecy to disguise that fact. Later in the summer, the CIA produced a special study of the Cambodian operation and concluded that it had not "substantially reduced" the North Vietnamese capability in Cambodia. Any supplies that were captured, the CIA said, could easily be replenished in two and a half months.* In early June, Le Duc Tho refused a Kissinger request for another secret meeting in Paris, telling the White House the talks were in "temporary suspension" because of Cambodia. (The public peace talks between the United States and North Vietnam continued to drag on in Paris, but those sessions—announced in advance to the press —were little more than propaganda forums, and remained so throughout the war.)

The CIA's analysis proved to be highly accurate, but it was not the whole

* Cambodia was another setback for Helms and the CIA, however, in the view of Nixon and Kissinger. The Agency's analysts had insisted for years that the Cambodian port of Sihanoukville, on the Gulf of Siam, was not a major supply conduit for the North Vietnamese and Vietcong. Military analysts disagreed, and the dispute, which reached into the President's Foreign Intelligence Advisory Board, was not resolved until after the May invasion, when captured documents showed that an estimated 23,000 tons of military supplies had been funneled through the port from 1966 to 1970, far higher than the 6,000 tons officially estimated by the CIA. The Agency had refused to upgrade its estimate during the controversy, despite heated Pentagon protests. Helms had sided with his analysts, and as a result his reputation was diminished further. Nixon considered the Agency soft on Vietnam.

story. Nixon's invasion of Cambodia had backfired in two important aspects: It had not damaged North Vietnam's military capability there, and it had also led to an improvement in Hanoi's relations with its difficult ally, the Khmer Rouge. Throughout the Vietnam War, the constant tension between those two guerrilla armies was never fully perceived by the policy makers and intelligence agencies in Washington.

The antagonism originated with Hanoi's support of the Sihanouk government. In his postwar interviews, Deputy Foreign Minister Thach explained that his country supported Sihanouk because of his stance against the United States and his insistence on keeping Cambodia neutral—and thus open to North Vietnamese infiltration. But Sihanouk was also relentless in his efforts to stamp out the Khmer Rouge, and this naturally led to and reinforced the Khmer Rouge's distrust of Hanoi. After Sihanouk was overthrown, Pol Pot, the Khmer Rouge leader, went to Peking for conferences with the Chinese. In his absence, Thach said, Pol Pot's deputy asked the North Vietnamese to help fight Lon Nol. "Within two weeks, we helped them liberate four provinces," the North Vietnamese official said. "When Pol Pot came back to Cambodia, he asked us to leave—and so we did." *

Thach's explanation of the early days of warfare after Sihanouk's ouster was no doubt self-serving, but his description of the poor relations between Pol Pot and North Vietnam was borne out by the hostile relations between the two countries after the Khmer Rouge took over Cambodia in 1975.

Congress, in the wake of Laos and Cambodia, became even more concerned about the war in Southeast Asia. The Cooper-Church Amendment, which had passed the Senate, was not acted upon in the House, but other senators were proposing end-the-war amendments that went even further. Senators George McGovern and Mark Hatfield jointly proposed an amendment to the Defense Procurement bill that would have cut off all funds for the Vietnam War by the end of 1970; it lost 55 to 39. "But the pattern was clear," Kissinger noted with resignation in his memoirs: "Senate opponents of the war would introduce one

* Sihanouk, meanwhile, had established an exile government in Peking, which the Chinese government recognized. This raised the specter—at least in Nixon's and Kissinger's eyes—of his possible return with a pro-Communist government to Phnom Penh. Despite the White House fears, such a move was highly unlikely, for Sihanouk's main popularity was in the Cambodian countryside, not in Phnom Penh. In addition, there is evidence that the Chinese were less than enthusiastic in their initial support for Sihanouk. Thach recalled that shortly after Sihanouk's ouster, China formally requested North Vietnam to recognize the Lon Nol regime. Lon Nol, whose grandfather was Chinese, was treated deferentially by the Chinese during a visit there in 1969, Thach said, and invited to visit the graves of his ancestors. Thach claimed that the Chinese decided to endorse Sihanouk's exile government only after the North Vietnamese, Vietcong, and Khmer Rouge began their successful counteroffensive in late March and early April. "The Chinese realized that Lon Nol was very weak and so they recognized Sihanouk," Thach said. There is independent evidence for Thach's allegations. In *Sideshow*, William Shawcross cited a CIA report, made within days of Lon Nol's ouster of Sihanouk, which said that the Chinese Ambassador to Phnom Penh had made it clear that China was prepared to accept the Lon Nol government as long as the North Vietnamese Army and Vietcong could continue to have access to the sanctuaries. The CIA also reported that the Chinese, as well as the North Vietnamese, initially tried to deal with Lon Nol, but—after Lon Nol rebuffed any negotiations over rights of passage—both countries turned to the Khmer Rouge and gave it active support. Nixon and Kissinger, by encouraging Lon Nol to abandon neutrality in the Indochina war, managed to bring the North Vietnamese and Khmer Rouge together.

amendment after another. . . . Hanoi could only be encouraged to stall, waiting to harvest the results of our domestic dissent."*

On August 30, the Pentagon supplied Senator Edmund S. Muskie's office with some statistics that had been requested months earlier. Nixon's and Kissinger's operation in Cambodia had resulted in the deaths of 344 Americans and 818 South Vietnamese soldiers; 1,592 American GIs were wounded, as were 3,553 South Vietnamese. There were "no reliable or comprehensive" statistics for civilian Cambodian casualties during the two-month operation, the Pentagon said, but there was an estimate of the number of Cambodian refugees—130,000. None of these figures was mentioned in Kissinger's or Nixon's memoirs.

* The invasion did not prevent the ultimate defeat of South Vietnam, but it did pay off handsomely for Kissinger. In his memoirs, Nixon reported that in mid-May he awarded hand-sewn Purple Hearts to Haldeman, Ehrlichman, and Kissinger "for all the wounds you have sustained in the line of duty over the past few weeks . . . This will be our secret," Nixon told his aides, "but I wanted you to know how much I appreciate what you have done." The Purple Hearts, Nixon said, were sewn by a girl friend of Bébé Rebozo. Truly, Kissinger had cracked the inner circle.

17

IN FULL CONTROL

By the summer of 1970, the secret life of Henry Kissinger was known throughout the Washington press corps in the classic Washington way; that is, it was known to reporters and editors but not to their readers. Every reporter who considered himself a serious journalist understood that Kissinger was the "senior White House official" who briefed reporters or gave interviews about foreign policy. He became the one man in the Nixon Administration whom foreign affairs correspondents *had* to see. A senior editor in the Washington bureau of the *New York Times* told a newly hired reporter that summer that he, the editor, had a private telephone number and immediate personal access to Kissinger, as long as he did not "abuse the privilege."

Kissinger's elevated status inside the White House was apparent to his visitors: He had moved from the basement office to far more luxurious quarters on the first floor of the West Wing, just a few yards from the Oval Office. He now had his long-desired private bathroom, as well as a Marine guard on full-time duty in front of his door. His social comings and goings could make or break a Washington party; the society pages of the *Washington Post* and the *Evening Star* invariably began an account of an embassy party or diplomatic ball with a quote from or comment about Kissinger, usually describing him as a "secret swinger." Kissinger was not unaware of his value—in terms of policies and publicity—to the Nixon Administration, and he began demanding, perhaps unconsciously, some of the perquisites that belonged only to Richard Nixon. One demand in 1969, eventually rejected, was for full-time Secret Service protection, which, under law, was to be provided only to the First Family. Later, in July 1970, he requested personal full-time military security; this, too, was vetoed.*

By June, Haig had finally become Kissinger's deputy, primarily in charge of

---

* At a congressional budget hearing in November 1970, J. Edgar Hoover made public the allegation that a group of Catholic antiwar activists, headed by Fathers Philip and Daniel Berrigan, had conspired to kidnap Kissinger and blow up electrical facilities and steam pipes under the Capitol. The sensational charge, based on letters obtained by the FBI from a prison informant, was abandoned by the government in April 1971, but not before the Berrigan brothers and others were indicted by a federal grand jury in Harrisburg, Pennsylvania, in an effort, as Mitchell put it, "to get Hoover off the hook." The Justice Department subsequently filed a new indictment in the case, focusing on Philip Berrigan's antidraft activities. Daniel Berrigan, whom Hoover had named as a ringleader, was not included in the new charges. In April 1972, after an eleven-week trial, a jury convicted Philip Berrigan only of the minor charge of smuggling contraband letters. The government formally abandoned the rest of its case, including the conspiracy charges, in July 1972.

the day-to-day work of the National Security Council—an appointment that confirmed a *de facto* arrangement—and Kissinger seemed to spend even more time with reporters. David R. Halperin, a young Navy officer (not related to Morton Halperin) recruited from the Pentagon in late 1970 to serve as Kissinger's personal aide, recalls that Kissinger spent as much as half of each working day in meetings or in telephone conversations with reporters, far more time than he seemed to spend reading NSC staff memoranda. The price of such systematic access to Kissinger was deference, and it was a price willingly paid by the journalists, who were unable to meet regularly or casually with Haldeman, Ehrlichman, or other top aides.

The routine resembled an implicit shakedown scheme, in which reporters who got inside information in turn protected Kissinger by not divulging either the full consequences of his acts or his own connection to them. Thus, a week after the invasion of Cambodia, James Reston wrote a critical column about Nixon's inability to utilize advice "from his oldest friends in the Cabinet," naming Rogers as one without much influence. "Increasingly," Reston added, ". . . Mr. Nixon has isolated himself with a few members of his White House staff and followed the advice of Attorney General Mitchell and Vice President Agnew." The White House staff member who was most influential, as Reston must have known, was Kissinger, but the columnist did not cite him by name.* A few days later, Robert B. Semple, Jr., the *Times*'s White House correspondent, wrote that Kissinger was "believed to have registered objections" to the Cambodian operation; a belief that Kissinger or one of his aides undoubtedly fostered. H. R. Haldeman, in his memoirs, recalled the attitude of the President's men toward such coverage: "We knew Henry as the 'hawk of hawks' in the Oval Office. But in the evenings, a magical transformation took place. Touching glasses at a party with his liberal friends, the belligerent Kissinger would suddenly become a dove—according to the reports that reached Nixon."

Kissinger's machinations with the Washington press corps had their political usefulness, especially in an election year, and thus it was Kissinger who on June 26 was trotted out by Richard Nixon to brief a group of editors and newspaper executives at the Western White House in San Clemente. Kissinger's appearance at the five-hour briefing was essential, because Nixon was seeking favorable press reaction to a televised report to the nation, planned for June 30, on the "success" of the Cambodian invasion. Kissinger's solemn assurances to that effect would carry more weight than those from the President himself.

Many reporters knew or sensed the truth about the situation, but few wrote it. There was quick retribution for those who tried. A few days after the

---

* Sonnenfeldt sought to emulate Kissinger's technique in dealing with the press, but he was not always as successful. Murray Marder, then the diplomatic correspondent for the *Washington Post,* recalls an angry conversation after publication of a dispatch for which Sonnenfeldt—as well as some senior State Department officials—had been interviewed on a background basis. Under the rules, Marder could publish the information but not attribute it directly to the men interviewed. Sonnenfeldt's complaint was not that he had been misquoted but that Marder had interviewed others. "I don't see why I should talk to you," he told Marder. "I talk to you and then you talk to other people . . . and then you write that some people say 'this' and others say 'that.' " Marder recalls telling him that such reporting is "what journalism is about." Sonnenfeldt replied, "I don't have to talk to people who do that to me. Others don't do it to me."

briefing in San Clemente, Stuart Loory, White House correspondent for the *Los Angeles Times,* published a sharply critical article; he noted—prematurely, as it turned out—that "the patina is beginning to wear off the Kissinger mystique." Loory raised questions about Vietnam and said that Kissinger "has lost the respect of many of his old friends and associates on the nation's campuses." The response was melodramatic. David J. Kraslow, the *Los Angeles Times* news editor in Washington, was abruptly summoned to Kissinger's office. "As Kraslow walked into the office," Loory says, "Henry jumped up from behind his desk, rushed at him, and said, 'I don't care who you send to cover the White House, but I don't ever want to see Loory again.' " It took months, and the intervention of Robert Donovan, the distinguished journalist who was then Washington bureau chief for the *Times,* before Kissinger would talk to Loory again. Loory left the White House beat the following spring.*

Perhaps the Washington newspaper corps would have been less fawning if it had been more informed. The real secret was not that Kissinger was the sole source for most of the inside foreign policy stories, but that the maze of duplicity and illegality continued to expand in that summer of 1970. More men were being wiretapped, more illegal bombing was taking place, and the Central Intelligence Agency was being told to increase its spying on American dissidents at home, as well as to step up its covert activities abroad to prevent the election of Salvador Allende Gossens, a Socialist, in the Chilean presidential elections on September 4.

Kissinger's power as Nixon's chief collaborator was another untold story. He and a small group of NSC aides were in sole charge of the secret Paris peace talks with North Vietnam. With yet another group of NSC aides, he had begun a series of private backchannel talks with the Soviet Union on the SALT negotiations. And with eager support from Admiral Moorer, who was formally appointed chairman of the Joint Chiefs of Staff in July, Kissinger was able to bypass Secretary of Defense Laird and directly order bombing operations in North Vietnam.

The power grab was so complete that some decisions normally made by presidents after careful consideration were delegated—almost casually—to Kissinger. His approval, and not Nixon's, was needed when it came time to find a replacement for Moorer as Chief of Naval Operations, the Navy's top job. Laird's choice was Elmo R. Zumwalt, Jr., then commander of the Navy's forces in Vietnam. In his memoirs, *On Watch,* published in 1976, Admiral Zumwalt told of being summoned back to the United States to a meeting with Kissinger: "Kissinger and I shook hands. I sat down. After two or three minutes of discussion the telephone rang. He talked for about fifteen minutes with great fluency and charm, evidently to an inquiring journalist. He hung up and

* Loory, ironically, had been one of the first reporters in close touch with Kissinger after his appointment in December 1968 as national security adviser. Earlier in the year, Loory and Kraslow had published a study of the secret Vietnamese negotiations, *The Secret Search for Peace in Vietnam,* and Kissinger had been among those who cooperated, on a background basis, in their research. So it was not unnatural for Kissinger to ask Loory to lunch at President-elect Nixon's headquarters in the Hotel Pierre. "At that breakfast," Loory recalls, "Henry questioned me carefully and unceasingly on the press in Washington." Loory naïvely assured Kissinger, "Henry, all you have to do is do your job, and you'll get your press." Kissinger then offered to leak Loory an advance copy of his forthcoming *Foreign Affairs* article on the Vietnam negotiations, thus beginning a modus operandi as well as a close association which ended only with the critical article in mid-1970.

said that he had hoped to get me in to meet President Nixon, but that the President was all tied up. He said that he had enjoyed talking with me and I left." After his appointment, Zumwalt learned from Laird that Kissinger had concurred in the choice. "Evidently," Zumwalt wrote, Kissinger "had expressed that 'well-founded' concurrence to the President, which persuaded the President he did not have to interview me for the job himself." *

In early June 1970, Nixon suddenly pulled Elliot Richardson out of the State Department and appointed him Secretary of Health, Education and Welfare. If the transfer had been made a year earlier, one of its bitterest opponents would have been Kissinger, who had utilized Richardson as a back-door conduit from State to the NSC since the first days of the administration. But by mid-1970, Joseph J. Sisco, the Assistant Secretary for Near Eastern and South Asian Affairs, had come to understand Rogers' impotence as Secretary of State, and was moving more and more into Kissinger's orbit. There was a distinct advantage in working with Sisco: He was far more willing than Richardson to work behind Rogers' back.†

Kissinger also continued to make extensive use of Alexis Johnson, the career Foreign Service officer and Vietnam hardliner who saw it as his duty to maintain a role for the Foreign Service in policy making. Johnson would do anything he was asked to do, but he would also keep Rogers fully informed, so it was the brighter, more ambitious Sisco who became more useful. Sisco was held in contempt by many Foreign Service officers, in part because of his fawning relationship with Dean Rusk, the former Secretary of State, and his ability to support any policy without hesitation. To the despair of the Arabists in the Near East bureau of the State Department, who knew otherwise, Sisco was not averse to passing himself off as an expert on the area.

Elliot Richardson towered far over Johnson and Sisco in independence and integrity, but if the Kissinger of early 1969 had to tolerate these traits, not so the Kissinger of 1970. Kissinger's weekly lunches with Richardson began dwindling by the end of 1969; he no longer urged every reporter to "see Elliot"

* Neither Nixon nor Kissinger wanted to contest Laird's recommendation of Zumwalt; there were far more important issues between the White House and the Pentagon. Zumwalt's appointment did distress Haig, however, as Morris recalls: "Haig was furious, and came into Henry's office saying, 'Laird can't do this; he can't do it.' Henry instantly said, 'Laird knows exactly what he's doing. When you bring junior men in, they're forever loyal to you.' " Kissinger went on to cite the loyalty of young officers in the Soviet Army to Joseph Stalin despite Stalin's harsh purges in the 1930s. The purged army became leaderless and the power thus passed to the loyal young officers. "Henry didn't like Laird's idea," Morris says, "but he understood."

† Richardson's transfer was a severe blow to the morale of the young Foreign Service officers who worked as aides and deputies in the State Department. His reputation as a liberal cloaked the fact that, as the aides came to learn, he was a strong believer in national security who invariably supported the Nixon-Kissinger escalations in the Vietnam War. Nonetheless, Richardson encouraged a free flow of ideas and dissent at the top level; equally important, he found time to read the memoranda submitted to him and to argue the issues with those who cared. It was his willingness to work that may have greased the skids. Raymond Garthoff, the SALT delegation official, recalls a Verification Panel meeting in March or April of 1970 at which Richardson demonstrated a firm grasp on a complicated ABM negotiating issue involving radar technology. Garthoff and two other arms control officials had briefed Richardson a few days earlier, and the Under Secretary was able to rattle off a series of statistics that left the room quiet. "It was one of those times that Henry was not on top," Garthoff says. "He clearly didn't expect to have someone from State know more about the radars than he did, and it was evident that he didn't like it at all." After that performance, Kissinger treated Richardson "with more respect—and more suspicion." There was another word for Kissinger's attitude, Garthoff added: "wary."

and get a canned briefing on how well the two men worked together. By then, he had established his own relationships with senior members of Congress, another area in which Richardson had been invaluable. Also, Sisco and Johnson were able and willing to supply Kissinger's other needs: for advance information on State Department initiatives and as sounding boards for diatribes against the—as Kissinger saw him—incompetent, lazy, and uninformed Rogers. By the spring of 1970, Richardson had, for all practical purposes, been cut off by Kissinger and the White House. He was not told of the Cambodian invasion in advance; and, along with the rest of the State Department, he would learn of the secret Paris talks with Le Duc Tho when they were publicly announced by Nixon and Kissinger.

By early 1970, Kissinger's control also extended to the world of intelligence. Richard Helms and the CIA had been tamed: The internecine warfare over the CIA's analyses and estimates of Soviet missile testing had convinced Helms that it was far safer to misrepresent the intelligence than to do battle with the White House. The CIA no longer automatically analyzed intelligence data on critical issues, but immediately turned over the raw information to Kissinger and the NSC for them to analyze as they saw fit and draw whatever conclusions they chose. Similarly, Kissinger was able to establish dominance, so he thought, over the National Security Agency and its director, Vice Admiral Noel Gayler, who seemed to be as much in awe of Kissinger as the rest of the bureaucracy was. One of the NSA's most sensitive areas of activity involved the intercepting and decoding of diplomatic communications from embassies in Washington back to their own foreign offices, including the embassies of close allies. The ambassadors often reported on the comments made by White House officials or members of Congress at dinner parties or during cocktails— comments that were likely to include personal opinions about Kissinger and Nixon. "In the old days, that kind of diplomatic traffic was handled by a few officials in each agency," according to Ray S. Cline, a former CIA official who became director of State Department intelligence in 1969, "but Henry laid down the law—everything that mentioned him by name had to be cleared through his office. If his name appeared, it was strictly NODIS [not for distribution inside the government]." *

Kissinger was withholding more than personal communications intelligence. Colonel Pursley recalls that he and Laird "always had the feeling we weren't getting all the [NSA] stuff the White House was. Very little intercept mail was going to Mel and most of what we got was so innocuous." Laird began holding full-scale intelligence review meetings, specifically inviting NSA officials to his office, every other Friday morning, Pursley remembers, in an effort to "break down those barriers. But we never knew what we didn't know. I doubt if I saw five or six intercepts that were that important" in the years in Laird's office.

This is not the whole story, however. Laird had indeed been cut off from the flow of NSA intercepts, but not from the flow of information. Laird acknowledged years later that he had begun his tour of duty as Secretary of Defense

* After Kissinger became Secretary of State in 1973, Cline says, he still insisted that all sensitive NSA intercepts be sent directly to his office instead of being routed, as Rogers' had been, through his intelligence office.

with the assumption that Nixon and Kissinger would try to keep vital information from him. One of his first moves, he recalls, was to appoint Admiral Gayler director of NSA and Army General Donald V. Bennett director of the Defense Intelligence Agency, which was responsible for coordinating the intelligence output of the military services. "I brought them into my office and told them they'd better be loyal to me," Laird says. "If they were, they'd get four stars after four years"—promotions to the highest rank in the service. "And goddamn it," Laird adds with a laugh, "they were loyal."* When possible, Laird met two or three times weekly with Gayler, to learn what the White House was doing in the backchannel. He thus had a steady stream of information about the secret talks in Paris, the early contacts with the Chinese, and the backchannel talks with the Soviet Union. Laird refused to discuss how much knowledge he had at the time about Nixon's and Kissinger's supposedly secret dealings, nor would he say what he did—if anything—with his knowledge. He did confirm, however, that his private relationships with Gayler and Bennett, which apparently were never known to the men running the White House, were not a one-way street: "I was sending stuff over there through Noel." Laird, who had dealt extensively with intelligence issues as a congressman, had deduced a vital truth about Nixon and Kissinger: They paid far more attention to information that seemed to be secret, or came from a clandestine source. The possibility remains that Laird was able to shape policy without the White House's realization.

It is not known whether Kissinger had any suspicion of Laird's channels. NSC aides recall that he always seemed to believe that the Secretary of Defense was wiretapping his telephones, but Kissinger believed that about many in the government.

One Kissinger relationship that remained close was with J. Edgar Hoover. Kissinger was still receiving national security wiretap reports in 1970—those emanating, for example, from the FBI's many wiretaps on foreign embassies in Washington—as well as politically sensitive FBI information on an "Eyes Only" basis. The special files in Kissinger's office were not limited, however, to salacious information on such black antiwar leaders as Martin Luther King, Jr. Laurence Lynn recalls that Kissinger and Haig were supplied by Hoover with "raw FBI files"—always replete with malicious gossip and unproven allegations—on people the NSC was considering for staff vacancies or as consultants. Other aides say that some of the FBI material was stored in a secure four-drawer safe kept under the direct supervision of Haig and his trusted secretary, Muriel Hartley.

Laird's gamesmanship did not alter the basic relationship between the intelligence agencies and Henry Kissinger. The national security adviser, with Haig's help, was able to assert his will over the intelligence bureaucracy and quietly and effectively go about getting what he wanted when he wanted it from the NSA, the CIA, and the FBI. No one, not even Richard Nixon, could be as effective. On June 5, 1970, after the mass protests over the Cambodian invasion, Nixon summoned the intelligence chiefs and demanded that they

---

* Laird kept his promise. Gayler and Bennett were promoted to four-star rank, the highest military peacetime level, on September 1, 1972, a few months before Laird left the Pentagon.

prove what he insisted was the fact: that the antiwar demonstrations were the result of outside Communist agitators carrying out the policies of America's enemies. The fall congressional elections were coming and proof of such a link would be of enormous value in the campaign.

The task of coordinating a new and aggressive domestic intelligence program fell to Tom Charles Huston, a young, wide-eyed conservative whose subsequent list of recommendations, known as the Huston plan, became a key element in the Watergate inquiries and in the impeachment proceedings against Nixon.* Huston urged that the intelligence agencies be authorized to conduct illegal and unconstitutional searches and buggings in an effort to get the kind of evidence Nixon wanted. Huston's planning, coordinated with that of Haldeman, quickly became a bureaucratic nightmare. Both John Mitchell and J. Edgar Hoover argued strongly against the plan—Hoover called Huston a "hippie intellectual"—and, faced with their protests, Nixon had no choice but to withdraw approval in August. In his memoirs, he explained why Hoover's objections carried so much weight: "There was even the remote possibility that he might resign in protest."

Such high-level indecisiveness would have been unthinkable if Kissinger had been brought in on the deliberations. Hoover and Mitchell would have been placated in advance and left with nothing to protest. But, as Huston recalls, Kissinger "just wasn't involved" in any of that summer's plans for domestic spying.†

Kissinger may have been reluctant to be tainted by such activities, as he implied in his later discussions of the NSC wiretaps. Or Nixon and Haldeman may not have trusted the ability of the NSC staff to protect the truly important secrets. It is also possible that Haldeman, jealous of Kissinger's influence, simply decided to take over the domestic spying that was linked to the fortunes of Nixon and the Republican Party in the fall elections. In any case, Haldeman's decision was a poor one: He could not handle the bureaucracy on Nixon's behalf as well as Kissinger could.

Kissinger, however, kept his link to domestic intelligence through his excellent liaison with Hoover, and he was among the few non-CIA officials to receive full briefings on that agency's illegal domestic spying program. The program, known as Project Chaos, had been set up in 1967 under President Johnson, and it grew under Nixon and Kissinger. Helms supplied Kissinger with a steady stream of highly classified reports on American radicals, many of them based on information from CIA agents who infiltrated dissident groups abroad and in the United States. The Helms-Kissinger link seemed to work

* Huston's credentials for his position at the top of the federal government's intelligence operations consisted of a stint in Army intelligence. His claim to a White House position originated with his services as organizer of the World Youth Crusade for Freedom in 1966, which tried to promote support for the Vietnam War, and his endorsement that year of Richard Nixon for President. Huston, who came to the White House as a speech writer in January 1969, took his later link to high-level intelligence very seriously; others recalled that he kept a scrambler telephone—for use in highly classified conversations—locked in a safe beside his desk.

† Huston remembers the FBI's close relationship with Kissinger's office. As he became more involved in the planning, he says, FBI couriers would flow in and out of his office with "Eyes Only" documents. "They used to stop at my office and then go across the street to Kissinger's," Huston says. "I used to wonder what was going on—but you don't ask about stuff that's none of your business."

independently. For example, Helms was one of the participants in the meetings on the Huston plan, and yet Huston was never informed of the CIA's domestic spying programs.

There is no evidence that Kissinger did anything other than receive intelligence from Project Chaos, although his involvement as a recipient of the information was used at least once in 1970 by top-level CIA officials in an attempt to curb dissent within the Agency. By that time, three years after Project Chaos began, many CIA officials involved in intelligence collection had become concerned about the obvious illegality of spying on American citizens inside the United States, and had expressed their concern to Helms and his deputies. In a memorandum dated May 20, 1970, Richard Ober, the CIA official in charge of Chaos, noted that he had justified the program by explaining that "members of the Administration, including Dr. Kissinger and Attorney General Mitchell, have been briefed on this program and have recently received papers on this subject."

Far from objecting to such spying themselves, Kissinger and Haig apparently encouraged the National Security Agency to engage in similar activities, even if they involved eavesdropping on members of the staff. Morris remembers that in the fall of 1969 he had a telephone conversation about Biafra with Sam Brown, the student antiwar leader who was one of the main organizers of the Vietnam Moratorium. "Two days later," Morris says, "an NSA transcript of the call showed up in my box. The NSA was up to its ass monitoring the peace movement." Morris thought he probably received the transcript because his NSC assignment dealt with Africa.

Nixon emerged from the turmoil over Cambodia even more enraged at his antiwar critics and more nervous about prospects for the congressional elections. His mood about Vietnam, as described by Kissinger, "oscillated wildly" in July and August. At a meeting on July 4, Kissinger wrote, Nixon was resolute and determined to stay the course and bomb massively if necessary to end the war. A week later, he confided to Kissinger that the war was "sapping his domestic support" and could jeopardize his reelection in 1972; his solution was to combine renewed bombing of the North with total American withdrawal. On July 22, at a breakfast meeting with Kissinger, Nixon was more optimistic about Vietnamization and vowed to "see it through if I'm the only person in the country to do it. . . . I came into office without the support of all the people who oppose me today and I can get re-elected without their support." On August 10, after a meeting with Senators Harry F. Byrd, Jr., of Virginia and Gordon Allott of Colorado, conservatives who nevertheless urged him to end the war, Nixon again suggested to Kissinger that the war be brought to an end by all-out bombing, a blockade of the North, and withdrawal.

Nixon's mood may have oscillated, but his basic solution remained constant: massive bombing. He was always prepared to bomb; his only ambivalence was over the question of a total withdrawal of American troops. Kissinger was against the bombing that summer, fearing the inflammatory impact it would have on the antiwar movement. He warned the President, Kissinger wrote, that "in view of the trouble we had . . . in Cambodia, we would not be able to stick to such a course unless there had been overwhelming provocation." Full-scale bombing of the North would not begin until April 1972, after the North Vietnamese offensive.*

For all their bellicose talk, Nixon and Kissinger still had only the basic policy —Vietnamization—and that was increasingly under attack in Congress and everywhere in the country. Nixon's strategy for coping with both the antiwar movement and the fall elections was to have the Soviet Union bail him out by agreeing to a summit meeting. "Tormented by the anti-war agitators," Kissinger wrote, "[Nixon] thought he could paralyze them by a dramatic peace move." Eventually, as time grew shorter, Nixon's desire for a summit "reached a point of near obsession. . . . What would more discomfort his shrill opponents than emerging unexpectedly as a peacemaker. . . . He decided to make an all-out effort for a summit before the Congressional elections." In his memoirs, Kissinger claimed that he disagreed completely with Nixon's desire for a summit, largely because there was no basis for believing that such a meeting would be more than a media event. But Kissinger, as he wrote, "plunged ahead, reservations and all," and began a series of meetings with Soviet Ambassador Dobrynin.

Though Kissinger and Dobrynin discussed a summit in at least six meetings between April and August in 1970, by September it was clear that such an event was not possible before the election. In late August, Nixon and Kissinger went so far as to provide the Soviet Embassy with an agenda for a proposed summit, listing SALT, European security, the Middle East, détente, and trade as possible items. They heard nothing in response. Kissinger speculated in his memoirs that the Russians "probably did not think they needed to deal with us urgently, calculating that the pressures which had made us press for a summit in 1970 would make us even more eager later."

A far simpler explanation for the Soviet Union's reluctance was the one Dobrynin repeatedly gave Kissinger: The invasion of Cambodia had made such a meeting in 1970 all but politically impossible for the top leadership of the Soviet Union, who were concerned with their standing among Third World allies.

Richard Nixon's memoirs do not mention his desire that summer and fall for a Soviet summit, although at one point in April he too met with Dobrynin and declared, according to Kissinger, that he was prepared to let bygones be bygones and engage himself in putting United States-Soviet relations on a new basis. His private reaction to the turndown was predictable, since he had put his prestige on the line: He would show the Communists. In September there were three crises, involving Chile, Cuba, and Jordan, and Nixon and Kissinger turned each into a confrontation with the Soviet Union. In Chile, they set the CIA upon Salvador Allende Gossens in an effort to prevent his election; when that failed, they began a three-year CIA process of making it impossible for him to govern. In Cuba, they turned some sketchy intelligence about crew stops for Soviet submarines into a Soviet attempt to create a permanent nu-

* It should be noted again that in none of these conversations, as reported by Nixon and Kissinger in their memoirs, was any concern expressed about the loss of civilian life in Southeast Asia. Bombing, even by B-52s in populated areas, never seemed to raise any questions of morality inside the White House.

clear submarine base. In Jordan, they culminated eighteen months of feuding with the State Department by deluding themselves that they had engaged in a confrontation with the Soviet Union.

In these three instances, Nixon and Kissinger may not have operated illegally, as in the wiretapping, but they were responsible for a series of reckless midjudgments. Nixon, whose dual goal was to punish the Soviet Union and confound his antiwar critics, decided to campaign on the anti-Russian policy that always made good election-year politics. Kissinger, for his part, saw Chile, Cuba, and Jordan not just as threats to U.S. policy, but also as expedient vehicles to further best Rogers and show the President that when it came to communism, he could be as tough as anyone.

Above all, looking tough was important. In his memoirs, Nixon depicted his attitude toward the Soviets that September: "Communist leaders believe in Lenin's precept: probe with bayonets. If you encounter mush, proceed; if you encounter steel, withdraw. I had feared that in our handling of the EC-121 incident in 1969 the Communists may have thought they had encountered mush. While our efforts to prevent Allende from coming to power failed, at least in 1970 in Jordan and in Cuba, their probing had encountered our unmistakable steel."

Nixon and Kissinger were not dealing in unmistakable steel that fall, but in damaging mistakes.

18
MIDEAST:
THE ROGERS PLAN

SPITE PLAYED A MAJOR ROLE in America's foreign policy in the Middle East in 1969 and 1970. Nixon had assigned the Middle East to Rogers, in part because of concern about Kissinger's Jewishness but also out of a belief that Rogers, whose office was being systematically stripped of its authority, should be left with some area of responsibility. In the early months of the Nixon presidency, Kissinger, whose NSC would still have prior review of all State Department policy papers on the Middle East, accepted the division of power.

Kissinger nonetheless did not hesitate to move in on Middle East policy shortly after the inauguration. He sent Nixon a memorandum on negotiating strategy in early February 1969, taking issue with the first set of State Department plans for a Mideast settlement. But, Kissinger wrote, Nixon was too eager "to comfort his old friend," the Secretary of State, who was already in the process of becoming Secretary of State in name only. Furthermore, Nixon "considered himself less obligated to the Jewish constituency than any of his predecessors had been and was eager to demonstrate that he was impervious to its pressures. He also had his doubts as to whether my Jewish faith might warp my judgment." Elsewhere in his memoirs, Kissinger noted cautiously that "the President was convinced that most leaders of the Jewish community had opposed him throughout his political career. The small percentage of Jews who voted for him, he would joke, had to be so crazy that they would probably stick with him even if he turned on Israel. He delighted in telling associates and visitors that the 'Jewish lobby' had no effect on him." And in truth, Nixon had never been able to reach American Jews as a voting bloc.

By the middle of 1970, however, with the help of Joseph Sisco, Kissinger was haunting the State Department's efforts in the Middle East, constantly second-guessing every negotiation and, in his customary fashion, establishing elaborate backchannel communications with important leaders in Israel. In his memoirs, Kissinger, still spiteful, wrote that until late 1971 he was cut off from day-to-day control of the Middle East negotiations and "Thus . . . our policy lacked the single-minded sense of direction that Nixon usually demanded and I normally imposed. [Nixon] let matters drift, confident that with my help he could always take over before matters got out of hand. He permitted a range of discretion to the State Department unthinkable in any other area." To Kissinger, any attempt by Rogers to act as Secretary of State was unthinkable.

Even without the Kissinger-Rogers rivalry, which was destructive in itself,

Nixon's approach to the Middle East was confused and complicated. He was generally contemptuous of Jews, an attitude he did not bother to conceal from Kissinger and other close associates, but his venom was directed primarily toward those who were part of what he thought of as the Eastern Liberal Establishment, whose opposition to him was real—and whom he feared. Outsiders got only rare glimpses of Nixon's anti-Semitism. King Hussein of Jordan paid a state visit to Washington in early April of 1969; he was the first foreign leader to do so since Nixon's inauguration. By all accounts, there was a constructive Oval Office meeting, with Kissinger and State Department officials in attendance. Nixon, following protocol, saw the King to his car and then, as Hussein drove off, suddenly became agitated and declared, "We've got to help the King. We cannot let the American Jews dictate policy." One senior official recalls that the President seemed to be "jumping up and down" as he talked. Nixon's comments "just sickened me," the official says. "It was as if he thought since I was an Arabist and an Ambassador [in the Middle East] that I was some kind of a Jew hater."

Nonetheless, Nixon had genuine admiration for the Israeli Army and its intelligence agency, Mossad, which Kissinger—and the CIA—considered the best intelligence service in the world. Roger Morris recalls that Nixon's esteem for the Israeli military seemed to grow as, in 1969, the Israelis retaliated instantly and brutally against terrorist attacks from the newly emerging Arab guerrilla force, the Palestinian *fedayeen*. As the Vietnam War dragged on, and as Nixon and Kissinger were forced to restrain their aggressive instincts to some extent, Nixon's admiration for the Israelis grew. "He had a real machismo thing for the Israelis," Morris says. "He liked to see them shed blood."*

Reinforcing this admiration was Nixon's belief that the basic goal of American policy in the Middle East was to counter growing Soviet influence in the Arab countries. Most of the Arab world had cut off formal relations with the United States in the aftermath of the Six-Day War in 1967, in which the Israelis, aided by American arms and supplies, defeated the Egyptian and Syrian armies, which had been aided by the Soviets. During the fighting, the Israelis seized and occupied vast territories—lands three times larger than Israel itself —from Egypt, Syria, and Jordan. In Egypt, Israel now controlled all of the Sinai Desert up to the western bank of the Suez Canal; on the other side of the canal lay Egypt, and the African continent. Israel had also conquered the Gaza Strip, a narrow coastal area jutting toward Tel Aviv from the Sinai that had been under Egyptian control up to 1967, and from Syria it had wrested the Golan Heights, a hilly strategic area from which, before the war, Arab guerrillas had lobbed artillery shells onto Jewish settlements in the Jordan valley. From Jordan Israel seized all the walled-in Holy City in East Jerusalem, site of the Jewish temples of biblical times, as well as all the fertile land west of the Jordan River—the so-called West Bank. The West Bank and the Gaza Strip

---

* Adding to the inevitable tension and danger in the Middle East was the fact that American intelligence reported as early as 1966 that Israel had built an atomic bomb. By the end of 1969, the Nixon Administration estimated that Israel had between twelve and sixteen nuclear warheads that could be deployed. That information was, of course, kept highly classified; equally classified, according to a CIA report in my possession, was the extent of American knowledge of Israeli efforts to deny nuclear capability to other countries in the Middle East by assassinating their most sophisticated nuclear scientists.

were teeming with settlements and refugee camps holding hundreds of thousands of Arabs, many of them Palestinian refugees from the 1948 and 1956 Israeli-Arab wars, who avidly supported Palestine Liberation Organization terrorist activities.*

After the 1967 war, the Soviet Union broke relations with Israel and increased its economic and military support for Egypt, Syria, and Iraq. The United States continued its policy of strong alliance with Israel—a policy that coincided with the 1968 elections and traditional heavy American Jewish support, in votes and political contributions, for the Democrats.

The conflict facing the Nixon Administration in early 1969 was stark: The Arabs insisted that Israel give up its conquered lands before serious negotiations could begin; the Israelis demanded recognition of Israel's right to exist as a state—a demand that had been consistently rejected by the Arab world— as their price for beginning to talk about disengagement. Another destabilizing factor was the growing radical *fedayeen* movement, led by Yasir Arafat, head of the PLO, which was demanding creation of a "democratic secular state" in Palestine, theoretically permitting Jews, Arabs, and Christians to live together with equal rights.† Arafat maintained his headquarters in camps along the Israel-Jordan border, from which he could launch guerrilla raids into Israel as well as eventually threaten the regime of Jordan's King Hussein. Hussein was the most moderate and pro-Western of the monarchs in the Middle East—in part, perhaps, because of his direct financial ties to the United States. Since 1957, after Britain withdrew from the Middle East, the CIA had covertly funneled millions of dollars to the King. The funds were used to help pay for the King's army and also to maintain Hussein himself in high style. The funding gave American policy makers an obvious advantage in their dealings with

---

* The West Bank refugees had been granted Jordanian nationality after the 1948 war by King Abdullah, Hussein's grandfather, when he proclaimed the annexation of the West Bank. Palestinians who could demonstrate residence in the West Bank were subsequently granted passports for foreign travel by the Jordanian government, a condition that existed until 1967 and the Israeli seizure and occupation. By 1980, the West Bank's Palestinian population was nearly one million, and 450,000 Palestinians were living in the Gaza Strip. The remainder of the world's estimated four million Palestinians were scattered throughout the Mideast.

† This position evolved and, so some experts thought, was modified in the early 1970s into a two-stage proposal that raised the possibility of the PLO's willingness to accept a Palestinian state *inside* historic Palestine—rather than insisting on control of all of Palestine. This implied to some the possibility of coexistence with Israel, once a Palestinian PLO state was created. Thus far, partly through the reluctance of the United States and Israel, the PLO's hint of coexistence has never been put to the test. Nearly all Israelis, it should quickly be said, remain highly skeptical of the PLO's willingness to coexist with Israel on any level. Complicating any discussion of Palestine is its history. The last Jewish state and temple were destroyed by the Romans in A.D. 70, although Jews continued to live there through the centuries. Modern Zionist resettlement of Palestine began in the 1890s, and Jews had become a political force in Palestine by 1917, when Britain, in the Balfour Declaration, pledged to establish in Palestine "a national home for the Jewish people," with safeguards for the other inhabitants. With the collapse of the Ottoman Empire after World War I, Britain obtained a League of Nations mandate over Palestine. In 1947, the United Nations voted to divide the country between a Jewish and an Arab state, but the Arab nations resisted that decision militarily. The Arabs were defeated in the 1948 war with the Israelis, who established a Jewish state in part of Palestine while the rest was taken over by Jordan. It can be argued that the modern Arab-Jewish conflict began in 1948, and that, like the similar conflicts in biblical times, it is between two peoples of kindred origin struggling for possession of the same land. What has made a resolution so difficult is the unwillingness of either side to recognize the national aspirations of the other. The Arabs have consistently treated Zionism as an artificial agitation among Jews, and the Jews have been unwilling to recognize that Arabs have the same deep attachment to their and their ancestors' homeland.

Hussein, but the King was far from a supplicant, and maintained his independence from his benefactors.

Arafat's bloody guerrilla attacks inside Israel, and Israel's equally bloody commando retaliations, in the late 1960s were complemented by a more formal undeclared war in the Sinai desert. In early 1969, the Egyptians, aided by Soviet arms, began a series of artillery barrages and commando raids against Israeli troops dug in along the Israeli side of the Suez Canal. Egyptian President Gamal Abdel Nasser, in need of a stance that would maintain his popularity with the masses in Cairo and elsewhere, visited his troops along the canal in February 1969, and called for constant military action against the Israeli troops. The raids and counterraids became known as the War of Attrition.

For the new Nixon Administration, intent on Vietnam, SALT, and the concept of linkage, the Middle East was a secondary issue in early 1969. There was an ongoing Middle East peace initiative sponsored by the United Nations, but neither Nixon nor Kissinger, as Kissinger's memoirs make clear, seriously considered the possibility of permitting the United Nations to resolve a crisis and thus get credit that could conceivably go to the administration. At the urging of Charles de Gaulle, with whom Nixon and Kissinger talked during their trip to Western Europe in February and March of 1969, the United States agreed to join in formal four-power talks—with France, England and the Soviet Union—to negotiate an Israeli withdrawal from the occupied lands. A subsequent peace agreement with Israel, if one could be arranged, would be guaranteed by the four powers.

Along with those talks, Nixon authorized a separate series of direct discussions with the Soviet Union on the Middle East, with Rogers and the State Department in charge of the American negotiating team. In Kissinger's and Nixon's view, the Soviet Union, if it chose to do so, could influence Egypt to sign a peace agreement. During those talks, Rogers and Sisco were in regular consultation with Dobrynin, and Kissinger was chafing at the thought of the State Department, and Rogers, dealing directly with the Soviets. Even without a direct role, Kissinger's influence was enormous—and negative. The national security adviser constantly urged the President to discourage the State Department from going ahead with any initiative that called for Israel to give up some of its occupied lands in return for a peace guarantee. Kissinger's reasoning was global: If Israel agreed to talks, it would appear to be a victory both for the Arab radicals, who would be seen as justified in their terrorist attacks, and for the Soviet Union, which would be seen as skillful and successful in its policy of rearming the Arab world. Kissinger continued to argue over the next four years that Israeli concessions in the Middle East would be seen by the Arab world as a victory for the Soviet Union. Nixon, too, linked peace in the Middle East to big-power politics. In his memoirs, he published a March 1970 memorandum to Kissinger that said: "We are *for* Israel because Israel in our view is the only state in the Mideast which is *pro*-freedom and an effective opponent to Soviet expansion. . . . [We are] the kind of friend that Israel needs and will continue to need, particularly when the going gets very tough. . . ."

This Nixon-Kissinger view—linking the Middle East to American-Soviet relations—was to preclude the possibility of any United States pressure on the

Israeli government to make territorial concessions in 1970. These concessions were not made until after a war in 1973 that, with a different American policy, might have been avoided. Even more tragic, the Israeli concessions that did not bring a peace in 1974 and 1975 would perhaps have been more effective if they had come in 1970.

One former NSC staff member who in 1969 worked very closely with Kissinger recalls that at the beginning Kissinger had "a real hesitancy" about being involved in Middle East negotiations. For one thing, Kissinger was aware that he had a profound lack of knowledge of the politics and personalities of the Middle East; he had never visited an Arab country and had made only a few short visits to Israel. Even more significant was his instinctive reluctance to get involved in a negotiation he did not believe in. "He just didn't see how it was going to work," the aide says, "and his attitude was: So why jump in and not be successful and make a lot of enemies in the process?" That reasoning had a built-in bonus for Kissinger, because the person trying to do what Kissinger considered the impossible was Rogers. But Nixon and Kissinger were not content simply to watch and wait as Rogers floundered; by the end of 1969 they were actively working behind the scenes to undercut him.

In July 1969, Israel escalated the War of Attrition and its air force began flying across the Sinai to bomb and strafe Egyptian forts and artillery emplacements. Air-to-air battles were fought with the Egyptian Air Force, and a dozen Soviet-supplied Egyptian planes were shot down. In January 1970, Israel's Ministerial Defense Committee authorized a series of "deep penetration" air raids far inside Egypt; some missions involved the bombing of civilians in the suburbs of Cairo, including the destruction of at least one school. Neither Kissinger nor Nixon made any attempt in late 1969 or early 1970 to halt the Israeli attacks. In private meetings with Israeli officials, including Yitzak Rabin, the Israeli Ambassador to Washington, Nixon repeatedly and explicitly encouraged such aggression. Moshe Dayan, Israel's Defense Minister at the time, described in his memoirs a White House meeting in early December 1969, in which he discussed with Nixon, Kissinger, Rogers, and Laird the Soviet Union's increasing arms support for Egypt. "They were very worried by what they called the Sovietization of the Egyptian War," Dayan wrote. "I gathered that if the Soviet Union actively intervened, the United States would not be able to stand aside. . . . They were anxious to prevent such a situation from occurring, but they took the view that on no account should they show signs of weakness. . . . No one criticized us for having shot down the Soviet planes. On the contrary, one of them said, 'Shoot the hell out of them!' " Months earlier, in fact, the same advice had been given to Ambassador Rabin by Nixon and Kissinger.

Rabin, who had been the Israeli Army's chief of staff during the 1967 war, had a special entrée into the White House because he had been among the few foreign leaders who paid attention to Richard Nixon on his 1966 world tour as a private citizen. At a time when others were shunning Nixon, Rabin invited him to Israeli Army headquarters and provided, as Rabin put it in his memoirs, "red-carpet treatment." Kissinger, alert to the likes and dislikes of his superior, was quick to set up a special relationship with Rabin, and the Israeli

Ambassador soon had a direct telephone line to Kissinger's desk. In September 1969, a few weeks after the Israeli Air Force began its bombing missions across the Sinai, Rabin privately cabled home this assessment, as recorded in his memoirs: "Some sources have informed me that our military operations are the most encouraging breath of fresh air the American administration has enjoyed recently. A man would have to be blind, deaf and dumb not to sense how much the administration favors our military operations, and there is a growing likelihood that the United States would be interested in an escalation of our military activity with the aim of undermining Nasser's standing. . . . Thus the willingness to supply us with additional arms depends more on stepping up our military activity against Egypt than on reducing it." It is possible, of course, that Rabin was dramatizing to some degree the amount of direct encouragement he had been given, but his cable reflected Nixon's personal views, which were known to only a few insiders—and a few Israelis—at that time.

One State Department official who was closely involved in the Middle East negotiations as an aide to Sisco confirms being told that Nixon "was encouraging a certain militancy and bellicosity on the part of the Israelis." He was not surprised at the report, the aide says, since "it didn't seem out of character."

By the early fall of 1969, the Rogers-Sisco talks with the Soviet Union about the Middle East had broken down, much to Kissinger's relief. In his memoirs, Kissinger remarked that he had personally rebuffed Soviet Ambassador Dobrynin in late September, when Dobrynin, using his private channel to the White House, urged Kissinger and Nixon to get involved in another Soviet proposal for a Middle East settlement. "I had no intention to act jointly with the Soviet Union when the Soviets clearly expected to get a free ride on our exertion," Kissinger wrote, referring to his belief that the Soviets would not compel their allies, the Egyptians, to make as many compromises as they expected the Israelis to make under pressure from Nixon. Dobrynin turned back to Rogers and Sisco, and by mid-October the State Department was reporting progress—to Kissinger's dismay. "I had my doubts about this 'progress,' " Kissinger wrote. He suspected that the Soviets were suddenly being agreeable in the Middle East negotiations "to make Nixon think twice about his threatened November 1 'deadline' over Vietnam," a reference to the Duck Hook plan. Kissinger thought he had convinced Nixon, as he wrote, that the administration should signal its resolve by engaging in no diplomatic discussions of any kind with the Soviet Union before the November 1 deadline. By this time, however, Nixon had decided not to go ahead with the bombing and mining of North Vietnam, and State Department representatives were permitted to meet with the Soviets again on October 28. Kissinger was obviously not yet in full control of Middle East policy. At the meeting, the genesis of what was to be American Middle East peace policy for the next decade was spelled out: Israel was to withdraw to its pre-1967-war borders with Egypt, in return for guarantees of peace and security from Egypt.

Throughout this period, everybody involved recognized that the struggle to begin serious negotiations between Israel and Egypt would be an uphill one. There was obvious merit to the positions on both sides. The Israeli leaders, many of them from families that had not escaped the Holocaust, could justifiably argue that Israel was being asked to give up land won during a war of self-defense—a demand not always made upon the victor in battle.* If there were to be negotiations, Israel wanted them face to face with the Egyptians; such talks would amount to a direct recognition of Israel's right to exist. The American solution, which was accepted by the Soviets, was to compromise: Israel and Egypt would house peace delegations in the same city or perhaps in the same building and talks between the two would proceed with the help of an intermediary from the United Nations. As the compromise was being shaped in discussions between the State Department and Soviet officials that fall, reports were published that direct negotiations had been agreed upon between Israel and Egypt. State Department officials recall that the Egyptians complained at once, saying they had agreed only to indirect talks and anything more would amount to an Egyptian concession. No one in the American government learned precisely what happened over the next days in Cairo, as the Soviets and the Nasser government held discussions, but Dobrynin informed Sisco that the Egyptians had backed away and negotiations were no longer possible.

The Israelis were known to be unhappy about the State Department's efforts to compromise on what was repeatedly described in the media and by American and Israeli officials as a basic security issue. But the issue was far more complicated. Many Israelis still harbored the dream of territorial expansion into the West Bank of Jordan; that dream had been one of the driving forces of the Revisionist Zionist movement led by such men as the late Ze'ev Vladimir Jabotinsky and his disciple, Menachem Begin, who in 1969 was a minority member of the Israeli Parliament. The disposition of the issue of the West Bank required not only a political decision by Israel's leaders but a religious and philosophical decision about Israel's future territorial and ideological claims. The various Zionist political forces inside Israel were unable to settle the issue among themselves, and thus were not prepared in late 1969 to accept the State Department's unyielding demand that Israel return to the pre-1967 boundaries. This complicating factor never did become widely known to the American public. Instead, Israel's reluctance to return to its previous boundaries was depicted solely as a security decision: a legitimate basis in itself, and one fully accepted as rational by Nixon and Kissinger.

In early December, faced with continuing complaints about his diplomacy from the Israeli Embassy and the American Jewish community, Rogers decided to make his plan public. Rogers' decision was obviously a hurried one: State Department aides recall a scramble to find a suitable public forum for the Secretary to announce the American policy for the Middle East. The speech was delivered December 9 to an adult education forum which had been scheduled to receive a routine foreign policy address by a low-level Foreign Service officer. The Rogers speech, outlining what became known as the first Rogers plan, explicitly said that Israel should withdraw to its pre-1967 boundaries in the Sinai Desert in return for recognition from Egypt and an end to belligerency. Rogers also called for a more broadly based settlement in the Mideast, involving negotiations between Israel and Jordan over the West Bank, the

* Some of the most intransigent Israeli leaders had illegally emigrated to Israel as passengers on overloaded ships that eluded British blockades after World War II. These men and women found it difficult to understand that the Arab desire for a homeland could be as intense, and seem as justified, as their own.

future of united Jerusalem, and the Palestinian refugee problem. The gist of Rogers' recommendations had been privately conveyed to Cairo a month earlier, according to Mahmoud Riad, the Egyptian Foreign Minister, whose memoirs, *The Struggle for Peace in the Middle East,* were published in London in 1981. Egypt found much merit in Rogers' attempt to seek a comprehensive settlement, Riad wrote, rather than one limited only to Egypt and Israel.

The Rogers plan caused a shock wave of opposition in Israel, which had received no advance word, official or unofficial, of his speech, and from Israel's supporters in Congress. There was a sense of crisis in Israel. The Cabinet was summoned to an emergency session the next day and formally rejected Rogers' initiative. Kissinger, in his memoirs, claimed that Rogers had not cleared his speech in advance with Kissinger or Nixon; on that day, at least, the Secretary of State had apparently usurped Kissinger's right to usurp him. Kissinger was furious as he and his aides read a news report on Rogers' speech as it came across line by line on one of the wire-service machines in the White House. There was the usual tantrum, one aide recalls; Kissinger railed not only at the substance of the speech but at what he said was Rogers' failure to clear it with his office.

It may have been more theatrics. Sisco recalls that Rogers' speech had been sent to the White House before it was given, and that Kissinger not only approved the text but made substantive comments and recommendations for changes. Sisco adds, "I don't know whether Henry showed it to the President." His implication is clear: Kissinger had not shown the speech to the President in advance, so that when the predictable Israeli protests came after it was given—the timing was left to Rogers—he could suggest to Nixon that Rogers had delivered it without clearance. Such maneuvering would explain Kissinger's elaborate performance before his aides at the first reports on the speech and his failure to acknowledge in his memoirs that the basic Rogers proposal—if not its timing—had received his blessing.

Over the next few weeks, Kissinger and Nixon worked in tandem to further undercut the Secretary of State. On the day after the speech, as protests from Israeli officials and American Jewish leaders began pouring into the White House, Kissinger criticized the Rogers approach at a National Security Council meeting, reiterating his thesis that the longer the stalemate in the Middle East, "the more obvious would it become that the Soviet Union had failed to deliver what the Arabs wanted." On December 17, Nixon ordered White House aide Leonard Garment, a Jew and a former Nixon law partner who served as an occasional intermediary with the Israelis, to give private assurances to Prime Minister Golda Meir that the State Department initiative would not have his full backing. Similarly, the word was quietly passed to American Jewish leaders, one such leader recalls, that there was nothing to worry about. Nonetheless, protests went on. Ambassador Rabin warned Kissinger that he was personally prepared to lead an attack against the State Department's Middle East position. Kissinger responded, according to Rabin's memoirs, "I beg you, under no circumstances should you attack the President. . . . How you act is your affair. What you say to Rogers, or against him, is for you to decide. But I advise you again: Don't attack the President."

In his memoirs, Nixon further confused the issue of prior White House clearance for the Rogers plan by acknowledging that he permitted the proposal to go ahead, although it "had absolutely no chance of being accepted by Israel" and "could never be implemented." On January 25, 1970, the President took a direct step in opposition to the proposal: He sent a message to an emergency meeting of Jewish leaders, assembled in Washington to protest the Rogers plan, in which he promised to continue supplying necessary military equipment to Israel. The message also backed off from the strong language in the Rogers plan about the necessity for Israel's withdrawal from the occupied lands.

Many Foreign Service officers and State Department experts privately agreed with the Kissinger-Nixon view that the Rogers plan stood little chance of acceptance by Israel—certainly in December 1969. The intense infighting between Kissinger's office and the State Department undoubtedly influenced Rogers' sudden decision to make the proposal public without full White House consultation. But if the presentation of the Rogers plan was a tactical mistake, it did provide a strategic base for America's Middle East policy in the years ahead. Its basic principle—an Israeli withdrawal—eventually became the underpinning for Kissinger's famed Middle Eastern shuttle diplomacy after the 1973 Yom Kippur War. "The Rogers plan was not necessarily wrong," one former NSC official explains, "but it had the flaw of all comprehensive plans: Rogers had to put too much in front"—including the fatal requirement that Israel be prepared to withdraw to the 1967 borders. The NSC official, who worked five years with Kissinger, adds: "The good thing about the Rogers plan was that it provided a comprehensive framework to be implemented on a step-by-step negotiating approach. Henry's approach in '73 and '74 was to do it piece by piece and not pay attention to the ultimate goal: not to look ahead. The tragedy of the Rogers plan was that it made American diplomacy look foolish to the world and it convinced the Israelis that the White House was highly subject to manipulation. Those guys"—Kissinger and Rogers—"allowed their personality problems to completely emasculate their diplomacy across the board. We showed the Israelis how to manipulate us."

Mahmoud Riad reached a similar conclusion, as he reported in his memoirs: "We had already observed that the U.S. would take the initiative and submit projects and proposals from which it would invariably retreat immediately [if] Israel rejected them. We felt that such procrastination was not worthy of our confidence." In late December, Riad led a delegation of Egyptian officials, including Vice President Anwar Sadat, to Moscow to plead for more military support. The Soviets were cautious. "At the very outset," Riad wrote, "I noticed that the Soviet leaders were worried at the escalating military operations on both sides of the Suez Canal and were apprehensive that we would undertake a premature military action to cross the waterway." Leonid Brezhnev's argument, as spelled out to Riad and Sadat, was that Egypt should refrain from battle until its military buildup was complete. The Soviet Union would continue to supply arms, Brezhnev said, but also would be "energetically seeking a political settlement." The Soviet leader assured the Egyptians that there was "no contradiction" in his government's policy of continuing to talk and continuing to arm. There also was preliminary talk of sending Soviet pilots, posing as technical experts, to Egypt, as well as a shipment of more sophisticated Soviet surface-to-air missiles.

In early January 1970, the USSR formally rejected Rogers' initiative, which by then had been all but formally disavowed by the White House. In their objection, however, the Soviets also criticized the Rogers plan on the ground that it provided for all the details and particulars to be negotiated directly between Israel and the Arab states, and not in the context of the four-power talks. If there was to be an agreement in the Middle East, the USSR wanted to play a role.

The first Rogers plan was thus moribund, consigned to a lingering death over the next year, as the stage was set for escalation in the Middle East. On January 7, Israel launched its deadly "deep penetration" air raids over the suburbs of Cairo; it also continued to broadcast repeated propaganda messages urging the Egyptian masses to overthrow Nasser. One State Department official then serving in Israel recalled that the top level of the Egyptian government had a "very hysterical reaction" in those days to the raids and the propaganda attacks; there was more than enough provocation, he thought, for Egypt to seek increased military support from its ally, the Soviet Union. In late January, as Nixon and Kissinger were trying to mollify the Israelis and the American Jewish constituency at home, Nasser flew to Moscow and formally persuaded the reluctant leadership to supply Egypt with advanced SAM-3 antiaircraft missiles capable of shooting down the American-made Israeli Air Force F-4 Phantoms.

The Russians also agreed, under duress, to provide MIG aircraft as well as Soviet crews to man the missiles and teach the Egyptian military how to use them. Soviet pilots would also be provided to fly the MIGs over the Sinai. Nasser's closest aide, Mohammed Heikal, later wrote that Nasser had extracted the advanced equipment from reluctant Soviet officials. A key factor, wrote Heikal, was Nasser's threat to turn to the United States for arms if the Soviet Union refused to supply them.* The Soviets were incredulous but agreed. By March, technicians, pilots, and Russian-made arms were flowing into Egypt; a month later, Soviet pilots began flying their first missions in MIGs against the Israeli Air Force.

Once the Soviet Union made its commitment to Egypt, Nixon and Kissinger were on familiar ground. The Middle East debate in the White House was no longer centered on forcing long-term concessions from Israel and the Arab states; instead, it became the familiar "us against them" proposition. The strong evidence that the Egyptians had turned to the Soviet Union in desperation and fear after Israel's deep-penetration bombing was not important, as Kissinger made clear in his memoirs: "My view was that if the Soviets intro-

* Heikal, in his *The Road to Ramadan* (1975), wrote that Nasser's request for advanced SAM missiles as well as Soviet crews to man them was a "bombshell" to the cautious Soviet leadership. Russian planes would be needed to protect the missile installation, the Soviet leaders explained. "Send the planes, too," Heikal quoted Nasser as saying. When Leonid Brezhnev, General Secretary of the Communist Party, replied that such a step would have serious international implications and could create a Russian-U.S. crisis, Nasser asked: "Why is it the Americans can always escalate their support whereas we sometimes behave as if we are scared?" At this point, Heikal wrote, Brezhnev interrupted: "We are not scared of anybody. We are the strongest power on earth. But you must understand that this will involve a considerable risk and I don't know that we are justified in making it." Nasser then told the Soviets, "As far as I can see, you are not prepared to help us in the same way that America helps Israel. This means that there is one course open to me: I shall go back to Egypt and I shall tell the people the truth. I shall tell them that the time has come for me to step down and hand over to a pro-American President. If I cannot save them, somebody will have to do it. That is my final word." According to Heikal, Nasser's words "electrified the room" and led to the Soviet decision to provide the missiles, technicians, and MIG aircraft.

duced military personnel we had no choice but to resist, regardless of the merits of the issue that triggered the action." Nixon's approach was equally single-minded. In one memorandum to Kissinger, as recorded in the latter's memoirs, Nixon instructed: " 'Even Handedness' is the right policy—But above all our interest is—what gives the Soviets the most trouble—Don't let Arab-Israeli conflicts obscure that interest." To a President bogged down in Vietnam and at home, the Middle East had suddenly become the background frieze for the continuation of the Cold War.

In early February, Alexei Kosygin, the Soviet Premier, sent Nixon a personal note warning against growing Israeli military "adventurism" and making it clear that the Soviets would increase their aid to Egypt if the deep-penetration bombings continued. The Soviets, in effect, were giving the Nixon Administration advance notice of their intent to send men and matériel into Egypt. Kosygin asked for immediate four-power diplomatic action to compel Israel to stop the raids. For Kissinger and Nixon, the letter was confirmation that they were in a confrontation: ". . . [T]his was the first Soviet threat to the new Administration," Kissinger wrote in his memoirs, adding, however, that Kosygin had "stopped short of threatening any specific action." In other words, it was a threat without a threat.

The Israelis were pleased with the mild American reaction to the raids. Ambassador Rabin, knowing more than he wrote in his memoirs about Nixon's private views, described the date of the first Israeli deep-penetration raid, January 7, as a turning point in the Middle East struggles: ". . . [F]rom then on the American administration was gradually to shake free of the depressing feeling that it was backing a loser in the Middle East and consequently losing its own standing in the region." Once again the Israelis were doing what Nixon dared not do in North Vietnam.

Rabin reported on a lunch early in January with Sisco, who "was not in a position to concede that Israel's air operations were [as] welcome to the United States [as they were in Israel]. There was no need for him to say it; he knew that I knew." In mid-March, after the first confirmation that Soviet missile technicians had arrived in Egypt, Nixon met with Rabin and others and, astonishingly, urged further Israeli aggression. Rabin wrote in his memoirs: "[Nixon] paused again, and when he continued speaking I thought I could detect a strange glint in his eyes. . . . 'How do you feel about those [Soviet SAM-3] missiles? Have you considered attacking them?' Totally flabbergasted, I blurted out: 'Attack the Russians?' Strange, I thought to myself, how complex are the motives of a great power."

Two months later, in the midst of the national outcry over the Cambodian invasion, Rabin met with Nixon again. By then, the Israelis had abandoned their deep-penetration raids because of the increasing frequency with which the Soviet missiles had begun to shoot down their aircraft. At issue was the administration's delay in replacing the lost planes—a delay caused, in part, by the enormous outbreak of antiwar feeling in the United States.* Rabin quoted

* Another reason for the administration's decision to delay the Israeli military aid request tells much about the irrationality of its decision making. In early March, pro-Israeli crowds in Chicago and New York demonstrated violently against French President Georges Pompidou, who had agreed in January to sell French-made Mirage fighters to the revolutionary government of Muammar el-Qaddafi in Libya; the planes were obviously intended for use by other Arab countries. One group

Nixon as explaining the delay in these terms: "If it were just a question of you and the Egyptians and the Syrians, I'd say, 'Let 'em have it! Let 'em have it! Hit 'em as hard as you can!' Every time I hear of you penetrating into their territory and hitting them hard, I get a feeling of satisfaction."

What had started out in 1969 as an almost routine exercise in bureaucratic gamesmanship by Henry Kissinger emerged, by mid-1970, as a full-blown crisis. Kissinger, operating on behalf of his President but against his own instincts and judgment—as he would demonstrate in his more successful negotiations after the 1973 Yom Kippur War—maneuvered relentlessly as the Nixon Administration turned away from the Rogers plan and moved toward an unnecessary and reckless great-power confrontation.

After some delays early in 1970, the United States would firmly commit itself to the military resupply of Israel. The only policy that seemed to work in all of this was Israel's: Its leaders had decided to proceed on the assumption that any aggressive military action taken against Egypt and its benefactor, the Soviet Union, had the explicit support of the United States. The policy of the Nixon Administration, with its yawing back and forth between Kissinger and Rogers, had only one constant in 1969 and early 1970: Nixon and Kissinger could, so it seemed, be counted upon to try to stop the Russians no matter what the merits of the issues were.

The men and women who serve in the Middle East for the State Department and the Central Intelligence Agency have traditionally been considered very highly qualified. A knowledge of Arabic is essential to career success in those regions, and the dedication needed to master that language seems to be reflected in career performance. The State Department's Arabists have invariably been written off by Israel and its supporters as pro-Arab and anti-Israel, an oversimplification that still exists. A Foreign Service officer, if he reports critically on Israeli policy in State Department cables, runs a risk of being labeled anti-Semitic. Many State Department officials acknowledge that since the 1950s the Israeli Embassy in Washington has been able to obtain routine access to secret internal communications and reports from the State Department and the Pentagon. One diplomat recalls that two days after he filed a critical report from Jerusalem, where he was posted in the late 1950s, the Israeli Embassy was privately complaining about his views to State Depart-

---

of demonstrators in Chicago broke through police lines, jostled Madame Pompidou, and, she thought, spat on her. Nixon had received Pompidou at the White House with a state dinner and full pomp and circumstance, and he was furious when the rest of the country did not show the same respect. In response, Nixon ordered an indefinite delay in approval of the Israeli arms package—an order given, it should be noted, before the White House knew of the pending Soviet infusion of missiles, men, and aircraft into Egypt. Nonetheless, Kissinger was much distressed: The President was throwing away a chance to show the Russians how tough he could be. He immediately warned Nixon that "the Soviets were bound to be emboldened by our visible disassociation from our ally." The State Department took a different view: Nixon's decision gave them some flexibility and room for further discussions with the Soviets. Once committed to his decision, Nixon found it awkward to back away; the arms were not authorized to Israel for months. Nixon's embargo was extremely bad news for the Israelis, and Kissinger and Nixon found a solution to ease the onus on the White House—the decision was announced by the State Department.

ment officials in Washington. Such knowledge has severely limited the independence and integrity of Foreign Service officers assigned to Israel; it also limits the scope of their reporting. The CIA, as well, was specifically barred, at least until the mid-1970s, from intelligence reporting on Israel from inside the country. In return, the Agency benefited from a long-standing and close relationship with Mossad, whose expertise on affairs in the Middle East and Africa is considered nonpareil.

The effect of these limitations has, at the very least, been severe self-censorship by American officials, in the field and at home, in dealing with Israel. For example, many State Department and CIA Middle East experts were convinced that Israel's reckless bombing of Egypt and its public campaign for the overthrow of the Nasser regime were directly responsible for the Soviet shipments of men and matériel to Egypt in early 1970. When their views, albeit tentatively presented, were rejected out of hand by Kissinger, they did not persist. One CIA official with long experience as a station chief throughout the Middle East says, "There is a long history of the United States government believing that the Soviets were able to bring all kinds of influence to bear in the Middle East, and especially in Egypt. When it comes right down to it, they couldn't do it." This official was at a key post in the Middle East at the time of the Israeli deep-penetration raids. When they began, "We tut-tutted and asked the Israelis, 'Are you sure you know what you're doing?' We relayed our possible concern that the Soviets would react [by sending Egypt more matériel] and they rejected it. They assured us that the Soviets would do nothing, but they were wrong, dead wrong. It was predictable that the Soviets would have to do something and that they would come in with massive equipment and personnel. That may really have been precisely what the Israelis wanted—because it was the Israelis that benefited the most when the Soviets were in there."

This official doesn't "believe that the Israelis were surprised by the subsequent Soviet decision to build up Egypt's air defenses. I think not because the Israelis never feared that step—it played right into their hands. If I were in their position, I'd have played it the same way. Their best weapon—and the one that Israel exploited most successfully—was that they were the only bastion against communism in the Middle East."

With the arrival of Soviet missiles, men, and aircraft in Egypt, the battle lines between the White House and the State Department were clearly and distinctly drawn. Though no one knew it at the time, this was to be the State Department's last bureaucratic gasp under Rogers, the last time it was to play a significant role in the great-power struggle between the Soviet Union and the United States, as perceived by Kissinger and Nixon.

What to do about the Soviet presence in Egypt was the problem. In the State Department view, that question could not be considered unless American decision makers also dealt with the fact of Israeli responsibility. Kissinger dismissed that opinion, as he noted in his memoirs: "[The State Department] 'solution' to the Soviet military move was to press Israel to be more flexible. Precious time was wasted debating irrelevancies"—that is, the question whether the Soviets had responded to Israeli aggression. Once the Soviets established themselves in Egypt, Kissinger wrote, "the political balance would be drastically changed, and the military balances could be overthrown at any moment of Soviet choosing. Israel was not free of responsibility for the present state of affairs, but we would be able to deal with the political problem only after mastering the military challenge.'' In Kissinger's view, then, it did not matter who was in the right or in the wrong, as long as the Russians were punished.

Kissinger wanted a showdown but Nixon wasn't ready. He was still hopeful of getting Moscow to agree to a summit meeting, in the hope of bailing out the Republicans in November. Rogers, who was, to Kissinger's dismay, continuing to hold fruitful—and private—discussions with Dobrynin, announced in late March that the President had decided to "hold in abeyance" an Israeli request for advanced aircraft. The State Department was thus keeping control of the Middle East negotiations after the Soviets began their buildup. In April 1970, as the first waves of what would be 15,000 Soviet soldiers and advisers began pouring into Egypt, Sisco met with Nasser in Cairo and insisted that the United States was committed to a "balanced policy" in the Middle East. Nasser decided to try again, according to Heikal, and on May 1 publicly invited the United States to take a new political initiative in the Middle East. Obviously under pressure from the Soviet Union, Nasser hinted that he would be willing to accede to a limited ceasefire, if the price were right. The Nixon Administration would have to cancel its planned shipment of new warplanes to Israel and also order Israel to withdraw from the lands seized after the 1967 war. "I say to President Nixon there is a decisive point coming in Arab-American relations," Nasser declared. "Our insistence on liberating our lands is the fundamental and legitimate right of any nation that values its dignity.''

Nixon, under intense pressure from Kissinger to get tough, continued to waffle. On April 30, Kissinger wrote, the day before the Cambodian invasion, the President authorized Kissinger to tell Ambassador Rabin privately that he would "provide more planes, despite his earlier decision.'' A few weeks later, still embroiled in the Cambodian invasion, Nixon met in the White House with Abba Eban, Israel's Foreign Minister, and assured him that the flow of arms and aircraft would be continued. But Nixon also spoke of halting the growing escalation in the Middle East and said that a new diplomatic initiative was being planned. There would be prior consultation, he assured Eban. On June 2, Rogers again met privately with Ambassador Dobrynin and learned that the Soviets had persuaded Nasser to make two significant concessions. If a ceasefire could be arranged, Rogers was told, Nasser promised a formal end to Egypt's state of war with Israel and also guaranteed that he would limit the activities from within Egypt of the *fedayeen,* who, intelligence analysts all agreed, were certain to do all within their power to obstruct any accommodation. Rogers also warned Dobrynin not to permit any Soviet missiles or personnel to enter the Suez Canal zone—that is, within thirty kilometers of the canal itself and the Israeli fortifications on the other side.

The Rogers-Dobrynin meeting seems to have been the last straw for Kissinger, whose status inside the Nixon camp had reached new heights after his strong defense of the President's policies in Cambodia and Vietnam. Kissinger's control of the SALT talks, with its backchannel through Dobrynin, was now total, but he had yet to dominate the Secretary of State completely. Rogers was still in charge of the Middle East negotiations, and Nixon, growing more and more inclined toward a face-saving summit meeting, seemed unwilling to confront the Soviets directly in Egypt. In his memoirs, Kissinger described his anger upon learning of the June 2 Rogers-Dobrynin meeting, not in personal terms but solely in the context of foreign policy: "What it really did, however, was to give the Soviets a blank check; it acquiesced in the Soviet combat presence in Egypt so long as they did not move them directly into the combat zone. . . . And within two months they were in a position to advance their units rapidly into the combat zone."

John Ehrlichman, however, recognized Kissinger's anger as an artifice in his long struggle for domination. Kissinger had gone to the President with yet another threat to resign over the Rogers problem, and Nixon, in turn, asked Ehrlichman and John Mitchell to see his national security adviser and calm him down. As the three men met, Ehrlichman recalls, Kissinger presented them with a typewritten note with three points:

1. Attacks on Henry Kissinger, direct or indirect, must cease. An attack on Kissinger is an attack on the President.
2. All cables with policy implications, including especially the Middle East, must be cleared in the White House. Sufficient time must be left for the clearance procedure to operate properly.
3. All contacts with Dobrynin must be cleared ahead of time. Talking points must be submitted before and a full report afterwards.*

Kissinger's threat did not work. Nixon refused to stop the State Department, which had decided to push for a ninety-day ceasefire in the Middle East. But the President did his best to placate Kissinger, telling him in early June, as Kissinger wrote, that "the current Middle East track would lead us into disaster." Kissinger, encouraged, made one final attempt to stop Rogers: On June 16 he sent the President a memorandum warning that the ceasefire proposal was "inopportune unless it settled the issue of the Soviet combat presence, which seemed to me the heart of the problem." Two days later, Nixon formally endorsed a second Rogers proposal, which was publicly announced on June 25 by the Secretary of State. The second Rogers plan was far less sweeping than the first. Its basic intent was to call on all of the involved parties to "stop shooting and start talking," and it called for international talks, under the auspices of the United Nations, to discuss Israel's withdrawal from the occupied lands in return for guarantees of recognition, peace, and territorial integrity. The plan had been privately forwarded to Israel, Egypt, the Soviet Union, and Jordan a few days before its public revelation.

Kissinger brooded over his inability to dominate the policy and over what he insisted was Rogers'—and Nixon's—weakness in not challenging the Soviet military presence in Egypt. At a news briefing on June 26, before any official response had been made to the Rogers initiative, Kissinger, in San Clemente with the President, told reporters on "background"—that is, not for direct attribution to him—that the initial intent of the Soviet Union in aiding

* Ehrlichman located Kissinger's typewritten list of demands in June 1980, when he was given access to his White House papers, which were then under the control of the National Archive. The Kissinger note was not dated, but a reconstruction of events pinpoints that meeting at some time after the Rogers-Dobrynin meeting of June 2, 1970. Talking about the long-forgotten note, Ehrlichman couldn't help laughing at Kissinger's priorities—that is, listing the criticism of himself as the first item of business. Ehrlichman later included the Kissinger note in *Witness to Power*, his 1982 memoir.

Egypt was "irrelevant" to his belief that the continued presence of the Soviet troops represented a "strategic threat to the United States." He added: "We are trying to expel the Soviet military presence" in Egypt. Kissinger also required the reporters not to publish or broadcast stories based on his briefing until after July 1. His remarks, carefully attributed to the "Administration's top officials," were published by only one newspaper, the *Washington Post*.* Nevertheless, the assertions enraged Rogers, who privately accused Kissinger of trying to sabotage his ceasefire efforts.

On July 11, during a news conference in London, Rogers publicly and specifically disavowed Kissinger's remark, stating that the United States had "never thought of expelling" the Russians from the Middle East.†

All this pushing and shoving had no impact on the Egyptians. According to Heikal, Nasser decided in mid-July, shortly before returning from a two-week visit to Moscow, to accept the American ninety-day ceasefire offer. The Egyptian decision, publicly announced on July 23, was a brave one. It brought harsh criticism for Nasser and immediate political benefits for Israel. Arab unity was shattered and the radical *fedayeen* split. A PLO radio station in Cairo began

---

* Kissinger later accused the *Washington Post*'s Murray Marder, who wrote the dispatch, of making him a "laughingstock of the world." Marder's article, published July 2, began with this sentence: "The Nixon Administration is now convinced that Soviet air combat forces must be expelled from Egypt before they can become a springboard for long-term Soviet domination of the Mediterranean and the Middle East." The apocalyptic assessment alarmed leaders in Western Europe and caused the White House to issue a formal statement clarifying its view that the Soviet planes and pilots should be removed by diplomatic, not military, means. How Marder came to be the only journalist to write the story tells much about the state of the White House press corps that summer. Not normally a White House correspondent, Marder flew to San Clemente on July 1, after convincing his editors that a foreign policy specialist should cover the many background briefings being given by Kissinger that week. In the press room in California, he noticed a large stack of transcripts—including Kissinger's embargoed briefing on the Middle East—and took them to his motel to read. The President had a press conference scheduled that week—his first outside the White House—and the national press corps had been preoccupied with it. When Marder read Kissinger's statement on the Middle East, "My eyes popped out and I did what any reporter would do—write a story." The next morning, as he arrived at the San Clemente press room, a colleague warned him, "You're in terrible trouble. You didn't report what Henry said." It turned out that Kissinger had recanted the word "expel" in a second backgrounder, on June 27, also embargoed until after July 1. The reporters gathered for Ziegler's press conference that morning, Marder says, fully expecting that the press secretary would deny the gist of Marder's story. He did not do so because he could not; instead he issued a "clarification" to the effect that the administration had "no plans" to inject American troops into the Middle East. During the first few days following publication of the "expel" story, Marder recalls, "Henry wasn't unhappy about it at all." After the European press began to criticize the statement—he was criticized for his insensitivity to diplomatic language—Kissinger *then* concluded that "I'd embarrassed him in the eyes of the world, and he literally did not talk to me for a year. And when he did start to talk to me again, it was always with a bitter remark, such as, 'Murray, am I using the right word?' " What upset Marder about the incident was the fact that it was Peter Lisagor of the *Chicago Daily News,* a reporter known to be on good terms with Kissinger, who raised a question about the word "expel" the day after Kissinger's June 26 background briefing. After Kissinger modified the word in the second backgrounder, none of the reporters—save Marder, who wasn't there on June 26—chose to report what Kissinger had said initially.

† Such a statement from Rogers was uncharacteristically defiant, and the attitude seemed to seep down through the ranks of the State Department that summer. Sisco, who had always seemed compliant, suddenly "switched horses," as one former Kissinger aide puts it, and began ignoring Kissinger's behind-the-back policy recommendations on the ceasefire negotiations. A challenge from Rogers was one thing, but defiance from Sisco? The aide recalls that "Henry just went batshit over Sisco. He would walk around his office and rant and rave—'If I ever become Secretary of State blood will run in the halls and the first one to go will be Sisco.' " Sisco's departure from Kissinger's sphere of influence was brief, however, and he was soon a Kissinger conduit again.

broadcasting denunciations of the decision and Nasser ordered the station shut down. Heikal quoted Nasser as later explaining to Yasir Arafat that he did not believe the ninety-day ceasefire stood more than a one half of one percent chance of success, but even that one half was worth a trial. In the meantime, Nasser said, the pause in warfare would give Egypt a chance to finish constructing its SAM missile sites and other defense positions.

Rogers and the State Department were surprised and delighted by Egypt's acceptance, which gave them a major victory in the struggle for peace in the Middle East and in the struggle against Henry Kissinger at home. In his memoirs, Kissinger noted, however, that he "was not loath" to seek some of the credit for himself in the days following Nasser's announcement. Kissinger's reasoning was that the Egyptians had simply backed off in the face of his strong remarks about expelling the Soviets from the Middle East. His reservations about the wisdom of that remark suddenly evaporated.

Once the smell of a diplomatic success was in the air, the White House scrambled for its share. Nixon and Kissinger both became personally involved in the crucial next step: compelling the Israeli government to assent to the ceasefire, which called for both sides to cease all military activities in a zone thirty miles wide on each side of the Suez Canal. Nixon, in a letter sent July 23 to Prime Minister Meir, made a series of commitments, including the promise that Israel would not be asked to withdraw any of its troops from occupied lands "until a binding contractual peace agreement satisfactory to you has been achieved." In addition, he committed the United States to the sale of more Phantom jets and, for the first time, sophisticated Shrike missiles capable of destroying the Egyptian missile sites. The commitments were necessary because of the hostile and, at times, hysterical reaction of the Israeli government to the ceasefire. Golda Meir and Yitzak Rabin had clashed over Meir's initial decision to reject the State Department ceasefire proposal as soon as it was proposed in late June—and before the Egyptians had a chance to reject it first. "When I received the draft of Mrs. Meir's reply to the President," Rabin wrote in his memoirs, "I froze in horror." The Israeli Ambassador urged a delay and, obviously working closely with Nixon and Kissinger, succeeded in reassuring Meir to the point where, by the end of July, Israel had agreed to participate in the ceasefire. That decision was immediately praised by Nixon, in an impromptu visit to the press office at San Clemente.

American frustration with Meir reached a peak during those weeks. In mid-July, shortly before the Egyptians agreed to the ceasefire, the Israeli Prime Minister suggested in an interview with *Der Spiegel,* the German news magazine, that NATO and the United States should force the Russians out of the Middle East in a confrontation similar to the 1962 Cuban missile crisis. Despite her bright public image among Jews in the United States and Europe, many Israelis and Americans did not think Meir was up to the intellectual requirements of her office. After her death, some leaders of the Jewish community in the United States privately acknowledged in interviews that she was narrow-minded and unimaginative in her approach to international negotiations. "She was intransigent," says one prominent leader, who served as president of a worldwide Jewish organization. "It was very difficult for her to conceptualize." An Israeli diplomat thinks that "Golda Meir was a poor Prime Minister. She had a great press, but did very poorly." Another official says that "many of the worst mistakes that Israel made diplomatically came as a result of Golda." It should be noted that these comments all came from Jews who strongly supported the Israeli cause and worked unceasingly for it.*

Shortly after Israel accepted the ceasefire on July 31, there was a new crisis. The Egyptians began moving their sophisticated missile sites and other equipment closer to the Suez Canal. Such moves continued after the ceasefire went into effect on August 7; in early September the United States formally protested to the Soviet Union and the Egyptian government that at least fourteen missile sites had been modified during the month of August. The military significance of moving the missiles forward was far less than the political one. Israel not only publicly denounced the moves but also demanded immediate delivery of antimissile weapons, including the Shrike air-to-ground missiles, which were capable of locking onto the radars of the Egyptian SAM sites. Nixon and Kissinger were quick to blame Rogers and his State Department for not providing adequate guarantees in the ceasefire agreement to prevent such violations.† Kissinger, as he noted in his memoirs, considered it "crucial" to take a hard line against the ceasefire violation "and to bring their responsibilities home to the Soviets." If the United States did not act immediately to stop further ceasefire violations, Kissinger told the President, it would have "serious consequences" for long-term American relations with the Soviet Union.

Needless to say, as Kissinger acknowledged in his memoirs, the Secretary of State did not take such interference lightly. "The Middle East ceasefire had seemed like a great triumph, the *first uncontroverted achievement of the Nixon Administration in foreign policy* [emphasis added]," wrote Kissinger. "Understandably, Rogers was reluctant to face the prospect that it might fail. . . . He tended to consider my concerns as an attempt to deprive him of his one field of glory."

The Egyptian moves were indeed egregious, a bad-faith violation of the ceasefire agreement. It could be plausibly argued, as many an Israeli did, that Nasser's surprising acceptance of the ceasefire was merely a ploy to permit him to move missile sites forward without Israeli Air Force interference. On the other hand, many State Department officials argued that it would be foolish to permit the violations, although serious, to destroy a working ceasefire.

* Michael Brecher, the Canadian political scientist whose prize-winning studies of Israeli foreign policy are considered seminal by Middle East scholars, was sharply critical of Meir's "pragmatic, short-sighted, purely reactive approach" to high policy issues in mid-1970. In *Decisions in Israel's Foreign Policy,* published by Oxford University Press in 1974, Brecher quoted Meir as telling an Israeli newspaperman in April: "Our foreign policy may be limited but it is limited to our interests. . . . We have to concentrate on a very limited subject, according to all of us—in the worry simply to remain alive. . . . I didn't know what people want of our lives when they demand of us a long-run view when, at the same time, we might be attacked and destroyed in the short run." Brecher wrote that what he called the "Holocaust fixation" had dominated Israel's foreign policy after its independence in 1948. "Justifiable in the early years, it began to lose credibility after the Sinai Campaign; and in 1970, when the Meir statement was uttered, it was remote from the reality of power in the Near East Core; Israel was the strongest actor in the area, amply capable of surviving an Arab attack. The Meir belief, widely shared among Israel's decision-makers, was a major psychological obstacle to intelligent and efficient decision-making."

† The American response to Israel's allegation of immediate and large-scale ceasefire violations was complicated by a serious intelligence failure. The American negotiators had not thought in advance to obtain either satellite or U-2 aircraft photographs of the Sinai area prior to the formal ceasefire, which, amazingly, was programmed to go into effect in the middle of the night on August 7. "We had no data base," one official recalls. "We really couldn't figure out what was going on out there."

There were also some legal questions. Egypt had deliberately delayed its initialing of the ceasefire agreement in an obvious effort to minimize accusations of cheating. The ceasefire text was vague as to which actions specifically were prohibited. Furthermore, the Soviet Union was not legally bound to the ceasefire or to its requirement for a military standstill. Finally, there was evidence that the Israelis had themselves been violating the ceasefire—although in a far less significant manner—by building new roads and new bunkers inside their thirty-mile standstill zone, as well as by flying unauthorized reconnaissance flights over Egyptian territory.

The choice of what to do was the President's, and Richard Nixon still wanted his summit. His solution was not to confront directly the issue of ceasefire cheating but instead to increase the shipment of military goods to Israel—including eighteen F-4 Phantom jet fighters—and to order the State Department to file pro forma protests in Cairo and Moscow. Nixon's soft approach was politically motivated: The congressional elections, not the Russians, were coming. At a meeting with Ambassador Rabin on August 17, in the Map Room in the White House, Nixon was accompanied not by Henry Kissinger, who still wanted to challenge the Soviets, but by Haig. As Rabin recalled it, "The President . . . reminded me that, like the prime minister, he too faced domestic political pressure. The American public was in a 'peace mood,' as he put it, and above all he felt obliged to encourage the start of negotiations to reach a political settlement."

Kissinger was upset and became even more so when Rogers, in a confrontation at San Clemente on August 25, accused him of seeking, as Kissinger wrote, "to foment a crisis by being so insistent on ceasefire violations." Rogers' success in bringing about the Middle East ceasefire and improving the administration's political position in the Middle East had obviously emboldened him, and Nixon responded to the controversy inside his Cabinet in his usual way, as Kissinger wrote, with "procrastination." The President, he added despairingly, "was still toying with the idea" of a Soviet summit meeting before the elections. As late as September 1, Nixon—under heavy pressure from Kissinger and the Israelis over the Egyptian ceasefire violations—was still insisting that Israel participate in the ceasefire talks that were to begin, under Rogers' second initiative, in early September at the United Nations in New York City. Those talks were to be held under the auspices of Gunnar Jarring, a Swedish diplomat who had been appointed by the United Nations late in 1967 to help negotiate a peace in the Middle East. Jarring had publicly announced on August 24 that delegates from Israel, Egypt, and Jordan would participate in the negotiations. Ambassador Rabin, in his memoirs, recalled informing his government late in August that Nixon would not consider Egypt's ceasefire violations a justification for an Israeli refusal to participate in the Jarring talks. There was a solution, Rabin wrote: "We could postpone appointing our representative to the talks while urging the United States to take diplomatic action to remove the missiles. . . ." Rabin had proposed exactly what Kissinger wanted.

On September 6, Israel announced that it could not take part in the Jarring talks because of the Egyptian ceasefire violations. Under normal conditions, Nixon, still hoping for his Moscow summit, might have been quick to pressure the Israeli government, but other events—involving the PLO—intervened and the Jarring talks never did materialize. Israel, concerned over the strengthening of Egyptian air defenses, made no effort to break the ceasefire; it held on both sides of the canal zone, and would continue to do so until the 1973 war.

As the White House's attention turned elsewhere, the State Department's diplomatic initiative was quietly allowed to wither, as the 1969 comprehensive plan had withered, but the mere fact of the two American peace initiatives offered hope to some Egyptians. Mahmoud Riad's memoirs describe the mid-1970 period as "the nearest the U.S. came to achieving genuine peace—nearer than at any time past. The Rogers initiative . . . was the first American step on the correct path. . . . There were two factions in the U.S. who had sponsored the initiative: Rogers and a group of State Department experts who were fully convinced of the need to establish peace in the area in order to safeguard American and Western interests. There was, however, an opposing faction led by Henry Kissinger which believed that it was in the interest of the U.S. to support Israel totally. . . . Kissinger was able to persuade Nixon to adopt his views under the pretext of confronting Soviet infiltration in the area. This was the real beginning of the failure of the initiative."

For a few months in mid-1970, Richard Nixon had turned his foreign policy inside out. He was so caught up in election-year politics that he retreated from his major foreign policy goal—confrontation with the Soviets—and tried to accomplish a settlement in the Middle East. By mid-September, however, having yet to hear from the Soviets on the possibility of a summit, Nixon was forced to face the bad news: No summit was possible. Playing soft on the Egyptian ceasefire violations had not worked, and Nixon was embarrassed, enraged, and, of course, ready to strike back. Inevitably, he turned to Kissinger, whose hardline advice was again in vogue. There was nothing subtle about Kissinger's view: The Russians had humbled the United States in the Middle East and had been allowed to do so without paying a price.

In early September, Joseph Alsop, the syndicated columnist who was Kissinger's closest newspaper confidant—as well as the newspaper columnist most often used by the White House—signaled Kissinger's view by publishing a harsh attack on Rogers and Dobrynin. Alsop was provided with access to the highly classified account of Rogers' June 2, 1970, meeting with Dobrynin, the meeting that had triggered a Kissinger resignation threat. In his column, Alsop wrote of the "black lies" that Dobrynin had told Rogers that day. Describing their talks as "Beel-and-Toli" chats—a snide reference to each man's use of the other's first name—Alsop characterized as "squalid" the violations of the Middle East ceasefire by the Soviets and "their Egyptian puppets," and added: "The reluctance of certain American officials to admit they had been shamelessly bamboozled quite obviously played a role in the shabby American shuffling about the reality of the ceasefire violations." As for Dobrynin, Alsop indirectly suggested that the United States should declare him persona non grata because of his "persuasive mendacity." No one in the State Department or in the Soviet Embassy had any doubt about the source of Alsop's documents or whose point of view his column represented.

In the Nixon-Kissinger White House, if there was to be no summit with the Soviet Union and no peace, there would be politically palatable confrontations and nuclear threats. The Egyptian ceasefire violations were no longer viable as a pretext for confrontation, but in September a long-brewing civil war broke out between Arafat's PLO and the CIA-aided army of King Hussein in Jordan. Before the month was out, Nixon and Kissinger had seized on the dispute as a vehicle for expiating their softness toward the Soviet Union during the cease-fire dispute. The President and his national security adviser managed to escalate that civil strife, with its local origins, into a direct big-power confrontation, involving military alerts, deployment of aircraft carriers, and a presidential order to commit an act of warfare in the Middle East that was ignored by his Secretary of Defense.

19

MIDEAST: MISPERCEPTIONS IN JORDAN

IN THE LATE SUMMER OF 1970, L. Dean Brown was a career Foreign Service officer in traditional flux—on the move from one overseas post to another. Brown had completed a three-year tour as Ambassador jointly to Senegal and Gambia in West Africa and was scheduled, he had been told by Joseph Sisco, for reassignment to Lebanon. Instead, in early September, he was abruptly ordered to report to the California White House to meet with the President, then in the midst of a lengthy working vacation in San Clemente. Brown, who hardly knew Nixon, was met at San Clemente by Kissinger, who quickly asked whether Brown would agree to serve as Ambassador to crisis-ridden Jordan. Of course the answer was yes; and now the President was ready to greet him.

Brown recalls being a little confused and apprehensive that day. He was not an Arabist, nor was he an expert on the Middle East. Far from it. After he and Kissinger were ushered in to see the President, "Nixon did most of the talking —he obviously thought I was an expert. Henry was at his most obsequious; taking notes on a yellow pad." Nixon's message was that he did not trust the State Department and its policies. In Nixon's view, the Russians were beginning to stir up trouble in the Middle East with their client states. In Jordan, the Soviet-aided PLO was directly threatening the moderate regime of King Hussein, and it would be Brown's job to shore up Hussein by whatever means possible. The King was then under renewed attack by the PLO for his support of Egypt after Nasser agreed to the July ceasefire in the Sinai with the hated Israelis.

Nixon made it clear he believed warfare was inevitable in the Middle East, a war that could spread and precipitate World War III, with the United States and the Soviet Union squaring off against each other. The President was impressive; he seemed to have a good grasp of Hussein's problems and a clear view of how to help the King. Like most American ambassadors who visited the President, Brown promised to relay any important information directly to Kissinger's office by backchannel.

Nixon's and Kissinger's misperceptions about the extent of Brown's knowledge of the Middle East were not significant; he turned out to be an excellent and effective ambassador. The more important misperception, and the tragedy of American policy in the Middle East in the early 1970s, lay in the White House's inability to understand that the Russians were not behind every sand dune in the Middle East.

By 1970, the PLO had carved out a virtually independent existence inside the small desert kingdom of Jordan; it was a state within a state. Arab refugees had been flocking to Palestinian settlement camps inside Jordan since the 1948 Arab-Israeli war. The number of such refugees increased dramatically after the 1967 debacle, when King Hussein, in a show of Arab unity, joined in attacking Israel and lost control of Jordan's West Bank. Hussein's position softened after the war, under American diplomatic pressure, and by 1968 he began talks with American officials in the hope of a negotiated return of the conquered area. As the PLO guerrillas, or *fedayeen,* became more organized and daring in the later 1960s, under Yasir Arafat, Hussein's rule grew more tenuous. By 1970, the *fedayeen* were operating with impunity inside Jordan, staging bloody guerrilla raids into Israel that could not be controlled or limited by Hussein and his central government in Amman. In June, a PLO faction tried to assassinate the King, and there was open—although brief—conflict between the guerrillas and Hussein's army, which was composed largely of British-trained Bedouin tribesmen intensely loyal to the King. Strong opposition to a protracted civil war inside Jordan came not only from the United States, which feared Hussein's overthrow and the emergence of a radical Palestinian state, but also from Egypt's President Nasser, who was convinced, as Mohammed Heikal wrote in his memoirs, that "civil war in Jordan would simply play into the hands of the Israelis and the Americans."

On September 6, 1970, two days after Dean Brown talked with Nixon and Kissinger, the Popular Front for the Liberation of Palestine, one of the most extreme factions in the PLO, hijacked a Swiss and two American passenger planes; three days later a British airliner was seized. Nearly 500 passengers from the aircraft were flown to an airport thirty miles outside of Amman and would not be released, the guerrillas declared, until all the PLO terrorists held in Swiss, German, British, and Israeli jails were freed.* A deadline of seventy-two hours was set. The hijackings and ransom demands were a precursor of terrorist acts by "Black September," a secret PLO terrorist wing, whose operations in subsequent years—triggered by the failed September war in Jordan—created outrage and anxiety throughout the world.

The hijackings did more than jangle nerves in Washington. Nixon, deciding that the time had come to destroy the *fedayeen,* ordered American Navy planes from the Sixth Fleet in the Mediterranean to bomb the guerrillas' hideaways. The strike was meant to be purely punitive, a warning blow. Nixon's goal was not to save the American hostages, but to demonstrate America's willingness to challenge the PLO and to aid its ally, King Hussein. There is no evidence that Kissinger raised any objections to the order, which the President himself verbally gave to Laird. But Laird did. "We had bad weather for forty-eight hours," Laird recalled years later, with a grin. "The Secretary of Defense can always find a reason not to do something. There's always bad weather."

At the time Nixon articulated his order, the *fedayeen* were still in control of

* One of the hijacked planes, a Pan American 747, was flown to Cairo airport, the passengers were released, and it was blown up by Popular Front guerrillas. The PLO was far from unified in support of the hijackings. On September 12, the Central Committee of the guerrilla movement, led by Yasir Arafat, suspended the Popular Front, a Marxist group led by Dr. George Habash, for having violated PLO discipline. The Central Committee also condemned all actions "that could affect the safety and security of the Palestinian resistance."

nearly 500 aircraft hostages. Asked what the President hoped to accomplish with the bombings, Laird admitted that he wasn't sure: "He probably wanted to show the Russians that, by God, they couldn't tell what he might do." The former Defense Secretary was reluctant to discuss the incident in detail, but in a conversation with a former government official not long after the incident, he expressed shock at the presidential order and at Kissinger's role in urging its execution. As the official remembers the conversation, Laird said, "Conducting an air operation would have been incredibly dumb," and he explained that he had been forced to move quickly to prevent the White House from going around his office to that of Admiral Moorer, who would have been only too willing to do what the President and Kissinger wanted. Laird telephoned Moorer and said, as he told the official, "Tom, I've gotten this order. . . . We're just going to have terrible weather out there for the next forty-eight hours." Laird managed to stall for days, although Kissinger telephoned to find out why it was not carried out. The White House seemed to accept the explanation of "bad weather," and eventually rescinded the order. Nixon had changed his mind.

The exact date of Nixon's order is not known, but the evidence—and Laird's recollections—suggest that the most critical moment came on or before September 8, two days after the first hijacking, and before the deadline for the release of the jailed PLO members. Nixon convened a high-level meeting of his advisers that afternoon, and also invited J. Edgar Hoover and John Mitchell. Kissinger, always eager to demonstrate his role as an insider, revealed in his memoirs that the President "had earlier told me privately that the hijacking should be used as a pretext to crush the fedayeen; in the meeting he made no such comment. He did say that in an extremity he preferred American to Israeli military intervention." At this point, Kissinger wrote, Rogers raised his usual objection, noting that an American involvement would result in the payment of an "enormous price for an essentially useless act." Nixon then turned to Kissinger, who—the President understood—knew far more than Rogers what Nixon wanted to hear, and Kissinger told the group that if "the fedayeen could use Jordan as their principal base and in the process destroy the authority of the king . . . the entire Middle East would be revolutionized. . . . We could not acquiesce in this by dithering on the sidelines, wringing our hands, urging the resumption of peace talks, and then proclaiming our importance."

It was a good show. If the weather "cleared" and the ordered air raids on the *fedayeen* did take place, the rationale had been laid out. If the raids did not come off, a possibility that must have seemed more likely to Nixon and Kissinger with each passing hour, the President and his top aide had managed in front of J. Edgar Hoover to look far more resolute than their Cabinet advisers.

Neither Nixon nor Kissinger mentioned the attack order in his memoirs. Some years later, Kissinger described the incident to at least one of his senior associates, but he depicted it solely as an example of Nixon's irrationality. He failed to mention that he was involved in reaffirming the order to Laird and in badgering the Defense Secretary about it on Nixon's behalf. Laird has steadfastly refused to talk about the incident in detail, explaining, "If I'm going to be insubordinate on a direct order, I'm not going to tell anybody about it."

With his Patton-type order to Laird out of the way, Nixon worked effectively with Kissinger during the rest of the crisis. The two refused to negotiate with the *fedayeen,* who were still insisting on the release of jailed terrorists. The President also made it more than a little obvious that the United States was prepared to take military steps, if necessary, to free the hostages. He ordered a carrier task force in the Mediterranean to deploy off the coast of Lebanon and placed some Army units in Europe on "semialert." Plans were drawn up in the Pentagon, and made known in some detail to the press, for the deployment of American paratroop units to the Middle East, where they would be within a short flight of the hostage sites. The *fedayeen* responded to the reports of American troop movements by destroying the three remaining aircraft on the ground on September 12 and shifting the hostages to a new hideaway. The American threats and the *fedayeen*'s response led to a new round of intense bargaining, with the International Red Cross involved, and with more deadlines set by the *fedayeen.* The situation remained highly volatile, especially since a superpower showdown in the Middle East seemed possible.*

As tensions grew, the Soviet Union decided to urge restraint on Jordan and Iraq, and to tell the Nixon Administration it had done so. A Soviet diplomat informed Sisco on September 9 that Moscow had sent diplomatic notes to Jordan and to Iraq, its closest ally in the Middle East, and urged them to practice restraint in the crisis. Conflict among the Arab nations would only help their enemies—"the Israeli aggressors and the imperialist forces behind them," the Soviet notes said. Given the fact that the notes were addressed to Arab countries, such language could hardly be construed as out of proportion, but Kissinger, as he made clear in his memoirs, viewed the Soviet attempt to be conciliatory as an act of provocation. He concluded that the notes were a "crude slap at us" that was "hardly calculated to douse any fires." It was a sign that "Moscow obviously did not believe that it was running a serious risk" in the Middle East. The Kremlin leaders had "made formally correct noises," Kissinger acknowledged, "but did nothing constructive to reverse the drift toward crisis."

Kissinger and Nixon were unable or unwilling to separate the Soviet Union from the actions of the PLO. Nothing the Soviets said or did in the next three weeks would change their view.

The Popular Front's continuing terrorist activities in September had little to do, in fact, with the Soviet Union's foreign policy, but were an angry reaction to Egypt's decision to participate in the ceasefire with Israel. The Popular Front's main goal was to provoke a military confrontation between Hussein and the more cautious wings of the PLO. In those efforts, the Popular Front was supported by the bitterly anti-Israel governments of Syria and Iraq, both of which ruled out the possibility of any negotiations with Israel. Syria also had long-standing grievances against King Hussein, whose moderate views it held in contempt. In none of this did the Soviet Union play anything amounting to a key role, although it was a major supplier of arms to Syria and Iraq.

Nonetheless, Nixon reported in his memoirs that on September 15, when

---

* A compromise, in which Israel played a key role, was eventually worked out and the hostages were freed. Israel agreed to release 450 Palestinian prisoners in return for a *fedayeen* commitment to begin releasing the hostages in small groups. The hostage release was concluded by September 29, without incident, despite the onset of the PLO war in Jordan.

King Hussein decided to initiate a full-fledged civil war between his 50,000-man army and the PLO guerrillas in Amman, Kissinger informed him: "It looks like the Soviets are pushing the Syrians and the Syrians are pushing the Palestinians." Nixon readily agreed that the Soviets were the villains. In his memoirs, he described the situation in Jordan as confused on September 15, but "[O]ne thing was clear. We could not allow Hussein to be overthrown by a Soviet-inspired insurrection." The prophecy that Nixon had raised earlier in the month in his talk with Ambassador Brown was now being fulfilled, less than seven weeks before the congressional elections. Nixon's memoirs presented the moment as the ultimate test of American resolve and courage: "It was like a ghastly game of dominoes, with a nuclear war waiting at the end. . . . If it [Hussein's overthrow] succeeded, the Israelis would almost certainly take pre-emptive measures against a Syrian-dominated radical government in Jordan; the Egyptians were tied to Syria by military alliances; and Soviet prestige was on the line with both the Syrians and the Egyptians. Since the United States could not stand idly by and watch Israel being driven into the sea, the possibility of a direct U.S.-Soviet confrontation was uncomfortably high." Nixon was determined to have his crisis and prove his mettle, as John F. Kennedy had in the Cuban missile crisis. If there was to be no summit, there would be nuclear dominoes.

Another major power that fully shared the Nixon-Kissinger view of the crisis in Jordan was Israel, whose army and air force, so the White House thought, would surely intervene if necessary to rescue Hussein's army. Hussein informed the British on September 15 that he was forming a military government and would begin combat operations in Amman and in other PLO strongholds. Word was immediately flashed to Nixon and Kissinger, resulting in another wave of Kissinger-dominated meetings in the White House Situation Room and a Nixon-Kissinger decision to order a second aircraft carrier to the Mediterranean. Full-scale warfare broke out in Amman on September 17, and continued for the next few days, although Hussein's troops—fighting well—always maintained control of the city.

As their memoirs show, Nixon and Kissinger spent much of the next week debating whether it would be wise to permit the Israelis to intervene to protect Hussein, if necessary, or whether American military units should be involved. Kissinger was in total command—he was finally getting a chance to act in the Middle East without State Department fetters. Secretary Rogers, as usual, was more cautious and more inclined to seek a negotiated settlement. He urged a diplomatic approach with the Russians, such as a joint American-Soviet intervention to prevent the spread of warfare in the Middle East. "Rogers thought calming the atmosphere would contribute to its resolution," Kissinger wrote. "I believe that it was the danger that the situation might get out of hand which provided the incentive for rapid settlement." The same threat policy that was not working against the North Vietnamese would now be put into effect in the Middle East.

Nixon, with Kissinger's support, rejected Rogers' conciliatory proposal out of hand. Russia was not to be a partner of the United States in a Middle East peace settlement; it was the enemy. One immediate Nixon-Kissinger goal was to "signal" the Russians to stay out of Jordan; within a week the United States had assembled in the eastern Mediterranean two aircraft carrier task forces with fourteen destroyers, a cruiser, and 140 aircraft, as well as a Marine landing force of 1,200 men. A third carrier task force and an additional 1,200 Marines were en route to the coast of Lebanon. Three Army battalions in Europe were also ordered to stand at full readiness and be prepared to parachute into Jordan within eight hours. The Army's 82nd Airborne Division at Fort Bragg, N. C., was also placed on full alert and ordered to be ready for airlifting to the Middle East. Eighteen F-4 Air Force fighter planes and crews had been assembled at a base in Turkey for possible combat, with refueling craft—although, as a Pentagon memorandum warned Nixon and Kissinger, "Turkey has *not* authorized us to use the base to launch these aircraft in strikes over Jordan."

In all of these military deployments and signalings, Kissinger was dominant. The Kalbs, in their biography, reported that Kissinger, the World War II intelligence sergeant, was in his element as he pored over military maps of the Mediterranean in the White House Situation Room, shifting about toy battleships and aircraft carriers, arguing with combat-seasoned admirals, and peremptorily picking up the telephone to demand that the Joint Chiefs of Staff change the deployment of the Sixth Fleet. "Henry adores power, absolutely adores it," one senior official was quoted as saying. "To Henry, diplomacy is nothing without it."

All this American military might had been assembled in the Mediterranean with almost no publicity inside the United States and no awareness among the public or the bureaucracy of the drastic steps being taken in the name of stopping the Russians. The military moves were kept secret because, as Kissinger wrote, "announcements would have backfired because they would have required too many public reassurances. . . ." The Russians, however, were to learn of the troop alerts and deployment, since Kissinger ordered the military units involved to move without any special communications security, insuring that the Soviet intelligence agencies would intercept their signals.

Nixon was far less interested in such secrecy; he wanted the American voters to know that he was standing up to the Soviets in Jordan. On September 16, shortly after learning from Kissinger of the renewed fighting in Amman, Nixon, then in the middle of a short campaign trip, told the editors of the Chicago *Sun-Times* that his administration was "prepared to intervene directly in the Jordanian war should Syria and Iraq enter the conflict and tip the military balances against government forces loyal to Hussein." Only Kissinger, Nixon, and a few military aides knew the extent of that preparation. The President's statements were meant to be off the record, but they were published by the *Sun-Times* for a few editions the next morning without any sign of presidential displeasure.* Kissinger's memoirs portray Nixon as almost jubilant because of the military maneuvers during those days, quoting him as saying: "The main thing is there's nothing better than a little confrontation now and then, a little excitement."

---

* In his memoirs, Nixon noted that Kissinger awakened him in his Chicago hotel room at 8:00 A.M. on September 17 with a report on the intensified civil war in Amman. At the time, however, the *New York Times* reported that Nixon had been awakened at 2:00 A.M. by the Kissinger call. The disparity can easily be explained as routine campaign drama, as the p.r. men who seemed to be incessantly around Nixon—including Kissinger, on occasion—sought to heighten the sense of crisis and presidential stamina.

The reality was far less exciting, and much less of the stuff by which political campaigns can be won. The most important misconception—or deliberate Nixon and Kissinger deception—concerned the Soviet position toward King Hussein and the Jordanians. Many senior United States intelligence officials and diplomats believed at the time that the Soviet leaders were as concerned as Nixon and Kissinger were at the possibility of Hussein's overthrow and the emergence of a Palestinian state in Jordan. "I don't think the Soviets wanted to see Hussein overthrown," one American diplomat, a Middle East expert, recalls. "They saw that as a very risky occurrence. I'm not a believer that the Soviet Union goes around the Middle East pushing buttons and making people react." The Soviets obviously realized that, if they did rush into Jordan on the side of the *fedayeen,* the Israelis would be difficult to restrain, and a major war could be triggered. Another limiting factor on the Soviet role in the Middle East, and one that seemed to escape Nixon's and Kissinger's attention, was the widely known fact that the Soviets' influence with the PLO had been diminishing—ever more so with the approval of the ceasefire agreement between Israel and Egypt in July. The PLO publicly condemned Egypt's participation, which was tacitly supported by the Soviet Union. By mid-1970, many of the PLO factions had far greater affinity for the People's Republic of China than for the Soviets.* A third restraining factor was King Hussein's careful determination to stay on good terms with Cairo as well as with Moscow. For example, Hussein sent a delegation to see Nasser before forming the new military government in Amman and beginning his offensive against the *fedayeen.* Mohammed Heikal reported in his memoirs that Nasser subsequently called a summit meeting of Arab leaders in Cairo, some of whom wanted to send men and matériel in support of the *fedayeen.* At a critical point in the conference, Heikal wrote, Nasser argued against the spread of war in the Middle East, stating that "the difficulty is that if we send troops to Jordan this will only result in the liquidation of the rest of the Palestinians."†

There was also evidence that the Soviets were advocating restraint on all

* Kissinger and Nixon seemed unaware of a basic fact: The Soviet Union's rivalry with China lessened its influence in the Middle East and elsewhere in the Third World.

† The sharpest advocate of Arab intervention in Jordan on behalf of the *fedayeen* was Muammar el-Qaddafi, the President of Libya, who was depicted throughout Heikal's memoir as an often-irrational gunslinger, always eager to commit his army to bloodshed. Heikal published excerpts from what seems to have been an unofficial transcript of the summit meeting, which took place September 22 and 23 at the Nile Hilton Hotel, in which Qaddafi argued with Nasser and King Feisal of Saudi Arabia:

Qaddafi: "I think we should send armed forces to Amman—armed forces from Iraq and Syria."
Feisal: "I think that if we are going to send our armies anywhere we should send them to fight the Jews."
Qaddafi: "What Hussein is doing is worse than the Jews. It's only a difference in the names. . . . If we are faced with a madman like Hussein who wants to kill his people we must send someone to seize him, handcuff him, stop him from doing what he's doing, and take him off to an asylum."
Feisal: "I don't think you should call an Arab King a madman who should be taken to an asylum."
Qaddafi: "But all his family are mad. It's a matter of record."
Feisal: "Well, perhaps all of us are mad."
Nasser: "Sometimes when you see what is going on in the Arab world, your Majesty, I think this may be so. I suggest we appoint a doctor to examine us regularly and find out which ones are crazy."
Feisal: "I would like your doctor to start with me, because in view of what I see I doubt whether I shall be able to preserve my reason."

240

factions throughout the crisis in Jordan. One explicit Soviet message was sent to Nasser's summit meeting, urging, as Heikal reported, that Egypt and other Arab nations "exercise the utmost restraint because . . . any miscalculation might result in the Arabs losing all the reputation which they have recovered over the past three years" (since the 1967 war). A few days earlier, the Soviet Union had warned, through a commentary in its official press agency, Tass, against any outside interference in Jordan, a declaration that seemed to be aimed at Iraq, Syria, and the United States. The Tass commentary specifically cited "the concentration of ships of the U.S. Sixth Fleet near the coasts of Syria and Lebanon . . . and other events," which it said were "alarming symptoms which in no way contribute to relaxation of tensions in the world." Western diplomats in Moscow subsequently told reporters they were "sure" that the Soviets were urging the Syrians—who were threatening to come to the aid of the PLO—to stay out of the fighting. Still another sign of Soviet caution was seen in the waters of the eastern Mediterranean. One American official with access to communications intelligence recalls that as the carriers and destroyers of the United States Sixth Fleet began their early September buildup off the coast of Lebanon, the Soviet fleet "started getting out of their way" and there was no harassment of the American forces, a clue that the Soviets did not believe their role in the Middle East was at stake in Jordan.*

It is possible that the Nixon Administration played a far greater role than is publicly known in King Hussein's decision on September 15 to form a military government and take on the *fedayeen*. Heikal wrote that Nasser sent a delegation of Arab leaders on a private visit to Amman shortly after Hussein's army began its attacks. The delegation came back "shaken by what they had seen," largely because of the size and scope of Hussein's military activities against the guerrillas. General Mohammed Ahmed Sadiq, chief of staff of the Egyptian Army, subsequently concluded that Hussein's operation had been planned far in advance. "By then," Heikal wrote without elaboration, "Nasser had information that the operation had been planned in cooperation with the CIA and some Jordanians, including Wasfi Tel," the Jordanian Prime Minister. No further evidence was cited by Heikal, nor could more be learned in subsequent research on the CIA's direct involvement in Hussein's decision, but Wasfi Tel did play a major role in the next phase of the Jordanian crisis, a role that neither Kissinger nor Nixon mentioned in his memoirs.

The most mysterious and controversial phase of the Jordanian crisis began early on September 20, according to Kissinger's account, when the United States received intelligence reports from the Jordanians and from Mossad of a large-scale tank invasion of Jordan by the Syrian Army. By late afternoon, Kissinger wrote, the United States was able to confirm—he did not say by what means—that two additional Syrian armored brigades had crossed the Jordanian border and were rolling toward the strategic town of Irbid, south of the Golan Heights. By that date, the Hussein regime was no longer facing a direct threat from the *fedayeen;* the Jordanian Army had performed well in the

---

* This official, who had been closely involved in United States defense planning since the Kennedy Administration, said of Nixon and Kissinger in the Jordanian dispute: "They were looking for a cheap Cuban missile crisis."

heavy fighting. The Syrian tank movement was obviously a destabilizing factor, as Kissinger wrote: "I had no doubt that this challenge had to be met. If we failed to act, the Middle East crisis would deepen as radicals and their Soviet sponsors seized the initiative." The rhetoric was familiar, as were the culprits.

Nixon's account offered different facts. The Syrians invaded with "at least a hundred tanks" on the night of September 18, and, after "a very stern note" was delivered to the Soviets, half of the tanks returned to Syria. Three days later, three hundred tanks crossed the border, broke through Jordanian defenses, "and were rumbling almost unopposed along the roads toward Amman." Nixon wrote that he placed 20,000 American troops on alert, moved more forces into the Mediterranean Sea, and told the Israelis that America would support its air force in strikes on the Syrian tank forces if necessary. The next day, most of the Syrian tanks, faced with the American troop movements and the possibility of Israeli intervention, withdrew.

The Nixon and Kissinger accounts differ so dramatically because neither told the full story. At the time, the United States had no independent means of intelligence in the crucial areas of Jordan and Syria; it relied almost totally on information supplied by Mossad and King Hussein—far from objective sources. Some tanks and armored cars, many of them bearing the markings of the Palestinian Liberation Army, did move into Jordan from Syria, but their numbers were not independently known by the American government. Kissinger listed a total of 120 destroyed Syrian tanks without revealing that the statistic was supplied by Israeli intelligence. Neither Nixon nor Kissinger described the extensive disarray inside the Syrian government over the tank attacks, nor did either report that a faction led by Lieutenant General Hafiz Asad, the Syrian Defense Minister, was in surreptitious and indirect contact with Wasfi Tel of Jordan. Asad would emerge in a bloodless coup two months later as Syria's new leader. And finally, Kissinger and Nixon, while praising Israel's willingness to come, if needed, to the aid of King Hussein's forces during the crisis, did not fully describe Israel's price for such support: a guarantee of American military intervention in case the Soviet Union or Egypt came to the aid of Syria or the *fedayeen*. Some NSC and State Department aides who were involved in the crisis recall that a fundamental American commitment was given to the Israelis: an explicit promise of support in case Israel attacked in northern Jordan and annexed portions of that area, considered vital to its defense.

The underpinnings of the American responses in Jordan were predicated on a series of mistaken assumptions that could have led to an American act of war whose consequences had not been fully thought out. Nixon's reaction to the reports of a Syrian tank invasion has not been described in any memoirs or contemporary news accounts, but the Syrians—and the Soviet Union, in Nixon's eyes—were defying his warning as published by the Chicago *Sun-Times* a few days earlier. Nixon had explicitly said then that he was ready to intervene if Syria or Iraq entered the war.

By Sunday night, September 20, there were intelligence reports that Syria had taken up his challenge. On Monday, a further report of a large-scale Syrian tank breakthrough in northern Jordan was relayed to the White House by the Israeli and British embassies in Washington. At the time, Pentagon contingency plans endorsed by Nixon and Kissinger called for an airborne battalion of the Eighth Infantry Division, on alert in West Germany, to parachute into Amman airport to set up perimeter defenses in support of Hussein, with a second battalion landing in transport planes. Both units, whose immediate goals were to save Hussein and rescue the American dependents and hostages in Jordan, would be protected by fighter planes from the Sixth Fleet. Would Nixon and Kissinger really have committed the forces in a showdown? Robert Pursley, Melvin Laird's military assistant, recalls that the White House was acting with a sense of panic on that Sunday night, relying exclusively on raw intelligence from the Israelis and Hussein's government, as relayed through the British. None of the intelligence had been evaluated by area specialists in the State Department or the Pentagon. "If there's one thing we'd learned, it's that you never believe the first story, and only one-half of the fourth story" during a crisis. "The White House was always reacting to the first story." The White House desire to use American forces in Jordan was shaped by the same lack of analysis that marked the EC-121 incident, according to Pursley. "What are you going to use if you get involved in a big war? Where are the forces going to come from if the other side, such as the Soviets and the Egyptians, decides to go to the aid of the Syrians?"

In a speech to a military meeting five months after the crisis, Alexis Johnson echoed Pursley's view. "[T]hose of us who were involved in planning and working on that contingency"—the rescue effort in Jordan—"were appalled at the . . . inadequacy or limited resources and capabilities that we had to bring to bear if we had been called upon to do so." There were immense logistical problems, as Johnson obviously appreciated, in getting fighting troops to the area and, if necessary, keeping them supplied on the ground. There were also immense conceptual problems: How do you land fighting troops in a guerrilla stronghold without severe casualties? Could any hostages be rescued under such circumstances?

Such problems were far removed from the Oval Office at the height of the crisis. Richard Nixon seemed once again to have personalized a confrontation with the Soviet Union. The Soviets were coming to the aid of Syria against Jordan to challenge *his* presidency and *his* authority. Henry Kissinger was a willing conspirator in perpetuating Nixon's attitude, for his power always expanded in such situations. Nixon was "at his best" in crises like that in Jordan, Kissinger wrote in his memoirs. "He did not pretend that he was exercising his responsibilities as Commander-in-Chief by nervous meddling with tactical details or formative deliberations; he left the shaping of those to the governmental machinery under my supervision. . . . [H]e had a great sense of timing; he knew instinctively when the moment for decision had arrived; and he would then act resolutely, especially if he could insulate himself from too much personal controversy."

During the crisis, one young NSC aide caught a glimpse of Nixon "at his best" that showed a great deal about the reality of life at the top. Kissinger had assigned the staff man, an expert on the Middle East and South Asia, to prepare overnight situation intelligence reports on the crisis. He quickly learned that Nixon would invariably first want to know about the Russians, and so he carefully included any possibly relevant items about the Soviet Union. "We always seemed to be dragging the Soviets into crises," he recalls. "It's almost as if the Soviets weren't there, but we were going to discover them anyway." An unusual routine was soon worked out. The aide prepared his intelligence briefing for the President and then waited outside the Oval Office while Kissinger and Nixon discussed policy in private. Upon being summoned, he was to give only an intelligence briefing and respond to Nixon's specific questions; not—according to Kissinger's repeated orders—to engage the President in any policy discussion. That was solely Kissinger's province. It was a rare chance for an aide to see the two men in action in an informal meeting, and he learned more than he had thought possible. "I'd walk in and begin to give a specific listing of what'd happened overnight and Nixon would interject, 'Bomb the bastards,' or some other wild remark." Normally the young man was shooed out of the office at such points, but "sometimes Henry would forget to move me out and so I stayed and listened."

The Arabists in the State Department knew nothing of Nixon's hope for a military intervention by someone—the United States or Israel—in the Jordanian crisis, but they did share increasing doubts about the intelligence upon which the White House was basing its diplomatic activity. One of the first to question the intelligence on the Syrian tank invasion was Andrew N. Killgore, a State Department desk officer in charge of monitoring developments in Arab Region North—Lebanon, Syria, Iraq, and Jordan. At the height of the crisis, after Hussein's troops seemed to have won their battle with the *fedayeen* in Amman, "We started getting CIA reports of a great Syrian tank movement. The Syrians were apparently going down to help the *fedayeen*." Killgore was suspicious, he says, because "I knew that Asad was a cautious man and he wouldn't commit his tanks across an open plain." Some tanks and armored cars did cross the border into Jordan, "but we started getting these reports as if it were El Alamein. They were invading in full force." Killgore subsequently learned that the CIA's reports were in fact supplied by Mossad and were being relayed directly into the White House. At one point the CIA was relaying reports on a tank battle Mossad said was taking place south of the city of Irbid, more than thirty miles inside Jordan.

Killgore was skeptical. "My theory was that the Israelis saw this as a possible opportunity," he recalls. "If the *fedayeen* got the best of Hussein, it would have created a dangerous situation and given Israel a chance to grab off some land in the north" of Jordan. Killgore himself believes that peace will not come to the Middle East until the Palestinian refugees have a separate state —a view that has marked him as an enemy of Israel in the view of many in the State Department. Yet his account is supported by one of Kissinger's NSC aides who was directly involved. "We were relying on the Israelis, who had a vested interest, and Hussein, who was panicked," for up-to-the-minute assessments of the battlefield situation. There was no American satellite coverage available and no reports from undercover CIA agents in Syria. There was even less information about the decision making there: "It was like the dark side of the moon. We knew very little about the dynamics of Syria's internal society. No one in the White House or who came to the meetings could tell us what was going on." If a major tank battle near Irbid did take place between Hussein's troops and the Syrians, the aide added, he saw no evidence of it in the White House.

In this aide's view, "The Israelis wanted the Irbid Heights"—the area surrounding the city of Irbid—"and they wanted the green light from us. And they almost got it. For the Israelis it was a strategic decision—Irbid is the high ground and you could control everything in the line of sight."

In his memoirs, Kissinger wrote that Nixon—in the hours after the Syrians began the tank "invasion"—agreed at one point to support Israeli ground actions inside Jordan, and the Israelis moved army units close to the border.* Kissinger agreed with Nixon in the use of Israeli rather than American forces, he wrote, because he thought the American forces "were best employed in holding the ring against Soviet interference with Israeli operations. . . . [I]f the situation in Jordan got out of control it could be remedied only by a massive blow against Syria, for which Israeli armed forces were best suited." Thus the White House was willing to challenge the Soviet Union in support of the Israelis in an attack against a tank force which may or may not have been Syrian, may or may not have totaled in the hundreds, and may or may not have been part of a Soviet-led plan aimed at overthrowing King Hussein and installing a Palestinian government. The only certainty in all this was the Israeli goal. In a 1977 interview with David Frost, Nixon explained that the Israelis saw a great military potential in the Jordanian crisis: "There's nothing they [the Israelis] would like to have done than to roll on those Heights [in Jordan] with their aircraft . . . and with their own tanks. They would have demolished the Syrians and gone right into Damascus, which they would have wanted to do." †

Nixon did not explain to Frost how he had come to hold that view, which is shared by former Egyptian Foreign Minister Riad. In his memoirs, Riad wrote that the real danger was not that of American intervention but the "possibility of Israel taking advantage of the opportunity to deal a military blow against Syria." If that had happened, he added, Egypt would have had no choice but to support Syria by resuming warfare against Israel in the Sinai, "which would have inevitably led to a new war.‡ Riad dismissed the American threats as

---

* Nixon later changed his mind about the Israeli ground action, Kissinger wrote, after Rogers expressed "serious reservations" and Laird asked to see further intelligence on the situation in Jordan. Kissinger once again maneuvered himself into the position of being the only senior adviser Nixon could trust to be consistently hard line.

† This Nixon-Frost interview took place on March 30; it was the fourth in an extensive series of tapings made in preparation for Frost's television interview with Nixon, which was broadcast later in 1977. Only a fraction of the interview was televised, but Frost kept a complete transcript. In those interviews, Nixon also gave the following explanation of the crisis in Jordan: "My feeling was that the conduct of the Russians in Jordan in 1970 should be used by us as one of the tests as to whether or not we could go forward and meet with the Russians later in a summit and expect them to keep their word and expect them to be helpful in reducing crisis. . . ." In reality, a factor in the White House's hysterical reaction to the crisis was precisely the opposite: Nixon's belief that the Russians had humiliated and embarrassed him by not agreeing to a summit before the congressional elections of 1970, despite his personal intervention with Ambassador Dobrynin.

‡ Riad also took issue with Kissinger's account of the crisis. "Kissinger had tried in his book," he wrote, "to picture the crisis as a confrontation between the United States and the Soviet Union, not between Jordan and the [PLO] Resistance." Kissinger ignored the fact that "the Soviet Union had no interest in coming to their [the PLO's] defense in Jordan. . . . The only role played by the USSR during the events in Jordan, as proved by its communications with us in Egypt and by its contacts with the Syrians and Iraqis, was to urge the containment of the crisis rather than accelerate it."

"muscle-flexing" because, he wrote, if the Nixon Administration had seriously considered deploying its naval power in the crisis, "it would have come face-to-face with the Soviet fleet in the Mediterranean . . . which Nixon would not have welcomed." Since the American threats and hints did not "intimidate anybody," Riad added, they could not "have been the decisive factor in the withdrawal of the Syrian tanks."

Kissinger's memoirs show that he and Nixon believed that the Soviet Union, impressed by the joint American-Israeli show of resolve, persuaded its client state Syria to begin withdrawing its tank force, thus ending the crisis and giving the White House a foreign policy victory. The American strategy—to create "maximum fear of a possible American move," Kissinger wrote—had worked. On September 21, Yuli Vorontsov, Dobrynin's chief deputy at the Soviet Embassy in Washington, visited Joseph Sisco at the State Department and presented a note urging all parties not to intervene inside Jordan—a reference not only to Syria, with whom the Soviets were in contact, but also to the Israelis and the United States. Kissinger could not resist a note of triumph in his memoirs: "The tone of the message was remarkably mild, considering the menacing, almost flaunting openness of our deployments. . . . Unless the Soviets were tricking us, they were saying that they were pressing the radical government in Syria to halt its invasion. And tricking us while our strength in the Mediterranean was growing daily and Israel was mobilizing would have been extremely foolhardy."*

Unquestionably the Israeli and American military movements played a role in the Syrian turnabout, but those maneuvers were not the whole story. The Syrians, it should be noted, had defied Nixon's public threat in the Chicago newspaper, and theoretically could do so again. Equally significant during those crucial days was the bitter feuding between the military and civilian wings of the ruling Baath party in Syria—a dispute that flared anew with the tank invasion into Jordan. At a critical point in that invasion, General Asad—a leading figure in the military wing of the party—refused to commit the Syrian Air Force to the defense of the tank force inside Jordan, thus permitting Hussein's weak air force to bomb and strafe the Syrian tanks unmolested. Asad's decision to limit the Syrian military involvement was a significant turning point

* Despite his expressions of satisfaction at the time and in his memoirs over the outcome in Jordan, there is evidence that Kissinger believed the American maneuvering and "signaling" had had less impact on the Soviets than desired. In 1972, citing Jordan as an example of the impotence of American nuclear planning, Kissinger asked senior Pentagon officials to study new options for the use of such weapons in, as one officer calls them, "non-central campaigns"—that is, not against the Soviet Union. Kissinger's comments came during a meeting with members of an ad hoc military panel on American nuclear-targeting strategy directed by Dr. John S. Foster, the Pentagon's director of defense research and engineering. Staff director for the study was General Jasper A. Welch, one of the Air Force's leading nuclear theoreticians. At the meeting, Kissinger spoke of Jordan as an example of an American threat that nearly failed. One participant recalls that he said, "We put everything on the line with the Soviet Union, and they didn't blink until the last day." Kissinger's complaint was that if he was unable effectively to threaten the use of nuclear weapons in such crises, "we weren't getting our money's worth out of them." He asked the planners to develop new options "to be sure that America's strategic forces really did cast a shadow on peripheral situations," as the participant says. "Kissinger's point was that even if the military situation on the ground is not interesting for nuclear use, the Def Con [America's military alert] has a different impact on the Russians if they know we have flexible options." The Pentagon's planning did eventually lead to more flexible presidential options for nuclear response, which were adopted by the White House in 1974.

in the crisis, American analysts concluded, since it forced the remaining Syrian and PLO tanks to return across the border to safety. State Department officials who were in the Middle East at the time have said it was also known in select diplomatic and intelligence circles that Asad had been in indirect communication with Wasfi Tel, the Jordanian Prime Minister, and had reassured Hussein in advance that the Syrian Air Force would not retaliate against Jordan's air force.

In November 1970, Asad joined with Mustafi Tlas, the Syrian Army chief of staff, and other military moderates in Syria to overthrow the more radical government of President Nuredin Attassi. The new government emphatically denounced the Attassi regime for having urged the commitment of Syrian tanks in the Jordanian war, and a number of radical officials were arrested, including Major General Salah Jadid, Asad's chief political rival, and Yussef Zaylin, a former Syrian Prime Minister who was commander of the Palestinian tank force that entered Jordan. Attassi, Jadid, and Zaylin had been among the leading advocates of Syria's stated policy—prior to the coup—of opposing any form of accommodation with Israel.

United States officials concluded at the time that the Soviet Union supported Asad's seizure of control, largely to insure that, as one Middle East expert puts it, "someone who would listen to the Soviets was installed." There was no evidence that the Attassi government had done so, at least to Moscow's satisfaction, these officials noted. Analyzing the 1970 war much later, one experienced CIA official, who was on duty as a station chief in the Middle East at the time, said that Nixon and Kissinger were simply wrong in their belief that the Soviet Union could control Syria's military and political decision making. "The Soviets don't have that much influence," he said, adding that the demonstration of Soviet impotence—though missed by the White House—had been carefully noted in Cairo. A senior State Department analyst similarly concluded, "It was a Jordanian victory and a Syrian defeat. It wasn't seen by the political officer [in the State Department] as primarily a Cold War issue." The real cost of the war, these officials understood, was not to be found in the failed political aspirations of the Soviet Union, imagined or not, but among the civilian populations of the cities and PLO camps in Jordan. Estimates of the Palestinian and Jordanian dead ranged from 5,000 to 20,000, with thousands of homes in Amman and elsewhere demolished.

The view was different in the White House, where Nixon and Kissinger began claiming the spoils of victory. Elaborate press briefings were held and photographers were allowed to take pictures of the President agonizing over strategic decisions in his Oval Office (as photographers had been permitted to photograph President Kennedy after his success in the Cuban missile crisis).*

By late September, Asad's intervention—not described in Kissinger's or Nixon's memoirs—had turned the tide and made Syrian withdrawal inevitable.

---

* In one interview after the crisis, Haig described the President's response to the pressure in these glowing terms: "He makes lonely decisions, sometimes after contrary advice, thoughtful decisions based on intellect, not emotions. In this crisis he contributed the extra ingredient of personal leadership. He stayed on it from the time it got white-hot until it was resolved. He had a firm hand on the controls. His success is a great tribute to him. Most of the country had no conception of the tenseness of the crisis. This also resulted from the President's decision. He showed cold calm. He didn't drain the American people with fears and emotions. . . . He refused to indulge in a phony publicity buildup to make himself a national hero."

The Soviet Union was active in passing messages to the Syrian government and Yuli Vorontsov took the unique step of approaching Kissinger at a cocktail party to reassure him that the Soviet Union had no vital interest in Jordan. But Kissinger kept up the pressure. On September 23, he ordered four more destroyers to leave the United States for the Mediterranean and redirected two attack submarines to the area. "Letting up now would surely leak and could convey the wrong signal at a critical moment," Kissinger wrote. "Contingency planning against Soviet intervention continued. . . ." Nixon later told Congress that the crisis in Jordan was "the gravest threat to world peace since this administration came to office." *

The major victors were the Israelis, who had joined in active partnership with Nixon and Kissinger in supporting Hussein's regime. On September 17, shortly before the Syrians sent their tank force into Jordan, Nixon had authorized $500 million in military aid for Israel and also agreed to accelerate the delivery of previously promised F-4 Phantom aircraft. There was also an unprecedented promise from Nixon and Kissinger: If Israel moved its troops into Jordan and they were engaged by Egyptian or Soviet forces coming to the aid of the Syrians, the United States would then intervene on behalf of Israel. The agreement, which has never been fully disclosed, was made in oral communications between Ambassador Rabin and Kissinger, who met and talked repeatedly during the crisis.† In his memoirs, Rabin told of a telephone call from Kissinger on September 25, conveying a message of victory and thanks from Nixon to Golda Meir: "The President will never forget Israel's role in preventing the deterioration in Jordan and in blocking the attempt to overturn the regime there. He said that the United States is fortunate in having an ally like

* There was a curious addendum to the Jordanian crisis that gave a hint, perhaps, of some presidential uncertainty. In late September, shortly after the threat to Hussein had subsided, Nixon began a previously planned nine-day trip to Europe, with stops in Italy, Spain, Yugoslavia, and Ireland. For obvious political purposes, a visit to a group of freed American hostages in Rome was tacked on to the presidential schedule, after the White House learned that the hostages would stop briefly at the airport there en route to the United States. The President met privately with the group for a few minutes and later described to the White House traveling press corps some of the key elements in the conversation. "I told them that . . . those of us with responsibility in government wanted to do something. We were naturally terribly frustrated because we realized that if we did the wrong thing, it would cost them their lives. . . . We had to show power and at the same time, we had to demonstrate restraint." The former hostages were sympathetic and supportive of his efforts, Nixon told the press: "They told me that was exactly the right policy, because they said that every day they had the feeling that their captors might do something irrational in the event that we triggered it, or somebody else triggered it." Nixon, having finished his summary of his conversation with the hostages, added: "This, of course, bore out the wisdom of our policy, and I am glad that we did show the proper restraint during this period while, at the same time, being very firm in our diplomacy and firm in the demonstration of our military strength." The President's description of his conversation with the hostages and their support of his policy was made out of whole cloth; such an exchange did not take place, as an official White House transcript of the meeting demonstrates. The transcript shows that Nixon engaged in small talk, as he had in May with the antiwar demonstrators at the Lincoln Memorial, asking various hostages, for example, to name their home states. At one point a hostage complained of being "so sick of that Red Chinese jam we had to eat," and Nixon responded: "Is that what it was? It is a little better if you could mix some pineapple with it." In *The Illusion of Peace* (1978), commenting on Nixon's curious account of the meeting, the journalist Tad Szulc asked: "Why did Nixon feel the need to invent this—since nobody in the United States seriously questioned his policies in the first place?"

† In *Decade of Decisions* (1977), an insider's account of the Nixon-Kissinger Middle East policy, former NSC aide William Quandt reported that Israel had asked for and received clarification of the American commitment on seven specific points—none in writing. Congress did not learn of the agreement at the time, because of the usual White House secrecy.

Israel in the Middle East. These events will be taken into account in all future developments." Rabin understood the significance of the Kissinger message, as he wrote: "This was probably the most far-reaching statement ever made by a president of the United States on the mutuality of the alliance between the two countries."

The legacy of Jordan was a new American policy in the Middle East—never formally stated—that would strangle diplomacy for the next three years. No longer would the White House seriously consider an "even-handed" American role in the Middle East, although Rogers, ever more isolated from real authority, still talked that way on occasion. The policy was tilted toward Israel. Kissinger and Nixon, exhilarated by their successful showdown with the Soviet Union, would continue—until forced otherwise—to view the basic problem in the Middle East as one of containing the Soviet Union and its client states, especially Egypt. Israel was seen as the bulwark of that policy, a regional American partner willing to intervene without question on behalf of the Nixon-Kissinger view of the world. More arms and economic aid also began to flow to King Hussein, who was perceived as an equally unquestioning ally for his seeming willingness to permit the Israelis to enter his country and, if necessary, do battle with the Syrians. By mid-1971, Hussein had fully reestablished his authority over Jordan and ousted the *fedayeen*. America's policy in the Middle East was now measured in terms of insuring that Israel and Jordan had enough hardware to maintain the military balance.

Egypt's President Nasser died in late September 1970, and his successor, Anwar Sadat, realized that Egypt and other Arab nations had been frozen by Nixon's and Kissinger's beliefs into a pro-Soviet—and thus anti-American— position. Sadat and his advisers, no longer inhibited by Nasser's distrust of the West, would try a new approach in 1971. But, knowing little of the real balance of power inside the Nixon Administration, Sadat would rely on William Rogers and the State Department to relay his proposals. His approach thus was marked for failure before it began.

20
CUBA:
A FALSE CRISIS

As H. R. HALDEMAN DESCRIBED the scene in his memoirs, Henry Kissinger burst into his office, slammed down a file of highly classified reconnaissance photographs on a desk, and said, "It's a Cuban seaport, Haldeman, and these pictures show the Cubans are building soccer fields. . . . These soccer fields could mean war, Bob." Haldeman asked why. "Cubans play *baseball*. Russians play *soccer*," Kissinger replied.

Kissinger's dramatic visit to Haldeman took place on September 18, 1970, at the height of the Jordanian crisis, and only hours before the Syrians, so the White House thought, began invading Jordan with hundreds of tanks. Now the evidence was clear, both Kissinger and Nixon wrote, that the Soviets were challenging Nixon's leadership not only in the Middle East but in Cuba. American reconnaissance intelligence, Kissinger wrote, had established beyond doubt that the Soviet Union had "rushed" in recent weeks to build a submarine service installation on a small island in the bustling harbor of Cienfuegos, on Cuba's south shore. A Soviet flotilla was tracked by satellite intelligence and U-2 spy planes as it sailed across the Atlantic in late summer and into the harbor on September 9; the small fleet included a submarine tender and two barges of the type normally used for servicing nuclear-powered submarines. Aerial photographs on September 15 showed "a fairly significant shore installation," Kissinger wrote, including two new barracks, administrative buildings, a new dock and a fuel storage depot, the beginnings of a major communications facility ("undoubtedly the radio link to Moscow"), and recreation facilities, including a basketball court and that soccer field. "In my eyes this stamped it indelibly as a Russian base," Kissinger went on, "since as an old soccer fan I knew Cubans played no soccer."*

Sometime after his meeting with Haldeman, Kissinger gave the senior White House staff a top-secret briefing on the crisis. John Ehrlichman recalls that Kissinger's introduction was "laden with crisis." The national security adviser warned that the Soviet Union had implanted "navigationally located" concrete

---

* Kissinger could not have been more wrong. The first Cuban soccer association was founded in 1924, and by the 1930s, Sunday afternoon soccer was so popular on the island that winter-league baseball games had to be rescheduled for morning. In 1938, a Cuban team reached the final eight of the World Cup international soccer competition in France. The sport declined in popularity in the 1950s, according to *Sports Illustrated* magazine, but revived after Castro's takeover in 1959. Cuba began fielding teams in the World Cup competition again, and by the late 1970s had seventy organized teams.

buoys inside the harbor at Cienfuegos and moored a submarine tender there in mid-September that could be utilized by Soviet nuclear submarines. "This was to be a precise location on the globe," Ehrlichman says, "and the missiles could be launched from that harbor, perhaps by remote control"—and thus have the impact of a permanent Soviet missile facility. All in all, Ehrlichman remembers it as a somber briefing.

Those who knew Nixon well had reason to suspect the worst: He was especially sensitive on the subject of Cuba. The President was convinced that John F. Kennedy had won the 1960 election by managing to suggest, as Nixon wrote in his memoirs, "that he was tougher on Castro and communism than I was." Nixon further believed that Kennedy had manipulated the Cuban missile crisis of 1962 for its effect on undecided voters in the congressional elections; a last-minute outpouring of Democratic ballots had prevented Nixon from becoming governor of California. Out of the missile crisis came an informal agreement between Kennedy and Soviet Premier Nikita Khrushchev in which the United States promised not to invade Cuba in return for a Soviet commitment not to install offensive weapons in Cuba.* There was nothing indirect or subtle about Nixon's views toward Cuba. Roy Burleigh, a CIA program analyst, recalls that one of Nixon's first directives to the Agency after taking office dealt with Cuba. "The first thing the administration wanted us to do was double our operations against Cuba. We couldn't believe it—we thought the American people had matured more than that." At the time of the order, the Agency had been in the process—long overdue, in the view of many CIA people—of cutting back on secret anti-Castro activities run by exile groups in Miami.

Kissinger was on safe ground in his toughness. Here was a chance, as in Jordan, to face down the Soviets, win a diplomatic victory for the President, and demonstrate that foreign policy should be controlled by the White House. "I saw the Soviet move as going beyond its military implications," Kissinger wrote. "It was a part of a process of testing under way in different parts of the world. The Kremlin had perhaps been emboldened when we reacted to the dispatch of combat troops to the Middle East by pressing Israel for a ceasefire"—the policy, of course, that Rogers had advocated. "I strongly favored facing the challenge immediately lest the Soviets misunderstand our permissiveness and escalate their involvement to a point where only a major crisis could remove the base."

There was one hitch, however: The President did not agree. "For Nixon," wrote Kissinger, "the coincidence of Cuba with an electoral campaign set off waves of foreboding and resentment. In his view, nothing was more to be avoided than a Cuban crisis in a Congressional election year. . . . A new Cuban missile crisis . . . would generate a massive public cynicism." Another

* Nixon and Kissinger had different views on exactly what was agreed in 1962. Kissinger wrote in his memoirs that the 1962 understanding prohibited "the emplacement of any offensive weapon of any kind or any offensive delivery system on Cuban territory." In his memoirs, Nixon described the 1962 understanding as barring the Soviet Union only from putting nuclear weapons in Cuba. Ironically, the 1970 confrontation over Cuba resulted in the Soviet Union and the United States formally acknowledging that there had been an agreement of some kind in 1962 and that, whatever it was, it was still in force. After the 1962 crisis, neither side took steps to prepare a formal written memorandum summarizing the agreement. It seems clear that if the agreement had been made formal, the continuing efforts against the Havana regime—including a CIA assassination plot against Fidel Castro in 1963, code named AM/LASH—would have been in violation of the 1962 agreement not to "invade" Cuba.

reason for caution was that Nixon had planned a nine-day trip to Europe in late September and wanted nothing to interfere with the publicity it was sure to bring. His solution, Kissinger wrote, was to delay two months and confront the Soviets after the election—by which time the public, cynical or not, could no longer vote. Kissinger demurred, but Nixon insisted that he did not want some "clown Senator" asking for a Cuban blockade in the middle of an election—as Republican Kenneth Keating of New York and other senators had done in 1962.

If the immediate issue for Nixon and Kissinger was how to deal politically and diplomatically with the alleged submarine base, for the rest of the bureaucracy there was a more fundamental question: Just what was going on in Cienfuegos? Intelligence experts in the State Department, the CIA, and even the Pentagon saw no tangible evidence of a major installation. In their opinion, Cienfuegos was meant to be a rest-and-recreation facility for Soviet submarines that would permit the Soviet Navy to lengthen its normal overseas tours. Over the next year, confirmation of this analysis began to emerge in previously classified intelligence testimony that was published by the House Foreign Affairs Subcommittee on Inter-American Affairs, whose chairman, Representative Dante B. Fascell, a Democrat from Miami, maintained a strong interest in Cuban activities. For example, in testimony taken a few weeks after the Cienfuegos crisis in 1970, but not publicly released until 1971, Colonel John Bridge, chief of the Soviet area office of the Defense Intelligence Agency, testified that "they [the Soviets] have established—we say it is a facility, at Cienfuegos, which might support naval operations, including those of submarines. It is by no means to be construed, I think, as a formal full-scale base. It is a support facility, a possible support facility." As for the barracks, he testified, they were built of wood, obviously temporary facilities for crew stopovers.* The concrete buoys which so alarmed Kissinger had been in place at least since 1968, well before the arrival of the Russians, Major Gerald Cassel, an analyst on Cuba for the DIA, told the Fascell subcommittee in a separate set of hearings in the fall of 1971. Similarly, the new dock Kissinger had noticed enclosed "a small area, perhaps . . . a swimming area, or something like that." The water was far too shallow for any other use, one officer said.

Fascell and his subcommittee tried to get transcripts of briefings on Cienfuegos that Kissinger gave to the press. In late November of 1970, Alexis Johnson was given the task of demonstrating that the administration's claim of victory in Cienfuegos was not overstated. He did not persuade anyone, because he testified honestly. Asked, for example, about the claim of a communications facility at Cienfuegos, Johnson said, "We have no conclusive evidence or proof" that such a facility exists, "but there is an assumption that they were going to use this [Cienfuegos] as a semi-permanent facility [and] that they might want to have a shore-based communications facility there." The White House subsequently refused to declassify Johnson's testimony.

Fascell told the struggling Johnson, "This is a confrontation without really being a confrontation; this is a victory without really being a victory. . . . It is really a good game. The only problem is that it hasn't settled anything." Speak-

* Another official later described the barracks as single-story units resembling chicken houses.

ing of the accounts of Nixon's firmness, he added, "The game is fine; I admire the game that has been played."

State Department officials did not realize that Kissinger was eager for a confrontation, whether justified or not, and thus were dismayed at his reaction. Many of them viewed the Soviet moves as essentially routine fleet exercises. The Russians had been expanding their naval operations in the Atlantic since July 1969, when a Soviet flotilla visited Cuba and the Caribbean. In May 1970, a larger group of Soviet ships, including three submarines, had visited Cuba for two weeks. There was nothing the United States could do about such visits, which were consistent with internationally recognized rights of free sea passage. The State Department also concluded that the Soviets had a political motive for such ostentatious visits: to challenge what seemed to be a double standard that permitted the United States Navy to sail anywhere with impunity, and to establish bases all over the world, while criticizing the Soviet Union for any similar expansion. The Soviet goal in building the temporary facilities in Cuba, these analysts concluded, was to ameliorate this double standard.

The increase in Soviet construction activity at Cienfuegos was first reported on September 15 by the CIA. A few days later, the State Department's Bureau of Intelligence and Research, then directed by Ray S. Cline, a former CIA official, provided a cautious assessment. Cline realized that any development inside Cuba would be nerve-wracking for Richard Nixon, particularly in the middle of a congressional election, and thus he decided to brief Alexis Johnson. "I remember clearly going to Alex and saying, 'Look, I don't think this is a crisis,' " Cline says, " 'but you ought to at least be aware that something new and unusual is going on in Cienfuegos and it has to do with Soviet submarines in Cuba.' " He concluded that the Soviets were seeking an elementary facility to give their submarine crews a chance to go ashore, relax, eat fresh vegetables, and perhaps mingle with Cuban women.

Johnson took Cline's findings directly to Kissinger's office, and the crisis began. "There's no doubt that Henry overplayed it for his own purposes," says Cline.

The irony of this affair is that Cienfuegos, unlike Jordan, may have been one crisis in which Kissinger had little ulterior motive. He truly believed that a permanent base was being built in Cuba which would be "a quantum leap in the strategic capability of the Soviet Union against the United States." It was a misreading of the available intelligence that was solely his responsibility; for once, Richard Nixon was willing to avoid a confrontation. "He accepted my analysis," Kissinger wrote, "but for the interim he chose Rogers' policy of soothing delay." There was the usual gamesmanship at a National Security Council meeting on September 23. Nixon had already decided to do nothing, but he asked for contingency plans for the mining of Cienfuegos Harbor, the blockading of Cuba, and the removal of all restraints on the CIA-led Cuban exile community in Miami. "In the interval," Kissinger wrote, he "ordered a very low-key public posture, confined simply to noting that we were aware of what was happening and were watching.''

Faced with a President who would not take the tough road, Kissinger treated him like any other bureaucratic enemy, and leaked to the press. In his memoirs, Cyrus L. Sulzberger, the *New York Times* columnist, recalled a breakfast on September 16, 1970, with Kissinger in which there were complaints about ''Soviet horsing around in Cuba these days.'' Two days later, at lunch with Richard Helms, Sulzberger was told in detail about Cienfuegos, which Helms depicted as a permanent base for sheltering Russian Y-class submarines, the Soviet equivalent of an American Polaris, the world's most powerful ballistic missile attack submarine. In their biography, the Kalbs reported that Kissinger also ''selectively'' briefed a handful of congressmen and columnists, warning of a ''grave confrontation'' unless construction at Cienfuegos ceased, and had still another argument with Rogers, whose basic point undercut the Kissinger thesis: Since Soviet submarines could fire at the United States from any point in the Atlantic or the Pacific, how could a facility in Cuba drastically alter the balance of power? And so far there was no evidence that a Soviet Y-class submarine had ever entered Cienfuegos Harbor.

Sulzberger's column on the possibility of a submarine base was published on September 25; Nixon was still hopeful, as he wrote in his memoirs, ''that the story might not be picked up for several days''—long enough so he could leave for Europe with no crisis on hand. But at the Pentagon, Jerry W. Friedheim, the Deputy Assistant Secretary of Defense for Public Affairs, told what he knew to reporters who asked: There was evidence of Soviet construction on Cienfuegos. As Friedheim remembers, ''All hell broke loose.'' ''Contrary to our carefully planned press guidance,'' Kissinger wrote, ''the spokesman of the Defense Department had filled in every detail when asked a question at his morning briefing.''

It was all in the day's work for Kissinger. Having leaked the story, he now managed to get one of his archenemies, the Pentagon, blamed for the leak.* In his memoirs, however, Kissinger wrote that ''the Pentagon bloopers . . . were actually our salvation'' because the President was forced ''to face the Soviets down.'' Nixon ''understood immediately that waffling could only increase our dangers,'' Kissinger wrote, and he was authorized to warn the Soviets in a background press briefing that afternoon that the United States ''would view the establishment of a strategic base in the Caribbean with the utmost seriousness.'' After the briefing, Kissinger summoned Ambassador Dobrynin to the White House for their second meeting of the day, and accused the Soviet

* Friedheim recalls that after the Sulzberger story, his office requested permission from the White House to brief reporters on the Soviet fleet movement: ''We said, 'We'd all look silly if we didn't know where it was.' '' After a White House meeting, a set of complicated instructions was relayed to the Pentagon press office, requiring some information to be placed on the record, other information to be provided on a confidential background basis, and yet other facts to be supplied only if the journalists ''pressed'' for answers. ''There was no military reason for us not to brief,'' Friedheim recalls, ''and we thought we could mention it [the Cienfuegos construction].'' Years later, Friedheim was still mystified by the White House reaction: ''Maybe it just could have been 'get mad at the Pentagon week.' '' The briefing soured Kissinger on him, and it was Kissinger's objection, according to Friedheim, that kept Gerald Ford from naming him White House press secretary after Nixon resigned the presidency and Ford took over in August 1974. ''Henry got me in the end,'' Friedheim says.

Union of building an offensive submarine base at Cienfuegos.* "Moscow should be under no illusion: we would view continued construction with the 'utmost gravity.' " As he wrote in his memoirs, he viewed Cienfuegos as "a test between major powers involving important national interest . . . [L]ess than forty-eight hours after the end of the Syrian invasion of Jordan, we were close to another confrontation, this time with a superpower."

On September 27, the President left on his high-profile trip to Europe, accompanied by Rogers and Laird. Kissinger, having met with the North Vietnamese in Paris the day before, joined the entourage in Rome, the first stop. During the next week, the President would meet with the Pope at the Vatican, spend a night aboard a Sixth Fleet aircraft carrier on patrol at sea, and enjoy well-publicized ceremonial visits to Yugoslavia, Spain, and Ireland. As Kissinger wrote, "To say that Nixon in deciding on his second European trip was unaware of the glow it might cast on the forthcoming Congressional elections would be to deny him the qualities that led him to the Presidency."

Laird and Rogers had been taken along, Kissinger wrote, "so that coherent press policy was easier to maintain than normally." Neither Kissinger nor Nixon wanted anyone left in Washington to tell the press just how unclear the evidence about Cienfuegos was. Some facts did emerge, nonetheless. On September 30, Tad Szulc of the *New York Times* reported that the United States "had only dubious and dated information to indicate that the Soviet Union might be planning to build a strategic submarine base in Cuba," and quoted intelligence sources as saying "they were at a loss" to explain the White House's action. When the Szulc story caught up with Kissinger in Madrid, he told Max Frankel, the *Times*'s Washington bureau chief, who was on the trip, that the account was an "act of treason." On the same day, the Soviet Union published a statement in *Pravda* accusing the Nixon Administration of fanning a "war psychosis." The *Pravda* article also criticized a piece by James Reston, in which the columnist—following the Kissinger line—accused the Soviets of provoking "the old cold-war game" by their approval of the Syrian tank invasion of Jordan and their attempt to move submarines into Cuba. "It is reviving Mr. Nixon's old anti-Communist instincts," Reston warned.

Nixon returned in early October; Dobrynin visited Kissinger the next day to present a note reaffirming the 1962 understanding on Cuba between the United States and the Soviet Union. He also told Kissinger that, as Kissinger wrote, "he was prepared on behalf of his government to affirm that ballistic missile submarines would never call there in an operational capacity." The Soviets

* That morning, the two men had held a scheduled conference, their first since Dobrynin returned from a seven-week home leave. In the interim, the White House had received no word on Nixon's much-desired summit, although a formal agenda had been submitted to the Soviets in mid-August. Nixon refused to attend the Dobrynin meeting, Kissinger wrote, partly because "to have kept the President waiting for six weeks for an answer to the summit proposal . . . was an act of discourtesy that did not deserve a personal audience." There was another reason, too: Nixon "was afraid the Soviets were turning down the summit and he did not wish to receive a rebuff personally." But Dobrynin's message held out hope: The Soviet Union agreed in principle to a summit and the White House's August agenda was acceptable. Nixon could no longer dream of a summit prior to the congressional elections, but even the announcement of such a meeting would win the Republican Party some peace votes.

were not going to make an issue of the facility at Cienfuegos; whatever they had been building there was not essential to their planning. Thus a major diplomatic victory—real or not—was in Kissinger's grasp. On October 9, he wrote, he presented Dobrynin with a formal memorandum, entitled "President's Note," which stated, in effect, that Soviet nuclear submarines armed with nuclear weapons were prohibited from using Cuba as a base of operations.* Four days later, the Soviet Union officially denied that it was constructing a submarine base in Cuba or in any other way "doing anything that would contradict" the 1962 understanding.

Kissinger claimed victory: "By great firmness in the early stages of construction, we avoided a major crisis, yet we achieved our objective. Military construction was halted . . . the communication facility never became operational." Nixon, in his memoirs, went further: "After some face-saving delays, the Soviets abandoned Cienfuegos."

And yet, nothing changed in Cienfuegos. The wooden barracks were not dismantled, the soccer field was not converted into a baseball diamond.† The shallow dock area still served Soviet swimmers. In the next four years, Soviet diesel-powered submarines, as well as nuclear submarines carrying missiles that were not strategic, visited Cienfuegos on more than a dozen occasions. In late April of 1974, a diesel-powered submarine of the Soviet "Golf" class, carrying three nuclear ballistic missiles capable of attacking American land targets, spent three weeks in harbor at Cienfuegos. In all these visits, however, the Soviets chose not to challenge the 1970 understanding directly by sending Y-class submarines to Cienfuegos or any other Cuban port.‡

* The note was drafted by Admiral Rembrandt Robinson of the NSC liaison office, who had worked so efficiently on the Duck Hook planning the previous fall. Robinson had taken an earlier version of the memorandum to Admiral Zumwalt for his guidance and approval, a step that would have surprised Kissinger, who even in late 1970 did not seem to realize that such contact went on all the time inside the bureaucracy. In his memoirs, Zumwalt, who had just begun to serve as Chief of Naval Operations, recalled asking Robinson why such an important policy document had not been routed through the Secretaries of State and Defense, as well as the Joint Chiefs of Staff. He was told that Kissinger "did not want any policy discussion on this matter. . . . Henry did not like to bring Secretary Rogers into foreign policy matters that were delicate." Zumwalt eventually learned not to ask such questions, but he remained troubled by the Kissinger memorandum. While it dealt firmly with nuclear-powered submarines carrying nuclear weapons, there seemed to be a loophole: What about the status of diesel-powered submarines with nuclear weapons? And suppose the Soviets decided to send into Cuba nuclear-powered submarines that were not carrying nuclear weapons? Were they excluded? Also, the memorandum did not really define what kind of base was permissible inside Cuba, other than to rule out the use of Cuba as "an operating base" for Y-class submarines. Admiral Robinson agreed with his concerns, Zumwalt wrote, and explained that "he had already brought the matter up with Kissinger, who had replied that it was too late to do anything about it."

† Alexis Johnson, informed later that he, Kissinger, and others in the government had been wrong in assuming that Cubans played no soccer, laughed heartily. "That was our hardest evidence." He said he had not been "as worked up" about the alleged submarine facility in Cienfuegos but viewed the American protests as worthwhile: "I had no problem at shaking my fingers at the Soviets and saying, 'Stay away.' "

‡ In early 1972, Kissinger ordered a special interagency study group assembled to review Soviet naval deployments throughout the Caribbean, with emphasis on the continuing, albeit occasional, Soviet submarine use of Cienfuegos. The group was to develop a series of "options" for the administration, which was then in the process of concluding a SALT agreement in Moscow that would give the Soviets the right to build as many as twenty more submarines than were deployed by the United States. Experts from the Joint Chiefs of Staff, the Defense Department, the CIA, and the State Department convened to review the data, under the chairmanship of Raymond Garthoff of the State Department, who was then assigned to the SALT delegation. There were no outcries

Kissinger acted precipitously, and perhaps recklessly, in the Cienfuegos affair, all the more so because he was not being pushed—as he had been in the Jordanian crisis—by the President. Once again American foreign policy had relied on threats in an attempt to convince the men in Moscow that Richard Nixon and Henry Kissinger meant business. "Moscow chose to test whether this willingness [to force the issue in Cienfuegos] reflected indecision, domestic weakness due to Vietnam, or the strategy of a serious government," Kissinger wrote. "Having been given the answer, Moscow permitted Cienfuegos to recede once more into well-deserved obscurity."

The Soviets, far from getting the message, seemed dumfounded by the American tactics. In his memoirs, *Doubletalk,* Gerard Smith, chief American negotiator at the SALT talks, described how in early 1971 a Russian delegate complained plaintively that "when one bloody little submarine goes to Cuba, everyone in America goes crazy."*

In any case, Cienfuegos marked a turning point for Kissinger: He had bypassed an indecisive and election-minded President to challenge the Russians and win. Whether it was a victory over what actually did exist, or over what he thought might exist in the future, did not matter. He was acting alone and on his own. It was a foretelling of what would come later, in the negotiations with North Vietnam at the end of 1972.

---

from the interagency panel over Soviet expansion. Instead, the group concluded that the Cienfuegos facility did not give the Soviet Union any significant new military capability, but would permit Soviet submarines to remain at sea for longer periods. They added that it was "a reasonable estimate" that the Soviet Union had been moving toward some kind of permanent facility at Cienfuegos in 1970 that would have given them a military benefit—"palpable but not dramatic"— in terms of getting more on-station use for each submarine. Garthoff concluded that the principal goal of the Soviets in Cuba was not strategic but political—to make some effort to match the seemingly unquestioned right of the United States to rim the Soviet Union with missiles and military bases. "In Cuba," Garthoff says, "one of the Soviets' goals was to obviate the double standard. The irony of it all is that the only military base on the island belonging to anyone else is ours [at Guantanamo Bay]—not the Soviet Union's."

* The possibility does exist that Kissinger thought he knew something no one else did. One of the most closely held secrets in the Nixon Administration revolved around a series of NSA intercepts emanating from the Soviet Embassy. Through such intercepts, Kissinger and Nixon were able to obtain what they believed to be reliable intelligence on the attitude and activities of Ambassador Dobrynin and others in the embassy. In addition, officials recall, the Nixon Administration was also able to obtain extensive communications intelligence from Cuba. At one point in mid-October, when there was speculation from some Democrats in Congress and some journalists about the authenticity of the crisis, Kissinger indicated to Max Frankel that, as Frankel wrote, "some secret development justified them [in the White House] in fearing the worst." Frankel subsequently acknowledged that he had been told, not by Kissinger, of the United States' ability to intercept and decode Soviet transmissions from Washington. Kissinger seemed to be suggesting, therefore, with his comment to Frankel, that there was secret intelligence on Soviet intentions in Cienfuegos. I have found no evidence to that effect, however, nor did Kissinger or Nixon even hint at the existence of such information in their memoirs, although the preparation of those books involved the constant use of highly classified government documents that have not been made available to the public. It also should be noted that in other equally sensitive areas, such as the administration's decision not to intervene in the India-Pakistan war, Kissinger and Nixon both freely acknowledged reliance on a CIA operative's report. Finally, even if such information did exist, that fact did not mean it was per se reliable. One of the constant problems of the NSA intercept programs dealing with Dobrynin and the Soviet Embassy, involved officials recall, was their significance. The fact that something was said and clandestinely intercepted did not make it a truth.

21

CHILE:
HARDBALL

YEOMAN CHARLES E. RADFORD did not want to be reassigned to Washington, but it was the fall of 1970 and he was in the Navy and his country was at war. Radford, twenty-seven years old and previously stationed in New Delhi, India, had been hand-picked by Admiral Rembrandt Robinson to serve as his confidential aide and secretary on the National Security Council staff in the White House. The bright and ambitious Radford was an obvious choice for the sensitive job: He was married and had young children; he was a devout Mormon who did not drink and would never consider using drugs; and he was fierce in his determination to earn a commission and become a Navy officer. He had also just completed a special Navy training course in stenography. The yeoman reported for duty on September 18, replacing a civilian secretary who had been on the job since 1966 and had been transferred, as were three other women employees. Admiral Robinson, in a move aimed at improving security, had ordered all his civilian employees replaced by military personnel. There was obvious tension in the office, and Radford recalls that in one of their first meetings, Admiral Robinson demonstrated why: "He made it clear that my loyalty was to him, and that he expected my loyalty, and that I wasn't to speak outside of the office about what I did in the office."

Robinson had become an insider by that fall; Kissinger had developed full confidence in his discretion and loyalty.* He had been among the very few in the White House to help draft the President's October note to the Soviets on the Cienfuegos crisis. He was also deeply involved in the secret Kissinger and Nixon operations against Salvador Allende of Chile, who had astounded the Central Intelligence Agency and the White House by winning the September 4 popular election for the Chilean presidency, although Allende received only 36.6 percent of the vote in a three-way race.

Radford, who arrived at his new post a few weeks after the Chilean election, vividly recalls the sense of crisis: "This wasn't supposed to happen. It was a real blow. All of a sudden the pudding blew up on the stove." Admiral Robin-

* Kissinger even began praising Robinson to his military superiors. In early November, Kissinger astonished Admiral Zumwalt, the newly appointed Chief of Naval Operations, by suddenly declaring during a discussion of Navy problems in the Mediterranean that, as Zumwalt recalled in his memoirs: "When I had a problem I should come straight to him, not go through Al Haig, because —here [Kissinger's] voice lowered conspiratorially—he did not trust Haig, who was always trying to go behind his back directly to the President. He told me that Rem Robinson was authorized to tell Tom Moorer and me *everything* he, Kissinger, was doing."

son and his superiors were "wringing their hands" over Chile, Radford says, "almost as if they [the Chileans] were an errant child." Over the next few weeks, Radford saw many sensitive memoranda and options papers, as the bureaucracy sought to prevent Allende from taking office. Among the options was a proposal to assassinate Allende.

One options paper "discussed various ways of doing it," Radford remembers. "Either we have somebody in the country do it or we do it ourselves. I was stunned; I was aghast. It stuck in my mind so much because for the first time in my life I realized that my government actively was involved in planning to kill people."

The options papers had been prepared for Nixon in the weeks after Allende's election. "They were exploring ways to get Allende out of there," Radford says, and murder was one of the ways: "I don't know if they used the word assassinate, but it was to get rid of him, to terminate him—he was to go."

By the mid-1960s Chile had become widely known in the American intelligence services as one of the CIA's outstanding success stories. The Agency had managed to penetrate all elements of Chilean government, politics, and society and took credit for insuring that Chile remained a progressive democratic nation that—not so incidentally—encouraged American multinational corporations to do business within its borders. The extent of American corporate involvement was a source of constant debate in Chile, however, and by the end of the decade it was a major political issue, pitting the Chilean right, with its support for continued American profit taking, against the left, which organized increasingly fractious labor strikes and public demonstrations against the American firms. Chile was a world leader in the mining of copper, but 80 percent of its production—60 percent of all exports from Chile—was in the hands of large corporations mostly controlled by U. S. firms, most prominently Anaconda and Kennecott Copper. Profits for the American firms were enormous: During the 1960s, for example, Anaconda Copper earned $500 million on its investments—generously estimated by the company at $300 million —inside Chile, where it operated the largest open-pit copper mine in the world. The most significant threat to Chilean democracy, in the view of American policy makers, was Salvador Allende Gossens, a member of the Socialist Party, who had unsuccessfully run for president in 1958 and 1964 on a platform that advocated land reform, nationalization of major industries (especially copper), closer relations with socialist and communist countries, and redistribution of income. National concern over the disparity of income was especially critical to Allende's campaigns: By 1968, studies showed that the 28.3 percent of the Chilean people at the bottom of the economic scale took in 4.8 percent of the national income, while the 2 percent of the population at the top received 45.9 percent of the income.

In 1958, Allende had lost the presidential election by less than 3 percent to Jorge Alessandri Rodriguez, an archconservative who was strongly probusiness and was heavily backed by American corporations. Neither Allende nor Alessandri received a majority vote, and under the Chilean constitution the election was resolved in a runoff election in the Chilean Congress, which voted Alessandri into office. Despite CIA aid, Alessandri and his party steadily lost popularity over the next six years, and the presidential elections of 1964 came down to a battle between Allende and his radical forces and Eduardo Frei Montalva, a liberal representing the Christian Democratic Party, which was pro-American and far more favorable to business than Allende's coalition.

The United States' influence on the 1964 election was more extensive than has been publicly reported. At least $20 million in support of the Frei candidacy—about $8 per voter—was funneled into Chile by the United States in 1963 and 1964, much of it through the Agency for International Development (AID).* Millions of dollars in AID and CIA funds were allocated, with the full knowledge of the Chilean and United States governments, to Roman Catholic organizations throughout the country whose objective was to oppose Protestantism and communism. Frei won handily with 56 percent of the vote. Fully aware of the source of his funding, Frei also received covert help from a group of American corporations known as the Business Group for Latin America. The group had been organized in 1963 by David Rockefeller, chairman of the Chase Manhattan Bank, at the express request of President Kennedy, who was directing his administration's fight against Castro and the spread of communism in Latin America. It included on its executive committee such prominent corporation executives as C. Jay Parkinson, board chairman and chief executive officer of Anaconda; Harold S. Geneen, head of the International Telephone and Telegraph Company, which owned and operated the telephone facilities in Chile; and Donald M. Kendall, board chairman and chief executive officer of PepsiCo, the soft-drink company, which had extensive business activities in Latin America.

The principal contact in Chile for the CIA as well as for the American corporations was the organization of Agustín Edwards, a close friend of Kendall's who was the owner of the conservative *El Mercurio* newspaper chain in Chile and a focal point for the opposition to Allende and the left. The CIA and the Business Group (which by 1970 had been reorganized into the Council of the Americas) relied heavily on Edwards to use his organization and his contacts to channel their covert monies into the 1964 political campaign. Many of the ties between the Business Group and the CIA in 1964 remained in place long after the election. For example, Enno Hobbing, a CIA official who had been assigned as liaison to the Business Group, later left the CIA and became the Council's principal operations officer.

The most profound issue for the American corporations was the threat of possible nationalization of their profitable subsidiaries in Chile. Allende's election would certainly lead to such a step. Frei, although his Christian Democratic Party included factions that insisted on nationalization, offered more hope: One of his major campaign promises called for a compromise known as "Chileanization," a procedure by which the state would be authorized to purchase large blocks of the stock of the Chilean subsidiaries of the American copper companies. By 1967, the Frei regime had purchased 51 percent of

* In a 1975 report on CIA clandestine activities in Chile, the Senate Intelligence Committee, relying on CIA-supplied documentation, listed the amount of CIA aid to the Frei campaign in 1964 at $3 million. The committee, set up in the wake of a *New York Times* exposé of illegal CIA spying inside the United States, conducted an extensive investigation into the CIA. But the committee often found itself at the mercy of information originating in the agency it was investigating.

Kennecott's Chilean company and 25 percent of the Chilean Anaconda firm.*
The stock transfers took place after negotiations with the companies, which
subsequently continued to generate high profits for their American-based owners. Frei's reforms did not affect other industries, and there was a general
increase of American business activity and profit taking inside Chile throughout the 1960s. Political pressure from the left increased, and the Frei regime
reopened its negotiations with Anaconda in 1969 and tried to begin a discussion
of total nationalization—the only process that would enable the state to gain
control of the huge profits, as the more radical supporters of the Christian
Democratic Party were demanding.

During the Frei years, the CIA continued to operate at will throughout the
country, primarily seeking to repress radical and leftist political activities. At
least twenty covert operations were mounted inside Chile between 1964 and
1969, according to a report of the Senate Intelligence Committee, which conducted an extensive investigation in 1975. Most of them were designed to
support moderate and conservative candidates in Chilean congressional elections. By the late 1960s, serious strains began to develop in the CIA's relationship with the Frei government. The most important reason for this change was
that the CIA station chief in Santiago, Henry D. Hecksher, believed that Frei
and his Christian Democratic Party had tilted dangerously far to the left.
Hecksher, a vigorous anti-Communist, as were his subordinates, incessantly
urged CIA headquarters to change American policy and formally turn from
Frei to Alessandri, who was planning to run for president again in the 1970
elections. Under Chilean law, Frei could not stay in office for consecutive
terms. Hecksher and others feared—correctly, as it turned out—that the
Christian Democrats would choose an even more liberal candidate in 1970. If
the CIA needed further evidence of the party's leftward drift, Frei soon gave
it: In 1969 he reestablished trade relations with Cuba.

Richard Nixon entered office with a profound dislike for Eduardo Frei. The
Chilean President's movement to the left and his attempts, albeit feeble, to
nationalize the American copper companies in the late 1960s were justification
enough, but Nixon had another reason: Eduardo Frei was a Kennedy man, a
social liberal who had risen to prominence with the aid of the Kennedys and
the Georgetown set in the CIA. The American Ambassador to Chile, Edward
M. Korry, was also suspect: A former newspaperman with impeccable anti-
Communist credentials, Korry had been appointed Ambassador to Ethiopia by

* The Frei government paid the Kennecott subsidiary, known as Braden Copper, $80 million for
its 51 percent share of the firm, although the book value for the whole of Braden was $67 million.
Braden claimed that the book value was unrealistically low, but one reason for the low value was
the Chilean government's willingness to permit the firm to depreciate its assets at a favorable rate,
and thus pay lower taxes. The Kennecott subsidiary thus was able, under "Chileanization," to
keep the company's book value artificially low for tax purposes, and yet enjoy the maximum value
when it was compelled to divest 51 percent of its stock to the government. Another stipulation of
the stock sale was the express condition that Kennecott and Anaconda would continue to manage
their investments inside Chile. All the copper produced would still be sold—as before—through
sales subsidiaries of the parent corporations, which would continue to make decisions on operations, accounting, administration, and geological surveys. "Chileanization" by no means gave the
government of Chile control of its copper.

President Kennedy in 1963, and had served in Chile since 1967. In December 1968, the month after Nixon's election, the CIA issued a National Intelligence Estimate on Chile. The NIE was critical of economic and social policies of the Frei government, and, so Ambassador Korry thought, played down the importance of democracy in Chile.

Nixon, once in office, quickly made clear his distaste for the current regime, Korry recalls, by striking Frei's name from a State Department list of foreign leaders being considered for future visits to Washington. He also ordered a further cutback in American aid to Chile, which had totaled more than $1 billion between 1962 and 1969, by far the largest per capita aid program in Latin America.* Whether intentionally or not, the White House moves weakened the moderates in Frei's Christian Democratic Party while strengthening the resolve of the CIA's anti-Frei position in Santiago. Right-wing attacks on the government in *El Mercurio* grew more frequent and harsher in tone, adding to the polarization of Chilean political forces. The Frei government responded by moving even further to the left. When Korry protested bitterly about the peremptory cutback of one $20 million aid program, which had been negotiated over an intense five-month period, he was told that his resignation would be accepted by the new President—he was fired. After some special pleading by Charles A. Meyer, the newly appointed Assistant Secretary of State for Latin America, Korry says, he was permitted to stay on in Chile and assigned the task of negotiating the future of the copper companies with the Frei government. Korry was cynical about Nixon's motives in reinstating him. He suspected that if the Christian Democrats moved ahead with their nationalization plans, Nixon would quickly mollify his corporate supporters by making Korry —as a Democratic holdover—a scapegoat.

The Frei government did little to increase its popularity with the White House. Early in 1969, Frei canceled a planned visit to Chile by Nelson Rockefeller. The visit, part of a highly publicized tour of Latin America that the New York Governor took at the express wish (so the public was told) of President Nixon, was meant to be a sign of amity of sorts between the Nixon and Rockefeller wings of the Republican Party, and Frei's cancellation—which was preordained by Nixon's aid cutback—was taken by the White House as further proof of his leftward drift. Even Korry had officially opposed the visit, however, since he was aware that Rockefeller's appearance would spark large-scale anti-American demonstrations. Until mid-1970, Korry and Frei were forced to resort to duplicity in communicating with the White House. "Any

---

* In his memoirs, Kissinger listed the date of the aid cutback as 1968, explaining that the Johnson Administration had decided "to terminate grant economic aid to Chile on the ground that the Chilean economy had become largely self-sustaining." Kissinger was, at best, confused. Economic aid to Chile, under the Alliance for Progress program initiated by President Kennedy, consisted of loans, to be repaid at favorable interest rates, and direct cash grants. The vast majority of economic aid to Chile was in the form of loans, with grants rarely exceeding $3 million—even in the mid-1960s, when Chile was receiving an average of nearly $70 million annually. State Department statistics show that the economic loan programs to Chile were reduced in the last years of the Johnson Administration, but the major cutbacks took place under Nixon. In 1968, for example, Chile received $57.9 million in economic aid (of which $54.3 million was in loans); that total dwindled to $18 million by 1970, the election year. In 1973, when Allende was overthrown, American economic aid to Chile totaled only $800,000. It should be noted that Nixon reduced economic aid programs throughout Latin America, a cutback that many in the government linked to Nixon's instinctive antagonism toward any Kennedy-sponsored initiative.

idea put forward by Frei had to be transformed into my idea," Korry says. "Otherwise, we reckoned it would be automatically disregarded or turned against him."

Any doubts in the Frei government about its standing with the White House were removed after an unusual face-to-face confrontation between Nixon and Gabriel Valdés, Frei's Foreign Minister. The occasion was a June 1969 meeting of Latin American ministers in the White House, at which Valdés, a member of an aristocratic Chilean family, chose to turn a formal ceremony into a seminar on North-South policy. In his account of the Allende years, *The Black Book of American Intervention in Chile,* Armando Uribe, a diplomatic officer at the Chilean Embassy in Washington, writes that Valdés had been scheduled to present Nixon with a formal policy statement on commercial and financial matters. Instead, "he spoke of the impossibility of dealing with the United States within the framework of inter-American relations; the differences in power were too great . . . and Nixon was caught off guard. . . . Masking his irritation, Nixon heard Valdés out, and then pulled himself together, lowering his eyelids, becoming impenetrable, withdrawn. Kissinger frowned."

Valdés recalls his impromptu talk as "the most difficult time in my life." He had come to the White House with the other Latin American officials knowing that the State Department had lobbied against his visit. At one point in his Oval Office talk, Valdés says, he told Nixon that Latin America was sending back 3.8 dollars for every dollar in American aid. When Nixon interrupted to challenge the statistic, Valdés retorted that the number had come from a study prepared by a major American bank. "As I delivered my speech," Valdés says, "Kissinger was looking at me as if I were a strange animal." The next afternoon, Kissinger asked for a private lunch with Valdés in the Chilean Embassy. The meeting was unpleasant. As Valdés describes it, Kissinger began by declaring, "Mr. Minister, you made a strange speech. You come here speaking of Latin America, but this is not important. Nothing important can come from the South. History has never been produced in the South. The axis of history starts in Moscow, goes to Bonn, crosses over to Washington, and then goes to Tokyo. What happens in the South is of no importance. You're wasting your time."

"I said," Valdés recalls, "Mr. Kissinger, you know nothing of the South." "No," Kissinger answered, "and I don't care." At that point, Valdés, astonished and insulted, told Kissinger: "You are a German Wagnerian. You are a very arrogant man." Later, to his embarrassment, Valdés learned that Kissinger was a German Jew, and suspected that he had gravely insulted him. Although it would have been impossible for Valdés to fathom, one aspect of Kissinger's motives in arranging the lunch was clearly to avenge Nixon's honor, to confront the Foreign Minister who had dared to tell the President something he did not wish to hear. Korry, still in Santiago, was subsequently informed that Nixon was "very angry" over Valdés' "arrogant and insulting" lecture. "Valdés went beyond the limits agreed to," Korry says.

The Valdés incident showed the White House attitude: Like a child, Latin America was to be seen and not heard. Those who defied Nixon, such as Valdés and Eduardo Frei—and, later, Salvador Allende—were to be treated harshly. In his memoirs, Richard Nixon devoted only seven paragraphs and a few hundred words to Chile, and said nothing at all about Latin American policy during his presidency. Kissinger, in his memoirs, defended his role in a long chapter on Chile but in no other way dealt with the administration's policies and problems in the South. Until 1970, Kissinger wrote, when he became involved in the planning against Allende, "Latin America was an area in which I did not then have expertise of my own." That may be so, but from the first months of the administration, he was an expert disciple of basic American policy: Latin America was to be permitted little independence. And the independence that did exist, Kissinger also understood, was to be controlled and manipulated by American intelligence.

Kissinger, with his long and varied experience in the world of clandestine operations, was able to assert almost total control over the intelligence community soon after he joined the Nixon Administration. His bureaucratic device was a high-level group known as the 40 Committee, formally chaired by Kissinger (and brought into being by NSDM 40). Its members included John Mitchell, Richard Helms, Admiral Moorer, Alexis Johnson, and David Packard, Melvin Laird's deputy in the Defense Department. The 40 Committee was, in theory, responsible for approving all sensitive covert operations by the CIA; it also supervised and monitored many intelligence-gathering activities by the armed forces. In practice, however, Kissinger and Nixon treated it as they did all the bureaucracy—as another office to be utilized or ignored at will. In Chile, for example, the CIA was ordered to conduct its activities aimed at overthrowing or assassinating Allende without any knowledge or involvement of the 40 Committee members, with the exception of Kissinger and Mitchell.*

Kissinger and Nixon were not the only ones to hide information from the 40 Committee. The CIA, in what amounted to routine operating policy, was also circumspect. For example, the Agency's extensive contacts with ITT officials throughout Latin America, and especially in Chile, were carefully shielded from the 40 Committee, whose members presumably did not "need to know" —as the CIA would put it—about them, although ITT played a major role in Chile before the 1970 elections.

Most sensitive intelligence decisions are made without a paper trail. In the case of Chile in 1970, many of the documents that did exist, even those in

---

* By all accounts, Mitchell's function on the 40 Committee was baffling: Officials recall that he sat through meeting after meeting calmly puffing on his pipe and saying little. Mitchell's demeanor and his presence at the highly classified meetings seems to have unnerved Richard Helms, who had problems enough with Nixon and Kissinger. Helms, as he later testified before an investigating committee, had first met Mitchell in late 1968, shortly after President-elect Nixon decided not to replace Helms as director of Central Intelligence. "He [Nixon] told me," Helms testified, "that anything that I . . . could say to him, I could also say to Mr. Mitchell; he had his total trust and confidence." Once in office, Nixon quickly appointed Mitchell to the secret intelligence monitoring group. "I assumed he was there as the eyes and ears of the President to keep an eye on Henry Kissinger, Dick Helms, and anybody else who was attending those meetings," Helms said. "He was here sort of as a shadowy figure, sometimes asking questions, sometimes being absolutely silent in meetings as these things went on." One 40 Committee member, asked to describe Mitchell's role, recalls: "He sat there nodding sagely, and listened to covert operations being discussed and thought that was the way things were. He fell for it." This official says he was not surprised when he learned later that Mitchell had played a direct role in the Watergate break-in in 1972: "Mitchell just heard enough of that wild talk in the 40 Committee, and he didn't realize that was over his head." As far as he could recall, this official added, he rarely heard Mitchell express his views on any operations. Mitchell, told of the comment, smiled broadly and said: "I never said very much since I knew what was going to be decided before the meetings began." His point was that he, Nixon, and Kissinger made their decisions about the proposals before the meetings, a procedure similar to that used for formal meetings of the National Security Council.

government files, remained secreted inside the Agency long after the Senate Intelligence Committee and the Justice Department conducted full-scale inquiries in 1975 and 1976. Justice Department attorneys concluded, according to files later made public under the Freedom of Information Act, that Kissinger went so far as to make his own personal minutes of the 40 Committee meetings, which presumably were more detailed, and kept them separate from the official minutes that were routinely distributed to the bureaucracy.*

The files of the 40 Committee, at least those the CIA turned over to the various investigating groups, showed that the pending election in Chile was discussed on at least four occasions between April 1969 and September 1970. In April 1969, the CIA warned that a major campaign to influence the 1970 elections would not succeed unless the CIA station in Santiago could begin assembling paid operatives in various political parties. No direct action was taken, the records show, until a 40 Committee meeting on March 25, 1970—a week after the overthrow of Prince Sihanouk in Cambodia—at which time $135,000 for anti-Allende propaganda efforts was approved. On June 27, the 40 Committee approved an additional outlay of $300,000—recommended by Ambassador Korry as well as the CIA—for more anti-Allende electioneering. It was at this meeting, according to the official minutes, that Kissinger signaled his support of the anti-Allende programs: "I don't see why we need to stand by and watch a country go Communist due to the irresponsibility of its own people."

In these early meetings, however, the State Department generally took a position against more direct interference in the Chilean presidential elections. On June 27, for example, the CIA had sought approval for $500,000 in contingency funds to begin buying votes in the Chilean Congress in case the September 4 election resulted in a runoff between Allende and Alessandri. When some State Department officials objected, approval was deferred, pending the election. One official who attended the early meetings as a backstop for Alexis Johnson remembers that he considered the operations against Allende "a stupid effort. It assumed too much reliability from people over whom we had no control. We were doing something culpable and immoral. Why take these risks?" His views prevailed that summer, but as the White House became more concerned, he soon found himself disinvited to the 40 Committee meetings. In his memoirs, Kissinger felt he had to explain his decision at the June meeting not to insist on approval of the postelection contingency plans, an authority he most certainly could have wielded. As usual, he blamed Rogers' State Department. The experts there, he wrote, "disparaged both the likelihood and the danger of an Allende victory."

There was another reason, surely: Chile was not yet vital to the President.

What the 40 Committee did approve in March and June was a series of anti-Allende "spoiling" operations—as they became known in the intelligence community—that used the media and right-wing civic groups to plant alarming allegations against the Allende political coalition, known as Popular Unity.

* Kissinger's attorney, William D. Rogers, told the Justice Department in 1977 on behalf of his client that no such personal 40 Committee files were kept. Rogers' letter was made available under the Freedom of Information Act.

Thousands of newsletters were mailed, booklets printed, posters distributed, and walls painted—under the aegis of the CIA and the Agustín Edwards empire—that equated Allende's election with such events as the 1968 Soviet invasion of Prague and Castro's purported use of firing squads. By 1970, according to data compiled by the Senate Intelligence Committee, the CIA was subsidizing two wire services and a right-wing newspaper, whose views were so extreme as to "alienate responsible conservatives."

Although he had recommended the propaganda programs, Korry says he soon grew disenchanted with the crude results and antagonized the CIA by criticizing, in writing, its "spoiling" campaign as counterproductive and, in effect, "making votes for Allende."

Despite his complaints, there was no panic about Chile in the Nixon Administration that summer (it was winter, of course, in Chile). Until election day, the CIA confidently predicted a huge Alessandri victory, on the basis of polls conducted by the organization of Agustín Edwards—polls that were based, as Korry understood and Washington perhaps did not—on outdated 1960 census data. Edwards had become more important than ever to the CIA in Chile. Hecksher recommended that the $300,000 approved on June 27 be floated into Chile via his organization; the CIA, Hecksher argued, had no other proven "asset" in Chile with Edwards' skills and discretion. He owned three daily newspapers in Santiago, and his business interests seemed to be constantly expanding: He was affiliated with Lever Brothers and with PepsiCo, and owned one of the nation's most successful granaries and a large chicken farm. At some point early that summer, the CIA reported that Edwards' polls showed Alessandri with 50 percent of the popular vote, which would obviate the necessity of a runoff election in the Chilean Congress.

Such predictions did little to soothe the American business community, which had been rebuffed earlier in the year in its efforts to persuade the Nixon Administration to join with it, as the Johnson Administration had in 1964, to make sure the right man won. In April, according to documents made available by Korry, members of the Council of the Americas approached the State Department and offered to give at least $500,000 to Alessandri's campaign. A small delegation of Council members, including C. Jay Parkinson of Anaconda, chose to relay the campaign pledge through Charles Meyer. Meyer was the logical choice; a former Sears Roebuck executive, he had been involved in the firm's operations in Latin America and had been an active member of the Council. Korry recalls that Meyer, shortly after assuming the State Department position, told a private Council luncheon that he had been "chosen" for the post "by David Rockefeller." The Council's cash offer had a condition: The funds would be contributed only if, as in 1964, the CIA also invested a significant amount of money in the Alessandri campaign. Meyer forwarded the proposal to Korry, who objected strongly. In a secret cable, Korry warned that such interference would be impossible to cloak and would lead to serious problems for the United States if discovered. He also asserted that any overt American opposition to the Christian Democrats, whose candidate, Romero Radomiro Tomic, was running third in the polls, "would doubtless produce a negative reaction that would do harm to immediate and longer term United States' interests." Korry's opposition was instrumental in the State Department's rejection of the Council's offer.

By that spring, Korry looked more and more like a wild card for both the CIA and the American corporations. He was fiercely anti-Communist and anti-Allende; his dramatic, inflammatory cables warning of the dangers that Allende posed to American national security interests were legendary throughout the State Department. One State Department official recalled Korry's briefings on Chile as "really terrible. If you didn't believe in Korry's concept of free enterprise, you were a Commie." Nonetheless, Korry was adamant on maintaining control over the CIA in his embassy, and he had flatly ruled out any contact by the CIA with those members of the Chilean military who were known to be eager to stage a military coup d'état in the event of an Allende victory. Korry and the CIA station chief, Henry Hecksher, who was bitterly opposed to Allende and the Frei regime, did not have a good working relationship—a fact that only Hecksher seemed to realize. One CIA operative working in Latin America at the time says that Korry "and the Agency were not on the same wave length. He was a difficult ambassador." Although Korry agreed enthusiastically with the CIA that a major propaganda program was needed to counter the growing drift to the left in Chile, he insisted that the propaganda be anti-Communist in nature—and not pro-Alessandri, as Hecksher and his superiors in Washington wanted.

ITT and its president, Harold Geneen, were still determined to give money to Alessandri's campaign. But Geneen, obviously aware of Korry's rejection of the Council's proposal in April, avoided the American Embassy in Santiago and worked directly with the highest levels in Washington.* Geneen's go-between was his good friend John A. McCone, a CIA director under Presidents Kennedy and Johnson, who in 1970 was a director of ITT; his wife was a major Anaconda stockholder. In May, June, and July, McCone repeatedly discussed the Chilean situation with Richard Helms. At least two meetings were at the CIA's headquarters—McCone was still a consultant to the Agency—and one was at McCone's home in San Marino, California. McCone, in 1973 testimony before the Subcommittee on Multinational Corporations of the Senate Foreign Relations Committee, said that he learned from Helms that the 40 Committee and the White House had decided that no major CIA programs in support of Alessandri were to be carried out in Chile—a decision obviously based on Korry's anticipated opposition as well as on the optimistic polls. Nixon and Kissinger also were distracted by the continuing crises in Cambodia and the Middle East.

The Senate subcommittee concluded in its final report that it was McCone's suggestion that led Helms to arrange for Geneen to meet in July with William V. Broe, then chief of the CIA's clandestine operations in Latin America. During that meeting, Broe told the subcommittee, Geneen offered to make a "substantial" contribution to the Alessandri campaign if the CIA would handle the funds. The subcommittee did not learn, however, that the Geneen-Broe meeting had been stimulated not by McCone but by Hecksher, who—working behind Korry's back—had met in Santiago with ITT operatives and given them

---

* While he was Ambassador, Korry met Geneen only once, in 1968, when Geneen flew to Santiago to confer with President Frei. Korry asked a local official of Chiltelco, the ITT subsidiary in Chile, to arrange the meeting and was told, Korry recalls, "Mr. Geneen is not in the habit of dealing with ambassadors." The two met, nonetheless, and had a pleasant hour's conversation, Korry says.

the name of a Chilean who could be used as a secure conduit for ITT's money. The Senate Intelligence Committee learned about Hecksher's role later on, but the information was censored from the committee's final published report.*

Hecksher's main ITT contacts inside Chile were with Harold V. Hendrix and Robert Berrellez, two senior company officials who had a close and long-standing relationship with the Agency's station in Santiago. The ITT men were considered "assets" of the CIA, and were described by special code names in encoded Agency communications.† The Senate Multinational Subcommittee, after hearing sworn testimony from Geneen, Broe, McCone, and others, was unable to find evidence that ITT had provided funds. In fact, Geneen did authorize at least one large contribution that summer from ITT to the Alessandri campaign, a payment of at least $350,000 that the firm did not make public until 1976, after the Senate Intelligence Committee discovered it. Geneen's offer established a precedent for anti-Allende activity that summer and fall: Hecksher and his colleagues in Santiago knowingly became involved in a policy of political support that had been specifically rejected by Korry and the 40 Committee.‡ No evidence has been found directly linking Kissinger or Nixon

* The subcommittee's inability to find out about Hecksher's role, and his close ties to ITT, indicated to what extent senior officials such as Helms and Broe would go to protect Geneen and his corporation—and, through Geneen, Nixon and Kissinger. Helms and Broe could rationalize their incomplete and misleading testimony by telling themselves it was vital to national security and the protection of CIA "sources and methods," a repeated catch-all excuse for not talking about Agency misdeeds. The willingness of the Senate Intelligence Committee to permit the CIA to monitor and censor its reports prior to publication—and in the process to delete mention of Hecksher's role and the specific involvement of Agustín Edwards at key meetings—is much harder to understand.

† Berrellez and Edward J. Gerrity, Jr., a senior ITT vice president, were later charged with obstruction of proceedings, false statements, and perjury in their misleading testimony in March 1973 before the Senate Multinational Subcommittee, which held hearings in March and April of that year on ITT's role in Chile in 1970 and 1971. The hearings were scheduled after Jack Anderson received and published a batch of internal ITT documents dealing with the company's efforts to prevent Allende's presidency in 1970. The subcommittee, led by its counsel, Jerome I. Levinson, a former AID employee in Latin America, independently learned of the role McCone and Geneen played with the White House in mid-1970 and successfully demanded the right to hear testimony from Broe, the first CIA operative to testify openly before a Senate committee. Helms's testimony in secret before the subcommittee on March 6, 1973, eventually resulted in felony perjury charges against him and his plea of guilty, after plea bargaining, to misdemeanor charges. The Justice Department's cases against Berrellez and Gerrity became possible when government attorneys persuaded Harold Hendrix to testify against his former associates in return for being charged with a misdemeanor for his false statements to the Multinational Subcommittee. Harold Geneen was also a subject of investigation of the grand jury, but was not charged. The accusations against Berrellez and Gerrity were dismissed in 1979 after ITT officials, according to senior Justice Department officials, threatened to make public all ITT activity worldwide on behalf of the CIA and the National Security Agency. It was a classic case of "graymail," those cases in which government prosecutors drop legal action for fear national security secrets would be compromised during a trial. The Justice Department attorneys could have initiated a criminal case that might have gone far to unravel the truth of the Nixon Administration's involvement in Chile. As late as December 1977, according to Justice Department documents made public under the Freedom of Information Act, potential defendants in the case included not only Harold Geneen but two other corporate leaders—C. Jay Parkinson and Donald Kendall, Nixon's close friend. Geneen, Parkinson, and Kendall were each under investigation on felony charges for perjury, obstruction of justice, and conspiracy. Parkinson and Kendall also escaped indictment.

‡ In May 1976, at the annual meeting of ITT stockholders, Geneen revealed that the company had received "recent information indicating that some $350,000 of ITT funds may have been sent to Chile in the year 1970" for political purposes. Geneen also declared, in a carefully hedged statement, that "it would appear from published reports" that the Nixon Administration "both knew of and encouraged funding of this type at that time by several corporations, as furthering the

to personal knowledge of the ITT support, but some senior officials in the White House surely had to know. It is inconceivable that the CIA, with its justifiable fear of crossing the White House, would have relayed to ITT Hecksher's information on how to slip money into Chile unless it had been authorized to do so. In August 1970, Charles Colson ran into Harold Geneen in John Ehrlichman's office. Colson recalls not being surprised at all when Geneen told him that ITT had "been funneling money to help us" in Chile. "Geneen was very happy to be in alliance with the CIA," Colson added. "He was bragging about all the money he had given to the Agency." At the time, Colson thought Geneen was working closely with Viron P. Vaky, a former State Department expert on Latin America who was then assigned to Kissinger's National Security Council staff.

ITT's money did not help. The boom fell on September 4. Salvador Allende defied the opinion polls and won the Chilean election by 39,000 votes out of the 3,000,000 cast, forcing a congressional runoff election on October 24—an election in which, if history repeated itself, Allende, as the winner of the popular election, was destined to defeat Alessandri. Washington reacted with despair, and with rage at Allende for having defied the wishes of American policy makers. At 6:30 on the morning of September 5, a Saturday, Richard Helms and a group of key assistants rushed into the Agency's operations center to look at the results. An official who was on duty that day recalls their attitude. "The CIA had had its nose rubbed in the dirt in Chile. We had staked our reputation on keeping Allende out. Alessandri's loss hurt the CIA's standing [in the White House] and its pride." The official, who monitored highly secret traffic from Santiago to Washington over the next few months, says that Helms and his deputies "just couldn't put up with Allende. He became part of a personal vendetta. They'd gone so far and got out on a limb."

Korry was also upset at Allende's victory in the popular election. He filed a dramatic cable noting metaphorically that he could "hear the tanks rumbling under my window" as Allende's socialism began to take over Chile. "We have suffered a grievous defeat; the consequences will be domestic and international. . . ." In his memoirs, Kissinger described that sentence as among those underlined by Nixon when he read the Korry report. But in a sentence Nixon left unmarked, the Korry cable also said: "There is no reason to believe that the Chilean armed forces will unleash a civil war or that any other intervening miracle will undo his victory."

That was not what Nixon and Kissinger wanted to hear. "Nixon was beside himself," Kissinger wrote, adding that the President blamed the State Department and Korry "for the existing state of affairs." In future planning in the Chilean crisis, Kissinger wrote, Nixon "sought as much as possible to circum-

---

U.S. Government's own objectives." He defended ITT's intervention as "lawful," and added: "In any case it would have only been for the purposes of seeking to preserve for the stockholders a major investment . . ." Until that statement, Geneen had repeatedly denied any ITT involvement in Chilean internal politics. In January 1978, after additional inquiry by a review committee set up by the ITT board of directors, it was revealed that the firm had also contributed $100,000 in 1970 and $125,000 in 1972 to *El Mercurio*.

vent the bureaucracy." Kissinger neglected to note that he too was beside himself, and as eager as Nixon to circumvent the bureaucracy.

There is compelling evidence that Nixon's tough stance against Allende in 1970 was principally shaped by his concern for the future of the American corporations whose assets, he believed, would be seized by an Allende government. His intelligence agencies, while quick to condemn the spread of Marxism in Latin America, reported that Allende posed no threat to national security. Three days after the popular election, the CIA told the White House in a formal Intelligence Memorandum that, as summarized by the Senate Intelligence Committee, the United States "had no vital interests within Chile, the world military balance of power would not be significantly altered by an Allende regime, and an Allende victory in Chile would not pose any likely threat to the peace of the region." Nixon's anger at failing his corporate benefactors—Jay Parkinson, Harold Geneen, and Donald Kendall—was passed directly on to Kissinger. Kissinger, many on his staff recall, seemed to be less interested in corporate well-being than in pleasing Nixon. "While he was their servant ideologically," Morris says, "Henry's attitude toward the business community was contemptuous."* But Kissinger also seemed to be truly concerned about Allende's election: "I don't think anybody in the government understood how ideological Kissinger was about Chile. I don't think anybody ever fully grasped that Henry saw Allende as being a far more serious threat than Castro. If Latin America ever became unraveled, it would never happen with a Castro. Allende was a living example of democratic social reform in Latin America. All kinds of cataclysmic events rolled around, but Chile scared him. He talked about Eurocommunism [in later years] the same way he talked about Chile early on. Chile scared him." Another NSC aide recalls a Kissinger discussion of the Allende election in terms of Italy, where the Communist Party was growing in political strength. The fear was not only that Allende would be voted into office, but that—after his six-year term—the political process would work and he would be voted out of office in the next election. Kissinger saw the notion that Communists could participate in the electoral process and accept the results peacefully as the wrong message to send Italian voters. In mid-September, in Chicago with the President, Kissinger talked privately with a group of midwestern reporters about the Chilean election, among other issues. He told the journalists, with apparent conviction, "I have yet to meet somebody who firmly believes that if Allende wins there is likely to be another free election in Chile." His real fear, of course, was precisely the opposite: that Allende would work within the democratic process.

His other fears about Allende were expressed more candidly. Convinced that the domino theory was true for Latin America, he went on to say, ". . . . [I]n a major Latin American country you would have a Communist govern-

* Morris also recalls the occasion, early in Kissinger's tenure, when he became upset with yet another request from Haldeman's office for favorable treatment for a multinational corporation. Haig was peremptorily ordered to go upstairs to Haldeman and warn the chief of staff that if his interference with Kissinger's operations did not end, Kissinger would resign. Haig duly went on his mission, returned thirty minutes or so later, shrugged his shoulders good-naturedly, and told his colleagues, "Well, I guess Henry's going to resign."

ment, joining, for example, Argentina, which is already deeply divided, along a long frontier, joining Peru, which has already been heading in directions that have been difficult to deal with, and joining Bolivia, which has also gone in a more leftist, anti-U.S. direction. . . . So I do not think we should delude ourselves that an Allende take-over in Chile would not present massive problems for us, and for democratic forces in Latin America, and indeed to the whole Western Hemisphere."

The first White House reaction to Allende's election was muted, perhaps because so much else was going on. On September 4, the day of the Chilean popular vote, Nixon and Kissinger had discussed the situation in Jordan with Ambassador Dean Brown at San Clemente, where the President was winding up his long vacation in California. On the sixth, PLO terrorists began hijacking commercial airliners in Europe and the Middle East, beginning what would become the crisis in Jordan. On September 8, Kissinger chaired a meeting of the 40 Committee at which he, Helms, and Mitchell agreed "that a military [coup] against Allende would have very little chance of success unless undertaken soon." According to a summary published later by the Senate Intelligence Committee, Kissinger ordered Korry to prepare a "cold-blooded assessment" of "the pros and cons and problems and prospects involved should a Chilean military coup be organized now with U.S. assistance. . . ." Korry's answer came back hot and anxious on September 12: The possibilities for such an event were "nonexistent." On September 14, with the crisis in Jordan in temporary hiatus, Kissinger summoned another 40 Committee meeting.

The meeting was dominated by serious discussion of what became known as the "Rube Goldberg" gambit. Alessandri had announced that if he was elected by Congress on October 24, he would resign the presidency after his inauguration on November 3. Under Chilean law, his resignation from the presidency would force another popular election, and Frei, having been out of office even briefly, could legally run again. The men in Washington somehow considered this scheme a constitutional solution to the Allende problem, but it hinged, obviously, on cooperation from Frei, as well as Frei's ability to get renominated by the Christian Democratic Party.

The scheme had begun in August. Korry had been approached by some leading members of the Christian Democratic Party, who reported Frei's willingness to run again if Allende won the October election and if a constitutional solution could be arranged. Korry reported the proposal to Washington, and, after Allende's surprise victory on September 4, the Nixon Administration— desperate for workable ideas—debated and approved the gambit at the 40 Committee meeting on September 14. In a top secret dispatch the next day, Korry was authorized to offer Frei and his supporters $250,000 and more, if necessary, for "covert support of projects which Frei or his trusted team deem important" to ensure Frei's election—such as buying votes in the Chilean Congress. Korry rejected the money out of hand, telling the State Department in a cable that under no circumstances should the United States do "Chile's dirty work for it." By that time, Korry recalls, he knew what Washington did not: The "Rube Goldberg" scheme was unworkable. It had become clear as early as September 15 that Frei could not win the nomination of his own Christian Democratic Party, even if Alessandri won the runoff election and withdrew, as announced. "I also suspected Frei wasn't going to *try* to win [his party's nomination]," Korry says, "so why should I go running around trying to buy up Chilean congressmen if Frei couldn't control his own party."*

Korry remained hostile to Allende's candidacy during this period, but he asserts that he repeatedly sought to prevent any direct United States intervention in the elections. "If Frei could win his party's nomination in an open, democratic way," Korry explains, "and then use the system constitutionally in an open way to become President, that was his business." During those hectic weeks, Korry enthusiastically backed some of Frei's more ardent supporters in a series of anti-Allende propaganda steps. When some of those supporters came to him, Korry recalls, and reported that they planned to help disrupt the economy, "I endorsed this in a cable to Washington." Korry's concern, he says, was to show Washington that he could be as tough as anyone else; his goal, he insists, was solely to prevent what he suspected was being considered: direct American support for a military coup. For a few weeks, then, in mid-September, if Korry's account is accurate, his world became as devious as Henry Kissinger's: He sent a stream of tough-sounding cables to Washington strenuously supporting a gambit he knew had no chance of success. In one such cable, he told of a stern warning he had given Frei's Defense Minister about the problems Chile would face if Frei did not act: "Frei should know that not a nut or bolt will be allowed to reach Chile under Allende. Once Allende comes to power we shall do all within our power to condemn Chile and Chileans to utmost deprivation and poverty, a policy designed for a long time to come. . . ." Korry insisted later, in testimony to the Senate Intelligence Committee and in interviews, that he had deliberately "overstated the message . . . in order to prevent and halt this damn pressure on me to go to the military." He did not know at the time he wrote the cable, he said, that such a policy was, in fact, being advocated by Nixon and Kissinger.†

The unworkable "Rube Goldberg" plan was not the only issue before the 40 Committee at its September 14 meeting. Approval was granted for a last-minute increase in propaganda activities to convince the Chilean Congress that an Allende election would mean financial chaos. Within two weeks, according to the Senate Intelligence Committee, twenty-three journalists from at least

---

* There was another reason for Korry's lack of interest in the "Rube Goldberg" approach. The American Embassy had learned, Korry says, that Radomiro Tomic, the Christian Democratic candidate who finished third on September 4, had secretly agreed before the election to switch his votes to Allende in case of a runoff. That agreement made any chance for Alessandri's election virtually impossible, and Alessandri could not resign the presidency if he could not win it.

† It is nevertheless difficult to understand Korry's explanation of his decision to file such inflammatory cables. For one thing, it is hard to conceive how a senior American diplomat could place himself in a more untenable position with his peers and superiors in the State Department than by sending deliberately misleading cables. Many others who served in the State Department during the Allende crisis and who had access to Korry's cables also remain skeptical of his explanations; for these officials, Korry's zeal in denigrating Allende seemed totally real. On the other hand, as a reporter for the *New York Times* in 1974 and 1975, I wrote many of the first newspaper accounts of the CIA's involvement inside Chile during the Allende period. At the time, I found Korry's repeated denials of any involvement in military coup plotting not credible, a belief buttressed by my awareness of his harsh anti-Allende reporting. It was not until my research on this book was nearly completed that it became clear that Korry had not been centrally involved with the military and had, as he insisted, been trying to prevent a violent coup d'état.

ten countries were brought into Chile by the CIA; they combined with the CIA "assets" already in place to produce more than 700 articles before the congressional election—a staggering total whose ultimate influence cannot be measured. By late September, a full-fledged bank panic had broken out in Santiago and vast funds were being transferred abroad. Sales of durable goods, such as automobiles and household goods, fell precipitously; industrial production dropped. Black-market activities soared, as citizens sought to sell their valuables at discounted prices.

The pressure was on. The screws had started turning in earnest on September 14 when the 40 Committee signaled that the Nixon Administration was willing to go to great lengths to keep Allende out of the presidency. Just how far the President would go was not yet fully clear. Ten days had passed since Allende's popular-vote election and Nixon had managed to control his rage. There had been no outbursts yet. The explosion came on the next day, the fifteenth, and the spark was the alarm of Nixon's friends and benefactors in the corporate world.

The corporate path to Nixon had begun in Santiago the day before Allende's election, when Agustín Edwards made his first and only visit to Korry's embassy. Edwards had been on friendly terms with Korry's predecessor, Ralph A. Dungan, a Democrat who served in Chile from 1964 to 1967, but had not developed a similar relationship with Korry. During their ten-minute talk, Korry recalls, he reassured Edwards that the latest polls still predicted that Alessandri would win. "Edwards seemed pleased and left," Korry said. "[He told me] that he had plowed all his profits for years into new industries and modernization, and would be ruined if Allende won." Three or four days after the election, Hecksher told Korry that Edwards wanted to meet with him again, but this time at the home of one of his employees, on the outskirts of Santiago. At the meeting, Korry says, he told Edwards he did not believe the Chilean armed forces would move to prevent Allende's election by Congress; he also acknowledged that the CIA propaganda programs had little chance of accomplishing their goal. Edwards agreed that Allende's election by the Congress seemed assured, and surprised Korry by announcing that he was leaving Chile immediately. He explained that he had been told by Allende's associates that he would be "crushed" by the new regime. He flew within days to see Donald Kendall in Washington, who immediately hired him as a PepsiCo vice president and invited him to be a house guest. On September 14, according to Kissinger's memoirs, Kendall met privately with Richard Nixon, a meeting that, like many others, did not appear on Nixon's daily log as maintained by the Secret Service. The next morning, Mitchell and Kissinger, at Nixon's direction, had breakfast with Kendall and Edwards; hours later, Kissinger asked Helms to meet Edwards for, as Kissinger wrote, "whatever insight he might have." Helms later told an interviewer that Kendall was with Edwards when they met in a Washington hotel. The two men appealed passionately for CIA help in blocking Allende—an argument, Helms realized, they must have made to Nixon. In the early afternoon, Nixon summoned Helms, Mitchell, and Kissinger to his office and gave Helms a blank check to move against Allende without informing anyone—even Korry—what he was doing.

The newspapers and networks would later make much of the fact, as published in the Senate Intelligence Committee's report on Chile, that Helms provided the committee with his handwritten notes of the September 15 meeting with Nixon. The notes included such remarks as "no concerned risks involved;" "full-time job—best men we have;" "make the economy scream;" "$10,000,000 available, more if necessary;" and "no involvement of Embassy." But CIA men who served closely with Richard Helms knew that he had much more than mere notes to turn over, if he chose to do so. "You don't take notes" in such meetings, one senior CIA man explains, "but as soon as you're in your car, you dictate a memo for the record." Helms was extremely careful about keeping such memoranda, this official says, which were never put into the official CIA record-keeping system.

In his testimony to the Senate Intelligence Committee, Helms said he left the Oval Office meeting with the "impression . . . that the President came down very hard . . . that he wanted something done, and *he didn't much care how* and that he was prepared to make money available. . . . This was a pretty all-inclusive order. . . . If I ever carried the marshal's baton in my knapsack out of the Oval Office, it was that day [emphasis added]." Asked specifically by Senator Gary Hart, Democrat of Colorado, whether assassination was included, Helms responded carefully: "Well, *not in my mind*. . . . I had already made up my mind that we weren't going to have any of that business when I was director [emphasis added]."

Helms's answer was carefully hedged and far from responsive. In a conversation later with a close associate, Helms provided a much more believable description of what took place on September 15; Nixon had specifically ordered the CIA to get rid of Allende. Helms told the associate that there was no doubt in his mind what Nixon meant. In the weeks following the meeting, Helms added, he was pressured on the subject at least once more by Kissinger. Helms also revealed that he had made and kept detailed memoranda of his talks with Nixon and Kissinger about Allende.*

Helms was no innocent in the matter of CIA assassinations, having been one of the few high-level Agency officials to be fully aware of the efforts, beginning in late 1959, to have Castro assassinated. Helms told the Senate Intelligence Committee in 1975, according to its published report on assassinations, that he fully believed in those attempts, some involving Mafia leaders, and that the CIA, as the committee put it, was "acting within the scope of its authority and that Castro's assassination came within the bounds of the Kennedy Administration." Asked by Senator Charles McC. Mathias, Jr., Republican of Maryland, whether an explicit presidential order to assassinate Castro was necessary, Helms was quoted as responding: ". . . I think that any of us would have found it very difficult to discuss assassinations with a President of the United States. I just think we all had the feeling that we were hired to keep those things out of the Oval Office." In a second appearance, a month later, Helms was pressed again on the issue, this time by Senator Frank Church, the

---

* It should be emphasized that the "close associate" cited above, who requested that his identity not be hinted at, was in a position to know the truth. This associate also reported that Helms had provided his attorney, Edward Bennett Williams, with similar information after being charged by the Justice Department with perjury in connection with the Allende matter. Williams has refused to comment.

committee chairman. Asked whether Robert F. Kennedy, President Kennedy's Attorney General, had ever ordered him to kill Castro, Helms responded: "Not in those words, no." Were less direct phrases used to make the same point? "Sir," he replied, discomfited, "the last time I was here, I did the best I could about what I believed to be the parameters under which we were working, and that was to get rid of Castro. I can't imagine any Cabinet officer wanting to sign off on something like that. I can't imagine anybody wanting something in writing saying I have just charged Mr. Jones to go out and shoot Mr. Smith."

Another senior CIA official, who spent years dealing with Cuba and Latin America, explained the technique more directly in an interview: "All a President would have to say is something innocuous—'We wish he wasn't there.' That much of a message, even if it were to appear on the famous [Nixon White House] tapes, would get no one in trouble. But when it gets down to our shop, it means to about six people, 'Don't ever come back and tell what happened.' "

Talking about assassination was not as dangerous in the White House in 1969 and 1970 as it would become five years later, at the height of the domestic uproar over revelations of the CIA's failed assassination attempts against Castro and its involvement in the murders of Patrice Lumumba of the Belgian Congo and Rafael Trujillo of the Dominican Republic. Roger Morris recalls at least two casual conversations with fellow Kissinger aides about the killing of Nguyen Van Thieu, South Vietnam's President, who was seen as a key stumbling block to the success of the Paris peace talks. In one case, Morris says, he mentioned plaintively to a colleague that Thieu's "assassination is one that the American government ought to look at with interest." To his amazement, his colleague, who worked in Kissinger's personal office in the White House, responded seriously: "They have."

There was boasting about assassination, too. Haig once told John Court, an NSC staff aide, that, as Court recalls, "if we have to take care of somebody, we could do it." Court linked Haig's remarks to the killing in late October 1970, two days before the congressional election, of General René Schneider, commander in chief of the Chilean Army, who was viewed as the only man capable of stopping a faction of right-wing officers from staging a coup to prevent Allende's election. In Chile too there was talk about assassination. Korry was directly approached by the ambassador of a West European nation and urged, in all seriousness, to arrange for the murder of Allende. Korry rebuffed the diplomat, he recalls, and carefully reported the gist of their conversation to the State Department.

Out of Nixon's meeting on September 15 emerged what the CIA would later call the "two-track" approach. Track I would include the anti-Allende propaganda and political programs voted by the 40 Committee and relayed to Korry and Hecksher. Korry was also to continue his support for a solution involving last-minute political chicanery by Frei or Alessandri. Track II was to be kept secret from Korry, the State Department, and even the 40 Committee. Specially recruited CIA agents, using forged foreign passports, would work their way into Santiago and make contact with a group of extreme right-wing military officers who were willing—if properly financed—to overthrow the government before the October 24 congressional election and prevent an Allende presidency. The goal of Track II was not only to encourage the Chilean military to initiate a coup but also to provide direct assistance in getting one under way. It was to be an American coup carried out by Chileans.

With Track II launched, the White House apparently decided to keep ITT, too, in the dark about the great lengths to which it was willing to go in Chile. A week after Allende's election, John McCone met with Kissinger and Helms and relayed yet another ITT pledge, this one for $1 million, to assist any CIA plan to stop Allende. Viron Vaky, the NSC aide for Latin American affairs, was separately informed of the offer by an ITT official in Washington, who added that Harold Geneen was available to fly to the White House to discuss the matter with Kissinger. ITT was taking no chances; its two top guns were making pitches to the White House in the same week. The Senate Multinational Subcommittee could not learn whether a Geneen-Kissinger meeting on Chile took place, nor could it find evidence that ITT passed funds to the Nixon Administration for use in Chile—a predictable failure, given the less than candid testimony in the hearings, which enabled the company to glide past the subcommittee in 1973.

In his memoirs, Kissinger went to great lengths to minimize the significance of Track II: ". . . [T]here was always less to Track II than met the eye. As I have shown many times . . . Nixon was given to grandiloquent statements on which he did not insist once their implications became clear to him. The fear that unwary visitors would take the President literally was, indeed, one of the reasons why Haldeman controlled access to him so solicitously." It is not clear from the memoirs whether Kissinger considered Richard Helms one of those "unwary" visitors who took the President at his word.

Helms tried his best. The men sent down to Chile included one agent who was a smuggler and black-market dealer, another described in CIA documents as an alcoholic suffering from a nervous breakdown, and a third who passed a large sum of cash to a Chilean desperado whose sole goal at the time, as the Agency knew, was to assassinate Allende.

If there was apprehension in the White House over what the administration was trying to do to Chilean democracy, Richard Nixon did not share it. On September 16, the day after his strained meeting with Helms, he flew to Kansas State University to give a lecture honoring Alfred M. Landon, the losing Republican presidential candidate in 1938.

Nixon praised Landon's graceful acceptance of defeat and added: "There are those who protest that if the verdict of democracy goes against them, democracy itself is at fault, the system is at fault—who say that if they don't get their own way the answer is to burn a bus or bomb a building. Yet we can maintain a free society only if we recognize that in a free society no one can win all the time."

Especially Salvador Allende.

22

CHILE:
GET RID OF ALLENDE

IN THE DAYS that followed Richard Nixon's emotional charge to Richard Helms, the CIA reached deep into its resources to perform what many of its senior officers believed was a real-life "Mission Impossible." Without itself being exposed, and within six weeks of a closely watched congressional election in Chile, the Agency had to increase its direct involvement with leading members of opposition groups and provide arms, money and promises in support of a coup d'état. The goal was to get rid of Allende, as the President demanded.*

CIA contact was immediately intensified with two separate groups of military plotters whose members, just two days before the October 24 election, ambushed and assassinated General Schneider, a strong constitutionalist, in hopes of creating a climate for more violence. A few days earlier, a CIA agent, operating inside Chile with a false passport and a carefully constructed "cover," had passed thousands of dollars to a fanatical right-wing military officer whose declared aim was to murder Allende. Other CIA agents, hand-picked by a newly set up Chilean task force inside the Agency, were inserted under cover into Santiago that October.

Throughout this period, the CIA was in close contact with the White House. Thomas H. Karamessines, the Agency's senior official in charge of clandestine activities, met and talked with Kissinger six to ten times, by his count, in September and October. Samuel Halpern, a long-time CIA official who was a deputy to Karamessines, also reported to the White House, but his contact was usually Haig; if Haig was not available, Halpern spoke to Thomas K. Latimer, a CIA liaison officer assigned to the National Security Council staff. In interviews and in testimony in 1975 before the Senate Intelligence Commit-

* In his 1980 autobiography, *Facing Reality*, Cord Meyer, one of Richard Helms's most trusted deputies, recalled attending a small meeting at the Agency on September 15, shortly after Helms's meeting with the President. "We were surprised by what we were being ordered to do, since, much as we feared an Allende presidency," Meyer wrote, "the idea of a military overthrow had not occurred to us as a feasible solution." Despite the doubts, however, the men at the top of the CIA were determined to carry out Nixon's "aberrational and hysterical decision," Meyer wrote. "The pride we might have felt at having been among the select few chosen by the President to execute a secret and important mission was more than counterbalanced by our doubts about the wisdom of this course." Meyer did not say so, but surely there were also doubts about the legality of the President's directive. In the eyes of many critics, the fact that a group of mature government officials would enthusiastically carry out such a policy without question provided an excellent reason for abolishing the CIA's authority to conduct covert operations.

tee, CIA officials repeatedly described White House pressure to stop Allende as intense, matched only by the pressure early in the Kennedy Administration to do something about Castro. It was perhaps natural, then, that Richard Helms would place responsibility for the operations against Allende in the hands of the same men who had worked against Castro.

As the various congressional investigations unfolded the story during the mid-1970s, official distortions and lies about Chile reached a point equaled by only one other issue in Nixon's first term: the June 1972 Watergate break-in, with its subsequent cover-up. With Chile as with Watergate, cover-up payments were sought for CIA contacts and associates who were caught in acts of crime. With Chile as with Watergate, records were destroyed and documents distorted. With Chile as with Watergate, much of the official testimony provided to congressional investigating committees was perjury. With Chile as with Watergate, the White House was in league with unscrupulous and violent men.

Nixon's sharply worded order to Helms elevated Chile to Kissinger's list of vital national security issues. It was September 16, the day after Nixon's outburst, that Kissinger told the midwestern journalists he had "yet to meet somebody who firmly believes that if Allende wins there is likely to be another free election in Chile." It was a ludicrous statement, in view both of Allende's graceful acceptance of defeat in the 1958 and 1964 elections and of Chile's long-standing commitment to democratic government, but none of his audience knew enough, or was bold enough, to challenge Kissinger.

By that time, Kissinger had wrested control of the Middle East from the State Department. In a few days, he would single-handedly run the response to the Cienfuegos crisis. It was a period in which Kissinger saw himself, and the presidency, as facing grave challenges from the Soviet Union and rising to meet them head-on. If he could mobilize Army divisions and deploy Navy task forces with a thirty-second telephone call, surely he could change the election result in a not-very-important Latin American country and demonstrate anew to the Communist world the authority of the Nixon White House. Kissinger was to be totally in control in Chile: Nixon's orders the day before had explicitly excluded the State Department, Ambassador Korry, and even the 40 Committee. Perhaps it was the totality of his command, as well as the eager meekness of his audience in Chicago, that prompted his bravado, for at the briefing on September 16, he proceeded to tell the journalists the essentials of Track I. "According to the Chilean election law," Kissinger said, in a section of the briefing that he did not reprint in his memoirs, "when nobody gets a majority, the two highest candidates go to the Congress. The Congress then votes in a secret ballot and elects the President. . . . In Chilean history, there is nothing to prevent it, and it would not be at all illogical for the Congress to say, 'Sixty-four per cent of the people did not want a communist government. A communist government tends to be irreversible. Therefore, we are going to vote for the No. 2 man.' " Kissinger was describing the "Rube Goldberg" ploy without, of course, revealing that $250,000 had been authorized by the 40 Committee to bribe members of the Congress. The failure of that ploy, because of Eduardo Frei's refusal to act, would not become clear to Washington for another week.

Kissinger gave no clue, however, about the other half of the White House operation, Track II. In his memoirs, as in his 1975 testimony before the Senate Intelligence Committee, he repeatedly suggested that Tracks I and II had been quietly merged. In Track II, Kissinger wrote, despite Nixon's promise to Helms of a fund totaling $10 million or more, "The expenditures, if any, could not have amounted to more than a few thousand dollars. It was never more than a probe and an exploration of possibilities, even in Helms' perception."

Kissinger's eagerness to downplay Track II is understandable, for the true extent of the Agency's activities inside Chile has still not been revealed.* Helms certainly knew that it was more than an exploratory probe: Within weeks, he approved the assignment of some of the Agency's most experienced men to Santiago. One such man, known in CIA dispatches only by his cover name, Henry J. Sloman, epitomized the Agency's best. By 1970, Sloman had spent more than twenty years operating in disguise throughout Latin America, Europe, and Asia. His cover was impeccable: He was considered a professional gambler and a high-risk smuggler directly linked to the Mafia. When Sloman retired in 1975, he had been inside CIA headquarters less than a dozen times in his career, occasionally meeting high-level officials there on a Sunday to avoid the possibility of chance observation by other CIA operatives. He was a fabled figure inside the Agency; there was repeated talk of his involvement in "wet ops," those involving the shedding of blood. Helms knew him well, according to other officials, and awarded him at least two CIA medals for his undercover exploits, which included other operations—mostly in Southeast Asia—staged expressly on Kissinger's orders. If there was a CIA "best and brightest," it was Henry J. Sloman.

He was not alone. At least three other senior operatives, who could also pass for Latin American natives, were carefully rotated into Santiago before the October 24 election. The mission of these operatives—known as "false-flaggers," for their phony Latin American passports—was not to help facilitate a constitutional solution to the Allende problem, but to pass money and instructions to those inside Chile who wanted to stage a military coup d'état.

In their briefings to the Senate Intelligence Committee, CIA people explained the false-flaggers as necessary to maintain security and minimize possible linkage of the United States government to anti-Allende plotting. There was a more important reason for their assignment, however: The false-flaggers were trained to do what they were told, and would not flinch, as many intelligence operatives based in Chile would, at having to deal with the men known throughout Chile as the most vitriolic haters of Allende—an assortment of extreme right-wing terrorists led by General Roberto Viaux. The American intelligence operatives stationed in Chile considered Viaux and his associate,

---

* It is worth noting that Kissinger's most trusted biographers, the Kalb brothers, to whom he gave many interviews, did not mention either Chile or Salvador Allende in their book. Not even Allende's downfall in 1973 was noted. The point is not that the Kalbs suppressed any information, because their book was written before the CIA's role in Chile was publicly known, but that Kissinger did.

former Captain Arturo Marshal, unstable and impossible to control; their fanatic group was also believed to have been infiltrated by Allende's forces. In 1969, Viaux had been relieved of command and Marshal cashiered for leading an anti-Frei coup attempt; ever since, they had been escalating their call for violence against the left. Marshal had gone so far as to tell supporters privately that he would assassinate Allende if given a chance—threats that led Allende's advisers to urge him, unsuccessfully, to wear a bullet-proof vest. There was strong opposition to any dealing with Viaux and Marshal in the CIA station in Santiago. The Agency's main contact with the Chilean military, Colonel Paul M. Wimert, Jr., the American Army attaché in Santiago, who had served in intelligence in Latin America since the 1950s, was adamant in his contempt for Viaux. "I always operated on the assumption that there's no substitute for brains and Viaux didn't have any," Wimert says. The colonel was as anxious as anyone in the embassy to provoke a military coup that fall, but not with Viaux.

The false-flaggers were ordered to have no contact with other Americans inside Chile. They were to get in, hide out in a hotel, pass money and instructions to Viaux, Marshal, and their men, and get out. Their only contact with the American Embassy and its CIA station was to be through Hecksher, who would relay instructions to them and forward their reports to Washington. All this scheming was routinely reported to the White House, as anything of significance inside Chile was after September 15. The heat was on and the CIA was letting the White House know that it was doing its best.

Kissinger was out of Washington from September 26 to October 5, traveling with the President on his electioneering visit to Europe; he also held another secret meeting in Paris with the North Vietnamese. Even before he left, however, there is evidence the White House knew that the "Rube Goldberg" ploy was not going to work. On September 23, according to documents published by the Senate Intelligence Committee, Henry Hecksher reported that there were "strong reasons" for thinking that Frei would not act. Hecksher urged that the CIA station in Santiago be authorized to begin approaching anti-Allende officers in the Chilean Army and Navy and inducing them to lead a military coup. The key contact point was to be Colonel Wimert, who was an expert horseman and had many close friends among the senior officer corps, many of whom shared his love for horses and competitive riding. Wimert had been granted the privilege of stabling his horses at the Chilean Military Academy in Santiago; his access to and influence with the military in Chile were unmatched by that of any CIA operative. But Wimert had also been ordered by Korry not to discuss politics with the Chilean officers—an order that, despite Wimert's intense dislike for Korry, he had obeyed.

In late September, Wimert was quietly approached by Hecksher and told that he had been assigned by a "high authority" to work directly with the CIA in contacting senior Chilean military men and urging them to lead a coup. Korry was not to be told of Wimert's new mission. Wimert asked for, and received, a highly classified cable from his direct superiors in the Defense Intelligence Agency confirming the arrangement. The cable was so secure, Wimert was told, that he could not keep it in his files. He was to report until further notice to Henry Hecksher and the CIA and do what they ordered. A few weeks later, when the danger of his mission had become clear to him,

Wimert was given a confidential assurance from Richard Helms—in another cable Wimert was shown but not permitted to keep—that his family and horses would be provided for in case he was killed while at work for the Agency.

Over the next three months, Wimert dutifully filed his reports and his assessments—for the CIA and also, he thought, to his superiors in the Pentagon—through Hecksher. It was not until 1975, at the time of the Senate Intelligence Committee hearings, that he learned that not one of his reports had made its way to the Defense Intelligence Agency. Chile was to be his last assignment for the DIA; when he returned to Washington, he was treated coldly by his superiors, who, Wimert learned later, had been distressed by his failure to file from Santiago during the Allende election period. "Nothing I sent went to the DIA; it went to Haig and Kissinger directly," Wimert recalls. "I was filing for three months and I thought everything I sent over there was going to the DIA and it wasn't—it was going over to the White House." While in Santiago, Wimert received cables of congratulations signed by Admiral Moorer and by General Donald V. Bennett, who was in charge of the Defense Intelligence Agency. Often Hecksher would present Wimert with orders that were signed by General Bennett, and the CIA would relay Wimert's responses, so Wimert thought, to the general. All those cables had been created somewhere outside the Pentagon, Wimert learned later, but they "had to have been written by someone with a military background." In 1971, Wimert managed to obtain an appointment to the Inter-American Defense College in Washington before retiring, as a disappointed colonel, to a horse farm in Virginia in 1973.*

When Kissinger returned to Washington on October 5, he could not have been surprised to learn that the "Rube Goldberg" approach was dead. A 40 Committee meeting was set up for October 6, and Kissinger once again dominated. Minutes of that meeting, as later published in part by the Senate Intelligence Committee, quote Kissinger as caustically criticizing those who "presumed total acceptance of a *fait accompli*"—that is, the election of Allende—and warning that "higher authority had no intention of conceding before the 24th; on the contrary, he wanted no stone left unturned." No one in the government was taking Richard Nixon's desires lightly at this point. Karamessines later told the Senate committee that the pressure was still intense and that Kissinger "left no doubt in my mind that he was under the heaviest of pressure to get this accomplished, and he in turn was placing us under the heaviest of pressures to get it accomplished."

By the second week in October, the CIA—with the aid of Colonel Wimert —had made contact with a military faction inside Chile that, along with the Viaux group, was considered the most likely to take the necessary violent steps. The group, headed by General Camilo Valenzuela, commander of the

* The Senate Intelligence Committee, in its report on Chile, declared that it was unable to decide who was to blame for Wimert's being duped; CIA officials testified that they had not tampered with his cables. In an interview in mid-1982, however, a senior CIA official acknowledged that Wimert's reports to the Pentagon had been derailed because officials there had no "need to know" of the intense plotting in Santiago. Such manipulation was routine, the official added, when an outsider such as Wimert was called upon to aid the CIA in a clandestine operation. "There isn't a military attaché I know of who isn't an amateur," the official said, adding that Wimert's participation had been necessitated by the intense White House pressure on the CIA.

main army garrison in Santiago, was composed of moderate conservatives on active duty in the Army and Navy. CIA officials, in their testimony before the Senate Intelligence Committee, sought to make a distinction between the Valenzuela and Viaux factions: Many senior officers on active duty in the Chilean Army and Navy were known to be opposed to Viaux's extremism and his terrorist activities. The Senate Intelligence Committee concluded, however, that there was close contact and coordination between the two groups. All the anti-Allende plotting throughout the preelection period was made riskier by the reports of clandestine CIA operations that repeatedly surged through Santiago; most of the rumors accurately linked Valenzuela and Viaux to the plotting of a coup and to the CIA. Another source of tension inside the Agency was Hecksher's view that Viaux was too unstable and too much out of control to be trusted. One of Viaux's first demands, rejected by the CIA, was for the Agency to deliver—via an airdrop—several hundred paralyzing-gas grenades for use in a coup attempt. Hecksher warned headquarters not to convey the impression to the White House that he had a "sure-fire method of halting, let alone triggering coup attempts." He was recalled to Washington and warned, as he later testified, that his superiors were "not too interested in continuously being told by me that certain proposals which had been made could not be executed, or would be counterproductive." If Nixon and Kissinger wanted it done, it was to be done—even if the best intelligence minds in Chile reported that dealing with Viaux would, in the long run, be inimical to the interests of the United States.

On October 13, the CIA station was authorized to pass $20,000 to Viaux—through a false-flagger—and to promise him a $250,000 life insurance policy in support of his efforts to lead a coup. Such large sums of money were kept on hand inside the CIA station in the American Embassy and disbursed with no receipts given or questions asked. Colonel Wimert, who was later authorized to pay out $100,000 to anti-Allende groups, recalled that the cash was too bulky to carry: "I kept it in my riding boots in the trunk of my car."

The complaints about Viaux from Hecksher and others in Santiago were not the only sources of anxiety for Washington: Korry also posed problems. Nervous about the constant rumors of CIA involvement in Chile, he filed a backchannel warning to Kissinger and Alexis Johnson at the State Department on September 25, the day before Kissinger left Washington en route to the Paris peace talks and his later rendezvous with the Nixon party. "Aside from the merits of a coup and its implication for the United States," Korry reported, "I am convinced that we cannot provoke one and that we should not run any risks simply to have another Bay of Pigs." Accordingly, Korry said, he had instructed the CIA station in Santiago "not to engage in . . . encouragement of any kind."* Korry followed the cable with a request that he be permitted to

* Korry did not report that a few days earlier he and Hecksher had engaged in a brief shouting match over Hecksher's complaint that Korry was not doing all he could to urge Eduardo Frei to involve himself in the Allende crisis. "Why the hell don't you twist Frei's arm?" Korry recalls Hecksher shouting. "You're telling Washington you're doing it and you're not." Korry was astonished by such an outburst from a normally quiet man, and warned the station chief that if he did not calm down in the next twenty-four hours, he would order him out of the country. What Korry did not know then was that Hecksher was defying Korry's orders and trying to organize a coup attempt that he did not think could succeed. Hence his eagerness to see Frei step in with the "Rube Goldberg" or some other Track I constitutional gambit and resolve the crisis. Hecksher's turning

return to Washington to brief the administration and members of Congress about events in Chile. He was told to stay in Santiago because his presence there was "too valuable."

By early October, Korry was suspicious that something was going on behind his back. In a second backchannel "Eyes Only" message to Kissinger and Johnson, dated October 9, he again warned: "I think any attempt on our part actively to encourage a coup could lead us to a Bay of Pigs failure. I am appalled to discover that there is liaison for terrorists and coup plotting. . . . I have never been consulted or informed of what, if any, role the United States may have." Korry further told Kissinger that he and his senior Foreign Service aides in the embassy in Santiago had reason to suspect that an anti-Allende coup was being plotted by the CIA with the Patria y Libertad, an extreme right-wing civilian group that advocated violent action against Allende and his political coalition. If this was true, Korry added, such efforts would not be successful and "would be an unrelieved disaster for the United States and for the President. Its consequences would be to strongly reinforce Allende now and in the future, and do the gravest harm to U.S. interests throughout Latin America, if not beyond."*

This time, there was an immediate reaction. Alexis Johnson filed an urgent cable ordering Korry to report for a meeting with Kissinger at the opening of business on Monday, October 12. Korry duly arrived at Kissinger's office at the appointed hour. "Henry greeted me and kept blaming 'those idiots at the State Department' for not providing earlier warning about the possibility of an Allende election," Korry recalls. He realized that he was in the difficult position—as an ambitious Democrat working for the Nixon Administration—of having to prove his loyalty while at the same time trying to convince the White House that nothing should be done militarily in Chile. After a few moments of talk, Korry says, he told Kissinger that "only an insane person would deal with a man like Viaux." Korry recalls describing Viaux as a "totally dangerous man" whose political faction had been penetrated by Socialists close to Allende, compounding the risk of American exposure. At this point, Kissinger asked Korry if he "would like to see the President"—an audience that had obviously been prearranged.

---

to Frei as a possible salvation in Chile would have amazed many of his associates inside the CIA, who knew Hecksher as consistently anti-Frei and anti-Christian Democrat during his service in Santiago. One former high-level CIA official recalls having lunch with Hecksher in Washington late in the 1960s, at which the station chief pronounced the Christian Democrats "a greater threat to American security than the Soviets." In the intervening months, Hecksher obviously had not changed his views toward Frei, but he must have been increasingly uncomfortable with his position: On the one hand, he was constantly deceiving not only his ambassador but a military attaché who was loyal to him and whose reports were deliberately misrouted; on the other hand, he was doing all that scheming to further a plot that he did not think would work—and when it failed, he would undoubtedly lead the Agency's list of scapegoats. Korry, when he learned all this later, concluded that Hecksher's outburst in October 1970 had been linked to the pressure that was being placed on him.

* Once again Korry's insistence that he did not know anything untoward was going on in his embassy seemingly defies belief. Yet he was able to establish beyond question the authenticity of his October 9 cable, and even testified about it in his 1975 appearance before the Senate Intelligence Committee without challenge from Kissinger, Haig, or other officials of the Ford Administration. Interviews with former Korry associates and aides in the Santiago embassy reveal that he was widely disliked for his arrogance and officious manner, and was therefore totally isolated from the corridor gossip in the embassy—a basic source of information.

The two men marched to the Oval Office. "When the door opened," Korry says, "Nixon was standing right inside. He smacked his fist into his hand and said, 'That S.O.B., that S.O.B.' I looked surprised and he said, 'Not you, Mr. Ambassador. I know this isn't your fault and you've always told it like it is. It's that son-of-a-bitch Allende.' "

Nixon, obviously aware of how careful he had to be with Korry, who was not to know of the White House coup planning, began to explain lucidly how his administration would apply economic pressure across the board to bring down the Allende government. When he concluded, he "turned to me, looking rather pleased—as if I were going to say 'yes, sir.' " But Korry had met Nixon in 1967 when Korry was Ambassador to Ethiopia and Nixon was out of office and on one of his many worldwide trips; the two had spoken frankly. Meeting Nixon for the first time since then, Korry felt he could continue to speak his mind and did so: "Mr. President, I know you won't take it amiss if I tell you that you're dead wrong." Not many people talked to Nixon that way. "I saw Henry's eyes bulge," Korry recalls. The Ambassador then proceeded to tell the President that he wanted authority to begin a series of wide-ranging discussions with Allende and his entourage as soon as his election was confirmed. "Which," he said, "is an absolutely foregone conclusion. Nothing on God's green earth can stop it." At that point, Korry again brought up Viaux, warning the President that "of course, there are madmen running around dealing with Viaux."

At the end of his monologue, Korry says, "the one who was steaming— quite obviously—was Henry. He looked daggers at me. When I left the office, Nixon was very nice. He got up and walked me to the door asking about my children." Kissinger stayed behind with the President, undoubtedly to join in the savaging of Korry that would take place.

Kissinger's dagger looks were merely reflecting Nixon's real feelings, the rage the President suppressed. In his memoirs, Kissinger minimized the Nixon-Korry meeting, merely saying, "I gave Korry an opportunity to present his views to Nixon."*

Korry, by his direct warning to Kissinger and Nixon, had thrown a monkey wrench into Track II. Track II's secrecy cut two ways: Not only would the White House be able to operate inside Chile without fear of exposure, but only a few key CIA officials, whose loyalty was unquestioned, would know that the two top men in the government were personally involved. Now the President and his top adviser could not deny any knowledge of the CIA's activities if something went wrong.

In Korry's view, some carefully orchestrated moves were made over the next few days to convince him and other administration officials that no secret CIA coup plotting was under way. On the thirteenth, if the White House logs for that day are correct, Karamessines was summoned to the White House to meet with Nixon, Kissinger, Alexis Johnson, and Laird. The never-to-be-

* Kissinger also wrote that the meeting took place on October 15, though Korry says his cables and travel documents show that he was summoned to an early-morning meeting on October 12. The official Secret Service logs of Nixon's daily meetings, which were not made available to the Senate Intelligence Committee, also show the Nixon-Korry meeting as taking place on October 15. Korry is convinced that the discrepancies are not accidental. He believes the logs were doctored to enable Nixon and Kissinger to claim that they had decided to order an end to Track II planning prior to the meeting, as they later insisted to the Senate Intelligence Committee.

trusted Laird had not been filled in on Track II; no plotting of coups would be discussed in front of him—a fact Laird could testify to, if need be, in later inquiries. Karamessines, in his testimony to the Senate Intelligence Committee, recalled being taken aside by Nixon as the meeting ended and being told again—Nixon had made a similar statement during the meeting—that "it was absolutely essential that the election of Mr. Allende to the presidency be thwarted." Karamessines understood the message, as he later told the Senate committee: The Track II pressure was still on. The next day, Wednesday, October 14, the 40 Committee met again. Also at the meeting were Korry and Charles Meyer, who were invited by Alexis Johnson, obviously with the prior approval of Henry Kissinger. Korry remembers that much of the session, held in the White House Situation Room, dealt with how to handle Chile in the post-Allende period. Characteristically, the irrepressible Korry was the first speaker to raise the possibility of a military coup. Speaking after Karamessines provided a generally negative intelligence assessment, Korry referred to rumors about General Viaux "only in passing," he recalls, and once again said, as he had two days earlier with the President, that "there was no chance for a military coup." Kissinger said little during the forty-five-minute meeting, which John Mitchell attended briefly. Korry later concluded that Kissinger had staged the meeting and invited Korry because "he wanted me to take responsibility for saying there's going to be no coup—so he wouldn't be the one accused of getting cold feet." *

The official minutes of that October 14 meeting, as provided to the Senate Intelligence Committee, quote Karamessines as saying General Viaux was "the only individual seemingly ready to attempt a coup and . . . his chances of mounting a successful one were slight." Viaux was "unpredictable." The official minutes also quote Kissinger as observing that "there presently appeared to be little the United States can do to influence the Chilean situation one way or another."

The other participants at the meeting, with the exception of Karamessines, Mitchell, and possibly Alexis Johnson, would have been shocked to learn that only the day before, CIA headquarters, after getting clearance from the White House, had agreed to provide Viaux with cash and a life insurance policy—despite explicit warnings about Viaux's instability from Korry and Hecksher. The pessimistic talk by Kissinger and Karamessines was clearly aimed at duping Korry and at improving the ability of Kissinger and Nixon to deny responsibility for what, they hoped, was to come.

The need for so much duplicity apparently did have some impact; the evidence is clear that Kissinger and Nixon suddenly began to have grave second thoughts. Any violent action by Viaux carried the considerable risk of exposing

* Korry says that two days earlier, in their brief talk before the meeting with Nixon, Kissinger asked him to write an "Eyes Only" memorandum documenting how the State Department had dragged its feet in the opposition to Allende. At the time, Kissinger claimed it was Nixon who wanted such a memo, but Korry was sure that Kissinger, afraid Allende's election could not be averted, was seeking ammunition to justify his actions to his President. Korry was later very bitter about Kissinger's role: "His interest was not in Chile but in who was going to be blamed for what. He wanted me to be the one who took the heat. Henry didn't want to be associated with a failure and he was setting up a record to blame the State Department. He brought me in to the President because he wanted me to say what I had to say about Viaux; he wanted me to be the soft man. He didn't have the moral courage to say to the President, 'Look, we're in over our heads. Let's get out of there.' "

CIA involvement with anti-Allende plotting; now there was a second, much more serious issue: the possible exposure of high-level White House involvement.

From all available evidence, the decision to turn primary efforts from Viaux to the Valenzuela group was made on October 15, the day of the White House meeting on Chile. Colonel Wimert had been reporting for days that his contacts with Valenzuela and the other plotters were substantial and he was convinced, so he reported to the Agency (and, he thought, to his superiors in the Pentagon), that the Chilean military men were ready to mount a coup that would have a far greater chance of success than any operation proposed by Viaux. On the fourteenth, Wimert received a dramatic order ostensibly signed by General Bennett: "High authority in Washington has authorized you to offer material support short of armed intervention to Chilean Armed Forces in any endeavors they may undertake to prevent the election of Allende on October 24." Karamessines later told the Senate Intelligence Committee that the "high authority" could only have been Kissinger or Nixon, for General Bennett had no authority to issue such orders. The CIA official also testified that the message must have been drafted in the White House—or at least cleared by Kissinger's office—before being routed to Wimert.*

On October 15, a Thursday, Karamessines again met with Kissinger and Haig at the White House. According to Karamessines' memorandum of that meeting, as supplied to the Senate, the officials closely reviewed the possibility of a military coup, focusing on Viaux and Valenzuela. In a decision that was clearly linked to the orders given Wimert the day before, Kissinger ordered Karamessines to stall Viaux, to persuade him to stand down for the present. The other plotters, the more reliable group headed by Valenzuela, were to be encouraged to proceed. Kissinger closed the meeting by urging the Agency to "continue keeping the pressure on every Allende weak point in sight—now, after the 24th October, after 3rd November [inauguration day], and into the future until such time as new marching orders are given."

The next day, CIA headquarters cabled Hecksher its understanding of the new White House orders: "It is firm and continuing policy that Allende be overthrown by a coup. . . . We are to continue to generate maximum pressure toward this end utilizing every appropriate resource." Hecksher was also told to warn Viaux not to move, since a "coup attempt carried out by him alone with the forces now at his disposal would fail," but to "continue to encourage" Viaux to join forces with other coup planners. "There is great and continuing interest in the activities of Valenzuela et al and we wish them optimum good fortune."

The White House decision to turn to Valenzuela was, without question, triggered by Korry's meeting with Kissinger and Nixon on October 12 and his articulation of the dangers inherent in dealing with the unstable Viaux. But the basic American policy remained the same: a military coup to prevent Allende's presidency. Over the next eight days, the CIA continued to report regularly to Kissinger and Haig about contacts with Valenzuela and other plotters, and they, in turn, continued to pressure the Agency to get something done.

---

* Karamessines, who had an extremely high reputation for integrity inside the Agency, died of a heart attack in September 1978 at his vacation home near Grand Lake, Quebec.

And yet Kissinger and Haig insisted in their testimony to the Senate Intelligence Committee in 1975 that they had "turned off" the CIA's coup planning against Allende in the October 15 meeting with Karamessines. After that day, Kissinger testified, "There was no separate channel by the CIA to the White House and . . . all actions with respect to Chile were taken in the 40 Committee framework. There was no 40 Committee [meeting] that authorized an approach to or contact with military people, no plots I am familiar with . . . and if there was any further contact with military plotting, it was totally unauthorized and this is the first that I have heard of it." Haig corroborated this testimony: "The conclusions of that meeting [on October 15] were that we had better not do anything rather than something that was not going to succeed. . . . My general feeling was, I left that meeting with the impression that there was nothing authorized."

Nixon, in a written response in 1976 to a series of interrogatories from the committee, went even further: He was not aware of any coup planning at all, not even Track II. "I do not presently recall being personally consulted with regard to CIA activities in Chile at any time during the period September 15, 1970 through October 24, 1970," he stated. The one exception to that statement, Nixon added, came in mid-October, when Kissinger "informed me that the CIA had reported to him that their efforts to enlist the support of various factions in attempts by Mr. Allende's opponents to prevent Allende from becoming president had not been successful and likely would not be." He then agreed, Nixon said, with Kissinger's recommendation that the CIA be ordered to abandon its efforts. Thus the basic thrust of the Nixon, Kissinger, and Haig testimony before the Senate committee was that the CIA had been operating on its own in continuing to move against Allende after October 15. The Senate committee made no effort to investigate the obvious contradiction between the Nixon-Kissinger and the CIA versions.*

In his memoirs, Kissinger, freed from the burden of sworn testimony, took the White House cover story a step further: "When I ordered coup plotting turned off on October 15, 1970, Nixon, Haig, and I considered it the end of both Track I and Track II. The CIA personnel in Chile apparently thought the order applied only to Viaux; they felt they were free to continue with the second plotters [led by Valenzuela], of whom the White House was unaware." The Agency's efforts in Chile were "amateurish, being improvised in panic and executed in confusion." What Kissinger could have added, of course, was that much of the panic originated with Nixon on September 15, and much of the confusion with White House fears of exposure that grew out of Korry's warnings. Blood was going to be shed in Santiago that October, and the White House wanted no part of the responsibility.

In later interviews, CIA officials were amused and almost philosophical about the Nixon and Kissinger testimony: "We're there as the whipping boy,"

---

* Kissinger was treated very gingerly by the Intelligence Committee members, who did not directly raise the possibility that he was not telling the truth in his testimony. "The Senators rolled over and played dead," said one committee staff member. "It was his celebrity status. When Kissinger came to testify [in the closed hearings], all of a sudden we let in the press and all the senators stood up and had photographs taken with him." Most of the staff members investigating Chile had no doubts about who was lying and who was not, but they were unable to do more in the published reports than note the many discrepancies, most of which pitted the CIA against the White House.

said one senior operative who was directly involved in Track II. "Kissinger and Nixon left us holding the bag, but that's what we're in business for. And if you don't like it, don't join up."

One of the problems in dealing with fanatics is their fanaticism. On October 17, the CIA station in Santiago informed headquarters that the White House's words of caution had been passed to Viaux by one of the false-flaggers but Viaux couldn't have cared less. He informed his contact that it did not matter what the CIA did, since he and his cohorts had decided to proceed with the coup with or without American support. During these last few days before the congressional election, the CIA, desperately trying to induce Valenzuela to act and at the same time keep Viaux from acting, sweetened its offer to Valenzuela. On October 19, he was promised three machine guns stripped of all identifying markings, six tear-gas grenades, and 500 rounds of ammunition, in support of a plan to kidnap General Schneider, the Army commander in chief, whom both the CIA and the Valenzuela plotters thought of as standing between the armed forces and a military coup.

The plan, which was supported by the CIA, was to grab Schneider as he left a military dinner October 19, and fly him to Argentina—thus removing from the scene the most ardent supporter of democracy in the armed forces. Frei would resign; one of Valenzuela's aides would be placed in charge of a military government and dissolve Congress; and thus Allende could not be elected. Without Schneider's presence, it was argued, the chances of military backing for a takeover were significantly increased.*

On the afternoon of the nineteenth, Karamessines met with Haig in the White House and, as he testified to the Senate, reported the new Valenzuela plan "very promptly, if for no other reason than that we didn't have all that much promising news to report to the White House." Haig, of course, denied hearing anything about the ambitious last-minute scheming, and Kissinger continued to maintain that he "was informed of nothing after October 15." Kissinger went so far as to tell the senators that, according to his daily calendar—which he did not turn over to the committee—he held no conversations with Karamessines or Helms between October 15 and October 19, a statement that did not rule out the obvious possibility that Karamessines met with Haig, as Karamessines testified, and Haig dutifully filled Kissinger in later. Haig and Kissinger both specifically denied hearing anything about the alleged kidnaping plot against General Schneider.

On the evening of the nineteenth, the Valenzuela group, bolstered by some of Viaux's thugs as well as the six tear-gas grenades Wimert had delivered, failed to kidnap Schneider when the general left the official dinner by private means instead of in his command car. With this overt act, the pressure from the White House became even more acute. Early on October 20, Henry

* One constant goal of the CIA station that fall was to "create a coup climate" in Chile. A headquarters cable dated October 19—only five days before the election—provided guidance: "It still appears that [the proposed] coup has no pretext or justification that it can offer to make it acceptable in Chile or Latin America. It therefore would seem necessary to create one to bolster what will probably be their claim to a coup to save Chile from Communism." The cable, reprinted in part in the Senate Intelligence Committee's report, makes clear that the CIA was aware that the citizens of Chile were prepared to accept an Allende presidency peaceably.

Hecksher received an urgent cable asking him to report anything he could because "Headquarters must respond during morning 20 October to queries from high levels."* After the failure became known, Wimert was authorized to promise Valenzuela and his chief associate, an admiral, $50,000 each if the two men would try again.

The second attempt, on the evening of the twentieth, also failed, and even more extreme steps were taken as constant White House pressure and Valenzuela's failures induced what must have been near-panic in the CIA station. On October 22, two days before the election, the sterile machine guns—shipped into Chile by diplomatic pouch—were delivered to Valenzuela.

General Schneider was assassinated that day by a group of military officers and thugs who did not use the American-supplied machine guns. Neither Valenzuela nor his senior associates were at the scene, but Chilean military courts later determined that the men who participated in the October 22 assassination, which was led by Viaux, also participated in the kidnaping attempts on October 19 and 20. The military courts eventually convicted Viaux of kidnaping and conspiring to cause a military coup for his role in the Schneider slaying; Valenzuela was convicted of the single charge of conspiring to cause a coup.

Just who was responsible for what in the Schneider assassination is impossible to determine; contradictions abound between the findings of the Senate Intelligence Committee and later statements made to the author by participants. For example, the Senate Intelligence Committee reprinted numerous CIA cables stating that no actual funds were passed to Valenzuela in the days before the October 24 election. Yet Colonel Wimert said in an interview that he indeed did pass Valenzuela and the admiral $50,000 each. After the failed kidnaping, Wimert recalls, he was determined to get back the $100,000 and thus shield, as best he could, his direct role in the plotting. The admiral returned the funds without comment, but Valenzuela resisted, Wimert says. Wimert recalls that he felt compelled to pull out his revolver, which he always carried with him in Santiago, wave it in front of the Chilean general, and say, "I'll beat the shit out of you with this if you don't get me the money." Valenzuela still hesitated, Wimert says, "and so I just hit him once and he went and got it." The exchange took place in Valenzuela's house. There is no apparent record in the CIA files of these financial transactions, which Wimert insists he reported to Hecksher.

Valenzuela's role was minimized in all the subsequent reporting, both in CIA cables and by the Senate Intelligence Committee. The underlying assumption was always that Viaux and the other plotters failed in a kidnaping attempt and were compelled to shoot Schneider when he resisted. The murdered general was said to have pulled out a handgun when first confronted. Yet the

* Karamessines, queried closely by the Senate Intelligence Committee about that cable, said he was certain that the "high levels" cited were a reference to Kissinger, who, he said, had undoubtedly been briefed on the pending kidnaping the evening before and was concerned the next morning to find out what happened. Kissinger, in his testimony before the Intelligence Committee, stood the cable on its head: He interpreted it as indicating that he had not been informed of the attempt in advance and, upon learning that a kidnaping had been attempted, would have asked an aide to "pick up a telephone and say, 'What is this all about?' " If he learned then—as he presumably would have—that the CIA was still supporting anti-Allende actions, despite his claim that he and Nixon had stopped all such activity on October 15, the next question is obvious: Why did he not again order a halt?

official report, on file in Santiago, of the military police officer who investigated the slaying depicts an execution; there is no mention of Schneider's alleged resistance. The report, signed by Major Carlos Donoso Pérez of the 24th Commissariat of military police in Las Condes, in east Santiago, noted that Schneider's car was struck and stopped by a second vehicle. The car was then "surrounded by five individuals, one of whom, making use of a blunt instrument similar to a sledgehammer, broke the rear window and then fired at General Schneider, striking him in the region of the spleen, in the left shoulder, and in the left wrist."

The Senate Intelligence Committee concluded that since none of the machine guns supplied to Valenzuela had been used in the assassination, and since the CIA had withdrawn direct support to Viaux, there was "no evidence of a plan to kill Schneider or that United States officials specifically anticipated that Schneider would be shot during the abduction."

Some of the CIA agents inside Chile knew better. In the months following, at least one of those who saw the most—the false-flaggers—feared that his action against Schneider would come to haunt him. The worried operative was Bruce MacMaster, a career CIA officer who had served throughout Latin America in the 1950s and 1960s under cover as a State Department Foreign Service officer. MacMaster apparently began having reservations about what he had seen and done in Chile, and also about the activities of Henry Sloman. On February 16, 1971, he walked into the office of John C. Murray, the branch chief for Mexico, at Agency headquarters in Washington. Murray was a career operations officer with a reputation for integrity—a straight shooter. MacMaster proceeded to tell the story of his involvement in Chile, acknowledging that he, Sloman, and others were ordered into Santiago in an effort to mobilize a coup. As Murray reported in a "Secret—Eyes Only" memorandum two days later, MacMaster "stated that [while in Chile] he ostensibly was representing American business interests such as the Ford Foundation, the Rockefeller Foundation and other unidentified business groups."*

MacMaster, who was born of American parents in Colombia, told Murray that he had traveled to Chile on a falsified Colombian passport to meet with the coup plotters and reassure them that, as Murray reported, "as a representative of American business interests he was most anxious to see the continuance of democratic institutions in Chile." MacMaster further said that he and Sloman had met with General Viaux and were involved in the plotting against Schneider. They learned that Viaux was also working with some right-wing students. It was the student group, MacMaster told Murray, that "was responsible for the machine-gun attack on General Schneider."

The main goal of Murray's memorandum, which he sent to William Broe, the chief of Latin American clandestine operations, was to warn of MacMaster's fear that some members of the Viaux group, many of whom were jailed following the Schneider assassination, "will possibly implicate CIA in the action taken against Schneider." MacMaster told Murray that he had met privately, outside Chile, with one of Viaux's associates and been informed that the men jailed were "seeking a large amount of money—somewhere in the

---

* The Agency had agreed in 1967, after widespread scandals about the use of philanthropic and educational foundations as CIA conduits, not to use the credentials of Ford, Rockefeller, and similar foundations to shield their agents on overseas assignments.

neighborhood of $250,000 for the purpose of providing support for the families of the members of the group jailed. . . . Mr. MacMaster said that we could probably get away with paying around $10,000 for the support of each family."

MacMaster had another complaint—about Sloman's black-market activities while in Santiago. He accused his colleague of smuggling clothing and jewelry out of Santiago for his personal profit, and reported that Sloman had been using diplomatic pouches to bring pornography into Mexico from the United States. The two men had been friends, but MacMaster had lost a bitter fist fight with him at a New Year's Eve party in Mexico City, and had retaliated by telling Mexican internal-security officials about Sloman's status as a long-standing CIA operative.

All these seamy doings, as reported by Murray, were hushed up by the Agency over the next few months and later kept from the Senate Intelligence Committee. Sloman, in a later interview, casually acknowledged that he had been involved in smuggling in Santiago, but described it as part of his CIA cover. "I've always been an outside man," he said. "I lived my cover in every place I've ever been. I was also known as a professional gambler—or as Mafia." Sloman confirmed that he had been reported to the police in Mexico City after a fight with MacMaster, but called his action justified: "He made a pass at my oldest daughter, and so I hit him in the mouth and knocked his teeth out."

Senior officials of the CIA were kept aware of the MacMaster-Sloman dispute in a constant series of highly classified official reports and communiqués in early 1971. Somehow the Mexican authorities were soothed and Sloman was routinely promoted, despite the serious questions raised about his activities, and the fact that his feud with MacMaster had blown his cover in Mexico and, more important, compromised the security of the Agency's plotting against Allende. In deciding not to reprimand or dismiss the two men, the CIA perhaps concluded that the character defects that got MacMaster and Sloman into hot water in Mexico City also made them good agents. The official memoranda detailing the incident reveal much, inadvertently, about the kind of men recruited to serve as undercover operatives. MacMaster was reported in official documents to be a heavy drinker; Sloman was admonished for having violated Agency rules about the purchase of duty-free liquor from American Embassy commissaries and the use of diplomatic pouches for the shipment of personal —and obviously contraband—goods. Sloman also told a senior Agency official in Mexico City who queried him about some of the MacMaster charges that— as a subsequent internal report noted—"he knew a great deal about the people in the Station and threatened to blow the Station out of the water."

Yet the only one to suffer in the incident was John Murray, who had forwarded the first official reports to his superiors. Murray, who died of cancer in 1979, began to investigate on his own and was told by one senior CIA operative that there were at least a few members of the CIA station in Santiago who realized that Schneider would never escape from the kidnaping attempt with his life. Murray was told that there had been a "panic" inside the station after General Schneider rebuffed the suggestion that he lead a military coup to prevent Allende's election. The fear was that, as a patriotic gesture, Schneider might tell Allende about the CIA-inspired plotting against him. For his efforts, Murray found himself categorized as a "squealer" and subsequently dumped into the bottom 5 percent of his rank in terms of future promotions. He retired in 1976, without receiving another promotion and after refusing a transfer to Haiti. By then he was fatally ill, bitter, and no longer willing or able to fight the bureaucracy.

Murray knew that his inquiries were bringing him to the brink of the most secret area of CIA activity: political assassinations. No document will ever be found, nor will there be an eyewitness, to describe CIA plans or White House directions to murder Salvador Allende. In interviews, nearly everybody involved, including the false-flaggers, has denied knowledge of any such planning. A few CIA operatives did acknowledge hearing talk of assassination from Chilean officers, but they said that was all they heard: loose talk. That the plans and pressures existed is confirmed by a senior member of the intelligence community, whose information on other sensitive activities—provided to the author when he worked for the *New York Times* in Washington—has been unfailingly accurate. This official learned while on a visit to Chile in 1971 of intense pressure even then to update contingency plans for the assassination of Allende. In subsequent conversations, in Washington, he was flatly told by the men at the top of the CIA that such planning was initiated in the fall of 1970 because "Henry wanted it."

The only involved American to state directly that the CIA may have been under instructions to assassinate Allende in the fall of 1970 is Wimert, who, as an Army officer, was perhaps not as steeped in the ways of secrecy as his CIA associates. Wimert says he did not know about the false-flaggers in Santiago until 1975, when he was asked about their activities during questioning by the Senate Intelligence Committee. In 1980 he told the author what he would never have volunteered in 1975: When Wimert heard about the false-flaggers, he "figured" they were there to arrange for Allende's death. "Why else would they be there?" The assassination of Allende "was always something everybody hoped would happen. It would have been the ideal thing."

The key contact in Santiago was made by a false-flagger we shall call Robert F.* He was a career CIA operative who had retired by 1970 but was persuaded, after appeals to his sense of patriotism, to return for one last mission. The more he learned about Chile, the less he liked; he told some of his colleagues that it was corporate security, not national security, that was involved in the anti-Allende operation. After testifying less than candidly before the Senate Intelligence Committee, Robert F. had second thoughts and later tried—without success—to warn a committee staff member that "you guys didn't get the real story."

Robert F. was ordered to spend two weeks in Santiago, make contact with Viaux and his group, and pass them money. He met Marshal, the fanatic who told friends of his desire to assassinate Allende, late one night in the National Cathedral, a few blocks from the Presidential Palace in the center of Santiago. Marshal struck Robert F. as being insane, but orders were orders. He gave

---

* Robert F. and Henry Sloman lived under deep cover during their service in Latin America; to reveal their real names, they argued, would jeopardize them and their families. Many other CIA men who took part in the Chilean operation also agreed to discuss it with me only under the condition that they not be identified.

him the money. A few days later, around October 19, Marshal was arrested by the Chilean police and spent the next two years in jail.* Sloman acknowledges that men such as Marshal were provided with funds and also talked about assassinations in conversations with him and the other false-flaggers. But Sloman insists that the Chileans were always told not to get involved in bloodshed: "Our answer to them was no—by no means." Yet, he said, "There is no way you can stop a Chilean from doing anything."

After the Schneider killing, fear gripped the CIA station. Wimert recalls that he collected not only the $100,000 he had paid to Valenzuela and his navy accomplice, but also the three sterile machine guns that had been provided to the would-be kidnapers. He and Hecksher then jumped into a car and drove seventy miles west, to the resort town of Viña del Mar, and threw the weapons into the Pacific Ocean. "You can say we really deep-sixed them," Wimert says with a laugh.†

Hecksher had reason to be afraid. He must have realized that, in the likely event of a full-scale investigation, Viaux and the other conspirators would be able to testify that the concept of Schneider's kidnaping had originated with the Central Intelligence Agency. A little-noted exchange of CIA cables published by the Senate Intelligence Committee shows that on October 13, Hecksher was queried by CIA headquarters about possible plans to prevent Schneider from exerting his influence to disrupt a coup. The response, filed within hours, was that the coup leaders—Viaux and Valenzuela—would first eliminate Schneider by kidnaping him, and then proceed with the coup.

The Schneider assassination, far from easing the way for a successful coup in the days before Allende's election, made it impossible. The Chilean military and citizenry, outraged by what was widely viewed as a right-wing attempt to disrupt the constitutional process, rallied around Allende; he easily won the congressional election on October 24 and was inaugurated without incident on November 3. Within a few days, Hecksher was summoned back to Washington and replaced—the first victim of the CIA's failure to do what the President wanted. Nixon and Kissinger were also furious with Helms, who had failed them once again. As for Korry, he was in the last ambassadorial post he would hold in the Nixon Administration, although he would not learn as much for another year.

None of this was described by Kissinger in his memoirs. In his version, he and Nixon sought on October 15 to stop the CIA excesses, and were deter-

* Ironically, it may have been Korry who provoked Marshal's arrest. He had learned that Marshal was responsible for the dynamiting of pro-Allende radio stations in Santiago and warned Eduardo Frei about his activities. "I told Frei that in my view he was a man who would be planning to kill Allende," Korry recalls. Frei promptly ordered Marshal's arrest. After his release from jail, Marshal made an unsuccessful attempt to assassinate Allende and then fled to Bolivia.

† The Senate Intelligence Committee, in its final report, concluded that no American officials authorized the assassination of General Schneider; it also found no evidence that "assassination was ever proposed as a method of carrying out the Presidential order to prevent Allende from assuming office." Toward the end of its inquiry, the committee staff seemed almost reluctant to learn of such goings-on. Ambassador Korry, in a private communication to the committee in early 1976, after publication of its main reports on CIA activity in Chile, asserted that the American Embassy did have reports of assassination planning in Chile. Korry, according to internal committee files made available to me, specifically cited Arturo Marshal as being involved in such planning against Allende. Committee officials handled the Korry "assertions" by summarizing his testimony in a letter "for the record" to a senior CIA official and requesting him to "please make the appropriate inquiries." The CIA's response is not known.

mined to adopt a "cool but correct" stance toward the new administration. But Allende, wrote Kissinger, was somehow not in the mood to accept the good wishes of the Nixon Administration; in greeting a Nixon envoy at his inauguration, he "gave no evidence of a conciliatory approach." The possibility that Allende might have been aware of some of the White House planning against him is not even suggested.

After the failure to stop Allende's election, the next step was economic: The administration would stop the flow of financial aid and loans from as many sources as possible, in an effort to cripple Chile's economy and force Allende out of office. On November 9, the White House promulgated National Security Decision Memorandum No. 93, "Policy Toward Chile," a top-secret paper that outlined the economic warfare. "Within the context of a publicly cool and correct posture toward Chile," the administration would undertake "vigorous efforts . . . to assure that other governments in Latin America understand fully that the United States opposes consolidation of a Communist state in Chile hostile to the interests of the United States and other hemisphere nations, and to the extent possible encourages them to adopt a similar posture."

The President ordered steps taken to:

A. Exclude, to the extent possible, further financing assistance of guarantees for United States private investments in Chile, including those related to the investment guarantee program or the operations of the Export-Import Bank;

B. Determine the extent to which existing guarantees and financing arrangements can be terminated or reduced;

C. Bring a maximum feasible influence to bear in international financial institutions to limit credit or other financing assistance to Chile;

D. Assure that United States private business interests having investments or operations in Chile are made aware of the concern with which the United States Government views the Government of Chile and the restrictive nature of the policies which the United States Government intends to follow.

The document also called for a review of possible steps to adversely affect the world price of copper, Chile's main export, and ordered a ban on all bilateral economic aid commitments. "Existing commitments will be fulfilled," NSDM 93 stated, "but ways in which, if the United States desires to do so, they could be reduced, delayed or terminated should be examined."

Nixon had authorized an economic death knell for Chile. In the next few weeks, Kissinger took charge of a series of interagency meetings, mandated by NSDM 93, to work out the policy of economic retaliation. The goal was to make sure that the State Department bureaucracy carried out orders and cut off Chile without a dollar. "It stuck in my mind because Kissinger, in effect, became a Chilean desk officer," says one senior State Department official. "He made sure that policy was made in the way he and the President wanted it. Henry was showing the President that he was on top of it." The cutoff was a success: No agency in the government and none of the multilateral lending banks dared cross Richard Nixon or Henry Kissinger. Before Allende's election, for example, the World Bank had lent Chile more than $234 million; afterward, not one loan was approved. Severe shutdowns took place at the

Export-Import Bank and the Inter-American Development Bank. American AID assistance to Chile, which averaged nearly $70 million annually during much of the 1960s, totaled just $3.3 million in the three years of the Allende presidency.

In his memoirs, Kissinger called NSDM 93, which he did not reproduce, "stern but less drastic and decisive than it sounded." Whatever policy the United States pursued between 1970 and 1973, Kissinger argued, "the credit-worthiness of Chile would have dropped dramatically." The cutbacks had been ordered, of course, before Chile's credit rating began to fall—a drop due in part to the Nixon-Kissinger economic warfare.

Economic pressure was buttressed by continued CIA activity against Allende. Within months, a new chief of station and a new network of agents were in place. By late 1971, there were almost daily contacts with the Chilean military and almost daily reports of coup plotting. By then, too, the station in Santiago was collecting the kind of information that would be essential for a military dictatorship in the days following a coup—lists of civilians to be arrested, those to be provided with protection, and government installations to be occupied immediately. The CIA, aware that its men and activities were being closely monitored by the new Allende government, turned to its allies. In response to a formal request from the Agency, two operatives from the Australian Secret Intelligence Service were stationed inside Chile; the Australians were told that outsiders were needed because of the government's close surveillance. By 1972, the Australians had agreed to monitor and control three agents on behalf of the CIA and to relay their information to Washington. The bare fact of such involvement became known after an internal inquiry by the Australian government in 1977; just what the ASIS operatives were doing inside Chile on behalf of the United States was not made public.

In its published report on covert action in Chile, the Senate Intelligence Committee acceded to the Agency's request and permitted details of the post-1970 operations to be censored. The eliminated material included the fact that in early 1971 the CIA began an elaborate disinformation and propaganda program, "to stimulate the military coup groups into a strong unified move against the government." In addition, the censored material included information on a "long-term effort" to collect operational data that would be necessary for a military coup, such as illicitly obtaining government contingency plans in case of a military uprising. More than $3.5 million was authorized by Nixon and Kissinger for CIA activities in Chile in 1971; by September 1973, when Allende was killed during a successful military coup, the CIA had spent $8 million, or at least had officially reported spending that much, on anti-Allende plotting.

After Allende's inauguration, the CIA believed that it still had a presidential mission to accomplish: the ouster of Allende. Track II was reduced in scope and in intensity over the next few years, but it continued—for there had been no cancellation. Karamessines was explicit about that in his Senate testimony: "As far as I was concerned, Track II was really never ended. What we were told to do . . . was to continue our efforts, stay alert, and to do what we could to contribute to the eventual achievement of the objectives and purposes of Track II. That being the case, I don't think it is proper to say that Track II was ended."

National security, in terms of a threat to the well-being of the United States and its citizens, played no significant role in Chile in 1970. And yet the election of Allende, with his open support for Cuba and other revolutionary countries, did pose a major problem for the National Security Agency, the elite group responsible for communications intelligence. There were at least two top-secret NSA facilities operating "in the black"—under cover—in Chile. One, disguised as an Air Force atmospheric testing station on Easter Island, in the Pacific Ocean, was responsible for monitoring and tracking Soviet and French nuclear tests and ballistic missile firings in the South Pacific. Easter Island's significance was in its location: Any Soviet missile strike from submarines in the South Pacific would have to pass within its radar range, strengthening the American early warning system. In addition, Chile—with its narrow coast and high mountain ranges—provided the perfect topography for the successful monitoring and interception of low-frequency Soviet submarine communications. At least one NSA facility, under cover at an offshore island, was operating round the clock to help keep track of the Soviet submarine fleet. When Allende won the congressional election, both bases were evacuated overnight, and their equipment was flown to a U.S. base in Panama.

The loss of such facilities, coming on the heels of the Cienfuegos crisis, in which Kissinger believed—or said he believed—that the Russians were seeking to expand their submarine operations in the Caribbean, could have helped explain or make more rational the White House hostility to Allende. Yet not one of the participants in the Chile crisis, including CIA men who attended meetings in the White House, can recall hearing any expressions of concern from Kissinger or Nixon about the bases. "The NSA played no part at all," one official says. "The bases were never mentioned in any meetings I heard or saw notes of. They weren't a reason for Nixon's and Kissinger's concern about Allende. There was genuine concern over his policies."

The President and his national security adviser had differing motives for their high-risk attempt to prevent Allende's election. Nixon was primarily protecting the interests of his corporate benefactors, Jay Parkinson, Donald Kendall, and Harold Geneen. For Kissinger the issue was more complicated, linked not only to his need to please the President and dominate the bureaucracy but also to his world view and his belief that no action to stop the spread of communism was immoral.

But Chile was also an interlude, an opportunity for the men who did not understand the limits of their power to make something happen, to get it done, to solve a problem with the appropriate blend of political, military, and economic force, applied in secrecy. It did not work that fall in Chile, just as it was not working in the most pressing issue before Nixon's administration—the war in Vietnam.

23

VIETNAM:
THE QUAGMIRE DEEPENS

RICHARD NIXON, the political hardball player, turned to Vietnam in late 1970 in an attempt to contrive a Republican sweep in the congressional elections. His promises to end the war had helped him win the presidency; now he would again talk peace to the American public. It was high-risk politicking, as Kissinger understood. He knew that his own fate hinged on his willingness to wring political benefit from national security problems. The crisis in September in Jordan and the hard line in Cienfuegos and Chile had been sustained far more for political purposes than anyone could guess.

In October, Nixon and Kissinger made a contrived peace offer, announcing a ceasefire-in-place proposal that would sit well with the East Coast press and moderate elements of the antiwar movement—even if it should be, as they correctly guessed, rejected out of hand. It was a departure for Nixon, who in his May 1969 peace offer, and even in the invasion of Cambodia, seemed to believe he was doing the right thing. And yet for all their new cynicism, Nixon and Kissinger would become hostages to that October offer, because it was predicated on a complex series of studies that concluded that the war was indeed winnable, and that Vietnamization was having a positive impact. The studies may have been misleading, like all such studies made during the course of American involvement in Vietnam, but the ones who were most misled were the men who had ordered them for their own political advantage.

By the end of 1969, there were incessant reports that something new was happening in South Vietnam. The enemy's presence seemed to be diminishing. Rural roads that had been considered unsafe for years were open. These reports came not only from the chronically optimistic American Embassy in Saigon, but from experienced hands recognized for their good judgment—men such as John Paul Vann, the former Army officer and military adviser who was considered by many the most knowledgeable American in South Vietnam.

Kissinger had moved quickly to establish a backchannel link to Vann, whom he apparently met on one of his mid-1960s visits to Vietnam. Vann was, he later told his good friend Daniel Ellsberg, excited at what he saw as the possibility that the Saigon army could hold its own, particularly in the wake of the Vietcong's disastrous "victory" at Tet in February 1968. Vann urged Ellsberg to make another visit to Vietnam, and later, while in Washington, Vann had a private meeting with Kissinger and Nixon to report on improving conditions in the South.* Vann, so he told Ellsberg later, explained to the men in the White House that he believed they could significantly reduce the number of American combat troops in the South without adverse effects, as long as American military and air support was maintained at present levels. He had concluded, after much first-hand observation, that South Vietnamese troops were performing as well as American GIs when they received sufficient artillery and air support. In a subsequent conversation with Ellsberg, Vann put it more bluntly: American GIs were being used as battlefield "bait"—just as the South Vietnamese were—to lure Vietcong and North Vietnamese troops into contact, so they could be attacked by air. Vann understood in late 1969, as he told Ellsberg, that the South Vietnamese Army would never be able to stand up by itself without air support.

In early 1970, Kissinger made his first attempt to learn what was really going on in South Vietnam: He authorized the Vietnam Special Studies Group to make an exhaustive study of pacification. The team of experts, all with first-hand experience as military or civilian advisers in Vietnam, was led by Charles Cooke, then still at work as an aide for Vietnam matters to Elliot Richardson, the Under Secretary of State. Cooke's team spent several weeks in twelve provinces of South Vietnam and concluded that the South Vietnamese forces had indeed made "dramatic progress" since early 1969. By the end of that year, Cooke told the White House, South Vietnam controlled 60 percent of the rural population, a 300 percent gain over its control in mid-1968.† But the report included many hedges. For one thing, it cited a slowdown early in 1970 in the rate of control gains by the South Vietnamese Army, perhaps due to the enemy's strategy, as outlined in COSVN Resolution 9, the Vietcong planning document that had been captured the previous fall. Under that resolution, the Vietcong had decided after Tet to begin operations in smaller units in an attempt to rebuild its control apparatus throughout the nation. Cooke further warned that the Vietcong, regardless of its level of activity, was still in control of the basic political structure throughout rural areas of South Vietnam.

John D. Marks, a Foreign Service officer who served on Cooke's team and then returned to Binh Duong province, near Cambodia—a focal point of fierce warfare in what was known as the Iron Triangle—distinctly recalls his reservations: "Yes, pacification was working in Binh Duong, but my conclusion was that the South Vietnamese government still hadn't put roots in the countryside. Pacification was working because of the American push, but the other side wasn't contesting."‡

Cooke's conclusions were circulated as usual through the bureaucracy; pre-

---

* The visit with Nixon was a "weird" experience, Vann told Ellsberg. After their talk, Kissinger informed him that "the President wants to meet you." Vann's first impression upon walking into the Oval Office was that Nixon's desk was absolutely clean. The President was sitting in what was obviously a carefully thought-out pose, Vann told Ellsberg, and every one of his gestures seemed to be studied and rehearsed. It struck Vann, then a relatively low-level AID employee, as bizarre that the President was trying to impress *him*. Vann was killed in South Vietnam in late 1972.

† The statistic appears in a secret report, "The Situation in the Countryside," that was submitted to the National Security Council on May 13, 1970, by the VSSG. Cooke's data were used in dozens of other studies submitted that spring.

‡ Marks left the Foreign Service a few months later to work as an aide to Senator Clifford Case, Republican of New Jersey, and in 1974 published, with Victor Marchetti, a best-selling exposé of the Central Intelligence Agency, *The CIA and the Cult of Intelligence*.

dictably, other agencies took exception to them. The American Embassy in Saigon, for example, accused him of being "more pessimistic than developments . . . justify" and of overstating "the enemy's current capabilities." His report, said the embassy, failed to take account of the invasion of Cambodia, depicted as a major success, and the constantly expanding Phoenix assassination and elimination programs aimed at Vietcong cadre throughout South Vietnam. Cooke worked through the spring and early summer of 1970 at revisions to meet the bureaucratic criticisms. When he moved over to the Department of Health, Education and Welfare with Richardson late that summer, he had no illusions about what was happening: "The report got massaged."

Nevertheless, Cooke believed that a ceasefire had a chance of success in the South, as long as the main problem was understood to be not military but political. "We had to concentrate on improving the political situation," he recalls. In early 1970, as the White House team spread throughout South Vietnam, President Thieu had been busily railroading a political opponent, Tran Ngoc Chau, into jail on trumped-up charges of dealings with the Vietcong. Chau, a member of the Vietnam National Assembly, had been among a small group of legislators to insist that the Thieu regime make political concessions to the Vietcong in an attempt to end the war.*

By early fall, Laurence Lynn and his group of analysts on the NSC staff concluded that there was indeed a favorable trend in the South and a ceasefire was possible. Lynn, then in the process of formally resigning from Kissinger's staff, recalls that various studies "showed there was an interesting pattern of erosion of Vietcong and North Vietnamese control associated very clearly with the presence of American and strong South Vietnamese forces nearby. . . . Something was happening out there." Similarly, a study directed by Wayne K. Smith, a former Pentagon analyst and instructor at West Point, who had joined Kissinger's staff early in the year, concluded that the invasion of Cambodia had given the United States another year to improve its Vietnamization programs. The year's grace period carried a high price tag—the destruction of Cambodia—but in the short run things seemed to be looking up.† And yet Lynn, a sophisticated analyst, was unable to say what everyone in the White House desperately wanted to hear: that South Vietnam could be viable under

* After his return from Vietnam, Cooke repeatedly urged Kissinger and others to intervene in the Chau case, arguing that Chau was a patriot and a nationalist and his jailing would be perceived as further evidence of a police regime in Saigon. It would also destroy the credibility of the proposed negotiated settlement to the war, Cooke insisted, since the Thieu government would be shown as not being willing to tolerate any true political compromise. Complicating the issue, Cooke noted, was Chau's widespread acceptance as a loyal anti-Communist by many of his American friends in the press corps and the American Embassy. If the United States refused to intervene in the persecution, Cooke argued in one of a stream of memoranda about Chau in March 1970, "it means the choice of an authoritarian regime based upon police repression and military power, upon the support of a narrow group of Vietnamese factions excluding all others, above all upon the continued support and presence of the Americans." All those factors, Cooke correctly believed, would be detrimental in the long run to any ceasefire solution. The White House refused to intervene.

† Smith, far more conservative than Lynn but equally honest, was placed in charge of the NSC's Office of Program Analysis in late 1970, after Lynn's departure. Like all those with influence inside the NSC at the time, Smith thought the United States could force the North Vietnamese into a political settlement; it was a point of view that seemed necessary for advancement. Nonetheless, Smith was well aware of the war's basic irrationality. At one point, he remembers, he and his staff analyzed two military warehouses at the Long Binh supply depot in South Vietnam—monstrous complexes jammed with equipment—and concluded it would be more efficient and practical to ship new supplies rather than "to do an audit and find out what was in there."

a ceasefire agreement. "I didn't say that because the central government was so piss-poor," he recalls.

Those with different perceptions on the increasingly hawkish Kissinger staff in late 1970 included Richard Smyser, the Foreign Service officer who had replaced Lake as Kissinger's principal deputy to the Paris peace talks. "The VSSG studies were good in terms of showing trends," Smyser recalls. "Roads were opening up. And I was looking at something else that I regarded as psychologically important—I felt Vietnamization would have the psychological consequence of giving the Vietnamese the sense of doing things for themselves." Smyser had served as a political officer in the Saigon embassy in the mid-1960s, where he was considered a sophisticated cold warrior who understood the complexity of the Vietcong's political movement. As a hardliner, he provided solace: "Henry was constantly asking for my assessment," he says.

Nixon was no doubt buoyed by the image of his strength and toughness that emerged from the Middle East, but that was not enough to carry the congressional elections. The American people were in a "peace mood," as he told Yitzak Rabin late that summer. And the peace they wanted was in Vietnam. In September, Kissinger held two more secret meetings with the North Vietnamese, the first since the invasion of Cambodia. They were unproductive. Le Duc Tho did not attend, an obvious sign that no progress would be made. At the first meeting, on September 7, Kissinger continued to talk about mutual withdrawal and the political makeup of mixed electoral commissions that, under the American proposal, would supervise national elections after the withdrawal of American and North Vietnamese troops. Both sides would get their prisoners of war returned, which was a key goal for the United States; by then the captured American pilots in North Vietnam had become a national obsession. That Hanoi would seriously consider a political arrangement with the Thieu regime was a preposterous assumption at that point, but Kissinger took comfort in the politeness of Xuan Thuy, the chief North Vietnamese negotiator. "In the never-never land of Vietnam negotiations," as Kissinger put it in his memoirs, "having negotiators from Hanoi listen to a proposal from us was considered progress; I drew from it the naïve conclusion that Xuan Thuy might go so far as to consider it." On September 17, the Vietcong issued an eight-point peace program calling for American withdrawal and the installation of a coalition government that could not include President Thieu. A subsequent ceasefire would begin only after a satisfactory political reordering took place and the other Vietcong and North Vietnamese conditions were met. Kissinger, in his memoirs, sounded unsure about what upset him the most, Hanoi's continued hard line or the fact that "Xuan Thuy had given me no advance word of this . . ." Ten days later, he secretly flew to Paris for another meeting, at which Thuy affirmed the Vietcong statement and, as Kissinger wrote, "elaborated" on the ceasefire aspects of the proposal. Hanoi's position was that a ceasefire would go into effect between the United States and the Vietcong and North Vietnamese forces during a unilateral American withdrawal, if the Americans agreed to that concession, but no ceasefire of any kind would take place with the South Vietnamese troops during the withdrawal. "We were being asked to withdraw even while our allies were being attacked," Kissinger wrote.

Xuan Thuy was telling Kissinger and the President that Hanoi's private position, as spelled out in the secret talks, was the same as the public position of the Vietcong. *"Our unilateral exit was not enough,"* Kissinger wrote in anguish. "We had to engineer a political turnover before we left, or else the war could not end, we would have no assurance of a safe withdrawal of our remaining forces, and we would not regain our prisoners. Our dilemma was that Hanoi maintained this position until October, 1972."

Kissinger's and Nixon's reaction to Hanoi's private rejection was to announce publicly a ceasefire-in-place offer on October 7—a proposal, as many in the White House quickly realized, that was aimed at producing votes for Republican congressional candidates. The extreme level of cynicism disturbed even William Safire, Nixon's speech writer and public relations aide, who managed at one point in his memoirs to dismiss South Vietnam and the whole of Southeast Asia as "a bone in the throat that had to be cleared before major-power peace construction could begin." Summoned to Ireland in early October to meet with Nixon and Kissinger on the final leg of the President's overseas trip, Safire was ordered to write the final draft of Nixon's ceasefire speech. "The proposal," Safire wrote, "was what Nixon would call 'grandstanding' or 'showboating,' presented primarily for its political impact in the States, buying Nixon some more time, with little chance of acceptance by the North Vietnamese, but with every chance of its embrace by editorial writers who wanted a dramatic offer." There was some discussion about the lead phrase in the speech, Safire recalled, but "[N]either the President nor Kissinger worried much about what it was called since it was not likely to be accepted. Kissinger could tell I was concerned about the President's broadcasting a proposal that was popular at home but not possible at the negotiation table—that was not Nixon's way. 'We want to get the proposals judged on their merits,' Henry told me, 'not on whether they are acceptable.' "

In the ensuing weeks, Nixon frantically tried to portray himself as the man of peace. Disenchantment was growing in the Congress. On September 1, thirty-nine senators voted for the McGovern-Hatfield Amendment, which set a deadline of December 31, 1971, for the complete withdrawal of American troops from South Vietnam. The amendment was defeated handily, but the trend was clear: Unless there were huge Republican gains in November, Congress might be able to do the unthinkable—legislate an end to the war. Nixon and Kissinger were fighting not only the antiwar demonstrators in the streets, but the Senate as well. Back in Washington on October 6, Nixon made a rare unannounced visit to the White House press room and plugged his ceasefire speech, telling the reporters it would be "the most comprehensive statement ever made on this subject since the beginning of this very difficult war. . . . I would like to indicate that we do not consider this to be a propaganda gimmick. We are not saying it simply for the record." His audience had no reason not to take the President at his word.

In his televised speech the next evening, Nixon called for an immediate ceasefire not only in South Vietnam but also in Laos and Cambodia, where the opposition was on the offensive despite ferocious American bombing. The Communist-led forces in Indochina were being asked to accept a ceasefire that would freeze them into diminished areas of control without a political settlement at the central government level. Nixon, in the speech, managed to describe the offer as one that could "break the logjam in all the negotiations . . . The United States has never sought to widen the war. What we do seek is to widen the peace," he said.*

The President, who made little effort to come to grips with the policies and intentions of the North Vietnamese or the Vietcong, may have indeed viewed his decision to formally concede some territory in South Vietnam to the NLF as a major concession. But Kissinger knew better when he participated in a series of misleading background briefings for the White House correspondents on VSSG studies. Max Frankel reported in the *New York Times* the day after Nixon's speech that various studies showed that American and South Vietnamese forces "have finally gained the upper hand in the most important and populated sectors of South Vietnam and that a ceasefire . . . would enable them to retain, and perhaps even extend, that position." Naming presidential aides as his sources, Frankel added that Nixon "clearly feels that he could indeed profit from a ceasefire and, with the end of the shooting, even enhance his staying power at the conference table."

The White House was having it both ways. It told reporters that the war was going better than ever, while Nixon announced a proposal to create "a generation of peace." No journalist seemed to question seriously why Hanoi, which had responded to the Johnson Administration's intense bombings by sending its forces to the South to fight, would suddenly agree to negotiate from weakness. Over the next three weeks, Nixon traveled more than 17,000 miles, making more than forty campaign appearances in twenty-two states. He repeatedly told audiences that, as he said on behalf of a local congressman on October 19 in Grand Forks, North Dakota, "The peace offer is on the table. . . . We are on the road to a just peace in Vietnam. And I say to you further that in order to get that just peace in Vietnam, we need support . . . in the House of Representatives." Nixon customarily concluded his speeches by suggesting that a vote for him was a patriotic vote because the question of peace in Vietnam "is bigger than whether you are a Republican; it is bigger than whether you are a Democrat. It involves the future of America. . . ."

* Kissinger would later tell journalists, notably the Kalb brothers, that the Nixon speech broke new ground in that it did not call for mutual withdrawal from the South by the United States and North Vietnam. In their biography, the Kalbs referred to that omission as a "key switch in American policy—the retreat from the previous negotiating proposal of 'mutual withdrawal' to the proposal for a ceasefire in place." In making such statements, Kissinger seemed to be rewriting history in an effort to show that the United States' negotiating position was more reasonable than was generally realized. No such offer was made, as was evident at the time. Nixon, in his October 7 speech, explicitly linked the American withdrawal to an overall "settlement based on the principles I spelled out previously"—which included mutual withdrawal. On October 8, Nixon told a reporter that "[W]e offered a total withdrawal of all of our forces, something we have never offered before, if we had mutual withdrawal on the other side." And in his memoirs, Kissinger commented that Nixon's speech was "in the context of mutual withdrawal, but in a language so deliberately fuzzy as to invite exploration." That Hanoi would be willing to explore a "fuzzy" offer by Nixon in late 1970 was, at best, a woebegone belief.

302

Even as Nixon advocated a ceasefire throughout Southeast Asia, his administration was secretly expanding the war inside hapless Cambodia. A White House decision—never fully analyzed in terms of its impact on the people of Cambodia—was made to build up Lon Nol's army and fully engage the Khmer Rouge and the North Vietnamese. Laird and Rogers objected, but Kissinger and Nixon believed that more resistance by the Cambodian Army would make the fighting there more costly for the North Vietnamese, and thus aid Vietnamization in South Vietnam. The Cambodian people were to become the cannon fodder of Vietnamization—a "sideshow," as William Shawcross's book so graphically reported, to the struggle for Saigon.* On October 26, as Nixon was preparing to campaign in Florida, National Security Decision Memorandum 89 went into effect. There was to be a drastic increase in American military and economic aid to Cambodia and a buildup of the Lon Nol army. Cambodia was now doomed.

In Hanoi that fall, the men running the war did not think twice about the Kissinger-Nixon ceasefire proposals. They had decided in 1969 to reduce the scope of the war, to regroup, and to prepare for an offensive in 1972, when Nixon would be up for reelection. "From 1969 on there was nothing serious in the secret talks," Nguyen Co Thach recalled in 1979, "because we knew that Kissinger and Nixon would like to have a strong position before election year. And so in 1969, '70, and '71 we gathered our forces; we prepared ourselves so that in case there was a peace agreement, it would be all right. But we also had to prepare for worse things, and so we must prepare our offensive." Thach said the positioning of supplies and arms for the 1972 offensive began in 1970, after the Cambodian invasion. "Of course there were differing views [in the Hanoi politburo], but in the end we all agreed on one offensive in 1972. You see, we could not prepare for this in some months. In America you are more sophisticated; you can prepare very quickly. In my country, we must prepare two or three years for a big offensive."

The congressional elections were most disappointing to the White House. The Republicans won only two Senate seats and lost nine House seats. Despite Nixon's extraordinary efforts, Congress might still legislate an end to the Vietnam War. Nixon professed to be satisfied, telling newsmen that the two additional Republicans in the Senate "enormously strengthen our hand . . ." but few journalists were taken in. John Osborne, the White House correspondent for the *New Republic* magazine, wrote that Nixon's performance in the last three weeks of the campaign "seemed to me and others to demean him and the Presidency and to diminish both his capacity for national leadership and his chances of re-election in 1972."

* Nixon was exceedingly frank about the American policy at a news conference on December 10, 1970, his first in four months. Asked about the new aid programs for Cambodia, the President noted that Lon Nol's army was engaging 40,000 North Vietnamese regulars inside Cambodia. "If those North Vietnamese weren't in Cambodia, they'd be over killing Americans," he said.

Nixon and Kissinger moved decisively in the next three months, in an attempt to show Hanoi that it was still dealing with a President unafraid to take risks. In November, Nixon authorized a daring but unsuccessful commando raid on the Son Tay prison west of Hanoi, where sixty-one American prisoners of war were thought to be captive. And in January, he authorized a major South Vietnamese assault into Laos in an attempt to sever the Ho Chi Minh Trail.

Planning for the prison raid had begun early in the summer, after military intelligence established that American prisoners—most of them shot down while on bombing missions over North Vietnam—were being kept at Son Tay. In late September, while he was out of the country, Nixon was informed that the operation, to be carried out by an elite force of volunteers from the Army and Air Force, was ready to go. The Son Tay planners gave Kissinger and Haig a full-scale briefing on October 8 and requested permission to stage the raid on October 21, when the weather would be advantageous. A few days later, they were dismayed to learn that the White House had decided to delay. As they later told Benjamin F. Schemmer, author of *The Raid*, the most authoritative account of the mission, the officers in charge could not understand the President's veto. Air Force General Leroy J. Manor, commander of the mission, was quoted as saying, "One reason I wanted to go in October was because I was very concerned about security."

Manor and his colleagues would have been appalled had they been at a dinner party in early January at the Harvard Faculty Club and heard Kissinger suggest that he and Nixon had weighed the Son Tay decision largely in terms of the November congressional elections. "Give us credit," Kissinger told one of his dinner companions, "that we decided to do it after the election." What Kissinger may have meant, of course, was that he and Nixon were fearful that a raid on a North Vietnamese prison camp, even if it was successful, would provoke charges of politicking with the lives of both the rescuers and those they were sent to rescue.

On November 18, two weeks after the election, Admiral Moorer met for more than an hour with Nixon, Kissinger, and others to review the raid, which was to take place in three days. Nixon was worried, according to a first-hand account provided to Schemmer. He couldn't afford any more near-riots in Washington, like those after Cambodia: "Christ, they surrounded the White House, remember? This time they will probably knock down the gates and I'll have a thousand incoherent hippies urinating on the Oval Office rug." As Moorer left the President's office, Haig took him aside. "Tom, you did one helluva job," Haig said. "The boss was visibly moved; I can tell you that. He'll approve it. One thing, Tom, if this thing fails, maybe we could find a way to let the Old Man off the hook? He's taken nothing but bum raps on every decision he's made about Vietnam. We can't let him down on this one. You know what I mean."

Moorer was bothered by Haig's remark. "I don't think the President knows about this one," he subsequently told one of the Son Tay planners, meaning that the armed services would take the heat if things went wrong. Moorer was new to his job as head of the Joint Chiefs, and he could not know whether Haig was in fact speaking for the President; but that the nation's leading military officer, a four-star admiral, would seriously listen to avuncular advice from a one-star Army general tells much about the power of Kissinger, and the aggressiveness of Haig.*

The mission was a failure. There had been an intelligence snafu and the prisoners were not there. It didn't matter. There would be no political hell. A raid in November was not a raid in October. More important, Kissinger and Nixon authorized two days of heavy bombings over North Vietnam by an armada of 200 aircraft. Targets were struck in the Hanoi area and near the port city of Haiphong. Other missions were flown against dozens of military supply depots, bridges, and mountain passes along the Ho Chi Minh Trail. It was a brief taste of the "madman theory," a signal of what was to come. The raids were carried out with no public announcement by the White House; later, as details of Son Tay became known, word was passed that the air attacks were "protective reaction" strikes designed to suppress possible antiaircraft attacks on the Son Tay mission as well as to divert the North Vietnamese military.†

Colonel Pursley recalls that before the Son Tay raiders began their mission he and Laird were informed by the Defense Intelligence Agency that the chance that prisoners were still at the camp was, at best, 10 or 15 percent. Last-minute reconnaissance overflights had been unable to find evidence that the camp was still in use. After some hesitation, Pursley says, Laird gave the order for the mission to proceed. It is not known whether Laird discussed the issue with Nixon, but he must have: Vietnam was the central issue facing the President. In his memoirs, Kissinger criticized the "egregious failure of intelligence" at Son Tay, and said nothing about knowing in advance that the prisoners had been moved: "[N]one of the briefings that led to the decision to proceed had ever mentioned the possibility that the camp might be empty."

* In his 1977 interviews with David Frost, Nixon gave a conflicting description of his reaction to Son Tay. He said he and Laird were at a White House meeting when the commando team took off from Thailand. Nixon said he could see that Laird was "a little nervous" that morning and slipped his Secretary of Defense a hand-written note saying: "If it succeeds, you get the credit; if it fails, I'll take the blame." Laird, Nixon said, reached under the table and grabbed his hand in a show of gratitude. Nixon's account may indeed be right, just as the account of Haig's special pleading with Moorer also may be accurate. Nixon often seemed to be anxiously playing the heroic commander in chief in public but—as Haig and Kissinger understood—he never stopped worrying in private about political effects.

† "Protective reaction" was the phrase invented to justify American bombing missions against North Vietnamese radar sites and antiaircraft batteries that fired on the reconnaissance planes that continued to be flown over North Vietnam in the aftermath of the Johnson Administration's 1968 bombing halt. The unarmed reconnaissance planes were escorted by fighter planes, which poses the chicken-and-egg question: Did the North Vietnamese open fire because of the fighter planes or because of the reconnaissance flights? At some point early in the Nixon Administration, the rules were expanded to permit attacks on North Vietnamese radar sites as soon as they began to lock onto the reconnaissance flights, on the assumption that such radar contact was the initiation of combat. At a news conference on December 10, 1970, in the wake of the failed Son Tay mission and amid reports of increasing infiltration into South Vietnam from the North, Nixon enunciated a new definition of "protective reaction": If, because of the increasing infiltration, he determined that the North Vietnamese could increase "the level of fighting in South Vietnam . . . I will order the bombing of military sites in North Vietnam. . . . That will be the reaction that I shall take." Nixon claimed that authority for the expansion of the war was inherent in the "understandings" about North Vietnamese actions that were implicit in the bombing halt agreement. Of course, according to the men who negotiated that agreement, including Cyrus Vance and Averell Harriman, there was no such "understanding." Queried about the contradiction in a January 4, 1971, interview with network correspondents, Nixon explained simply, ". . . [T]he other understanding is one that I have laid down. It is a new one . . . if the enemy at a time we are trying to de-escalate, at a time we are withdrawing, starts to build up its infiltration, starts moving troops and supplies . . . then I, as Commander-in-Chief, will have to order bombing strikes on those key areas."

Nixon, in his memoirs, was more plausible: "Even if I had known when the operation was being planned that the reports were out of date, I believe I would still have given my approval." Over the next few weeks, however, Laird would join with other senior officials in publicly denying that the administration knew the Son Tay camp was empty.*

The fact that an American invasion team was able to penetrate Hanoi's air defenses, land inside North Vietnam, and return with no casualties provided a psychological lift, a reminder to the other side that the United States was capable of such derring-do at any time. Kissinger wrote that he viewed the heavy bombings, in part, as retaliation "for the abrupt rejection of our peace proposal."

The message got through. In Hanoi, there was concern over the commando team's ability to penetrate North Vietnam's air defenses. "This was to prove to the Vietnamese that they can operate in our rear," Nguyen Co Thach told the author. "So we must be careful." Thach said that—as Nixon and Kissinger had hoped—his government perceived the commando raid as part of an over-all policy. "This was a true activity but designed to show that their false threat is true. So we were aware of the threat strategy."

The raid caused the North Vietnamese to move the more than four hundred American prisoners of war from scattered camps into one central location in Hanoi, an old prison that became known to the captives as the Hanoi Hilton. For many, the move meant the end of isolation. Conditions inside the POW camps had eased since the bombing halt in 1968, which ended the more extreme deprivation and torture many prisoners endured, treatment that the almost daily bombing of the North made more harsh. In one Air Force survey conducted after the prisoners were released in 1973, 70 percent of the former prisoners who responded said that the Son Tay raid, despite its failure, had a "major positive effect" on their morale.

The most senior American prisoner in the Hanoi Hilton was Air Force Colonel John P. Flynn, who was shot down in October 1967. Flynn told Schemmer he was exuberant about the Son Tay raid when he and his fellow prisoners learned of it through North Vietnamese propaganda broadcasts. But Flynn was wise enough to understand the full implications. "We asked ourselves," he

* There was a bizarre postscript to the Son Tay raid. Shortly after the mission, Schemmer, a West Point graduate who was then editor and publisher of the *Armed Forces Journal,* was summoned by one of Kissinger's NSC staff members to a meeting. Nixon had somehow heard that one of the commandos had in frustration seized a baby water buffalo at Son Tay and had taken it back to his base as if it were a stray puppy. The President was incensed over the report, believing that if it got into the newspapers it would undermine the integrity of the rescue mission. "We've got a serious problem," one of Kissinger's deputies said. Schemmer, whose contacts with the military were excellent, was asked to check it out privately for the White House. "Do you realize how insane this nation would look if the word got out that the White House was looking for a baby water buffalo?" the aide asked. He added that he had never seen the President so preoccupied as he was over the incident. Schemmer duly asked around and was roundly denounced by the Son Tay planners for posing such idiotic questions. In his book, Schemmer did not reveal that he was the journalist who had been summoned to the White House. Kissinger acknowledged in his memoirs that he had "jokingly" queried whether the Pentagon had brought him back a water buffalo from North Vietnam, since they had not returned with prisoners of war. "The Pentagon refused to believe I had made my comment lightly," Kissinger wrote. Schemmer stands by his account: that it was Nixon who precipitated the minicrisis.

told Schemmer, "why would the U.S. resort to such an extreme? We concluded that the U.S. had lost its leverage at the bargaining table in Paris. Son Tay, we speculated, was a 'court of last resort'—a last chance to get us out, or to get enough of us out to regain some bargaining power, by focusing attention on the prisoner situation and showing the world how badly we were being treated." Flynn and other captives became discouraged by such reasoning. "Our original estimate had been that the war would last eight years," he told Schemmer. "We said to ourselves, 'Maybe we'd better think of fifteen years if we've lost that much bargaining power.'"

Nixon and Kissinger had the same fears. The administration had begun a deliberate public relations effort, beginning in late 1969, to emphasize the mistreatment of the American prisoners of war. The policy had some immediate short-term benefit in terms of rallying public opinion, but by late 1970 it began to backfire. The downed American pilots were an important bargaining chip for the North Vietnamese; their presence made it impossible for Nixon and Kissinger to consider a unilateral withdrawal without a political settlement. Unless there was an agreement on the future of Saigon, it was clear that Hanoi would never return the pilots. Hanoi seemed willing to wage war forever; the White House had no such luxury. Nixon's main bargaining card, as 1971 rolled around, again seemed to be his unpredictability, his "irrationality." It was to be set loose once more in early February.

The invasion of Laos in early 1971 was a classic military failure: poorly planned, poorly executed, and based on poor intelligence. The Nixon White House somehow concluded that the South Vietnamese Army had improved to the point where it could invade and block the Ho Chi Minh Trail in a strategic area of Laos known to be heavily defended by the North Vietnamese. The South Vietnamese troops were to invade the Laotian panhandle, overcome the North Vietnamese forces defending the Ho Chi Minh Trail, and then engage in a wide-scale search-and-destroy operation that would disrupt any North Vietnamese plans for a dry-season offensive in 1971, and also make such an offensive more difficult in 1972. Instead, the South Vietnamese forces, which included some of the most battle-tested Marine units, found themselves ensnared in a trap of their own making. Once they had gotten into the dense Laotian foliage, they were ambushed by well-armed North Vietnamese and suffered enormous casualties. The battle, which began in early February, lasted five weeks, with the South Vietnamese in retreat within three weeks. At the end, in mid-March, America's ally was in desperate flight. The invasion, designed to prove to the South Vietnamese—and to Hanoi—that Vietnamization was working, did precisely the opposite.

"It was a splendid project on paper," Kissinger wrote. "Its chief drawback, as events showed, was that it in no way accorded with Vietnamese realities. South Vietnamese divisions had never conducted major offensive operations against a determined enemy outside Vietnam and rarely inside." To make matters more difficult, there could be no American ground help, since American troops were forbidden by the Cooper-Church Amendment to serve even as advisers in Laos. The only American support had to be airborne.

However, Kissinger's reservations about the operation, code named "Lam

Son 719" by the South Vietnamese, were limited to his memoirs. At the time, he joined Richard Nixon in enthusiastic support. The only opposition came from Rogers, yet another sign of his "softness." Rogers' basic complaint was elementary—the risks were too high. The North Vietnamese would learn in advance of the invasion, as they always seemed to learn about secret South Vietnamese Army planning. And what factors had changed, Rogers asked, that enabled the United States to approve an operation which had been rejected years earlier when the American combat presence was 500,000, double the size it was now? Finally, Rogers argued that the mission, if it failed, would threaten the Thieu regime, which faced a national election in the fall.

By the time Rogers was permitted to voice these objections at a meeting with Nixon on January 27, it was too late. Planning for the operation was completed and Nixon had decided to proceed. He had only to issue the final order. In addition, Kissinger wrote, "Nixon simply did not believe that his Secretary of State knew what he was talking about." Planning for the operation was, as usual, restricted to a few key officials in Washington and Saigon, and those outsiders who might raise questions—such as the experts in the CIA— were kept in the dark. One senior intelligence official recalls that the CIA was not asked to write an official estimate paper on the proposed invasion, although it could have a drastic long-term impact on North Vietnam's planning. Not even such trusted NSC aides as Richard Smyser were involved. Smyser recalls being in Haig's office the day before the mission was to begin and learning that the South Vietnamese Army was going to be sent into Laos to cut the Ho Chi Minh Trail. "Al asked me what I thought," Smyser says. He concluded that the mission had been secretly planned and evaluated by Haig with the aid of Admiral Moorer and the Joint Chiefs of Staff, and perhaps John Holdridge, the hawkish West Point graduate who was Richard Sneider's replacement for Asian matters.

There was immense irony in the secrecy, for North Vietnamese documents captured after the operation showed that Hanoi's planners had been fully aware of its most minute details. "Hell, they had every goddamned order, every change of plans," says Samuel Adams, who was a CIA analyst. He recalls that the captured documents indicated that the North Vietnamese knew weeks in advance where every helicopter landing zone would be located— obviously a factor in their great success against the helicopters, which suffered a 60 percent loss rate.

In his memoirs, Kissinger revealed why the planning had to be so secret: "Nixon was determined not to stand naked in front of his critics as he had the year before over Cambodia." His solution was to make Laird the fall guy; to manipulate and entrap him into appearing to be the advocate of the operation in an attempt to "get around [Nixon's] reluctance to give orders to his subordinates." Kissinger then described in astonishing detail how the President of the United States spent hours play-acting in front of his senior Cabinet officials about an act of war that led to the death or wounding of 317 Americans and 9,000 South Vietnamese Army allies: "Nixon conceived the idea of first maneuvering Laird into the position of proposing what Nixon preferred, and then letting his Secretary of Defense become the advocate of the plan within the National Security Council." The Nixon plan, as Kissinger described it, had three stages. First, Haig was sent on a secret mission to Saigon in mid-December, where he met with General Abrams and President Thieu, both ardent advocates of the invasion as a means of stemming Hanoi's increasing infiltration of men and matériel down the Ho Chi Minh Trail. Laird then made a fact-finding trip to South Vietnam in early January, where—in the second stage of the Nixon plan—he received the same briefings from Abrams and Thieu.* Laird returned to Washington and, in stage three, formally reported to Nixon on the Abrams-Thieu recommendation in the presence of Rogers and Helms. Laird, in his report, emphasized factors Nixon and Kissinger knew were also essential to Rogers—the continuing progress of Vietnamization and the probability that the invasion of Laos would lead to a more rapid withdrawal of American troops. Throughout Laird's presentation, Kissinger wrote, "Nixon made encouraging noises, asking questions with feigned amazement while steering the conversation to its ordained conclusion." By that time, mid-January, Kissinger added, "I had heard the same briefing at least three times and was approaching battle fatigue. Nixon was earning himself high marks for his acting ability. He listened each time with wide-eyed interest as if he were hearing the plan for the first time. His questions—always the same—were a proper mixture of skepticism, fascination and approval. . . . And since everybody else had already agreed, it took a strong individual to stand his ground in opposition." Left undescribed by Kissinger was his role in the sham.

Pursley, who made the trip as Laird's chief military aide, had heard nothing of the proposed invasion in Laos until he got to Saigon. "Abrams was talking about it and he talked as if it was his idea," Pursley says, "and it was not to be a high-risk operation. He came on as if it was a reasonable operation, and laid it on with enough assurance so that Laird came back as a proponent for it." In the spring, Pursley had been disturbed at signs of backchannel communications between the White House and Abrams that excluded Laird from key elements of the Cambodian planning, but any doubts he might have had about Laird's approval of it were now swept away. "In the Secretary of Defense's point of view," Pursley recalls, "when Abrams comes on that strong, we went along with it." Among other things, Abrams had stalwartly supported Vietnamization, and in Laird's eyes he deserved more credit for that than he would ever get. After the failure of the operation in Laos, Pursley says, Laird, still protecting Vietnamization, made it clear to all in the Pentagon that there would be "no recriminations" toward Abrams or any other officers involved.

Thus the ill-fated Laos operation was approved in advance by Nixon, Kissinger, Haig, Laird, and Abrams, a general with a brilliant reputation as a combat leader. Kissinger wrote in his memoirs that he had been among the strongest proponents of the invasion: "I strongly encouraged the concept of a

* In a subsequent written report to Nixon about his trip, Laird quoted Thieu as saying he knew the invasion of Laos would cause some political problems for the White House from critics who would claim that the war was again being widened. Thieu offered Nixon the following public relations advice, Laird said: "He suggested our reply should be that we are widening the peace"— parroting the line Nixon had used in his October 7 ceasefire speech. The tone of Laird's report to Nixon, released under the Freedom of Information Act, was unctuous—the only tone, apparently, that aides were permitted to use with the President. "In retrospect," Laird said, in discussing Vietnamization, "your decisions in 1969 constituted a true watershed. . . . The Nixon Doctrine has taken form. Major, if not virtually incredible, progress had been made."

dry-season offensive in 1971. . . . A campaign to weaken Hanoi's campaign to launch attacks for as long as possible would give us a margin of safety. Faced with the prospect of yearly spoiling offensives, Hanoi might prefer to negotiate." There is no evidence that anyone in the White House conducted a post-mortem to try to learn why all had gone so wrong. In his memoirs, Kissinger disavowed much of the blame by criticizing President Thieu's indecisiveness and demeaning the capability of the South Vietnamese generals. He also suggested to such friendly journalists as the Kalbs that, as they wrote, he "had little enthusiasm for the Laos operation." The after-the-fact posturing was only to keep his public reputation unsullied; he knew he had not been tarnished within the Nixon White House.* No one could go wrong there by advocating more war.

The most compelling reason for Laos had nothing to do with failure or success, but with the reelection of Richard Nixon in 1972. The North Vietnamese had been resupplying at a furious rate through the Ho Chi Minh Trail and it was clear that their goal was an election-year offensive, another Tet that could shatter political chances. Laos thus became a no-lose proposition. Even if the South Vietnamese Army stumbled into a trap and took severe losses, the cost to the North Vietnamese in ammunition and fuel would be great, and would delay their supply plans. The more than 9,000 South Vietnamese soldiers who were killed, wounded, or missing in Lam Son 719 were hostage to Nixon's reelection ambitions, and more cannon fodder for the White House.† In a private press briefing in Washington months later, Kissinger depicted the "strategic" goal of Lam Son 719 as being "to gain as much time as possible for Vietnamization," so that the American troops would be able to leave South Vietnam without "riot or collapse." The interruption to the North Vietnamese supply lines, he said, would deter an enemy offensive for 1971 and 1972. Talk about "strategic" goals was spurious; Laos was a tactical operation, a short-term affair designed primarily to strengthen the chances for Thieu's reelection in the fall of 1971 and for Nixon's in 1972.

The firestorm over Cambodia had taught Nixon and Kissinger a lot about how to expand the war. In January and February of 1971 there were no dramatic presidential speeches, no early morning visits to demonstrators, no White House staff resignations. And some of the immediate advantages of the Vietnamization program became clear. There were no photographs of American GIs being shot at or shooting inside one more foreign country, no television footage of National Guardsmen shooting protesters in America. Lam Son 719

* Haig had his own villain: Laird. He had been sent by Nixon and Kissinger to monitor the operation in Laos and saw the basic problem as a lack of aggressive American leadership. In an interview for Michael Maclear's *The Ten Thousand Day War*, a history of the war published in 1981, Haig complained about "our preoccupation with the Vietnamization concept. . . . And the American leadership on the ground, I am sure directed by the Secretary of Defense, was to be one of benign overwatch when it should have been very active management, and had that been applied, it would have been a successful operation." Once again Laird wasn't obeying White House dicta.

† Senator Eugene J. McCarthy, the antiwar candidate for the Democratic presidential nomination in 1968, was by this time publicly describing Nixon's Vietnamization policy as merely aimed at "changing the colors of the corpses" in the war.

was blacked out, officially censored for the American press in Saigon—allegedly by the South Vietnamese—for national security reasons. The South Vietnamese mobilized for a week on the Laotian border, and the Washington press corps, carefully provided with information by the White House, was permitted to conclude that an invasion was in the works. When the troops finally crossed the border into Laos, on February 8, it came as no surprise; there was no spectacular announcement as in Cambodia, and no reports of captured enemy headquarters. On the day of the formal invasion, Nixon released a lengthy and generally praiseworthy White House position paper on ecology and the environment. He also taped a statement on the environment for distribution to television stations that began with a quotation from T. S. Eliot's *Murder in the Cathedral:* "Clear the air! Clean the sky! Wash the wind!"*

By early March the Laotian invasion was a shambles, and the press was no longer under the control of the White House. American television viewers watched with growing horror as retreating South Vietnamese soldiers were shown clinging desperately to the landing skids of American evacuation helicopters. The South Vietnamese fled in panic, a badly defeated army, and they did so in front of the cameras. Many soldiers seized bandages from wounded colleagues and, with their feigned injuries, were among the first to be evacuated. Word of such malingering passed quickly among the American helicopter crews and medical personnel, and they reacted badly. Stephen W. Genetti, an Army corpsman assigned to the 64th Medical Group headquarters in Danang, recalls what took place all too often: "Some of our boys would find these fake injuries and they gave them real ones." One of Genetti's colleagues, in rage and panic, used a long screwdriver to injure those he found uninjured. Sometimes more direct means were taken. Genetti says, "We had to eliminate some of these"—that is, throw them, alive, out of the helicopters.†

The leadership in Hanoi fully understood the significance of Lam Son 719. "It was a big defeat," Nguyen Co Thach said. "You see, Lam Son was the test—to have the Saigon army go alone against the Revolutionary forces [of North Vietnam]. But it was the first test and the biggest failure; so it was the defeat of Vietnamization." Until the Laos invasion, Thach said, Hanoi's leadership had been worried about what seemed to be the steady progress of the

---

* Copyright 1935 by Harcourt Brace Jovanovich, Inc.; renewed 1963 by T. S. Eliot. Reprinted by permission of the publisher. Daniel Ellsberg, in his 1972 *Papers on the War*, noted that Eliot's lines did not deal with the physical environment but were "a chorus of horror chanted as murder is being done." Ellsberg reproduced the passage:

> Clear the air! clean the sky! wash the
>   wind! take stone from stone and wash
>   them.
> The land is foul, the water is foul, our
>   beasts and ourselves defiled with blood.
> A rain of blood has blinded my eyes.

† Genetti and his colleagues at the 64th Medical Group learned of the invasion of Laos a month in advance, when they were ordered to reopen the Khe Sanh fire base, near the Laotian border, and set up a medical station there. "That was like sending the North Vietnamese a telegram," Genetti says. "We knew the South Vietnamese were going in, and if we knew, the NVA [North Vietnamese Army] damn sure knew it."

Saigon army under Vietnamization: "We were sure that Vietnamization wouldn't succeed, but we had to see whether it would or not. We were sure because if, with the presence of the American Army, they couldn't succeed, why should they now succeed without the Americans?"

After Lam Son, Thach said, his government concluded that the Saigon army would not be able to defeat the North Vietnamese and Vietcong. "For Vietnamization to succeed," he added, "there had to be four things: First, mutual withdrawal of foreign forces and a ceasefire. Second, the successful improvement of the South Vietnamese Army. Third, destruction of the Ho Chi Minh Trail and the sanctuaries, and fourth, a stopping of the resupply of the North. If one fails, all fail."

By early 1971, Thach said, there had been no mutual withdrawal, Lam Son had raised questions about the Vietnamization program, movement down the Ho Chi Minh Trail had not been stopped, and the supplies of arms and food to the North from its allies in China and the Soviet Union continued to flow. Lam Son, he said, made North Vietnam's politburo more determined to resist a political compromise in the South.*

Nixon and Kissinger spent the spring of 1971 insisting publicly that the Laos operation had been a major victory. Nixon indeed may have believed it. On March 22, in a television interview, he said that the Laos invasion showed that the South Vietnamese Army could "hack it" and added, quoting General Abrams, that the majority of South Vietnamese soldiers were coming out of Laos "with higher confidence, with greater morale, despite the fact that they have taken some very severe losses. . . . We have now concluded . . . that the South Vietnamese have now passed a milestone in their development." What Kissinger believed was, as usual, much less clear. At a meeting with reporters in late March, as both he and Nixon were striving to mount a public relations campaign over Laos, Kissinger claimed success. Within a few minutes, however, he grew defensive and, aware that he was not to be quoted, told the reporters: "Look, we didn't have to do this. We knew there were other options that would have involved less risk and less cost, but this was the most effective step we could take. We knew what the reaction would be here, in the press and so on. This war is a tragedy; it has made everyone completely emotional. . . . The malaise in this country is so terrible—the best people have had it with

* When I went to Hanoi in March of 1972 for the *New York Times*, I was taken immediately to the National Military Museum, where much of the exhibit space had been given over to a reconstruction of Lam Son 719. The battle was viewed as an epic turning point in the war, second only to Tet. Dozens of combat photographs were on display, as well as hundreds of captured artillery shells—all bearing American manufacturing marks—seemingly undamaged heavy guns, and jeeps and other vehicles. North Vietnamese officials said that American helicopter pilots responsible for evacuating South Vietnamese troops during the retreat from Laos in March had resorted to applying heavy coats of grease to their landing skids in an effort to prevent the Vietnamese from clinging. The battle was seen then—and it should be remembered that my visit came before Hanoi's successful spring offensive of 1972—as the ultimate defeat of Vietnamization. Museum officials claimed that North Vietnamese troops shot down or damaged some 700 American helicopters during the operation and killed or wounded 23,400 South Vietnamese troops. Those figures were, of course, inflated, but no more so than the official number of North Vietnamese killed or wounded claimed by the South Vietnamese—put more modestly at 19,360. The South Vietnamese also officially claimed that they had destroyed more than 176,000 tons of North Vietnamese ammunition stockpiled along the Ho Chi Minh Trail; the credibility of that statistic was not enhanced by the fact that it jumped by 162,000 tons during the last weeks of the operation, when the South Vietnamese troops were in their panicked retreat.

the war. And now they are trying to end it, no matter what the rationale. . . . They just want it ended."

In his memoirs, Kissinger described the Laos operation as a "watershed," but only because it was the last major offensive operation involving the direct participation of Americans. Lam Son 719 did not achieve its main goal, he wrote, which was to prevent Hanoi from mounting its election-year offensive in 1972, and it revealed many "lingering deficiencies" among the South Vietnamese commanders: "In retrospect, I have even come to doubt whether the South Vietnamese ever really understood what we were trying to accomplish." No such doubts were expressed to Richard Nixon. In his memoirs, Nixon quoted Kissinger as telling him in late March, "If I had known before it started that it was going to come out exactly the way it did, I would still have gone ahead with it."

Years later, the Pentagon asked a former South Vietnamese Army division commander, Major General Nguyen Duy Hinh, who fled Vietnam after the fall of Saigon in 1975, to compile an exhaustive after-action report.* General Hinh concluded that the troops who participated in the mission "almost without exception . . . did not believe they were victorious." The South Vietnamese had met with much more resistance than expected, Hinh said—including North Vietnamese tank forces, which were not known to be in the area—and they did not achieve their basic objective of destroying Hanoi's main stockpiles.

Hinh was able to describe only a few positive aspects of the Laos invasion. One infantry unit, the First Infantry Division, lived up to its reputation as the leading combat team in the South Vietnamese Army, and coordination between some of the artillery units supplying support for the infantry teams was "extremely flexible and effective." Many senior South Vietnamese combat officers, going into battle for the first time without their American advisers nearby, handled themselves "quite professionally," Hinh noted. But he could not escape the overall assessment: "In summary, Lam Son 719 was a bloody field exercise. . . . [Thousands of] soldiers and millions of dollars worth of valuable equipment and matériel were sacrificed." The most profound repercussion of Lam Son 719, Hinh wrote, was found among the civilian population of the South: "Despite official claims of a 'big victory' and mass demonstrations to celebrate . . . the people still were shocked by the severe losses incurred. Perhaps the greatest emotional shock of all was the unprecedented fact that the [South Vietnamese] forces had to leave behind in Laos a substantial number of their dead and wounded. This came as a horrendous trauma for those unlucky families who, in their traditional devotion to the cult of the dead and their attachment to the living, were condemned to live in perpetual sorrow and doubt. It was a violation of beliefs and familial piety that Vietnamese sentiment would never forget and forgive."

* The report, made available through a Freedom of Information request, was prepared under contract for the Army's Office of Military History.

24

PROTECTING
THE SECRETS

BY EARLY 1971, Henry Kissinger's daily life as national security adviser had a staggering complexity. There were the bad secrets, the continuing effort to undermine Salvador Allende in Chile and the continuing White House wiretaps. There were the good secrets, such as the backchannel negotiations with China and the Soviet Union that would lead to breakthroughs—without any State Department involvement—before the year was out. And there were the routine secrets, the enormous flow of documents and cables that Kissinger and his staff handled as the national security adviser expanded the influence of his office. Even in early 1971, the full sweep of Kissinger's authority was still unknown to much of the public; some newspaper correspondents were still capable of believing that Rogers had a major role to play in the foreign affairs of the Nixon Administration.*

As the flow of secrets intensified, so did Kissinger's concern about the security of his own office. His telephones were still repeatedly swept for signs of wiretapping, but Kissinger insisted that such surveillance not be placed on a routine basis with any single agency. Special Secret Service, CIA, FBI, or National Security Agency teams would be summoned at random and on short notice to inspect the telephones. This raised the inevitable question: Who was the enemy? David Halperin, the former Navy officer who became Kissinger's personal aide in late 1970, recalls Kissinger's constant fear that he was being wiretapped. And yet, asked why Kissinger did not simply assign the FBI to monitor his phones, Halperin responded: "Who trusted Hoover?" Rumors about Kissinger's paranoia were rife among the NSC staff. One senior NSC aide remembers being told that Kissinger's office telephones were swept immediately after every meeting with Ambassador Dobrynin. He was convinced it was so.†

---

* Many reporters and bureau chiefs knew of Kissinger's primacy and his hatred for Rogers, but they paid a price for their insight. Max Frankel, concluding a *New York Times* series on Nixon's foreign policy in late January 1971, correctly reported that Nixon and Kissinger were in firm control of all aspects of policy making. Frankel was also a conduit for much White House misinformation in the dispatch. For example, he reported that Nixon did not "act on—or even betray—his private fear and sense of challenge when Chile elected a Marxist government last fall." Frankel also described the SALT talks with the Soviet Union as having been briefed with "extreme care" to America's allies in Europe, at a time when not even Gerard Smith, the head of the American delegation, was aware of what was really going on.

† Believing the worst seemed to be a widespread phenomenon among the NSC staff. Andrew J.

By his own account, the first months of 1971 were dark ones for Richard Nixon. The congressional elections in November had not produced a Republican triumph. Vietnam was still politically damaging, despite the unilateral withdrawal of more than 250,000 American GIs. In his memoirs, Nixon spoke of early 1971 as "the lowest point of my first term as President. The problems we confronted were so overwhelming and so apparently impervious to anything we could do to change them that it seemed possible that I might not even be *nominated* for re-election in 1972 [emphasis added]." There was much basis for his concern. By early spring, the Gallup poll reported that Nixon's midterm popularity had sunk to the lowest level of any President's since Harry Truman. And the Harris poll showed him losing ground to Edmund G. Muskie, the Democratic senator from Maine, in the early months of the year. George Wallace, the Alabama governor, was another potential headache. He was expected to wage a strong fight for the presidency in 1972 and cut deeply into Nixon's strength among southern and conservative Democrats.

Nixon found succor that winter in his national security adviser—as well as a path to reelection. Political success would lie not in Vietnam but with Communist China and the Soviet Union. In early December, the Chinese climaxed months of public and private gestures by secretly inviting Nixon to send a personal envoy to Peking. Nixon and Kissinger, of course, kept the message to themselves. A breakthrough in China meant everything: more leverage against the Soviets in the SALT talks, more leverage against the North Vietnamese in the secret peace negotiations, and a political triumph. A few weeks after the message from China, Kissinger won Nixon's approval for backchannel negotiations with Dobrynin that might bring a private agreement on SALT and also get the White House more involved in the ongoing four-power talks in Bonn with the Soviet Union, France, and England. Those talks, which were initiated by Willy Brandt, the West German Chancellor, were aimed at finally resolving the Berlin crisis by legitimizing access rights for West Berliners and establishing the city's formal ties to the Federal Republic. If there was to be a diplomatic resolution of the Berlin problem and a breakthrough in SALT before 1972, however, the White House wanted to be sure that it, and not Rogers' State Department, received full credit.

By early 1971, Kissinger wrote, he had been granted free rein in the backchannels by Nixon: "[W]e had talked at length almost every day; we had gone through all crises in close cooperation. He tended more and more to delegate the tactical management of foreign policy to me. . . . He did not believe that the conductor need be seen to play every instrument in the orchestra."

The bureaucracy was the most important part of this orchestra, and Kissin-

---

Hamilton, formerly a reporter for the defunct New York *Herald-Tribune,* joined the staff in 1970 to handle NATO and force-structure issues. These were areas of minor significance to Kissinger, and Hamilton thus had little direct contact with him—a common situation for many staff aides. One afternoon, he bumped into Kissinger returning from his lunch, surrounded by the usual retinue of Secret Service men. "I said, 'Hello, Mr. Kissinger.' I had a beard and he didn't recognize me. He looked startled." Hamilton thought nothing more of it until, months later, as he was briefing an interagency meeting, Kissinger interrupted to say, "My Secret Service agent nearly shot that man." Hamilton realized that Kissinger was joking, but he also suspected there was an element of truth in the remark. Dismayed at the "bad atmosphere" inside the NSC staff, Hamilton resigned in 1971.

ger turned to an old standby, Morton Halperin's revised National Security Council system. By early 1971, NSC staff aides had long realized that Kissinger was using the Halperin plan to create make-work for State and Pentagon officials that got them out of the way. "What we did was kill them with NSSMs," one NSC aide recalls. Kissinger had given up dealing seriously with such studies, but the secret negotiations with China and Russia called for more analyses than his staff could manage. He ordered State and Defense to prepare elaborate studies of policy options that, unbeknownst to them, were no longer options but policy. "The control of interdepartmental machinery . . . enabled me to use the bureaucracy without revealing our purposes," Kissinger wrote. "I would introduce as planning topics issues that were actually being secretly negotiated." Kissinger blamed the President for such deviousness: "These extraordinary procedures were essentially made necessary by a President who neither trusted his Cabinet nor was willing to give them direct orders. Nixon feared leaks and shrank from imposing discipline."

Nixon and Kissinger were conducting the orchestra together, of course, as they had been for two years. In mid-January, Kissinger, acceding to Harvard's rule barring its faculty from extended sabbatical leaves, resigned his tenured professorship. Nixon issued a public letter of gratitude in response: "Frankly, I cannot imagine what the Government would be like without you. Your wise counsel and strong support over the past two years have meant a great deal to me."

There is no reason to doubt that the President meant what he said. And yet a month later, as the South Vietnamese invasion of Laos was beginning to flounder, Nixon decided to install the infamous taping system in the White House; he did so, according to Haldeman's memoirs, largely because of Henry Kissinger. "Nixon realized rather early in their relationship that he badly needed a complete account of all that they discussed . . ." Haldeman wrote. "He knew that Henry was keeping a log of those talks, a luxury in which the President didn't have time to indulge. And he knew that Henry's view on a particular subject was sometimes subject to change without notice." Haldeman wrote that only he, of all the senior advisers to the President, was to know about the system. Kissinger, so warmly praised in January, was to be tape recorded in February.

Kissinger apparently did not learn of the taping until May 1973, along with other senior members of the Watergate-besieged White House staff, and once again was outraged at someone else's successful use of his methods. Even in early 1971, there was little about Nixon's personality that Kissinger did not know, understand, and emulate. David Halperin, who monitored many of Kissinger's telephone conversations with the President in this period, describes Nixon as "swinging from trust to lack of trust" in his dealing with Kissinger—a description that perfectly matches Kissinger's attitude toward Nixon. If the President coped with their unstable relationship by secretly tape recording all conversations in his office and on his telephone, Kissinger coped by tape recording *his* telephone talks with the President—and with everybody else—and by continuing to smuggle important national security documents and papers to Nelson Rockefeller's estate in New York. Both men soon accumulated far too much—in writing and on tape—on each other.

Kissinger had yet another means of insuring his importance to Richard Nixon; he continued to try to exclude his staff from any contact with the President. He was able to do so, with one exception: Alexander Haig. Haig's relationship with Nixon had become close because of the Cambodian invasion, when Haig was outspoken in the White House in defense of the invasion. His militarism and his hardline approach to foreign policy problems, which Kissinger had seized upon as a shield, were attractive and reassuring to Nixon. Haig began appearing more frequently on Nixon's appointments calendar in early April of 1970; there were days—when Kissinger was also in Washington—when Haig would spend more time alone with the President. David Halperin recalls with a visible shudder the first time the President directly telephoned Haig: "There was more tension than I can ever recall in that office," he said. Kissinger was in his outer office, conferring with his secretary, Julie Pineau, when Nixon's direct line rang. "Julie picked it up," Halperin says, "and Henry started walking back to his office [Kissinger always took the President's calls in privacy]. Julie said, 'It's for you, General Haig.' Haig went to his office and Henry stood by the door [of Haig's office] as Haig and Nixon talked." After a moment or two, Kissinger resignedly "walked into his office and shut the door. He stayed in there for hours." Haig, meanwhile, was "drenched in sweat" by the time he hung up. Halperin is convinced that neither Haig nor Kissinger discussed the call that day. "From Henry's point of view, someone else now had access to the President," Halperin says—and thus Kissinger had suffered a loss of personal power.

By late 1970, Haig had become the indispensable man on the National Security Council staff, the man whom everyone else had to see to get position papers and cables approved. Kissinger, caught up with backchannel negotiations and his eternal cajolery of the press, stopped even pretending to administer day-to-day operations. What began after Cambodia as a delegation of power to Haig became an abdication. Young men such as Chester A. Crocker, an African expert with a doctorate from Johns Hopkins University, were added to the NSC staff without even a perfunctory interview by Kissinger.* Haig moved quickly to set up firm command. Jonathan T. Howe, a bright Navy officer who had earned a doctorate in international relations at Tufts University, was recruited to serve as his personal aide, and Richard T. Kennedy, a soon-to-be-retired Army colonel, became his main operative. It was Kennedy, fervently loyal to Haig and his values, who controlled the flow of documents and papers to Haig, just as Haig had once controlled it for Kissinger. New staff members soon learned that nothing could get to Haig's desk, let alone to Kissinger's, without first being cleared by Colonel Kennedy.

Kissinger was aware of the loss of control, and made at least one effort to

* Crocker, after being hired to replace Morris as the NSC staff expert on Africa, was unceremoniously shoved into an office in the Executive Office Building that was shared by Rodman, Kissinger's personal amanuensis, and Kissinger's long-time friend, Nancy Maginnes. Maginnes, then working for Nelson Rockefeller, was being provided with free office space. Crocker met Kissinger for the first time only when he "came to see Nancy and made some jokes before we were introduced."

do something about it. In early 1971 he urged Laurence Lynn, then teaching at Stanford University's graduate school of business, to write an "Eyes Only" proposal for redesigning the functions of the NSC staff, just as Morton Halperin had done in late 1968. Kissinger made it clear, Lynn remembers, that if he would rejoin the staff he could create his own supervisory position. "Henry knew what was happening in the Executive Office Building. He knew what Haig was doing behind his back and he knew he was letting it get away from him." Kissinger also remembered, obviously, Lynn's dislike for Haig. "The thing that Henry stressed to me," Lynn says, "was his fear that Haig would take it over. He didn't think Haig was that smart; he thought he was an ideologue. He told me he needed someone who was strong enough to stand up to Haig." Kissinger told Lynn that if he returned, "I could, in effect, run the whole substantive side of the staff."

Despite the enticing offer, Lynn balked. He'd had enough of the bad smell in Washington. But he did write a four-page critique of the NSC staff system, urging Kissinger to create two deputies—one for operations and another for policy evaluation and analysis—as a means of avoiding overreliance on Haig. Having made it clear he would not take either of these jobs, Lynn heard no more from Kissinger.

The possibility exists that Kissinger had no intention of making any changes and sought Lynn's advice simply to flatter him and insure that he would not begin to talk.* Despite his doubts over Haig's growing influence, Kissinger could not afford to turn openly on Haig, just as Nixon would not be able to turn on Kissinger; each knew too much about the other. Kissinger knew that Haig was a double-dealer who had ingratiated himself with Nixon, Haldeman, and other senior aides by savaging Kissinger behind his back and spying on him. But Kissinger also knew that Haig's expertise on the Pentagon was invaluable if he and Nixon were to maintain their ability to circumvent Melvin Laird and Robert Pursley and directly order military action in the Middle East or Southeast Asia. Haig could also be trusted, as he had demonstrated during the CIA's efforts in Chile, to execute orders in the backchannel conscientiously and discreetly. Haig, for his part, was aware of the complications in the Nixon-Kissinger relationship in a way no one else in the White House could be, since he constantly heard each man's complaints about the other. Nixon did enjoy the savaging of Kissinger that went on in his office, Haig knew, but the President also realized that among his aides only Kissinger had the intellectual stamina and the nerve to successfully conduct simultaneous backchannel negotiations with the Soviets and the Chinese. Still a one-star general, Haig understood in early 1971 that future promotions lay with Kissinger as much as with the President.

Kissinger and Haig also shared knowledge about the White House wiretapping that, they knew, would cause serious—perhaps fatal—problems for themselves and the Nixon presidency if made public. The wiretapping must have

* By 1971, Kissinger had developed what amounted to a pattern of flattering his former aides. Thus, bumping into William Watts and his wife at a Washington party, he told Watts's wife that her husband had "behaved with great dignity and honor." Watts was pleased, despite his lingering suspicions about Kissinger's motives. Later, after Kissinger became Secretary of State, he unfailingly sent Roger Morris personal notes of praise for his commentaries on foreign affairs—some of them exceedingly critical of Kissinger—when they appeared in magazines such as the *New Republic*.

been particularly sensitive for Kissinger in early 1971, because the main target of the White House program, Morton Halperin, was a constant reminder to Nixon, Mitchell, and Haldeman of Kissinger's poor judgment in initially filling his office with liberals and Democrats who were not loyal to Nixon and his policies. Kissinger was saying little by early 1971, at least to the NSC staff, about Halperin and the three close aides who had resigned over Cambodia. But Haig could be irrational about them. Watts, Lake, and Morris were "traitors" to Kissinger and the NSC staff, Haig told one NSC newcomer in a rage, and Halperin was a "Communist." Haig had a special reason for being exceedingly angry about Halperin; he knew what the former Kissinger aide was saying about him on the telephone. In one conversation with a former colleague, for example, Halperin referred to Haig as a "blabber mouth who hears everything . . . all phone conversations to the President and everything."

The wiretapping remained an important program for Kissinger and Haig through early 1971, although both men later denied any significant involvement after May 1970, when Nixon ordered Haldeman to assume full responsibility. Kissinger no longer received direct "Eyes Only" letters from J. Edgar Hoover summarizing important conversations, but he was still very much in the flow. The conduit was Haig, who continued to maintain the NSC's wiretap files and to visit FBI headquarters to read verbatim transcripts of conversations. William Sullivan, in charge of the wiretap program for Hoover, told the Senate Foreign Relations Committee in 1974 that Haig had visited his office "about 12 to 18 times between May, 1969 and February, 1971," when the wiretaps were turned off at Hoover's request. Sullivan, whose memory seemed to grow more vague every time he was ordered to testify, also told the committee that his estimate of the number of Haig's visits was a "guess," and could be off by as much as ten visits. Asked specifically whether Haig continued to visit his office to read transcripts after May 1970, Sullivan said, "Yes, he did come to my office after May, 1970."*

Just why Haig and Kissinger were so adamant in denying involvement with the wiretap program after that date is not clear. Whatever moral or legal stigma they incurred would not be mitigated by their having stopped midway. In an Oval Office tape recording supplied to the Watergate Special Prosecutor's Office in 1975 but not made public, Nixon briefly discussed Hoover's desire in early 1971 to stop the taping and said the taps were "knocked off after the hullabaloo out there." The Special Prosecutor's Office was unable to learn what that "hullabaloo" was all about.†

* Attorneys for the Watergate Special Prosecution Force later came to doubt that Haig had visited the FBI building as often as Sullivan suggested. The prosecutors were unable to find memoranda noting each of Haig's visits; such important missions, they believed, would have been recorded somewhere in the files. Another argument against the extended series of visits was their awkwardness. It was unlikely, given Haig's growing prominence in official Washington, that he would have been able to visit Sullivan's office regularly without someone raising questions.

† The Senate Foreign Relations Committee looked into the Hoover decision in late 1973, before its hearings on Kissinger's nomination as Secretary of State, and concluded that the wiretaps were stopped shortly before Hoover was to testify before Congress at the annual FBI appropriations hearings. Hoover traditionally discontinued wiretaps before congressional hearings, the Senate report said, so "he could report minimum taps in effect if he were questioned." Nine White House wiretaps were in existence as of February 10, 1971, the cutoff date. Another factor in the decision to cut off the wiretaps may have been the chronic Nixon anxiety over Edward M. Kennedy, chairman of the Senate Judiciary Subcommittee on Administrative Practice. On February 5, the

The wiretap on Halperin's home telephone, which continued for twenty-one months, was in many ways the most significant. Halperin, no liberal when he joined Kissinger's staff, had become increasingly outspoken in his opposition to Nixon's and Kissinger's Vietnam policies since leaving the White House. By mid-1970, he was a member of the foreign policy group advising Senator Muskie, the Democrat who was considered Nixon's strongest challenger for the presidency in 1972. FBI summaries sent to Haldeman in the fall and early winter of 1970 showed that Halperin was heavily involved in Democratic and anti-Nixon politicking. On October 14, for example, Hoover told Haldeman that Halperin had discussed publishing an article on the workings of the National Security Council with a reporter for *Der Spiegel,* the German weekly news magazine—a prospect that must have filled Kissinger with dread. A few weeks later, Halperin published a trenchant analysis of Vietnam policies in the *New York Times.* Nixon was refusing to force a political settlement upon Saigon, Halperin wrote, and his Vietnamization policy "will at best lead to an indefinite presence in Vietnam of thousands of American troops. It could well drive the President to massive escalation, the mining of Haiphong Harbor and saturation bombing of North Vietnam." Such escalation, the cornerstone of the 1969 November ultimatum, was still a constant subject of debate among Nixon, Kissinger, and their key aides. The men at the top in the White House had to conclude that Halperin had somehow learned of the 1969 Duck Hook planning. Halperin's essay undoubtedly helped insure that the wiretap on Winston Lord, the former Halperin protégé who had become one of Kissinger's closest aides after Cambodia, would remain active until the very end. Six days after the Halperin piece appeared, Hoover reported to Haldeman that Halperin had been in frequent contact with Leslie Gelb, his former Pentagon deputy whom he had rejoined at Brookings; the two, Hoover said, had discussed a Muskie advisory group meeting on "China policy." The FBI report came to the White House just as Kissinger's secret contacts with China through the Pakistani government were reaching fruition. In December came another FBI report on Halperin, this one dealing with a visit to Moscow that Senator Muskie was planning. The trip had been recommended, so Halperin told Gelb, by Averell Harriman, Nixon's nemesis, who was to go with Muskie. Harriman so alarmed the White House that the FBI was instructed to report verbatim every conversation in which his name was overheard.

On December 30, another FBI report on Halperin and Gelb came to Haldeman: Robert Pursley, Laird's military assistant, who had been promoted to brigadier general in late 1969 and was still being wiretapped at his home, had sent some papers over to Clifford's law office. Gelb told Halperin that Clifford had asked him to look over "about 20 pieces of paper that Pursley sent over." Gelb, Halperin, and Pursley had worked together in the Pentagon during the last years of the Johnson Administration, and also shared detailed knowledge

subcommittee requested FBI statistics on the number of wiretaps that had been authorized since June 1968. The information supplied did not include the White House wiretaps. Charles Colson dates this period—when the White House wiretaps were cut off—as the time when Nixon began to demand a special internal police unit. By June 1971, when the *New York Times* published the Pentagon Papers, Colson recalls, "Nixon had been asking Haldeman, Ehrlichman, and Kissinger for four months to get an intelligence and operational capability in the White House." A few days later, Colson heard Nixon complain bitterly to Haldeman about his failure to "get this capability in place."

of the conclusions of the Pentagon Papers. The Papers, a 7,000-page top-secret study of the history of America's involvement in Vietnam, had been under-taken in 1967 at the request of Robert McNamara and assigned to Gelb, then deputy director of the Pentagon's policy planning staff.*

The Halperin wiretap reports were useful not only to Haldeman, who main-tained strong control over all White House political operations, but also to Kissinger, who learned through them that approaches to China and Russia were being discussed by Muskie's advisers and that Halperin was still in touch with at least one NSC staff member. In early November, the FBI reported that Winston Lord had made uncomplimentary remarks about Kissinger and Nixon on his home telephone. A summary published by the House Impeachment Committee did not give details, but Lord was still in touch with Morton Hal-perin, and, according to Halperin's wiretap logs, would occasionally share some gossip with him. David Halperin, Kissinger's personal aide, remembers this period as one of "general paranoia" inside Kissinger's office. A steady flow of FBI reports was hand carried into the office by Russell Ash, the NSC official in charge of staff security, and Kissinger and Haig each carefully read them.

"Ash would come in with a folder," David Halperin says, "wait outside, and then go in and out of Henry's office with the folder in his hands." Halperin never learned what was in the folders, he says, but assumed the Ash docu-ments had to do with leaks of classified information. In 1974 testimony to the Senate Foreign Relations Committee, Kissinger repeatedly sought to minimize his interest in such unseemly issues. "After May of 1970," he said, "I had no basis for knowing whether a tap had been initiated or was continuing. . . . I construed my instructions from Mr. Haldeman to mean that my tangential connection with the program was being terminated." In mid-October 1970, Kissinger testified, when a second wiretap was authorized for Helmut Sonnen-feldt, who was then Kissinger's closest friend on the NSC staff, his role was

* Gelb, who taught a foreign policy course at Harvard in the early 1960s, immediately tried to involve Kissinger as a consultant. The two had been colleagues for years. Gelb earned his doctorate in 1964 at Harvard's Government Department, was Kissinger's assistant there, and helped teach his Defense Policy seminar. He had worked as a Senate aide before joining the Pentagon's Office of International Security Affairs in 1966, which was then one of the most powerful offices in the Defense Department. The office was headed by Assistant Secretary of Defense John T. McNaughton, a former Harvard Law School professor (McNaughton was killed in an airplane crash in 1967). Ellsberg had served earlier as McNaughton's special assistant, a position Halperin had also held. Gelb, suddenly handed the responsibility for the Pentagon Papers, instinctively reached out for Kissinger. "It was utterly natural to think of him," Gelb says. "He was my professor at Harvard and I wanted somebody outside the system to get involved." Kissinger spent a day in Gelb's office discussing the project with Gelb and Halperin, and, although he decided against joining Gelb's staff, he maintained a special status with the project. Later in 1967, Kissinger began his first negotiations with Hanoi through the two Frenchmen in Paris, as part of the Johnson Administra-tion's secret efforts to end the war. As a matter of necessity, he was later given access by Gelb to the most sensitive volumes in the study, those dealing with previous negotiations with the North Vietnamese. These studies were considered so secret that many of Gelb's thirty-six-member staff were denied access to them. When Ellsberg decided to make the Pentagon Papers public in 1971, he did not release any of the diplomatic volumes and, as of mid-1983, some portions still remain classified. Ellsberg and others presumably withheld those volumes because many non-U.S. citizens had been involved in trying to negotiate an end to the war, and public disclosure of their activities might have embarrassed them. (The diplomatic volumes, ironically, were routinely available to newspaper reporters covering Ellsberg's trial in 1973, but were later placed under court seal.)

even more tangential.* "[I]t is hard to imagine the flood of material that goes across my desk. I am apt to look at something and say this is for somebody else and throw it into my out basket. Most of these documents are not noted for extraordinary precision." The less than precise document in question in Sonnenfeldt's case, however, was a summary of a wiretap on the Israeli Embassy in which Richard N. Perle, a foreign policy aide to Senator Jackson, was overheard discussing classified information that had been supplied to him by someone on the National Security Council staff.

Haldeman and Nixon must have hit the roof. In a telephone call to Hoover on October 15, 1970, Haldeman invoked the name of Henry Kissinger in asking for another wiretap on Sonnenfeldt. Hoover, in a subsequent memorandum to William Sullivan and other FBI officials, quoted Haldeman as explaining that Kissinger—perhaps seeking to ward off a Nixon explosion—had handed him the FBI wiretap on the Israeli Embassy and requested that the FBI be assigned to determine which NSC staff member was in contact with Richard Perle. Kissinger had to realize that Haldeman and Hoover would suspect Sonnenfeldt, who was known from previous wiretaps to have close ties to the Israelis as well as to Perle. Sonnenfeldt had been repeatedly investigated by the FBI for other suspected leaks early in his State Department career, and Kissinger, as he told the Senate Committee, was aware that Sonnenfeldt had "been the subject of a malicious campaign by a group of individuals who had been out to get him for a long time." But Haig was now part of that group, too—another fact Kissinger surely knew. Sonnenfeldt had been among Haig's early rivals in 1969 for the job as assistant to Kissinger; that, plus Sonnenfeldt's continued closeness to Kissinger—despite the mistreatment Kissinger handed out—was enough for Haig to mark him permanently as an enemy.†

At a minimum, then, Kissinger had to know that Haig was still actively plotting against Sonnenfeldt as of midsummer 1970; he also had to know the consequences of turning over the Israeli Embassy wiretap to Haldeman, who would certainly link Sonnenfeldt, a Jew, to the intercepted conversation. Kissinger was, in essence, turning in his closest remaining friend on his staff. It must have been a painful moment. Kissinger handled questions about the Sonnenfeldt wiretap from the Senate Foreign Relations Committee in his usual fashion. "I have no recollection of this at all," he testified. "All that could have happened is that the FBI sent over something off a tap on the Israeli Embassy which I did not think was relevant to my concern and on which I

* Sonnenfeldt was first wiretapped May 12, 1969, in the wake of the May 9 *New York Times* report on the B-52 bombing of Cambodia. That wiretap was removed after five weeks.

† Earlier in 1970, Haig had sought out Donald Lesh, Sonnenfeldt's former NSC aide who was then working on Capitol Hill, and urged him to come to a meeting with Kissinger. Lesh went to the White House but found only Haig waiting. "Sonnenfeldt's got to go," Lesh recalls Haig's exclaiming. "Henry wants you to come back to take over the European area. We can't do this right from the start," Haig added. "You'd come back in about six months. Hal will be gone and you'll be the man." Lesh was tempted, but only briefly. He decided to turn down the proposal in a letter to Kissinger but realized that he had no evidence Kissinger even knew of the offer. Lesh decided to "sandbag" Haig, and on July 24 sent a courteous letter of rejection to Kissinger, pointedly noting that he had been "very flattered by the invitation recently extended to me on your behalf by Al Haig . . ." Lesh heard no more but, describing the incident later, concluded that it could well "have been another of Al's machinations." If so, Kissinger did nothing about it.

wrote, 'Give this to Haldeman.' " The committee members apparently accepted that explanation at face value.*

Kissinger's handling of the Sonnenfeldt wiretap epitomized his attitude toward such eavesdropping after two years in the White House. He was still very much a Nixon team player, but far more aware than anyone else of the public relations disaster that could result if the wiretapping ever became known. It was clear by late 1970 and early 1971 that the wiretaps had little to do with national security. There had been no significant leaks of highly classified information in 1970; publication of the Pentagon Papers was yet to come. Far more significant was the fact that some of those who were still being wiretapped in 1971 were now dealing not in national security secrets but in presidential politics. Halperin and Lake had become deeply involved in Muskie's foreign policy planning; through Halperin's wiretap, the White House was also learning a great deal about Leslie Gelb's political activities. The continuing wiretap on Lake was particularly ironic, since Lake had been one of the few on the NSC staff to have good reason to suspect the wiretapping of Halperin. Kissinger and Haig must have had similar thoughts: Would Lake tell? Wiretapping him was one means of finding out. Equally difficult to explain would be the continuing wiretaps on Pursley at the Pentagon and Richard Pederson and William Sullivan at State. None had been even remotely linked to a significant national security leak, and all were close associates of Henry Kissinger's key competitors inside the bureaucracy. Two journalists were also among those wiretapped until February 1971, but for differing reasons. William Beecher, the *New York Times*'s expert on strategic military issues, was perhaps the one reporter capable of penetrating the backchannel negotiations with the Soviets. But how could a wiretap be justified in terms of what a reporter *might* do? Beecher was not wiretapped until May 1970, fully a year after he wrote the B-52 bombing story that helped trigger the wiretap program. The other journalist, Henry Brandon of the London *Sunday Times,* was a mainstay on the Washington social scene and a friend of many of Kissinger's newly won friends in Georgetown. When Brandon was first wiretapped, in late May of 1969, it served multiple purposes: appeasing Hoover, Haldeman, and others in the White House who saw Brandon as a dangerous liberal and potential foreign spy, and

* David Halperin recalls that Kissinger "knew Sonnenfeldt was a double agent" in terms of his personal loyalty, a colleague and friend who was capable of ridiculing Kissinger with other White House aides behind his back. Kissinger in turn seemed to get pleasure from teasing Sonnenfeldt, and he was the permanent butt of many of Kissinger's jokes. By late 1970, Sonnenfeldt—always anxious for social success—had taken to hanging around Kissinger's office in the White House on the afternoons of formal White House dinners waiting to see if he could obtain a last-minute invitation, Halperin says. (Such waiting was known as "rug time" among NSC staffers.) Sometimes Sonnenfeldt's goal was simply to cadge a ride to an embassy party in Kissinger's White House limousine. Kissinger would respond in kind by permitting Sonnenfeldt to read and analyze only a portion of a backchannel document, making it clear there was more that was not being shown. Nevertheless, according to Halperin, Kissinger valued Sonnenfeldt's analytical ability very highly, perhaps because the two men had similar views about the Soviet Union. Trying to summarize their complex relationship, Halperin put it this way: "Henry had bested Sonnenfeldt in life. He went to Harvard; Hal went to Johns Hopkins. Henry got a doctorate; Hal stopped at an M.A. Henry had an appointment at Harvard; Sonnenfeldt went into the bureaucracy."

also providing Kissinger with a chance to learn what was being said about him as well as about others important to the White House, such as Senator Kennedy.

Brandon's wife, Mabel, whose first husband had been a Washington newspaperman, was extremely friendly with Joan Kennedy, the wife of Senator Kennedy, and many of their most intimate conversations were monitored by the FBI. Not everything got to the White House, however. The Watergate prosecutors later learned that one discussion of Joan Kennedy's "problems with Teddy" was typed up and delivered to Courtland J. Jones, a supervisor in the FBI's Washington Field Office, for transmission to higher officials. Jones told the prosecutors that he destroyed the transcript instead of sending it to the White House. "I knew what those people would do with this stuff," he explained.

Kissinger had no fears about what he said over the telephone: He knew that William Sullivan and the others involved in the FBI would be terrified, as would any careful bureaucrat, at the prospect of confronting a superior in the White House with evidence of indiscretion. Even after May 1970, when the wiretap summaries were provided directly to Haldeman, Kissinger continued to talk—and gossip—on the telephone with Brandon and others he knew were wiretapped; to do otherwise might possibly have provided a clue that a wiretap was in place. A review of some of the transcripts shows that Sullivan and his FBI subordinates were indeed careful to protect Kissinger by not including some of his remarks—such as his words of praise to Morton Halperin in August 1969—in the summaries prepared for the White House. Similarly, none of Haig's telephone conversations with Pursley, many of them dealing with classified material, was included in the telephone summaries Pursley obtained from the government after the wiretapping was made public in 1973.* The FBI's Sullivan was clearly responsible for protecting Kissinger and Haig in the first year of the wiretaps, and apparently he protected them throughout the twenty-one-month program. If so, the only person outside the FBI to know what Kissinger was actually saying—and what wasn't being reported to Haldeman and the President—was Haig, the tireless deputy who made trips to the FBI to read the verbatim transcripts. It is not known whether Haig's knowledge played a part in the increasing tension between the two men, but there is a possibility that Kissinger suspected Haig of making some of his more outrageous statements—as overheard by the FBI—available to Haldeman.

The wiretap on Morton Halperin was useful not only because it provided valuable political information about Senator Muskie's foreign policy planning, as discussed with Gelb and others. The tap also kept the White House informed about one former insider who was capable of leaking genuinely major secrets—Daniel Ellsberg.

Ellsberg, like Halperin, was a source of embarrassment for Kissinger. He

* In mid-1970, Pursley took a brief sailing vacation with his wife, the first such trip they had taken together in years. The morning after his return to Laird's office, his wife telephoned and asked him how it felt to be back. Miserable, said Pursley, not unnaturally. "I wish I wasn't here." At this point in the transcript of the call, an FBI agent noted: "He appears to be a disgruntled employee." Morton Halperin's wife, Ina, constantly told callers that her telephone was wiretapped. In a conversation in the fall of 1969, Mrs. Halperin suddenly exclaimed, "You hear that beeping?" At this point the agent noted: "There isn't any beeping on the line. Ina has a complex her phone is being tapped."

had, after all, permitted Ellsberg—dovish reputation and all—to write some of the Nixon Administration's early Vietnam option papers and to be involved in the preparation of NSSM 1, the exhaustive Vietnam study. During the twenty-one months of the Halperin wiretap, Ellsberg was overheard fifteen times. The conversations between the two men revolved around Vietnam, and what both correctly perceived as the administration's secret plan to escalate the war. The close-mouthed Halperin was careful, of course, on his telephone but Ellsberg was not. He talked openly about drug use and sex. On August 30, 1969, for example, Ellsberg, visiting Halperin in Washington, was overheard talking about a "trip" and urging someone named Harry, "who may be his brother," not to take a trip at the same time as his wife. "Ellsberg subsequently mentioned to another individual," the FBI summary said, "that he had left a satchel filled with 'stuff' at his friend's house. . . ." Four years later, the FBI clerks who monitored that conversation were able to recall it clearly.*

It is not known how Nixon, Haldeman, or Mitchell reacted to the link between Ellsberg, drugs, and Morton Halperin; such revelations, however, could not have enhanced Kissinger's reputation as an employer of prudent aides. Halperin and Ellsberg knew hundreds of government secrets, ranging from the most specific information about America's nuclear targeting procedures to the working of the NSA's far-flung electronic eavesdropping operations. The White House's concern, however, was not limited to past secrets that Ellsberg and Halperin could expose; the men at the top were worried about what Ellsberg and Halperin thought the administration's future policy in the war would be. Late in the summer of 1969, Ellsberg had visited Halperin, who was in the process of resigning from the NSC, to discuss war policy, and it was then, Ellsberg recalls, that Halperin first told him of the B-52 bombing of Cambodia and of Kissinger's direct warning to the Soviets about escalation in Vietnam. Halperin also described Kissinger's repeated studies on the mining of Haiphong Harbor, and speculated that Richard Nixon would not go into the 1972 election campaign without putting his escalation plan into effect.

Both men knew, from their work on the Pentagon Papers, that the Johnson Administration had tried to bully North Vietnam into accepting a defeat in the South. Diplomatic documents, still unpublished then, showed that Ho Chi Minh was warned in August 1964 that unless his nation ceased its support of the Vietcong in the South, "it can expect to continue to suffer the consequences." The warning, delivered by J. Blair Seaborn, the Canadian member of the International Control Commission, came a few days after American warplanes bombed the North for the first time, in retaliation for what Washington said was a North Vietnamese attack on American warships in the Gulf of Tonkin. Ellsberg had known of the Seaborn mission, and he recalled the response to the threat: Within months, one of the best North Vietnamese battalions had begun infiltrating into the South. "They did it when they were staring right down the barrel at LBJ's threats," he said. He was convinced, after his

* Ellsberg later told me that the telephone call was to his brother, Harry, who was living in a New York suburb. It was no secret to Ellsberg's friends and associates that he and other Rand employees had participated in a series of UCLA-sponsored research tests into the effects of psychedelic drugs, including LSD, in the early 1960s. In the later summer of 1969, Ellsberg recalled, he had been given a gift of mescaline and it was that drug which he proposed to give to his brother, who did not use such substances and declined the offer.

talks with Halperin, that Nixon and Kissinger were going to make the same threats, with the same results. Ellsberg began to brood about doing what Halperin would not—talk publicly against the war.

At this point, another Vietnam scandal broke. Stanley R. Resor, Secretary of the Army, announced on September 29 that he had decided not to file charges against six U. S. Special Forces men accused of assassinating an alleged South Vietnamese double agent. Ellsberg recalls his rage at reading Resor's insistence that he had taken the action on his own authority, and not —as the media reported—at the direction of the President. "This is a system that I had served for fifteen years," Ellsberg thought. "It is a system that lies automatically from top to bottom to protect a cover-up murder. I've got a safe full of documents that are full of lies." He was talking about the Pentagon Papers, and his top-secret safe at the Rand Corporation. It was in the aftermath of Resor's announcement, Ellsberg says, that he telephoned a colleague at Rand, Anthony Russo, "and asked him if he knew where there was a photocopying machine." Russo knew he was taking an enormous risk in photocopying top-secret documents: "I expected with certainty that what I was doing would put me in jail for the rest of my life." (He would become a codefendant in the Pentagon Papers case.) A few days later, Ellsberg flew to Washington and met with J. William Fulbright, the Senate's leading dove. He told the Senator about the papers and what they revealed about the American involvement. Fulbright had already scheduled a series of public hearings on Vietnam before his Foreign Relations Committee; Ellsberg could be a witness, if he chose, and make public what he wished. Ellsberg did not know that Fulbright was still in close contact with Henry Kissinger.

In October, a few days after the first Moratorium, Fulbright abruptly backed away from his commitment to stage the hearings and publicly voiced his support for the President's policies. "I believe the President's own statements that he is trying to wind down the war in Vietnam and I assume his November 3 speech [which had been announced on October 13, two days before the Moratorium] will provide further evidence of his determination to liquidate the war," he declared. The Foreign Relations Committee hearings were to have explored legislation to cut off congressional funding for the war. At the time, Washington was full of rumors, many of them the work of Henry Kissinger, suggesting that a new peace initiative was in the offing. After the Nixon speech, Fulbright again delayed his hearings, telling Ellsberg that there was no support for critical testimony on the war "in my own committee." At that moment, Ellsberg was carrying the first 1,000 pages of the Pentagon Papers in his suitcase. The *New York Times* subsequently quoted Fulbright as explaining that he had delayed the hearings for a second time because "We want to be responsible and careful. . . . [The committee] didn't want to do anything at this stage that might be interpreted as antagonistic. These are very difficult times."

Frustrated by Fulbright, Ellsberg took the next step and began meeting privately with influential journalists and business groups, trying to describe the real Nixon strategy of coercion and escalation. "People knew my reputation on Vietnam," he recalls. "No one questioned my credentials; that was no problem. But when it came to my assertions that Nixon's policy was not a disguised retreat but a plan for staying in and escalating as necessary, I discovered that I couldn't make anyone believe it." Ellsberg told all those he met with that Nixon's coercion strategy was a contingency plan that would go into effect only if the threats against the North Vietnamese did not work. "I wasn't saying that they had a conscious plan that on a certain date they would enlarge the war. Escalation was not in their thoughts, but they were committing themselves to threats that would fail." The administration, he said, was being honest, to a degree, in publicly claiming that it did not want to enlarge the war and did not expect to do so. But there was a missing link, one he sought futilely to provide to his listeners: "They were making explicit threats which they expected to be effective without being carried out and it was this that they were not hinting at or telling anybody."

No one paid much attention.

It is not known how much the White House was able to learn about Ellsberg's contacts with Fulbright and his private warnings. In mid-1969, however, Ellsberg and five Rand colleagues published their letter attacking the administration's Vietnam policy. Although the letter received little publicity, it appeared at a critical time for Nixon and Kissinger: Was it to be yes or no on the November ultimatum, with its provisions for intensive B-52 bombing and the mining of the harbor at Haiphong?

By early 1970, Ellsberg had repeatedly photocopied relevant sections of the papers and had given thousands of pages to Senator Fulbright for storage in the classified safe in the Foreign Relations Committee office.* Ellsberg's two children from his first marriage helped photocopy the papers; his former wife thus heard of the project and told the FBI that Ellsberg had given a set of documents to Fulbright. Two months later, Ellsberg learned from his fiancée, Patricia Marx, that FBI agents had been around to question him. "I assumed I'd be arrested within days," Ellsberg recalls, "and I didn't want to embarrass myself or Rand by being arrested while at work." He resigned and accepted a long-standing offer to become a research associate at the Massachusetts Institute of Technology in Cambridge. The FBI got to Rand on April 27, twelve days after Ellsberg had resigned, and was told by senior officials that the papers were merely a history of the Vietnam War that did not involve national security. If Senator Fulbright had asked for a copy of the study, the FBI was told, he would have been routinely given it. Fulbright, as the FBI agents obviously did not know, had been doing just that—asking Laird's office for a copy—with no success. Ellsberg filed a Freedom of Information request years later and learned why the FBI dropped its inquiry so quickly in April of 1970: out of fear of the link to Fulbright. It wouldn't do to investigate such a powerful senator. Officials decided, the FBI documents showed, that further inquiry could "embarrass the bureau."

Throughout this period, the FBI never questioned Ellsberg, nor did his Rand colleagues tell him they had been questioned. Continuing his seemingly futile efforts to alert the country to Nixon's and Kissinger's real plans, he took his antiwar belief to the public on May 8, 1970, just after the invasion of Cambodia. His denunciation of the war at a teach-in at Washington University, in St. Louis, marked an evolution; years earlier, he had been sent to teach-ins by the Johnson Administration as a defender of the war.

* Fifteen copies of the papers had originally been distributed inside the government, and only two men—Ellsberg and Gelb—had read all the papers and analyses as of early 1970.

On May 13, Ellsberg finally testified before the Foreign Relations Committee, and discussed with Senator Fulbright the significance of the Pentagon Papers. Once again no one paid much attention—except the Rand Corporation, whose officials finally removed all the classified materials, including his original copy of the Pentagon Papers, from Ellsberg's safe. By mid-June, Ellsberg was back at Rand for a visit and—still unaware that the FBI had been around—had the Pentagon Papers retrieved from Rand's top-secret files and again began photocopying. Ellsberg says the reckless invasion of Cambodia reinforced his conviction that Nixon and Kissinger "were going to go all the way on the escalation." He had spent much of the past ten years studying presidential behavior for government officials, and had concluded that presidents, once having issued threats, were compelled to carry them out.

That summer, Ellsberg was obsessed with the thought that the papers he was photocopying could alter that conclusion by provoking a massive antiwar reaction. He continued his talks with journalists and others who would listen. They listened, but did not believe. In August, while in Los Angeles, he chanced to visit Lloyd Shearer, the editor of *Parade* magazine, just as Shearer was about to drive to San Clemente to interview Kissinger. Ellsberg asked if he could come along. Shearer, who was friendly with both men, hesitated for only a few seconds before telephoning the California White House. Kissinger was adamant, Shearer recalls: "No, under no circumstances. I don't want to talk to him. He's a madman; he likes to argue." When Shearer insisted, Kissinger relented: "All right, Lloyd, we'll stick him with Al."

Arriving at San Clemente, Ellsberg got a glimpse of Nixon, driving a pink golf cart, "scowling and looking very grim." Behind him came Bébé Rebozo in another pink cart. Kissinger appeared and began the conversation with his usual flattery, telling Shearer, "I have learned from Dan Ellsberg more than from any other person on the subject of bargaining." Ellsberg, with surprise and some unease, remembered his lectures on bargaining theory to Kissinger's Harvard seminar, lectures that had dealt with Hitler's use of madness to take over other nations without firing a shot. "The very thought that an adviser to a President had those lectures in his mind in 1970 . . . It was one of those moments with the hair rising on the back of my neck." A few weeks earlier, Kissinger had announced that the United States was seeking to "expel" the Soviets from the Middle East—a word he later retracted—and Ellsberg had speculated at the time that the overreaction was linked to the Vietnam War. And Kissinger himself had written on the use of bargaining with threats. What all this meant, Ellsberg concluded, was that he had been right—the White House was consciously using a threat strategy and Kissinger had been unable to resist alluding to it.

At lunch, Shearer tried to discuss the Vietnam War, a subject Kissinger obviously didn't want to talk about in front of Ellsberg. Moments later, Ellsberg was indeed shunted off to Haig, who said little as Ellsberg recited his views. Before the visit ended, Kissinger agreed to see Ellsberg when he was next in California.

Why Kissinger agreed to the second meeting is not clear—needless to say, Ellsberg is not mentioned in the Kissinger memoirs. In any case, there was nothing outwardly unseemly about their meeting. As of September 1970, Ellsberg had yet to be linked to any leak of classified materials and he was widely known inside the government as a leading theorist on decision making. Ellsberg took the meeting, for which he interrupted his honeymoon (he and Patricia Marx were married on August 8), very seriously. His goal was "to scare Henry with the thought that his strategy might not be viable. I was going to leak into the White House what I had been saying outside."

The evening before, Ellsberg recalls, he went to a party in Los Angeles with some friends from his days at Rand, including Konrad Kellen, the Rand expert on the North Vietnamese. Did he have any advice for Kissinger? "Tell him that he does not understand the enemy," Kellen responded. "Tell him he is confronting the most popularly supported government in the world."

Ellsberg's appointment in San Clemente coincided with the burgeoning crisis over the PLO and Jordan in the Middle East. Kissinger began, Ellsberg recalls, by saying, "I'm very worried about Bill Rogers' policy in the Middle East. I'm afraid it's going to explode." Ellsberg responded: "Well, Henry, I'm here to talk about your Vietnam policy. I'm afraid *it* may explode." For the next ten minutes or so, Ellsberg summarized his view of the White House threat strategy in Vietnam, which hinged on a series of escalations that included an invasion of Laos and the mining of Haiphong Harbor. "I thought to myself," Ellsberg recalls, "if I'm right, he's got to be hemorrhaging inside." Kissinger was silent, drumming his fingers on a table and staring intently as Ellsberg talked. When Ellsberg stopped, Kissinger said only, "I do not want to discuss our policy; let us turn to another subject." Ellsberg, who was not easily put off, turned the talk to the Pentagon Papers. He remembered that Kissinger had been invited to be a consultant in the initial stages. Kissinger acknowledged that there was a copy in the White House safe but said he had not looked at it. Should he? Ellsberg urged him to "at least read the summaries." Kissinger obviously did not want to: "Do we really have anything to learn from this study?" he asked. At this point, Ellsberg says, "My heart sank. The major lesson of the study was that each person repeated the same patterns in decision making and pretty much the same policy as his predecessor without even knowing it. I thought, 'My God! He's in the same state of mind as all the other makers of decision in this long process, each of whom thought that history had started with his administration, and had nothing to learn from earlier ones.' "

Kissinger seemed anxious to set the date for another meeting and Ellsberg agreed to call for an appointment, but over the next few weeks three dates were fixed and canceled by Kissinger. Ellsberg stopped calling. He decided that Kissinger had wanted to see him "so he could say he listened to 'everyone —a whole range of opinion—for example, Dan Ellsberg.' "*

* Kissinger, it turned out, did drop Ellsberg's name a few months later. In an interview with Don Oberdorfer of the *Washington Post*, who was writing an assessment of the first two years of the administration's Vietnam policies, Kissinger cited Ellsberg and Halperin as being among those who were "great critics" of the administration who "had been crucial in the development of the policy." Oberdorfer telephoned Ellsberg to ask his reaction. "I was absolutely amazed by this," Ellsberg says. "I asked, 'What did Kissinger say the policy was?' Oberdorfer said, 'It's the policy of negotiating in Hanoi while withdrawing the troops from Vietnam.' I said, 'Look, if that were the policy, I would still be at Rand and Mort Halperin would still be in the White House. This guy is trying to smear me as being implicated in *his* rotten policy.' "

The futile raid on the empty Son Tay prison camp near Hanoi in late November of 1970, and the heavy bombing of North Vietnam that accompanied it, convinced Ellsberg once again that he and Halperin were right in their perceptions. He began working closely with antiwar activists, and continued his efforts to get someone in the Senate to publish the Pentagon Papers in the *Congressional Record*. When it was clear that Senator Fulbright was not prepared to act, he went to others. Gaylord Nelson, the liberal Democrat from Wisconsin, turned him away; so, after a week of hesitation, did George S. McGovern, the Democrat from South Dakota. Senator Mathias of Maryland expressed eagerness to do something, but lost interest when he learned the Pentagon Papers dealt largely with the Kennedy and Johnson administrations: "Can't you get me something on this administration?" he asked. Ellsberg's final step, months away, would be to approach a newspaper reporter he knew from Vietnam—Neil Sheehan of the *New York Times*.

On November 22, two days after the Son Tay bombing raids, Ellsberg telephoned Halperin again. The FBI wiretap logs reported that the two men agreed, "This is the time to act, to get people activated; that if this doesn't move people nothing will until the holocaust—the destruction of Hanoi or the *invasion of Laos* [emphasis added]." At that point, White House plans for the Laos invasion were not yet completed, but the men running the war knew that more escalation was coming. "The enemy had to be prevented from taking over Cambodia and Laos if Vietnamization was to have any chance of success," Kissinger wrote in his memoirs, summarizing his views as of late 1970. Kissinger first thought "the best place" for an offensive in early 1971 would be Cambodia, he wrote, but he was persuaded, without too much difficulty, by Haig and the military in Saigon that an attack on Laos would be more damaging to the North.

Kissinger and Ellsberg met face to face once more before publication of the Pentagon Papers, at a private conference on the war held at MIT during the last weekend in January of 1971. The meeting was sponsored by a group of moderate student leaders, academics, journalists, businessmen, and former government officials. Kissinger, still carrying the banner for the administration with such groups of Establishment liberals—as Nixon viewed them—flew from Washington to speak. It was a tour de force at first, with Kissinger being charming and disarming as usual, confiding to the group that Richard Nixon had not been his first choice for the presidency, and telling a questioner that he would resign his position when the "whole trend of the policy became morally reprehensible to me." Even then, he added, he would not publicly attack the President if he did resign—"unless gas chambers were set up or some horrendous moral outrage." Finally Ellsberg rose. The NSC staff, he said, was known to have made estimates on the number of Americans who would be killed during the next year of the war. "What is your best estimate of the number of Vietnamese who will be killed in the next twelve months as a consequence of your policy?"

Derek Shearer, a Yale University student who attended the conference, described in the *Nation* magazine what happened next: When Kissinger responded "his voice sounded suddenly less certain; he hesitated, then called Ellsberg's question 'cleverly worded.' 'I answer even if I don't answer,' he said. Ellsberg interrupted to say that he had no intention of being clever, that this was a basic question—were such estimates made? Kissinger started to say that one had to consider the options. 'I know the options game, Dr. Kissinger,' said Ellsberg, 'can't you just give us an answer or tell us that you don't have such estimates?' Kissinger again evaded the question; he said the question had racial overtones. Ellsberg pressed him again. For the first time the meeting took on the air of confrontation—then the student moderator stood up abruptly and ended the questioning, saying that Dr. Kissinger was tired, and thanked him for coming. The audience, save a few of us, applauded."

A few weeks later, Ellsberg published a bitter essay, "Murder in Laos," in the *New York Review of Books,* in which he again criticized the administration's failure to estimate civilian casualties of the war. "How many will die in Laos?" he asked. "What is Richard Nixon's best estimate? . . . He does not have an estimate. He has not asked Henry Kissinger, and Kissinger has not asked the Pentagon."

Ellsberg's continuing attacks on the administration's policy created a stir in the academic community in Cambridge, and in March 1971, the *Boston Globe* published a front-page story by Thomas Oliphant on his emerging role in the antiwar community, focusing not only on the Laos article but also on Ellsberg's role in preparing the Pentagon Papers, and the fact that only a few had actually read all of the secret study. Within days, Kissinger's office asked the *Globe*'s White House correspondent for a copy of the story. Ellsberg, told about that by Oliphant, immediately began making more copies of the Pentagon Papers. "My nightmare had been that someday the FBI would come to get all my copies," Ellsberg says. He and his wife spent thousands of dollars making as many as eight more complete sets of the Papers.*

Ellsberg and his complaints about the lack of civilian casualty estimates were of more than passing interest to Kissinger that spring. Ellsberg's name was raised, for example, at a small off-the-record lunch with a group of Washington journalists on March 21. "Dan Ellsberg never worked for me," Kissinger said, "except on one project during the transition. He has no idea what records are kept. As a matter of fact, no civilians are in the area of Laos where this operation has been conducted." † Ellsberg's criticisms, Kissinger went on, were "the new line of attack—that we are causing the civilian casualties. No one mentions that the only place the fighting is occurring is where the North Vietnamese have invaded first."

Questions about civilians may have been upsetting to Kissinger at the time, but they were quickly rationalized. Kissinger was able to tell journalists during

* It was those extra sets, whose photocopying was inspired by the call from Kissinger's office, that were provided by Ellsberg and a group of friends to seventeen newspapers across the United States after the Justice Department obtained a temporary restraining order on June 15 barring the *New York Times* from continuing to publish the Pentagon Papers. The *Times,* which had begun publishing the papers on June 13, acceded to the order after some internal debate over the unconstitutionality of such prior restraint. The Supreme Court ruled on June 30 that the government had failed to prove the necessity of prior restraint in the case, permitting the *Times* and other newspapers, including the *Washington Post,* to publish the remainder of the Papers.

† None of the reporters challenged that statement, although Kissinger had acknowledged to them moments earlier that the intelligence was poor for the Laos operation; the North Vietnamese were found to have dozens of tanks that were not anticipated, and had committed four divisions to the battle when only one and a half were reported to be in the area. Why the Pentagon's intelligence on civilian settlements in the area would be any better than its intelligence on the enemy's military forces was a question unasked and unanswered.

the lunch that attacks by Ellsberg and other critics were the result of a conspiracy of the left: "What they really want us to do is to conspire to defeat Saigon and that is something I cannot justify."

The full range of Kissinger's influence and his extraordinary ability to manipulate the press while wiretapping two of its leading members were impossible to comprehend at the time, mainly because so much of what he did was skillfully hidden. On March 22, the day after he seemed so open in discussing the Laos operation at the press lunch, he chaired a meeting of the 40 Committee in which the CIA was given an additional $185,000 for its ongoing campaign against the Allende government. Allende had been President for less than five months, but the 40 Committee, at Kissinger's and Nixon's continued urging, had already approved $2 million in covert funds for the CIA to put to use against the new Chilean government. Allende had defied the White House by winning the election and becoming President in the fall of 1970, but the CIA—always sensitive to the orders of the men at the top—was still trying.

On March 23, a seemingly relaxed and friendly Kissinger received Orlando Letelier, the Chilean Ambassador to Washington, at the White House. In a report cabled later that day to Santiago, Letelier was enthusiastic about Kissinger, who, he wrote, "reflected a more positive attitude than could have been expected."

Kissinger emphasized, Letelier reported, that "his government did not desire for any purpose to interfere with the actions that the Government of Chile adopted internally. In this context he commented that the United States already had too many enemies abroad and did not want to do anything to turn Chile into an enemy." Letelier took advantage of the meeting's warmth, he wrote, to inquire gently about newspaper stories speculating that the Nixon Administration had promulgated a "secret document" calling on the international financial community to shun Chile—a reference, although Letelier of course did not realize it, to NSDM 93. "Kissinger told me he was aware of that information and called it 'absolutely absurd and without grounds of any kind,' " Letelier reported.

"At the end of the conversation," Letelier added, Kissinger "was emphatic in indicating his desire to maintain a permanent dialogue with me, not only for the purpose of discussing specific issues but also as a way to get to know better the Chilean political process, which he repeatedly described as of the most extraordinary interest."

Letelier, with his old-world manners and civility, was no match for Kissinger. But even a tougher, more diabolical emissary from Santiago would have been in a difficult position in Washington.* Nixon and Kissinger, determined

* Letelier was serving as Chile's Defense Minister at the time of the military overthrow of Allende in 1973. He survived that event and his subsequent imprisonment by the ruling junta, headed by General Augusto Pinochet, and eventually returned to Washington, where he became active in the Chilean exile community and a fellow at the Institute for Policy Studies, a liberal think tank. In 1976 he was assassinated by a car bomb while driving two colleagues to work; one of the passengers was also killed. Federal investigators determined, after a lengthy investigation, that the killings had been authorized by DINA, the secret police agency of the Pinochet government.

to have their way in Chile, left nothing to chance. By early 1971, the CIA had installed a wiretap inside Letelier's embassy. The White House was learning —and passing on to its friends in the corporate world—the nationalization steps contemplated by the new socialist government in Chile. The wiretap would stay in place for the next eighteen months.

25

SALT:
A GRAIN DEAL

IT WAS MAY 19, 1971. A clear, warm spring evening in Washington. Nixon and his top aides—H. R. Haldeman, John Ehrlichman, John Mitchell, Charles Colson, and Henry Kissinger—were enjoying dinner and a private celebration aboard the presidential yacht, the *Sequoia*. The next day, at noon, Nixon was to appear on nationwide television and announce that the United States and the Soviet Union had made a breakthrough in the SALT negotiations; an unprecedented disarmament treaty between the two nuclear powers was within reach. His announcement would create a sensation, Nixon knew, the kind of splash he needed for reelection. There had been antiwar rioting on the streets of Washington on May 1, May Day, and the announcement of a pending SALT agreement would neutralize the impact of the Vietnam War protests.

The rivalries and suspicions among the aides seemed to dissipate as the *Sequoia* sailed along the muddy Potomac River. At one point, Colson proposed a toast to Henry Kissinger, who—as the men sipping drinks knew—had negotiated the SALT agreement in direct, backchannel meetings with Ambassador Dobrynin. No members of the American SALT delegation, not even Gerard Smith, had been aware of the high-level White House involvement. Nixon talked about his foreign policy plans, Colson remembers, as the men drank their scotches and ate their steak. (Ehrlichman and Haldeman, both Christian Scientists, stuck to ginger ale.) At one point, the President turned to Colson and asked, with a wink, "Do you think, Chuck, you'll get me an SST to fly to China?" Kissinger blanched, Colson recalls—in fear that Nixon would spill the beans about the scheduled trip to Peking, at that point known only to him, Nixon, and Haldeman. "Relax, relax," Nixon said to Kissinger. "If those liberals on your staff, Henry, don't stop giving everything to the *New York Times,* I won't be going anywhere. The leaks; the leaks; that's what we've got to stop at any cost. Do you hear me, Henry?"

Nixon turned to Colson. "Chuck, your job is to hold off those madmen on the Hill long enough for Henry to finish his work in Paris [with the North Vietnamese]. Then go for the big play—China, Russia."

Colson recalls learning of one other assignment that night: with the maritime unions. Nixon made it clear what would be involved in the SALT talks—the Soviets had been promised liberalized trade. That country needed corn and other livestock feed to maintain its commitment to supply more meat for its

240 million citizens, and America's corn supply in 1971 was overflowing, literally, on the streets of several towns in Iowa. "I knew that the grain trade would be one of the key issues in SALT," Colson says. "I also knew I was going to work very hard" with the leaders of the maritime unions, fervent anti-Communists who since 1963 had refused to permit longshoremen to load Soviet cargo ships unless 50 percent of the grain was carried on American ships.

The link between the grain trade and the May 20, 1971, SALT announcement remained one of the most carefully kept secrets of the administration. Neither Nixon nor Kissinger hinted at such a possibility in his memoirs. One reason, of course, is obvious: Within months of the May 1972 summit meeting, the Soviet Union, capitalizing on the administration's eagerness to negotiate a SALT agreement in Moscow, secretly began to purchase more than $1 billion worth of wheat from American grain companies, depleting existing stockpiles and driving up the price of wheat—and bread—to consumers in America and around the world.

Another reason for Nixon's and Kissinger's caution had to do with the nature of the bargaining that lay behind the breakthrough, which was widely treated as an American negotiating success. Members of the SALT delegation soon learned that Kissinger had made significant concessions to the Soviets in the backchannel. There were those on the delegation—including Gerard Smith and Raymond Garthoff—who believed that the May 20 agreement, far from being a breakthrough, was in some sense a step backward. They kept their silence at the time. Nixon and Kissinger kept their silence, too, about the link between grain and SALT.

The SALT talks, rotating between Helsinki and Vienna, had bogged down in mid-1970 when the Soviets refused to discuss any limitations on their rapidly growing force of offensive missiles unless the United States agreed to reduce its fleet of fighter-bomber aircraft, all with nuclear capability, stationed at land bases and on aircraft carriers throughout Europe and Asia. Without such reciprocity, the Soviets argued at the SALT talks, only a treaty banning antiballistic missile systems (ABMs) was possible.

By early 1971, the SALT talks had become sharply politicized: Senate liberals and arms control advocates were urging the administration to settle for a treaty limiting ABMs, theorizing that such an agreement would be a worthwhile achievement in itself, and a solid basis for future negotiations to limit offensive missiles. The Nixon Administration insisted that the ABM system was vital as a "bargaining chip" to be negotiated out of existence or downward only if the Soviets would agree to a freeze or some constraint on their offensive strategic forces. As in 1969, Nixon and Kissinger had no interest in limiting *qualitative* improvements in Soviet or American offensive missile systems, such as the MIRVs, but were seeking a *quantitative* limit or freeze on the number of missile launchers each side would be permitted to build. The American position amounted to a unilateral freeze for the Soviets, for they were still increasing their strategic land-based and submarine-based missile launchers. The United States had stopped deploying new missile launchers in 1967, after reaching a total of 1,054, and was instead concentrating on increasing the number of MIRVed warheads that could be placed on each missile.*

Another key element of the SALT debate in early 1971 was that the American ABM system was in political jeopardy. Its critics were able to demonstrate, far more persuasively than the administration could counter, that the system's complicated mélange of interceptor missiles and radars simply would not work. In 1970, the administration barely beat back a Senate attempt to kill the planned expansion of the ABM system, which had received congressional approval to begin construction at two sites. The vote, 52 to 47, was won only after Smith, the chief American negotiator and thus the main target of Nixon's and Kissinger's scheming, was prevailed upon to intervene with a few senators to help switch their votes.†

Thus in early 1971 the Nixon Administration was in the position of offering to reduce its widely criticized ABM system, whose funding was barely surviving Senate votes, as a bargaining chip to make the Soviet Union unilaterally stop increasing its fast-growing offensive missile fleet. Complicating this weak negotiating position was the fact that the President had staked his reputation, and the integrity of the SALT talks, on his public insistence that any acceptable arms agreement had to limit offensive missiles. In late February, in his second annual report to Congress on foreign policy, Nixon declared that "to be stable and satisfactory, an agreement should include limitations on both offensive and defensive systems. . . . To limit only one side of the offense-defense equation could rechannel the arms competition rather than effectively curtail it." Whether that view was wise or persuasive was not the issue in early 1971; determined, as usual, to face down his liberal critics in the Senate, the President continued to insist that the ABM system was essential to national security, if for no other reason than as bait for Soviet SALT concessions. "Congressional doves," Nixon wrote in his memoirs, "were treating the Soviet ABM-only proposal as a way to chalk up a belated victory over the administration. . . . I felt it would be disastrous to go into the final SALT

---

* The proposed freeze had another, less obvious, advantage for the United States. The Soviets, by agreeing to a freeze on missile launchers, would be unable to offset—if they chose to do so—the constantly expanding American lead, aided by MIRVs, in deployed warheads. The Soviets were not capable of deploying MIRVs until 1975, and thus could increase their number of deployed warheads only by adding more missile launchers, which an agreement would prohibit.

† In his memoirs, Kissinger warmly praised Smith for his support, quoting a *New York Times* article to the effect that Smith's intervention was decisive in carrying the ABM vote. Smith, in his memoirs, acknowledged that he had offered to discuss the importance of the ABM with certain key senators, if the President thought the risk was worth it. "I was not soliciting Senatorial calls," Smith wrote, since "It was important that the delegation not appear to be lobbying for the ABM programme." Instead, Smith agreed to send a classified message to Kissinger reaffirming the delegation's view that a negative vote on the ABM in the Senate would "prejudice prospects for SALT agreement." Kissinger, expressing the President's gratitude, asked and received Smith's permission to show the cable to some senators should there be any questions. Smith was now in over his head. Several senators did telephone him and, after receiving assurances that the calls were confidential, Smith proceeded to lobby them for a favorable vote on the ABM. "To my disgust," Smith wrote, "several days later I read in the *New York Times* that my written views had been given to certain senators," one of whom mentioned his lobbying efforts during the ABM debate. "I complained to Kissinger about this breach of confidence," Smith went on, "but the best I could get from him was that somebody in the White House had goofed." It was obvious just who had goofed and Smith resolved never again to get involved in such lobbying. During a briefing to the Senate a year later, before another vote on ABM, Smith recalled, one senator "expressed the hope" that a proponent of the ABM would "not at the last moment come up with a letter from me that he could use to support the ABM in the forthcoming debate. Touché."

negotiations in this position." The ABM also had continued support from the Pentagon.

The May 20 announcement seemed to meet Nixon's criteria. The Soviets agreed to discuss "certain measures" regarding the limitation of offensive weapons while also continuing to discuss a limit on ABMs. There would be no formal treaty dealing with offensive limitations, both sides agreed, but there would be an interim freeze on ICBM launchers, with details to be worked out in later negotiations. The Soviets, in a second major concession, further agreed that American forward-based aircraft stationed in Western Europe and Asia would not be included in the freeze (although they explicitly reserved the right to include a limit on such aircraft in later SALT negotiations). In his television statement, Nixon was hyperbolic: "This agreement is a major step in breaking the stalemate on nuclear arms talks. . . . If we succeed, this joint statement that has been issued today may well be remembered as the beginning of a new era." In his memoirs, Kissinger depicted the breakthrough, "despite an obviously weak bargaining position," as a vindication of his personal backchannel negotiating technique. Another key factor, he claimed, was his decision to link SALT with the continuing four-power talks over the status of West Berlin and with the pending ratification of Brandt's peace treaty between the Soviet Union and West Germany, which established diplomatic relations between the two nations and formally ratified the European border changes imposed by the Soviet Union after World War II.

There is no evidence, however, that the linkage had any significant influence on the Soviet compromises. Far more important were the American concessions.*

Two of the concessions involved technical issues important to SALT. Kissinger agreed to exclude submarine-launched ballistic missiles (SLBMs) from the pending negotiations, in effect freeing the Soviets to continue their major submarine-building programs. He also promised the Russians that the "modernization" of their land-based missile system would not be included in the talks, freeing them to pursue MIRVs and other qualitative improvements. Nixon and Kissinger were no longer interested in negotiating a full-scale treaty limiting both offensive and defensive weapons. Instead, there would be a treaty only for ABMs, plus an interim agreement, not requiring the ratification of the Senate, that would seek a short-term constraint on Soviet ICBM launcher construction. All the other major issues in SALT were left unresolved by the backchannel "breakthrough."

The administration's poor bargaining position—relying on the ABM to force Soviet offensive missile concessions—stemmed in part from a series of White

* Raymond Garthoff, in an analysis of SALT published in the spring 1977 issue of *International Security*, argued that the Russians repeatedly rejected the Nixon-Kissinger notion of linkage and the implicit assumption that the Soviet Union needed or wanted a SALT agreement more than the United States did. That is why, Garthoff wrote, the Soviets did not agree to proceed with the SALT negotiations until late in 1969, after the early Nixon rhetoric about linkage had dwindled. During the more than two years of negotiation, there was "a remarkable absence" of propagandizing and extraneous ideology by the Soviet delegates, in part because the Soviets may not have wished to "open the door to the earlier American propensity for linkage." Garthoff added, however: "But this is not the main explanation; a similar businesslike approach has also characterized other negotiations with the Soviet Union in recent years on a number of subjects, for example, on the status of Berlin . . . When the Soviets see sufficient intrinsic value in a negotiation, and seek an agreed outcome, they negotiate seriously." Garthoff's views were diametrically opposed to Kissinger's.

House negotiating misjudgments in 1970 and early 1971. In the space of a year, the United States had formally offered the Soviets three separate positions on ABM limitations, one of which was accepted by the Soviets and subsequently ignored by the American delegation, as if the offer had not been made. Such skirmishing astonished the Soviet negotiators and worked against American interests. On April 20, 1970, the American delegation—operating, as usual, under Kissinger's tight control—formally proposed that both sides be limited to one ABM system to protect their national capitals, known as NCAs, national command authorities. Seven days later, the Soviets—aware that the United States Congress was unlikely to approve funds for the ABM defense of Washington—accepted the offer. In his memoirs, Kissinger acknowledged that he had made a serious mistake: ". . . the proposal . . . was a first-class blunder; it made no substantive sense whatever." Both the State Department and the Arms Control and Disarmament Agency were in favor of the program, Kissinger added, since it would lead to a total ban on ABMs, which many civilians in the bureaucracy thought was the most sensible approach to the problem. After wistfully noting that "I find it hard to explain how this option could ever be considered, much less adopted," Kissinger came up with an answer—it was Nixon's fault: "I . . . acquiesced despite my better judgment for the not very elevated reason that over an issue so technical I knew the President would be reluctant to do battle with the agencies responsible for implementing it." The technical discussions about SALT and the political infighting over various positions invariably took place "before a President bored to distraction," Kissinger wrote. "His glazed expression showed that he considered most of the arguments esoteric rubbish; he was trying to calculate the political impact and saleability of the various options, of which only the broad outlines interested him."

As Kissinger viewed Nixon with contempt, so did Gerard Smith view Kissinger. Smith, a diplomat of the old school, did not publicly take issue with Kissinger until late 1980, when his political memoir, *Doubletalk,* was published. His was a story, told in understated fashion, of being constantly lied to and manipulated by Kissinger. "A serious flaw" in the negotiation process, Smith wrote, "was that Kissinger . . . had too much influence. I must say that he had us all buffaloed. Nothing could go forward without his approval, be it a press release, a briefing of the North Atlantic Council or an interagency study. . . . Time and again meetings he had called were canceled and set for a later day. It got to be a joke—but not a very funny one. At times, he seemed to be the only one in the cast of SALT characters who was free to take initiatives."

Kissinger has justified his heavy-handed treatment of Smith and the SALT delegation by writing that "Nixon was seized by the fear that Gerard Smith, rather than he," would get credit for any successes in SALT. As early as June 1970, Kissinger wrote, "Nixon opened his three-year-long contest with Smith over who would get the credit for SALT by asking me to convey to Dobrynin that a SALT settlement should come at a summit and not in Vienna."

None of the officials in the SALT delegation had any basis for knowing that such opportunism existed at the highest levels in the White House. On August 4, 1970, Kissinger, aware of his mistake in the offer that limited each side to one ABM site, tried to recoup by ordering the SALT delegation to propose a total ban on ABMs. At the time, he wrote in his memoirs, he and the President actually preferred that both sides keep on building their ABM systems, but "I thought it essential to get off the NCA proposal." The new offer "was certain to be rejected," especially since the White House coupled it with a demand that the Soviet Union agree to freeze construction of all its offensive missile systems. A Soviet rejection, Kissinger said, would free the United States "to move from there to insisting that the existing [ABM] sites be continued." In December, the Soviets responded to the two American offers by formally proposing at the Helsinki talks that, as a first step in the SALT process, a treaty limiting ABM systems be signed, with the more complex and difficult issues of offensive limitations deferred for a second round of SALT. In March 1971, two months after Kissinger and Dobrynin began their backchannel communications, and with the SALT talks now moved to Vienna, the Soviets submitted the text of a draft treaty limiting ABM deployment to one site for each nation. A week later, at Kissinger's direction, the American delegation introduced its third position on ABMs—calling for the United States to have four ABM sites to defend its missile fleet and the Soviet Union to have one ABM system to defend its NCA (Moscow).

Gerard Smith was outraged by the Kissinger machinations, but dutifully suppressed his feelings and followed orders. "The hardest job I had that year," Smith wrote, "was to try to understand Washington's reasoning on the ABM negotiations. . . . We [had] three proposals on the table at once, without anyone in the delegation and probably not even in Washington knowing which was the preferred United States position. People in the delegation compared this somewhat irreverently to a shell game, with no one knowing under which shell the pea was—or whether in fact there was a pea."

The Soviets were also confused. Garthoff, one of the most knowledgeable members of the American delegation, wrote about their response to Kissinger's third ABM offer: "The . . . delegation was astonished. They pointed out that the United States had earlier offered an NCA limitation to which they had agreed. The United States had then offered two alternatives, on an equal basis, and the Soviets had chosen and accepted one of them—an NCA level. Now the United States had proposed yet a third alternative." Garthoff described the American position as "marked not only by inconsistency and instability, but by unreliability. Both sides at times changed positions; only we withdrew proposals once accepted. We pulled back from an agreement on an NCA level, and we slapped down the idea of a complete ABM ban *after* a Soviet show of interest which was not even pursued. Proposals should *never* be made on the expectation they will be rejected by the other side and gain points on the record for their advocacy."

Garthoff's conclusion was that "clarity and consistency did not characterize our negotiating position on ABM levels, and evidently not our negotiating objectives." He, like everyone connected with the SALT talks, remains convinced that the ABM agreement signed at the 1972 Moscow summit was a "truly significant arms limitation." That agreement, however, Garthoff wrote, clearly could have been reached in 1970.

But Nixon was not running for reelection in 1970.

In his memoirs, Kissinger reported that he conceived the idea of discussing the SALT issue privately with Dobrynin in mid-December of 1970, and then raised the issue with the President. He told Nixon, he wrote, "that the moment had come to test the channel between Dobrynin and me. I conjectured that the Soviets might be ready to break the deadlock on a number of negotiations," including SALT. Kissinger did not tell the President, however, that his "test" was based on more than conjecture. Kissinger knew that Garthoff and Smith had been privately approached early in December by their Russian counterparts at the SALT talks and told that the Soviet Union was willing to continue negotiating offensive weapons limitations while the ABM treaty was being worked out. These would be "parallel" talks, Smith wrote in his memoirs. On December 9, 1970, Smith said, he was reminded that the Soviets would be interested in the "possibility of an ABM treaty accompanied by a moratorium on certain offensive force developments." Two days later, Smith dutifully reported to Kissinger that the Soviets were signaling the possibility of an ABM agreement combined with an agreed understanding regarding certain offensive forces. This was, Smith wrote sardonically, to be the "much-touted 'breakthrough' negotiated in the backchannel in 1971."

There were many reasons for Kissinger and Nixon to act unilaterally. Foremost was the fact that only through backchannel negotiations could Nixon— and not Gerard Smith—emerge as the peacemaker at a summit that, as the presidential election drew nearer, became politically essential. A second reason was Kissinger's constant need to dominate; permitting a SALT delegation to conclude an arms treaty would diminish his importance, no matter how thoroughly he controlled its deliberations. Nixon and Kissinger also believed, as their memoirs made clear, that their personal involvement in the detailed negotiation would lend substance to the American negotiating position, for the President would have the freedom to make concessions elsewhere in return for Soviet acceptance of American proposals. The SALT I agreement in Moscow, they both wrote, was the product of their use of such linkage.

The Soviet Union had its own needs. In mid-December of 1970, workers' riots had broken out in Poland, triggered by a large government increase in the price of meat products. There had been poor harvests and the nation was short of the grain needed to feed cattle and other livestock; hence meat was in short supply. Within a few days troops with tanks were called out to restore order in industrial cities such as Gdansk on the Baltic coast. Wladyslaw Gomulka, the Polish party leader, was replaced on December 20 by Edward Gierek, who promised improved conditions for the Polish citizens. The message from Poland was not lost on the economic planners in Moscow, who had begun their drive to produce more meat in 1968. By 1971, the Soviets had increased their use of feed grains for livestock by 40 percent. Moscow leaders, like their comrades in Warsaw, promised increases in the supply of meat. More grain would have to be imported.

In their memoirs, Kissinger and Nixon published only excerpts from the backchannel communications with the Soviets, and there is reason to doubt the integrity of the record. NSC staff aides recall that Kissinger ordered revisions in at least some portions of the secret transcripts of his meetings with Dobrynin. One such instance, according to NSC aides, occurred when Ambassador Smith found out about the backchannel and demanded to see the records.

The request was a disturbing one, for Smith had inadvertently provoked a backchannel crisis in early May by enthusiastically cabling the White House that the Soviets were hinting at a compromise. Smith reported that Vladimir S. Semenov, the chief Soviet delegate in Vienna, had suggested that his country would accept an ABM agreement and some understandings on offensive limitations, to be negotiated after the ABMs. What Semenov was trying to accomplish isn't clear; perhaps he wanted to alert Smith to the negotiations between Dobrynin and Kissinger, which were near conclusion. Semenov, after all, was also a victim of the backchannel, which diminished his role as chief Soviet disarmament negotiator. In any case, Kissinger and Nixon hit the roof. "Semenov's move," Kissinger wrote, "as well as raising doubts about Soviet good faith, in effect circumvented the Presidential channel." Kissinger did not try to explain how Semenov's conversation with his American counterpart in the SALT negotiations could possibly raise doubts about Soviet "good faith." The Soviet Ambassador obviously thought he was acting properly, for he raised the issue a second time with Smith a few days later, and his two principal aides discussed it at least four times with Garthoff. Nonetheless, Dobrynin was promptly summoned to the White House and warned that unless Semenov stopped making serious proposals to Smith, all hell would break loose: "The President's anger at what he could only construe as a deliberate maneuver to deprive him of credit would be massive," Kissinger wrote.

After Dobrynin and Kissinger reached their agreement, but before it was publicly announced, Kissinger had the task of breaking the news to Gerard Smith, who had been abruptly recalled to Washington after Semenov began his overtures.* Their meeting took place on May 19 in the White House, before Kissinger joined Nixon and the other aides for the evening cruise on the *Sequoia*. "It was not a pleasant assignment," Kissinger wrote, but he did the best he could: "I showed Smith all the exchanges with the Soviets and a summary of my conversations."

Smith didn't remember it quite that way. In his memoirs, he recalled only being given a look at the formal Kissinger-Dobrynin statement to be delivered the next day by Nixon. He expressed dismay at the ambiguity of the language and the fact that nothing in the statement or in the backchannel records he saw mentioned submarine-launched ballistic missiles. He was further convinced, Smith wrote, that the language in the announcement was of "obvious Russian origin," indicating that Kissinger, in his reluctance to involve the bureaucracy, had left the drafting of the statement to the Soviets—and thus was more vulnerable to subtle shifts of interpretation. Smith also did not view the announcement as quite the awesome breakthrough that Nixon and Kissinger described, since the Soviets had begun the SALT process two years earlier by insisting that defensive and offensive strategic weapons be limited.

---

* There was also the problem of how to deal with Rogers, who had once again been pushed aside. Nixon's first instinct, wrote Kissinger, was "to claim that a sudden Soviet communication had unexpectedly produced a breakthrough." That excuse would be used in July to explain how Kissinger suddenly wound up in Peking. Instead, after some discussion, Kissinger wrote, Nixon left it up to Haldeman to tell Rogers.

Kissinger tried to salvage something from the encounter. "I was told," Smith wrote in his understated style, "that Secretary Laird would be advised of the agreement at one o'clock that day and the President was just then advising the Secretary of State. I suppose I should have been pleased to be advised before the Secretary of Defense: There was no need for me to tell Kissinger what I thought of his procedure in negotiating behind the back of all responsible Administration officials save the President."

Smith's distaste would have been more acute if he had known that the backchannel records he saw were not complete. Kissinger aides recall that the documents shown Smith had been carefully "sanitized" of any possibly embarrassing information. Some portions had been hastily rewritten before Smith's arrival, apparently by Sonnenfeldt and William Hyland, Kissinger's trusted Soviet experts. The practice was not new. Earlier that spring, Kissinger, always anxious to have sources inside what he believed were enemy camps, had begun showing memoranda of some of his backchannel conversations with Dobrynin to Paul Nitze, the arms control skeptic who was a Pentagon representative on the SALT delegation. Kissinger insisted that Nitze could see the material only if he promised to report on the internal machinations of the delegation. Nitze, consistent in his loyalty to Gerard Smith, again refused to spy for the White House, and a compromise was reached: Nitze would not tell Smith about the existence of the backchannel, but would tell him as much as he could about the substance of the Kissinger-Dobrynin exchanges without describing the source of his information. Nitze was aware that he wasn't seeing every document generated in the backchannel, but he did believe he was seeing the full reports of certain conversations. Even those reports had been substantially altered, however. David Halperin vividly recalls the hasty rewriting that went on before the documents were shown to Nitze. "He only saw excerpts," Halperin said, "but the documents were characterized to him as being the whole record."

Such chicanery did not hide the fact that Kissinger, to the surprise of both Smith and Nitze, had not made any effort to include submarine-launched missiles in the agreement. As it stood at the time of Nixon's announcement on May 20, the Soviets were required only to discuss certain unspecified limits on their land-based ICBMs. Nitze vividly recalls the backchannel exchange at which SLBMs were discussed: "At one point Dobrynin asked Henry whether the freeze would apply to ICBM and SLBM launchers. Henry told him, 'I don't know.' He checked with the President and came back and said, 'I don't care.'" The Soviets, then building submarines at the rate of eight per year, of course opted to exclude the SLBMs from any subsequent freeze negotiations. "Henry didn't understand," Nitze says. "He knew the difference [between the sea-based and land-based missiles] but didn't realize the significance of the difference and the problem that a large Soviet advantage in SLBMs was going to cause the Joint Chiefs of Staff."

Over the next year, as the American and Soviet SALT delegations strove to implement the backchannel agreement, a major emphasis would be placed on restoring some SLBM limits. And in April 1972, only a month before Nixon was to arrive in Moscow for the summit, Kissinger would have to negotiate in the backchannel again. Once again there would be questionable bargaining in private.

Smith, who made no public complaints while serving in the Nixon Administration, wrote in his memoirs: "An autopsy may be in order to see how the May 20 agreement was reached. . . . The backchannel negotiation, as it had been called, followed an entirely different procedure from that which governed the delegation. There were no building blocks, no analytical work, no strategic analysis in the agencies concerned. There were no Verification Panel or National Security Council discussions. There were no consultations with congressional committees or with allies. It was a one-man stand, a presidential aide against the resources of the Soviet leadership. . . . It is not a pleasing contrast —one American . . . ranged against the top Soviet political and technical authorities."

Later that summer, when the delegations were back at work, Smith would learn informally from Semenov about Kissinger's second significant backchannel concession: to waive any constraints against modernization, a decision that would permit the Soviets to make huge qualitative improvements in their missiles. They would be able to hurl more powerful nuclear warheads farther and more accurately without the expense and difficulty of significantly enlarging the size of the missile silo.

In the Pentagon, where the Joint Chiefs of Staff received even less information about the backchannel talks than the SALT delegation did, there was confusion and suspicion over the sudden breakthrough on May 20. Admiral Elmo Zumwalt recalled a JCS meeting that week at which the military's representative on the SALT delegation, Lieutenant General Royal B. Allison, was at as "much of a loss as we to explain the Soviet shift," which had the effect of "letting us off the NCA hook we had caught ourselves on." Zumwalt and his colleagues realized that the Nixon announcement meant that the administration and the Soviet Union had come to some kind of political agreement in the SALT talks; a deal had been struck. "Now we faced the probability," Zumwalt wrote in his memoirs, ". . . that if we could not negotiate an agreement favorable to the U.S., we would sign one that was unfavorable." Although he and his colleagues would strongly oppose the SALT I agreements, Zumwalt had a grudging admiration for Kissinger's continued ability to manipulate the bureaucracy: "The old prestidigitator's hand continued to be quicker than our eyes."

The key to the White House's hidden agenda was to be found in the link between grain and the SALT talks. Interviews with Colson and the union leaders he negotiated with, including such stalwarts as Jay Lovestone of the AFL-CIO, Thomas W. (Teddy) Gleason of the International Longshoremen's Association, Frank Drozak of the Seafarers International Union, and Jesse M. Calhoon of the Marine Engineers' Beneficial Association, produced extensive evidence that Nixon had accomplished his backchannel SALT breakthrough only after assuring Moscow that he would end the grain embargo and once again sell American wheat to the Soviet Union. To accomplish this, as Nixon knew, he would first have to arrange to ship most of the wheat on Soviet freighters, whose operating costs were far lower; he would have to persuade the maritime unions to accept the increased use of Soviet ships and drop their long-standing political objections to loading Russian vessels. Government policy at the time called for fully half of all grain shipments to the Soviet Union to be on the unionized and more costly American freighters. The President, working primarily through Colson, got his way, but only after making a series of private economic and political concessions to the unions that somehow did not become public.

In his memoirs, Kissinger wrote little about his role in the sale of American grain to the Soviet Union, which he said began only after the Moscow summit in 1972. "Every President since Kennedy," wrote Kissinger, "had considered that it would be a major political success to demonstrate the superiority of our system by selling the Soviet Union what it could not grow for itself. For a while our labor unions had prevented such sales by refusing to load Soviet ships and by requiring shipment in American bottoms, which were far too expensive for the Soviets. But those issues were resolved soon after the summit. . . . Fundamentally, the Soviet purchase of grain in our markets was seen as a domestic matter, an element of our agricultural policy; the NSC staff was kept informed only in general terms."

Kissinger was in fact involved in the grain sale every step of the way, beginning less than three weeks after the May 20, 1971, "breakthrough." It was not until late fall, when Kissinger was still unable to persuade the maritime unions to drop their objections to loading Soviet ships, that Nixon turned to Chuck Colson, who made a series of secret commitments and won over the dock workers.

Kissinger's first known involvement was on June 8, 1971, when he telephoned Lovestone, the AFL-CIO's virulently anti-Communist director of international affairs. There was a problem with the maritime unions, Kissinger said, and an immediate meeting was necessary. Lovestone arranged for Teddy Gleason, the tough-talking ILA president, to attend the meeting at the White House the next day. Gleason, another fervent anti-Communist, had led his union in refusing to permit the loading of Soviet merchant ships; in 1964 he was quoted in a Maritime Administration hearing as saying, in reference to a pending Soviet grain sale, "Let the Russians go to hell. Let 'em starve."

The June 9 meeting in Kissinger's office did not go well, according to the union men. Kissinger discoursed on international conditions until Gleason, who obviously had more sources of information than Kissinger anticipated, spoke up: "Dr. Kissinger, I don't see why the hell we're beating around the bush. There's a big grain deal involved. We're against it but you people have the power." The longshoremen would not load the grain, Gleason insisted, unless half the shipment was made on American vessels.

At this point, an eyewitness recalls, Kissinger affected surprise upon hearing that a grain sale was pending. He pushed a button on his desk, picked up his telephone, and briskly asked about a pending Soviet grain deal. It seemed to the union men that no one was on the other end of the telephone. Finally putting it down, Kissinger announced that Gleason was right—a Soviet grain deal was in the works. Then he got around to hinting that the administration wanted Gleason and his workers to load the Soviet ships. "Dr. Kissinger," Gleason exclaimed, "I want to tell you something: We won't let you sell the American people down the Volga or down the Yangtze."

Kissinger was never able to have his way with the maritime union leaders as he could with the press and diplomatic corps. There would be more private meetings in the next few months, and appeals to patriotism and national security, but they would fail to move the longshoremen. One union leader who was exceptionally unimpressed by Kissinger was Paul Hall, president of the SIU, which in 1971 represented a majority of America's merchant seamen. Hall, who died in 1980, talked in 1971 about the pressure Kissinger applied to the maritime unions with two close associates, Frank Drozak, who succeeded him as president, and Herbert Brand, chairman of the board of directors of the Transportation Institute of Washington, a maritime research organization. Both remember Hall's anger at Kissinger's request that the unions, for dimly defined national security reasons, drop their objections to the easing of Soviet trade restrictions, a request that did not include the promise of something in return. Brand quotes one of Hall's complaints: "Kissinger thinks that when he walks into a room, he's 60 percent there already."

"We had a view of this guy," Brand says. "There are labor mediators who are professionals and, in my book, this is what Kissinger is—he's a mediator. What he wants to do is make a score. He wants to make the agreement. We've seen these guys. They have no commitment to protecting either side. All they want to see is what you give up." Hall and the other waterfront union leaders, including Gleason, were impervious to Kissinger's charm—or his intimidation. Hall thought he was being taken for granted by a "superintellect." Brand says, "Hall told me: 'I don't like to be punked.' "

Apparently, Kissinger still did not anticipate any serious problems with the maritime unions, for on June 10, the day after his meeting with Lovestone and Gleason, the White House announced that it had removed export controls on a wide array of nonstrategic American items, including metals, electronic goods, communications equipment, agricultural products, and automotive and consumer goods. In a formal statement and a series of press briefings, the White House presented the President's action as being designed to end the twenty-one-year embargo on trade with Peking. But the order went much further: It also ended the policy, in force since 1963, that called for half of all grain trade to the Soviet Union and Eastern Europe to be carried on American flag vessels. This policy change, which received far less attention, made it clear that the move was aimed at least as much at the Soviet Union, and SALT, as at the Chinese.

The White House's action in lifting the shipping restrictions was publicly criticized by maritime union officials and by George Meany, president of the AFL-CIO, who sent Nixon a letter on June 15 pointing out that American merchant vessels had been carrying less than 5 percent of the nation's foreign trade, with little prospect for improvement, even before the removal of the sanctions. The language of the protests was moderate, but a union official was quoted in the *Baltimore Sun* as saying that the lack of strong rhetoric did not indicate any softening of the unions' resolve not to load Soviet ships.

Kissinger, however, had a different interpretation, telling reporters through his aides that Gleason and Lovestone had produced "no fuss" at the meeting. "They said they'd keep their mouths shut and they did," the *Washington Post* later quoted a White House official as saying. That view found its way to Meany, who called in Lovestone and Gleason and asked each of them to report separately; he had been told, Meany explained, that "Kissinger had put out the word that Lovestone and Gleason had gone along." After comparing notes, the three officials concluded that Kissinger had deliberately chosen to distort the gist of the private meeting. As one involved union official recalled, "We were furious at Henry for what he said and did."

Such tactics, commonplace for Kissinger in the day-to-day world of bureaucracy and diplomacy, proved to be an egregious error with the union leaders during the next few months. The summer of 1971, with a crisis over the Pentagon Papers, internal dissent over SALT, the always festering situation in Vietnam, and a first trip to China, was an exceedingly busy period for Nixon and Kissinger, but the question of which union would or would not load American wheat on Soviet ships remained a high priority in the White House.

Grain purchases were also a priority for the Soviet Union, and by July its export officials were in contact with the Continental Grain Company of New York. In early October, the Soviets placed an order for nearly three million tons of barley, corn, and oats. A second order went to another major grain company, Cargill, Incorporated, of Minneapolis, calling for at least 800,000 tons of barley and oats. The two sales totaled nearly $200 million, roughly 15 percent of American grain exports for all of 1970. And by the end of the summer, the Soviets had placed orders for millions of dollars worth of manufacturing goods, machine tools, and road-building equipment. Only Teddy Gleason and Paul Hall stood in the way.

In late October, representatives of Continental and Cargill met in Washington with the maritime unions, who again refused to load Soviet merchant ships unless American ships were promised half the cargo, as would have been mandatory before Nixon lifted the 1963 sanctions. One union official privately told the *Baltimore Sun* after the meeting that "I think more is at stake than they [the administration and grain companies] let on in the long run." If the government thinks the grain shipments are *that* important, he added, "let's see what we can get for them."

By late October, the grain sales had become more than important; they were a presidential obsession. On October 12, 1971, Nixon announced that his long-desired summit would be held in Moscow in late May of 1972—perfect timing for his reelection drive. Its success, Nixon, Kissinger, and the Soviet Politburo knew, would hinge on a successful resolution of the outstanding SALT issues. And SALT, in turn, would hinge on the sale of American feed grains to Russia. It was up to Colson. The call for help came late one night from an agitated President. "Henry has been cold-shouldered by Gleason," the President explained. "SALT depends on it. Can you save it?" Nixon was worried, Colson recalls; it would be a tough job. If the Democratic unions had refused to load Soviet ships for John F. Kennedy, why would they load them for Nixon?

Colson had already begun his political romancing of the maritime unions as part of Nixon's reelection campaign. He knew that Gleason had told Kissinger "to go fuck yourself," as Colson puts it, "and loved doing it." Colson promptly approached his oldest acquaintance in the maritime union movement,

Jesse Calhoon, president of the Marine Engineers' Beneficial Association. "I thought this guy Calhoon was really great," Colson says. "He was tough—no liberal. I called him in and I said we've got to make a deal. He said, 'What's in it for us?' " Calhoon recalls the meeting and remembers Colson's explaining "that the whole Soviet SALT agreement hinged on the trade agreement. He said he'd been assigned by Nixon to see if we could work out a satisfactory agreement with the maritime industry."

The first concession was relatively easy for the White House, Calhoon says. Colson agreed to have the federal budget revised and funds freed to permit the immediate construction of more merchant ships, thus speeding up a planned revitalization of the dwindling American cargo fleet. Such intervention in the budget process, without revealing what was at stake, was far more complicated than Calhoon could appreciate. A second concession was more important and even more difficult: Colson promised the unions, on behalf of the President, that Nixon would not veto legislation pending in the Senate that would require 50 percent of all oil imported to the United States to be carried on American ships. This legislation was an amendment, offered on behalf of the maritime unions, to the 1954 Cargo Preference Act, which declared that half of all federally subsidized shipments—such as those under Food for Peace or AID grants—must be carried, whenever feasible, on American flag vessels. Colson's promise meant that the Nixon White House was committed to an extension of the Cargo Preference Act to the private sector. The amendment was not considered likely to pass the Senate (it did, in fact, lose by eight votes in July 1972), but Nixon's gamble was still an extraordinary one. If the legislation had somehow passed the House and Senate before the election, as did a similar amendment in 1974, Nixon's refusal to veto it would have astounded and infuriated his supporters in the oil and banking industries, who had raised millions of dollars for his campaign.*

Calhoon, in an interview in 1981, confirmed that the deal, as described by Colson, was accepted by the maritime unions; he was convinced, he said, that "Nixon would have signed the legislation" if it had been passed by Congress.† Calhoon recalled something else about his meetings with Colson and other White House officials that fall. "There was one quote that sticks in my mind," he said. One of Nixon's aides, stressing the urgency of the situation, solemnly cited the words of Anatoliy Dobrynin, telling the union leader that Dobrynin had threatened "that there would be no SALT agreement unless the grain deal was worked out."

* The 1974 amendment, which was vetoed by President Gerald R. Ford late in December, provided for 20 percent of all privately imported foreign oil to be carried on American flag carriers, with an increase to 30 percent by 1977. In his autobiography, *A Time to Heal,* Ford wrote of his difficulty in telling Paul Hall he had decided to veto: "I knew that my decision would come as a blow to Hall and when I telephoned him . . . our conversation was strained. He was terribly disappointed." Most of the union anger was directed at Kissinger, who, so Hall, Calhoon, and other maritime leaders believed, was instrumental in getting the veto. Their anger stemmed in part from their awareness of Kissinger's role in the 1971 negotiations. The union leaders felt that Kissinger had doublecrossed them.

If the Cargo Preference Act amendment had passed Congress in 1972, it would have affected only 25 percent of privately shipped oil, since roughly half the oil imported into the United States then was residual fuel oil and No. 2 fuel oil, which were exempt, under federal rules, from the provisions of the Cargo Preference Act.

† Teddy Gleason, in a 1981 interview, also confirmed that such an agreement was struck, as did Frank Drozak, Hall's replacement as SIU president.

Calhoon and the other union officials agreed to keep quiet about their politicking with Colson and their decision to do a turnabout and permit the loading of grain and other American export goods on Soviet ships. "We didn't like the fucking Russians to start with," Calhoon explained. "No union guy wants to be seen as a friend of the Russians, and so we kept our mouths shut." To do otherwise, of course, would have spilled the beans. The unions' decision was announced in early November 1971, at a White House news conference staged by a group of aides, including Andrew E. Gibson, Assistant Secretary of Commerce for Maritime Affairs. Gibson, who had worked closely with Colson in the negotiations, told the assembled reporters, according to an account in the *New York Times,* that the unions had not "asked for anything in return for permitting the grain to be loaded on foreign vessels."

The successful resolution of the shiploading crisis in 1971 was the beginning of a beautiful friendship between Richard Nixon and the maritime unions. In September 1972, Teddy Gleason became the first member of the AFL-CIO's executive committee to endorse Nixon's reelection. Gleason also praised the administration's plan to sell hundreds of millions of dollars' worth of wheat to the Soviets, telling a news conference—in what amounted to a self-serving version of linkage—that expanded trade with the Russians and the Chinese was the best way to get increased pressure put on North Vietnam to release the American prisoners of war.*

Kissinger, notwithstanding his published denials, continued to play a key role in American-Soviet trade talks throughout 1971 and 1972. On January 31, 1972, for example, in a directive to the Secretaries of State, Commerce, and Agriculture, he cited agricultural products as "one of the possible areas for increased trade with Russia . . ." Two weeks later, he directed the Agriculture Department to begin work on a "negotiating scenario" that would provide American credits in dollars to the Soviet Union for the purpose of buying grain.

The most immediate payoff for the secret SALT and grain concessions was political, and it had come on August 10, 1971, when the Soviets at long last invited Nixon to Moscow for a summit in May or June 1972. The summit thus would take place within weeks of the Democratic National Convention in Miami. The Soviet Union had decided to help reelect Richard Nixon, and it was permitting him to successfully negotiate the world's first significant arms control agreement just before the Democrats nominated a candidate who would have one basic issue in the presidential campaign—peace.

Nixon and Kissinger would continue to have acute negotiating and personal problems with the American SALT delegation. The men doing the day-to-day

---

* The possibility exists that there was more to the relationship between the White House and the unions than the public record shows. Early in 1973, the Nixon reelection campaign, fulfilling its reporting obligations to the General Accounting Office, listed a last-minute $100,000 contribution from the Seafarers International Union in a year-end statement. The $100,000 was borrowed from the Chemical Bank of New York, whose executive committee chairman was a Nixon campaign finance official. The SIU contribution came within weeks after a Justice Department decision not to appeal a federal judge's order dismissing charges against the union for illegal 1968 campaign contributions to the Democrats and Republicans. The judge based his ruling on the lack of a speedy trial in the original case.

bargaining with the Soviets were confounded by many of the President's decisions, and would continue to be.

In the months after the May 20, 1971, "breakthrough," the SALT delegation and the bureaucracy managed to convince Kissinger that some limits on Soviet SLBMs would have to be included in any summit agreement, if only to protect the agreement from severe and possibly fatal criticism from Congress and arms experts. Kissinger's backchannel negotiating error on the SLBM issue was never fully rectified, nor was the SALT delegation able to rebound from Kissinger's agreement to permit the Soviet Union to modernize its missile weaponry without restrictions. In August, the delegation ran up against another backchannel agreement, also of dubious merit, that became known only after Nixon had abruptly refused to permit Gerard Smith to begin formal discussions of a total ban on ABM systems, despite hints from the Soviet delegation that such a ban would be seriously considered. "The opportunity to eliminate a central weapons system from strategic arsenals and from the competition between the two sides was lost," Smith wrote in obvious despair.*

Kissinger later made clear that he and Dobrynin had ruled out a total ABM ban in the backchannel, a move that would mollify the military in Russia and America. After that pronouncement, it was obvious to the American negotiators that each side would eventually agree on a limit of one or two sites, and Nixon and Kissinger left the ABM issue, with its complicated negotiations over radars and futuristic weaponry, to the SALT delegation. There would be no sense of urgency in the White House over the winter and early spring of 1972 to reach final agreement on the other outstanding issues, those dealing with the proposed interim limits on offensive missile systems. Members of the delegation and Kissinger's staff aides understood that Nixon and Kissinger were deliberately stretching out the SALT negotiations to insure that some issues would be left to the summit for triumphant presidential resolution.

---

* Nixon sent Smith a personal note in mid-August in an effort to explain his decision against a total ABM ban. After reviewing the record, Nixon said, "it is my conclusion that pressing for a complete ban on ABMs would risk jeopardizing the understanding already achieved with the USSR. This is all the more true because if we went to a zero ABM proposal we would have to ask for more sweeping offensive limitation than seems immediately negotiable." Smith reprinted the letter in his memoirs, noting that he was unable to "see the logic" in Nixon's claim that there was a connection between an ABM ban and further reductions in offensive arms. That there was no such connection was subsequently made very clear, when Nixon traveled to Moscow in 1974, shortly before he was forced out of office, and agreed to reduce the two SAM sites permissible under the SALT treaty to one, without negotiating any further limitations on offensive arms. Nixon was consistent in his manipulation of the ABM issue for political purposes. In July 1970, when he was desperate for a Soviet summit before the 1970 congressional elections, Nixon told Kissinger that he was willing to negotiate an ABM-only agreement with the Soviets, and worry about offensive limitations in subsequent arms talks. "I shudder at how a summit would have unfolded in 1970," Kissinger wrote.

26
CHINA:
OPENING MOVES

THE AMERICAN RAPPROCHEMENT with China was the high point of Richard Nixon's presidency and the most positive product of his collaboration with Henry Kissinger. China was Nixon's vision and triumph; somehow Nixon understood—as John Kennedy and Lyndon Johnson had not—the possibility and the importance of triangular diplomacy. An opening to China would not endanger relations with the Soviet Union, he sensed, but improve them, as well as further isolate North Vietnam from one of its main suppliers. Nixon also understood the immense political potential a China opening offered: A prime-time visit to Peking would astonish and neutralize American liberals and assure his reelection.

As a congressman, Nixon had railed against the Chinese Communists and joined in criticizing the Truman Administration for "losing" China in 1949, when Chiang Kai-shek fled in defeat to the island of Formosa (known to the Communist Chinese as Taiwan), leaving Chairman Mao Tse-tung and his movement in control of the mainland. However, as with other major foreign policy issues, Nixon's views on China had always been more pragmatic than ideological. In 1960, the year after his highly successful visit to Moscow—where his "kitchen debate" with Khrushchev brought much publicity at home—Vice President Nixon tried to get a visa to Peking. His theory, as Paul Dixon, a columnist close to Nixon, wrote at the time, was "that if it worked once it can work twice and that if he can achieve a 'breakthrough' into the forbidden country that holds one-fourth of the earth's people his 'image' will be so gigantic he'll overshadow any stay-at-home Democratic opponent." In his memoirs, Nixon, while not mentioning his 1960 scheme, recalled his trip around the world in 1967 in which he learned, he said, that many foreign leaders "had come around to the view that some new and direct relationship between the two nations [America and China] was essential if there were to be any chance at all . . . to build a lasting peace in Asia. . . ." Nixon sounded that theme in a much-quoted article on Asia published in late 1967 in *Foreign Affairs* magazine. "In the long view," Nixon wrote, "we simply cannot afford to leave China forever outside the family of nations, there to nurture its fantasies, cherish its hates and threaten its neighbors." At the time, the official United States position was, in essence, that China—with its eight hundred million residents—did not exist; the Taiwan government of Chiang Kai-shek was the

350

only China formally recognized by Washington. In August 1968, just before his nomination at the Republican convention in Miami, Nixon described China, according to the Associated Press, as "the next superpower"; he also said he might visit Peking "if they would give me a visa." Nixon stayed with these views after the election, telling members of his transition team that one of the goals of his administration would be to recognize China.

There is no evidence that Kissinger seriously considered the question of an American-Chinese rapprochement before his appointment as Nixon's national security adviser. In the first few contacts with the Chinese, Nixon emerged as the grand theoretician and Kissinger as his occasional operative, the agent who found some of the backchannels and delivered a few of the messages. Within months after Nixon's inauguration, the increasingly bitter Sino-Soviet dispute made Nixon's private hopes more credible. By the end of the summer, Kissinger—not surprisingly—had become convinced that Nixon was right about the possibility of a rapprochement with China, and about the great strategic potential of such a move. In his memoirs, he cited November 1969 as the beginning of "an intricate minuet between us and the Chinese so delicately arranged that both sides could always maintain that they were not in contact, so stylized that neither side needed to bear the onus of an initiative. . . ."

The American "signals" to China were far from delicate. China was barraged with hints, messages, and clues from Washington attesting to Nixon's desire to change relationships. Most of these contacts were hidden from the bureaucracy, but the backchannel at times seemed to veer out of control. By late 1970, at least five, and perhaps more, different groups of diplomats were funneling messages from Washington to Peking, via Pakistan, France, Romania, and even Norway. Kissinger, always a master at disciplining the backchannel approaches, had a unique problem with China—the President. Nixon, far more than in any other area, was personally involved in these communications, and he seemed intent on establishing his own backchannels, notably with the French, Romanians, and Pakistanis.

Nixon made his initial move in early 1969, while on his first overseas trip as President. In Paris, he brought up China during a private meeting with French President Charles de Gaulle, whose Foreign Ministry continued to maintain diplomatic relations—strained as they were—with the Peking regime during the ragged years of China's Great Proletarian Cultural Revolution. Exactly what Nixon said to De Gaulle is in some dispute. In their biography of Kissinger, the Kalbs quoted Nixon as telling De Gaulle that he envisaged the admission of Peking to the United Nations and the "normalization" of relations between China and the United States. Nixon was also said to have asked De Gaulle to relay word to the Chinese through the French Ambassador in Peking that he would put an end to the American involvement in Vietnam. In his memoirs, Nixon quoted De Gaulle as bringing up the subject of American normalization with China. He and De Gaulle had agreed on the need for more communication with China as it became a nuclear power and grew in strength, and De Gaulle had added: "It would be better for you to recognize China before you are obliged to do so by the growth of China." Nixon wrote that he had agreed with De Gaulle's suggestion that direct negotiations between North Vietnam and the United States be initiated in an effort to end the war. Kissinger's memoirs depicted the Nixon–De Gaulle talk as a much more general conversation, in which Nixon's intent was only to "keep his options open." Nixon's remarks to De Gaulle could not have been extensive, Kissinger added, because "the new Administration"—preoccupied with Vietnam—"had no clear-cut plan."

China must have been a sensitive policy area for Kissinger in early 1969. Still new to his job, he knew little of the political makeup of China and had yet to begin to reevaluate his stereotyped view of it as a brooding and violently xenophobic society immune to diplomatic approaches. The Kalbs quoted him as saying to an aide, "I can't recall anyone ever inviting me to dinner to hear my views about *China*." Roger Morris, who joined Kissinger at the Hotel Pierre in late 1968, recalls the staff's amazement at learning of Nixon's plans for China. "You're not going to believe this," Morris quoted another aide as saying after a staff meeting, "but Nixon wants to recognize China." For Nixon, Morris says, the move toward China "was there from the beginning," while Kissinger had neither the interest nor the "political bureaucratic inclination to raise it." In his memoirs, however, Kissinger suggested that Nixon at first shared his skepticism but that, as events proceeded, both came to change their minds. "We took even ourselves by surprise," Kissinger wrote of the subsequent breakthrough. "Originally we had not thought reconciliation possible."

The evidence is clear, nonetheless, that Nixon was alone in understanding very early in his administration that an approach to China would be possible after he began the Vietnamization program. He played his hand quietly at first. Nixon did indeed make a number of far-reaching statements to De Gaulle, as the Kalbs reported and Kissinger denied. The French Ambassador to China, Etienne M. Manac'h, who took up his assignment in April 1969, carried Nixon's message to Peking with him. In mid-1971, Manac'h met with Ross Terrill, the Australian journalist and China expert, and told Terrill he had informed the Chinese that Nixon planned to withdraw from Vietnam and was going to begin a process of normalization with Peking. Manac'h also told Terrill that Peking had been impressed by Nixon's statements and the subsequent withdrawals of American troops from Vietnam. Peking came to understand, Manac'h said, that Nixon had meant what he told De Gaulle. And thus Nixon, whose words and deeds on Vietnam were already being denounced at home, was viewed as a man of integrity 12,000 miles away. China's image of Nixon would not change, even after Watergate.

Nixon and Kissinger conducted their pursuit of China without seeming to perceive the full extent of the economic, cultural, and political disarray caused by the Cultural Revolution, which erupted—with Mao's approval—in 1965. Within months, the country was in upheaval, with millions of self-styled "Red Guards" attacking intellectual and social life, shutting universities, and triggering mass purges of those thought to harbor bourgeois thoughts or intellectualism or "modernism." China, always aloof, sealed itself more deeply from the world during the revolution, recalling all but one of its ambassadors from foreign capitals (the sole ambassador to stay on was in Cairo).* After Mao's death in 1976, Chinese leaders became increasingly critical of the excesses of the Cultural Revolution, and claimed that its incessant purges and internal feuding had brought China to the brink of economic disaster. In late 1980, Chiang Ching, Mao's wife, who was a militant leader of the Cultural Revolution, was brought to trial by the government. She and nine other defendants were formally accused of responsibility for the deaths of 34,380 citizens and the persecution of more than 80,000 members of the People's Liberation Army. The indictment further charged that Defense Minister Lin Piao, one of Mao's oldest associates and another leader of the Cultural Revolution, had unsuccessfully plotted to assassinate Mao in September 1971, two months after Kissinger's secret visit to Peking in 1971. The attempt failed, and Lin reportedly was killed when his plane crashed while attempting to flee China for the Soviet Union. All the defendants were found guilty in early 1981 in a staged event that, by implication, tried the leadership of Mao himself during the years of the Cultural Revolution. There was no independent verification of the number of beatings and deaths allegedly triggered by the Cultural Revolution and the Red Guards, but the violence of the upheaval was greater than Nixon and Kissinger, with their limited knowledge of China, could comprehend. Lin Piao's threats had so unnerved Mao and his immediate aides that by early 1970 he was forced to flee his home inside the walls of the Imperial City in Peking, where he and his wife, Chiang Ching, had lived since his Communist forces seized control of the city in 1949. Chiang Ching's American biographer, Roxanne Witke, wrote that the two fled because "constant threats, divisiveness among the people, and conspiratorial actions made it almost impossible for them to work—even at their home . . . which had also become infiltrated by the enemy. Nor could they sleep or eat there safely." Witke, who interviewed Chiang Ching extensively, also wrote that Mao did not receive foreign guests at the Imperial City until February 1972, when he met there with the unsuspecting Richard Nixon.

Little of the tension inside China at the time was reflected in Nixon's and Kissinger's memoirs. For political reasons and because it made good "p.r.," the White House had decided to humanize and romanticize Chairman Mao and Premier Chou En-lai, who directed the Chinese negotiations during the Kissinger and Nixon visits. The China to which Nixon and Kissinger wanted to expose the American people was not the China that existed; for many of the masses, Mao Tse-tung did not always represent serenity and continuity but, far more often, turmoil, paranoia, and human suffering. The serene, ancient Peking that Kissinger and Nixon visited and described in their memoirs was, to some extent, a Potemkin Village that successfully concealed the true state of China's internal affairs.

China made the first approach, just after Nixon's election and three months after the Soviet invasion of Czechoslovakia, in August 1968. Most China schol-

---

* Although its ambassadors were withdrawn, China kept the embassies open where possible. The ambassador who stayed on the job was Huang Hua, who later became Ambassador to Canada. Huang Hua emerged as the spokesman for China after it was voted a seat at the United Nations in late 1971, and in 1976 he became China's Foreign Minister, serving until his retirement in 1982.

ars agree that the invasion was a key factor in China's turn to Washington; officials in Peking must have begun to wonder who would be next. By late 1968, two main factions had emerged in the People's Republic. The moderates, headed by Chou En-lai, believed that the growing dissent in America and the hopelessness of the Vietnam War had reduced the American threat to China to the point where negotiations with Washington could begin. The military faction, led by Lin Piao, Chou En-lai's chief rival, argued that China's future lay with the Soviet Union, despite the difficulties between the two countries that had been increasing since 1959. In Lin Piao's view, the United States would sooner or later expand the Vietnam War into China. There were, of course, many other political factions in China, including a radical sect that had led the Cultural Revolution and that argued angrily against rapprochement with either Moscow or Washington, but the main political struggle inside China was between the Lin Piao and Chou En-lai groups, with Chairman Mao's role not always clear.* At a Communist Party meeting in October 1968, Chou En-lai and his pragmatic approach seemed to win, and the next month China sent its first diplomatic signal to Washington, proposing on November 26 that the long-standing ambassadorial talks between China and the United States, which had been held intermittently in Geneva and later in Warsaw, be resumed for the first time since their suspension in May. The Johnson Administration, after checking with President-elect Nixon, agreed that the talks would be reconvened in Warsaw on February 20, 1969. In a Foreign Ministry statement, China made it clear that the new initiative was aimed at Nixon, declaring that by the date of the meeting "The new U. S. President will have been in office for a month, and the U. S. side will probably be able to make up its mind" about the course of future relations.

Most China scholars agreed that Chou En-lai and the moderates, by taking the initiative with Nixon, had exposed themselves and their point of view to harsh criticism from the military and radical factions in China. By early 1969, there were signs of heated political feuding inside China, stimulated by the proposed resumption of the Warsaw talks. Nixon, however, seemed oblivious to the dispute. In his early news conferences he said nothing that could encourage the Chou En-lai faction, and emphasized instead the need for closer American relations with the Soviet Union on such issues as disarmament and Vietnam. Many scholars think that Nixon's failure to provide some public support for China's November 26 initiative doomed the chances—remote as they may have been—for an early resumption of negotiations. The President did not neglect China deliberately; he and his advisers were simply too overwhelmed by the immediate responsibilities of the presidency. On February 18, China canceled the Warsaw meeting, and over the next few months the Chou En-lai faction was in retreat. China was again belligerent about the United

* A 1977 Rand study of Chinese foreign policy, prepared for the Pentagon, concluded that Mao deliberately held back from the internal feuding of the late 1960s, giving the impression to some scholars that he was "little more than a powerless shuttlecock bouncing back and forth between rival factions. . . . We would argue," the study added, "that a more accurate representation would have Mao as the arbiter among various leadership factions—simultaneously manipulating the debate by seemingly throwing his support first with one group and then another. . . . In this manner, Mao cannily awaited the appropriate moment before fully revealing his hand." The truth seems to be that no one really knows where Mao stood.

States, at one point comparing Nixon, while he was on his first presidential trip to Europe, to a "rat crossing the street."

In his memoirs, Kissinger glossed over the early Chinese initiative, stating instead that "by March 1969, Chinese-American relations seemed essentially frozen in the same hostility of mutual incomprehension and distrust that had characterized them for twenty years." He and Nixon, who would later be justifiably proud of their skill in negotiating the Chinese rapprochement, had simply missed a signal whose importance was so great that a China scholar, preparing a private report for the Rand Corporation in 1977, would conclude, "With Nixon ambivalent and without Mao's backing, it was not difficult for the military and the radicals to overturn the [Chou En-lai] initiative and cancel the scheduled Warsaw meeting. As a result, what might have been the Peking Agreement of 1969 instead became the Shanghai Communiqué of 1972."*

Over the next months, two issues emerged that were to lead the way to the American-Chinese rapprochement. For one thing, China and the Soviet Union moved from polemics to shooting along their shared borders in the far reaches of northeast Asia, with large-scale military operations and scores of casualties. The fighting was quickly limited, but each side continued its military buildup and verbal provocations. Each also blamed the other for initiating the fighting, and there were hostile Soviet demonstrations against the Chinese Embassy in Moscow while thousands of Chinese marched against the Soviet Embassy in Peking. The moderate faction in China, fully aware of the economic, political, and social disarray created by the Cultural Revolution, inevitably began looking toward the United States once again. The second issue was Vietnam.

By the summer of 1969, the early Nixon-Kissinger dream of a quick settlement to the war, aided by the Soviets, had vanished. Nixon's speech on May 14, 1969, in which he made what he and Kissinger thought was the generous offer of mutual withdrawal, had produced no positive response from either the Hanoi government or the increasingly restless domestic antiwar movement. The Soviets, perhaps in reaction to the heightened tensions with China, became even more supportive of Hanoi's war effort. On June 13, the Soviet government formally recognized the Provisional Revolutionary Government of South Vietnam, the government-in-exile of the Vietcong's National Liberation Front. In October, as the White House was clearly moving closer to China, the Soviets signed a communiqué fully endorsing the Liberation Front's ten-point peace program, which called for a new coalition government in Saigon. Another factor in the Soviets' strong support for the NLF was the death of Ho Chi Minh in September 1969. Ho had been close to Chairman Mao since their early days as outlaw revolutionaries; his successors were considered more friendly to the Russians.

These developments made an opening to China more attractive for Kissinger and Nixon. Not only would they punish the Soviets for refusing to behave (as the White House viewed it), but perhaps they could also induce China to do what the Soviets never would—cut off or slow down the flow of arms and supplies to Hanoi. As the antiwar movement grew in America, with the success

* Quoted from "Chinese Foreign Policy Factionalism and the Origins of the Strategic Triangle," by Thomas M. Gottlieb, an unclassified report prepared in November 1977 by Rand for the Director of Net Assessment, Office of the Secretary of Defense.

of the student-led Moratoriums in October and November, Nixon became more aware of the political respite that a rapprochement with China could provide.

Within weeks of the Soviet recognition of the PRG, signals to China suddenly began pouring out of the White House.* On July 21, the administration announced a relaxation of passport restrictions on travel to China and also permitted the purchase abroad of up to $100 worth of goods originating in China. Two days later, Nixon told a group of students on the White House lawn, "I want the time to come when the Chinese people and Russian people and all the peoples of this world can walk together and talk together."

In late July and early August, while on his around-the-world trip, Nixon met privately with President Yahya Khan of Pakistan and President Nicolae Ceauşescu of Romania, whose countries had close ties to China and a sometimes frosty relationship with the Soviet Union. The exact nature of Nixon's assurances, for relay to Peking, are not known, but Kissinger, according to his memoirs, set up a backchannel to Peking via Pakistan as soon as he got back to Washington. In August, Secretary of State Rogers made a speech in Australia, not much noticed by the press, in which he explicitly stated that "we have been seeking to open up channels of communication" with China. Even in that early period, anything Rogers was permitted to say in public had already been conveyed to Peking by Nixon or Kissinger in a backchannel message. While all this signaling was going on, Nixon enunciated his Vietnamization policy and began to do what he had asked De Gaulle to tell the Chinese he would do: pull American troops out of South Vietnam. In midsummer he also spelled out the Guam Doctrine, in which he resolved to reduce the American military presence around the world. If the men in Peking needed further confirmation that changes were in the air, it came in early November 1969, when Nixon ordered a suspension of American Navy patrols in the waters between Taiwan and China, thus ending a military surveillance that had begun at the outbreak of the Korean War. Kissinger wrote in his memoirs that the patrols were ended to meet a request of the Pakistanis for something positive to tell Chou En-lai in advance of his scheduled visit to Islamabad, Pakistan's capital.

The significance of these White House moves was generally missed by the press, preoccupied with the furor over the Vietnam War and unable to imagine that Nixon, the cold warrior and original member of the Who Lost China Club, would actually consider a visit to Peking. Despite the carefully kept secrecy, there was still, in the White House view, a basic flaw in the China strategy: The State Department was involved. Kissinger simply did not know enough about China and was forced to rely on the experts in State. The working group there, centered in Richardson's office, was under strict orders to limit information about the China initiatives. Kissinger ordered State and Defense to

* Nixon reacted to the Soviet recognition of the PRG by instructing Kissinger to find a way to give a direct signal of American interest in rapprochement with China. Such requests would normally have been discussed with Morton Halperin, who had written widely on China and its policies toward the West. But Halperin was already a marked man in the White House, and could not be allowed to handle such a sensitive issue. Instead, Kissinger turned to Elliot Richardson, who was ordered to develop a series of proposals for relaxing trade controls. Halperin learned of Kissinger's request immediately, for one of Richardson's deputies promptly telephoned him, among others, to ask for advice.

prepare a series of studies on all aspects of China's foreign policy and the Sino-Soviet split, with the aim of increasing his knowledge to the point where the White House could take control. Roger Morris recalls the China negotiations as "one of the few places where Henry really felt intellectually insecure and could be educated. He was aware of his limitations and approached China in a relatively scholarly way." Morris had been brought in on the China initiative to help analyze the flow of papers from Defense and State on such critical issues as the Chinese-Russian border disputes because, he says, Kissinger believed that John Holdridge, the former West Pointer who was the senior White House aide, "simply couldn't handle it."

One of the few outsiders who ever played an important role in the White House policy, Morris recalls, was Allen S. Whiting, a former State Department official who was then teaching at the University of Michigan.* Whiting, a Democrat, was a critic of the Vietnam War but was also one of the leading intelligence experts on China, having served from 1962 to 1966 as director of the State Department's Office of Research and Analysis for the Far East. On visits to Washington in the summer of 1969, Whiting repeatedly met with his former intelligence colleagues and learned, he says, that they felt "cut off from the White House. They felt useless and unwanted. Henry wasn't asking any questions, because if he asked, the bureaucracy might know what he was planning." During that summer, Whiting learned that senior intelligence officials believed a Soviet bombing attack—with conventional weapons—against Chinese nuclear production facilities was possible. The March battles between Soviet and Chinese border guards had died down by early spring, but the Russians, so Whiting's former colleagues told him, had immediately begun serious preparations for air raids inside China. In May, late-model Soviet aircraft were transferred from Eastern Europe to newly enlarged airfields in Outer Mongolia, within easy reach of China. By June, the Soviets seemed to have completed planning for conventional air strikes against the Chinese nuclear production facility at Lanchow. There were other, equally ominous, military moves. The number of Soviet infantry divisions near China's borders began to increase, and would eventually double from fifteen to thirty; there was also reliable intelligence showing that Soviet missiles, which were probably nuclear-equipped, were being installed near Manchuria, in northeast China, for possible retaliation in case the Chinese fired a nuclear weapon in response to the conventional bombing attack. The ground troops were poised to respond to a nonnuclear retaliation by China. The American experts realized that all these preparations had to be known to the Chinese, who were able to monitor

* The necessity for a change in American policy toward China was clearly felt throughout the academic community. As early as November 6, 1968, the day after Nixon's election, eight prominent China scholars from Harvard University, Columbia University, and the Massachusetts Institute of Technology drafted a memorandum for the President-elect urging his administration to "move more positively toward the relaxation of tensions between China and the eventual achievement of reconciliation." The group, chaired by Professor Jerome A. Cohen, a professor of law at Harvard, urged, among other moves, sending an emissary to meet in secret with the Chinese to discuss prospects for a normal relationship. In February 1969, some members of the group met with Nixon and Kissinger at the White House, but of course none was included or consulted when the American-Chinese contacts began. "Henry didn't give much of a clue as to his thinking," A. Doak Barnett, one of the group, recalls.

Soviet communications.* Whiting learned that the Soviets had even begun making simulated low-level conventional bombing strikes apparently aimed at Lanchow, where, so American intelligence officials thought, the Chinese were operating a centrifuge and gaseous-diffusion plant. The concern of the officials, whose views were not getting to the White House, was that the Chinese would believe the United States had tacitly approved such an attack.

Whiting, who was also a consultant to the Rand Corporation at the time, discussed his findings with Fred Iklé, who insisted that Whiting brief Kissinger. A meeting was arranged in late August at San Clemente, where Kissinger and Nixon were resting after their around-the-world trip. At the time the White House was concerned about the possibility of a Soviet nuclear attack on China. Whiting, in his meeting with Kissinger and John Holdridge, argued that the real threat was not from a nuclear attack but from a conventional attack by the Soviet planes that had been transferred to airfields near the Chinese border.

At that point, Whiting says, Kissinger turned to Holdridge, who acknowledged that he did not know such airfields existed. Whiting then emphasized his belief that the President, by privately assuring the Chinese that the United States would not condone a Soviet attack, nuclear or otherwise, on its nuclear facilities, could improve chances for Chinese concessions on the major issue blocking American-Chinese rapprochement—Taiwan. China's position had seemed eternally intractable: Taiwan was a province of China; the government of the People's Republic was the sole legal government of China and there could be no "two Chinas" policy. Whiting argued that the threat to China from the Soviet Union was so great that Taiwan—although China would never say as much—would be less important and thus there would be some room for bargaining. The flow of world events had put a rapprochement within reach of the White House.

At the close of his presentation, Whiting recalls, Kissinger asked him to write a report for the President. "No one must know of this," Kissinger told Whiting. "You must type it up yourself and bring it back yourself." Whiting, who was working temporarily at Rand's offices in Santa Monica, drove back to his office, wrote his report in a few hours, and late that evening delivered it to the California White House. After that, "I never heard another word."

How important was Whiting's visit? Kissinger did not mention the briefing in his memoirs, although he told the Kalb brothers that he had been influenced by Whiting's analysis. "Years later," the Kalbs wrote in their biography, Kissinger "was to admit its influence on the development of his thinking about China." Morris recalls that Kissinger "respected" Whiting, who became one of the "rare exceptions" to Kissinger's general contempt for academics.†

---

* American intelligence officials believe that the Chinese Communists were among the pioneers in electronic intelligence gathering, having developed a capability to intercept signals by the early 1930s.

† One reason for Kissinger's neglect of Whiting in his memoirs may have to do with Whiting's decision to testify as a witness for Daniel Ellsberg in the 1973 Pentagon Papers trial in Los Angeles. His testimony, as a former senior government intelligence official, was essential: He told the court that publication of the Pentagon Papers did not jeopardize national security—one of the prosecution's key allegations. The government's attorneys were so concerned about his testimony—and similar testimony from Morton Halperin—that they flew in Alexander Haig as a rebuttal witness. Haig, then Vice Chief of Staff of the Army, appeared in the courtroom in uniform, with four stars on each shoulder and eight rows of medals across his chest. Seeking to diminish Whiting's influence

There is other evidence suggesting that Whiting's notion that China might be willing to soften its position on Taiwan was a major new element in the Nixon-Kissinger approach. On September 5, 1969, a few weeks after Whiting met with Kissinger, Elliot Richardson delivered what was, in essence, Whiting's proposed message to the Chinese. Speaking at a meeting of the American Political Science Association in New York, Richardson warned the Soviet Union that the United States "could not fail to be deeply concerned . . . with an escalation" of the Sino-Soviet quarrel. The warning came at the height of reports about Soviet plans for a nuclear strike inside China and its meaning was immediately clear. The United States would not side with the Russians against China. The possibility exists that, as with Rogers' speech in Australia, Kissinger and Nixon had first used the newly created Pakistani backchannel to communicate their position to Peking.

There was another major step. On September 9, Nixon and Kissinger summoned Walter J. Stoessel, Jr., the American Ambassador to Poland, who was returning to Warsaw after a home leave, for what Stoessel thought would be a routine review of American-Polish problems. Instead, Nixon promptly turned to the Chinese issue, and asked the Ambassador to establish secret contact with the Chinese Ambassador in Warsaw. The President told Stoessel, according to Tad Szulc's *The Illusion of Peace,* that the American feelers put out through Pakistan, Romania, and France were not working as rapidly as the White House wished. Stoessel was to take action to renew the Warsaw talks. Nixon and Kissinger apparently did not realize that there was no Chinese Ambassador in Warsaw at the time, another lingering effect of the Cultural Revolution. It took Stoessel nearly three months to make an informal contact with Lei Yang, the chargé d'affaires, who was, of course, startled and unsettled.* Two days later, on December 5, the Chinese telephoned Stoessel and invited him for tea the next week at the Chinese Embassy—an unprecedented event, since none of the previous Chinese-American encounters in Warsaw had taken place on Chinese ground. Kissinger was exultant over the Chinese invitation, for, as he excitedly told Haldeman, Stoessel had been specifically invited to arrive at the front door—a clear signal to the Soviets.† Triangular

---

as an adviser to Kissinger, Haig testified that Kissinger had met with him only four times, to discuss "the political situation in Communist China." But he acknowledged, under cross-examination, that the two men could have had telephone discussions he had not known about.

* Kissinger was unsettled too, believing that Stoessel was deliberately defying his instructions. The Kalbs quoted Kissinger as claiming that he had to send Stoessel three cables and warn him, "Either you do it or we will get somebody who will," before Stoessel made the approach. Stoessel's version, as he gave it to Szulc, was that he had been unable to approach the Chinese official privately at any party or diplomatic reception that fall and winter. When he did make contact, on December 3, he did so by running after the Chinese delegation as they left a reception and explaining his purpose to the chargé's interpreter.

† In his memoirs, Haldeman reprinted portions of his diary in which he had noted Kissinger's "great state of excitement" over the Chinese invitation. Kissinger also volunteered his "personal opinion that the Russian/Chinese situation was very serious and that he expected that there was a very strong probability that the Russians would attack China by April 15th [1970]." Kissinger did not mention any such personal opinion in his memoirs. As we have seen, there were repeated rumors in the late summer of 1969—apparently started by the Soviets—of a possible strike against China's nuclear facilities, but such talk dissipated by October, when the Chinese and Soviets began negotiations in Peking about the border disputes. Did Kissinger really believe in December that such an attack was still possible? Or was it merely his manner of dealing with men such as Haldeman, whom he considered ignoramuses about foreign policy? Haldeman declared in his book that

diplomacy suddenly sprang to life, and the Nixon Administration held the upper hand. Stoessel and Lei Yang agreed at their meeting to set January 20, 1970, as the date for renewing the formal ambassadorial meetings.

By early 1970, China's foreign policy was in the midst of a metamorphosis. Public statements about the United States became far more flexible, beginning with a statement on September 29, 1969—a few weeks after Under Secretary Richardson's New York warning to the Soviets—declaring that Washington had become "more and more passive" toward China in recent years. China was also renewing its contact with the world, reopening its embassies and its diplomatic relations with nations in Eastern Europe, such as Yugoslavia, and in the Middle East.

There were two Warsaw meetings in 1970, in January and February, and these were far more important than either Kissinger or Nixon has ever acknowledged. Despite these successes, the Warsaw forum would never do, for the State Department was involved there and Kissinger and Nixon were, as usual, determined not to share any foreign policy triumphs. Nixon, of course, had his vision of a dramatic trip to Peking and his subsequent reelection. Kissinger had his dreams of glory, too: By early 1970, Morris remembers, there was talk of Kissinger—not some faceless bureaucrat—attending the Warsaw meetings to negotiate face to face with the Chinese. But Kissinger was ambivalent about Warsaw, as he told his staff, because the meetings there were mired in the failures and biases of the past—the same assortment of failures, he believed, that doomed the public peace talks in Paris.

In his memoirs, Kissinger complained steadily about the State Department, whose Asian experts, he suggested, frustrated the White House's wishes for a quick accommodation with Peking. Some of those experts, in subsequent interviews, have expressed astonishment at the portrayal and described their group as pleased and excited about the new policy. Paul H. Kreisberg, considered among the most knowledgeable China specialists in the State Department, was assigned to draft the guidelines for Stoessel's first meeting with the Chinese: "We constructed what we thought we ought to be saying, and sent it up to the White House for approval. It came back unchanged. Whatever we were doing, they must have liked it." Stoessel was instructed to propose that a high-level administration representative fly to Peking for more detailed talks, and Kreisberg recalls that the basic goal was "to normalize relationships. The objective was to find a way of putting Taiwan on the back burner, to give the Chinese the face-saving out they were looking for, and to give us flexibility." Stoessel was further instructed—this was a major concession—to make it clear that some American forces would be removed from Taiwan, thus meeting one of the main requirements of the Chinese. In his secret summary cabled to Washington after the meeting, Stoessel reported that he had followed orders and told Lei Yang that "the limited United States military presence on Taiwan is not a threat to the security of your government, and it is our hope that as peace and stability in Asia grow, we can reduce these facilities on Taiwan that

the Nixon-Kissinger intervention had prevented a Chinese-Soviet nuclear war. In gratitude, Haldeman added, the Chinese leaders invited Nixon "to visit their country and resume relations at a time just before Nixon's reelection campaign in 1972, when it would have the greatest political effect in his favor." Haldeman, at least, had no doubt what the 1972 summit was all about.

we now have." Nothing further had to be said. "What we did," Kreisberg recalls, "was to turn the key in the door."

After Stoessel's presentation, Lei Yang read a formal statement that, as Stoessel reported, included a Chinese offer for continued meetings in Warsaw at the ambassadorial level or "at a higher level or through other channels acceptable to both sides." When the two diplomats met again, a month later, this time in the American Embassy in Warsaw, both were primed with strong signals that the talks were on the right track. Lei Yang promptly accepted the American proposal to continue the talks in Peking, telling Stoessel that the Chinese government "will be willing to receive" a special presidential envoy "for further exploration of the questions of fundamental principle. . . ." In his remarks, Stoessel carefully shifted the American position on Taiwan. No longer was it a "hope" that the troops could be reduced; instead, Stoessel told Lei Yang, "It is my Government's intention to reduce those military facilities which we now have on Taiwan as tensions in the area diminish."

The breakthrough had been made. The United States had made it explicit that it was willing to withdraw from Taiwan in return for a commitment to future high-level talks in Peking. A summit loomed. The speedy Chinese acceptance of the American offer startled the State Department's Asian experts, one of whom later acknowledged that when he and his colleagues heard about Lei Yang's initial proposal in January, they suspected that the White House was conducting simultaneous backchannel negotiations. In December, as the State Department knew, Gheorge Macovescu, the Deputy Foreign Minister of Romania, had met privately in Washington with Nixon, obviously to relay a message about China policy. Kissinger said nothing about the Romanian visit in his memoirs, nor did he mention the use of backchannels in connection with the Warsaw negotiations, but private communications were certainly flying back and forth. One clue did appear in the memoirs. Kissinger wrote that between the first and second meetings in Warsaw, "[W]e redoubled our search for less constrained channels. One of the penalties of twenty years of isolation was that we had no idea how to approach the Chinese leaders." That he could hold such a view amidst the most productive American-Chinese talks since World War II reflected the real White House issue: how to seize control. The chance came after the February meeting, when Marshall Green, Assistant Secretary of State for East Asian and Pacific Affairs, expressed disquiet over the amazingly quick pace. To have ambassadorial meetings in Warsaw was perfectly appropriate and useful, but to jump suddenly into wide-ranging diplomatic negotiations in Peking was risky. Such a course, Green told Kissinger in a memorandum in March, would "weaken our ability to press the Chinese now to commit themselves further on their own intentions and negotiation position at higher-level meetings." Kissinger and Nixon disagreed and—apparently unable to get responses quickly enough via the backchannel—pushed hard for an immediate third meeting in Warsaw. Stoessel was instructed to accept the Chinese offer and discuss travel plans and agenda. The men in State envisioned that a special emissary would be sent, someone like Green or Alexis Johnson, the Under Secretary of State for Political Affairs. Or perhaps a special envoy from outside the government would be asked to represent Richard Nixon in Peking. Kissinger knew better: He sought the third meeting because he would be the one to prepare the path for a presidential summit. Hanoi would be devastated when he appeared in Peking. As he wrote in his memoirs, "The United States should choose to be not an impotent bystander but rather the purposeful shaper of events."

Unfortunately for their secret dreams, Nixon and Kissinger were not yet in full control of the bureaucracy. Some China experts in the State Department believed that Peking wanted to use the United States in the struggle against the Soviet Union; they argued that some unilateral gesture of good will by Peking was necessary before a high-level visit was planned. The dispute made it impossible to schedule another Warsaw meeting in March, despite Kissinger's insistence. Any chance for a resumption of the talks in April disappeared when the State Department announced on April 3 that Chiang Ching-kuo, Deputy Premier of Taiwan and son of Chiang Kai-shek, would visit Washington in three weeks to meet with Nixon, Rogers, and Laird. Peking, obviously distressed (as Kissinger was), waited until Chiang Ching-kuo's visit was over before renewing the planning discussions in Warsaw. By then, the invasion of Cambodia had begun, and an American visit to Peking in 1970 became impossible. The Chinese denounced the invasion and canceled the third Warsaw meeting, which had been set for May 20.

In his memoirs, Kissinger found a bright side in all this: At least he was able to get the State Department out of the planning for China. "The White House's interest in talking to Peking about common geopolitical concerns could not be dealt with—or perhaps even understood—there [in Warsaw]," he wrote. "The Warsaw talks never resumed. When we re-established contact later in the year, it was in a different channel, with a sharper focus." Only with a personal visit, only in Peking, and only without any participation by the State Department, could Kissinger and Nixon negotiate the American-Chinese rapprochement.

27
CHINA:
KISSINGER'S SECRET TRIP

THERE WAS A PROFOUND CHANGE in the relationship between Washington and Peking over the summer of 1970. Nixon was reeling from a series of political reverses that included the Senate's rejection of two Supreme Court nominations, the disastrous invasion of Cambodia, and the shootings at Kent State University. His administration was on the defensive and would remain so for another year. In November, the President put his political ego on the line in the 1970 congressional elections in an effort to achieve significant Republican gains and insure continued House and Senate support for his Vietnam policies. He failed. Later that November, there was another failure, at the Son Tay prison camp in North Vietnam. In early 1971, the poorly conceived South Vietnamese invasion of Laos turned into a setback for Vietnamization. By then, Nixon's concern was primitive: He might be on the way to becoming a one-term President.

His political revival began in mid-1971, with the SALT breakthrough and the rapprochement to China, both negotiated in the backchannel. In their memoirs, Nixon and Kissinger described these events solely in terms of foreign policy and diplomacy, without any mention of domestic considerations. Yet, as with SALT, rapprochement with China had become a political necessity. The important questions debated by Nixon and Kissinger in late 1970, as they tried to pick up the political pieces, were those of expediency. What concessions would have to be made to get to Peking and Moscow? Could China and Russia be maneuvered into presidential summits within the first six months of 1972? Could the Russians and the Chinese reelect the President?

How much Chairman Mao and Premier Chou En-lai knew about the disarray in Washington is not clear. China scholars have concluded that the Nixon invasion of Cambodia—with its overtones of the "madman theory"—was a setback for the pro-American moderates in Peking. Lin Piao's military faction again seemed to move into the ascendancy by midsummer, as China broke off the scheduled third round of Warsaw talks in May without setting a date for resumption, and as negotiations began with the Soviet Union over the disputed Chinese-Russian border areas. For reasons not fully known to scholars, Chou En-lai's faction seemed by early fall to have finally won a clear victory in the internal feuding that culminated at a plenary meeting of the party's Central Committee in August. After the meeting, Peking renewed its strident attack on the Soviet Union and Mao permitted the senior party officials to make speeches for broadcast abroad suggesting that improved relations with the United States were possible and spelling out the ideological justification for such a shift. Some scholars believe that it was not until this meeting, proceedings of which are still secret, that Mao fully grasped the extent of Lin Piao's plotting against the regime. Few details of the internal warfare are known in the West, but Chiang Ching, Mao's wife, told her biographer in 1972 that Lin Piao "not only wanted to assassinate Chairman Mao and drew up many plots to do so, but he also intended to kill all the comrades of the Politburo. His men drew up a sketch map of our residences [in the Imperial Palace] and were going to attack and bomb them and finish us off all at once." Mao apparently moved out of his home sometime in 1970.

Nixon's persistent dream of a prime-time visit to Peking may have played a role in developments inside China. Ten days before the invasion of Cambodia, he announced the withdrawal of 150,000 more troops from Southeast Asia in an obvious effort to limit domestic dissent; the withdrawals also may have been aimed at reassuring China. Further reassurance came in mid-June, when Nixon and Kissinger, realizing that the breakdown of the Warsaw talks offered an opportunity to get the State Department out of the picture at last, authorized Lieutenant General Vernon Walters to approach a Chinese official in Paris with an offer to open direct channels between Washington and Peking. There was no response, although Walters' efforts were undoubtedly reported to the Chinese leadership. Walters, an intelligence officer who had served as Nixon's trusted interpreter during the 1950s, was instructed by an anxious White House to try again in September. The Chinese, caught up in their internal problems, still did not respond, causing Kissinger to complain in his memoirs: "[O]ur backchannel system, which had so intrigued the Soviets, held as yet no attraction for the Chinese. Perhaps they did not understand how a serious government could be run in that way. . . ." Walters' intercession was meant not only to eliminate the State Department from the discussions with China but to bypass the governments of Romania, France, and Pakistan. Nixon and Kissinger so clearly wanted to get rid of all the middlemen that the Walters assignment raises the possibility that they had decided as early as mid-June 1970 to begin making whatever concessions Peking deemed necessary. If so, the central problem would have been how to communicate that decision in private.

Since they had not responded to the two Nixon messages, it fell to the Chinese leadership, once they resolved their internal difficulties, to make the next move. On October 1, Communist China's National Day, Mao permitted Edgar Snow, the American journalist, and his wife to join him at a reviewing stand in Peking's Tien-An-Men Square while hundreds of thousands of Chinese paraded in the traditional patriotic celebration. Snow, a friend of the Chinese who had begun reporting on Mao and his movement in the 1930s, was the first American ever permitted on the stand with Mao on National Day; it was, as he later wrote, a clear signal that "something new was happening. . . . Nothing China's leaders do publicly is without purpose." Chairman Mao was putting his personal imprimatur on a future Chinese-American relationship; it was his way of responding to the hints from the White House.

Unfortunately, Mao's message was too indirect; in his memoirs, Kissinger wrote that "[W]e had missed the point when it mattered. Excessive subtlety had produced a failure of communication." Though the Chinese news agencies duly reported Edgar Snow's presence at the ceremonies and the dispatches were routinely noted by the CIA and other intelligence services, little attention was paid. One former CIA official explains the thought process: "Edgar Snow is visiting China again? Fine. He's visited it many times in the past. Who cares? Without any guidance from above that this issue [China] is especially important, you wouldn't highlight it."

By early October, as Nixon's popularity fell, his anxiety about China became acute. There is no evidence that he or Kissinger was briefed about the end of China's internal struggles and the apparent defeat of Lin Piao; little reliable information was available anywhere in Washington. No further messages arrived from Mao Tse-tung or Chou En-lai. Nonetheless, the White House kept its signals flashing. Early in the month, Nixon was quoted in *Time* as declaring that "[I]f there is anything I want to do before I die, it is to go to China. If I don't, I want my children to." On October 25, Nixon met privately for fifty-five minutes with President Yahya Khan of Pakistan and told him, according to the Nixon memoirs, that "we had decided to try to normalize our relations with China." Kissinger was not at the meeting, but he accompanied President Ceauşescu of Romania to a meeting the next day at which Nixon again relayed a message to China. That evening, in a toast to President Ceauşescu at a state dinner, Nixon publicly described China as the People's Republic of China, the first use of China's official name by an American President.*

There is evidence that Nixon and Kissinger went even further in their discussions with the presidents of Pakistan and Romania. In their biography, the Kalb brothers quote Romanian diplomats as having privately claimed that Nixon made a significant concession to the Chinese, telling Ceauşescu that "so far as he was concerned, Taiwan was not an international but an internal problem, to be resolved by the Chinese themselves in a peaceful way." That was China's view on the Taiwan issue, as expressed at the Warsaw meetings and in its propaganda broadcasts. Similarly, G. W. Choudhury, a former member of Yahya Khan's cabinet who had access to the flow of backchannel messages from Washington to Peking, recalls that Nixon "made it clear" in the private communications in late 1970 that he would give recognition to China's Taiwan policy. Choudhury says this commitment was made in the backchannel. "The Chinese would not have received either Nixon or Kissinger without a commitment to one China."

On November 5, Edgar Snow had a four-hour meeting with Chou En-lai and learned that China also would demand in return for rapprochement that the United States reduce its troop levels on Taiwan. "Taiwan is China's affair," Snow quoted Chou En-lai as reaffirming. "We will insist on this." A week later, Snow wrote, Yahya Khan arrived in Peking for a state visit, fresh from

---

* Although the business of diplomatic "signaling" was invariably overstated by Nixon and Kissinger in their memoirs, Nixon's toast at the state dinner was discreet and effective. The toast was not mentioned in any of the press reports of the dinner, nor, apparently, did any of the Americans at the dinner perceive its significance. Nixon and Kissinger hoped that Ceauşescu would grasp the import and relay the President's words to the Chinese after his return to Bucharest. Kissinger saw to it the next day that the signaling was not so indirect. ". . . [J]ust to make sure that the Rumanians got the message," he noted in his memoirs, "I reiterated Nixon's themes and language in a private conversation with Ceauşescu at Blair House." Ambassador Dobrynin also got the message. He telephoned Kissinger after the dinner, according to the Kalbs' book, to ask for an explanation. Kissinger assured him that Nixon's language had no special meaning.

his private meetings with Nixon. He brought with him a personal letter from Nixon which formally raised the question of a presidential visit, to be preceded by a visit from Kissinger, who was authorized "to discuss the Taiwan question." The Pakistani President was received by Mao during his five-day visit to Peking, and repeatedly conferred—for as much as eighteen hours, Choudhury recalls—with Chou En-lai. Later in November, Chou also received a ranking Romanian Foreign Ministry official, who obviously was bearing more of President Nixon's messages as relayed to Ceauşescu.

The response that was relayed through the Pakistani backchannel reached the White House on December 9. Kissinger was handed a letter from Chou En-lai to Richard Nixon, in which the Chinese Premier agreed that "In order to discuss the subject of the vacation of Chinese territories called Taiwan, a special envoy of President Nixon's will be most welcome in Peking." A similar message from Chou was received in January of 1971, this time passed through the Romanians as the Chinese struggled to keep up with the various backchannels.

Chou's message was the first direct confirmation that things were on track and that, if he avoided any pitfalls, Nixon could be welcomed in Peking before the election. But Nixon was still troubled, Kissinger wrote. He wanted to be the first senior member of his administration to visit Peking; a prior Kissinger visit might detract from the political gloss. Thus Chou En-lai's straightforward invitation was rejected and a counteroffer made: The President proposed that the preliminary meeting of Chinese and American representatives be held not in Peking but in Pakistan. In his memoirs, Kissinger cited part of Nixon's letter to Chou but did not mention the suggested change of venue, a proposal that necessarily confused the Chinese and added to their suspicions about the sincerity of the White House.*

On December 18, Snow—in China on a five-month visit—was permitted to meet with Mao. He later wrote that Mao told him that China had received "several urgent and authentically documented inquiries" from Nixon requesting permission for a presidential visit. "Mao would be happy to talk with him," Snow wrote, "either as a tourist, or as President. . . . Discussing Nixon's possible visit to China, the Chairman casually remarked that the presidential election would be in 1972, would it not? Therefore, he added, Mr. Nixon might send an envoy first, but was not himself likely to come to Peking before early 1972."

Snow, who had agreed in advance to submit the interview for clearance, initially was not to mention Mao's comments about Nixon's preelection tactics, and did not quote Mao on that subject until Kissinger's secret visit to Peking became known. A few months after his return from China in early 1971, Snow was fatally stricken with cancer and was unable to write extensively about his meeting with Mao. However, in tape recordings made immediately

* Later in his memoirs, however, Kissinger noted that Nixon had repeatedly urged him to make the initial contact with the Chinese in a place other than Peking. "I did not know how to put this to either the Pakistanis or the Chinese," Kissinger wrote. "We had already raised suspicions by insisting on secrecy. . . . So I procrastinated, as Nixon could tell from the messages to Peking . . . none of which suggested a different venue." Even as he left Washington in mid-1971, en route to his secret rendezvous in Peking, Kissinger wrote, he was "still being urged to find another site." Kissinger, in essence, had defied the President on an issue dear to Nixon's heart—reelection publicity. He would pay later for that defiance.

after the interview, he told his wife, Lois, many more details of the private communications from the White House. Asking Snow not to quote him, Mao revealed that Nixon had sent "several messages" saying he wanted to arrange a private visit—obviously the one undertaken by Kissinger—"without the State Department even knowing about it." The Chinese leader, who found the request puzzling, suggested that "maybe Nixon's got something up his sleeve. If he comes over in an airplane and lands in Peking, we'll welcome him," Mao said. "We can guarantee him security if he wants to come." But, Mao added, "He can't come unless he wants to talk about Taiwan."*

"If you see him," Mao finally told Snow, "tell him he's welcome."

Despite the many missed signals, it seems clear that, by communicating through intermediaries, the White House and Peking were able to resolve a number of critical issues by the end of 1970. Nixon had specifically sought permission to make a presidential visit to Peking. The two countries had tentatively agreed on the need for a previous meeting involving a Nixon emissary —obviously to be Henry Kissinger—and senior Chinese officials. That meeting would take place in Peking, unless Nixon got his way and it was transferred to another site in China or in a nearby country. Mao and Chou En-lai understood the relevance of the Vietnam War and the 1972 presidential elections to the negotiating process, and undoubtedly viewed Nixon's anxiety as a bargaining asset. There had even been some preliminary discussion of presidential security, with Peking reassuring the White House that Nixon would be safe. In return for China's invitation and guarantees, Nixon and Kissinger had made clear that Taiwan would not be a stumbling block and that some concessions, some American enunciation of a "one-China" policy, would be forthcoming. The White House also made it clear that it would agree—at a summit—to a public commitment to withdraw all American troops from Taiwan. One American official who had access to the backchannel communications recalls that the White House "recognized right from the start that you couldn't even begin to negotiate until you got that out of the way. We couldn't quibble over that." The proposal for withdrawal was conveyed in writing to Chairman Mao and Chou En-lai via Pakistan.

In return for the concession on Taiwan, Nixon and Kissinger would seek Chinese support for a negotiated settlement in the Vietnam War. As with the Soviet Union, there would also be a summit whose timing would help guarantee the President's reelection. Each side was asking the other to betray an ally. The United States would walk away from its commitment to Taiwan, an emotional issue for the Nixon political constituency, which—if it somehow learned of his plan—would do everything possible to sabotage it. The Chinese had an easier task: to begin to turn their backs on their future rival for dominance in Southeast Asia, the North Vietnamese.

* The Chinese asked Snow not to publish Mao's direct invitation to Nixon, but Mao and the other leaders assumed he would be able to relay their important communication privately to the White House. At this point there was another snafu. Allen Whiting, who had been consulting regularly with John Holdridge on China policy, thought there was a possibility that Snow, whose views on China were anathema to the White House, had been given a private message. He volunteered to fly to Switzerland, where Snow lived, and debrief him. "John told me no," Whiting recalled. "He viewed Snow as a leftist." It was sometime later that a CIA official, operating under cover, visited Snow and learned the significant fact that Mao Tse-tung himself had expressed a willingness to welcome and meet with Nixon.

None of the Nixon-Kissinger concessions on Taiwan would have distressed the majority of academic and bureaucratic China watchers in the United States, who saw their country's policy toward China as counterproductive. They would have applauded the White House's moves as a moral act of statesmanship. Nixon and Kissinger, however, did not make their concessions in late 1970 to right a historical wrong, or even primarily to increase their diplomatic leverage on the Soviet Union. Their goals were to have a 1972 summit in Peking and to get China's help in achieving "peace with honor" in South Vietnam, sustaining Nguyen Van Thieu in power. In their memoirs and elsewhere, both men have repeatedly denied that any commitments to China were made prior to Nixon's visit. Presumably they believe these denials are justified, if only to insulate themselves from criticism by supporters of Taiwan.

The full extent of the administration's eagerness for the rapprochement became obvious only in the last half of 1971, as Yahya Khan's government mounted a war of genocide inside East Pakistan in a futile effort to stop a rebellion and prevent the emergence of the independent nation of Bangladesh. Hundreds of thousands of Bengalis were massacred by Pakistani troops in the spring and summer, as the United States looked away out of fear that any intervention would distress China, Pakistan's ally, and mar the President's summit. Nixon and Kissinger, refusing to listen to the bureaucracy, which came close to open rebellion on the issue, chose to support Pakistan. They maintained that position in the famous "tilt" of late 1971, even as the war escalated to a near-showdown with the Soviets, who were supporting India, Pakistan's perennial enemy, in its objection to the terror tactics in Bangladesh. In his memoirs, Nixon quoted Kissinger's statement at a key point in the conflict, as the potential for a Soviet-American clash deepened: "We don't really have any choice. We can't allow a friend of ours and China's to get screwed in a conflict with a friend of Russia's."

Nixon's invoking of the "madman theory" in the Vietnam War intruded into the Chinese rapprochement for a second time late in January 1971, when the South Vietnamese invasion of Laos began. The action was deemed essential because the White House believed that, win or lose, it would slow down the North Vietnamese resupply efforts along the Ho Chi Minh Trail and thus delay Hanoi's election-year offensive. In his memoirs, Kissinger wrote that he and his advisers in the White House were "convinced" that China would not intervene in Laos because "China was playing a bigger game"—with the United States. In other words, China would do in Laos what the United States would do in Bangladesh—look the other way. China, however, despite many profound disagreements with Hanoi, did not permit its much-desired improvement of relations with the United States to diminish its steady supply of arms and matériel to North Vietnam. Most China scholars believe, in light of China's continued support of Hanoi even after Nixon's visit took place, that the Peking leadership also responded, albeit reluctantly, to Vietnamese calls for help in Laos with increased shipments of aid. The Chinese government was known to be far more concerned than the Kissinger memoirs show about the invasion of Laos and what it suggested about the rationality of the Nixon Administration. In his book *800,000,000*, published in 1972, Ross Terrill reported that in late

January 1971, as the South Vietnamese began their troop buildup for the Laos invasion, "China was concerned at the possible use of tactical nuclear weapons in conjunction with the buildup. . . ." When the invasion began, Terrill said, China alerted substantial forces in the border province of Yunnan.*

It was the failure of the Laos invasion, Terrill was told, that permitted the American-Chinese rapprochement to get back on track. "Peking was buoyed," Terrill reported, and its leaders viewed the failed invasion as a measure of the inevitability of the decline of American influence in Southeast Asia. Terrill quoted a Chinese proverb to summarize the view in Peking: Saigon had "picked up a stone to throw against the people's forces only to drop it on its own feet." Adding to China's relief was the fact that the White House had done nothing dramatic—Richard Nixon had not escalated the war in revenge or in an attempt to salvage the invasion, once its failure became clear.

China was at this time in the midst of a delicate balancing act whose significance eluded the White House. The Chinese were not at all committed to a North Vietnam victory in the South, for they viewed a reunified Vietnam as threatening. The enmity between China and the Vietnamese was profound, and had been for two millenniums; the nations began their struggle against each other at least as far back as III B.C.†

As the Laos threat receded, Washington and Peking began to signal each other anew. In early April of 1971, Mao and Chou En-lai took the initiative and suddenly decided to grant visas to an American ping-pong team competing in a tournament in Japan; the team members and some American journalists who accompanied them were greeted warmly in Peking by Chou En-lai. The Kalbs reported that immediately upon hearing of the ping-pong invitation, Nixon convened an NSC meeting at which Kissinger summarized the administration's China policy. It was another bit of theater, designed to keep the State Department and other agencies at bay, for Kissinger did not discuss the real negotia-

---

* There is no evidence that in early 1971 Nixon and Kissinger did more than talk about the use of tactical nuclear weapons, although that possibility was repeatedly raised by the President in his late-night telephone calls to Kissinger. Former aides to Kissinger recall that such talk, which some aides directly overheard, went on throughout the Vietnam War. The only indication that more than just talk was involved came during an interview I had in late 1980 with a CIA official who had knowledge of the Agency's activities in Chile. While serving in the CIA's operations center in the winter of 1970–71, the official recalled, he learned that the Air Force had issued a top-secret "standdown" order forbidding all intelligence and other operations in and over an area in North Vietnam. "A stand-down did exist and it's a standard indicator for a nuclear attack," the CIA official said. "We were talking about it—that if the Soviets had done this on the Chinese border, we'd be scared stiff." He and his colleagues always understood, the official said, that a stand-down "means that they've reached the point of activating" a nuclear weapon. The official, who did not keep a personal diary or take his files with him when he retired, was unable to set the time or place of the standdown any closer than somewhere in North Vietnam—perhaps near Laos—during the winter of 1970–71. It is possible that the Chinese had some specific evidence for expressing concern, as they did to Terrill, about nuclear attack. I have found no documentation of an official order to arm a nuclear device.

† During my visit to Hanoi in 1972, at the height of the Vietnam War, my North Vietnamese hosts insisted that I visit a museum where the ancient wars against the Chinese were depicted. Their pride in not having acceded to Chinese domination was surprising to me, for I had assumed a steadfastness between the two nations. Asked about the Nixon summit, which took place a month before my arrival, one government official dryly noted that China was prepared to support North Vietnam "until the last Vietnamese is killed."

tions in the backchannel. (For that matter, none of the participants at the meeting, including Admiral Moorer, chairman of the Joint Chiefs of Staff, was authorized to know that the White House was secretly negotiating a SALT agreement in the backchannel with the Soviet Union.) A week after the ping-pong invitation, Nixon and Kissinger announced the end of a long-standing trade embargo with China. Scores of goods, including truck and automobile parts, could be shipped to China; American vessels were now free to dock there and also to refuel inside China.

There was one more contretemps before Kissinger's secret visit. By early spring, so the Chinese told Terrill, they had decided to grant visas to Senators Edward M. Kennedy and Edmund S. Muskie, leading Democrats who were viewed with anxiety by Nixon as possible opponents in the 1972 elections. Senator George McGovern, another possible presidential candidate, was also on China's list. The White House first learned of such a possibility sometime in April, after a Chinese official said as much to Tillman Durdin, a *New York Times* correspondent who had gone into China with the American ping-pong team. Durdin apparently did not file a dispatch based on the information, but instead relayed its essence to the American Consulate in Hong Kong. Also to be invited, the Chinese said, were three senior American journalists, James Reston of the *Times*, Walter Cronkite of CBS, and Walter Lippmann, the columnist. The consulate, unaware of the significance of its report, filed a routine cable to the State Department that somehow got to the White House. Kissinger became extremely upset, one State Department specialist on China recalls. "Nobody knew he was planning to go. He responded by telling the Chinese that 'You can't invite any American politicians but us.' He had to close off the Democrats going before Nixon," the specialist says, "to protect the political use of this for Nixon in '72." * It is not clear how close the Chinese were to issuing the visas, but the incident shows that Peking was well aware of Nixon's eagerness to exploit the rapprochement, and also aware of the bargaining power provided by that eagerness.

China had not been officially heard from since the beginning of the Laos operation, and in late April of 1971, Nixon and Kissinger dispatched a courier to France in another attempt to open a communications link. It was on that day, dramatically, that Chou En-lai's invitation for a high-level visit arrived, via the Pakistan Embassy. Nixon toyed with Kissinger over the next few days, while they discussed who would be the appropriate emissary. Such names as Nelson Rockefeller, David Bruce, Elliot Richardson, and George Bush, then the Ambassador to the United Nations, were bandied about, but it was always clear to John Mitchell who would make the trip. "Who else could he send?" Mitchell says. "I was Attorney General; I couldn't just disappear." As for Rogers or some other State Department envoy, "The whole point was to keep

---

* In his memoirs, Kissinger referred to the incident as one that primarily affected Nixon, who, he wrote, "was still concerned that the Chinese might . . . bring pressure on us by inviting other American political figures in opposition to us. . . . I questioned that. . . . Peking would not want the opening to China to appear extorted. . . ." Nixon asked, nonetheless, that Kissinger raise the issue with Peking in the backchannel, and, Kissinger wrote, he agreed with reservations, since it was "difficult to know what to do about it." Kissinger, of course, could simply have ignored Nixon's order, as he had chosen to do with Nixon's request that the first secret meeting be held anywhere but Peking. But in this case, as he wrote—still suggesting it was solely Nixon's concern —he urged the Pakistanis to tell the Chinese to "make no other initiatives."

it out of the State Department." After debating the issue at length, Kissinger related, Nixon chose him.*

Once that issue was resolved, Nixon and Kissinger decided to play it cool. "Having been kept waiting for four months," Kissinger wrote, "we did not wish to return a formal response immediately, lest we appear too eager." It was too late for games. Mao and Chou En-lai knew that Nixon was hooked: The President would be coming to Peking—for political and strategic purposes —and he would need to negotiate a positive diplomatic agreement.

In his memoirs, Kissinger reprinted much of the White House's response, which was handed to the Pakistanis on May 10 and which included more evidence of the extensive backchannel bargaining. Once again, the White House declared that Nixon was prepared to accept what the note termed the Chinese "suggestion" that he visit Peking. Nixon's commitment to a summit thus became unconditional. Kissinger "would be authorized to discuss the circumstances which would make a visit by President Nixon most useful, the agenda of such a meeting, the time of such a visit and to begin a preliminary exchange of views on all subjects of mutual interest." All of this was to be done in strictest secrecy.

The secrecy played into Nixon's and Kissinger's sense of the dramatic, but it was also imperative if they were to protect their flanks from the China lobby. Taiwan was an emotional issue for America's conservatives, and Nixon, suddenly confronted with an opportunity to improve his political standing, could not afford to have a debate over "Who lost Taiwan?" He was already nervous about Kissinger's trip, and about the fact that it would be his aide who would enter China first. "The trip heightened the nervous sensitivity of Nixon's public relations antennae," Kissinger wrote. "Having made the decisions without executive or congressional consultation, Nixon had left himself quite naked should anything go wrong . . . [I]n his complicated personality high motives constantly warred with less lofty considerations." In other words, the President, who was taking all the risks, wanted to keep Kissinger out of the limelight as much as possible. At one point, he insisted that the first official communiqué announcing Kissinger's visit not mention Kissinger at all, but instead bracket the President's name with Chou En-lai's. "Reality took care of this problem," Kissinger noted caustically. "He did not explain how one could announce the visit of an American emissary to Peking without revealing the emissary's name unless one wanted to get a reputation in China for complete inscrutability." Nixon also remained hopeful that he could somehow prevent Kissinger from preceding him into Peking, if not into China; the White House note specifically suggested that the Kissinger meeting was to take place "on Chinese soil" without specifying where.

The Chinese response, also published in part in the Kissinger memoirs, arrived in Washington on June 2, and provided more evidence of the importance of the backchannel. Signed by Chou En-lai, the hand-written letter adroitly conceded the question of who invited whom—an issue far more important in Washington than in Peking—and also raised the possibility that

---

* Kissinger got some measure of revenge in his memoirs by writing that Thomas Dewey, the old-line Republican leader, was among those considered as possible emissaries. Nixon raised his name several times, Kissinger wrote, "and waxed eloquent about his ability; unfortunately, Dewey was no longer available, having died a few months previously."

Nixon would meet with Mao Tse-tung, who was said to be looking forward to "direct conversation" with the President. The Chinese had done their homework well; they knew that Nixon would be unable to resist the prospect of a highly visible meeting with Mao. With the flattery out of the way, Chou En-lai returned to business: "It goes without saying that the first question to be settled is the crucial issue . . . [of] the question of the concrete way of the withdrawal of *all* the US Armed Forces from Taiwan and the Taiwan Straits areas [emphasis added]." Clearly, at some point in the backchannel exchange of messages—most likely in those messages sent through Pakistan in late 1970 —Nixon and Kissinger had committed themselves to the total withdrawal of American forces from Taiwan.

Nixon was euphoric over Chou En-lai's response. In his memoirs, he recalled Kissinger telling him: "This is the most important communication that has come to an American President since the end of World War II." Triangular diplomacy had begun. Nixon would get to meet with Chairman Mao. There would be pressure from all sides on the North Vietnamese. And the President's standing in the Gallup poll, which had sagged below 50 percent by midyear, would go up.

Advance word of what Kissinger planned was the highest secret of the state in late June 1971, as Kissinger prepared for what was publicly announced as an "information trip" to Asia, his first such trip as national security adviser, with scheduled stops, beginning July 2, in Saigon, Bangkok, New Delhi, and Islamabad. He was to fake a stomach illness in Pakistan and fly from there into Peking on July 9 for two days of talks, returning in time to fly on to Paris for a secret meeting with Le Duc Tho. The critical issue was, as usual, what to do with the Secretary of State. The solution was shoddy. Rogers, echoing the advice of his senior aides, had protested Kissinger's proposed visit to South Asia, a visit—as the regional experts in the State Department understood— with no readily conceivable usefulness and one that could deepen the already severe criticism of the Nixon Administration for its reluctance to condemn Yahya Khan's brutal and continuing suppression of the Bangladesh revolution. Even in the face of such well-founded opposition, Nixon decided he could not risk sharing his secret with the Secretary of State. As Kissinger related in his memoirs, Haldeman was called upon to handle Rogers. Rogers was not to be told of the real purpose of Kissinger's trip until Kissinger was safely on his way; he learned at that point, Kissinger wrote, only because Nixon "conceived the idea of inviting Rogers to San Clemente for the major part of my Asian trip; he would thus be able to break the news under the best, or at least most controlled, circumstances." Nixon pretended, Kissinger wrote, that the visit to Peking had been a last-minute thing, a spur-of-the-moment response to an invitation received in Pakistan. How Rogers tolerated all this remains one of the most poignant aspects of the Nixon White House. His solace, if any could be had, lay in the fact that none of the other senior Cabinet officials were officially told at all until after Kissinger's return.* Laird, who had his own

* Rogers was soothed, perhaps, by White House "p.r." efforts after the summit announcement to depict him as a major player in the Chinese rapprochement. The Kalb brothers, for example, reported that in the months before Kissinger's first trip to Peking, Kissinger and Nixon met often in the Lincoln Sitting Room in the White House to review the negotiations. "Haldeman would occasionally join them, sometimes Rogers—but no one else," wrote the Kalbs. In his memoirs, Kissin-

sources of information through the NSA, acknowledged later that he had known in advance of Kissinger's plan but not precisely when the trip would take place.

Only five senior members of Kissinger's NSC staff made the trip: Winston Lord and John Holdridge, who handled the China negotiations; Richard Smyser, who prepared the papers for the meeting with Le Duc Tho; Harold Saunders, the South Asian expert; and Wayne Smith, who had worked on security assistance agreements with the Thais that were to be discussed during the stopover in Bangkok. David Halperin was also on the flight, along with Yeoman Radford, who was scheduled to be left behind in Pakistan during the visit to Peking. In his memoirs, Kissinger exalted Lord's role and unblinkingly described his function: "Not only had he supervised the substantive preparations, he also had to keep track of the distribution of documents within my party. This was a monumental task. For there were three levels of knowledge. Some knew where I was going and what I would say when I got there. Others knew of my destination but not of my agenda, being along to assist me on the other stops. Still others were aware of neither."

Kissinger's recollection notwithstanding, the fact is that all his staff aides, once they boarded the aircraft, knew that one of the stops would be inside China, and the one man—Yeoman Radford—who was not scheduled to make the Chinese trip probably knew the most. Radford went through Kissinger's briefcases during one of the stops, duplicated many of the seemingly more essential documents, and on stopovers in Asia calmly shipped the purloined materials to his White House office via diplomatic pouch.*

One last-minute change of plans cast a pall over the staff. While still in the United States, Wayne Smith had argued with Kissinger over the proposed assistance package that was to be presented to the Thai government in Bangkok, explaining that the proposal was too complicated and would infringe on the Thais' national sovereignty. Kissinger dismissed the protest and the matter was dropped. Smith learned of its ultimate destination after he boarded Kissinger's plane in California for the trip to Saigon; he was also told that he was to fly into Peking. Bangkok was an intermediate stop, and it was there, at a state dinner, that a Thai official informed Kissinger that the proposed agreement was far too complicated and violated Thailand's sovereignty. Smith and the other aides listened as an obviously annoyed Kissinger responded, "Mr. Minister, one of my colleagues told me you might say that. His name is Wayne Smith. He's the one at the end of the table smirking." Before leaving Bangkok,

---

ger accepted the puffery about Rogers without complaint but objected to the White House insistence that he promote Nixon's role in the planning for the summit. At one point, he "begged Haldeman to spare me," and quoted Haldeman as saying, in agreement, "You can only lie so far." Nixon, according to Kissinger, did not substantively involve himself in the initial negotiations, spending—as usual—just a few hours reviewing all the various briefing books that had been prepared.

* Radford also recalled seeing a memorandum on the desk of one of Kissinger's key aides before the Peking trip that evaluated the possibility of surreptitiously bringing a small high-powered tape recorder into the meetings in China. The memorandum specifically talked about placing the recorder on the inside of Kissinger's leg. Radford later recalled discussing the proposal with another high-level NSC aide, who expressed surprise that he knew of the plan. Both Kissinger aides said in subsequent interviews that they could not recall any such proposal and that, to the best of their knowledge, Kissinger did not plan to secretly record his meetings in Peking. It should be noted that Radford has supplied considerable information to me since 1974; invariably his information has been demonstrated to be accurate.

Kissinger pulled Smith aside and ordered him to remain in Thailand to negotiate a new agreement. Smith and the others were convinced that he was being punished not only for having been right but for having had the audacity to say as much to Kissinger. A few months later, Smith resigned from the NSC staff.

The public announcement on July 15, 1971, of Kissinger's secret trip to China stunned the world and led to encomiums for his diplomacy. He was suddenly an international celebrity, a publicity boon that enraged the President and his loyalists. Most historians have ascribed Nixon's anger to envy, but he was also disturbed because he was not being fully recognized for his own role in the rapprochement. In his memoirs, Nixon said little about the substance of Kissinger's talks in Peking, but depicted the mission as aimed primarily at paving the way for the presidential summit. "Kissinger's description of his time in China was fascinating," Nixon wrote. "The Chinese had agreed to virtually everything we proposed regarding the arrangements and schedule for my trip."

Kissinger, on the other hand, described the secret visit as the highlight of the rapprochement. A fifty-five-page chapter in his memoirs is devoted in large measure to a detailed review of the step-by-step planning, as well as an at times awestruck description of Chou En-lai, with whom he met three times in Peking.*

But what was said? In their memoirs neither Kissinger nor Nixon specifically spelled out the bargaining in Peking, although there was much to bargain about.

* Kissinger's fascination with Chou En-lai and with Mao Tse-tung, whom he met with Nixon in February 1972, did not surprise those who had more experience of Asia. John K. Fairbank, the Harvard professor considered by many the dean of America's academic experts on China, wrote in 1960 that "Chinese politics are more subtle and sophisticated, if less vocal, more personal and less ideological, than Western politics, which explains why so many American envoys have been frustrated, flattered, confused, or enthusiastic in the course of their negotiations, but seldom victorious over the Chinese interests." Fairbank, in a 1960 lecture at the University of Connecticut, described some of what he called Chinese "operating principles" for such negotiations:

1. The cardinal Chinese principle in dealing with a non-Chinese is to use friendship as a halter. Admit the outsider to a guest membership in Chinese society. Compliment him on his knowledge of aspects of Chinese culture or of the Chinese language. Entertain him with informality and frankness. Establish the personal bonds of friendship. . . . Become really intimate friends and understand his unspoken assumptions and personal motivations.
2. Ask the foreigner's advice so as to ascertain his aims and values and to enlist his sympathy and support.
3. Disclose to him those Chinese vital interests which are allegedly more important than life itself, so as to pre-empt a position ahead of time and warn him it is not negotiable.
4. Build up the peculiar uniqueness of Chinese values and conduct. . . .
5. Find out the foreigner's friends, enemies and other circumstances so as to avoid offense to him and also to know where to find allies if necessary to mobilize against him. . . .
6. Use the foreigner's own rules to control him, especially the Western legal concept of sovereignty.

Kissinger's comments in his memoirs about Chou En-lai demonstrate that he was no more immune to such principles than other Westerners. "So it happened," Kissinger wrote, "that the talks between Chou and me were longer and deeper than with any other leader I met during my public service, except possibly Anwar Sadat. . . ." At another point: "Chou never bargained to score petty points. . . ." And a few paragraphs later: "I could work with a great man across the barriers of ideology in the endless struggle of statesmen to rescue some permanence from the tenuousness of human foresight." And lest anyone misunderstand his parity as a statesman with Chou, Kissinger wrote that the fact that the common interests of Washington and Peking "were perceived clearly and acted upon decisively was due to leadership that—on both sides—skillfully used the margin of choice available."

Kissinger arrived in China with a major political concession on Taiwan's status, as well as a commitment to announce the withdrawal of all American troops from the island. He would receive China's pledge of cooperation to urge North Vietnam not to end the war by force and to accept a negotiated settlement that would leave the reviled Nguyen Van Thieu still in power. Kissinger also received a commitment for a presidential summit in February, three months before the summit in Moscow. China was endorsing Richard Nixon for reelection.

It is not known how these agreements were reached. The only hint of what Nixon sought from the secret meeting came in Kissinger's memoirs, when he described, with no special emphasis, a presidential conversation just before Kissinger's around-the-world flight began. Nixon "wanted me to stress that if pressed he would 'turn hard on Vietnam,' " Kissinger wrote. "He thought I should keep in play a 'possible move toward the Soviets.' . . . He wanted me to emphasize that China's fears of Japan could best be assuaged by a continuing U.S.-Japanese alliance." In subsequent comments in his memoirs, Kissinger downplayed Nixon's instructions as just "boilerplate on which I knew Nixon would not insist. . . ." Once in Peking, Kissinger wrote, he and Chou held a series of philosophical and contemplative discussions, as would any world statesmen of equal wisdom. ". . . [T]he necessities that brought us together would set the direction for our future relationship, provided neither side asked the other to do what its values or interests prohibited. Thus ensued a conversation whose easy banter and stylized character, as if it were a dialogue between two professors of political philosophy, nearly obscured that the penalty of failure would be continued isolation for one side and sharpened international difficulties for the other."

Again, what was said? There is evidence that Kissinger did, in fact, follow Nixon's advice. Not only was China warned of further escalations of the war against the North, if necessary; it was also presented with a bill for America's concessions on Taiwan: Chinese acquiescence in the escalations. China was being asked to look the other way. It would do so in the spring of 1972, when American B-52 bombers mauled Hanoi and Haiphong. In his memoirs, Kissinger insisted that Taiwan was discussed only "briefly" in Peking, with more attention paid to the status of the secret talks with Le Duc Tho. Nothing was settled, Kissinger wrote. Yet the North Vietnamese, in interviews and in subsequent publications of its Ministry of Foreign Affairs, have depicted the July 1971 Kissinger-Chou meeting as a watershed in their relations with China.

Three days after Kissinger left Peking, Chou En-lai flew to Hanoi to reassure his worried allies. He told Hanoi that the withdrawal of American troops from Taiwan was a secondary issue to his government, and that, as a Foreign Ministry publication later put it, "As far as China is concerned, the withdrawal of U.S. troops from South Vietnam is problem No. 1. . . ." Nguyen Co Thach, North Vietnam's Deputy Foreign Minister, has said that he and other officials simply did not believe Chou's assurances. They were convinced, as a 1979 Foreign Ministry publication said, that Peking, "at heart, wanted to make use of the Vietnam question for the settlement of the Taiwan issue first." China subsequently did begin to exert extreme pressure on Hanoi to accept a political compromise in Saigon, and thus to accept a continued Thieu regime. On July 18, a week after Kissinger left Peking, China communicated a four-point American peace proposal to Hanoi. The proposal was old hat: It offered the withdrawal of all U.S. troops within a year after August 1, 1971, in return for the release of all prisoners and a ceasefire throughout Indochina. (Thus American involvement would end before the 1972 presidential elections.) The Thieu regime would stay in power, and for "face-saving" purposes, China told Hanoi, the United States wished to retain a number of technical personnel in the South. A few months later, Peking was more direct with the North Vietnamese, according to Foreign Ministry documents published by Hanoi: "Vietnam should take advantage of the opportunity to settle the question of withdrawal of US troops first and should consider the settlement of the POW problem. The overthrow of the Saigon puppet administration is a long-term issue." Such comments were considered betrayals by the North Vietnamese—evidence that the Nixon rapprochement with China was going to succeed.

Kissinger obviously did more than discuss generalities in Peking when it came to the Soviet Union; after all, the common ground for the two nations was distrust of Russia. But almost nothing was said in Kissinger's memoirs about his talks with Chou on that subject. It is also unlikely, given Kissinger's bent for editing transcripts, that any full account exists in government files today. At one point in his memoirs, Kissinger noted that "I soon found that the best way to deal with him was to present a reasonable position, explain it meticulously, and then stick to it. I sometimes went so far as to let him see the internal studies that supported our conclusions." Those "studies" were far more significant than Kissinger suggested: They undoubtedly included highly classified American satellite reconnaissance photographs and communications intelligence concerning the Soviet buildup on the Chinese borders. Aides who worked closely with Kissinger in 1971 recall that a black-bound intelligence notebook, containing some of the nation's most sensitive information regarding the Soviet Union, was prepared by Alexander Haig and Jonathan Howe, one of Haig's assistants, before Kissinger made a second trip to Peking in late October, to settle the basic arrangements for Nixon's early 1972 summit meeting in Peking. Documents provided for Kissinger's first trip included, according to the aides, information gleaned from top-secret National Security Agency intercepts of encoded Soviet communications as well as high-resolution satellite photographs.

China paid a diplomatic price among Third World allies for its decision to negotiate directly with Nixon and Kissinger. One of the bitterest attacks came in late 1971, from Enver Hoxha, First Secretary of the Central Committee of the Communist Party in Albania, which had supported China in its ideological struggle against the Soviet Union. Hoxha, whose collected diary entries were published in 1979, was contemptuous of China's decision to renege on its ally, North Vietnam. He accused Mao and Chou of practicing "opportunism" and warned: "We do not believe that the United States of America will withdraw the troops and dismantle the bases which it has in the world without being forced to do so by war. . . . In no way should they have agreed that Nixon should go to Peking." The Albanian leader also correctly summed up the importance of rapprochement to Nixon: "With what it has done China has helped the fascist Nixon, given him great possibilities of triumphing again in the presidential elections, has brought about that he can pose as a 'president of peace, a great president.' With this Nixon gains the role of 'arbiter' between the Soviet Union and the People's Republic of China."

China handled Hoxha's protest by ignoring it, and refused to send an official delegate to the Sixth Congress of the Albanian Communist Party in November. China was playing for higher stakes. It and the Nixon Administration had much to offer each other in mid-1971. Nixon needed a summit in Peking, with live television back home, to assure reelection.* China needed instant world recognition that it, like the Soviets, was in a position to bargain on equal terms with the United States—although, even by mid-1971, China's might was primarily in its potential. The Cultural Revolution had shattered the economy, weakened the political structure, demoralized the armed forces, and even jeopardized the physical safety of Chairman Mao. As China viewed the bargain, Nixon would make his state visit, the United States would publicly agree to withdraw all its troops (at some unspecified time) from Taiwan, and it would be publicly announced that the Taiwan issue was an internal question for the Chinese to solve among themselves. Such developments, especially Nixon's appearance in Peking, would be a blow to Chiang Kai-shek and would mark a fundamental change in the Asian balance of power. Rapprochement could restore much of what had been lost in the dark days of the Cultural Revolution.

* One clue to the extent of the understanding in China regarding Nixon's political motive for pursuing rapprochement showed up after Kissinger's July visit in two poems that were found by a Dutch scholar tacked up on a factory bulletin board in the ancient city of Sian, southwest of Peking, where the Cultural Revolution flourished. The first, entitled "Nixon's Personal Statement," was a parody of one of Mao's poems and included the following lines, as translated:

Blazing fires of revolution burn the world over
Boiling oil is poured on the Pentagon
The raging fire in Coconut Grove startles the universe
War drums along the Equator shake the heavens
As the economy takes a further downward turn every day
A tide of rebellion rises up in waves
A visit to China is the only way out
For a brief respite from blazing flames that singe
   the eyebrows.

The second, also translated by the foreign visitor, read:

For next year's national presidential elections
Two promises made have not at all been redeemed
The key to capture votes is a visit to China
He will not hesitate to use grease paint and to
   peddle his sex-appeal
The CIA brain trust is at its wits' end
The Ping-Pong game let through a glimmer of hope
Kissinger's trip to Peking brought a joyful message
He drinks fine wine and eats crab's legs, pulling
   his happiest grinning face
That Nixon may go down in history, the most famous
   president in two hundred years
With painted face-mask, disguised as a beauty, he
   comes to negotiate
But the demons-demasking-mirror in the city of Peking
   is truly inexorable
A fear grows that his true image will be revealed and
   his great cause will fail
There is no way out but to go to church, and in profound
   worship
Pray to high heaven and beseech God: "Protect me through
   this difficult passage!"

Behind these trade-offs, the leaders of both nations understood, was a shared hostility toward the North Vietnamese and a shared need to limit their influence. The conversations between Chou En-lai and Henry Kissinger, if they were ever to be made public in uncensored form, would be marvels in realpolitik—"hardball," as Nixon would put it. The two nations were willing to deal cynically with each other and with the life and death of the peoples of Vietnam.

Kissinger's and Nixon's reluctance to describe what really took place in Peking that July extended even to lesser issues. There is evidence that Kissinger softened some rough talk about Japan's possible future as a nuclear power with a concession on the question of China's seating at the United Nations. Kissinger's solution was simple enough: The United States would no longer actively campaign against China's admission to the General Assembly and its replacement of Taiwan on the Security Council.* It was clear that the administration's *de facto* one-China policy would be bitterly attacked by Taiwan and its supporters, and thus it was left to Secretary of State Rogers to enunciate it in early August. The White House, meanwhile, sealed the fate of the UN vote when it announced on October 5, a few weeks beforehand, that Kissinger would make a second visit to Peking. He left on October 16, after once again overcoming protests from Rogers, who argued, Kissinger wrote, "that it would interfere with our strategy on Chinese representation in the United Nations. He was right in principle," Kissinger added. "Presidents should not send emissaries who are independent of the Secretary of State . . . [but] we could hardly change the date of a visit agreed to for two months without some cost to our new relations with Peking."

Kissinger arrived in Peking on October 20 for what had been announced as a four-day visit and stayed six days, although, as Ross Terrill noted, "business was not so pressing as to prevent Kissinger from going sight-seeing and to the theatre." Photographs of his sight-seeing in Peking made page one in New York and obviously affected the UN delegates, who voted on October 25 to seat China.† "The grief in Washington was not searing," wrote Terrill. However, Taiwan's ouster brought a wave of criticism from conservatives in the House and Senate, who began talking about retaliation against the United Nations. Nixon took the high ground publicly, sending Ron Ziegler out to tell the press that the President was outraged by the "cheering, handclapping and dancing" that had broken out on the floor of the General Assembly after China's admission. In his memoirs, Nixon spelled out his ambivalence: "It had not been easy for me to take a position that would be so disappointing to our old friend and loyal ally, Chiang. . . . I have never believed in bowing to the

* Up to then, the official American position had been that Taiwan was the sole representative of China in the United Nations; American diplomats lobbied extensively each fall, when the issue of representation arose in the UN, to keep China from being seated. The American position had held in 1970, but it was clear, as more Third World nations were admitted to UN membership, that Taiwan would eventually be ousted.

† China's satisfaction at its adroit handling of the Nixon Administration was made clear in September 1971 by Huang Hua, who had aided Chou En-lai in his negotiations with Kissinger. "The Americans say they are going to step down from some of their high responsibilities in Asia," Huang told the journalist Wilfred Burchett. "We are happy to provide a small stool for them."

inevitable just because it is inevitable." The President summoned that old stand-by, national security, to justify his decision: "In this case, however, I felt that the national security interest of the United States lay in developing our relations with the PRC." There was a convenient scapegoat for Nixon's conflicting emotions: Henry Kissinger. ". . . I was asked to stop over in Alaska on the way back so that I would not arrive home on the day of the UN vote . . . a virtual acknowledgment that my trip was responsible for the outcome," Kissinger lamented in his memoirs. "And I was disembarked at a distant corner of Andrews Air Force Base [near Washington], inaccessible to newsmen and photographers. It was not a heroic homecoming. . . ."

The timing of Kissinger's second visit to Peking was not an accident. Peking had proposed October knowing that the General Assembly of the United Nations convenes that month and, prior to its opening, must settle all seating questions. Kissinger, by not urging a different time, made a major concession. So was the decision to provide Chou En-lai with more American intelligence information on the Soviet Union. In return, the Chinese gave the White House a very special gift: live television coverage for Nixon's summit. On July 19, only four days after the announcement of Kissinger's first trip, Ziegler met with the Washington bureau chiefs of the three major networks. According to the *Washington Post,* the network officials were told that some television coverage for the summit would be available in Peking. The TV men urged the White House to request permission for live satellite coverage, which would necessitate the construction of a satellite relay station in China. On Kissinger's second trip, in October, the *Post* reported, the Chinese, "to everyone's surprise . . . agreed to a ground station and live coverage."

As his shunting to a distant corner of Andrews Air Force base indicated, Kissinger emerged from his stunning successes in China with increased attention from the public and increased resentment from the White House; aides noted that Nixon seemed, from that period on, to feel directly competitive with Kissinger about poll ratings and crowd responsiveness. Kissinger's success with the press, which had done so much in the early years of the administration to limit antiwar dissent, was no longer seen as a glowing asset.

Nixon, in fact, did more than merely brood; he ordered his aides to spy on Kissinger, who in turn began to lie to him about contacts with reporters. One senior Nixon aide dates Kissinger's troubles to the first few days after Nixon's July 15 announcement of Kissinger's first trip to Peking. At a meeting of the senior staff in San Clemente, Nixon issued an edict: "From this point on, no one in the White House should say another word about the China trip." Kissinger was quick to say me-too. "Henry's line," the aide recalls, "was that 'If we start talking about this, the Chinese will start to think we're not serious people. It could destroy the initiative.' " In subsequent weeks, however, Nixon learned that Kissinger considered the edict to apply to others but not

himself, and in early September, John Scali was summoned to Nixon's office.*
There was no love lost between Kissinger and Scali, a former television news-
man who had been brought onto the staff by Haldeman to handle foreign affairs
briefings for the President—in obvious competition with Kissinger's role.
Nixon wanted to know who was leaking. Scali answered promptly: Kissinger.
Nixon affected surprise: He had asked Kissinger about the stories, and been
assured that he had not seen "a single reporter on China." Scali understood
his assignment. He checked the various White House logs and registration
slips and compiled a list of twenty-four reporters who had been in Kissinger's
office and had subsequently written some details on the trip to Peking.

The aide, remembering the scene years later, sympathized with the President's role: "It was so tough for Nixon because Kissinger was lying so much
that he never knew what to believe. This was why Al Haig was so indispensable. He had to talk to Haig to find out what the truth was." Needless to say,
it was far more complicated than that.

Amid the secrecy that dominated—and still dominates—those first two Peking trips, one overwhelming mystery remains: Nixon's insistence that he and
Kissinger specifically warned Chou En-lai that they would permit Japan to
develop nuclear weapons if China did not agree to rapprochement. Nixon made
the claim in late June of 1975, nearly a year after his resignation, during secret
testimony before the Watergate Special Prosecution Force. The prosecutors,
trying to conclude their grand jury inquiries into presidential misconduct, had
asked a series of questions about Yeoman Charles Radford, who triggered a
major scandal late in 1973 when it became known that, while working for
Admiral Robinson in the Joint Chiefs of Staff liaison office in the White House,
he had been routinely stealing highly classified documents for the Pentagon.
One of the documents Radford stole was a "President's Eyes Only" summary
of Kissinger's meetings with Chou En-lai, which was subsequently passed on
to Admiral Moorer, the chairman of the Joint Chiefs of Staff. Nixon became
extremely agitated when asked about Radford, one of the Watergate prosecutors recalls, and testified that "Radford knew everything. He was in all the
sensitive meetings." Nixon went on, "We had these tough negotiations with
China over the Mutual Defense Treaty [of 1961] with Japan. You have to be
tough. And we told them that if they tried to jump Japan then we'll jump
them." The Watergate prosecutor further remembers Nixon as testifying that
"We told them that if you try to keep us from protecting the Japanese, we
would let them go nuclear. And the Chinese said, 'We don't want that.' "
Nixon did not make clear when these alleged threats were made, but Radford's
only direct involvement with China came on Kissinger's first visit in July 1971.
The prosecutor, who knew few details of the diplomatic negotiations with
Peking, was amazed at Nixon's account. "The impression I had was of a real

* It was a Joseph Alsop column, published a few days after Kissinger's return from China, that
especially distressed the White House apparatus. Kissinger had provided Alsop, an enthusiastic
amateur archaeologist, with an account of a major new Chinese find: the tomb of a brother of Han
Wu-ti, a great emperor of the second century B.C. The brother and his wife were covered with jade
bodystockings and the emperor was wearing what, as Alsop wrote, could only be described as a
jade jockstrap.

street fighter," he says. "Nixon said he'd 'put it to' the Chinese—like some-one out of Hell's Kitchen." The President's point was, as the prosecutor saw it, that America could "deal with China by warning that nuclear arms for Japan would be in the balance."

Neither Nixon nor Kissinger mentioned such a threat to China in the mem-oirs, but many of their aides recall that both men were known to have been intrigued since early 1969 with the possibility of an independent Japanese nu-clear deterrent. Kissinger had been hostile to the Non-Proliferation Treaty, which was signed by Japan in 1970 (but not ratified for six years), in part because there seemed to be no bargaining gain for Japan and other allies in giving up something—the possibility of going nuclear—for nothing. In late 1969, Roger Morris was pulled from his NSC staff duties on Africa and as-signed to China, where he summarized and rewrote many of the early White House and State Department studies on the border dispute between China and the Soviet Union. Morris recalls being asked to write the "scenario" for a possible China-Soviet war and, along with that, to discuss a scenario on Ja-pan's future. "Henry's query was what would the United States do if there was a military takeover in Japan," Morris recalls. Kissinger's concern was "freewheeling," Morris says. "Henry said what if Japan became an indepen-dent nuclear power? What if it became militarized? I remember our joking in the staff that we could, in these policy papers, totally restructure the world."*

Nixon and Kissinger took their theoretical views a step further at a Novem-ber 1969 meeting in Washington with Prime Minister Eisaku Sato; at issue was the Mutual Defense Treaty, which hinged on agreement on the reversion of Okinawa and American imports of Japanese textiles. At that meeting, Nixon and Kissinger broadly hinted to Sato that the United States would "under-stand" if Japan decided to go nuclear. The only other person present, a State Department interpreter, was troubled by such talk, and leaked his notes to senior officials in the State Department; the notes eventually made their way to Richard Sneider, the former Kissinger NSC aide then serving as Deputy Chief of Mission in the American Embassy in Tokyo. "These guys [Nixon and Kissinger] thought they were being cute," Sneider says. "Sato and his aides walked away confused. We had to go cleaning up the mess and had to tell the Japanese they'd misunderstood what Nixon and Kissinger were saying. We just quietly sabotaged the whole thing."†

* A nuclear option for Japan was not a new concept in the American government; similar discus-sions had taken place in 1964 after China detonated its first nuclear bomb. The issue was how to reassure India, then America's ally and China's enemy. Dean Rusk, the Secretary of State, was among those recommending that India be encouraged to develop its own nuclear weapon in re-sponse. Daniel Ellsberg, who was then working in the Pentagon's Office of International Strategic Affairs, recalls that he and fellow aide Alvin Friedman objected vigorously to Rusk's proposal, which had not been challenged by Secretary of Defense Robert McNamara. The issue was reopened at high levels after intervention by John McNaughton, the Assistant Secretary of Defense, who later told his aides that Rusk's attitude was that "India needed a nuclear weapon as a deterrent and there was no reason for them not to have it." Confronted with the obvious rebuttal—that an Indian weapon would lead to a Japanese weapon—Rusk reportedly answered, so Ellsberg was told, "Why shouldn't Japan have a nuclear weapon." The aides were told that Rusk's general approach to nonproliferation was, in essence, "Why shouldn't our friends have nuclear weapons now that our enemies have them?" Rusk's view did not prevail in the bureaucratic debate, Ellsberg recalls, and American policy continued to be hostile to nuclear proliferation.
† It is not known whether Kissinger learned of the interpreter's action, but no State Department

381

Despite the efforts of Sneider and his State Department colleagues, China may have learned something about the Nixon-Kissinger approach to Sato. By 1971, just before Kissinger's first visit to Peking, Chou En-lai and other Chinese officials were extremely upset about the possibility of Japan's going nuclear. On July 5, Ross Terrill interviewed Chou En-lai and, as he later wrote, found the Premier "very agitated indeed about Japan." Chou accused the United States of joining forces with reactionaries in Japan to revive "Japanese militarism"; America, he charged, was debating the possibility of giving the Japanese tactical nuclear weapons.

There is no evidence, despite Nixon's statements to the Watergate prosecutors, that Kissinger relayed any kind of threat to China during his first meeting with Chou En-lai in Peking. By late 1971, as the American summit with Moscow neared, China prudently sought to improve its relations with Japan and gradually diminished its protests against Japanese militarism. Yet Nixon and Kissinger, having settled relations with China, began to talk in private during Nixon's second term about the inevitability of a nuclear Japan. For example, in March 1974, Kissinger gave a secret briefing to the Joint Chiefs of Staff to win their support for a second round of SALT negotiations. According to notes taken by one senior officer, he presented the following analysis: "The Japanese are mean and treacherous but they are not organically anti-American; they pursue their own interest. . . . It is essential for the U.S. to maintain a balance of power out there. If it shifts, Japan could be a big problem. [Kissinger] said, 'Don't mistake me about the Chinese. They would kill us if they got the chance and they would pick up Japan if they thought they could get away with it, but right now they are so concerned with the Russians that they'll cooperate.' He said that he believed that Japan will go nuclear at some time; the oil crisis has accelerated that. He said that the Chinese would worry if the Japanese began to increase their defense expenditures. He said that it is all right; we ought to let the Japanese do so without being publicly linked with it. He said it is good to keep the Chinese concerned."

---

interpreters were used in his subsequent backchannel meetings with Soviet officials and in the meetings in China with Chou En-lai and Mao Tse-tung.

28

THE PLUMBERS

IN THE EARLY EVENING of June 17, 1971, four days after the *New York Times* began publication of the Pentagon Papers, Henry Kissinger held forth in the Oval Office, telling his President, John Ehrlichman, and H. R. Haldeman all about Daniel Ellsberg. Kissinger's comments were recorded, of course, on the hidden White House taping system, and four years later a portion of that tape was heard by the Watergate Special Prosecution Force, then investigating the internal White House police unit known as the Plumbers. The Special Prosecution Force had agreed with the White House early in the Watergate inquiry that all the Nixon-Kissinger meetings were prima facie concerned with national security matters; hence none of their conversations was ever subpoenaed. Prosecution files show, however, that Kissinger, who took part in the fifty-minute meeting on June 17, expressed concern not only about Ellsberg's disclosure of the Pentagon Papers but also about other documents and secrets he might release. On that day, or perhaps the day before, the White House also learned that Ellsberg had provided Senator Charles Mathias of Maryland with a copy of the top-secret NSSM 1, one of the administration's first studies on Vietnam. Nixon was anxious about the Brookings Institution, a liberal think tank in Washington to which Morton Halperin had gone after leaving Kissinger's staff. Also at Brookings was Leslie Gelb, the former Pentagon official who directed the Pentagon Papers project and who, many in the White House believed, had been involved in getting the papers to the *Times*. At one point during the meeting, Nixon and Kissinger agreed that top-secret documents not available to the White House from the Pentagon might possibly be stored in Halperin's or Gelb's safe at Brookings, awaiting future release. "They've got the stuff over there," Nixon said. "Stuff that we can't even get out of there from the Pentagon." Kissinger responded: "Can't we send someone over there to get it back?"

Kissinger was not a target of the Special Prosecution Force and no attempt was actually made to get access, legally or by other means, to the documents believed stored by Halperin and Gelb—although many plans were discussed over the next few weeks. The June 17 tape itself was not relevant to the Watergate prosecution, and knowledge of it was tightly held inside the Special Force, but its importance was obvious to the few investigators who did know about it: Kissinger was involved. "There was incredible ambivalence about the whole thing," one Watergate attorney recalls. "Do you want to go up against him? Kissinger was being promoted by everybody as the one guy in the administration who's solid—and he's threatening to resign. I got a sense that if I found something that finished Henry, the country was going to be in bad shape.''

Kissinger escaped any serious investigation during Watergate, as those attorneys who suspected that Kissinger knew far more than he could admit about the workings of the Nixon White House soon found themselves immersed in the prosecution of the President's men. One prosecution official, discussing that White House tape recording years later, recalled a quality of Kissinger's conduct in front of Nixon, Ehrlichman, and Haldeman that made him wish he had listened to more. ''He was like one of the boys, talking tough. One says, 'Let's bring knives.' Another says, 'Let's bring bats.' And Henry pipes up, 'Let's bring zipguns.' '' The prosecutor was surprised: ''I thought he might have been classier.''

Kissinger dominated the meeting on June 17 with his description of Ellsberg and the threat to the national security he posed. Ehrlichman's notes for that day, as published by the House Impeachment Committee, showed that Kissinger depicted Ellsberg as a half-crazed genius whose views on the war had turned dovish with excessive drug use and aberrant sexuality. It was a shrewd performance that played perfectly to the prejudices of Nixon and his two top aides. It was also an exercise in character assassination, similar in intent, if not degree, to Kissinger's performance in maligning Morton Halperin in front of the President when Halperin was suspected of leaking in May 1969. Kissinger described Ellsberg as a ''genius'' who was the ''brightest student'' he ever had at Harvard. (Kissinger had, in fact, never taught Ellsberg.) Ellsberg was further described as one who ''shot at peasants'' while assigned as an embassy aide in Vietnam and who seemed ''always a little unbalanced.'' (Ellsberg has emphatically denied ever shooting at civilians while in Vietnam.) Kissinger then spoke of Ellsberg's use of drugs, information that he could have learned only from the White House wiretaps, and suggested that this was what had turned Ellsberg from ''hawk to peacenik.''* Kissinger told the President that he hadn't seen Ellsberg in a year and a half, except for the meeting at MIT at which Ellsberg had ''heckled'' him. (The two had met the previous August at San Clemente and again a month later when Ellsberg urged Kissinger to read the Pentagon Papers.) Ehrlichman's notes included the phrase ''Murder in Laos,'' a reference to Ellsberg's 1971 article in the *New York Review of Books* in which he restated the theme that the White House made no estimates and took no account of civilian casualties in the Vietnam War.

Kissinger's description was vivid, and the men in the Oval Office would remember it clearly. Three years later, in an affidavit filed before he obtained access to his personal notes, Ehrlichman was able to describe the presentation accurately: ''We were told that he [Ellsberg] was a fanatic, known to be a drug abuser and in knowledge of very critical defense secrets of current validity, such as nuclear deterrent targeting. Having never heard of Ellsberg before the

---

* The tape of the June 17 meeting, according to Special Prosecution Force files, has Nixon asking whether Kissinger was sure about Ellsberg's use of drugs. Kissinger responded: ''There is no doubt about it.''

theft of the papers, my impression from Kissinger's description was that the ation was presented with a very serious potential security problem beyond theft of the largely historical Pentagon Papers . . . In these meetings both the President and Dr. Kissinger were deeply concerned. The latter was quite agitated at times."

Kissinger's seemingly emotional performance on June 17 was all the more remarkable because he had run through practically the same allegations the day before. On June 16, Charles Colson took two young Vietnam veterans, John O'Neill and Melville L. Stephens—both supporters of the White House war policies—to visit the President, and after a few moments Nixon summoned Kissinger. Responding to the cue, Kissinger gave what Colson recalls as "one of his most passionate tirades. He described Ellsberg as a sexual pervert, said he shot Vietnamese from helicopters in Vietnam, used drugs, had sexual relations with his wife in front of their children. Henry said he was the most dangerous man in America today. He said he 'must be stopped at all costs.' " Melville Stephens, who later joined the White House staff, confirms this account and says he left the Oval Office convinced that Ellsberg "obviously had access to lots of other sensitive documents."

These must have been nerve-wracking days for Kissinger, poised on the eve of his secret trip to China. He had to distance himself decisively from Ellsberg to insure the President's continued trust. After all, he had brought Ellsberg into the National Security Council staff as a consultant and encouraged him to work on NSSM 1, the major review of Vietnam policy in early 1969. Furthermore, Kissinger himself was cited in the Pentagon Papers as seeking diplomatic contact with the North Vietnamese during the Johnson Administration. He also knew far more about the project than anyone in the White House; he had even read some of its most secret volumes. Thus publication of the Papers served as yet another example of his poor judgment in the staffing of his office. Nixon remained convinced, as he had been since the days of Morton Halperin, that most of the serious leaks emanated from the NSC staff, which even in mid-1971 he still considered disloyal and overpopulated with liberal Democrats. Kissinger's reaction to the Pentagon Papers was as much a response to those pressures as to the potential national security threat. Ellsberg was a personal security threat.

Harrison E. Salisbury, in *Without Fear or Favor,* his book on the *New York Times,* describes Haig as being hard at work on the night of June 12 trying to learn all he could. One of the first people he called was Walt Rostow, Lyndon Johnson's national security adviser.

"What is this Vietnam study which is going to be in the *New York Times* tomorrow?" Haig asked.

"Who leaked it?" Rostow responded.

"We think it is a guy named Ellsberg."

"The son-of-a-bitch," Rostow said. "He still owes me a term paper." *

---

* Rostow, who confirms Salisbury's account, says that his use of the phrase "term paper" was "half in jest"; the overdue paper was not an academic report but a highly classified study of nuclear crises that Ellsberg, as a Rand consultant, had agreed to undertake for the State Department Policy Planning Group in 1964. Ellsberg recalls spending more than six months on the study, which focused on communications in potential nuclear crises, such as the U-2 incident, the 1956 Suez dispute, and the 1962 Cuban missile crisis. During his research he maintained an office in the Pentagon and was

Kissinger was in California that weekend, but he and Haig always stayed in close touch. Both men knew that Ellsberg had become more outspoken in his opposition to the administration's war policies, and they may have heard that in late 1970 he tried to persuade Anthony Lake to become active in the antiwar movement. They surely would have recalled Ellsberg's near-obsession with the Pentagon Papers during his visit to San Clemente the previous year. Although Ellsberg loomed as a logical suspect, there is no evidence that Kissinger or Haig told either the President or the FBI of their suspicions. Ellsberg's name did not come to light until June 16, when Sidney Zion, a former *Times* reporter, revealed his role on a radio talk show. By that time Senator Mathias had informed the Justice Department that Ellsberg had visited him earlier in the year and given him a copy of NSSM 1.*

The Pentagon Papers posed no threat to national security but provided a vital opportunity to score political points against the antiwar movement and the liberal Democrats. Nixon made his views explicit during a meeting in late July to discuss another newspaper leak, this one dealing with the SALT negotiations. "This does affect the national security—this particular one," Nixon said, according to a published House Impeachment Committee transcript. "This isn't like the Pentagon Papers. This one involves a current negotiation." Through the Pentagon Papers, Nixon could strike at a small group of Muskie advisers, including Halperin, Lake, and Gelb, who had been overheard repeatedly on the wiretaps denigrating the White House. Nixon's obsession, in fact, had been focused on Gelb from the early days of his administration. In his memoirs, Haldeman told of a Nixon demand in 1969, shortly after the inauguration, that the White House obtain the Pentagon files on the Johnson Administration's last-ditch peace initiative late in October 1968, which almost won the election for Humphrey. Late that year, he learned that Gelb had taken a pertinent document to the Brookings Institution, where he had a fellowship.†

---

the first person outside the Joint Chiefs of Staff to read all the command and control studies of those incidents. Before he could finish, he was hired by the Pentagon and became involved in Vietnam. There was another reason, he says, for his not providing Rostow with the written report: "It would have been so highly classified nobody would read it." His point is that he was reluctant to write a paper that would not be widely disseminated.

* Mathias informed John Mitchell almost immediately after publication of the Pentagon Papers that Ellsberg had visited him a few months earlier and left a copy of NSSM 1 with an aide. Mitchell was "all excited," Mathias remembers, and asked him to bring the documents to the White House. The Senator did so. Over the next six months, however, Mathias told no one, not even Ellsberg, of his decision to inform the White House. His role became known to Ellsberg and his attorneys late in 1971, when the FBI, seeking permission to search Ellsberg's personal belongings that were in storage in California, submitted documents in camera to William M. Byrne, Jr., the federal district court judge hearing the Pentagon Papers case, in support of their claim that Ellsberg had possession of other classified materials. The FBI documents outlined Mathias' role. Mathias acknowledged his distress at what he had done at a later meeting with two Ellsberg attorneys, Charles Nesson, a Harvard law school professor, and Charles E. Goodell, the former New York Republican senator. "He was very embarrassed because he'd wanted to help," as Goodell remembers it. "He was obviously torn." The lawyers had visited Mathias to determine whether he would be a witness at Ellsberg's trial. At one point, Mathias took his former Senate colleague aside and explained, "Charlie, I have to be careful. They may try to do the same thing to me that they did to you." Goodell was widely known to have been successfully targeted by Nixon and his political aides for defeat in 1970. Samuel Goldberg, who was then Mathias' aide for national security affairs, confirmed that the pressure was acute. Mathias, says Goldberg, "had heard that he was next on the shit list. The word in our office was that Chuck Colson had let it be known that Mac was next on the list."

† Gelb categorically denied taking any sensitive files from the Pentagon when he left his Pentagon post on May 1, 1969. He said that he did move three or four volumes of the Pentagon Papers to

Nixon was irritated by the information, Haldeman wrote, and said, slamming down a pencil, "I want that goddamn Gelb material and I don't care how you get it." Over the next few months, Haldeman worked closely with Haig, "who had helped to compile other material," in an attempt to develop "various James Bond-type techniques to retrieve the documents." One proposed solution was simply to have them stolen from Gelb's safe, Haldeman wrote, but nothing ever came of the planning "as far as I was concerned."

Nixon saw the Pentagon Papers as providing further justification for an assault on Brookings. In his memoirs, he candidly admitted that the Ellsberg leaks renewed his interest in Gelb's bombing halt report—without, of course, mentioning that he had sanctioned illegal means to obtain it in 1969: "I saw absolutely no reason for that report to be at Brookings, and I said I wanted it back right now—even if it meant having to get it surreptitiously. . . . I wanted to know what had actually happened; I also wanted the information as potential leverage against those in Johnson's Administration who were now trying to undercut my war policy."

Kissinger, with his frantic desire to show up Ellsberg as a national security threat, was playing right into the President's hands. By mid-June of 1971, the White House had already been threatened with exposure for its wiretapping, albeit indirectly, by J. Edgar Hoover, who understood only too well that national security had little to do with the twenty-one months of wiretapping.* If there was to be a break-in at Brookings, or other clandestine activities against the Democrats, the justification would have to be airtight. In 1970, Hoover had stopped the Huston plan, which called for the FBI, with the aid of other intelligence agencies, to make use of wiretapping, illegal break-ins, and other techniques to combat the antiwar movement. Kissinger, with his diatribes against Ellsberg, was now providing Nixon with the rationale to try to initiate such actions again.

Brookings, but they were merely unclassified summaries of the public statements of the Kennedy and Johnson administrations. In addition, he asked a Navy enlisted man who worked in his office to pack and move a number of public documents and personal books. The Navy man had also been involved in shifting a classified set of the Pentagon Papers to the Rand Corporation, under the appropriate regulations for such transfers. After publication of the Pentagon Papers, Gelb added, everyone who had worked in his office was interviewed by government security agents, and the possibility exists that the enlisted man may have confused what was classified and unclassified. Even so, Gelb remains baffled by Haldeman's comment that he took classified documents to Brookings in 1969.

* Hoover, aware that Nixon and his top aides wanted him retired, was making it clear by early spring that he fully understood the implications of the White House wiretaps and the grave political problem their revelation could cause in an election year. On April 12, 1971, according to the records of the Watergate Special Prosecution Force, Hoover sent a memorandum to all assistant directors of the FBI, ordering them no longer to provide any domestic intelligence information to Robert C. Mardian, an Assistant Attorney General who was Mitchell's close confidant and a political operative. The reason for Hoover's order was made clear in *Will*, the autobiography of G. Gordon Liddy, a member of the White House's secret investigation unit, the Plumbers, that was set up in mid-1971. Liddy quoted Mardian as telling him that Hoover had become enraged at what he considered criticism about the FBI in the spring of 1971. Hoover telephoned Richard Kleindienst, John Mitchell's deputy in the Justice Department, and declared, with Mardian being permitted to overhear, that if Congress launched an investigation into the FBI and ". . . if I am called upon to testify . . . I will have to tell *all* that I know about this matter." Mardian, so he told Liddy, quickly telephoned the President to report the threat, which obviously dealt with the White House wiretaps. Nixon, Haldeman, and Ehrlichman subsequently discussed the "Hoover problem" in the White House, as prosecution records show.

In late June of 1971, Kissinger was busier than anyone else in the White House. His travel plans, even aside from the trip to China, were demanding. He was scheduled to meet with Le Duc Tho in Paris on June 26, to receive Hanoi's response to a revised American peace offer that had been made secretly in May. He arranged for a public two-day visit to London beginning on June 24, in part to disguise his mission. He was also under attack inside the SALT bureaucracy for his backchannel concessions on the SLBM issue, and he was beginning to perceive the extent of his error. And there were other issues: the fall presidential elections in South Vietnam, in which the administration was determined to help Nguyen Van Thieu win reelection; the United States role in the nearly complete negotiations with Russia, England, and France, as well as East and West Germany, over the future status of Berlin; and the continuing efforts by Rogers and Sisco to work out a Middle East settlement.

Rogers was still a source of insecurity and another reason the China trip was all-important. A successful visit to Peking would deal a near-fatal blow to Rogers' prestige. There was nothing in the Pentagon Papers that would jeopardize the China rapprochement, Kissinger knew; the far greater threat came from Ellsberg and the President's obsessive belief that the NSC staff was not trustworthy. Over the next few months, as Nixon continued to focus on the Pentagon Papers and other leaks, Kissinger would not dare to do other than to support his President wholeheartedly.

Kissinger's heavy schedule often prevented his participation as the White House organized a secret internal police unit in early July and began domestic operations aimed at destroying the credibility of Ellsberg and others in the antiwar movement. But when Kissinger did participate in discussions of how to deal with the publication of the Pentagon Papers, he was enthusiastic. At the Oval Office meeting on June 17, for example, according to Ehrlichman's notes, Nixon conceived the idea of asking Lyndon Johnson to denounce publication of the Papers and thus make the attack bipartisan. The President, as he often did, turned to Colson and urged him to call Texas. Nixon's request came as Colson was meeting with Bryce Harlow, the former White House adviser then working as a high-priced lobbyist. It was thought that Harlow would have better luck with Johnson, but the former President refused to get involved, insisting that the *New York Times* and the *Washington Post*, which had begun publishing its own set of Pentagon Papers after the Justice Department successfully (though temporarily) enjoined the *Times*, were trying to "reexecute him."

Johnson's refusal escalated a routine presidential request to a crisis. "Nixon was calling me all the time," Colson recalls. "He was obsessed about Johnson." After renewed tries by Colson and Harlow, Kissinger sought to move in. "Henry called and said it was foolish to call Johnson directly. He said, 'I can get to him through Walt Rostow. I'll take care of it.' " But Kissinger also demanded that Harlow and Colson stop any further efforts to reach Johnson. Colson viewed the squabble as business as usual in the White House: "Kissinger wanted the credit." So did Colson. "I told him the President wants me to do it." Kissinger then announced that he would telephone Nixon and resolve the issue. Nixon had gone to bed by that time, and Colson proposed a compromise: "I'll make a deal with you," he told Kissinger. "If you promise me that you won't call the President tonight, I promise you I won't do anything more tonight to reach Lyndon Johnson." Kissinger agreed, but Colson "knew" that Kissinger would not abide by their agreement. He waited a few minutes, then picked up the telephone and asked the White House operator whether anyone had called the President that evening. "Dr. Kissinger called three or four minutes ago and is talking now," she responded.

Few outsiders were aware of the extent of the top aides' eternal scrambling to curry favor with the President. During the 1973 Senate Foreign Relations Committee hearings into wiretapping, Kissinger was asked—almost casually —about White House attempts in mid-1971 to make political use of the Pentagon Papers. Kissinger's response seemed plausible: ". . . [T]here were a number of individuals in the White House who occasionally made requests of various kinds, which, as a matter of principle, I refused. . . . I frankly thought there were a few Boy Scouts who were trying to win some points, and I always rejected them."

In his memoirs, Kissinger again suggested that the political opportunism provoked by the Pentagon Papers had little to do with him: ". . . The sudden release of over 7,000 pages of secret documents came as a profound shock to the Administration. The documents, of course, were in no way damaging to the Nixon Presidency. Indeed, there was some sentiment among White House political operatives to exploit them as an illustration of the machinations of our predecessors and the difficulties we inherited. But such an attitude seemed to me against the public interest: Our foreign policy could never achieve the continuity on which other nations must depend, and our system of government would surely lose all trust if each President used his control of the process of declassification to smear his predecessors."

Kissinger found it easy to take the high road in his memoirs, but the reality of the White House in 1971 did not permit such indulgence. To allow a group of political operatives, including Colson, to become involved in an investigation of national security leaks involving his office was unthinkable—especially in the days before the China trip. The delicate task of defending both the National Security Council staff and Henry Kissinger inside the Oval Office fell to Haig, and it was he who played a pivotal role in the summer and fall of 1971, as the White House began its illegal activities against Daniel Ellsberg and the Muskie advisers conveniently believed by John Mitchell and others in the Justice Department—as well as by the President—to be involved in a political conspiracy against the White House and the Vietnam War. Haig had been loyal to Kissinger during the nearly two years of White House wiretapping. He directly exposed himself by regularly consulting with FBI officials and he was responsible, in large measure, for drafting and signing documents that relayed Kissinger's wiretap instructions to the FBI. Haig believed in the wiretapping as much as he believed that Daniel Ellsberg was a traitor whose goal was to see the United States defeated in South Vietnam. He held similar views toward Halperin and others at Brookings, and such beliefs gave him credibility with the President. In Kissinger's view, Haig had one other essential trait: He was bureaucratically sophisticated, as an ambitious Army officer had to be, and he would know how to protect Kissinger when things got rough behind his back —as Kissinger knew they would. The issue was how to limit the damage.

Nixon began his attacks on the National Security Council staff within days of Kissinger's departure for Peking. On July 2, Ehrlichman was assigned full responsibility for the Ellsberg case and ordered to appoint a staff aide to devote full time to the "conspiracy" involving Ellsberg and his fellow Democrats. A continuing Nixon concern was Hoover and the FBI, which, so the White House believed, was less than enthusiastic about the investigation of Ellsberg and his fellow conspirators. On July 6, Ehrlichman's notes quoted Nixon explicitly expressing his feeling about Kissinger's staff: "can't assume NSC staff not participants" in the assumed conspiracy. The President suggested that Laurence Lynn, the former Kissinger aide then teaching at Stanford University, be given a lie-detector test to determine his involvement. Ehrlichman was also told, his notes showed, to "put a nonlegal team on the conspiracy"—and thus the internal police unit, which would become infamous as the White House Plumbers, was born.*

There was also talk that day of a "Communist" link to Ellsberg—a connection that no government agency was ever able to demonstrate. Three days later, while Kissinger was at meetings in Peking, the President told Ehrlichman and Haldeman that Kissinger's "staff must be cleaned out." By that day, too, Ehrlichman had found the right man to direct the "nonlegal" team sought by the President—David Young, Kissinger's former personal aide, who, dissatisfied with his lack of status in the NSC, had transferred to Ehrlichman's Domestic Council staff early in the year. Nixon approved the choice and asked Ehrlichman to bring Young in for a face-to-face meeting. Kissinger, in China, was not to be bothered about the new "special duty" for Young, but Haig would be informed.

By July 6, there was another element at work: renewed presidential insistence that the Brookings Institution be penetrated and that Gelb's and Halperin's files be removed and brought back to the White House. The catalyst in Nixon's renewed anxiety was Colson, who had obtained a 1969 Brookings brochure announcing a two-year history project on the Vietnam War by Leslie Gelb, which was to culminate with the publication of a "balanced and accurate history . . ." Daniel Ellsberg, according to the brochure, was on an advisory panel for the study.† The timing indicated, Colson told Ehrlichman in a memorandum, that "another installment of the Pentagon Papers" would be made public in a few months. More top-secret documents were headed for America's newspapers. When Nixon learned of the new study, Colson recalls, he "blew up at Haldeman" and said, "Goddamnit, Bob, haven't we got that capability in place? How many times am I going to have to tell you. Get'em back." After the meeting, Haldeman took Colson aside and said, as Colson remembers it, "Well, you heard the President. Take care of it." Over the next two months

---

* So called because, obviously, its role was to stop leaks.
† The advisory panel was far from a revolutionary group. Gelb recalls that it included Walt Rostow and William L. Langer, the Harvard historian who had served as historian for the Office of Strategic Services during World War II. Gelb's study, *The Irony of Vietnam: The System Worked*, was not published until 1980.

there was repeated and serious talk inside the White House of a possible firebombing of Brookings in an effort to steal the classified papers believed to be stored there. The project eventually came to the attention of G. Gordon Liddy, the former FBI agent, and E. Howard Hunt, the former CIA operative, who had been hired, with Ehrlichman's eventual approval, for the Plumbers unit. In his memoirs, Liddy wrote that he and Hunt developed a plan in September to buy a used fire engine and firemen's uniforms for a squad of Cubans who would be trained in firefighting techniques "so their performance would be believable." Brookings would "be firebombed" with delayed timing devices; the Cubans would respond, "hit the vault [where Nixon believed the documents were held], and get themselves out in the confusion . . ." The plan was rejected as being too expensive, Liddy wrote.*

Kissinger was being protected in all this by Haig, who over the summer became more indispensable than ever. Whether Haig was involved in the proposed firebombing of Brookings in mid-1971 is not known, but in 1969 he had joined Haldeman in similar planning to retrieve documents that, so Nixon believed, Leslie Gelb had removed from the Pentagon. Far more significant than such planning and talking is evidence that in the summer of 1971 Haig was involved in an effort, triggered by the President, to further violate Ellsberg's constitutional rights by destroying evidence that Ellsberg had been overheard on the White House wiretaps.†

According to the still unpublished records of the Watergate Prosecution Force, Haig first became directly involved in the White House campaign against Ellsberg on July 12, 1971, at San Clemente, although Haig himself was not present when Nixon and his top aides gathered to discuss the question of Ellsberg's repeated appearances on the White House wiretaps. On June 28, Ellsberg had been indicted by the Justice Department and charged with violations of the theft, espionage, and conspiracy statutes for his act in photocopying the Pentagon Papers. Within a few days, the Internal Security Division of the Justice Department, following routine practice, requested the FBI to check

---

* All this scheming took place after Liddy, Hunt, and the Cubans broke into the Beverly Hills office of Dr. Lewis J. Fielding, Ellsberg's former psychoanalyst, in early September, in a futile effort to find Ellsberg's psychiatric records or other possibly detrimental information.

† Private notes kept by a key Kissinger aide, which summarized many conversations between Kissinger and the President as well as Kissinger and Haig, were made available to me on condition that their author not be named. These notes show that Haig was receiving reports on the Plumbers' activities throughout mid-1971 and was reporting fully to Kissinger. They further reveal that by the time of the Watergate scandal in 1973, David Young had become a constant cause of concern for Kissinger. In early June, after Haig was brought into the White House as chief of staff, the NSC notes show that Kissinger was openly worried about Young and whether he was truly loyal to Kissinger or was just saying he was "a Kissinger man." At one point in 1973, Kissinger even considered reinstating Young as an aide on the NSC staff, a step that he knew would please Young and, presumably, help insure his loyalty.

Kissinger also became convinced over the summer that *he* was one of the targets of the President and his aides, and he said as much to outsiders. In August 1971, amid the public acclaim for his secret trip to Peking, Kissinger lamented to Allen Whiting, "This has been a very difficult time for me. When I took this job I expected to get it from the left," but Haldeman and Ehrlichman were "passing on to the President all kinds of mail about me—about my business life and my sex life. It's very difficult." Whiting was astonished at the remark and concerned that Nixon and his aides might force Kissinger to resign. In a 1975 interview with Watergate prosecutors, Kissinger said that in 1971 he "assumed additional taps may have been used to investigate the Pentagon Papers leak and that he himself may have been tapped," according to a summary of the interview.

391

its wiretap logs to determine whether Ellsberg had been overheard. On July 9, the Internal Security Division filed a second request, asking the FBI also to check its records on potential grand jury witnesses in the case, including Morton Halperin, Leslie Gelb, and Neil Sheehan, the *New York Times* reporter to whom Ellsberg provided access to the Papers. On July 6, Nixon, Mitchell, Ehrlichman, and Haldeman met in the Oval Office and discussed—almost casually—the importance of reviewing the illicit wiretap records to see whether some detrimental information about Ellsberg and his suspected collaborators could be found. "In light of this," Haldeman said at one point, according to a Prosecution Force transcript, "some of that stuff may be a hell of a lot more meaningful now . . ." Mitchell responded, "I've had them reviewed in the Bureau." Haldeman recalled "a lot of conversations with Sheehan in them, to my recollection." Mitchell, after some discussion, acknowledged, "Bob is right. You never know what those taps mean. . . ."*

The revived interest in the White House wiretaps also prompted William Sullivan, who was then in the midst of a power struggle with J. Edgar Hoover, to visit Robert Mardian, head of the Justice Department's Internal Security Division, and warn him, as Mardian later testified, that Hoover could not be trusted and might try to blackmail Nixon, as he had blackmailed other presidents, because of the wiretap material. Sullivan, who suspected Hoover would soon fire him from his post as an assistant FBI director and who had his own ambitions to be Hoover's successor, also told Mardian that he had physical possession of the FBI's set of wiretap logs and summaries. On July 11, Mardian flew to the California White House for a meeting with Nixon and his closest aides the next morning. By then, the FBI had still not responded to the Justice Department's request for wiretapping information on Ellsberg and potential grand jury witnesses.

John Ehrlichman's notes for the July 12 meeting, which have not been made public until now, suggest that Mardian raised the issue of the Hoover threat directly with the President, for Nixon and his aides spent much of the meeting discussing problems that could be caused by a formal admission that Ellsberg had been overheard. To make such an admission would reveal the Kissinger wiretaps. Nixon, according to Ehrlichman's notes, ordered Haldeman to "recover documents from Haig"—that is, the set of wiretap summaries and logs in Kissinger's office. The President then said, "O.K. Obtain and destroy all logs . . . Tell Hoover to destroy." A few minutes later, according to the notes, the President, again discussing the wiretap records, ordered that Haig be instructed to return the White House copies of the summaries and logs to Sullivan's office in the FBI. Sullivan was then to forward all the documents to Mardian's office "for destruction." There was to be an additional role for Haig, Nixon said, according to Ehrlichman's notes: "Haig request the FBI (Sullivan) to destroy all special coverage." Thus Haig, who had played a role in setting up the White House wiretaps, was to help get rid of the evidence, along with Mardian, the senior Justice Department official who had signed the formal letter to the FBI requesting all wiretap information on Ellsberg and the

* Nixon, obviously aware of the Oval Office taping system, said little in the conversation but did interject at one point: "In light of current history who's got the time to read it. I haven't. I naturally never saw any of that stuff." The conversation was subpoenaed and transcribed by the Prosecution Force in 1975.

others.* Haig, even more than Kissinger, was a presidential insider that summer, one who could be trusted to play "hardball," even on an issue as sensitive and potentially damaging as the destruction of evidence relevant to the government's prosecution of the Pentagon Papers case.

Kissinger returned from Peking and Paris early on the morning of July 13, the day after the fateful decision on the wiretaps. Did Haig tell Kissinger what was going on? It is inconceivable that he did not—that he did not remain loyal to Kissinger at this critical juncture, with Kissinger in sole control of China policy, the SALT talks, and the secret Vietnam negotiations. Haig and Kissinger both repeatedly glossed over their involvement with the Plumbers in their later testimony on the wiretapping before the Senate Foreign Relations Committee, but Haig did insist to the senators that "I never viewed myself as anything but an extension of Dr. Kissinger, an agent of Dr. Kissinger." Former National Security Council staff aides, in scores of interviews, unanimously praised Haig for serving Kissinger faithfully, at least until late 1972, when the relationship between the two men was destroyed over Vietnam. Kissinger's frequent denials of any knowledge of the White House's Watergate activities involving Daniel Ellsberg or the Plumbers unit were taken at face value by much of the general public and the media during the Watergate inquiry in the mid-1970s largely because so little was known about the full extent of Haig's complicity. Haig not only knew what was going on in the White House but was a part of it. And Kissinger knew all—or nearly all—that Haig did.

Later on July 13, two days before the announcement of Kissinger's visit to Peking, Ehrlichman told Kissinger that Young was leaving his staff to work on the Ellsberg investigation—news Kissinger must have learned earlier from Haig. Ehrlichman recalls that Kissinger resisted: "Henry had no objection to the activity, but he didn't want to give up Young." The President decided that Young would join forces with Egil (Bud) Krogh, Jr., one of Ehrlichman's deputies on the White House Domestic Council, to set up the "nonlegal" internal investigations unit. Kissinger's concern about Young's departure was almost reflexive; aides such as Young, who were permitted access to many of the backchannel secrets and some of Kissinger's private telephone conversations, knew far too much. Young knew, for example, about the White House wiretaps, and he took copies of some of the wiretap summaries and perhaps some of the original FBI logs of the Halperin-Ellsberg conversations to his new office in the basement of the Executive Office Building, where he was soon joined by Howard Hunt and Gordon Liddy.

By mid-1971, Young was one of the few remaining members of the National

---

* The Watergate Special Prosecution Force concluded that there was evidence of a conspiracy to obstruct justice in connection with Mardian's removal of the wiretap documents from the FBI. No criminal indictment was sought after Nixon resigned the presidency in August 1974. In a memorandum three weeks later summarizing the status of the case, Francis J. Martin, the assistant special prosecutor in charge of the wiretap inquiry, wrote: ". . . [T]he evidence indicates that the former President gave a direct order to Robert Mardian that he should cause the records of these wiretaps to be concealed . . . This was clearly a major obstruction of justice and if the present evidence is corroborated . . . it is likely we will recommend prosecution of Mardian, Ehrlichman and three or four present or former officials of the FBI. We also, of course, would strongly recommend prosecution of Mr. Nixon . . . the former President's actions were designed not to try to save his friends from embarrassment [as Nixon had claimed in the Watergate cover-up cases] but rather to deny his enemy, Daniel Ellsberg, his constitutional rights." Martin's memorandum was released to me in March 1983, under the Freedom of Information Act.

Security Council staff who had worked closely with Kissinger and had known him before Nixon's election. Young, then thirty-four years old, had met Kissinger while working on Nelson Rockefeller's 1968 presidential campaign. His credentials were impeccable: He was an associate of a prominent Wall Street law firm who had attended Oxford University after graduating from Cornell University Law School in the early 1960s. After Nixon's election, Young volunteered his services to Kissinger and was brought onto the NSC staff in early 1970 to help handle Kissinger's scheduling and other personal matters. By all accounts, the balding, seemingly self-assured lawyer was dutiful in his loyalty to Kissinger. Young's wife handled Kissinger's laundry and he, according to other former aides, was responsible for purchasing some of Kissinger's clothes. One aide remembers accidentally seeing a note from Young to Kissinger asking: "Did you like the tie? I thought it would go well with your blue suit." When the Kissinger-Young relationship soured, as did most of Kissinger's relationships with his personal aides, David Halperin was brought onto Kissinger's personal staff. Young had been unable to outmaneuver Haig, and by late 1970 he had begun to complain to friends in the White House about his desire to assume a more substantive role in the government.

In the second volume of his memoirs, *Years of Upheaval,* Kissinger wrote that Young had run "afoul" of Haig, and said that he had been shifted in January of 1971 "from my immediate office to a make-work job of research in the White House Situation Room." There is evidence, however, that Young—his "make-work job" notwithstanding—continued to be directly involved in some of the most sensitive and closely held issues in the White House, a measure, perhaps, of Kissinger's confidence in Young's discretion. On January 25, 1971, for example, Kissinger brought only Young to a meeting with the chairman, general counsel, and chief security officer of the Atomic Energy Commission to discuss the security clearance of the operator of a privately owned nuclear fuel processing plant in Pennsylvania, who was suspected of helping to divert 200 pounds of highly enriched uranium to the Israelis. Adding to the sensitivity of the meeting was the fact that agents from Mossad, the Israeli intelligence service, were believed by the CIA to have engineered the diversion of the plutonium—enough material to make five to ten nuclear bombs.

Within months, however, Young's role had eroded to the point where he approached John Ehrlichman and appealed for a job on the Domestic Council staff. As Ehrlichman tells it, "Young came to me and literally broke down and cried. He felt he'd been badly treated by Kissinger and didn't know what to do." Young complained that Kissinger was no longer seeing him "and Haig was bedeviling him." Ehrlichman had proposed Young for the Plumbers job believing that Kissinger would not object. Young later told a friend on the NSC staff that Kissinger's heated objection created a "major battle" that, after Nixon's intervention, was settled with a compromise. Young's friend, one of the few in whom Young confided, says the compromise was that "David would be on loan to other people but Kissinger could call on him whenever he wanted. He did see Henry from time to time; he said Henry still had some kind of a claim on him." Young escaped prosecution in the Ellsberg case by cooperating with the Watergate Prosecution Force's investigation of Ehrlichman, who was convicted in 1974 of violating Ellsberg's civil rights and lying to a grand jury; no investigator from the Prosecution Force or the House impeachment inquiry ever queried him on his link, as co-director of the Plumbers, to Henry Kissinger.*

In his public statements, Kissinger has insisted that in 1971 he did not know that Young had left his staff to set up Nixon's special investigation unit and begin working on the Ellsberg case as well as national security leaks. In a private briefing to a group of *Time* executives in early 1974, Kissinger declared: "Let me put David Young's relationship to me in perspective. He was not a big man in my life, and I was in his life." As far as he was concerned, Kissinger said, Young had been reassigned only to handle declassification matters for the President. That, of course, was the cover story Young used to explain his new job to his friends and associates.† Kissinger, despite his denials, not only knew the full truth about Young's important new role but must have suspected that Young's most urgent assignment would be to investigate his NSC staff and even his personal involvement with White House leaks.

The President and all his senior advisers—with the exception of Kissinger, who kept any doubts to himself—were enthusiastic about the Plumbers and about the plan for the White House to take charge of "national security" investigations. Richard Allen, the former Kissinger aide, who had returned to the White House in 1971 to help handle foreign trade issues, recalls hearing Haldeman describe Howard Hunt that summer as a "balls-out" CIA operative. Nixon was then moving to the right politically as part of his drive to capture the hard-hat Middle America vote, and punishing Daniel Ellsberg for releasing the Pentagon Papers fit right in. As 1972 drew nearer, Nixon became increasingly demagogic on the issue of school busing, took a narrower stance on the

* Young was able to provide the Watergate Prosecution Force with an intact copy of a Plumbers' memorandum on which Ehrlichman specifically approved the covert entry into the office of Ellsberg's psychoanalyst. No other complete copy of that memorandum could be found in the Plumbers' files in the White House, apparently because Young had gone through the files and scissored the most damaging paragraphs. He and his attorney then used the intact document to bargain for immunity, since the prosecutors were far more anxious to bring Ehrlichman to trial than Young. Amazingly, Young all but telegraphed his intentions to Ehrlichman in a meeting on March 27, 1973, just as the first wave of Watergate panic flooded the White House. In a summary of his talk with Ehrlichman which he supplied to the prosecutors, Young wrote that the meeting took place after Ehrlichman requested a review of the files. Before that meeting, Young said, he had sent a briefcase with the documents to Ehrlichman's office. When they finally met, Ehrlichman insisted that he had not known of the break-in in advance. Young, according to his notes, set him straight: "I said no, I had known about it beforehand and my clear recollection was that he also had known of it . . . in fact, his approval of the matter was reflected in a couple of the memos in the envelope in the briefcase." Ehrlichman then acknowledged that "there was no question about what had actually happened, but that he had taken those memos out and thought he should keep them because they were a little too sensitive and showed too much forethought." Young solicitously warned, he wrote, that Hunt or Liddy "or someone else might have copies." Ehrlichman said that he "would have to take that chance."

† The cover story worked perfectly when Young was interviewed by the FBI in the weeks following the June 1972 Republican-led break-in into the Democratic Party offices in the Watergate apartment and office complex. Young portrayed himself as being solely involved with classification and declassification questions, including investigation of leaks. Howard Hunt had been added to his staff, Young said, to evaluate cables "to determine if the 'Pentagon Papers' accurately represented the facts and circumstances at that time in history." Gordon Liddy's function was to "maintain close liaison with the Justice Department . . ." All these lies were accepted at face value by the FBI and the U.S. Attorney's Office in Washington. It seems ironic that Young, who lied about almost everything in his 1972 statement to the FBI, was willing to acknowledge that he was investigating leaks—something Kissinger publicly claimed that he did not learn until he read it in the newspapers in 1973.

395

abortion question, promised federal aid for parochial schools, and renewed his law-and-order proclamations against the "era of permissiveness." He also began relying more on John Connally, the conservative Texan who had been appointed Treasury Secretary in late 1970 and who was emerging—to Kissinger's dismay—as a rival for the President's ear.* Men such as Gordon Liddy and Howard Hunt were viewed as exciting additions to the Plumbers unit; they were tough, experienced agents ready to operate clandestinely on behalf of the President and his reelection. Egil Krogh, the Ehrlichman deputy who was assigned to direct the Plumbers along with David Young, could also be tough when it came to the President and national security.

Charles Cooke, Elliot Richardson's aide, initiated a series of casual lunches with Krogh shortly after moving with Richardson to the Department of Health, Education and Welfare in 1970. Although he and Krogh had many domestic issues to discuss, Cooke recalls, they invariably talked about Vietnam. Late in the year, after Nixon ordered the resumption of bombing in the North, Cooke started to summarize all the reasons against it, beginning with the fact—obvious to him—that the war was in the South and could be won only on the ground there. "Krogh just blew up," Cooke recalls. " 'My God, don't you people understand—the man [Nixon] is going to blow them off the face of the earth unless they cave in.' "

Cooke says, "That was our last lunch."

Krogh knew little about foreign policy in 1971. He had been brought onto the White House staff by Ehrlichman in early 1969, after working part-time for Ehrlichman's Seattle law firm while a student at the University of Washington Law School. Krogh's primary responsibilities on the Domestic Council were in narcotics control, crime prevention, and transportation policy; he also ran the White House command post during the antiwar rallies that convulsed Washington in the early years of the administration.

Krogh and Young knew each other casually in mid-1971, but they were not close friends; both were members of a group of White House aides who met occasionally in a Georgetown bar for drinks and free-wheeling gossip.† Shortly after their assignment as co-directors of the Plumbers, Krogh recalls, Young began doing exactly what Kissinger feared: gossiping about the Kissinger-Nixon relationship. Krogh says that in one of their first extended conversations, Young "told me of the time he was on the phone [listening in] when Nixon and Kissinger were talking. Nixon was drunk and he said, 'Henry, we've got to nuke them.' " The anecdote was chilling, Krogh remembers, and added a sense of urgency to his mission: The Vietnam War had to be won and

* Connally ran the Democrats-for-Nixon operation during the 1972 campaign. He was subsequently promised, Colson recalls, that if he switched his party affiliation to Republican, Nixon would support his drive for the Republican presidential nomination in 1976. Kissinger must have realized, even in mid-1971, that Connally could offer Nixon an irresistible chance to make political inroads with conservative Democrats, while Kissinger's main domestic usefulness was much less significant: the containment of the liberals and the neutralization of the press.

† Just how much each member of the group confided in the others is not clear, but their relationship was strong. Besides Young and Krogh, who was a teetotaler, the group included Dwight Chapin, Nixon's appointments secretary; Gerald L. Warren, Ziegler's deputy in the press office; Henry C. Cashen II, a Colson aide; Edward L. Morgan, a legal aide who was later convicted of a Watergate-linked offense; Tod Hullin, Ehrlichman's appointments aide; and Kenneth R. Cole, Jr., Ehrlichman's deputy on the Domestic Council. Colson and John Dean sought membership but were blackballed in a secret ballot.

Daniel Ellsberg had to be stopped. "We were going after an espionage ring, not just Daniel Ellsberg," Krogh explained to Ehrlichman in 1973, during the Watergate crisis. "We had guys like Warnke, Gelb, and Halperin . . . Halperin had even been tapped when he was on the NSC staff because they didn't trust him. They thought he was a traitor. We didn't know if there were spies all over this country at that point."

Krogh, inexperienced in foreign policy, may well have believed that such a conspiracy existed. David Young's beliefs are more difficult to assess. Young knew, as Krogh, Hunt, and Liddy did, that a success in the Plumbers job would put him in line for a senior appointment in the Nixon Administration—perhaps, as he once mentioned to Coleman S. Hicks, Kissinger's personal aide in 1971 and 1972, an assistant secretaryship in a Cabinet-level department. Did Young really suspect that Ellsberg was part of a conspiracy involving Halperin and other Democrats? Young had access to the Halperin wiretaps, and he knew that Ellsberg was as hostile privately about Nixon's and Kissinger's policies as he became in his public statements and writings by 1971. But the wiretaps were devoid of any disclosures of national security information; Ellsberg may have been able to predict correctly the administration's future course of action in the Vietnam War, but he was not violating any laws in so doing. Most of the significant leaks of national security information, as Young knew, originated in Henry Kissinger's office. Young was also aware that Ellsberg had met with Kissinger and Haig in the late summer of 1970 to urge an end to the war, and he may have known that Kissinger asked Ellsberg to meet with him again. Young must have understood that the Ellsberg matter was far more complicated than Krogh, Ehrlichman, and the President believed. Yet Young joined with alacrity in the White House machinations against Ellsberg.

Kissinger's concern was Young's knowledge and what he would do with it. As a former personal aide, Young was aware that the really important secrets in the National Security Council concerned not code words and operators but who had been told what about which backchannel. He had also been exposed to Kissinger's frequently expressed contempt for the President and his senior advisers, notably Haldeman and Ehrlichman, and the possibility existed that he would choose to relay some of these comments.

Young's anger at Haig and his bruised feelings about Kissinger did not prevent the Plumbers from working closely with Haig to investigate still another leak to the *New York Times,* a dispatch by William Beecher published July 23, 1971, that outlined the administration's revised SALT negotiating position. The *Times* story, which revealed that the administration had decided, after all, to seek controls over SLBMs, submarine-launched ballistic missiles, enraged the President and the disarmament specialists. Nixon summoned Egil Krogh and Ehrlichman to an Oval Office meeting the next day, a Saturday, and ordered widespread polygraph tests and a revision of the classification system. A few hours later, Krogh called a meeting of his own to discuss the Beecher story; those in attendance included two senior FBI officials, Robert Mardian, Alexander Haig, Howard Hunt, and David Young, among others. According to an FBI summary of the meeting, Krogh described the President as being "up on the ceiling" about the leak and wanted the sources located within thirty-six hours. General Haig then reported "the results of his coordinating and he found that over 200 persons in various agencies, excluding clerical personnel, had access to the [National Security] Decision Memorandum relating to the U.S. proposals." Haig was thus more than just participating in the leak inquiry, he—along with Krogh, Young, and the other Plumbers—was one of its administrators. Five days later, W. Donald Stewart, chief of the Pentagon's Investigation Division, provided further evidence of Haig's role. Stewart reported to Haig on the results of the Defense Department's inquiry into Beecher's story, which involved interviews with more than a hundred officials.*

Kissinger's anxiety about the SALT leak cannot have been acute, because he knew the Beecher article had compromised very little in the SALT talks: Gerard Smith's delegation had already advanced the main elements of the new proposals to the Soviets. Furthermore, as members of the American SALT delegation later came to realize, Kissinger had undoubtedly broached the administration's revised position in advance to Ambassador Dobrynin. Haig certainly knew everything Kissinger did, but he was the model of efficiency that weekend, trying to help Egil Krogh meet the President's deadline for finding the culprit.

Kissinger himself got directly into the internal security business once more, a few days after his return from Paris, where he had another secret meeting with Le Duc Tho. On July 29, William Beecher had done it again, reporting that the Nixon Administration had ended its long-standing spy flights over China in an effort to avoid any serious incident before the President's trip to Peking in early 1972. In a memorandum for the record, Donald Stewart, the Pentagon official in charge of investigations, reported that Kissinger had telephoned William Sullivan of the FBI to relay "his great concern" about Beecher's new story and to urge a full investigation. Such a request would have been perfectly appropriate for the President's national security adviser, but it was one more contradiction of Kissinger's repeated testimony during the Watergate inquiries that he had stopped dealing in internal security matters as of May 1970, when the White House ordered all wiretap summaries to be sent only to Haldeman's office.†

On August 5, just a few days after Kissinger's call to Sullivan about the Beecher story, one of the final steps in the wiretap saga was taken in Kissinger's office. Robert Mardian, who shared with Haig the assignment of getting rid of the White House wiretap records, visited the National Security Council to inspect Kissinger's wiretap records. Mardian had discovered that some copies of the FBI summaries had disappeared from the Justice Department; the suspected culprit was none other than J. Edgar Hoover, who had made it clear to the President that he would stop at nothing to save his job. Exactly what happened to all the wiretap documents is not known. The Watergate

---

* The FBI summary and Stewart's memorandum were released to Beecher under the Freedom of Information Act; he made them available to me.

† One intriguing issue is why Kissinger telephoned Sullivan when he must have known that David Young and Egil Krogh were investigating leaks. Kissinger's reliance on Sullivan may have been intuitive, since the two men had been involved in internal security investigations since early 1969. The call may also suggest that Kissinger was fully aware of how busy the Plumbers were on the SALT leak and the continuing political operation against Ellsberg, areas in which Haig was keeping him fully abreast. A third reason may simply have been a desire to head off any Plumbers inquiry into any aspect of the Chinese rapprochement, whose main elements were, of course, hidden in the backchannel.

prosecutors did learn, according to unpublished files, that sometime in mid-July, just after the crucial July 12 meeting in San Clemente, the White House files of Kissinger, Haldeman, and Nixon were stripped of all wiretap summary letters and logs. Those documents were returned to the FBI, and they eventually came into Mardian's control, as Nixon had ordered.

Mardian and his aides subsequently determined that a few of the FBI summary letters were missing, and it was this fact that prompted Mardian's visit to Kissinger and Haig. His goal, apparently, was to account completely for Kissinger's copies of the FBI documents, and to insure that Kissinger's records were consistent with the FBI's tally. It wouldn't do to have such papers floating about the bureaucracy. Mardian, as the FBI account of the interview reported, "specifically remembered the incident because when he came into the office, Dr. Kissinger addressed a remark which Mr. Mardian felt was in extremely poor taste under the circumstances . . . Kissinger said something to the effect, 'Do you have what I said on the phone?' implying, according to Mr. Mardian, that Mardian had results of a wiretap on Dr. Kissinger . . . Dr. Kissinger also said that he had been keeping logs for the time when he writes his memoirs, but laughed and said he doesn't keep them anymore."*

Kissinger and Haig then got down to the business at hand, and carefully went through Kissinger's set of the wiretap records. It was not clear from Mardian's interview with the FBI whether Kissinger kept a set of the wiretap summaries and logs in his office, or whether he merely had a summary of what had been in his possession and previously returned. Mardian later delivered all the collected wiretap records to Nixon, who instructed Ehrlichman to bury them in his files, where they were discovered a few days after Ehrlichman's resignation from the White House in 1973. In his August 5 meeting with Kissinger and Haig, Mardian acknowledged that the careful checking was necessary to insure that Hoover did not have access to any of the documents and thus was not in a position to blackmail the White House. Kissinger, in his interview with the Special Prosecution Force in late 1975, also acknowledged that he was aware of Hoover's blackmail threat, although he denied being present when Mardian and Haig went through his office wiretap records. In a report on the interview, the Prosecution Force further quoted Kissinger as conceding that he was aware that "the nature of this [Hoover's] blackmail threat related to the embarrassment that would be caused if it were known that newsmen had been tapped."

"Embarrassment" was hardly the word. Such a revelation would have been devastating, not only to Kissinger himself, but even perhaps to Nixon's reelection campaign. It would also have heightened the resolve of the antiwar forces in the United States. Kissinger suffered through the meeting with Mardian and the distasteful comparing of wiretap documents for the same reason that everyone in the White House did—fear of exposure.

The wiretaps remained secret until early 1973, just before the Watergate onslaught, when *Time* reported that the Nixon White House had wiretapped journalists as well as administration officials. The *Time* story, written by Sandy Smith, the magazine's senior investigative reporter, must once again have

---

* Mardian told the FBI that he considered Kissinger's comment about the logs to be merely a joke, and let it go. In fact, Kissinger was keeping logs, but chose in his memoirs not to discuss the incident or his belief at the time that he too had been a target of the Plumbers.

created severe anxiety. Revelation of the wiretapping could lead to revelation of the secret B-52 bombing of Cambodia, as well as to some glimpse of the intense turmoil of Nixon's first term, which led to the successful White House spying effort by Yeoman Radford, working for the Joint Chiefs of Staff. Even more threatening was the fact that Daniel Ellsberg had been repeatedly overheard on the wiretap on Morton Halperin's telephone. Ellsberg's trial in the Pentagon Papers case had been delayed late in 1972 after a highly publicized dispute over the trial judge's refusal to permit Ellsberg and his attorneys to read the transcript of a wiretapped conversation involving Leonard Boudin, one of the attorneys in the case. Kissinger and Nixon had to fear the damage that would result if the public learned that summaries of Ellsberg's wiretapped conversations had been passed around by the top officials in the White House nearly four years earlier. Such information could also expose the existence of the Plumbers unit.

William Sullivan understood how far Kissinger would go to avoid embarrassment. He suddenly emerged in early May of 1973, at the height of seemingly never-ending Watergate revelations, as Kissinger's and Haig's candidate for the newly vacant post of FBI director. L. Patrick Gray III, Nixon's choice to replace J. Edgar Hoover after Hoover's death in May 1972, had run afoul of the Senate Judiciary Committee during tumultuous hearings in the spring of 1973, and the job was wide open. Sullivan sent Kissinger a memorandum summarizing his understanding of the White House wiretapping, which was still not publicly known. Kissinger was furious, according to a close aide, but he knew what to do without being told. It was Haig, Nixon's new chief of staff, who in early May telephoned the office of Elliot Richardson, the newly nominated Attorney General, to recommend Sullivan strongly for the FBI job.* Richardson's senior aides, J. T. Smith and Jonathan Moore, moved quickly to block Sullivan's nomination. Moore says that he had no special knowledge about the wiretapping; he argued against Sullivan because "he was the wrong guy with the wrong history."

Sullivan, rebuffed, turned to the author, then working in Washington for the *New York Times*. In mid-May, after the existence of the Ellsberg overhearings had become known and helped force the judge's dismissal of all charges against him on May 11, Sullivan made available to me copies of the White House wiretap authorizations, which directly linked Kissinger to the requests for wiretaps on his own staff aides. Kissinger, meanwhile, had spent the days following the dismissal of the Ellsberg case in a desperate attempt to avoid being linked to the wiretapping. He told reporters during a White House briefing on May 12 that he "never received any information that cast any doubt" on Morton Halperin's loyalty and discretion; the statement caused problems, because its clear implication was that he had seen some logs or summaries from the Halperin wiretaps, Two days later, in an interview with R. W. Apple of the *New York Times,* Kissinger confirmed that he had seen summaries from several wiretaps that were in place in 1969 and 1970. When Apple asked him

---

* Richardson served as Secretary of Health, Education and Welfare until November 28, 1972, when Nixon nominated him to replace Melvin Laird as Secretary of Defense. He was named Attorney General, replacing Richard G. Kleindienst, on April 30, 1973, as part of a Watergate-related administration shakeup. Mitchell had resigned as Attorney General on March 1, 1972, to take over the Nixon reelection effort.

whether he had taken any action to inform the appropriate authorities upon discovering that Halperin's telephone was wiretapped, Kissinger refused to comment. He did tell Apple, however, that he had not heard the word "Plumber" until it began appearing in the news media. Three days later, on May 17, Sullivan's information appeared in a *New York Times* dispatch of the author's, which stated that "Kissinger personally provided the Federal Bureau of Investigation with the names of a number of his aides on the National Security Council whom he wanted wiretapped."

There was panic in Kissinger's office. "Haig is running from the whole question," according to the private note of one of his aides. "Kissinger keeps insisting that he was not involved in Watergate, that he didn't know about the wiretaps. Haig now monitors Kissinger." The Kissinger note taker understood that Kissinger's definition of Watergate was not limited to the break-in at Democratic Party headquarters and its subsequent cover-up, but included far more. "Dave Young has unbelievable constraints on him," the diarist had reported in a notation dated March 15, 1973. "Kissinger is worried concerning the 'Plumbers' work. Young is still on the NSC staff for pay purposes." At that date there was still no public revelation of the existence of the Plumbers unit.

Kissinger managed to survive it all. If anything, his stature rose as Nixon's plummeted over the next year. He escaped serious investigation by the Watergate Special Prosecution Force and, for that matter, by the nation's press. By October 1975, when Kissinger finally agreed to be interviewed by the Watergate prosecutors, it was safe to do so. Gerald Ford was President and Watergate seemed far removed. The fact that Kissinger had minimized his role in the wiretapping and his relationship to the Plumbers was taken for granted in the Washington press corps, and even the Watergate Prosecution Force, but Kissinger was permitted to get by.

In retrospect, Kissinger had made a wise choice in deciding to deny any knowledge whatsoever of the Plumbers' operation. His public explanation for his activities, although chipped, never crumbled as Haig and David Young kept their silence. If Kissinger had taken another tack and admitted to having some idea of what David Young and Egil Krogh were doing, he would have exposed himself to further inquiries and, inevitably, more admissions of knowledge. Only a few Watergate Prosecution Force attorneys fortunate enough to have listened to the White House tapes understood the truth: Kissinger was involved.

29

MIDEAST: FINAL DEFEAT FOR ROGERS

CHINA WAS NOT Henry Kissinger's only triumph in the summer of 1971. He also triumphed, once and for all, over William Rogers. The victory did not have to do with the opening to Peking, however, for Rogers seemed resigned by then to his lack of involvement in significant foreign policy matters. Kissinger won, rather, by undercutting Rogers in the complicated negotiations in the Middle East and in Berlin, areas in which the Secretary of State made a last stand for his department's rightful role in foreign policy and for his personal dignity.

Rogers' final humiliation had its beginnings in March 1971, when Senator Stuart Symington, the Missouri Democrat, declared in a Senate speech that Kissinger was "Secretary of State in everything but title" and Rogers was the object of ridicule in official Washington. "It is rather sad that wherever one goes in the afternoon or evening around this town," Symington said, "one hears our very able Secretary of State laughed at, because they say he's only the Secretary of State in name." The Senator was careful to limit his criticism, however, by telling his colleagues that he had nothing but the highest admiration and respect for Kissinger, "one of the ablest men it's been my privilege to have as a friend." Symington's assessment made headlines, although many in the government and in the press corps understood that he had done little more than say the obvious. Despite that understanding, or perhaps because of it, the White House pulled out all the stops to deny what was true.

Nixon told a news conference that Symington had taken a "cheap shot" by belittling Rogers' role, and depicted the Secretary of State as "my oldest and closest friend in the Cabinet." James Reston wheeled into the issue the next day, acknowledging in his column that Kissinger was exercising "advisory powers normally reserved for the Secretary of State," and doing so without any congressional review. Having conceded that much, he was quick to add that Kissinger really wasn't responsible for any of the administration's wrongdoings: Senators Fulbright, Symington, and the other Senate critics of the administration's policy in Vietnam, he wrote, "are not saying that Mr. Kissinger is responsible for that policy or that he is playing some devious Rasputin role." Six weeks later, in a second column on the issue, Reston pronounced the bureaucratic warfare resolved: "Secretary of State Rogers is beginning to play an increasingly significant role in the Nixon Administration's foreign policy planning."

Salvaging Rogers became an important crusade for the President, and that decision reflected an astute judgment: Rogers would go along, and be content to be Secretary of State in title only, as long as he did not suffer too much humiliation in public. Nixon's goal was not only to protect Rogers but to hold on to the White House's ability to make policy on its own.

White House preoccupation with China, Russia, Vietnam, and reelection left Rogers with a free hand in the Middle East in the first half of 1971. In those months, the first signs of a peace agreement between Israel and Egypt suddenly became visible as Anwar Sadat, Egypt's new President, made a series of significant concessions. In response to initiatives from Washington, Sadat was willing to reopen the Suez Canal if the Israelis were willing to withdraw some forces from the east bank of the canal and permit some Egyptian soldiers or police to cross over to Israeli-held territory. There were some influential figures in Israel, notably Moshe Dayan, the Defense Minister, who privately insisted that the reopening of the canal would stabilize the region and make it more difficult for Egypt to violate the ceasefire which was still in effect. At a critical point in July 1971, Kissinger—despite his intense involvement with other issues—heatedly warned Nixon of the danger of continued American support for the Rogers initiative, and it was quickly stifled.*

Nothing is sure in the Middle East, and it is impossible to say that the Rogers plan, calling for the partial disengagement of both sides along the canal, would have been accepted. The distrust between Israel and Egypt was deep, and each government could find persuasive arguments for avoiding an accommodation. What can be said is that when confronted with the opposition of Henry Kissinger, Rogers' disengagement plan failed—and that in 1974 and 1975, after a bloody war, Kissinger adopted the Rogers plan as his own and won its acceptance.

Anwar Sadat, a former Egyptian Army officer who was involved in the overthrow of King Farouk in 1952, was a political unknown in early 1971. In his memoirs, Kissinger recalled telling a journalist shortly after Sadat was named President that he considered him ''an interim figure who would not last more than a few weeks.'' Kissinger's view was at first shared by many in the State Department and intelligence agencies. Over the next few months, however, the bureaucracy would begin to perceive Sadat as a leader willing to make compromises and take chances to obtain peace. Kissinger, in a crucial mistake in judgment, continued to write him off as pro-Soviet and pro-Communist.

In February 1971, Sadat announced two policy changes aimed at encouraging the United States to intervene in the dispute over Israel's continued occupation of the Sinai Desert and its refusal to give up any territory seized in the 1967 war. In return for a partial Israeli withdrawal from the east bank of the Suez Canal, Sadat said Egypt would clear, rebuild, and then reopen the Suez Canal to commercial shipping. A few days later, Sadat offered to sign a peace

---

* One NSC aide for the Middle East says that he and his colleagues often had great difficulty getting Kissinger to turn away from the Vietnam War and other, more pressing issues, to focus on the Arab-Israeli negotiations. ''We couldn't get Henry's time,'' the aide recalls. ''Hal Saunders [Kissinger's special assistant for the Middle East] would plead for five minutes and not get it.''

agreement with Israel if Israel would withdraw to the boundaries that existed prior to the 1967 war. This made Egypt the first Arab nation willing even to discuss such a commitment. The offer was per se unacceptable to the Israelis, except as a possible starting place for extended negotiations.

The rationale behind the Egyptian proposals was most clearly described in the memoirs of Mohammad Heikal, the Nasser aide and confidant who for a short time played a similar role with Sadat. Sadat realized, Heikal wrote, that he had "a chance of moving the Americans toward an understanding of Egypt's position that, to be realistic, Nasser had never had. The mistrust between Nasser and the Americans ran too deep. Sadat was free of that legacy." Heikal's view, which he successfully urged upon the new Egyptian President, was that "no problem in the Middle East could be solved without the active participation of the two super-powers, but that there was no need for the Arab-Israel problem to become polarized between the Soviet Union and the United States." The goal of the new policy was to accept the unarguable fact that America and Israel "were closely linked" while striving "to ensure that they did not become completely identified with each other."

Sadat's first step was to let the United States know privately that Egypt's ties with the Soviet Union, which had an estimated 15,000 troops and advisers in Egypt in early 1971, did not preclude direct negotiations with Washington over the critical issues in the Middle East. At the time there was no official American presence in Cairo. Egypt had cut off relations with the United States as soon as the 1967 war broke out, but had permitted a small group of diplomats to remain in Cairo under the aegis of the Spanish Embassy. The ranking American, Donald C. Bergus, was considered one of the most knowledgeable Middle Eastern experts in the State Department; Eugene W. Trone, the CIA station chief who worked under cover in the American Interests Section of the Spanish Embassy, was also very highly rated. Both men would find many of their dispatches—reporting Sadat's new willingness to compromise—ignored at the White House throughout 1971.

Early that year, Bergus recalls, he was summoned to a private meeting with Sadat and given a message for President Nixon: "Sadat said that if he could come to an agreement about disengagement and reopening the canal, he would remove the Russians from Egypt." Bergus relayed the Sadat initiative in an immediate "Eyes Only" cable to Nixon. Sadat knew, as Bergus did, that Moshe Dayan had been discussing a partial Israeli withdrawal from the Sinai, in the belief that such a move made military sense, since it would be extremely difficult to defend against an Egyptian offensive from the unfortified Israeli positions along the Suez Canal. Sadat's proposal to open the canal after an Israeli pullback was a breakthrough, in Bergus' view: "As I saw it, it was a major step toward peace." Sadat would have to spend millions to clean the canal and rebuild the war-torn cities along it. Once he made that commitment, and began accepting the inevitable international plaudits for it, Bergus says, "My thought was—you can write off war as a viable alternative in the Middle East."

If there was optimism over Sadat's flexibility, there was also a strong sense, shared by Bergus and his colleagues, that the bargaining would be difficult, and perhaps impossible. Sadat's proposal called for Israel to withdraw at least two-thirds of the way across the Sinai Peninsula, roughly 100 kilometers, setting up a demilitarized zone that would include the strategically important Mitla and Giddi passes. He also demanded the right to move Egyptian troops and arms, including tanks, across the canal, and insisted that any withdrawal be linked to a timetable for full disengagement. In return, he offered to extend the ceasefire indefinitely. His eventual goal was to negotiate Israel's withdrawal back to the 1967 prewar borders.

Despite Sadat's stiff demands, which he made it clear were negotiable, his willingness to pick up on Dayan's thesis—that Israel would be more secure militarily with a demilitarized Sinai and a reopened Suez Canal—shook the leadership in Jerusalem, which had become adept at putting Nasser's bellicosity to good public relations use. There was little immediate applause for Dayan inside Israel. The Defense Minister was at his most controversial at the time, and many members of Golda Meir's cabinet disliked him intensely. The official Israeli view of Sadat's offer, as expressed over the next few months, was that a partial disengagement, or "thinning out" of the opposing forces on both sides of the canal, was possible, as long as there was an *explicit* dissociation between the Sadat plan and any future negotiations. The disengagement was not to be part of a long-term step-by-step negotiating process, as Sadat envisioned, but a one-time agreement. The Israeli government was contemplating, at best, a pullback of up to ten kilometers from the Suez Canal, a far more limited withdrawal than that envisioned by the Egyptians.

At this point Kissinger and Nixon were preoccupied with the disastrous failure of the Laotian invasion; it was a time of mutual recrimination and finger pointing inside the bureaucracy. Kissinger, as his memoirs made clear, blamed Laird and the Pentagon for the collapse in Laos. By late February, he wrote, "It became embarrassingly difficult to explain our policy when the facts were so elusive and I began to suspect that even the Pentagon had no idea what was going on." Nixon, in his memoirs, depicted the first few months of 1971 as the gloomiest period of his first term. Symington's criticism of Rogers, which was really an indictment of the administration's foreign policy procedures, was undoubtedly a factor in Nixon's decision to see—for at least a few weeks— whether a Middle East compromise was possible.

In his memoirs, Kissinger repeatedly declared that Egypt's insistence that the disengagement be negotiated as part of a continuing process invalidated it from the start: "Disengagement had no chance of success as long as it had to be negotiated together with an overall settlement. And if there was no chance of success, I saw no reason for us to involve ourselves. . . . My aim was to produce a stalemate until Moscow urged compromise or until, even better, some moderate Arab regime decided that the route to progress was through Washington." This, of course, did happen after the 1973 Arab-Israeli war.

The only problem with Kissinger's analysis is that it didn't happen this way. There is clear evidence that Nixon and Kissinger, in the wake of the Laos fiasco and the embarrassing Senate attack on Rogers, made a strong effort in March and part of April to persaude the Israelis to compromise on the Sinai and begin serious negotiations with Sadat. A quick settlement in the Middle East would be a public relations coup for the White House and would buy more time in Vietnam. In his memoirs, Yitzhak Rabin, then the Israeli Ambassador to Washington, graphically described private meetings in which Kissinger raged about Golda Meir's inability to match Sadat's flexibility. "No one knows what you want," Kissinger exclaimed. "There is serious fear that what you *really* want is to evade any settlement that requires concessions on your part so that you can remain along the lines you hold at present." Kissinger did not mention these talks with Rabin in his memoirs, but it seems clear that if there was to be a disengagement in the Sinai, as well as the possible ouster of the Soviets, the White House wanted to play its usual backchannel role. Any public credit for a disengagement agreement would have to be given to Rogers, who was still angered by the Symington attack.

In these weeks, Kissinger seems to have lost control of the Middle East negotiations to the State Department. Rogers was being strongly supported by Sisco, although the cautious Assistant Secretary continued to maintain close contact with Kissinger. "He played an awfully good game," Donald Bergus says. "He convinced Rogers of his loyalty, but he knew that Rogers was not long for this world." Nonetheless, NSC aides recall, this was a period of frequent Kissinger outbursts against Sisco, who was Rogers' most effective aide. The diplomatic successes with Peking and Moscow had yet to emerge from the backchannels and Nixon seemed unwilling to stop the Secretary of State's efforts to carry out his responsibilities: "It was becoming increasingly difficult to find out who was proposing what to whom," Kissinger complained in his memoirs. "The White House could no longer tell whether the parties were putting forward their own views or else interpretations of ours to force us into supporting publicly what we had told them privately."

Nixon was dealing directly with Rogers on the Middle East, and Kissinger and his staff did not know what was being negotiated. Sadat and Nixon exchanged personal letters in March, in which there were discussions of the disengagement and possible compromise. Kissinger did not mention the letters in his memoirs, and may not have been involved in the exchange. But Kissinger understood that no matter what Nixon hinted in private to Sadat and Rogers, and no matter what he said publicly in an effort to hide the stranglehold he and Kissinger had on the bureaucracy, the President would never take the political risk of *imposing* a settlement on the Israelis.

Nixon might decide to urge the Israelis to make a forward-looking proposal to Sadat and to begin serious discussions on disengagement, but he would push only to a certain point and no further. The American involvement was complicated by the fact that Sadat's offer to kick the Russians out of Egypt would never be taken seriously by Nixon and Kissinger, who continued automatically to view Egypt as part of the Soviet bloc. "As long as Egypt was in effect a Soviet military camp," Kissinger wrote, "we could have no incentive to turn on an ally [Israel] on behalf of a Soviet client." Those in the State Department who thought and reported otherwise—such as Donald Bergus—were simply diregarded. "There was a real ideological difference between State and the NSC on Middle East policy," one closely involved Foreign Service officer says. "Henry viewed the world as a chessboard with black and white Soviet and U.S. pieces. He was persuaded that the professionals in this building were dead wrong."

Kissinger's function throughout this period soon evolved into the familiar one: to quietly sabotage Rogers' efforts. If in March he urged the Israeli government, through Ambassador Rabin, to be more positive in its response to Sadat's offer, he also warned the President in May that reopening the Suez Canal to shipping would primarily aid the Soviets, whose oil tankers would no longer be forced to steam around the Cape of Good Hope in South Africa. He repeatedly played on the Soviet threat in his analyses to Nixon. "Not knowing Sadat, I had to conclude that he was still playing Nasser's game," Kissinger wrote in his memoirs. "Furthermore, Sadat's impatience was becoming evident in repeated declarations that 1971 had to be the 'year of decision' in the Middle East. Our strategy had to be to frustrate any Egyptian policy based on military threats and collusion with the Soviet Union." It was, of course, precisely to avoid that kind of stereotyped thinking that Sadat had made his initiatives.

At this point, it is difficult to sort out Kissinger's legitimate policy concerns, as expressed in his memoirs, from his constant refusal to permit Rogers to achieve *anything*. He must have been aware that Sadat's flexibility, despite his ties to the Soviets, posed a major opportunity for the first serious peace negotiations between an Arab country and Israel. Kissinger also understood that Richard Nixon was still not willing to give him the free hand in the Middle East that he had obtained in his dealings with the Soviets and the Chinese. On its face, forcing Israeli disengagement in the Sinai posed immense political risks for the President, who was counting on heavy Jewish financial and electoral support in the 1972 elections—support he had never had before. And yet Sadat was giving the United States and its President a chance for a wondrous triumph —the kind of opportunity Kissinger and Nixon had seized in other parts of the world. Middle East peace would isolate the Soviet Union and further disarm the administration's antiwar critics.

Why didn't Kissinger join Rogers and Sisco in trying to increase the possibility of a breakthrough? "I have a hard time believing that the balance wasn't tilted by personal feelings," says one former NSC aide who was directly involved in Middle East affairs. "It's such an unflattering thing to say, but I think there was a lot of not wanting State to do it—rationalized, to be sure, by Henry. If Henry would have had a shot at it, he might have attempted it. It was the one genuine missed opportunity in that period. It was a step that would have prevented the '73 war from taking place. We almost challenged Sadat to do something more dramatic—and he did."

The White House's ambivalent attitude toward a Middle East agreement did not seem to be clearly communicated to Rogers in this period; Nixon was willing, as in so many other instances, to deal disingenuously with his Secretary of State. Rogers also seemed unaware of the extent to which Kissinger would invoke the Soviet bogeyman. On March 16, at a State Department news conference, Rogers suggested that an international peacekeeping force, which would include Soviet troops, could be assembled to guarantee any revised borders in the Middle East. Senator Henry Jackson, the conservative Democrat from Washington who was viewed as a potential presidential candidate, immediately accused the Nixon Administration of "courting disaster" with such proposals. "We should be trying to get Russians out of the Middle East," the pro-Israel Senator said in a speech, "not designing plans to dig them in." Neither Kissinger nor Nixon discussed these events in his memoirs, but the criticism must have caused consternation in the White House. Jackson was the most influential member of the Senate on strategic arms issues, and his approval would be essential to the passage of a SALT treaty.

Nixon's and Kissinger's reluctance to accept the inherent weakness of the Soviet Union's position inside Egypt insured a quiet death for the Sadat initiative. Kissinger, in his anxiety to undermine the State Department, had to ignore a steady stream of reports in 1971 from Donald Bergus and Eugene Trone in Cairo. "The Egyptians knew all along that they were not pro-Communist," Trone, the CIA station chief, recalls. "They were accused of that because they accepted help from the Soviets. Sadat knew he was not going to win a war [with Israel] by military means, and so he tried to rearrange the strategic situation by lining up the United States on his side diplomatically."

Another major factor was the omnipresent Israeli lobby. Once again, Israeli officials and leaders of the Jewish community in the United States were up in arms against what they perceived as the pro-Arab bias of Rogers and Sisco. Sisco was particularly suspect. "Sisco was the author of the Rogers plan," one senior Israeli official recalls, "and we don't forget that for a minute."

Rogers kept the Sadat initiative on center stage within the administration throughout the spring and early summer of 1971, in part because of his determination to have at least one issue in which he could play a major role. Israel, despite entreaties from the White House and a promise of twelve more F-4 fighter planes, was unable to make a substantive response to the Egyptian offer. The government of Golda Meir obviously knew what Rogers did not: that the White House would not force any concessions. Nixon would not provoke a fight with American Jews—and potential campaign contributors— by punishing Israel for not negotiating. Israel's formal response, when it was finally presented to Sadat in late April, did not even specify how far it was willing to pull back from the Suez Canal. There was no question inside the administration that the response was, as Kissinger wrote, "a total non-starter" which was "certain to be unacceptable to Egypt."

Rogers persisted in his peace effort and about this time won permission from Nixon—eager to find something for his old pal to do—to visit Egypt as part of a Middle East tour. He would be the first American Secretary of State to visit there since John Foster Dulles had gone in 1954. In a memorandum to Nixon, Kissinger sought to undermine the trip: "It would be especially worrisome were his presence to accelerate the diplomatic process and further to intensify the current stalemate between Israel, the Arabs, the US and USSR." Before Rogers arrived in Cairo, Bergus and Michael Sterner, the State Department desk officer for Egypt, held a preliminary meeting with Sadat at the Egyptian President's country home at the Barrages, north of Cairo on the Nile River. "Sadat was sitting with a map," Bergus remembers, "and he drew a line midway in the Sinai. 'If you can get me a retreat to this line,' he said, 'I'll open the canal. And if the canal opens, do you think I'll ever start another war?' "

Sadat's line still extended halfway across the Sinai and still called for Egyptian troops to cross the canal in force; a UN peacekeeping force perhaps would serve as a buffer between the two armies. The plan would not be acceptable to the Israelis. By early May, when Rogers and Sisco arrived in Cairo for their two days of meetings with Egyptian officials, Sadat had backed off a bit and made clear his willingness to compromise. He directly promised Rogers that he would begin removing Soviet troops, for whom he was paying in hard currency, as soon as the Israelis began their disengagement. Sadat also agreed to restore diplomatic relations with the United States after disengagement. Rogers flew on to Jerusalem and ran into a stone wall. Israel did not want Egyptian troops to cross the Suez Canal. Nor was the Israeli government willing to retreat very far in the Sinai. On May 9, Sisco was sent back to Cairo to discuss further compromises. His role was difficult at best: trying to present the position of both sides in the best possible light without the authority of the White House to help force a solution.

In his eagerness to emerge with an agreement, Sisco overplayed his hand during an extended private meeting with Sadat at the Barrages. Sisco left the meeting convinced that, with another concession or two, disengagement could be reached. The Egyptian President told Bergus a few days later that he and Sisco had taken a map and worked out possible Egyptian and Israeli positions on the east side of the Suez Canal. It was more information than had been provided to Bergus by Sisco. In a December 1971 interview with *Newsweek,* Sadat went public: "I said I was ready to compromise. So Joe drew two theoretical lines—Egyptian forces, he said, would be on line A to B on the eastern side of the Canal and Israeli forces on line X to Y also on the eastern side. That was his own terminology. . . . More than that, I said I was ready to agree that between these two lines U.N. forces or troops from the four powers should take up positions. Sisco said: 'I think we can work something out on this basis. It sounds reasonable to me.' "

In his 1977 study on the Middle East, William Quandt, a former Kissinger aide, added another detail: Sadat cabled Sisco a few days after their meeting, asking whether he was correct in assuming that the Israelis would be willing to withdraw to the Israeli side of the vital Mitla and Giddi passes in the Sinai. Sisco, back in Washington, responded that "such a line was not precluded, that there was some flexibility in the Israeli position." In fact, there was no such flexibility, as Sadat was to discover and Sisco should have known.

Kissinger's analysis of the Rogers and Sisco mission was merciless. He wrote in his memoirs that the "trip had no result except to get Dayan in some trouble at home. . . ." At the time, he continued his private criticism, repeatedly telling the President that the State Department's stumbling in the Middle East was helping the Soviets.

In early May, just before Rogers' visit, Sadat had purged many of his political opponents, including Ali Sabri, Secretary General of the Arab Socialist Union. The Ali Sabri group was pro-Nasser, pro-Soviet, and violently opposed to Sadat's ceasefire with Israel and his peace initiatives. A few weeks later, Sadat signed a friendship treaty with the Soviet Union, obviously aimed at mollifying Moscow after the purging and jailing of many of its strongest supporters in Egyptian politics. Rogers, in a memorandum to Nixon, depicted the treaty for what it was, "a move to solidify Sadat's standing with his own military that possibly would give him even more flexibility on the disengagement issue." Kissinger saw the treaty as a "bombshell," as he wrote Nixon, that "reflected a new Soviet boldness and Sadat's frustration with erratic American diplomacy."

Another chance for criticism came in June, when Bergus took it upon himself to summarize the disengagement negotiations, from the Egyptian point of view, in a private memorandum to the Egyptian Foreign Ministry. Bergus took the initiative, he recalls, after Sisco's second visit to Cairo in early May, when he and Sadat discussed Israel's intransigence and possible compromises on the Sinai withdrawal issue. On May 20, Mahmoud Riad summoned Bergus to the Foreign Ministry and handed him a stiffly worded summary of the revised Egyptian position, in the wake of Israel's resistance. Bergus was convinced that the Egyptian note was far too negative; he was worried that the talks would be broken off before any real bargaining could begin. He thus won permission from the Egyptians to redraft their message in a more positive manner, changing its tone but not its substance. As summarized by Bergus, the Egyptian position still required the Israelis to withdraw roughly halfway across the Sinai, conceding the passes at Mitla and Giddi. Egyptian troops would be permitted to cross the Sinai; and there would be a United Nations peacekeeping force in place between the two armies. Sadat accepted the Bergus draft with little modification and assumed, not unnaturally, that his government's revised position, as drafted by Bergus, had been officially sanctioned by the State Department. When there was no response to his new proposals, Sadat felt betrayed not only by Jerusalem but also by Washington. Within a week, the Bergus memorandum was leaked by Egyptian officials to a French newspaper and eventually made its way into the American news media, where it created a brief sensation, outraging the Israeli Embassy and embarrassing the State Department. The incident had a Keystone Kops quality to it that was quickly seized upon by Kissinger, who made it clear in his memoirs that he believed Bergus could not have been acting on his own but must have received private instructions from the bumbling and pro-Arab State Department. "It was an extraordinary procedure," Kissinger wrote, "which I remain convinced no professional diplomat of Bergus' experience would have undertaken without authorization from higher-ups. . . . I was annoyed—to put it mildly—that none of these moves had been disclosed to the President of the United States." Bergus ended up with everyone angry at him, he says. "Rogers was furious at me for giving Henry some ammunition. Henry didn't believe that I had sat down on my very own and written the Bergus paper, simply trying to state the Egyptians' ideas in a positive way. The whole idea that a Foreign Service officer would take an initiative is one that Henry just can't understand."*

By June, when the Sadat-Bergus proposal reached Washington, any desire that Nixon or Kissinger may have had to urge a compromise upon Israel had dissipated. The President was always open, of course, to persuasion on the basic political premise that what would not be good for Israel would not be good for his reelection in 1972. Kissinger left that approach to others and utilized the Egyptian-Soviet friendship treaty to do in Sadat: "Sadat's Friendship Treaty . . . whatever its motives, did not galvanize us to help him as he might have hoped," he wrote in the memoirs. "On the contrary, it reinforced

---

* Bergus suffered for his boldness. Although held in high repute by his peers for his knowledge and understanding of Egypt, he was ordered out of Cairo early in 1972, and spent the next six months as a diplomat in residence at the University of South Carolina. He was then named deputy director of the Foreign Service Institute in Washington, which provides language training and specialized area instruction for reassigned State Department officers. "I was in limbo," Bergus acknowledges. In 1974, he was reassigned as Deputy Chief of Mission of the American Embassy in Ankara, Turkey. He was named Ambassador to the Sudan in 1977, in the Carter Administration, and served there until his retirement from the Foreign Service in 1980.

my determination to slow down the process even further to demonstrate that Soviet threats and treaties could not be decisive."

Kissinger was only days away from the secret trip to China now, and his authority was at a peak. The tiresome question of Middle East policy seemed far removed from the glamour of Peking and the pending summit meeting in Moscow. Forcing the Israelis to begin disengagement in the Sinai would only lead to protracted and messy negotiations and disputes that could hurt Nixon politically. But Rogers, clinging to the only foreign policy issue over which he still had some say, refused to let go of the possibility of an Israeli-Egyptian settlement. A few days after Kissinger had left the country, Rogers won Nixon's permission for another try. Donald Bergus and Michael Sterner would meet with Sadat in Cairo in early July and Joseph Sisco would fly to Jerusalem later in the month for a talk with Golda Meir. Kissinger learned of the new effort while airborne. "Within hours of my leaving town," he wrote, "Rogers showed that he had learned some bureaucratic lessons. He attempted to use my absence to obtain Presidential authority for a trip by Joe Sisco to the Middle East for another round of negotiations. . . . It was too transparent a maneuver. From Saigon I cabled [Nixon] that such a trip now would only accelerate tensions in the Middle East and should be deferred. I suggested the device of scheduling an NSC meeting on the Middle East for a date soon after my return. The President agreed."

Kissinger's cable was too late to stop Sterner, the Egyptian desk officer, who joined Bergus on July 6 in Cairo for the meeting with Sadat. The Egyptian President reassured the Americans that the friendship treaty with the Soviet Union was, as he described it in his later *Newsweek* interview, "only a new frame for already existing relations—nothing really new." Sadat repeated his promise to restore full diplomatic relations with Washington and again said that he intended to begin shipping Soviet military personnel out of Egypt. In the interview, Sadat recalled that Sterner told him the President had made a major decision on the Middle East: "But before the U.S. took an official stand, President Nixon needed some clarification. 'The President is waiting for my telegram,' Sterner said to me. 'And if the answers are satisfactory, the President's plan will be in effect as of this evening.' 'Shoot,' I said." Bergus, confirming Sadat's description of the meeting, says that he and Sterner "thought we had this thing back on track. We'd been instructed to say that we were speaking with the authority of the President."

Kissinger returned to the Western White House early on July 13, preoccupied with the drama of his visit to Peking. He still managed to spare time to denigrate Rogers. Charles Radford, the Navy yeoman who had handled Kissinger's secretarial work on the China trip, was assigned the last-minute task of typing a memorandum from Kissinger to Nixon recommending which administration official should notify which foreign head of state prior to public announcement of the China opening. "In the memo I typed," Radford recalls, "Rogers was specifically given only three minor countries to call. He was excluded from everything. My gosh, he was Secretary of State." *

---

* Nixon overruled Kissinger on his wish list and Rogers was permitted to notify foreign governments of the astounding change in American foreign policy. Kissinger's account of Rogers' role in this trivial area was cruel in its matter-of-factness. He, Nixon, and Haldeman had spent hours

Kissinger's "device," the NSC meeting on the Middle East, was scheduled for July 16. Any final vestige of Rogers' plan had to be snuffed out, once and for all, and Kissinger left little to chance. Sometime that day, just before the meeting, the NSC staff specialists for the Middle East received an urgent order from the California White House: They had to produce within an hour ten reasons why the United States could not become involved in a Suez Canal disengagement. "I got my marching orders," as one NSC official puts it. "Destroy this thing. It's got to be destroyed. Henry wants it cut down." The message from Kissinger was passed along by Haig, who ordered the staff members to make no copies of their recommendations. The NSC aides did as they were told and quickly compiled their list of reasons, emphasizing, of course, the potential gains to the Soviets in the Middle East in case of a settlement. "We played heavily on the Soviet angle," an aide recalls. "That was one thing you could always turn the President around with—he was determined to keep the Russians out." The aide says, "I felt badly about it. I wasn't sure we were really serving the national interest. Rogers' proposal, I thought, had some merit, and here we are destroying it because of bureaucratic rivalry. We knew we were on a destruction mission [against Rogers]. The Middle East was the only action Rogers had."

In his memoirs, Kissinger made no mention of his staff's last-minute memorandum to Nixon and described the NSC meeting on July 16 as routine: "At the end of the meeting, Nixon authorized the Sisco trip to explore whether there was any flexibility in the Israeli position." Sisco duly flew to Israel on July 28 to meet with Golda Meir and others during a week-long stay. He accomplished nothing; the Israelis refused to make a good-faith offer. As Kissinger wrote, "His trip produced so little that Sisco did not even bother to stop in Cairo on the way home."

William Quandt apparently had access to the NSC minutes of the July 16 meeting, and provided an important new element in his book, *Decade of Decisions, 1967–76*. "Sadat was apparently still interested in a limited agreement," Quandt wrote, "but his patience was wearing thin. Nixon agreed that Sisco should travel to Israel to learn whether the Israelis would drop their objection to a token Egyptian force on the east bank of the canal. He pointedly refused, however, to promise that he would exert pressure on Israel if Sisco encountered difficulty. In brief, Sisco was on his own." *

Without Nixon's direct intervention, as all understood, Israel would never begin serious negotiations on the disengagement. Nothing was said to Sadat officially, as he bitterly recalled in the *Newsweek* interview: ". . . We had a

---

discussing how to announce the Peking visit. Kissinger wrote: "Finally Rogers joined us. I gave him the 'sanitized' version of my trip that Nixon had suggested. We discussed his role in the unfolding events. Notifying foreign governments would be the State Department's role. Rogers ably took charge."

* Bergus remains convinced that Sisco was not an unwitting dupe of Kissinger and Nixon but was fully aware of the situation at the California White House. "I think this is where there was real double-dealing," Bergus recalls. "In this period, Henry got word to Sisco that the canal disengagement is a nonstarter. Joe then went through the negotiations [in Israel] just doing enough so that Rogers wouldn't catch him red-handed." Sisco insisted in a subsequent interview that he had not played a duplicitous role in the mid-1971 negotiations: "I had no evidence or no feeling that I was being undermined." At least one former NSC aide recalls Sisco's rage at the orders from Nixon. "He claimed that we cut his balls off," the aide says, "and that he was mortified in front of the Prime Minister of Israel. He was livid and he had Rogers behind him."

70-day blackout from America. Absolutely nothing from anyone. We were never told what Sisco had done in Israel. Nothing from Don Bergus, nothing from our embassy in Washington. . . . It was quite obvious that Sisco's mission had been a complete failure.''

Even with Nixon's and Kissinger's explicit support, Israel and Egypt might not have been able to overcome their mutual mistrust and reach an accord that summer. But Bergus, for one, believes that success was possible: "I think we would have gotten it because you had a divided Israeli cabinet. If it had been push-and-shove on a continued U.S.-Israeli relationship, they would have done it." After July, however, the chances for a beginning of disengagement—and a possible end to warfare in the Middle East—"were all washed up." Rogers continued to try, but Bergus and his counterparts in Egypt knew that a vital chance had been missed. Desultory talks continued in late 1971 in Washington between the State Department and Ambassador Rabin of Israel, but "by that time they'd gotten so far away that I didn't even give the messages to Sadat, but to the Foreign Ministry. Everything went back to square one."

In his memoirs, Mohammad Heikal has described Sadat's disappointment over the American failure to insist that Israel begin serious negotiations, a disappointment heightened by his unilateral offers in early July 1971 to begin ousting Soviet troops and to reestablish full diplomatic relations with Washington. Sadat learned his lesson, perhaps even more thoroughly than Kissinger might have anticipated, as Heikal wrote: ". . . [F]rom this time [Sadat's] feeling grew that nothing was to be achieved through the State Department: if there were going to be any results they would only come via the 'other channel,' Henry Kissinger." Private contacts with Kissinger would be initiated by 1972, and Sadat, still eager for a settlement in the Middle East, would "expel" —as Kissinger had urged—the Soviet military from Egypt. Many in Egypt had doubts about Sadat's decision to deal with Kissinger, notably Mahmoud Riad, the Foreign Minister, who had become increasingly skeptical of Sadat's peacemaking efforts after witnessing Nixon's and Kissinger's repeated abandonment of Rogers during the peace initiatives. Riad's basic argument was that the United States would change its policy and endorse Egypt's demand for a comprehensive settlement in the Middle East only after a show of force. As long as Egypt and Israel continued to respect the Sinai ceasefire, Riad wrote in his memoirs, Washington would feel "no urgency, nor even a desire to speak in terms of a comprehensive settlement." Riad also scoffed at Rogers' explanation that the Soviet presence in Egypt was an obstacle to American peace efforts. "Kissinger had already used that logic," Riad wrote. "The fallacy of this logic would be exposed [in 1972] when the services of Soviet experts and advisers in Egypt were terminated without the U.S. making any progress towards a comprehensive peace." The hardline Riad was shunted aside by Sadat in 1972.

In his memoirs, Kissinger maintained the myth that he was not involved in Middle East diplomacy until late in 1971, after the failed disengagement negotiations: "What finally got me involved in the execution of Middle East diplomacy was that Nixon did not believe he could risk recurrent crises in the Middle East in an election year. He therefore asked me to step in, if only to keep things quiet."

Kissinger accomplished the goal: Things were quiet not only past the 1972 elections but for another year. Sadat and many of his colleagues eventually came to understand what Mahmoud Riad had been telling them: Only a cataclysmic action could break the diplomatic logjam. It came in October 1973—a war that Kissinger, by his need to dominate Rogers and his willful misunderstanding of the limits of Soviet influence inside Egypt, helped to make inevitable.

30

A BERLIN SETTLEMENT

NIXON'S AND KISSINGER'S DIPLOMATIC SUCCESSES with Peking and Moscow were not the only foreign policy breakthroughs of the early 1970s. In late August of 1971, Willy Brandt, Chancellor of West Germany, culminated two years of diplomatic initiatives with the Soviet Union, Poland, and East Germany—his *Ostpolitik*—by stage-managing a far-reaching agreement that finally removed Berlin as a perennial source of controversy between East and West. Brandt had been elected Chancellor in September 1969, and immediately set out to redeem his campaign promise to accept the postwar division of Germany as permanent and to negotiate final peace treaties with the East. In August 1970, he signed the first and most important of these agreements, with the Soviet Union, acknowledging the West German government's acceptance of Russia as a peaceful partner of Central Europe. In a speech televised throughout West Germany, Brandt declared that "Europe ends neither at the Elbe nor at the eastern frontier of Poland. Russia is inextricably involved in the history of Europe, not only as an opponent and a peril, but also as a partner, historically, politically, in culture and economics . . ." In his 1975 biography of Brandt, *The Other German,* David Binder, a former *New York Times* correspondent in Bonn, wrote that for "the Germans and the Russians . . . the Moscow Treaty had a far deeper impact—something to do with the texture of their national souls, after the shedding of so much heart's blood between them. This was why . . . everyone on both sides spoke of the 'historic' nature of the treaty."

The Moscow treaty began the unraveling of many of the old enmities between Western and Eastern Europe. Eventually there were successful West German negotiations with Poland, the recognition of East Germany, and discussions on East-West troop reductions. An equally successful negotiation over West Berlin, assuring freedom of access for its 2.2 million residents living more than a hundred miles inside East Germany, was the legacy of Brandt's initiatives. Until the Berlin question was settled, senior officials in Moscow understood, there could be no formal ratification by the West German parliament of the German-Moscow Treaty. The linkage was Brandt's and the impetus was his, although West Germany was not technically involved in the negotiations over West Berlin, which were conducted by the four postwar occupying powers—the United States, England, the Soviet Union, and France.

415

Brandt's plans to reunite East and West politically in Europe became one of Kissinger's obsessions in late 1969 and early 1970. "He hated *Ostpolitik* and Willy Brandt from the beginning," says Roger Morris, who sat through many staff meetings when the West German initiatives were discussed. "Henry thought the Germans were flirting with historical tragedy; that *Ostpolitik* would be a prelude to internal fascism, a turn to the right, and the emergence of another Weimar Republic." Robert E. Osgood, who directed the NSC staff's policy planning group, submitted an analysis of Brandt's maneuvers to the East that found merit in the German approach. At a subsequent staff meeting, Morris recalls, Kissinger, in his half-joking manner, announced, "My staff should understand who I really detest in the world. . . . Osgood thinks he is really Willy Brandt." Osgood too remembers Kissinger's "great fear and distrust of the Germans, particularly those who wanted closer relations to the East in what he considered a fuzzy-minded and dangerous way."

Haig supported Kissinger in his distrust, Morris says, but Nixon was much less hostile to Brandt. Morris thought "Nixon liked Brandt better than most European politicians," which forced Kissinger to conduct a "charade in which his real feelings and irrational attitude toward Brandt were never transferred upstairs to the Oval Office. With Nixon, he couldn't insult the Germans." In *The Other German,* Binder quoted a Kissinger aide as recalling that Kissinger and Sonnenfeldt, the two refugees from Nazi Germany, intensely disliked Brandt and his chief aide, Egon Bahr. They were regarded as "pernicious," Binder wrote, because they had dared to move on their own and "embodied instability in Germany." In his memoirs, Kissinger said as much in a milder way: "Brandt's *Ostpolitik,* which looked to many like a progressive policy of quest for détente, could in less scrupulous hands turn into a new form of classic German nationalism."

Brandt had begun to do in late 1969 exactly what Nixon and Kissinger decided to do a year later: open negotiations with the Soviet Union. In addition, as Kissinger had to know, the West German initiatives to the East had been repeatedly urged upon the Bonn government by the Johnson Administration. One senior German diplomat recalls that Johnson told Kurt G. Kiesinger, Brandt's predecessor as Chancellor, that the United States "would no longer fight a war of unification [of the two Germanys]. If you want to live in peace in Europe, you have to look for an alternative." The German official says that such discussions were no secret inside the top strata of the governments in Washington and Bonn in the late 1960s. "The notion [in the Nixon White House] that it was the Germans who all of a sudden had this mad lust for dealing with the East is just historically not true," according to this diplomat. "The first steps came at the initiative of the United States and the West."

Willy Brandt shared one trait with the Nixon White House: a distrust of his foreign office. In 1970 and 1971 much of his negotiation with Russia, Poland, and East Germany was carried out in the backchannel, through Egon Bahr, his political colleague and personal brain trust, who had long favored closer ties to the East. Bahr was sent to Washington in October 1969, after Brandt's election but before his installation, and met privately with Kissinger and Sonnenfeldt.* "Obviously they were skeptical," Bahr recalls dryly, of Brandt's

---

* Bahr's visit to the White House had been scheduled in advance, but Rogers objected on the ground, Kissinger wrote, that any negotiations should be held in the State Department. After some

ambitious plans for *Ostpolitik*. The West Germans had quickly perceived that the important foreign policy decisions of the Nixon Administration would be made in Kissinger's office, not in Rogers', and Bahr agreed to maintain close liaison with Kissinger. "I made clear we'd inform them in advance of what we would do," he says, "but we would do it anyway."

By the fall of 1970, Brandt had signed the historic agreement with the Soviet Union, and Kissinger no longer wasted energy trying to diminish *Ostpolitik* but instead sought to capitalize on it. Bahr became another player in the Nixon-Kissinger operation, making clandestine visits to the White House and elsewhere to describe to Kissinger—but not to the State Department—the progress of *Ostpolitik* and to discuss the four-power Berlin negotiations that began in early 1970. Brandt was anxious to speed those talks along; in his and Bahr's view, the ambassadors involved were far too legalistic. "It was impossible," Bahr recalls. "We faced the possibility that the whole four-power negotiations could break down." Such complaints were gratifying to Kissinger, who, as the West Germans knew, was always eager to denigrate the State Department and its diplomacy. Yet another backchannel was set up, involving Nixon, Kissinger, and Kenneth Rush, the American Ambassador to West Germany, who was a close friend of John Mitchell's and had been Nixon's professor at Duke University Law School. Bahr, Willy Brandt's backchannel expert, recalls his satisfaction with the arrangement: "I had the NSC, the President and the Ambassador—all the people I needed. It's not my business to coordinate the State Department."

In February 1971, just as Kissinger and Nixon were beginning their backchannel activities with Ambassador Dobrynin on SALT, trade, and other issues, Rush flew to Washington on a pretext arranged by Mitchell and met Kissinger at Mitchell's apartment at the Watergate complex. "Nobody trusted Bahr," Rush recalls, "and we agreed to try and have a secret channel. After the meeting, I talked to Nixon and he told me to report to Henry and to say nothing to anyone in the State Department or my embassy."

Such manipulations had a multitude of purposes. Primarily, of course, Kissinger was carrying out Nixon's wishes in insuring that the State Department had a minimal role in any important negotiations. In addition, there was the continuing battle with Rogers, which drove Kissinger to seize control of all possible issues. The Berlin negotiations, steeped in complex questions of access rights and other legalisms, were technical and not very glamorous, but Kissinger, as a native German who had written extensively on European issues while at Harvard, viewed himself as the ultimate authority on Berlin and the overall German questions.* Willy Brandt and the Soviets obviously understood

---

discussion, it was agreed that Kissinger would receive Bahr but not negotiate with him, and Martin J. Hillenbrand, Assistant Secretary of State for European Affairs and an expert on Germany, would attend the meeting. "There was not insignificant deviation from my compact with Rogers," Kissinger wrote, "in that Bahr, after leaving the White House by the front door, re-entered through the basement for a private talk with me, primarily to establish a channel by which we could stay in touch without the formal procedures."

  * Martin Hillenbrand was widely respected throughout the department for his competence and knowledge of German affairs. Kissinger's treatment of him during the Nixon years can only be described as brutal: He was a constant target of Kissinger's backchannel manipulation, even after he became Ambassador to West Germany in 1973. In a meeting with the JCS in March 1974, for example, Kissinger depicted him as soft on the Soviets, according to a transcript made available to me.

Kissinger's need to be perceived as a leading expert on German affairs and played on that need in a highly primitive—and highly successful—fashion. "The Soviet leaders were delighted that I was willing to engage myself in the Berlin talks," Kissinger wrote. "They had been told by Brandt and Bahr that of all the American leaders I understood German conditions best. (This was probably true; at the same time Moscow must have decided that playing on my vanity could do no harm.)"

Kissinger's vanity, as reflected in his memoirs, was staggering to officials in both Washington and Bonn. In his view, he, Bahr, and Rush, consulting together in private, would formulate negotiating positions and proposals on such issues as access procedures and Soviet guarantees for West Berlin, and would coordinate those positions with the other negotiating powers. "I would then explore them with Dobrynin," Kissinger wrote, "and then Rush or Bahr would put them back into regular channels. Against all odds, this three-dimensional chess worked. We achieved within seven months an agreement that has stood the test of time." What made this unusual methodology work, he wrote, was the leverage posed by the American diplomatic success with China and the ongoing SALT negotiations, not necessarily Willy Brandt's policies. At one point in his memoirs, however, Kissinger did come close to acknowledging Brandt's importance. "What we had going for us in 1971," Kissinger wrote, "was Moscow's concern to achieve ratification of Brandt's Eastern treaties." Having made that concession, Kissinger depicted Brandt's bargaining in *Ostpolitik* as essentially one-sided—"after all, Bonn was accepting the division of its country in return for nothing more than improvement in the political atmosphere [in West Berlin]." Thus the price of *Ostpolitik* had to be a favorable settlement on Berlin. "It was a classical case of linkage," Kissinger wrote, adding ungenerously: "The practical consequence of this linkage, however, was that in the process we became responsible for the ultimate success of Brandt's policy." The view from Washington was still Ptolemaic; Nixon and Kissinger were still running the world.

Nixon had an even more self-centered analysis: Progress in the Berlin talks did not come until after the July 15, 1971, China announcement. It is not clear from his memoirs or from his few public comments at the time whether he had any appreciation at all of the immense complexity of the negotiations. Such details, to a President preoccupied with domestic economic problems, China, Vietnam, and reelection, did not deserve much personal attention. Nor did Kissinger, according to the men who dealt with him on Berlin in 1971, fully understand the issues. He chose, at the time and in his memoirs, to make light of those who took the legal questions seriously: "Berlin exceeded even SALT in its intricacy and esoteric jargon," Kissinger wrote. ". . . [T]he negotiation was encrusted by years of haggling over legalisms. There was scarcely any topic, from the exact form of a stamp on a pass to the legal status of the entire city, that had not been squabbled over with the Soviets in the 1950s and 1960s."

However, Kissinger and Nixon perceived by early 1971 that Brandt's *Ostpolitik* was going to pay off with a negotiating success. The White House wanted in and the backchannel gave them the entrée.

The basic American negotiating positions on the various complexities involved in the Berlin talks were drawn up not by Kissinger in the backchannel but by the State Department and its leading experts on Germany, Martin J. Hillenbrand and James Sutterlin. Hillenbrand, as Assistant Secretary for European Affairs, headed the interdepartmental group dealing with the American recommendations, and Sutterlin directed the Berlin desk. They both realized, as the French and British negotiating teams did, that the White House had set up a series of backchannels to Bonn and to Moscow; it was widely assumed that the French, as was their custom in negotiations involving Germany, were equally circumspect. Concern inside State over the existence of backchannels was eased somewhat by the knowledge that the American negotiating stance, which was based on staff papers prepared by Sutterlin, among others, had been presented to the White House in early 1970 and formally endorsed by Nixon and the NSC staff. Sutterlin and Hillenbrand were convinced that the critical factor in the Berlin talks would not be a backchannel between Washington and Bonn, or Washington and Moscow, but the influence of Willy Brandt's *Ostpolitik*. "The most important aspect of the Central Europe agreements was Brandt," Sutterlin recalls. "He was the one who saw it. We in State understood from the beginning that East Germany would eventually be recognized by the United States and this would mean its membership in the United Nations." The Soviet Union and East Germany had too much at stake to refuse a Berlin settlement.

One of the sticking points in the negotiations was the Soviet Union's demand that its concessions on guaranteed access rights for the residents of West Berlin be balanced by Western approval of a Soviet Consulate in West Berlin, a step to which State Department officials vehemently objected on grounds that the Soviet Union already had a consulate in East Berlin. The American position had been that all of Berlin, East and West, was occupied by the four powers and all of it had special status. To give the Soviets diplomatic offices in both East and West would provide them with a political foothold in the Western sector and diminish the legal argument that both sectors shared the same occupation status. The Defense Department and CIA also argued against a second consulate, on grounds that it could provide a base for intensified spying and military actions against the West. The Nixon Administration's fallback policy, as outlined in the White House-approved National Security Decision Memoranda, was that a Soviet Consulate, if agreed upon, could not be an intrinsic part of the overall Berlin agreement but must be handled in a separate understanding. The reasoning was that in case of improper Soviet behavior—such as spying—the Western powers must be able to shut down or expel the consulate without doing away with the whole agreement. Most important, the operating NSDM explicitly ordered the Berlin negotiators not to accede to a Soviet Consulate in West Berlin without the express approval of the President. Such a requirement was considered appropriate by the State Department, since it provided the President with assurance that he could maintain control.

The American negotiators did not know, however, that Nixon, Kissinger, and Rush had privately agreed to the Soviet demand for a consulate. Nixon had countermanded his own orders without telling his State Department. Kenneth Rush would argue later that the duplicity was essential "because of the hardliners" in the Defense Department, the CIA, and the State Department. "You had to backchannel from the top," Rush recalls, to avoid premature leaks about the White House's concessions. "If they'd told Bill [Rogers] about this, he'd probably have gotten some people [aides] in on it—and we'd have been finished." *

Rush's concern, obviously shared by Kissinger, was that Rogers would not do what the President told him to. Others disagreed. James Sutterlin argued that no one would have countermanded Nixon: "All the President needed to do was to call the Secretary of State and say it's time to take the agreement. If they had said 'Do it'—we'd have done it." The refusal of the White House to deal straightforwardly with Rogers led to an embarrassing confrontation between Rogers and Rush, with a loss of face for Rogers. In mid-August 1971, when the key issue of a Soviet Consulate in West Berlin was conceded in the backchannel by Rush, Kissinger, and senior Soviet officials, "I had an agreement," Rush says, "and my problem was—how could I get it accepted by State?" Rush managed to disguise the major American concession in his cabled reports to the State Department; meanwhile, the British and French delegations acceded to the Soviet Consulate and agreed to the final four-power draft agreement on Berlin. Rush was jubilant, Kissinger wrote, sending a backchannel telegram to the White House "claiming that the bureaucrats 'have been foiled.' " In the Berlin talks, as with SALT and the China initiative, Nixon and Kissinger had managed to isolate the State Department bureaucracy. Berlin was different in one significant aspect, for the final text of the agreement had to be reviewed by the Secretary of State. Kissinger wrote, "Somehow we had to see to it that our own State Department did not complicate matters . . . There is no agreement that cannot be picked to death by professionals not involved in negotiating."

Kissinger's memoirs notwithstanding, the State Department was not the only agency picking away at the Berlin agreement that August; Kissinger's own NSC staff also did. There was a sharp dispute inside his office over what was perceived as Kissinger's and Nixon's willingness to yield on the consulate issue. "The bargaining could have been a little better," says one Kissinger aide, who was directly involved in coordinating the White House's backchannel to Rush. "It was a tough issue and a big dispute." Sonnenfeldt, Kissinger's European expert, was convinced that the Soviets would have agreed to the quadripartite agreement without getting a consulate. The dissent apparently troubled Kissinger, for he took the time—a rare move by 1971—to hear objections and smooth ruffled feathers. One NSC official remembers the criticism as sharp—"it was one of the six times Sonnenfeldt threatened to resign that year." Another official has a different recollection: "There was a concern, but not a deep concern. I don't think it was a major issue."

Rogers thought it was. Upon being told that Rush had agreed to a Soviet

* Rush also acknowledged in an interview that the real linkage involved in the Berlin negotiation came from Brandt's *Ostpolitik,* not from the White House's involvement in SALT and China: "While we were negotiating, Vietnam, SALT, and China had nothing to do with it. Obviously, all of our relations with the Soviet Union are intertwined, but that doesn't mean that you can't make progress on any one unless you make progress on all." When the China announcement came on July 15, Rush recalls, "There wasn't a whisper about that at all" in the negotiating sessions. "Henry really didn't understand the Berlin agreement very much because he was spread so thin," said Rush.

Consulate in West Berlin, he exploded. Rush received an urgent cable instructing him to "stop everything. I had violated the NSDM. Let everybody know I did not agree." At that point, Rush says, "All I could do was ignore the cable and go ahead." Rogers subsequently ordered Rush to return to Washington for a two-week consultation to enable the State Department experts to review the agreement. "We were in a serious quandary," Kissinger wrote. ". . . [T]he State Department could scarcely be told that it had no right to review an agreement of such importance. We could not guarantee that some bureaucratic nitpicker might not force us to reopen issues settled already . . ." Sutterlin recalls that Rush was summoned to a hostile meeting at Rogers' office: "It was an unpleasant confrontation. There was a feeling that Rush was going too fast and we didn't see why we couldn't take more time to check for loopholes. It was clear the Soviets wanted the agreement." In the middle of the meeting, Rogers was called out to take a telephone call from John Mitchell, who relayed the word that the President wanted Rush to fly to San Clemente and be at Nixon's side when the Berlin agreement was made public. Rogers was not to go. It was yet another humiliation. "We went public the next day in San Clemente," Rush says. "Rogers was still in Washington."

The final Berlin agreement, all experts agreed, was a remarkable accomplishment, a capstone to Brandt's *Ostpolitik*. It provided a Soviet guarantee of unimpeded access from West Germany to West Berlin, and it gave West Berliners the right to visit East Germany and East Berlin. It also permitted West Berlin to retain its ties to the Federal Republic of Germany, including the right to travel on West German passports, while assuring the Soviets that the Bonn government would refrain from conducting presidential elections and other constitutional business in West Berlin, thus reducing some aspects of the federal West German presence there. A few days after the announcement, the White House put out the word that President Nixon had been personally responsible for keeping the negotiations going at critical junctures by intervening directly with Andrei A. Gromyko, the Soviet Foreign Minister. In a *New York Times* dispatch, Nixon was said by American diplomatic sources to have "provided the initiative for getting the talks started originally, proposing them in a speech in West Berlin in February 1969." It was a lackluster "p.r." effort, by White House standards, but Nixon got what he wanted: a few political points.

Kissinger also got what he wanted: another ignoble defeat for Rogers. The residue at the State Department and its European affairs secretariat was bitterness together with a firm belief that the backchannel was not used as a device to facilitate negotiations, but as an instrument to impose humiliation. "We didn't need the backchannel," insists David Klein, who was the American Minister in Berlin during the negotiations. "The deal would have come out not a great deal differently." Klein was among those who argued against granting a Soviet Consulate in West Berlin, on the grounds that it would undermine the key legal issue—that all of Berlin, East and West, was occupied, and must continue to have that status. "Kissinger can claim that everybody is picayune," Klein says, "but the history of Berlin is a history of badly drawn agreements and the Soviets, in a crisis, can always point to a dropped stitch. Historically, the Soviets have been able to take advantage of loopholes."

The final treaty became formally known as the Quadripartite Agreement; at no place was the word "Berlin" used. The American view was that Berlin, as defined in the post–World War II peace agreements, was an area—located geographically inside East Germany—that was one separate political entity. The Western negotiators agreed, prior to the final settlement, that describing the area discussed in the treaty as West Berlin or the Western sector would tend to establish it as a separate entity, and thus diminish the legal right of the occupying powers to maintain access to East Berlin—which, after all, was what the negotiation was about. In the final agreement, the Western sector was invariably described as the "relevant area." With all this care, State Department officials were understandably dismayed in May 1972, at the close of Nixon's summit meeting in Moscow, when the final joint American-Soviet communiqué depicted the 1971 Quadripartite Agreement as "relating to Western Sectors of Berlin . . ." "I couldn't believe it when I saw it," Sutterlin remembers. "Neither could the British or the French." Rush, who had been named Melvin Laird's deputy at the Defense Department in early 1972, well remembers his efforts during the late summer of 1971 to "never use the term West Berlin" in negotiating the agreement. "I was upset" about the 1972 gaffe. "How the hell it ever happened I don't know."

For most of the State Department's "nitpickers," the mistake at Moscow was just another example of Kissinger's poor judgment in excluding the bureaucracy from such complex issues as a four-power treaty involving postwar Berlin. Men such as Sutterlin and Klein acknowledge that their fears over the possible adverse legal ramifications turned out to be unfounded, as the Quadripartite Agreement worked remarkably well over the next decade. But their job and their obligation was to raise such issues. The State Department's German desk was also responsible for coordinating the concerns of specialized government agencies, such as the CIA, whose day-to-day operations could be affected, and reflecting those concerns in the position papers. "The fact is," Sutterlin recalls, "we maintained total consensus within the government on the negotiations. The cooperation and general agreement in Washington was greater than in any other issue I know of. There were no leaks. This meant going slower than the people in Bonn wanted, but we had to keep the legal department involved. They were meticulous." By mid-1971, however, maintaining bureaucratic consensus and coordinating legal issues were of little interest to the White House. Conducting the nation's and the world's business in the secrecy of the backchannel had become a way of life, a means of reaffirming the authority of the President and his chief adviser.

William Rogers had now been mauled in the Middle East and Asia, and he had been unable to protect himself and his aides from humiliation in Berlin. Sometime late that summer, with State Department morale continuing to sag, he blew up. It came at one of his morning senior staff meetings. The usually stoic Rogers declared with rare anger that he was upset by the criticism from inside the department. "If anybody doesn't like the way things are being done," Rogers told his senior advisers, "they ought to quit." Perhaps he was talking to himself.

The summer's successes brought Kissinger celebrity status around the world and much private gratification over his domination of the bureaucracy. But all of his and the President's successes, even in Peking, would be diminished unless the Vietnam War was brought under control. The Nixon presidency would be judged by history—and by the electorate in November 1972—on that issue.

31
VIETNAM:
A MISSED CHANCE

HANOI OFFERED THE WHITE HOUSE a chance for a negotiated peace in mid-1971, but the price was too high: an honest election in the South.

Nixon and Kissinger clung to Nguyen Van Thieu, the increasingly repressive and unpopular President of South Vietnam; keeping him in power became a face-saving mechanism more important than ending the war. Stung by the failure of the Laos invasion and fearful about reelection, Nixon agreed in May 1971 to hint at a significant concession in the secret Paris peace talks: North Vietnam would be allowed to keep its troops in the South. Mutual withdrawal, the negotiating stance adopted by the Nixon Administration with so much hope two years earlier, was no longer cited as a precondition for a settlement. But the new White House position did not lead to progress either. Both sides continued to talk past each other. The concession on Hanoi's troops was never specifically spelled out in Paris in 1971, and Hanoi's leaders, always wary of American "tricks," adopted the legal position that the revised proposals hinged on the withdrawal of their troops. In Hanoi's view, even an explicitly worded commitment that its troops had the right to remain in the South would only concede diplomatically what Washington could not prevent militarily. The White House proposal was still contingent on Hanoi's willingness to accept a ceasefire in Cambodia and Laos, where Communist gains had been greater and ultimate victory was more assured, as well as in South Vietnam; and it did not provide the National Liberation Front with any guarantee of participation in the political life of the South. In essence, the United States proposed to withdraw its troops from South Vietnam if Hanoi would accept a political defeat and a military stalemate.

But Kissinger also began talking, during six secret meetings in Paris between May and October, of America's willingness to accept a neutral South Vietnam and political competition among Communists and non-Communists in Saigon. This *was* something new, and North Vietnam responded that summer with what it considered a significant modification of its demands: The United States would not have to depose Thieu and his coterie, whose ouster Hanoi considered essential if there was to be open political life in the South, but instead could negotiate an end to the war by remaining neutral during the Vietnamese presidential elections, scheduled for October 3, and allowing the South Vietnamese voters to do what Nixon and Kissinger would not—get rid of Thieu. It was a solution the White House never considered. Thus Nixon made a military concession that the other side deemed misleading, and Hanoi made a political suggestion that the White House found untenable. Hanoi was misjudging Nixon's determination not to lose in South Vietnam as much as Nixon had misjudged Hanoi's determination not to let his threats and coercion—the "madman theory"—drive it out of the South.

That summer Nixon and Kissinger publicly continued to insist that America's honor remained synonymous with Nguyen Van Thieu—pending a better offer from Hanoi. The South Vietnamese President had no intention of campaigning honestly and holding a fair election, nor did his benefactors in the White House press him to do so. For them, the 1971 election, called for by Vietnam's 1967 constitution, which had been shaped by American advisers, was merely an unfortunate nuisance that arose at an awkward time. Nixon and Kissinger repeatedly assured the world that America would remain neutral in the election, but few in Saigon and Washington expected the administration not to do all it could to maintain its man in power in Saigon.

There was immense irony in the White House's backing of Thieu, for Hanoi, in seeking a political end to his regime, found itself in league with non-Communist American and Vietnamese critics of the South Vietnamese government, including Vietnamese politicians who were members of the "Third Force" in Saigon, as well as dozens of junior- and middle-level American diplomats assigned to the embassy in Saigon and to district and provincial offices throughout the South. These dissidents shared with Hanoi an understanding that the 1971 elections offered the White House a chance to get out of Vietnam without an immediate Communist takeover. In their view, an honest election, far from endangering the future of South Vietnam, would strengthen the political structure of the government and enable its demoralized military to perform more effectively against the North Vietnamese. They argued that a rigged election would end legitimate political life in the South and make the eventual collapse of Thieu's regime inevitable. By spring 1971, after the failure in Laos, a military concession by the United States became essential if an agreement was to be negotiated: Hanoi could keep its troops in South Vietnam. The one unresolvable issue in the secret talks thus became Hanoi's insistence that Thieu be ousted. If the White House would not do it by fiat, Le Duc Tho began telling Kissinger, the next-best solution would be to let Thieu take his chances with the people.

Thieu had been challenged by his Vice President, Nguyen Cao Ky, the ambitious head of the South Vietnamese Air Force, but Ky's candidacy posed no threat; his commitment to continue the war offered little real choice for the electorate. The compromise candidate who became most acceptable not only to Hanoi but to many Vietnamese and American dissidents was General Duong Van Minh, who had been sent to Thailand as South Vietnam's Ambassador—and kept out of the country until 1968—for his role in the 1963 coup d'état against Ngo Dinh Diem. With his suggestion about an honest election, Tho was telling the White House that, as a minimum, Hanoi was willing to sign a peace agreement on the basis of a divided Vietnam whose political future would be resolved after a decent interval. General Minh, known as "Big Minh" in Saigon, also had the support of many American Foreign Service officers as a candidate of conciliation who could bring together the fragmented political and religious forces in South Vietnam. Equally important was the belief that while Minh was willing to negotiate with the Provisional Revolutionary Government, the Vietcong's government-in-waiting, he would not accept a peace that would hand over the South to the Communists. General Minh had enlisted in the French Army at the age of twenty-four and risen rapidly through the ranks in the 1940s and early 1950s during the war against the Viet Minh, the Communist insurgents led by Ho Chi Minh, who defeated the French in 1954 at Dien Bien Phu. Many of his associates in 1971 were also retired South Vietnamese officers who had fought for the French against the Vietnamese Communists. His support among the various peace movements in Saigon was genuine; he was perceived as a hero for his role in the 1963 assassination of Ngo Dinh Diem and his equally despised brother, Ngo Dinh Ngu. Minh joined with two other senior South Vietnamese Army officers in the coup, which was carried out with the prior knowledge and acquiescence of the American Embassy and the White House. The job of assassinating Diem and Ngu fell to Minh's personal bodyguard, who shot both men as they were supposedly being driven to safety. In 1971, the anniversary of Diem's assassination was still celebrated as a national holiday throughout the South. Minh's most significant support came from those elements in Vietnamese politics known as the "legal opposition," or the "Third Force," which included the influential Buddhist groups. The coalition was highly patriotic and far more interested in obtaining the endorsement of the American Embassy than in negotiating a compromise with the North Vietnamese; nonetheless, Nguyen Van Thieu and many in the American Embassy were convinced that it was little more than a front for the Communists. Minh's campaign platform in 1971 specifically ruled out negotiations with the National Liberation Front unless it agreed to give up its political and military fight for a neutral coalition in the South and, as Minh declared in mid-June, agreed to "accept the rules of democracy."* Recognition of North Vietnam, he said, would be "possible only when North Vietnam recognizes the non-Communist nature of South Vietnam and accepts division for the time being."

None of this seemed to carry any weight with Nixon or Kissinger, who viewed Minh merely as a Communist dupe. In his memoirs, Kissinger complained about the timing of the 1971 elections, which had been fixed by the 1967 Vietnamese constitution: "Thus, at a crucial point in the history of America's involvement in Vietnam, an event imposed on Vietnam essentially by American choice [in 1967] turned into a new source of turmoil and anxiety. . . . Many in the bureaucracy were hoping that Thieu would be defeated by a candidate prepared to accept a coalition government. I hoped that a democratic election would increase support for an ally." As for the candidacy of General

* There was a constant shuffling of names for the Communist forces and political movements in the South in anticipation of serious negotiations between North Vietnam and the United States. American and South Vietnamese officials repeatedly referred to the opposition as the National Liberation Front, and depicted the NLF as a front group for the Lao Dong Communist Party, whose headquarters were in Hanoi. In 1969, the NLF created its Provisional Revolutionary Government, an alliance of NLF and pro-Communist forces in the South. The PRG was not a political party but an opposition government ready to assume a share of the power in Saigon. Hanoi officials, in their interviews and writings on the 1969–1972 negotiations, described the proposals of the South Vietnam Communists as emanating from the PRG, not from the NLF.

Minh, "If Hanoi accepted him—which was unclear—it would be because he was the easiest of all candidates to overthrow should he become President." Kissinger's disdain for General Minh seemed irrational even to some of his close aides. Richard Smyser, the NSC staff specialist on Vietnam, who was one of the few staff people involved in the secret Paris peace talks, suggested to Kissinger that summer that he and other officials were underestimating Minh, but such views were disregarded. "The United States government always mistrusts our friends," Smyser says in hindsight. "It also distrusts neutral solutions, because we would lose control." *

Nixon's decision in May 1971 to consider the inevitable—North Vietnamese troops in the South—arose from domestic political necessity. Vietnamization may have been working to some degree in the field, but it had failed to provide lasting political benefits in the United States. Every withdrawal of American troops seemed to be offset by a reverse. In early April of 1971, Nixon announced the withdrawal of another 100,000 American fighting men by December 1, 1971, increasing the total withdrawn to 365,000 since mid-1969. The political benefit was more than offset, however, by a renewed media controversy over the My Lai massacre. On March 29, Lieutenant William L. Calley, the hapless officer who took part in the 1968 massacre, was found guilty by a military court-martial of the premeditated murder of twenty-two Vietnamese civilians. The Calley case had created controversy when the atrocity first became known in 1969, with many Americans refusing to believe that the massacre was as deliberate and systematic as the initial news reports said. Calley's conviction, by a group of Army officers—his peers—was a blow to those Americans who had refused to accept the implications of the My Lai incident, those Middle Americans whose support Nixon and previous presidents had been able to rally by appeals to patriotism. Nixon, with his excellent political instincts, understood the danger of Calley's conviction and intervened to insure that Calley was not immediately put into an Army stockade, pending his appeal. It was good politics, but not good enough. Senator Edmund Muskie, viewed as the leading contender for the Democratic presidential nomination, had begun to match Nixon's strength in public opinion polls early in the year; by May, the Harris poll reported that Muskie was running well ahead of Nixon, by a margin of 47 to 39 percent.

---

* Dislike and lack of respect for Minh were widespread throughout the top echelons of the American government. One senior diplomat who served as Deputy Ambassador in Saigon described Minh in a 1981 interview as "a very inferior personality, a nullity with vague ideas. Minh was not a peace candidate, but a patsy for the other side. He was an image created by an unwitting combination of neutralists, Communists, and American press people who disliked Thieu very much." This official acknowledged that there were many junior officers who had different views, but he had been convinced, he said, that the United States was forced to "put its money on Thieu" in the 1971 elections. Kissinger and Nixon obviously shared that view, and Ambassador Ellsworth Bunker, in some of his cables to Washington, seemed to encourage that predisposition. In February 1971, for example, at a time of press speculation in Saigon about the possibility of General Minh's candidacy, Bunker discussed that issue with Thieu at the palace. "When I asked if he thought that Minh had made up his mind to run," Bunker cabled, Thieu gave "a most amusing account of Minh's indecisive character. . . . He described Minh's way of working. When an operation was contemplated, Minh would call a meeting. There would be briefings, and then Minh would pick out all the weaknesses on his side and all the strong points of the enemies. He would then conclude that 'the situation is not ideal,' 'further study or further action is needed,' 'we will have to meet again to consider what to do.' " It was left to others in the embassy to report on the significance of General Minh's candidacy. Bunker's cable was made available under the Freedom of Information Act.

Something had to be done about Vietnam. Richard Smyser recalls Nixon's decision to make a move in the secret Paris peace talks—to find a way to get all the American troops out of Vietnam. "We all understood what we were doing," Smyser says. "For domestic and political reasons, American troops had to be gotten out of there."

On April 24, with the outcry over his intervention in the Calley case barely behind him, Nixon authorized Kissinger to renew contact with the North Vietnamese in Paris. There was no immediate response. On April 29, at a news conference, Nixon was asked about growing congressional demands that he set a date for withdrawing all American troops from Vietnam if Hanoi would agree to release the American prisoners of war. In response, he recapitulated his peace proposals, carefully noting that "they included, as you know, a mutual withdrawal of forces. . . ." It was the last time he was to use such language in public. Hanoi, obviously believing it held the upper hand, waited until May 14 before agreeing to secret talks, which were then set for May 31. Between those dates, Kissinger somehow convinced Nixon that the time had come for a military concession.*

There would be a new American peace proposal offered in Paris on May 31, one that did not specifically call for the withdrawal of Hanoi's troops from the South. That point would simply be left unstated. The decision to drop mutual withdrawal would not be made known in Saigon, where Nguyen Van Thieu was being told as little as possible about the secret talks. Kissinger was optimistic. In his memoirs, he described the new proposal as "the most sweeping plan we had yet offered." Nixon considered it a "final offer." The North Vietnamese had a different view. In return for the vaguely hinted-at military concession, they believed the White House had set a high price: America would set a date for total withdrawal, but that withdrawal would not begin until the other side had agreed to a general ceasefire throughout South Vietnam, Laos, and Cambodia. The Thieu regime would also be left in place to

---

* On the crucial issue of how the compromise was agreed upon, Nixon's and Kissinger's memoirs are silent. Kissinger's repeatedly portray Nixon as skeptical and often inconsistent about the Paris negotiations. Once having agreed to a negotiating plan, or a concession, Kissinger wrote, Nixon "would deluge me with tough-sounding directives not always compatible with the plan, and some incapable of being carried out at all. The reason may have been his unease with the process of compromise or the fear of being rejected even in a diplomatic forum." Vietnam seemed constantly to bring out the irrational in Nixon. In September 1981, I obtained and published in the *New York Times* a transcript of an Oval Office conversation between Nixon and Haldeman on May 5, 1971, at the height of the May Day antiwar demonstrations in Washington. At one point, the President endorsed Haldeman's suggestion that "thugs" from the teamsters union be hired to beat up the demonstrators. "They, they've got guys who'll go in and knock their heads off," Nixon said enthusiastically. "Sure," Haldeman responded. He added: "Murderers. Guys that really, you know, that's what they really do . . . it's the regular strikebuster types and . . . they're gonna beat the shit out of some of these people. And, uh, and hope they really hurt 'em. You know, I mean go in . . . and smash some noses." Such talk must have occupied much of Kissinger's time in the Oval Office. Nixon's distress over the demonstrations may also have been a factor in his decision later in May to permit Kissinger to hint to the North Vietnamese that they might be able to maintain some of their troops in the South as part of a negotiated settlement. In the May 5 tape recording, the President was almost beseeching Haldeman to see the bright side of the protests, to which the White House had responded with orders for mass arrests: ". . . we may have more goin' for us than we think here, Bob. Yah. We shouldn't be frightened about it. . . . Stay firm and get credit for it. That's my point. . . . I don't want to be doing on the basis, well, we're sorta sitting here embattled and doing the best we can. I think the idea here is to lead a noble—it may be that we're setting an example, Bob, for, uh, for universities, for other cities, and so forth and so. Right? . . . Let 'em look here. These people try somethin', bust 'em."

continue to operate under the 1967 South Vietnamese constitution, which barred Communist participation in the political life of the South. In addition, the American formula would leave the Thieu regime's police force and army intact while the North Vietnamese and the PRG, having agreed to the ceasefire, were to negotiate the final political solution. Hanoi would already have released its American prisoners of war, one of its main bargaining chips in forcing the United States to withdraw unilaterally.

Hanoi had no way of perceiving it at the time, but there was another unstated assumption in the American proposal: A ceasefire would be buttressed by Richard Nixon's commitment to return with air power to both North and South Vietnam.

The new American offer came at a time of lowered military activity in South Vietnam. Kissinger and many of his aides, among them Richard Smyser, were convinced that the South Vietnamese could hold up well on their own, with American air support. In mid-1971, a series of upbeat reports from the American Embassy and the CIA station in Saigon noted that the Thieu regime had been generally able to improve internal security conditions. The North Vietnamese and the National Liberation Front had come to a similar conclusion. In an analysis prepared in early 1971 by the Central Office for South Vietnam, the Communists conceded that "The enemy has achieved some temporary results. . . . During the past two years, the U.S. and puppet focused their efforts on pacifying and encroaching upon rural areas, using the most barbarous schemes. They strengthened puppet forces, consolidated the puppet forces, consolidated the puppet government, and established an outpost network and espionage and People's Self-Defense Force organizations in many hamlets and villages. They provided more technical equipment for, and increased the mobility of, puppet forces, establishing blocking lines, and created a new defensive and oppressive system in densely populated areas. As a result they caused many difficulties to and inflicted losses on friendly forces." The analysis, published after a political conference somewhere in the jungles of South Vietnam and known as COSVN Directive 10, nonetheless concluded on an optimistic note, pointing out that the speeded-up Vietnamization program was compelling the Saigon government "to expedite its dictatorial and fascist policies on conscription" in order to send Vietnamese troops to the battlefields "to die in the place of U.S. soldiers." The directive predicted that as Vietnamization continued, the contradictions between the policies of Saigon and the aspirations of the people "would ripen the political awareness" and force increased demands for the replacement of the Thieu regime. But, as COSVN 10 made clear, the Vietcong and North Vietnamese understood that victory was not around the corner.

The North Vietnamese, their forces on the defensive in the South, were skeptical about the May 31 peace proposal. Any agreement would have to be carefully negotiated. Nguyen Co Thach, Le Duc Tho's aide throughout the secret peace talks, later characterized the new White House offer as "no change. It was a wording change." Thach's point was that the May 31 proposal did not explicitly give North Vietnam the right to keep its troops in the South;

that concession, he said, was never really spelled out during the talks over the summer of 1971. Legally, Thach said, the United States "stuck to its demand that we withdraw our troops." What Nixon and Kissinger viewed as a subtle change in their negotiating position was too subtle for the North Vietnamese. The proposal, as published in Kissinger's memoirs, made no mention of North Vietnam's right to maintain its troops in the South but simply stated that the Vietnamese and "the other peoples in Indochina should discuss among themselves the manner in which all other outside forces would withdraw from the countries of Indochina." That was far too ambiguous for the circumspect and suspicious men from Hanoi.*

What did interest the North Vietnamese, Thach said, was Kissinger's suggestion, made during a conversation with Le Duc Tho on May 31, that the White House was willing to discuss seriously a possible coalition government in Saigon. Kissinger "touched on the question of the 'decent interval,'" Thach recalled. "He said that the withdrawal of American troops would have a big effect on the internal political processes of South Vietnam, and the USA would accept a neutral South Vietnam." It was the first time such language had been heard in the secret talks. Kissinger guaranteed that the United States would not impose one side on another; he said that he would "accept two sides and both sides will have competition." Thach said Le Duc Tho and the Hanoi leaders were intrigued by the new guarantee, although they did not find it "credible or believable" because of the Nixon-Kissinger insistence that all political competition in the South be "within the framework of the Saigon constitution. They would like to put the PRG into the framework of the constitution of Saigon. This was not possible. We were fighting to abolish this constitution."

Despite the suspicions that permeated the secret peace talks, Xuan Thuy, Hanoi's chief delegate at the May 31 meeting, understood that a major new element had been added. A second secret session was agreed upon for June 16, and Le Duc Tho came to take over. (Throughout this period, the public peace talks were continuing, and there was no public clue to the intense activity in secret.) Richard Smyser knew there had been a change in North Vietnam's attitude as soon as he arrived with Kissinger and Winston Lord: "Instead of all of us sitting in easy chairs opposite cocktail tables, we suddenly were sitting on hard chairs opposite a green cloth table. It was something that told us, 'Okay, folks, this is bargaining.'" The North Vietnamese offered a nine-point peace plan, the first concrete proposal that included a change in their demands about Thieu. Instead of demanding that Thieu be ousted, Hanoi asked the Nixon Administration to "stop supporting" him and his allies, so

* There was perhaps another reason for Hanoi's caution. Samuel Adams, a CIA official who specialized in analyzing the Vietcong, concluded in a highly classified 1970 paper that there were as many as 30,000 Communist agents permeating every aspect of the South Vietnamese government. Adams recalls that his paper, which was disavowed by everyone in the CIA and the White House, concluded that the Vietcong penetrations in the South "called into question the basic loyalty of the South Vietnamese government and armed forces." One Vietcong agent, Adams insists, was a high official of South Vietnam's intelligence service. If Adams's thesis was correct, the White House's decision to cut Thieu out of the secret talks may have undermined the May 31 proposal; it would have been difficult for the North Vietnamese to believe that the United States would agree to leave Hanoi's troops in the South without informing its ally in Saigon.

that "a new administration standing for peace, independence, neutrality, and democracy" would be set up.* As a further inducement, Hanoi agreed for the first time to release the American prisoners of war and all civilian detainees simultaneously with American troop withdrawals. Both the withdrawals and the release would be completed on the same date. Hanoi was now telling Nixon and Kissinger that they could get their prisoners of war back in return for the withdrawal of all American troops—a process already under way—and a fair election in the South. In such an election, Hanoi knew, Thieu would be hard-pressed to defeat General Minh, especially if the third major candidate, Vice President Ky, remained in the race. The flamboyant Ky had wide support among the Catholics and the military, two of Thieu's main constituencies, and he was sure to drain votes from the South Vietnamese President. On July 1, the PRG publicly released a more detailed peace plan, calling for a three-segment "government of national concord" and urging Nixon and Kissinger to "really respect the South Vietnamese people's right to self-determination." The proposal also called on the White House to "stop all maneuvers, including tricks on elections, aimed at maintaining the puppet Nguyen Van Thieu." Washington no longer had to be responsible for the replacement of the Thieu regime, the PRG proposal said; instead, it must "put an end to its interference in the internal affairs of South Vietnam."† During this period, the National Liberation Front began urging its supporters not to boycott the presidential elections, as had been recommended in 1967, but to defeat the Thieu regime by voting against it.

After the June 26 meeting, Kissinger thought he and the North Vietnamese were on the verge of an agreement. "In the fairy-tale atmosphere of Vietnam negotiations, after two years of Communist stonewalling and domestic flagellation," he wrote of Le Duc Tho's proposal, "my colleagues and I were elated that Hanoi had for the first time responded to a proposition by us. . . ." But there was no elation in the White House over the July 1 proposal, for it had been made publicly and raised the possibility—echoed in newspaper editorials across the nation—that a White House decision to withdraw all the troops could bring home the prisoners of war and close out America's involvement in Vietnam.

On July 7, Anthony Lewis of the *New York Times* published an interview with Le Duc Tho in which the North Vietnamese official reinforced that thesis. Tho declared that the prisoner of war issue could be isolated from the political issue of Saigon's future if Nixon withdrew his insistence on a total ceasefire in Vietnam, Cambodia, and Laos. Hanoi, obviously eager to prod the White House on the election issue, had decided to appeal directly to the antiwar element in the United States. "Once Mr. Nixon sets a date" for total with-

* Hanoi's offer came amid the furor in Washington over the *New York Times* publication of the Pentagon Papers, which indicates that the publication had no impact on the secret peace talks. One of Nixon's and Kissinger's arguments in their campaign against Daniel Ellsberg and the *New York Times* for its publication of the Pentagon Papers was the threat such leaks posed to secret diplomacy.

† Both Hanoi and the PRG stood firm in three important aspects of their mid-1971 peace proposals: The final withdrawal of American troops had to take place before the end of the year; the withdrawals would not be contingent on a prior political settlement in Saigon; and the American prisoners of war would be released as American troops were withdrawn, with both the troop withdrawal and the POW release to be completed at the same time.

drawal of the American troops, Tho told Lewis, "agreement on the modalities of troop withdrawal and prisoner issue will not be difficult." But, Tho added, if Nixon accepted the offer and insisted on linking it to a ceasefire—which, as Tho knew and Lewis did not, had consistently been done in the secret talks— "then it cannot be settled in that way because the ceasefire throughout Indochina will raise many other problems." In addition, Tho said, the United States, if it accepted the North Vietnamese proposal, must stop supplying military aid to Saigon and also must renounce the right to use military force in any way in South Vietnam, and thus would be barred from bombing and shelling in support of Saigon's troops. Tho was, in essence, offering the White House two ways out of the Vietnam War. It could have what its critics in Congress, the press, and the antiwar movement demanded: a total withdrawal of American troops and support elements—including aircraft—by a fixed date in return for the release of the American prisoners of war and a North Vietnamese and Vietcong ceasefire against all Americans to insure their safe withdrawal. If Nixon and Kissinger chose to seek a more comprehensive settlement, involving a political settlement in Saigon and their much-desired ceasefire throughout Southeast Asia, Tho suggested, the United States could take advantage of the presidential elections in Saigon. "The election in South Vietnam will be decided by the United States," Tho told Lewis. "It is . . . an opportunity for Mr. Nixon to change Thieu. It is a yardstick to show whether Mr. Nixon desires a peaceful settlement to this war or not." * Tho's proposal for a quick end to American involvement, as given to the *Times,* was obviously unacceptable to Nixon and Kissinger. They feared that without a ceasefire and without the right to use air power, Thieu's regime would collapse within weeks. Not even the return of the prisoners was worth that; maintaining Thieu in power had become the *raison d'être* of the war. Hanoi, by making its proposals public, had put the White House on the spot. There was a chance to end American involvement and get the prisoners back without a prior dissolution of the Thieu regime, but the risks were too great for the President and his adviser.

Nixon and Kissinger in their memoirs depicted the Tho interview as being a misleading attempt by the North Vietnamese to suggest to the American antiwar movement that Nixon would not accept a prisoners-for-withdrawal trade, even if one were possible. In the White House view, Hanoi had abused the secret talks.† It was in this period that some of Kissinger's NSC aides first

---

* In an interview six months later, Xuan Thuy explained that his government was convinced that if the Nixon Administration had agreed to set a precise date for withdrawal prior to the Vietnamese elections, and if an honest election had been held, President Thieu would not have been reelected. It was on the basis of that belief, Thuy said, that Hanoi was willing to separate the military and political issues of the war, and permit the Americans to withdraw and get back their prisoners of war. Thuy, who was interviewed by Richard Barnet and Peter Weiss in early February 1972, shortly after the Nixon Administration made public the secret peace talks in Paris, depicted the 1971 Vietnamese elections as a "farce" and added that the United States did not "seize the opportunity" to get out of the war "with honor." By early 1972, North Vietnam had again hardened its demands, and insisted that Thieu must be removed before any agreement could be reached.

† Nixon, who spent much of the summer falsely reassuring the American people that the United States would remain neutral in the Saigon elections, seemed to be perpetually surprised that Hanoi would try to interfere directly with *his* propagandizing. By 1971, it was widely understood among those who knew of the secret peace talks that Hanoi, merely by agreeing to the talks, had provided the White House with a major political asset. Smyser recalls that he was always aware of

heard talk of making the secret negotiations public. "It was our eagerness for a breakthrough," Kissinger wrote, "that made us preserve a secrecy which enabled our cynical adversaries to whipsaw us between a public position we dare not rebut and a private record we could not publish." In their memoirs, Nixon and Kissinger both insisted that they had formally proposed what the antiwar movement sought in mid-1971—a direct prisoners-for-withdrawal trade—and been turned down by Hanoi. In fact, no such deal had ever been offered, in public or in private, by the White House. The American offer of total withdrawal was always preconditioned on an immediate ceasefire throughout Indochina, and it was that offer that had been repeatedly rejected by the North Vietnamese.

Nixon and Kissinger must have understood the real message of the Le Duc Tho interview and the Communist peace offer in mid-1971: There was a way out if the White House insured a fair election in Saigon. They chose not to respond.

The American position was at odds with itself. Kissinger had insisted during the nearly two years of secret talks with Hanoi that a settlement could be reached in the South if North Vietnam's leaders would agree to abide by the results of an "internationally supervised" election. Now that Hanoi indicated some willingness to chance the electoral process, Kissinger's attitude underwent a metamorphosis. The United States had no faith in the South Vietnamese electoral process, and those who did, Kissinger wrote, were naïve: "In the United States there were many sincere and concerned individuals who thought that a fair democratic process in South Vietnam would unlock the door to negotiations. Why this should be so was never explained."

The North Vietnamese would come to understand the extent of American manipulation of the election process during the first peace talks in 1971. By late June, when Le Duc Tho and his colleagues were suggesting that there was a political way out of the Vietnam morass, the South Vietnamese election had already been fixed. The large CIA station in Saigon, then headed by Theodore G. Shackley, a hard-nosed careerist, had been preparing for more than a year, pouring millions of dollars into Thieu's private campaign treasury and helping him set up political support groups to give his candidacy the appearance of broad-based endorsement. All this was approved by Kissinger and Nixon, who were receiving the usual backchannel messages from Shackley and others that summer. The CIA and the top layer of the American Embassy, led by Ellsworth Bunker, the senior Foreign Service career officer, who was then seventy-five years old, agreed with the White House that Thieu had to be reelected and that the administration had to do all it could privately to make it happen. The risk of such an undertaking was high, and Bunker and the White House knew it.

In early 1971, the political section of the American Embassy had begun reporting that Thieu would be an easy reelection winner in a two-way race against General Minh, but would be seriously imperiled if Vice President Ky

---

the leverage such talks gave Nixon and Kissinger, for they could decide to make them public at a time of their choosing, describe them in any manner they saw fit, and reap the political benefits.

also ran. Thieu's response was to propose legislation that would require presidential candidates to have the endorsement of either forty members of the South Vietnamese National Assembly or one hundred provincial officials. Once this bill was rammed through the legislature, Thieu, aided by the CIA and its seemingly inexhaustible supply of money, planned to bribe those legislators most likely to support Ky and thus keep him off the ballot. By early spring, the embassy's political officers, unaware of the Thieu-CIA plotting, were warning of potential trouble if the election was rigged. They predicted that if the Thieu government excluded Ky from the race, the probability was high that General Minh would also withdraw, leaving Thieu unopposed. ". . . [S]uch a situation would intensify Vietnamese cynicism toward the political system," one classified embassy report said on March 31, "undercut Thieu's legitimacy and invite plotting against him. The political instability that would ensue could represent a serious threat to American policy objectives."

The unconstitutionality of Thieu's election-law gambit further distressed many of the junior pacification and Foreign Service officers in Vietnam, who were convinced that an honest election was essential to the survival of South Vietnam. A small group of AID workers in South Vietnam, who had resigned their government jobs, got together in early 1971 and formed the Vietnam Elections Project to lobby Congress and the White House for honest elections. Headed by Theodore Jacqueney, who had spent eighteen months in the Danang City Advisory Group, the Project meant to convince Washington that the defeat of Thieu in the election would not turn the South pro-Communist. Jacqueney and his colleagues believed that General Minh, if he were the victor in a three-way race with Ky and Thieu, would immediately seek an accommodation with the PRG. But, Jacqueney argued in one analysis prepared in early 1971, Minh "is not a supporter of the [Communist] 'Front,' nor is he likely to simply knuckle under to the will of Hanoi." Later that spring, Jacqueney met with Frank Mankiewicz, the former press aide to the late Senator Robert F. Kennedy who was then writing a syndicated newspaper column with Tom Braden, one of Kissinger's close friends. Jacqueney wanted advice on where to go with his Project, and Mankiewicz arranged a meeting with Kissinger. "I did it," Mankiewicz recalls, "because I believed—perhaps naïvely—that Jacqueney might have some impact and that Henry might be scared that these guys would talk openly." *

Four members of the Project, which was operating on a shoestring out of Jacqueney's apartment, attended a session on May 8 in Kissinger's White House offices. Taking notes for Kissinger was Sven Kraemer, a junior NSC aide who was among the most fervent hardliners on the staff. The naïveté of the former AID workers was considerable. "We thought maybe he [Kissinger]

---

* Mankiewicz had met Kissinger early in 1968, when Kissinger was working in the Rockefeller campaign. After Kennedy was assassinated in June 1968, Mankiewicz had some further meetings with Kissinger before the Republican convention. "I gave him a few ideas on the [Vietnam] war for Rocky. After Nixon was elected," Mankiewicz says, "I talked to Henry again because it occurred to me that he was getting no advice on Latin America and didn't know anything about Latin America." Mankiewicz had been Latin American director for the Peace Corps before joining Kennedy's staff. He met secretly with Kissinger throughout the spring and summer of 1969, Mankiewicz recalls, by slipping through a side door in the Executive Office Building and walking to his White House basement office. That relationship ended in the fall, when the Nixon Administration's policy on Vietnam became clear.

wasn't in control'' and didn't realize what was happening at lower levels in Vietnam, says Richard Winslow. The men gave the unusually quiet and attentive Kissinger a summary of the importance of the Third Force in Vietnam, and described the ways the United States representatives were working to rig the election in favor of Thieu. "We were telling the guy who made the policy that this was his policy—in case he didn't know it," Winslow remembers ruefully. Another participant, Oliver Davidson, describes the meeting as the "high point" of the group's lobbying activity. "You could really see Kissinger at work. He listened and listened and then he asked very pointed questions to determine whether we had anything he wanted to know." Kissinger's goal, as Davidson quickly sensed, was to find out "who we were and what was behind us, who was funding us. He was evaluating first of all the information we were giving him, and second of all who we were, and whether we had any influence on anyone and whether he should pay attention to us."

Jerry Ruback, the fourth participant, says that Kissinger portrayed himself as " 'Here I am lonely and brilliant, holding out against all my peers.' He seemed to be surprised about what we were telling him, but it was impossible that he didn't know it." At one point, Ruback was struck with how theoretical and abstract the issue seemed to Kissinger, who told the group: "You know, of course, it won't be a perfect election; these people aren't like us. . . ." The ground rules for the meeting were one-sided: Jacqueney and his colleagues were committed to secrecy, but Kissinger was free to make any use he wanted of the session. The Kissinger meeting was indeed a high point of sorts for the Project, whose members watched dispiritedly as everything they urged not to have happen in the Vietnamese elections did happen, and as they found it impossible to arrange a promised second meeting with Kissinger. Despite commitments from prominent liberal Democrats, funds were hard to come by, and within months the Vietnam Election Project was no more.*

In the late spring and summer of 1971, a stream of official announcements attested to American neutrality in the elections. On April 24, Secretary of State Rogers declared that "we are working diligently on plans to make sure that we are not only fair and impartial, but that we appear to be fair and impartial."

---

* For the next eighteen months, Jacqueney continued to lobby Congress and testify whenever asked on the necessity for a coalition government in Saigon, but he got little media attention. He committed suicide in 1979. Oliver Davidson remains bitter about the failure of antiwar liberals to support the Project. "Here we were—all of us out of work—all back from Vietnam; having really put our guts on the line. We were just asking for small contributions to keep the project going. We thought it was doing some good." At one point, Davidson says, the group visited Sargent Shriver, the former Ambassador to France, who was to be George McGovern's running mate in 1972. Shriver had encouraged the formation of the Project, and they were distressed to hear him "complain about all the bills and all the obligations he had to meet." Ironically, the only senior Nixon Administration official who paid the group any attention was Secretary of State Rogers. Jacqueney and his colleagues managed that spring to get resolutions introduced in the House and Senate calling for American supervision of the Vietnamese elections. The resolutions did not pass but won support from Rogers, who seemed to have no idea what the real Nixon-Kissinger policy toward the Vietnamese elections was. On May 24, 1971, Rogers sent Nixon a secret memorandum recommending that the administration "discreetly encourage passage" of the resolutions. If they did not pass Congress, Rogers added, the President should consider the appointment of a "national commission of distinguished citizens" as his personal representatives to demonstrate "the deep and legitimate interest of the US government in the survival of constitutional government in Vietnam." The President, of course, did no such thing.

On May 19, Ambassador Bunker issued instructions for American personnel in Vietnam directing them to "avoid implying by word, deed or acts of presence that the United States supports any individual candidate or group of candidates or political party for elective office." Kissinger, en route to China in early July, visited Saigon for highly visible meetings with Vice President Ky and General Minh. The *Washington Post* reported that Saigon was "buzzing" with rumors about the real reason for Kissinger's stopover. South Vietnamese politicians told the *Post* they did not accept the official explanation that Kissinger had come only to listen, and not to suggest or dictate. "It's the same old story," the *Post* quoted an American official as saying. "The South Vietnamese believe that everything that happens is according to an elaborate American plan. We only wish it were that simple."

Of course it was. With the tacit concurrence of the White House, President Thieu had been encouraged to utilize all of his government's apparatus to insure his reelection. The Vietnamese secret police organizations, including the much-feared Phoenix program, were instructed to reach into the hamlets and villages and threaten citizens with arrest or unfavorable reports if they opposed Thieu. Other steps were less dramatic but equally effective; for example, the government simply did not distribute voting cards in the areas where Thieu was not popular.* Like Richard Nixon, Nguyen Van Thieu ran scared. So did the CIA. Frank Snepp, then a political analyst for the CIA in Saigon, recalled in an interview that the station was deeply involved in aiding President Thieu's successful attempt to legislate Vice President Ky out of the election. By then, the embassy had informed Washington that Thieu's insistence on getting rid of Ky would undoubtedly result in a decision by General Minh to withdraw, leaving Thieu unopposed and making a mockery of the process. Despite such warnings, which proved accurate, the CIA became directly involved in bribing members of the National Assembly to insure that the legislation was passed and that Ky could not obtain enough signatures to run. The CIA had a special reason for working against Ky: He was considered an unstable opportunist who could not be controlled. "The antagonism toward Ky was unabating," Snepp says; the Agency was genuinely afraid of him. By mid-1971, according to Snepp, Theodore Shackley was repeatedly boasting in his backchannel messages to Kissinger—known as "Shackleygrams" in the station—that the CIA's effort had produced the votes needed for approval of Thieu's election law. The many junior Foreign Service officers in the embassy and throughout Saigon who were reporting rising discontent with Thieu were apparently cut out of the action. "If Bunker told the [CIA] station to go out and pay people off," Snepp says, "they did it. The State Department might not even have known what was going on." The CIA's role in easing Ky out

* American pacification workers, under the supervision of William E. Colby, a career CIA official who later became Agency director, had conducted extensive surveys throughout South Vietnam in an attempt to measure security as well as political support for Thieu. In one such survey, in November 1970, Vietnamese citizens were asked, "What kind of man should be elected next September?" and "What issue will you consider most important in deciding who to vote for in the next election?" The results were classified and submitted to President Thieu and his political advisers, who made use of the information in the 1971 elections. Such overt abuse of the surveys created dissension inside the pacification effort, and eventually led to an exposé in the *New York Times* in early 1971, written by Gloria Emerson.

was known to only a few Americans; even the normally well-informed Kissinger aide Richard Smyser said later that he had been unaware of the Agency's deep involvement.

The PRG and the North Vietnamese, who had infiltrated most levels of the South Vietnamese government, must have suspected some, if not all, of the American moves. In his memoirs, Kissinger made a feeble effort to cover his tracks: "As the [Saigon] campaign progressed, I thought that Thieu was acting unwisely in using his incumbency to discourage rival candidacies." It was with that in mind, as well as the Paris talks, that he decided to visit Saigon in early July—"to emphasize our interest in a contested election. . . . But neither Nixon nor I was prepared to toss Thieu to the wolves; indeed . . . there was no practical way to do so." Kissinger seemed to believe that Hanoi—then heavily involved in the Paris talks—would accept his visit to Saigon at face value and ignore the evidence of American bad faith in the election process. The delusion continued during the next Paris meeting, which took place on July 12, as Kissinger was on the way back from Peking. There were three more hours of detailed and serious negotiations with Le Duc Tho that ultimately came down to the question of political power in Saigon. Kissinger quotes Le Duc Tho as saying to him: "I tell you in a serious way that you have to replace Thieu. . . . You have many means"—an obvious reference to the pending elections. Kissinger remained convinced that a settlement was in the offing: "For some intoxicating weeks we thought that we might have a simultaneous breakthrough toward peace in Vietnam and toward China; Winston Lord and I on the way back from seeing Le Duc Tho [on July 12] had sufficient hubris to speculate on which would be considered historically the more significant achievement." Kissinger, with his dreams of glory, seemed unable to understand the link between what he and Nixon were doing on Thieu's behalf in Saigon and the success or failure of the peace talks.

Kissinger and the North Vietnamese agreed upon a fourth meeting in Paris on July 26. In a memorandum delivered to Nixon a few days before the meeting, Kissinger told the President what he wanted to hear: Peace must not come at the price of overturning the South Vietnamese government. "It is obvious that we cannot do their political work for them," Kissinger wrote. "For all his faults, Thieu has been a loyal ally." Somehow the two men continued to miss the point: that the election offered a way around the Thieu dilemma. By late July, nonetheless, chances for a contested election in Saigon were becoming remote. Vice President Ky would be forced to withdraw if the South Vietnamese Supreme Court ruled, as the Thieu regime had made sure it would, that he was not eligible because of his inability to collect enough valid signatures, and General Minh announced that he would withdraw if Ky did. This would leave the White House spending millions in covert support of Thieu in a one-candidate election. The July 26 meeting in Paris produced nothing. "Le Duc Tho and Xuan Thuy had no interest in an American pledge of neutrality or in a free political process that they disdained," Kissinger wrote, as if the American promises of neutrality and fair elections were credible.*

---

* At the July 26 meeting, Kissinger wrote in his memoirs, Le Duc Tho took him aside and suggested "that if we did not know how to replace Thieu by means of the presidential election, assassination would do admirably." He protested vehemently, Kissinger wrote, flustering Le Duc Tho. Later, when I mentioned the allegation, the men in Hanoi grew very angry. "It's not true,"

Washington's response to the stalemate in Paris was more public relations. Much of the political panic of early 1971 was over: Nixon and Kissinger had not only pulled off the backchannel SALT negotiations with the Soviet Union but had delivered China. The President's popularity climbed dramatically after the July 15 announcement of the China breakthrough, and by September he was running well ahead of Muskie in the Gallup and Harris polls; he would increase his lead steadily until the end of the year. Kissinger was famous as the man who made the secret trip to mysterious Peking. It was the optimal time, both men knew, to tough it out in Vietnam. At a news conference on August 4, Nixon said, "Our position is one of complete neutrality in these elections. We have, under Ambassador Bunker's skillful direction, made it clear to all parties concerned that we are not supporting any candidate, that we will accept the verdict of the people of South Vietnam." Such bald assertions always seemed to work—at least in the first term.

On August 6, to the surprise of no one in the White House, the Supreme Court of South Vietnam ruled that Vice President Ky was disqualified from the campaign. The political situation was ideal for President Thieu and his backers in Washington: a campaign against General Minh, with Thieu in full control of the nationwide election apparatus. Over the next few weeks, the election process became even more farcical. In mid-August, General Minh obtained a twenty-page document, marked "Top Secret," which outlined a systematic election-fraud scheme on the part of the Thieu regime. It described how the bureaucratic apparatus of the Saigon government, with the police forces and the Army, would insure Thieu's reelection. Minh met with Ambassador Bunker and demanded that he publicly support his charges of fraud. Bunker refused. "My feeling was that it was not authentic," he said of the document. There was a very basic reason for his belief, Bunker recalled in an interview: "It wasn't necessary to write it. [Thieu] had control of the apparatus of government anyway." Other embassy officials recalled that the CIA was assigned the task of evaluating the document and concluded that it was authentic.

On August 20, General Minh withdrew from the presidential race. Bunker, apparently responding to backchannel orders from the White House, visited Minh at his home and, according to evidence that came to light years later, offered him a bribe of $3 million to remain in the race.* Bunker's visit with

---

Nguyen Co Thach said. "It went something like this: he [Le Duc Tho] told Henry Kissinger that they have replaced their stooges many times in many places in the world, so they have enough imagination to do it again. Le Duc Tho said nothing about this assassination of Thieu."

* The most specific documentation for the bribe offer, which was known in Saigon at the time but was heatedly denied by Bunker and others, came in a 1978 deposition taken in a Freedom of Information Lawsuit filed by Frank Snepp, who left the CIA in 1976 and subsequently published a brilliant book, *Decent Interval,* about the last years of American involvement in South Vietnam. It was widely known that the CIA had wiretapped both Thieu's private quarters and his office in the Presidential Palace, but the Agency's efforts—as the lawsuit made clear—also extended to the residence of General Minh. Ambassador Bunker had been careful to speak privately with Minh in August 1971, when the bribe offer was made, but in a deposition in the Snepp case, a CIA official acknowledged that the Agency had tapes "in which Ambassador Bunker offered to finance [national security deletion] race for the Presidency. [deletion] notes that the amount of $3 million was not mentioned in that conversation, although the basic report by Snepp is true." Snepp alleged in his book, published in 1977, that the bribe offer was $3 million.

General Minh came shortly after the Ambassador's return from a brief trip to Washington. His orders also apparently included the simple assignment of persuading President Thieu to get the Supreme Court of South Vietnam to reverse itself. After Bunker saw Thieu at the palace, Thieu did order the Supreme Court to change its decision, but it was too little, too late even for Ky, whose tolerance of official corruption was known to be high. Most American journalists seemed resigned to the corruption in Saigon, perhaps because they did not know how deeply Washington was involved in it. In a column published August 24, 1971, Joseph Kraft wrote: "There is no point in getting angry about the fix that has so obviously been put in on the South Vietnamese presidential election. Rigging elections is as usual for Vietnam as hot weather in August." The White House, in the person of Ron Ziegler, struck an upbeat note: Thieu's subsequent decision to go ahead with the election and depict it as a vote of confidence, Ziegler told the press on September 2, was an attempt "to introduce an element of popular choice to the election." Few in South Vietnam agreed. Protest riots broke out in Saigon and Thieu ordered his National Police to "shoot down anyone who attempts to burn vehicles in the street."

All this was closely watched, of course, by the North Vietnamese, who had listened politely at the fifth secret meeting of the year, on August 16, when Kissinger offered what he termed a "specific proposal for American neutrality" in the Vietnamese presidential elections. The promise of neutrality was accompanied by a restatement of the May 31 proposal with one modification: America now offered to withdraw all its troops nine months after the signing of a final peace agreement. Hanoi was still being asked to agree to a ceasefire throughout Indochina before a final political agreement was reached, and to attempt to carry out its political operations in the South under the Thieu regime and the constitution of South Vietnam.* On September 13 the two sides met again, in secret, with the negotiations in deadlock. Le Duc Tho had missed the August meeting and chose to stay away again in September, an expression of Hanoi's contempt for the election process in Saigon. It was left to Xuan Thuy to make clear that nothing could be accomplished.

Nguyen Co Thach later insisted that his government was willing to settle for a coalition government in Saigon in late 1971, at a time when military conditions in the South were not favorable. "At that time we had many, many losses in the South," he said. "The control of the biggest part of the South was under the South. Our offer was in good faith because we would like to have the withdrawal of the American troops" from South Vietnam. "But Nixon and Kissinger were not wise," Thach said. "With a coalition government they could have withdrawn with a ceasefire"—the ceasefire that the White House so badly desired throughout 1971. "When the United States refused to let Thieu face an honest election in 1971," Thach added, "by this we realized that the biggest goal of Nixon and Kissinger was the maintenance of the Saigon government, and not the sharing of power with the PRG. We see that they would like to have all the cake."

* Frank Snepp remembers that at about this point in August the NLF began an unusually large recruitment drive in the Vietnamese countryside, going so far as to lower the age requirement for enlistment. Hanoi had written off the 1971 elections and was planning its 1972 offensive.

In his memoirs, Kissinger expressed satisfaction with the 1971 election results in Saigon: "We considered support for the political structure in Saigon not a favor done to Thieu but an imperative of our national interest. We weathered the storm. It would be preposterous to maintain that Hanoi lamented the absence of a fair election in Saigon. What bothered it was our refusal to use the election as a pretext to decapitate the leadership of the non-Communist political structure in South Vietnam." To arrive at that conclusion Kissinger had to overlook the warnings issued not only by the critics but by some of the administration's leading experts on South Vietnam. On August 17, for example, Samuel D. Berger, the Deputy Ambassador in Saigon, who seemed far less willing than Bunker to go along blindly with the White House's backchannel directives, cabled in all seriousness that if Thieu decided "to go through with a one-man sham election, he will become subject to growing opposition which would soon require repressive measures. . . . The outlook therefore would be for growing political instability." *

Nixon's concern was not political instability in South Vietnam but in the United States. On September 10, Senator Henry Jackson threatened in a Senate speech to oppose further aid to Saigon if the Nixon Administration did not help arrange a "genuine" election in Saigon. Jackson's statement was prompted by expediency as much as by morality; as his political aides told the New York Times, his speech represented a new and more liberal approach to the Vietnam problem in his unannounced drive for the Democratic presidential nomination. Jackson was important to the White House; he had been a bulwark for the administration against liberal attempts to cut off funding for Vietnam and against a concerted effort that fall to stop the draft. A week after the Jackson speech, Kissinger warned Nixon that "the momentum for rapid disengagement was rising. We now faced the real danger that Congressional legislation would set an obligatory date for our withdrawals and perhaps limit our assistance to South Vietnam." He proposed a new offer to the North Vietnamese in Paris: a commitment to a presidential election in the South six months after the signing of a final agreement. The election would be run by an electoral commission that would include Communists, and Thieu would resign the presidency one month before the election. Alexander Haig was sent to Saigon on September 22 and obtained Thieu's acquiescence, but Haig, carrying out orders, did not tell the South Vietnamese President that the election commission proposal would be presented to the North Vietnamese at the Paris peace talks

* In August also, Berger informed the State Department of a constitutional ploy that could be invoked in an effort to avoid a one-man election. Under Article 56 of the constitution, if the nation's president were to resign from office, new elections could be ordered by the chairman of the Vietnamese Senate. If Thieu could be persuaded to resign, Berger told Washington, "presumably Vice President Ky would be willing to cooperate in the hope that he would be able to present his candidacy under the new election law that would then become necessary." Although it was totally clear to all involved that Thieu would never agree to such a scheme, Berger and his counterparts in the State Department seriously debated the pros and cons of the suggestion in a series of cables over the next week. The debate came to an end when Bunker returned to Saigon, after his brief visit to Washington, and reported that Thieu would have nothing to do with the proposal. "It has been and remains our view, however," Bunker added sharply, "that an uncontested election is viewed with greater concern in the US than in SVN [South Vietnam]." Kissinger also got involved in the debate, an NSC aide recalled, and again warned the Saigon embassy to do nothing to undermine Thieu. The State Department cables about Article 56 were declassified in 1981, after a Freedom of Information Act request.

within a few weeks.* Washington's new offer was submitted in writing to the North Vietnamese by Nixon's old friend, General Vernon Walters, on October 11, eight days after Thieu's reelection, reportedly with 94 percent of the ballots cast.† Hanoi considered the new proposal insolent. "It was meaningless," Nguyen Co Thach said. "One month is not enough when they [the Saigon government] are working all the time to decide the election outcome."

The intent of the Nixon-Kissinger offer on October 11 is open to question. Hanoi's rejection of the proposal is described in harsh phrases in Kissinger's memoirs: ". . . Hanoi's grim and implacable leaders would compromise only as a last resort; protracted warfare was their proposal. . . . They were determined on another military throw of the dice." But by October it was the Nixon Administration that had decided on another "throw of the dice" and had ordered increased bombing raids over North Vietnam, under the increasingly thin veneer of "protective reaction," in what Kissinger described as an attempt to punish Hanoi for not responding in Paris. At his meeting in Paris with the North Vietnamese, General Walters formally requested another secret negotiating session for November 1. November 20 was agreed upon, but shortly before then, Nixon and Kissinger were informed that Le Duc Tho had "suddenly become ill" and only Xuan Thuy would be available on the twentieth. Xuan Thuy wouldn't do, and the talks were suspended by Washington. Nguyen Co Thach later acknowledged that—as Kissinger had to know—Hanoi considered further talks after Thieu's reelection to be useless. "Le Duc Tho was sick, really," Thach said, "and that was one cause. Another cause was that we saw in the context of the time that it was not propitious after the election of Thieu. The Nixon government was going ahead with its plan, and so it was useless of us to meet at this time." Hanoi's next move would be military.

If the October 11 peace offer made no diplomatic sense, it did make good domestic politics. With the failure of the 1971 negotiations, Nixon and Kissinger knew that they were going to take the secret peace talks public at a time in 1972 when such a relevation would have the most impact. Both men believed (and apparently still believe, according to their memoirs) that the American peace offers in 1971 were good enough—if not for the North Vietnamese, then at least for the American public. Nixon especially seemed convinced that he and Kissinger had offered a straightforward trade—American troop withdrawal for American prisoners of war—and that Hanoi had turned them down in private, while publicly telling reporters and visiting politicians that they would accept such a deal, if only one were offered.‡ One early sign of Nixon's

---

* In his memoirs, Kissinger wrote that although Thieu approved of the revised peace offer, he was not told that it had been presented to the North Vietnamese until shortly before Nixon decided to make the secret talks public in late January 1972. The White House's handling of the issue led to some "touchy encounters in Saigon," Kissinger wrote.

† Kissinger cited that statistic, given out publicly by the Saigon government, as a demonstrable fact in his memoirs, and also reported that 87 percent of those eligible voted across the country. Robert Shaplen, the *New Yorker* magazine's correspondent in Southeast Asia, noted a few weeks after the election that "Very few observers here, Vietnamese or foreign, believe . . . the official figures. The best estimates are that in the countryside fifty or sixty percent of those eligible voted, and in Saigon and other major cities something like thirty or forty percent." Shaplen's statistics raise obvious questions: Did Kissinger know the true results but suppress them in his memoirs? Did he fall victim to his/Thieu's propaganda machine?

‡ In his memoirs, Nixon cited a talk Senator George McGovern had with Xuan Thuy in September 1971. "Afterward," Nixon wrote, "McGovern told reporters that he had been assured

desire to go public may have come at a news conference on August 4 when the President, asked about the peace talks, said: "The record, when it finally comes out, will answer all the critics as far as the activity of this Government in pursuing negotiations in established channels." By then, NSC aides recall, Kissinger had repeatedly discussed the merits of making the secret talks public. Were that to be done in an election year, the October 11 proposal, with its seemingly bold offer of a one-month presidential resignation by Thieu, would play well in the media. That the offer came eight days after the farcical election in Saigon, the White House correctly foresaw, would not attract much comment.

By late fall of 1971, Nixon and Kissinger had reason to believe they had weathered another potential crisis in Vietnam. The Vietnamese constitution had been ignored and the White House choice had stayed in power. Politically, Nixon had emerged from the intensive secret negotiations with an ace in the hole: He would go public with the secret negotiations at a time of his choosing, to present the image of a frustrated man of peace who was willing to go more than halfway. The pending summit meetings in Peking and Moscow were essential factors in his political revival. Nixon began a news conference on October 12, just after Thieu's reelection, by announcing that a date had been set for the summit in Moscow. He had achieved his goal with China and Russia, and those aspects inevitably dominated. Only two questions about Vietnam were asked. At a news conference a month later, Nixon announced another withdrawal, of 45,000 men over two months, reducing the troops that would be left in Vietnam by early 1972 to 140,000. He also warned that American bombing in support of the South Vietnamese would continue indefinitely, "until there is a negotiated settlement or . . . until the South Vietnamese have developed the capability to handle the situation themselves." The withdrawals dominated the news.

All this had a positive effect on Nixon's rating in the polls, in which he continued to lead all Democratic challengers, including Senators Muskie and Kennedy. "We had made the two great Communist powers collaborators in holding our home front together," Kissinger exulted in his memoirs. On his second trip to Peking, in October, Kissinger discussed Vietnam at length with Chou En-lai, and explicitly told the Chinese what he had never said to Le Duc

---

that the North Vietnamese would return all our POW's as soon as we agreed to set a date for our withdrawal." The next line, printed in italics for added emphasis, is: "These were exactly the terms that we had offered on May 31, 1971, and they had rejected on June 26, 1981." Nixon added that when Kissinger asked Xuan Thuy about "this duplicity" at the next secret meeting, Thuy replied, "What Senator McGovern says is his problem." Nixon believed that Hanoi had somehow been treacherous, but in fact the White House, as noted earlier, always insisted that a ceasefire throughout Indochina accompany any agreement providing for the exchange of prisoners and a complete American pullout. Nixon's terms called for Hanoi to cease its activities in Laos and Cambodia, as well as in South Vietnam. McGovern remembers that he and his aides found it nearly impossible to get the American press to report that important precondition. "I knew what was going on," he says, "but it was like beating into a fog. None of this was getting on the network news." McGovern, one of the leading opponents of the Vietnam War, marveled at the White House's ability to manipulate the American press: "They orchestrated this thing to the point where they almost had the public convinced we went to see the Vietnamese to bring back some prisoners from Hanoi. Time after time I tried to explain, but somehow they always seemed to be able to market it to the press."

Tho. Nguyen Co Thach recalled that a message from Peking came within days of Kissinger's visit: "The Chinese told us that Kissinger had told them the United States would accept the withdrawal of [North Vietnamese] troops from Laos and Cambodia, but not from South Vietnam." North Vietnam could keep its troops in the South. Hanoi told Peking, Thach said, that "The Americans must say this directly to us." Hanoi had been stung by Kissinger's first secret mission to Peking in July; China, along with the Soviet Union, had been a firm ally and major supplier of food and weaponry during the long war. China's policy turnaround was difficult for the Hanoi leadership to comprehend, because the Peking government had protested vehemently when North Vietnam agreed to begin the negotiations with the Johnson Administration that led to the November 1968 bombing halt. Hanoi later said that Peking—then at the height of its Cultural Revolution—had even cut back on its flow of military goods in protest. Shortly after Kissinger's first visit, however, Peking had begun pressuring Hanoi to accept a political compromise in Saigon and thus accept continued control by the Thieu government. China also increased its shipments of supplies after Kissinger's visit, in an apparent attempt, as Hanoi saw it, to increase its leverage on North Vietnamese decision making.

In November 1971, after Kissinger's second visit to Peking, Prime Minister Pham Van Dong of North Vietnam agreed to visit the Chinese. He had turned down an earlier invitation, proffered within days of the first Kissinger visit, Nguyen Co Thach recalled. Thach, then the leading specialist on North American affairs in Hanoi, accompanied his Prime Minister. There was a tense meeting with Mao Tse-tung, Thach said. "Mao told my Prime Minister: 'Your victory has forced Nixon to come to Peking.' He said Nixon was coming [for the summit meeting in February 1972] to discuss Vietnam and Korean questions." Discussing the Vietnam War, Mao cited what he said was an old Chinese proverb: "If the handle of your broom is very short, you cannot wipe out a spider high on the wall of a closet. So you must allow it to stay." Thach supplied the translation: "The Chinese broom is very short and we must let Chiang Kai-shek stay on in Taiwan, and so Vietnam has a short broom and so Pham Van Dong must let Thieu stay on."

"He was arguing for Nixon," Thach said. "Mao was telling us to maintain the status quo." Pham Van Dong replied: "Excuse me, but the handle of the Vietnamese broom is long enough to sweep all of these dogs out of Vietnam." Mao wasn't happy, Thach recalled, but neither were the North Vietnamese. Pham Van Dong asked Mao not to receive Nixon, but he was told that the visit was a commitment. Hanoi had also asked its Soviet allies not to receive Nixon, Thach said, but they too declared the visit to be a commitment.

Nixon and Kissinger were pleased with their triangular diplomacy. If this was Nixon's secret plan to end the war—bringing political pressure from Russia and China on the North Vietnamese—he got what he wanted. There were other pressures. In November 1971, the Seventh Air Force, then under the control of "protective reaction" General John D. Lavelle, began a series of strikes on strategic targets in the southern parts of North Vietnam, including fuel depots and airfields. Full-scale American bombing raids, authorized by Nixon, took place over a two-day period in December in the same areas.

Strongly worded diplomatic notes were also sent that month to Moscow and Peking, warning, as Kissinger wrote in his memoirs, that "an offensive would evoke the most serious retaliation." The threat strategy was at work again.

Nixon and Kissinger had missed an opportunity to ease Nguyen Van Thieu out of office and negotiate a settlement of the war before Hanoi's military offensive began. Now they were forced to return to a bankrupt and brutal strategy that offered victory only at the cost of the ultimate destruction of Vietnam by American bombers. Hanoi may have misjudged Nixon once again. He was prepared—perhaps even eager—to respond to an offensive by ordering B-52 bombers to target the most populated areas of North Vietnam. "We knew we would face an offensive in 1972," Kissinger wrote. "The outcome of the war would then depend on whether the South Vietnamese, aided only by American air power, would be able to blunt the assault." It was, in truth, not a strategy but a gamble.

In Hanoi, there was distress at the success of the Nixon-Kissinger triangular diplomacy, and anger at what was perceived as American arrogance in passing up a chance for a political solution in South Vietnam by refusing to allow a legitimate election. "Once Nixon went to Peking," Nguyen Co Thach said, "we knew that he would go also to Moscow and be received, because the question of Vietnam is not the sole question discussed between them. We Vietnamese, we always prepared for the worst. Never did we think things would come in an easy way, and if we are prepared for the worst, and the worst doesn't come—well, then?" Thach, who spent five hard years in a French prison near Hanoi as a Communist leader in the early 1940s, shrugged fatalistically.

"We reaffirmed our assessment that Kissinger and Nixon could not have good will with Vietnam," Thach recalled, "and so we must go forward with the offensive. We knew this will get Nixon very angry, because it will spoil his election, and he will return to his threats. But we also knew this one element must be considered: Big bombing [of the North] could not save Nixon in South Vietnam."

32

THE INDIA-PAKISTAN WAR

ON MARCH 25, 1971, President Yahya Khan of West Pakistan, who had been so useful in Washington's secret negotiations with Peking, ordered his army to begin a war against secessionist forces in East Pakistan. It was a war that many in South Asia considered inevitable, but the violence of the West Pakistani attack shocked the world. Yahya Khan's troops went on a rampage inside East Pakistan to eliminate the opposition systematically—by genocide. Pakistan's tensions and its violence were exacerbated by its unique geography: It was a partitioned nation of Moslems separated by more than a thousand miles of India, which has a Hindu majority. There had been elections in Pakistan the previous December that gave a strong rebuke to Yahya Khan's leadership. The Awami League, East Pakistan dissidents, who sought autonomy from the central government in the West, captured a majority of the seats in the national assembly. Yahya Khan responded by postponing the seating of the new government and ordering his army to make its sudden attack. Within days, all foreign correspondents were expelled from Dacca, East Pakistan's capital, and communications to the outside world were shut off. Over the next weeks and months, the West Pakistan Army expanded its march of horror, slaughtering Awami League supporters, students, and intellectuals on a scale not seen since the Third Reich. All Hindus, whether or not they were engaged in East Pakistan's political life, also became victims. Estimates of the killing ranged from 500,000 to three million. Within days, despite attempts at censorship, reports began appearing , many of them in London newspapers. There were accounts of mass graves, the murders of college students in their dormitories, and repeated descriptions of random assassination. The brutality was appalling. "Women were raped, or had their breasts torn out with specially fashioned knives," one West Pakistani journalist who fled reported in the London *Times*. "Children did not escape the horror: the lucky ones were killed with their parents; but many thousands of others must go through what life remains for them with eyes gouged out and limbs roughly amputated."

The State Department did not need the newspaper reports to learn what was going on. The American Consulate in Dacca maintained a clandestine radio transmitter and was able to send out graphic reports during the early days of the extermination. In one account, widely circulated in the State Department and to Henry Kissinger's aides on the NSC staff, Archer Blood, the ranking Foreign Service officer in Dacca, told of West Pakistani soldiers setting fire to

444

a women's dormitory at the University of Dacca and then calmly machine-gunning the students as they ran out.

Most nations immediately denounced the atrocities in East Pakistan, but the United States—at the specific direction of the White House—remained mute. On April 6, twenty Americans assigned to the consulate in Dacca filed a formal dissent from the American policy. "Our government has failed to denounce the suppression of democracy," the cable, transmitted as a priority message to Secretary of State Rogers, said. "Our government has failed to denounce atrocities . . . while at the same time bending over backwards to placate the [West Pakistan] government. . . . Private Americans have expressed disgust. We, as professional public servants, express our dissent with current policy and fervently hope that our true and lasting interests here can be defined and our policies redirected in order to salvage our nation's position as a moral leader of the Free World." A copy of the cable was endorsed by nine officials in the State Department and AID and forwarded to Rogers. By early April, even the Soviet Union had sent Yahya Khan a note defending democracy in East Pakistan and calling for an end to the bloodshed. One of Khan's first orders had been for his troops to arrest Sheik Mujibur Rahman, the popular leader of the Awami League. Many of Mujibur's political followers were less fortunate, and were immediately slaughtered.

For Nixon and Kissinger, there was no issue. Yahya Khan held the key to Nixon's reelection; their conduit to the Chinese would not be challenged. The policy was easy to rationalize: Those who were against Yahya Khan were pro-India and pro-Soviet Union. India, under Prime Minister Indira Gandhi, was drawn into the tragedy as millions of refugees, most of them Hindus, poured across the Indian border to sanctuary. India was a nation led by Hindus, and the Hindus of East Pakistan, roughly 10 percent of the population, had nowhere else to flee. The American Ambassador to India, former New York Senator Kenneth Keating, had been quick to express his shock and anger at the "massacre." In a dramatic cable to Washington on March 29 he urged the Nixon Administration to avoid "association with reign of military terror. . . . This is a time when principles make best policies." He recommended that the administration "promptly, publicly and prominently deplore this brutality. . . . It most important these actions be taken now, prior to inevitable and imminent emergence of horrible truths. . . ." There was no question where Nixon stood. He ordered Archer Blood transferred out of East Pakistan and, as Kissinger reported in his memoirs, ridiculed Keating for having been "taken over by the Indians." In his memoirs, the President said nothing about Yahya Khan's genocidal attack and wrote only of the "almost unbelievable cruelty of the fighting on both sides . . ."*

For many in the State Department, the tragedy was compounded by what seemed to be an appalling ignorance in the White House of the realities of

---

* Kissinger wrote, "There was no doubt about the *strong-arm tactics* of the Pakistani military [emphasis added]." Some of those in America who objected to the administration's silence about events in East Pakistan, he suggested, were not all that concerned about some dead South Asians but "had a vested interest in undermining their government's standing on whatever issue came to hand in the belief that this would collapse our effort in Vietnam."

South Asia. Unity had always been fragile in Pakistan, because the ethnic and political differences between West and East were far more important than their shared religion. The nation's economy was controlled by an elite minority of twenty-two families in West Pakistan who lived in royal style and educated their children at preparatory and military schools abroad. Political control also lay in the West, which had declared Urdu, its language, the national language of the East; in the West also, hundreds of millions of dollars were being spent constructing a lavish new capital at Islamabad. Pakistan's army was dominated by the Punjabis of the West, experienced warriors who had been trained by the English and fought with distinction for the British Empire. The Punjabis were taller and more fair-skinned than the Bengalis, their countrymen in the East, a tolerant, gentle and cultivated race that formed the largest part of the East's 75 million residents. After the British withdrawal in 1947, Hindus living in what was to become West Pakistan had fled in panic to India to avoid a wave of racially inspired assaults and murders. Hindus were far more easily assimilated in the East, and were able to remain there safely, though with occasional tension. There were strong feelings of racial superiority on the part of the Punjabis, who held the Bengalis of the East in contempt.

Life was harsh for the peasants of East Pakistan, who eked out meager livelihoods as farmers and fishermen threatened by monsoons, cyclones, and floods that struck regularly, killing thousands. The East, with its low-lying alluvial plains, was smaller but far more fertile than the West and produced nearly 80 percent of the world's jute crop and 50 percent of Pakistan's foreign currency. The political leaders of the East, led by the Awami League, felt that the absentee leaders in the West took far more than they returned.* Disease and illiteracy dominated peasant life, and by the late 1960s, the political leaders and the masses came to believe that it was time for East Pakistan to declare its autonomy from the military dictatorship of the West. In 1970, Yahya Khan, fulfilling a promise he had made—under political duress—to return the nation to civilian leadership and democracy, permitted national elections. The West was taken aback when candidates sponsored by the Awami League won 167 of 169 contested seats in the National Assembly, a victory that, theoretically, should have enabled Sheik Mujibur, the Awami leader, to become Prime Minister. But Yahya Khan, unwilling to allow a Bengali in such a high post, postponed the seating of the new National Assembly until late March and, late on the evening of March 25, ordered his army to arrest Mujibur and purge East Pakistan of his supporters.

Thus the genocide began. It would lead, by the end of the year, to a disastrous war with India, the end of Yahya Khan's regime, and the emergence of an independent Bangladesh led by the Awami League. It would also lead to a decision by Richard Nixon and Henry Kissinger to risk world war in a South Asia showdown with the Soviet Union. Nixon and Kissinger totally misread

* The Pakistani government, in a five-year planning study published in 1970, reported that per capita income was 61 percent higher in West Pakistan than in the East for the years 1969 and 1970. The Pakistani document was cited in a 1971 study circulated in Washington shortly after West Pakistan's assault by Edward S. Mason, Robert Dorfman, and Stephen A. Marglin, all of whom were advisers to the American government on foreign economic development. In their study, the professors also reported that East Pakistan had transferred about $2.6 billion in resources to the West in the twenty-year period ending in 1969. At the time, the population in West Pakistan was 55 million, six times larger than that of the East.

the situation, and the showdown they expected never took place. But if it had begun, and if China had decided to intervene on the side of West Pakistan, as Nixon and Kissinger convinced themselves it would, the United States was ready to do battle allied to China and against the Soviet Union. It was a series of misjudgments not equaled since the Jordanian crisis in the fall of 1970.

Yahya Khan's suppression of East Pakistan and his subsequent war with India managed again to bring out the worst in the White House. The basic Nixon-Kissinger goal was, of course, to protect the prospective opening to China, but there were other factors. Nixon hated Prime Minister Gandhi and viewed her as a deceitful "bitch," a view that Henry Kissinger was careful to emulate. Nixon had visited New Delhi in 1967, on his private tour around the world, and had been treated there with little ceremony, to his everlasting dissatisfaction. He remembered best a dinner with a leading Indian politician who was a vegetarian and did not drink. In Pakistan, however, it had gone much better. Yahya Khan, with his patrician manner and his military background, knew how to throw a good party with plenty of scotch. Nixon was a VIP.

Two years later, as President, Nixon visited Pakistan on another world tour and, in a ninety-minute private meeting with Yahya Khan, brought him a secret only a few would share—the United States wanted to normalize relations with China and wanted his help in exchanging messages. "It was almost a God-sent gift for Pakistan," G. W. Choudhury, one of Yahya Khan's close aides, later wrote. "Pakistan was greatly delighted to have this opportunity, as the Sino-Pakistan relationship was not only approved by the United States but the U.S. President sought to utilize it for improving ties with Peking. . . . I cannot say why Nixon chose the Pakistani President. . . . Yahya was altogether unknown to Nixon and he [was] also a novice in diplomacy."* In their memoirs, both Nixon and Kissinger saw their support for Yahya Khan during the upheavals as being global in nature. West Pakistan, China, and the United States were lined up against India and the Soviet Union, with East Pakistan serving as the battleground. ". . . Mrs. Gandhi had gradually become aligned with the Soviets," Nixon wrote, "and received substantial economic and military aid from Moscow. . . . With Moscow tied to New Delhi and Peking tied to Islamabad, the potential for the subcontinent's becoming a dangerous area of confrontation between Communist giants was great." He viewed the dispute between India and West Pakistan as essentially a question of whether "big nations supported by the Soviet Union would be permitted to dismember their smaller neighbors." The analysis was more than merely wrong: It was phantasmagorical. To protect his link to China and, later, the summit meeting in Peking, no price was too great, not even the butchery of hundreds of thousands of civilians in East Pakistan. Kissinger's function was to rationalize White House support for West Pakistan, and in his memoirs he devoted nearly eighty tortured pages to the attempt.

* Choudhury, who was Minister of Information in President Yahya's cabinet, fled to the United States after Yahya's demise. His analysis appeared in "Reflections on Sino-Pakistan Relations," *Pacific Community*, January 1976.

Yahya Khan began his violent attack on East Pakistan in March of 1971 convinced, he told close associates, that his special relationship with the United States and China would insulate him from retaliation. In October 1970, he had been pampered by Nixon and Kissinger during a visit to Washington; Yahya told Choudhury, who was part of his entourage, that Nixon assured him that "nobody has occupied the White House who is friendlier to Pakistan than me." A few weeks later, Yahya was given another effusive reception in Peking, where he relayed Nixon's message that the White House considered closer relations with China to be "essential." Choudhury later came to the conclusion that "If Nixon and Kissinger had not given him that false hope, he'd have been more realistic." Yahya Khan's decision to begin the attacks in the East were his own responsibility, "but there was a hope that the United States would bail him out if he did something stupid."

There was a firm basis for Yahya Khan's trust; the White House "tilt" began even before West Pakistan's invasion. On March 6, 1971, the Senior Review Group of the National Security Council was summoned by Kissinger to a meeting on the impending political crisis. There was blood in the air and the American officials knew it. Christopher Van Hollen, then the senior State Department specialist for South Asia, recalls that Alexis Johnson expressed the prevailing State Department view that the United States should try to discourage President Yahya Khan from using force against the Awami League. But Johnson did not "press the point," Van Hollen says, "after Kissinger cautioned SRG members to keep in mind President Nixon's 'special relationship' with Yahya. . . ." The officials, unaware of the negotiations through Pakistan with China, were confused: What "special relationship"? Kissinger also said that the President "would be reluctant to suggest that Yahya exercise restraint in East Pakistan" because the Pakistanis "wouldn't give a damn" if the American Ambassador, Joseph Farland, a political appointee, were ordered to express his disapproval to the Pakistani dictator.* Van Hollen, describing these events in a scholarly analysis published in 1980, added that the review group took Kissinger's not so subtle hints and concluded that "massive inaction" was the best policy.†

In his memoirs, Kissinger wrote that "We wanted to stay aloof from this if we could. . . . We had, moreover, every incentive to maintain Pakistan's good will. It was our crucial link to Peking; and Pakistan was one of China's closest allies." A few paragraphs later, Kissinger elevated West Pakistan to "our sole channel to China; once it was closed off it would take months to make alternative arrangements." Kissinger knew that China was perfectly willing to communicate through Romanian President Nicolae Ceauşescu. In fact, in late 1970 and early 1971, Peking and the White House were sending messages easily

---

* Farland, a former FBI agent whose first ambassadorial appointment was made by President Dwight D. Eisenhower, was reported to spend hours drinking with Yahya Khan, whose alcoholic and sexual excesses were well known in the State Department. By the end of Yahya's regime, Farland was in daily contact with him, and was said to be the only ambassador with whom Yahya would meet. Farland, a conservative Republican, was a former coal owners' lobbyist whose diplomatic abilities were held in low esteem by many in the Nixon Administration. One NSC aide, who saw much of the daily cable traffic from Farland to the State Department, described the Ambassador as having "groveled before the guy [Yahya Khan]." Farland had been Ambassador to the Dominican Republic and Panama before his appointment in 1969 to Islamabad.

† See "The Tilt Policy Revisited," *Asian Survey*, April 1980.

through both Pakistan and Romania: "Obviously," Kissinger wrote in an ear-
'ier section of his memoirs, "the Chinese were no more certain how to communicate with us than we with them." It was Nixon and Kissinger who decided
in late January to deal exclusively through Pakistan and its compliant dictator.

Kissinger, aware of the weakness of his rationale—that protecting the China
link through Pakistan justified inaction toward genocide—tried his best to explain it away in his memoirs: "I considered a policy of restraint [toward Yahya
Khan] correct on the merits, above and beyond the China connection . . . In
the case of Pakistan it seemed appropriate because its government was an ally
that, we were convinced, was bound soon to learn the futility of its course."
Unfortunately, the slaughter of the Bengalis was completed, Pakistan suffered
a military defeat, and Yahya Khan was forced to resign his presidency before
any lessons could be learned.

In mid-April, with the State Department in open dissent over the White
House's policies, an interagency group of South Asia specialists, including
Harold Saunders of Kissinger's staff, met to assess policy and concluded that
the crisis in East Pakistan had reinforced the importance of good relations with
India. According to Van Hollen, the specialists concluded that India "seemed
to be moving into a period of new political stability and was demonstrating a
renewed willingness to develop a cooperative relationship with the United
States." A group of State Department desk officers were also urging the White
House to authorize an immediate embargo on the shipment of military arms
and economic aid to Pakistan. The men in the bureaucracy did not perceive
the extent to which they were swimming upstream, against a White House on
the verge of a breakthrough with China. In early April, the Chinese invited an
American ping-pong team on tour in Japan to visit the mainland, and on April
27, the Pakistani Ambassador in Washington, Agha Hilaly, relayed Chou En-
lai's long-awaited formal invitation for a visit by Kissinger or any other "special envoy" to Peking. The President and Kissinger were grateful to Yahya
Khan, Kissinger wrote, "for his delicacy and tact"—unusual praise for a dictator in the midst of genocide—and formally told him so in a diplomatic note.
In early May, Ambassador Farland flew from Pakistan to meet secretly with
Kissinger and help plan his July trip to Peking from Islamabad. This would
involve the closest cooperation of Yahya Khan, who would be responsible for
the cover story.

On May 2, Nixon made a gesture toward appeasing those in his administration who wanted a strong stand against the Pakistani terror by signing an order
limiting American aid to spare parts and nonlethal equipment, but even that
step was mitigated when the President added in his own handwriting: "To all
hands. Don't squeeze Yahya at this time. RN."*

At this point, a miraculous new element emerged to buttress the seemingly
incomprehensible White House policy: highly classified evidence that Mrs.
Gandhi was planning to attack East Pakistan. In mid-May, Kissinger wrote, he

* On March 25, 1971, the day West Pakistan invaded the East, the Nixon Administration issued
a blanket ban on the delivery of military equipment to Yahya Khan. The ban was not strictly
enforced, and millions of dollars' worth of ammunition and arms that had been authorized prior to
the cutoff date were shipped in June, enraging Pakistan's critics in the media and Congress and
raising renewed questions about the administration's policies. Pentagon officials also continued to
meet with their Pakistani counterparts through the year to discuss that nation's arms needs.

and Nixon learned "from sources heretofore reliable" that "Mrs. Gandhi had ordered plans for a lightning 'Israeli-type' attack to take over East Pakistan." The evidence, taken at face value in the White House, confirmed his and Nixon's view that as "Pakistan grew more and more isolated internationally, she [Gandhi] appeared to seek above all Pakistan's humiliation." There was no doubt, Kissinger added, that the millions of refugees fleeing from East Pakistan and certain death were a factor in her concern, but "as the weeks passed, we began increasingly to suspect that Mrs. Gandhi perceived a larger opportunity."

For the next six months, until the final defeat of Yahya Khan at the hands of India, Nixon and Kissinger constantly invoked their "reliable sources" to justify the White House's hard line toward India. The source was never named, for an obvious reason: The informant was reporting from India through the Central Intelligence Agency. Nixon and Kissinger may have been honorable in protecting the man, but the few in the American government who knew his identity must also have known that his information was highly biased. The informant was undoubtedly Moraji Desai, a prominent Indian politician who was fired from the post of Deputy Prime Minister by Indira Gandhi in 1969—but stayed in her cabinet—after a bitter political dispute. Desai was a paid informer for the CIA and was considered one of the Agency's most important "assets." He had been in public life since the late 1940s, serving as chief minister of the state of Bombay, as Finance Minister, and, briefly, as Deputy Prime Minister. He was a political reactionary and a bitter opponent of Prime Minister Gandhi; his hostility showed repeatedly in his three-volume *The Story of My Life,* published in India in the mid-1970s. Former American intelligence officials recall that Desai was a star performer who was paid $20,000 a year by the CIA during the Johnson Administration through the 303 Committee, the covert intelligence group that was replaced by the 40 Committee under Nixon and Kissinger. One official remembers that Desai continued to report after Nixon's election, much of his information having to do with contacts between the Indian government and the Soviet Union. According to this official, Kissinger was "very impressed with the asset. He couldn't believe it was really in the bag." During meetings with CIA and other officials dealing with international crises, he would occasionally smile knowingly and say to Helms or one of his deputies, "Why can't you have a source in the cabinet?" *

Kissinger's visit to New Delhi in early July 1971 was part of his carefully worked out scheme to get into Peking secretly. His meetings with Prime Minister Gandhi and other officials were part of a ruse whose ultimate purpose would become known within days. The price of such duplicity, renewed Indian distrust of the American role in the East Pakistan crisis, was, in the view of the White House, a small one to pay for the entry to China. While in India,

* I have been able to establish firmly that Desai was reporting through 1970. After that year, the officials who were willing to discuss Desai's information with me were no longer in a position to see his reports, which presumably continued to flow to Washington. American officials inadvertently provided another hint that the reports were continuing by stressing the high position and proven reliability of the source they used in late 1971 to try to justify the administration's policy in the war. Desai became Prime Minister in March 1977; Mrs. Gandhi returned to office in July 1979.

Kissinger went out of his way to mislead the Gandhi government. At one meeting, he told a group of Indian officials that the United States, while bent on improving relations with China, "would take a grave view of an unprovoked Chinese attack on India. . . . We must await the memoirs of our interlocutors," he added in his memoirs, "to see whether the Indian ministers considered my reassurances the best we could do given our constraints, or an effort at deception."

Of course it was deception, but the White House had already decided where it stood in the India-Pakistan dispute. "I left New Delhi with the conviction that India was bent on a showdown with Pakistan," Kissinger wrote. "It was only waiting for the right moment. The opportunity to settle scores with a rival that had isolated itself by its own shortsightedness was simply too tempting." In his view, India was not emotionally or morally troubled by the carnage in East Pakistan, but would cleverly seize on it to justify military action against a long-time enemy.

By early July, American policy toward that carnage was twofold: to authorize millions of dollars in relief for the Pakistani refugees slowly starving to death in India, and thus mitigate protests from liberal senators such as Kennedy; and to urge Yahya Khan to establish civilian control in the East and reduce tensions to the extent that the refugees, who eventually reached a total of ten million, could begin returning to Pakistan. It was a policy that had no chance of resolving the basic issues, for the demands of the Awami League included the immediate release of its jailed leader, Mujibur Rahman, and the guarantee of an independent East Pakistan that would defer to the West only on defense and foreign affairs issues. Yahya Khan, as Kissinger knew, had no intention of meeting such demands. Nonetheless, Kissinger wrote, he made his recommendations to the Pakistani dictator and was satisfied when "Yahya promised to consider these suggestions."*

In Peking, Kissinger and Chou En-lai discussed their mutual distrust of India and their support for Pakistan. Chou told him, Kissinger wrote, that "China would not be indifferent if India attacked Pakistan." Kissinger added, "I returned to Washington with a premonition of disaster." India would almost certainly attack Pakistan and "China might then act. The Soviet Union might use the opportunity to teach Peking a lesson. For us to gang up on Pakistan— as our media and Congress were so insistently demanding—would accelerate the danger; it would give India an even stronger justification to attack. It would jeopardize the China initiative."

Events over the next five months would prove every aspect of Kissinger's analysis wrong. Pakistan initiated the war with India; China did not move; and the Soviet Union urged restraint on the Indians.

On July 17, two days after Nixon's announcement of the China breakthrough, Kissinger took the first step in what can only be described as a reckless attempt to provoke the worst possible case. He summoned L. K. Jha, the

* Kissinger staged his famous disappearance in Islamabad, aided by a false report of a stomachache, to fly into China. While he was gone from public view, some critics of the administration's South Asia policy hoped he was secretly visiting Sheik Mujibur, who was known to be held somewhere near Islamabad. Kennedy told of those hopes in a Senate speech on December 10, 1971, at the height of the India-Pakistan war. "As we now know, Mr. Kissinger was neither negotiating nor primarily concerned about the root cause of the conflict in South Asia," Kennedy said.

Indian Ambassador to Washington, to a private meeting at San Clemente. Jha, an economist and a prominent Indian civil servant, had been posted to Washington in 1970 and had quickly understood the importance of a working relationship with Kissinger. Jha recalls that the day before Kissinger left Washington for the trip to Peking, the two men had lunch, and Kissinger asked, seemingly in earnest: "Do you think I'll get a chance to see the Himalayas?" Jha gave him a serious answer about how best to see the mountains. There was no such jousting on July 17. Kissinger gave the Indians a direct warning, as Jha reported in an urgent cable to New Delhi: If war broke out between India and Pakistan, and China became involved on Pakistan's side, "We would be unable to help you against China." Jha added in his summary of the meeting: "He [Kissinger] could not but express the most serious anxiety and concern about an India-Pakistan conflict resulting from the present crisis. While India would have no problem in East [Pakistan], Pakistanis were bound to counterattack in the West. While he did not know what the Chinese would do, it would be unsafe for us to assume that they would not come to Pakistan's help. The consequences would be the most serious and would spread beyond the subcontinent."

Government officials in New Delhi were angry when they learned Kissinger's real purpose for his earlier visit. "Here we were," one diplomat recalled, "faced with a tremendous human problem"—the flood of East Pakistan refugees. "We thought he had come to discuss it with us, and then we found that we were just stepping stones on the way to China. This turned New Delhi against him." Jha's cabled warning of the new power alignment in South Asia led to a reevaluation at the top levels of the Indian government and played a major—if secret—role in India's decision to sign a friendship treaty with the Soviet Union. The twenty-year agreement, announced on August 9, had been discussed two years earlier in Moscow, but the Indian government had hesitated to sign it for fear of alienating the United States. "After Jha's cable reached Delhi," one Indian official said, "we recognized that the United States was moving into a strategic alliance with China. Some of our analysts thought that the Nixon Administration may even have encouraged China to put military pressure on us." Indira Gandhi sent one of her close advisers to Moscow, and India and the Soviet Union agreed to include a provision in the treaty calling on the two powers to consult each other before going to war to remove a threat.

Unlike the Soviet Union's treaties with Egypt, North Vietnam, and Iraq, the Indian-Soviet pact included no specific clauses on defense and emphasized India's nonaligned status. Cooperation was pledged on economic, scientific, technical, and cultural matters. The bureaucracy in Washington took the treaty in stride, generally viewing it, as Christopher Van Hollen wrote, as not meaning "unequivocal Soviet support for India nor a cessation of Moscow's effort to encourage a political settlement." The Soviet Union continued to pressure India not to recognize an independent Bangladesh, and it continued to urge restraint, both in published commentaries in Tass and in private communications to New Delhi.*

* On August 13, Tad Szulc of the *New York Times* reported that the United States had received intelligence information from New Delhi that the Soviet Union had agreed to sign the friendship

Such complexities held no interest for the White House. Nixon and Kissinger insisted on seeing the friendship treaty as confirmation of all their worst fears: India was now aligned with the Soviet Union against West Pakistan and China. Kissinger described the agreement in his memoirs as "the bombshell. . . . The Soviet Union had seized a strategic opportunity. To demonstrate Chinese impotence and to humiliate a friend of both China and the United States proved too tempting. If China raised the ante, it risked Soviet reprisal. With the treaty, Moscow threw a lighted match into a powder keg."

Kissinger's anger may have been real, but it was irrational. He chose simply to ignore the effect of his July 17 warning to Jha. There is no evidence that he informed anyone in the bureaucracy or on his staff about it, and Jha recalls that no Kissinger aides were at the meeting. The warning, and its immense impact on American-Indian relations, was also omitted from his memoirs. India's first reaction to the President's July 15 announcement on China had been favorable, Kissinger wrote, and New Delhi praised the visit to Peking as a "significant, positive development." But by the twentieth, Kissinger added, "India began to display second thoughts; it started to invoke fictitious Sino-Soviet designs on the subcontinent. . . ." By then, Jha's account of his meeting with Kissinger had reached New Delhi, and the Indians, already angry at Kissinger's deception, may well have had second thoughts. Kissinger, still ignoring the July 17 meeting with Jha, characterized the friendship treaty as one that "for all practical purposes gave India a Soviet guarantee against Chinese intervention if India went to war with Pakistan." He cited a memorandum from two of his staff aides, Sonnenfeldt and Hyland: "The India-Pakistan conflict becomes a sort of Sino-Soviet clash by proxy."

At this point, Kissinger and Nixon were doing more than misjudging a situation; they were deliberately deceiving their government in an attempt to create the conditions that they thought existed. Of course India would move closer to the Soviet Union, if it was warned that the United States would side with China and Pakistan in case of a dispute. India's predictably tougher line after the Kissinger warning was also used by the White House in an attempt to beat back opposition from the bureaucracy and Congress to the Nixon-Kissinger policy in South Asia.

The China announcement had provided some comfort to the confused officials in the State Department, for the White House's apparently suicidal policy was shown to have at least some conceptual basis. Kissinger and Chou En-lai had agreed in Peking to establish direct communications through Paris, and Pakistan was no longer needed as a go-between. What the bureaucrats could not envision, however, was the extent of Nixon's and Kissinger's anxiety about the 1972 summit in Peking, whose final details would not be worked out

---

treaty as "the price for an indefinite delay in India's plan to recognize East Pakistan." The story upset Richard Helms, who telephoned the White House Plumbers, Egil Krogh and David Young, and urged them to investigate the leak, which he said put the agent's life in danger. The story also had the effect of diminishing the White House argument that the Soviet Union had joined India in seeking to "humiliate"—Kissinger's favorite verb—China and West Pakistan. The "endangered" agent was obviously Moraji Desai, and Nixon and Kissinger thus continued to head into a crisis on the basis of intelligence that had been contradicted by a man they considered one of their best operatives.

until Kissinger's second trip to China in October. After July 15, Christopher Van Hollen wrote, "Hopes rose among some officials" that the Nixon Administration would now be in a position to encourage Yahya Khan to make some real political concessions to the Awami League. Those hopes were dashed at a Senior Review Group meeting on July 31, Van Hollen wrote, when Kissinger sharply rejected a proposal that the Pakistanis be urged to remove their army from relief duties in East Pakistan to enable more economic aid to flow to the starving Bengali peasants. Van Hollen recorded Kissinger's response: "Why is it our business how they govern themselves? . . . The President always says to tilt toward Pakistan, but every proposal I get [from the bureaucracy] is in the opposite direction. Sometimes I think I am in a nut house."

Every move the White House made in this period seemed to backfire. On August 4, Nixon, seeking to ease the continuing attacks on his policy in Congress and from editorial writers, told a news conference that the administration would continue to supply food and economic aid for the millions of East Pakistani refugees in India. But he also publicly signaled a continuation of the "tilt" toward Yahya Khan: "We are not going to engage in public pressure on the Government of West Pakistan. That would be totally counterproductive. These are matters that we will discuss only in private channels." Five days later, President Yahya made an attempt at reconciliation all but impossible by announcing that his government would try Mujibur Rahman in secret for treason. Sixty-nine members of Congress immediately demanded that the White House urge Pakistan to show compassion. Ambassador Jha was extremely active during this period, working closely with Senator Kennedy, who was chairman of a Senate subcommittee on refugees.

In his memoirs, Kissinger praised Jha's skills in "getting the Indian version of the issues to the press" and added: "I was supposed to be skillful in dealing with the press. On the India-Pakistan issue Jha clearly outclassed me." Kissinger did not, however, describe an extraordinary warning he gave Jha at another of their private meetings in San Clemente, this one on August 25, at the height of the outcry over American policies. "You must realize," he said, as the Ambassador reported to New Delhi, "that no matter how much you succeed in influencing important senators, you have to deal with this administration and that means the President. As for bringing about any change in the U.S. attitude, the President is angry with the Indian Embassy's efforts with the Congress. The President does not feel that apart from the East Coast intellectuals, among whom I used to be counted at one time, there are many people in this country who are genuinely interested in or excited about the affairs of the [Indian] subcontinent. The congressional leaders who support you do so because they want to use any excuse for attacking the President and not because they have any deep sympathies." Despite the warning, Jha and his aides in the embassy maintained their contacts on Capitol Hill.

As the situation in South Asia remained deadlocked during the late summer and fall, American officials were aware that open warfare between India and West Pakistan was inevitable. They also knew that Pakistan could not win such a struggle. Indian elections were scheduled for early 1972 and Gandhi knew she had to resolve the staggering refugee problem before then. However, the refugees would not return to East Pakistan as long as the hated army of Yahya Khan was in control. Bangladesh guerrilla activities, supported by India, grew more and more successful in the East. Indian diplomats acknowledged later that their army, aided by the rebels, could have seized East Pakistan with ease at any time that fall but chose not to do so because it was clear that the Bangladesh insurgents were bound to win. Mrs. Gandhi's government also felt it had its own interests to protect by maintaining close liaison with the Bangladesh rebels, who, it was feared, might otherwise become radicalized. Most of the refugees were near Calcutta, in East India, a traditional center of radical activity. "If we did not maintain contact," one senior diplomat said, "there was every possibility of the moderates in the Awami League being replaced by radicals and Marxists who would spill over India." None of this reasoning penetrated the White House; in its view, India, backed by the Soviet Union, was fomenting the crisis in East Pakistan to humiliate China and West Pakistan.

There was one attempt by the White House to negotiate a settlement. Kissinger authorized a series of contacts through the State Department with the Foreign Minister of the Bangladesh government-in-exile, Khondakar Mustaque Ahmed, the Awami League's third-ranking official. In his memoirs, Kissinger accused Mrs. Gandhi of breaking up the talks, which had been approved by Yahya Khan, because "once discussions between Pakistan and the Awami League started, some sort of compromise might emerge; India might then lose control of events. Mrs. Gandhi was not willing to risk this." Once again the national security adviser seemed to be out of touch with reality.

The contacts with Mustaque, who was not cited by name in Kissinger's memoirs, were made clandestinely in Calcutta, without the advance knowledge of the Indian government. The relatively junior State Department official in direct charge of the talks in Calcutta, George G. B. Griffin, was put under surveillance by the Indian government. Mustaque, as subsequent accounts made clear, was meeting without the approval of the two senior officials of the Awami League, Syed Nazrul Islam and Tajuddin Ahmed. Indian officials and the Awami League leadership in exile later concluded that the goal of the Yahya-approved contacts was to split the Awami League. President Yahya then planned to negotiate directly with Mustaque, who would be willing to modify some of the League's demands—notably its requirement that Mujibur Rahman be immediately released from prison. Mustaque was summarily removed as Foreign Minister after the talks became known, and Indian officials later characterized him and his followers as "quislings" willing to sell out their compatriots.*

* Kissinger's reluctance to name Mustaque in his memoirs is understandable in terms of subsequent events in Bangladesh: In 1975, a coup d'état headed by Mustaque led to the assassination of President Mujibur Rahman and the jailing of his two top aides, Nazrul Islam and Tajuddin Ahmed. Prior to the coup, Mustaque had been Commerce Minister in Mujibur's cabinet; he emerged afterwards as the Acting President of Bangladesh. Three months later, Nazrul and Tajuddin were executed by bayonet in their jail cells. Griffin, who by all accounts was merely following instructions, suffered as a result. In July 1981, the Indian government vetoed his appointment as political counselor to the American Embassy in New Delhi. No official reason was made public, but an Indian official privately acknowledged that his government's unusual step had been taken in part because of lingering suspicions over American contacts with Mustaque. Griffin had served as the second-ranking diplomat in the American Embassy in Kabul, Afghanistan, prior to his aborted reassignment to India.

In early November, Indira Gandhi arrived in Washington for meetings with the President. Her goal was straightforward: to convince the White House that unless Yahya Khan could be persuaded to modify his policies, war was inevitable. Beneath the diplomatic smiles, there was icy rage. "She was there to tell Nixon," one of her aides recalled, "and his bloody lackey, Yahya Khan, not to commit murder." Gandhi's poise broke almost immediately, when Nixon in his short welcoming speech referred sympathetically to recent floods that had devastated parts of India. She was to have responded politely in Hindi but instead went directly to the issue at hand: "To the national calamities of drought, flood, and cyclone has been added a man-made tragedy of vast proportions. I am haunted by the tormented faces in our overcrowded refugee camps reflecting the grim events which have compelled the exodus of these millions from East Bengal. I have come here looking for a deeper understanding of the situation in our part of the world, in search of some wise impulse. . . ." Nixon had been rebuked and he knew it. In his memoirs, he accused the Prime Minister of duplicity: ". . . [E]ven as we spoke, Mrs. Gandhi knew that her generals and advisers were planning to intervene in East Pakistan and were considering contingency plans for attacking West Pakistan as well. . . . Those who resort to force, without making excuses are bad enough—but those who resort while preaching to others about their use of force deserve no sympathy whatever." Kissinger, in his memoirs, described Gandhi as listening to one of Nixon's "better" presentations with "aloof indifference." As he analyzed it, India had already decided to go to war out of fear that American pressures on Yahya Khan would produce a negotiated settlement in East Pakistan. "India had to act before this sequence came to pass," Kissinger wrote. "Mrs. Gandhi was going to war not because she was convinced of our failure but because she feared our success." At that point, only Nixon and Kissinger believed there was any chance of a negotiated settlement between Yahya Khan and the Bengalis. During the fall, the Awami League had escalated its demands as well as its guerrilla activities against the West Pakistani Army, and nothing short of total independence for Bangladesh was negotiable.

On the second day of Gandhi's visit, Nixon repaid the perceived insult by keeping her waiting for forty-five minutes before their meeting. One of Kissinger's aides realized something was up when Kissinger didn't make his usual appearance just before the appointed hour: "I didn't know what to do. First I sat with her in the diplomatic entrance, and then I walked her upstairs to the Roosevelt Room." No apology was given.*

What had begun as a "tilt" to protect the China opening had become national policy, and what had been Nixon's visceral dislike of ascetic Indians had been elevated to a personal vendetta against Indira Gandhi. With her quick tongue and uncompromising manner, she was perceived not only as a symbol of America's previous misguided policy in South Asia but also as a threat to

* In a newspaper interview in late 1979, Prime Minister Gandhi described her curious meetings with Nixon eight years before: ". . . [I]t was not so much Mr. Nixon talking as Mr. Kissinger, because Mr. Nixon would talk for a few minutes and would then say, 'Isn't that right, Henry?' and from then on Henry would talk on for quite a while and then Nixon would say two words and then he would say, 'Wouldn't you say so, Henry?' I would talk with Henry rather than Nixon." When she and the President did talk, Gandhi added, Nixon "was unwilling to accept my assessment of any situation."

the Chinese summit in early 1972. The date of the summit was announced by the White House on November 29. Few outsiders could realize how much that event was shaping the White House's policy in South Asia.

The war began in earnest on December 3, when Yahya Khan, for strategic reasons known only to him, ordered the Pakistani Air Force to launch a surprise attack on eight Indian airfields in the north and west. The attacks failed to do serious damage to the Indian Air Force, but they provided justification for Mrs. Gandhi to order a full-scale offensive in East Pakistan and a more limited retaliation in the West, where Indian troops seized thousands of square miles of territory within a few days. The war in the East was over, as most experts predicted it would be, in two weeks. Yahya Khan capitulated and a new government, soon to be headed by the released Sheik Mujibur Rahman, assumed control of Bangladesh. The day after the surrender in the East, Gandhi offered Yahya Khan an unconditional ceasefire in West Pakistan, and in negotiations concluded a month later, she agreed to withdraw her troops from the occupied areas of the West.

In their memoirs, Nixon and Kissinger insisted that the Prime Minister's decision to accept peace in the West was not of her own doing. The real story, Kissinger wrote, was the courage that he and Nixon exhibited in early December by escalating the regional crisis into one between the world powers. It was to prevent the dismemberment of West Pakistan, Kissinger wrote, that he, Nixon, and Haig agreed a Third World War might not be avoidable. He and Nixon were convinced "that Mrs. Gandhi was not motivated primarily by conditions in East Pakistan" but had decided sometime in mid-1971 "to use the opportunity to settle accounts with Pakistan once and for all." Nixon did not directly discuss in his memoirs the possibility of all-out war, but in 1975, during his secret grand jury testimony to the Watergate Special Prosecution Force, he shocked the lawyers by insisting that the United States had come "close to nuclear war" during the India-Pakistan dispute. He said, one attorney recalled, that "we had threatened to go to nuclear war with the Russians."* There is evidence that he and Kissinger believed they had indeed done so. Nixon's language was indirect in the memoirs, but the message was the same: "The Indo-Pakistan war involved stakes much higher than the future of Pakistan—and that was high enough. . . . If we failed to help Pakistan, then Iran or any country within the reach of Soviet influence might begin to question the dependability of American support." Kissinger's comment to Nixon, as transcribed in the presidential memoirs, bears repeating: "We don't really have any choice. We can't allow a friend of ours and China's to get screwed in a conflict with a friend of Russia's."

In a rare on-the-record interview, Winston Lord, who by 1971 was one of Kissinger's key aides, explained the theory behind the White House's South

---

* The Prosecution Force attorneys, who did not know how to evaluate Nixon's comments, sealed those portions of his testimony and sent them to the White House for safekeeping. In an interview years later, John Mitchell spoke of Nixon's grand jury remarks as "an exaggeration. It was more the preliminaries in the game of chess than it was a confrontation." Senior Indian officials, told of Nixon's recollection, similarly dismissed it. As in the Jordanian crisis in the fall of 1970, what actually happened and what threats actually were made became less important to Nixon and Kissinger than what they *thought* was happening.

Asia policy to a researcher for the Carnegie Endowment for International Peace: "We had to show China that we respect a mutual friend and opposed the crossing of international borders. So it was not so much a 'thanks, Yahya, for helping us with China' as demonstrating to China we were a reliable country to deal with. . . ."

In the two weeks it took India to defeat Pakistan, Nixon and Kissinger pursued a provocative course of strategic mistakes. Their basic error was the belief that the Soviet Union, which had agreed in August to a summit with Nixon in the spring of 1972, was now urging Indira Gandhi to dismember Pakistan—although such a move would jeopardize the Moscow summit. They compounded that error by concluding, also in error, that China was prepared to enter the war militarily at any moment. The White House's policy was to force the Soviet Union and India to pull back from their attempts to "humiliate" China and Pakistan, and thus to preserve Yahya Khan's regime—and America's credibility. That no one else in the administration shared their view did not matter, and undoubtedly gave them an added sense of bravado.

By the end of the first week of December, Congress and the press were in an uproar over the White House's continued "tilt" toward Pakistan. The White House's animus toward India had become progressively more obvious. On December 1, the State Department had suspended the licensing of arms shipments to India; on the third it canceled all remaining export licenses for military goods for India; on the fourth, Joseph Sisco, ordered to carry Nixon's message to the press, declared that "India bears the major responsibilities" in the war; on the sixth, Secretary of State Rogers complained that the Indians had attacked an American merchant vessel; and on the seventh, in a press briefing, Kissinger suggested that a political compromise had been in the process of being negotiated between West Pakistan and the Awami League when India initiated the war.*

The public briefings were complemented by Kissinger's private efforts to minimize dissent inside the bureaucracy. At a meeting of the Washington Special Action Group on December 3, a summary of which was made public later by Jack Anderson, Kissinger was recorded as saying: "I am getting hell every half hour from the President that we are not being tough enough on India. . . . He does not believe we are carrying out his wishes. He wants to tilt in favor of Pakistan." The next day, he told the group, "Everyone knows how all this will come out and everyone knows that India will ultimately occupy East Pakistan." No one directly challenged the "tilt" policy, according to the doc-

* Kissinger's briefing was to have been on background, but it was made public two days later by Senator Barry Goldwater, the conservative Republican from Arizona. The backgrounder seemed to reflect Kissinger's belief that he could say anything to the press and get away with it. "There have been some comments that the Administration is anti-Indian," Kissinger declared. "This is totally inaccurate. India is a great country. . . . As for the President, I was not aware of his preference for Pakistan leaders over Indian leaders, and I, therefore, asked him this morning what this might be based on. He pointed out . . . the warmth of the reception that we extended to the Indian Prime Minister two weeks before the attacks on Pakistan started should make clear what enormous value we attach to Indian friendship." Kissinger was equally misleading in discussing the abortive negotiations in Calcutta between Khondakar Mustaque Ahmed and the American Consulate: "We took the view that once negotiations started, the release of Mujibur would be an inevitable consequence after some period of time, and therefore, we felt that the most important thing was to get the negotiations started." There was no basis, as Kissinger had to know, for his suggestion that the regime of Yahya Khan ever considered the release of Mujibur before the December defeat.

458

uments published by Anderson. In his memoirs, Kissinger acknowledged that at this point "we were playing a weak hand, but one must never compound weakness by timidity." The goal, with American policy collapsing in South Asia, Kissinger wrote, was for the United States "to act in a manner that would give pause to potential Soviet adventures elsewhere, especially in the Middle East. . . ."

Throughout this period of crisis, however, the Soviet Union—far from urging India to dismember Pakistan—was still cautioning the New Delhi government to avoid conflict. One Indian diplomat then stationed in Moscow recalls high-level meetings at which the top Russian leaders—Premier Alexei Kosygin, Party leader Leonid Brezhnev, and President Nikolai Podgorny—all urged the Indians not to take the offensive. "The strongest voice of this view was Kosygin. . . . He told us: 'You Indians don't know what a war is. We've been through the Second World War. You don't know how our people have suffered.' " There was nothing mysterious about the Soviet position as far as the State Department was concerned. "Once the military issue in East Pakistan was resolved," Christopher Van Hollen says, "the Soviet Union was also counseling India in the direction of the ceasefire in the West. . . . Moscow . . . was anxious to prevent further military conflict and to retain its political relationship with Pakistan. . . ."

At this point, Nixon and Kissinger were engaged in a breathless rush toward confrontation. The formal contacts with the Soviets began on December 5, when Ambassador Dobrynin's deputy, Yuli Vorontsov, was summoned by Kissinger and told, Kissinger wrote, "that we were at a watershed. . . . Vorontsov was soothing. The crisis would be over in a week; it need have no impact on US-Soviet relations. If the Soviet Union continued on its present course, I snapped, it would not be over in a week, whatever happened on the subcontinent." Vorontsov had been there before; he had played a key liaison role in the 1970 Middle East crisis, when Nixon and Kissinger insisted that the Soviet Union had been behind Syria's alleged tank invasion of Jordan.

On December 6, Mrs. Gandhi finally recognized the republic of Bangladesh, a step India had delayed for five months at the behest of the Soviet Union. Kissinger and Nixon interpreted the recognition as further evidence for their thesis: "We decided that the best hope to keep India from smashing Pakistan," Kissinger wrote, "was to increase the risk for Moscow"—that is, publicly and privately to threaten the 1972 summit. "Fundamentally, our only card left was to raise the risks for the Soviets to a level where Moscow would see larger risks jeopardized." Vorontsov was handed a letter from Nixon, for delivery to Brezhnev, in which the President, as he recorded in his memoirs, wrote that "Indian military forces are being used in an effort to impose political demands and to dismember the sovereign state of Pakistan." The President requested the Soviets, "in the spirit" of the forthcoming summit in Moscow, to urge the Indians to use restraint—which was precisely what the Soviets had been doing since March.

Amid all the blustering by the men at the top of the American government, the CIA received a report—allegedly from inside the New Delhi cabinet—that was full of tough talk from Prime Minister Gandhi. The source, as described by Kissinger, could only have been Moraji Desai: "A report reached us from a source whose reliability we had never had any reason to doubt and which I do not question today, to the effect that Prime Minister Gandhi was determined to reduce even West Pakistan to impotence." Kissinger said that the intelligence showed that Gandhi would proceed with the "liberation" of the southern part of the Pakistani province of Kashmir, long an area of dispute between Pakistan and India, "and continue fighting until the Pakistan army and air force were wiped out." The raw report, handed directly to Kissinger without any evaluation, was seized by the White House to justify its policies; Nixon and Kissinger still relied heavily on it in their memoirs. They did so with the knowledge that the information turned out to be incorrect, since India did not invade West Pakistan. There was another flaw in the intelligence: By late 1971, according to Ambassador Jha and other officials, the Indian cabinet as a whole did not discuss sensitive military issues; Mrs. Gandhi instead relied on a small subcabinet committee into which the CIA was not likely to penetrate.

A government expert on South Asia recalls the arrival of the new Desai report in the midst of a WSAG meeting on the India-Pakistan war: "Dick Helms rushed in with this paper in his hands and Henry picked it up. I had seen the report earlier in the day: Mrs. Gandhi was talking to somebody she knew to be a hawk and she was blowing it up a bit. At the time, it didn't wake me up. If you knew enough about India, you knew there was no point to it [the report of expanded war]. India doesn't want Pakistan. Probably what she means is that she'd just knock out their armor and then forget about them. Helms read the report or summarized it for everybody around the table— Admiral Moorer, Alex Johnson, Joe Sisco, and David Packard. You can shudder for the Republic. It was terribly scary. Sisco was the brightest, but he was playing his own game. If it meant kowtowing to Henry, he did it. The intelligence fitted right into a prejudice. It gave Henry and Nixon a chance to do what they wanted to do." In his analysis of the intelligence, Christopher Van Hollen noted: "Nixon and Kissinger were virtually alone in the U.S. government in interpreting the report as they did."

Kissinger and Nixon found additional dubious evidence for their thesis in a conversation between Ambassador Jha and John Irwin, the Under Secretary of State. Irwin had summoned Jha to a meeting on December 9, and requested assurances that India would not attack West Pakistan. On December 11, Jha refused to provide such a one-sided guarantee, and in turn asked Irwin whether the United States was in a position to give India its assurance that if Pakistan succeeded in occupying Indian territory, it would not be annexed. Irwin, Jha reported to New Delhi, could provide no such assurances. Nonetheless, Jha's refusal to provide what amounted to a unilateral guarantee was enough for Nixon and Kissinger. A Navy Task Group with the aircraft carrier *Enterprise* as its center was ordered to steam toward the Bay of Bengal. Admiral Elmo Zumwalt, Chief of Naval Operations, had no advance notice of the Task Group's deployment. In his memoirs, Zumwalt also revealed that the White House orders "did not specify what [its] mission was, nor could anyone, including the Chairman of the Joint Chiefs, tell me. . . . I sought to be sure that these ships either had a mission or were not sent in harm's way."*

* Zumwalt thought that Nixon and Kissinger, perhaps "frustrated by their inability to influence events on the subcontinent, impulsively organized [the Task Group], and sent it on its way in a final effort to show the world that America was not to be taken lightly." A more likely possibility, he added, was that the White House wanted to show China that the United States "was a relevant

Nixon and Kissinger were operating on their own because they had to; the bureaucracy was united in opposition. Nixon was "beside himself," Kissinger wrote, over repeated stories in the press in which senior officials were being quoted anonymously in opposition to the White House "tilt." Once again, rather than deal with the root cause of the opposition, they chose to shape the world to their own sense of reality. On the morning of December 10, a few hours after ordering out the Navy Task Group, Kissinger arranged a meeting with Huang Hua, the newly appointed Chinese Ambassador to the United Nations; the Chinese Mission to the UN was yet another contact point between Washington and Peking. Before that meeting could take place, Kissinger learned that the West Pakistani commander in Bangladesh had given up the battle and proposed a ceasefire. The war seemed to be over and there was relief in the State Department.

But there was dismay in the White House—ending the war without some face-saving confrontation would not do. "I was disconcerted," Kissinger wrote, because he and Nixon believed that a separate ceasefire in the East would leave Gandhi and the Indian Army free to attack the Yahya Khan regime. Kissinger then proceeded to urge the Pakistanis to withdraw their proposal, at least for a few days or until the Pakistani troops in the East were reduced in effectiveness to the point where a ceasefire was academic. That evening, having averted what he and Nixon obviously viewed as a calamity, Kissinger met with Huang Hua and came away, he wrote, with an errant impression, "an indication that China might intervene militarily even at this late stage." Huang Hua had been tough in his anti-Indian rhetoric and in pledging Peking's determination to supply Yahya Khan as long as feasible, and Kissinger had taken his remarks at face value.

It was a major blunder. There was no known evidence suggesting that China, then still in the midst of its Cultural Revolution upheavals, would under any circumstances intervene in the India-Pakistan war. Kissinger himself suggested earlier in his memoirs that Gandhi had delayed the showdown with East Pakistan until winter so that the main mountain passes from China to India would be blocked with snow. As Christopher Van Hollen viewed it: "Even if the Chinese internal political tensions had not acted as a restraint, any government in Peking would have thought carefully before attacking across the Himalayas in winter." There is also evidence that Peking had been distressed with Yahya Khan's decision to invade East Pakistan in force. When Yahya Khan sent his foreign minister, Zulfikar Ali Bhutto, to Peking just before the war with India, G. W. Choudhury recalls, "the Chinese left him with no doubt about their disapproval of the policy of repression in Bangladesh." Bhutto was handed "a list of sixty prominent pro-Peking Bengali leaders who had been slaughtered by Yahya Khan's troops." Despite these indications of disapproval, Choudhury recalls, Yahya Khan remained convinced that Peking would join the United States in coming to his aid in case of military reverses; possibly he was a private source of reassurance on this point to Kissinger and Nixon.

___

military actor in that part of the world and had the will to deploy military power in a situation in which a Soviet client was defeating a Chinese ally." In either case, the admiral said, "my hunch is that the gesture was untimely and futile." At its largest, the Task Group included seven destroyers and a helicopter carrier with two companies of Marines aboard.

The most critical step took place at a White House meeting on December 12, when Richard Nixon decided to risk war with the Soviet Union to salvage his policy. Haig was also at the meeting, but not Laird or Rogers. "It was symptomatic of the internal relationships of the Nixon Administration," wrote Kissinger, who did as much to isolate Rogers and Laird as the President, "that neither the Secretary of State nor of Defense . . . attended this crucial meeting, where, as it turned out, the first *decision to risk war* in the triangular Soviet-Chinese-American relationship was taken [emphasis added]." Both Kissinger and Nixon wrote that they left the meeting convinced that a great-power struggle could take place. "History's assessment of Nixon, whatever its conclusions," Kissinger wrote, "must not overlook his courage and patriotism in making such a decision, at risk to his immediate political interest, to preserve the world balance of power for the ultimate safety of all free people." Kissinger stated it incorrectly. Nixon was willing to risk world war *for* his immediate political interest: for the safety of his 1972 summit in Peking.

While at the meeting, Kissinger wrote, he received a message from Peking. Nixon and Kissinger guessed that China was entering the war on Pakistan's behalf. Nixon decided, Kissinger wrote, that "if the Soviet Union threatened China we would not stand idly by." Huang Hua's message, when Kissinger finally received it, said only that Peking was willing to assist in reaching a standstill ceasefire in East and West Pakistan. At that point, Prime Minister Gandhi was also under pressure from Moscow to offer an unconditional ceasefire in the West, where the Indian Army had made substantial ground gains. Moscow's repeated assurances to the White House that India sought no wider war was not enough for Kissinger and Nixon, who chose to believe their hardline intelligence from inside the Indian cabinet. Nixon and Kissinger had another, more immediate, goal in all of this: If there was to be a successful ceasefire in East and West Pakistan, credit would be theirs.

On December 14, Yuli Vorontsov delivered a nine-page handwritten note to Haig, once again relaying India's assurances that it had no intention of permanently seizing territory in West Pakistan—but such notes did not matter. Kissinger was then with the President at an economic summit in the Azores; on the way home he summoned a group of journalists and warned that the President might have to reconsider his plans for a May 1972 summit meeting in Moscow if the Soviet Union did not restrain India from attacking West Pakistan.* Kissinger's remarks, which made headlines, were on "deep back-

---

* The Azores meeting was a triumph for Kissinger, who, working with Georges Pompidou, the French President, resolved an international monetary crisis in less than two days. The crisis had begun on August 15, 1971, when Nixon, with the encouragement of John Connally, Secretary of the Treasury, announced a tough new economic policy in an effort to rectify the balance-of-payments deficit. His proposals, which provided an immediate political boost for the administration, included a devaluation of the dollar and a 10 percent surcharge on all imports. The new sanctions shocked America's trading partners in Europe and Asia, and posed a diplomatic threat. Connally, in a subsequent meeting with a group of independent economists, including C. Fred Bergsten, a former member of Kissinger's NSC staff, heightened everyone's concern by declaring, Bergsten recalls, "My philosophy is that all foreigners are out to screw us and it's our job to screw them first." Bergsten, who says he was "shocked" by the remark, arranged a meeting with Kissinger. "Henry," he recalls saying, "do you know you're dealing with a xenophobe? You're going to have to turn this thing around." Kissinger replied, "I'll wait my time." By December, Kissinger had managed

ground," meaning that the journalists could publish the information but not attribute it in any way to the administration.*

Two days later, Gandhi offered West Pakistan an unconditional ceasefire which was accepted immediately. Nixon and Kissinger seemed to believe, as they claimed in their memoirs, that their tough policies had been responsible. "By using diplomatic signals and behind-the-scenes pressure we had been able to save West Pakistan from the imminent threat of Indian aggression and domination," Nixon wrote. "We also once again avoided a major confrontation with the Soviet Union." Kissinger also credited the White House policy: "There is no doubt in my mind" that Gandhi's offer of the unilateral ceasefire "was a reluctant decision resulting from Soviet pressure, which in turn grew out of American insistence, including the fleet movement and the willingness to risk the summit. . . . We had avoided the worst—which is sometimes the maximum statesmen can achieve."

Nixon and Kissinger were alone in their view that they had salvaged a victory from the crisis. Christopher Van Hollen, in his later analysis, concluded, "There is no support for the claim that India had decided upon an all-out assault on West Pakistan; there is certainly no support for the contention that the two countries [India and the Soviet Union] were working in tandem toward that goal." The White House's policies represented "the domino theory raised to global heights—and to the heights of incredulity," he said. Indira Gandhi later expressed amazement at Nixon's and Kissinger's belief that their intervention with Moscow had prevented an Indian assault in the West. "The Soviet Union did not speak to me about the matter," she told a journalist. "We had no intention of doing anything with West Pakistan."

The available evidence in the crisis supports the Indian position; Nixon and

---

to convince Nixon that Connally's approach would lead to diplomatic chaos, and it was Kissinger who joined Nixon at the Azores summit with Pompidou. The two men negotiated away the surcharge, agreed on a 9 percent devaluation of the dollar vis-à-vis the franc, and also worked out exchange rates for most of the world's important currencies. It was a tour de force for Kissinger, who once again awed his associates with his ability to come immediately to grips with the essence of an issue—an ability he seemed unable to use in dealing with the Vietnam War or great-power issues. Bergsten, who became an Assistant Secretary of the Treasury in the Carter Administration, recalls admiringly that Kissinger "had understood the theory of fluctuating international exchange rates in thirty seconds." Connally was bitter about the incident and the ease with which Kissinger muscled him aside, but he held his peace during Nixon's first term. Later he would tell reporters he had been "stabbed in the back."

* Kissinger's threat about the summit led to a row with the *Washington Post,* whose editor, Benjamin C. Bradlee, decided that the summit statement was too significant to publish without direct attribution to the national security adviser. Kissinger had made the remark, which was to be on "background"—his standard form of public communication—to a five-man White House press pool aboard the presidential aircraft on its return from the economic summit meeting. The news made immediate headlines and Bradlee decided to name Kissinger as the source. "We are convinced," Bradlee was quoted as saying at the time, "that we have engaged in this deception and done this disservice to the reader long enough." Other journalists, who were convinced that Kissinger was the best source of information in the administration, bitterly disagreed. David Kraslow, then Washington bureau chief of the Los Angeles *Times,* publicly accused the *Post* of "unprofessional, unethical, cheap journalism" in naming Kissinger. The internecine argument among the press came less than a week after Senator Barry Goldwater had inserted the text of Kissinger's December 7 backgrounder in the *Congressional Record.* Kissinger's pattern of success with the press seemed about to become a casualty of the administration's wrong-headed policies in South Asia, but the crisis was eased by Nixon's announcement in early 1972 of Kissinger's role in the secret peace talks with Hanoi and by the President's trip to Peking. The *Washington Post* returned to the fold and began once again reporting Kissinger's backgrounders the way the White House wished.

Kissinger have done nothing to substantiate their claim that they successfully threatened the Soviets. The hot-line messages that were relayed between Nixon and the Soviet leaders were not published; Nixon's characterization of them as "threats" to begin a nuclear war—as he told the Watergate Special Prosecution Force in 1975—was not repeated in his memoirs. Kissinger similarly provided few details of the President's "decision to risk war."

In a letter to Nixon at the close of the war, Indira Gandhi cited the American Declaration of Independence, with its call for man's right to life, liberty, and the pursuit of happiness, as a "great moment" of history "which has inspired millions of people to die for liberty." She then pointedly turned to America's role in supporting Yahya Khan in his war on East Pakistan. "The fact of the matter is," she wrote, "that the rulers of West Pakistan got away with the impression that they could do what they liked because no one, not even the United States, would choose to take a public position that while Pakistan's integrity was certainly sacrosanct, human rights, liberty, were no less so. . . . Lip service was paid to the need for a political solution, but not a single worthwhile step was taken to bring [it] about." *

American policies would provide support in the next years for those officials in India who advocated nuclear development. They argued that the *Enterprise* must have been carrying nuclear weapons when it sailed into the Bay of Bengal; if India had its own arsenal, the argument went, the White House might not have been so quick to deploy its warships. India was undoubtedly intent on developing the nuclear option before the crisis, but American pro-Pakistan policy can only have expedited that process. India's first successful nuclear test took place in May of 1974.

For Yahya Khan, the White House "tilt" led to military disaster and to his decision, taken in late December of 1971, to resign the presidency of West Pakistan and to turn the government over to Zulfikar Ali Bhutto, the Foreign Minister. Bhutto released Sheik Mujibar Rahman early in January 1972, and Mujibar returned triumphantly to Dacca to become the first President of the new nation of Bangladesh.

Richard Nixon would later rationalize the "tilt" toward West Pakistan as being an act of morality, telling David Frost during one of their interviews in 1977 that "basically we saved West Pakistan because it was right. . . . We had to do something to keep India from gobbling up Pakistan. . . ." There was another reason, he conceded: "What we did in saving West Pakistan built up a lot of credibility with the Chinese."

No amount of presidential posturing could hide the truth: Richard Nixon, facing what he feared would be a most difficult reelection campaign, had been sullied by the India-Pakistan war. His administration had been looking the other way as Yahya Khan carried out his policy of genocide—and had been caught doing so. There was little doubt who would pay for the mistake.

---

* She later told a reporter, "I can't understand a country like America being so afraid of the Soviet Union. I don't know whether they have an inferiority complex or what it is. This is what distorts the whole view of what is happening everywhere in the world. . . . America could have a tremendous influence in the world because in its technology it is so far ahead. But it is not able to play that role because of their wrong assessments, whether it is Mr. Kissinger's or anybody else's."

33

SPYING ON KISSINGER

HENRY KISSINGER SUFFERED through the most serious crisis of his three-year association with Richard Nixon during the Christmas and New Year's holidays of 1971–72. Although the policy in South Asia was Nixon's, Kissinger was the fall guy: He had failed in his most essential function, control of the press and the bureaucracy. Senior officials of the State Department dared to criticize the White House's policies toward India and Pakistan in conversations with reporters, and as public dissatisfaction mounted, Kissinger became more distressed and erratic. When he told his subordinates, "I am getting hell every half hour from the President that we are not being tough enough on India," he was not exaggerating. The tension inside the White House was acute. One aide remembers a day in early December when Nixon ordered Kissinger to hold a background briefing to defend the White House policies: "It was one of the worst days I had in my years there. Henry was screaming and yelling at us. He was supposed to provide an explanation of why it wasn't a 'tilt'—a mission impossible."

The rift between Nixon and Kissinger deepened on December 13, when Jack Anderson began publishing a series of classified documents dealing with this "tilt." By early January, Anderson had distributed copies of some of his documents to the *Washington Post* and the *New York Times*, and the White House's insistence that the President had been even-handed in his approach to the war had been discredited. Here, too, Kissinger was vulnerable. In the past, his NSC staff, which had once included Morton Halperin and other Jewish "liberals," had been automatically blamed for every significant leak. Not surprisingly, Nixon again suspected the men around his national security adviser. Kissinger's personal standing lessened with each Anderson revelation, but Nixon went further than merely blaming him for the leaks. He seems to have decided that Kissinger's inability to handle the press—one of Kissinger's great successes up to now—was responsible for his problems with Anderson and the India-Pakistan war. Kissinger suddenly found himself denied access to his boss.

At this same time, a far more serious problem emerged: The White House Plumbers discovered that Charles Radford, the Navy stenographer attached to the NSC, had been stealing all the significant documents he could get his hands on and passing them to Admiral Moorer's office. It amounted to an internal spy ring targeted against Kissinger—but Nixon chose to do nothing about it.

By Christmas week, when the full extent of Moorer's spying became known, Kissinger was in despair. The White House, he wrote in his memoirs, began "to deflect onto me the attack on our conduct during the India-Pakistan crisis. The policy became *my* policy." His comments about his relationship with the President were even more bleak: "Nixon could not resist the temptation of letting me twist slowly, slowly in the wind. . . . It was a stern lesson in the dependence of Presidential Assistants on their chief."

Yeoman Radford had arrived at the White House in the midst of the crisis in September 1970 over the possible election of Allende as President of Chile. Radford's assignment was to be a stenographer and clerical aide to Admiral Rembrandt Robinson, the officer in charge of the NSC liaison office set up to facilitate communications between the White House and the Joint Chiefs of Staff. Robinson was more than just a facilitator, however, as Radford was quick to perceive. He was held in high esteem and trusted by Alexander Haig and Henry Kissinger and was personally involved in the most secret of the White House activities. He was a breathing "backchannel" capable of carrying orders from Kissinger via Haig to Admiral Moorer, thus bypassing the Secretary of Defense. Admiral Moorer was more than willing to do what his predecessor, General Earle Wheeler, would not: carry out a combat mission or a planning study for the White House without informing Melvin Laird, who in late 1971 was more than ever viewed as the enemy.

Radford learned that there was more to his job than merely helping to subvert the chain of command. Within weeks, Admiral Robinson informed the yeoman that he was to begin spying on the NSC itself. Radford later described their talk in testimony before a Senate investigating committee: "He told me that I would be seeing things that, in some cases, he would not see and that, as I became more familiar with his files, I would know what he was interested in; that I should make sure that he saw or knew about what I had seen. He stated that if I was able to make a copy, to do so and give it to him. He made it clear that my loyalty was to him, that he expected my loyalty, and that I wasn't to speak outside of the office about what I did in the office."

Radford's testimony was given in 1974, when he was still on active duty in the Navy.* In later interviews with this author he said what he felt he could not say at that time. He had taken the job in the White House principally because he was informally told that a good performance there would enable him to obtain a commission as a Navy warrant officer; that ambition helped sustain him throughout his fifteen months as a member of Kissinger's staff. During that time, he purloined five thousand or more documents for Admiral

* The hearings were held in February and March of 1974 by the Senate Armed Services Committee, as the result of repeated newspaper stories and the urging of committee member Harold Hughes, the liberal Democrat from Iowa who had been instrumental in 1973 in getting hearings on the Air Force's allegedly unauthorized bombing of North Vietnam. Only four days of hearings were held by the notoriously pro-military committee, whose chairman was John C. Stennis, Democrat of Mississippi. None of the conservatives who comprised the majority on the committee had any stomach for pursuing the inquiry, which dribbled away by the spring with few of the relevant witnesses having been summoned. At one stage, Senator Stennis told me in a telephone conversation that if he continued the investigation, it would "destroy the Pentagon." There was little public pressure on the committee, in that hectic post-Watergate period, to do a more thorough investigation.

Moorer and the Joint Chiefs. "I took so darn much stuff I can't remember what it was," Radford said. "It was a perfect thing: I had everybody's confidence." Radford made it a point to be polite, well-groomed, self-effacing, and willing to do all the annoying jobs that have to be done in any large office: getting coffee, running the copying machine, and filling in for secretaries on coffee breaks. As a military man, he was assumed to be above suspicion, and Kissinger's secretaries often relied on him to copy special documents. He would do so, and make an extra copy for his admiral. He managed to make himself a permanent coffee-break fill-in for the secretary to Colonel Richard Kennedy, who handled all White House sensitive materials, including 40 Committee documents and data on the secret Paris peace talks. Radford would copy those materials daily or as often as possible; the secretary knew that she could stay an extra few minutes on her coffee break and not irritate the polite yeoman. At night Radford would calmly enter the White House area where burn bags—full of classified documents earmarked for destruction—were stored pending their shredding and incineration. Those documents included carbon copies of personal memoranda from Kissinger to Nixon and drafts of various foreign policy messages. They must also have included copies of Kissinger's personal policy recommendations to the President after National Security Council meetings; those recommendations, as everyone had learned, shaped the policy far more than the deliberations of the NSC Cabinet members, who were rarely given access to all that Nixon and Kissinger knew.

Radford followed a procedure designed to insulate Admiral Moorer from culpability in case the spy operation was discovered. Admiral Robinson instructed him to cut off any identification markings, including the letterhead, from the purloined papers and then copy the document with a plain piece of white bond paper behind it. The idea for the procedure may have come from Moorer. In his memoirs, Admiral Zumwalt quoted Moorer as describing to him a NSC meeting at which David Packard, the Deputy Secretary of Defense, glanced into Moorer's briefing book and saw a document with a White House letterhead that had not been sent to either his or Laird's office. "From then on," Zumwalt wrote, "the [White House] liaison office made sure to cut off the letterhead before photocopying NSC documents for Moorer." Since Admiral Robinson maintained offices in both the JCS and the NSC, a special safe was kept near Admiral Moorer's office in the Pentagon for the stolen materials. Occasionally, Radford recalls, he obtained copies of documents so sensitive that the JCS chairman decided not to keep them in his safe but had them shipped back to the liaison offices. There was no doubt that the senior military officers around Admiral Moorer also knew what was going on, Radford says, for they would often go out of their way to compliment him after he had turned over some especially valuable materials, such as notes on Kissinger's private memorandum to the President on his first talk with Chou En-lai in July 1971. He knew what he was doing was wrong, Radford recalls, but he also believed that it would lead to a possible commission or, at the least, quick advancement. There was another reason, too: "I was loyal to the 'cause'—the Navy. And I was eager to please and would go to extra lengths to get a pat on the head." *

* It was widely understood that the military men assigned to the NSC had special loyalties and ambitions. Admiral Robinson was renowned as among the most assiduous of the "corridor cruis-

Besides approval, Radford was interested in self-protection. He began taking some of the most significant documents home.

Haig was the first direct victim of Radford's spying. In early December 1970, Admiral Robinson informed his yeoman that he was to accompany Haig and a small team of NSC aides on a fact-finding mission to Southeast Asia; it was on this trip that Haig laid the groundwork for the February 1971 invasion of Laos. Haig, a military man, felt more comfortable with an all-male entourage, and Radford served as the chief stenographer and typist. Robinson gave the yeoman a shopping list of documents to steal, including, Radford later testified, any "Eyes Only" cables from Haig to Nixon and Kissinger. There was concern in the JCS about further American troop cuts in Vietnam, and Radford was urged to watch for any information on that subject stemming from Haig's private talks with President Thieu. Radford did his job well; by the end of the trip he had accumulated a thick sheaf of materials.

When Radford was back in Washington, the efficient Robinson instructed him to note carefully the name of the official who had written each document, Radford testified, "as this would make it more useful. . . ." Robinson was cautious with the material and usually delivered it to Admiral Moorer's office himself. Haig made a second trip to Southeast Asia in March 1971; again Radford was assigned, and again he stole hundreds of pages of documents. The trips were hard-working affairs, with Haig constantly reporting back to Washington in "Eyes Only" messages.*

Radford's most daring thefts took place in July, when he accompanied Kissinger on the around-the-world flight that included the secret trip to Peking. By that time, Admiral Robinson had been reassigned and his replacement, Admiral Robert O. Welander, who was hand-picked by Admiral Moorer for the job, made it plain that there was to be no change in Radford's spying. Welander's basic advice, Radford recalls, was "Don't get caught." Before he left Washington with Kissinger, Welander asked him to keep an eye out for documents dealing with negotiations with China—someone inside the Pentagon obviously had a hint of what Kissinger and Nixon were up to. The yeoman managed to obtain so many contraband documents that by the time the Kissinger entourage reached New Delhi, midway in the trip, his own suitcases were overflowing. Radford had served in the American defense attaché's office in New Delhi before his assignment to Washington, and he turned to a friend still on duty

---

ers,'' those who kept their eyes open in the perennial struggle for a greater share of the Pentagon's budget for their branch of service. John Court, then working for Laurence Lynn's program and analysis staff in the NSC, sought Robinson's help for a study of Navy force structures. Later, the admiral asked Court for permission to read the study. "I said there was 'no way' Robinson could review it and he got mad and stalked out,'' Court says. "I went to lunch. While I was out, Robinson went to my secretary and said I'd approved giving him the memo. She said no and Robinson then tried to physically take it away from her.'' When he returned, Court said, she was still sobbing. Most of the NSC staff thought it was only on that clumsy level that the game was being played. Even Haig was involved in trying to protect his service, the Army, from budget cuts or reorganizations and sometimes exercised his influence with the President. Haig handled his problem in a direct manner, however, and his activities on behalf of the Army inside the NSC were so extensive that Kissinger developed a standing joke with which to demean his military assistant, telling his aides, John Court recalls, that he was planning to telephone General William Westmoreland, the Army Chief of Staff, "to see if he would let Haig work for the NSC for a day or so.''

* The trips also included a lot of hard drinking by Haig and others, Radford recalls. Apparently each of the men aboard Haig's plane was permitted to bring back one case of duty-free liquor, and Radford, as a favor to Haig, purchased a case in his name for the general. "We did it all the time.''

with the embassy to whom he entrusted three large manila envelopes crammed with documents. The friend was instructed simply to drop the envelopes, addressed to Radford at his White House office, into the diplomatic mail pouch from the embassy. They arrived unmolested on Radford's desk—"I coded the envelopes so I could tell whether they'd been tampered with." During the group's stop in Pakistan, Radford got into Kissinger's room and rummaged through his suitcases and briefcases, learning, to his astonishment, that Kissinger planned to fly secretly to Peking for his meetings with Chou En-lai. Radford rejoined the Kissinger group for the flight back to the United States, via Paris, where Kissinger was to hold more secret talks with the North Vietnamese. On that flight, Radford again ransacked Kissinger's personal luggage looking for material. He was able to take notes on Kissinger's private report to Nixon dealing with the first meetings with Chou En-lai in Peking.

A few days after Kissinger's return from Peking to the California White House, Admiral Moorer flew out for an NSC meeting and high-level briefings on the new China policy. Welander ordered Radford to drive to the Naval Air Station at El Moro, California, bringing the stolen papers. He arrived at Moorer's quarters with a stack of stolen documents as well as a smuggled copy of the agenda for the next day's meeting with Nixon and Kissinger. "I went into the bedroom and gave everything I had to Admiral Welander. I laid it out on the bed and explained where everything came from and what some things meant," Radford recalls. "I saw Welander go into the next room, a living room, and saw Admiral Moorer receive it." Some of the material he gave the admirals eventually arrived in the normal flow of documents to the Pentagon —"but very little of it."

Some weeks later, Radford was complimented by Admiral Moorer's executive assistant, Captain Arthur K. Knoizen, who told him to "keep up the good work." Radford knew exactly what he meant. Knoizen's predecessor in the job, Captain Harry D. Train II, had also praised the yeoman, telling him after one of the earlier trips with Haig that "you do good work."*

In September 1971, Radford went on another trip to Southeast Asia, with Haig, and again Admiral Welander gave him a specific request for information. Haig's trip came at the height of American antiwar unrest over the corruption of the presidential elections in South Vietnam, and Radford was instructed to look for documents dealing with the secret peace negotiations or "any messages" to President Thieu from Kissinger or Haig. Once again Radford went the extra step and rummaged through at least one of Haig's briefcases while on the trip.

Throughout this period, Radford accumulated a vast store of knowledge about the secret doings of the White House, ranging from illegalities, such as the proposed assassination of Salvador Allende, to the various contingency plans for the defense of U.S. allies, such as Israel, in case of nuclear war. He knew many of the sensitive intercept and decoding programs run by the National Security Agency; he also knew how the government's secret spy satellites operated, and how the satellites were targeted by a small group of officials,

* Knoizen and Train went on to brilliant Navy careers. By 1981 Rear Admiral Knoizen was the Navy's chief of legislative affairs and Admiral Train was commander in chief of the U.S. Atlantic Fleet, based in Norfolk, Virginia. Neither officer was summoned to testify before the Senate Armed Services Committee in 1974.

headed by Kissinger, who made up the executive committee, or Ex-Com, of the National Reconnaissance Office, the still-secret agency responsible for purchasing and targeting American satellites. He knew of such secret CIA operations as Project Jennifer, the multimillion-dollar effort to retrieve a Soviet submarine from the bottom of the Pacific Ocean, where it had mysteriously sunk; he also knew that Howard Hughes' Summa Corporation was cooperating with the CIA in providing a "cover" for the operation.

Asked in an interview why he thought he had been required to steal documents, Radford said simply, "The government stank. The JCS weren't getting all the information that they wanted and were forced to steal their information." Radford also didn't like what he saw of Kissinger's treatment of his personal staff; the rages and tantrums helped him to rationalize his thievery. "He frightened me," Radford recalled. "I was afraid of him. He just seemed too power hungry. I equated it this way: If things didn't go right in his office and he was a tyrant—what if he gained control of the nation?" Nixon was a mystery man rarely seen by the young Navy aide, but he did recall one evening when Nixon, accompanied by six Secret Service men, entered the White House from his offices in the Executive Office Building. "He seemed white and almost frightened," Radford said. "Imagine being afraid in your own home."

Another source of disenchantment was Admiral Welander, who was given to insults and unpleasantness. If there had been respect for Robinson, there was contempt for Welander, who, as Radford told the Senate, "seemed to come apart at the seams" during crises. In December, after what he viewed as months of loyal service to the Navy, Radford discovered that he had been passed over for a commission as a warrant officer, despite receiving the highest possible rating from Admiral Robinson and personal commendations from Haig. There was additional disenchantment with the White House "tilt" policy in the India-Pakistan war and the many lies to the public about its goals in South Asia. Radford had enjoyed his service in New Delhi with the American Embassy; he and his wife had made good friends among the Indians. All of this, investigators later concluded, led Radford to continue doing what he had been trained to do—surreptitiously obtain and pass along highly classified documents. Sometime in December, however, he apparently turned from Admiral Moorer to columnist Jack Anderson. Radford had met Anderson's parents in India, where they were traveling, and he was assigned to help them obtain visas. The Andersons were devout Mormons, as Radford was, and a friendship was struck. A year later, when he was in Washington, Radford and his wife were invited to dinner with the elder Andersons at the home of their son, Jack. In December 1971, at the height of his personal and professional uneasiness, Radford and his wife had dinner in a Chinese restaurant with Jack Anderson and his wife. A few days later, Anderson published the first of his columns on the Nixon "tilt" toward Pakistan that would earn him the 1972 Pulitzer Prize for national reporting.

Subsequent investigations left Pentagon and White House officials with little doubt that Radford had provided Anderson with huge files of White House documents, but in mid-December 1971, there was no conceivable reason for anyone in the National Security Council to link the yeoman to the leaks. Welander later told the Senate Armed Services Committee that he had begun to suspect Radford after realizing that Anderson's second column on the India-Pakistan war, published December 14, had accurately quoted from Pentagon documents that were available to his NSC liaison office. Welander recalled that Radford had talked favorably about his service in India, and that an Indian student had stayed in Radford's house over the summer. Radford had also told Welander he was concerned about the President's decision to move the Navy Task Group, led by the *Enterprise*, into the Indian Ocean.

The basis of Welander's defense, as it emerged during the inquiries, was that he had been the one to turn in Radford, and obviously he would not have done so if he had anything to fear. Radford knew who had turned him in. He remembers a stony car ride from the Pentagon to the White House the day the second Anderson column appeared. Welander, sitting alone in the back seat, "asked me pointedly if I gave the papers to Jack," Radford recalls. "There was a lot of tension in that car." A few hours later, he was relieved of duty. Whatever Welander's motives, the admiral obviously did not anticipate that the yeoman would begin discussing with outsiders his activities on behalf of the chairman of the Joint Chiefs of Staff. Welander may have rationalized that he was, in some way, less responsible for Radford's thievery since it had been initiated by his predecessor, Admiral Robinson, and since he and Radford had held no serious conversation about it. He may also have assumed that no independent investigation would be able to penetrate the secrecy of the White House.

In any case, Welander testified that he visited Haig on the morning of December 14 and told Haig why he thought Radford should be interrogated. Haig was the obvious person to turn to, since Welander knew that Haig had been involved—on Kissinger's behalf—in the July 1971 investigation of William Beecher's SALT story. Haig had worked closely with David Young and Egil Krogh, the White House Plumbers, on that inquiry. Shortly after his meeting with Welander, Haig telephoned John Ehrlichman, who still had overall responsibility for investigating leaks. Ehrlichman says that he was in a Domestic Council staff meeting across the street from the White House when the urgent call came. "Haig said that Jack Anderson was running a column about the movement of Navy vessels, in relation to the Pakistan crisis, and the President had said that I was to help Henry and Al in the development of the facts," Ehrlichman recalls. At that moment Kissinger was with Nixon at the economic meetings in the Azores; the White House secure telephone system must have been in heavy use that morning. Krogh was also at the Domestic Council meeting, and Ehrlichman ordered him to initiate the investigation with Young. The White House Plumbers were back in business.

Radford was not mentioned in the first Haig-Ehrlichman conversation, but he was apparently the first suspect to be interviewed. He was summoned to the Pentagon on December 16 and underwent the first of what would be four long interrogations over the next week by, among others, David Young, Kissinger's former personal aide, and W. Donald Stewart of the Defense Investigative Service, who had also worked on the SALT leak. At some early moment in that first interview, Stewart asked a question he had routinely posed to hundreds of suspects in his career: Did the yeoman know Jack Anderson? Radford admitted he did, and things suddenly became tense. Within a few hours, Radford—insisting, as he would throughout, that he had not turned over documents to Anderson—began talking about his work for Admirals

Moorer, Robinson, and Welander. "We had no idea what was going on," Stewart recalls. "We walked out thinking this was *Seven Days in May.*" Radford confessed to having obtained files from Kissinger's briefcases after the secret trip to China; Stewart immediately suggested that Young see Kissinger and find out what documents he had had. Radford could not be accused of theft unless the government could establish what had been stolen. When Young returned, Stewart got his first hint of trouble: The former Kissinger aide stalled and said he had not been able to meet with Kissinger. Stewart found it impossible to believe that Kissinger would not respond immediately to a report that a trusted clerk had been stealing from his briefcase, particularly in view of the White House's obsession with leaks. "This was top priority," Stewart recalls. "I knew that he [Young] had talked to him, because he had other orders"—to do all possible, so Stewart thought, to keep Henry Kissinger's office out of the investigation.

The next day, December 17, the yeoman was relieved of his duties in the military liaison office, and was also advised by Admiral Welander to hire a lawyer and stop talking to Stewart and Young about his role in purloining White House documents. Stewart was furious at Welander's interference and the admiral's insistence—during his own interrogation by Stewart—that the documents Radford had referred to were "too secret" to be discussed with the Pentagon and White House investigators. Radford kept on talking to Stewart and Young, however, and by December 21, Ehrlichman gave the President an account of the yeoman's activities. Haldeman and Mitchell also attended the briefing. There was the strong possibility of a far-reaching and politically devastating scandal—whose ultimate target might become the immense power and secrecy of the White House decision-making mechanism—and Nixon wanted his top aides to help him make an assessment. Nixon reacted to the briefing cautiously, Ehrlichman recalls, and at the end asked Ehrlichman to interview Welander, who was still on the job in the NSC. Ehrlichman knew that Nixon had an excellent reason for caution: "He and Henry had had a backchannel with the Joint Chiefs of Staff to cut out Laird and here they find that Moorer's been doubledealing on them."

On December 22 Ehrlichman and David Young interrogated Welander, using a tape recorder. The admiral "made a clean breast of it," Ehrlichman recalls. "He admitted everything but blamed it all on Robinson," his predecessor, who had "set it up." In his later testimony to the Senate Armed Services Committee, Welander characterized his response to Ehrlichman in far milder terms: "I found myself trying to put gross distortions of fact and circumstance into some reasonable and rational perspective," he said. He testified, however, that he did tell Ehrlichman that Radford had passed documents through him to Admiral Moorer.* Ehrlichman urged Welander to sign a statement describing his role in the spying, but Welander refused to go that far.

---

* Welander's 1974 Senate testimony was prepared with care, as Admiral Moorer was still chairman of the Joint Chiefs of Staff; all concerned, including Kissinger, worked together to whitewash the significance of the Radford incident. There is evidence that Welander, who hoped to avoid a permanent blemish on his record, was much more forthcoming in his December talk with Ehrlichman than he later admitted. W. Donald Stewart recalls that he and J. Fred Buzhardt, the Pentagon's general counsel, also had an interview with Welander in late December 1971, in which they learned many details of Admiral Moorer's role in the spying. Welander agreed to talk with the two men,

Ehrlichman's enthusiasm for the inquiry was based in part on self-preservation. The scandal came at a crucial time for the domestic affairs adviser, whose influence inside the White House had steadily dwindled during 1971, and he was determined to make the most of it.* What he failed to perceive was the lack of enthusiasm for such an investigation in the Oval Office. Nixon, Mitchell, and Haldeman were not willing to jettison the compliant Admiral Moorer merely for spying on Henry Kissinger. John Mitchell recalls his own attitude: "I only got in on the very top side of it—the problem of whether Admiral Moorer or somebody was trying to do a number on the President. Moorer was totally uninvolved and blameless. There wasn't any military junta doing a number on Richard Nixon, which was my concern. As for spying on Henry Kissinger, this goes on all the time." Mitchell, of course, knew that Admiral Moorer was far from blameless, but to prosecute the admiral would jeopardize the President and his backchannel maneuverings. Moorer, a native of Alabama, was also known to be a close friend of Governor George Wallace, who was being taken very seriously by the White House as an adversary in the 1972 elections.†

After his productive interview with Welander, Ehrlichman hurried to another meeting with Nixon, Mitchell, and Haldeman. The President raised an additional point: If Admiral Moorer and the White House's excellent backchannel arrangement suffered, it would mean more influence for Laird. Nixon told Ehrlichman that he had been relying on Moorer because "he was not sure Laird would follow his orders." To punish Moorer would give Laird a "whip hand" over the Joint Chiefs of Staff—which, of course, was the relationship Laird was legally obligated to have. Nixon's problem was not that Laird wouldn't follow orders, but Laird's awareness that some of the orders—such as the directive to bomb the PLO hideaways during the 1970 war in Jordan— should not be carried out.

Mitchell, assigned the role of covering up the mess, was sent to visit Moorer, who promptly denied any involvement and, Ehrlichman recalls, told the Attorney General that if the material he received from Radford was stolen, Admiral Welander was responsible and should be punished. On December 23, Ehrlichman and Haldeman were sent to brief Kissinger about the activities of Yeoman Radford. At this point, Ehrlichman was still the eager investigator, and he, as well as Stewart in the Pentagon, considered the spying on Kissinger as serious as the leaking of documents to Jack Anderson. Kissinger's initial response to the briefing baffled Ehrlichman; he was "calm, almost sleepy" as he listened to a preliminary report of Radford's spying.

Kissinger was far from calm. Nixon had been unavailable to him for days

---

who were conducting an investigation for Laird, after receiving what Stewart characterized as "an implicit deal. We got all his information but promised not to prosecute."

* Ehrlichman had been scheduled to serve as the advance man for Nixon's summit trip to Peking, but had been set aside for Dwight Chapin, the presidential appointments secretary, who was close to Haldeman. By early 1972, Ehrlichman had also lost the right to see any reporter he wished, and instead had to clear such meetings through Haldeman. He decided not to serve as domestic adviser in Nixon's second term and claims he probably would have left the White House by early 1973 if the Watergate scandal had not developed.

† Nixon was still in trouble in the polls, with Wallace clinging to as much as 15 percent of the potential votes, many of which would probably go to Nixon if Wallace stayed out of the race. There may have been concern that Wallace would make a campaign issue out of it if Moorer were forced to resign.

and Kissinger was convinced that the Radford investigation was directed at him—in part, as he told the Watergate Special Prosecution Force in 1975, because "Haldeman wanted to prove that Kissinger's people were unreliable and that only people hired by Haldeman were reliable." If Nixon and Haldeman refused to act, Kissinger would. One senior NSC aide recalls exchanging pleasantries with Admiral Welander late in the afternoon of December 23. "Two hours later they [security officials] were taking his safes away," the aide said, "just carting them out of his office. He didn't know he was going." The office was shut down by nightfall. Kissinger then arranged with Ehrlichman to listen to the tape of Welander's confession. Nixon had already decided to do nothing. The Pentagon's inquiry into the Radford-Welander spying had been quashed, on the President's orders, with Welander put into limbo, pending reassignment, and the yeoman hurried out of Washington to a new assignment in Oregon. Radford recalls getting only a few hours to pack, and spending much of that time frantically shredding documents and flushing them down a toilet in his home before the moving trucks arrived.* Kissinger and Haig spent ninety minutes listening to the Young-Welander interview the next morning, December 24, Ehrlichman recalls, and Kissinger finally vented his anger—at Richard Nixon as much as at the JCS machinations. "He won't fire them. If he won't fire Rogers—impose some discipline in this administration—there is no reason to believe he'll fire Moorer."

In turn, Nixon saw Henry Kissinger as his main problem in those last days of 1971. He complained bitterly to Ehrlichman that Kissinger had been behaving irrationally and offering almost daily tirades against Rogers. At one stage, as Ehrlichman reported in his memoirs, Nixon "wondered aloud if Henry needed psychiatric care." Ehrlichman was ordered to talk to Kissinger and Haig about such a possibility, a step he knew he could not take. Haldeman told Ehrlichman that Nixon was considering firing Kissinger, but such talk was little more than presidential musing. It would have been impossible for Nixon to dismiss his foreign policy collaborator before the summit meeting in Peking and before the 1972 elections. On Christmas Eve, Ehrlichman did raise the question of Kissinger's frame of mind with Haig, who knew—perhaps from Haldeman or from the President himself—that Nixon was talking about firing Kissinger. "The President needs Henry," Haig told Ehrlichman. "You've got to realize that the President isn't doing his homework these days. It's only Henry who pulls us through the summit conferences."

Kissinger had many ways of learning the full scope of Admiral Moorer's spying on his relationship with Richard Nixon. It is inconceivable that he

---

* Zumwalt, in his memoirs, described with considerable contempt the eagerness of the White House to accommodate Radford, who had requested that his new assignment be in the Northwest, where his family lived. Radford apparently did not like his first assignment, to the Seattle area, and asked for a change. Zumwalt, who had been pointedly told that Radford's orders were being issued at the specific direction of Richard Nixon, could only observe as Radford pronounced himself "pleased" with the reassignment to Oregon and the fact that his security clearances were not revoked. A few weeks later, after Radford had arrived in Oregon, the Pentagon learned he was not happy. Zumwalt was told that Radford did not think his new assignment provided him with a proper opportunity for advancement. The Navy tried to reassure him, Zumwalt wrote: "General consternation. Gnashing of teeth and rending of garments. Unbearable suspense. At 18.30 the telephone rings. It is the Under Secretary of the Navy [John W. Warner, later the Republican Senator from Virginia] calling the Chief of Naval Operations to tell him that . . . Charles Radford has agreed to obey his orders."

would have relied only on Ehrlichman's taped interview with Welander for his information; there was Haig, who was moving closer and closer to the Oval Office, and there was David Young, who would have viewed it as his duty to brief Kissinger fully on what was going on behind his back. Kissinger also knew that his relationship with Nixon had undergone a significant deterioration, signaled by the fact that the White House minions, directed—so Kissinger thought—by Haldeman and Ehrlichman, now felt free to be direct and heavy-handed in their attacks on him and the NSC staff. In his memoirs, Kissinger wrote, "I did not take kindly—or even maturely—to my first experience of sustained public criticism and Presidential pressures." Kissinger was more specific with the Kalbs, who describe him as feeling that "Haldeman and Ehrlichman, always on the lookout for an anti-Kissinger opportunity, were then engaged in an intensive effort to undermine his position in the White House." The President made it clear to all inside the White House that his national security adviser was out of favor. As late as 1974, Kissinger was still complaining about his treatment, telling a group of *Time* editors and reporters that "for four weeks I was not allowed to have a press conference and Ziegler said not a word to defend me. . . . I debated for several weeks at that time whether I should go on, and decided to." Kissinger made no mention in his memoirs of an internal debate at that time about resignation.

What Kissinger did in his moment of crisis was characteristic: He turned to the press. If the White House apparatus would not defend his honor, he would do it himself, via background interviews with trusted reporters. Coleman Hicks, Kissinger's personal aide at that time, recalls Kissinger's distress over Nixon's refusal "to step out front" and take the heat for the controversial decisions in the India-Pakistan war. "Henry started calling in journalists and putting his side out. He was talking to people and threatening to resign," Hicks says. "He would use that threat to get good coverage. He was extraordinary."

The columns began flowing in early January. Tom Braden's was one of the first, declaring that the leaks to John Anderson suggested "that somebody in the United States government—and at a high level—is opposed to the new China policy and is not averse to destroying Kissinger in the process of opposing the policy." Joseph Kraft concluded that the Anderson disclosures did not affect Nixon Administration policy but "The chief consequence was to impugn the integrity of Dr. Kissinger." Kissinger went even further with Marquis Childs, to the point of making it clear that the President knew who had leaked the documents to Jack Anderson and had refused to take action. "The leak of the Anderson papers seems to have come from a desire to 'get Henry' and put him in the worst possible light in trying to execute a dubious policy," wrote Childs. "The source of that leak is known. What to do about it is another matter, with no one in the administration prepared as yet to take action." Childs added that the documents "seem to have come out of the Pentagon. . . ." Kissinger, no amateur in the uses of the press, must have understood that some in the White House would view that leak to Childs as a threat. Childs concluded his column by noting that "much of what the President's adviser has done in three years in the White House is still secret. . . . It is no wonder he is target for tonight by the resentful and by those who fear that peace may break out." By early February, Kissinger had largely managed to expunge the negative criticism over India-Pakistan and the Anderson columns. Both *Time* and *Newsweek* made him—not the President—their cover story in the same week; the magazine accounts dealt largely with his role in the secret Vietnam peace negotiations, which had been made public by Nixon on January 26. The war in South Asia was barely mentioned in the magazine stories, and there was no hint of a major internal scandal.* The White House was still the dark side of the moon for much of the American press.

Nixon's decision not to prosecute Yeoman Radford or the admirals for their military spying was not only politically expedient but also had a short-term gain: added control over Admiral Moorer and the Joint Chiefs of Staff. The summits in Peking and Moscow lay ahead, with the pending concession on an American pullout from Taiwan and the approval of SALT I, and the President needed steady support from the military. Ehrlichman says that Mitchell again visited Moorer on behalf of the President "to let him know that we had the goods." At the same time, Moorer was informed that he would be renominated in the spring to serve a second two-year tour as JCS chairman. Asked why Nixon chose to reappoint Moorer to the nation's highest military post, Ehrlichman smiled and said, "After this, the admiral was preshrunk."

There was a lingering problem: Melvin Laird. According to Ehrlichman, Nixon was fearful that Laird, who had different standards from the White House for senior military men, might react to the spying scandal by preemptively firing Moorer. Nixon's decision to retain the admiral prevented that possibility, but Laird had ordered Admiral Welander to turn over to him the contents of his personal safe. Welander asked Haig what to do. That a one-star admiral would not respond to an order from the Secretary of Defense distressed no one in the White House. The problem was funneled to Ehrlichman, who ordered Haig to tell Welander that any documents in his possession were to be delivered to the White House, and not to Laird. "We assumed Welander still possessed copies of some of the material he'd sent to Moorer," Ehrlichman recalls. "Some of it might be dangerous in Mel Laird's hands." The documents stayed in the White House.

If there was any concern in the White House over the decision not to take legal action against Radford, Nixon eased it by authorizing wiretaps on the yeoman's home telephone in Salem, Oregon, and at his new duty assignment at a Naval Reserve Center there. (Radford was also wiretapped in Washington before he was shipped west.) The wiretaps stayed in place until June 20, 1972, a few days after the Watergate break-in, and produced little of significance

* There was apparently one leak that Kissinger did not manipulate. Kissinger obviously had complained bitterly and in some detail about the military spying to Dr. Fritz Kraemer, a senior Army adviser who had befriended Kissinger during World War II and served as his mentor in the early days of the Nixon Administration. Kraemer shared Kissinger's outrage, and at one point, during one of his regular meetings with a group of Pentagon correspondents, mentioned the military spying. One of the reporters, Lloyd Norman of *Newsweek*, immediately tried to follow up the story, but Admiral Moorer refused to be interviewed and his aides denied the account. Other senior officials in the Pentagon, including Laird, also refused to discuss the allegation. "They were scared to death," Norman recalls. "It was the most tightly held secret in my thirty-two years in the building."

except a congratulatory telephone call from Radford to Jack Anderson in early May, when Anderson won his Pulitzer Prize.*

Donald Stewart, the Pentagon investigator, recalls being urgently summoned to David Young's White House office on December 23, shortly after Nixon had decided to take no action in the military spying case. Young shocked Stewart by ordering him to "establish" a homosexual relationship between Anderson and Yeoman Radford; it was clear from Young's tone that Stewart was not merely to investigate such a relationship but find one. Stewart, a former FBI agent who was nearly fifteen years older than Young, objected emphatically. As Stewart protested, Young jumped up and shouted, Stewart recalls, "Goddamn, the President wants this and every time we tell him we can't do something!" Later, as the Watergate scandals unfolded, Stewart came to realize that Young had indeed been passing along a presidential order.

A few weeks later Nixon tried again, this time working through Charles Colson, who in turn went to E. Howard Hunt, another of the Plumbers. Precisely what Nixon wanted done to Anderson later became a source of dispute, but as first reported by Bob Woodward of the *Washington Post,* Hunt told associates that he had been ordered late in 1971 or early in 1972 to assassinate Anderson "because he was publishing sensitive national security information." In his autobiography, G. Gordon Liddy, who refused to testify about the matter to the Senate Intelligence Committee, wrote that Hunt told him early in 1972 that Anderson had to be stopped because he had compromised a top American intelligence source overseas—an apparent reference to Moraji Desai, the Indian whose reports had been so heavily relied upon by Nixon and Kissinger in the India-Pakistan war.

In his memoirs, Nixon claimed that he had decided not to prosecute Radford for leaking the documents to Anderson solely because of the fear that too many state secrets would come to light during judicial proceedings. The real concern was to avoid a scandal that might compromise both his reelection and his and Kissinger's control over the foreign policy apparatus. On December 29, at the height of the Radford crisis, the Justice Department reindicted Daniel Ellsberg on twelve charges for his alleged role in the theft and unauthorized possession of the Pentagon Papers. The press and the public could never have been made to understand how a President who so assiduously prosecuted Ellsberg could do nothing when documents far more sensitive than the Pentagon Papers were stolen by a Navy yeoman from the personal effects of his national security adviser. There had to be yet another worry: that the revelation of the military spying could lead to public knowledge of the existence of the White House Plumbers, whose leaders, David Young and Egil Krogh, had been directly

---

* Local police officials in Salem were not told about the FBI wiretaps, which were authorized by John Mitchell. The secrecy led to some consternation when the taps produced evidence that one of Radford's co-workers was making a series of obscene telephone calls to the wife of a colleague. It was decided not to pass along the information, for fear of compromising the wiretaps on Radford. The Radford wiretaps also led to the removal of Egil Krogh from the White House Plumbers. Krogh recalls that he had been ordered by Ehrlichman to seek authorization from John Mitchell for wiretaps on Radford and another enlisted White House aide. Krogh chose not to make the request for a variety of reasons, one of them being that he simply "didn't want anything to do with it any more." A few days later, Krogh says, Ehrlichman telephoned and abruptly ordered him off the investigation.

involved in the illegal break-in at the office of Ellsberg's psychiatrist in Beverly Hills, California, a few months earlier. All the Plumbers' activities, including their attempt to concoct cables suggesting that John F. Kennedy had a direct role in the assassination of Ngo Dinh Diem in 1963, would be compromised. And the journalist who would undoubtedly begin the unraveling was Jack Anderson.

Nixon's fear of Anderson, of what he knew, or could learn, about the workings of the White House, was acute by the end of 1971, and yet, Ehrlichman recalls, the President refused to grant John Mitchell permission to wiretap Anderson's telephones at the time the taps were placed on Radford's. Nixon apparently feared that Anderson's contacts inside the FBI were so extensive that he would be tipped off about a legally authorized wiretap. Perhaps Anderson would also be told of other wiretaps that had not been legally authorized.

Given the fear and anger in the Oval Office, if Richard Nixon could not move legally to stop Anderson, he would certainly seek to damage his antagonist in other ways. Liddy wrote that he and Hunt had lunch with an active-duty CIA physician and discussed various techniques for drugging Anderson. The three men reached apparent agreement, so Liddy wrote, that Anderson should "become a fatal victim of the notorious Washington street-crime rate." He learned later, Liddy added, that assassination had been ruled out by Hunt's "principal," an obvious reference to Charles Colson. Colson, in testimony before the Senate Intelligence Committee, denied any knowledge of assassination plans but said that Nixon had asked him "many times" to take action to discredit Anderson. He also said that he could not "discount the possibility of having said something in jest" to suggest that Anderson should be eliminated. In its final report in 1976, the committee concluded that there was no available evidence of a plan to assassinate Anderson, but it stated that, at a minimum, Hunt and Liddy had considered means of drugging Anderson to discredit him in public.

There was a third stage in Nixon's private campaign against Anderson. In mid-February of 1972, the CIA mounted a major surveillance operation against the columnist and his chief aides, spending the next two months following them by car and foot in an attempt to learn their sources. The inquiry, given such code names as "Mudhen" and "Celotex," used as many as twenty agents to follow Anderson and his family around suburban Washington and elsewhere. The illegal domestic surveillance was conducted at the direct order of Richard Helms, who later claimed, in response to a lawsuit filed by Anderson, that he had done it because of Anderson's reporting on India and Pakistan. The CIA failed to learn any of Anderson's sources, although agents filed a photograph of Les Whitten, an Anderson associate, walking down the street with a woman they could not identify. Whitten was shocked when he saw the photograph, which he obtained in 1976 under the Freedom of Information Act, because the woman with whom he had been walking was one of his best sources at the time. "We were with them [sources for the column] all the time," Whitten said. "You'd think the CIA would be able to do better than that."

The only certainty in the White House at this period was that whatever Richard Nixon wanted, his aides strove to accomplish. A chastened Henry

Kissinger spent January trying to work his way back into Nixon's good graces, a job made easier by the approaching Chinese summit and the President's decision to make the Paris peace talks public. Nevertheless, Kissinger had a constant reminder all that month of the President's wrath. At the height of his rage, Nixon had ordered Ehrlichman to initiate a detailed investigation into NSC security practices. Kissinger later told a friendly reporter that Ehrlichman had planned to assign the inquiry to David Young, but decided not to when Haig threatened to resign. If true, this is the first known instance in which Haig made such a direct threat, which was a standard Kissinger gambit. Ehrlichman eventually turned to Charles A. Sither, a retired Air Force colonel and White House security expert, who spent much of January interviewing more than a hundred NSC aides. Sither concluded that there was a serious morale problem among the Kissinger staff and said as much in a written report submitted to the President, through Haldeman, in mid-February.

No one paid much attention. By then the Nixon-Kissinger tandem was back on course. The Peking summit matched the President's dreams as a political bonanza; so did the revelation of the secret Paris peace talks. There were Vietnam, the Moscow summit, and reelection to worry about. The Kissinger problem would be dealt with later. The overt feud was over, but the lesson was reinforced: Pleasing the President was the first priority.

Kissinger, by surviving his New Year's crisis, underscored a basic reality in the White House. Nixon, for all his ambivalence about his national security adviser, had few options. Kissinger still dominated the press in a way Nixon never could. To move against him would create a firestorm of media protest; it could also lead to revenge from one who—as the President must have known—assiduously continued to ship files and documents to Nelson Rockefeller's estate in New York. Those files were not only the raw material for Kissinger's memoirs but also his protection.

34

VIETNAM: GOING PUBLIC

CONVINCED BY EARLY 1972 that he was in deep political trouble, Richard Nixon gambled on a quick fix: He would go public with the Paris peace talks, a surefire public relations success that would give him a boost in the polls. Whatever long-run damage such maneuvering would do to the talks would be far outweighed by the short-run political gain. Kissinger loyally supported his President in that decision, although he certainly understood that it would doom any chance for a negotiated settlement before Hanoi's anticipated spring offensive. That such an offensive was being planned was no secret in Washington, but there were divisions over when and where the North Vietnamese would strike. It was a high-stakes political game but a familiar one. Both men knew there would be no one else to blame if some part of the truth emerged.

Vietnam and the secret threat policy was not the only danger in early 1972. The White House was continuing to wage secret wars elsewhere. In Chile, Nixon and Kissinger were still pressuring the CIA to force Salvador Allende out of office. In late 1971, Ambassador Korry had been replaced by Nathaniel M. Davis, a career Foreign Service officer who understood his real mission all too well. In one of his first "Eyes Only" cables to Washington, Davis described his initial impression of Santiago in words more appropriate to a battlefield commander than a diplomatic envoy: "What is significant now is growing conviction in opposition parties, private sector and others that opposition is necessary. . . . Reports of discontent and plotting in the military services have been substantially greater during past two months than before." The military potential for "playing a role in forthcoming months," he added, "is perhaps slightly increasing." By early 1972 there was a new tactic in the covert war against Allende. The CIA had begun heavily subsidizing the Institute of General Studies, a right-wing think tank in Santiago that became, according to a still-classified portion of the 1975 Senate Intelligence Committee report on Chile, "the brain center for all groups opposed to the Allende government. A steady flow of economic and technical material went [from it] to opposition parties and private sector groups," including anti-Allende unions. During 1972, the 40 Committee, still directed by Henry Kissinger, authorized more than $2.5 million in secret CIA subsidies to anti-Allende forces.

Nixon and Kissinger realized the necessity of avoiding any public hint of their real intent toward Chile in an election year. It was an intent easy to hide, since the CIA operations were known to very few. It was more difficult in

Cambodia, where the President and his chief adviser, ignoring reports of high-level corruption and evidence of massive civilian dislocation, continued to support the Lon Nol regime in its futile war against the Cambodian Communists, the Khmer Rouge. In late 1971, Lon Nol's army suffered a horrendous defeat—the toll was never fully calculated—in an attempt to mount an offensive against the Khmer Rouge. By early 1972, the Cambodian Ministry of Health estimated that more than 20 percent of the property in the country had been destroyed in the war; by then, too, more than two million of Cambodia's seven million residents had been displaced. This information was readily available in Phnom Penh but did not seem to get as much attention as similar statistics did in South Vietnam; Cambodia was still a sideshow. Nixon was asked about the war in Cambodia only once in his six 1972 news conferences, and even then the question was in the context of further withdrawals of American troops.* By the end of the year, a basic administration aim was to keep the war going in Cambodia. That struggle, Nixon and Kissinger believed, was aiding the progress of Vietnamization in South Vietnam. The Cambodians who had been killed already, and those who would be slaughtered in the next three years, were bargaining chips.

Nixon's feud with Kissinger soon yielded to his political problems. Senator Edmund Muskie had pulled even in the Harris and Gallup polls in the first week in January. Harris reported the two men at 42 percent each, with Governor George Wallace a distant third at 11 percent. Gallup reported Nixon with 43 percent of those polled, followed by Muskie with 42 percent and 12 percent for Wallace. The President's mishandling of the India-Pakistan war was a short-run factor; the basic problem was Vietnam.

Nixon tried to shake the Vietnam bogeyman in the first weeks of the new year. On January 7, he announced his candidacy by authorizing his supporters to enter his name in the New Hampshire primary. A week later he announced the scheduled withdrawal of 70,000 more troops from South Vietnam by May 1, reducing the number of American combat soldiers to 69,000. In a subsequent news conference, coordinated by the White House, Laird declared, "We no longer will have, with this announcement, any active U. S. military divisions in Vietnam." All combat responsibilities, he explained, had been turned over to the South Vietnamese. At the same time, "We will continue to use American air power to protect the remaining forces. . . ." The American policy had

* During this period, the CIA was confronted with another internal dispute over the size of enemy forces in Southeast Asia. Samuel Adams, the CIA analyst who had provoked controversy with his estimates of Vietcong penetration of the South Vietnamese government, had moved on to Cambodia and discovered major discrepancies. Adams, as he later wrote in an essay for *Harper's,* concluded that the number of Khmer Rouge had reached more than ten times the official estimate. He slipped a memorandum of his new findings to John Court the day before he officially turned over his report to his superiors in the Agency. The CIA was unable to suppress the study, but Adams was punished; he was taken off all studies dealing with the Khmer Communist Army. The CIA assigned the problem to a junior analyst, Adams wrote, who was instructed to hold the official estimate of Khmer Rouge to under 30,000. "I spent the rest of 1971 and a large part of 1972 trying to get the CIA to raise the Cambodian estimate," he wrote. "It was useless. The Agency was busy with other matters, and I became increasingly discouraged. The Cambodian affair seemed to me to be a repeat of the Vietnam one; the same people made the same mistakes, in precisely the same ways, and everyone was allowed to conceal his duplicity." Adams resigned from the CIA in 1973.

come down to an equation: The South Vietnamese Army, aided by American bombs and matériel, was to equal the North Vietnamese and Vietcong forces.

The dwindling support for Nixon in the polls was reflected in Congress, where Democratic opponents of the war had become more outspoken. In November, the House and the Senate had agreed on a compromise version of the Mansfield Amendment declaring it was the "policy of the United States" to end military operations in Vietnam and withdraw all troops pending North Vietnam's release of the prisoners of war and its accounting of all missing in action.* The amendment seemed to match precisely the offer that Hanoi had secretly made in the Paris peace talks before the South Vietnamese elections. Congress was asking the White House to accept a proposal it had already rejected. North Vietnam correctly read the mood of the American public and Congress, but Nixon and Kissinger still wanted to end the war on their terms —with "honor." In the memoirs, neither of them took note of the similarity between Hanoi's offer and the Mansfield Amendment, but Kissinger did say he realized Congress would not hold out much longer: "The day when the Congress would legislate a deadline was clearly approaching." The pending presidential trip to Peking would not be enough to hold off Congress, he added, for a North Vietnamese offensive in the spring of 1972 was imminent and "our domestic position was sure to be under assault again." Kissinger did not add that Hanoi's offensive was made all but inevitable by the circumstances surrounding Nguyen Van Thieu's reelection in Saigon, by General John Lavelle's "protective reaction" bombing of the North, by the secret escalation of the White House's peace terms, and by Richard Nixon's decision to make the secret peace talks public.

The peace talks were now deadlocked. North Vietnam was no longer hinting at the possibility of a separate military settlement. As before, Hanoi was saying that no peace was possible until Thieu and his claque were out and a three-tiered coalition government, including Communists, was installed. The United States was still insisting that any settlement be linked to a ceasefire in South Vietnam, Laos, and Cambodia, with the political future of the South left to the South Vietnamese. Thieu would resign a month before a new presidential election, to be handled by an independent commission, but his police and military forces would not be disbanded.

The exact date when Nixon and Kissinger decided to publicize their version of the peace talks is not clear. In his memoirs, William Safire told of being summoned from the Super Bowl game in Miami on January 16 to work on the President's speech, which was given on January 25. By the sixteenth, Nixon had already received a lengthy draft from Kissinger's office. The goal, Safire clearly understood, was political, and Kissinger was very much part of the effort. He described Kissinger as expressing bitterness at the way Hanoi had manipulated the liberal Democrats: "For the first time," Kissinger said, as if it were justification for going public, "they've used the secret talks to create confusion, and we cannot permit that." †

---

* Nixon subsequently declared that he would disregard the compromise amendment, which he depicted as a "judgment" about how to withdraw from Vietnam that "is without binding force or effect." Senator Frank Church, the Idaho Democrat, angrily denounced Nixon's statement: "What is he going to do next? Dispatch Henry Kissinger . . . to Capitol Hill and disband the Congress?"

† Hanoi, as Kissinger and Nixon knew, had been steadfast in its determination to keep the Paris

The cynicism of the decision to go public was all but impossible even for a trusted insider such as Safire to perceive.* Nixon and Kissinger controlled the information about the issues involved, and could present them in any manner they wished. Safire, in his memoirs, did show the President as being aware that the high drama of Kissinger's secret trips in and out of Paris would titillate the news media and thus "overshadow the news stories of who offered what and when." He quoted Nixon as telling him on January 17: "There's good cops and robbers stuff here."

Nixon's and Kissinger's theme was that the United States had been offering in the secret talks what its critics were publicly insisting should be offered: a withdrawal of American troops in exchange for the return of prisoners. In his memoirs, Kissinger described none of the internal discussions leading up to Nixon's January 25 speech, but he did quote a criticism by Senator McGovern in the first week of the new year. "It is simply not true—and the President knows it's not true," McGovern said, "that our negotiators in Paris have ever discussed with the North Vietnamese the question of total American withdrawal from Indochina in conjunction with the release of our prisoners." Kissinger's implication was that McGovern was wrong, and that Nixon's January 25 speech was intended to rectify such errors. "The fact was," Kissinger wrote, "that most opponents of the war were at this point beyond caring about the particular issues in dispute; they simply yearned for the war to end. . . . [I]t seemed to be taken for granted that the Administration which had arranged summits with Peking and Moscow within a three-month period was lax in negotiating with Hanoi."

McGovern *was* right, however. The White House had never proposed a troops-for-prisoners trade, but had always linked a ceasefire throughout all of Southeast Asia to its withdrawal offer. There had been one brief period, in the weeks before the corruption of the South Vietnamese election became apparent, in which the Hanoi government was suggesting—to Anthony Lewis and others—that a withdrawal-for-prisoners deal would be possible without a prior political settlement and with a ceasefire. But Hanoi's offer presumed total

---

talks secret. The previous October, shortly before his second trip to Peking, Kissinger had invited Wilfred Burchett to an early morning White House meeting. Burchett was close to the leadership in Hanoi and Peking and, as he wrote in *At the Barricades* (1981), had just talked with Xuan Thuy in Paris. Burchett had breakfast with Kissinger and a long conversation about the Vietcong's seven-point peace plan that had been made public the previous July, which Kissinger dismissed as a "bore." At one point, Burchett recommended that Kissinger seek private talks with the North Vietnamese. Burchett later concluded, he wrote, that Kissinger had been able to confirm from their conversation that Le Duc Tho and Xuan Thuy indeed "were observing the pact on total secrecy for the private talks. . . ."

* In his memoirs, Nixon did not mention political exigencies in describing his decision to go public, but declared that the talks were jeopardized by Yeoman Charles Radford and Anthony Lake, Kissinger's former personal aide. There was "no way of knowing," Nixon wrote, whether Radford had provided Jack Anderson with details of the secret Paris talks and no way to insure that Lake, who had joined Senator Muskie's campaign staff late in 1971, would not tell Muskie. "If the American people learned about the secret negotiations through a newspaper lead," Nixon wrote, "there would be political and diplomatic hell to pay." Nixon's analysis was extremely self-serving, for the difference—as far as the North Vietnamese were concerned—between deliberately betraying the peace talks for obvious political reasons and having them become public because of an unavoidable newspaper leak was enormous. Radford acknowledged in one of his interviews with me that he had access to the secret talks but said that he would have considered the release of that information a betrayal of his country. And there was never any evidence that Lake discussed White House business, as Nixon had to know, for Lake was among those wiretapped in 1970 and 1971.

American neutrality in the Vietnamese election, the end to all American bombing in the South, and a very limited ceasefire that would have protected only the American troops during their withdrawal from the South. And yet Kissinger told reporters, in a news conference on the day after the President's January 25 speech, that "We [Hanoi and Washington] may well differ about how we define the ceasefire, but that is not a contentious issue." He also stated that the North Vietnamese had at no time suggested in the secret talks that a ceasefire would be "difficult" to negotiate, adding that "the ceasefire is not in itself an issue in the negotiations, the principle of the ceasefire." The sole purpose of Kissinger's comments was political; he, like Haldeman, Colson, and the others, was trying to help the President score political points.

Neither Kissinger, in his on-the-record news conference—the first of his White House career—nor Nixon, in his speech, made clear that the ceasefire Washington was proposing had been rejected out of hand by the North. The deception was aimed not only at the public but at the White House staff. Safire, in his memoirs, reported that Nixon's chief justification for going public was to counter the Democratic liberals who were berating him for not making an offer that, so he told Safire, he had made in the secret talks—setting a date for American withdrawal in return for the release of prisoners and a ceasefire. Safire did not grasp that the White House's demand for a ceasefire had as little chance of being accepted in 1972 as did the standstill ceasefire offer Nixon made shortly before the congressional elections in 1970. Safire had also helped to write that speech, but at the time, as he reported in his memoirs, he realized the offer was a meaningless gesture made to get more votes for Republicans.

In his January 25 speech, Nixon also made public the main points of Kissinger's October 11 secret peace offer. That proposal, whose new feature was a guarantee that President Thieu would step down from office one month before a new election, was taken at face value by most in the United States. Few could perceive the extent to which the offer, made barely a week after the uncontested reelection of Nguyen Van Thieu, had insulted the North Vietnamese. Nor were there many who understood that the October 11 offer had reinstated the demand for mutual withdrawal. Hanoi was again being told that its forces in the South, augmented in the last few months of 1971 by more than 100,000 men who walked down the Ho Chi Minh Trail, must leave. The text of the October 11 peace proposal, released by the White House shortly after Nixon's speech, called for North and South Vietnam to settle by negotiation "the implementation of the principle that all armed forces of the countries of Indochina must remain within their national frontiers." *Time* subsequently reported in its cover story on Kissinger that Hanoi had specifically been told that it would have to withdraw its troops from Laos and Cambodia as well as from South Vietnam.

Thus the American position had hardened significantly since May 31, 1971, when Kissinger renewed the stagnant peace talks with a much more forthcoming proposal. The May offer, which was not made public in full until Kissinger did so in his memoirs, depicted the withdrawal question this way: "The Vietnamese and the other peoples of Indochina should discuss among themselves the manner in which all other outside forces would withdraw from the countries of Indochina." The ambiguity was deliberate, and meant to pose an invitation for further negotiations on the issues to Hanoi, whose leaders, as Nguyen Co Thach explained, remained skeptical nonetheless.

The October 11 offer was considered a step back by North Vietnam and never received serious consideration. It was that offer, as Thach said, that played a role in Le Duc Tho's decision not to meet again with Kissinger on November 20. One skeptic, I. F. Stone, the independent journalist, described the October 11 peace proposal as ". . . the first time we ever heard of a con man offering the Brooklyn Bridge at half-price twice in a row to the same visiting hayseed." But the overwhelming majority of the media fell in line, as the President had anticipated they would, emphasizing Kissinger's exotic role in the secret diplomacy far more than the substantial issues of the negotiations. The President's decision to have Kissinger give his first on-the-record news conference also resulted in extensive accolades. *Newsweek* declared that Kissinger was a "skilled and cool negotiator—a fact dramatically underscored again last week when it was revealed that he had been the President's 'secret agent' in a dozen meetings with the North Vietnamese in Paris, meetings that, almost incredibly, went totally undetected by the world's press." It wasn't made clear why Kissinger's ability to deceive the press "underscored" his skill at negotiating. The *New York Times,* in its first reports on the news conference, did not mention the ceasefire requirement but reported that the Nixon plan called "for the eventual withdrawal of American troops in exchange for the release of the prisoners of war, and a political settlement to be determined by the Vietnamese people themselves in new presidential elections." That, of course, was precisely the offer Nixon and Kissinger wanted the American public to believe had been rejected by the North Vietnamese.

Some Democratic critics began to back off. Senator Mike Mansfield, whose withdrawal amendment had caused so much grief to Nixon and Kissinger, applauded the President's proposals as a "long step forward." Hubert Humphrey was quoted as saying, "So what, there are plenty of other issues" for the Democrats in the 1972 elections. Far less prominently reported was Senator Edward Kennedy's assessment: "As long as we try to condition our withdrawal on things like free elections, a ceasefire, or any of the other trappings . . . reasonable as they may seem, we shall be pursuing the same blind alley in public negotiations that we have followed with such futility in private."

The success of Nixon's speech and Kissinger's news conference was immediate. The Harris poll showed that Nixon had opened up a four-point lead, 44 to 40, over Muskie by early February, *before* he made his trip to Peking. Nixon moved promptly to continue taking advantage of the hoopla. Two nights after his speech, he sent Haldeman and Colson a detailed four-page memorandum, which has never before been made public, outlining a divisive two-week campaign "to sustain a massive counterattack on the partisan critics of our peace proposals." The White House propagandists were to go after Senators Muskie, Humphrey, and Kennedy by repeating "over and over again . . . that those who got us into the war are now trying to sabotage Nixon's efforts to get us out."

Nixon further instructed his aides that the White House attack should be structured not in political but in patriotic terms: "[I]t is essential that this not be presented as a Republican versus a Democratic issue . . . any converts who stay in our corner should always come in for a word of praise. That will enable our speakers to sharpen themselves on those who continue to badger us even after we have gone 'as far as we can go.' " There were instructions for Safire and Patrick Buchanan, another favorite in-house writer, to "Get a few very sharp lines and keep nailing them with them." One suggested Nixon "line": "We have done everything but offer surrender to the enemy. They want the United States to surrender to the Communists." Another "line": "Now his proposal has been made and has so clearly shown that the United States has offered everything that any honorable government could offer, they are con- sciously giving aid and comfort to the enemy. They want the enemy to win and the United States to lose. They want the United States to surrender." Nixon further suggested that some "positive lines" could be used, focusing on "how the President took heat for 30 months from his critics on the war when he had information in his possession which would have demolished them." But he told Haldeman and Colson not to invest too heavily in these: "I cannot empha- size too strongly, however, that the attack line will be more effective than the positive line. . . . [I]t will tend to keep the critics from getting out too far and also because it simply makes more news." Senator Muskie, the President's main challenger in the public opinion polls, was to be a particular target, Nixon wrote, because of his previous support for the Vietnam War as a presidential aspirant in 1968. Kissinger's role in all this was that of a loyal henchman: "You should inform Kissinger, Scali, and others who may be putting out our line how they should proceed. Try as much as possible to get Rogers to get into the act."

Colson remembers the memorandum as one of the many that Nixon would draft late at night, often when drinking by himself in his hideaway in the Executive Office Building, and have typed by his personal secretary, Rose Mary Woods.* By early 1972, with the election looming, Colson had assumed new standing in Nixon's eyes. He was receiving copies of such memoranda, formerly sent only to Haldeman. Kissinger, despite the success of his news conference, was viewed as a novice by the White House political operatives, but he was determined to change that. As the White House became more involved with political matters early in 1972, Colson recalls, "Henry would call me every morning and . . . pump me for information and then walk in on the President and talk as if he knew what was going on." †

Nixon ordered in the memorandum that Muskie should be a "particular tar- get," and his orders were followed. When Muskie scheduled a major Vietnam

---

* Nixon's control over his senior staff at this point was nearly total. On January 28, a few hours after he received Nixon's memorandum, Haldeman participated in an interview with Barbara Walt- ers, of the NBC *Today* show. The loyal aide parroted Nixon's words, telling Walters that the Vietnam antiwar critics "are consciously aiding and abetting the enemy of the United States. . . . The only conclusion you can draw is that the President's critics are in favor of putting a Communist government in South Vietnam and insisting that that be done, too." The interview, broadcast ten days later, created a storm and forced the White House to claim that Haldeman's comments were "his own personal point of view," not necessarily that of the President.

† Kissinger, concerned about Lake's decision to begin working for Muskie, did his best to make sure there were no more embarrassing defections from his staff. Arthur T. Downey, a lawyer who worked on European problems for Sonnenfeldt, began in late 1971 to talk about leaving the NSC to begin a law practice. Kissinger quickly let it be known that the young aide did not have the luxury of procrastination—he had to agree to remain through the election or leave right away. Kissinger would not have his aides quitting in the middle of an election. Downey left within a few months.

speech for February 2 at a church in Northwest Washington, the "attack" lines went out promptly.*

Muskie's speech, drafted by Lake and others, was front-page news as newspaper editors realized that a classic confrontation was in the making. Muskie articulated what amounted to a two-point peace proposal, calling for unilateral American withdrawal from South Vietnam and a clear requirement that the Thieu regime be compelled to seek a political accommodation with the PRG or face the loss of indirect American military support after the withdrawal. In return for the withdrawal, which included the removal of all American ships and bombers, Muskie called for the release of all American prisoners of war and Hanoi's guarantee of safe passage for the returning soldiers. No ceasefire was required.

Once a copy of the Muskie speech got to the White House, Colson recalls, there was a meeting with the President and Kissinger. "The goal was to cut down Muskie," Colson says. "He attacked and we dropped the shoe on him." The shoe was wielded by William Rogers, who, at the President's request, accused Muskie of jeopardizing the prospects for a negotiated peace by rejecting the President's peace proposal before the North Vietnamese responded. Rogers attacked Muskie's peace proposals as coming at an "inappropriate and harmful" time that did not serve the national interest. "Rogers resisted doing it," Colson recalls. "He said that he had never used the State Department for political attacks, but I psyched him up and he banged the hell out of it. He did a very tough and effective job." At the time of the speech, Colson says, Muskie had been running neck and neck with Nixon in the polls. "From that day he did nothing but drop."†

Muskie continued to drop in the polls, another victim of White House manipulation of foreign policy and reliance on "dirty tricks." Neither tactic was to let up. In late February, Muskie shed tears of anger when he responded to allegations—in the infamous "Canuck" letter published in the archconservative *Manchester Union Leader*—that his wife had made racial slurs against

---

* In the hours before Muskie spoke, there was near-panic in Chuck Colson's office. Colson had been ordered by Nixon to get an advance copy of the text so the White House propaganda experts could prepare a rebuttal for distribution before or just as Muskie's speech was delivered. Such gimmickry always had a high priority in the Oval Office. Colson ordered a group of his aides, headed by Noel Koch, a speech writer, to attend the meeting and obtain a copy of the speech. Even that seemingly routine task was turned into derring-do. In the Colson group was a White House secretary who had worked with Lake in Kissinger's office. Koch, convinced that Lake had recognized her, decided to grab a copy of the speech, which Lake was casually handing around, and flee. He ordered another aide to impede Lake or anyone else who might get in the way. Of course, no Muskie aide tried to prevent the Koch group from leaving, and Lake, in a later conversation, could recall nothing unusual. Koch remembers that the secretary resigned over the incident.

† Colson's ascendancy in the White House's political hierarchy coincided with the demise of John Mitchell as a trusted insider. Nixon, as his handling of the politicking over the secret peace talks made clear, chose—at least in early 1972—to address his tough-talking memoranda to Haldeman and Colson, who would do what he wanted without an argument. Mitchell, who was in the process of taking over the President's reelection campaign that January, had left specific orders to ignore Senator Muskie, on the theory that any White House attack would only add to his credibility. Colson, in his 1976 memoir, *Born Again,* wrote that Mitchell telephoned him in a rage after the Rogers attack on Muskie: "I'm going to the President unless you promise never to attack Muskie again." Colson made the promise, but his success with Rogers did little to diminish his standing with the President. Kissinger had his own reasons for helping Colson: Mitchell, as Kissinger had to know, had little confidence in Kissinger's political views. "Henry had his ideas, but what could he do?" Mitchell recalled. "He had no feel for politics." Little did Mitchell know.

New Hampshire's French-Canadian population. The letter, whose author was never located, was certainly spurious, but its impact, abetted by Muskie's dramatic response, was devastating. During the various Watergate investigations of the mid-1970s, Colson repeatedly denied any responsibility for the letter, but he did admit in an interview with the author in 1981 that his office had forged other denigrating letters in early 1972 as part of the White House campaign. None of those other letters, which Colson would not talk further about, ever became a public issue.

35

CHINA:
A PRIME-TIME VISIT

RICHARD NIXON AND HENRY KISSINGER left Washington for the Peking summit in midmorning, February 17, 1972. There was a brief departure ceremony, televised live coast to coast, on the South Lawn at the White House. The President, although he would be half a world away, would remain live on television for the next ten days. In his remarks, Nixon compared his flight to Peking to that undertaken by the first group of American astronauts to the moon. His "historic mission," Nixon said, was also being made as a journey of peace. If Nixon was heavily dramatic, it may have been because he was burdened with an additional secret: He was flying to China *without* a commitment that Mao Tse-tung would receive him. The fact that no such appointment existed was a state secret that February morning, but China's leaders knew that Nixon and Kissinger were putting themselves into their hands while all the world watched.

Adding to the drama was another secret: The Nixon mission was not really a journey of peace, but a chance to seal a bargain to accomplish what American and South Vietnamese armies could not do—to end the war in the South without displacing Nguyen Van Thieu. China was far more prepared than the White House realized to join in such a pact. The rapprochement would also benefit both countries in their war of words with the Soviet Union; each could foresee enormous strategic advantages in being able to play the other off against the Russians. The only concern, then, was China's persistent refusal to commit Chairman Mao to a formal meeting. There had been frantic telephone calls between Dwight Chapin and Ronald H. Walker, the senior White House advance man who had flown to China a month earlier to check out security arrangements. Was Mao in Peking? Had he set a date to see Nixon? "We couldn't talk about it on the open [telephone] line," Walker recalls. "We had to do it by code." He knew that any Chinese official listening in would understand exactly what he and Chapin were discussing, and that Nixon and Kissinger wanted nothing to endanger the trip.

John Mitchell said in a later interview that he wasn't perturbed about the lack of an appointment. "Henry talked to me about how the protocol wasn't complete before the trip," was Mitchell's laconic comment. That things worked out was enough for him. Rogers was far more concerned and ordered Roger M. Sullivan, one of the China experts in the State Department, to prepare an elaborate justification of Nixon's summit goals for public release in case things went awry. "He decided it was going to be a fiasco," Sullivan says. Nixon and Kissinger knew long before the trip began, however, what Rogers would not learn until the visit was nearly completed: that the White House had agreed in the backchannel to remove all American troops from Taiwan. Keeping Rogers in the dark led to a sharp confrontation on the sixth day of the summit, and to some frantic last-minute revisions in the joint American-Chinese communiqué that was issued at its close. All this furor was hushed up before the presidential party left the People's Republic of China, and remained unreported.

For the White House the most important summit issue was television. Dwight Chapin had gone along on Kissinger's second mission to Peking in October to arrange as much live coverage as possible. Kissinger had been reluctant, one of his aides recalled: "Henry was saying, 'The Chinese are serious people. We don't want them to think we're using the summit for political purposes.' " Kissinger turned out to be, as the aide put it, "more Chinese than the Chinese. They turned out to be understanding." Peking not only agreed to live television coverage but also constructed the ground satellite relay station for it.

In the last months of 1971, the public relations side of the White House, led by Haldeman, Chapin, and Ziegler, was immersed in the issue. There were morning staff meetings to discuss the media aspects, meetings so secret they were held in the presidential bomb shelter under the East Wing basement.

By early 1972 Richard Nixon had all but given up on dealing with the nation's newspapers; he had participated in only nine press conferences in all of 1971, and he had managed to avoid any meaningful contact with the press between November 12, 1971, and January 31, 1972—a period that embraced the India-Pakistan war; a presidential order freeing James R. Hoffa, the former teamsters union president, from prison; high-level conferences on international trade and monetary issues with Canada, Great Britain, France, West Germany, and Japan; and Jack Anderson's disclosure of the White House "tilt" in South Asia. In early January, when Ziegler joined Chapin and Haig on a third American trip to Peking to work out final details, the White House entourage included seven network officials and technicians but no one representing a newspaper. Unbeknownst to reporters covering the White House, the President's men had decided that while the three networks could have sixty-eight technicians on the 155-member press delegation that would accompany the President, it would include fewer than forty print journalists, including only twenty-one reporters to represent all the daily newspapers of America. Among the newspapers left out were the *Boston Globe* and the Long Island *Newsday*, both critical of Nixon's policies. There were no complaints from the newspapers or agencies that were invited, nor from the three television networks, whose employees made up two-thirds of the media delegation. China was a land of romance and mystery, and the visit of a President who came to power as an enemy of communism was a wonderful story, sure to grab the nation's attention—and high Nielsen ratings. That the White House was exercising total control over who could cover it seemed at worst a minor snag.*

Television coverage had another potential advantage. It would, perhaps, obscure one of Kissinger's most worrisome issues—how to justify the American concessions on Taiwan. It was obvious that China would find it politically impossible—despite its successful bargaining on Taiwan—to announce publicly that it favored a negotiated solution to the Vietnam War. But without such a stated concession, the Nixon-Kissinger bargain struck in Peking would appear lopsided, and those who did not know the White House secrets would wonder why the United States hadn't gotten more out of the Peking summit.

In fact, Peking's immediate strategic problems were, if anything, more acute than Washington's. The Soviet Union, with its troop buildup along the border areas, was a constant threat, and one that would be buttressed by any disarmament agreement with the United States at the May summit in Moscow. The rubles saved because of arms control with the West would be spent, Peking had to assume, along Russia's eastern borders. China was also obsessed with the idea that Japan harbored dreams of becoming a military power in the area again, a belief that Nixon and Kissinger had fostered. A reconciliation with the United States, so Peking thought, would lessen tensions in the area and persuade America not to encourage Japan in a military buildup or the development of nuclear arms. Finally, China was concerned over North Vietnam's impending success in the Vietnam War and a shift in the balance of power just when the central government in Peking was becoming stable after the disarray of the Cultural Revolution. Chou En-lai's position as Premier had become secure only with the death of Lin Piao the previous September, after Lin's alleged attempts to assassinate Mao.

Nixon and Kissinger made no public attempt to capitalize on China's strategic needs. Instead, the President was content to arrive as a supplicant and engage in daily television spectaculars. The men running the government in Peking couldn't resist bragging about their diplomatic skills in enticing him. In an interview with the London *Sunday Times,* published in December 1971, Chou En-lai seemed more than a little self-satisfied: "Nixon himself knocked on the door, saying that he wished to come to Peking himself. So well and good. We invited him to come for talks." Chou then referred to the October 1971 vote admitting China to the United Nations: ". . . [T]he talks [with Nixon] have not yet started, but we are already in the United Nations. This is a victory, and we have not bartered away any principles." Chou also knew that Nixon would make concessions on Taiwan, and he hinted as much: ". . . [I]f he comes to China and yet the Taiwan question remains unsettled, how will he account for himself when he gets back?"

However, Richard Nixon and Henry Kissinger understood that China was also paying a price: It was in league with the White House and the Soviet Union to pressure North Vietnam into a political compromise. It is not clear

* One protest did appear in the *Bulletin* of the Washington news committee of the Associated Press Managing Editors Association. In addition to criticizing Nixon for not meeting more regularly with the press, the news committee also focused on the China trip, pointing out that many more newspaper reporters had been permitted to travel on Nixon's three major trips to Europe and Asia in 1969 and 1970—forty-nine in one case—than were allowed to go to Peking. The APME bulletin, unfortunately, attracted little attention.

whether Washington learned of the tough stance taken by Mao and Chou at their meetings with Phan Van Dong and Nguyen Co Thach after Kissinger's second visit to Peking in November. If there were any last-minute doubts about the Chinese position, however, they were washed away early in January 1972, when Alexander Haig met with Chou En-lai in Peking. In his memoirs, Kissinger tried to play down the significance of the Chinese concessions on Vietnam. In the talk with Haig, Kissinger wrote, Chou only "reiterated his moral support for Hanoi and urged a rapid settlement of the war in order to reduce Soviet influence in Indochina." Years later, Haig gave Michael Maclear, the Canadian television journalist, a more meaningful summary: "I left that discussion with a very firm conviction that what he [Chou] was saying indirectly was, 'Do not lose in Vietnam, and do not withdraw from Southeast Asia.' " There was little moral support for Hanoi in that message.

Nixon and Kissinger had no choice but to minimize the extent of China's willingness to pressure the North Vietnamese on Washington's behalf. To describe such goings-on publicly would amount to a betrayal of the Chinese and lessen China's impact on the Hanoi leadership, as well as the rest of the Third World. The men running the White House thus had no choice but to accept publicly what looked to others like a flimsy bargain: a troop concession on Taiwan in return for a presidential visit to Peking. Not unnaturally, Nixon and Kissinger coped with their predicament by dramatizing the Chinese and ascribing to them the highest qualities of political sophistication and intellect. There was an element of honest awe in all this. A few weeks before the summit, Kissinger met with James C. Thomson, a Harvard specialist on Asia who was providing analysis for the American Broadcasting Company's coverage. Thomson recalls Kissinger's remarks vividly: "This man Chou En-lai. Never in all my years have I met anybody as impressive, except maybe Charles de Gaulle. What a mind. You know, Jim, the Chinese are different. The Russians tell you where they are moving in their negotiations—it's always a process of going from one fallback position to another. But the Chinese—they tell you right away what their ultimate fallback position is. Right away." Thomson thought, "Oh brother! If he believes the Chinese immediately tell you their ultimate negotiation position . . . then Henry is about to give away the Crown Jewels." But he made no attempt to caution Kissinger. "I'd waited twenty-two years for this opening and I didn't care how it came out. I rather applauded the Chinese. If they did a snow job on us for a change, it was about time."

In the months before the summit, Kissinger realized that the Asia experts on his NSC staff, headed by John Holdridge, would be unable to produce all the papers needed, and he turned to an outsider, Alfred Jenkins of the State Department. Jenkins was one of the few China hands who had escaped the purges of the "Who lost China?" lobby in the early 1950s, because he had been unrelentingly hostile to the Communist Chinese. Over the winter of 1971–72, Jenkins became a trusted insider and was provided with copies of the back-channel communications between Washington and Peking and the transcripts of Kissinger's meetings with Chou En-lai. His basic assignment was to draft a communiqué to be made public at the close of the summit. Jenkins, unable to handle all Kissinger's demands, in turn recruited two other State Department

Asia experts, Roger Sullivan and William A. Brown. The three men were given office space in a hideaway on the top floor of the State Department. It is not clear whether Kissinger realized that Sullivan and Brown were actually writing most of the papers, or indeed if he knew of the three-man operation. The secrecy extended everywhere. William Rogers and his top aides, Alexis Johnson and Marshall Green, knew of the special office, but they were not told that the Jenkins group had access to the backchannel messages and the transcripts of the Kissinger-Chou meetings. At one point Kissinger ordered a secretary from the National Security Council assigned to the office he thought was occupied solely by Jenkins; his fear was that one of the regular State Department stenographers who was loyal to Rogers would provide some clue about what was really going on. Sullivan recalls that most of the specific Kissinger requests for reports came late in the afternoon, with a deadline early the next morning. "That way," Sullivan said, "Marshall Green or any of the others wouldn't get to see it." Sullivan soon learned that he and his two colleagues knew more about what was going to happen in Peking than anyone in the State Department, including the Secretary.

Sullivan was fascinated by Kissinger's ability to absorb information. He knew little about China's history and its internal politics, Sullivan said, "but he managed to internalize the strategic issues that were important to the Chinese, and that's a great intellectual strength. When he asked for papers, they were good requests." Kissinger was unfazed by China's internal turmoil, announcing caustically at one point that he had been to Peking after the demise of Lin Piao, which had had no discernible effect on the arrangements. Sullivan was convinced that Kissinger was right in plowing ahead with the preparations without formally involving the State Department: "If he'd tried to do it on the usual interagency basis, the trip would never have taken place." For all his braggadocio, however, Kissinger's hip-pocket group of China experts quickly learned that he was sensitive. "You had to be very careful not to give the impression that you had some kind of expertise he didn't," Sullivan said, adding that Kissinger once became enraged at an aide who reproduced a phrase in Chinese script in one of the staff papers. Nine drafts of the proposed communiqué were prepared by Jenkins, Sullivan, and Brown before the mid-February summit, and Kissinger flew to Peking with a copy of each in his briefing books.

Nixon and his entourage arrived in Peking before sparse crowds but with an audience of hundreds of millions throughout the world. The Chinese leaders used their diplomatic leverage skillfully, as the President was granted an audience with Chairman Mao within a few hours of his arrival: The summit would be a success; Mao Tse-tung, having just solved his own political problems, would now solve Richard Nixon's. Kissinger, in his memoirs, implied that the invitation, which was relayed to him by Chou En-lai, was predictable. Instead of immediately accepting, on behalf of Nixon, he wrote, "I decided to play it somewhat cool by asking Chou whether he would read his toast at the evening's banquet or speak extemporaneously. . . . I inquired whether ours should be muted or tough, to respond to his mood." China's psychological dominance extended, obviously, to the formal toasts. It was only after Chou offered to send the text of his toast in advance, Kissinger wrote, that "I said I would fetch Nixon." Nixon's memoirs depict a Kissinger who was no longer playing it cool: "I was getting ready to take a shower when Kissinger burst in with the news that Chairman Mao wanted to meet me." The meeting with Mao was primarily a courtesy call, albeit a most significant one; by early 1972, China's foreign policy seemed to be firmly in the hands of Chou En-lai. Mao had suffered a series of strokes and had been living—in part out of fear for his life—outside of Peking. Yet he still exuded immense power and authority, and Kissinger and Nixon, who had spent more than three years desperately seeking to acquire those attributes, were impressed. "I have met no one," Kissinger wrote, "with the possible exception of Charles De Gaulle, who so distilled raw, concentrated willpower." Nixon described in his memoirs how he and Mao exchanged jokes over Kissinger's reputation as a lady-killer; the President also proudly told how Mao characterized *Six Crises* as "not a bad book." In the original draft of his memoirs, Nixon had much more to say about the meeting with Mao, telling how Kissinger had embarrassed everyone by suddenly and gratuitously making a scathing reference to Golda Meir, Israel's Prime Minister. Mao, though he did not comment, was obviously nonplused, and the President quickly moved in to "save the moment." Nixon deleted the section from the published version of his memoirs, but the incident, and Nixon's anger at what he considered Kissinger's boorish behavior, were widely known among his immediate staff.

At Nixon's direction, William Rogers and Marshall Green were excluded from that first session with Mao.* Nixon was accompanied only by Kissinger and Winston Lord, who—to forestall even more anger from Rogers—was cropped out of the official photographs as released by the Chinese government.† The Chinese, ever the courteous hosts, went along with the White House machinations. Nixon and Kissinger had carefully arranged for Rogers and his staff to negotiate trade agreements and cultural exchanges with their counterparts in Peking, while the more serious business of power politics was discussed at the presidential level with Mao Tse-tung and Chou En-lai. "These meetings . . . served the purpose of keeping the State Department delegation occupied . . ." Kissinger wrote. "The major problem was to prevent the Chinese, whose internal communications were less constrained than ours, from revealing in the foreign ministers' meetings matters that had already been settled in other forums. . . ." He added that before the various meetings took place, "Chou and I had to sort out the scenario to make sure who would participate in which meetings and who knew what."

Over the next five days, there would be televised formal banquets, televised walks along the Great Wall, and televised visits to the Chinese ballet. Richard

* Ronald Walker recalls the distress among the senior White House aides over the exclusion of Rogers. "It was a great big cow turd in Rogers' face," Walker says. "There was real resentment that Henry had gone." Adding to the resentment was the fact that Kissinger and Nixon had slipped away to visit Mao without informing either Walker or any other official on the advance team, whose function was to protect the President and accompany him at all times. Walker, who had been unable to learn in the weeks before the trip just when—or if—Nixon would meet with Mao, had been astonished two weeks before the summit to learn from a Chinese official that Mao had only then arrived in Peking. Mao's decision to see Nixon so quickly "was a high," Walker recalls. "Nixon was on a high from that time on."

† Lord kept a copy of the original photograph, which shows him sitting at Kissinger's left during the meeting.

Nixon was finally getting the kind of "p.r." he had sought for more than three years. Back in Washington, the White House press office was working overtime, sending copies of the daily news summary to Peking and photocopying front-page headlines from newspapers all over the country to relay to the President's quarters. "The White House was playing this as a pageant, not as news story," says Stanley Karnow, the *Washington Post* Asia expert who—after a struggle within his newspaper—had been granted permission to cover the summit. Most of the major newspapers and magazines, limited to only one reporter, had ended up sending a bureau chief or senior correspondent, not their Asia expert. "It was the big social event of the year," as Karnow puts it.* It was also a wonderful story and Nixon's finest week in the presidency. Nixon had defied one of America's post-World War II taboos and ended America's estrangement from the 800 million people of China. Karnow, with his *Washington Post* dispatches raising questions about the substantive diplomatic issues, felt that he was the odd man out. The press and the American public, as Nixon understood, were caught up in the cops-and-robbers aspect of the presidential visit to the mysterious Orient—just as they had the month before virtually ignored the diplomatic subtleties of the Vietnam peace talks while reporting in detail on Kissinger's ability to fly secretly in and out of Paris.

The story that everyone missed during the summit concerned the Shanghai Communiqué, the joint statement that was released in Shanghai by the White House and the Chinese government on the afternoon of February 27, the last day of Nixon's visit. Kissinger and Chiao Kuan-hua, the Deputy Foreign Minister, had worked hours each night on the final language of the communiqué, which both sides understood would be the only significant document to emerge from the summit. The form of the document, with both sides presenting their views serially, had been agreed upon in the Kissinger-Chou talks in October 1971. Both nations had made compromises to get to the summit, and both were anxious to hide the full extent of their private dealings. Kissinger's goal was somehow to negotiate a document that did not reflect all the American concessions on Taiwan. Peking, for its part, wanted nothing said of its willingness to intercede with Vietnam but insisted that Kissinger publicly state an American commitment to withdraw all its troops from Taiwan. It was a symbolic commitment, and both sides knew it: The final American troops would not leave Taiwan until 1979, but Mao and Chou had their political problems, too.

The pressures on Peking from the Communist world must have been acute, if Enver Hoxha's diaries are in any way typical. Commenting on a Chinese band that played "America the Beautiful," the Albanian leader sounded apoplectic: "The orchestra at the banquet played the song 'America the Beautiful'! The beautiful America of millionaires and multimillionaires! America, the center of fascism and barbarous imperialism! America, the murderer of Vietnamese and Arabs, the suppressors of the peoples' freedom. . . . And they sing to this America in Peking so ardently that Nixon, in his reply to Chou En-

---

* In an essay on the trip, published in *Foreign Policy*, Karnow listed only three other reporters on the trip who had concentrated on Chinese affairs: Henry Bradsher of the *Washington Star*, R. H. Shackford of the Scripps-Howard newspapers, and Robert Keatley of the *Wall Street Journal*. "I am inclined to believe that most newsmen who went to Peking unprepared for their task came home with egg foo yong on their faces," Karnow wrote.

lai at the banquet, said: 'I have never heard American music played better than this in a foreign country.' "

There is no way of calculating whether Nixon's potential problems from the China lobby on the right were more acute than the pressures on Mao and Chou from their left. The overall impact was enormous, however: Bargaining over the communiqué revolved not around the issues themselves but over how to best present them. In his memoirs, Kissinger described the initial Chinese position as unequivocal: "The Chinese wanted us to commit ourselves unconditionally to the total withdrawal of American forces from Taiwan." The impasse was solved, Kissinger wrote, when he "hit upon the idea" of separating the issue of phased withdrawals of American troops, which Nixon was willing to talk about in public, from the issue of total withdrawal, which the White House desperately sought to keep secret. "My proposal was to tie the final withdrawal to the premise of peaceful settlement, and to link the progressive reduction of forces to the gradual diminution of 'tension in the area.' " The Chinese expressed interest in this suggestion, which eventually was adopted. "I was convinced that we had made our breakthrough." Kissinger added didactically: "In every negotiation a point is reached where both sides have gone too far to pull back."

As finally published, the critical paragraph of the communiqué summarized the American position on Taiwan as follows:

The United States acknowledges that all Chinese on either side of the Taiwan Strait maintain there is but one China and that Taiwan is a part of China. The United States Government does not challenge that position. It reaffirms its interest in a peaceful settlement of the Taiwan question by the Chinese themselves. With this prospect in mind, it affirms the ultimate objective of the withdrawal of all U. S. forces and military installations from Taiwan. In the meantime, it will progressively reduce its forces and military installations on Taiwan as the tension in the area diminishes.

There is no doubt that Kissinger was adroit in his last-minute bargaining, but the fact remains that the basic language he proposed was more than two years old. Jenkins and his colleagues had borrowed the key formula from State Department staff papers prepared for the second Warsaw meeting in February 1970, in which Ambassador Walter Stoessel told the Chinese that "it is my Government's intention to reduce those military facilities which we now have on Taiwan as tensions in the area diminish."*

* Stoessel also broke significant ground in that second meeting in Warsaw by telling the Chinese that the Nixon Administration was willing to discuss a joint declaration confirming the nonaggression and noninterference principles of Peking's Five Principles: mutual respect for territorial integrity and sovereignty: mutual nonaggression; noninterference in the internal affairs of others; equality and mutual benefit; and peaceful coexistence. The Chinese had made that doctrine public in 1955 at the unaligned nations' conference in Bandung, Indonesia, at the height of the Cold War. The United States had consistently avoided expressions of support for the Five Principles on the grounds that the statement would somehow support Peking's claims over Taiwan. Stoessel, in the second meeting in Warsaw, significantly changed American policy by declaring that he believed the revised American position on Taiwan was "consistent" with the Five Principles. He also directly expressed official willingness "to discuss with you a joint declaration incorporating the principles . . . and affirming our two governments' adherence. . . ." It should be noted that Stoessel, by agreeing to discuss the Five Principles, was responding, in effect, to the Chinese. In November 1968, Peking had proposed in its seminal overture to the Nixon Administration that the two nations

Nixon, in his memoirs, acknowledged what was ultimately at stake in the negotiations: domestic politics. "We knew that if the Chinese made a strongly belligerent claim to Taiwan in the communiqué, I would come under murderous crossfire from any or all of the various pro-Taiwan, anti-Nixon, and anti-PRC lobbies and interest groups at home," Nixon wrote. "If these groups found common ground on the eve of the presidential elections, the entire China initiative might be turned into a partisan issue. . . . In the official plenary session with Chou, therefore, I spoke very frankly about the practical political problems a strongly worded communiqué on Taiwan would cause me." One of Nixon's arguments to the Chinese was that if he lost the election because of the American concessions on Taiwan, "my successor might not be able to continue developing the relationship between Washington and Peking." It was that argument, surely, that carried the day.*

As the summit neared its close, Nixon and Kissinger learned that their main problem would be not the Chinese, but the State Department. The completed communiqué had been initialed and approved by Nixon, Kissinger, and the Chinese politburo, including Mao and Chou, before it was shown to Secretary of State Rogers. Rogers and Marshall Green were seething by the end of the week, for they had been visibly and brutally shunted aside; the *Washington Post* later called the summit a "bad trip" for the Secretary. Adding to Green's dismay was the fact that he had been designated to tour the capitals of Asia after the summit to explain the rapprochement to America's anti-Communist allies. On Saturday, February 26, the Nixon party concluded its stay in Peking and flew to Hangchow, at the mouth of the lower Yangtze River southwest of Shanghai. It was there, in one of China's most beautiful cities, Green recalls, that Rogers permitted him to read the draft of the communiqué. "I thought it was disastrous," Green says, because it did not mention America's treaty obligations, still in force, with Taiwan. The omission was all the more glaring, as Green told Rogers, because the communiqué specifically cited America's continued support for South Vietnam, South Korea, and Japan. "The implication was that we were going to abrogate or overlook" the obligation to Taiwan, Green explained. "Why mention the others when you don't mention this obligation?"† Rogers, who had told Nixon he saw no major problems with

conduct their foreign policy toward each other on the basis of the Principles. It was the first time China had raised the issue since the beginning of the Cultural Revolution. A joint statement supporting the Five Principles was included in the Shanghai Communiqué.

* Kissinger's initial version of the dispute, as provided to the Kalb brothers for their biography, was extremely misleading. "Kissinger felt the Chinese needed a communiqué more than the Americans did, for two reasons: first, to justify Nixon's presence to the Chinese people, and, second, to present the Russians with a tangible example of Chinese-American cooperation," the Kalbs wrote. "Therefore, he felt that it was up to the Chinese to break the deadlock."

† Green recalls that the Kissinger version of the Shanghai Communiqué instantly reminded him of Dean Acheson's famous "mistake" in early 1950 when, in a speech before the National Press Club in Washington, the Secretary of State defined America's "defensive perimeter" as extending from the Ryukyus Islands in the West Pacific to the Philippines in Asia. He did not specifically mention South Korea. The Republicans made a major political issue of that speech in the 1952 presidential campaign, with Eisenhower, the candidate, accusing Acheson of "incompetence" and suggesting that his failure to include South Korea might have encouraged the North Koreans to go to war. In his memoirs, *Present at the Creation,* published in 1969, Acheson accused his critics of "specious" reasoning, noting that "the first of all our mutual defense agreements was made with

the proposed communiqué, "became more and more concerned" about the adverse impact the document could have on Nixon's supporters in the United States. "There were a lot of people in the Republican Party who had strong feelings about Taiwan," Green says, "and not honoring a commitment could wreck all the things he wanted to do. There were two basic issues: We don't sell out Taiwan, and our reliability as an ally willing to stand by all our commitments."

Rogers, always reluctant to disturb the President with bad news, finally decided to telephone Nixon with Green's caveat. He moved into the next room to make his call, but Green recalls overhearing him fail to persuade Haldeman to rouse the President, who was resting, though "he literally pleaded with him."

Rogers somehow got to Nixon later in the evening, triggering a scene that can only be described as chaotic. Nixon and Kissinger finally decided they would have to reopen the negotiations, and the next morning Kissinger told Green he was outraged at Green's "poormouthing" of the communiqué. Green, by then equally angry, recalls responding, "Since when is constructive criticism 'poormouthing'?"

Nixon did not discuss the impasse in his memoirs and Kissinger minimized it. The complaints from Green and Rogers, he wrote, were the price that must be paid for excluding the professionals from a negotiation. "Unfamiliar with the obstacles overcome, those not participating can indulge in setting up utopian goals . . . and can contrast them with the document before them. Or they can nitpick at the result on stylistic grounds, pointing out telling nuances, brilliantly conceived, which the world was denied by their absence." Some of Green's quibbles were indeed legalistic and dealt with minor phrasing, but his chief reservation posed a potentially important political problem, and Nixon and Kissinger knew it. However, the validity of the objections didn't matter. Rogers had been deliberately excluded from the real bargaining, and now the President and his advisers were convinced they were paying for that exclusion. In their view, it would have been impossible to inform Rogers of the real import of the negotiations, for he might have shared that information with Green, who, Nixon suspected, had been involved in anti-administration leaks during the Cambodian invasion of 1970. If Green had been able to learn before the summit that Nixon and Kissinger were in the process of isolating Taiwan in return for television coverage and Chinese pressure on North Vietnam, he might have tipped off those senior congressmen and retired diplomats who made up the China lobby. And what Nixon and Kissinger were doing the China lobby would have seen as heresy: They were cutting off Taiwan to save South Vietnam.

The Rogers-Green complaints also provoked presidential rage. Kissinger depicted Nixon storming around his quarters in Hangchow late at night in his underwear, swearing to "do something" about State: "Nixon was beside himself. He recognized his political dilemma. He was already edgy about the reaction of his conservative supporters to the trip; he dreaded a right-wing

Korea." Furthermore, he wrote, neither Australia nor New Zealand was cited in his definition of America's "defensive perimeter," although both had strong ties to the United States.

assault on the communiqué. And he could see that leaks that the State Department was unhappy about American concessions might well be the trigger."

Nixon did more than storm around his suite. He decided to fire Rogers. He picked up the telephone (with little concern, obviously, about electronic eavesdropping) and called John Mitchell in Washington. "Nixon said, 'Get rid of him,' " Mitchell recalls. The Attorney General shared the President's anger. "That was a very serious thing that Rogers did," he explains. "Nixon had control of it and was going to do it. Rogers shouldn't have intervened." Mitchell was soothing, however; firing Rogers in an election year over a communiqué wouldn't do. "We'll talk about it when you get back," he told the President.

Nixon ordered Kissinger to meet again that night with Chiao Kuan-hua in an attempt to accommodate Rogers and Green. When the Chinese official refused to reopen discussion of the portions of the communiqué dealing with Taiwan, Kissinger's solution was ingenious. An on-the-record news conference had been scheduled for him that afternoon in Shanghai, where the President would conclude his China trip. When the question of America's commitment to Taiwan arose, he would orally reaffirm that commitment. Satisfied that nothing different would appear in the formal communiqué, the Chinese agreed.*

Rogers and Green discussed the communiqué once again at a breakfast in Hangchow that included John Scali. "I said that impact in the United States would be that it's a sellout of the Taiwanese," Scali recalls. "Not only do you have a foreign policy problem," he told Rogers and Green, "you have a political problem."

Kissinger's lack of candor with his colleagues was paralleled once again in his dealings with the press. At the news conference in Shanghai, he was at his best, giving no hint of the dissension inside the American delegation, or, for that matter, of the real issues at stake in the Peking summit. The question dealing with the status of America's treaty commitments to Taiwan was asked by David Kraslow of the *Los Angeles Times*.† In his reply, Kissinger reaf-

* Kissinger went to elaborate lengths in subsequent interviews to distort and minimize the significance of the textual changes Rogers and Green proposed. The Kalbs, obviously relying on Kissinger, reported in their biography that Rogers "argued that a few words in the draft language had to be changed"—including a sentence in which the word "stressed" was to be changed to "stated." The Kalbs added that "Kissinger felt that Rogers was quibbling, but the lawyer in Nixon supported the quibble of a fellow lawyer. . . ." Henry Brandon also reported the switch from "stressed" to "stated" in his *The Retreat of American Power*. Brandon, in his account of the incident, dutifully noted that "some thought later that Mr. Rogers' request had been more embarrassing than useful to the United States."

† Kraslow, like most senior Washington correspondents, had his own story of a friendship gone sour. Kraslow had first met Kissinger in 1961, while he was studying at Harvard on a Nieman Fellowship. The two men remained in contact and their personal friendship became a professional one when Kissinger came to Washington. Kissinger soon became one of Kraslow's—and the *Times*'s—principal sources of information. Kraslow even worked out an arrangement whereby the busy Kissinger promised to return any "most urgent" query as soon as possible, to prevent Kraslow from publishing wrong information. Sometime in the middle of Nixon's first term of office, the *Los Angeles Times* received advance word on a pending ground operation by American and South Vietnamese soldiers across the demilitarized zone straddling North and South Vietnam. Kraslow was hesitant about the story and telephoned Kissinger late on a weekend night with a "most urgent" query. The return call came immediately, and Kissinger warned Kraslow that if the article were published, the *Times* would be "terribly embarrassed." Kraslow, without hesitation, ordered the

firmed the American commitment to Taiwan and then added with great seriousness, "I would appreciate it if that would be all that I would be asked to say about it in these circumstances." The reporters complied. Kissinger referred to the news conference in his memoirs as "surely one of the most paradoxical events to take place on Chinese soil since the revolution. A foreign official explained that his country would continue to recognize a government which was rival to that with which he had been negotiating, and would defend it with military force against his hosts." The event looked very different to the Chinese, for whom Nixon and Kissinger had demonstrated their *bona fides* by secretly agreeing to collaborate on a Vietnam settlement, negotiating a compromise on the troop issue in Taiwan, and previously supplying detailed and sophisticated intelligence about the Soviet Union.

Many of the reporters in Shanghai sensed that there was far more to the story. Karnow led his dispatch to the *Post* by saying that Nixon had "acceded" to Chinese Communist demands on Taiwan and added that the ever omniscient "many observers here"—invariably a reflection of the reporter's own view—"feel that the Chinese got the better of the bargain." Karnow wrote that the Chinese officials appeared to be "pleased" by the summit and quoted one as saying: "We don't owe the Americans anything, but the Americans owe us much. Now they are redressing the balance." David Kraslow's account in the *Los Angeles Times* noted that the communiqué had contained "an oblique and ambiguous statement on the status of Taiwan that is certain to stir controversy in Asia and at home, both because of what it said and what it did not say." But if some of the first reports were less than enthusiastic, White House disappointment was short-lived. What saved the day was television. "For once," Kissinger wrote, "a White House public relations strategy succeeded, and performed a diplomatic function as well. Pictures overrode the printed word. . . ."

Richard Nixon returned in triumph on February 29. His press staff, so adept at turning out crowds and manufacturing favorable post-event telegrams to the White House, was not needed. The President realized once again that, as he had written in *Six Crises,* his first political memoir, "where voters are concerned . . . one TV picture is worth 10,000 words." The war-weary American public responded with warmth and enthusiasm to television's account of Nixon's heroic visit to the far reaches of Asia, and thousands came to the airport to greet him. There was no such consolation for Kissinger, who seemed compelled to demonstrate that he had not been a poor bargainer in China. At a Cabinet meeting assembled by Nixon hours after his return—at which the President received the expected homage—Kissinger talked obsessively about the Shanghai Communiqué. William Safire, in his memoirs, described him as

---

story killed. A few days later the operation took place, and Kraslow's reputation among his colleagues was damaged. He telephoned Kissinger for an explanation. "I lied to you," Kissinger confessed, because of national security. "I can no longer trust you, Henry," Kraslow remembers saying, "and that's a hell of a price to pay for one lousy story." If Kissinger had told him the truth, Kraslow added, and asked him not to publish it for national security reasons, he, of course, would have honored the request. The two men remained outwardly friendly and Kissinger remained a good source for the newspaper. "But it was never the same."

being unsure and "shaken" when he complained that "We are asked why
didn't affirm our commitment to Taiwan. An equally pertinent question wo
be why they did not denounce our commitment to Taiwan?" It was a gloo
performance, Safire recounted, and Kissinger "seemed to feel guilty" about
the communiqué.

It was more than gloom. Kissinger was determined to defend his record
without resorting to any hint of the Chinese decision to aid in Vietnam. Next
day, March 1, at a meeting with most of the reporters who had gone to China,
he gave a background briefing in which his basic purpose was to protect his
reputation as a brilliant bargainer. It was an act of defiance, for he must have
been aware that Richard Nixon was insisting on receiving all the adulation.
The President had been angry when Kissinger continued to meet with journal-
ists after his secret trip to Peking in July of 1971; certainly the same rules
would apply after the summit. Kissinger went ahead, nonetheless, and it was
another bravura performance, all the more remarkable because, less than two
months earlier, he had been exposed as a manipulator of the press by Jack
Anderson. Kissinger's confidence was supreme. He seemed to be sure that
Rogers and Green would not leak their version of the events in Hangchow and
Shanghai, or that, if they did so, he would be able to mitigate its impact. He
must also have weighed the possible adverse effects his statements could have
on Peking's leadership and concluded that his immediate needs were greater.*

Two weeks after the return from China, Kissinger wrote in his memoirs,
Haldeman sent him a memorandum "whose thrust was that my briefings de-
voted too much time to substance; I would serve the President by stressing to
the press and above all on television the great personal qualities [of Nixon]
that made the achievements possible." Kissinger's campaign of self-justifica-
tion was less than pleasing to a President who, in a memorandum five days
earlier, had urged Kissinger to stop talking about his personal role and to
embellish that of the President: "You could begin by pointing out that I made
the decision [in the Shanghai Communiqué] with regard to the tone of the
statement of our position. . . ."

Kissinger was repelled by Nixon's attempt to seize the limelight: After all,
it had been *his* backgrounder and *his* assiduous work with the press that had
elevated the stature of the communiqué. "Nixon, of course," he wrote, "de-
serves full credit for the Shanghai Communiqué. A President is always respon-
sible for the policy, no matter who does the technical labors." It was Nixon's
"tendency to confuse illusion with reality" and even starker character traits,
Kissinger added acidly, that "at first flawed, and later destroyed, a Presidency

---

* Kissinger also managed to get away with a simplistic explanation of the Chinese state of mind
in his background briefing at the Federal City Club. ". . . [H]ere we are dealing with people of
profound ideological motivation," Kissinger said, according to the transcript. ". . . [T]o them prin-
ciple is a reality and they may be confirmed in this by the tradition of Chinese society in which
virtue has always been considered power. So that Maoism is the new version of Confucianism
combined with the psychological motivation of a revolutionary experience. These were the people
we were dealing with and they are people who are living by values which are really quite different
than ours. We think of peace. They think of justice. We think of compromise. They think of
principle. We think of stability. They think of struggle." Robert G. Sutter, a China scholar at the
Library of Congress and a former research analyst for the CIA, was consulted later about Kissin-
ger's assessments—which were taken at face value by the assembled press—and found it "a lot of
gobbledegook. It's a mix of all sorts of concepts. He's trying to say that China's leaders view the
world in different ways than we do. So what else is new?"

so rich in foreign policy achievements. . . . It caused him to seek to embellish his most incontestable achievements, or to look for insurance in the face of even the most overwhelming probability of success. It was the psychological essence of the Watergate debacle."

Thus at a moment when Nixon and Kissinger were receiving plaudits from all sides, including the academic and liberal community, the President and his national security adviser were engaged in a squalid argument over who should get the most credit. Perhaps both men sensed that the publicity would be the summit's most tangible short-run asset.

The China trip did accomplish its basic goals. Richard Nixon and Henry Kissinger broke a twenty-four-year taboo on dealing with the People's Republic of China. They made triangular diplomacy a reality and, so they thought, permanently tipped the balance of power to their advantage. China would help with Vietnam. And finally, they opened the political gateway. Although the President would continue to use dirty tricks and illegalities in the campaign, none of the Democratic candidates, after the summit, would pose a serious threat to his lead in the polls.

Not every problem was solved. The North Vietnamese, despite pressure from Peking, went ahead with their election-year offensive in late March. The Chinese had continued to pour high levels of arms and war matériel into the North (to do otherwise would have been extremely damaging to their standing in the world), but were not told in advance of the Vietnamese offensive, and thus were not able to warn the White House, as Hanoi apparently feared they might. Enver Hoxha wrote of a report he received a few days after the offensive began that made him dubious about the relationship between Peking and Hanoi. The Albanian Ambassador to North Vietnam had met with the Chinese military attaché in Hanoi and had been told that "We [the Chinese] know nothing about these offensives because the Vietnamese do not inform us. We do not know whether this is a serious action which will be carried through to the end, or an adventure which will cost them dear." The comments, wrote Hoxha, especially the use of the word "adventure," created "doubts on the issue: are the Chinese for or against the present offensive?" Hoxha wrote further of a strange tableau at a diplomatic dinner in Peking, as reported by Albania's Ambassador to China. Chou En-lai was rudely ignored when he beckoned to two Vietnamese diplomats to join him. After a moment's hesitation, Chou walked over to the men to chat. "They listened to him with marked indifference," Hoxha wrote, "which struck the eye of all those who were watching." The Vietnamese eventually summoned an interpreter, insultingly suggesting that they found it difficult to understand what was being said. The incident "made a big impression," Hoxha noted.

Hoxha guessed correctly: China had altered "its main support of Vietnamese aims" in the Southeast Asian war. Now, as he wrote in his diary, he understood the real import of Sino-American rapprochement: "The situation between China and Vietnam appears to be unhealthy. The Soviet revisionists and the American imperialists are benefitting from this situation to the detriment of the Vietnamese people, who are fighting heroically." The Nixon-Kissinger policy was working.

36

VIETNAM:
HANOI'S OFFENSIVE

HANOI BEGAN ITS OFFENSIVE on March 30, 1972. Three North Vietnamese regular army divisions, supported by tanks and artillery, crossed the demilitarized zone separating North and South Vietnam and began to rout Nguyen Van Thieu's troops. The offensive had been expected much earlier, and when it did not take place, Richard Nixon and Henry Kissinger had permitted themselves to believe that Hanoi would not act. Triangular diplomacy had worked, so they thought; Hanoi had responded to pressure from Moscow and Peking, whose governments presumably had relayed Nixon's threats.

At first the offensive seemed to be no more than a local probe. When the full scope of the North Vietnamese operation became clear four days later, Nixon took it personally. He perceived Hanoi's offensive not only as an attack on the government of South Vietnam and the Vietnamization program, but also as a direct challenge to his presidency. The offensive was Hanoi's attempt to deny him reelection, as a similar offensive had done to Lyndon Johnson four years earlier. The President responded erratically, alternately blaming the Russians, who continued to supply North Vietnam, and those on his immediate staff— notably Melvin Laird—whose advice, he feared, had put his presidency in jeopardy. Nixon was suspicious and irritable on the morning of April 3, the day after the South Vietnamese were forced to evacuate fourteen bases south of the demilitarized zone. There was a meeting in the Oval Office with Kissinger and two Pentagon officials, Admiral Moorer and Kenneth Rush, the former Ambassador to West Germany who had just been confirmed as Deputy Secretary of Defense. Both men, Nixon knew, were loyal aides. Before moving to the Pentagon, Rush had been privately told by John Mitchell that he was to be Secretary of State in Nixon's second term.

Surrounded by such cronies, Nixon still could not control himself. "He accused the Pentagon of concealing the fact that we knew the offensive was going to blow up and didn't tell him," one participant recalls. "He said he had left the Pentagon with strict instructions about alerting him to everything." Nixon insisted that it was impossible for the North Vietnamese to have assembled three divisions and support facilities without the Pentagon's knowing about it. Laird, so the President made clear, had deliberately withheld the information. Rush nervously assured Nixon that he had not had an inkling that the offensive was to begin. The Deputy Secretary of Defense then threw the ball to Moorer: Did the chairman of the Joint Chiefs of Staff have anything to add? Moorer replied lamely that he and his colleagues "had kept the President fully informed." Kissinger said nothing throughout the eerie scene, but there is evidence that he agreed with Nixon about duplicity in the Pentagon. In his memoirs, he noted that civilian officials there—an obvious reference to Laird —had been reluctant to inform Nixon of the full scope of the offensive, perhaps in part because they were afraid "Nixon might be tempted to implement his oft-repeated threat of an all-out response if this was *the* long-awaited Communist offensive." Nixon's threat strategy had not deterred the North Vietnamese but was alive and well in the Pentagon.

Over the next few weeks, Nixon was increasingly distrustful of Laird, relying on Kissinger, Haig, and Moorer to carry out his military instructions. In early May, the President explicitly ordered that Laird not be included in the planning for the mining of Haiphong Harbor, which was implemented on May 8. Admiral Moorer, as he later confided to Admiral Zumwalt, was present on at least two occasions when Nixon ordered the dismissal of Laird. Nixon's rage was that much greater because he and Kissinger had once again misjudged the staying power of the North Vietnamese. Kissinger told the Kalb brothers that he had expected an attack at the time of Tet, in late January. When it did not materialize, and after Nixon's summit meeting in Peking had gone so well, Kissinger began to think, the Kalbs wrote, "that the North Vietnamese might have changed their minds . . . In a moment of self-delusion, he began to believe that there wouldn't be a Communist offensive after all."

In their memoirs, both Nixon and Kissinger wrote about repeated warnings to Hanoi relayed through Moscow and Peking. It was the same old strategy but with new urgency: Richard Nixon did not want to be driven from office by a Hanoi offensive. On January 25, Nixon sent a letter to Brezhnev with advance word of his speech that evening unilaterally revealing the secret peace talks. "The Soviet Union should understand," Nixon wrote, "that the United States would have no choice but to react strongly to actions by the North Vietnamese which are designed to humiliate us." A similar message was sent to the Chinese, via Paris. To back up the threats, Nixon and Kissinger ordered a significant increase in the bombing of the North. Some of the raids, as announced by Radio Hanoi and reported by American journalists in Saigon, made headlines. Just before Christmas of 1971, there were five days of heavy air raids on fuel depots, airfields, and antiaircraft missile sites over wide areas of North Vietnam, ranging from the demilitarized zone to the Twentieth Parallel, about seventy miles south of Hanoi. Other missions made less news. As the air war expanded in the North, the number of officially reported "protective reaction" strikes—bombings in response to North Vietnamese attacks on American reconnaissance planes—began to soar. The North Vietnamese were moving an increasing number of Soviet-built MIG aircraft to airfields in the southern portions of the country, and those fields became prime targets. By December, "protective reaction" missions were reported almost daily and amounted to an unannounced policy of systematic bombing of North Vietnamese airfields, fuel stockpiles, and air defense sites. In some cases, the reconnaissance aircraft sent on intelligence missions were accompanied by no less than sixteen fully armed fighter-bomber planes, whose pilots had been briefed in advance on their assigned targets. Many of these missions were conducted by Air Force units under the direction of General John Lavelle, commander of the Seventh Air Force, who had been visited by a stream of high-level travelers —including Admiral Moorer—late in the fall of 1971 and encouraged to bend the rules as much as possible. In mid-February, two more days of concentrated raids over the southern part of North Vietnam were authorized. Nixon and Kissinger were taking no chances that the North Vietnamese would embarrass them with an offensive before the summit later that month in China.

Once in Peking, Nixon made more threats. In his memoirs, Kissinger described a Nixon-Chou conversation in which the President, in the midst of redefining the American commitment to Taiwan, declared that the United States "would not impose a political solution on Vietnam, as Hanoi wanted. If we did, no country would ever trust us again . . . He warned that we would react violently if Hanoi launched another major offensive in 1972." Kissinger and Nixon got what they wanted from Chou En-lai, Kissinger wrote: "We indeed understood each other; the war in Vietnam would not affect the improvement of our relations . . . Peking's priority was not the war on its southern border but its relationship with us." The message was clear: China would not interfere if Nixon carried out his threats.

Throughout this period, Hanoi prepared for the worst. Concrete bunkers, many of them built during the earlier air war waged by the Johnson Administration, were refurbished, and plans for civilian evacuation were updated. In its daily broadcasts, Hanoi depicted far more extensive bombing than that reported by the American press. In one summary, issued February 10, the North Vietnamese alleged that during January there had been more than five hundred violations of air space by American reconnaissance planes, which resulted in 138 attacks by American jets on populated areas. Many of the aircraft, Hanoi said, were dumping antipersonnel bombs, some of them capable of spewing out 250,000 steel pellets over an area the size of four football fields. The Pentagon officially reported twenty-seven "protective reaction" missions that month.

Richard Nixon's rage on April 3 was premature; the attack across the demilitarized zone was only the beginning of a coordinated offensive whose full scope did not become apparent for weeks. By April 7, a second front had been opened northwest of Saigon, as three more North Vietnamese divisions raced across the border from their sanctuaries in Cambodia. A third major operation began two weeks later in the mountainous Central Highlands area in north-central Vietnam, where the Vietcong had established a strong grip on the indigenous population, or what was left of it. The Highlands area, which included such cities as Kontum and Pleiku, had in the late 1960s become a focal point for American "pacification" efforts, which included the forced relocation of peasants and farmers, followed by unrelenting bombing and artillery attacks on the evacuated areas.

Hanoi's offensive was an instant military and psychological success. By April 2, North Vietnamese units had overrun the northern half of Quang Tri Province, near the demilitarized zone. By April 15, the city of Danang, roughly fifty miles down the coast, was being shelled. The city of Quang Tri, a provincial capital, fell on May 2. In the South, near Saigon, North Vietnamese troops laid siege to the city of An Loc, and round-the-clock American bombings destroyed the city but prevented its fall. By April 25, there was fighting near Kontum in the Highlands. Reserve units of the South Vietnamese Army were pulled out of "pacified" areas throughout the South, notably in the rice-rich Delta region south of Saigon, and rushed into combat. As those units pulled out, North Vietnamese and NLF troops were again able to infiltrate into the rural areas, the traditional base of operations that had been denied to them by the American "pacification" efforts.

Nixon and Kissinger responded to the offensive by increasing the bombing of North and South Vietnam. More than a hundred additional B-52 aircraft were ordered to Southeast Asia in April and May, causing a traffic jam on Guam so severe that one runway had to be shut down and turned into an aircraft parking lot. Hundreds of smaller tactical aircraft were also rerouted to bases in Thailand and in South Vietnam, along with additional aircraft carriers. The Seventh Fleet, charged with waging the air and sea war against North Vietnam, was within weeks increased from 84 to 138 ships, draining resources from Navy fleets throughout the world. By mid-May, American and South Vietnamese aircraft were flying more than 500 missions daily over the battle-grounds in South Vietnam. Those flights were buttressed by a steady stream of B-52 raids concentrated in the South that often reached seventy-five a day, with each aircraft capable of dropping 48,000 pounds of bombs.

From the first days of the offensive, Nixon became intensely involved in a role that, in earlier crises, he had left to Kissinger: armchair commander. Suddenly, more than ever, it was *his* war and it was going to be fought *his* way. There was poor weather over Vietnam in early April, and Nixon chafed. "Damn it," he told Mitchell and Haldeman during a late-afternoon meeting on April 4, "if you know any prayers say them . . . Let's get that weather cleared up. The bastards have never been bombed like they're going to be bombed this time, but you've got to have weather." "Is the weather still bad?" Mitchell asked. "Huh!" responded Nixon, according to an Oval Office tape recording made public during the impeachment proceedings. "It isn't bad. The Air Force isn't worth a—I mean, they won't fly."

On April 6, as the bombing was beginning to intensify, Nixon met briefly in his hideaway office with Air Force General John Vogt, who had been ordered only days before to assume command of the Seventh Air Force in Vietnam. Nixon was "wild-eyed" as he told Vogt that his predecessors in Saigon had lacked aggressiveness and failed to take advantage of opportunity. "He wanted somebody to use some imagination—like Patton," Vogt says. Nixon turned to that theme repeatedly during their thirty-minute talk, exclaiming at another point: "I expect you to turn back the invasion and we will emerge with a victory. We will not abandon Vietnam."* The President also told his new

---

* Nixon asked Vogt if he needed anything. To the President's surprise, the general said yes. Vogt recalls giving Nixon a brief seminar on the complexities of the command-and-control arrangements for the air war, under which he had as many as five or six separate authorities to coordinate before getting final permission to stage a raid. For example, Vogt said, approval for Air Force raids on North Vietnam came from Washington via Pacific Air Force headquarters in Honolulu, which was under the control of the Commander in Chief of the Pacific. For raids in the South, orders were relayed from Washington through the military assistance command of General Creighton Abrams in Saigon. Various parts of North Vietnam were divided into different "route packages," some of which were controlled by the Navy through a different command structure. In Laos and Cambodia, the air operations were controlled in part by the American ambassadors on duty there. Pilots thus

commander that the United States would continue withdrawing troops, "ultimately to zero." At no time during the fiery talk did Nixon, Kissinger, or Vogt mention Vogt's predecessor, John Lavelle, who had been relieved of command a few days earlier and demoted, without a hearing, after a sergeant in his command wrote a letter to Congress complaining about falsified "protective reaction" raids.*

By the second week of April, Nixon had authorized the B-52 bombing of targets inside North Vietnam that had been on the restricted list since the fall of 1967. More than 700 B-52 raids were flown at Nixon's insistence over the North in April, including a two-day series of sustained attacks in the Hanoi

---

found themselves flying by one set of rules in the morning and under different authorities in the afternoon. Vogt pleaded for a revision of the command structure so there would be only one official to whom he had to report. Kissinger attended the meeting as usual, Vogt recalls, and Nixon, who seemed to be unaware of the complications, turned to his national security aide and ordered, "You get him the necessary command instructions and make sure it happens." Of course, as Vogt suspected even when he was leaving the White House, "The command structure never changed." He almost paid a price for his impertinence, however. In the draft of his memoirs, Nixon included a brief description of his meeting with Vogt and depicted the general as demanding full authority to run the whole war, in the air and on the ground. Vogt was privately shown the passages in question by a Nixon aide who doubted that the general would have dared make such a request. After Vogt's protest, the material was deleted.

* Lavelle, certain that his superiors in the Pentagon and the White House were aware of and supported his action, authorized at least twenty-eight bombing missions on restricted targets in the North in late 1971 and early 1972. After some of those missions, he ordered the pilots and the ground-based intelligence teams that debriefed the pilots and crews to report falsely that the strikes were in response to enemy attacks—that is, that they were "protective reaction" missions. It was double bookkeeping, a procedure not unlike that ordered by the White House in early 1969 to help disguise the B-52 bombings of Cambodia. The issue arose in early March, when Lonnie D. Franks, a young Air Force sergeant stationed in Thailand, wrote his senator, Harold Hughes, Democrat of Iowa, a letter detailing the falsification of official reports. Sergeant Franks wrote that, under Lavelle's direction, he and others in the Seventh Air Force spent literally hundreds of hours after missions compiling falsified operational and intelligence reports for higher headquarters. The Senator asked for an investigation, and within three weeks Lavelle was relieved of command, shipped home, and retired. Nixon personally approved that decision, and he also approved Lavelle's punishment: He was demoted one full rank, to lieutenant general, the first such demotion for a general officer in modern military history. The President, who had done so much to bend the rules and norms of the command structure, and who had seen fit to reduce the sentence of Lieutenant William Calley for his role in the My Lai massacre, was now a stern disciplinarian. By early April, when General Vogt reached Southeast Asia, the restrictions on American bombing had been lifted and protective reaction was no longer necessary as a smokescreen. Nonetheless, the reasons for Lavelle's abrupt disappearance were kept secret. On April 7, reporters at the Pentagon were handed a cryptic memorandum noting Vogt's appointment and adding that Lavelle was retiring "for personal and health reasons." Fear of scandal diminished over the next few weeks, as Lavelle chose to retire quietly and the press and Congress were absorbed by Hanoi's offensive and the pending Moscow summit. In early May, someone inside the government began to talk to Representative Otis G. Pike, a New York Democrat who was a ranking member of the House Armed Services Committee. In early June, Pike privately urged me to follow up on the Lavelle story. I found the general on a golf course in a Washington suburb. He told of being relieved for the unauthorized bombing and claimed that higher authorities were aware of his bombing and did nothing to stop it. In my first dispatch on the issue for the New York Times, published June 12, I wrote: "If General Lavelle's superiors in Saigon or elsewhere knew that his planes were conducting bombing missions . . . who authorized such missions?" For the next six months I continued to report on the Lavelle story, convinced that it would lead me to secret orders from the White House or somewhere in the Pentagon. Richard Nixon and Henry Kissinger were suspects, with Admiral Moorer the conduit. It was not until mid-1973, amid the Watergate scandal and after the disclosure of the secret B-52 Cambodian bombing, that Congress and the public learned the full extent of the disarray in the military. Witnesses told the Senate Armed Services Committee of the ease with which the Air Force and the Navy could preplan "protective reaction" raids and bomb with impunity. By then, of course, direct Air Force and Navy involvement in the Vietnam War was over, and Richard Nixon was on the run.

and Haiphong area. In his memoirs, Admiral Zumwalt quoted an obviously unhappy Melvin Laird as saying, "The President is personally insisting on massive strikes—personally sent the [additional aircraft] carriers. . . . The President said, 'I sent them—no one else asks for them.' " Zumwalt also quoted a message from Nixon in which the President reassured General Abrams, through General Vogt, that "everything he needs will be given to him . . . [Nixon] said that we will use every carrier in both fleets and all our tactical air if that is what is needed to get the job done . . ."

During these first days of the Vietnamese offensive, one of Kissinger's new NSC aides got his first look at the President. The aide had gone with Kissinger to a midmorning meeting in Ziegler's office to discuss press coverage of the offensive. The President suddenly stormed in, kicked Ziegler's desk, and demanded that the North Vietnamese always be referred to as "the enemy." Then he left as abruptly as he had arrived, without saying a word to Kissinger or the aide, who had watched in silence. It was Ziegler who said the obvious: "The Old Man's really high again."

It was at this point in the Vietnam War—and in his extraordinarily complex relationship with Richard Nixon—that Henry Kissinger began to travel his own path inside the White House, a divergence that would lead months later to a dishonored peace agreement, the Christmas bombing of Hanoi and Haiphong, and a breach between the two men that would never be healed. Kissinger shared Nixon's rage over North Vietnam's offensive and agreed in principle with the President's decision to escalate the bombing. Kissinger was far more concerned than Nixon, however, about the effect of that escalation on the May summit and the SALT talks in Moscow. He had been invited months earlier by Ambassador Dobrynin to make a secret trip to Moscow in late April to resolve some of the outstanding SALT issues, most significantly the proposed limits on submarine-launched ballistic missiles. Kissinger, eager for a breakthrough in the SALT talks the year before, had naïvely conceded the issue in his backchannel negotiations with the Soviets. But the SALT delegation, headed by Gerard Smith, was insistent on including SLBMs in the final agreement, and Kissinger realized that the fate of the summit rested on resolving that issue and thus removing any possibility that he and Nixon would face charges of poor bargaining. Kissinger knew from his private talks with Dobrynin that the Soviet leaders were more than willing to change policy and include the SLBMs in the final agreements if their demands were met.

All this intense last-minute maneuvering, the main purpose of which was the April visit to Moscow, was jeopardized by Nixon's insistence on escalating the war against North Vietnam. Sometime in early April, Kissinger unilaterally decided to make a prodigious effort to negotiate an end to the Vietnam War. To do otherwise, he explained in his memoirs, would have led to "a simultaneous crisis in Vietnam and in relations with the Soviet Union. Down the drain would have gone our strategy of creating a triangular relationship to stabilize the global equilibrium and to foster a Vietnam settlement . . . Vietnam would have consumed our substance after all—the nightmare that we, and not only our critics, feared."

His goal was somehow to convince the Soviets of his intent to achieve a final settlement of the war. He would become allied, at least during the few weeks before the summit, with the Soviet leadership against his President.

Once in Moscow, Kissinger offered a major concession to Hanoi in an effort to reach a settlement before the 1972 presidential elections. He sent word through Soviet channels that North Vietnam would be permitted to keep its troops in the South. Kissinger's correct perception that a negotiated peace was attainable was all the more remarkable in that there is little evidence in his memoirs or in any of his published remarks in 1972 that he fully perceived one of the major goals of Hanoi's military effort: to seize and gain political control of large areas of South Vietnam, especially in the Delta. Hanoi's strategy, as its leadership openly declared in mid-1972, was to reinstate its dominance over the countryside in preparation for a negotiated settlement. A fuller explanation of Kissinger's thinking in the spring of 1972 would emerge, perhaps, if he decided to publish his extended backchannel conversations with Dobrynin, who by 1972 was a major broker not only on SALT and related issues but on the Vietnam War.* It is inconceivable, however, that Kissinger did not accurately perceive how parlous his own situation was by the spring of 1972. He must have known that, despite the success of the Peking summit, his days in the White House were numbered. Nixon's personal dislike of him was becoming more acute, and was reflected in the antipathy of the closest Nixon aides. Despite the increasing tension and Nixon's faith in the bombing, Kissinger insisted that summer and fall on trying to negotiate an end to the Vietnam War.

His motives in all of this were not entirely geopolitical. Much impetus, of course, was provided by his *realpolitik* view of the world: He believed that the United States, through a series of shrewd trade-offs and concessions to the Soviet Union and China, could settle all outstanding world issues, including the Vietnam War and the Middle East dispute, on favorable terms. His other concerns were more self-serving. Nixon increasingly favored John Connally, his Secretary of the Treasury, whom, Kissinger was aware, Nixon considered the ideal choice to succeed him as President in 1976 and, in the interim, perhaps to serve as Secretary of State (the job already promised to Kenneth Rush). Kissinger desperately wanted the latter job for himself, as his staff knew all too well, and the problem of how to get Nixon to appoint him seemed herculean. To negotiate a successful end to the Vietnam War—"peace without honor"—would help reelect the President and give Kissinger the leverage he needed to win the State Department job.

Another factor in Kissinger's effort was his insatiable need for adulation; each success created the need for more. A military end to the Vietnam War, whether through ignominious defeat or through a Hanoi collapse caused by B-52 bombing or worse, would offer his talents little scope. Only a negotiated peace could keep Kissinger at center stage.

Hanoi's offensive had set the stage for negotiations, assuming the success of the bombing and the South Vietnamese Army's ability to hold off the North Vietnamese. By mid-April of 1972, Kissinger's diplomacy would be needed not only with the North Vietnamese and the Soviet Union, but also with his President.

---

* During my 1979 interviews in Hanoi for this book, Vietnamese officials would not discuss their diplomatic contacts with the Soviet Union except in generalities.

In his memoirs, Kissinger carefully minimized his areas of disagreement with the President as of early April. "North Vietnam had brutally and cynically chosen a test of arms," he wrote. "It had played with us for months, using negotiations as a smokescreen for a massive invasion. Nixon and I both sought to end the war as rapidly as possible. But there was a nuance of differences between us over the strategy for doing do . . . Though favoring a strong military reaction, I never wanted to rely on power alone or, for that matter, on negotiation by itself. In my view diplomacy and strategy should support each other . . ." Those innocuous words masked a major disagreement. Richard Nixon had become unnerved; he had concluded that he could not politically survive a defeat, or even the appearance of a defeat, in South Vietnam. He was convinced that his political future rested on the resolution of the Vietnam War, and not on a Moscow summit. Laird and others in the Pentagon were up to their old tricks, and had deliberately not informed him of the North Vietnamese offensive. And only he had the daring and the guts—like General Patton—to challenge the Hanoi government with increased bombing. Hanoi had been treacherous, but so had its ally, the Soviet Union, whose matériel had, so he believed, made the offensive possible. The Vietnamese and Russians had conspired to humiliate him, and he wanted to move boldly against Moscow.

Kissinger, on the other hand, thought that Nixon, bolstered by successful summits in Peking and Moscow, could politically survive even a debacle in Vietnam. Shortly after the offensive began, Nixon recorded the following entry in his diary, as reprinted in his memoirs: ". . . Henry, with all of his many virtues, does seem too often to be concerned about preparing the way for negotiations with the Soviets. However, when he faces the facts, he realizes that no negotiation in Moscow is possible unless we come out all right in Vietnam. What really matters now is how it all comes out. Both Haldeman and Henry seem to have an idea—which I think is mistaken—that even if we fail in Vietnam we can survive politically."

The major difficulty in determining what really happened over the next few months is the fact that neither Nixon nor Kissinger has told the full story, either to aides at the time or in the memoirs. For example, there is evidence that Nixon acted unilaterally in ordering the weekend wave of B-52 attacks in mid-April on the Hanoi and Haiphong Harbor area. In his memoirs, he described the decision as his, taken over the strenuous opposition of Laird and Rogers, and quoted himself as telling Haldeman after the raids, "Well, we really left them our calling card this weekend." Senior Pentagon officials told William Beecher of the *New York Times* that the B-52s had initially been targeted to bomb sites as far as seventy-five miles south of the Hanoi-Haiphong area, but the mission was revised by the President at the last minute—"some time between Friday night and Saturday morning." Kissinger, in his memoirs, presented a far different account: "To make sure that both Hanoi and Moscow understood our determination, I had recommended—and Nixon had approved—a dramatic two-day attack on fuel storage depots in the Hanoi-Haiphong area. . . ."

Kissinger may have gone along with some B-52 bombing, as part of the price he paid for continued influence with the President, but his thoughts were reflected by James Reston in a column dated April 18. Undoubtedly, he wrote, the heightened bombing was "a temporary expression of Presidential frustration and anger rather than a calculated plan to force a showdown with the Soviet Union in Indochina . . . Mr. Nixon usually cools down after he blows off, especially when calmer minds begin working on the problem." By then, Nixon was conducting the war by temper tantrum, and Kissinger could do little more than complain to a columnist about it.

Adding to Nixon's distrust was Hanoi's manipulation of the American offer for a renewal of the secret Paris peace talks between Kissinger and Le Duc Tho, which had been suspended since October. Kissinger made his proposal for a further meeting on January 26, 1972, only a day after Nixon had revealed the existence of the previous secret meetings. The North Vietnamese leadership, which by then had made its commitment to begin the offensive in late March, at the height of the spring monsoon, promptly accepted a date for March 20. A few weeks later, Hanoi asked for a postponement to April 15, but readily agreed with Kissinger to meet instead on April 24. While these lulling negotiations were going on, the North Vietnamese continued to plan for their offensive—an action that Nixon and Kissinger later viewed as duplicitous. In his memoirs, Kissinger claimed that "it had become evident to us that it was the forthcoming offensive which controlled the timing of North Vietnamese diplomacy . . . Our record of having sought negotiations would now be impeccable when we made it public."

Kissinger's analysis of the record would have been more credible if he had also mentioned that Ambassador William Porter, who had been named earlier in the year as Nixon's ambassador to the official peace talks in Paris, had decided unilaterally to break off those talks on March 23. Porter's decision, which was not cleared in advance in Washington, created headlines and forced the President, at a news conference on the next day, to suggest that the Ambassador's hard line was on Nixon's orders. "What we are trying to do here . . . and this has been done under my direction, is to break a filibuster."*

Over the next few weeks, Hanoi linked resumption of the secret talks to a resumption of the weekly official meetings, a serious complication in the American strategy. By then, the Soviet Union had been dragged into the negotiations by Nixon, who insisted that officials at State and the Pentagon publicly stress the Soviet Union's responsibility for supplying the North Vietnamese. ". . . [W]e held Moscow accountable for Hanoi's offensive," Kissinger wrote.

* When he was offered the job as David Bruce's replacement, Porter did not know of the secret meetings involving Kissinger and Le Duc Tho. He recalls a breakfast meeting with Kissinger at San Clemente when he was told of the secret talks and promised information on their progress as well as authority to change tactics in the open talks if he saw fit. Porter was also told that after the 1972 elections Nixon planned to name him Under Secretary for Political Affairs, the highest ranking State Department post for a Foreign Service officer. Being tough about the Communists, he knew, always played well with Nixon, and when he finally saw the President, "I expressed the belief that we should go after the other side" in the open talks. Nixon said it sounded like a good idea. "When I pounded them publicly," Porter remembers telling the President, "Henry could see what could be achieved in the secret sessions." Porter also recalls receiving the President's authority "to jerk them around and out of the conference if that seemed desirable." It was on the basis of that authority, Porter said, that he decided to walk out of the Paris peace conference on March 23, to the White House's dismay.

Nixon recalled in his memoirs, "I was determined not to indulge the Soviet fiction that they could not be held responsible for what North Vietnam did . . ."

These were difficult days for the Russians, who had far less influence with Hanoi than the White House suspected. On April 9, Kissinger wrote, he warned Dobrynin that drastic actions were possible in the North. Dobrynin, whose government had a vast economic and diplomatic stake in the summit, tried to be reassuring: His government had informed Hanoi, he told Kissinger, that it would be extremely interested in a successful meeting between Kissinger and Le Duc Tho. The next day, Dobrynin, who understood the way to Nixon's and Kissinger's hearts, casually mentioned that the President would be permitted to accredit as many as a hundred journalists to the May summit.

In mid-April, a few days before Kissinger was to leave for the secret meeting in Paris, the North Vietnamese rejected the scheduled April 24 meeting with Le Duc Tho, insisting that the secret talks could not reconvene until early May, and not then unless the United States agreed to resume the weekly official meetings. Ambassador Porter's walkout was now a major diplomatic hindrance. In his memoirs, Nixon claimed that the Soviets "had hinted" that the April 24 meeting "might be the decisive one for reaching a settlement." The President subsequently told Kissinger, he wrote, that he should not take his secret trip to Moscow "until we found out what kind of a game they [the Soviets] were playing." In a diary entry, Nixon noted with some irony that "Henry obviously considered this a crisis of the first magnitude." The President was confident that he understood Kissinger's real priorities. "I laid down the law hard to him that under these circumstances he could not go to Moscow. . . . I can see that this shook him because he desperately wants to get to Moscow one way or the other." Later in the day, Nixon turned apocalyptic: He had a mournful talk with Kissinger "about what we had to look forward to in the future. . . . [W]hat we were really looking at was a cancellation of the summit and going right hard on Vietnam, even up to a blockade. I said under these circumstances, I had an obligation to look for a successor. I ran down a list," Nixon wrote, naming Nelson Rockefeller, Ronald Reagan, Warren Burger, and John Connally, among others. "Henry threw up his hands and said that none of them would do," Nixon went on, "and that any of the Democrats would be out of the question. . . . He made his pitch that the North Vietnamese should not be allowed to destroy two Presidents." Having once again demonstrated his fealty, Kissinger waited until after dinner to inform the President that Dobrynin had agreed to make Vietnam the first subject on the agenda for Kissinger's secret trip. "There was some talk," Nixon recorded in his diary, "even of having the North Vietnamese Foreign Minister there." The President told Kissinger that he had "reconsidered" and Kissinger "should go to Moscow."

The North Vietnamese Minister never showed up, of course. Nevertheless, Kissinger left for Moscow on April 20, armed with concessions to break the deadlock in the Vietnamese negotiations. He spent four days talking with Leonid Brezhnev and others, and, according to two Kissinger aides who attended the meetings, was able to clear up one of the long-standing ambiguities of the secret peace talks with a declaration that the North Vietnamese could maintain their troops in the South after a negotiated settlement—if they agreed to withdraw the three divisions that had crossed the demilitarized zone in late March to attack Quang Tri Province. Kissinger also made a significant political concession—or at least hinted at the possibility—by indicating that those North Vietnamese troops who were permitted to remain in the South could consider some of the area they controlled territory of the Provisional Revolutionary Government. In other words, Hanoi was being indirectly told that the United States was willing to discuss the possibility that the government of Nguyen Van Thieu was not the sole legitimate power in the South. The United States had reached a turning point in its negotiations with North Vietnam, and Kissinger's aides understood its import: The goal was no longer to win the war, but to end it. What the aides did not perceive at the time was Kissinger's daring in all of this; he, alone, had decided to change American policy. One aide recalls hearing Kissinger declare for the first time, while in Moscow, that the United States could not stay in South Vietnam forever and could achieve nothing more than an exit with the South Vietnamese Army as strong as possible and Hanoi as weak as possible.*

The four days Kissinger spent in Moscow were tortured ones for Nixon, who seemed obsessed with the notion that the Soviet Union could deliver a peace agreement with the North Vietnamese. In his memoirs, Nixon claimed that he had instructed Kissinger to insist on a Vietnamese settlement prior to any discussions in Moscow on SALT and other summit issues. "In our last meeting" before Kissinger took off on his trip, Nixon wrote, "I had even told Kissinger that if the Soviets proved recalcitrant on this point, he should just pack up and come home."

Kissinger didn't come home, and his memoirs provide a vivid account of a President becoming increasingly irate. Secret Service logs show that Nixon spent a long weekend at Camp David with no official appointments while Kissinger was in Moscow. His only officially recorded visitors were Haldeman and Haig. Kissinger noted in his memoirs, however, that Bébé Rebozo spent much of the weekend with Nixon—information that would have come from Haig. It was a boozy weekend. Nixon grew more difficult each day, threatening the renewed bombing of Hanoi and Haiphong as well as insisting that Kissinger return immediately to Washington if the Russians did not guarantee some concessions from Hanoi. Nixon was making these threats not to the Soviets but to Kissinger. He was treating his foreign policy adviser as he and Kissinger had treated Laird for more than three years, and Kissinger didn't like it.

---

* Kissinger felt freer to make his deals with the North Vietnamese through Moscow than in Paris. In Paris, he had to summarize each day's developments in a memorandum for Nixon and Haldeman; there did not seem to be such stringent reporting requirements in Moscow, where Kissinger could strike bargains—as he did that April on SALT—without explaining his actions to anyone. Junior NSC aides such as David Engel, a Vietnamese-language expert, had seen much less of Nixon and, understandably, did not realize the extent to which Kissinger was operating on his own in Moscow. Engel, who was involved in translating many sensitive negotiations in 1972, acknowledged later that he was aware of the significance of the Moscow concessions but considered them, as he privately told an interviewer (not this journalist), decisions that had to have been made by Nixon. The junior aides' belief that Kissinger was coordinating his negotiating steps with the President diminished their willingness to dispute negotiating tactics with Kissinger, for their assumption was that any challenge to Kissinger's position was also a rebuttal of the President's view.

"Nixon wanted to use the threat of canceling the summit to obtain Soviet cooperation in Vietnam; I judged it wiser to . . . use Moscow's eagerness for the summit as a device for separating Moscow from Hanoi," Kissinger wrote, justifying his unilateral decision to stay at the talks. In addition, he added lamely, there was a mix-up in communications, so that Nixon's encoded instructions to him often arrived, due to the time-zone difference, after he had begun the next negotiating session. "This would have made it hard for me to carry out his instructions even in the best of circumstances."

Circumstances clearly were not the best, as Haig dutifully reported to Kissinger from Washington. Nixon had demanded that Kissinger leave Moscow as soon as the discussions on Vietnam were ended, but later he endorsed Kissinger's decision to stay on. Then he seemed to change his mind again, apparently fearing that the Soviets and the North Vietnamese would see Kissinger's continued presence as signs of weakness. In his memoirs, Kissinger raised the possibility that Nixon's ambivalence may have been "merely needling." Perhaps in retaliation, Kissinger's memoirs were explicit and merciless on the President's subsequent vacillation. Shortly after he received the authority to remain in Moscow, Kissinger wrote, Haig sent the following warning: "[T]he President just called again and added that he views Soviet positions on South Vietnam as frenzied and frivolous and, therefore, is determined to go forward with additional strikes on Hanoi and Haiphong. . . ." Kissinger, who seemed to have no Moscow-Washington communications problems, urged Haig to "Please keep everybody calm. . . . I am reading your messages with mounting astonishment. I cannot share the theory on which Washington operates. I do not believe that Moscow is in direct collusion with Hanoi." Recounting the exchange in his memoirs, Kissinger explained Nixon's real concern: "Nixon was very obsessed with the fear that we might be tricked into the very kind of bombing halt for which he had attacked Johnson in 1968 and which he believed nearly lost him the [1968] election." He was afraid, Kissinger added, that "we had been 'taken in' by the wily Soviets."

The President, who downplayed his views on Kissinger's Moscow insubordination in his memoirs, was eventually persuaded by his national security adviser to delay the renewed bombing of Hanoi until Kissinger met again with Le Duc Tho in Paris. Kissinger had assured the Soviets that the United States would return to the open peace talks, as Hanoi was demanding, and the secret negotiations were scheduled to resume in Paris on May 2. In a final cable to Kissinger in Moscow, Nixon warned that if Hanoi did not make concessions at that meeting, "We will have to go all-out on the bombing front." Once again Kissinger had become the enemy. The President apparently did have some second thoughts about the tone of his message, and concluded it on what was meant to be a reassuring note: "However it all comes out, just remember we all know we couldn't have had a better man in Moscow at this time than Kissinger. Rebozo joins us in sending our regards."

Kissinger, who well knew what the President's real views were, commented icily in his memoirs: "In the light of the previous catalogue of errors, one could only conclude that the Administration was in parlous shape indeed if its best man could do no better than that."

The bickering could not hide the reality: The American problem was not in Moscow, but on the ground in South Vietnam. Just as Kissinger was leaving Moscow on April 24, the North Vietnamese opened up their third front in the Central Highlands, threatening Kontum and Pleiku. The South Vietnamese, confronted once again with their enemy, performed disgracefully. General Vogt, who had been on his new job barely two weeks, recalls being awakened at his Saigon quarters by a midnight telephone call from General Abrams, who exclaimed: "Jesus, we've got a major catastrophe on our hands. The [South Vietnamese] 23rd Division . . . has been attacked by armor, and it's fleeing in the face of the enemy. They've thrown down their arms, and we're going to lose Pleiku." Vogt flew to the area for a first-hand look and recalled seeing undamaged South Vietnamese tanks "sitting there, completely untouched, where they had been abandoned by these little guys who ran. . . . [T]hese little guys knew they were up against something they couldn't handle and they just fled." Vogt had realized during his flight over the battlefield that the North Vietnamese troops had only feinted a full-fledged attack, panicked the South Vietnamese, as expected, and then pulled back. Hanoi had not accompanied its tanks with infantry troops for an obvious reason, Vogt says: "It was never meant to gain ground or the whole territory or to pursue. And we had misinterpreted." And yet, "These little guys . . . were crying, 'Alarm! Alarm! Alarm! We're being pursued!' This was the nature of the war."

Nixon and Kissinger chose to believe that the May 2 secret session with Le Duc Tho would be a turning point. Brezhnev had all but guaranteed to do as much as possible—short of curtailing aid—to insist that the North Vietnamese come to Paris ready to compromise and end the war. As he reported in his memoirs, Kissinger had warned Dobrynin earlier that the Soviets had put themselves in a position "where a miserable little country could jeopardize everything that had been negotiated for years." On April 26, as battlefield conditions in the South grew more tense, Nixon announced in a nationally televised speech from the Oval Office that he was ordering yet another withdrawal of 20,000 men, reducing the American troop level to 49,000 by July 1. The continued reductions, a major facet of the Vietnamization program, were patently illogical at a time when the South Vietnamese Army was being mauled by the North. But Nixon, who knew what escalation lay ahead if the May 2 meeting didn't produce, was paying extraordinary homage to the American peace movement. He did so despite private polls that showed his popularity climbing dramatically with the onset of the heavy bombing of the North.* The polls reflected a truth that became clearer as the war continued to escalate in mid-May: The antiwar movement had significantly diminished. Nixon had been able to undermine much dissent by eliminating the draft and emphasizing the Vietnamization program. Many of those who had taken to the streets in earlier years chose not to do so in 1972. Others continued to march and protest against

* In mid-1971 Charles Colson had begun relying on polls supplied by Albert E. Sindlinger, a private market analyst and Nixon supporter whose clients included Detroit's Big Three and other large corporations. Sindlinger had proved reliable in dealing with domestic economic issues; his polling took on new importance after the escalation of the war in April of 1972, when he reported a twelve-point rise in Nixon's popularity immediately after the B-52 bombing of Hanoi and Haiphong.

the administration's policy; the antiwar movement may have been reduced, but it would not go away.

Nixon also announced in his April 26 speech that Ambassador Porter would resume the weekly peace talks, but he did not, of course, reveal that the renewal of public talks was a concession demanded by Hanoi before it would meet again in secret. Anxious to buttress his improved public standing, Nixon also expressed an optimism about the progress of the war that few in official Washington shared. General Abrams, whose reputation for personal integrity was high, was cited by name no less than five times on April 26, and he was quoted as reporting that the South Vietnamese were "fighting courageously and well in their self-defense."

The tepid speech, which included the usual threats of continued bombing, made little impact, but Nixon grabbed the world's attention a few days later during a highly publicized appearance at a barbeque at John Connally's Texas ranch. Answering questions from the guests, he responded provocatively to a query about bombing North Vietnam's dikes and dams: "Just let me say that as far as the targets in North Vietnam are concerned, that we are prepared to use our military and naval strength against military targets throughout North Vietnam, and we believe that the North Vietnamese are taking a very great risk if they continue their offensive in the South. I will just leave it there, and they can make their own choice." There were some isolated bombings of dikes and surrounding irrigation systems in the next few months which may have been intended to warn of Nixon's willingness to carry out his threats, but American warplanes did not systematically target North Vietnam's waterworks. Nixon's apocalyptic threat was aimed primarily at Le Duc Tho, his colleagues in Hanoi's politburo, and the May 2 secret peace talks.

On May 1, Quang Tri fell to the North Vietnamese [it was May 2 in Vietnam]. Nixon, aware of his aides' reluctance to confront him with adversity, described a nervous Kissinger skulking into his office with a cable from Abrams telling of the losses. "What else does he say?" Nixon asked. Kissinger "cleared his throat uncomfortably," Nixon wrote, and said: "He feels it is quite possible that the South Vietnamese have lost their will to fight, or to hang together, and that the whole thing may well be lost." Nixon was shocked: "I could hardly believe what I heard. How can this have happened?" Kissinger gave a vague response and Nixon once more made his national security adviser the enemy. "I don't want you to give the North Vietnamese a thing," he quoted himself as telling Kissinger. "They'll be riding high because of all this, so you'll have to bring them down to the ground by your manner. No nonsense. No niceness. No accommodations. And we'll just have to let our Soviet friends know that I'm willing to give up the summit if this is the price they have in mind to make us pay for it. Under no circumstances will I go to the summit if we're still in trouble in Vietnam."

Nixon still thought the ground lost in South Vietnam could be won in Moscow. Kissinger, who had managed to defy the President on that issue a few days earlier, knew better than to try again. And so it was off to Paris with essentially the same peace proposal, modified by the formal American concession—as spelled out to the Russians—on the right of Hanoi to keep its troops in the South. It was a major improvement over the last American offer, on October 11, 1971, which had returned to a demand for North Vietnamese withdrawal, stated ambiguously, by declaring that "all armed forces of the countries of Indochina must remain within their national borders."

There is no evidence from his memoirs or from other accounts of the May 2 meeting that Kissinger raised the issue of shared political control in the South, as he had tentatively done in Moscow. It was clearly not the time, in the middle of the successful offensive and with Richard Nixon's tough words from the day before still ringing in his ears, to bring up another concession. Instead, Kissinger clung to Nguyen Van Thieu: Any settlement would have to leave the South Vietnamese President, his political structure, and American "honor" intact. What Kissinger basically proposed was to trade a unilateral American troop withdrawal and an end to the bombing of the North for a POW exchange, a ceasefire throughout Southeast Asia, and an election—at some undetermined date—in the South. Thieu would step down from office a month before the election, but would still, obviously, control the political apparatus. In addition, those North Vietnamese troops who had entered the South after the offensive would have to withdraw, a provision Kissinger had described earlier in his memoirs as a "throwaway" that would be discarded when Hanoi was "ready for serious negotiation . . ." Behind all the American proposals were the threats that had been made in public and to the Chinese and the Soviet Union.

Kissinger ran into a stone wall in Paris. Le Duc Tho, seemingly oblivious to the bombs that were falling and could fall, continued to insist on a sharing of political power in the South. North Vietnamese officials, describing the talks in later interviews with the author, acknowledged that the American concession on Hanoi's troops was essential and was one of the factors that led to their subsequent decision to offer a draft peace treaty in October. But May was not the time to talk peace. By early May, barely a month after the offensive began, the North Vietnamese had seized one provincial capital, eight district capitals, and more than forty military bases around the country. Even where there were not fierce fighting and retreats, North Vietnamese and Vietcong troops had been able to work their way back into positions of control throughout the countryside. In his memoirs, Kissinger called the May 2 meeting with Le Duc Tho "brutal." He saw the North Vietnamese as "implacable revolutionaries" who were negotiating at the end of a gun barrel. "For all Le Duc Tho knew, a complete South Vietnamese collapse was imminent." Indeed it would have been, without the American bombing, but Kissinger seemed to regard Hanoi's willingness to take advantage of Saigon's weakness as unfair. What he did not seem to perceive in early May was that the North Vietnamese, obviously aware of the retaliatory power of the American bombers and the American President, were hedging. If their offensive did not work, there was a fallback position—renewed negotiations, but from a far stronger posture. Over the next few months, as the war on the ground moved toward a stalemate, official Washington would persist in interpreting Hanoi's spring offensive as aimed primarily at the American presidential election— ignoring the reality that leaders of North Vietnam knew how to read and interpret public opinion polls. Another reality ignored was the fact that the two previous American presidential elections, despite pious claims of peacemaking by the winning candidate, had done nothing to alleviate the intensity of the conflict. By May 2, the North Vietnamese offensive had already pried free a critical American concession on the right of Hanoi's troops to remain in the South. Hanoi had nothing to lose by continuing to fight.*

One NSC aide who attended the May 2 meeting came to believe that Kissinger had not really expected any progress in Paris, but wanted to be sure that "nothing was overlooked" before proceeding with his plans (left over from the aborted Duck Hook ultimatum of November 1969) to mine Haiphong Harbor and bomb Hanoi. Kissinger had ordered Haig to review and update the Duck Hook studies early in April, after the intensity of the North Vietnamese offensive became clear. In his memoirs, Kissinger sought to leave the impression that he was merely going through the motions in his meeting with Le Duc Tho: "I had advocated delaying an all-out response until we had explored every diplomatic avenue. I had thought it desirable to make sure that we had assembled enough power for a massive blow. I wanted to bring about the greatest possible diplomatic isolation of Hanoi. And it was crucial that our negotiating record be above reproach to withstand the domestic fury ahead."

The truth was not so Machiavellian. Nixon and Kissinger managed to convince themselves in the days before the May 2 meeting that the Soviet Union had enough influence to compel the North Vietnamese at least to slow down their offensive. Emotions ebbed and flowed in the Oval Office during those days, and the two most powerful men in the United States seem to have maintained their faith in triangular diplomacy and the threat of American bombings. Perhaps Leonid Brezhnev would compel Hanoi to agree to a cease-fire before any agreement was reached on the political issues. Nixon's and Kissinger's faith in Brezhnev was justified, for there is evidence that he did all he could to get Hanoi to negotiate. But what he could accomplish was far less than what Washington believed. During that spring in Moscow, Brezhnev wistfully remarked to the French Ambassador at a reception, "I wish our Vietnamese comrades were as wise at the negotiating table as they are brave on the battlefield." Word of Brezhnev's comment soon spread through the diplomatic community with the inescapable conclusion, as reported in cables home to capitals: The North Vietnamese had rebuffed Soviet efforts to pressure them to negotiate an end to the war.

Nixon's misconception that May about the influence of the Soviets was not unique. He had badly misjudged their influence during earlier crises in Jordan, Cienfuegos, Chile, and Pakistan. Kissinger's reasoning was more complicated: A conclusion that the Soviets were unable to influence policy in North Vietnam would undermine the crux of the administration's grand strategy. The conces-

* There was no mystery to many Americans about Hanoi's two-stage strategy. Robert Shaplen, the New Yorker magazine's well-informed correspondent in Southeast Asia, reported on May 13, 1972, that the North Vietnamese offensive had, as a second purpose, the creation of "a military vacuum in some places [which] has led to reinfiltration by Communist agents and Viet Cong armed bands into a good many rural areas, especially in the Mekong Delta, previously rated by the government as secure and pacified." Shaplen went on to explain that if the offensive, "or at least this phase of it, fails and the Communists cannot seize and hold certain key area cities, they will, as they have always been able to do, revert to small-unit and guerrilla warfare." By early July, there were repeated North Vietnamese broadcasts in which the offensive was explained as being aimed at the development of liberated zones. One such broadcast on July 2, monitored by the United States, noted that the newly liberated zones "can serve as very favorable springboards from which to launch offensives and to advance the resistance toward complete victory." By that point, the concentrated American bombing had prevented a complete rout of the Thieu government forces and the North Vietnamese had obviously reverted, as Shaplen predicted, to a difference phase of warfare.

sions to Peking and Moscow that were essential to insure presidential summits in an election year were not justifiable on that ephemeral basis alone, but would be acceptable if considered as the price of restructuring world order. That Moscow was unable to force its views on North Vietnam was an assessment that Kissinger adamantly refused to make. He concluded his discussion of the Vietnam War in the first volume of his memoirs by insisting that the United States "would use our new relationships with Moscow and Peking to foster [North Vietnamese] restraint" in the months after the signing of the 1973 Paris peace agreement. Even then, he still saw the North Vietnamese as chattels of the Communist world powers.

Kissinger's dilemma after the May 2 meeting was acute. He was convinced that the Duck Hook plan, if put into effect, would force Nixon into preemptively canceling the Moscow summit lest the Soviet Union cancel first. He did not dare try to convince the President otherwise: He was already in the doghouse for his insistence on the Le Duc Tho meeting. The Haig problem was also ominous. During the crisis, Haig's star had been on the rise almost in direct proportion to Kissinger's decline, and Nixon had begun to lean on Haig as well as Connally for foreign policy advice. He told Colson at one point after the Le Duc Tho meeting, "Only Al and John understand. They're the only ones in the whole government, besides you and Bob [Haldeman], who favored this decision [to escalate]. You know, Chuck," Nixon added, "those are the only two men around here qualified to fill this job when I step down."

One reason for Haig's increased stature becomes apparent in Nixon's diary for this period, as excerpted in his memoirs: "Haig emphasized that even more important than how Vietnam comes out is for us to handle these matters in a way that *I can survive in office* [emphasis added]." Haig was now openly more loyal to the President than to Kissinger. "I had a long talk with Haig," Nixon wrote, "in which we concluded that we had to have a two-day strike rather than the one-day-separated-by-another-day as Henry had recommended earlier in the week. We have very few cards left to play."

For more than three years Henry Kissinger had helped shape American foreign and military policy as the President's closest collaborator. Nixon was now making basic strategic decisions with Kissinger out of town, conspiring with Haig against Kissinger just as he and Kissinger had conspired against Laird and Rogers. At this point in his memoirs, the President began to depict Kissinger as a liability: "He is so understandably obsessed with the idea that there should be a negotiated settlement and that we ought to be able to obtain it with everything that we have set in motion, that he cannot get himself to see clearly there really isn't enough in it for the enemy to negotiate at this time."

Returning from Paris on May 2, late in the day, Kissinger was summoned to join a cruise aboard the *Sequoia* with the President. Haig was also aboard. Kissinger's deputy was finally cracking the inner circle. No longer would he have to sneak in a visit with Haldeman or wait in his office for Kissinger to return from a late-night meeting to learn what was going on.

There was much tough talk aboard ship that night. The Kalbs, in their biography, reported that a range of sharp escalations was discussed, including the bombing of North Vietnam's dike system, an American ground invasion of the North, and the use of nuclear weapons. Nixon rejected all of them, the Kalbs added, obviously basing their description on an account provided by Kissinger.

The boat ride did produce one agreement, however: There would be renewed B-52 bombing of Hanoi, and Haiphong Harbor would be mined for the first time in the war. The mining had been explored as an option at least twice by Kissinger's staff early in 1969, and criticized as expensive to maintain and unlikely to effectively curtail Hanoi's ability to conduct the war.*

Similar studies questioning the effectiveness of the bombing of the North had been routinely supplied to the White House for years, with no effect on the decision makers. Whatever Nixon's motive in wanting to mine Haiphong Harbor in early May—whether it was a facet of his "madman threat" or caused by personal affront at the offensive—no senior official was prepared to tell the President that the bombing would not be effective.† During the cruise on the *Sequoia*, Kissinger wrote, he argued that the President should cancel

---

* NSSM 1, the initial Nixon-Kissinger study of the Vietnam War, concluded that mining the harbor would have no significant long-term effect on the ability of North Vietnam to resupply its forces and the Vietcong in the South, because there were many waterways and roadways from China into North Vietnam that could easily absorb the volume of needed supplies. The NSSM study further concluded that it would be impossible to stop all traffic along the waterways, since there was far more capacity for shipping supplies south than was needed. Bombing the railways from China also would not be significantly effective, the study showed, since it would be difficult to cause permanent disruption. Similar conclusions were independently reached by the CIA, the State Department, and the Systems Analysis Office of the Defense Department, with the Joint Chiefs of Staff dissenting. Kissinger, not satisfied with the results of NSSM 1, ordered Richard Sneider, then his assistant for East Asia, to prepare a second analysis with the aid of the JCS. That study, Sneider recalls, also came out negatively, in part because of the ease with which the North Vietnamese could offload cargoes into smaller vessels, such as fishing boats. To insure that the mining was effective, the United States would have to consider attacking Soviet and other nations' freighters that remained outside the harbor, a separate and major escalation that would bring new international problems.

† Some Watergate prosecutors would later conclude that the *Sequoia* cruise also produced conversation about Daniel Ellsberg, who had remained a White House obsession. Ellsberg, facing trial for his role in making the Pentagon Papers public, had reacted to the April bombing of Hanoi and Haiphong by leaking yet another document—NSSM 1. Portions of that top-secret paper were published in *Newsweek* and by Jack Anderson late in April, and it was then that Senator Mike Gravel, the maverick Democrat from Alaska, began what would be an unsuccessful two-week fight on the Senate floor to get the study published in full in the *Congressional Record*. During debate on the issue, Gravel made a vitriolic attack on the integrity of the President: "[O]ne can only come to the conclusion that the President of the United States had only one concern—and that concern was foremost—to save face. Today we are locked in a war that has been reescalated. We are killing thousands and hundreds of thousands of people only to save face, the political face of one individual." Within days, Ellsberg was once again a target of illegal activity by the White House. Files still kept under seal by the Watergate Special Prosecution Force strongly suggest that Nixon was responsible for an attempted assault on Ellsberg and disruption of an antiwar rally scheduled for May 3 in Washington. Ellsberg had been publicly warning for months that Nixon had planned since 1969 to escalate the war by mining Haiphong Harbor; he was also asserting that the President knew that the mining would not work and that it would do nothing to end the war. The White House recruited a team of six Cubans, led by Bernard Barker (the same group that would stage the Watergate break-in six weeks later), to assault Ellsberg at the rally. The Cubans' attempt was inept and counterproductive—a failure that obviously did not diminish their future value to the White House. Ellsberg was never touched, although at least one bystander was punched, apparently by Barker. Two of the Cubans were seized, but escaped arrest when two unidentified men, believed to be Howard Hunt and E. Gordon Liddy, showed some kind of official identification to the police. For some Watergate prosecutors, the significance of the May 3 incident was in its chain of command. The attack on Ellsberg, one of Nixon's enemies, was marked by a line of authority that extended from the President through Colson to the Nixon reelection committee. During the various Watergate investigations, Nixon and Colson repeatedly insisted that they had not known of or authorized the break-in at the Watergate apartments. The May 3 incident implicitly challenged that account. May 3 also raised questions—to which answers were never sought—about how much Haig and Kissinger knew. Would a tape recording of the May 2 cruise on the *Sequoia*—no such tape existed, of course—have found Nixon talking about Vietcong flags and Daniel Ellsberg? Some

the summit at the same time he announced the Vietnam escalation. No final decision was made, Kissinger wrote, but he was ordered by Nixon to plan "on the assumption that he would preempt Moscow." The SALT talks would continue at a lower level, and any agreement would be signed by the negotiators. Kissinger depicted the proposed cancellation in his memoirs as a joint decision —"our cancellation," he wrote. Over the next few days, however, Nixon apparently discussed the issue repeatedly with Haldeman and Connally, and changed his mind: He could bomb and also go to the summit. One factor appreciated by the Treasury Secretary was economic: The Moscow meetings would result in significant trade agreements, as well as a commitment by the United States to grant most-favored-nation status to the Soviet Union, giving the Russians assurances that they would not be penalized in trade dealings with the United States.

Nixon's estrangement from Kissinger was acute at this point, and the President could not bring himself to have another contentious discussion with his adviser. Instead, he arranged to have Haldeman participate in a long conversation on May 4, at which word of the President's change of mind was conveyed. In his memoirs, Haldeman told of being in Nixon's office when Kissinger again argued for a summit delay. "To Henry's surprise, and mine," Haldeman wrote ingenuously, "when Henry concluded Nixon said to me, 'What do you think, Bob?' " Nixon, who as usual had arranged the scene, was now interjecting his right-hand domestic operative into foreign affairs.

Kissinger's argument had been modified since the cruise two days earlier. Instead of a lower-level signing of the SALT agreement—neither he nor the President could endure the prospect of Gerard Smith or William Rogers getting

---

of the Watergate prosecutors thought so, but no questions were ever asked of Kissinger. "He was an untouchable," one prosecutor recalls, "and the sad thing is that everyone in our office believed it. It was never said, but certainly people were afraid to question him."

There were serious problems in investigating and prosecuting the case, but the impasse was broken in December 1973, when William F. Rhatigan, a young Colson aide who had also denied any knowledge of the May 3 incident, failed an FBI lie detector test. Rhatigan subsequently testified under a grant of immunity before the Watergate grand jury and told of a Colson order to disrupt the demonstration. Rhatigan quoted Colson as telling aides that "it would be fine if a couple of heads are knocked." The Watergate prosecutors eventually received a tape recording, one of the last to be turned over by the White House under subpoena, which included a presidential discussion of the May 3 demonstration and showed that Nixon knew that Colson and Rhatigan had been involved in seamy activities against demonstrators that day. The recording, not made public by the Justice Department, was of an April 25, 1973, Oval Office meeting attended by Nixon, Haldeman, and Ehrlichman, in which the President's two senior advisers seemed to be pleading for their jobs. Both were fired five days later. At one point, Haldeman reminded Nixon that Kenneth Clawson, a former *Washington Post* reporter who was working for Colson, "was heavily involved in the Colson-type activities as was Bill Rhatigan, I think." Ehrlichman interjected: "Bringing the Cubans to rough up the demonstrators . . . Then Bill Rhatigan someday becomes just as big a problem to you as I might be, if I were here. Because they haven't got me to focus on." After obtaining the new evidence late in 1974, the Watergate attorneys in charge of the May 3 inquiry formally proposed to their superiors that perjury charges be filed against Colson and his senior aide, W. Richard Howard, who also had testified that he knew nothing of an order to assault Ellsberg. By then, however, Nixon had resigned the presidency, Colson was in jail, and the men running the Prosecution Force considered their most important work over. "The office was winding down," one attorney recalled. "The momentum was not to do more." Henry S. Ruth, Jr., who succeeded Leon Jaworski as Watergate Special Prosecutor after Nixon's resignation, decided not to file any charges in the May 3 matter. The Watergate prosecutors remain convinced today, however, that the key to May 3 was Daniel Ellsberg and his involvement in the leaking of NSSM 1. "We were certain that a lot of it was related to the NSSM and the fact that he had it," one attorney recalls. "That was the outstanding factor that got you over the obvious pettiness of that act."

credit for the treaty—the summit could perhaps be saved for later in the year if a postponement was announced immediately. "I argued with Henry to this effect," Haldeman wrote, "he was *assuming* the Soviets would cancel the conference . . . *Maybe* we could still have the summit conference despite the bombing." Haldeman added that he supposed "Henry might have been angry at my intrusion into affairs in which I was far from expert. . . ." At this point, Haldeman added, Nixon interrupted with a mild comment, "Well, there seems to be a disagreement." Haldeman quoted the President as asking, "Why don't you both go to John Connally and see what his view is?" Connally, of course, echoed Haldeman's line; the summit did not have to be canceled. Kissinger chose, in his memoirs, to accept the day's events at face value. "As soon as Connally had spoken I knew he was right," Kissinger wrote. "I had gone along with Nixon's preliminary decision in deference to his superior knowledge of domestic political consequences. But when the Cabinet officer generally believed to have the best political brain in the Administration considered cancellation a domestic liability, I guiltily realized that on the *Sequoia* I had fallen into that cardinal sin of Presidential Assistants: permitting oneself to be seduced by arguments because they comported with Presidential preference." It was certainly a familiar sin for the national security adviser; all the same, one can hardly imagine that Kissinger was not stunned at the President's seeking the advice of outsiders on such issues.

At a meeting with Kissinger, Haig, and Haldeman later that day, Nixon, pacing up and down and gesturing with a pipe, authorized the mining of Haiphong. Nixon was actually smoking the pipe, Kissinger noted, which was a new twist, ". . . yet one more from my chief's inexhaustible store of surprises. On one level he was playing MacArthur." On another level, Kissinger added, "It was one of the finest hours of Nixon's Presidency." In Kissinger's view, Nixon "risked his political future on a course most of his Cabinet colleagues questioned. He was willing to abandon the summit because he would not go to Moscow in the midst of a defeat imposed by Soviet arms. And he had insisted on an honorable withdrawal from Vietnam because he was convinced that the stability of the post-Vietnam world would depend on it. He was right on all counts." William Safire was equally excessive in his memoirs: "The spring of 1972 was the apex of Richard Nixon's career. . . . In a six-week span, Nixon rose to the final challenge of his Vietnam policy by a foe that never wanted to negotiate and always wanted to win; he reacted with the application of enough power to counter that bid for victory, but with enough coolness in its presentation to the American public to be accepted without another Kent State. He came back with enough restraint in his choice of weapons and targets to permit a summit conference to be held and with enough power so that his display of nerve helped achieve the kind of arms limitation agreement he wanted."

What Nixon really did was lash out at an enemy and trust that the Soviets would expediently choose to ignore Hanoi long enough to conclude a profitable series of trade and diplomatic negotiations. Nixon had escalated the war in the North when the fighting was in the South. His only act of courage in all this was the decision not to cancel the summit out of fear that the Soviets would cancel first. He had defeated his own fear of rejection. Politically, he was aware that the Sindlinger polls showed that the public consistently supported his escalations. As for the notion that America's honor was synonymous with the prosecution of the war, Haig and Kissinger both realized that there were moments when Nixon was willing to sign anything—short of jettisoning Nguyen Van Thieu—if an agreement that did not immediately signify "humiliation" could be reached with the North Vietnamese.

No such signs of weakness were presented to John Connally, whose toughness was so much admired by the President. Connally was telling Nixon in those days what the President needed to hear: that his political future rested solely on the Vietnam War. In his memoirs, Nixon quoted Connally as telling him, "Most important—the President must not lose the war! And he should not cancel the summit. He's got to show his guts and leadership on this one. Caution be damned—if they cancel, and I don't think they will, we'll ram it right down their throats."

Gloomy about his loss of influence, Kissinger remained convinced that the Soviets would cancel. His aides saw a different Kissinger, one who was not comfortable with the decision to escalate in early May. "I heard Henry say that he didn't want to become the Walt Rostow of the administration," one close aide remembers. "It was not his idea" to bomb and mine North Vietnam, "but Nixon's." Kissinger not only feared for the summit, the aide theorizes, but saw the escalation as capable of leading to the unthinkable—bringing the Chinese and the Soviet Union together in a common policy on behalf of North Vietnam. Such a move could lead to a bridging of the Sino-Soviet split. Kissinger may also have learned by May 1972 what his predecessors took equally long to find out: Bombing does not end wars.

As Kissinger brooded, it was left to Haig to seize control of the NSC and carry out the President's planning. The general summoned the NSC senior members to the White House Situation Room and informed them that Nixon was prepared to order the escalation. The staff's function was to analyze the operations in advance to make sure nothing had been overlooked. On the next afternoon, a Saturday, an obviously torn Kissinger summoned a few members of his staff to a meeting. There was no Roger Morris, Anthony Lake, or William Watts to protest and then resign in outrage. Kissinger's NSC staff, under Haig's direction, had been militarized. Four of the eight men at that session—Haig, Jonathan Howe, John Holdridge, and Richard Kennedy—either had been or were on active military duty. Of the four civilians, only Winston Lord expressed any reservation about the escalation. And Lord, as everyone in the room realized, was prepared—after making his opposition known—to draft a speech for the President outlining and explaining the escalation. The CIA's George Carver expressed support for the bombing and mining; so did Helmut Sonnenfeldt and John Negroponte. Kissinger was surprised at Negroponte's strong endorsement; he had been known to oppose the earlier bombings of North Vietnam. This escalation was different, Negroponte explained; now the White House was going for the jugular. Kissinger would later summon Negroponte and Carver to his office to continue the discussion. Both men were known to have advocated softer lines than the military men who now dominated his staff, and he wanted their approval. Kissinger, in his memoirs, recalled acknowledging to Winston Lord, the NSC staff member he then considered his closest friend, that "all we had patiently put together over three years might go down the drain in a twenty-minute speech. But we had no choice. Seeing the President toasting Brezhnev while we were being defeated by Soviet arms in Vietnam would not be understood by Americans whose sons had risked or given their lives there. It would be better to stand firm, gain respect, and pick up the pieces later.''

It is impossible to believe that Kissinger saw the issues quite as simple-mindedly as that. No amount of mining or bombing of the North could possibly have any short-term effect on the battlefields in the South. If stopping the offensive were the priority, the bombs dropped on Hanoi over the next few weeks would be far better used on Hanoi's troops in the South. Since early April, the bombing of supply depots and of the Ho Chi Minh Trail in North Vietnam had continued around the clock in an effort to slow up the Hanoi offensive; the bombing of Hanoi and the mining of Haiphong Harbor could only be considered punitive. When Hanoi did choose to seek a compromise in the South, it did so after a careful analysis of presidential politics in America and the battlefield situation in South Vietnam—not because of bombing in the North. Hanoi's 1972 offensive ground to a halt by early summer, largely because of the bombing in the South, but Nixon's "finest hour" was his action in the North. He had bombed and mined to save face and insure votes.

There was genius in Nixon's diplomacy. He understood, as Kissinger did not, that if he could force the Soviets to accept the bombing and not cancel the summit, it would be a triumph bright enough to efface the humiliation being inflicted on the battlefields of South Vietnam. He also understood that the Soviets might well be willing to swallow an immense attack on their allies in Hanoi in order to get American grain and the SALT agreement.

Aware that his loyalty to the President was on the line, Kissinger was again eager to please. He spent part of the weekend working with Nixon on various drafts of the speech announcing the Vietnam escalation and, as Nixon reported in his memoirs, found Nixon's assessment of the Soviet position brilliant: ". . . Henry was very impressed with what I finally came up with on my own. It had to be done with great subtlety and I think we have stated the case as well as we possibly can to give them a way out if they want to find one." Kissinger reported optimistically on his staff meeting, Nixon wrote, adding that only one aide dissented.

On Monday, May 8, Nixon held a lengthy meeting with the National Security Council to present his plans for escalation. It was another dog-and-pony show, as everyone involved realized. Kissinger said little; it was left to Rogers and Laird to express opposition.*

* Rogers was urgently summoned back from Europe for the NSC meeting and Nixon was apparently "walking on the ceiling" over the subsequent newspaper accounts of his return, so Kissinger told Alexis Johnson. One account, published May 8 in the *New York Times,* was headlined, "Call of Urgency to Man of Calm," and it quoted the Secretary as "suggesting strongly . . . that Mr. Nixon was ready to risk his career and his reputation to stem the North Vietnam invasion of South Vietnam, and was ready to use everything short of nuclear weapons to do so." Kissinger shared Nixon's rage and perhaps inspired it. "Henry was making trouble for Rogers," Johnson says. It would have been impossible for Rogers not to have created a stir, since he had abruptly canceled a series of scheduled meetings and flown home with a contingent of State Department correspondents on his plane. Having tipped Johnson off to Nixon's ire, Kissinger then asked a favor. "He hoped that Rogers would oppose" the proposed mining of Haiphong, Johnson recalls. "He said that John Connally was pushing Nixon on the mining and he was against it. Henry said he didn't like to take a position against Nixon at a meeting of that kind." Would Johnson please make sure that Rogers argued against the mining? "I told Rogers," Johnson recalls, "and he was skeptical that Henry really was against it." The Under Secretary of State added: "It seemed like straight lying to me to set up Rogers." Crisis or not, it was business as usual in the White House.

One participant recalls that Rogers told the President, "You've done enough." Laird once again argued that the war was in the South; his point was that the real test was not of Nixon's courage or his ability to face up to the Soviets, but of the ability of the South Vietnamese Army to stand up to the North Vietnamese battalions. Laird also argued, as he usually did, that the costs of the offensive were excessive and would further ruin the Pentagon's budget. At some point in all this, one eyewitness recalls, John Connally all but jumped out of his chair, pointed his finger at Nixon, and declared, in essence: You will not be a real President if you don't do it.

There was a bizarre indignity for Kissinger soon after the NSC meeting, when Nixon asked him to personally deliver the executive order for the mining to the President's hideaway office. Haldeman was there also, and he suddenly began to complain about the planned escalation and warn that it would have a dire impact on public opinion. "If the President were defeated as a result of this," Kissinger quoted Haldeman as saying, "we would have lost every-thing." Kissinger, perhaps sensing some sort of ploy, heatedly defended the policy, of which President Thieu and others in Saigon had already been noti-fied. Nixon chose that moment to leave the room, Kissinger wrote, and "I whirled on Haldeman . . . and castigated him for interfering at a moment of great crisis. . . . Haldeman grinned shamefacedly, making clear by his bearing that Nixon had put him up to his little speech." Kissinger described the game as being beyond his comprehension until he learned of the taping devices in the President's offices. Nixon was apparently seeking to insure that the colum-nists would not write, as they had after the Cambodian invasion in 1970, that Kissinger had argued against the escalation.

A few hours before Nixon's speech, Kissinger briefed Ambassador Dobry-nin. He was terribly agitated, Kissinger told the President, and asked: "Why are you turning against us when it is Hanoi that has challenged you?" His point, lost on the Nixon-Kissinger White House, was that America would have to solve its problems with the Vietnamese in Vietnam, not in the Soviet Union.

Nixon's speech was remarkable for its fuzziness. It embraced both an esca-lation of the terms for settling the war and a significant concession. The lan-guage was demagogic. The President had decided to mine Haiphong Harbor because "There is only one way to stop the killing. That is to keep the weapons of war out of the hands of the international outlaws of North Vietnam." At the time, of course, United States warplanes were bombing the South and the North in unrelenting attacks. The President further declared that the renewed bombing and the mining would cease only when two conditions were met: the return of the American prisoners of war and an immediate ceasefire throughout Southeast Asia. After Hanoi met those demands, the United States would stop all acts of war and withdraw its troops within four months. Nixon said nothing directly about his significant concession—the fact that his new peace terms did not compel Hanoi's withdrawal from the South—and the net effect was ambig-uous. He repeatedly called the North Vietnamese attack an "invasion," a word suggesting that the North had no legal basis for being in the South. Safire, who helped prepare an early draft, characterized the President's concession as being "nearly as dramatic" as the mining of Haiphong Harbor. "Nixon did not want to play up the concession in a speech taking punitive action," Safire wrote in his memoirs, "so Kissinger put out the word in backgrounders."

Kissinger did no such thing. Called upon by Nixon to brief the press next morning, Kissinger said nothing in his opening statement about a ceasefire in place. The first question dealt with the essential issue: Would Hanoi's troops have to withdraw? Kissinger fudged. "We will be delighted to spell out the details of our proposal as soon as a serious negotiation starts," he said, "but I can only repeat that we would approach negotiations in a generous spirit and with the attitude of bringing about a rapid end to the war." The issue of Hanoi's ability to remain in the South did not arise again in a meaningful public forum until the fall.

There was great tension in Kissinger's office over the next few days as he and his aides waited for the Soviet Union to cancel the summit. The Russians, however, just as John Connally had predicted, made it clear that it was business as usual. Tass, the Soviet news agency, denounced the bombing but the Soviet government went out of its way to indicate that the summit would be held. Throughout the crisis, a White House advance team headed by General Brent Scowcroft, a military aide to the President, had remained in Moscow to work out security and communications arrangements for Nixon's visit, with the full cooperation of the government. Senior Soviet officials began to seek out journalists in Washington to give reassurances. Shortly after Nixon's speech, Stanley Karnow, the *Washington Post*'s expert on China, was abruptly approached while at lunch by a senior Soviet official. "I guarantee you that the summit will not be canceled," he told Karnow. "Listen, we've done enough for those Vietnamese," the official added. "We're not going to let them interfere with our relationship with you." Throughout these days also, Soviet specialists in the State Department were assuring their counterparts in the NSC that there was no reason to believe the Russians would permit the Vietnam issue to interfere with their much larger interests as a world power.*

In his memoirs, Kissinger dramatically described the few days after Nixon's speech: "In every crisis tension builds steadily, sometimes nearly unbearably, until some decisive turning point." The decisive event was a visit on May 10 from Ambassador Dobrynin, who wished to know if the President was planning to meet personally with a visiting trade official. Moscow was making it plain where its interests lay.

Vietnam lingered as an unofficial issue at the week-long Soviet summit that began May 22, which was publicly dominated by the final negotiations on the SALT treaty, as well as by a series of agreements on scientific cooperation and economic matters. And despite its low profile, Vietnam was the subject of at least two intensive meetings in Moscow, at which tentative American concessions on the war were presented. Neither Kissinger nor Nixon described any of these concessions in his memoirs; both focused instead on a May 24 "confrontation," as Kissinger put it, in which the ranking Soviets, Brezhnev, Kosygin, and Podgorny, took turns denouncing the American policy in Vietnam.

---

* Another factor not mentioned by Nixon or Kissinger was the ongoing NSA intercepts of diplomatic communications from the Soviet Embassy on Sixteenth Street in Washington to Moscow. Those intercepts, which, according to well-informed officials, continued to be decoded at least until 1973, must have reflected the reassuring words expressed to Karnow and others as anxiety built up over the possibility of a cancellation.

Kissinger rationalized the three-hour meeting, with its "bombast rudeness . . . [as] a charade . . . The Soviet leaders were not pressing us except with words. They were speaking for the record, and when they had said enough to have a transcript to send to Hanoi, they would stop."

The next day, Kissinger and a small group of aides met with Andrei Gromyko, the Soviet Foreign Minister, and, according to an account provided by one of Kissinger's aides, outlined two significant concessions on Vietnam. Kissinger began by noting that the bombing of North Vietnam did not necessarily have to continue until all the American prisoners of war had been returned, as Nixon had stated in his May 8 speech. He was thus presenting Hanoi, through the Soviets, with a softer position in private. He further told Gromyko that he was willing to discuss an electoral commission with three components, representing the Thieu government, the PRG, and the Third Force, the loose amalgamation of neutralists, nationalists, and Buddhists. In meetings with the North Vietnamese in Paris, Kissinger had avoided any specific discussion of the makeup of the electoral commission lest such a three-tiered group be interpreted as a step toward a coalition government, which Kissinger had strongly deplored as recently as two weeks before, at his press briefing the morning after Nixon's May 8 speech.

Now, however, he was secretly telling Gromyko that the United States would be willing to meet, at least partway, Hanoi's insistence that any settlement in South Vietnam include a political as well as a military element. Obviously aware of the significance of Kissinger's remark, Gromyko said at one point, "Let me make quite sure I got it right what you said." Kissinger obliged, according to a participant, explicitly acknowledging that he was departing from his government's public position.

On the last day of the summit, Nixon and Brezhnev agreed that Podgorny would go to Hanoi in June to tell the North Vietnamese the details of the new American position. Nixon also agreed, Kissinger noted in his memoirs, not to bomb Hanoi and Haiphong during Podgorny's stay. Kissinger was pleased with the negotiating progress, and with the Soviets' decision to continue to relay messages from Washington to Hanoi. "Did we do all right?" he repeatedly asked his aides. John Negroponte raised a question about the new American concession on the tripartite commission. "Well, they bought it, didn't they?" Kissinger responded. "They're going to help us."

The bombings had done the job by summer. Nixon and Kissinger could conclude that they were a success: The offensive had been stopped and perhaps Hanoi would now begin to compromise at the peace talks. The men in Hanoi also had reason for satisfaction. Their offensive had not overthrown the Thieu regime, but their troops were once again in position to conduct a long-term guerrilla war and begin stockpiling for another offensive. Furthermore, the Nixon Administration had finally indicated that it was willing to discuss a political settlement. Henry Kissinger was specifically talking about power sharing in the South. Much hard bargaining was to come, for the tripartite election commission envisioned by Kissinger was still to be within the framework of the South Vietnamese constitution, viewed by the North Vietnamese as a major impediment to any solution. Nonetheless, the Hanoi politburo, buttressed by its renewed military deployment in the South and encouraged by Kissinger's willingness to begin a political dialogue, decided in midsummer to explore seriously a sharing of power in the South with Nguyen Van Thieu.

In all of this maneuvering, the bombing of Hanoi and the mining of Haiphong Harbor had little effect. Nixon had bombed and mined out of rage, and had enjoyed a political bonanza. His violence had increased his public standing, and the Soviet Union's decision to hold the summit and sign a disarmament agreement, despite the escalation in Vietnam, had propelled him into the front ranks of pragmatic, hard-nosed leaders.*

The May 15 shooting of George Wallace solved most of the White House's remaining political problems. Barring a catastrophe in Vietnam, Nixon would achieve a landslide reelection. The Democratic nomination would be worthless.

---

* Nixon, having subdued the Soviets, turned to his critics in the press corps. Kenneth W. Clawson, deputy director of White House communications, recalls the President, obviously intoxicated, ordering him to attack the *New York Times* shortly after Anthony Lewis, the columnist who seemed to provoke the White House constantly, reported from Hanoi that the Navy's initial mining of Haiphong Harbor had been ineffective. The Pentagon immediately denied the report (which Lewis modified a few days later). "I got a call from Al Haig at Camp David and I hear the President in the background saying, 'Give 'em hell, give 'em hell,' " Clawson says. He asked Haig what they wanted him to do and he said, "I want you to take on the *New York Times* . . . Here's this guy talking to me and Nixon's saying 'Give 'em hell.' " Clawson immediately did as he was told, issuing a White House statement that accused the *Times* of being "a conduit of enemy propaganda to the American people."

37

SALT:
THE MOSCOW SUMMIT

RICHARD NIXON CAME HOME from the May summit in Moscow with reelection in hand and his reputation as a peacemaker assured. He and Kissinger had successfully negotiated the first disarmament agreement with the Soviet Union and had, so Nixon would triumphantly tell a joint session of Congress on June 1, "witnessed the beginning of the end of that era"—of the nuclear arms race—"which began in 1945."

The SALT I agreements were in two parts. There was a Treaty, which would require ratification by two-thirds of the Senate, in which the United States and the Soviet Union agreed to limit to two the number of antiballistic missile (ABM) defense sites each would construct. There was also an Interim Agreement, requiring congressional approval but not ratification, in which the two nations agreed to stop building land-based intercontinental ballistic missile (ICBM) launchers and to accept a constraint on the maximum number of submarine-launched ballistic missile (SLBM) launchers that could be assembled. The freeze on offensive weapons had been desperately sought by Nixon and Kissinger in the months before the summit and seemed to work solely in favor of the United States, since there were no plans to augment the American nuclear missile force during the five-year life of the agreement. The hurrah of the summit obscured the fact that the Interim Agreement did not call for a *reduction* in offensive weapons systems, but merely imposed a limit, a cap, on the number of missile launchers each country could build. No restraint of any kind was placed on the number of independently targeted warheads—MIRVs —that could be placed on each missile.*

For all its weaknesses, the Interim Agreement established the principle that the two nations could negotiate limits on offensive weaponry. SALT I was, as

* At the time of the signing of SALT I, the United States had an estimated 3,500 MIRVed warheads, far more than the Soviets' 2,350. By 1977, when the Interim Agreement was to end, the American lead in MIRVs was 9,000 to 4,000, with both sides continuing research and production programs. The SALT I agreements, however, certified the Soviet lead in offensive missile launchers. The United States agreed to freeze its missile launchers at its current total of 1,710, of which 1,054 were land-based and 656 deployed aboard the Polaris nuclear submarine fleet. The Soviets were limited to their current total of 2,328 launchers over the next five years, but were permitted to continue building nuclear submarines—with additional modern SLBM launchers—as long as they decommissioned an older land-based missile launcher for each additional new SLBM launcher. The Soviets had 1,607 land-based ICBMs, and it was agreed at the summit that the Soviets had an estimated 740 SLBMs as of July 1, 1972, the date the Interim Agreement went into effect (the exact number of Soviet SLBMs was a constant source of internal debate among American negotiators).

the *New York Times* headline said, "A First Step, but a Major Stride." Nixon and Kissinger envisioned further SALT negotiations in the second term, with the aim of systematic control and eventual reduction of MIRVed offensive missile systems. The goal was that the two superpowers, in future agreements, would begin to rationalize military spending and divert some of the billions spent each year on weapons into more socially productive uses. SALT I should thus have been a momentous first step, a triumph that left the American government willing and able to do more.

It was not. Nixon and Kissinger could not resist overselling and exaggerating what had been accomplished at Moscow. They insisted, as usual, on taking all the credit, once again upsetting the SALT delegation members who had quietly gone about the business of negotiating the ABM agreement in which both sides agreed not to deploy the systems "for a defense of the territory of its country." That two superpowers could agree not to try to defend themselves from the nuclear attack of the other was an unprecedented achievement that made tolerable, so members of the SALT delegation believed, most of the White House abuse. By the spring of 1972, Gerard Smith and his staff had tacitly agreed to suffer in silence. Far more disturbing to them was the fact that Nixon and Kissinger went beyond merely humiliating them in Moscow: They cheated their way to a summit, accepting less than what could have been achieved in the bargaining, and then lied to the press and public about what they had accomplished.* These lies would haunt SALT I and hurt its successors. The Moscow agreement did not lead to a "new era" of arms control, as Nixon

---

* Kissinger took an extraordinary step in 1971 to minimize any future difficulty on the issue of who accomplished what in SALT: He ordered his staff to cooperate with a journalist who would write an inside account. The journalist was John Newhouse, a former member of the Senate Foreign Relations Committee staff who had written widely on military and European affairs. Newhouse had known Kissinger since the early 1960s and was also friendly with Guido Goldman, Kissinger's former assistant at Harvard. Kissinger agreed to help, and authorized Helmut Sonnenfeldt and Wayne Smith to provide as much information as possible without compromising any classified documents or revealing the current negotiating positions. Newhouse, in turn, was not to indicate in his book that he had received briefings. This covert agreement was made only a few months after the *New York Times* SALT leak of July 1971, which revealed that the United States, Kissinger's backchannel agreement to the contrary notwithstanding, would seek a limit on submarine-launched ballistic missiles in the SALT negotiations. That story, written by William Beecher, was still under active investigation by the White House Plumbers. Newhouse had no illusions about the open-door policy. "Henry is totally shrewd," he says. "He'd read my other stuff. He was only going to do something that would make him look good." Newhouse was determined, nonetheless, to do as much research as possible throughout the government. Shortly after he began, one Kissinger aide recalls, Gerard Smith told Kissinger that Newhouse was coming to Geneva and wanted to interview him. Back came an urgent telegram telling Smith that "under no circumstance" could he or anyone on his delegation talk. Kissinger's strictures on providing Newhouse with current information soon turned into a farce, one aide remembers, "since what was current eventually becomes not current." By May of 1972, Newhouse had received briefings from at least six NSC staff members involved in the SALT process, including William Hyland, Philip A. Odeen, Barry E. Carter, and Lieutenant Colonel Jack H. Merritt. As the summit neared, Newhouse requested the most recent intelligence estimates of Soviet missile strength and also sought a briefing on the latest American position paper. By this time the chore of handling Newhouse had become Barry Carter's, and the young aide asked Kissinger in writing for permission to release the sensitive information. He also made clear in his memorandum that he had doubts about the propriety of the briefings. Kissinger signed his approval without comment. Newhouse's book, *Cold Dawn,* was published in 1973, after excerpts appeared in the *New Yorker*. The highly accurate excerpts were the first authentic account of the internal governmental debates on SALT, and their view—not surprisingly—often reflected that of Henry Kissinger and the White House. Kissinger would later deny, during the confirmation hearings in 1973 on his nomination as Secretary of State, that he or his office had anything to do with supplying classified materials to Newhouse.

assured Congress it would. Instead, the SALT process was damaged, another victim of White House abuse of power and the Nixon-Kissinger instinct for the politically and personally expedient. The two men chose not to permit Gerard Smith or his aides to participate in the actual negotiations; instead, Nixon and Kissinger would themselves face the Soviet leaders. Neither could resist the chance to appear heroic, to have battled the Soviet bears in their lair and emerged with diplomatic victory. For Nixon, it was good politics; he would demonstrate that his reputation as a savant in foreign affairs was justified. For Kissinger, it was a chance to demonstrate his skills anew to his President, to show Richard Nixon that there were no limits to what they could accomplish, as long as they worked together.

The Soviets, of course, were not innocents. They were careful not to disrupt the Nixon honeymoon in the months after the summit; there were no claims of triumph from Moscow that summer, as Nixon's reelection seemed assured. The Soviet price for the summit had included a presidential assurance of favorable trade terms and easy credit, as well as an Interim Agreement that focused attention on the imposing Soviet numerical lead in offensive missile launchers. The agreement also permitted Soviet scientists—as well as their American counterparts—a free hand in the continued development and deployment of the far more strategically important MIRVs.

Another element was grain. The Russian winter wheat crop had been severely damaged and the Soviet need for grain was acute. Soviet buyers were active inside the United States after the summit, purchasing more than $1 billion worth of grain at subsidized prices, eventually driving up the price of bread and related foodstuffs for American consumers. The full amount of the Soviet purchases was apparent by midsummer, but somehow it never became a political issue for the White House. In his memoirs, Kissinger described himself as uninformed about such economic matters and wrote that the grain purchases were an example of the American government being "outwitted" by the Soviets. Neither he nor his aides, he claimed, had received prior intelligence about the "catastrophic" crop failures in the Soviet Union. "No report accurately pointing to the scale of the Soviet failure reached the White House then [before the summit] or until long after the unprecedentedly massive purchases of that crop year had been completed," he wrote.

The truth of the matter could be found in a column published by Joseph Alsop in late May of 1972, just as the summit was getting under way. Alsop reported that after the secret trip to Moscow in April, Kissinger told the President of his "perfect astonishment" at the "vast importance" the Soviet leaders placed on concluding a comprehensive trade agreement at the summit. "He came home," Alsop wrote, "convinced that such an agreement was one of their highest priorities. . . . Because of the Soviet *crop failure*, there will surely be a big, immediate grain deal [emphasis added]." Making no attempt to shield Kissinger as his source, Alsop also accurately predicted that the Soviets would include a constraint on submarine-launched ballistic missile launchers in the final treaty.

Information about a Soviet crop failure would have been essential to Kissinger in the spring of 1972, for he was seeking any possible leverage to help

531

recoup his mistake of not insisting that SLBMs be included in SALT I. This was not his only problem: He had also agreed in the backchannel that "modernization"—that is, MIRVing—of the Soviet missile fleet would not be in any way limited by SALT I, a concession he was unable to rectify in later negotiations. There had been repeated complaints during the winter of 1971–72 from Gerard Smith and others about Kissinger's concessions, as well as direct warnings that any SALT agreement that did not limit Soviet submarine building would be politically suspect. In November 1971, as the American and Soviet SALT negotiators met in Vienna for the sixth round of negotiations, the White House had formally changed its views on modernization and SLBMs: Gerard Smith's delegation was instructed to develop a "precise understanding" of what would be permitted under modernization and also to "make a strong effort," Smith recalls, to include SLBMs.

The Nixon Administration was now in the diplomatic posture of trying to get the Soviet Union to restrain its submarine building programs as well as to slow down any qualitative improvements in its ICBM forces. The only quid pro quo offered by the United States, which had no missile building programs of its own, was the ABM agreement. Nixon and Kissinger seemed to believe, to the amazement of the SALT delegation, that the ABM agreement could serve as leverage to force the Soviets to reduce their ICBM and SLBM buildups. Kissinger had not dared to make such a demand in his backchannel negotiations early in 1971; the agreement to permit modernization and to ignore Soviet SLBMs had been the inducement that persuaded the Kremlin to negotiate offensive constraints as well as limits on ABMs—the essence of the May 20, 1971, "breakthrough" that had been so breathlessly announced by Nixon. Gerard Smith was less than pleased with his new negotiating instructions in November, as he noted in his 1980 memoir, *Doubletalk*. As soon as he introduced modernization and the SLBM inclusion at Vienna, Vladimir Semenov, the chief Soviet negotiator, declared that the May 20, 1971, agreement was dominant. Those issues had been decided at the highest levels, he told Smith, and "we were not called on to revise." Smith wrote simply, "This was another case of locking the stable door after the horse was gone."

With the delegation deadlocked, Kissinger and Nixon were forced to return to the backchannel and undo the damage. To convince the Russians at such a late date that SLBM launchers must be included, as well as *some* understanding on modernization, would require major concessions. The solution was an American willingness to finance a large sale of grain, but neither Kissinger nor Nixon could hint at such a link later on. To have done so would have suggested that much of the earlier backchannel bargaining had been faulty, and also would have exposed each of them to allegations of responsibility for the secret Soviet grain purchases and the resultant scandal over rising wheat prices.

In early 1972, before the full scope of the Soviet crop failure was clear, Nixon and Kissinger had much more than wheat to offer the Russians: easy credit, most-favored-nation trading status, and a congenial settlement of the World War II lend-lease debt, whose repayment was insisted upon by Congress before American loans could be granted. The first known link between potential grain sales and Kissinger's need to reopen the backchannel SALT talks came in December 1971, at the height of the India-Pakistan war. Nixon spent an hour with Vladimir Matskevich, the Soviet Minister of Agriculture, who was in Washington for discussions with Earl L. Butz, the Secretary of Agriculture. Kissinger told reporters on July 8, 1972, a few weeks before the public outcry over the extent of Soviet wheat purchases, that high-level discussions on grain sales had been initiated at the Nixon-Matskevich meeting. "As in all other negotiations that took place prior to the summit," he said at a news conference in San Clemente, "the discussions about the agricultural field occurred in two channels: one, the regular channel . . . and secondly, the direct presidential channel to Brezhnev . . ."*

There is evidence that Kissinger was telling the truth in July 1972 about the link between the Matskevich meeting and grain sales. On January 17, at about the time he must have accepted the invitation to visit the Kremlin, Kissinger had sent a National Security Study Memorandum to the bureaucracy asking about the advantages and disadvantages of a five-year Soviet commitment to purchase feed grains, utilizing American credit. The NSSM also demanded an evaluation of granting the Soviets most-favored-nation status as well as access to Export Import Bank credits. Less than a month later, Kissinger signed NSDM 151, calling for the Agriculture Department to develop a "negotiating scenario for handling the issue of grain sales to the USSR." The sales were to be made by private grain companies in the United States utilizing a federal line of credit and a Soviet commitment to draw on that credit. The NSDM also ordered the State Department to develop recommendations for resolving the lend-lease negotiations. Both Agriculture and State were given authority to begin direct negotiations with the Soviet Union on trade and debt issues.

The backchannel was clearly operative once again, and remained so until the May summit. Throughout those early months of 1972, Kissinger remained personally involved in the pending grain sale and other commercial transactions with the Soviet Union, including the arrangement of credit. In that same period, the United States began to receive its first reports on the Soviet wheat failure. On February 9, 1972, the agricultural attaché at the American Embassy in Moscow reported that the winter crop had suffered considerable damage; he cabled a similar dispatch nine days later.

On February 10, the Soviet newspaper *Izvestia* reported that the grain crop had been damaged; it also became known at about that time that the Soviets had negotiated a 3.5-million-ton wheat purchase from the Canadian Wheat Board. On March 31, the American Embassy in Moscow specifically noted that twenty-five million acres of winter wheat had been lost in the Soviet Union and that prospects for the spring planting were poor because of low soil moisture. *Foreign Agriculture*, a publication of the Agriculture Department, wrote in its March 20, 1972, issue that the Central Committee of the Communist Party had been called into session to discuss the poor harvest, indicating the

* In his memoirs, Kissinger depicted the Matskevich meeting as dealing solely with India and Pakistan and a warning by Nixon that American-Soviet relations were endangered by the war. The confused Soviet trade official protested, Kissinger wrote, "that such matters of high policy were outside his province." In this account, Matskevich was at the last minute summoned to the White House to underscore the importance Nixon was placing on a ceasefire in the South Asian war. Kissinger, perhaps seeking in his memoirs to minimize the significance of Matskevich's meeting with Nixon, caricatured the Soviet official: "Bullet-headed, hearty, bubbling with innocent good will . . ." No mention of the India-Pakistan war was made at the news conference in July 1972, when Kissinger and the President were in a desperate race with Earl Butz to obtain public credit for the grain sale. Matskevich may thus owe his unflattering description in the memoirs to Kissinger's later decision to remove himself as far as possible from the grain deal.

severity of the situation and suggesting that the Soviets would be forced to depend heavily on the West for grain imports. In early April, a team of Agriculture Department officials, in Moscow to discuss the proposed grain sale, toured the major wheat-growing areas in the Ukraine and saw, according to a subsequent American Embassy dispatch, "a significant amount of grain winter kill and a general lack of moisture . . . ."

Later that month, on his secret trip to Moscow to discuss Vietnam and the summit, Kissinger also raised trade and credit issues. William Safire quoted him as telling Brezhnev that "billions of dollars in business activities" could result from closer American-Soviet relations. Kissinger's speech was explicit: "The President wants to be candid with you: he cannot make commitments, say, for credits or tariff concessions, if these measures do not command wide support among our public and in the Congress. And this depends critically on the state of our political relations. . . . I say this not because we want you to 'pay a price' for economic and other relations with us or because we expect you to sacrifice important political and security interests for the sake of trade relations. I say it as an objective fact of political life."

Despite all this, Kissinger's position in his memoirs is that he was unable to learn about the Soviets' desperate need for American grain. It seems clear that this need, far from being overlooked in the White House, was one of the factors that kept the summit alive as Nixon escalated in Vietnam. During the extensive bombing of Hanoi and Haiphong in mid-April, American bombs sank one Soviet freighter and damaged three others. The Soviet Union protested publicly the fact that its four freighters had been struck by bombs, but kept silent about one having been sunk.

Grain was not the only inducement offered by Kissinger in return for a Soviet willingness to include SLBM launchers in the summit. The American and Soviet SALT delegations had agreed that only the ABM limitation would be dealt with in the formal Treaty; the proposed constraints on offensive missile launchers, which were being constructed only by the Soviets, were to be handled in the separate Interim Agreement, which would be in force for five years. By early 1972, American intelligence believed that the Soviets had forty-one or, at best, forty-two modern nuclear submarines of the Y-class in operation or under construction, carrying about 640 missile launchers. Without any constraints, the Soviets were believed to be planning to build—at the most—an additional twenty Y-class submarines over the next five years.

"If there had been no agreement at all," Elmo Zumwalt wrote in his memoirs, "the Soviets could not have had in operation very many more than sixty-two boats by 1977, which is when the agreement expires." Kissinger's most suspect negotiating came on his April trip to Moscow, when—unaccompanied by any member of the SALT delegation—he obtained agreement to reinstate SLBMs as an agenda item in the Moscow summit in return for granting the Soviet Union the right to build, over the five years of the Interim Agreement, as many as sixty-two submarines with 950 missile launchers. In other words, Kissinger asked Moscow to agree to a limit that set no limit. Kissinger also agreed, as the SALT delegation would later learn, to a generous accounting of the number of Soviet submarine-launched missiles "under construction" at the time of the agreement. He accepted at face value the Soviets' claim that they had forty-eight modern submarines at sea or under construction, six more than could be verified by American intelligence. Each submarine had as many as sixteen missile launchers on it. The Kissinger concession meant that any submarine or SLBM limit reached at the Moscow summit would not take effect, at least for the Soviet Union, until it had built the additional six submarines. Kissinger was granting the USSR what amounted to a bonus for its willingness to include the issue of submarine control in the Interim Agreement.

Even more disturbing than the poor bargaining were the subsequent attempts to conceal its significance. Upon his return to Washington, Kissinger arranged for a series of makeshift intelligence estimates that presented the agreed-upon limits of sixty-two submarines and 950 missile launchers as far less than the Soviets would have built by 1977; he would tell the press after the summit that without the Interim Agreement the Soviets would have been able to build as many as eighty or ninety submarines by 1977. It was a distortion that left prudent men like Gerard Smith nonplused: To manipulate the record about the Soviets' submarine buildup seemed reckless beyond belief. Kissinger would escape with his reputation intact, but the SALT process would suffer.

Once again it is not clear how much Richard Nixon knew. Kissinger and Haig complained to their aides and others that the President had not even tried to learn the intricacies of the SALT negotiations.* Raymond Garthoff, Smith's key aide on the SALT delegation, learned firsthand, during a visit to the White House in 1971, just how little Nixon knew. "It wasn't intended to be a business discussion," Garthoff recalls, but the talk inevitably turned to a new ABM proposal which was then being negotiated. "It's not that he just didn't know the details, but he didn't even realize what proposal we had on the table. He didn't even know what anyone reading the newspapers would know. He really was so removed from the substance of SALT."

By May 22, the first day of the summit, Kissinger and Nixon were involved in what amounted to a monumental public relations operation in which the press and the public were informed that the President had brilliantly and successfully negotiated major Soviet concessions on SALT.

There were no Soviet concessions during the Moscow summit. None of the issues negotiated in Moscow was, in fact, essential to America's national security, or even to the final SALT agreements. The only major concessions had been made by Henry Kissinger during his April visit to Moscow.

Kissinger's account in his memoirs of how he reached the SLBM understanding with the Soviets is impossible to credit. The key role, he wrote, was played by Secretary Laird, who, with Admiral Moorer, anxiously sought Nixon's approval of an accelerated construction program for the Trident submarine. The Trident was a multibillion-dollar advanced generation of nuclear submarine that, even if approved by the President and authorized by Congress

---

* One typical comment was made to Peter G. Peterson, then Secretary of Commerce, during an Oval Office meeting on economic and trade issues less than two weeks before the summit. Nixon, despite a careful agenda, began to "go off on some tangent," and Peterson recalls leaning over to Kissinger and whispering sarcastically, "He sure is a master of detail." "My God," Kissinger responded, "you should see him on SALT."

in 1972, was not scheduled to become operational until the late 1970s. There was much debate over the proposed vessel, and many strategic planners were convinced that it was unnecessary and far too expensive. For these experts and many in Congress, the Navy's Polaris and Poseidon fleet of nuclear submarines, then numbering forty-one, was more than adequate for nuclear protection into the 1980s. Kissinger did not deal fully in his memoirs with the questions posed by the Trident, but he did acknowledge that its long production time created a bargaining dilemma. "Unless there was a freeze on offensive weapons, including SLBMs, the numerical gap would widen with every passing month," Kissinger wrote. "But how could we induce the Soviets to stop a program when we had none and could not have one for five years?" —the earliest possible date for the promised delivery of the Trident. Laird supplied the answer, in Kissinger's account, by developing the "ingenious solution" of permitting the Soviets to build submarines at a slower rate and compelling them to dismantle older missile launchers for each new submarine on a one-for-one basis. Thus the Soviets theoretically would have to trade in sixteen SS-7s or SS-8s, their oldest land-based ICBMs, or sixteen missile launchers from diesel-powered submarines, for each newly commissioned Y-class nuclear submarine, which could carry as many as sixteen SLBM launchers.* Laird's scheme won quick approval of the Verification Panel, Kissinger wrote. He then casually proposed the scheme to Dobrynin (as if he were "thinking out loud") at one of their regular meetings before the April trip. Once in Moscow, Kissinger claimed, he was summarily handed a paper by Leonid Brezhnev. "It turned out," Kissinger wrote ingenuously, "that Brezhnev's new paper in effect accepted Laird's formula. . . . The Soviet Union agreed to a ceiling of 950 submarine-launched ballistic missiles (at least 200 less than our estimate of their capacity to reach over that period) and would 'trade in' older SLBMs and older ICBMs to stay under that figure. . . ." Kissinger depicted Brezhnev's acceptance as a major Soviet concession.

It is clear that Laird reluctantly agreed to include the SLBMs in the final agreement in return for a presidential commitment to build the new Trident submarine on an accelerated basis. The speeded-up procurement program ran into billions of dollars in cost overruns as well as a multitude of construction difficulties; it proved to be as foolish a decision as its many critics inside and outside the government had predicted.† Laird had bargained hard on SALT;

---

* One significant distortion in Kissinger's account was spotted by Garthoff, who remembers that the replacement proposal was not put forward by Laird, as Kissinger wrote, but by a Kissinger staff member. The concept was apparently "planted" by Kissinger in the Pentagon for bureaucratic reasons. The military would get its new submarine, and Kissinger a viable SALT agreement.

† For an example of criticism from a member of Kissinger's systems analysis staff, see "The Problems of Reform," in *Daedalus* magazine, Summer 1975, co-authored by Barry Carter, who wrote that ". . . in terms of strategic analysis, the Trident was not the most logical choice to be made from the options available." Even worse, Carter added, was the decision—made in the spring of 1972—to accelerate the program: "The accelerated schedule burdens shipbuilding capacity, doubtless increases cost, runs the dangers that result from concurrent development and procurement, and locks up the ship design at a time when the United States is ignorant of the technical characteristic of the threat [from Soviet submarines] that the Trident is supposedly designed to offset." The first Trident was not commissioned until November 11, 1981, more than two and a half years behind schedule and costing 50 percent more than had been budgeted for the vessel in 1974. Seven other submarines then under construction were reported to be at least fourteen months behind schedule, with similarly high cost overruns. By early 1981, after repeated delays, congressional inquiries, and allegations of fraud, John F. Lehman, Jr., the former Kissinger aide who was

he had won a presidential commitment late in 1971 to increase strategic spending by more than 16 percent—some $1.2 billion—in the 1973 Pentagon budget, the largest such increase since the Vietnam War became a major financial issue in the mid-1960s. More than $940 million was to be budgeted for the accelerated production of the Trident, whose hoped-for deployment by 1977 would theoretically put the White House in the position of being able to threaten an increased deployment of the submarine if the Soviets did not agree to an SLBM constraint. Gerard Smith watched all this maneuvering with distaste. "I saw no evidence that this acceleration would have any effect on the negotiation," he wrote. "It was just a case of increased military spending because an arms control negotiation was in train."

It was exactly that. Laird, having won his struggle for the Trident and for increased spending, was now willing to close his eyes to the SLBM deal that Kissinger had struck in Moscow. He was joined by Admiral Moorer, whose endorsement was less difficult for the White House to obtain. Moorer, as Kissinger and Nixon knew only too well, had just squeaked through the military spying scandal the previous December and was, as John Ehrlichman put it, "preshrunk." Other members of the Joint Chiefs were far less in the know, and were deliberately kept that way. Zumwalt, who favored a Soviet constraint on SLBMs, recalled in his memoirs that the issue had divided the government, with the Pentagon in favor and the SALT delegation opposed. "The White House's position was less easy to ascertain," he wrote. He and his colleagues received the impression from Moorer, who alone attended the key meetings, that the President was seriously considering the SLBM problem, "while Kissinger was searching for a tactic that would enable him to wriggle around the issue." On March 17, Zumwalt wrote, Moorer returned from a White House meeting with a report that Kissinger had informed him that Nixon might order the Joint Chiefs to support a no-SLBM decision. By this time, of course, the White House concession had already been relayed in the backchannel by Kissinger to Ambassador Dobrynin. "Needless to say," Zumwalt declared, "neither I nor any other Chief participated in a meaningful way in the discussion leading to the appalling SLBM numbers. . . . I can add that I thought it necessary to watch with a very keen eye any agreement being negotiated by Henry Kissinger. Unfortunately from where I sat it was not always possible to see Henry at all."

Smith was also kept in the dark. Before leaving for the Vienna talks in November 1971, he wrote in his memoirs, he told Kissinger "that if there were any more 'unknown negotiations' I would resign and I asked him to tell that to the President." Those were strong words from the usually diplomatic Ambassador, and Kissinger assured him "that there would be no such negotiations." In March 1972, shortly before the final round of SALT talks, Smith, who by this time was adamantly opposed to including SLBMs at the Moscow summit, once again asked Kissinger about other channels. His fear was that Nixon and Kissinger would try to use the pending agreement to extract some Soviet concessions on SLBMs, an attempt that was doomed since, as Smith wrote, "We had extracted about all we could reasonably expect for agreeing to limit

---

then Secretary of the Navy, publicly served notice that "it may be necessary to consider alternatives to the Trident class submarine." The Polaris submarine fleet was still playing a major defense role as of mid-1983.

our domestically unpopular ABM program." At the SALT talks, which had returned to Helsinki, Smith was tipped off on April 22 by Vladimir Semenov that the SLBM question was under serious study in the Kremlin. This was gratifying news, for it indicated that there would be no last-minute hitch involving the ABM Treaty. At the time, Smith had no idea that Kissinger was in Moscow negotiating directly with Brezhnev and other Soviet leaders. Perhaps he was suspicious or perhaps he was simply acting on intuition, but Smith had broached the issue of backchannel negotiations yet a third time with Kissinger, and had been reassured, in writing, "You will be kept fully informed if anything develops here." Kissinger did not say just when Smith would be informed, and the beleaguered Ambassador learned of the Kissinger visit on April 24, the day before it was publicly announced.

The White House viewed Gerard Smith as anything but a victim during this period. He had sent an urgent cable to Secretary Rogers in Washington describing Semenov's suggestion of a breakthrough on the SLBM issue; the report provoked a crisis akin to that in early May 1971, when Semenov and his aides had described the essentials of the backchannel breakthrough to Smith and Garthoff before it was announced by the White House. Smith's report of progress was immediately telephoned to Nixon by Rogers, who did not, of course, know that Nixon was in almost constant communication with Kissinger in Moscow. The cable provoked hysteria. Nixon concluded, Kissinger wrote, that "the wily Soviets were trying to deprive him of personal credit for a potential SALT agreement. . . . Smith's cable and Rogers' phone call compounded Nixon's nervousness about my Moscow talks"—which Nixon had insisted be limited to Vietnam—"and reinforced his suspicions about Soviet motives." The President of the United States "was now convinced that it was all an elaborate collusion by Moscow and Hanoi to make it more difficult for us to take strong action on Vietnam. . . . Moscow was using the summit prospects as leverage against us to prevent our bombing of the North. . . ."

It seems clear that Kissinger shared at least some of the hysteria over the activities of Semenov and Smith. In his memoirs, Kissinger raised the possibility of Soviet duplicity: "What possessed Semenov again to play our two channels against each other just as he had done the year before can only be answered from Soviet sources. It seemed either Soviet bureaucratic disarray or a calculated effort to exert pressure." Kissinger had disregarded Nixon's instructions to limit his Moscow talks to Vietnam because, as he wrote, he believed that "Brezhnev in his eagerness to get Nixon to Moscow was accepting *our* positions on SALT. . . ." At this point, Kissinger's goal seemed to be to convince himself—and his President—that it was the Soviets, and not the United States, who had made concessions in SALT.

That he should have sought to do so is not difficult to understand. From early April on, as the North Vietnamese offensive mounted, Kissinger was, as we have seen, in a constant struggle with the President to prevent the collapse of the summit. Nixon was convinced that he could not survive politically if he flew to Moscow without responding to Hanoi's attack in the South; he was also insistent that he receive full credit if he did go. Kissinger somehow came to believe that if he could remove the SLBM issue as a stumbling block, Nixon would be able to envision the glory that could be his in Moscow. He could now deliver on his promise of May 1971, when he announced the SALT "breakthrough," to negotiate a freeze on offensive missile forces as well as the ABM agreement. To accept less in Moscow, Kissinger could argue, regardless of events in Vietnam, would have been a political liability.

Out of Nixon's ambivalence toward and lack of understanding about SALT emerges a portrait of Kissinger almost totally in charge that spring, dealing single-handedly (with the help of Lord, Sonnenfeldt, and Hyland) with a full range of critical issues in Moscow. If he decided to initiate a concession on SLBMs, he did so. And if he decided to depict that concession as a victory for the American position, he did that. Nixon, who rarely read the newspapers, watched television, or talked to outsiders these days, had no independent basis for judging the accuracy of Kissinger's assertions.

Once Kissinger returned to Washington, he and Nixon stood as one to defend the SLBM agreement from Gerard Smith's criticism. Aware of the potential liability of his concessions, Kissinger turned for help to his aides, but there were few now whom he would trust. Wayne Smith had left the previous fall, and his replacement, Philip Odeen, who was in charge of SALT analysis, had only recently joined the White House from the Pentagon's Office of Systems Analysis, where he had been one of Laird's most valued aides. Odeen's chief deputy, Barry E. Carter, a Yale Law School graduate (and one-time son-in-law of Robert McNamara), had said earlier in the year that he intended to resign. Neither of them was close to Kissinger, and neither had been informed in advance of his secret trip. Instead they had been asked by Sonnenfeldt to prepare a series of working papers on the SLBM issue, allegedly for use at a meeting with the President at Camp David. Carter was chagrined to learn that Kissinger had flown to Moscow with Anatoliy Dobrynin aboard Air Force 1; obviously Kissinger trusted the Soviet Ambassador more on some SALT I issues than his own staff.*

Carter and Odeen were summoned to a small staff meeting by Kissinger after the secret trip to Moscow and told what had really been going on. Kissinger also explained his new approach to the SLBM issue, which he said had originated with Brezhnev. The meeting proceeded smoothly, one participant remembers: "Kissinger asked us what we thought. We said, 'We're not sure.' He said, 'I want it,' and we said, 'Okay.' " Kissinger ordered Carter and Odeen to prepare a study that would make the limits of sixty-two submarines and 950 launchers appear to be somewhere in the middle of the number of boats and missiles that the Soviets would be able to build without any SALT

* Also left in the lurch was Jacob Beam, who had been Nixon's personal choice in 1969 for Ambassador to the Soviet Union. Beam did not learn of Kissinger's presence in Moscow and his high-level negotiations until the last day of the April visit. Kissinger had communicated with Nixon via his presidential aircraft, and not through the secure facilities in the American Embassy. Beam was shunted aside with equal abruptness during the summit in May, when he was unable to get a formal meeting with the President. "It was really quite embarrassing for me," he says. When he did finally get a chance to talk with the President, at a ceremonial wreath laying at Moscow's Tomb of the Unknown Soldier, Beam offered his resignation. Nixon waved it away at the time, but Beam was through. He retired from the Foreign Service in early 1973, after spending his last three months as Ambassador traveling around the Soviet Union. "I was really mad at the way they treated me at the summit," Beam recalls, but, in the tradition of the Foreign Service, he said nothing publicly, and did not allude to his mistreatment in his memoirs, *Multiple Exposure*, published in 1978.

constraints. "My clear task," says a former NSC staff member, "was to make sure the Soviet proposals came up in the middle range." A White House study group was assembled and the CIA was pressed to estimate how many submarines the Soviets were planning to build by 1977. The Agency was also told to "come up with a high option," the official recalls, "as if the Soviets went into a crash building project." The NSC aides had no illusions about what they were being asked to do: falsify national intelligence estimates. "I felt awkward as hell," one participant acknowledges. "What it was was Henry having struck a deal with the Soviets and then manipulating the bureaucracy to accept the deal." He was convinced, the aide adds, that the numbers allegedly supplied by the Soviets—sixty-two and 950—had originated with Kissinger, not Brezhnev.*

The CIA's first report wouldn't do—the estimate was not high enough—and the Agency was ordered to revise the study with a new assumption: that the Soviets had decided to increase their submarine production efforts by 50 percent. There was, of course, no basis for believing that any such increase was being planned. On the second round, the Kissinger proposal emerged in the prescribed mid-range; the CIA now estimated that the Soviet Union could build eighty to ninety submarines over the next five years, and would be able to field 1,150 submarine-launched missiles. "The numbers were not a complete sellout," the NSC aide insists, "but they were close to a worst-case analysis of what the Soviets could do."

Kissinger also moved to head off the Pentagon. There was at least one private meeting with Admiral Moorer, at which Kissinger warned that he would withdraw his support for the accelerated Trident submarine unless the JCS chairman supported the SLBM launcher limits at the next meeting of the Verification Panel on April 29. Smith was among those at the Verification Panel meeting who spoke out strongly against including SLBM in SALT I on the basis proposed by Kissinger. The young NSC staff members watched as Kissinger and Moorer engaged in an extended colloquy. "We sat there," one aide recalls, "and said, 'The fix is in.' " The aide went on to recount the conversation: "Henry turned to Moorer and asked, 'Tom, what can we do [to counter the CIA's estimated Soviet submarine-building capacity]? Can we build subs faster?' " Moorer dutifully made it clear that he, as JCS chairman, was all for the new Trident submarine and did not want any more funds spent on the Polaris fleet.

Kissinger: "When is the fastest we can get the Trident?"

Moorer: "1978."

Kissinger: "If we can't build any more now, might we be able to stop the Soviets?"

Moorer: "No. They're building and there is no reason to think they'd stop building."

* So were many members of the SALT delegation, who realized, Garthoff recalls, that there was a correlation between the numbers Kissinger claimed had been supplied by Brezhnev and the CIA's 1971 analysis of Soviet submarine-building capacity. The CIA had estimated, in its annual National Intelligence Estimate on Russia, that it could reach a total of sixty-two submarines in a five-year period and 966 SLBMs only with a *maximum* effort. Kissinger subsequently acknowledged to John Newhouse at a Washington dinner party that he had supplied Brezhnev's SLBM numbers.

The point of the Kissinger-Moorer exchange was clear to all, an aide recalls: "The SLBM agreement isn't going to hurt and it might help."

Kissinger's target in all this was not Gerard Smith and his colleagues, who would quickly see through the White House estimates. The main goal was to convince Richard Nixon that the private agreements Kissinger had worked out with Brezhnev in April were well founded and fully justified his defiance of Nixon's order to limit the discussions to Vietnam. The President may indeed have left the meeting with Moorer convinced that Kissinger's SLBM settlement would be a milestone in curbing the arms race and in preventing the USSR from escalating its lead in submarine and missile launchers.

Gerard Smith, upon his return to Washington from Helsinki, was dismayed at the SLBM agreement. There was a brief, unsatisfactory meeting with Kissinger. "I pointed out some of the difficulties involved . . ." Smith wrote. "I asked to study the interpreter's notes of the Moscow conversations. None were available. A Soviet interpreter had been used. I asked if there were memoranda of the conversations. Kissinger said that 'eventually' there would be. I never saw them. Kissinger seemed elated at this turn of events. I had the impression he felt the Brezhnev papers were a major breakthrough." Kissinger showed the same elation at the April 29 Verification Panel meeting, telling Smith beforehand: "I'll deliver the Joint Chiefs and DOD. I worked on Moorer all week." At a National Security Council meeting chaired by the President a few days later, Rogers argued forcefully against the SLBM proposal, "both on principle and because of the numbers . . ." Smith also objected, only to be told later by Kissinger that his and Rogers' position had been "unbelievable." Kissinger's state of mind was clear, Smith wrote: "Now that he had gotten a SALT agreement we were trying to block it."

Kissinger's performance in these days was brilliant. He was fighting off attacks that he knew to be valid and that, indeed, he had tried to undermine with distorted intelligence reports. Did he really find Smith's and Rogers' objections that unbelievable? Smith returned to Helsinki with, he wrote, mixed feelings. "I was glad that SLBMs were to be included in the freeze but not with the terms of their inclusion. . . . I was flabbergasted that Kissinger once again had gone off on his own and bypassed the delegation and other government officials with SALT responsibilities. . . . There had been no preparation for this negotiation in the National Security Council machinery, no building blocks or Working Group consideration, no Verification Panel meetings or consultation with allies." But despite his unease, Smith flew back to the SALT talks in Helsinki "determined to make the best of the situation. . . ."

The ABM Treaty was resolved by the morning of May 22, as Nixon and Kissinger, with more than a hundred journalists in tow, arrived in Moscow for an eight-day state visit. The SALT delegation, working with almost no guidance from Washington, had just completed its negotiation on the joint text for the Treaty, which included the essential concept that neither side would deploy "ABM systems for the defense of the territory of its country." Each nation was permitted only two ABM sites under the Treaty and those sites would be limited to area defense. The delegation was pleased with the final agreement, and became even more so when, at the last minute and after persistent bargaining by Paul Nitze, the Soviet Union made a significant concession and agreed to stronger radar controls.

The summit was an artifice, as the senior officials on both sides understood, but an important one. The American President and his top national security aides would meet face to face six times during five days of intense negotiations with the leaders of the Soviet Union. It was an event that would dominate the newspapers and television of America and the world, leaving little room for the Democrats or presidential politics. The news media would be surfeited with the signing of no less than five major bilateral agreements, dealing with issues of trade and scientific cooperation, during the second, third, and fourth night of the summit. The ritual would culminate, but not end, on the fifth night of the summit, May 26, with the signing of the SALT agreement. Nixon would remain in the Soviet Union three more days, mostly sightseeing—with the press along—and would also make an unprecedented speech on Moscow television to the Soviet people.

Spirits were high as Nixon and Kissinger flew toward Moscow on the twenty-second. Nixon would get his SALT agreement and Kissinger would establish, once again, just who the President's right-hand man was. As he and Nixon approached Moscow, the only troublesome note, Kissinger wrote in his memoirs, was the formal statement of American-Soviet "Principles of Relations" that was to be signed on the last evening in the Soviet Union. Rogers did not yet know of the document's existence.* "I told Nixon that I would try to get Brezhnev to bring it up in a manner that made it appear to emerge from the summit," Kissinger wrote. He also told the President, however, that he did not rate "Soviet subtlety sufficiently high to be sure that we could bring it off." Nixon was morose at hearing that, wrote Kissinger, and "reconciled himself to an explosion as in Hangchow when the Shanghai Communiqué had been surfaced suddenly."

Once in Moscow, the American reporters were forced to rely on the White House's press apparatus; it was impossible to learn precisely what hard bargaining Nixon and Kissinger were facing. In fact, only two significant issues remained to be resolved. The SALT delegation was still up in arms over Kissinger's decision to permit the Soviets to claim more submarines and SLBM launchers in operation or under construction than could be accounted for by

* The "Principles" were a series of positive statements on the importance of maintaining peaceful and honorable relations between the two superpowers. Both sides agreed, as Kissinger explained at a news conference on May 29, the last day of the Moscow trip, that "they will seek to promote conditions in which all countries will live in peace and security and will not be subject to outside interference." The next day, Nixon and Kissinger flew to Tehran and made a secret commitment to the Shah to clandestinely supply arms to the Kurdish rebel faction inside Soviet-supported Iraq, the Shah's neighbor and bitter enemy in the Middle East. Over the next three years, more than $16 million in CIA funds was funneled to the Kurds, despite determined opposition from the State Department and the CIA, which had previously rejected the Shah's request for aid to the Kurds. Nixon's and Kissinger's action, aimed at intensifying a civil war, was a clear—albeit secret— betrayal of the high-minded statement of principles that had been signed in Moscow. In his news conference in Moscow, Kissinger had said that both nations had agreed to defuse the tensions in the Middle East and "to contribute what they can to bringing about a general settlement . . . [S]uch a settlement would also contribute to a relaxation of the armaments race in that area . . . Speaking for our side," he added a moment later, "I can say we will attempt to implement these principles in the spirit in which they were promulgated." The American "spirit" lasted about twenty-four hours.

American intelligence. The accounting was important, for if the Soviets were permitted to start with an artificially high number of SLBM launchers, they would not have to begin decommissioning their old missile launchers until they had actually built up to the numbers Kissinger allowed them. The SALT delegation considered the process, unless altered, one that would give the Russians a "free ride" during the first years of the Interim Agreement and would also undermine the public's confidence in the SALT process. It would be difficult to justify an arms freeze that gave the Soviets the right to unilaterally construct and deploy SLBM launchers—a process that would take two years—without dismantling an equal number of older missile launchers. The delay was not seen as a vital strategic issue but as a potentially embarrassing political one.

The other unresolved issue, dealing with the modernization of Soviet silos, also stemmed from the backchannel. The SALT delegation, despite intensive bargaining and a directive from Nixon, had been unable to persuade the Soviets to include a specific limit on the missile volume of its next generation of weapons. A missile's volume is its most critical measurement, for volume controls the size of the nuclear warhead that can be carried. Increasing the volume of a MIRVed missile means that more warheads can be carried by the missile, and delivered to targets. It was widely known in the intelligence community by May 1972 that the Soviets were in the process of developing one or more new MIRVed missiles to replace its SS-11 "light" missile. Work on these, which were to be installed in the SS-11 silos, obviously was far along and the Soviet SALT delegation took pains to inform their American counterparts privately that in the Interim Agreement they would resist any formal definition of modernization that would prevent the new weapons' installation. Similar missile improvements, as the Soviets knew, were being continuously undertaken by the United States, which was then in the process of emplacing a MIRV capacity on the warheads of its Minuteman I missile fleet. One Soviet official privately informed Garthoff, during a talk in late April in Helsinki, that his country's new missile would have a volume of "less than half" the volume of the Soviets' "heavy" SS-9 land-based missile, which had a much larger warhead—or nuclear "throw weight"—than the Minuteman I or SS-11.

As proposed, the Interim Agreement would specifically bar the conversion of lighter missiles into "heavy" ICBMs, but included no language defining either light or heavy. The American negotiating team at Helsinki had sought to reach agreement on a definition of a "heavy" missile that would bar the new generation of Soviet MIRVed missiles while leaving the United States free to continue to deploy its MIRVs, but the Soviets, as many on the American delegation expected, categorically refused to agree to any such definition. The American delegation also sought, on instructions from the White House, to negotiate a limit on ICBM silo modification to help curb increases in missile size. (No attempt was made in SALT to flatly bar any increase in silo dimensions, since such an agreement might preclude the modernization of the American Minuteman missiles; in effect, a MIRV ban.) The issue was negotiated at length by Gerard Smith and his aides, and a few days before the summit some consensus was finally reached: The Soviets would agree to language in the Interim Agreement calling upon both sides not to "significantly" increase their silo dimensions. That offer, all parties understood, was cosmetic, and would not preclude the deployment of the new MIRVed missiles. Kissinger's backchannel commitment to the Soviet Union early in 1971 barring any limit in the SALT negotiations on the development of MIRVs—that is, barring any restrictions on the "modernization" of the Soviet and American missile forces—was yet another complicating factor. The delegation, convinced that no meaningful agreement on silo volume was possible without a significant Soviet concession, left the final reckoning to the Nixon-Brezhnev talks in Moscow.

During the summit week, the press was unable to learn just which SALT issues were being negotiated. Ziegler played his role perfectly, solemnly assuring reporters at the various briefings that the talks were "serious" and "productive." On the second day of the summit, the *New York Times* reported that it was unclear whether a last-minute dispute over ABM sites was at issue or whether Nixon and Brezhnev had spent five hours, as their spokesmen told reporters, "engaged primarily in meticulous review of the hard negotiations of the last 30 months that have brought the agreement to the point of signing." Safire had been brought along to draft toasts and progress statements, but even he was largely dependent on Kissinger for information. In his memoirs, Safire described the bargaining in the way Nixon and Kissinger wanted it seen: "In negotiating technique, Nixon and Kissinger put on a formidable display, like a two-man interrogation team where one man holds a truncheon and the other offers a cigarette. Nixon's way was to appear rigid, sit tight for a long, long time, and then go for a 'bold new approach' that can be considerably different from his original position. Kissinger, on the contrary, was willing to invest heavily—in money and, if necessary, in lives—to achieve bargaining credibility. . . ."

Nixon and Kissinger had obtained in Moscow what they could not in Washington—complete control of the press. It was their account that made the front pages and the television broadcasts. Neither would permit outsiders, not even a State Department interpreter, to attend the negotiating sessions. Translations were handled by the Soviets. Gerard Smith and his experts were forbidden to come to Moscow, and had the frustrating experience of monitoring the talks through cables. Kissinger had flown to Moscow without any SALT experts, even those on the NSC staff. Philip Odeen and Barry Carter, who had coordinated much of the technical work, were left behind in Washington with Haig to answer queries and run errands. Kissinger's insistence on negotiating alone was not as reckless as it may seem, for he perceived that the issues he and Nixon were discussing, while significant, were not essential to America's strategic position. And for all his anger at being excluded, Gerard Smith was also aware that the SALT agreements had been virtually completed before Moscow. The remaining issues were extremely technical and far beyond the ken of the President, as Smith explained in his memoirs: "What would be permitted in the way of modernization and replacement under the freeze? When in the course of new launcher construction would older launchers have to be dismantled?" Smith viewed it as "out of keeping" for the President to become involved in such intricacies. "It is hard to avoid a conclusion," he wrote, "that there was some pretense about the nature of these Moscow negotiations. They were tense. They lasted well into the night. But they concerned secondary, not central issues."

Nixon and Kissinger were able to accomplish nothing on the modernization issue at the summit, but their attempt to resolve such a sophisticated issue at the highest levels led to confusion, some panic, and a sense of the blind leading the blind. The SALT delegation had recommended that if no agreement on the definition of a "heavy" missile could be reached, a possible fallback position would be a stipulation by both parties that no "significant" increase in silo size was permissible. On the more critical issue of missile volume, the United States would evade the issue simply by stating its views on the definition of "light" and "heavy" missiles, and hope for the best. The negotiations immediately became tense when, at the first summit meeting on SALT, Leonid Brezhnev declared that his nation had no intention of increasing the size of its silos.

Gerard Smith wrote that Kissinger and Nixon apparently misunderstood what Brezhnev was saying, and concluded that the Soviets were not planning to develop a new missile with larger dimensions. In fact, as Smith knew, both sides were capable of increasing the volume of a missile—and its "throw weight"—without necessarily increasing the size of the silo housing it. Smith wrote that Kissinger excitedly sent a cable to the SALT delegation summarizing the Brezhnev statement as a unilateral Soviet offer to prohibit any silo enlargement. If that was indeed what Brezhnev had said, Smith wrote, Kissinger and his aides should not have reported the proposal as one to be taken seriously. "We had sent three cables reporting the status of the silo dimension and the heavy missile definition issue," Smith wrote in anger. "The President and Kissinger perhaps had been too busy to read these reports. . . . Evidently one or both sides did not understand the differences in substance and status between the heavy missile and silo dimension issues. . . . I had often read about the fog of war. This was the fog of negotiation."

Part of Smith's dismay was linked to the fact that he was in Helsinki and Nixon and Kissinger were in Moscow conducting the negotiations to which he should have been a party. There was a more substantive reason for concern, however: If Brezhnev was proposing that the Interim Agreement ban any increase in silo dimensions, as Kissinger seemed to believe, the United States would be precluded from proceeding with the MIRV conversion of Minuteman I. The men in Moscow might have blundered into a MIRV ban. ("Some people say we should have kept quiet at Helsinki!" Smith couldn't help noting in his memoirs.)*

* Smith's amusement, if it was that, over the clumsy negotiations may have been increased by the cool reception accorded his own suggestion to freeze all development of land-based and sea-based offensive and defensive strategic forces. Smith's proposal, "Stop Where We Are (SWWA),'' came on June 11, 1969, at a time when ACDA was seeking White House endorsement of a MIRV ban. In his memoirs, Smith recalled: "SWWA was based on a simple concept that the way to stop arms competition was to stop strategic construction programs on both sides. Both now had sufficient strategic forces to deter nuclear war. Instead of trying to elaborate agreed levels for strategic forces and other complex arrangements, why not just freeze things at the 1969 level?" A key element of the proposal, as presented to the White House, was its elimination of a first-strike threat against the U. S. Minuteman force by freezing Soviet development of MIRV. SWWA got nowhere. "The President seemed to think SWWA was intended as propaganda," Smith wrote. "But he said he would give it serious consideration, perhaps as the basis for a speech—a speech he never gave. I felt and still do that such a mutual stop in strategic construction programs would have been very much in the United States's security interests." At the time, a freeze, if agreed to by the Soviets— a big if—would have insured American strategic superiority. Garthoff acknowledged much later that SWWA, despite its obvious advantages, was too radical for the Nixon-Kissinger White House and also posed too much of a political risk, in terms of opposition from conservatives and the JCS. There was another reason for Kissinger's indifference to Smith's idea, Garthoff said: "This would

Kissinger, aware by the time he wrote his memoirs of the distinction between silo size and missile volume, handled the *faux pas* by criticizing Nixon and Brezhnev. "Neither Brezhnev nor Nixon had mastered the technical issues," Kissinger wrote, and they wandered "into the bog of seeking to define 'heavy' missiles." Kissinger would have his readers believe that his role at the summit had suddenly diminished, at least during the modernization issue, to that of a back-bencher. It should be noted that Nixon's memoirs are useless in terms of the intricacies of the SALT negotiations; the only firsthand account of what actually took place is Kissinger's. At no point, however, did he claim that Brezhnev specifically mentioned silo dimensions; instead he wrote that Brezhnev "implied" or "seemed to go along" with the concept of barring any increases. "I cannot understand what Brezhnev thought he was doing," Kissinger wrote. "Was he offering us genuine concessions? Did he know enough about our Minuteman conversion program to expect us to turn his suggestion down? Or did he simply become confused by the technical details and fail to grasp the distinction between silo dimension and missile volume?"

Kissinger's rhetorical queries would have amused the American SALT delegation, who knew that it was Kissinger and Nixon who were confused. At one point during the flow of messages between Moscow and Helsinki, Kissinger cabled his thanks for the delegation's help and added: "You should understand that we are operating in a situation where we never know from hour to hour with whom we are meeting or what the topic will be." It seemed to be "a blueprint for how not to conduct a negotiation of any sort," Smith noted.*

Brezhnev's offer, or nonoffer, of a ban on silo enlargement was soon put aside, and it was agreed that the issue of silo dimension would be handled by declaring that ICBM launchers could not be "significantly" increased. The Soviets, at Kissinger's insistence, also agreed to define a "significant' increase as one that would be not greater than 10 or 15 percent, large enough for deploying MIRVs. Kissinger told the delegation members in a cable that the choice was up to them; did they want a formal quantification or a "significant" increase in terms of percentage? The delegation thought the term "significant" was clearly preferable, Smith wrote, since it could imply a smaller increase, and said as much in a return message. "But the next day we were to be informed that the other version had been agreed upon at Moscow. No expla-

---

be a matter of solving a major problem on its own merits, when Henry's approach was to have as much string as he could to manipulate. There was no promise in a freeze in terms of a useful card for future negotiations." The Federation of American Scientists publicized Smith's SWWA proposal shortly before the 1982 congressional elections, in which there were nine statewide and thirty local referenda on a proposed nuclear freeze.

* Paul Nitze expressed his disgust at Kissinger's antics, Smith wrote, by drafting a bogus memorandum entitled "The Last Twenty Minutes of a Negotiation Are the Most Important." Nitze included the following "guidelines": "Arrange for the negotiations to be conducted at several levels. Then try to pocket the optimum for your side arising at any one of the levels. Subtechniques include: (a) General statements at top subsequently withdrawn at lower level; (b) Introduction, without prior notice, of added starters at an intermediate level, to swing situation in your favor; *e.g.*, at political meeting, introduce 'expert' prepared to use his special knowledge to your advantage under circumstances where those on other side not in a position to contradict him." Nitze had other bits of advice: " . . . arrange to have top negotiations in your capital. Have their delegation split between Kremlin, Spasso House and Rossiya Hotel [in Moscow]. Use your interpreters for both sides. Have no typewriters nor Xerox machines available when needed. Give other side as minimum secure communications facilities as possible."

nation was given. I guess it was another case of, having been given a choice, we made the wrong choice—just one in a series of Moscow curiosities!''

It was this event—the decision to define a significant increase as one measuring 10 to 15 percent in dimension—that Kissinger presented in *his* memoirs as one of the major Soviet concessions at the summit. "When he agreed on 10-15 percent in dimension," Garthoff explained years later, "he didn't realize he was allowing an increase of 32 percent in volume, because there are two dimensions—volume and depth."

The basic modernization issue—how to define a "heavy" missile—was left unresolved, with Kissinger, Smith, and their aides aware that the Soviets were planning to install a new, heavier missile with MIRVed warheads in the SS-11 silos. It was agreed that a unilateral statement would be added to the published Interim Agreement, expressing American "regrets" that the Soviets were unwilling to agree on a common definition of a "heavy" missile and noting that the United States considered any weapon significantly larger in volume than the SS-11 to be "heavy." Kissinger had sought the statement, Smith wrote in his memoirs, as a fallback in case no agreement could be reached. Smith cautioned at the time that the statement would perhaps have "some slight deterrent effect . . . but I wouldn't put a very high estimate on the value of such deterrence."

The SALT delegation did not view the failure to resolve the definition issue as strategically important—after all, both sides were left free in the Interim Agreement to make qualitative improvements to their missile systems. On the last day of the summit, the National Security Agency intercepted a radio-telephone conversation in Moscow between Brezhnev and a senior military official in which the party chief, talking from the back seat of his limousine, received assurances that the commitment to limit increases in silo dimension to 15 percent would not preclude the employment of the new Soviet missile system. The highly classified intercept, code named "Gamma Guppy," was initially routed to Washington, one senior aide recalls, where it was marked by intelligence officials in the State Department for immediate dispatch, via Haig, to Kissinger in Moscow.

By the end of the summit, therefore, Kissinger not only had assurances from the American SALT delegation that a new Soviet weapon was to be installed; he also had firsthand confirmation from Leonid Brezhnev. And he understood that nothing in the Moscow agreement barred the Soviets from deploying their new missile system. Nonethless, Kissinger assured Congress in mid-June, as the ABM Treaty was submitted for ratification, that the Interim Agreement included "a prohibition on conversion of light ICBMs into heavy missiles." Asked specifically about the issue by Senator Jackson, one of the most knowledgeable members of Congress on strategic matters, Kissinger said: "There is the safeguard that no missile larger than the heaviest light missile now existing can be substituted. . . . We have adequate safeguards against a substantial substitution of heavy missiles for light missiles." The "safeguard" to which Kissinger was referring was the American unilateral statement, a fact that he did not make clear to Jackson and his colleagues at their White House briefing. In his memoirs, Kissinger lamented in a footnote that "We overestimated the restraining effect of such a unilateral statement."

Jackson and other critics of the SALT process would later insist that the

Soviets had "cheated" on the May 1972 agreement by installing their new SS-19 missile system in SS-11 silos. Kissinger's lie had spawned a criticism that would remain to mar future SALT discussions: that the Soviets could not be trusted on a disarmament agreement. Much of the criticism, as Jackson and other legislators could not know, was directed at the wrong party.

The modernization issue, for all its complexities, was a relatively straightforward negotiating matter. It had become clear in the weeks before the summit that no common definition of a "light" or "heavy" missile would be attained, and Gerard Smith and his aides did manage to have a role via cable in the Moscow talks. But on the SLBM issue, the delegation found itself floundering in a sea of misinformation and lack of information. Smith and his colleagues realized that before the summit they had been given only the minimum details of the Kissinger-Brezhnev arrangements worked out in the April meetings. It was understood that the Soviet Union would be permitted to increase its submarine forces over the five years of the Interim Agreement by decommissioning as many as 210 older land-based ICBMs. But which submarines and which submarine systems were to be counted? And where was the counting to begin? American negotiators could not answer such questions, and they weren't sure Kissinger knew the answers, either.

In the weeks before the summit, the delegation had sought means to finesse what seemed to be Kissinger's poor bargaining. Smith's goal was to protect the ABM Treaty—which he and his colleagues viewed as an essential step forward—from being damaged by what they saw as the inequity of the Interim Agreement. Neither Smith nor his aides, it should be noted once again, believed that the strategic balance between the United States and the Soviet Union hinged on the additional submarines or missile launchers that Kissinger had bequeathed to the Soviets. America's national security would not be threatened by one—or even six—additional Soviet submarines. His concern, Smith wrote, was for the arms talks of the future; he was eager to avoid "explicitly registering a large Soviet advantage in number of submarines in addition to SLBM launchers . . . especially if after this Moscow meeting negotiators were to continue looking toward offensive arms limitations . . . based on equality." Congress and the American public, already wary about negotiating with the Soviets, might balk at an agreement that seemed to give the Russians the right to operate more submarines than the Americans.

In early May, Smith proposed to Washington that only missile launchers on submarines, and not submarines themselves, should be covered by the Interim Agreement. If the Soviet submarines were not negotiated downward, ". . . what would appear in certain quarters to be an inequitable submarine arrangement could sour the whole deal." That proposal went nowhere. A few days later Smith was surprised to learn from a Soviet SALT negotiator that the USSR was claiming it then had forty-eight submarines in operation or under construction. The Soviets further claimed that any trading in of older missiles on a one-for-one basis could not begin, in their interpretation of the Interim Agreement, until the deployment of the forty-ninth Soviet submarine. Smith knew that United States intelligence was able to confirm the existence of no more than forty-two Soviet submarines on duty or under construction.

He considered the Soviet claim absurd and raised it directly with Semenov, who, however, "insisted that the number 48 had originated with us." Suspicion immediately turned to Kissinger and his private talks with Brezhnev in April, but Kissinger denied knowledge of any such concession. Semenov, queried again, told Smith that his country had not been the first to cite the number forty-eight. "Perhaps there had been a breakdown of U.S. communications," he remarked. Semenov had told Smith a few days earlier that the Brezhnev paper, which had been given to Kissinger during their talks in April, had specifically declared that the number of submarines for each side "could not be equal" because the Soviets "had to take account of U.S. forward submarines and allies' [French and British] submarines." Smith and his colleagues had been anticipating some hard bargaining on that question, but they had no clue that Kissinger had agreed to concede a significant Soviet lead. Smith later learned, he wrote, that in their April talks Kissinger and Brezhnev had agreed that the Soviets could have roughly a hundred additional SLBM launchers "as an offset"—apparently against the stationing of American submarines in Europe. The additional missiles would enable the Soviets to construct as many as seven more Y-class nuclear submarines which would not be covered by the Interim Agreement.

The SALT delegation, in the days before the summit, was now confronted with a major new problem, and Smith's goal was to somehow insure that every SLBM launcher deployed on new Soviet submarines over the five years of the agreement was balanced by the dismantling of a land-based missile launcher. The Soviets could not be permitted to spend the next two or three years building new launchers and submarines without being forced to decommission any missiles, or there would be hell to pay politically with Congress. Another approach was devised: to establish a threshold number of Soviet missile launchers and insist that any new missile launcher above that number required the dismantling of an older missile. The delegation fixed the threshold number at 740 by computing that the Soviets had 640 SLBM launchers aboard its forty-two Y-class submarines, and an additional one hundred launchers on its older G-class and H-class submarines in service. Smith was determined to stand fast, but he had few illusions: The replacement issue would be worked out at the Moscow summit and neither he nor any of his skilled aides would be there. "My central concern," Smith wrote, "remained that the Soviets claimed that replacement should start only with their forty-ninth boat. This free ride struck me as completely unacceptable. I knew of no way to justify such a bonus for them and recommended to the President that it not be accepted."

Kissinger was feeling the heat as he arrived in Moscow. In his memoirs, he acknowledged that there "was no dispute that it was in our interest to bring about the dismantling of the largest number of older Soviet missiles." He argued, as he must have done with the President, that if the freeze on submarines and launchers was dropped from the Interim Agreement, as Gerard Smith still thought advisable, the Soviets would be able to build forty more submarines over the next five years, and also reach a level of 1,150 SLBM launchers —two hundred more than would be permitted under the freeze. That all of those statistics were in serious dispute was, of course, not mentioned. Kissinger's problem in Moscow, and the reason he had to concoct such distorted estimates of Soviet buildups, lay in his April concessions to Brezhnev, and the

Soviet leaders were now refusing to budge. In their view, Henry Kissinger had permitted them to claim a base of forty-eight submarines, six more than actually existed, as a bonus for agreeing to include the submarine issue in the Interim Agreement. They further insisted on the right to add these launchers to their missile fleet before decommissioning any older ICBMs.

The backchannel from Moscow to Washington was humming as word of Kissinger's concessions on the SLBMs spread through the bureaucracy. Gerard Smith's warning about political fallout was proving all too prescient. On Wednesday, May 24, Representative John M. Ashbrook, a conservative from Ohio who had announced a challenge to Nixon for the Republican presidential nomination, took to the House floor to denounce the proposed Interim Agreement as one that would "lock the Soviet Union into unchallengeable superiority, and . . . plunge the United States and its allies into a decade of danger." Ashbrook also inserted in the *Congressional Record* a very precise summary of the SALT agreement, as published in *Newsday,* the Long Island newspaper. Someone in the administration had provided Martin Schram, *Newsday's* White House correspondent, with an accurate summary of the pending ABM Treaty and Interim Agreement, which, Schram wrote, would give the Soviets a numerical edge in missile launchers. The *Newsday* story, published on May 20, while Nixon was on his way to Moscow, caused little stir until Ashbrook took it up and told his colleagues that the proposed summit agreements "would doom the United States to nuclear inferiority." *

* Schram had gotten onto the story through his contact with David Young, Kissinger's former personal aide who was then assigned to the Plumbers unit in the Executive Office Building basement. Schram had no idea of Young's secret police work in the White House, nor did he realize that Young had just completed an inquiry into the 1971 *New York Times* SALT leak. Schram assumed that the young aide was still a full-time member of the NSC staff, a belief that Young encouraged. The two men had met at a Washington party early in the spring of 1972, and Schram had subsequently telephoned Young a few times at the Executive Office Building. "I'd ask him about NSC stuff and he was able to call someone on the staff and steer me the right way," Schram recalls. Young was loyal to Kissinger, constantly telling Schram that "Henry was a 'force for good' in a White House for hardhats. He was one of Henry's men, as far as I was concerned." Young "didn't know much about SALT, but he knew who did"—Barry Carter, his good friend on the NSC. An interview was arranged on May 19. Carter rarely dealt with the press while in the White House, and for good reason. A Democrat who was widely known for his relationship to Robert McNamara, he felt he would be an automatic suspect in case of a leak. He saw reporters only when explicitly ordered to do so. Carter, interviewed later, could not recall just how Schram happened to call upon him for the briefing, but was not surprised to learn that Young was involved. Carter understood that Young was still close to Kissinger in early 1972, although he knew Young was no longer Kissinger's personal aide or on the NSC staff. Carter realized why he was being permitted to discuss the SLBM negotiations in advance of the summit. He and others involved in the SALT process were concerned—as Kissinger was—about the adverse publicity over the Soviet SLBM lead that was built into the Interim Agreement. Carter knew the leak would not be damaging to the SALT negotiations or the summit. Nonetheless, Carter remembers that he was careful to check, either with Philip Odeen, his immediate superior, or with Peter Rodman, Kissinger's close aide, before seeing Schram. When approval was given, Carter, always conscientious, thoroughly outlined the SALT agreements to the reporter. Schram's story noted in its opening paragraph that the pending arms agreement would give the USSR "a decided edge in offensive submarine-based missiles . . ." and included the following caveat: "U.S. officials acknowledged that they were concerned about the possibility of initial negative reaction from U.S. hawks, who may be less than satisfied with the submarine-based missiles agreement. . . ." Within a few days, Schram's dispatch was reprinted in the *Congressional Record* and his basic facts, after confirmation by other government officials, were being reported anew. In Moscow, Kissinger waited until the criticism from Congress and other newspapers had mounted, and then won Nixon's permission to stand firm

There were some second thoughts in the Pentagon, too. The Joint Chiefs of Staff forwarded through Haig a series of increasingly sharp complaints and seemed ready to abandon their carefully arranged support for the terms of the inclusion of submarines and SLBM launchers in the offensive freeze.

Kissinger, with no technical experts in Moscow, fell back on Smith's approach to the critical questions of how and when to replace the old missiles with the new. He accepted the threshold number of 740 for Soviet SLBM launchers (suggesting, in his memoirs, that the approach was his). The Soviets had also accepted 740 as a threshold number, but they insisted on omitting both the seventy launchers on their G-class and the thirty launchers on their H-class submarines from the total. Kissinger, anxious to conclude the negotiations and having promised the Soviets in April that he would grant them additional submarines and missile launchers as a bonus for including the SLBM issues, was prepared to concede that the Soviets could exclude the seventy launchers aboard G-class submarines from the threshold number. In his memoirs he claimed that he consulted with Nixon on the new approach, which would permit the Soviets to add seventy modern SLBM launchers without replacement, but there is no evidence that Nixon understood the complex issue. The President was in the position of knowing only those facts—or fictions—that Kissinger told him.

The testy exchanges with Haig, who was working closely with Odeen and Carter, added to Kissinger's travails. One official recalls that the basic problem, as the men in Washington saw it, was that Kissinger and his aides in Moscow "just didn't understand the issues." Odeen and Carter were astonished at times by Kissinger's confusion and that of his key SALT aides, Sonnenfeldt and Hyland. "One night," a participant says, "there was an exchange of cables about the difference between G-class and H-class submarines. The group in Moscow didn't know which tubes were which." One Haig message prophetically warned of potential loopholes that the Joint Chiefs, as well as Odeen and Carter, saw in the SLBM agreement.

Facing a loss of support from the right, Kissinger turned to Nixon for protection. "We had no choice but to proceed," Kissinger wrote; his goal was to convince the President. It was easy. Nixon viewed the issue in the context that Kissinger supplied: Without a freeze on Soviet buildups, the USSR would be able to field at least thirty more submarines and as many as 600 more missile launchers by 1977. The freeze would limit the Soviets to a total of sixty-two submarines over the next five years instead of the eighty or ninety they could build without it. In his memoirs, Kissinger unabashedly praised Nixon for agreeing with him. The President, who was getting a back massage as they talked, had made "one of the more courageous decisions of his Presidency" in ordering the negotiations to continue. "He would not be swayed by politics at home, and he would not be pushed by the Soviets beyond what I suggested," Kissinger wrote, as if it had been conceivable that the President could leave Moscow without a SALT agreement. Nixon told his national security adviser

against *their* critics. In his memoirs, Kissinger praised the President for not being affected by "politics at home." Nixon, of course, had no way of knowing that the politics at home may have been manipulated by his national security adviser.

to ignore the Pentagon opposition and to "stand firm against Smith," who—more than any Russian—was the real enemy. Alluding to Nixon's massage, Kissinger wrote that "Nixon took a heroic position from a decidedly unheroic posture." The Kissinger-Nixon meeting was elevated to Great Moments in History in Safire's memoirs. "You'll be alone on this," Safire quoted Kissinger as telling the President. The President "decided to tough it out . . . He took one of the most fateful decisions of his presidency, and of the postwar generation, there on the massage table." Safire, whose source was surely Kissinger, further quoted the President as saying, "Go to your negotiations, Henry. Do the best you can. But we don't have to settle this week."

It was Nixon who described the scene most believably. Kissinger burst in during his massage and reported that "the Pentagon was in almost open rebellion and the Joint Chiefs were backing away from the SALT position to which they had previously agreed. Kissinger did not have to remind me—although he did so in the most urgent terms—that if word of this split reached the press, or if the Pentagon refused to support a SALT agreement I brought back from the summit, the domestic political consequences would be devastating." Nixon says he told Kissinger: "The hell with the political consequences. We are going to make an agreement on *our* terms regardless of the political consequences if the Pentagon won't go along."

The President wanted to accept the Soviet offer on the SLBM issue. If the Soviets insisted on excluding the G-class, so be it. The heroic presidential stand was taken not against the Soviets but with them, and against the SALT delegation and the Pentagon, who were insisting on stiff SLBM terms. Fortified by Nixon's trust, Kissinger turned harshly on Haig. "I sent him a sharp cable," he wrote in his memoirs. "His job was to rally support, not simply to transmit concerns." One White House aide has a more specific recollection: Kissinger told Haig that the President felt his criticisms had verged on personal disloyalty.

One question lingers: What did Nixon really know? Did he suspect that Kissinger was fabricating the statistics on the potential Soviet submarine and missile launcher buildup? In his memoirs, he gave no hint of any understanding of the complex issues but wrote vaguely of "critical questions," "their position," and "our terms." He described the final settlement of SALT I with this sentence: "Later, Kissinger and I were meeting in my apartment when Dobrynin arrived with the news that the Politburo had held a special session and agreed to accept our final position." The President did not seem to realize that the "final position" was another American concession.

The SLBM situation was still deadlocked on May 25, with the SALT delegation and the Joint Chiefs insisting that all the Soviet G-class and H-class missile launchers had to be included in the threshold SLBM figure of 740. That afternoon, shortly before the official party was to attend the Bolshoi ballet, the Soviets suddenly agreed to include in the agreement their nine H-class nuclear submarines, which carried a total of thirty SLBM launchers. The seventy launchers aboard the G-class boats would continue to be excluded. It was more than enough for Kissinger. Gerard Smith's first reaction was also one of approval, and he cabled as much to Kissinger. Smith assumed, as he wrote, that the Soviets would agree not to deploy modern SLBM launchers aboard any of the G-class submarines. In his memoirs, Kissinger depicted the Soviet concession on the H-class as coming almost as an aside, when a senior Russian negotiator "innocently stated" that the Soviets had always intended to count the H-class submarine launchers in the threshold total of 740 SLBMs.

It must have been more complicated. There is evidence that the Soviet compromise was linked to a new, final American concession, made in writing by Nixon on the last day of the summit and mentioned only in passing in Kissinger's memoirs. The Kissinger-Brezhnev arrangement in April gave the United States the theoretical right, under the proposed Interim Agreement, to trade in its outmoded Titan ICBM launchers and build three additional modern nuclear submarines carrying sixteen missile launchers each. The United States had kept its total of fifty-four older Titans on line for use as a possible bargaining chip, but there was never any intent to take advantage of the option in the agreement. The Navy would have no interest in building three additional submarines by 1977 when its new Trident-class boat would be beginning deployment. Despite repeated American assurances to that effect, Gerard Smith wrote, the Soviets still sought to include language in the final agreement that would rule out the American right to exercise its option to cash in its Titan missiles for more submarines. The matter was left for the summit, with Smith recommending that the United States resolve the dispute by declaring that it had no intention of asserting its right to cash in the Titans for submarines. If more were demanded by the Soviets, Smith added, "we would be better off not to have this 'right' at all."

Smith later learned, to his dismay, that Nixon, in a letter delivered to the Soviets on the last day of the summit, had explicitly backed down on the "right" to dismantle Titans for more submarines. Nixon's retreat was all the more distressing to the SALT delegation because it was unilateral; the United States was giving up a right to convert old missiles into additional submarines in exchange for nothing. The Soviets continued to have the right to convert their old missiles into modern SLBMs. The Interim Agreement would now seem even more asymmetrical. That such a concession was made remained a highly classified secret throughout the congressional hearings later in 1972, as the White House repeatedly insisted that there were no secret codicils to the SALT I agreements. Its existence was finally made known by the Soviet Union to an American negotiator in 1973, and was first reported in the *New York Times* in June 1974, shortly before Kissinger was to begin intensive negotiations—which were ultimately unsuccessful—on SALT II.*

---

* The *Times* story was written by Leslie Gelb, who also raised questions about the exclusion of the Soviet G-class submarines in the 1972 Interim Agreement. At a news conference a few days after the Gelb account, Kissinger, then Secretary of State, described Nixon's unilateral commitment not to convert the Titans as "not a concession the United States made to the Soviet Union. It was a relatively minor gesture designed to retain general confidence." The Titan option had not initially been written into the basic agreement, Kissinger went on, because "We did not think it was desirable to put into an agreement a Soviet right to convert old missiles into submarine-launched missiles without maintaining an American right to convert old missiles into submarine-launched missiles; and therefore to maintain the formal symmetry of the agreement we put into the agreement

Gerard Smith began to have doubts about Kissinger's decision to exclude the seventy G-class submarine launchers from the replacement threshold. Merely insisting that the Soviets give up the right to install modern launchers aboard their G-class boats seemed not to be enough. Smith, in last-minute discussions with Garthoff and other SALT delegation members, determined that Nixon and Kissinger had damaged the credibility of the agreement by excluding the G-class submarines and their seventy launchers from counting toward the limit of 740 launchers for each side. The Soviets would now be able to construct at least five more submarines, each with at least twelve launchers, before they would reach the 740 limit and be required to begin decommissioning older ICBMs. At the Soviets' estimated construction rate of five or more submarines per year, with each boat taking at least two years to build, it seemed clear to Smith and his aides that the Soviets could theoretically be deploying SLBMs three years *after* signing the SALT agreements, without taking any older ICBMs out of action. "It was no longer a freeze," Garthoff recalls arguing. Aware of the anger his change of mind would provoke in Moscow, Smith nonetheless sent a second cable to Kissinger, urging that he negotiate a revised missile replacement formula "that would not be a clear admission of a free ride for the Soviets." The conflicting advice predictably enraged Kissinger, who was convinced, he wrote, that Smith was acting out of personal pique at being excluded from the summit. There was a bullying telephone call to Smith. "Kissinger told me on the phone that everyone in Washington approved of the line he was pressing and that only I was objecting to it," Smith wrote. Smith found out through queries of his own that he was one of many with objections. In his memoirs, he acknowledged that he and others on the delegation may have "exaggerated the significance of the need for immediate decommissioning and inclusion of the diesel G-class submarines. But . . . I thought I was doing what the President wanted—to have the views of his chief arms control adviser before he made the final decision."

Smith made one final attempt to change the SLBM outcome. Shortly before five in the morning on May 26, the last day of actual negotiations at the summit, he urged Kissinger to persuade the Soviets to begin dismantling their older land-based missiles at the very start of the Interim Agreement and build their last seventy SLBM launchers without decommissioning any older weapons—as Kissinger had promised Brezhnev in April. The "free ride" would thus come at the end of the agreement instead of the beginning.

Nothing more was heard in Helsinki until Kissinger cabled at noon that all the issues had been resolved and Smith should fly to Moscow to attend the signing ceremony that night. The Soviets, having received Nixon's written assurance on the Titan, did agree on the last morning to accept Smith's proposed language, submitted before he had second thoughts on excluding the G-class, barring them from deploying modern SLBM launchers on the G-class. Kissinger depicted that agreement in his memoirs as yet another concession: "Without further ado Gromyko *accepted* . . . our position on the G-class . . . ." In return, the Soviets insisted on staging the formal signing ceremonies for the ABM Treaty and Interim Agreement that evening. "Whatever

a right which we had no intention to exercise." Kissinger's explanation inadvertently provided a motive for keeping the Nixon letter a secret: to preserve the appearance of symmetry.

the Soviet reasons, we had little basis for refusing," Kissinger wrote. "After all, they were accepting *our* proposals in *our* formulation." There were few, if any, in the SALT delegation who would have agreed.*

It was not known until the last few hours whether Nixon and Kissinger would permit any members of the delegation to attend the signing ceremonies. "In retrospect," Kissinger wrote in his memoirs, "it would have been better to have brought both [the Soviet and American] delegations to Moscow and let them continue their work there in synchronization with the summit. Given Nixon's feeling about who should get credit, I doubt that he would have agreed if I had proposed it. We shall never know because I did not put forward the idea, not uninfluenced by vanity and the desire to control the final negotiations."

Nixon's and Kissinger's conduct toward Smith and his delegation remained ungenerous to the end. Only in the last hours was Smith invited to Moscow, in part because Nixon decided he wanted Paul Nitze of the Pentagon and Air Force General Royal Allison, who represented the Joint Chiefs of Staff on the SALT delegation, to provide the appearance of unity at the final ceremony. Allison was ordered to appear in uniform. Garthoff, who had provided much of the intellectual leadership for the delegation and served loyally as Smith's executive officer, was expressly not invited. Kissinger seemed to link Garthoff to much of his difficulty with the delegation, and it took a protest from Smith to William Rogers to win last-minute approval for Garthoff to come to Moscow. "Don't tell Henry," Rogers cautioned Smith.

Some members of the delegation were wary of the Russian insistence on an immediate signing ceremony; their suspicion, not unnaturally, was that the Soviets wanted the agreements signed before the SALT experts could get a look at them. It was a hectic end to a hectic negotiation, not unlike the final hours of the Peking summit. When Kissinger—in a frantic rush—asked the American SALT delegation to put the summit texts in final form, the only copy of the Interim Agreement available in Helsinki was the Russian-language version received by the Soviet delegation. The English-language version eventually had to be transmitted, in the backchannel, from Haig in Washington. There were inconsistencies between the two texts that had to be reconciled, and some errors were not discovered in time to correct them before the formal signing, so Nixon and Brezhnev had to sign the real text in private the next morning.

When Smith and his aides landed in Moscow there were no American Embassy cars to meet them. It took hours, and a series of wrong stops, including one at the Kremlin, before the chief SALT negotiator finally arrived at the embassy, moments before he was to participate in a news conference with Kissinger. "I paced up and down a dark alley outside . . ." Smith wrote, "trying to keep my temper. . . . I had had nothing to eat or drink during this day which had started about 3:00 A.M. Here I was in the Soviet capital for the signing of SALT agreements on which I worked so long and I felt like an alley cat looking for a scrap to eat." In his memoirs, Kissinger expressed regret that

---

* In a final message to Smith, the American delegation in Moscow magnanimously decreed that, "if any substantive points still deeply concerned me, I was to contact Kissinger at once," Smith wrote. "The expression 'You must be kidding' came to me when I read this contrived record of how Kissinger valued the delegation's judgment."

Smith had been victimized by "honest bungling" that had prevented the official embassy cars from meeting his aircraft. "Having stated that Smith had a case," Kissinger added, "I must also recount that he wore his unhappiness on his sleeve. Wounded pride and rage were so ill concealed that he nearly turned the briefing into a shambles. . . . I began, but Smith in a stage whisper grumbled that he did not know exactly what the treaty contained. This was not likely to inspire confidence in the press; so I interrupted my presentation to take Smith in an anteroom to try to calm him down."

Kissinger's account is simply untrue. There was no shunting of Smith to an anteroom for calming. Smith was furious, and he was not about to gloss over the inadequacies of the SLBM agreement. He was convinced that Kissinger had tried to keep him away from the press conference in order to avoid sharing any credit: "I expect he thought I was safely parked at the Kremlin waiting for the signing ceremony." When the questioning began, Smith was there, and when the press focused on the Interim Agreement and the Soviets' right to increase their submarine forces, Smith acknowledged that the Soviets, if they "want to pay the price . . . can build additional submarines." One journalist, after a series of questions, declared: "You are leaving open the possibility of a very large superiority in the SLBM field." Smith did not rule out the possibility in his answer, stating that "There is no doubt that under this arrangement they could at a high price increase their submarine fleet."

It was too much for Kissinger, who abruptly ended the news conference and announced that he would meet with the press again after the formal signing ceremony. At the ceremony, Smith found himself standing next to Kissinger. "What were you trying to do," Kissinger demanded, "cause a panic?" Smith wrote that he was told a few minutes later by Herbert Klein, head of White House communications, that the President did not wish him to take part in the reconvened press conference. Smith had his suspicions. "I sensed that this was probably a case of the President's name being used without his knowledge. . . ." But he did not protest. Kissinger, in his memoirs, blamed it all on Ziegler, who had attended the news conference and relayed word to Haldeman, and thus to the President, of Smith's perfidy. "Haldeman was near panic that the treaty would not be properly received," Kissinger wrote. "Nixon feared a revolt by his constituency on the right, and saw in Smith's conduct an example of the Georgetown and Eastern Establishment conspiracy against him. . . . Nixon and Haldeman therefore insisted that I alone give another briefing to place the treaty in better context."

Whether they initiated the idea or not, Haldeman and Nixon were undoubtedly right to turn to Kissinger to get things in "better context." Kissinger's subsequent press conference before a fact-starved group of reporters facing a deadline across the ocean was an assortment of misstatements and half-truths. The event was staged at 1:00 A.M. in the night club of Moscow's Intourist Hotel, where most of the journalists were quartered. Kissinger's basic claim was the one he had been presenting to the President for the past month: that the SLBM agreement prevented the Soviets from building up to eighty or ninety submarines by 1977. He further said that the Soviets had been building "missiles at the rate of something like 250 a year. If I get arrested for espionage, gentlemen," Kissinger told the titillated journalists, "we will know who is to blame."

Kissinger's sin was not espionage. He had to know, for such estimates were essential, that the CIA and other intelligence agencies had been able to confirm the construction of only eighty new Soviet ICBM launchers since the SALT talks began in late 1969. It was a fact that, in the thirty months prior to the opening of the SALT talks, the Soviets had constructed an estimated 650 launchers, roughly 250 per year, but Kissinger did not indicate to the reporters that his estimate of the Soviet ICBM construction level was three years out of date. In response to other queries, Kissinger fudged the issue of how the base line of 740 was reached for Soviet missiles, and did not explain that the exclusion of the G-class submarines gave the Soviets the right to add seventy new modern missile launchers without dismantling seventy older weapons. Indeed, he posed the whole G-class issue as one in which the United States, in shrewd bargaining, had sought to exclude the submarines. ". . . [W]e think that the G-class submarines are bound to get retired simply because they wear out. They are the oldest missile-carrying submarine they have." *

There was no obligation, of course, for a presidential aide in the midst of a political campaign to present honestly all the ambiguities of an international arms agreement to the press and the public, but Kissinger's distortions were more extreme—and far more counterproductive—than the usual bureaucratic dissembling. By not revealing that he had conceded the Soviets a bonus in submarines and submarine launchers to obtain the SLBM agreement, Kissinger left SALT I open to allegations that the Soviets had deceived the United States about such basic issues as the numbers of their strategic forces. Claims that the Russians had "cheated" on SALT I by developing a new missile system lingered throughout the 1970s, as critics of the SALT process, many of them in the military, pointed to Kissinger's assurances that there were adequate "safeguards" against the deployment of new, "heavy" missile systems. Kissinger, and the SALT process, would be plagued for years by his misstatements. In March 1974, at a time when he was urgently seeking Pentagon support for his SALT II proposals, he agreed to a private meeting with the Joint Chiefs of Staff at the Pentagon. "If he were in Russia, and opposed Brezhnev today," Kissinger was recorded by an officer as telling the military men, "he thought he could make an overwhelming case [regarding SALT I] against him; that the U.S. had gotten the better of Brezhnev in everything except the wheat deal." Three months later, however, the *New York Times* reported on Nixon's secret SALT I assurances—made in writing in Moscow—in which the United States recanted its right to cash in Titan missiles for three new submarines, as permitted under the Interim Agreement.

The chronic disputes over various clauses and understandings in the Interim Agreement also served to minimize the significance of the ABM Treaty, in which two opposing nations accepted limits on each other's ability to defend

* Gerard Smith, in his memoirs, explicitly quoted Kissinger as telling the reporters that night that "We wanted to prevent the USSR from trading in a weapon [G-class submarine] which we were certain they would have to retire in any event for a modern weapon." The fallacious statement was apparently edited out of the official transcript of the briefing, as printed later by the "Weekly Compilation of Presidential Documents," published by the National Archives and Records Service. Such editing happened routinely. For example, Smith's brief question-and-answer session with the journalists that so annoyed Kissinger and Nixon was not included in the official summit transcripts. Smith, in his memoirs, quoted from the original, uncensored transcripts of his and Kissinger's news conference.

itself on the basis of parity, equal security, and mutual deterrence. The irony of that successful agreement was its distance from the Moscow machinations of Nixon and Kissinger. The essential first article of the Treaty "was never discussed at the Verification Panel or other senior levels in Washington," Garthoff noted in a published analysis of the ABM Treaty. "For a basic provision often cited by later commentators as fundamental, it is striking that it was at no time addressed in guidance from Washington to the Delegation!" And yet, in his private meeting at the Pentagon in 1974, it was the ABM Treaty that received the brunt of Kissinger's criticism. "We were up against a conspiracy between Congress and the Soviet Union," he was quoted as saying, "and we gave away too much. But the alternative would have been to have given away everything and not have any ABM Treaty." Such statements, he obviously believed in early 1974, would stand him well with the—as he seemed to think—unsuspecting military.

Manipulation was at the heart of what went wrong with Kissinger's attempts to advance the SALT process. The difficulties of SALT II did not stem from the Interim Agreement itself, which demonstrated that the two superpowers could rationally discuss limits on offensive weapons systems, but from the constant misleading of colleagues and the distortion of intelligence that Kissinger deemed necessary to obtain the agreement.*

Manipulation did not end with the final ceremonies in Moscow. Within days of their return, Nixon and Kissinger were plotting against their own agreement. Sometime in June, Nixon met in the White House with Senator Jackson, who had been outspoken in his distrust of the SLBM agreement and had also raised questions about the new Soviet missile that Kissinger and Nixon knew was to be deployed within months. Nixon did not need Jackson's support for the SALT I agreements, which were then pending in Congress and were assured of passage. But he did need his vote on the Trident submarine and he got it. In exchange, the President agreed to support Jackson's controversial amendment to the Interim Agreement, which declared that the United States should not accept "levels of intercontinental strategic forces inferior" to those of the Soviet Union. Jackson was complaining, as members of the SALT delegation had suspected he and other arms control skeptics would, about what seemed to be disparity in the numbers reached at Moscow. In mid-August, he would accuse the Soviets of lying about the number of submarines they had under construction at the time of the agreement. Jackson's accusations had to be two-edged, as the White House understood, for—with his uncanny ability to obtain highly classified information from within the government—he had to realize that Kissinger knew exactly how many Soviet submarines were under construction at the time of the summit. The real message of his amendment, as

* The Soviets did not actually begin dismantling older ICBMs to build new SLBM launchers until late 1975, more than halfway through the period of the Interim Agreement. Kissinger's concession on the 740 level, which resulted in the exclusion of the Soviet G-class submarines, and the fact that roughly two years are needed to construct and fully test the boats, were responsible for the three-year delay. By 1977, however, the Soviets had been forced to decommission nearly two-thirds of their arsenal of SS-7 and SS-8 missiles to continue their SLBM buildup—a reduction of arms, although no longer strategically important, that would not have taken place without the agreement.

an aide subsequently acknowledged, was a warning to Nixon and Kissinger not to manipulate the numbers in future arms talks. Gerard Smith, who despite his specific objections had testified in favor of the Interim Agreement, and had tried to convince Congress that the offensive freeze was not inequitable, was appalled to learn of White House support for the Jackson amendment. "I questioned General Haig as to why the Administration in effect was thus vomiting on its own much-vaunted SALT freeze agreement," Smith wrote. Haig, telling the truth, explained to Smith that it had been done "to assure Jackson's vote" on the Trident. A victim of too many White House lies, Smith concluded in his memoirs that Haig's answer was "hard to believe."

Over the next months, fourteen senior officials involved with SALT I would resign, be reassigned, or be dismissed as what can only be called a purge swept through the SALT delegation and the upper ranks of the Arms Control and Disarmament Agency, whom the White House considered emotionally committed to disarmament. Garthoff, who received the State Department's highest award for his work on SALT, was exiled to the Inspector General's office at State and languished there until the Carter Administration took office in 1977, when he was finally offered an ambassadorial post. The new generation at ACDA, of which Fred Iklé became director, was far more skeptical and chary of negotiations with the Soviet Union. By mid-1974, ironically, Kissinger had become convinced of the necessity of placing some limits on MIRVs in the SALT II bargaining, but was firmly opposed by the men at the top of ACDA. Once known for its strong support of arms control, ACDA emerged from the Nixon years transmogrified into a counterweight to the SALT process.

Many of those who were forced to resign after SALT I, or who watched the purge from within the government, became convinced that it was the work of Senator Jackson. There were reports that Nixon, at his White House meeting with the Senator, had promised to "get a whole new team" for the SALT negotiations, and to get rid of those who were "soft" on arms control. Nixon and Jackson may indeed have agreed on the need for changes in the SALT delegation and in ACDA, but Jackson knew that the real decision making was taking place in the White House. One aide close to the Senator cited the obvious: "Scoop had been in Washington thirty years. He never believed that these large issues of policy were settled by the Ray Garthoffs or Royal Allisons."*

When it was all over, there was little doubt that if Richard Nixon did promise Senator Jackson he would clean out those who were "soft," the real beneficiaries would be in the White House. Smith, Garthoff, and the others knew the

---

* Jackson did claim at least one victim, however—Royal Allison. The Air Force officer had angered Jackson during his SALT testimony by disputing assessments of the Minuteman's vulnerability to a Soviet nuclear attack. Allison, cruelly, would not be told of his reassignment, which Jackson had demanded of Admiral Moorer, until early 1973, after he had assembled a staff and made plans to move to Europe again for the opening round of SALT II. In Jackson's view, Allison had forgotten that his mission was to represent the military on the SALT delegation. Allison's supporters contended that his willingness to remain open-minded and his grasp of the issues made him an effective contributor. "Working in arms control is a dangerous business," Gerard Smith noted in his memoirs, "but one in which expert and courageous military advice is badly needed. The Allison example is not likely to encourage top military officers to take on arms control responsibilities."

secret: that, in the crunch at Moscow, it had not been the dovish "arms control types" from ACDA and the SALT delegation who had eagerly agreed to make concessions, but the two men at the top of the government. It was that knowledge that made the arms control specialists expendable.

38

VIETNAM:
INTENSE NEGOTIATIONS

EARLY IN THE SUMMER of 1972, the men who ran North Vietnam's politburo made the critical decision that would lead to the signing of the Paris peace accords and finally get the United States out of Vietnam. No record of the discussions is available, but it is known that the politburo emerged from its meetings with a far-reaching consensus: There would be a political compromise in the South. North Vietnam would drop its demand for a coalition government in Saigon. Nguyen Van Thieu would be permitted to remain in office and retain his control over the South Vietnamese Army and the police forces. Richard Nixon and Henry Kissinger would be able to proclaim "peace with honor."

The senior Communist Party officials in Hanoi understood that Nixon and Kissinger would pay dearly for their insistence on keeping Thieu. There would be a settlement in principle, before the presidential elections in November. Hanoi would be permitted to keep its 100,000 troops in the South. American soldiers and, most important, American bombers would stop all operations in the South and leave the country. There would be a ceasefire in place, but only in South Vietnam—not in Cambodia and Laos, as Nixon and Kissinger had demanded throughout the peace talks. There would be a stated commitment to a sharing of political power in the South, with two governments. The Provisional Revolutionary Government, the NLF's government-in-exile, would legally be in control of cities and rural territories it and Hanoi's troops had seized during the spring offensive and earlier; Nguyen Van Thieu would maintain his control in Saigon and elsewhere. The promise of political legitimacy had a special significance for the PRG—its followers would no longer be barred from public life under the constitution of South Vietnam, which had been put into effect, with American support, in 1967.

North Vietnamese officials, in 1979 interviews with the author in Hanoi, acknowledged that their government accepted less than they had publicly demanded as a minimum to end the war. There were a number of elements behind the decision to compromise. By June, Hanoi's spring offensive had failed to achieve its short-range goal, a rout of the South's forces and the overthrow of Nguyen Van Thieu. Nevertheless, the men in Hanoi pronounced themselves satisfied with the offensive in terms of its long-range objectives. Most significant was the renewed infiltration of men and matériel into the countryside of the South, especially in the Delta, where the American-led pacification effort, with its emphasis on body counts and assassinations, had by 1970 severely diminished the Communist presence. The military stalemate came at a time when Nixon had huge leads in the public opinion polls. The President had mined Haiphong Harbor, used B-52s to bomb Hanoi, and yet managed to pull off the Moscow summit, with its successful SALT agreement. By midsummer, with George Wallace out of the presidential race, Nixon opened up a two-to-one lead over George McGovern in some polls. Richard Nixon would have his Four More Years, and Hanoi knew it.

Kissinger had supplied the basic incentive for compromise during his visit to Moscow in April, when he made it known to the Soviets that the Nixon Administration would be willing to accept the permanent deployment of North Vietnamese troops in the South. A month later, during the SALT summit, Kissinger went further and indicated that he would be willing to discuss a three-tiered election commission with the North Vietnamese. It was a direct suggestion that the administration realized that there would have to be a sharing of the political power with the PRG in the South. Hanoi was cautious about such talk, for Kissinger's proposed election commission would still be operating in a South Vietnam controlled by a constitution that outlawed the Communist Party. During the spring and early summer of 1972, therefore, the North Vietnamese continued to insist, as they had throughout the secret talks in Paris, that Thieu must be ousted and a coalition government installed in Saigon.

Kissinger's willingness to initiate talk of a tripartite election commission, despite Thieu's heated opposition to such proposals, was a significant step toward peace, for the United States was beginning to bargain on political issues without consulting its allies in South Vietnam. There were other factors that played a role in North Vietnam's decision to compromise and settle the war. Continued war meant continued American bombing, both in the North and in the South. Nixon's ability to achieve successful election-year summits in Peking and Moscow raised an element of uncertainty over the long-term relationship between the two largest Communist nations and North Vietnam. The Chinese and the Soviets might be reluctant, four years hence, to supply a North Vietnamese election-year offensive once again. Perhaps the spring offensive of 1972 would be Hanoi's last.

North Vietnam had social and cultural fears, too. The growing domination of American values in Saigon and elsewhere in the South, accompanied by the denigration of Vietnamese culture, alarmed the leaders of the North, who had profound contempt for the prostitution, motorcycles, and miniskirts of Saigon. They also feared that the intense American bombing in the South would ultimately make rebuilding there almost impossible after North Vietnam managed to outlast the United States and the Thieu regime and win the war—a victory thought inevitable by the leadership of the North.

As Hanoi struggled with the political and military realities, Nixon and Kissinger continued to emphasize triangular diplomacy. In mid-June, Kissinger made his fourth trip to Peking, with the goal, he noted in his memoirs, of reassuring Chou En-lai that the success of the Moscow summit would not dampen the Nixon Administration's ardor for normalization of relations with China. Kissinger also sought, by the mere fact of his presence in Peking, to put additional political pressure on Hanoi to compromise. The trip, which came just before the Democratic convention in New York City, also had clear domestic political overtones. As the White House had learned in its dealings with Chou En-lai and Mao Tse-tung, China was more than willing to urge a negotiated settlement in the South; it did not want to deal with a unified Vietnam in Southeast Asia.

In mid-September, when negotiations with the North Vietnamese were moving toward a settlement, Kissinger returned to Moscow for four expensive days, in which he granted the Soviets liberal trade and credit concessions in return for continued Russian pressure on Hanoi's diplomacy. One of the agreements called for the United States to supply up to $750 million in credit, at an interest rate of 6 percent, to help the Soviets finance their earlier bargain-basement purchase of American wheat. The American taxpayer, already facing huge increases in the price of bread and related foods, was now being required to subsidize the purchases that had driven up the cost. Linkage had evolved into a device for paying off the Soviets in return for their intervention with Hanoi.

Triangular diplomacy was far less significant in Hanoi's account of the final months of negotiation. North Vietnam's concern was not with the messenger, whether Chinese or Russian, but with the message. In mid-June, shortly before Kissinger arrived in Peking, Nikolai Podgorny, the Soviet President, flew to Hanoi to tell of Kissinger's willingness to accept a tripartite election commission in the South and, perhaps, to bring word of a new Nixon-Kissinger threat. As promised, American bombers stayed away from the center of Hanoi and Haiphong during the visit. Later that month, after Kissinger left Peking, a senior Chinese official also visited Hanoi, presumably to relay once again China's view that a compromise was essential.

That Hanoi would have sued for peace in the South solely on the basis of pressure from Peking and Moscow is inconceivable; Hanoi's 2,000-year history and its subsequent independence after achieving its war aims in 1975 belie that theory. And despite constant pressure from Washington, China and the Soviet Union continued to supply North Vietnam after the American withdrawal in 1973 that made President Thieu's defeat inevitable. What is conceivable, however, is that the urgings from the Soviet Union and China, when combined with the military stalemate in the South and the American political concessions privately conveyed by Kissinger, created a climate in which Hanoi decided to accept a continued Thieu regime. In one move, Hanoi could get rid of the Americans and gratify the Chinese and Russians, leaving itself free to bargain vigorously with Kissinger on the other outstanding issues of the war. When the fighting between North and South entered a new phase after the peace agreement, as all involved realized was inevitable, North Vietnam would have dramatically increased its chances of victory by negotiating the return home of all the American military.

Nguyen Co Thach, the North Vietnamese Foreign Ministry official who served as a chief aide to Le Duc Tho during the secret peace talks with Kissinger, acknowledged in the 1979 interviews that American acceptance of the PRG as a valid government in the South was an essential element in Hanoi's acceptance of Thieu. By midyear, he said, with the spring offensive stalemated by American bombs in the South, "We came to the decision that it was time to deal with Thieu. It was a difficult decision, but not hard to make. I must tell you this: The most important thing was the American withdrawal. Second, is that they allow our troops to stay in South Vietnam.'' These were the military conditions that had to be met before the political decisions could be discussed, Thach said. The Hanoi official, who became North Vietnam's Foreign Minister in 1979, would not describe the inner workings of the politburo, but he said that Hanoi's leadership had prepared three "options" for dealing with political questions in the South.

The first option, which was vigorously pursued by Le Duc Tho during August and September in his negotiations with Kissinger in Paris, provided for the removal of Thieu and the imposition of a coalition government, including members of the PRG, in Saigon. When that proved unacceptable to Kissinger, as Hanoi apparently expected it to be, Le Duc Tho was authorized to negotiate for a coalition government with two regional governments, the PRG and Saigon, operating at lower levels. "On the top is a coalition," Thach explained, "and the lower elements are the two local governments—one controlled by the PRG and the other by Saigon." That also was rejected by Kissinger. Hanoi's fallback position was the one finally presented in its draft of the peace agreement, as turned over to Kissinger in Paris on October 8, 1972, less than a month before the American presidential election. It called for "two governments with a loose form of government on top—the Council for Concord and Reconciliation." Kissinger then watered down the option to suggest that the council's main function would not be governmental but merely to work jointly with Saigon to prepare for elections. With that significant modification, Hanoi's draft proposal of October 8 became the basis for the final settlement.

Thach said that all three options, including the modified version that emerged in the Paris peace agreement, had one significant thread: "It is to not have the Saigon government *uniquely* lawful. That is the one important thing for all the options—there is to be no lawful Saigon government. There are to be two lawful governments and not only one."

"This was the minimum," Thach said of the third option. "This reflected the reality of the time."

North Vietnam's negotiating logic was understood by Kissinger and eventually led to a settlement, but not until the White House went through an astonishing, and heretofore secret, spasm of recrimination and betrayal that was triggered by Kissinger's and Hanoi's insistence on resolving all issues before the election. Nixon, despite his seemingly insurmountable lead over George McGovern, was unable to decide whether a Vietnam settlement would be good or bad for his reelection. His fear was that, as in 1968, last-minute talk of agreement would help the Democrats. In late October, as Kissinger was on the verge of a settlement, Nixon maintained contact with his private pollster, Alfred E. Sindlinger, who insisted that a reelection mandate was possible without a settlement; in fact, he said, a peace would be detrimental to Nixon's election margin. Sindlinger's track record inside the White House was excellent; he had accurately predicted in the spring that Nixon's popularity would rise with the bombing of Hanoi and Haiphong.*

* Sindlinger had been brought into the White House during the domestic economic crises of 1971, when he met with Nixon and John Connally. He and Colson struck a bargain before the 1972

In the hectic days between October 20 and October 26, when Kissinger was forced to announce the breakdown of the peace talks with Le Duc Tho in a nationally televised news conference, Richard Nixon came unglued. He had accepted, in full and in writing, all of Hanoi's terms and relayed that acceptance to Hanoi's leaders. But political operatives such as Charles Colson suddenly found themselves playing a foreign policy role as it became clear that Nguyen Van Thieu could not be cajoled, bribed, or threatened into accepting the peace agreement. At a critical moment, when Kissinger was in Saigon pressuring Thieu, Nixon backed down. The President simply changed his mind, doublecrossing not only the North Vietnamese but Henry Kissinger. It was a betrayal that Kissinger, for reasons of his own, chose not to describe at the time or in his memoirs, although he has recounted a bitter version to many of his aides and friends.

Kissinger also chose not to tell of a second betrayal, by Alexander Haig, who summoned members of the National Security Council staff to a rump meeting in late October and announced that Kissinger had "gone too far this time." Haig had joined with Colson, Haldeman, and others in the White House to help convince Nixon that the peace terms to which the President had agreed were not good enough. Haig demonstrated no ambivalence about the negotiations while in Kissinger's presence, but, fortified with the knowledge that Haldeman and Colson disapproved of the agreement, became a leading critic behind Kissinger's back. Ever the apt pupil, Haig had learned well how to manipulate great-power issues for personal aggrandizement.

Kissinger's silence about all of this is not surprising, for the truth would undermine one of the basic fictions of the Nixon-Kissinger White House: that the Paris peace agreements were "peace with honor." Kissinger had an additional reason for holding back: the knowledge that Nixon and Haig had a story of their own to tell, one that would severely diminish his image as a brilliant negotiator. Kissinger, as Nixon, Haig, and Haldeman fully understood, had permitted his desire for another international triumph and his ambition to become Secretary of State to mislead him. He had deluded himself into thinking that Nguyen Van Thieu, in return for remaining in power in Saigon, would accept North Vietnam's troops in the South as well as permit the PRG to share in the tripartite election commission. It was a profound misjudgment. The corrupt President of South Vietnam disagreed strongly with the White House's plans for ending the war, and repeatedly said so in meetings and memoranda. Thieu's reward for his bluntness was to be handled the way Kissinger handled others who stood in his way: He was manipulated.

These sordid intrigues culminated in a series of secret commitments to Thieu and a presidential order to bomb Hanoi that Christmas. Thousands lost their lives to rectify decisions that were made out of political and personal expedience. None of these machinations brought honor to the United States.

The key player in the final stages of the peace talks was Hoang Duc Nha, a brassy thirty-one-year-old who was a second cousin to Nguyen Van Thieu.

campaign: Sindlinger would conduct special polls for the White House, but not for pay. He would finance the research himself. His reward would be long-term contracts after the election from the Commerce, Labor, and Treasury departments, and from the Federal Reserve Board.

Sent to the United States for his college education, Nha earned an electrical engineering degree at Oklahoma State University in 1965 and took a postgraduate course in management at the University of Pittsburgh. He returned to South Vietnam just before Thieu's election and joined the government, working primarily on land reform. A year later he became Thieu's private secretary. Laurence Stern of the *Washington Post* described him in late 1972 as Thieu's equivalent of a Haldeman, the President's "most influential personal adviser on the entire range of military, political and diplomatic problems that confront the Saigon regime." Fox Butterfield of the *New York Times* noted in 1973 that "Mr. Nha has quietly become the closest confidant of President Nguyen Van Thieu, and in the view of most knowledgeable Vietnamese, the most powerful man in the country after the President."

Nha played an essential role in blocking the Nixon-Kissinger peace initiative in October 1972. In his memoirs, Kissinger dismissed him with contempt: "America had to take some responsibility for the egregious Nha; he had been educated in the United States and in the process had seen too many movies of sharp young men succeeding by their wits; he came on like the early Alan Ladd in a gangster role. He was dressed in the fanciest Hollywood style, spoke American English fluently, and had retained from his Vietnamese background only an infinite capacity for intrigue. He reinforced Thieu's inherent suspiciousness. Both Bunker and I were convinced that he did much mischief in exacerbating every misunderstanding."

Nha takes great pride today in his willingness to stand up to Kissinger at those tense moments of confrontation in Saigon. He kept a private diary of his daily meetings with Thieu, as well as a complete file of the various peace initiatives that began flowing to Saigon via Kissinger in the summer and fall of 1972.* His account of the peace process begins on January 2, 1972, when Nixon hinted, in a television interview with Dan Rather of CBS, that the United States would be willing to withdraw all its troops if the North would release the American prisoners of war. "Thieu and I had a meeting," Nha recalls, "and we agreed that if the United States agreed to such an exchange, there was not much we could do about it." A few days later, on January 10, Ambassador Bunker and General Abrams met privately with Thieu for two hours and informed him that a previous peace proposal, which called for his resignation one month before general elections, had, in fact, been secretly broached the previous October to the North Vietnamese in Paris. Thieu had agreed that fall to the essentials of the proposal, but this was his first inkling that it had been presented to the North Vietnamese. He also learned that Nixon would repeat the proposal in a speech on January 26.

Deeply upset, Thieu summoned Nha to a midnight meeting at which both men, Nha recalls, discussed their fears of an American sellout. Thieu's agreement to step down had been made on the assumption that the offer was mere "posturing," a proposal not meant to be seriously conveyed. "We didn't think Hanoi would accept it," Nha says. "We knew they were pressuring the United States to topple Thieu." After Nixon went public with the proposal on January

---

* Nha left South Vietnam after its fall in 1975 and, when interviewed, was a successful employee of a large American electronics firm in New York City.

26, "We had to chime in and concur," Nha says. It was only one of many negotiating issues in dispute.

Nha insisted in later interviews that neither he nor Thieu understood the full seriousness of the secret talks in Paris until the January 10 meeting. "The only guy who was talking to us was Bunker," Nha says, "and we thought the private talks were part of the weekly public talks. We thought it was the same old thing" as in the days of the Johnson Administration's private meetings in Paris. The January 10 meeting also produced evidence that Nixon was willing to strike a deal that would permit Hanoi's troops to remain in the South. "It was the first time that we knew that the United States had made that concession," Nha recalls. Thieu had never agreed to such a concession, Nha insists, nor would he.*

In early spring, just after the North Vietnamese offensive was launched, Saigon learned that Kissinger was planning to go to Moscow in late April and would discuss Vietnam. Ambassador Bunker was asked about the meeting and replied, Nha recalls, "We've got to find a comprehensive view of the conflict." In early May, however, Nixon sent Thieu a warm letter of support and reported that the Kissinger–Le Duc Tho meeting had been the "least productive" of the secret talks. A few days later, Thieu was given advance word by Bunker and Abrams of the May 8 mining of Haiphong Harbor and the renewed bombing of the North. Abrams stayed on a few moments to discuss privately with Thieu—on White House orders—the possibility of a South Vietnamese invasion of the North. "We've got to bring the war to the enemy's camp," Nha quotes the American general as saying. Such an invasion, as Washington knew, was one of Thieu's fondest wishes. Later he would tell Oriana Fallaci, the Italian journalist, that "only a few million" of the residents of North Vietnam were Communists; ". . . the great majority of them would rise up if there were a landing."

Excited by the prospect of American support for such an invasion, Thieu told Nha, "If we do it, we've got to do it differently than in Lam Son"—the disastrous South Vietnamese invasion of Laos in early 1971. A few weeks later, however, Saigon got a different message. It learned, as did the rest of the world, that Podgorny had gone to Hanoi. After that visit, Nha recalls, the North Vietnamese politburo convened a meeting, which continued into July. "By then," Nha says, "the American Embassy was not telling us much." There was a brief visit by Haig in late June, but his message—that China would help the United States leave Saigon with honor—provided no great solace to

* Kissinger, in his memoirs, claimed that Thieu had explicitly agreed to the abandonment of mutual withdrawal prior to Nixon's May 31, 1971, peace offer. As we have seen, however, Hanoi and Saigon were not explicitly told in 1971 that the Nixon Administration envisioned a final peace agreement that permitted North Vietnam to keep its troops in the South. That offer was not directly posed to the North Vietnamese until Kissinger's visit to Moscow in April 1972. Kissinger, in a footnote, also minimized as "only a pretext" Thieu's anger at not being told that Hanoi had been forwarded his alleged offer to resign one month before an election. Thieu's real anger, Kissinger said he learned later, was over the basic proposal itself. In one of the most remarkable sentences of the first volume of his memoirs, Kissinger further wrote that Thieu "gave us no hint" that he would be opposed to an American proposal that he leave the presidency one month before an election—at a time when his staying in office was the most significant issue blocking the progress of the negotiations. That Kissinger needed such a hint, or could write seriously that he did, demonstrates an insensitivity to Thieu that perhaps made the impasse in October inevitable.

Thieu. The South Vietnamese viewed Haig as an errand boy, Nha says, and had far less faith than Washington in the basics of triangular diplomacy. (It was on that trip, according to an American official who accompanied Haig, that Haig—obviously on orders from Kissinger—once again raised the question of a possible South Vietnamese invasion of the North with a senior Vietnamese corps commander.) In mid-July, Thieu was informed that Kissinger would meet again, in secret, with Le Duc Tho on the nineteenth. "We thought something important was coming," Nha says, "but we were never told."

Hanoi began its slide toward compromise on August 1, when Le Duc Tho presented Kissinger with a revised ten-point peace proposal that dropped the long-held North Vietnamese demand that Washington, after signing a peace agreement, must abide by an unconditional timetable in arranging for a cease-fire, the withdrawal of its troops, and the staging of general elections. Under the new requirement, discussion of the political arrangements would proceed, but no longer against a deadline. It was a major step toward a settlement.

There was still the Thieu problem, however. Le Duc Tho continued to insist that Thieu must resign immediately upon the signing of a peace agreement, to be replaced by a three-segment "provisional government of national concord." The August 1 proposal, not revealed at the time and mentioned only in passing in Kissinger's memoirs, provided for the new government's function to be that of a caretaker, "to carry out the tasks of the period from the restoration of peace to the general elections and to organize general elections in South Viet-nam." It would include members of the PRG; any officials, other than Thieu, of the current Saigon administration; and a third segment of neutralists who supported neither the government nor the Communists. North Vietnam was proposing that power be shared equally between the two contending forces in the South. Kissinger was skeptical, as he wrote: "The concept of a coalition government, even on the terms suggested by Hanoi, remained unacceptable. It gave the side that controlled perhaps 10 percent of the population 50 percent of the power. And a fifty-fifty split between groups that had been killing each other for two decades was bound to be a sham."

Kissinger's caveats did not change the fact that Le Duc Tho had made a significant concession and obviously was prepared to go further. Nixon, sud-denly confronted with the prospect of a settlement, began to waffle. Charles Colson recalls that Nixon's attitude toward a preelection settlement hardened as his standings in the polls increased. In the spring, Nixon had been urging Kissinger to invoke the old "madman theory." "Henry," Colson quotes Nixon as saying, "you tell those sons of bitches that the President is a madman and you don't know how to deal with him. Once reelected I'll be a mad bomber." By late summer, however, "he stopped saying that. He began to have doubts."

Kissinger, however, was convinced that the November election would be, as he put it in his memoirs, "an unchangeable deadline for Hanoi. The equiv-alent of an ultimatum. Its fear of what the 'hawk' might do with a new mandate for four years might lead it to prefer a settlement before our election." The President and his national security adviser were on different tracks. Neither was telling the other what he had in mind. Kissinger continued to rush and Nixon to worry.*

On August 14, Kissinger held his third meeting in a month with the North Vietnamese in Paris. In a subsequent memorandum to Nixon, he reported that during the peace process "we have gotten closer to a negotiated settlement than ever before; our negotiating record is becoming impeccable; and we still have a chance to make an honorable peace." With that, Nixon became even more nervous. Haig was once again the middleman. In a note to Haig in mid-August, the President declared, "Al—it is obvious that no progress was made and that none can be expected. Henry must be discouraged . . ."

The gap between the President and his chief foreign policy aide could not have been wider at that moment, for Kissinger was exultant over the secret talks with Tho. The newspapers were full of reports of a diplomatic break-through, and Kissinger added to the urgency of that speculation by going to Saigon for meetings for Nguyen Van Thieu on August 17 and 18. Nixon's real concern was clear in his comments to Haig: "We have reached the stage where the mere *fact* of private talks helps us very little—if at all. . . . Disillusionment about K's talks *could* be harmful politically—particularly in view of the fact that the Saigon trip, regardless of how we downplay it, may raise expectations."

The President was confronted with an adviser who was every bit as popular as he was, whose popularity served as a significant benefit in an election year, and who was clearly out to end the war before the election, regardless of Nixon's political fears. Kissinger was intent, as Nixon understood, on making it difficult, if not impossible, for the President to dump him in the second term. Nixon, aware that he was not getting the whole story from his national security adviser, was still using Haig—as he had ever since Kissinger's secret trip to China—as a checkpoint.

Kissinger's optimism about the prospects for a settlement before the election may have been based on informal contacts with Le Duc Tho, or, more likely, on private messages relayed by Ambassador Dobrynin, or on both. During this period, a close Kissinger aide maintained an informal journal which was carefully shared with at least one senior member of the government outside the White House. Shortly after the August 1 meeting, this journal reported that "Hanoi wants to move fast. . . . There is discussion of international supervision [after a ceasefire]. There is an effort to get a ceasefire on the first of October with the announcement made by all parties." Thus by early August

---

* Kissinger said different things to different people about the men in Hanoi during this intense period of negotiation. At a lunch on August 2 or thereabouts with the novelist Norman Mailer, Kissinger described the North Vietnamese as all but impossible to threaten. "I know this has to sound unendurably callous to you," he told Mailer, then on assignment for *Life* magazine, "but the North Vietnamese are inconceivably tough people, and they've never known peace in their lives. So to them the war is part of the given. They are able to live with it almost as a condition of nature." Mailer included an account of the lunch in his book on the 1972 political conventions, *St. George and the Godfather.* Kissinger's comments about the North Vietnamese and their ability to live in harmony with war were similar to those of General William Westmoreland in a 1973 interview with Peter Davis, the writer and film maker. "The Oriental doesn't put the same high price on life as does the Westerner," Westmoreland told Davis. "Life is plentiful, life is cheap in the Orient, and as the philosophy of the Orient expresses it, life is not important." The general's comments appeared in *Hearts and Minds,* Davis' 1975 movie on the Vietnam War that won an Academy Award.

Kissinger was aware that within two months or so Hanoi was planning to move decisively to settle the war.

It is not clear how much of this information was relayed to Nixon. What is clear, however, is that Kissinger's optimism was not shared with Nguyen Van Thieu in their August meetings. Kissinger, whose primary concern was the successful manipulation of his President and the outmaneuvering of Le Duc Tho, seemed to pay little heed to the views of those running the South Vietnamese government. On August 1, the day Kissinger met with Le Duc Tho in Paris, President Thieu, whom Bunker informed of the meeting in advance, made a bitter speech questioning the American commitment to the war. He called on Washington to keep up the "relentless bombing" of the North for at least six more months and warned that the North Vietnamese spring offensive had been aimed at creating a "stalemate" that would threaten Nixon's reelection, as had happened with the Tet offensive in 1968.

Nha's increasing doubts were heightened, he recalls, when his office received an erroneous report in early August that Kissinger had reached a settlement on a coalition government with Le Duc Tho. He rushed the information to Thieu, sensing that such information, whether right or wrong, would not hurt his standing inside the palace.

Kissinger arrived in a Saigon thick with rumors of an imminent peace agreement.* Shortly after Kissinger's arrival, Thieu was given a copy of Hanoi's August 1 peace proposal, along with a copy of Hanoi's proposed "Modalities of Discussions," which had also been handed to Kissinger by Le Duc Tho at the August 1 meeting. The paper proposed that the main military and political questions about the future of South Vietnam be decided in private meetings between the United States and North Vietnam, with secondary issues of implementation handled, in some cases, by the Saigon government and the PRG.

Nha vividly recalls his and Thieu's anxiety about Kissinger's delay in showing them Hanoi's August 1 proposal until his arrival in Saigon. At a second meeting with Thieu, Kissinger also presented a draft of the American counterproposal, which again offered the North Vietnamese and the PRG a tripartite election commission whose function would include the monitoring of elections and overseeing the revision of the South Vietnamese constitution. In a blistering critique of both Hanoi's proposal and the American counteroffer, which he later made available to the author, Nha focused on the proposed election commission: ". . . this is the most important point which concerns not only the legal regime of our nation but also determines the life and death of all the people of SVN [South Vietnam]." The commission, Nha argued, given its power to revise the constitution, "can be viewed then as an elected coalition government." To have the Thieu regime share power with "this government would generate a parallel government and a duality of power. This in turn would cause serious unrest and a political crisis." Nha was enunciating a concern, shared by Thieu, that did not diminish during the months of intensive

---

* Amidst the rumors, Jonathan C. Randal published a highly accurate account in the *Washington Post* of August 17, noting that "some South Vietnamese and foreign analysts" were interpreting Kissinger's presence as a sign that "Hanoi had softened its terms"—which Hanoi had. Randal went on to note that some "cynical Vietnamese suggest that Hanoi might even drop its demand for Thieu's immediate resignation, reasoning that a more widely based government would represent a more dangerous rival to the National Liberation Front than the present isolated military regime." Hanoi would not make that offer until early October.

negotiations that followed. It was a concern that eventually led Thieu, who had repeatedly given notice of his intention, to refuse in late October to accept Hanoi's final compromise, which offered him a chance to stay in power as long as he shared some authority with the PRG in the election commission.

The significant issue here was not the merit of Thieu's position, which was dubious from Kissinger's point of view, but the fact that his complaint was made known to Kissinger, and in writing. There was little ambivalence in the documents. Nha's memoranda, which flowed steadily through Bunker to Kissinger over the next two months, further questioned the right of Washington to negotiate political issues directly with the North Vietnamese; such issues, Nha said, should be settled by the Vietnamese themselves. In other words, Nguyen Van Thieu wanted to have his say in the Paris peace talks.

Kissinger, in his memoirs, dismissed Nha's criticism of Hanoi's August 1 proposal as one "crafted in meticulous, nitpicking detail," but he did not cite any of the detail. Few of Nha's subsequent criticisms are mentioned in Kissinger's memoirs, which go to great lengths to cover up the extent of his misjudgments in Saigon. It is obvious that any balanced settlement of the war would have been difficult for Thieu and his aides to accept, but that fact does not minimize the extent of Kissinger's mistake. He negotiated an agreement with Le Duc Tho in early October that included provisions that he had every reason to suspect Nguyen Van Thieu would not accept. And yet he managed to delude himself that Thieu would be not only willing but eager to ratify the agreement.

Kissinger's inability to perceive the truth was based on two factors: first, his condescending attitude toward the South Vietnamese, and second, anxiety over his own standing. He had traveled to Saigon in mid-August, not to bring Thieu into his confidence but to manipulate and appease him, to find some means of keeping him quiet during the election period while he negotiated secretly with Le Duc Tho. One aide who participated in some of the Saigon meetings remembers Kissinger's explaining to Thieu that he was not to worry about forthcoming Nixon Administration positions, for they were designed to be rejected and thus place the onus for the continued war on the North Vietnamese. After the elections, Kissinger told Thieu, it would be a different story and the United States would do everything possible, including more intensive bombing, to bring Hanoi to its knees. Kissinger again raised the possibility of a South Vietnamese invasion of the North; he and Thieu discussed various cities in the North that could be attacked after the election, the aide recalls, with Kissinger recommending a South Vietnamese landing in Vinh or Dong Hoi and Thieu talking about an attack farther north, at the important transshipment point of Thanh Hoa.

Kissinger further urged Thieu to accept some form of tripartite election commission, although he did not inform the South Vietnamese President that he had already broached the concept with Hanoi. Kissinger, according to his memoirs, presented the election commission as representing "only the thinnest pretense of a joint body" and as one whose influence was nil. "It never occurred to me," he wrote, "that Thieu might object. . . . We did not grasp what was happening right away. We still thought we were operating in tandem with Thieu and therefore blamed his reserve on drafting difficulties and shortsighted advisers."

Nha has a very different recollection. He had been formally introduced to

Kissinger that August, and listened quietly as Kissinger made his pitch. His message, Nha recalls, was that "You have to help us because the elections are near." Kissinger remarked that when he left Saigon he would fly to Miami Beach and the Republican convention. There were reassurances, too, about any future elections in the South after a settlement, with Kissinger telling Thieu that "in an election with the NLF, you would not lose." Neither Thieu nor Nha, as Kissinger had to know, had any intention of letting those elections take place.

Henry Kissinger and Nguyen Van Thieu were thinking along different lines, but Kissinger in his memoirs claimed not to be aware of it: "I left Saigon with a false sense of having reached a meeting of the minds. Thieu and I had decided that we would settle the few remaining disagreements over our draft proposal by exchanging messages through Bunker. There was plenty of time—nearly four weeks until my next meeting [with Le Duc Tho] on September 15."

Kissinger's optimism was necessary; he had to believe in his success, because without it, his future in Washington would be severely curtailed. After a brief stop in Japan, he returned to Washington and a series of meetings with Nixon before going to the convention. Kissinger also briefed Rogers on the Paris and Saigon talks. Both men got a very upbeat message: Talking peace in the days just before the Republican convention was good politics. In mid-week, Rogers gave an interview to James McCartney of Knight Newspapers and revealed that he was "convinced" that a negotiated peace would be reached in the Vietnam War either before the November election or "shortly thereafter."* The White House press office denied that Rogers had spoken on the basis of any specific information, but on August 22, Richard Nixon, en route to Miami Beach for the Republican convention, confidently assured Stewart Alsop, the *Newsweek* columnist, "I'm sure of one thing. The war will be over. The war won't be hanging over us in a second term." In his eagerness to give the White House good news before the convention, Kissinger had gone too far.

Nixon's political position was more than secure at that point: On August 12, it was announced that the last American ground combat troops had left Saigon. The White House continued to report more withdrawals; there would be fewer than 25,000 American soldiers in Vietnam by the end of the year. In another week, Nixon would announce the end of the draft as of July 1973, doing away with a focal point of student antiwar dissent. The polls that showed Nixon far ahead of McGovern also indicated that the public was overwhelmingly in support of his handling of the war, and that a vast majority believed he was doing

* Rogers had thrown in the towel by mid-1972, and seemed to be intent primarily on keeping the truth of his eclipse from the public. The published transcript of a Nixon meeting with Bob Haldeman on June 23, 1972—the meeting in which the President ordered the CIA to be drawn into the Watergate cover-up—also provided evidence of Rogers' reduced status. Kissinger was en route to Washington from his visit to China. "I told Haig today that I'd see Rogers at 4:30," Nixon said. ". . . Rogers doesn't need a lot of time, does he?" Haldeman said no. "Just a picture?" Nixon asked. "That's all," Haldeman responded. "He called me about it yesterday afternoon and said I don't want to be in the meeting with Henry. I understand that, but there may be a couple of points Henry wants me to be aware of." It was agreed that Rogers could stop in the Oval Office later in the day to be photographed as a participant in the Kissinger-Nixon meeting.

everything possible to end it. If there was any danger, it came from peace. A Harris poll in early September showed that 47 percent of those interviewed said they opposed a coalition government in Saigon.

Kissinger's appearance at the Republican convention created the usual splash, and the President's most visible adviser was accorded the same degree of Secret Service protection—five agents—that Vice President Agnew received.* At one party, a *Washington Post* society reporter overheard a woman ask Kissinger, who was known to have just returned from Saigon, whether he "would go on to Hanoi like some of those other Americans after he left Saigon?" Kissinger hesitated a moment, eyed the woman seriously, and said, "Oh, I am saving that for later."

Indeed he was.†

President Thieu, with Nha's strong support, continued to protest the proposed tripartite election commission in late August and early September. Haig, accompanied by John Negroponte, had been sent to Saigon after Kissinger's visit in another attempt to sell the concept, but Thieu emotionally denounced the commission. Kissinger was outraged at Thieu's refusal to do what Kissinger thought best for him. "Insolence is the armor of the weak; it is a device to induce courage in the face of one's own panic," Kissinger wrote. ". . . [O]ur own ally . . . had managed to generate in me that impotent rage by which the Vietnamese have always tormented physically stronger opponents." Thieu was digging himself in "on a point so peripheral to the final result" that it would emerge as a serious political liability if the peace talks broke down and the public learned of Thieu's position. Left unmentioned was another reason behind Kissinger's anger: his personal timetable. Thieu's reluctance could prevent a settlement before the election.

Adding to Kissinger's frustrations was a sudden barrage of signals indicating that the North Vietnamese would back down and permit Thieu to remain in office if the election commission could be worked out. In an address on September 1, Vietnam's National Day, Premier Pham Van Dong of North Vietnam recounted the list of his country's negotiating demands for a ceasefire in the

* Kissinger had earlier filmed a brief interview for a fawning film portrait of Nixon that was shown at the convention. "I, like most of my colleagues," Kissinger said of Nixon, "had always been opposed to him and had formed certain images about him and I found that he was really . . . totally different from the image intellectuals have of him. He's very analytical but quite gentle in his manner. . . . There's a certain, you know, it's a big word, but it's a certain heroic quality about how he conducts his business . . ."

† Daniel Ellsberg also attended the Republican convention, and drew reporters' attention by accusing the Nixon Administration of having planned, since late 1968, the escalation of the Vietnam War. Ellsberg also revealed that the White House had authorized the B-52 bombing of Cambodia and had authorized the Marines to engage in combat inside Laos in early 1969. Ellsberg refused to tell reporters who had given him the information—he was protecting Morton Halperin—and his allegation, while reported extensively, led to no follow-up stories. I had lunch with Ellsberg later that summer and concluded that there was no evidence to support the assertion that the administration had been waging secret war in Cambodia. The bombing did not become generally known until the Watergate scandals the following May. Ellsberg was under federal indictment at the time for his role in the release of the Pentagon Papers and was in the process, ironically, of suing John Mitchell and other senior administration officials for damages stemming from what he contended was illegal wiretapping. At issue was the government's admission that one of Ellsberg's attorneys, later revealed to be Leonard Boudin, had been overheard on a foreign embassy wiretap. There was no reason to believe, in mid-1972, that the White House had been involved in secret wiretapping—which, in a further irony, stemmed from the *New York Times* account in 1969 of illegal B-52 bombing in Cambodia.

South—and pointedly omitted any mention of Thieu's resignation. Frank Snepp, then the CIA's principal analyst for political trends in the North, considered Dong's address "the sign we had been waiting for" and wrote an analysis predicting a breakthrough very soon.* On September 11, the PRG made the new position public, releasing a statement on Radio Hanoi that, for the first time, explicitly noted that a settlement in South Vietnam would have to reflect the "reality" of "two administrations, two armies, and other political forces." The message was clear to Kissinger: Not only could Thieu stay in office, but Hanoi would no longer demand that a tripartite government, the coalition Thieu feared, supersede the two existing governments that were, even then, sharing power in the South. The new PRG position, which became known four days before Kissinger's next scheduled meeting with Le Duc Tho, attracted surprisingly little attention. Its significant nuance—that the overthrow of Nguyen Van Thieu was no longer sought—was missed by the American press. The official United States response, coordinated by Kissinger, was to depict the PRG statement as posing "absolutely no change," as one official told the *New York Times*. The *Times* account ran ten paragraphs and was tacked onto another story from Saigon on page 12. Its last paragraph said: "One ranking American analyst said he thought this statement simply repeated the thought, if not the wording, of the last major peace statement of the Provisional Revolutionary Government, issued February 2."

Kissinger's control of the media was never more of an asset than over the next few months. The PRG statement was not important news because he chose not to make it so.

On September 10, the day before the PRG statement, Kissinger had flown to Moscow for three days of consultations, with economic issues at the forefront. While there, aides remember, Kissinger was privately assured by Leonid Brezhnev that the September 11 PRG statement presaged a breakthrough. Frank Snepp, in his memoir, reported that Brezhnev further told Kissinger that Pham Van Dong's National Day speech was yet another signal that Thieu's removal was no longer a precondition for achieving a ceasefire and releasing the American prisoners of war.

Kissinger had to believe that Nixon's ambivalence about a settlement before the election would evaporate when a peace agreement was reached. At that point, he understood, his standing inside the administration would be unassail-

---

* Despite his sensitive position, Snepp was not privy to Kissinger's secret negotiations and did not realize that the Paris talks had moved into a critical phase. He was stunned to find himself severely reprimanded for his analysis, which had found its way into the President's daily CIA briefing paper—and thus, perhaps, into the hands of Henry Kissinger. Snepp, as he wrote in *Decent Interval*, was accused by his superiors of foul play in releasing such a sensitive item over a weekend, when the details of Pham Van Dong's address reached Washington. The CIA's briefing papers were subjected to far less rigorous clearance during weekends, and Snepp, by immediately releasing his analysis, had denied Kissinger's office a chance to censor it. Snepp was accused of deliberately avoiding the Kissinger clearance process by not withholding the information until a weekday. His quick work meant that, to Kissinger's anger, word of North Vietnam's change of position was spread throughout the upper reaches of the administration. His CIA superiors "were frightened of offending Kissinger," Snepp wrote, "and they lowered the boom." Within twenty-four hours, Snepp was barred from writing any more analyses for the CIA's Vietnam Task Force. "I would have to find another job elsewhere in the agency," Snepp wrote. He eventually worked his way back to Saigon, where in 1975 he was on hand for its fall, the focal point of his memoir.

able: China had been broached; the SALT agreement had been signed; and now American participation in the Vietnam bloodletting was nearing resolution.

Thus the Thieu dilemma was acute, and Thieu was rapidly emerging as Kissinger's greatest enemy. While Kissinger was in Moscow, Ambassador Bunker made another attempt to persuade Thieu to drop his opposition to the election commission. One of Kissinger's aides recalls the flash of anger from Kissinger when, on September 13, the last day of the Moscow meetings, he heard from Bunker that Thieu had again refused to accede. It was at this point that John Negroponte urged Kissinger to fly to Saigon and confront Thieu once again. "I don't want your stupid State Department advice on going back to South Vietnam!" Kissinger exclaimed. After a midnight walk around his dacha, Kissinger decided to go ahead and formally propose the election commission to Le Duc Tho in Paris without prior approval from Saigon. Nixon had to be sold on the idea, and Kissinger handled that problem by cabling the President that he did not expect the North Vietnamese to accept the offer. At this point, with the election less than two months off, Kissinger knew that Nixon, who paid scant attention to detail anyway, would be preoccupied with politics. Nevertheless, it took great daring for him to deceive the President on such a critical issue. He was playing the kind of hardball that Nixon respected, the kind that had initially brought him to Nixon's attention in late 1968, when there had also been a flurry of peace talks. Only now Kissinger was playing hardball against his President.

In his memoirs, Kissinger cited portions of his cable: "If the other sides accept our [election commission] proposal, which we believe quite unlikely, then the fact that GVN [Government of South Vietnam] was not totally on board to the last detail will be obscured by myriad other complexities. . . . In such an eventuality, it is inconceivable that GVN would find it in its interest to surface what few differences we may have had. . . ." Kissinger further told Nixon that if Hanoi rejected the proposal, Thieu would "have absolutely every incentive to go along with us" in publicly castigating the North for its intransigence. What Kissinger did not say was that he had received private assurance from Soviet leaders that Le Duc Tho was prepared to compromise on the issue.

Kissinger had no choice but to trust Haig—who had remained in Washington —to sell his views to the President. Haig later told colleagues on the NSC staff that Kissinger was giving away too much, but from all available evidence, he played his role straight this time.* Kissinger, in his memoirs, quoted from Haig's cable in which Nixon gave his approval for proposing the election commission to Le Duc Tho. Nixon "finally agreed," Haig cabled, "but in-

* Haig, after years of silent obedience, was beginning to talk openly about his dissatisfaction. At lunch with Admiral Zumwalt on August 2, Haig began gossiping, as Zumwalt recorded in his memoirs, about "his difficulties as the intermediary between the President, who didn't trust Henry, and Henry, who felt uncomfortable with the President." Haig said that Nixon "vacillated between a strong impulse to get out of Vietnam as fast as possible at almost any price and an equally strong impulse to 'Bomb North Vietnam Back to the Stone Age,' " as General Curtis LeMay, former Air Force Chief of Staff, once put it. Zumwalt went on: "Al said that he had to exercise considerable dexterity to stiffen the President's backbone when the President was in a bug-out mood, and that he lived in dread that some day the President would be with Henry instead of him when the bug-out mood came on and Henry would be unable to handle it."

sisted that in conveying his approval to you that I emphasize to you his wish that the record you establish tomorrow be a tough one which in a public sense would appeal to the Hawk and not to the Dove.'' If the negotiations did have to be made public, as Kissinger had hinted, Nixon wanted to be sure he would get good press notices. Nixon also complained, Haig cabled, that Kissinger and others on his staff did ''not seem to understand that the American people are no longer interested in a solution based on compromise, favor continued bombing and want to see the United States prevail after all these years.''

One lingering mystery is why Nixon agreed to such gamesmanship. Did he really believe the North Vietnamese would reject the election commission offer, leaving the White House free to go public, as it had done in early 1972 when it unilaterally revealed the existence of the secret Paris talks? The major basis for Kissinger's belief that his ploy would work was his perception of the extent to which the President was *not* involved in the day-to-day aspects of the secret negotiations.

Early September 1972 was a period of distraction for the President. On the fifteenth of that month the federal grand jury in the District of Columbia would indict the Watergate break-in team, and Nixon, through Haldeman and John W. Dean III, was closely monitoring the Justice Department's investigation. The President's men had authorized a series of illegal spying activities against the Democrats that culminated in mid-June with the arrest of a team of con-spirators, headed by Howard Hunt and Gordon Liddy, inside the Democratic National Headquarters in the Watergate office complex in Washington. The operatives had been trying to repair a previously installed wiretap on the tele-phone of Lawrence F. O'Brien, the party chairman. There had been a major effort during the summer, under the direction of Nixon and Haldeman, to insure that the full story of the White House involvement did not emerge in the subsequent FBI inquiry into the break-in. Adding to the urgency of the White House effort was the fact that four of the men arrested were Cuban-Americans and former CIA operatives who had been recruited by Hunt from the Miami area and who had also been involved in the September 1971 break-in at the office of Daniel Ellsberg's psychoanalyst in Beverly Hills, California. The Watergate arrests could thus begin to unravel more than Richard Nixon could afford.

To Nixon's immense relief, only Howard Hunt and Gordon Liddy were indicted, along with the Cuban-Americans and a former CIA official, James W. McCord, Jr., who had been in charge of the break-in at O'Brien's office. The indictments did not reach more deeply into the Republican reelection commit-tee or the White House. The cover-up was working. It was during these weeks that Nixon held the first of what would be a series of fatal meetings with Dean, who, as the White House counsel, had become the President's fair-haired boy for his handling of the crisis. Those close to the Oval Office understood that the Watergate problem was consuming huge chunks of the President's time and energy during this period. Watergate, by giving Kissinger an even freer hand with which to take diplomatic chances, had begun to make its mark on foreign policy.*

---

* Kissinger and Haig had their own dirty linen to hide. Robert Pursley, Laird's military assistant, decided that summer that, after four years of vendetta and intrigue, there had to be a better way to

While Nixon celebrated his Watergate reprieve on September 15, Kissinger and Le Duc Tho prepared to exchange peace proposals in Paris, with each side continuing to make concessions. Le Duc Tho, presenting Hanoi's second offer within six weeks, still insisted on Thieu's removal and a coalition government, but conceded the right of the Thieu regime to continue administering the regions under its control, pending general elections, when a newly elected government would take over. Hanoi's offer was movement in the right direction, in Kissinger's view, just as Moscow had predicted. The new North Vietnamese offer also called on the United States to pay $9 billion in war reparations, to be equally divided between North and South. It was the first time Hanoi had used any specific dollar amount in making such a request—which raises the possibility that private conversations on the issue had been held between Kissinger and the North Vietnamese, or through the good offices of the Soviet Union. Kissinger did not reprint Hanoi's September 15 proposal in his memoirs, nor did the American proposal, as presented on the same day to Le Duc Tho, make any reference to reparations.

Kissinger's offer did, however, formally provide for the establishment of an election commission, to be called the Committee of National Reconciliation, whose functions would include a review of South Vietnam's constitution. Kissinger was committing the Nixon Administration to a ceasefire whether or not Thieu agreed. It was, perhaps, the most fateful moment of the secret negotiations: Hanoi was being assured that its allies, the PRG, would have legal standing in the South. A meeting of minds was reached on another significant issue that day—the timing of a settlement. Both sides were in a hurry. Hanoi was fearful that Richard Nixon, after his reelection, would be less willing to compromise on his support for Thieu. Henry Kissinger's fear was more personal: His role would diminish after November, he suspected, if a settlement could not be reached. The two men agreed on a private timetable. "I saw no harm in agreeing to a target date," Kissinger wrote, as if the thought had been

---

make a living. "I was just so fed up," Pursley recalls. "The whole atmosphere had changed so much. All of this sinister back-biting just wore you down." After some brooding, he decided to give it one more try, and arranged a heart-to-heart with Haig. "I thought if we just sat down and talked openly" about the problems, Pursley says, "maybe we could come to a conclusion." The meeting with Haig, which took place in the White House, began well. "Al listened sympathetically. 'Look,' I said, 'we're just not getting along well. How can we do things better?' Al then said, 'Yeah, you've been under the gun since Nixon came in. Buz Wheeler [chairman of the Joint Chiefs of Staff in 1969 and early 1970] used to complain about your access to Laird and Wheeler told this to the President.' " Haig suddenly reached into his desk, pulled out an oversized green binder notebook, and waved it at Pursley. "We started keeping notes right away on you!" he exclaimed. The implication was clear to Pursley. "It was a dossier." If Pursley began to talk after leaving the government, Haig seemed to be suggesting, the White House was in a position to retaliate. It was an ugly moment. "I thought, 'Holy Hell. I'm busting a gut for my country and all these guys are doing is keeping a book on me. These guys are trying to hang my ass.' " Pursley told Laird about the scene and received permission to retire right away, despite being offered a promotion to lieutenant general and a chance to head an Air Force command, one of the most attractive jobs at his level in the service. There was a formal retirement ceremony at the Pentagon, with a high-powered guest list that included Henry Kissinger, whose remarks were captured on a tape recorder: "I am very grateful to him and so also is the President—for the tremendous role he has played in the decisions that have been taken . . . I must say that while life may be a little more comfortable we will miss you deeply. And the only consolation we have is that, knowing General Pursley's sense of public service, he'll be no further away from us than the end of the telephone." Pursley, who was subsequently talked out of retiring and promoted by Melvin Laird, learned the next year that his telephone had been wiretapped twice by Kissinger and Nixon—in May 1969, for fifteen days, and in May 1970, until all the taps were terminated on February 10, 1971.

entirely Le Duc Tho's, "as long as we were making no additional concessions. We settled on October 15.*

There is no evidence that Le Duc Tho was aware of the circumstances of the American offer of an election commission—that it was being proposed with the certainty that President Thieu would object vigorously. Hanoi, as a senior official explained later, consistently took the position that it did not consider Thieu's prior approval necessary for the settlement of the war. "In the talks," the Vietnamese official told the author, "we considered all the demands as American demands, not as South Vietnamese demands—because the talks were between two sides. So there was no program for the South Vietnamese." At a moment of crisis some weeks later, when Kissinger raised the question of prior South Vietnamese approval, the official recalled, Le Duc Tho was unyielding; he told Kissinger: "The USA is the dog and South Vietnam is the tail and the tail cannot wag the dog."

Kissinger's goal, in the days following the September 15 meeting, was to conceal the intensity of the negotiations from the Thieu regime and the American press, which was informed only that the private meetings were taking place. It is not clear how much Kissinger told the President, either. In his memoirs, Nixon did not mention Hanoi's August 1 and September 15 offers. Nixon may have been ambivalent about Kissinger's pursuit of peace before the election, but he must have enjoyed his own public position: The White House, while repeatedly acknowledging that the private talks had reached a "sensitive" point, was refusing to discuss any specifics. The effect was to weaken George McGovern's ability to capitalize on the peace issue, and the Democratic challenger was reduced to accusations against Kissinger, who enjoyed immense popularity and prestige. In mid-August, when Kissinger flew to meet Thieu in Saigon, McGovern accused him of manipulating public opinion by appearing "to be negotiating when actually he has been stalling to prop up General Thieu and his corrupt military regime in Saigon." But attacking Kissinger, as Nixon understood, was not good politics in 1972.

Kissinger, as usual, found it easy to overwhelm the White House press corps, which continued to rely almost totally on his version of events. In a briefing on September 16, a few hours after returning from Paris, he would concede only that the continued existence of the talks "indicated" that they had a "certain seriousness." Asked whether the PRG's proposal of September 11 provided a new element, in view of the Communists' statement that neither

* Nixon, as Kissinger knew, would have much preferred to wait until after the elections and then, if no agreement could be reached, once again escalate the war to try to force a solution. In his memoirs, Kissinger sought to explain his haste by arguing that he had moved precipitately only because he was convinced that Nixon had made a serious misjudgment about his postelection position. A combination of budgetary pressures, congressional complaints, and "media demands" for continued withdrawal, Kissinger wrote, would serve to make the presidency more vulnerable, not less: "If we did not strike while the iron was hot *before* November 7," Kissinger wrote, "Hanoi would soon see the fragility of our position." Kissinger did not justify his desire to end the war quickly on humanitarian or moral grounds—to stop the killing and prevent a future escalation. Instead, he insisted that Nixon was at the height of his strength—and thus his bargaining position —before the election, and would be less able to push through his escalation policies afterward. This argument, as stated in the memoirs, did not take into account Nixon's decision to initiate the Christmas bombing of Hanoi. The President obviously did not share Kissinger's view that his political and military position had been weakened by his overwhelming reelection.

side should dominate, Kissinger responded: "The question is not what was said, but what the actual consequence of it is."

Two days later, Joseph Alsop was in print in the *Washington Post* with a column that reported what Kissinger would not say: that the odds were improving on "an acceptable settlement in Vietnam before election day." Alsop added: "At best, at least a month will be needed to work out the details. . . . Thus the next fortnight or so is the crucial, last-chance period."

Kissinger's goal in this maneuvering is impossible to fathom. Was he trying to tip off other reporters that something was in the wind? Was the leak to Alsop meant to lay the groundwork inside the White House for a quick settlement? Was he continuing to curry favor with Alsop, a dominant figure in Nixon's much-hated Georgetown set? Or was he simply unable to stop himself?

There was nothing careless in his approach to Saigon. Nguyen Van Thieu was still in the dark about the real progress being made in Paris, as Richard Nixon was. On September 18, Kissinger authorized Ambassador Bunker to forward Hanoi's September 15 offer to Thieu. "The plans, of course," Bunker told Thieu in a brief note, "are not acceptable to us and we have no intention of moving away from our present position." Thieu's response, as drafted by Hoang Duc Nha, was pointed. The Thieu government rejected North Vietnam's proposals as "an insolent demand for surrender. . . . Their 'proposal' amounts to requiring from our side unconditional surrender while they are the aggressors and are unable to achieve their aims on the battlefield." Nha's memorandum proposed once again that the Thieu government be included in the private Paris peace talks; it called for the "Vietnamization of peace." Hanoi should be told, Nha wrote, that "it should negotiate directly with the GVN for a negotiated solution." The sentence was underlined. Nha's memorandum also made clear that the Saigon government would protest any agreement that rewarded Hanoi's "aggression" by permitting its troops to remain in the South.

There was nothing vague about the South Vietnamese response. Whatever Thieu found it difficult to say in face-to-face meetings with Bunker, Nha was saying in writing. Yet in his memoirs Kissinger was able to write that at this point he was "still half-believing that Thieu's hostility must reflect a misunderstanding . . ." On September 23, he sent Bunker a message for Thieu pleading for his support. "If Thieu is genuinely worried that we might settle prematurely," Kissinger told Bunker, "he must understand that the appearance of differences between Washington and Saigon could have the practical consequences of influencing Hanoi toward a rapid settlement in the private talks so as to exploit what they might perceive as a split between the US and GVN . . . it is essential that Thieu stay close to us so that we demonstrate solidarity to Hanoi."

At the time, of course, Kissinger *was* in the process of settling the war, precisely as Thieu suspected.

On September 26, Kissinger returned to Paris for another private meeting. Once again Le Duc Tho put a peace offer on the table, Hanoi's third since August 1. Le Duc Tho still insisted on Thieu's resignation, but the new offer made an important stride toward the Kissinger position. After a ceasefire, a Provisional Government of National Concord would emerge to coordinate the election process and to draft a new constitution. It would not serve as a coalition government, however, but would operate in conjunction with the two existing administrations. Hanoi also conceded that the Saigon government, as well as the PRG, would both be able to "maintain their respective existing foreign relations that are not at variance with the foreign policy of peace and neutrality of South Vietnam . . ." Hanoi, in another concession to Kissinger, also agreed that the new Provisional Government would operate on the principle of unanimity. Thus the Saigon regime, if it chose, could block any action by the commission with its veto. These concessions convinced Kissinger, he wrote, that the new "Provisional Government of National Concord" would be limited to endless and frustrating squabbles over procedural issues.

The final stumbling block, Kissinger realized, was Hanoi's continued insistence on Thieu's resignation. Another meeting with Le Duc Tho was scheduled for early October; under the timetable to which both sides had agreed, a breakthrough, if one was to come on that issue, was imminent. Haig was dispatched to Saigon for another attempt to persuade Thieu to drop his opposition to the election commission. By then, Nha was convinced that Kissinger was in the process of making an agreement behind Saigon's back. Nha had gotten hold of dispatches to left-wing newspapers in Japan, from reporters stationed in Hanoi, which reported that a ceasefire in place in the South was imminent, and would not include ceasefires in Laos and Cambodia.

There was good reason to believe that Hanoi was ready for a compromise. The heavy American bombing of the North, which since late May had involved more than two hundred B-52s, was creating massive supply backups and delays that could not be easily alleviated. The mining of Haiphong Harbor was further limiting the North's ability to deliver supplies by sea. On September 15, the South Vietnamese Army had finally managed to recapture Quang Tri, the only provincial capital North Vietnam had seized in its spring offensive.

Haig arrived for his first meeting with Thieu armed with a set of American counterproposals that were centered on the tripartite election commission. One ambitious scheme called for the election of a constituent assembly that would draft a new constitution; the assembly would be in lieu of a presidential election. Under the counterproposal, which Kissinger could not have seriously expected Hanoi to accept, the PRG and the Thieu regime would continue to govern areas under their control until the new constitution went into force. Nha would "present us with a new proposal for [assembly] elections, with a new Constitution." The new Kissinger offer also called for a program of postwar development for "all the countries of Indochina"—thus fulfilling a commitment, as Thieu and Nha had no way of understanding, to pay reparations to Hanoi.

Haig's meetings went badly, as he cabled Kissinger. In his memoirs, Kissinger quoted Haig as reporting that he met on October 4 for nearly four hours with Thieu, Nha, and other senior officials, and "It was evident from the outset that we were being confronted by solid, unified GVN opposition . . ."* Saigon

---

* At one point, Kissinger quoted Haig as reporting, Thieu broke into tears of distress. Nixon, in his memoirs, provided an added detail: Thieu's tears came after he had "railed against Kissinger, who, he said, did not 'deign' to consider Saigon's views in his negotiations."

went further in its protests than reported by Kissinger, who has thus far written the most extensive account of this period, and has based much of that account on documents to which only he and Haig and a very few others have had access. Haig was also handed a caustic four-page memorandum, drafted by Nha, that repeated many of the South Vietnamese government's objections. Hanoi's peace proposals of August 1, September 15, and September 26 were each "even more arrogant and absurd than the previous ones," Haig was told. There was a new demand, based on the Japanese press dispatches, that any settlement of the war in the South must include ceasefires in Cambodia and Laos. Nha took issue again with the exclusion of Saigon from the Paris peace talks between Kissinger and Le Duc Tho, and there was a complaint about the speed with which Washington was proceeding: ". . . we should avoid giving to the other side the impression that we need to have a certain agreement within a given frame of time."

To emphasize their dismay, Thieu and Nha presented the memorandum to Haig in an insulting fashion. "We gave it to him sealed," Nha recalls. "We were so mad. We just wanted him to know that he was just a messenger." Nha says he and Thieu knew that Haig would tear open the envelope as soon as his car left the palace "and curse us under his breath."

Kissinger could not really have been surprised by the failure of Haig's mission, for his office had received nothing but protests from Saigon since the peace process intensified late that summer. Haig's inability to convince Thieu played into Kissinger's hands, for Haig represented the hard line inside the White House, and Thieu's rebuff would force Nixon to do what he might not choose to do if the victim were Kissinger—to defend his man. In a critical meeting on October 4, described differently in each of the memoirs, Kissinger brought Haig's report to the attention of the President. Kissinger quotes Nixon as being offended at Thieu's obstinacy: "Nixon told me that Haig had made a mistake returning home as had always been planned; he should have stayed to work over Thieu." The President authorized Kissinger to proceed with his October 8 meeting with Le Duc Tho, "consoling himself that Hanoi would probably turn down our proposals anyway." Nixon clearly "wanted to stall" the peace negotiations "until after the election," Kissinger wrote. The President, in his memoirs, however, suggested that he completely understood Thieu's apprehension: "I sympathized with Thieu's position," since a ceasefire would leave Hanoi's troops in place in the South. "I shared [Thieu's] view that the Communists' motives were entirely cynical. . . . But I felt that if we could negotiate an agreement on our terms, those conditions could be met."

Nixon's concern in early October was focused on the margin of his reelection victory, not on Thieu. If Hanoi was willing to sign a peace agreement on American terms, as Kissinger repeatedly suggested, Nixon realized he had no choice but to go along. To rebuff his own peace offer would be bad politics, since Hanoi might decide to publicize the details of the negotiations and embarrass the administration. Charles Colson, who dealt with the President on political matters all that fall, believed at first that Nixon was far too worried about a settlement prior to the election. "I thought he'd be a hero with an agreement," Colson recalls, even one that came just before election day. Colson changed his mind by early October, a decision perhaps made inevitable by his eagerness to please the President. Throughout the last months of the campaign, Colson recalls, Kissinger also seemed to be an enthusiastic member of the team. When in Washington, the national security adviser would telephone the President's chief political operative at least twice a day "to ask me, 'How is it going?' Henry was as much of a sniveling politician as I was." As the election drew nearer, however, and Nixon continued to dominate the polls, the President became more outspoken, accusing Kissinger—"that son-of-a-bitch" —of "wanting me to be in his debt for winning this election." Colson never directly overheard a conversation about the negotiations between Kissinger and Nixon, but he remembers Nixon "telling me what he'd told Henry: 'If we get it, great. Right now, it won't help and it might hurt. We don't want to get it just to get it.' "

In public, Nixon took the high road. Shortly before noon on October 5, he called in a group of White House reporters and declared: "The election, I repeat, will not in any way influence what we do at the negotiating table." He was far ahead of McGovern then, but, as usual, he was running scared. His fear was that another last-minute foreign policy development would affect the election. His nervousness was not alleviated, apparently, by the Sindlinger polls, which reported a steady increase in the percentage of voters who believed that Nixon would be reelected. By October, 80 percent of those polled were predicting his victory. On the afternoon of October 5, at Colson's insistence, Nixon met privately with Samuel Lubell, another pollster who had discovered sharp rises in Nixon's popularity stemming from his escalation of the war. In mid-August, Lubell had reported in a syndicated newspaper article that Nixon's "mining of Haiphong harbor in May gained him the sweeping voter support he needed to exercise a free hand in Indochina until after the election . . . [M]any of the new Nixon supporters, while talking of 'getting out,' are really searching for some way of staying in Indochina indefinitely, if it can be done without losing American lives." The validity of Lubell's conclusions, which were based on a small sample of personal interviews, was not debated by the White House. Lubell recalls a long meeting with Nixon, Colson, and Haldeman; it was Haldeman who brought up Lubell's August reports: "Had I changed my mind?" Lubell assured the President and his political advisers that he considered his finding still valid. When he returned home, Lubell recalls, "I told my wife, 'Something has gone wrong in Vietnam.' "

Something had gone wrong, in Nixon's view. Kissinger was insisting on trying to end the war before the election. "I can't convince Kissinger to slow down," Colson recalls the President telling him again after the Lubell meeting. "Please tell him it will hurt—not help us—to get the settlement before the election." Nixon's goal, Colson realized, was "to downplay Henry."

It was not until he wrote his memoirs that Kissinger could bring himself to acknowledge that Nixon did not want a settlement before the election. His cover story, as provided to the Kalb brothers for their biography, was that he believed, even at the time of Nixon's October 5 press conference, that "despite private and public disclaimers, [Nixon] would be delighted to see a workable agreement reached before election day. . . ." Kissinger's major problem, as he prepared to fly to his rendezvous with Le Duc Tho on October 8, was that he would have to convince the President that any negotiated settlement was a total victory for the Nixon policies. Kissinger took the unusual step of taking

Haig with him for the meeting with Le Duc Tho because, he wrote, "he would be able to help me to sell any possible agreement to Nixon." There was another reason, of course: Having Haig in Paris would make it easier for Kissinger to sell Haig on the settlement. Haig's presence also meant that little information would be relayed to the White House, for Kissinger would not take a chance on having one of the political aides, such as Colson, sabotage the agreement. "Both Haig and I knew that Nixon might show a particularly interesting cable to whoever happened into his office," Kissinger wrote. "If that person were Charles Colson—with whom he was spending an increasing amount of time—there was no telling what would happen."

Le Duc Tho made the final compromises on October 8. He presented a draft treaty in English, the first such document offered by either side during the secret talks, that accepted the notion of two governments and two administrations with an election commission, an "Administration of National Concord," whose precise functioning was left unclear. Nguyen Van Thieu could stay in office. The American prisoners of war would be returned. The Nixon Administration could resupply its allies. In return, Hanoi would have the right to keep its troops in South Vietnam, legal acceptance by the Saigon regime of the legitimacy of the PRG, assurance that the United States would stop all acts of force against South and North Vietnam, and also the right to continue its military operations in Cambodia and Laos. The compromise reached in Paris called for a ceasefire only in South Vietnam.

Le Duc Tho, perhaps understanding Kissinger very well, also agreed that Kissinger should fly to Hanoi late in October to initial the agreement. The trip, like the one to Peking the year before, would be staged in secret but announced to the world's press within days. Kissinger did not say in his memoirs how or when the idea of the trip to Hanoi arose; Le Duc Tho, he wrote, "urged" such a trip after the breakthrough. North Vietnamese officials later insisted that it was the United States which had proposed "several times" that the agreement be initialed by Kissinger in Hanoi before its formal ratification in Paris. One Kissinger aide, who attended the Paris meetings in October, confirms Hanoi's account, saying that the North Vietnamese "could not have cared less" where the peace treaty was initialed. Kissinger also agreed to a precise timetable. The schedule, as of October 11, called for the United States to stop the bombing and mining of North Vietnam by October 21, with Kissinger's arrival in Hanoi on the next day. The formal signing of the peace treaty would be left to William Rogers and the various foreign ministers in Paris on October 30, with the ceasefire in place beginning twenty-four hours later throughout South Vietnam.

In his memoirs, Kissinger depicted the receipt of Le Duc Tho's offer as "my most thrilling moment in public service. I have participated in many spectacular events . . . But the moment that moved me most deeply has to be that cool autumn Sunday afternoon . . . At last, we thought, there would be an end to the bloodletting in Indochina. We stood on the threshold of what we had so long sought, a peace compatible with our honor and our international responsibilities."

The Kissinger office journal, in an entry made a few weeks later, took a less exalted view: "It's taken for granted that Hanoi will cheat. The question is how to set up communications, intelligence and command arrangements." Such arrangements would be needed to enable the United States, after the complete pullout of its forces, to help coordinate the military activities of the Saigon regime after the ceasefire. The command and control facilities would also be necessary to help coordinate renewed American bombing in South and North Vietnam, if such bombings, after the peace agreement went into force, were deemed necessary by the President. Both sides would violate the ceasefire, and all involved in the Paris talks understood it. Blood would continue to flow in South Vietnam, but it would no longer be American blood.*

Kissinger's euphoria was not shared by everyone on his staff. It was recognized, of course, that there had been a major breakthrough, but some aides— notably John Negroponte—also realized that Nguyen Van Thieu would object vehemently. The South Vietnamese were told nothing from Paris, and neither was the White House. Kissinger's first move after the October 8 session was to order Negroponte and Winston Lord to draft a counterproposal emphasizing the need for ceasefires in Laos and Cambodia and improving the language controlling the replacement of war matériel. Kissinger kept a dinner date, and, upon his return, was enraged to discover that Negroponte and Lord had drafted a relatively tough set of demands. "You don't understand," Kissinger shouted, according to an eyewitness. "I want to meet their terms. I want to reach an agreement. I want to end this war before the elections." Negroponte got upset in turn and accused Kissinger of "trying to do too much with too much risk." Kissinger insisted that the United States had to "seize the opportunity"—as De Gaulle had done in settling the Algerian war, he said—by imposing a deadline and meeting it. A timetable had been set, Kissinger told his young aide, and he was going to keep to it. Negroponte concluded that for

---

* Kissinger's memoirs repeatedly denigrated Senator George McGovern's peace plan, offered in a televised campaign address on October 10, as a program that "asked much less of Hanoi than Hanoi had already conceded to us." McGovern's plan called for an immediate end to all American acts of war in "all parts of Indochina," followed by the withdrawal of all American forces from Southeast Asia. In return, he would expect North Vietnam to return all American prisoners of war within ninety days, as North Vietnam and the PRG had offered in their previous peace proposals. No political solution in the South would be imposed, leaving the way open for a coalition government. What Kissinger saw as McGovern's failure—his lack of support for the Thieu regime—was, in fact, the centerpiece of McGovern's plan. The Democratic candidate based his program on the immorality of the Thieu regime: "I say General Thieu is not worth one more American prisoner, one more drop of American blood . . . Our problem is that we have asked our armed forces to do the impossible—to save a political regime that doesn't even have the respect of its own people." McGovern's peace platform also focused on the war's immorality. "The reality of this war," McGovern said in his address, "is seen in the news photo of the little South Vietnamese girl . . . fleeing in terror from her bombed-out school. She has torn off her flaming clothes and she is running naked into the lens of that camera. That picture ought to break the heart of every American. How can we rest with the grim knowledge that the burning napalm that splashed over [her] and countless thousands of other children was dropped in the name of America?" McGovern's thesis—that no peace that maintained Thieu in power was morally just—was an issue that did not exist in the Nixon-Kissinger White House, and one that made Kissinger's empirical point-by-point comparison of the peace terms irrelevant. McGovern ran, and lost, as a candidate who believed that the American involvement in Vietnam had become immoral and undemocratic, and that the nation's first goal was to stop its Vietnamization program and the support of Thieu. "Now," McGovern noted in his speech, "there are those who say that you will accept this because the toll of suffering now includes more Asians and fewer Americans. But, surely, conscience says to each of us that a wrong war is not made right because the color of the bodies has changed. We are all created in the image of God."

Kissinger "the scenario was almost more important than the words. He got so excited about going to Saigon and then going to Hanoi to announce the signing." *

Over the next three days, the American delegation, working with English and Vietnamese versions, made some improvements in the draft treaty, but the basic spirit and substance of the North Vietnamese proposal was not altered. Two issues were not immediately resolved. Kissinger refused to accept Hanoi's demand that civilian prisoners in Saigon, who included thousands of Vietcong cadre, be released simultaneously with the American pilots after the ceasefire. He also insisted that the agreement permit military goods to be replaced on a one-to-one basis, a ratio that favored the South Vietnamese Army since it was so much larger. "I had no illusions," Kissinger wrote. "Whenever we or Hanoi were looking for an elegant way to bury an issue, we left its resolution to the two South Vietnamese parties, who we knew might never agree to anything."

No such cynicism was displayed to Nixon or Haldeman. Kissinger continued to keep the White House in the dark; the President would not learn of the breakthrough until October 12, when Kissinger returned to Washington. Kissinger acknowledged all this in his memoirs, but once again he was careful at the time to put out a cover story to the press. In the Kalbs' biography, Kissinger claimed that he had delayed the second meeting with Le Duc Tho, on October 9, because he had been forced to wait "for the President's response" to his breakthrough report the night before. There had indeed been a delay before that meeting, but only because Kissinger, as he wrote in his memoirs, insisted that Negroponte and Lord redraft the American counterproposal to soften its tone. The Kalbs, relying on Kissinger, reported that he chose not to begin the October 9 meeting until "the President's approval was flashed by Haldeman . . ."

Kissinger was operating on his own in Paris, and it left a sour aftertaste in the mouths of some of his aides. It was not until the fourth Paris meeting, on October 12, Negroponte later told friends, that he learned that Kissinger's flight to Hanoi would be a secret one. Negroponte had other concerns: "Nobody really knew what was happening in Saigon. Ambassador Bunker was only vaguely aware. . . . There was nothing in Saigon to tell Thieu that we were close to an agreement. We now had a virtually complete document . . . but a document on which Thieu had not been consulted." Negroponte expected the South Vietnamese President to defend himself "like a trapped tiger."

Kissinger's report to Nixon on October 12 was upbeat. "Well, Mr. President," Nixon quoted his adviser as saying, "it looks like we've got three out of three"—meaning the China breakthrough, the SALT agreement, and now a

---

* Negroponte paid dearly for his independence. Kissinger, after becoming Secretary of State in the fall of 1973, ordered the Foreign Service officer banished to the American Embassy in Quito, Ecuador. Another factor in the reassignment was undoubtedly Kissinger's belief that Negroponte had been one of Tad Szulc's main sources in his account of the Vietnam negotiations published in the Summer 1974 issue of Foreign Policy, "Behind the Vietnam Cease-Fire Agreement."

settlement in Vietnam. Kissinger "was smiling the broadest smile I had ever seen," Nixon wrote. The North Vietnamese, Kissinger told the President, had made concessions that "amounted to a complete capitulation by the enemy; they were accepting a settlement on our terms." The only hint of doubt came from Haig. "I noticed that Haig seemed rather subdued . . ." Nixon wrote. "I asked him directly how he felt about these terms from Thieu's point of view. He replied that he honestly felt this was a good deal for Thieu. He was worried, however, about how Thieu himself would react to it."

Kissinger, in his memoirs, did not recall the colloquy: "Nixon remembers Haig was worried; I have no such recollection. It made no difference, for Haig strongly endorsed the agreement." Haig did endorse the agreement, and continued to do so in front of Kissinger. The evidence is clear, nonetheless, that Haig, like Negroponte, had grave doubts about Thieu. Haig's role in this period is difficult to trace, because he did not express his opposition to Kissinger's policy for another week, and then only after forming an alliance with Haldeman and Colson. As for the main participants, Nixon and Kissinger, they did not come close to telling the extent of the infighting that undermined the chances for a preelection peace agreement.

The Kalbs, in their biography, described Haig as joining Negroponte in the belief that Kissinger had pushed too quickly for an agreement in the October talks. "The smartest thing we could have done," one official told the Kalbs, "was fly back to Washington, get a good night's sleep, clear the fog out of our minds, check out the draft carefully . . . and then return to Paris for another hard look. . . . But no, Henry would have none of that. He wanted the deal, and he wanted it then."

Kissinger was euphoric by the time he returned to Washington. He was convinced, as he wrote, that "Thieu would happily go along with an agreement better in almost all essentials than the terms we had been offering with his concurrence for two years." In reaching this conclusion, which all evidence indicates he honestly held at the time, Kissinger chose to ignore the fact that Thieu's "concurrence" to the previous peace approaches had been granted in the firm belief that no settlement would be reached. If the White House wanted to posture with a peace offer, Thieu had been ready to accommodate. Kissinger also ignored the stream of increasingly hostile memoranda from Nha; and he ignored a mid-October CIA assessment, later described by Frank Snepp in *Decent Interval*, which predicted that Thieu would "never support any cease-fire agreement that demanded political accommodations with the Communist or left NVA [North Vietnamese Army] forces in the South." Kissinger read the assessment, Snepp wrote, and then "impatiently tossed it aside. Too much gloom, he declared." Kissinger must have thought that Hanoi's concession in granting Thieu a continued reign as President would be more than enough. He decided to deliver that news himself.

On October 14, Thieu—who already knew Kissinger was planning another visit—received a memorandum from Ambassador Bunker that was, at best, misleading. The two-page note did not inform the South Vietnamese that an agreement had been reached, but described the four days of talks in Paris as demonstrating "decided movement" by North Vietnam. "Dr. Kissinger's judgment is that the other side may be ready to accept a ceasefire in place in the not too distant future," Bunker wrote. Thieu was also given a copy of

Hanoi's "Administration of National Concord" proposal—the essential element in the Paris breakthrough—but the South Vietnamese were not informed that a few days earlier Kissinger had accepted the proposal in the name of the United States and South Vietnamese governments. Kissinger's decision to mislead Thieu was instinctive; apparently he convinced himself that during face-to-face meetings he could persuade Thieu, as he had persuaded Nixon, that Hanoi's concessions had been basic.*

By that point, however, President Thieu and Hoang Duc Nha were convinced that they had been betrayed. They had been told on October 11, while Kissinger was still in Paris, that he would fly to Saigon for another series of consultations. Once again, rumors of a Kissinger–Le Duc Tho settlement were rife. The rumors soon turned into fact. Nha recalls that late in the evening of October 17, two days before Kissinger's meeting with President Thieu, he received intelligence that a copy of ceasefire orders had been found on the body of a slain North Vietnamese soldier. Nha was convinced that the long-rumored settlement between Kissinger and Le Duc Tho "was already set up. We had our heads on a chopping block." He and Thieu both came to believe, he said, that Kissinger had been secretly working with Le Duc Tho since early August to resolve the war in a manner that favored the North. All the various North Vietnamese peace offers that had been provided to the South Vietnamese had been "cooked up just to keep us busy." Kissinger and Nixon had betrayed their ally.

Kissinger seems still to have had little insight into the suspicions of the South Vietnamese. Unable to restrain his sense of triumph, he spoke confidently to his favorite columnists during the five days he spent in Washington between negotiating sessions. He was to meet briefly again with the North Vietnamese in Paris on October 17 to settle the few outstanding issues, and then fly directly to his October 19 date in Saigon with Thieu. James Reston and Joseph Alsop both published optimistic columns shortly after he left Washington. Alsop was the most specific: ". . . the chances for an honorable, early settlement of the Vietnamese war appear to be reasonably good—and for the first time during the long, cruelly hard effort in which Henry Kissinger has been the President's other self from start to finish." Alsop also raised the question of who would be Secretary of State in Nixon's second term, and came down strongly for Kissinger. "Obviously," wrote Alsop, "he would like to assist in the completion of the grand design for world relationships that the President has already so successfully sketched out."

The few days between October 12 and October 17 would mark a high point for Kissinger. Most of the senior aides in the American government, including Secretary of State William Rogers, shared his enthusiasm for the settlement that would permit Thieu to stay in power. Few, obviously, understood the high price Hanoi had exacted for that concession. Within days, Kissinger would discover that neither his personal charm not the peace accord was enough for

---

* Kissinger, in his memoirs, made it clear that he was misleading Bunker as well as Thieu. In a message sent shortly before his trip to Saigon, Kissinger informed Bunker that he would visit Paris on October 17 and "anticipate that the other side will propose a political formula which will require far less of Thieu . . ." At that point, of course, the agreement had been struck. Bunker, in relaying Kissinger's information to Thieu, was himself victimized. Deception is routine in diplomatic life; the point here is that Kissinger's decision not to take Thieu into his confidence immediately was another mistake in judgment that helped stiffen South Vietnamese resistance to the settlement.

Nguyen Van Thieu. The South Vietnamese President saw what Kissinger somehow could not: that the legalization of the PRG, coupled with the permanent presence of Hanoi's troops in the South and the cessation of American bombing, spelled his eventual doom. Over the next few weeks, however, as Kissinger frantically pressured Thieu to sign the peace agreement, the South Vietnamese President would have a secret ally—Richard Nixon.

39

VIETNAM: POLITICS BEFORE PEACE

ON OCTOBER 16, Kissinger prepared to leave Washington for the mission on which, he wrote, "all our hopes had been concentrating for four years: the end of the war in Indochina." The plans were all in order: He would stop briefly in Paris to settle the few outstanding issues of the peace treaty, move on to Saigon and the expected endorsement by Nguyen Van Thieu, and then, in keeping with the schedule worked out with Le Duc Tho, fly secretly to Hanoi and initial the treaty. Then a return to Washington by October 24, where his trip would be dramatically announced to the world by the President. It would be his ultimate achievement, one to match his secret trip to Peking and propel him into the Cabinet as Secretary of State in Nixon's second term.

Nixon's attitude continued to veer. To his political advisers he intensified his bitter complaining about Kissinger, often railing against the national security adviser for his insistence on trying—in Nixon's view—to win the election himself. There is no evidence, however, that Nixon ever directly confronted Kissinger, or even saw to it that Kissinger was privately told his real attitude. More significant, there is no evidence that Nixon challenged Kissinger's authority to negotiate with Hanoi in the name of the presidency during the critical third week in October, when Kissinger and Nixon assured Hanoi in a cable that they considered the peace agreement complete. In this tense and dramatic period, Haig was totally devoted to Nixon, and representing the President's views in the constant exchange of messages with the traveling Kissinger. Kissinger was alone in trying to rush an end to the war.

Nixon's problem was to stop Kissinger without being caught at it, because as long as Kissinger persisted, the President could not afford to appear to be obstructing his efforts. Nixon was also afraid of derailing the peace process permanently; as Colson puts it, he did not want to "upset the apple cart and lose the peace" after November 7. The President's solution was to do all he could to delay the negotiations, even if it meant that he had to doublecross Henry Kissinger in the process. The doublecross must have seemed by far the easiest solution. To instruct Kissinger formally not to conclude a peace treaty by election day would be an invitation for him to leak word to his friends in the press and in Georgetown. But Kissinger cannot have had any illusions about what was going on. Every presidential act had a hidden meaning. Kissinger quoted in his memoirs, without comment, a hand-written note from the President that he found aboard his White House plane before departing for

Paris. "First," the President wrote, "do what is right without regard to the election. Second, we cannot let a chance to end the war honorably slip away. As far as the elections are concerned, a settlement that did not come unstuck would help among young voters, but we do not need it to win. A settlement that became unstuck would hurt, but would not be fatal . . . do what is right to secure an honorable peace, but do not let the timing be affected by the election."

The note, which was leaked to the press by the White House, was not a noble gesture of support. John Scali, the President's public relations aide, is matter-of-fact about its real purpose: "What Nixon was doing there was basically making it impossible for Kissinger to say that if the negotiations failed, it was because Nixon was on his back, making impossible demands." Nixon wrote it by hand, Scali added, "to protect himself."

In these critical weeks, as the *Washington Post* relentlessly investigated the Watergate scandal, political fear was strong in the White House.* The Presi-

---

* On October 10, 1972, for example, Bob Woodward and Carl Bernstein of the *Post* reported that there was a link between the Watergate break-in and an extensive White House-directed campaign of political sabotage. On October 15, the *Post* tied that sabotage operation, led by Donald Segretti, to Dwight Chapin, Richard Nixon's appointments secretary and H. R. Haldeman's close aide. Surprisingly the *Post* articles did not create a serious political problem for the President; the other news media—and therefore the public—did not yet find them credible. The men in the White House, however, knew how damaging the full story could be: All the Segretti activities had been authorized by Haldeman, obviously with the President's approval. On the fifteenth, a Sunday, John Ehrlichman summoned a number of top aides to a White House meeting, according to John Dean's 1973 testimony before the Senate Watergate Committee, at which Ronald Ziegler, the President's press secretary, was extensively coached on how to respond to press queries. A partial transcript of the session was provided by Dean to the Senate. In it, Ehrlichman suggests at one point that Ziegler parry queries by saying "We are going to see all kinds of Presidential friends, Presidential staff, Presidential relatives, dogs, etc., pictures on the front page of local newspapers to counteract the fact that McGovern is two to one behind. I am not going to try to cope with these unfounded stories." Chapin, who had withheld mention of Haldeman's role in the Segretti operation during an interview with the FBI, then offered his suggestion: "I am not going to dignify desperation politics." Another Ehrlichman suggestion for Ziegler: "Dwight Chapin is terribly offended at the treatment he got over the weekend. I approached him to the possibility of coming out here [to a press briefing]. He said he would never again speak to any member of the press and he would like your apologies." The attitude closely paralleled that of the President. In his memoirs, Nixon quoted a diary entry from October 15: "The big story on Chapin broke today and it was certainly guilt by association, hearsay, etc. McCarthyism at its very worst. In any event, as I told Haldeman, we could not be knocked off balance by these stories . . . Haldeman indicated that Chapin felt he was expendable. I said under no circumstances would we move in that direction because it was not fair since the press were simply using a double standard on all of this." Chapin was forced to resign early in 1973, a decision, according to Dean's testimony, that the President made in mid-November.

Nixon's diary entries, as reprinted in his memoirs, show the extent of his obsession with Watergate before the election. On October 25 the *Post* linked Haldeman to control of the slush fund that financed the Watergate break-in. The real White House fear at this point, less than two weeks before the election, was not of the press, but of the FBI agents who—in obvious frustration over the high-level cover-up—were leaking information to Woodward and Bernstein. In their 1973 book, *Watergate,* a team of London *Sunday Times* reporters concluded that by mid-October "the *Post* was outgunned" by the White House on the story and "was in no position to detail the evidence for the truth of its allegations"—largely because of the need to protect sources. "Moreover," the English journalists noted, Woodward and Bernstein were "practically alone" on the story. "The *New York Times* routinely followed up the *Post*'s stories but never mobilised an independent investigation of its own. . . . And the *Los Angeles Times,* the only other paper with the necessary investigative resources, did not show strongly until well after the election. . . . Six months later, in the afterglow of justification, the 'American press' took credit for the exposure of Watergate, but only a very narrow segment deserved it." The White House, then knowingly in the midst of a criminal cover-up, escaped immediate exposure because the press failed to accomplish what history has ironically recorded it as accomplishing—the end of a presidency.

dent's advisers continued to warn against a last-minute settlement. "Our great fear," Colson recalls, was that a settlement "would let people say, 'Well, thank goodness the war is over. Now we can go on and worry about peace and we will elect a Democrat because Democrats always do more in peacetime.' The other thing," Colson adds, "was that we didn't want to appear to be exploiting, as Johnson had done in '68 with the bombing pause, which was so blatantly and transparently political. After the fifteenth of October it was definitely contrary to our interest to get an agreement." These views, which were shared by Haldeman, also won support from Haig, who met regularly with the President and Haldeman during Kissinger's absences. Haig's argument was that Nguyen Van Thieu would never agree to the terms negotiated by Kissinger, and it was a point of view the general had not yet imparted to Kissinger. John Connally was also called in and spent more than three hours, according to Secret Service logs, with the President and others on the afternoon of October 17.

Kissinger spent that day in discussions with Xuan Thuy in Paris; the two men were unable to resolve at once the still outstanding issues of weapons replacement and civilian-prisoner release. Nonetheless, Kissinger claimed in his memoirs, all seemed to be going well. He had heard the day before from Haig that Laird and General Abrams had voiced their support for the proposed agreement in meetings with the President. In a later cable, wrote Kissinger, "Haig reported that Nixon was enthusiastic" and had even offered some advice: "The President suggested that I treat the forthcoming meetings with Thieu as a 'poker game' in which I should hold back the 'trump card' until the last trick." *

In his memoirs, Kissinger provided no hint of his real feelings at this point. The fact that John Connally spent an afternoon discussing who knows what with the President must have been disconcerting.† One hint can be found in the Kalbs' biography, which says that Kissinger became "almost hysterical" as the talks with Xuan Thuy dragged on. Kissinger had to leave Orly airport in France by 11:00 P.M. on October 18 to arrive in Saigon by the next day and thus maintain his rigid timetable. "I'm leaving. I must go to Saigon," the Kalbs quoted Kissinger as announcing shortly before 10:00 P.M. "Dr. Kissinger," Xuan Thuy replied, "if you go to Saigon, we'll never settle it." Kissinger gathered his papers and fled, telling the Vietnamese, "We'll solve it by cable."

North Vietnam was subsequently warned by Kissinger that the date for Kissinger's visit to Hanoi to initial the agreement would be delayed until the outstanding issues were resolved. Another meeting was proposed between Kissinger and Le Duc Tho, perhaps in Vientiane, Laos, with the timetable for formal signing moved back. Nguyen Co Thach later described Hanoi's suspicion: "We have a time schedule and now he says that they could not keep the

---

* Nixon and Kissinger, by now both high-stakes international gamblers, were obviously not poker players.
† Connally, with his tough talk in early May urging the bombing of North Vietnam, had emerged as the chief beneficiary, among Nixon's close aides, of the Moscow summit. Much of Kissinger's worry over his—and Connally's—future was captured in the informal office journal of one of his personal aides. In mid-June, the journal quoted Kissinger as resolving to resign if Connally were named Secretary of State in Nixon's second term. Kissinger's doubts had intensified when Nixon made Connally his personal envoy on a three-week tour of eleven nations in the Middle East, the Pacific, and Asia that summer. "Kissinger is petrified of Connally," the journal noted.

schedule. We smelled something. . . . It's a very difficult time for Nixon. He must accept or not accept."

Officials in Hanoi obviously sensed that negotiations were moving into a critical phase, for on October 18 they decided to accept the White House formulations on the outstanding issues: The Vietcong prisoners in the South would not be immediately released and Washington would be permitted to resupply its allies on the one-for-one ratio. Hanoi, as Thach explained, was operating on the assumption that Nixon wanted a Vietnam settlement before the election for political reasons; Kissinger's urgency, they thought, reflected that view. The extent of the Nixon-Kissinger estrangement was not at all clear in Hanoi, because Kissinger continued to conduct the negotiations in Nixon's name without challenge from the White House and the effect was to give the appearance of business as usual. "As in all other negotiations I conducted on his behalf," Kissinger wrote, "Nixon was given a copy of everything sent in his name; he certainly had an opportunity to countermand any message. He never did so. Once he had given general guidelines, he had no desire to involve himself in the process of negotiations. Nor would the text of documents interest him."

It was an astonishingly ambivalent position for the President. He had become violently opposed to a settlement prior to the election, yet he did not say as much to his national security adviser. He also permitted Kissinger to negotiate, in his name, with North Vietnam over the issue of when Kissinger would arrive in triumph in Hanoi to initial the peace agreement.

Kissinger seemed to understand how to work his will with Nixon. In a meeting in Washington, the President agreed with Kissinger on the need to reduce the level of American bombing north of the Twentieth Parallel in North Vietnam. Hanoi was further assured that all bombing of the North would cease the day before Kissinger's arrival there to initial the treaty. In his memoirs, Nixon acknowledged these concessions but recounted how he had "told" Kissinger that "there would be no bombing *halt* until the agreement was signed." The pause, of course, was more than ample demonstration of Kissinger's ability to deliver what he promised, for, as he noted in his memoirs, "I had already agreed with Le Duc Tho that we would decrease the bombing of the North during the final phase of the negotiations." Kissinger had made a commitment for a bombing pause, not a halt, before clearing it with the President. His ability to manipulate Nixon, who remained convinced he had turned down a proposed halt, remained intact even during this period of acute distrust. "I was not going to be taken in by the mere prospect of an agreement," Nixon wrote proudly, "as Johnson had been in 1968."

There was much irony in all this. Nixon's reluctance to share his honest feelings with Kissinger gave Kissinger the free hand he needed, while at the same time Nixon's private hostility to a preelection settlement was dooming Kissinger's efforts.

There was no possible way for Hanoi to perceive what was going on, to understand that its concessions on the prisoner and resupply issues had been wasted. Kissinger, with his insistence on maintaining the timetable, was playing into the hands of his enemies in the White House and Saigon.

The South Vietnamese leadership had become more than suspicious of Kissinger by the time of his arrival in Saigon; he was seen as an enemy of the state, as a man whose contempt for Asians was acute, and as a negotiator desperately eager to sell a bad bargain.

His tactics did little to change that view. He was convinced, his aides recall, that Nguyen Van Thieu would share his enthusiasm for the agreement. "The mood on the long ride to Saigon was optimistic," Kissinger wrote. "All of us except John Negroponte thought that Thieu would be overjoyed by the agreement." Winston Lord later acknowledged to a journalist that "It was naïve and somewhat unfair to Thieu to think we could get him to sign off on it." It was more than naïve: It was a monumental error, one of Kissinger's most profound as national security adviser.

John Negroponte was not alone in predicting that Thieu would be hostile to the peace treaty. In a meeting in the American Embassy, Kissinger finally permitted the long-suffering Ellsworth Bunker and other officials to review the agreement. Bunker, not surprisingly, assured Kissinger, as Kissinger wrote in his memoirs, that it "exceeded what he had thought attainable; less would still have been practically and morally justifiable." However, Charles S. Whitehouse, Bunker's deputy, was quick to warn Kissinger, "It's not going to fly." Asked later about the other officials who professed their admiration for the agreement, Whitehouse stated the obvious: "What else could they say? What good would it do? Kissinger was there and it was pretty close to what might go. Henry had his ass on the line."*

There was no dearth of clues to South Vietnamese feelings. In his memoirs, Kissinger complained that upon his arrival at the Presidential Palace "I was kept waiting for fifteen minutes in full view of the press." He was then greeted by Hoang Duc Nha, who had drafted the most stinging memoranda attacking North Vietnam's proposals. It was agreed that Nha would serve as interpreter for Thieu during the meetings with Kissinger, an obvious rebuke to Kissinger, who did not miss the point. "Considering that every Vietnamese present at least understood English," Kissinger wrote, "this indicated that Thieu was not going to make things easy for us."

Kissinger, who was in the position of having negotiated an agreement a week earlier without telling his allies in Saigon, began by presenting a letter from Nixon that said the proposed agreement was "the best we will be able to get and . . . meets my *absolute* condition—that the GVN must survive as a free country." Thieu listened quietly as Kissinger described a huge stockpile of

---

* Whitehouse later assembled all the embassy's junior officers, told them essentials of the agreement, which Thieu had refused to sign, and ordered them to suspend all other activities and concentrate on lobbying their Vietnamese counterparts and friends. One junior officer recalls that Whitehouse told them to explain the agreement as "the best they could get." Many of the young Foreign Service men shared Whitehouse's skepticism, and one called his lobbying missions "Operation Big Lie," a reflection of his view that the agreement was a sellout of the South Vietnamese. Another saw the draft treaty as "a formula for defeat" for the South. These officials also shared the opinion, it should be noted, that the Thieu regime was undemocratic and very much part of the problem in the failure to win the war. Kissinger acknowledged Whitehouse's objections in his memoirs but went on to quote Philip C. Habib as saying that the treaty "exceeded his highest hopes . . . every American senior official familiar with the negotiations and with Vietnamese had endorsed our effort." Habib, then Ambassador to South Korea, was in Saigon at Kissinger's request during his meetings with Thieu. The sharply differing views of the junior Foreign Service officers simply did not reach Kissinger.

arms—part of an enhanced resupply operation that had begun during the North Vietnamese offensive in May—that would flow into the South. Within a few months, South Vietnam would emerge with the fourth-largest air force in the world, as more than five hundred helicopters and fighter aircraft were supplied by the Nixon Administration. Huge numbers of tanks, armored personnel carriers, artillery, jet engines, and spare parts would also be shipped.

Thieu said little about the proposed peace treaty in that first meeting. Years later, in an interview with a Canadian television crew, he summarized, in his imperfect and often vulgar English, his sense of betrayal: "What happened Mr. Kissinger have negotiated over our head with the Communist and try to impose on us a peace that he has agreed with the Communist . . . North Vietnam troops has been allowed to stay forever in South Vietnam and no clause at all in the draft of that treaty had mentioned how and when the North Vietnamese troops will leave South Vietnam to go back to North Vietnam. That's the point we have fought from the beginning . . . The second point, in the treaty even though they use the very elegant terminology maybe to shit the United States [citizenry], but they cannot shit us, the Vietnamese . . . there's a coalition government, camouflaged under a form of National Council. Now for years I say never, never, never a coalition, never accept a coalition . . . I say that the life of South Vietnam rely on those two main points."

Kissinger somehow managed to leave that first meeting, as he claimed in his memoirs, "very optimistic" about progress: "Thieu's questions and his eagerness to discuss Enhance Plus [the stepped-up resupply program] suggested that he was moving toward a settlement." Such optimism could have been based only on Kissinger's inherent contempt for the South Vietnamese, who had gone along with Nixon's stratagems in the past without serious complaint. Perhaps he thought it inconceivable that Nguyen Van Thieu would challenge his, and Nixon's, authority. Perhaps he viewed the American resupply effort as a good enough bribe. If Thieu continued to balk, Kissinger was obviously convinced that some sharp words from Nixon would bring him around.

He would spend four more testy days in Saigon, but the peace proposal was dead by the end of the lunch hour. Hoang Duc Nha and a small group of other Saigon aides, including Tran Kim Phuong, the South Vietnamese Ambassador to Washington, took the document with them to a nearby restaurant and gave it close scrutiny. "To our horror," Phuong recalls, "we saw a lot of things we could not accept. We saw that Kissinger had been tricked by Le Duc Tho because he was so eager to sign the document." There was angry talk of Kissinger being in league with Le Duc Tho and the North Vietnamese "to trick us." Phuong thought differently: "My judgment was that Nixon and Kissinger just wanted out from Vietnam. I'm one of the rare Vietnamese who believes that Kissinger was not trying to sell us out."

Later that afternoon, Hoang Duc Nha attended a meeting of the Vietnamese National Security Council and began compiling what would become a list of sixty-nine specific objections to the proposed treaty. The agreement "was a total contradiction to what Bunker told us," Nha says. "We were never consulted. During the past two months, the U.S. had led us to believe they were talking, but when in the hell did they negotiate this?"

That evening, Kissinger learned of Hanoi's decision to concede the two outstanding issues of the peace agreement. "Hanoi accepted not only the substance of our position but also the text we had sent from the plane" en route to Saigon, Kissinger wrote. In Nixon's name, Kissinger cabled Hanoi that "The text of the agreement is considered complete." Nixon, in his memoirs, acknowledged the message without noting that it was drafted by Kissinger: "I sent a cable to Pham Van Dong saying that the agreement was now considered complete." There were lesser issues still unresolved, dealing with the return of American prisoners from Laos and Cambodia and the technical issues of the ceasefire; the United States proposed to resolve those by making a series of unilateral declarations that would have no legal force. Within twenty-four hours, Hanoi cabled its agreement. Nixon also reassured North Vietnam that Kissinger was still planning to fly to Hanoi to initial the agreement, although his arrival would have to be delayed a few days—a concession to the problems in Saigon. Finally, the Nixon cable emphasized that the ceasefire throughout South Vietnam would begin, as planned, on October 31.

As far as North Vietnam was concerned, it had a deal.

Nixon's performance in acceding to Kissinger's October 19 cable defies rational recounting. He was telling Hanoi that the peace treaty was complete, that nothing Nguyen Van Thieu would say or do could affect the agreement. It was a position that he did not accept, and one that his political aides were beginning to deny in public. That morning the *Los Angeles Times* had reported from Washington that "no breakthrough in the talks has occurred . . . No dramatic change in the situation can be expected before the U.S. election." The dispatch, by Robert C. Toth, accurately summarized the prevailing political views: "[T]here is some belief at the White House that Mr. Nixon is better off politically with the status quo than with a settlement before election day." Toth acknowledged later that his information for the dispatch came from senior White House officials, which raises the simple question: What was Nixon thinking?

Did he consider the cable to Hanoi just another easily disregarded campaign promise? Did he believe, on the basis of Kissinger's unrealistic reports from Saigon, that Thieu would go along? Was he reluctant to confront Kissinger with his indecision while Kissinger was still in Saigon, and still capable of causing great damage to the reelection campaign? Finally, did Nixon understand all along that at the critical moment he would *not* join Kissinger in pressuring Thieu to sign, thus avoiding a settlement that could limit his reelection margin and also inflicting grievous damage to Kissinger's international reputation as a negotiator? Was he setting up Henry Kissinger?

Whatever the answer, it was a reckless and dishonest moment in Nixon's presidency—akin, perhaps, to his decisions about the Watergate cover-up.

As Nixon was assuring the North Vietnamese that all was well, the tension mounted in Saigon. On the evening of the nineteenth a copy of the Vietnamese-language version of the draft treaty was delivered to Hoang Duc Nha in the palace. There were discrepancies that led him to conclude that Hanoi had taken even greater advantage of Kissinger than he had first thought. Hanoi's phrase to describe the powers of the National Council suggested that the election commission would be a "governmental" structure rather than an "administrative" unit, a distinction that loomed large to the suspicious South

Vietnamese. Hanoi had also used a pejorative slang expression for American soldiers that, as interpreted on the streets of Saigon, meant "dirty Yankee." It was more ammunition for use against the draft treaty.

The roof began to fall in at the third meeting, when Thieu, finally dealing with the main issue, reeled off a stream of specific complaints. The key issues were the presence of North Vietnamese troops in the South, the coalition government, and the policing of the ceasefire. "He told the Americans," Nha remembers, "that unless we discuss the principles we refuse to discuss the details." At one point, Nha recalls, "Kissinger told us a story. He said Le Duc Tho had made so many concessions that he 'cried with me. He was so sad about having to sign that he cried.' "

"It was pure bullshit," Nha says coldly, and even the much less cynical Thieu was aware that it was an improbable scene.* During the meeting, as Kissinger acknowledged in his memoirs, he extended the promise of swift American retaliation in case of North Vietnamese violation of the ceasefire. It was a promise, later reinforced by Nixon, that would cause consternation in Congress. Under the circumstances, however, at a time when Thieu and his aides were discounting much of the American rhetoric, the promise was hardly persuasive. Saigon had no interest in agreeing to the peace treaty, with or without such promises.

Again Kissinger's report to Nixon emphasized optimism. "They undoubtedly feel they need more time, but one senses they will always feel that way," he cabled. "They know what they have to do and it is very painful. They are probably even right. If we could last two more years they would have it made. . . . I have the sense that they are slowly coming along and are working themselves into the mental frame of accepting the plan, but their self-respect requires a sense of participation."

Kissinger was telling his President that the problems were merely cosmetic; once Saigon got its "sense of participation," all would be settled. In fact, Kissinger was barely hanging on in Saigon and Nixon knew it. In his memoirs, he accurately characterized Thieu as wanting to make it clear that "he was neither surrendering any of South Vietnam's vital interests nor accepting terms dictated to him by Washington. The problem was that this would take time," Nixon wrote, "and time was the one thing we did not have if we were to keep to the agreed signing schedule." Kissinger's trip to Hanoi was in jeopardy.

Haig now moved openly. Knowing that Nixon, Haldeman, and Colson were in agreement on not wanting a settlement before the election, he gave them a rationalization in the shape of a chestnut from the early Johnson Administration: the threat of a Communist bloodbath. Nixon, in his memoirs, quoted from a diary entry at this time in which he cited Haig's report that the North Vietnamese were moving "very, very strongly around Saigon . . . to get as much territory as they can." He quoted Haig as further telling him that the intelli-

* Other South Vietnamese officials who were interviewed remember that Nha was as intimately involved as he claims in rebuffing Kissinger. These officials invariably commented on Nha's brashness but corroborated much of his account. For example, Le Chi Thao, a junior Foreign Ministry official, described Kissinger as a man who had acute contempt for Asians. "It seemed to me that Kissinger didn't care whether you knew he was lying or not," Thao said. "When he lied, it was so obvious that it was humiliating to us—even a child wouldn't believe him. Too obvious lies do not make you angry, but humiliate you. That's what made Thieu very upset."

gence indicated that the North Vietnamese and Vietcong had "instructed their cadres the moment a ceasefire is announced to kill all of the opponents in the area that they control. This would be a murderous bloodbath, and it's something that we have to consider as we press Thieu to accept what is without question a reasonable political settlement but which must also be justified on security grounds."

There was no bloodbath in the South after Hanoi's victory in 1975, and there were no serious reports of Communist bloodbaths in the fall of 1972. Both the Saigon regime and Hanoi were involved in land grabbing, as American correspondents reported, but these had little to do with Thieu's objections to the peace agreement. In relaying such allegations to Nixon, Haig was sabotaging Kissinger, and in his treachery he was doing no more to Kissinger and his peace efforts in 1972 than Kissinger himself had done to Lyndon Johnson in 1968. Kissinger had posed as a friend of the Democrats in the critical days of the negotiations before the 1968 elections, and had then relayed his information to the enemy, the Nixon camp. Haig, in turn, was relaying Kissinger's secrets to Kissinger's enemies, the President and his political cronies. Kissinger's reward had been the security adviser's job; Haig sought a similarly high reward, an eventual nomination as chairman of the Joint Chiefs of Staff.*

By October 20, Kissinger's second day in Saigon, all the senior aides in the White House seemed to be dissociating themselves from the peace process. In his memoirs, General William Westmoreland, the retiring Army Chief of Staff, recalled Nixon's assurances that "he was not to be pressured by the forthcoming election into premature signing of an agreement." Westmoreland joined with Haig and the President's political advisers in urging that Nixon reopen the Paris negotiations and insist that Hanoi's troops be compelled to withdraw from the South. The general also wrote of a conversation with Haig in which Haig complained that "Mel Laird had turned 'Dove' and that he, Haig, was the only person in the Administration advising the President to take a tough stand." After the meeting with Westmoreland, Haig drafted a cable to Kissinger for the President warning anew of the danger of a "pre-election blow-up with Thieu . . . Thieu's acceptance must be wholehearted so that the charge cannot be made that we have forced him into a settlement which was not in the interest of preventing a Communist takeover of a substantial part of the territory of South Vietnam."

Kissinger understood only too well. ". . . I began to be nagged by the unworthy notion that I was being set up as the fall guy in case anything went wrong," he wrote. "Nixon ironically was implying the same charge against me that others were to make against Nixon—that I was rushing it for the elec-

---

* Such an appointment was impossible for Haig so long as Laird was Secretary of Defense, but the President tried his best early in 1973 with Elliot Richardson, Laird's replacement. The Kissinger office journal quotes Nixon as telling Richardson that "he wanted a new Chairman of the Joint Chiefs of Staff—someone on the Haig model. The President mentioned someone along the Haig model three or four times to Richardson." Haldeman was also said to have supported Haig's nomination. Richardson, from all available evidence, ignored Nixon's hints; not even his close aides in the Defense Department recall any conversation about naming Haig to the top military job. Another factor may have been Kissinger, who was doing all possible in early 1973 to prevent Haig's appointment. The office journal reported that Haig was "in trouble" over the appointment because "Kissinger has been talking to the President presenting evidence . . . that Haig has been leaking to the press." How serious Nixon was in all this is not known.

tion," he added. Kissinger, who most certainly was rushing the negotiations for the election, took the offensive, telling Haig and Nixon in a return cable that "If I am being told to stop this process, then this should be made unambiguous. . . . I am prepared to stall this operation if I receive a clear signal to do so." It was a challenge he could make with impunity: Richard Nixon would never hand him such direct evidence.

On October 21, as the third day of meetings began, Kissinger was given a list of twenty-three proposed changes in the agreement that had been drawn up by South Vietnamese officials, including Nha and Ambassador Phuong. The objections included continued opposition to the election commission and to Hanoi's troops in the South. "Kissinger was angry," Phuong recalls, "but he thought that our level was not important. He entertained the hope that he could swing Thieu," who had not attended the meeting. In his memoirs, Kissinger professed to have been "quite optimistic" after the meeting, a state of mind that defies belief. The blowup came that evening at the American Embassy, when Nha telephoned Kissinger to cancel a conference between Kissinger and Thieu that had been delayed all afternoon. Kissinger became even angrier when, during the conversation, Thieu's motorcade passed the embassy, sirens at full blast, more than two hours after the two men were to meet. Nguyen Van Thieu was treating Kissinger as Kissinger had treated so many others. Nha describes the reaction: "I am the special envoy from the United States President, I am not an errand boy." In his memoirs, Kissinger acknowledged his loss of temper: "Whatever their concerns, no ally had a right to treat an emissary of the President of the United States this way. . . . We felt that impotent rage so cunningly seeded in foreigners by the Vietnamese."

Later that night, Thieu telephoned Bunker to accuse Kissinger and Haig of trying to organize a coup d'état against him. "The phone calls from the Palace could leave no doubt that the mood was turning hostile and, in the absence of specific objections, we did not even know how to resolve matters or what there was to resolve," Kissinger wrote. "We were locked into a schedule that was to take me to Hanoi in seventy-two hours while our Vietnamese ally was disintegrating emotionally."

Kissinger and Thieu did meet again for three hours the next morning. Nha recalls the format: Thieu would raise an objection and Kissinger would try to explain it away. The tripartite election commission thus became, in Kissinger's words, "a miserable little council." In his memoirs, Kissinger insisted that he left the session "encouraged;" he also cabled Washington: "I think we finally made a breakthrough."

Kissinger fled the meeting with Thieu to fly to Phnom Penh, his only visit to Cambodia during the war, to discuss the pending agreement at a lunch with Lon Nol. It was a farcical meeting. Hoang Duc Nha heard later that Lon Nol, believing the war would be over, "broke out champagne" during the meal. The compliant Cambodian leader somehow accepted at face value Kissinger's suggestion that the North Vietnamese had promised to leave Cambodia, when in fact Le Duc Tho had explicitly ruled out a ceasefire in Cambodia on the ground that Hanoi's influence over the Khmer Rouge was insignificant. A Kissinger aide who attended the lunch recalls that Lon Nol, who was not shown a copy of the draft treaty, effusively thanked Kissinger for arranging the ceasefire and asked at one point, "When are the North Vietnamese leaving?" Cambodia was still a sideshow.*

Back in Saigon for a late afternoon meeting, Kissinger finally faced up to Thieu's opposition. He reported to Haig afterward that "Thieu has rejected the entire plan or any modification of it and refuses to discuss any further negotiations on the basis of it." Nixon's memoirs have him saying: "I need not tell you the crisis with which this confronts us."

Hoang Duc Nha recalls Kissinger's anger. "I have to tell you," he exclaimed, "we have a deadline to meet. I have to be in Hanoi to initial this." Nha insists that it was the first time he or Thieu realized Kissinger was negotiating under a deadline. At the end, there was nervousness, with Kissinger characteristically biting his fingernails. He announced that he would return to Washington but requested a brief farewell meeting the next morning, October 23, "to give the impression that the talks are proceeding." Neither side was to tell the press anything about his visit.

Personal recollections of the participants in such emotional proceedings are bound to be open to challenge on specific issues, but one conclusion does seem clear: Henry Kissinger did not need four days to understand the depth of Nguyen Van Thieu's opposition. A few months later, in his interview with Oriana Fallaci, Thieu described one of his meetings with Kissinger: "You are a giant, I told him. You don't care about anything because you have nothing to be afraid of. You weigh two hundred pounds, and if you swallow the wrong pill you don't even notice it . . . But I'm just a little man, maybe a little sick. I weigh hardly a hundred pounds, and if I swallow the same pill I can die of it. . . . You can allow yourself the luxury of accepting such an agreement. . . . For me, it's a matter of life and death. . . . What are 300,000 North Vietnamese to you? Nothing. What is the loss of South Vietnam to you? . . . For me it's not a question of choosing between Moscow and Peking. It's a question of choosing between life and death."

That evening Kissinger made a last-ditch effort to save his timetable, and in so doing triggered a near-mutiny in his National Security Council staff. He sent a cable to Nixon recommending that he keep his appointment in Hanoi and try to broker some revisions there. He also went a huge step further, according to an aide, in recommending that all American air support to the South Vietnamese be stopped, pending Thieu's agreement to the peace treaty. He was asking for a separate peace.

It was, perhaps, the ultimate moment of truth in the Nixon-Kissinger rela-

* In his memoirs, Kissinger praised Lon Nol because he had exhibited "none of the nitpicking of Saigon, or the insolence." He insisted, however, that Lon Nol's support for the agreement came "even though he understood that his was the one country in Indochina not given a specific date for a ceasefire . . ." Lon Nol had no such understanding. There is also evidence, as William Shawcross has pointed out, that a ceasefire in Cambodia—even if Hanoi had agreed—would have been questioned by Thieu. Any negotiated settlement in Cambodia would have involved the replacement of the Lon Nol government with a coalition that included the Khmer Rouge. The new government would thus not have been an ally of President Thieu, who believed that an anti-Communist government in Cambodia was essential. Nixon's and Kissinger's policy after the ceasefire in South Vietnam was to resupply the Cambodian Army and to divert American bombers from the South. In March, April, and May of 1973, B-52 bombers dropped some 95,000 tons of bombs over Cambodia; in all of 1972, when the war was still active in South and North Vietnam, less than 27,000 tons had fallen there.

tionship. Kissinger was badly exposed; it was *his* trip to Saigon and *his* desperate negotiating. If a settlement did not emerge, it would be *his* failure. Nixon, who had approved—or at least reviewed—Kissinger's cable telling Hanoi that the peace treaty was complete, was now being asked to pressure Thieu into acquiescence. Kissinger's misjudgment was not only of Thieu but of the President. He had vastly overestimated the President's willingness to force Thieu to sign, and he would pay the price for his misjudgment: a public defeat.

Nixon reprinted in his memoirs part of one message in which Kissinger pleaded for permission to go on to Hanoi: "We have obtained concessions that nobody thought were possible. . . . Washington must understand this is not a Sunday school picnic. We are dealing with fanatics. . . . We cannot be sure how long they will be willing to settle on the terms that are now within our grasp. To wash out the final leg could cost us dearly."

Nixon, however, had no intention—at least by the third week in October—of pressuring Thieu into a settlement. He would do so after the election, with the help of the mass bombing of Hanoi and Haiphong. At this point, he did what he had been unable to do earlier—he made it clear to Kissinger just where he stood. Kissinger noted in his memoirs that "Nixon vehemently rejected the option of going to Hanoi;" there was also "a flood of cables" from Haig with the same message. "Tempers rose dangerously on both sides of the Pacific Ocean," Kissinger wrote. Although very little of the White House's cable traffic was reproduced in the various memoirs, Kissinger published a portion of one of his rejoinders to Haig, cabled as he was flying home in defeat on October 23: "Many wars have been lost by untoward timidity. But enormous tragedies have also been produced by the inability of military people to recognize when the time for a settlement has arrived."*

The ever cautious Haig, while challenging Kissinger directly in cables, also struck at him inside the National Security Council, a step that could only reflect the extent of Nixon's anger. "Haig called in a group of us," one NSC aide recalls, "and, in essence, said, 'This time Henry's gone too far. He's through as a negotiator.' " The staff members, who included Jonathan Howe, Sven Kraemer, and William L. Stearman, were told that Kissinger's insistence on going to Hanoi had severely undermined his standing in the Oval Office.

"It was a unique experience," a participant recalls. "It looked like a mini-mutiny of the NSC staff. Haig put us in a difficult position. I witnessed something I'd never witnessed in all my years of public service." Haig's demeanor heightened the sense of unreality. "He looked a little elated," the aide recalls, "and there was an implication—he just didn't say it—that he was taking over. I never totally understood the point of the meeting." †

---

* Haig had initiated the internecine warfare, Kissinger seemed to suggest, by cabling a few days earlier that, in case of a blowup in the peace talks, the White House should denounce the National Council of National Reconciliation and Concord as a "coalition government" and characterize the agreement as Hanoi's attempt to improve its security without giving anything in return. Kissinger "considered this inconceivable," and he lectured Haig in a subsequent cable that we should not "poormouth an agreement that we will not be able to improve significantly and which we should use instead as a tremendous success."

† On March 30, 1981, moments after President Ronald Reagan was wounded in an assassination attempt in Washington, Haig, then Secretary of State, would stage another takeover attempt,

There was one last issue. Kissinger had promised Le Duc Tho that, assuming an agreement was reached, all bombing of North Vietnam would cease one day before his scheduled visit to Hanoi on October 24. "I did not think that we could fail to carry out this promise and continue full-scale bombing after Hanoi had accepted all our proposals," Kissinger wrote. Nixon, buttressed by Haig, bitterly opposed the halt. More cables were exchanged, which also did not appear in the memoirs. Kissinger backed off. "Nixon was right," he wrote. "I had overreached." The bombing of the North would continue.

At this point, Kissinger's essential toughness kept him going. There were few options. He could resign, and emerge as the scapegoat for the failed negotiations. Or he could somehow keep the negotiations alive, and save his job and his reputation in the process. He must have feared that Hanoi, outraged at its betrayal, would take its case to the court of world opinion—as Richard Nixon had done in January of 1972. His immediate need was to get back to Washington before Hanoi made the record public. The evening of October 22, Kissinger cabled Hanoi that he would be returning to Washington because "the difficulties in Saigon have proved somewhat more complex than originally anticipated." Hanoi was also told that it had erred in granting an interview on October 18 to Arnaud de Borchgrave, a *Newsweek* correspondent, in which Pham Van Dong spoke optimistically about the chance for a ceasefire. Kissinger seized on the interview, with its use of the word "coalition," as being a significant factor in Saigon's truculence. "The President must point out," Kissinger cabled in Nixon's name, "that the breach of confidence committed . . . with respect to the Arnaud de Borchgrave interview bears considerable responsibility for the state of affairs in Saigon."

Hanoi's leadership understood, however, that whatever problems Kissinger was having in Saigon had little to do with the *Newsweek* interview, in which Pham Van Dong had also acknowledged that his government was accepting what it publicly had insisted for years it would not: the continued existence of the Thieu regime. "One must accept that there are two administrations each in control of their own zones," the North Vietnamese Premier told de Borchgrave. "It's an undeniable fact. Everyone must respect this state of affairs." *

Kissinger's disingenuous cable to Hanoi included a reaffirmation of the American "commitment to the substance and basic principles of the draft agreement." Hanoi was also told that there would be a "longer message,"

---

declaring at the White House, "I am in control here." As in 1972, his actions were considered bizarre.

* De Borchgrave spent less than a week in Hanoi, leaving immediately after his interview with Pham Van Dong, and thus missed the real story: that the peace talks were breaking down. Michael Maclear, then a Canadian television correspondent based in London, was also in Hanoi at the time and, upon leaving, filed a dispatch for CBS News revealing that Hanoi no longer considered an agreement possible before the presidential elections. He quoted senior officials as saying that Washington "shows no positive sign of wanting to settle right now" because of opposition from Saigon. Maclear recalls that he interviewed Pham Van Dong two hours after de Borchgrave and was told of the perilous state of the talks on an off-the-record basis. "The point is," Maclear says, "that while everybody was believing that peace was at hand, he was telling me that the negotiations were very delicate and he still had grave doubts. I'd interviewed Pham Van Dong at least two times before. What he says on the record is never as significant as what he says off-record, and it's the off that you must go by."

explaining what had gone wrong, within a day. It was a stall, designed to hold off Hanoi's public denunciation until Kissinger could get back to Washington and repair the damage with his President and with Haig, who was now a force to be reckoned with. On October 23, his fifth day in Saigon, Kissinger made a brief farewell visit to Nguyen Van Thieu and sought to smooth over their dispute. "Outrageous as Thieu's conduct had been," he wrote, "our struggle had been over a principle: that America did not betray its friends. I agreed with Nixon that turning on Thieu would be incompatible with our sacrifice." The full retreat was on: "My duty was to manage affairs, and not let them slide deeper into chaos."

Shortly before leaving Saigon, Kissinger finally cabled the bad news to Hanoi: It would be "impossible" for him to go to North Vietnam to initial an agreement to which both sides had not agreed. Another meeting in Paris was needed "to reconcile the remaining issues." He also warned that if Hanoi chose to announce the terms of the peace agreement, it would "only lead to prolongation of the negotiations." In his memoirs, Kissinger reprinted much of the cable, which was dated October 23, but not all of it. The key paragraph, which was not published, included Kissinger's list of the "difficulties" that had caused the cancellation of the visit to Hanoi. "First, there is the excessive speed with which the DRV has sought to proceed. Second, the interview between the Prime Minister and the 'Newsweek' correspondent had a devastating impact at the crucial moment in Saigon. . . . Third, there is the problem which Dr. Kissinger has repeatedly mentioned to Special Advisor Le Duc Tho, represented by the DRV forces in the South. Fourth, there are several technical points which have arisen, but which could be readily solved in one more session. . . ."

Kissinger's motives for not publishing the operative paragraph of the cable seem obvious: It was hardly credible. Nguyen Co Thach, Le Duc Tho's senior aide, supplied the full text of the document to the author during interviews in 1979 in Hanoi. Thach said his government viewed the cable as "a threat to renew the bombing," as well as evidence of betrayal. "We knew that they would only like to have this understanding to move smoothly through the elections, and not to sign a peace agreement," he said. "They would like to have it settled but not signed, so they can say there is no more to the Vietnam War. . . . They would like to change it after the election.

"And they explain," Thach added caustically, "there is an interview with Pham Van Dong."

Eager to return to Nixon's good graces, Kissinger sent a message from his aircraft volunteering to take the heat in Washington, to explain publicly why the peace talks, which had dominated so much of the preelection news, had broken down. In his memoirs, Kissinger wrote that he agreed to hold a press conference "if Hanoi went public . . . [to] acknowledge the agreement, indicate that it represented major progress, but insist that some details remained to be worked out free of any artificial deadline."

Nixon, however, had a different recollection. Kissinger's news conference did not hinge on Hanoi's going public, because the White House did not expect that dreaded step immediately. "Kissinger had already planned to hold a press conference on October 26," Nixon wrote, "in order to reassure the North Vietnamese . . . as well as to distract attention from Thieu's obstructionism." The White House press apparatus, tightly controlled by Haldeman and the President, decided that Kissinger's news conference could take place before television cameras. It was the first time the whole country would be permitted to see Kissinger in action, and to hear his accent. Under the circumstances, as Kissinger had to suspect, it was a dubious honor.

In Saigon, Nguyen Van Thieu's aides, including Hoang Duc Nha, advised him to denounce the proposed peace agreement publicly. Kissinger's anger was still vivid to the men in Saigon; they were convinced he would retaliate. "After Kissinger left," Nha recalls, "we knew they'd accuse us of obstructing the peace. I urged Thieu to preempt the issue."

It was impossible, of course, for Thieu and Nha to realize how quickly Kissinger could change his point of view. He was already in the process of preparing for a news conference in which he would defend Nguyen Van Thieu. Thieu, unable to keep pace with the personalities in the White House, declared in a rambling two-hour televised speech that all the peace proposals discussed by Kissinger and Le Duc Tho were unacceptable. He would never agree to a coalition government, nor would he permit Hanoi's troops to remain in the South. He would agree to a ceasefire only if fighting ceased in Cambodia and Laos. He also proposed, as he and Nha had been insisting, that his government be permitted to participate in the negotiations with North Vietnam and the PRG. He further authorized the South Vietnamese Army to begin full-scale military activities against Vietcong forces, who had begun emerging from underground hideaways all over South Vietnam in anticipation of a ceasefire. "The Communist infrastructure must be wiped out quickly and mercilessly," Thieu announced. It was a renewed declaration of war on Hanoi.

These were Kissinger's most trying days. He was back in Washington, seeking to regain some measure of influence with the President. But the bitterness was acute. He turned to his most dependable friends, the press, to complain about his betrayal at the hands of the White House. "You can't believe how hard it is, especially for a Jew," he told one senior journalist, who was also Jewish. "You can't begin to imagine how much anti-Semitism there is at the top of this government—and I mean at the top." There was a somewhat different complaint to James Reston, whose column on October 25 called for an immediate ceasefire in South Vietnam, to be followed by a "long pause to give time for really careful and private negotiations." Reston did not explain why North Vietnam would agree to stop fighting without first obtaining some guarantee of legal standing for the PRG in South Vietnam. Kissinger, while obviously not fully describing the political realities to Reston, did convey an accurate sense of the personality conflicts inside the White House. Reston wrote: "And it is also true that there are influential men around the President who are arguing that he doesn't need a ceasefire before the election and will get a better settlement later on. . . . Well, nobody knows in this capital these days because—and this is the heart of the Washington problem—there is mistrust in the President because he trusts no man, even many of the men in his official family."

At midmorning on October 25, with Hanoi still silent, Kissinger initiated a lunch date with Max Frankel, Washington bureau chief of the *New York Times,* and outlined the essential details of the agreement. The meeting was in direct violation of the President's orders: Kissinger, as he wrote, had been emphatically told by Nixon shortly after his return from Saigon "to keep things quiet." Kissinger's lunch with Frankel was not an act of defiance but of anxiety, to insure his continued role in the peace process and also to put Thieu on notice. Kissinger knew he would be holding a news conference the next day, and he warned the South Vietnamese President, through Frankel, that he would have to live with the peace agreement. Thieu, wrote Frankel, though not ready to accede to the agreement, nonetheless "is believed here to have no logical alternative and his public position is thought to be mostly preparation for a final acquiescence."

One can only speculate at Kissinger's ultimate intentions in briefing Frankel and having his version of the peace treaty splashed all over the *Times*'s front page. One factor may have been political: Frankel's upbeat article, which was given the headline "Aides See a Truce in Few Weeks, Maybe by Election Day," continued to place the Nixon Administration in a position that had neutralized George McGovern since the secret talks began intensifying in midsummer. The Frankel dispatch also put the President far above the fray: "Mr. Nixon, feeling confident of re-election, is said to be insisting that the election is irrelevant, justifying neither haste nor delay."

Whatever the reason, Kissinger obviously felt he had done well by the President. Charles Colson remembers being with Nixon shortly after five on the afternoon of October 25, when Kissinger walked into the President's office and announced, "I've just briefed Max Frankel on the general agreement." Nixon "was so mad his teeth clenched," Colson recalls. "He was furious." The President complained later, according to Colson, that "I suppose now everybody's going to say that Kissinger won the election." The men at the top in the White House, faced with the imminent collapse of the most important negotiations of their administration, were still bickering over who would get the credit.

Shortly after midnight on the morning of October 26, Radio Hanoi began broadcasting a summary of the text of the peace agreement as approved by Nixon, Kissinger, and Le Duc Tho, as well as a lengthy history of the secret talks in Paris. "[W]hat we had been fearing happened," Nixon wrote. "They broadcast the general provisions of the agreement over Radio Hanoi, including the October 31 signing timetable. They revealed two of my cables to Pham Van Dong. . . ." Those two cables, Nixon did not add, dealt with his assurances that, as Radio Hanoi put it, "the formulation of the agreement could be considered complete." Kissinger's press conference now had an added importance, Nixon wrote: "We had to use it to undercut the North Vietnamese propaganda maneuver and to make sure that our version of the agreement was the one that had great public impact." North Vietnam's broadcast was *not* propaganda, as Nixon knew.

Kissinger had done it—his fiddling with the peace talks had put the President in political jeopardy. There was panic in the White House. The world would know that Nixon had agreed to end the war without consulting Thieu. No honest account of the early-morning anxieties has been made public, but Colson recalls meeting a weary Haldeman shortly before 8:00 A.M. "He had big circles under his eyes, and he told me that at midnight Hanoi blew the agreement. He said he was up all night and Henry was angry and was furious. He said he'd never spent a night like that in his life. 'We almost lost Henry last night.' " Haldeman's implication was clear to Colson: Kissinger had been on the verge of a breakdown.*

In his memoirs, Kissinger wrote that his October 26 news conference had two objectives: "One was to reassure Hanoi that we would stand by the basic agreement, while leaving open the possibility of raising Saigon's suggested changes. The second was to convey to Saigon that we were determined to proceed on our course." The most important objective of all was to protect the President, to somehow slide by the fact that Nixon had not once but twice reassured Hanoi that the peace agreement was "complete." Kissinger was also seeking, of course, to keep alive the chance, no matter how slim, that a settlement could be reached within days. It was for all these reasons that he declared, "Peace is at hand"—the same message, in essence, that he had given to Frankel the day before. Kissinger apparently still believed, or wanted to believe, that a preelection settlement would be well received by the President regardless of his disclaimers. "And despite all the opprobrium heaped on it later," Kissinger wrote in his memoirs, "the statement was essentially true—though clearly if I had to do it over I would choose a less dramatic phrase."

Nixon was furious, although he would undoubtedly have found some other statement to dispute if Kissinger had not used the "dramatic phrase." Upon hearing from Ziegler that the news lead from the press conference was "Peace is at hand," Nixon "knew immediately that our bargaining position with the North Vietnamese would be seriously eroded and our problem of bringing Thieu and the South Vietnamese along would be made even more difficult." In one of his interviews with David Frost years later, Nixon described Kissinger's statement as having "boxed us a bit into a corner. Because, by saying 'peace is at hand,' it put the North Vietnamese in a position where they realized that, ah, we had to have peace. That we had to negotiate. We had no choice, no option. And, ah, it put the American people . . . it gave them a euphoric view that, ah, another meeting or so, and it was over."

There may have been a penitent meeting between Nixon and his national security adviser, for the President in his memoirs declared that "Kissinger himself soon realized it was a mistake to have gone so far in order to convince the North Vietnamese of our bona fides by making a public commitment to a settlement."

* Kissinger made no attempt in his memoirs to describe the early-morning White House scene, claiming that he did not learn of the Hanoi broadcast until 5:30 A.M. The Kalbs, in their biography, reported that Kissinger learned of the broadcast at 2:00 A.M., when Haig telephoned. For the next three hours, the Kalbs wrote, Kissinger, Haig, and William H. Sullivan, the State Department official who had been assigned to the negotiations earlier in the month, discussed ways of responding. Haldeman would tell John Ehrlichman six weeks later, according to Ehrlichman's memoirs, that Kissinger had accepted Hanoi's peace proposal in Nixon's name "over Al Haig's strong objections and beyond any Presidential authority." No evidence for that assertion can be found in the various memoirs or elsewhere. Many of Kissinger's closest NSC aides, including those who had left the White House by this time, doubt that Kissinger, despite his occasional recklessness, would have dared go so far as to accept a peace offer without Nixon's approval.

Whatever Kissinger told Nixon, he did not view "Peace is at hand" as a mistake. The Kalbs described the reaction across the country: "The families of POWs and servicemen rejoiced. Congress cheered. The stock market soared. . . . Even on such a triumphant day, Kissinger could not relax. From 3 to 4 p.m. he briefed TV reporters . . . from four to five, he returned calls from columnists, accepting congratulations and dispensing additional insights. From five to six, he conferred with columnist Joseph Kraft. From six o'clock on, he took calls from reporters." The next day, the Kalbs wrote, Kissinger talked to senior representatives from the news magazines, the wire services, and the *New York Times*. "No other official was allowed to brief, not even the handful who knew about the negotiations. 'Call Henry,' they would counsel."

While Kissinger was being fêted as the peacemaker, Nixon and Colson were having frantic conversations with Sindlinger. The pollster, who made his reputation as an analyst of economic issues, had been among the first to measure accurately the extent of Nixon's strength among Democratic working-class voters. Sindlinger had predicted to Colson that Nixon would win at least seventeen million votes from that group. "Nixon had the hardhat labor members who figured that he was a tough guy who could handle Congress and all the other crooks," Sindlinger says. "I figured Nixon was a smart crook."

Over the summer and fall of 1972, Sindlinger was in close contact with Colson and Colson's deputy, Richard Howard. Early on the morning of October 26, Colson telephoned Sindlinger about the Kissinger press conference, which Sindlinger watched. "Peace is at hand" stunned him. "I grabbed the telephone and called Chuck. I was angry. 'You've just elected McGovern. My God. There are seventeen million Democrats who will vote for Nixon because he's a crook and he's tough. All the polls have Nixon so far ahead that these fellows will now vote straight Democratic.' " Twenty minutes later, Colson called back and put Nixon on the line. "Chuck says we made a mistake." "Made a mistake?" Sindlinger told the President. "You've lost the election." The pollster went through his reasoning, emphasizing that the hardhats would no longer feel the need to vote for Nixon. Then he asked Nixon directly: "Do you have an agreement? Is peace at hand?" Nixon said no and Sindlinger urged him to "let it hang. McGovern would never figure out what's going on."

An hour later, Nixon telephoned again. "He asked me," Sindlinger says, "what would be the public reaction if we bombed Hanoi?" Sindlinger promised to research the issue.* Before the end of the day, there was at least one more telephone call from the President. Sindlinger concluded that there were problems between Kissinger and Nixon. Nixon had somehow conveyed that the concept of a settlement was "Kissinger's idea," and there was a curious moment during one of their talks when Nixon asked how Kissinger's popularity compared with his. "I said, 'You're almost equal,' " Sindlinger remembers. "He gulped."

The excitement over Kissinger's pronouncement was reflected in the press.

---

* Ten days later, Sindlinger recalls, he told the White House that the public would overwhelmingly support the bombing. His polls continued to be treated with reverence by Nixon and his advisers; Sindlinger's huge gaffe in predicting Nixon's loss of support among the hardhat voters—a loss that did not materialize in the election—seemed to make little difference.

On October 27, in a column titled "The End of the Tunnel," James Reston wrote, "It has been a long time since Washington has heard such a candid and even brilliant explanation of an intricate political problem as Henry Kissinger gave to the press on the peace negotiations." Reston would write two columns that week on the "Kissinger compromise" without raising any questions about Nixon's two cables to Hanoi, as made public by North Vietnam, in which he pronounced the negotiations complete. The serious allegations broadcast by Hanoi were effaced, and North Vietnam's account of Nixon's perfidy was treated as Communist propaganda. Kissinger's persuasiveness had made Hanoi's notion that it was the United States which was engaged in wholesale distortion seem impossible. The *Los Angeles Times* breathlessly described Kissinger's announcement as a "dramatic negotiating breakthrough," although Kissinger was really describing a negotiating breakdown. Many other key issues were also obscured. No reporter saw fit to ask Kissinger to elaborate on what he meant when he acknowledged that the agreement called for "the existing authorities with respect to both internal and external policies [to] remain in office . . ." Kissinger did not tell the journalists the essence of the bargain: that the Thieu regime would have to share political and legal authority with the PRG. That issue would remain fuzzy—deliberately so—for the next three months.

Kissinger also managed to obscure the fact that the United States was seeking to reopen the negotiations after having reached a final agreement with the North Vietnamese. He did this by telling the journalists that there had been a "misunderstanding" on Hanoi's part: "It was, however, always clear, at least to us . . . that obviously we could not sign an agreement in which details remained to be worked out simply because in good faith we had said we would make an effort to conclude it by a certain date." Nixon and Kissinger had done much more than commit themselves to a "good faith" effort to sign by October 31; they had reassured Hanoi in two cables that they would do so. Hanoi's leaders were now being told that the Nixon Administration reserved the unilateral right to reopen the negotiations. They also were being told that it was their "misunderstandings," and not Kissinger's ambitions, Nixon's treachery, and Nguyen Van Thieu's categorical opposition, that had created difficulties.

October 26 was Kissinger's last hurrah on the Vietnam issue. He would be celebrated again after the signing of the agreement in January 1973, but that triumph would be tarnished by the Christmas bombing. In October, there were no cries of genocide; Kissinger emerged from his news conference as a skillful negotiator trapped between two difficult parties. There was no hint to the public that he and Nixon had been engaged in a brutal struggle over the timing of a settlement in South Vietnam, a struggle that did not deal with the morality of the war or even the merits of the settlement. Nguyen Van Thieu's complaints were, in part, an excuse seized by Nixon to justify delay; after the election, the President would not hesitate to use both inducements and coercion to force Thieu to sign the treaty. Kissinger, for all his concern about the escalations Nixon "might" order if he were reelected, understood that the President was more than willing to find a way to accept the October settlement and declare it "peace with honor." Nixon simply wanted to do so on his terms and at his timing.

After the election, the role of the President and his collaborator would begin to reverse: Kissinger would emerge as the one most avid in urging the use of bombs to force an agreement with Hanoi. Having failed in his attempt to improve his status inside the White House by delivering a preelection settlement, he now fought to cling to his job. Under severe pressure, he would do what had worked before; he would again endorse the "madman theory."

Meantime, Nixon moved promptly to undercut the promise of "peace is at hand." Before leaving on a brief campaign trip in the late afternoon of October 26, he told Colson he would find a way to "back off" from Kissinger's already famous statement. That evening, in a speech given without notes at Ashland, Kentucky, the President acknowledged the reports of progress toward peace in Southeast Asia, but he added: "The day has not yet come. There are still some differences that must be resolved." The war would not be settled, he said, until he was satisfied that its terms would "discourage aggression in the future rather than encourage it."

Kissinger had not only moved too fast, Nixon seemed to be suggesting, but had agreed to terms that were too soft. The public did not realize that Nixon's comments were aimed not only at Hanoi and Saigon but at his national security adviser, but Kissinger surely did. A few days later, on October 31, the original target date for formally signing the peace treaty, Nixon, speaking through his press secretary, told the White House press corps that he would not be rushed into an agreement to end the war that did not offer "the best hope for lasting peace." Ziegler told the reporters that the "only deadline we're operating under is the one that will bring about the right kind of an agreement . . . a peace that does not leave the seed of a future conflict." Nixon himself, in a televised campaign address two days later, declared that "we are not going to allow an election deadline or any other kind of deadline to force us into an agreement which would be only a temporary truce and not a lasting peace." The President was virtually in open warfare with Kissinger.

Kissinger also backed off. On November 1, he arrived, amid much fanfare, at the South Vietnamese Embassy for its National Day reception. The *New York Times* concluded that his appearance, which was replete with jostling journalists, busy photographers, and pretty women, was a public demonstration of the Nixon Administration's support for Nguyen Van Thieu's government.

In fact, Kissinger was isolated inside the White House. Nixon was in the process of disavowing an agreement he had approved, and the President's aides were beginning to spread stories that Kissinger had gone too far in his negotiations with Le Duc Tho; that he had exceeded his authority. His long-time ally, Alexander Haig, had defected, and he had few confidants inside the NSC staff. There was always the press, but Kissinger knew that he could not dare tell his newspaper friends the truth, for the full story would jeopardize his job. His only option was to join the President's betrayal of the peace accord, and somehow find a way to bring Nguyen Van Thieu into line.

This behind-the-scenes maneuvering in the White House helps to clarify the meaning of Kissinger's interview with Oriana Fallaci on November 4. Fallaci asked Kissinger to explain his immense popularity; Kissinger's response was to create an international sensation. "I'll tell you," Kissinger responded. "What do I care after all? The main point stems from the fact that I've always acted alone. Americans admire that enormously. Americans admire the cowboy leading the caravan alone astride his horse, the cowboy entering the village or city alone on his horse. Without even a pistol, maybe, because he doesn't go in for shooting. He acts, that's all: aiming at the right spot at the right time. A Wild West tale, if you like."

Of course. Kissinger had sought to visit Hanoi, amidst a bitter war, unannounced and alone. He would settle the war and win the election for his President. Without a pistol. Nixon had pulled the rug out from under the Wild West tale, and Kissinger couldn't hide his bitterness. "This romantic, surprising character suits me," he told Fallaci, "because being alone has always been part of my style. . . . Independence, too. Yes, that's very important to me and in me."

There was more. A few moments earlier in the interview, asked about his future plans, Kissinger responded, ". . . I've by no means decided to give up this job yet. You know, I enjoy it very much. . . . You see, when one wields power, and when one has it for a long time, one ends up thinking one has a right to it."

Within weeks, as his enemies gleefully circulated copies of the interview throughout the White House, Kissinger would reach the nadir of his days in the Nixon Administration. Nixon would begin bragging to his aides about his plans to fire Kissinger, to force him to go back to Harvard. Kissinger would plead for the renewed bombing of Hanoi—and survive. And Nguyen Van Thieu would be assured by the President of the United States that the political provisions of the peace agreement were nothing more than "pieces of paper."

40

VIETNAM:
THE CHRISTMAS BOMBS

HENRY KISSINGER HAD EVERY REASON to know, in the first week of November 1972, that he would be the scapegoat for the failed settlement of the Vietnam War. He had been betrayed by the President, who, at the most critical moment of the negotiations in Saigon, had refused to pressure Nguyen Van Thieu into accepting an agreement. Nixon had chosen instead to dupe the leaders of North Vietnam, to whom Kissinger, in Nixon's name, had sent two cables affirming his final acceptance of the peace treaty. And now Kissinger was being subjected to unrelenting criticism from Nixon and his two leading advisers, H. R. Haldeman and Charles Colson, for his October 26 declaration, "Peace is at hand."

Kissinger responded to what he considered an unfair assault in characteristic fashion: He toadied to the President. He had little immediate hope now of becoming Secretary of State, the ambition that had driven him to a reckless speed-up of negotiations in Paris and Saigon. He simply wanted to keep his job. On election day, as Nixon was preparing to accept his overwhelming mandate, Kissinger arranged for a hand-written note to be left on the President's pillow:

Dear Mr. President—

It seems appropriate before the votes are counted to tell you what a privilege the last four years have been. I am confident of the outcome today. But it cannot affect the historic achievement—to take a divided nation, mired in war, losing its confidence, wracked by intellectuals without conviction, and give it a new purpose and overcome its hesitations, will loom ever larger in history books. It has been an inspiration to see your fortitude in adversity and your willingness to walk alone. For this—as well as for the unfailing human kindness and consideration—I shall always be grateful.

Nixon reproduced the note without comment in his memoirs.

One public sign of Kissinger's fall from grace appeared in the *Washington Post* two days after the election. Murray Marder, the newspaper's diplomatic correspondent, reported that Nixon never intended to settle the Vietnam War by October 31, the deadline day, because he would have been exposed to a "messy" situation in the week just before the election. Marder's accurate source for the story was Haig, who was now Nixon's closest national security aide. Haig, interviewed on condition that he not be cited by name, told Marder that Nixon, by deciding not to go ahead with a settlement, had deliberately chosen "to expose himself to what he regarded as the lesser hazard of a charge of duplicity by North Vietnam." Kissinger had been left high and dry.

In his memoirs, Kissinger acknowledged that he met with Nixon only twice during a nine-day stretch in mid-November. He ascribed his difficulties, however, not to the Vietnam situation but to the President's jealousy over his high standing with the media and the public. There were only "vague clues" about the President's feelings toward him, Kissinger wrote: "They were never made explicit in our personal contacts, which were unfailingly courteous and in which no disagreement surfaced." Kissinger further insisted that he and Nixon "never differed on the substance of our negotiating position" during the last phases of the Vietnam negotiations.*

In mid-November, Nixon decided to go ahead with his plan to nominate Kenneth Rush, Laird's deputy in the Pentagon, as Secretary of State. Rush had been promised the job by John Mitchell early in the year, in reward, partly, for his loyalty to Nixon during the Berlin negotiations. On the sixteenth, Rogers took the helicopter ride to Camp David; he had no illusions about the purpose of the visit. Haldeman, in his memoirs, recalled that he was left with "the unenviable task of telling Richard Nixon's closest personal friend in the government that Richard Nixon had decided it was now time for him to leave." Rogers insisted on staying; being forced out now, he told Haldeman, would appear to be a victory for Kissinger, and that he could not accept.† There was

* Kissinger was almost in a panic at this time—as he had not been since his early days in the White House—to please his patron. There had been some ugly racial disturbances aboard the aircraft carrier *Constellation* a few days after the election, with network camera crews recording a group of militant blacks on deck giving the clenched-fist "black power" salute. Richard Nixon flew into a rage at such dissent and turned to Kissinger, who was eager to pass along the President's displeasure to Admiral Zumwalt. "Kissinger all but shrieked at me," Zumwalt recalled in his memoirs: " 'The President . . . feels strongly that there are to be no further negotiations with people who do not carry out orders no matter what the price.' " Kissinger demanded, in the name of the President, that the protesters be given dishonorable discharges, "immediately, if not sooner." There was a basic problem with the President's order, Zumwalt wrote—under the Code of Military Justice, it was illegal. The protesters were entitled to courts-martial to determine whether their actions warranted such dismissal. The conversation with Kissinger shocked Zumwalt: "Even though a professional military man has been prepared by training . . . to obey unhesitatingly the orders of his superiors, including specifically orders he disagrees with, he cannot but be taken aback when his Commander-in-Chief, of all people, relays to him a peremptory, angry, illegal order such as that had been given me." Zumwalt concluded that Nixon viewed the sailors' "clenched-fist salutes as he tended to view all disagreement, not to say opposition, as mutiny." The admiral, who had earlier made a widely publicized plea for racial tolerance at a meeting of senior Navy officers, to their everlasting resentment, was also suspect. He was subsequently told that Kissinger had been ordered by Nixon to fire him, and had relayed that order to Laird. Laird, wrote Zumwalt, "told Kissinger that if Kissinger wanted me fired he should try firing me himself." He was spared early retirement, Zumwalt wrote, because "Kissinger was not up to knocking that chip off the shoulder of a man Laird's size."

† Rogers, in a later interview, did not take serious issue with Haldeman's account, although he said another motive for staying was his desire to be in office when the Vietnam War was settled. Months later, when Rogers was back in his private law practice in New York and Washington, Haldeman paid a surprise visit to ask for advice on what he should do. The former Secretary of State laughed disdainfully as he recalled the meeting. "I didn't know what to tell him," he said. Rogers had turned down a chance for revenge in late April 1973, when Nixon asked him to inform Haldeman that it was his turn to resign in the Watergate scandal. The Secretary of State refused to

611

a meeting with the President and, as Haldeman had suspected, the President "was not up to fighting it out with his old friend." Rogers would stay, at least through June, and Haldeman had to inform Kissinger of that fact. "The explosion was predictable," Haldeman wrote, "but nonetheless searing. 'You promised me, Haldeman. You gave me your *word*. And now he's hanging on just like I said he would. Piece by piece. Bit by bit. He stays on and on and on!' " At that point, Haldeman added, Kissinger turned away and declared: "There is a price you must pay, I suppose. Mine is Rogers. He will be with me forever —because he has this President wrapped around his little finger."

Rush was told five days later that he would be nominated Deputy Secretary of State. The top job was again promised to him, to be bestowed after Rogers' resignation. Kissinger, distressed at Nixon's decision to keep Rogers on the job, and aware of Rogers' reasons for staying on, soon had a more serious worry: His interview with Oriana Fallaci was published just as he prepared to resume his negotiations with Le Duc Tho. It was, he wrote in his memoirs, "without doubt the single most disastrous conversation I ever had with any member of the press." It was also one of his most honest. He went to Paris under a cloud: ". . . Nixon could give me no direct sign of his displeasure," but there were some clues. "He would not see me on November 18, the day before I took off, even though he was in the White House; we only spoke briefly on the telephone."

Colson bore the direct brunt of Nixon's rage. The President was spending much of his time at Camp David in meetings with Haldeman and Ehrlichman, planning to place Nixon loyalists in every agency. Every Nixon appointee, including Cabinet members, had been required to submit a resignation in writing, and the President was choosing his new team. Kissinger had been told by Haldeman shortly after the election that his letter of resignation would be considered a "mere formality." It was another lie, for Nixon was seriously considering dismissing Kissinger. On November 20, at Camp David, Nixon took Colson aside; the two men, with Nixon leading the way, walked into a wing of the main presidential quarters. Nixon revealed that he had decided to get rid of Kissinger. "It's time for Henry to go back to Harvard, Chuck," Colson recalls the President telling him. "It's the best thing for him. He needs to do it." Kissinger would leave, Nixon said, as soon as the peace talks were over.*

At this juncture, Vietnam was a problem in public relations. Nixon had reneged on the agreement out of political fear; his immediate problem was how to put the package back together without losing face. In a diary entry for November 20, reproduced in his memoirs, he outlined the dilemma: "[A]ssuming we get what we consider to be a good agreement—well, as a matter of fact, we consider the present one to be good . . . then we have to put it to Thieu hard: he either accepts the agreement and goes along with it, or we will have to go our separate ways." He was now willing to tell the South Vietnamese what he would not before the election, assuming that Hanoi cooperated in Paris.

do what Haldeman had so willingly done to him, and told Nixon he would have to fire his chief aide himself.

* Much later, Colson says, he realized that Nixon, by walking out of the living room to discuss his plans for Kissinger, was avoiding Camp David's tape-recording system.

The South Vietnamese continued to insist that they would not sign an agreement that included an election commission or permitted Hanoi's troops to remain in the South. And in November a new demand was added: Nguyen Van Thieu wanted assurance from Hanoi that his regime still had sovereignty over all of South Vietnam. If the PRG were to occupy some portions of the South, Thieu wanted a guarantee that it would be considered an illegal occupation. Thieu understood, as the American public did not, the real significance of the proposed agreement: legal standing for the PRG.

Nixon picked Haig, not Kissinger, to fly to Saigon after the election with a warning. Nixon's overwhelming election triumph had done little for the Republican Party. The Democrats had gained two seats in the Senate while easily maintaining their control of the House. A congressional cutoff in Vietnam spending was now far more likely. "There was no question," Nixon quoted himself as telling Haig, "that if we did not have a settlement completed before Congress returned in January, and if it appeared that Thieu was the obstacle to achieving one, the Senate would cut off the funds that South Vietnam needed to survive. The situation was as simple, and as certain, as that."

Hoang Duc Nha recalls Haig's message as being blunt: "Haig said, 'If you don't sign, the United States will take brutal actions.' Thieu said, 'We understand how Nixon feels, but this is the destiny of our nation.' " Haig did not prolong the conversation, Nha added, telling Thieu that "we have to help the President."

Nha says he and Thieu realized "we'd taken a big gamble, but we had to do it. I told Thieu, 'Either Haig will take a brutal reaction—overthrow, assassination—or the Communists will get the bombs. That's the only way we can break the impasse.' "

Again Nha's account may have some elements of self-aggrandizement, but his basic analysis was correct. The South Vietnamese were gambling that Nixon, who had refused to cut them off a month earlier, would back down again. The White House could not claim "peace with honor" if the Thieu regime had to be dragged into the agreement. And there was an additional advantage to a renewal of the bombing in the North—it would demonstrate to Hanoi and to the Soviets that Richard Nixon, having been reelected, was as unpredictable and as much of a "madman" as ever.

Kissinger's goal as he flew to Paris for the November 20 meeting with Le Duc Tho was to salvage an agreement. If the North Vietnamese could somehow be induced—or threatened—into making an additional concession, the White House would have some leverage with Thieu. Without a concession, Nixon and Kissinger, facing an impasse of their own making, would be forced to turn either on Thieu or on the North Vietnamese. The choice would surely be the North Vietnamese.

Kissinger got off on the wrong foot in Paris by bringing an assortment of gifts, including a photographic study of the Harvard campus. Years later, members of Hanoi's peace delegation were still amazed at his belief that he could mollify them with trinkets. He added to the insult by presenting, on behalf of Saigon, a series of sixty-nine proposed changes to the October draft agreement. "This proved to be a major tactical mistake," Kissinger acknowledged in his memoirs. "The list was so preposterous, it went so far beyond what we had indicated both publicly and privately, that it must have strengthened Hanoi's already strong temptation to dig in its heels. . . ."

Kissinger was following orders. Two days later, he withdrew the vast majority of Saigon's objections, a bargaining tactic that did little to improve his position. The demands he kept were substantive, however, and amounted to a reopening of the October agreement. He now wanted to add a clause guaranteeing respect for the demilitarized zone separating North and South Vietnam, a statement that would suggest that any presence of northern troops below the DMZ was illegal. Kissinger also proposed that civilian traffic across the DMZ be severely limited, in effect denying the North Vietnamese and the PRG, who controlled both sides of the line, their claim of sovereignty. He further sought to reopen the issue of ceasefires in Laos and Cambodia, a dispute that had been resolved in October in North Vietnam's favor.

Over the next few days, Le Duc Tho responded in kind, and began retracting many of North Vietnam's earlier concessions. He demanded again that Vietcong prisoners held by the Thieu regime be released, and also that all American civilian technicians be withdrawn from the South, along with American military men (the technicians were to have stayed behind, under contract to South Vietnam, to maintain Saigon's rapidly growing air force). Le Duc Tho's bitterness was extreme; "Hanoi felt they were victims of a con game," as one of Kissinger's aides puts it. Nixon's decision to cancel the October agreement had left thousands of Vietcong cadre badly exposed in the South, where Thieu's forces, buttressed by the vast American resupply of arms, had been grabbing land for nearly a month. There was little incentive for Hanoi to rush a second agreement now. Its leadership was not prepared to begin a ceasefire —which would merely be another phase of the war—until its forces could recoup in the South. The North Vietnamese had also begun a major program to upgrade their surface-to-air defenses around Hanoi and Haiphong, in case Nixon and Kissinger tried again to bomb their way to victory.

As Hanoi refused to submit, Kissinger got tougher. North Vietnamese officials recall that warnings of escalation were issued. In his memoirs, Kissinger cited a cable from Nixon, sent on November 22, after two days of fruitless negotiations, which proposed that North Vietnam be "disabused of the idea they seem to have that we have no other choice but to settle on their terms. You should inform them directly without equivocation that we do have another choice and if they were surprised that the President would take the strong action he did prior to the Moscow summit and prior to the election, they will find now, with the election behind us, he will take whatever action he considers necessary to protect the United States' interest." The cable was marked, Kissinger wrote, "not a directive—for possible use with the North Vietnamese."

Kissinger suggested that he did not deliver the message: ". . . [T]hreats seemed premature after only forty-eight hours of negotiation." North Vietnamese negotiators later stated, however, that such warnings became an integral part of the American tactic. On November 23, according to Nixon's memoirs, Kissinger offered two options. "Option One would be to break off the talks at the next meeting and dramatically step up our bombing," Nixon wrote. "This was the option Kissinger favored. Option Two would be to decide upon fall-back positions on each of Thieu's major objections and present them as our final offer." If the North Vietnamese agreed, "we could still claim to have improved on the October terms." That step, Kissinger cabled, would call for a complete break with Thieu. At this point, Nixon, obviously unsure of how best to resolve the diplomatic impasse, rejected the bombing: "I strongly opposed breaking off the talks and resuming the bombing unless it was absolutely necessary to compel the enemy to negotiate. I was also becoming irritated by some of Thieu's tactics."

Kissinger had now moved to the President's right, which could only improve his status. The White House was still a place where no one could go wrong advocating escalation. In his memoirs, Kissinger denied making any recommendations at all in the November 23 exchange of cables, explaining in a footnote that he "hinted" at a preference for the second option; but there is strong evidence that Nixon's recollection is right. On November 23, the day of Kissinger's options proposal, Nixon forwarded a top-secret letter to Thieu in which he directly expressed the irritation alluded to in his memoirs. "I am increasingly dismayed and apprehensive over the press campaign emanating from Saigon," he wrote Thieu. "The unfounded attacks on the draft agreement have continued with increasing frequency. In addition, I am struck by the dilatory tactics which we are experiencing from your side in Paris." The letter, not cited by Nixon or Kissinger in their memoirs, was provided to the author in 1979 by the North Vietnamese. It makes clear that, as of the twenty-third, as Nixon claimed in his memoirs, he was intent on making one last try before breaking off the Paris talks and escalating the war. His goal, at least on that day, was to convince Thieu he must compromise. "I will proceed promptly to a final solution if an acceptable final agreement is arrived at in Paris this week," Nixon wrote. ". . . [A]ny future delay from your side can only be interpreted as an effort to scuttle the agreement. This would have a disastrous effect on our ability to support you and your Government. . . . If the current course continues and you fail to join us in concluding a satisfactory agreement with Hanoi, you must understand that I will proceed at whatever the cost."

As Kissinger insisted on introducing at least some of Thieu's changes into the draft agreement, however, North Vietnam stiffened its public position. An editorial that week in *Nhan Dan,* the party newspaper published in Hanoi, warned that the United States, by insisting on major changes in the October agreement, would force Hanoi to return to the battlefield and "fight on until total victory."*

Kissinger's attitude had already hardened. Nixon, in a diary entry quoted in his memoirs, described a conversation with him after his return from Paris on November 25: "I had to back him off the position that we really had a viable option to break off the talks with the North and resume the bombing for a period of time. It simply isn't going to work. . . ."

Thieu, ignoring Nixon's warning, was meanwhile doing his best to make things difficult. According to Hoang Duc Nha, in late November his government mounted a "p.r. campaign" against the peace agreement. One goal was to exploit the division between Nixon and Kissinger. After extensive negotiations, a meeting was arranged in Washington for November 29 between Nixon and two Thieu aides, Ambassador Phuong and Nguyen Phu Duc, South Viet-

* The Hanoi correspondent for Agence France-Presse, Jean Thoravas, reported a few days later that the American negotiating stance in Paris had "resulted in the hardening of the attitude of the North Vietnamese . . ."

nam's national security adviser. The Vietnamese brought a long letter, drafted in part by Nha, in which they again raised the issue of being allowed to participate in the Paris talks with Le Duc Tho. "Our position was: Why should you guys sit in the dining room while we're cooling our heels in the kitchen?" Nha recalls. The Vietnamese were told, however, according to Nixon's and Kissinger's memoirs, that the White House was prepared to sign a separate peace with Hanoi if the Thieu government did not drop its public opposition to the agreement. "I said it was not a question of lacking sympathy for Saigon's predicament, but we had to face the reality of the situation," Nixon wrote. "If we did not end the war by concluding a settlement at the next Paris session, then when Congress returned in January it would end the war by cutting off the appropriations."

The signals were more than mixed; they were interwoven. Nixon and Kissinger, working together once again, needed a compromise somewhere—either from Hanoi or Saigon—or they would begin their second term with the war still raging and a new, more liberal Congress ready to impinge on their control of foreign policy. Hanoi's ploy of recanting some of its concessions in the October settlement added to the dilemma. The threats of renewed bombing accomplished little: Hanoi ignored them and Saigon used them as a further rationale for making trouble. The "p.r." problem was growing more acute.

The record is far from complete, but there is clear evidence that Nixon came to a significant decision by the end of November: He would make a secret agreement with Nguyen Van Thieu. In return for Thieu's acceptance of the peace agreements, he would assure Thieu that the Nixon Administration would view the political agreements—which called upon Saigon to share power in the South with the PRG—as meaningless. Thieu would still be considered the sovereign ruler of all South Vietnam and would not be censured if he continued his military and political activities. If the North Vietnamese chose to retaliate, as was inevitable, the President would unleash American bombers, which would have retreated, under the peace agreement, to aircraft carriers offshore and bases in Thailand.

Just when Nixon conveyed his secret agenda to Thieu is not known, but the policy first came to light during his annual briefing with the Joint Chiefs of Staff on November 30, the day after Nixon's meeting with Duc and Phuong.

"The President, Kissinger and Al Haig already were in their armchairs when we Chiefs trooped in," wrote Elmo Zumwalt in his memoirs, "sober of mien, highly beribboned and, I fear, a little like performing poodles or trained seals. Our annual meeting always included a picture-taking session and so, before we got down to business, photographers materialized and we all assumed the expressions and stances of statesmanship." Zumwalt took copious notes. If the talks with Le Duc Tho were broken off, Nixon told the military men, there would be violent retaliation: ". . . [I]f they get hardnosed, then we will mine and hit more targets with B-52s."

Nixon was clearly seeking support from the Joint Chiefs for an agreement. "The left will debunk his deal," Zumwalt paraphrased his remarks. "DOD must support it . . . after all the blood, the sacrifices, the military must be for it . . . We need to make the point that no paper is worth a damn, what really matters is the economic and military support . . . whether the war resumes or not depends on the PRC and the USSR . . . but they've got other fish to fry.'' Nixon continued, according to Zumwalt's notes: North Vietnam "faced resumed hostilities from the U.S. and South Vietnam if they violate the deal. We have told the Soviets and the PRC of our concern . . . he urged that *we not worry about the words, we will keep the agreement if it serves us*—their interests require them to obey [emphasis added].''

Zumwalt was distressed at Nixon's duplicity. "[I]t was perfectly obvious to all of us at the time," he wrote, "that the promise of massive American assistance to South Vietnam and of prompt U.S. retaliation to serious truce violations [would be] the critical elements in securing the cease-fire and that the fulfillment of these promises would be the critical element in maintaining the cease-fire." He criticized the administration's decision not to inform the American people fully of the obligation, in case of ceasefire violations, to renew military support to the Thieu regime and added: "There are at least two words no one can use to characterize the outcome of that two-faced policy. One is 'peace.' The other is 'honor.' ''

The American negotiating policy, then, was to wait for either Saigon or Hanoi to crack. Thieu would be offered a guarantee of sovereignty, an ambitious resupply program, and a promise of American retribution in case Hanoi violated the ceasefire agreement; Hanoi would be offered threats. The fact that bombing had not solved any of the basic problems of the war thus far seemed not to be a factor in the reasoning.

In all of this, Nixon was dominant; he was taking an active role, finally, in the negotiating process. Kissinger, having once again been shown who was boss, continued negotiating in Paris on the basis of the October breakthrough. If he disagreed with Nixon's policy of planning to pay only lip service to the essential political provision in the proposed settlement, he did not say so.

Over the next few weeks, the first signs of Nixon's secret policy began filtering into Saigon. The word was passed by Ambassador Bunker, who began reassuring President Thieu that the Nixon Administration would continue to consider his regime to be sovereign, no matter what the final peace agreement said. Hoang Duc Nha recalls that a similar message was also conveyed to Thieu in November and early December by American military authorities. The men in Saigon were still skeptical of Nixon's promises; not even the Christmas bombing would convince them they should accept a negotiated settlement.

Kissinger, perhaps sensing that renewed bombing of the North was inevitable, and perhaps aware that it would not influence either side in the war, could not control his rage at Thieu. There was violent talk. William Porter, the ambassador to the public peace talks in Paris who joined Kissinger's personal negotiating team in the late fall, recalls hearing Kissinger threaten Thieu's life. "We'll kill the son-of-a-bitch if we have to," he told his aides late one night in his quarters at the American Embassy, after hearing that Thieu was still insisting on the removal of all North Vietnamese troops from the South. There was talk on another occasion of "strangling" Thieu, Porter says, in front of Peter Rodman, Winston Lord, Alexander Haig, and himself. "I was upset" at Kissinger's remarks, Porter recalls. He told Kissinger at one point, "Oh, Christ, don't talk about that. We've been through this before.''

Kissinger's dilemma became worse as the negotiations floundered in Paris.

He confided to a few of his newspaper friends that he had been doublecrossed by the President before the election; in a strong column in the *Washington Post* on November 25, Tom Braden declared flatly that the President had "undercut" Kissinger. At the same time, Colson and Scali began briefing a few selected journalists on Kissinger's follies. Some reporters were told that Kissinger had exceeded presidential authority in negotiating the October agreement with Le Duc Tho. Kissinger's mistakes, the story ran, had been repaired by Nixon, who was aided by his legal training in reviewing the documents. "Failure in Washington requires a sacrificial offering," Kissinger wrote in his memoirs. "I was the logical candidate."

He managed nonetheless to turn the attacks to his advantage. In his memoirs, he cited an argument that presumably was also made directly to the President: "All this was good clean bureaucratic fun, but it had a massively pernicious impact in the negotiations. It encouraged Thieu in his intransigence and in his seeking to exploit the presumed split between Nixon and me. And it was bound to tempt Hanoi to stonewall in its talks." On December 2, the White House announced that Kissinger would continue to serve as Special Assistant for National Security in Nixon's second term; it was, as the Kalb brothers reported in their biography, "a much-needed psychological boost" for Kissinger. Nixon, in his memoirs, recalled that Kissinger was optimistic, gratefully so, as he returned to Paris on December 4: "[I]t would take only a few days to conclude an agreement; in fact, he said there was 70–30 chance that he could have the whole thing 'wrapped up' " within two days. Kissinger "blamed his 'peace is at hand' statement for having caused many of our present troubles," Nixon wrote, "and he talked about resigning if he was unable to conclude an agreement. I told him that he should not even be thinking in such terms."

So it went in the White House. Having been formally renamed national security adviser, Kissinger offered to resign a few days later. It was posturing but effective, this penitent recanting. Nixon would continue to hear only what Kissinger thought best for his career. In his memoirs, Kissinger did not mention any of the 70–30 optimism he had shared with the President. Instead, he wrote, "Amid looming Congressional disenchantment, caught between two implacable Vietnamese sides . . . stung by leaks at home that my position as negotiator was not all that secure, I was not in a brilliant position from which to resume the negotiations."

His position was, in fact, untenable. He was asking the other side to reopen negotiations on issues that had been settled, and offering them no incentives to do so. Nguyen Co Thach recalls that North Vietnam's policy at the November-December round of negotiations was simple: to insist on the October accords. In early December, Le Duc Tho went a step further: He began to withdraw some of the changes he had accepted two weeks earlier. He also continued to retract the basic concessions that had led to the October breakthrough, once again insisting, for example, that Vietcong prisoners be released from Saigon's jails and that all American civilians be withdrawn from the South. Kissinger, in his memoirs, reprinted a portion of a December 4 cable to Nixon: ". . . Tho stuck firmly by his intransigent position. The only alternative he offered to his presentation this afternoon was to go back to the October agreement with no changes by either side." At this point, the newly reappointed national security adviser joined Nixon in opposition to the October accords: "Though I considered the agreement a good one then, intervening events would turn acceptance of it into a debacle. If we could not bring about a single change requested by Saigon . . . it would be tantamount to wrecking the South Vietnamese government. . . . Thus our only real choice was to pursue a course that involved a high risk of break-off."

Colson, who was among a small group of aides who read the three-page cable, remembers other parts of it as apocalyptic: "Start the bombing immediately. These madmen have doublecrossed us. Go on national television tomorrow night and announce to the American people that we're resuming bombing of the North."* Kenneth Rush was also shown the cable and also recalls its toughness: "Henry wanted Nixon to start bombing again and lower the boom." Nixon, in his memoirs, did not cite the most inflammatory sections of the cable. "The central issue," he quoted Kissinger as reporting, "is that Hanoi has apparently decided to mount a frontal challenge to us such as we faced last May. If so, they are gambling on our unwillingness to do what is necessary . . . we are faced with the same kind of hard decision as last spring." Kissinger was now assuming the role that John Connally had played the previous spring; he would be Richard Nixon's tough guy. He proposed, as restated by Nixon, that a few of Saigon's minimum demands be insisted upon, and if the Communists refused to accept them and the talks broke off, "we have no choice but to step up our bombing as a means of making them agree to a redefined negotiating position."

Being urged to renew the bombings would not trouble Nixon, but the recommendation that he announce it to the public was something else. Nixon was not about to go on television and take the heat for that decision. He later told David Frost why: "The main reason you couldn't go on and make a public statement with regard to the bombing, was that in making that statement, it would have to be said, 'We are doing this because they have not agreed to settle on certain terms that they agreed to earlier and that we believe are reasonable now.' " What Nixon did not tell Frost, of course, is that the United States had joined with North Vietnam in reaching an agreement in late October, only to renege a few days later. In his acknowledgment to Frost that he viewed the "agreed to" October settlement as "reasonable" in early December, Nixon made it clear that he and Kissinger understood what they have been unable to admit elsewhere: The duplicity was not Hanoi's but Washington's.

When he got the cable, Nixon turned to Haldeman (Haig was in Paris with Kissinger) for help in handling Kissinger. "I have talked to a very few of the hardliners here in total confidence," Haldeman cabled Kissinger, "and it is their strongly unanimous view that it would be totally wrong for the President to go on TV and explain the details of why the talks have failed." Kissinger

* Colson first talked about the Kissinger cable in a television interview in February 1975, shortly after serving a seven-month prison term for his role in Watergate. In the second volume of his memoirs, *Life Sentence*, published in 1979, he wrote that a few days after his television appearance, Nixon, then living in exile in California, telephoned him about the interview and said, ". . . uh, well, Henry called . . . You know we only have one President now. One Secretary of State. So we need to support them, you know, Chuck. They are all we have. I mean, you and I know Henry's faults, but as Americans we support our leaders and our country, right?" Colson wrote a letter of apology to Kissinger.

sent a second message urging the President to announce the renewal of bombing. Nixon, in response, urged Kissinger to keep on negotiating. "It was my firm conviction," he wrote in his memoirs, "that we must not be responsible —or be portrayed as being responsible—for the breakdown of the talks." Once again self-protection and public relations were vital factors. Kissinger, in his memoirs, acknowledged as much: "Fundamentally, Nixon's and my attempts to shift responsibility back and forth were as meaningless as they were unworthy. If the negotiations succeeded, there would be the same scramble for credit as there was now to avoid blame. If they failed, I was the logical victim. . . ."

Kissinger continued to insist that Le Duc Tho agree to a new definition of the demilitarized zone that would have the effect of making it illegal for northern troops to enter the South; the new language also implied Saigon's sovereignty over the DMZ. Hanoi continued to find Kissinger's demands preposterous. It was a stalemate.

Kissinger wanted out of Paris. The talks, he realized, would break down. Hanoi also had no illusions. Its leaders authorized the evacuation of children from the capital on December 4. "We didn't know concretely about the B-52 bombing," one senior North Vietnamese official recalls, "but we had a smell." On December 6, after another fruitless meeting with Le Duc Tho, Kissinger cabled Nixon that he had "reached a crossroads," as Nixon wrote, and proposed two options. One involved making a minimum demand to Le Duc Tho, and, if it was accepted, running the risk of a public break with Nguyen Van Thieu. The second called for provoking the North Vietnamese to break off the talks by making an unacceptable demand, and then resuming massive bombing until the North agreed to return American prisoners in exchange for an American withdrawal from the South. Nixon quoted Kissinger as believing "that if we could keep up the bombing for six months—through the summer of 1973" —the policy might work. "If we are willing to pay the domestic and international price," Kissinger cabled, "rally the American people, and stay on our course, this option has fewer risks than the other one, given the [South Vietnamese] attitude."

Kissinger's options again called for the President to explain policy publicly. Nixon wanted nothing to do with that. In a return cable, printed in his memoirs, he urged Kissinger to keep on trying to seek a compromise. Each man was eager to set the other up. "I realize," Nixon cabled, "that you think if I go on television that I can rally the American people to support an indefinite continuation of the war simply for the purpose of getting our prisoners back. . . . But that can wear very thin in a matter of weeks, particularly as the propaganda organs—not only from North Vietnam but in this country—begin to hammer away at the fact that we had a much better deal in hand, and then because of Saigon's intransigence, we were unable to complete it." Kissinger, of course, knew the "intransigence" was not only Saigon's but Nixon's. He had refused to do in October what he was preparing to do in December: force Thieu into an agreement. Kissinger dutifully stayed in Paris, but accomplished nothing. He would tell Nixon a few days later, as Nixon recounted in his memoirs, that the North Vietnamese were "just a bunch of shits. Tawdry, filthy shits. They make the Russians look good, compared to the way the Russians make the Chinese look good when it comes to negotiating in a responsible and decent way!"

The best account of the internal tensions in the White House over the next week was kept in the Kissinger office journal, whose author had firsthand exposure to the infighting. The journal, it should be stressed, was maintained by a close Kissinger associate; the world he saw was one in which suspicion and intrigue were the pivotal factors in foreign policy decisions. "Kissinger thought he had a deal . . . then Hanoi stalled. Kissinger stayed until Wednesday December 14. The President, whose mind is being poisoned by Haig on the subject, feels that Kissinger is screwing up the negotiations. Haig told the President that Kissinger would be yo-yoed by the North Vietnamese. Haig called Kissinger to relay this as the President's judgment. Kissinger was furious. Al reported to the President that Kissinger wouldn't come home. The President held firm; Kissinger said he'd come if he must. Kissinger got back . . . he acted defeated. Haig got with Haldeman and Ehrlichman to get their support for B-52 bombing of Hanoi." The journal went on to note that it was unclear whether it was Haldeman who originated the idea of using B-52s to raid Hanoi. "Before the elections, the idea had been discussed of using B-52s to destroy the water treatment plant. Kissinger had said that he would prefer to bomb with tactical air since it creates a less bloody image, but Kissinger had to go along with B-52s.

"When Haig was away," the journal added, "Kissinger went to the President about Haig," whose appointment as the Army's Vice Chief of Staff, under General Creighton Abrams, had been announced months earlier. "[Kissinger] said it was important to get Haig back in the Army because nobody was watching Abrams from within the Army . . . Haig is trying to use Scali to get Henry, to send word to the President that Kissinger is whipped as a negotiator. Haig is playing the 'sinking ship' routine very skillfully. He plays both sides, working Henry and telephoning the President." *

"The President was in a very low mood today," the journal noted shortly after the B-52 bombing of Hanoi had begun. "He seems to swing back and forth between getting out and his fear of what this will make him look like historically." There was "some thought" inside the White House that Nguyen Van Thieu might have played a key role in disrupting the negotiations by "leaking to Hanoi . . . The Soviets have told us that we can't handle Saigon and that they're having trouble handling Hanoi."

Nixon's insistence that Kissinger continue the stalemated negotiations for another week was both a sign of his displeasure with Kissinger and a diplomatic shot in the dark. He was hoping that his threats, relayed by Kissinger, could accomplish what they had been unable to do all during the Vietnam War —make the North cower. He would wait until the bombs started falling before

---

* Haig told one NSC colleague, according to the Kissinger office journal: "Henry is trying to promote me out of the White House." Haig's promotion in September to full four-star general, a two-rank jump within six months, enraged his fellow Army officers, as did his continued access to the President after he began the Pentagon job in early 1973. He and Nixon continued to talk via a direct secure telephone line that was installed in his Pentagon office, to the annoyance of General Abrams, who had become Army Chief of Staff on October 16, 1972.

dealing with Thieu. On December 14, the President authorized the reseeding of mines in Haiphong Harbor and extensive B-52 strikes against Hanoi and Haiphong. Some two hundred aircraft, more than half of the Strategic Air Command's B-52s, were pressed into service for around-the-clock bombing despite monsoon weather. The bombing was to begin in three days. Nixon quoted himself as telling Admiral Moorer: "I don't want any more of this crap about the fact that we couldn't hit this target or that one. This is your chance to use military power effectively to win this war, and if you don't, I'll consider you responsible."*

Kissinger was quick to give reassurance. In a diary entry of December 13, Nixon quoted him as talking "rather emotionally about the fact that this was a very courageous decision. . . . I pointed out to him that there was no other choice." It was agreed that Kissinger would brief the press about the state of the negotiations on December 16, two days after Nixon's order to attack and one day before the first bombs fell.

In this moment of crisis, Kissinger was careful to reinforce his ties to the liberal press. His main vehicle once again was James Reston, who had flown to Paris during the December round of talks with Le Duc Tho and been granted a series of private meetings with Kissinger.† On December 13, the day before the talks broke off and more than a week after Kissinger had secretly urged Nixon to renew the bombing of the North, Reston published a dispatch describing Thieu's insistence on sovereignty as being the most difficult unresolved issue in the talks. Reston's dispatch was essentially accurate on the point, but its message was that Kissinger or some other presidential envoy was planning to make one more trip to Saigon "in a final effort to persuade President Thieu to sign the cease-fire agreement and avoid a separate peace . . ." Kissinger did not tell Reston about the warnings to Hanoi. His goal in talking to the columnist was to deflect the criticism that was bound to come when the bombs started falling. Kissinger's credibility with the *Times* remained high enough to prevent the newspaper from publishing a mid-December dispatch from the reliable William Beecher reporting that the private Paris talks had broken down and that renewed bombing of the North was being considered. A Washington editor of the *Times* remembers Beecher's account of an enraged President "throwing stuff against the wall" and calling for a resumption of the bombing; but the *Times* editors in New York consulted Reston, so the Wash-

* Just what Admiral Moorer honestly understood about the negotiations remains a mystery. In 1981, analyzing the Christmas bombing in a Navy journal, Moorer wrote that the bombing had been authorized by Nixon after it became "quite clear that the North Vietnamese had no intention of either releasing the POWs or abiding by the agreement which Dr. Kissinger thought he had made. The President was increasingly determined to take some action that would convince them they must release the POWs." He recommended the B-52 bombing of Hanoi and Haiphong, the admiral wrote, "because I felt then, and feel today, that the historians of the future are going to shake their heads in bewilderment when they remember how the United States was literally outmaneuvered by a third-rate country with a population of less than two counties in one of the 50 states of the United States." Unfortunately, it seems possible that the admiral was as ignorant of the negotiating issues as his account suggests.

† William Porter was amused to learn, after joining Kissinger's personal staff for the final round of negotiations, that Reston was sharing occasional breakfasts with Kissinger in the embassy. Invariably Kissinger would assemble his staff before such meetings, Porter says, and "We'd all catch hell about leaking. All of us. He'd tell us that the *New York Times* was going to break this or that story. Every damned time there'd be a breakfast with Scotty [Reston], Henry would gather the staff to warn about leaks."

ington bureau was told, and Reston insisted that the talks were on track, and Beecher's story was shelved. "The Pentagon's trying to sabotage the agreement," one senior editor told the Washington bureau.

Kissinger also took steps to deny that he and Nixon were at each other's throat, as much of official Washington believed. Nick Thimmesch, a conservative columnist known for his close ties to Haldeman and Colson, was summoned to Kissinger's office shortly after Kissinger returned from Paris and scolded about two recent columns in which a Nixon-Kissinger estrangement was mentioned. "I don't care who you talked to," Kissinger told Thimmesch. ". . . [The] President and I are in complete agreement, we are in immediate and constant contact. There are absolutely no differences between us." Kissinger made the same point a few days later in a talk with John Osborne, White House columnist for the *New Republic*. Kissinger's motive in issuing such denials was self-protection, of course; he was a creature of the President and his authority was derivative. He would need all his authority and all his skills to explain away the administration's bumbling of the negotiations and convince the world that it was Hanoi, not Saigon—or Washington—that had made a settlement impossible.

The purpose of Kissinger's December 16 news briefing was to place the blame on Hanoi for the breakdown of the talks, and thus prepare the way for the heavy bombings that would follow within hours. Kissinger, of course, did not remind the press that Richard Nixon had twice approved the October agreement (nor was he asked about Nixon's approval). He blamed the failure in October on three events: an alleged Communist buildup, the Arnaud de Borchgrave interview with Pham Van Dong, "and thirdly . . . we encountered some specific objections from Saigon." In response to a question, he insisted that "the obstacle to an agreement at this moment is not Saigon because we do not as yet have an agreement that we can present to them." Kissinger's astonishing implication, unchallenged by any reporter, was that the Nixon Administration would not discuss a proposed treaty with Nguyen Van Thieu prior to a final settlement. Kissinger once again argued on behalf of Thieu's claim of sovereignty: ". . . [W]e cannot accept the proposition that North Vietnam has a right of constant intervention in the South." Kissinger did not remind his audience, however, that such concerns had not prevented him from negotiating the October agreement. The real issue—Hanoi's insistence that the October agreements be ratified—was never broached on December 16. Instead, Hanoi was accused of spuriously raising new issues to frustrate Kissinger's attempt to reach agreement. "It was very tempting for us to continue the process which is close to everybody's heart . . ." Kissinger said. "But the President decided that we could not engage in a charade with the American people."

The press was hopelessly outgunned. Kissinger had negotiated in secret, and relentlessly controlled information about those negotiations. He had fought with Nixon and his aides in secret. He had spoken sternly with the hawks and softly with the doves. It was impossible for the press to trip him up.

Kissinger, in his memoirs, expressed no regret over the B-52 bombing of Hanoi and Haiphong; his main concern was Nixon's decision to link him publicly to it. "If I admired Nixon's decision," Kissinger wrote, "I was less enthusiastic about his refusal to explain it to the public . . . These events were bound to produce a tremendous furor. But Nixon was determined to take himself out of the line of fire . . . [I]f there was a major uproar, only the President would be able to quiet it and give the public a sense of where we were headed." Kissinger did find a way to duck the limelight a little: He mentioned the President fourteen times during his December 16 briefing.

Much of the nation and the world immediately denounced the B-52 bombings as a military and moral outrage. As protests rolled into the White House, Hanoi reported the destruction of the Bach Mai Hospital, the city's largest, which was hit by an estimated one hundred bombs. There were eyewitness accounts of the almost total destruction of a workers' housing area, and fiery statements of defiance from North Vietnamese government officials. The real target of the bombs, however, was in Saigon, where Nguyen Van Thieu would soon be handed a presidential ultimatum. Nixon was bombing to convince Thieu that America's secret promises were credible. He was bombing so that a corrupt dictator who had been supported for four years in the name of American credibility would allow him to claim "peace with honor." He was bombing in the belief that the combination of American aircraft and secret agreements would be enough to keep South Vietnam non-Communist forever. Kissinger apparently supported Nixon's policy without qualms, though he also understood that the North Vietnamese were being punished for insisting that he and Nixon sign an agreement that had been negotiated two months earlier and considered complete.

Kissinger perhaps could have taken consolation in the knowledge that the bombs over Hanoi would at last force a showdown in Saigon, and leave the White House free to return to the October agreement. This did, in fact, take place, but there is no evidence in the memoirs that the men running the government ever explicitly discussed the fact that the target of the bombs was in Saigon. Nixon's and Kissinger's memoirs are replete with the fiction that Hanoi, faced with B-52 bombing, capitulated and returned chastened to the Paris talks. Hanoi did return to Paris, but only after Nixon and Kissinger made it clear that the October agreement would once again be on the table, without additional demands; Kissinger, in a cable to Hanoi in late December, also held out a promise of "normalization"—the establishment of full diplomatic and economic relations—with the North Vietnamese.

The Nixon-Kissinger policy was one that, as the memoirs made clear, neither man seemed capable of describing to the other. Nixon authorized the bombing knowing it would force Nguyen Van Thieu to accept his assurances of continued sovereignty, increased aid, and renewed bombing. He was bombing the North in order to continue the war. Kissinger supported the bombing policy aware that its real purpose was to convince Thieu he should accept a peace agreement he would be able to disavow.

Over the Christmas holidays, as the bombings and the protests continued, Kissinger began dissociating himself. He told his favorite columnists that he had disagreed with Nixon. James Reston put it most directly: "It may be, and probably is, true, that Mr. Kissinger as well as Secretary of State Rogers and most of the senior officers in the State Department are opposed to the President's bombing offensive in North Vietnam. And also, that Mr. Kissinger would be more willing than the President to take a chance on signing the ambiguous truce terms of October 26. But Mr. Kissinger," Reston wrote loyally, "is too much of a scholar, with too good a sense of humor and history, to put his own thoughts ahead of the President's." In his memoirs, Kissinger perfunctorily denied indicating to journalists that he had opposed the B-52 decision. "But," he added, "I did little to dampen the speculation, partly in reaction to the harassment of the previous week [from press attacks instigated by Nixon's aides], partly out of a not very heroic desire to deflect the assault from my person. Some of the journalists may have mistaken my genuine depression about the seeming collapse of the peace efforts for a moral disagreement."*

* Kissinger never quite seemed to make up his mind about the bombing. In his memoirs, he denigrated the notion, widespread as it was throughout the world, that the bombing was indiscriminate and aimed at terrorizing the residents of the North. He quoted at length from an analysis by historian Guenter Lewy of the University of Massachusetts, whose *America in Vietnam*, published in 1978, was extremely critical of American press coverage of the war. Lewy suggested that part of Hanoi's death toll of up to 1,600 (most residents had been evacuated from the city before the bombing began) was caused by North Vietnamese surface-to-air missiles that had impacted in Hanoi and Haiphong after being fired at American aircraft. Yet while in the White House Kissinger repeatedly bragged about the bombing's devastation. After he had flown to Hanoi for his first visit, in early 1973, he told Nick Thimmesch that he had been anxious at landing near Hanoi because of the damaged airfield. "You should have seen it," Thimmesch quoted Kissinger as exclaiming. "It looked like a lunar landscape." He told South Vietnamese Ambassador Phuong that "if he had known that the B-52s were that effective, he would have recommended it four years earlier. He was surprised by the effectiveness." Kissinger had a different description for President Nixon, who shared his nervousness over the reports of "carpet bombing" of the North. Nixon quoted Kissinger as telling him there was little damage to the nonmilitary areas. Nixon, in one of his conversations with David Frost in 1977, added that Kissinger had made his own estimates of civilian casualties— "perhaps no more than 400–500 civilians were killed." It was not clear how Kissinger reached that conclusion. One American military estimate, cited by *U.S. News & World Report* early in 1973, quoted intelligence analysts as concluding "that between 5,000 and 10,000 North Vietnamese soldiers may also have died in the raids . . ." The magazine also quoted officials in Hanoi as reporting that "fewer than 2,200 persons [civilians] were killed in the capital." One military man was quoted as saying, in response to allegations of indiscriminate bombing, "When you compare the lives lost in the December raids with the hundreds of thousands who died in a single fire-bomb attack during World War II, then it can be seen that the strikes were not aimed at inflicting casualties." General John Vogt, the Seventh Air Force commander, was perhaps the best informed of any official American witness about the accuracy of the B-52 bombers. In a 1978 interview with the Air Force's oral history program, made available under the Freedom of Information Act, General Vogt acknowledged that the Christmas bombing demonstrated that the "accuracy of even our strategic forces is not all that good, and we had lots of problems in using B-52s in bad weather . . . The equipment was designed for nuclear weapons, where it didn't make much difference if you were 1,500 feet off the target, you were still in the blast areas. But with conventional bombs, trying to drop them to do some damage and effectively hit a target with accuracies less than 500 feet simply couldn't be done." In a subsequent interview, Vogt emphasized that the SAC forces did everything possible, given the constantly poor weather over North Vietnam, to minimize civilian casualties. He blamed much of the nonmilitary damage to Hanoi and Haiphong on the "notoriously bad" internal radar systems of the B-52s. "The missed distances were great," the general added. "Misses of 1,000 feet or more were common." The accuracy of the B-52 bombsights was so unreliable, Vogt recalled, that the White House refused to authorize a B-52 raid on a plant in the heart of Hanoi at which SAM missiles were being constructed overnight. Knocking out the facility was considered one obvious way to reduce the high loss rate of the American bombers, but the estimate of civilian casualties from a B-52 strike was in the thousands. Vogt requested authority to attack the plant with tactical fighter-bomber planes instead and was told by Admiral Moorer, he recalled, "You've got authority to do it, but you are not authorized to kill any civilians." "Can you believe it?" Vogt added in disgust. The fighter-bombers withstood intense fire and destroyed the plant, he said, but the mission came far too late to prevent the B-52s from "going down like flies."

There was little rejoicing, either, at the top of the Saigon government. Tran Kim Phuong, Saigon's Ambassador to Washington, recalls his fear that the "bombing was to put pressure on us to sign. After the bombing, the United States would have grounds to go it alone." Le Chi Thao, the young South Vietnamese national security aide, says, "Our analysis was that the Christmas bombing was not good for the Vietnamese government at all. It was done to press the signing of the agreement." Hoang Duc Nha remembers his disappointment when the White House announced the end of the bombing on December 30: "We said, 'They have no intention to bomb Hanoi off the earth.' I understood they had broken the impasse. Now it was our turn to be ready to negotiate." Haig, still viewed as Nixon's errand boy by the South Vietnamese, arrived in Saigon on December 19 to deliver a tough letter to Nguyen Van Thieu. "It was imperative," Nixon wrote in his memoirs, that Thieu "join us in offering reasonable terms Hanoi would be willing to accept. We considered Agnew, Laird, and Connally for this unenviable job, but finally I said, 'Haig is still the man to carry the message to Garcia.' " Thieu was at last going to get the ultimatum that Nixon had refused to give in late October. "Let me emphasize," Nixon's letter, as drafted by Kissinger, declared, ". . . that General Haig is not coming to Saigon for the purpose of negotiating with you. The time has come for us to present a united front in negotiating with our enemies, and you must decide now whether you desire to continue our alliance or whether you want me to seek a settlement with the enemy which serves U.S. interests alone." Thieu understood that Nixon was offering secret guarantees of sovereignty and continued economic and military aid, plus a commitment to retaliate in case of North Vietnamese ceasefire violations, in return for his acquiescence in the continued presence of Hanoi's troops in the South.

The next day, Kissinger reported in his memoirs, the bombing paid an immediate dividend: Thieu withdrew his objections to the political provisions as presented in the October agreement. But he again restated his opposition to Hanoi's troops being granted a legal right to stay in place. "Haig and I both recommended to Nixon that we proceed with the negotiations with Hanoi anyway," Kissinger wrote. After two months of travail, and the mass bombing of the North, Kissinger had come full circle; he was concluding a settlement behind the back of Nguyen Van Thieu. Now, however, he had Richard Nixon with him. The President, convinced that the bombing would hide his retreat, was suddenly eager to do Thieu in. "Thieu leaked word to reporters," Nixon wrote in his memoirs, "that we had tried to force him to accept an ultimatum and that he had refused. I was shocked when I learned this, and I felt we would now be justified in breaking with him and making a separate peace with Hanoi." What stopped him, Nixon added, was his reluctance to "allow our annoyance with him to lead us to do anything that might bring about Communist domination of South Vietnam." At this point, the President still believed that the October agreement would not lead to Hanoi's eventual victory in the South. The agreement Nixon had in mind, of course, was the secret one. Those aides, such as Haig, who had harshly criticized Kissinger's peace plan in October shared Nixon's understanding; they remained silent about what seemed to be the same agreement in late December. Nguyen Van Thieu's published complaints must have appeared all the more insulting, for he was denigrating

Nixon's secret peace plan, with its promise of retaliation, which, if carried out, offered him a real chance to stay in power.

Over the next ten days, Nixon and Kissinger, having wrung some concessions from Thieu, began to back down with the North Vietnamese. The bombing, which would continue for twelve days, had accomplished its major mission —with Nguyen Van Thieu—by its third day; the President now needed a graceful way out. The political heat was intense. A poll of seventy-three senators by *Congressional Quarterly* magazine showed that, as of December 21, only nineteen were in favor of the renewed bombing. The senators also declared that they would vote, forty-five to twenty-five, in favor of legislation to end American involvement in South Vietnam. Nixon, in his memoirs, acknowledged that he expected the newly seated Congress, which was to go into session on January 2, 1973, to vote immediately to cut off American spending. The bombing had to end before Congress acted.

As usual, the White House retreat was shielded from the press. On December 19, the day after the first wave of bombings, a tough-talking Ziegler told reporters that the raids over the North would "continue until such time as a settlement is announced." Four days later, after the ultimatum to Thieu, Ziegler, now in Florida with the President, had a much softer message. The President, he declared, was "determined" to continue the bombing until North Vietnam decided to resume the negotiations "in a spirit of good will and in a constructive attitude." No one in the press seemed to notice the change in terms. It was Kissinger's memoirs, ironically, that provided the most detailed account of how Washington backtracked. On December 22, Kissinger wrote, he sent a cable to Hanoi proposing another meeting with Le Duc Tho: "The choice is whether to slide into a continuation of the conflict or to make a serious final effort to reach a settlement at a time when agreement is so near." If Hanoi agreed to a meeting, Kissinger cabled, the B-52 bombings of Hanoi and Haiphong would cease as of December 31. Kissinger did not publish the full text of the message in his memoirs, but there is little doubt that Hanoi was also told then—as it was five days later—that the negotiations would be reopened on the basis of the October draft. On December 26, Hanoi cabled that talks could be resumed as soon as the bombing stopped. Kissinger had proposed a meeting with Le Duc Tho on January 3, but Hanoi, describing Tho as being in poor health, instead suggested January 8.

At this point, Kissinger wrote, Nixon wanted reassurance that the talks would be back on track before Congress returned. Kissinger depicted the President as suddenly "enthusiastic" about a possible television appearance should the peace negotiations finally succeed. To meet Nixon's desire for a speedy return to the bargaining table, he sent another message to Hanoi on December 27 offering to stop the bombing within thirty-six hours if Hanoi would confirm that Le Duc Tho was prepared to meet in Paris on January 8. Hanoi was reassured that the treaty to be discussed was the October draft. "If both sides now return to the attitude of good will shown in October," Kissinger cabled, "the remaining problems can be rapidly solved. This will be the spirit with which the U.S. side will approach this final effort to conclude *the October negotiations* [emphasis added]." Hanoi agreed on December 28, and, according to Kissinger's memoirs, the Vietnamese were formally told that the bombing would stop by evening on December 29. Still another inducement was offered in Kissinger's cable of December 29, as reprinted in his memoirs: "The decision must be made now whether it is possible to move from a period of hostility to one of normalization. This remains the US goal. . . ."

Hanoi had thus been promised that the B-52 bombing would stop if it agreed to return to Paris to discuss normalization—full diplomatic relations—as well as to negotiate within the October framework, which of course had been Le Duc Tho's basic demand ever since October. Yet Nixon, in his memoirs, described Hanoi's cable of December 26 as "the first signal that they had had enough. . . ." He knew better. The doubts showed up in his diary, as excerpted in his memoirs: "The real question is whether the announcement today [ending the bombing] will be interpreted in the public mind as having been the result of a policy that worked. Of course, it will not be so interpreted by our opponents in the media and the Congress." He was confident Kissinger would say the right thing, however. "Henry always looks at it in terms of the merits," Nixon wrote, "and on the merits we know that what this is is a very stunning capitulation by the enemy to our terms."

The military men weren't fooled. They knew it was Nixon, and not North Vietnam, who had capitulated. Even Haig acknowledged, in a television interview years later, that "I felt as a military man that could we have applied that pressure, ah, somewhat more extensively for a great period of time—that the conditions which we could have imposed on Hanoi would have been somewhat more binding. . . . I was, ah, frankly uncomfortable about the aspect of the negotiations at the time that it would have been a good idea if we had continued until they did exactly what we wanted them to—until we got every North Vietnamese soldier out of South Vietnam. . . ."

It was left to Gerald Warren, the deputy press secretary, to announce the end of the bombing. Everyone else had run for cover over the Christmas holidays, leaving Warren and two other junior officials—Richard Kennedy of Kissinger's staff and Alexander Butterfield of Haldeman's—nominally in charge. Nixon flew to Key Biscayne on December 20, two days after the bombing began, where he wallowed in self-pity as the protests mounted. "It was the loneliest and saddest Christmas I can ever remember," Nixon told David Frost, "much sadder and much more lonely than the one in the Pacific during the war. I didn't get many calls from members of the Cabinet . . . and some of our friends in the media, the few that we had, were raising serious questions about the wisdom of what had been done . . ."* Nixon had all but

* Fifteen B-52s were shot down over North Vietnam during the twelve days of bombing, with ninety-three American airmen officially listed as missing. Hanoi reported capturing thirty-one pilots. The high loss rate resulted in part from the major air defense improvements in November and early December, as hundreds of additional SAM units were dug in around Hanoi and Haiphong. There were immediate repercussions over the loss of the aircraft, not only in the press and in Congress but in the Strategic Air Command. Many pilots and crew members refused to fly, a fact that was carefully kept from the public by the Air Force. "In any event," Nixon wrote after learning of the loss of three B-52s on the first day of bombing, "the decision is made and we cannot turn back . . . I have called Moorer to be sure to stiffen his back with regard to the need to follow through on these attacks. I suppose we may be pressing him too hard, but I fear that the Air Force and the Navy may in carrying out orders have been too cautious at times . . ." Kissinger, in his memoirs, described the B-52 bombings as Nixon's "last roll of the dice." The bombing further demoralized the young airmen flying intelligence operations for the Air Force Security Service, whose mission was to monitor North Vietnamese communications constantly and help the B-52s dodge the SAM

retreated from direct public view. His last presidential news conference had been on October 5, shortly before North Vietnam's breakthrough in the Paris peace talks. His last Cabinet meeting had been on November 8, the day after his overwhelming reelection. His easy reelection, he acknowledged in his memoirs, triggered a depression. "I am at a loss to explain the melancholy that settled over me on that victorious night," he wrote. "To some extent the marring effects of Watergate may have played a part, to some extent our failure to win Congress, and to a greater extent the fact that we had not yet been able to end the war in Vietnam." Aside from a brief victory statement, at which no questions could be asked, Nixon had appeared in person only on November 27, when he met briefly with reporters in California to announce Cabinet changes. He answered no questions.

There was, as usual, much brooding in the President's isolation; and, as usual, much of the concern was over Henry Kissinger. Nixon's resentment of Kissinger, which ebbed and flowed during this period, was basic. It was Kissinger's insistence on rushing the peace agreement in October and then declaring, "Peace is at hand," that had gotten him into the mess. As a result, Kissinger was constantly unsure of his standing. He had, for example, flown with Nixon to Key Biscayne and told his staff he would be there a week, until Nixon returned to Washington on December 26. Two days later he was back in Washington, and he did not meet with Nixon again until January 2, 1973. After Christmas, Kissinger joined other senior members of the White House staff, including Haldeman, in Palm Springs, California, for a brief vacation.

missiles. The airmen were able to eavesdrop on the North Vietnamese SAM batteries in "real time" —that is, as the communications took place—and were responsible for alerting the heavy, slow-flying aircraft to potential danger. Many of the airmen had been serving during the alleged "protective reaction" missions of General John Lavelle earlier in the year, and they staged a work stoppage to protest the December bombings.

In early 1973, I learned of the protests, which centered on members of the supersecret 6990th AFSS unit at Torii Station in Okinawa. My interviews then showed that in the fall the men of the 6990th had concluded, on the basis of their monitoring of the North, that the Hanoi government was preparing for a major air show in late October to celebrate the expected peace. Some of Hanoi's MIGs had been disarmed in preparation for the show when Kissinger issued his "Peace is at hand" statement. Over the next six weeks, members of the 6990th said in interviews, bombing continued in northern sections of North Vietnam, despite the White House announcement of a ban on such missions. Angry at the continued heavy bombing, which the unit was forbidden to report, the airmen simply refused to monitor SAM traffic and other communications over Christmas. Charles Terry Iverson, who served more than three years with AFSS, recalled: "I took the first messages on the Christmas blitz. That was a hard time for me. What we were doing was providing security for them [the B-52s]—monitoring North Vietnam's SAM sites and their ground operations. And it was like we were putting them up there. A lot of guys felt the same way. It was a funny feeling: like what the B-52s were doing wasn't right. Rather than working, guys were refusing. If the men would have been motivated, if they had wanted to do their job, we wouldn't have lost as many B-52s as we did. It was a sick feeling I had personally. My father was a military man, so I did what was expected of me. But it was the hard part, because my conscience told me not to." Courts-martial for some members of the 6990th were held later, in Taiwan, amid stringent secrecy. Some members of the unit (I interviewed more than ten in early 1973) described the work stoppage as a virtual mutiny, with cheers arising every time a B-52 was shot down. Tom Bernard, also of the 6990th, recalled that "the unit was in a state of shock, with all that talk that had been going on about 'Peace is at hand.'" Thomas E. Eskelson said that the shock of the Christmas bombing was heightened by "our mostly certain knowledge that the North Vietnamese were fully ready to abide by a ceasefire on the first of November." Most of the malcontents were immediately pulled off AFSS duty and reassigned to menial military tasks, pending reassignment and judicial proceedings. At least one member of the 6990th was found guilty after a court-martial of refusing to report to work and was sentenced to loss of pay, reduction of rank, and a month's confinement at hard labor. Others received only minor punishments.

Before leaving, he spent an hour with Ross Terrill, the China scholar, then doing research at Harvard University. Terrill had been prepared to fly to Florida for the meeting but was summoned instead to Washington; it was clear from the confusion, Terrill recalls, that Kissinger's relations with the President were strained. Kissinger was anxious, not surprisingly, to talk about Vietnam. "The Vietnamese are all the same," he told Terrill. "They are quite impossible to deal with." At another point, when Terrill praised him for the China initiative, Kissinger responded, "Now I hope we can sustain it for four more years." He paused and added: "I won't be here for four more years. I couldn't." Asked whether he would return to Harvard, Kissinger described it as "impossible . . . No job could be as important as this. There is nowhere to go."

Kissinger's intent in these days was to keep not just his job but his reputation with the press and the liberal community.* In Palm Springs, he talked incessantly to reporters, unaware that Charles Colson, on behalf of the President, had ordered that copies of his telephone logs, which were maintained by the Secret Service, be sent to his office. "We weren't listening to Henry's conversations," Colson recalls. "We were learning who he called." John Scali was also involved in the snooping, Colson says. By New Year's Day, there was no attempt to hide what they were doing. After Kissinger had an extensive telephone conversation with Joseph Kraft, Colson reminded him of Nixon's orders that he not deal with the press. "Kissinger told me, 'I wouldn't talk to that son-of-a-bitch'—and he had just hung up from him," Colson recalls.

Kissinger struck back. He understood the peril of his situation. The privately maintained NSC office journal describes him as being aware that week that "his job is on the line . . ." Reston again was the vehicle for a message to the man on top. On December 31, Reston published a detailed analysis of Kissinger's bargaining leverage: "Mr. Kissinger is a servant of the President and has never pretended he was anything else. He has carried out the President's instruction in Paris to the letter. He has put all the blame on Hanoi for the impasse in the Paris cease-fire negotiations, and has said nothing in public

---

* Kissinger justified the bombing to some reporters by suggesting that it had been necessary to convince the "hawks," or pro-Soviet faction in Hanoi's politburo, to accede to the peace agreement. Reporters were told that the "hawks," in a dispute with the pro-Chinese "doves," had resisted a negotiated settlement in favor of mounting another wide-scale offensive in 1973. The thesis of a split inside Hanoi's Communist Party had been bandied around by American intelligence officials, notably in the CIA, since the early 1960s, but there was no real evidence. In NSSM 1, the Nixon Administration's first review of the issues in the Vietnam War, the various analysts were unable to agree whether such factions did exist. Foreign Service officers in the American Embassy in Saigon reported then that information about the politburo was "very limited and speculative." One official, who helped coordinate the initial responses to NSSM 1, recalls each agency agreeing that there were at least two or three factions in the politburo. But each cited different members in different factions, with some senior politburo members being listed in both the Soviet and Chinese camps. "The point is," the official says, "these guys didn't have a clue." Nguyen Co Thach, asked about the alleged split, acknowledged that there had been extensive discussions in the politburo in mid-1972, when the decision to compromise over Nguyen Van Thieu was made, but that decision, once made, was unanimous, he said. Kissinger's last-minute adoption of the hawk-dove thesis in late 1972 in an attempt to help justify the Christmas bombing was patently self-serving, for there is no evidence in his memoirs or elsewhere that he found it plausible. For a more complete discussion of the issue, see "How Scholars Lie," by D. Gareth Porter, in *Worldview* magazine for December 1973. Porter reviews the literature on the alleged split in the politburo and concludes that "it has been based not on historical evidence but on politically inspired speculation."

about the bombing in North Vietnam, which he undoubtedly opposes. . . . He is avoiding a break with the President, and the President is avoiding a break with him. For if the bombing goes on and there is an open split between the President and his principal foreign affairs adviser and negotiator, Mr. Kissinger will be free to resign and write the whole story of the Paris talks and why they broke down, and this would probably be highly embarrassing to Mr. Nixon at the beginning of his second term."

The President of the United States was being warned, and not subtly. Haldeman, in his memoirs, recalled the reaction. "Find out what the hell Henry's doing," Nixon ordered from his retreat at Camp David, where he was spending the New Year's holiday. Haldeman and Nixon understood that Reston's "inside information," as Haldeman put it, could only have come from Kissinger. But Kissinger, Haldeman wrote, denied talking "about bombing to *anyone*." In particular, he vehemently claimed that he had never talked to the *Times* columnist. "He said, 'I did not give Reston an interview.' " Haldeman checked around, he wrote, and, not mentioning the Colson-Scali monitoring, said to Kissinger, "You told us you didn't give Reston an interview but in fact you did talk to him." Kissinger's response: "Yes, but that was only on the telephone."

Nixon abruptly decided to return to the White House early on New Year's Day. "He was so angry that he couldn't stay at Camp David," Colson says. Colson and Steve Bull, the President's appointments secretary, spent much of the day with the President—"babysitting him," as Colson puts it—watching various football bowl games on television. There was no direct confrontation with Kissinger. There never would be. Neither Nixon nor Kissinger wanted the truth of the peace negotiations made public.

By early January, Nixon and Kissinger were forced to go a step further with Thieu. On January 2, the House Democratic caucus voted 154 to 75 to cut off all funds for the Vietnam War as soon as the orderly withdrawal of American GIs and the prisoners of war had been arranged. On January 4, the Senate Democratic caucus passed a similar resolution 36 to 12. The next day, Nixon put his secret commitment in writing to Nguyen Van Thieu: "Should you decide, as I trust you will, to go with us, you have my assurance of continued assistance in the post-settlement period and that we will respond with full force should the settlement be violated by North Vietnam." Nixon had made a similar, if less specific, guarantee in a letter to Thieu in mid-November, but the January letter was more significant, for it came only days after Nixon had concluded the bloody and divisive Christmas bombing. His promise was now credible.

Having made his commitment, and having previously reassured Thieu that he would maintain his sovereignty—in America's eyes—in the South, Nixon was ready to settle the war. On January 6, he met with Kissinger—their personal differences temporarily put aside in the face of danger—to discuss strategy for Kissinger's meeting with Le Duc Tho in Paris on January 8. "Adding it all up," Nixon wrote in his memoirs, "I put it to Henry quite directly that even if we could go back to the October 8 agreement that we should take it, having in mind the fact that there will be a lot of details that will have been ironed out so that we can claim some improvement.''

The North Vietnamese were stunned, Nguyen Co Thach later recalled, when Kissinger opened the January 8 meeting by insisting to Le Duc Tho as they shook hands: ''It was not my responsibility. It was not my fault about the bombing.'' Nevertheless, much of the meeting was spent rebuking Kissinger for it. At one point, Tho declared, ''You have come to Hanoi by bombing with B-52s.'' Kissinger requested that Tho not speak so loudly, according to the North Vietnamese, out of fear that the reporters outside the villa would over-hear. At the close of the meeting, Kissinger urged Le Duc Tho to join him in walking out in view of the press: ''Now we must forget all that has happened,'' a Vietnamese official quotes him, ''and walk out and smile.'' Kissinger, in his memoirs, painted a far different scene: ''Le Duc Tho,'' he wrote, seeking ''to play to our media's outrage at the bombing . . . avoided any joint public hand-shakes with me at all . . . In fact, relations on the inside, out of sight of the press, were rather warm.''

It took only a few hours on the next day, January 9, to resolve the few outstanding issues and return to the October agreement. There were some cosmetic compromises on the DMZ and the tripartite election commission, but Kissinger, following Nixon's orders to reach a quick settlement, did not insist on any basic changes. One compromise called for civilian traffic across the demilitarized zone to be regulated by ''North and South Vietnam.'' This did nothing for Thieu, since the PRG controlled the areas south of the DMZ and could be construed under the compromise to represent ''South Vietnam.'' The language was deliberately left ambiguous. Le Duc Tho agreed to drop the phrase ''administrative structure'' from the language describing the tripartite election commission, but the commission still stood, and still remained as a dramatic improvement—at least on paper—in the status of the PRG.

In his memoirs, Richard Nixon did not deal at all with the substantive issues of the peace agreement, nor did he discuss the negotiated compromises and the secret commitments at the end. He accepted Kissinger's account, as cabled late on January 9, of a ''major breakthrough'' and quoted Kissinger's obse-quious final paragraph: ''What has brought us to this point is the President's firmness and the North Vietnamese belief that he will not be affected by either Congressional or public pressures. Le Duc Tho has repeatedly made these points to me. So it is essential that we keep our fierce posture during the coming days. The slightest hint of eagerness could prove suicidal.''

Kissinger did not hesitate to cite phantasmagorical statements allegedly made by Le Duc Tho. He could also tell Nixon on his own, after a day of making concessions, that it was ''our fierce posture'' that had brought results. Nixon, by accepting such pabulum at face value, was sharing in the lie. The two men were dealing in fantasy—toward the public. Privately, both must have understood that much of what took place in those final negotiations was a charade that would produce no ceasefire, no election, and no peace. Nguyen Van Thieu, bolstered by American arms and secret promises, would continue to wage the war. South Vietnam would continue to be non-Communist.

By January 11, the final drafting was complete, and four days later Nixon ordered all bombing over North Vietnam to cease. "The bombing had done its job; it had been successful, and now it could be ended," he wrote. Haig was sent on another mission to Saigon, to wring Thieu's final consent to the treaty. Nixon was determined to prevail, Kissinger wrote. " 'Brutality is nothing,' he said to me. 'You have never seen it if this son-of-a-bitch doesn't go along, believe me.' " In his diary, as quoted in his memoirs, Nixon tried to convince himself that he was merely providing Thieu with strong medicine that would soon be curative: "Thieu's choice is simply whether he wants to commit suicide or go along with a settlement that could save his country as well as himself." Thieu, facing a threatened cutoff of all economic and military assistance, gave in within days. In his farewell speech in South Vietnam on April 21, 1975, shortly after he resigned as President, Thieu explained why he had finally consented to the Paris peace agreement: "There was untold menace and pressure [in late 1972 and early 1973]. With regard to pressure, let me say frankly, that Mr. Nixon told me as follows, 'All accords are, in the final analysis, mere sheets of paper. They will be worthless if they are not implemented and if North Vietnam violates them. Therefore, the important thing is what you will do after the agreement, and what facilities we will make available to you if North Vietnam reneges or violates the agreement and renews its attacks against the South. So, you should not be concerned about the signing of this agreement . . .' " He had concluded at the time, Thieu went on, that South Vietnam's survival "depended on bombs and ammunition . . . on economic facilities and on U.S. backing. This was more practical than having a beautifully worded agreement." *

Nguyen Van Thieu had been told that he could ignore the Paris peace agreement and would receive continued American support in so doing. No senior official in the White House or in the Presidential Palace was taking the political provisions of the agreement seriously on January 23, when the treaty was finally initialed in Paris.

On that day, three days after his second inauguration, and while he and Kissinger were being celebrated as peacemakers, Richard Nixon announced the end of the war in a television interview. He claimed peace with honor and then fulfilled one of his secret commitments to Thieu by declaring: "The United States will continue to recognize the Government of the Republic of Vietnam as the sole legitimate government of South Vietnam." With that sentence Nixon was broadcasting his intention not to abide by the agreement, which had established the right of the PRG to share power in the South with the Saigon regime.† It was, of course, not the end of the war. Both sides fought

* At least one reporter grasped the significance of Thieu's remarks. Tom Wicker, the *New York Times* columnist, wrote on the day of Thieu's speech that Nixon's pledge, if made, "was bound to have had the effect of underwriting Mr. Thieu's policy of ignoring the American-sponsored peace agreement while continuing hostilities . . . [Thieu] was virtually guaranteed his security . . . Why should he enter a negotiation that if honestly pursued could only lead to compromise with Hanoi and his own departure from power?" Thieu's speech, Wicker added, "does tend to confirm that it was not Hanoi that reneged on the October agreement but Saigon that at first refused to accept the agreements negotiated by Mr. Kissinger and Le Duc Tho. That is almost entirely contrary to the official version given the American people . . ."

† Kissinger went on a forced march of press briefings during these days, meeting reporters privately and also at a news conference on January 24 that dispensed considerable misinformation. The final accords were invariably presented as being full of complexities (that, presumably, only Kissinger and few others understood). Kissinger suggested that the agreement barred the infiltration

on, but Nguyen Van Thieu now had a presidential promise of American air support, continued aid, and carte blanche to violate the peace agreement.

Thieu began his attacks on the political aspects of the agreement immediately. On January 24, he told the citizens of the South that "if Communists come into your village, you should immediately shoot them in the head," and that people who suddenly "begin talking in a Communist tone . . . should be immediately killed." New orders were issued to South Vietnam's police and military forces, ordering them to shoot to kill those who "urge the people to demonstrate . . ." Police were also ordered to arrest and detain anyone trying to travel between PRG-controlled areas and those controlled by the Saigon government.

The North Vietnamese and the PRG, aware that the peace agreement—if carried out in full—was to their advantage, urged their supporters to demand the specific freedoms needed for the political struggle ahead, such as freedom of movement. Communist officials also sought to publicize throughout the country the text of the peace accord, with its acknowledgment of two political authorities in the South; its terms were repeatedly broadcast over Radio Hanoi. Saigon's newspaper published the text of the agreement, but that was the extent of the Thieu regime's effort to inform the public. Military men were supplied with a distorted summary of the agreement and were ordered to inform villagers, as one soldier told a reporter for the *Christian Science Monitor,* that "this is nothing more than a cease-fire in place, and the people are supposed to stay in place."

It was inevitable that war would continue.

---

of men and matériel across the DMZ; he further suggested, without ever quite saying as much, that it was significant that the DMZ was cited in the final agreement as serving as a boundary line between North and South Vietnam. The suggestion was that Saigon had survived the agreement intact. That was doubletalk. Kissinger did not tell the journalists that the agreement clearly depicted the demarcation line at the DMZ as being "only provisional and not a political or territorial boundary . . ." and he did not say that there was little he, or Nguyen Van Thieu, for that matter, could legally do about it. "We had to place stress on the issue of the Demilitarized Zone," Kissinger disingenuously said at the news conference, "because the provisions of the agreement would have made no sense whatsoever if there was not some demarcation line that defined where South Vietnam began." There was more doubletalk: "If we had accepted the proposition that would have in effect eroded the Demilitarized Zone, then the provisions of the agreement with respect to restrictions about the introduction of men and matériel into South Vietnam would have been unilateral restrictions applying only to the United States and only to our allies. Therefore, if there was to be any meaning to the separation of military and political issues, if there was to be any permanence to the military provisions that had been negotiated, then it was essential that there was a definition of where the obligations of this agreement began." *Newsweek* also declared, incorrectly, that the peace agreement specifically mentioned the "sovereignty" of the Thieu regime. "Hanoi finally conceded," *Newsweek* wrote, "that, in Kissinger's words—'there is an entity called South Vietnam.' In one important sense, the dispute over that question was what the war in Vietnam was all about." Such wrong information, repeated in differing forms by the news media, left readers with the belief that the final agreement really was between North and South Vietnam, with the Thieu government assured of sovereignty in the South. North Vietnam never disputed the existence of the South, of course, and the "entity called South Vietnam" also included the PRG. The agreement seemed simply to overwhelm the press. *Newsweek* depicted it as "incredibly complex" and noted that the formal signing ceremony involved the signature of American and North Vietnamese officials "no fewer than 144 times." The magazine went on: "Buried deep within the convoluted phraseology of the agreement and its protocols were the terms most Americans had long hungered for—a quick end to U.S. involvement in the war and an equally speedy return of the POW's. For Richard Nixon, that alone was a diplomatic triumph; he had made good on his pledge not to be the first U.S. President to preside over a humiliating military defeat abroad." Such coverage was not a triumph for American journalism.

Nixon and Kissinger were driven into collaboration once more that January in an effort to protect the secret commitments that were the foundation of their "peace with honor." Each, again, had too much on the other. There would be no resignation, and Kissinger, his hopes renewed, would again begin plotting his takeover of the State Department. The alliance was renewed on the afternoon of January 25. "I had a good talk with Kissinger," Nixon wrote in his diary that night. "I told him what a superb job he had done. He told me about his daughter, who had been approached in Cambridge to sign a resolution against the bombing. He said that to try to involve a thirteen-year-old was a terribly vicious thing." Kissinger made his *mea culpa*. "He seems at the moment convinced that he should talk to our friends and not try to pander to our enemies," Nixon wrote. "I told him that . . . we had to recognize—and that's one of the things that our terribly difficult decision in December meant—we had to recognize that our enemies had now been exposed for what they really are. They are disturbed, distressed and really discouraged because we succeeded, and now we have to start to play to those who are willing to give us somewhat of a break in writing the history of these times."

Kissinger escaped Vietnam with his reputation largely intact. Most Americans chose to believe what he and Nixon told them: The war was over. With the return of the prisoners in early 1973 and the end of direct American involvement, the struggles between South Vietnam and the PRG moved to the back sections of the newspapers and off the nightly television news. Soldiers continued to be killed in battle but they were no longer American soldiers.

The bombers never returned to South Vietnam, despite constant threats by Nixon and Kissinger. Kissinger would later insist that the all-consuming Watergate scandal prevented Nixon from carrying out his commitment, expressed in his personal letters to Nguyen Van Thieu, to bring back the bombers if necessary. "We were determined," Kissinger wrote in his memoirs, "to do our utmost to enable Saigon to grow in security and prosperity so that it could prevail in any political struggle. We sought not an interval before collapse, but lasting peace with honor. But for the collapse of executive authority as a result of Watergate, I believe we would have succeeded."

Watergate did intervene, however, and Kissinger soon joined Nixon in scrambling to avoid its stain.

41

THE PRICE OF POWER

RICHARD NIXON'S COLLAPSE began early in 1973. Within weeks after his second inauguration, he became obsessed with the incessant plotting and lying about Watergate that eventually destroyed his presidency. In his memoirs of this period, discussion of foreign policy issues all but disappears. At one point, he wrote, in mid-March of 1973, "I needed desperately to get my mind on other things." He knew by then, as his aides did also, that it would take all his abilities to keep the various White House illegalities from leaching into print.

It was sometime in these first few months of 1973 that Nixon's active collaboration with Henry Kissinger came to an end. No longer would there be elaborate scheming over Soviet policy and Soviet "threats." The "madman theory" died a natural death, as Nixon and Kissinger began their separate attempts to hide their secrets.

Kissinger had one shining moment before the crisis of Watergate set in. He made his fifth visit to Peking in mid-February and agreed with the Chinese leadership on an exchange of liaison offices in Peking and Washington. But the official American-Chinese relationship froze there, and full diplomatic relations were not established until the Carter Administration came into office.

Foreign affairs became all but moot in the remaining months of the Nixon Administration. SALT I did not lead to SALT II. A Kissinger attempt to proclaim 1973 the "Year of Europe" and reaffirm American dominance among its NATO allies turned into a fiasco as Europe's leaders assailed Kissinger's opinion, enunciated in April 1973, in his first major public address, that "The United States has global interests and responsibilities. Our European allies have regional interests."

Middle East policy remained stagnant; Kissinger and Nixon simply did not understand the message Anwar Sadat was sending in late 1972 and early 1973 —that he would be forced to invade Israel unless there were serious negotiations on Israeli disengagement from the Sinai. Sadat had ordered Soviet troops and advisers out of Egypt in mid-1972 in an attempt to convince the Nixon Administration that his government was not pro-Communist. The White House did more than miss the signal: Sadat was reviled as a fool who, by unilaterally ousting the Soviets, had thrown away an opportunity to bargain. If anything, Kissinger saw Sadat's move as a victory for his policy of support for Israel, a view he held throughout much of 1973. In October 1973, the Middle East war broke out, and Kissinger began what the press began to call his shuttle diplomacy, negotiations in which he managed to achieve the basic underpinning of the various Rogers plans that he had helped sabotage for years: an Israeli disengagement. Kissinger's much-vaunted success in the Middle East would be short-lived, for the negotiations never came to grips with the real issue at stake: a future homeland for the Palestinians.

Vietnam remained a quagmire but no longer a front-page quagmire. The Vietnam peace was, of course, not a peace but a continuation of war. The bloodshed, which was initially provoked by Nguyen Van Thieu and his army, surprised no one, except those Americans who wanted to believe that "peace with honor" had been established. In June 1973, Congress finally voted to ban funds for all military activity throughout Indochina, including the bombing of Cambodia, which was to cease on August 15. Lon Nol thus joined Nguyen Van Thieu as a doomed leader. Throughout the spring, Nixon and Kissinger could do little more than repeatedly threaten to unleash the B-52s once again on North Vietnam. In their memoirs, both would blame Congress and Watergate for the failures of American policy. "With every passing day," Kissinger wrote, "Watergate was circumscribing our freedom of action. We were losing the ability to make credible commitments, for we could no longer guarantee Congressional approval." Kissinger's basic complaint was, astonishingly, not even disguised: Watergate had returned the American Constitution to the making of foreign policy.

There is little doubt that in early 1973, as Nixon and Kissinger insisted in their memoirs, the President was indeed prepared to live up to his secret commitment to Thieu and renew the bombing in North and South Vietnam. The Kissinger office journal, in an entry in mid-March, discussed the bombing decision as a *fait accompli;* the only issue was whether to wait for the final batch of American troop withdrawals. There was a series of leaked stories to the usual columnists that March in an attempt to mitigate what everyone in the White House realized would be another postbombing wave of public condemnation. At a news conference on March 15, Nixon alluded to Hanoi's resupply efforts—which were not barred by the Paris peace agreements—and issued a warning: ". . . I would only suggest that based on my actions over the past four years, that the North Vietnamese should not lightly disregard such expressions of concern when they are made, with regard to a violation."

Watergate stopped Nixon. As the scandal flared in late March and April, with the first reports that the White House had made cover-up payments to buy the silence of the Watergate break-in team, renewed bombing became impossible. It would only have increased the pressure for full-scale investigations into the President's conduct, and such investigations would turn up—as Nixon, Kissinger, and others had to fear—the illegal wiretapping and spying that had been authorized by a President trying to hide his real policies in Vietnam and elsewhere from the public and his own administration.

It had come full circle. Nixon and Kissinger had designed a policy for Southeast Asia of secret threats and secret military activities. To protect those secrets they had resorted to illegalities. And then, years later, those illegalities had become a public issue just at a time when the administration was finally on the verge of achieving a stalemate in Vietnam. There is a strong possibility that the White House's secret peace agreement—based on a guarantee of continued bombing and aid on behalf of the South Vietnamese—might have succeeded in keeping the South non-Communist for many more years. Congress, which had refused throughout Nixon's first term to legislate an end to funding for the war, was now anxious to strike at the President, and Nixon knew that more bombing would lead to a congressional vote to cut off the money at once. Nixon's and Kissinger's contempt for Congress' delayed courage could only have been heightened by their belief that the vast majority of the American public, as the White House polls had shown in 1972, would have supported the bombing in the name of stopping communism and salvaging "peace with honor."

For Nixon and Kissinger, there could only be bitter irony: A war they could have won with a secret agreement had been lost because of the illegal steps that had been taken years earlier to win. As both the memoirs showed, neither man ever came to grips with the basic vulnerability of their policy: They were operating in a democracy, guided by a constitution, and among a citizenry who held their leaders to a reasonable standard of morality and integrity.

There was one notable foreign policy success for the Nixon-Kissinger team in 1973. Salvador Allende, who had been a target of the Nixon Administration and the CIA since his election in 1970, was finally overthrown and killed in a bloody coup d'état in September, just as Kissinger was undergoing confirmation hearings before the Senate Foreign Relations Committee on his nomination as Secretary of State. In the hearings, Kissinger was quick to deny any United States involvement in the overthrow. His answer was far from the whole truth—as some of the committee senators, who kept their peace, well knew. Allende's presidency had been complicated by severe economic and political problems, to be sure, but those problems were compounded by clandestine CIA interference, as the Senate Intelligence Committee discovered in 1975.

Chile was a Pyrrhic victory for Kissinger's foreign policy. In September 1974, the author published in the *New York Times* the first account of CIA involvement, and Kissinger began yet another scramble to repair his reputation.

Kissinger's long-sought appointment as Secretary of State was inevitable by the fall of 1973. He was again threatening to resign, according to the private journal kept by one of his office staff, and such a threat amidst Watergate carried weight. The President treated Kissinger shoddily in the weeks before announcing the nomination. It was clear to those on the inside that he was naming Kissinger only as part of his Watergate defense. In early August, according to the second volume of Kissinger's memoirs, Nixon told Haig that he would make the appointment, "provided he did not have to dismiss Rogers personally." Haig then sought Rogers' resignation but got nowhere.* It took a

---

* It was the second time Rogers had spurned a Haig order to resign. Some weeks after Haig became chief of staff, Rogers recalled years later, Haig telephoned and urged Rogers to issue a public statement in support of Nixon's refusal to permit his staff to testify on grounds of executive privilege; at the time, it was a basic White House strategy in the Watergate defense. He pressed Rogers on the issue. "It made me angry as hell," Rogers says. "He tried to get me to say it in public and I didn't want to. Haig finally came one night to my home and said that 'The President wants

week for Nixon to get around to meeting with Rogers, who—much to Nixon's (and Kissinger's) relief—at once offered his letter of resignation. "And still Nixon said nothing to me," Kissinger complained in his memoirs, adding that he was not officially told about his nomination until less than a day before it was announced.

Richard Nixon understood, as few did in the government, the full price Kissinger had paid to remain in power. In the end, it was Henry Kissinger who survived and Richard Nixon who did not. Kissinger would lose little of his immense public standing as he careened from crisis to crisis—many of them self-inflicted—as Secretary of State. There would be serious misjudgments in Cyprus, Portugal, and Angola, many of them well reported but none that undermined Kissinger's basic credibility. South Vietnam would finally fall, in the face of the long-awaited attack by North Vietnam, and America would watch on the nightly news as its Ambassador was helicoptered from the besieged American Embassy in Saigon hours before the end. There would be few television reports about the fall of the Lon Nol government in Phnom Penh to the ragtag and crazed troops of the Khmer Rouge, whose leader, Pol Pot, would seal Cambodia's borders and begin a program of retribution and genocide whose final death toll reached into the millions.

Kissinger would demonstrate how little he had learned within a few days after Saigon's collapse. On May 12, 1975, Cambodian gunboats forcibly seized the S.S. *Mayaguez,* an American merchant ship, in international waters sixty miles south of Cambodia. The crew of forty was taken to Koh Tang island, also under Cambodian control and closer to the mainland. The Ford Administration viewed the ship's seizure as an arbitrary act of defiance, although the new government in Phnom Penh had repeatedly proclaimed that its territorial waters extended ninety miles offshore and had been detaining vessels in the area for the past ten days. Kissinger argued for immediate retaliation—air strikes against the mainland and a Marine invasion to free the *Mayaguez* crew. He got his way, as he usually did with President Ford. The invasion was a slaughter: Eighteen Marines were killed and fifty more wounded out of an assault force of 110; twenty-three Air Force men also died in an offshore crash. The Marines, in their desperate evacuation, detonated a 15,000-ton bomb on the island, the largest nonnuclear weapon in the U.S. arsenal. Heightening the tragedy was the fact that the *Mayaguez* crew members were no longer on the island; they had been set free by the Cambodians hours before. Later congressional investigations revealed that Ford and Kissinger had behaved during the crisis just as Nixon and Kissinger would have. They had waited ten hours after learning of the *Mayaguez*'s seizure before making an effort to reach the Cambodian government to arrange a diplomatic solution. They had failed to act after learning of a Cambodian broadcast announcing the release of the *Mayaguez* crew, a broadcast that reached the White House just as the Marine invasion was beginning. They had ignored a confidential communication delivered fourteen hours before the U.S. assault in which a foreign government revealed

you to either make the statement or resign.' I said no, I wouldn't resign unless the President asked me to. 'This is an order from your Commander in Chief,' Haig said. I said, 'You can tell the Commander in Chief to go fuck yourself.' Haig was shocked. 'Are you telling the President to go fuck himself?' 'No,' '' Rogers replied, " 'I'm telling *you* to tell the Commander in Chief to go fuck himself.' '' After that, Rogers had few problems with Haig.

that it was intervening in Cambodia and expected an early release of the ship and crew. And, finally, they chose to publicly celebrate the crew's release as an American victory—the result of their use of force.

Kissinger and Nixon would repeatedly claim that the failures in South Vietnam and Cambodia were not their responsibility but the fault of Congress, which had cut off funding for the war. Even the public release of the secret Nixon-Thieu commitments in the spring of 1975, as Saigon fell, failed to provoke a reexamination of the Nixon-Kissinger war strategy. America proved a sore loser in Vietnam, and quickly turned its back not only on its policies but also on its young men who had fought, suffered, and died there.

In the end, as in the beginning, Nixon and Kissinger remained blind to the human costs of their actions—a further price of power. The dead and maimed in Vietnam and Cambodia—as in Chile, Bangladesh, Biafra, and the Middle East—seemed not to count as the President and his national security adviser battled the Soviet Union, their misconceptions, their political enemies, and each other.

EPILOGUE

RICHARD NIXON PAID A HIGH PRICE for his misuse of power. On August 9, 1974, after the House of Representatives Committee on Impeachment had recommended impeachment proceedings, and ten days before the full House was to open debate, the thirty-seventh President of the United States resigned. He was the first President to do so. On September 8, 1974, Nixon was spared the possibility of an extended criminal trial by a jury of citizens when President Gerald Ford, his successor, granted him a "full, free and absolute pardon" for any offenses against the United States from January 20, 1969, his first inaugural, through the date of his resignation. Ford himself had become Vice President the preceding December, after financial scandals forced Spiro Agnew to resign and, later, to plead no contest to an income tax evasion charge. The pardon to Nixon embraced not only Watergate offenses but all the Nixon-Kissinger foreign policy activities, including those known at the time, such as the illegal B-52 bombing of Cambodia, and those still secret, such as the CIA operations against Salvador Allende. After years of self-imposed isolation in California, New York, and Saddle River, New Jersey, Nixon began to be active in public affairs once again in the early 1980s; he was received as a former President, Republican elder statesman, author, and expert on international relations.

Alexander Haig served as chief of staff for Nixon and for Ford until his appointment, in the fall of 1974, as Supreme Allied Commander of NATO, one of America's highest military assignments—and one that did not require Senate confirmation. Haig resigned from that post in 1978 after publicly expressing displeasure with the foreign policy of President Jimmy Carter's administration, which had taken office in January 1977. Haig then became a director and chief operating officer of the United Technologies Corporation, in Hartford, Connecticut. In 1980 he campaigned for the Republican nomination for President. That campaign floundered, but Haig was named Secretary of State by President-elect Ronald Reagan. Haig's ability to manipulate other bureaucrats and the press, which was among his greatest strengths in the Nixon White House, was increasingly seen as a liability by Reagan and his aides. In June 1982, after a series of public controversies, Haig was forced out as Secretary of State and returned to private life. He became a senior fellow of the Hudson Institute for Policy Research and a consultant to United Technologies. He is considered still to have presidential aspirations.

Henry Kissinger served as Secretary of State under Nixon and then under Ford. When Carter took office, Kissinger began a new career as an international consultant, writer, speech maker, and part-time university lecturer. He was a personal consultant to the Shah of Iran after his exile, and is associated with many prominent firms as an adviser or consultant, including Goldman Sachs & Co., an investment house, and the Rockefellers' Chase Manhattan Bank. He is also a consultant for many foreign firms, including the General Electric Company of Britain. Kissinger is constantly portrayed by the news media as an adviser and consultant on foreign policy issues to the Reagan Administration, but as of spring 1983, he had not rejoined the government.

NOTES

As noted in the Introduction, this book is based primarily on interviews with men and women who worked in the American government during Nixon's first term. Many of those officials were interviewed two, three, or more times, often in different locations. For example, Richard V. Allen, who played a prominent role in bringing Henry Kissinger to the attention of Richard Nixon during the 1968 presidential campaign, was interviewed five times at length in 1979 and 1980, before he became national security adviser to President Ronald Reagan. Allen was one of more than thirty people who were interviewed for the material in Chapter One; only a few of those interviewed, however, ended up being cited by name in the chapter. In some cases, those who were interviewed requested anonymity; sometimes names were deleted for reasons of editorial simplicity. The information itself, once cross-checked and verified, was more significant than the names of all those involved in providing it. Also, rather than listing the date and location of each interview, I have chosen in these notes to describe where the quoted person was living and/or working at the time of our last contact.

The memoirs of Richard Nixon and Henry Kissinger were basic sources. *RN: The Memoirs of Richard Nixon* (Grosset & Dunlap, 1978) is much less detailed than the two volumes of Kissinger memoirs, *The White House Years* (Little, Brown, 1979) and *Years of Upheaval* (Little, Brown, 1982). Three other foreign policy studies were very useful: *Kissinger,* by Marvin and Bernard Kalb (Little, Brown, 1974); *The Illusion of Peace,* by Tad Szulc (Viking, 1978), and *Uncertain Greatness,* by Roger Morris (Harper & Row, 1977). All references to these works are attributed as they occur in the text, and no further attribution will be included in these notes.

Another essential source was the daily reporting in the *New York Times* and the *Washington Post* on Nixon-Kissinger foreign policy. I relied heavily on dispatches in these two newspapers in describing the background of the events of the period; footnoting each article would obviously add little of substance to these notes. I have chosen instead to cite only those articles—usually by Washington columnists —of special significance.

1. The Job Seeker

Richard Allen, when last interviewed, was an international business consultant in Washington. A brief description of his early contacts with Henry Kissinger can be found on page 52 of *Before the Fall* (Doubleday, 1975), Nixon speech writer William Safire's account of the Nixon presidency. Kissinger's colleagues at Harvard were correct in recalling that he was a Democrat in the early 1960s; the town clerk of Belmont, Massachusetts, where Kissinger lived, listed him as a registered

Democrat as of September 18, 1962. Max Kampelman, Humphrey's former aide and adviser, was practicing law in Washington when interviewed. The anecdote about Nixon and Lansdale can be found on page 196 of *Papers on the War* (Simon & Schuster Touchstone, 1972), by Daniel Ellsberg. Daniel Davidson was practicing law in Washington when interviewed; so was Paul Warnke. Morton Halperin was director of the Center for National Security Studies in Washington. John Negroponte was, as of early 1983, the American Ambassador to Honduras. John Mitchell was a Washington consultant. The quote from Jack Valenti can be found on page 374 of his memoir *A Very Human President* (W. W. Norton, 1975). A full transcript of Joseph Kraft's public-television interview, with station WETA in Washington, is in my possession. The Theodore White anecdote on Nixon and Kissinger can be found on page 270 in *The Making of the President, 1972* (Atheneum, 1973). For a full discussion of the intrigues during the last days of the 1968 presidential campaign, see *The Man Who Kept Secrets: Richard Helms and the CIA*, by Thomas Powers (Alfred A. Knopf, 1979), pages 197–200. Also see pages 727–735 in *An American Melodrama: The Presidential Campaign of 1968* (Viking, 1969), by three London *Sunday Times* journalists, Lewis Chester, Godfrey Hodgson, and Bruce Page. Thomas W. Ottenad of the *St. Louis Post-Dispatch* did excellent reporting on the issue of who did what in the last few days before the 1968 election. Anna Chennault's memoir was published by Times Books. She was president of an international consulting firm in Washington at the time of our interview. Clark Clifford's postelection criticisms of Thieu can be found in "Clifford Asserts Talks May Go On Without Saigon," by William Beecher, *New York Times*, November 13, 1968. William Buckley's memoir was published by G. P. Putnam's Sons. Edward Rozek's review, entitled "Whitewashing the White House," was published in *Survey*, an English quarterly, Spring 1980. Rozek was a professor at the University of Colorado when interviewed. Buckley and Frank Shakespeare were reached through their offices in New York City. Carl Kaysen was teaching at Harvard University when interviewed.

2. A New NSC System

The revised Nixon-Kissinger NSC system has received relatively scant academic study. One exception is a two-part analysis published in *Foreign Policy*, the quarterly magazine, in the Winter 1971–72 issue, "Kissinger's Apparat," by John P. Leacacos, and "Can One Man Do?," by I. M. Destler. Kissinger's early 1950s intelligence background is outlined in *Who's Who*. His service with the 970th CIC unit in Germany is cited in *The Belaris Secret* (Alfred A. Knopf, 1982), by John Loftus; see page 117. Morton Halperin supplied me with his unpublished manuscript on the NSC system, as well as many of the original planning papers, all unclassified, that he prepared for Kissinger in late 1968 and early 1969. Bryce Harlow was living in retirement near Harper's Ferry, West Virginia, when interviewed. Roger Morris was a free-lance writer in Santa Fe, New Mexico. Daniel Ellsberg was active in the nuclear freeze movement and living in Berkeley, California. William Rogers was practicing law in Washington and New York; Elliot Richardson was practicing law in Washington. U. Alexis Johnson was retired from the Foreign Service and living in Washington. Richard Moose was an investment counselor in New York and Washington.

3. Consolidating Authority

The interview that caused Richard Allen's troubles was with *U.S. News & World Report*, November 18, 1968, and was titled " 'We Must Present a United Front to the Soviet Union.' " The December 26, 1968, Evans & Novak column was also published in the *Washington Post* and was headlined "Nixon's Appointment of

Assistant to Kissinger Raises Questions." The columnists described Allen as considered a member of the "sandbox right." Donald Lesh was executive director of the U. S. Association for the Club of Rome, in Washington, when interviewed. Martin Anderson was interviewed while he was working in Ronald Reagan's presidential campaign; he subsequently joined Reagan's White House staff. Patrick Buchanan was a newspaper columnist living in McLean, Virginia, when interviewed. Jacob Beam described some of his encounters in the Nixon White House in his memoir, *Multiple Exposure* (W. W. Norton, 1978). Retired from the Foreign Service, he was living in Washington. Paul Nitze was still involved in strategic planning in Washington when interviewed; in 1981 he was named by President Reagan as Ambassador to the Intermediate Range Nuclear Force negotiations in Geneva. William Porter was retired and living in West Point, Massachusetts; he provided me with portions of an unpublished memoir. Robert Finch was living in Los Angeles. Richard Sneider was a business consultant in New York City.

4. Vietnam: The Policy

Kissinger's private lunch in Saigon was held at the home of Barry Zorthian, then the senior American spokesman in Saigon. The lunch produced a dispatch by Jack Foisie, a correspondent for the *Los Angeles Times,* that was disputed by Kissinger and Clark Clifford. Their subsequent letters were made available by the Lyndon B. Johnson Library in Austin, Texas. Foisie's story, as published November 2, 1965, in the *Washington Post,* was headlined "Saigon Political View Dismays LBJ Envoys." Mathew Meselson was teaching at Harvard University when interviewed. Joseph Kraft's praise for Kissinger's *Foreign Affairs* article can be found in the *Washington Post* of December 19, 1968: "Kissinger Article on Vietnam Hailed as Best Augury to Date." William Kaufman was teaching at the Massachusetts Institute of Technology when interviewed. John Court was a businessman in Cincinnati, Ohio. NSSM-1, when made public through the efforts of Ellsberg in late April of 1972, produced many newspaper dispatches. Among the best were those on consecutive days beginning on April 25, 1972, by Murray Marder, Michael Getler, and Stanley Karnow of the *Washington Post.* Eisenhower's *Mandate for Change* was published by Doubleday in 1963; see pages 179–182. More on the Korean War threat can be found in *Firsthand Report,* by Sherman Adams (Harper and Brothers, 1961); see also *Eisenhower: Portrait of the Hero,* by Peter Lyon (Little, Brown, 1974) pages 535–536. The footnoted study of the Korean War bombing can be found in the Winter 1953 issue of the Air University *Quarterly Review,* "The Attack on the Irrigation Dams in North Korea," a study prepared by the magazine's staff. It was cited in "U.S. Involvement in Vietnam," by Noam Chomskey, in *Bridge: An Asian-American Perspective,* October-November 1975. A blow-by-blow account of the destruction of the North Korean dam system was published on pages 623–629 of *The United States Air Force in Korea, 1950–1953,* by Robert Frank Futrell, Brigadier General Lawson S. Moseley, and Albert F. Simpson (Duell, Sloan and Pearce, 1961). For a partial text of Nixon's off-the-record talk to the southern delegates in Miami Beach, see pages 461–464 in *An American Melodrama: The Presidential Campaign of 1968,* by Lewis Chester, Godfrey Hodgson, and Bruce Page (Viking, 1969). The *Herald* published its transcript, "What Dick Nixon Told Southern Delegates," on August 7, 1968. Richard Whalen's memoir is *Catch the Falling Flag* (Houghton Mifflin, 1972); the Nixon quote is on page 27. Nixon's "madman" threat to Bob Haldeman is reported on page 122 in Haldeman's memoir, *The Ends of Power* (Dell, 1978).

5. Cambodia: The Secret Bombing

Colonel Ray Sitton later served, as a three-star general, as director of the Joint Staff of the JCS in the Pentagon; he was living in retirement in Calhoun, Georgia, when I talked with him. Roger Morris, the former Kissinger aide, assembled much of the known literature on Haig, including congressional testimony, in his 1982 biography, *Haig: The General's Progress* (Playboy Press, 1982). See also "Mr. T & Colonel Haig," by Lucian K. Truscott IV, in the New York *Village Voice*, May 17, 1973. Robert Houdek was serving in the State Department when interviewed. The Buckley anecdote about Haig can be found on page 57 in *United Nations Journal: A Delegate's Odyssey* (G. P. Putnam's Sons, 1974). For the "Kissinger's Kissinger" reference, see "The Rise of Dr. Kissinger's Kissinger," by Fred Emery, London *Times,* January 20, 1973, page 15. Kevin Buckley's article on "Speedy Express" was published in *Newsweek* June 19, 1972. Many official documents dealing with the secret B-52 bombing of Cambodia, some of them marked top-secret before declassification, were made available to me under the Freedom of Information Act. Some of these documents had earlier been supplied by the Department of Defense to William Shawcross, the British journalist, when he was researching his acclaimed study of the Nixon-Kissinger policy toward Cambodia, *Sideshow* (Simon and Schuster, 1979). Shawcross supplied me with other documents he had accumulated on the bombing. Harold Knight's testimony was given on July 16, 1973, before the Senate Armed Services Committee. I had written an extensive account of his activities which was published the day before the *New York Times*'s "Cambodian Raids Reported Hidden Before '70 Foray." Former Green Beret Randolph Harrison was an editorial writer for a newspaper in Orlando, Florida, when interviewed. Kissinger's comment deploring the falsification of the B-52 bombing records came in an interview with me that was published in the *New York Times* on July 20, 1973.

6. Korea: The First Crisis

Nixon's never delivered Vietnam speech of March 31, 1968, can be found on pages 283–294 of Whalen's *Catch the Falling Flag* (Houghton Mifflin, 1972). Melvin Laird was a senior counselor in the Washington editorial office of the *Reader's Digest* when interviewed. Robert Pursley was retired from the Air Force and working as an investment analyst in New York City when interviewed. William Rogers' speech before the American Society of Newspaper Editors was reported in the *New York Times* on April 17, 1969: "U.S. to Emphasize Diplomatic Steps on Loss of Plane," by Max Frankel. Patrick Anderson's profile of Kissinger for the *New York Times Magazine,* "Confidence of the President," was published on June 1, 1969; the discussion of the EC-121 incident can be found on page 42. The quote from the *Times* about diplomatic action can be found in Frankel's April 17 dispatch. See page 124 of Haldeman's *The Ends of Power* (Dell, 1978) for the quote about Kissinger's overreaction in the crisis. Donald Riegle's account of his 1969 meeting with Kissinger can be found on page 25 of his memoir, *O Congress,* with Trevor Armbrister (Popular Library, 1975). Riegle gave me copies of his October 1, 1969, correspondence with Kissinger. Nguyen Co Thach was Deputy Foreign Minister of the Democratic Republic of Vietnam when interviewed in Hanoi in August 1979; he was named Foreign Minister later in 1979 and a member of his nation's ruling politburo in 1982. I first interviewed Thach for "The Talk of the Town" in the *New Yorker;* see "Observer from Vietnam," October 23, 1978, pages 29–32.

7. The Wiretaps

The basic sources for this chapter were the hearing record entitled *Dr. Kissinger's Role in Wiretapping,* published by the Senate Foreign Relations Committee on September 29, 1974. The volume includes the censored text of eight days of secret hearings on the wiretapping in 1973 and 1974, as well as public testimony.

Many of the relevant documents not published by the Senate can be found in the proceedings of the Impeachment Panel of the House Judiciary Committee, especially the volumes of Book VII, *White House Surveillance Activities and Campaign Activities,* May-June 1974. An excellent summary of the wiretapping imbroglio can be found in *The American Police State,* by David Wise (Random House, 1978), especially the first three chapters. Walter Pincus wrote effectively on Alexander Haig's role in Watergate and the White House cover-up in a series of articles in 1973 and 1974 for the *New Republic;* see especially "Alexander Haig," October 5, 1974. The pleadings of Morton Halperin and his attorneys, especially Mark Lynch of the American Civil Liberties Union, provided much new information, as did the depositions in the Halperin case, which are on file at Lynch's office at the Center for National Security Studies, in Washington. Kissinger's statement that his office logs were "sporadic and undeveloped" was made in a written response, filed January 18, 1976, in the Halperin case. The FBI document on Kissinger's early contacts cited in the footnote was printed in the *Nation* magazine, November 10, 1979, in an article by Sigmund Diamond, who obtained it under the Freedom of Information Act. John Ehrlichman was working as a novelist and living in Santa Fe, New Mexico, when interviewed. The Goldwater letter to John Mitchell and other documents cited here—such as those from the FBI and the White House—are now part of the Halperin wiretapping case on file in federal court in the District of Columbia and are also available through Mark Lynch. In some cases, documents were also published by the Senate Foreign Relations Committee or the House Impeachment Committee. Beecher's *New York Times* dispatch of May 9 was headlined "Raids in Cambodia by U.S. Unprotested." The story was positioned, under a one-column headline, at the bottom of the right-hand column of the front page—far from dramatic display. Beecher's May 6 dispatch dealing with the EC-121 incident was headlined "Aides Say Nixon Weighed Swift Korea Reprisal;" that story received much bigger play at the bottom of page one, with its headline running across three columns. Laurence Lynn was teaching at Harvard University when interviewed. Charles Cooke was a state education official in Sacramento, California. Jeb Stuart Magruder's memoir, written with Washington journalist Taylor Branch, is *An American Life: One Man's Road to Watergate* (Atheneum, 1974). See David Wise's *The American Police State,* at pages 63–64, for a discussion of the Romanian "spy" allegations against Marvin Kalb.

8. Decay

In *The Final Days* (Simon & Schuster, 1976), their study of Nixon's fall from power, Bob Woodward and Carl Bernstein, aided by Scott Armstrong, graphically described the day-to-day atmosphere inside the National Security Council in a chapter on Kissinger, pages 184–201. Their reporting was of course focused on the Watergate scandal and not on the foreign policy of the Nixon Administration. Spurgeon Keeny was living in Washington when interviewed. Anthony Lake was teaching at Amherst College, Amherst, Massachusetts. Guido Goldman's comments about Kissinger's office were provided in an interview with WETA, the Washington public television station, as part of its research into the Kissinger years for a 1977 documentary; I have a copy of the transcript. William Watts lived in Washington; as did Ivan Selin. Dr. Roger Egeberg was working for the federal government.

9. Intrigues

Charles Colson was directing a prison reform project in Great Falls, Virginia, when interviewed. *Uncertain Greatness* (Harper & Row, 1977), Roger Morris' study of Kissinger, has a discussion of White House racism that, amazingly, was not noted by the press upon the book's publication; see page 131. Jeanne Davis was living in Warrenton, Virginia. Richard Pederson was president of the American University of Cairo. The quote from William Safire's *Before the Fall* (Doubleday, 1975) can be found on page 170.

10. Vietnam: Planning for Götterdämmerung

Robert Ellsworth was working as a consultant in Washington when interviewed. Kissinger's quote about Vietnam protesters can be found in "Strategist in the White House Basement," by Gerald Astor, *Look,* August 12, 1969, page 53. The Halperin article that seemed to presage the Nixon Doctrine is "After Vietnam: Security and Intervention in Asia," in the *Journal of International Affairs,* Volume XXII, Number 2, pages 236–246; see especially page 243. The letter from Ellsberg and five Rand colleagues protesting the Vietnam War was published October 12, 1969, in the *Washington Post.* Joseph Kraft's criticism of it, "Breaching the Code," was published on the same day in the same paper; Kraft had been given a copy of the letter prior to its publication. Kissinger's suggestion to Donald Riegle that he had made a mistake in not trying to make a deal with "sincere" doves can be found on page 25 in *O Congress* (Popular Library, 1975). Seth Tillman was a fellow at the American Enterprise Institute when interviewed. Joseph Urgo was working in a New York City restaurant when interviewed. The *Newsweek* cover story was published on October 20, 1969. Dwight Chapin's memorandum is reproduced in part on pages 81–83 in Magruder's *An American Life* (Atheneum, 1974). Vice President Spiro Agnew's speech criticizing the news media was given extensive play in the nation's press; a full transcript was published in the *New York Times,* November 14, 1969, beginning on page one. William Gulley's memoir, *Breaking Cover* (Simon and Shuster, 1980), written with Mary Ellen Reese, describes the White House fears of demonstrators on pages 165–169. Alexander Butterfield was an executive of an insurance company in Los Angeles when interviewed.

11. A Greek Tragedy and a Civil War in Africa

For a full account of the Greek civil war and the "Truman Doctrine," see *Intervention and Revolution,* by Richard J. Barnet (World Publishing Company, 1968), especially Chapter Six. Elias Demetracopoulos was Washington correspondent and North American editor for the Greek newspapers *Makedonia* and *Thessaloniki* when interviewed. The cited *Boston Globe* article was "Thomas Pappas: portrait of a wealthy immigrant, political kingmaker," by Christopher Lydon, October 31, 1968. Pappas' close links to Ambassador Tasca were reported August 14, 1974, by Steven V. Roberts in the *New York Times,* "U.S. Is Replacing Envoy to Athens." One source told Roberts that Pappas would see the Ambassador "three or four times a week" when in Athens. (Tasca's information about the junta's campaign contributions to the 1968 Nixon election campaign raises the question whether the CIA, which was financing the Greek intelligence operations at the same time, was aware that some of its funds were being returned to the United States for use in the presidential election. This question was not looked into by the Senate Intelligence Committee during its CIA inquiries in 1975 and 1976. Sources close to the committee have said that its investigation was abruptly canceled at Kissinger's direct request. He urged the committee to drop the investigation, one official said, on the ground that relations between the United States and Greece could be "severely harmed.") Demetracopoulos' confrontation with Murray Chotiner was first reported by Jack Anderson in his column distributed for release on

February 12, 1975. Harold Saunders was a resident fellow at the American Enterprise Institute in Washington when he discussed his role in Greek affairs. William Rogers testified before the Senate Foreign Relations Committee on July 14, 1969; Laird testified one day later. The quote from Laurence Stern can be found on pages 66–67 in *The Wrong Horse* (Times Books, 1977), his study of American policy in Greece and Cyprus. The *New York Times* article announcing the end of the arms embargo was "U.S. to End Restriction on Arms Aid for Greece," by Neil Sheehan, September 19, 1970. See a report from Washington by Elizabeth Drew in the *Atlantic Monthly,* June 1970, which discussed the Biafran war and referred to Nixon's campaign remarks on the war. Dr. Jean Mayer was president of Tufts University when interviewed. Justice Louis Mbanefo's comments can be found in "Biafran Leaders Grow Bitter Over U.S. Role in War," by Jim Hoagland, *Washington Post,* November 8, 1969.

12. SALT: A MIRV Mistake

The best account of the Nixon-Kissinger manipulation of the SALT process can be found in *Doubletalk: The Story of SALT 1* (Doubleday, 1980), by Gerard C. Smith. John Newhouse's *Cold Dawn* (Holt, Rinehart and Winston, 1973) is also insightful. Herbert Scoville, Jr., and George W. Rathjens have written widely on various SALT issues. Jack Ruina was teaching at MIT when interviewed. George Rathjens was a State Department consultant. The Ruina-Rathjens paper outlining the MIRV issue was provided to me by Rathjens. Paul Doty's praise for Kissinger was in his paper given at the International Colloquium on "Science and Disarmament" in Paris, January 15–17, 1981. Walter Slocombe was a senior arms control official for the Department of Defense when interviewed in late 1979. Sidney Drell was teaching at Stanford University. Richard Garwin was an IBM executive in Westchester County, New York. Herbert Scoville was retired from government service and was living in McLean, Virginia.

13. SALT: A Mistake Becomes a Policy

The quotation from Henry Brandon's book, *The Retreat of American Power* (Doubleday, 1973), can be found on page 304. The internal intelligence debate over whether the Soviets had tested a MIRV is discussed in Thomas Powers' *The Man Who Kept the Secrets* (Alfred A. Knopf, 1979), pages 211–212; it was also the subject of a series of excellent analyses by Representative Les Aspin, Democrat of Wisconsin. See especially Aspin's press statement of February 7, 1980, available from his office. John Huizenga was retired from the CIA and living in Washington when interviewed. Alton Frye was a Washington arms control consultant. He described his experiences on the MIRV issue in *A Responsible Congress,* published for the Council on Foreign Relations by McGraw-Hill in 1975. See Chapter Three, "Congress and MIRV: An Exercise in Legislative Catalysis," pages 47–66. Gerard Smith was a partner in a Washington consulting firm. Phillip Farley was teaching at Stanford University. Raymond Garthoff was at the Brookings Institution. The first American MIRV contract was made known by the *Baltimore Sun,* "Contract for MIRV's Reported," by Nathan Miller, June 27, 1969. See the *Washington Post* for March 13, 1970, "MIRV Disclosure a Slip, Officials Say," for an account of Secretary Seaman's role. Senator Albert Gore's complaints were reported in the *New York Times* on November 13, 1969, "Nixon Said to Bar Arms Testimony," by Robert B. Semple, Jr. Lawrence Weiler was living in Washington when interviewed. Two papers by Raymond Garthoff were especially useful: "SALT: An Evaluation," in *World Politics,* October 1978, and "Negotiating with the Russians: Some Lessons from SALT," *International Security,* Spring 1977.

14. Southeast Asia: Policy Change and Escalation

The "secret" war in Laos began to be exposed in the press in late 1969; see a series in the *New York Times* in October, especially reports by Henry Kamm on October 21 and 28. For an account of the American combat deaths in Laos, see "Deaths of 27 Americans in Laos Disclosed by U.S.," by James M. Naughton, *New York Times*, March 9, 1970. Jerome Doolittle was working for the Federal Aviation Authority when interviewed; in 1982 he published a novel, *The Bombing Officer* (Dutton), based on his experiences in Laos. Richard Barnet wrote about his visit to Hanoi in the *New York Review of Books* for January 29, 1970, "How Hanoi Sees Nixon," page 19.

15. Cambodia: The Coup

William Shawcross' *Sideshow* (Simon and Schuster, 1979) is essential to an understanding of the Cambodian situation in the spring of 1970. Prince Sihanouk gives his view of events leading to his ouster on pages 49–59 of his memoir, *My War with the CIA*, as related to Wilford Burchett (Pantheon, 1972, 1973). The Pentagon publicly released statistics on its secret operations inside Cambodia and Laos on September 10, 1973. The John McCarthy trials were thoroughly covered by the *New York Times* and the *Washington Post*. Two articles stand out: "U.S. Is Reported to Have Hired Sihanouk Forces for '67 Missions," in the *Times*, January 28, 1970, and " 'Terminated' Agent May Haunt U.S.," by Murray Marder, in the *Post*'s "Outlook" section, February 8, 1970. Forrest Lindley was living in Washington when interviewed. Samuel Thornton's account of the Navy's anti-Sihanouk activities was first made available to William Shawcross, who shared the material with me. When I talked with Thornton later, in Phoenix, Arizona, he was able to demonstrate that he had indeed served in sensitive intelligence offices in South Vietnam. As of late 1982, he was working in La Jolla, California. Gerald Hickey's memorandum of October 1970 was prepared as "A Working Note" for the Pentagon's Advanced Research Projects Agency. The document, though unclassified, is marked "Not for Public Release"; a copy is in my possession. Professor George Kahin's testimony can be found beginning on page 79 of Senate Foreign Relations Committee hearings, *Supplemental Assistance to Cambodia,* February 24 and March 6, 1975. Stephen Linger was working in Frederick, Maryland, when interviewed.

16. Vietnam: A Spring Invasion

For a good example of how the White House, led by Kissinger, handled the press on the crucial question of Hanoi's intentions, see "Cambodian Decision: Why President Acted," by Hedrick Smith, in the *New York Times* of June 30, 1970. Smith wrote that Nixon was "haunted" by the intelligence reports of North Vietnamese movement against Cambodia. The CIA analysis expressing doubt on the efficacy of the Cambodian invasion became a case study for the Senate Intelligence Committee. See pages 79–83 in Book 1 of the committee's final report on foreign and military intelligence, published April 26, 1976. A copy of Roger Morris' and Anthony Lake's resignation letter was provided to me. The citation from *Before the Fall* (Doubleday, 1975), William Safire's memoir, can be found on page 186. The quotation from Haig is on page 187. William Beecher was the national security correspondent for the *Boston Globe* when interviewed. Jonathan Moore was director of the John F. Kennedy Institute of Politics at Harvard University. The best account of Nixon's early-morning visit to the Lincoln Memorial is on pages 202–211 of *Before the Fall*. The anecdote about Kissinger's April 17, 1970, appearance at the Johns Hopkins School of International Studies in Washington was provided by one of the students who arranged the demonstration. Walter Pincus was a reporter for the *Washington Post* when interviewed. For specific details on the B-52 and other bombings in Cambodia, see the 1973 Senate Armed Services Committee hearings, *Bombing in Cambodia*. The CIA dispute over the significance of Sihanoukville is discussed on pages 216–219 in *The Man Who Kept The Secrets,* by Thomas Powers (Alfred A. Knopf, 1979). The Pentagon statistics supplied to Senator Muskie's office were made available to me under the Freedom of Information Act.

17. In Full Control

A critical account of the government's action in the Berrigan case can be found in *The Age of Surveillance* (Alfred A. Knopf, 1980), by Frank J. Donner, pages 87–90. David Halperin was working for a New York law firm when interviewed. H. R. Haldeman's quote on Kissinger can be found on page 135 in the paperback edition of his *The Ends of Power* (Dell, 1978). Murray Marder was still reporting for the *Washington Post* when interviewed. Stuart Loory's assessment, "Kissinger Image Shows Signs of Wear and Tear," was published on July 5, 1970, in the *Los Angeles Times.* Loory was managing editor of the *Chicago Sun-Times* when interviewed. Admiral Elmo Zumwalt's memoir, *On Watch* (Quadrangle, 1976) is among the most honest books by those who served in the Nixon Administration. An account of his job interview with Kissinger can be found on page 46. Ray Cline was retired from the government and associated with Georgetown University's Center for Strategic and International Studies when interviewed. Tom Charles Huston was an attorney in Indianapolis, Indiana. The CIA's Operation Chaos, a facet of its domestic spying program, was investigated by the Senate Intelligence Committee; see its 1976 published reports.

18. Mideast: The Rogers Plan

A detailed summary of American policy in the Middle East can be found in *Decade of Decisions, 1967–1976* (University of California, 1977), by William Quant, a former Kissinger NSC aide. Two memoirs were especially useful: *The Rabin Memoirs* (Little, Brown, 1979), by Yitzhak Rabin, who was Israel's Ambassador to the United States during much of the Nixon-Kissinger era, and *The Road to Ramadan* (Quadrangle, 1975), by Mohammed Heikal, a confidant of both Nasser and Sadat. See Chapters Eight through Ten in Rabin, pages 143–218, for his views of the early White House diplomacy. For an insight into Israeli-Arab tensions in Palestine immediately following World War II, and a plea for understanding on both sides, see I. F. Stone's *Underground to Palestine and Reflections Thirty Years Later* (Pantheon, 1978). Much, obviously, has been written about Jabotinsky and other founders of Revisionist Zionism, but one recommended newspaper analysis, by Mark Bruzonsky, a Washington consultant on the Middle East, appeared in the *Washington Post*'s "Outlook" section, November 16, 1980, titled "The Mentor Who Shaped Begin's Thinking: Jabotinsky." Egypt's early notification of the first Rogers plan, is reported in Mahmoud Riad's memoir, *The Struggle for Peace in the Middle East* (Quartet, London, 1981), page 109. Joseph Sisco was a Washington consultant when interviewed. Riad's meeting in Moscow is described on pages 112–114 of his memoir, Nasser's meeting in Moscow on pages 84–89; Nasser's attempt to "try again" with another initiative in May 1970 can be found on page 92. Murray Marder's controversial article in the *Washington Post,* "U.S. Seeking to Oust Soviet Troops in Egypt," was published July 3, 1970. Nasser's problems after agreeing to the ninety-day American ceasefire proposal are outlined in Heikal, pages 95–97. The quotation from Michael Brecher's work, *Decision in*

Israel's Foreign Policy (Oxford University Press, London, 1974), can be found on page 514. Mahmoud Riad's quote on the nearness of peace in the Middle East can be found on pages 156–157 of his book. The cited column by Joseph Alsop was published September 9, 1970, in the *Washington Post,* under the title "Dobrynin on Mideast."

A special sensitivity about the Middle East should be noted. Dozens of American officials, ranging from NSC aides to Nixon Administration ambassadors, were interviewed for the chapters dealing with the Middle East, but only a few officials agreed to be quoted by name—not out of lack of conviction or fear of retribution, but solely in an attempt to avoid losing any influence on policy making.

19. Mideast: Misperceptions in Jordan

L. Dean Brown was affiliated with the Middle East Institute, in Washington, when interviewed. The war in Jordan has been very much overlooked by scholars. In its Spring 1973 issue, *Foreign Policy* carried two opposing accounts of the war, the only such studies that could be found in American periodical literature. Henry Brandon of the London *Sunday Times* summarized the Nixon-Kissinger view in "Were We Masterful . . ." and University of Iowa historian David Schoenbaum wrote ". . . Or Lucky?" Schoenbaum's article raised direct questions about what actually had taken place in the war, questions to which there were, at the time, no answers. Nasser's concern about the war was reported on pages 98–103 of Mohammed Heikal's *The Road to Ramadan* (Quadrangle, 1975); those pages also include the footnoted exchange involving Qaddafi. Alexis Johnson's speech after the crisis was reported by Schoenbaum. Andrew Killgore had retired from the Foreign Service and was a Washington consultant when interviewed. The full text, or outtake, of Nixon's 1977 interviews with David Frost was made available to me with Frost's approval. Mahmoud Riad's account of the war in Jordan can be found on pages 158–166 of his *The Struggle for Peace in the Middle East* (Quartet, London, 1981). Kissinger's concern about the lack of nuclear options in the Jordanian crisis was reported by John Edwards in *Super Weapons: The Making of MX* (Norton, 1982), pages 67–69. Haig's praise of Nixon's leadership can be found on page 87 of *Nixon's Quest for Peace* (Luce Books, 1972), by Frank van der Linden. The author, a conservative columnist who reflected the White House's view, was granted an unusual amount of access to Nixon and his top aides for his book, which was published during the presidential campaign.

20. Cuba: A False Crisis

Kissinger's excitement over the reconnaissance photographs was described on pages 125–126 of *The Ends of Power,* by H. R. Haldeman (Dell, 1978). The reference to Cuba's love for soccer can be found in *Sports Illustrated,* November 5, 1979, page 25. Roy Burleigh was interviewed in Tallahassee, Florida, where he went to live after his retirement from the CIA. He died of cancer in 1980. Representative Dante Fascell's hearings were released on September 26, 1971; the testimony was given in September, October, and November 1970. Major Gerald Cassell's testimony was taken September 28, 1971, and published immediately by the Fascell subcommittee. Cyrus Sulzberger's comments on his meetings with Kissinger and Helms can be found on pages 655 and 660 in his memoirs for 1963–1972: *An Age of Mediocrity* (Macmillan, 1973). Jerry Friedheim was working in Reston, Virginia, when interviewed. Tad Szulc was interviewed in Washington. James Reston's *New York Times* column in defense of the Nixon-Kissinger policy, "Back to Cuba and the Cold War," was published September 27, 1970. Elmo

Zumwalt's account of the Cienfuegos affair can be found on pages 310–313 of *On Watch* (Quadrangle, 1976). The Soviet complaint about Cienfuegos, as relayed to Gerard Smith, was reported on page 215 of his *Doubletalk* (Doubleday, 1980). The reference to "fearing the worst" is in "U.S.-Soviet Ties: An Uncertain Crisis," by Max Frankel, *New York Times,* October 15, 1970. For an overview of the dispute, see "Soviet Submarine Visit to Cuba," by Barry M. Blechman and Stephanie E. Levinson, in the *Proceedings* of the United States Naval Institute, September 1975, pages 30–39. The authors conclude that even a Soviet submarine base in Cuba "would not pose qualitatively new military threats . . ."

21. Chile: Hardball

The major sources for the chapters on Chile are two reports of the Senate Intelligence Committee: *Covert Action in Chile, 1963–73,* published December 18, 1975, available in Volume 7 of the Committee's publications, and *Alleged Assassination Plots Involving Foreign Leaders,* a separate volume published November 20, 1975; see pages 225–254. Background material on the Allende election and economic conditions can be found in *Allende's Chile,* by Edward Boorstein (International Publishers, 1977), and *The Breakdown of Democratic Regimes: Chile,* by Arturo Valenzuela (Johns Hopkins, 1978). For a different view, see *The Overthrow of Allende and the Politics of Chile, 1964–76,* by Paul E. Sigmund (University of Pittsburgh Press, 1977). Another basic source for much of the information about the CIA's role in Chile during the Frei years was former Ambassador Edward Korry, whom I interviewed extensively in late 1980. Korry also made available to me copies of his sworn statements to the Justice Department and the Senate Intelligence Committee; many of his assertions were subsquently confirmed. He published some of his account in the March 1978 issue of *Penthouse* magazine, "The Sell-out of Chile and the American Taxpayer," beginning on page 70. For a discussion of my complicated reportorial relationship with Korry, see "New Evidence Backs Ex-Envoy on His Role in Chile," by Seymour M. Hersh, *New York Times,* February 9, 1981. For a different point of view, see "The 2,300-Word *Times* Correction," *Time* magazine, February 23, 1981, page 84. Charles Radford was working in Kelso, Washington, prior to his reenlistment in 1982 in the submarine service of the Navy. Kissinger's remark to Admiral Zumwalt is on page 318 of Zumwalt's *On Watch* (Quadrangle, 1976). Statistics on American aid to Chile can be found on page 34 of the Senate Intelligence Committee's *Covert Action* report. Charles Meyer was a business executive in Chicago when interviewed. The Nixon-Valdez meeting is described on pages 30–33 of Armando Uribe's memoir, *The Black Book of American Intervention in Chile* (Beacon Press, 1975). Gabriel Valdez was interviewed in New York, where he was an official with the United Nations Secretariat. Walt W. Rostow was a professor at the University of Texas when interviewed. The Senate Multinational Subcommittee of the Foreign Relations Committee held hearings in March and April, 1973, into the ITT–White House link; its report was issued on June 21, 1973. The subcommittee also published, in a separate appendix, all the available ITT correspondence and files. For a good overview of the ITT issue, see "Reflections: Secrets," by Richard Harris, in the *New Yorker,* April 10, 1978, pages 44–86. Data on ITT's Special Review Committee, chaired by Terry Sanford, former Governor of North Carolina, are available from the corporation; these reports are undated. For more data on the CIA's disinformation programs inside Chile, and their impact on American newspapers and magazines, see "Halperin Alleges 4 Instances of CIA Exploitation of Media," by John Jacobs, *Washington Post,* January 5, 1978; the article was based on Morton Halperin's testimony to a House subcommittee. Former Ambassador Ralph Dungan was living in Washington when interviewed.

22. Chile: Get Rid of Allende

The Cord Meyer anecdote can be found on page 185 in his memoir, *Facing Reality* (Harper & Row, 1980). Samuel Halpern was living in Alexandria, Virginia, when interviewed. Kissinger's Chicago backgrounder with the press is reprinted, beginning on page 541, in the appendix to the 1973 Senate Multinational Subcommittee hearings, published June 21, 1973. Paul Wimert was interviewed at his Waterford, Virginia, farm. Major Carlos Donoso Perez's report in Santiago of the Schneider shooting is reprinted on page 50 of *The Murder of Allende* (Harper & Row, 1975–76), by Robinson Rojas Sandford, a Chilean journalist. Copies of some of John J. Murray's documents are in my possession. See "The Multilateral Development Banks and the Suspension of Lending to Allende's Chile," by Jonathan E. Sanford, a research monograph of the Library of Congress' Congressional Research Service, published August 6, 1974, for data on lending cutbacks in Chile. The role of the Australian Secret Intelligence Service in Chile was initially reported in the *National Times* of Australia, March 15–21, 1981, page 11.

23. Vietnam: The Quagmire Deepens

John Marks was a fellow at Harvard's Institute of Politics when interviewed. Charles Cooke made many of his files available to me. Wayne Smith was a managing partner of a major accounting firm in Washington. Richard Smyser was still in the Foreign Service, assigned in Washington. The quotation from John Osborne was published as "Love That Pap!" in the *New Republic*, November 28, 1970; it was reprinted on page 179 of Osborne's *The First Two Years of the Nixon Watch* (Liveright, 1971). Benjamin Schemmer's *The Raid* (Harper & Row, 1976) is the best source by far on the failed Son Tay mission; see also my report "POW Site Raid Based on Data Six Months Old," distributed by the Reporters News Service and reprinted in the *St. Louis Post-Dispatch* and other newspapers on January 29, 1971. Kissinger's comment at the private Harvard Faculty Club dinner was relayed by a participant, who kept a journal. Schemmer was interviewed in Washington in early 1981. Samuel Adams was a farmer and livestock breeder in Waterford, Virginia, when interviewed. Laird's top-secret trip report to Nixon, released under the Freedom of Information Act, was dated January 16, 1971, and is available from the Pentagon. Michael Maclear, author of *The Ten Thousand Day War* (St. Martin's Press, 1981), made many of his raw interview notes, transcripts, and outtakes available to me; an extensive interview with Alexander Haig was among them. Daniel Ellsberg's comment about T. S. Eliot can be found on page 273 of his *Papers on the War* (Simon & Schuster Touchstone, 1972). Stephen Genetti was interviewed at Radford, Virginia, where he was a college student. General Nguyen Duy Hinh's after-action pamphlet, "Lam Son 719," was published under an Army contract on July 31, 1977, by the General Research Corporation of McLean, Virginia.

24. Protecting the Secrets

The Max Frankel article, "U.S. Foreign Policy: A Firm Nixon Style," was published January 24, 1971, as the seventh in a *New York Times* series on U.S. foreign policy. Andrew Hamilton was living in Washington when interviewed. H. R. Haldeman's analysis of Nixon's reasons for installing the White House taping system—a fear of Kissinger—can be found on pages 258–259 of his *The Ends of Power* (Dell, 1978). Nixon's appointment calendars for the years 1969–1974, as maintained by the Secret Service, are in my possession. Chester Crocker was a research fellow in Washington when interviewed; he joined the Reagan Administration in 1981 as an Assistant Secretary of State for African Affairs. Morton Halperin's essay in the *New York Times,* "Vietnam: Options," was published November 7, 1970, on the Op-Ed page. Many of the FBI summary letters and much of the FBI documentation cited in this chapter are on public file in Halperin's wiretapping lawsuit, which was still pending as of early 1983 in federal court. Leslie Gelb was a foreign policy reporter for the *New York Times* in Washington when interviewed. J. Blair Seaborn's warning to Hanoi can be found on page 291 of *The Pentagon Papers,* as published by the *New York Times* (Bantam, 1971). For a full account of the *Times*'s role in publishing the Pentagon Papers, see *Without Fear or Favor* (Times Books, 1980), by Harrison E. Salisbury, especially pages 70–133. Lloyd Shearer was still editor-at-large of *Parade* and living in Los Angeles when interviewed. Derek Shearer's report on the Ellsberg-Kissinger confrontation was included in "An Evening with Henry," in the *Nation,* March 8, 1971, pages 296–299. Tom Oliphant's story, "Only 3 Have Read Secret Indochina Report; All Urge Swift Pullout," was published March 7, 1971, in the *Boston Sunday Globe.* Orlando Letelier's cable to Santiago was made available by his widow, Isabel.

25. SALT: A Grain Deal

Charles Colson's recollection about the ride to the Sequoia can be found on pages 43–45 of his memoir, *Born Again* (Chosen Books, 1976); he elaborated further in interviews with me. Gerard Smith's aborted lobbying effort in behalf of Kissinger is reported on page 149 of *Doubletalk.* (Doubleday, 1980). See Garthoff's articles "SALT 1; An Evaluation," in *World Politics,* October 1978, and "Negotiating with the Russians: Some Lessons from SALT," *International Security,* Spring 1977, for an analysis of the Nixon-Kissinger misjudgments in the 1970–1971 SALT negotiations. Smith's criticism of Kissinger's manipulations at SALT strategy meetings is on page 108 of *Doubletalk.* Smith's memoir, especially pages 121–445, is essential for an understanding of the issues and personalities involved, and will not be specifically cited further. Elmo Zumwalt's criticisms of the backchannel SALT negotiation can be found on pages 348–353 of his *On Watch* (Quadrangle, 1976). Teddy Gleason of the International Longshoremen's Association was interviewed by telephone in his New York office. The best account of the 1971 grain transactions with the Soviet Union is in "U.S.-Soviet Grain Deal: Case History of a Gamble," by Murray Marder and Marilyn Berger, in the *Washington Post,* December 7, 1971. Their article dealt extensively with the various political and economic problems inherent in the negotiations between the White House and the anti-Communist unions, but did not link those dealings to SALT. The most thorough analysis of U.S.-Soviet grain trading can be found in *Merchants of Grain* (Viking Press, 1979), by Dan Morgan, who was reporting on international agricultural and economic matters for the *Washington Post.* The anti-Soviet quotes from Gleason can be found in Marder and Berger. Jay Loveston, the AFL-CIO director of international affairs, was interviewed in Washington. Frank Drozak was president of SIU when interviewed. Brand was still with the Transportation Institute of Washington. Day-by-day reporting on the grain sale negotiations was provided by Richard Basoco, maritime editor of the *Baltimore Sun;* see especially his articles of mid-June 1971. Jesse Calhoon was still president of the MEBA when interviewed. See the *Congressional Record* for July 26, 1972, pages 25443–25467, for the close Senate vote on the Cargo Preference Act. President Gerald Ford's veto late in 1974 is described on pages 226–227 of his memoir, *A Time to Heal* (Harper & Row/Reader's Digest, 1979). Andrew Gibson's news conference remark can be found in "U.S. to Let Russians Buy $136 Million in Feed Grain," by William M.

Blair, *New York Times,* November 6, 1976. The legal action over the SIU's $100,000 political contribution was reported in the *New York Times,* February 4, 1973, "Seafarers Gave $100,000 to Nixon."

26. China: Opening Moves

For an insider's account of Nixon's long-held wish to visit China, see pages 266–267 in Safire's *Before the Fall* (Doubleday, 1975). Nixon's desire to visit China, expressed to Paul Dixon, the columnist, in 1960, was cited by the Kalb brothers in their biography at pages 217–218. Nixon's *Foreign Affairs* article, "Asia After China," was published in October 1967. His comments at the Republican National Convention in 1968 were cited by Stanley Karnow in *Mao and China* (Viking, 1972), on page 493. Ross Terrill's reporting on China was particularly useful; he kindly supplemented his writings with additional notes and documents. Ambassador Manach's comments to Terrill can be found in *800,000,000* (Atlantic Monthly Press, 1972), beginning at page 144. Roxanne Witke's revealing biography of Chiang Ching, *Comrade Chiang Ch'ing* (Little, Brown, 1977), discusses Mao's fear of the Imperial City at page 372. Two well-researched monographs on China's foreign policy strategy in the late 1960s and early 1970s were prepared by the Rand Corporation for the Director of Net Assessment in the Defense Department. See "Chinese Foreign Policy Factionalism and the Origins of the Strategic Triangle," by Thomas M. Gottlieb, November 1977, and "Sino-Soviet Conflict in the 1970s," by Kenneth G. Lieberthal, July 1978. The unclassified studies were approved for public release. Another useful study is *China-Watch* by Robert G. Sutter, a former analyst for the CIA (Johns Hopkins, 1978). Sutter was a researcher for the Library of Congress when interviewed. Allen S. Whiting was a professor at the University of Michigan when interviewed; he discussed his meetings with Kissinger in "Sino-Soviet Détente," published in the June 1980 *China Quarterly,* pages 334–341. The memorandum presented to President-elect Nixon in late 1968 was published in the *Congressional Record* on August 6, 1971, beginning at page 30765. Its publication was part of a right-wing attack on Nixon's China policy. Haldeman's diary note about Kissinger's excitement over China appears on page 129 of his memoir, *The Ends of Power* (Dell, 1978); Haldeman's strange thesis concerning imminent warfare between China and the Soviet Union takes up the next six pages. Stoessel's classified cables reporting on his Warsaw meetings are in my possession. He was assisted in his discussions with the Chinese by Paul H. Kreisberg, the State Department expert on China, who was director of the Office of Asian Communist Affairs, and by Donald M. Anderson, a Foreign Service officer. Kreisberg was director of studies at the Council on Foreign Relations, in New York City, when interviewed. Marshall Green was retired from the Foreign Service and living in Washington when interviewed.

27. China: Kissinger's Secret Trip

Edgar Snow's seminal role in the signaling between China and the United States is well documented. See Snow's *The Long Revolution* (Random House, 1972); his June 30, 1971, essay in *Life* magazine, "China Will Talk from a Position of Strength," and two articles in the *New Republic* magazine: "The Open Door," March 27, 1971, and "Aftermath of the Cultural Revolution," April 10, 1971. His widow, Lois Wheeler Snow, provided me with Snow's private reflections, including some of Chairman Mao's off-the-record comments, as tape recorded by Snow in Peking in December 1970. G. W. Choudhury was teaching in Durham, North Carolina, when interviewed. China's concern about nuclear weapons in Vietnam is reported on page 136 in Terrill's *800,000,000* (Atlantic Monthly Press, 1972). The advice from Professor John Fairbank can be found on pages 59–61 in his *China:*

The People's Middle Kingdom and the U.S.A. (Harvard University Press, 1967). Hanoi's Foreign Ministry documents on its dealings with China during the period of détente with the White House were provided to me during a visit to Hanoi in July-August 1979, and subsequently made public. See "The Truth about Vietnam-China Relations over the Last Thirty Years," as reproduced in the U. S. government's Foreign Broadcast Information Service for Asia and the Pacific, October 19, 1979. Enver Hoxha's memoirs were produced by the Albanian government in two volumes, the first dealing with 1962 to 1972 and the second with 1973 to 1977. They are available in English from the Albanian Mission to the United Nations in New York. Both volumes were published in Tirana, Albania, in 1979. The poems found on a factory bulletin board in Sian were included in Ross Terrill's *The Future of China: After Mao* (Delacorte Press, 1978), pages 296–297. Huang Hua's comment to Wilfred Burchett was relayed by Burchett to Terrill. The White House's adroit maneuvering with the television media was reported by Don Oberdorfer in "The China TV Show," *Washington Post,* February 20, 1972. John Scali was a television reporter for ABC News when interviewed. The Alsop column, "Jade Body-Stockings," was published July 21, 1971, in the *Washington Post.* Chou Enlai's fears about the revival of Japanese militarism were reported by Ross Terrill, beginning on page 133, in *800,000,000.* The notes of Kissinger's secret briefing in 1974 to the Joint Chiefs of Staff are in my possession.

28. The Plumbers

Many White House and Watergate Special Prosecution Force documents dealing with the Plumbers unit and the official investigation of its activities can be found in Book VII of the House Impeachment Panel's *White House Surveillance Activities and Campaign Activities,* May-June 1974. See also two of my *New York Times* articles, "The President and the Plumbers: A Look at 2 Security Questions," December 9, 1973, and "Nixon's Active Role on Plumbers: His Talks with Leaders Recalled," December 10, 1973. The journalist Nick Thimmesch has also been a persistent critic of Kissinger's role in the Plumbers affair. See, for example, "How Kissinger Fooled Us All," *New York* magazine, June 4, 1973, beginning on page 48, and his "Henry and the Plumbers," in *New Times* magazine, July 12, 1974. The Ellsberg article on Laos was published in the *New York Review of Books* as "Murder in Laos" on March 11, 1971. Melville Stephens was working in London when interviewed. Walt Rostow's conversation with Haig, as quoted by Harrison Salisbury, can be found on page 210 in Salisbury's *Without Fear or Favor* (Times Books, 1980). The anecdote about Senator Mathias' role in making the Nixon Administration aware of the NSSM 1 leak was described in interviews by Ellsberg and his attorneys and subsequently confirmed by Mathias. Mathias was still in the Senate, Charles Goodell a Washington attorney, and Charles Nesson a professor at Harvard Law School when interviewed. Haldeman's account of Nixon's rage at "the goddam Gelb material" can be found on pages 286–287 of his memoir, *The Ends of Power* (Dell, 1978). G. Gordon Liddy's report of Mardian's threat can be found on pages 155–156 of his *Will* (St. Martin's Press, 1980). John Ehrlichman's office notes, as censored for national security material, were published in Appendix III of the House Impeachment Committee, May-June, 1974, pages 89–263 (including some telephone transcripts). Additional notes were supplied to me by Ehrlichman. I also obtained access to internal Special Watergate Prosecution Force records and transcripts, which included some previously censored Ehrlichman notes. Liddy's discussion of firebombing the Brookings Institution is on pages 171–172 of *Will.* The Kissinger aide's office notes are in my possession. Kissinger's briefing to *Time* magazine was held February 4, 1974; a declassified transcript was made public under the Freedom of Information Act. Egil Krogh was teaching law in San Francisco when interviewed. W. Donald Stewart was a private investigator in suburban Virginia. The cited *Time* article, "Questions About Gray," which gave details of the White House wiretapping, was published March 5, 1973. J. T. Smith was practicing law in Washington when interviewed. The FBI's William Sullivan had been discussing intelligence matters with the author for six months before Watergate.

29. Mideast: Final Defeat for Rogers

For Senator Symington's attack on Rogers, see "Symington Hits Kissinger Role As the 'Real' Secretary of State," by Murray Marder, *Washington Post,* March 3, 1971. James Reston's immediate defense of Kissinger, "The Kissinger Role," was published the same day. Reston's second column on the issue, which praised Rogers, was published April 25, 1971, under the title "The Quiet One." Anwar Sadat's decision to make concessions and seek a settlement was extensively reported in Mohammed Heikal's *The Road to Ramadan* (Quadrangle, 1975), especially pages 114–155. See also Chapter Five, "Standstill Diplomacy," in William Quandt's *Decade of Decision* (University of California, 1977), pages 128–164. Sadat gave his view of the negotiations in an extraordinary interview published December 13, 1971, in the international edition of *Newsweek:* "Sadat: 'We Are Now Back to Square One.' " Donald Bergus was retired from the Foreign Service and on an academic fellowship in Washington when interviewed. Eugene Trone was living in suburban Virginia. Michael Sterner was in the Foreign Service, assigned to Washington. The Bergus incident was extensively reported by the *Washington Post:* see Marilyn Berger's "Envoy 'Paper' Compromises U.S. in Mideast," June 29, 1971, and "Rabin Meets Rogers on Cairo 'Paper' Flap," the next day. Quandt's reporting on the July 16, 1971, NSC meeting is on page 143 of *Decade of Decision.* Mahmoud Riad's skepticism about Kissinger's policy is spelled out on page 201 of his memoir; see Chapter Ten, "The Year of Decision," pages 182–208, for Riad's shrewd analysis of the continuing power struggle in Washington.

30. A Berlin Settlement

David Binder's study of Willy Brandt and his *Ostpolitik* is *The Other German: Willy Brandt's Life and Times* (New Republic Books, 1975); the quoted excerpt is from page 272. Kissinger's and Sonnenfeldt's dislike of Brandt is mentioned on page 266. Egon Bahr was retired from public office in the Federal Republic of Germany when interviewed in Washington. Kenneth Rush was also retired from public life when interviewed in Washington. Martin Hillenbrand and James Sutterlin were retired from the Foreign Service when interviewed. The cited *New York Times* dispatch hailing Nixon's role "President Broke a Berlin Impasse," by Lawrence Fellows, was published August 31, 1971. David Klein was retired from the Foreign Service when interviewed.

31. Vietnam: A Missed Chance

See "The General' Gambit," *Newsweek,* November 16, 1969, at page 54, for an account of General Minh's early start in the 1971 presidential campaign. D. Gareth Porter, who was bureau chief in Saigon for Dispatch News Service in 1971, provided me with a full file of his articles on the South Vietnamese election; Porter's political coverage was more thorough than that provided by the major United States newspapers, which focused on the battlefield. Much of the detail about Minh's campaigning and his popularity in the South came from Porter. For additional information, see his study of the war, *A Peace Denied* (University of Indiana, 1975), at pages 95–97. Nixon's tough talk about antiwar demonstrators was published September 24, 1981, in the *New York Times:* "1971 Tape Links Nixon to Use of 'Thugs.' " The complete transcript of the tape is in my possession. The Xuan Thuy interview with Peter Weiss and Richard Barnet was published in the *New York Times* on February 6, 1972: "Hanoi Rules Out a Partial Accord." For details of the CIA's attitude toward the 1971 elections, see Frank Snepp's *Decent Interval* (Random House, 1977), especially Chapter Two. The embassy documents obtained under the Freedom of Information Act are in my possession. The Vietnam Elections Project, headed by the late Theodore Jacqueney, received little press coverage at the time. Family members and former associates provided many of Jacqueney's papers to my researcher, Jay Peterzell. Peterzell also interviewed Richard Winslow, Oliver Davidson, and Jerry Ruback. Frank Mankiewicz was president of National Public Radio when interviewed. The "same old story" quotation is in "Kissinger Talks to Ky, Minh," by Peter A. Jay, *Washington Post*, July 6, 1971. Gloria Emerson's article was "Thieu Using U.S. Surveys in Vote Campaign," *New York Times*, February 2, 1971. The deposition revealing the American bribe offer to General Minh was taken by the ACLU's Mark Lynch in Washington, and is available through him. The Joseph Kraft column appeared August 24, 1971, in the *Washington Post*, under an apt headline, "The Fix in Saigon." For Senator Jackson's election-eve warnings, see "Jackson Warns on Aid to Saigon," by John W. Finney, *New York Times*, September 11, 1971. Robert Shaplen's dispatch, "Letter from Vietnam," was dated November 1 and published in the *New Yorker* November 13, 1971, beginning at page 77. Former Senator George McGovern was interviewed in Washington.

32. The India-Pakistan War

The most comprehensive and questioning account of American policy in the India-Pakistan war was written by a former senior State Department official, Christopher Van Hollen, and published in *Asian Survey*, April 1980, as "The Tilt Policy Revisited: Nixon-Kissinger Geopolitics and South Asia." Jack Anderson has published his "how I did it" account in *The Anderson Papers* (Random House, 1973), written with George Clifford; see pages 205–269. The imminence of war between India and Pakistan was hardly a little-known fact in mid-1971; see, for example, "India vs. Pakistan: Is This the Next War?" in the August 23, 1971, edition of *U.S. News & World Report*. See also "Pakistan Seems Likely to Push Its Repression of Bengalis in the East," by Peter Kann, *Wall Street Journal*, September 20, 1971. A full account of the various atrocities of the war, and the incidents leading up to it, was published in two volumes of *Bangla Desh Documents*, by the Indian government. Many of the foreign newspaper accounts cited in this chapter were reprinted in those volumes. A copy of the April 6, 1971, State Department dissent cable is in my possession. Ambassador Kenneth Keating's cable was made public by Jack Anderson in late 1971, along with dozens of other classified cables and memoranda on the India-Pakistan war. Anderson gave me copies of all his materials, including a number of documents that he did not publish at the time. G. W. Choudhury's comment about "false hope" from Nixon and Kissinger was made in an interview with me in Washington. For evidence of continued arms shipments after the March 25, 1971, West Pakistani invasion of the East, see "Kennedy Bares 2 Arms Deals with Pakistan," by Lewis M. Simons, *Washington Post*, October 5, 1971. Morarji Desai shows his intense feelings about Indira Gandhi most explicitly in the third volume of *The Story of My Life* (S. Chand & Company, New Delhi, 1979); see especially Chapter Fourteen, "Indira Gandhi Dilutes Democracy," beginning on page 57. The volumes are available from the Indian Embassy in Washington. There have been some reports alleging that Mujibur Rahman's assassination in 1975, when he was President of Bangladesh, may have had an American involvement. See "The intrigue behind the army coup which toppled Sheikh Mujib," by Lawrence Lifschultz, *The Guardian*, London, August 15, 1979, page 13. And see Lifschultz' book on Bangladesh (with Kai Bird), *Bangladesh: The Unfinished Revolution* (Zed Press, London, 1979; distributed in the United States by Monthly Review Press). Indira Gandhi's caustic comments about Kissinger came in an interview with Jonathan Power, "Indira Gandhi's Quest," published in the *Washington Post*'s "Outlook" section December 30, 1979. Winston Lord's interview is reprinted in part on page 156 of *Bangladesh: The Unfinished Revolution*. Senator Barry Goldwater inserted the Kissinger backgrounder in the *Congressional Record* for December 9, 1971, at page 45734. See "Goldwater Identifies Kissinger as 'Sources,' " by Bernard Gwertzman, *New York Times*, December 11, 1971. Admiral Zumwalt's detailed account of the crisis begins on page 360 of *On Watch* (Quadrangle, 1976). Gandhi's letter to Nixon at the close of the war is included in the Indian government's *Bangla Desh Documents*. Her footnoted comment raising questions about the American "inferiority complex" is in the "Outlook" interview with Power.

33. Spying on Kissinger

For a detailed account of Yeoman Radford's White House spying, see three publications of the Senate Armed Services Committee in 1974, with the overall title *Transmittal of Documents From the National Security Council to the Chairman of the Joint Chiefs of Staff*. Part 1 was published February 6; Part 2, February 20 and 21; Part 3, March 7, 1974. The committee's final report, *Unauthorized Disclosures and Transmittal of Classified Documents*, was published December 19, 1974. See pages 369–376 in *On Watch* (Quadrangle, 1976) for Admiral Elmo Zumwalt's version of the military spying. Admiral Welander, who was living in Annapolis, Maryland, after his retirement from active duty, refused to discuss the spying. Kissinger's private lunch with the *Time* editors and reporters took place on February 4, 1974. Coleman Hicks was general counsel of the Navy Department when interviewed. Tom Braden's column, "Net Effect of the Anderson Leaks," was published January 11, 1972, in the *Washington Post*. Kraft wrote of "Undermining Kissinger" in the *Post* on the same day, and Marquis Childs's column, "Kissinger—New Target," appeared in the *Post* on January 20, 1972. Bob Woodward's disclosure of the alleged plot to kill Jack Anderson "Hunt Told Associates of Orders to Kill Jack Anderson," was published September 21, 1975, in the *Washington Post*, G. Gordon Liddy's similar understanding can be found on pages 207–214 in *Will* (St. Martin's Press, 1980). Les Whitten, Jack Anderson's associate, was interviewed in his suburban Washington home. Whitten also made available the CIA's files on project "Mudhen," as declassified under the Freedom of Information Act. Charles Sither had left the White House and was working in Los Angeles, as a security official for the Occidental Oil Company, when interviewed.

34. Vietnam: Going Public

Samuel Adams' article in *Harper's* magazine, "Vietnam Cover-up: Playing War with Numbers," was published in May 1975. Adams later aided CBS television in the production of its controversial 1982 special report on the issue. Kissinger's caustic comment to William Safire about Hanoi's manipulation can be found on page 401 in Safire's *Before the Fall* (Doubleday, 1975). See pages 272–281 in Wilfred Burchett's *At the Barricades* for an account of his private breakfast with Kissinger. I. F. Stone's trenchant and perceptive analysis, "The Hidden Traps in Nixon's Peace Plan," was published in the March 9, 1972, *New York Review of Books*, beginning on page 13. *Newsweek*'s praise for Kissinger can be found in "Talking with the Enemy," its cover story for February 7, 1972. The cited *New York Times* dispatch, published January 27, 1972, was "President's Adviser Asks Public to Back Initiatives," by Robert B. Semple, Jr. Nixon's private memorandum to Haldeman and Colson is in my possession. Arthur Downey was practicing law in Washington when interviewed. Noel Koch was a public relations consultant in Washington. Secretary of State Rogers' attack on Muskie, as orchestrated by Nixon and Colson, was page one news in the *New York Times:* "Rogers Says Muskie Hurt Prospects of Peace Talks," by Terence Smith, February 10, 1972. Colson told of the John Mitchell complaint on pages 66–67 of *Born Again* (Chosen Books, 1976).

35. China: A Prime-Time Visit

Ronald Walker was an employment consultant in Washington when interviewed. Roger Sullivan, the National Security Council's expert on China during the Carter Administration, was an international trade consultant. Chou En-lai's interview with the London *Sunday Times* was published December 5, 1971, as "Midnight Thoughts of Premier Chou," by Neville Maxwell. James Thomson was curator of the Nieman Foundation at Harvard University when interviewed. Alfred Jenkins was living in Bennington, Vermont. Stanley Karnow was a free-lance journalist. For a good example of Karnow's reporting during the summit, see "Nixon Pledges Pullout of Forces in Taiwan," *Washington Post,* February 28, 1972. His cited article in *Foreign Policy* magazine, "Playing Second Fiddle to the Tube," was published in the Summer 1972 issue; it was paired with an equally critical piece by John Chancellor of NBC television, "Who Produced the China Show?" Dean Acheson's "mistake" is discussed on pages 355–365 of his *Present at the Creation* (Norton, 1969). For Eisenhower's attack, see "Eisenhower Scores Acheson 'Mistake,'" by James Reston, *New York Times,* September 23, 1952. See page 192 in Henry Brandon's *The Retreat of American Power* (Doubleday, 1973) for Kissinger's account of Rogers' role as told to Brandon. David Kraslow was publisher of the *Miami News* when interviewed. Summit coverage in the *Los Angeles Times* also led to immediate questions; see "Nixon Seen as Giving More Than He Got—in Short Run," by Robert C. Toth, February 28, 1972. Kraslow's lead story that day described the Shanghai Communiqué as "oblique and ambiguous" on Taiwan's status. Safire's account of the Cabinet meeting is on pages 409–416 of his *Before the Fall* (Doubleday, 1975). A copy of Kissinger's background briefing at the Federal City Club is in my possession.

36. Vietnam: Hanoi's Offensive

A perceptive account of North Vietnam's and the NLF's strategy in the spring offensive can be found in a monograph by David W. P. Elliott, "NLF-DRV Strategy and the 1972 Spring Offensive," Interim Report Number 4, January 1974, published by Cornell University's International Relations of East Asia Project. Elliott's general conclusions about what the North Vietnamese were trying to do were borne out by their interviews with me in 1979 in Hanoi. General John Vogt was retired from the Air Force and living in Annapolis, Maryland, when interviewed; his oral history was taken August 8–9, 1978, by the Air Force and declassified in part early in 1982, at the general's request. For a full account of the Lavelle incident, see the September 1972 hearings before the Senate Armed Services Committee, *Nomination of John D. Lavelle, General Creighton W. Abrams, and Admiral John S. McCain,* published October 10, 1972. Otis Pike retired from Congress and was a Washington journalist when interviewed. See page 380 in Zumwalt's *On Watch* (Quadrangle, 1976) for his quotes from Laird. The cited William Beecher dispatch was "On the Side of Restraint in Vietnam, an Aide says," *New York Times,* April 18, 1972. James Reston's April 18 column was aptly titled "Mr. Nixon's Temper." Shaplen's article was "Letter from Vietnam," dated May 6 and published in the May 13, 1972, *New Yorker.* Representative Ronald V. Dellums,

California Democrat, inserted much of NSSM 1 in the *Congressional Record* of May 10, 1972; see pages E4975 to E5005. See pages 297–299 in *The Ends of Power* (Dell, 1978) for Haldeman's account of his and Nixon's machinations against Kissinger. Safire's assertion that Kissinger put out the word in backgrounders can be found on page 402 of his *Before The Fall* (Doubleday, 1975). Tad Szulc was the first journalist to describe fully the Vietnam negotiations that took place during Kissinger's two Moscow visits in the spring of 1972; NSC aides and North Vietnamese officials subsequently confirmed the main points of Szulc's reportage. See "Behind the Vietnam Cease-Fire Agreement," in *Foreign Policy*, Summer 1974, pages 21–69. Kenneth Clawson was interviewed in his suburban Washington home. His attack on the *Times* was issued May 18, 1972, by the White House.

37. SALT: The Moscow Summit

It should be noted again that I have relied heavily on Gerard Smith's memoir, *Doubletalk* (Doubleday, 1980), and found it to be exceedingly accurate. John Newhouse was a Washington free-lance journalist and author when interviewed. Joseph Alsop's column linking SALT and grain, "A View of the Summit," was published May 24, 1972, in the *Washington Post*. See Safire's memoir, *Before the Fall* (Doubleday, 1975), pages 432–439, for an account of Kissinger's discussion of trade with Leonid Brezhnev. Elmo Zumwalt's comments about the SALT process in 1972 are on pages 400–410 of his *On Watch* (Quadrangle, 1976); the quote about Soviet boats is on page 403. For Navy Secretary John Lehman's 1981 complaints about the Trident, see "Trident Woes Put Military-Industrial System in Doubt," by Philip Taubman, *New York Times*, April 4, 1981. Philip Odeen was interviewed in Washington, where he was working for an accounting firm. Barry Carter was a professor at the Georgetown University law school. Interviews with Raymond Garthoff—and his published analyses—continued to be invaluable in providing an insight to the actual bargaining at the summit in 1972. Safire's praise for the Nixon-Kissinger negotiation team is on pages 442–443 of *Before the Fall*. Gerald Smith's 1969 freeze proposal was released to the Federation of American Scientists under the Freedom of Information Act and made public by the federation October 30, 1982. See "1969 study called freeze verifiable," *Columbus Dispatch*, Columbus, Ohio, October 31, 1982. Kissinger's briefing of Congress and his colloquy with Senator Henry Jackson took place June 15, 1972, in the White House; a complete text of questions and answers was on file in the White House press office. For an example of Senator Jackson's subsequent complaints, see "Jackson Raps Arms Curbs," by George C. Wilson, in the *Washington Post* of July 19, 1972. Representative John Ashbrook's attack on SALT can be found in the *Congressional Record* for May 24, 1972, beginning at page 18687. The cited *Newsday* newspaper article was "Details of Missile Treaty," by Martin Schram, May 20, 1972. Schram was reporting for the *Washington Post* when interviewed. See page 451 in *Before The Fall* for Nixon's heroics in Moscow as reported by Safire. For Gelb's SALT challenge to Kissinger, see "Soviets Said to Get Missile Concessions," by Leslie H. Gelb, *New York Times*, June 22, 1972. The dispute simmered in the *Times* for a week. Royal Allison was a consultant in Washington when interviewed. For a lively account of Kissinger's extraordinary press conference in Moscow, see "Kissinger's Nightclub Act," by Murray Marder, *Washington Post*, May 28, 1972.

38. Vietnam: Intense Negotiations

Essential information in this and subsequent Vietnam chapters was provided by Huang Duc Nha, Nguyen Van Thieu's close aide. Nha supplied copies of previously unavailable—and unknown—draft peace agreements, many of them marked top secret, that were exchanged between Washington and Hanoi in the late summer and early fall of 1972. Copies of this material are in my possession. For more on Nha, see "Thieu's Top Emissary," by Lawrence Stern, *Washington Post,* November 30, 1972, and "Saigon's New Chief Spokesman," by Fox Butterfield, *New York Times,* January 11, 1973. He was also interviewed by the Kalb brothers. Kissinger's lunch with Norman Mailer was described in Mailer's *St. George and the Godfather* (Signet Special, 1972), pages 114–121. The Westmoreland quote from *Hearts and Minds* was provided by Peter Davis. Rogers' interview before the Republican convention in Miami Beach was the lead story in the *Miami Herald* on August 20, 1972: "Vietnam Peace This Year Is Predicted by Rogers," by James McCartney, of Knight newspapers. A White House denial came quickly; see "U.S. Discouraging Hints of Success at Peace Parley," by Bernard Gwertzman, *New York Times,* August 22, 1972. For Nixon's comment about ending the war, see "A Conversation with President Nixon Aboard Air Force One," by Stewart Alsop, *Newsweek,* September 4, 1972, pages 24–25. Kissinger's comment about going to Hanoi was made to Dorothy McCardle of the *Washington Post* and published in the newspaper's "Style" section August 24, 1972. Ellsberg's activities at the Republican convention, cited in the footnote, were page-one news in the *Washington Post* for August 23, 1972: "Ellsberg Says Nixon Tried Frogman Ploy," by Chalmers M. Roberts. The *New York Times* also treated Ellsberg's allegations seriously: "Ellsberg Says Escalation Was Part of Nixon's Plan," by R. W. Apple, Jr., August 23, 1972. See page 25 of his *Decent Interval* (Random House, 1977) for Frank Snepp's assessment of Pham Van Dong's National Day Speech and Brezhnev's alleged comment to Kissinger about it. Haig's complaints to Zumwalt about Nixon can be found on page 399 of Zumwalt's *On Watch* (Quadrangle, 1976). Joseph Alsop's September 18, 1972, column in the *Washington Post* was headlined, "Imaginable Hat Trick," a reference to ending the Vietnam War and the summits in Moscow and Peking. Albert Sindlinger was interviewed in his Media, Pennsylvania, offices; the pollster gave me copies of some of the material he had given the White House through Charles Colson. Colson subsequently verified much of Sindlinger's account. Samuel Lubell's column, "How the 'Psych War' Affects Everyone," was distributed for publication August 16, 1972, or thereafter; a copy of the original release is in my possession. Lubell briefly described his White House meeting in a letter to me dated January 20, 1982. The transcript of Senator George McGovern's speech on Vietnam was published in full on October 11, 1972, in the *New York Times,* page 29. A reference to Frank Snepp's ignored intelligence report can be found on page 26 of his *Decent Interval* (Random House, 1977). The cited Joseph Alsop column, "A Niche for Kissinger," was published in the *Washington Post* on October 23, 1972. James Reston's upbeat column was published October 18, 1972, in the *New York Times,* "Don't Cheer Yet, But . . ."

39. Vietnam: Politics Before Peace

John Dean's description of the White House coaching session for Ronald Ziegler was given on June 25, 1973, his first day of public testimony before the Senate Select Committee on Presidential Campaign Activities, known as the Senate Watergate Committee. Dean's testimony was published in Book 3 of the committee's hearings into *Watergate and Related Activities,* June 25 and June 26, 1973, at page 965. The volume also includes a set of notes from the coaching session that Dean submitted into evidence, at pages 1200–1209. The caustic comments about the American press and its role in Watergate can be found on page 204 of *Watergate: The Full Inside Story,* by the London *Sunday Times* team, Lewis Chester, Cal McCrystal, Stephen Aris, and William Shawcross (Ballantine, 1973).

The Kalbs' account in *Kissinger* of the Kissinger-Thieu meetings was especially useful in this chapter. Charles Whitehouse had retired from the Foreign Service and was living in Washington when interviewed. The Canadian television interview with Nguyen Van Thieu was conducted by Michael Maclear in London, in early 1980, for his book on Vietnam, *The Ten Thousand Day War* (St. Martin's Press, 1981), and for his subsequent syndicated television series; the full text of Thieu's remarks was made available by Maclear. Tran Kim Phuong was interviewed at his home in suburban Washington, where he has lived since the fall of Saigon in 1975. The *Los Angeles Times* dispatch was "U.S. Sources Deny Viet Breakthrough," by Robert C. Toth, October 19, 1972. Le Chi Thao was living in suburban Virginia when interviewed. Westmoreland's advice to Nixon can be found, beginning at page 393, in his memoir, *A Soldier Reports* (Doubleday, 1976). Thieu's interview with Oriana Fallaci was held in Saigon in January 1973; it can be found, beginning on page 45, in a reprint of Fallaci interviews, *Interviews with History* (Houghton Mifflin, 1977). Arnaud de Borchgrave's interview with Pham Van Dong was published in the October 30, 1972, issue of *Newsweek,* "Exclusive from Hanoi." Michael Maclear's contrasting dispatch in the *New York Times* was published in late editions of October 22, 1972, on page 4. Maclear was interviewed in Toronto, where he was an independent film producer. The full text of Nixon's October 23, 1972, cable to Hanoi was supplied to me by the North Vietnamese government. Reston's column dealing with Nixon's lack of trust was titled "First Things First," *New York Times,* October 22, 1972. John Ehrlichman's account of the final negotiations can be found on pages 313–316 of his memoir, *Witness to Power* (Simon & Schuster, 1982). Kissinger's interview with Oriana Fallaci was first published in the November 16, 1972, issue of *L'Europeo* magazine; its first publication in the United States was in the December 16, 1972, issue of the *New Republic,* beginning at page 17. Kissinger's bureaucratic enemies began circulating inside the White House the text of the *L'Europeo* interview, including Fallaci's personal report and analysis of her subject. One copy of Fallaci's personal notes, which appeared in *L'Europeo* but not in the *New Republic,* was made available to me. It was believed to have been prepared in John Scali's office. The five-page memorandum was dated November 20, 1972, and reproduced on White House stationery, with no other indication of where it originated.

40. Vietnam: The Christmas Bombs

For Murray Marder's report that Nixon did not want to settle the war before the election, see "Deliberate Stall Seen on Peace," *Washington Post,* November 9, 1972. Zumwalt's account of Nixon's rage at the black power issue begins on page 239 of *On Watch* (Quadrangle, 1976). The *Nhan Dan* editorial and Jean Thoraval's dispatch for *Agence France-Presse* are cited on page 152 of *A Peace Denied* (Indiana University, 1975), by Gareth Porter. Zumwalt's description of the Joint Chiefs of Staff meeting with Nixon begins on page 412 in *On Watch.* The Tom Braden column, headlined, "Vietnam Stalemate," appeared in the *Washington Post,* November 24, 1972. Laurence Stern of the *Washington Post* ably summarized many of the rumors about the Nixon-Kissinger dispute in a dispatch published December 3, 1972, "Rumors on Kissinger's Status Rush into Peace News Void." Colson's public comments about Kissinger's role in the bombing were aired February 7, 1975, in an interview with Barbara Walters on the NBC-TV *Today* show; see the account in the *Washington Post* for February 8, subtitled, "Kissinger Urged Bombing, Colson Says," by Douglas Watson. Colson's second volume of memoirs, *Life Sentence* (Chosen Books, 1972), describes the incident on pages 27–30. For an account of Haig's rapid rise to the rank of full general, see "Kissinger Aide Given No. 2 Army Post Over 243 Senior Generals," by Michael Getler, as published in the *Los Angeles Times,* September 8, 1972. For Admiral Moorer's puzzling analysis of the Christmas bombing, see "The Christmas Bombing of Hanoi—or How the POWs Got Home," in *foundation,* a publication of the Naval Aviation Museum, March 1981, beginning at page 18. James Reston's column of

December 13, 1972, was headlined, "Mr. Kissinger in Paris." Kissinger's remarks to Nick Thimmesch were reported in his June 4, 1973, *New York* magazine article, "How Kissinger Fooled Us All," at page 52. Kissinger's comments to John Osborne were reported in the *New Republic* for December 16, 1972, "Kicking Sand." Reston's column loyally suggesting that Kissinger was opposed to the Christmas bombing was titled "Nixon and Kissinger" and published in the *New York Times*, December 31, 1972. Kissinger's remark to Thimmesch about the effectiveness of the bombing is in Thimmesch's *New York* article. The military's accounting of the number of casualties in the B-52 bombing of Hanoi can be found in "What Christmas Bombing Did to North Vietnam," *U.S. News & World Report*, February 5, 1972, page 18. The Haig television interview was with Michael Maclear. Admiral Moorer's desire to continue the Christmas bombing was expressed in his *foundation* magazine article, page 24. Gerald Warren was editor of the *San Diego Union* when interviewed. While working in the Washington bureau of the *New York Times*, I spent several months investigating the link between the demoralized 6990th Air Force Service Service unit and the high loss rate of B-52 bombers over Christmas. I have partial transcripts of some of the subsequent courts-martial. Charles Iverson, Tom Bernard, and Thomas Eskelson were interviewed after they concluded their Air Force careers. James Reston's New Year's Eve warning was in his "Nixon and Kissinger" column. Haldeman's account of Nixon's rage at the Reston column is on pages 135–136 in *The Ends of Power* (Dell, 1978). Some of Nixon's secret pledges to Thieu, contained in top-secret letters, were made public by Nguyen Tien Hung, Saigon's former Minister of Planning, at a news conference in Washington on April 30, 1975, as the South Vietnamese government was being overthrown. See "Thieu Aide Discloses Promises of Force by Nixon to Back Pact," by Bernard Gwertzman, *New York Times*, May 1, 1975. The *Times* carried the full text of the cited letters. Thieu's April 21, 1975, farewell speech in Saigon was major news in the United States, but no reporter followed up the implications of Thieu's revelation that Nixon had considered the peace agreement "mere sheets of paper." Tom Wicker's column, "Mr. Thieu Tells His Side of It," was published April 22, 1975, in the *New York Times*. A full text of Thieu's speech was translated and distributed by the U.S. government's Foreign Broadcast Information Service on April 22, 1972. *Newsweek*'s effusive—and misleading—description of the January peace agreement, "At Last, the Vietnam Peace," was published February 5, 1973, beginning on page 18; the specific quote about Saigon's "sovereignty" is on page 23. Thieu's immediate moves against his opposition following the peace agreement are summarized on pages 179–184 of Gareth Porter's *A Peace Denied* (Indiana University, 1975).

41. The Price of Power

Gerald Ford's account of the *Mayaguez* incident can be found on pages 275–285 of *A Time to Heal* (Harper & Row/Reader's Digest, 1979). The most thorough study of the bungling was prepared by the Comptroller General of the United States and published on October 4, 1976, by the Subcommittee on International Political and Military Affairs of the House Committee on International Relations, as *Seizure of the Mayaguez*, Part IV. The subcommittee held investigatory hearings in May, June, July, and September 1975, published as Part I, May 14 and 15, 1975; Part II, June 19 and 25 and July 25, 1975; Part III, July 31 and September 12, 1975.

ACKNOWLEDGMENTS

This book owes its being to James Silberman, publisher of Summit Books, who approached me in 1976 with the idea of doing a definitive study of Henry Kissinger in the Nixon White House. Jim waited three years for me to agree, and then was generous with his advice, his money, and his editing skills. Arthur H. Samuelson, a senior editor at Summit, also had many useful suggestions. On Jim's staff, Elizabeth Kaplan, Kate Edgar, and Kathy Hurley were constantly forthcoming and supportive. Mary Heathcote, the copy editor, was caring and intelligent in her work.

William Whitworth, editor of the *Atlantic,* was the first outsider to read the work, and his support, and that of the *Atlantic,* were essential. David Halberstam gave the right advice at the right time.

My colleagues in the newspaper business were unfailingly helpful, most notably Tad Szulc, David Wise, Stanley Karnow, Courtney R. Sheldon, Seth Kantor, Jack Anderson, Les Whitten, Joe Spears, and Dale Van Atta. Mrs. Sunday Fellows, chief librarian for the Washington bureau of the *New York Times,* and Mark Hannah, head of the library at the *Washington Post,* permitted me virtually unlimited access and treated me as one of their own. Josephine Kirks, librarian for the Knight-Ridder newspapers, and Diana Moore, in the Washington bureau of the *Los Angeles Times,* responded to all requests with alacrity. My neighbors in the National Press Building, in the Washington bureaus of the *Baltimore Sun* and *Chicago Sun Times,* permitted me constant access to their photocopying machines and reference works.

My assistant and colleague throughout the four years it took to research and write this book was Jay Peterzell, who prepared position papers on most of the major issues and did voluminous chronological studies that made my work much easier. Peterzell also expertly handled my Freedom of Information Act requests, and became a self-made scholar on Vietnamese election law. David Karpook, formerly a librarian in the Washington bureau of the *New York Times,* spent hundreds of hours photocopying files after work and on weekends; he has a valued ability to discern what is important from what is not. Gail Lynch and M. Jane Cumberlege typed and retyped the manuscript cheerfully and well. My agent, Sterling Lord, remained his usual unflappable and loyal self throughout.

Finally, special thanks to Mrs. Miriam Borgenicht Klein, whose help came at a critical moment.

SEYMOUR M. HERSH

March 1983
Washington, D.C.

INDEX

in MIRV debate, 158–59, 187n
Mossad and, 214, 225, 394
Nixon's objections to, 28, 159, 187n
Office of National Estimates of (ONE), 159, 162
Paris negotiation leaks investigated by, 21, 22
Phoenix Operation of, 80–81, 178, 299, 435
Soviet submarine potential estimated by, 540–41
"two-track" approach of, 275–76, 278–279, 282n, 284–88, 295
Vietnamese elections influenced by, 432, 433, 435–36, 437
Vietnam War and, 50, 80–81, 133, 168, 169, 170, 178n, 179n, 308, 481n, 520n, 574, 630n
in Watergate cover-up, 572n
wiretaps and, 314, 333
Central Office for South Vietnam, see COSVN
Chaos Project, 209–10
Chapin, Dwight, 22, 130, 132, 473n, 489, 490, 590n
Chau, Tran Ngoc, 299
chemical weapons, Nixon-Kissinger ban on, 35n
Chennault, Anna, 21–22
Chiang Ching, 353, 364
Chiang Ching-kuo, 362
Chiang Kai-shek, 350–51, 377, 379
Chiao Kuan-hua, 495, 499
Chicago Sun-Times, 239, 242
Childs, Marquis, 475
Chile, 258–96, 314, 318
  anti-Allende "spoiling" operations in, 265–66, 275
  CIA role in, 180n, 205, 211, 258–62, 264–69, 270, 272n, 273–96, 332–33, 480, 638, 641
  Congress in, 259, 265, 266, 271, 272–273, 278–79, 288
  democracy in, 259, 262, 270, 276, 288
  economic pressures on, 294–95
  elections of 1958 and 1964 in, 259–60
  40 Committee and, 264–66, 267, 271–273, 275, 278, 281, 285, 287, 332, 480
  Frei government in, 260–63
  income distribution in, 259
  investigations of U.S. role in, 264n, 276; see also Senate Intelligence Committee
  in Kissinger memoirs, 262n, 264, 269, 276, 284, 287
  nationalization of copper in, 259, 260, 261, 262

in Nixon memoirs, 263–64
Pinochet junta in, 137n, 332n
"Rube Goldberg" gambit and, 271–72, 278–79, 280, 281, 282n
U.S. contributions to elections in, 260, 265, 266, 267–69
U.S. corporate involvement in, 183n, 259, 260–61, 267–69, 270, 276, 296
U.S. economic aid to, 262, 263
U.S. national security and, 270, 278, 296
Watergate compared to, 278
"Chileanization," 260–61
China, People's Republic of, 73n, 123, 314, 315, 350–82, 398
  Albania and, 376–77
  backchannel and, see backchannel messages, China policy and
  Cambodia and, 201, 362, 363
  Cultural Revolution in, 351, 352–53, 354, 355, 359, 377, 442, 461, 491
  end of U.S. trade embargo with, 370
  Five Principles of, 496n–97n
  French relations with, 351–52, 359, 364, 370
  India-Pakistan war and, 368, 447, 451–452, 453, 458, 461–62
  in Kissinger memoirs, 351, 352, 353, 356, 360, 361, 362, 364, 366, 368, 370, 371, 374–75, 376, 379, 492, 493, 494, 496, 498, 505
  Kissinger's visits to, 353, 366n, 367, 370–79, 382, 388, 411, 441–42, 451n, 453, 454, 467, 468–69, 490, 562–63, 636; see also Peking summit
  Korean War and, 51, 52
  moderate vs. military faction in, 354–55, 363–64
  in Nixon memoirs, 350, 351, 353, 368, 372, 374, 378–79, 494, 497
  Nixon's messages to, 352, 356, 366, 367
  Nixon's views on, 350–52
  Nixon's visit to, 176n, 353, 360n, 489–502, 505; see also Peking summit
  as nuclear power, 53, 357–58
  nuclear threats against, 357–58, 359, 369, 380–82
  "operating principles" in negotiations of, 374n
  Pakistani relations with, 356, 365–66, 368, 447, 451–52
  PLO and, 240
  Sihanouk's exile government in, 201n
  Soviet relations with, 353–54, 355, 357–358, 359, 363, 381, 453, 489, 491, 523
  U.S. ping-pong team invited to, 369, 449
  Vietnam War and, 120, 126, 129, 312,

674

China policy and, 314, 315, 350–82,
388, 441–42, 489–502
in Cienfuegos affair, 211–12, 250–57,
296, 297
as Democrat, 13
Democratic assassination plots alleged
by, 23–24
disdain for non-Western world of, 145–
146, 263, 571, 630
in Duck Hook planning, 120, 124n, 125–
127, 218
EC-121 incident and, 69–77, 84, 88
elevated status of, 203–12, 314
Fallaci's interview with, 608–9, 612
first on-the-record press conference of,
484, 485, 486
as flatterer, 40, 42, 43, 67, 103n, 318,
328, 573n
foreign policy views of, 76–77
40 Committee and, 264–66, 271–73,
281, 285, 287, 332, 480
as go-between in election of 1968, 12–
24, 38, 44, 597
Greece and, 137, 138n, 140–41
Hanoi's offensive and (1972), 504–28
India-Pakistan war and, 257n, 368, 445–
464, 465–66, 533n
intellect of, 151, 172, 318, 493
intelligence background of, 26–27, 84
intelligence controlled by, 207–10, 264–
266
as Jew, 84–86, 89n–90n, 91, 213, 263,
603
in Jordanian crisis, 211, 212, 232–49,
297
Laos invasion and, 304, 307–13, 405
leaks and, 91, 92, 98, 160, 205n, 254,
379–80, 397, 579, 603–4, 631
"lollipop treatment" of, 99
"madman theory" endorsed by, 607–8,
614–15, 619–20
on making of history, 263
memoirs of, 22, 394; see also specific
topics
Middle East policy and, 85, 213, 216–
218, 220, 222–49, 402–14, 636–37
Moscow press conference of, 555–57
Nixon's relationship with, see Nixon,
Richard M.
office journal of, 583–84, 621, 637
"peace is at hand" statement of, 602–8,
610, 618, 629
post-governmental career of, 642
power as goal of, 13, 25, 37, 67, 147,
243, 470
press favorable to, 25, 31, 38, 44, 76–

77, 98–99, 118, 127–28, 203–5, 379,
465, 475–76, 479, 574, 578–79
press problems of, 205, 463n, 465
private diary of, 108, 112
private files of, 112–13, 316, 479
proving loyalty as obsession of, 77, 84,
90, 91–92, 116, 212, 384, 388
racism of, 110, 111
realpolitik world view of, 509
renamed national security adviser, 618
resignation threats of, 227, 232, 270n,
383–84, 475, 591n, 618, 638
as scapegoat for failed peace settlement,
596–98, 601, 610, 618
as Secretary of State, 101n, 137n, 207n,
318n, 402, 565, 585n, 589, 610, 638–
639, 642
secret bombing of Cambodia and, 54–65,
84, 121–22, 175
sexual innuendoes about, 115
Shanghai news conference of, 499–500
in shift to Republican Party, 13
shuttle diplomacy of, 221, 636–37
Sihanouk's overthrow and, 181–83
social life of, 99, 109, 203
Son Tay raid and, 304–6
temper of, 99, 103, 115, 191, 228n, 465,
470, 598
as trusted adviser to Democrats, 14, 16,
17
Watergate and, 383–401, 635
White House tapes and, 316, 383
wiretaps and, 82, 83, 86–87, 89–90,
91–97, 103, 116, 193–94, 197–99,
314, 318–26, 391n, 398–401
in World War II, 23, 26, 84
Kissinger, Nancy Maginnes, 83, 317n
Klein, David, 421, 422
Klein, Herbert, 92n, 556
Kliendienst, Richard, 387n, 400n
Knight, Andrew, 180n
Knight, Hal, Jr., 62
Knoizen, Arthur K., 469
Koch, Noel, 487n
Korean War, 51–53, 56
Korry, Edward M., 261–63, 266–68, 271–
273, 275, 278, 280, 282–87, 293, 480
Kosygin, Alexei N., 40–41, 223, 459,
526–27
Kraemer, Fritz, 476n
Kraemer, Sven, 433, 600
Kraft, Joseph, 19, 99, 116, 122, 438, 475,
606, 630
Kraslow, David J., 205, 463n, 499–500
Kreisberg, Paul H., 360, 361
Krogh, Egil, Jr. (Bud), 393, 396, 397, 398,

Lon Nol, 175–83, 184, 186–87, 303, 481, 598–99, 639
Look magazine, 119
Loory, Stuart, 205
Lord, Winston, 114, 125, 188, 373, 436, 494, 523, 539, 593
  American counterproposal drafted by, 584, 585
  on South Asia policy, 457–58
  wiretap on, 197, 198, 320, 321
Los Angeles Times, 38–39, 46n–47n, 171, 205, 499–500, 590n, 595, 607
Lovestone, Jay, 343–46
Lubell, Samuel, 582
Lumumba, Patrice, 275
Lynn, Laurence E., Jr., 90, 115, 116, 125, 135, 186, 299–300, 390
  Cambodia invasion and, 188–89
  NSC critique by, 318
  resignation of, 117, 199, 299
  SALT and, 100, 101, 153–54, 158

MacArthur, Douglas, 56
McCarthy, Eugene J. 14, 310n
McCarthy, John J., Jr., 178–79
McCartney, James, 572
McCloskey, Paul N., Jr. (Pete), 79, 82
McCloy, John J., 163–64
McCone, John A., 267, 268, 276
McCord, James W., Jr., 576
McGovern, George S., 201, 330, 370, 440n–41n, 483, 564, 604, 606
  accusations against Kissinger by, 578
  peace plan of, 584n
  in political polls, 562, 572, 582
McGovern-Hatfield Amendment, 301
Maclear, Michael, 310n, 492, 601n
McLucas, John L., 163n
MacMaster, Bruce, 290–91
McNamara, Robert S., 15–16, 46, 49, 50, 71, 89n, 321, 381n, 539
McNaughton, John T., 30n, 321n, 381n
Macovescu, Gheorge, 361
"madman theory," 53, 60, 75, 119, 126n, 130, 133, 173n, 368, 568, 636
  Cambodia invasion and, 185, 188, 192, 363
  Hanoi's offensive and (1972), 504–5, 516, 520
  Kissinger's endorsement of, 607–8, 614–615, 619–20
Maginnes, Nancy S., 83, 317n
Magruder, Jeb Stuart, 92n, 130n
Mailer, Norman, 569n
Manac'h, Etienne M., 352
Manchester Union Leader, 487–88
Mandate for Change, 1953–56

(Eisenhower), 51
Manila formula, 78, 80
Mankiewicz, Frank, 433
Manor, Leroy J., 304
Mansfield, Mike, 176–77, 485
Mansfield Amendment, 482, 485
Mao Tse-tung, 350, 354, 355, 363–67, 369, 371, 376, 442
  Cultural Revolution and, 352–53, 377
  internal threats against, 353, 364, 377, 494
  at Peking summit, 489, 493–94, 496, 497
Marchetti, Victor, 298n
Marder, Murray, 99, 204n, 228n, 610–11
Mardian, Robert C., 387n, 392, 397, 398–399
Marglin, Stephen A., 446n
Marks, John D., 298
Marshal, Arturo, 280, 292–93
Martin, Francis J., 393n
Martin, William H., 74
Marx, Patricia, 327
Mason, Edward S., 446n
Mathias, Charles McC., Jr., 169, 274, 330, 386
Matskevich, Vladimir, 532–33
Mayaguez, seizure of, 639–40
Mayer, Jean, 143, 145
Mayo, Robert P., 135
Mbanefo, Sir Louis, 143
Meany, George, 345–46
Meir, Golda, 220, 229–30, 248–49, 406, 411, 494
"Menu," *see* Cambodia, secret bombing of
Mercurio, 260, 262, 269n
Merritt, Jack H., 530n
Meselson, Matthew, 47n
Meyer, Charles A., 262, 266, 285
Meyer, Cord, 277n
Miami Herald, 52n
Middle East affairs, 213–49, 402–14
  in Kissinger memoirs, 85, 220, 225, 227, 229, 230, 238, 239, 243, 245, 246, 405, 407, 409, 413
  in Nixon memoirs, 216, 220–21, 237–238, 239n
  as Rogers's responsibility, 85, 213, 216, 217, 403
  role of spite in, 213
  see also Arab-Israeli wars; *specific countries*
Middle East peace policy, 213, 216–32, 403–14
  American solution in, 218, 219
  Holocaust as influence on, 218–19, 230n
  linkage and, 216–17

685

Poseidon submarines, 536
Pravda, 255
Present at the Creation (Acheson), 497*n*–498*n*
President's Foreign Intelligence Advisory Board, 200*n*
President's Science Advisory Committee (PSAC), 100, 150*n*, 151
PRG (Provisional Revolutionary Government), 428, 429, 436, 513, 561, 568, 580, 613, 614
  creation of, 425*n*
  in Hanoi's peace options, 564
  legitimizing of, 561, 562, 563, 577, 583, 588, 607, 616, 633–34
  Minh's willingness to negotiate with, 425, 433
  Soviet recognition of, 355, 356
  in tripartite election commission, 527, 565, 570, 571
"Principles of Relations," American-Soviet, 542
prisoners of war, 300, 301, 376, 428, 566, 583
  in Laos and Cambodia, 595
  Son Tay raid and, 304–7, 330, 363
  as trade for withdrawal, 430–32, 440, 482, 483–84, 517, 525, 620
  Vietcong as, 585, 592, 618
"protective reaction" bombing, in Vietnam War, 305, 482, 504–5, 507, 629*n*
Provisional Government of National Concord, 568, 580
Provisional Revolutionary Government, *see* PRG
Psychological Strategy Board, 27
Public Health Service, U.S., 143–44
Pueblo, seizure of, 69
Punjabis, Bengalis compared to, 446
Pursley, Robert E., 71–73, 75, 90, 106, 109, 121*n*, 185, 207, 243, 305, 318
  Cambodia invasion and, 185, 186, 191–192
  Laos invasion and, 309
  retirement of, 576*n*–77*n*
  wiretap on, 91, 193, 194, 320, 323, 324, 577*n*

Qaddafi, Muammar el-, 223*n*, 240*n*
Quadripartite Agreement (1971), 421–22
Quakers, Kissinger's meeting with, 119
Quandt, William, 248*n*, 409, 412

Rabin, Yitzak, 217–18, 220, 223–24, 226, 229, 231, 248–49, 405–6, 407
racism, 110–11

Radford, Charles E., 258–59, 373, 411, 483*n*
  Kissinger's trip to China and, 467, 468–469
  as spy for military, 380, 400, 465–74, 476–77
  wiretap on, 476–77, 478
Radio Hanoi, 129, 193*n*, 504, 505, 604–5
Raid, The (Schemmer), 304
Randal, Jonathan C., 570*n*
Rand Corporation, 47, 48–49, 122, 160, 173*n*, 325*n*
  China studies and, 354*n*, 355, 358
  Pentagon Papers and, 326–28, 385*n*, 386*n*
Rather, Dan, Nixon's interview with, 566
Rathjens, George W., 150–52, 154–55
Reagan, Ronald, 152, 512, 600*n*, 641
Reagan Administration, 152*n*, 641
Rebozo, Charles G. (Bébé), 109, 110*n*, 111, 190, 191, 201*n*, 328, 513, 514
refugees:
  Cambodian, 202
  Pakistani, 445, 450, 451, 452, 454–55, 456
  Palestinian, 215, 220, 235, 244
Republican National Convention (1968), 12, 13, 14, 52
Republican National Convention (1972), 572, 573
Republican Platform Committee, 13
Resor, Stanley R., 326
Reston, James, 31, 99, 132, 204, 255, 370, 402, 511, 603
  on Christmas bombing, 624–25
  Kissinger's bargaining leverage analyzed by, 630
  on Vietnam peace talks, 587, 607, 622–623
Retreat of American Power, The (Brandon), 157*n*, 499*n*
Rhatigan, William F., 521*n*
Riad, Mahmoud, 220, 221, 232, 245–46, 410, 413
Richardson, Elliot L., 33, 34, 76, 169, 206–7, 298, 299, 396, 400, 597*n*
  Biafra relief efforts and, 142, 143, 145–146
  China policy and, 356, 359, 360
  compliant behavior of, 107*n*
  Nixon's attacks on, 106–7
  SALT and, 158, 160, 164
Richardson, John H., 137
Ridenhour, Ronald, 135
Riegle, Donald W., Jr., 79, 82, 122
Road to Ramadan, The (Heikal), 222*n*

Robert F. (CIA false-flagger), 292–93
Robinson, Rembrandt C., 120n, 125, 256n, 258–59, 380, 466, 467, 470, 471, 472
Rockefeller, David, 260, 266
Rockefeller, Nelson, 27, 32, 37, 106, 112, 262, 316, 317n, 433n, 479, 512
  Kissinger as adviser to, 12, 13, 18, 22–23, 27
  Nixon files of, 14, 21
Rodman, Peter W., 112, 125, 317n, 551n
Rogers, William D., 265n
Rogers, William P., 111, 129, 133, 139, 249, 303, 314, 388, 416n–17n
  alleged incompetence of, 32, 33, 206, 207
  in anti-Muskie campaign, 486, 487
  Berlin talks and, 420–21, 422
  bombing opposed by, 61, 63, 624–25
  Cambodia invasion and, 187, 190, 191, 195, 197
  China policy and, 356, 362, 372, 378, 489–90, 493, 494, 497–99, 501
  Cienfuegos affair and, 253, 254, 255, 256n
  Dobrynin and, 67–68, 216, 226–27, 232
  EC-121 incident and, 69, 72, 73, 74–75, 113
  firing of, 498–99, 611–12, 638–39
  Hanoi's offensive and (1972), 510, 524–525
  in Jordanian crisis, 236, 238, 245n
  in Kissinger memoirs, 68
  Kissinger's bypassing of, 32, 39, 40–43, 60n, 76, 81, 114, 174, 206, 256n, 417
  Kissinger's criticism of, 67–68, 113–14, 409
  Kissinger's final triumph over, 402–14
  Kissinger's jealousy and anxiety about, 111, 113–14, 212, 213, 216, 226–27, 388
  Laos invasion opposed by, 308
  Middle East issues as responsibility of, 85, 213, 216, 217, 403
  in Middle East peace talks, 216, 218, 219, 226–27, 232, 406–9, 411
  Middle East toured by, 408–9, 411
  Nixon's friendship with, 32, 41, 113, 213, 402, 611–12
  Nixon's salvaging of, 402–3
  NSC reorganization and, 25, 31–34
  NSC staff views on, 106
  SALT and, 147, 157, 158, 164, 521, 538, 539, 555
  sexual innuendoes about, 108, 109, 113
  social graces of, 32–33
  South Asia policy and, 445, 458, 462

Vietnamese elections and (1971), 434
  in Vietnam peace initiatives, 572, 583, 587
Rogers plan, 403, 408, 637
  first, 219–22, 224
  second, 227–32, 251
Romania, 39
  China and, 356, 359, 361, 364, 365, 366, 448–49
  Nixon's visit to, 123, 356
Rostow, Walt W., 26, 27, 28, 33n, 37, 385, 388, 390n
Rowen, Henry, 48–49
Rozek, Edward J., 23n
Ruback, Jerry, 434
"Rube Goldberg" gambit, 271–72, 278–79, 280, 281, 282n
Ruina, Jack P., 150–55, 156, 163
Rush, Kenneth, 417, 418, 419–21, 503–4, 509, 619
  Cabinet position promised to, 503, 611–612
Rusk, Dean, 163–64, 206, 381n
Russo, Anthony, 326
Ruth, Henry S., Jr., 521n

Sabri, Ali, 409
Sadat, Anwar el–, 221, 249, 403–14, 636
Sadiq, Mohammed Ahmed, 241
Safeguard system, 150n, 154, 158–59
Safire, William, 192, 195, 522, 525–26
  as Nixon's speech writer, 114, 301, 482, 525, 544
  SALT and, 534, 544, 552
  on secret peace talks, 482–83, 484
  on Shanghai Communiqué, 500–501
Sainteny, Jean, 120
St. George and the Godfather (Mailer), 569n
Salisbury, Harrison E., 385
SALT (strategic arms limitation talks), 147–167, 314n, 334–49, 408
  backchannel and, see backchannel messages, SALT and
  breakthrough in, 334–35, 337, 341–42, 532
  Doty group recommendations and, 151–155, 156, 160, 162
  effects of U.S. bombing escalation on, 508–9
  in Kissinger memoirs, 337, 339, 340, 536, 546, 549–50, 551, 552, 553, 554–55
  Kissinger's dominance of, 147, 148, 152–56, 160–61, 162, 164–67, 338–343, 348, 537–42, 544–48, 551

691

Shawcross, William, 180*n*, 183*n*, 201*n*, 303, 599*n*

Shearer, Derek, 330

Shearer, Lloyd, 328

Sheehan, Neil, 116, 330, 391, 392

Shriver, Sargent, 434*n*

shuttle diplomacy, 221, 636–37

SI (Special Intelligence) clearance, 92*n*

Sideshow (Shawcross), 180*n*, 183*n*, 201*n*, 303

Sidey, Hugh, 99

Sihanouk, Norodom, 54, 60, 61, 64, 122
  overthrow of, 174, 175–83, 185–86, 201
  U.S. assassination plan and, 179–80

Sihanoukville, as Vietcong supply conduit, 200*n*

Sindlinger, Albert E., 515*n*, 522, 564, 582, 606

Sino-Soviet split, 355, 363, 381, 491, 523
  nuclear threat in, 357–58, 359

Sisco, Joseph J., 206, 207, 213, 220, 223, 226, 234
  Jordanian crisis and, 237, 246
  in Middle East peace talks, 216, 218, 219, 228*n*, 388, 406, 408–9, 411, 412–13
  South Asia policy and, 458, 460

Sither, Charles A., 479

Sitton, Ray B., 54, 69, 124
  in secret bombing of Cambodia, 59–63, 64–65, 75, 121–22

SLBMs (submarine-launched ballistic missiles), 337, 342, 397, 508, 548–57
  ICBMs traded for, 536, 548, 550, 553–554, 558*n*
  Kissinger's backchannel negotiating error on, 341, 349, 388, 532
  in SALT I, 529, 532, 534–41, 532, 543, 548–59
  "under construction," 534–35

Slocombe, Walter B., 154, 165–66

Sloman, Henry J., 279, 290–91, 292*n*, 293

Smith, Gerard C., 113, 147, 314*n*, 334, 398, 544–56, 560
  Kissinger's opposition to, 161, 162, 336, 338–43, 349, 521, 530–31, 537–39
  memoirs of, 257, 338, 340, 532, 545, 546*n*, 557*n*, 559
  MIRV ban advocated by, 158, 161–62, 164
  at Moscow summit, 555–56
  Nixon's scheming against, 42, 161–62, 336, 338, 521, 530–31
  SALT agreement as viewed by, 335, 341–42
  SLBM issue and, 341–42, 508, 532,

535, 537–39, 541, 548–56
  staff selected by, 100, 162
  SWWA proposal of, 545*n*–46*n*

Smith, Hedrick, 92, 93–95, 116

Smith, Ian, 115*n*

Smith, J. T., 400

Smith, Sandy, 399

Smith, Wayne K., 299, 373–74, 530*n*, 539

Smith College, antiwar movement at, 184

Smyser, W. Richard, 172–73, 300, 308, 373, 426, 427, 429, 436

Sneider, Richard L., 55, 57, 58, 60, 64, 84, 86, 105, 381–82, 520*n*
  EC-121 incident and, 70, 73, 86, 101
  resignation and post-NSC career of, 101, 102
  wiretap on, 91, 92, 94

Snepp, Frank W., 435, 437*n*, 438*n*, 574, 586

Snow, Edgar, 364–67

soccer fields, as intelligence evidence, 250, 256

Sonnenfeldt, Helmut, 23, 85, 88, 98, 204*n*, 416, 420, 453, 523
  in Duck Hook planning, 125, 126
  on Kissinger's fear of war-crimes trial, 116
  Kissinger vs., 114–15, 322, 323*n*
  racism of, 110–11
  SALT and, 100, 153, 158, 162, 342, 530*n*, 539, 551
  wiretap on, 87*n*, 91–92, 321–22

Son Tay raid (1970), 304–7, 330, 363
  intelligence failure in, 305
  water buffalo minicrisis in, 306*n*

South Korea, 51, 497
  EC-121 incident and, 70, 72

South Vietnam, 497
  Americanization of, 562
  ceasefire in, 482, 483–85, 517, 525, 561, 573–74, 577, 580, 581, 583–84, 595, 596, 597, 603
  Central Office for, *see* COSVN
  Christmas bombing as viewed by, 626
  Communist Party outlawed in, 47, 562
  constitution of, 47, 424, 425, 428, 439*n*, 441, 562, 570, 577, 580
  "decent interval" and Communist take-over of, 47, 48
  diminished enemy presence in (1969), 297–99
  election in (1971), 423–26, 430, 432–440, 443, 482
  fall of, 597, 639, 640
  Hanoi's demand for coalition government in, 482, 561, 562, 564, 568, 577

South Vietnam (*cont.*)
  Kissinger's visits to, 14–15, 16, 46–47, 435, 569, 570–72, 578, 589, 593–602
  National Assembly in, 433, 435
  North Vietnam's infiltration of, 15, 74n, 80–81, 561–62
  Phoenix Operation in, 80–81, 178, 299, 435
  p.r. campaign against peace agreement by, 615–16
  Provincial Reconnaissance Units in, 135
  Supreme Court of, 437, 438
  "Third Force" in, 424, 425, 434, 527
  tripartite election commission envisioned for, 527, 562, 563, 565, 570–71, 573–76, 577–78, 580, 598, 632
  see also Paris peace talks; Vietnam War
South Vietnamese Army, 50–51, 77–78, 118, 121, 297–98, 513, 585, 603
  in Cambodia invasion, 175, 186, 187n, 192, 199
  in Laos invasion, 307–13
  Quang Tri recaptured by, 580
  in response to Hanoi's offensive (1972), 506, 509, 515, 516, 525
  see also Vietnamization
Soviet Union, 12, 26, 35n, 39, 40–41, 73n, 74, 108, 115, 123
  Berlin talks and, 315, 337, 388, 415, 417–22
  Brandt's negotiations with, 415, 416, 417
  Chile and, 211, 212, 296
  Chinese relations with, 353–54, 355, 357–58, 359, 363, 381 453, 489, 491, 523
  Cienfuegos affair and, 211–12, 250–57, 296
  Czechoslovakia invaded by (1968), 48, 148, 149, 266, 353–54
  EC-121 incident and, 70, 212
  Egypt and, *see* Egypt, Soviet Union and
  India-Pakistan war and, 368, 446–47, 451, 452–53, 455, 457, 458–59, 462–464, 533n
  India's friendship treaty with, 452–53
  Jordanian crisis and, 211, 212, 233, 234, 237–49
  Korean War and, 51
  Navy of, 252, 253, 256n–57n
  Rogers plan and, 221–22, 230, 231
  U.S.-Chinese relations and, 350, 359–60, 363
  U.S. grain deal with, 334–35, 343–48, 531–34, 557, 563
  U.S. trade and credit concessions to, 563
  Vietnam War and, 48, 51, 53, 59, 66–68, 77, 120, 124, 147, 149, 211, 218, 312, 334, 350, 355, 442–43, 491–92, 503, 504, 508–10, 511–15, 518–19, 525–26, 562, 563
  see also Moscow summit; SALT
Speedy Express Operation, 59n
Spiegel, Der, 229, 320
Sports Illustrated magazine, 250n
SS-9 land-based missiles, 151, 543
SS-11 "light" missiles, 543, 547
SS-19 missiles, 548
Staats, Elmer B., 27
Stalin, Joseph, 206n
Standard Oil of New Jersey, 137
State Department, U.S., 31, 47, 50, 68, 206, 403, 406, 520n
  Arab-Israeli conflict and, 213–14, 216–22, 224–32, 404–11, 413
  Arabists in, 206, 214, 224, 244
  Berlin talks and, 417, 419, 420–21, 422
  Biafra rebellion and, 141–46
  Bureau of Intelligence and Research in, 253
  Cambodia invasion and, 187, 191
  Chile policy and, 263, 265, 266, 267, 272n, 275, 278, 283, 285n, 294
  China policy and, 356–57, 360–62, 364, 367, 369–71, 372, 378, 381–82, 489–490, 492–93, 496, 497–99
  Cienfuegos affair and, 252, 253, 254, 255
  end-of-the-year report of (1969), 114
  Jordanian crisis and, 212, 234, 236, 238, 243, 244–45
  Kissinger as consultant to, 13, 14–16, 47
  morale problems in, 33–34, 422
  Nixon's lack of confidence in, 27, 33, 42, 43
  NSC reorganization and, 25, 27, 29, 30, 31–35, 316
  path to success in, 33n
  SALT and, 147, 154, 157, 158, 159, 164, 338, 521, 538, 539, 555
  secret bombing of Cambodia and, 61, 63
  Senior Interdepartment Group of, 33, 34
  South Asia policy and, 444–45, 448, 449, 453, 455, 458, 461, 465
  U.S.-West German relations and, 416n, 417
  Vietnamese elections and, 434, 435, 439n
  war in Laos opposed by, 169–70
Stearman, William L., 600
Stennis, John C., 466n
Stephens, Melville L., 385
Stern, Laurence, 140, 566
Sterner, Michael, 408, 411
Stewart, W. Donald, 398, 471–72, 477

ABOUT THE AUTHOR

SEYMOUR M. HERSH was born in Chicago in 1937 and graduated in 1958 from the University of Chicago. He began his newspaper career as a police reporter for the City News Bureau in Chicago. After Army service, he was hired by United Press International in Pierre, South Dakota. In 1963 he joined the Associated Press in Chicago and in 1965 went to Washington for the AP to cover the Pentagon. He served as press secretary and speech writer for Senator Eugene H. McCarthy in the famed "Children's Crusade"—the 1968 New Hampshire Democratic primary campaign against Lyndon Johnson. In 1969, as a free-lance journalist, Mr. Hersh wrote the first account of the My Lai massacre, distributing five newspaper stories on the atrocity through Dispatch News Service. He joined the *New York Times* in 1972 and worked out of both Washington and New York until his resignation in 1979 to begin *The Price of Power*. In early 1983, he joined the *Atlantic* magazine as National Correspondent.

Mr. Hersh has won more than a dozen major journalism prizes. For his account of the My Lai massacre he earned the 1970 Pulitzer Prize for International Reporting, the George Polk Award, the Sigma Delta Chi Distinguished Service Award, and the Worth Bingham Prize. For his reporting on the secret B-52 bombing of Cambodia, he was accorded the Roy M. Howard Public Service Award and a second Polk Award in 1974. The next year he won the Drew Pearson Award, the John Peter Zenger Freedom of the Press Award, the Sidney Hillman Foundation Award, and a third Polk for his stories on the CIA and Chile and on CIA domestic spying. And in 1981 he received a second Sigma Delta Chi Award and his fourth Polk Award for two articles in the *New York Times Magazine* on the involvement of former CIA agents in arms sales to Libya.

Mr. Hersh's previous books are *Chemical and Biological Warfare: America's Hidden Arsenal*; *My Lai 4: A Report on the Massacre and Its Aftermath*; and *Cover-up: The Army's Secret Investigation of the Massacre of My Lai*. His articles have appeared in the *New Yorker, Saturday Review*, the *New York Review of Books* and the *New Republic*. He lives in Washington with his wife and three children.

This book is to be returned on or before
the last date stamped below.